Y0-CAD-374

THE 1971 Compton Yearbook

A summary and interpretation of the events of 1970 to supplement Compton's Encyclopedia

F. E. Compton Co.
Division of Encyclopædia Britannica, Inc.

William Benton
PUBLISHER

CHICAGO • LONDON
TORONTO • GENEVA
SYDNEY • TOKYO
MANILA

Contents

Library of Congress Catalog Card Number: 58-26525
International Standard Book Number: 0-85229-159-0

Printed in U.S.A.

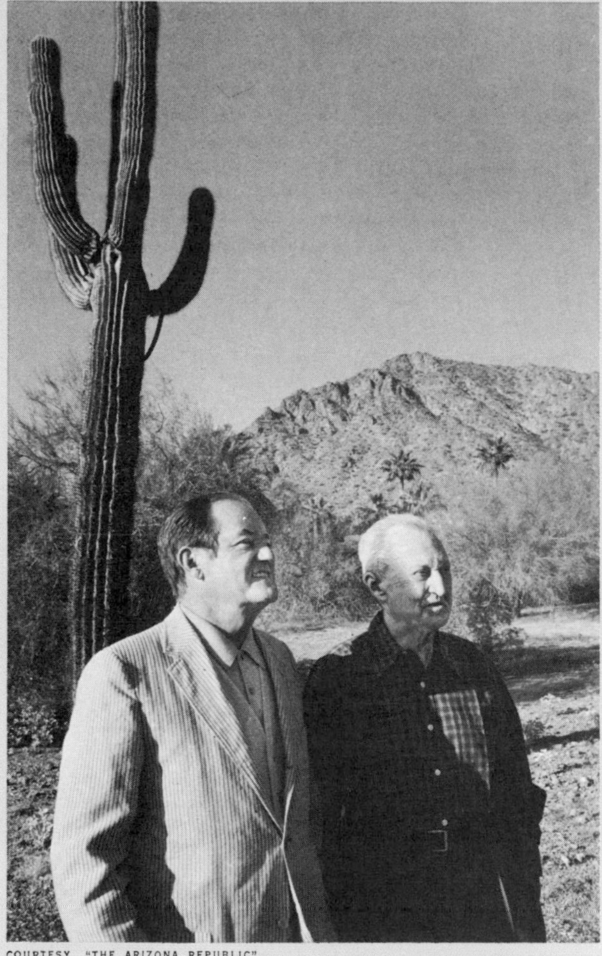

COURTESY, "THE ARIZONA REPUBLIC"

Senators William Benton and Hubert H. Humphrey confer in Arizona. Humphrey was a board member of Encyclopaedia Britannica, Inc., and Encyclopaedia Britannica Educational Corp. in 1969 and 1970.

The Quest for Change

by Senator William Benton, Publisher

Like a great university, an encyclopedia enjoys an inner structure of authority and an external sense of purpose.

Our purpose at Compton's is to be authoritative, but also contemporary; to be historic but also current. *The Compton Yearbook* is a primary tool of that purpose. It provides contemporaneity in an historic setting. Its goal furthers that of the Encyclopedia: not only to offer a great diversity of significant information but to offer it with current insight that helps provide the reader with opportunity for historical judgment.

A dilemma is to keep pace with a society in ferment. The events recorded in the Yearbook must reflect not only the turbulence within our society but also the substance of its quest. They must suggest the "something historic" that is happening to us: so sweeping is the impetus of change in our times that we find ourselves passing through a New Reformation. It has of course been going on for quite a while, at least since World War I. But increasingly we seem to experience—or endure, if you will—the phenomena of centuries in the period of decades, of decades in the period of months.

"A cosmos without known cause or fate is an intellectual prison," observed historian Will Durant of the "first" Reformation. "We long to believe that the great drama has a just author and a noble end." Here is where we are today.

We seek to achieve our goals, in this volume, in a multifaceted manner.

First, the editors recognize the fact of change. A good example of this is our special section on the U.S. census. Every census is an event, yet some censuses have acquired a character and dimension all their own. The census of 1890, for instance, was the official farewell to the American frontier; it was from its statistics—after three years of study and contemplation—that Frederick Jackson Turner arrived at his theories of the significance of the frontier in American life and gave to history a new vision of the emerging nation. Now, in 1971, as 10,000 miles of electronic census tape begin to spew out new patterns in American life, we offer here in the Yearbook the raw facts of change—the basis of a census that promises to be of the importance and vast dimensions of 1890's.

What the census cannot tell us is how the *style* of American life is changing. Traditional values of our society are being challenged, and the nation faces what historian Theodore H. White describes as a "clash of cultures"—the new versus the old. Part of the new culture, for many young Americans, is the abuse of drugs. It is a phenomenon worthy of the careful and objective analysis given it in the feature article written by Dr. Stanley F. Yolles, Assistant

Surgeon General, U.S. Public Health Service.

Second, we recognize not merely the fact of change but the desire for change. That desire is in the newest but also the oldest traditions of society. Perhaps a good example in the Yearbook is our feature article on international travel: the flights of the new 747; the expansion of the travel industry (one company has not only erected a resort complex in Abidjan, capital of the Ivory Coast, but has also provided it with the first ice-skating rink in all of Africa). Perhaps a better example is a new report on an old experience—the reading of the Bible—through the changes in translation that were completed in 1970. Is a new translation necessary, or justifiable? "We already had," observes our special report, "in the 1611, or King James, version"—sometimes called the Authorized Version—"a translation . . . whose words, phrases, and rhythms have long enriched the very bloodstream of English language and literature." And yet—despite the hold that this luminous volume had on the hearts and minds of English-speaking people—the modern translation pushed ahead. To me, some of it sounds like the *Saturday Evening Post* and I do not relish the sound of the *Saturday Evening Post* in church. What would prove to be its value, its enduring attraction? "It was not likely," says our special report, "that any version in 20th-century English, however 'timeless', however scholarly, and however free from colloquialism or cliché, would have anything like the literary merit of the King James Version." Would this desire for change reduce the spiritual significance of the text? Or would it bring home the Biblical message to more people? All these questions—many of them so personal, so intimate, so questioning of the traditional and the familiar—are but reflections of the dynamics of change. Whether it is to be? How it is to be? What is its value?

Thirdly, we recognize the roots and the directions of change. These now increasingly center in man's demand for better use of our earthly resources. They are seen in the growing human concern over conservation and the environment; both these issues are the substance of our Yearbook's report on Alaska and the opportunities and problems of the oil deposits on its North Slope. They can be seen also in our reports on tenants' rights, on the abuse of our civic and intellectual rights by certain TV commercials in election campaigns, and perhaps above all in our feature article on the population crisis.

What is the potential impact of the explosive growth in world population? Will there be enough living space for all if present trends continue? Statisticians tell us that the number of people on earth will quadruple—to 14.4 billion—during one man's lifetime at the current growth rate. Can we feed and house that many? Can we provide medical care? These are basic questions we must face, and our feature article by Dr. Paul Ehrlich of Stanford University and Anne Ehrlich provides the kind of information on which we can base our judgments.

Another direction of change in 1970 was the intense activity of women's liberation groups. Our feature article by Jacqueline Wexler, president of Hunter College of the City University of New York, goes beyond the public demonstrations to examine the traditional role of women in American life, and how that role is changing. As with so many social protest movements, too much attention is given to the confrontations in the streets which dominate the newspapers and television.

Finally, and most of all, our editors try to express the substance and spirit of change through those sensitive, intuitive, almost visceral antennae that touch all of us as human beings. We do not talk simply of the apocalyptic nature of the drug abuse problem, or yield simplistically to the division of the young into the children of darkness and the children of light. Instead, we speak of the "lonely empties"—an affliction of the age—and the drifting spirit in human affairs which gave them character. We do not speak trivially of the fight for "women's liberation" but of—in the words of our authoress—"the rising expectation, demand, quest and hunger of every emerging group in the world today . . . for recognition as persons within a community of persons." We do not talk simply of the problem of overpopulation but of the deep and historic trends that reflect not only the present cultural objections to control of the birthrate but more ancient objections to reduction of the death rate. " . . . If undertakers are miserable," wrote Will Durant, "then progress is real."

There is a passage in Emerson that says that the time to live is not when everything is quiet and serene but when all is tumult. If there is a particular sense of hope in these times, does it not spring from man's awakened determination to meet science on its own terms and to cope with its once unyielding imperatives? This dawning moment of the tumultuous 1970's is the spirit-lifting time of change when everything is fresh and exciting and the demand on man is for new qualities of mind and spirit, for the "emancipation"—in Woodrow Wilson's words—"of the generous energies of a people."

The vigor, the fortitude, the resourcefulness of those who shape those qualities of change and bear them into the future is the essence of what we offer you in these pages of *The Compton Yearbook*.

How to Use the Yearbook

In order to make the best possible use of the Yearbook, the reader is advised to make frequent use of the Index and of the cross-references within articles. The Index can save a great deal of time and effort for a reader who is looking for specific information. In addition to cataloging all the articles in the current Yearbook (see below), the Index notes whether a given topic has been covered in Yearbooks of the past five years. Many articles in the Yearbook contain cross-references to other articles of related interest within the Yearbook—for example, the CAMBODIA article might have a cross-reference to INTERNATIONAL RELATIONS. At the end of an article, the reader will usually find a cross-reference to articles in Compton's Encyclopedia, which should be consulted if more background information is needed or wanted—for example, (*See in* CE: Honduras.).

The Yearbook is divided into several sections—feature articles and special reports, main text, new words, census summary, reprints, index, and family record.

FEATURE ARTICLES AND SPECIAL REPORTS
The feature articles discuss topics of special current interest. Each one is written by an expert in his field. Each is a full-length survey piece. The special reports are two- or three-page supplements to nine main-text articles—covering the news in greater depth.

MAIN TEXT
The main text of the 1971 Compton Yearbook is an alphabetical arrangement of articles on all the subjects that made news during the year. At the end of this section is a useful 1971 calendar. Most of the articles are accompanied by outstanding news pictures, diagrams, maps, or graphs.

NEW WORDS
The New Words section in this Yearbook comes in two parts. The first is a list of words newly accepted for inclusion in Merriam-Webster dictionaries. This list is a valuable reference source and could be a great aid in schoolwork. The second part of this section is an interesting essay on some of the new words of recent years and how they came to be used.

INDEX
The Index lists alphabetically all the subjects and illustrations in the Yearbook. It shows the exact page on which information can be found. In addition, bracketed numbers, such as [69], [67], indicate that material on this subject can also be found in the Yearbooks of those years.

FAMILY RECORD
The last section of the Yearbook is a unique one with Compton's. Family affairs can be recorded under convenient headings.

THE 1971 COMPTON YEARBOOK

Feature Authors

Paul R. Ehrlich, Professor of Biology, Stanford University, and **Anne H. Ehrlich,** Senior Research Assistant, *THE NEED FOR POPULATION CONTROL*

Horace Sutton, Associate Editor, *Saturday Review, LET'S TRAVEL*

John Szarkowski, Director, Department of Photography, Museum of Modern Art, New York City, *THE ART OF PHOTOGRAPHY*

Jacqueline Wexler, President, Hunter College of the City University of New York, *WOMEN IN SOCIETY: THE SEARCH FOR "PERSONHOOD"*

Dr. Stanley Fausst Yolles, Assistant Surgeon General, U.S. Public Health Service, and Associate Administrator for Mental Health, Health Services and Mental Health Administration, U.S. Department of Health, Education, and Welfare, *DRUGS AND YOUTH*

Contributors and Consultants

These authorities either wrote the articles listed or supplied information and data that were used in writing them.

Stener Mørch Aarsdal, Economic Editor, 'Børsen', and Press Officer, Chamber of Commerce, Copenhagen, *Denmark*

Rudy P. Abramson, Science and Technology Correspondent, Washington, D.C., Bureau, 'Los Angeles Times', *Space Exploration SPECIAL REPORT: After Apollo*

Joseph John Accardo, Washington Columnist for several publications, *Fuel and Power* (in part)

Jacob Bernard Agus, Rabbi, Beth El Congregation, Baltimore, Md., *Religion* (in part)

John Anthony Allan, Lecturer in Geography, School of Oriental and African Studies, University of London, *Libya*

Gustavo Arthur Antonini, Associate Professor, Center for Latin American Studies, University of Florida, *Dominican Republic*

Miguel Aranguren, Deputy Director, Department of Information and Public Affairs, Pan American Union, *Latin America* (in part)

Bruce Arnold, Free-Lance Journalist and Writer, Dublin, *Ireland SPECIAL REPORT: The Two Irelands*

Robert M. Ball, Commissioner of Social Security, U.S. Department of Health, Education, and Welfare, *Social Services* (in part)

Kenneth de la Barre, Director, Montreal Office, Arctic Institute of North America, *Arctic*

Paul Charles Bartholomew, Professor of Government, University of Notre Dame, *Supreme Court of the United States* (in part)

Howard Bass, Winter Sports Correspondent, 'The Daily Telegraph' (London) and 'Christian Science Monitor', *Ice Hockey; Ice Skating; Skiing*

David H. Beetle, Special Correspondent, Gannett Newspapers, Albany, N.Y., *State Governments, United States* (in part)

William Beltrán, Economic Research Officer, Economic Intelligence Department, Bank of London and South America Ltd., London, *Argentina*

Clyde Richard Bergwin, retired U.S. Air Force Information Officer, Author of 'Animal Astronauts', *Aircraft*

David Lynn Bickelhaupt, Professor of Insurance, College of Administrative Science, The Ohio State University, *Insurance* (in part)

Victor Gordon Charles Blackman, Staff Photographer, 'Daily Express' (London), Columnist, Amateur Photographer, *Photography*

Alan Geoffrey Blyth, Music Critic, London, *Music; Opera*

William Charles Boddy, Editor, 'Motor Sport', Full Member, Guild of Motoring Writers, *Auto Racing* (in part)

Dick Boonstra, Member of Staff, Department of Political Science, Free University, Amsterdam, *Netherlands*

Kooman Boycheff, Supervisor of Physical Education and Coordinator of Recreation, University of California at Berkeley, *Hobbies; Toys and Games*

Mary Beatrice Boyd, Senior Lecturer in History, Victoria University of Wellington, New Zealand, *Fiji; Tonga; Western Samoa*

Charles Leofric Boyle, Lieutenant Colonel, Royal Artillery (Ret.), Chairman, Survival Service Commission, International Union for Conservation of Nature and Natural Resources, 1958–63, *Conservation* (in part)

Arnold C. Brackman, Writer and Consultant on Asian Affairs, *Indonesia*

Lewis Braithwaite, Research Associate, Centre for Urban and Regional Studies, University of Birmingham, England, *Cities and Urban Affairs*

William A. Bresnahan, President, American Trucking Associations, Inc., Washington, D.C., *Transportation* (in part)

Jack Brickhouse, Vice-President and Manager of Sports, WGN Continental Broadcasting Co., *Baseball* (in part)

D. A. Brown, Agriculture Librarian, University of Illinois, *Animals and Wildlife; Conservation* (in part)

Thomas M. Brown, Reporter, 'Anchorage Daily News', *Conservation SPECIAL REPORT: The Alaska Pipeline*

Charles G. Burck, Associate Editor, 'Fortune' Magazine, *Business and Industry SPECIAL REPORT: Franchising*

Ardath W. Burks, Professor and Director, International Programs, Rutgers, The State University, New Brunswick, N.J., *Japan*

M. Dallas Burnett, Associate Professor of Communications, Brigham Young University, Provo, Utah, *Newspapers; Television and Radio SPECIAL REPORT: News and Views*

Allen D. Bushong, Associate Professor of Geography, University of South Carolina, *El Salvador; Honduras*

Frank Butler, Sports Editor, 'News of the World', London, *Boxing*

Alva Lawrence Campbell, Regional Director, Institute of Life Insurance, *Insurance* (in part)

Henry Cummings Campbell, Chief Librarian, Toronto Public Library, Toronto, Ont., *Literature, Canadian* (in part)

Joanna A. Carey, Assistant Director, Bureau of Public Information, American Dental Association, *Dentistry*

Lucien Chalmey, Adviser, International Union of Producers and Distributors of Electrical Energy, Paris, *Fuel and Power* (in part)

Robin Chapman, Economic Research Officer, Bank of London and South America Ltd., London, *Cuba; Haiti; Portugal*

Robert Chaussin, Government Civil Engineer, Department of Technical Studies on Roads and Highways, Bagneux, France, *Engineering Projects* (in part)

Hung-Ti Chu, Expert in Far Eastern Affairs, United Nations Area Specialist and Chief of Asia-Africa Section and Trusteeship Council Section of the United Nations Secretariat, 1946–67, and Professor of Government, Texas Tech University, *China, People's Republic of; Taiwan*

Max Coiffait, Correspondent, Agence France-Presse, Vientiane, *Laos*

Rufus William Crater, Editorial Director, 'Broadcasting', New York City, *Television and Radio* (in part)

Norman Crossland, Bonn Correspondent, 'Manchester Guardian', *Germany* (in part)

Gloria Clare Cumper, Chairman, Council of Voluntary Social Services, and Member, Judicial Services Commission, Kingston, *Jamaica*

Krsto Franjo Cviic, Leader Writer and East European Affairs Correspondent, 'Economist', London, *Yugoslavia*

Hiroshi Daifuku, Chief, Section for the Development of the Cultural Heritage, United Nations Educational, Scientific, and Cultural Organization, Paris, *Landmarks and Monuments*

David Keith Davies, Economic and Political Research Officer, Bank of London and South America Ltd., London, *Bolivia; Uruguay*

Ernest Albert John Davies, Editor, 'Traffic Engineering and Control', 'Roads and Their Traffic', and 'Traffic Engineering Practice', *Transportation* (in part)

Patricia B. Davis, Associate Editor, Gaines Dog Research Center, *Pets* (in part)

Philippe Decraene, Member, Editorial Staff, 'Le Monde', Paris, *Cameroon; Central African Republic; Chad; Congo, People's Republic of the; Dahomey; Gabon; Guinea; Ivory Coast; Malagasy Republic; Mali; Mauritania; Niger; Senegal; Togo; Tunisia; Upper Volta*

Lyle William Denniston, Supreme Court Reporter, 'Evening Star', Washington, D.C., *Blackmun, Harry A.*

Frances C. Dickson, 4-H Information Specialist, Extension Service, U.S. Department of Agriculture, *Youth Organizations* (in part)

Elfriede Dirnbacher, Austrian Civil Servant, *Austria*

Jim Dunne, Detroit Editor, 'Popular Science Monthly', *Automobiles*

François Duriaud, Reuter's Correspondent, Algiers, *Algeria*

Raul d'Eca, formerly Fulbright Visiting Lecturer on American History, University of Minas Gerais, *Brazil*

Herbert Leeson Edlin, Publications Officer, Forestry Commission of Great Britain, *Conservation* (in part)

Harold Ellis, Professor of Surgery, Westminster Medical School, University of London, *Medicine* (in part)

N. R. Ellis, formerly of the Agricultural Research Service, U.S. Department of Agriculture, *Agriculture* (in part)

Jan Robert Engels, Editor, 'P.V.V. Flitsen' (Journal of the Belgian Party for Freedom and Progress), *Belgium*

Kathleen M. Engle, Assistant Editor, 'Nation's Schools' Magazine, McGraw-Hill, Inc., *Education*

David M. L. Farr, Professor of History, Carleton University, Ottawa, Ont., *Canada*

Robert Joseph Fendell, New York Editor, 'Automotive News', New York City, *Auto Racing* (in part)

Melba M. Ferguson, Media Specialist, Public Affairs Division, Girl Scouts of the United States of America, *Youth Organizations* (in part)

Ronald W. Ferrier, Company Historian, British Petroleum, *Fuel and Power* (in part)

Robert Moore Fisher, Senior Economist, Board of Governors, Federal Reserve System, and Professorial Lecturer, American University, Washington, D.C., *Building Construction*

Rita Marie Flynn, Assistant Director, Public Information, Boys' Clubs of America, *Youth Organizations* (in part)

David Fouquet, Staff Writer, 'Congressional Quarterly', *Immigration and Citizenship*

Robert John Fowell, Research Associate, Department of Mining Engineering, University of Newcastle upon Tyne, *Fuel and Power* (in part)

David A. Fredrickson, Assistant Professor of Anthropology, Sonoma State College, Rohnert Park, California, *Archaeology*

Fabio Galvano, Correspondent, 'Epoca', London, *Italy*

Albert Ganado, Lawyer, Malta, *Malta*

S. N. Geal, retired Assistant Director, American Camping Association, *Camping*

Thayil Jacob Sony George, Assistant Editor, 'Far Eastern Economic Review', Hong Kong, *Asia; Cambodia; Korea; Thailand; Vietnam* (in part)

Donald LeRoy Gilleland, Public Affairs Officer, Secretary of the U.S. Air Force Office of Information, *Armed Forces, United States* (in part)

Harry Golombek, British Chess Champion, 1947, 1949, and 1955, and Chess Correspondent, 'The Times' and 'Observer', London, *Chess*

Robert Goralski, Correspondent, NBC News, Pentagon, Washington, D.C., *Vietnam* (in part)

Jarlath John Graham, Editor, 'Advertising Age', *Advertising*

The Rev. Arthur R. Green, Pastor, Good Shepherd Parish, Chicago, *Religion* (in part)

Anthony Royston Grant Griffiths, Lecturer in History, Flinders University of South Australia, *Australia; Nauru*

Jack A. L. Hahn, President, American Hospital Association, *Hospitals*

William D. Hawkland, Provost and Professor of Law, School of Law, State University of New York at Buffalo, *Supreme Court of the United States* (in part)

John Arnfield Heap, Member of the British Antarctic Survey, *Antarctica*

Phyllis West Heathcote, Correspondent on Women's Topics, 'Manchester Guardian', Paris, *Cosmetics; Fashion*

The Rev. Peter Anthony Hebblethwaite, Editor, 'The Month', *Religion* (in part)

William Dale Hickman, Jr., News Correspondent, McGraw-Hill Publications, Inc., Washington, D.C., *Telephones*

Edison L. Hoard, Attorney at Law, *Law*

Robert David Hodgson, Assistant Geographer, U.S. Department of State, *Luxembourg; Monaco*

Jerome Holtzman, Sportswriter, 'Chicago Sun-Times' *Basketball; Football*

Oscar H. Horst, Professor of Geography, Western Michigan University, *Guatemala*

Louis Hotz, formerly Editorial Writer, 'The Johannesburg Star', *South Africa*

Audrey M. Hudson, Assistant to National Public Relations Director, Camp Fire Girls, Inc., *Youth Organizations* (in part)

David Huelin, Manager, Economic Intelligence Department, Bank of London and South America Ltd., London, *Latin America* (in part)

Stephen Hughes, Reuter's Correspondent, *Morocco*

Kenneth Ingham, Professor of History, University of Bristol, England, *Congo, Democratic Republic of the; Equatorial Guinea; Kenya; Malawi; Rhodesia; Tanzania; Uganda; Zambia*

(William) Harold Ingrams, formerly Adviser on Overseas Information, Colonial Office, London, *Gambia, The; Sierra Leone*

Stanley S. Jados, Ph.D., Professor of Political Science, De Paul University, Chicago, *United States* (in part)

Bernard R. Kantor, Chairman, Division of Cinema, and Associate Dean, School of Performing Arts, University of Southern California, *Motion Pictures* (in part)

William A. Katz, Professor, School of Library Science, State University of New York, *Magazines*

John Arnold Kelleher, Editor, 'The Dominion', Wellington, *New Zealand*

Lotte Kent, Editor, 'Cooperative News Service', International Cooperative Alliance, London, *Cooperatives*

Peter Kilner, Editor, 'Arab Report and Record', *Sudan*

Jon Kimche, Editor, 'The New Middle East', and Expert on Middle East Affairs, 'Evening Standard', London, *Israel*

Joshua B. Kind, Associate Professor of Art History, Northern Illinois University, De Kalb, *Museums*

Resa W. King, Contributing Editor, 'Business Week', *Business and Industry*

Alfred Paul Klausler, Executive Secretary, Associated Church Press, *Religion* (in part)

Jean Marcel Knecht, Assistant Foreign Editor, 'Le Monde', Paris, *France*

Ole Ferdinand Knudsen, Editor, 'Norway Exports', Oslo, *Norway*

Philip Kopper, Free-Lance Writer, Washington, D.C., *Agnew, Spiro T.; Awards and Prizes*

Valdimar Kristinsson, Editor, 'Fjármálatidindi', *Iceland*

Geoffrey Charles Last, Adviser, Imperial Ethiopian Ministry of Education and Fine Arts, Addis Ababa, *Ethiopia*

Wilma Laws, Journalist, London, Member of International Association of Art Critics, *Painting and Sculpture* (in part)

Chapin R. Leinbach, Public Relations Officer, Air Transport Association of America, *Transportation* (in part)

Arnold E. Levitt, Senior Associate Editor, 'Chemical and Engineering News', *Chemistry*

Raymond Basil Lewry, Senior Research Officer, Bank of London and South America Ltd., London, *Colombia; Ecuador*

Chaim U. Lipschitz, Vice-President, Mesivta Torah Vodaath; Managing Editor, 'The Jewish Press'; and President, National Information Bureau for Jewish Life, *Religion* (in part)

Jerry Lipson, Reporter, 'Chicago Daily News', *Post Office, United States*

J. Anthony Lukas, Staff Writer, 'The New York Times'; Author of 'The Barnyard Epithet and Other Obscenities', *Law SPECIAL REPORT: Chicago Conspiracy Trial*

Virginia Rose Luling, Historian, *Somalia*

Warren P. McClam, Economist, Bank for International Settlements, Basel, Switzerland, *Money and International Finance*

Captain Terry McDonald, Chief, Public Information Division, U.S. Coast Guard, *Armed Forces, United States* (in part)

Irene McManus, Assistant Editor, 'American Forests' Magazine, *Forest Products* (in part); *Recreation*

Katharine A. Mahon, Public Relations Director, Girls Clubs of America, Inc., *Youth Organizations* (in part)

Andrew J. A. Mango, Orientalist and Broadcaster, *Turkey*

Peter (John) Mansfield, formerly Middle East Correspondent, 'The Sunday Times', London, *Iraq; Jordan; Kuwait; Lebanon; Middle East; Oman; Saudi Arabia; Southern Yemen; Syria; United Arab Republic; Yemen*

Aldo Marcello, Civil Engineer, *Engineering Projects* (in part)

Edward L. Marcou, Assistant Public Relations Manager, American Bowling Congress, *Bowling*

Joseph William Marlow, Lawyer, *Pictured Highlights and Chronology of 1970*

Jerome Mazzaro, Author and Professor of English, State University of New York at Buffalo, *Literature*

Arthur M. Mikesell, Assistant Director, Public Relations, American Bankers Association, *Banks*

Raymond Spencer Millard, Deputy Director, Road Research Laboratory, Ministry of Transport, *Engineering Projects* (in part)

Richard F. Miller, Professor of English, Washington State College, *Stamps*

Sandra Millikin, Assistant Curator of Drawings, Royal Institute of British Architects, London, *Architecture; Painting and Sculpture* (in part)

Marilyn M. Milow, Staff Writer, Magazines and News Features, Bureau of Communications, National Board, Young Women's Christian Association, *Youth Organizations* (in part)

Mario Modiano, Athens Correspondent, 'The Times', London, *Greece*

Hazel Romola Morgan, *Popular Music*

Horace Denton Morgan, Senior Partner, Sir William Halcrow and Partners, *Engineering Projects* (in part)

Molly Mortimer, Journalist on Commonwealth and International Affairs, *Botswana; Burundi; Commonwealth of Nations; Ghana; Lesotho; Maldives; Mauritius; Nigeria; Rwanda; Swaziland*

John Moss, Barrister-at-Law, Editor of 'Local Government Law and Administration', *Social Services* (in part)

George Saul Mottershead, Director-Secretary, Chester Zoo, England, *Zoo*

Pauline G. Mower, Information Director, Future Homemakers of America, Washington, D.C., *Youth Organizations* (in part)

Stephanie Mullins, Historian, *Heath, Edward*

Leonard M. Murphy, Chief, Seismology Division, Coast and Geodetic Survey, Environmental Science Services Administration, U.S. Department of Commerce, *Earth Sciences* (in part)

Edward Harwood Nabb, Vice-President, Union of International Motorboating, *Boats and Boating*

National Oceanic and Atmospheric Administration, U.S. Department of Commerce, Office of Public Information, *Weather*

Raymond K. Neal, Assistant to the Director, Editorial Service, Boy Scouts of America, *Youth Organizations* (in part)

John Neill, Author of Climbers' Club Guides 'Cwm Silyn and Tremadoc' and 'Snowdon South' and Alpine Club Guide 'Selected Climbs in the Pennine Alps', *Mountain Climbing*

Bert Nelson, Publisher, 'Track and Field News', *Track and Field*

Edwin Bohannon Newton, formerly Manager, Advanced Rubber Technology, B. F. Goodrich Co., *Rubber*

Laurence H. Nobles, Professor of Geology, Northwestern University, *Earth Sciences* (in part)

Harold Stanley Noel, Editor, 'World Fishing', London, *Fish and Fisheries*

Julius Novick, Assistant Professor of English, New York University, Guest Lecturer, Drama Division, Juilliard School, and Dramatic Critic, 'Village Voice', *Theater*

Arden W. Ohl, Instructor of Geography, Modesto Junior College, Calif., *Nicaragua*

Frederick I. Ordway, Director, Science and Technology Applications and Evaluation, Research Institute, University of Alabama, *Space Exploration* (in part)

Sidney Arnold Pakeman, Author of 'Ceylon', *Ceylon*

Rafael Pargas, Computer Operator, National Geographic Society, *Philippines*

Sandy Parker, Fur Editor, 'Women's Wear Daily', *Furs*

Vernon John Parry, Reader in the History of the Near and Middle East, School of Oriental and African Studies, University of London, *Cyprus*

Sheila Caffyn Patterson, Research Fellow, Centre for Multi-Racial Studies, University of Sussex, Brighton, England, *Barbados*

Robin Charles Penfold, Public Relations Executive, Carl Byior and Associates Ltd., London, *Synthetics* (in part)

Virgil W. Peterson, Executive Director, Chicago Crime Commission (1942–70), *Crime; Police*

Eugene Edwin Pfaff, Professor of History, University of North Carolina at Greensboro, *International Relations*

David Kemsley Robert Phillips, Editor, 'World Sports', *Sports Champions of 1970*

Otto Pick, Reader in International Relations, University of Surrey, England, *Czechoslovakia; Union of Soviet Socialist Republics*

Frederick H. Pittera, Chairman, International Exposition Consultants Co., and Director, New Nations Exposition and Development Corp., *Fairs and Shows*

F. N. Plowman, *Fuel and Power* (in part)

Simeon Potter, Professor Emeritus of the English Language and Philology, University of Liverpool, England, *New Words* (in part)

Holenarasipur Y. Sharada Prasad, Director of Information, Prime Minister's Secretariat, New Delhi, *India*

Manuel Pulgar, Senior Economic Research Officer, Bank of London and South America Ltd., London, *Mexico; Spain*

Howard Pyle, President, National Safety Council, *Safety*

Margaret H. Quinn, Reporter, 'Sun-Gazette', Williamsport, Pa., *Baseball* (in part)

Charles Edgar Randall, Assistant Editor, 'Journal of Forestry', *Forest Products* (in part)

Mahinder Singh Randhava, Subeditor, 'The Straits Times', Kuala Lumpur, *Malaysia; Singapore*

Vivian Foster Raven, Editor, 'Tobacco', *Tobacco*

Randolph Richard Rawlins, Journalist and Broadcaster, *Guyana; West Indies* (in part)

Joseph Lee Reid, Research Oceanographer, Scripps Institution of Oceanography, La Jolla, Calif., *Oceanography*

A. Daniel Reuwee, Director of Information, Future Farmers of America, *Youth Organizations* (in part)

Richard K. Richards, Professor of Pharmacology, Northwestern University Medical School, Chicago, *Drugs*

Wallace B. Riley, Computers Editor, 'Electronics', McGraw-Hill Publications, Inc., *Computers; Electronics*

David Jonathan Robinson, Economic Adviser, Petroleum Press Service, London, *Peru*

David Julien Robinson, Film Critic, 'The Financial Times', *Motion Pictures* (in part)

Leif J. Robinson, Associate Editor, 'Sky and Telescope' Sky Publishing Corp., *Astronomy*

Evelyn Gita Rose, Cookery Editor, 'Jewish Chronicle', and Home Economics Consultant, Broadcaster, and Food Historian, *Home Economics; Interior Decoration*

John Kerr Rose, Senior Specialist in Natural Resources and Conservation, Legislative Reference Service, Library of Congress, Washington, D.C., *Agriculture* (in part)

Robert L. Ross, Vice-President, Adela Investment Co., Washington, D.C., *Chile*

Philip Morton Rowe, Press Officer, British Man-Made Fibres Federation, Manchester, England, *Synthetics* (in part)

Nicholas Ruggieri, Assistant Public Affairs Adviser, U.S. Arms Control and Disarmament Agency, *Disarmament*

Al Salerno, Press Director, American Heart Association, Inc., *Medicine* (in part)

Carl Fredrik Sandelin, Foreign News Editor, Finnish News Agency, and President, Society of Swedish-Speaking Writers in Finland, *Finland*

Alex Sareyan, Executive Director, Mental Health Materials Center, *Mental Health*

Stephan E. Schattmann, Economist, London, *Germany* (in part)

Albert Schoenfield, Editor, 'Swimming World', *Swimming*

William Scholz, Director of Public Relations, American Hotel & Motel Association, *Hotels and Motels*

Byron T. Scott, Editor, 'Today's Health' Magazine, American Medical Association, *Medicine* (in part)

Mitchell R. Sharpe, Science Writer, *Space Exploration* (in part)

Harvey R. Sherman, Environmental Policy Division, Legislative Reference, Library of Congress, *Agriculture* (in part); *Food*

James R. Shields, Staff Writer, 'All Hands' Magazine, Bureau of Naval Personnel, *Armed Forces, United States* (in part)

Glenn B. Smedley, Governor, American Numismatic Association, and President, Society of Paper Money Collectors, *Coin Collecting*

John Jervis Smith, Research Officer, Economic Intelligence Department, Bank of London and South America Ltd., *Paraguay*

Raymond Daniel Smith, Publisher, 'Cats Magazine', *Pets* (in part)

J. Frederick Smithcors, Associate Editor, American Veterinary Publications, Inc., Santa Barbara, Calif., *Veterinary Medicine*

Kazimierz Maciej Smogorzewski, Founder and Editor, 'Free Europe', London, and Writer on Contemporary History, *Albania; Bulgaria; Hungary; Intelligence Operations; Mongolian People's Republic; Poland; Romania*

Frank Smothers, former Director of Publications, Council of State Governments, *State Governments, United States* (in part)

Leonard M. Snyder, Director, Interpretation Services, Young Men's Christian Association, *Youth Organizations* (in part)

Wallace Sokolsky, Associate Professor, History Department, Bronx Community College, the New School for Social Research, New York University, Division of Adult Education, *Africa*

Melanie F. Staerk, Editor, 'UNESCO Press', Swiss National Commission for UNESCO, *Switzerland*

Phyllis B. Steckler, Project Director, CCM Information Corp., *Publishing, Book*

Robert Stent, Economic and Political Research Officer, Bank of London and South America Ltd., London, *Costa Rica; Venezuela*

Douglas R. Stephenson, Manager, Information Services, Public Relations Department, Association of American Railroads, *Transportation* (in part)

Tom Stevenson, Garden Columnist, 'Baltimore News American', 'Washington Post', and 'Los Angeles Times', *Flowers and Gardens*

David Lloyd Streiner, Assistant Professor of Psychiatry, McMaster University, *Psychology*

Peter C. Stuart, Staff Correspondent, Washington, D.C., 'Christian Science Monitor', *Housing SPECIAL REPORT: Tenants on the Move*

John H. Stumpf, Special Projects Editor, Atomic Industrial Forum, Inc., *Nuclear Energy*

Zena Bailey Sutherland, Editor, 'Bulletin of the Center for Children's Books', University of Chicago, and Editor, Books for Young People, 'Saturday Review', *Literature, Children's*

Richard N. Swift, Professor of Politics, New York University, New York City, *United Nations*

Sol Taishoff, President, Editor, and Publisher, 'Broadcasting', *Television and Radio* (in part)

Harold Anthony Taylor, Air Transport Editor, 'Flight International', London, 1964–69, *Transportation* (in part)

Walter Terry, Dance Critic, 'Saturday Review', *Dance* (in part)

Adrien Therio, Professor of Lettres Françaises, University of Ottawa, *Literature, Canadian* (in part)

William Harford Thomas, Managing Editor, 'Manchester Guardian', *Great Britain and Northern Ireland, United Kingdom of*

Anthony Thompson, General Secretary, International Federation of Library Associations, *Libraries* (in part)

Norman Samuel Thompson, Professor of Business Education and Chairman, Department of Business Education, Eastern Washington State College, *Consumer Protection; Economy*

Lancelot Oliver Tingay, Lawn Tennis Correspondent, 'The Daily Telegraph', London, *Tennis*

Edward Townsend, Associate Editor of 'Business Week', *Labor Unions*

Melvin M. Tumin, Professor of Sociology and Anthropology, Princeton University, *Race Relations*

Govindan Unny, Special Correspondent for India, Nepal, and Ceylon, Agence France-Presse, *Burma; Nepal*

John R. Vosburgh, Chief, Branch of Features, Division of Information, National Park Service, U.S. Department of the Interior, *National Park Service*

David McCall Walsten, Senior Editor, 'Britannica Junior Encyclopaedia', *Insects and Pesticides; Ships and Shipping; Stocks and Bonds*

Percy Ainsworth Ward-Thomas, Golf Correspondent, 'Manchester Guardian', *Golf*

Anne R. Warner, Director, Public Relations Department, American Nurses' Association, *Nursing*

Basil Willey, Professor Emeritus of English Literature, Cambridge University, England, *Religion SPECIAL REPORT: The New English Bible*

Laurence Frederic Rushbrook Williams, C.B.E., Professor of Modern Indian History, Allahabad, India, 1914–19; Editor of 'Handbook to India, Pakistan, Burma, and Ceylon', *Afghanistan; Iran; Pakistan*

Peter Williams, Editor, 'Dance and Dancers', *Dance* (in part)

Trevor Williamson, Sports Subeditor, 'The Daily Telegraph', London, *Soccer*

Alan David Wilson, Assistant Editor, 'Sweden Now', *Sweden*

Philip Windsor, Reader in International Relations, London School of Economics and Political Science, University of London, *Germany SPECIAL REPORT: East Meets West*

Richard Worsnop, Writer, Editorial Research Reports, Washington, D.C., *Foreign Policy, United States; Liberia; Nixon, Richard M.; United States*

Almon R. Wright, retired Senior Historian, U.S. Department of State, *Panama*

Peter Frederick Yopes, Mining Engineer, Bureau of Mines, U.S. Department of the Interior, Washington D.C., *Mines and Mining*

Paul Ziemer, Night Chief Caption Writer, 'Chicago Today', *Congress, United States; Elections; Political Parties*

Arnold J. Zurcher, Professor of Comparative Politics, Graduate School of Arts and Sciences, New York University, *Europe*

Vietnam
Cambod
Laos

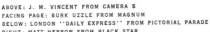

ABOVE: J. M. VINCENT FROM CAMERA 5
FACING PAGE: BURK UZZLE FROM MAGNUM
BELOW: LONDON ''DAILY EXPRESS'' FROM PICTORIAL PARADE
RIGHT: MATT HERRON FROM BLACK STAR

Compton's Pictured Highlights and Chronology of 1970

JANUARY

1 U.S. President Richard M. Nixon signs legislation creating the three-member Council on Environmental Quality.

Jordan announces that for the third time Israel has knocked out the vital East Ghor Canal on the east bank of the Jordan River.

2 Full-scale fighting resumes in South Vietnam after the expiration of two separate New Year cease-fires.

5 An increase from 7.5% to 8.5% in the interest rate ceiling on mortgages guaranteed by the U.S. government goes into effect.

8 The U.S. Army charges two more of its soldiers with premeditated murder in connection with the slaying of South Vietnamese civilians at My Lai 4 hamlet in the village of Song My in March 1968.

9 South Vietnam's President Nguyen Van Thieu says that it would be impossible to withdraw all U.S. combat troops from his country in 1970.

The government of France acknowledges that it will sell about 50 Mirage jet fighters to Libya.

11 The Kansas City Chiefs defeat the Minnesota Vikings 23–7 to win professional football's Super Bowl game.

12 Biafra surrenders to Nigeria, ending the 30-month-old civil war.

14 The U.S. Supreme Court rules that school integration in six Deep South states must take place not later than Feb. 1, 1970.

15 The Republic of Biafra officially ceases to exist when a formal surrender is signed in Lagos, Nigeria.

19 President Nixon nominates Judge G. Harrold Carswell of Florida to be an associate justice of the Supreme Court.

U.S. Vice-President Spiro T. Agnew returns to Washington, D.C., from a three-week tour of 11 Pacific and Asian countries.

20 The United States and Communist China resume formal ambassadorial talks in Warsaw, Poland, after a two-year suspension.

Albania announces the signing of a new trade and financial agreement with Communist China that will establish closer ties between the two nations.

22 An Israeli task force captures the Egyptian Shadwan Island at the entrance to the Gulf of Suez.

President Nixon, in his 1970 State-of-the-Union message, designates world peace (including a "just" settlement in Vietnam) as his major priority and commits his Administration to an attack on environmental pollution.

28 The U.S. House of Representatives fails by 52 votes to override President Nixon's veto of a $19.7-billion health and education appropriations bill.

New uniforms for the White House guard were introduced in January. Reaction to the uniforms, especially the hats, was essentially humorous, and the outfit was later modified.
UPI COMPIX

UPI COMPIX

An abandoned hospital in the Eastern Region of Nigeria, attended by relief workers, became a refuge for homeless, starving children at the end of the Nigerian civil war in January.

Oldrich Cernik, one of the leaders of Czechoslovakia's 1968 liberal reform movement, is replaced as premier by Lubomir Strougal, a conservative.

30 The United Nations (UN) Security Council, by a vote of 13–0, condemns South Africa's presence in South-West Africa (Namibia).

Lesotho's constitution is suspended and a state of emergency is declared by the prime minister, Chief Leabua Jonathan.

FEBRUARY

1 Israeli and Syrian tank and artillery units fight their heaviest battle since 1967, in the Golan Heights, Syria.

Pope Paul VI declares that celibacy of priests is so fundamental a principle of the Roman Catholic church that it cannot be questioned.

Communist China pledges support to the Arabs in their struggle against Israel.

Former President José Figueres Ferrer of Costa Rica is again elected president in national elections.

2 President Nixon submits to Congress his budget for the fiscal year beginning on July 1, 1970, estimating expenditures at $200.8 billion and revenue at $202.1 billion.

The U.S. Supreme Court approves, by a 7–0 vote, the merger of the Great Northern, Northern Pacific, and three of their subsidiaries.

3 Japan signs the nuclear nonproliferation treaty.

6 The European Economic Community (EEC), or Common Market, signs a trade agreement with Yugoslavia, the first commercial treaty between the EEC and an East European nation.

Students from the University of California at Santa Barbara burned a Bank of America branch office in nearby Isla Vista on February 25.

WIDE WORLD

Israeli jets sink a United Arab Republic (UAR) vessel in the Gulf of Suez after UAR frogmen sink an Israeli supply ship in the port of Elath, Israel.

7 Northern Ireland's two-day-old Public Order Act is defied by Roman Catholic groups charging that the act is aimed at suppressing their civil rights movement.

12 Israeli fighter-bombers attack a scrap-metal-processing plant in El Khanka, a suburb of Cairo, Egypt, killing 70 civilians.

14 Federal Judge Julius J. Hoffman sentences four defendants to lengthy prison terms for contempt of court in the trial of seven persons charged with conspiracy to incite a riot during the 1968 Democratic National Convention in Chicago.

17 Israeli jets bomb targets near Cairo, and Israel warns the UAR that there will be no letup in the attacks until the latter agrees to abide by the cease-fire of 1967.

18 An estimated 2,000 youths attack the U.S. Embassy in Manila, Philippines, with stones and fire bombs.

After nearly 40 hours of deliberation, a jury in the Chicago Conspiracy trial acquits the seven defendants of conspiring to incite a riot but convicts five of seeking to incite a riot through individual acts.

21 North Vietnamese troops capture the last Laotian government stronghold in the strategic Plain of Jars, Laos.

23 Prime Minister Forbes Burnham declares Guyana a cooperative republic, severing its ties to the British Crown.

26 The U.S. Marine Corps command in Saigon, South Vietnam, announces that five Marines have been charged with murdering 16 South Vietnamese women and children while on patrol south of Da Nang.

27 National Guardsmen patrol the area around the Santa Barbara campus of the University of California in the wake of three nights of student violence.

MARCH

2 Rhodesia's white minority government declares the country a racially segregated republic, formally dissolving its last ties with the British Crown.

4 Great Britain announces that it will return to West Germany a brigade of 4,500 troops, withdrawn as an economy measure in 1968.

The U.S. Department of Defense announces that it will either eliminate or reduce activities at 371 military bases by June 30, 1971.

5 The U.S. government moves to void the reelection of United Mine Workers of America (UMW) President W. A. Boyle and to require a new election under federal supervision.

A large group representing the "American Committee in Rome for Peace in Vietnam" staged a demonstration in March on the Spanish Steps in the center of the city, to protest the expansion of U.S. military involvement into Laos and Cambodia.

WIDE WORLD

PAOLO KOCH FROM BLACK STAR

The Swiss pavilion was one of the most dazzling buildings at Japan's Expo '70, which was opened to the public on March 15.

U.S. postal workers went on strike in March. In New York City the U.S. Army was brought in to handle the mail.

WIDE WORLD

FRANK LEONARDO FROM PICTORIAL PARADE

On Earth Day in April the black and white flag of death appeared on Fifth Avenue in New York City. The names and insignia of companies identified as polluters appear on the flag.

6 Sean M. Holly, a political secretary with the U.S. embassy in Guatemala, is kidnapped by a guerrilla group.

12 The U.S. Senate approves, by a vote of 64–17, legislation that would lower the voting age to 18 years in all elections.

Edgar J. Benson, Canada's finance minister, submits a budget for the fiscal year ending March 31, 1971, with estimated revenue at $13.15 billion and expenditures at $12.9 billion.

14 The Japan World Exposition, Expo '70, opens in Osaka.

16 The U.S. Department of State removes most of the barriers against travel to Communist China by U.S. citizens.

17 The U.S. Army accuses 14 officers, including Maj. Gen. Samuel W. Koster, superintendent of the U.S. Military Academy, of involvement in the suppression of information concerning the alleged massacre of civilians at My Lai.

The United States uses its veto for the first time in the UN Security Council and joins with Great Britain in rejecting an African-Asian resolution that would have condemned Britain for not forcibly overthrowing Premier Ian Smith's white minority government in Rhodesia.

18 Prince Norodom Sihanouk, while on a journey abroad, is overthrown as Cambodia's chief of state.

19 West Germany's Chancellor Willy Brandt and East Germany's Premier Willi Stoph hold a historic meeting in Erfurt, East Germany.

Postal workers in New York City go on strike to protest lack of Congressional action on pay legislation.

20 Newspapers in the UAR confirm the reported arrival of Soviet SAM-3's (surface-to-air missiles) and military personnel to operate them.

Joseph Honoré Gerald Fauteux is appointed chief justice of Canada.

23 President Nixon declares a state of national emergency and orders federal troops into New York City to help handle the mail.

24 A U.S. air attaché in the Dominican Republic is kidnapped by guerrillas who demand the release of 21 prisoners being held by the government.

26 The United States, Great Britain, France, and the Soviet Union meet in West Berlin in their first combined attempt in 11 years to ease some of the tensions over the divided city of Berlin.

27 Israel reports that its planes have shot down five UAR MiG-21 jets over the Suez Canal.

APRIL

1 The Cambodian government denounces all foreign incursions into its territory.

The first labor contract covering U.S. table-grape pickers is signed in Los Angeles.

President Nixon signs the bill outlawing cigarette commercials on radio and television effective Jan. 2, 1971.

2 An agreement on wage increases is reached by the U.S. government and seven national postal unions.

3 The official death toll is listed at 1,089 as western Turkey suffers its sixth straight day of earth tremors.

An additional 500 British troops are flown into Northern Ireland, raising the total there to 7,000.

5 The body of Count Karl von Spreti, West Germany's ambassador to Guatemala, is found, following his kidnapping by a Guatemalan Marxist group called the Rebel Armed Forces.

6 The U.S. Supreme Court rules, by a 5–3 vote, that a state can constitutionally limit the amount of welfare benefits payable to a family.

8 The U.S. Senate rejects, by a 51–45 vote, the nomination of Judge G. Harrold Carswell to be an associate justice of the Supreme Court.

The UAR claims that two Israeli jets bombed an elementary school at Bahr el Bakr, about 20 miles from the Suez Canal, killing 30 children.

9 The United States rejects Canada's claims to jurisdiction over extensive areas of Arctic waters.

11 Florida's Gov. Claude R. Kirk, Jr., is fined $10,000 a day by a federal district judge for disobeying court orders to desegregate the Manatee County public schools.

13 The U.S. spacecraft Apollo 13, which was successfully launched on April 11, is forced to abort its flight to the moon because of a serious oxygen leak.

President Nixon signs "with considerable reluctance" a bill authorizing the appropriation of $24.6 billion for education.

14 President Nixon names Adm. Thomas H. Moorer, the chief of naval operations, to succeed Gen. Earle G. Wheeler as chairman of the Joint Chiefs of Staff.

15 British Columbia becomes the first Canadian province to lower the age of legal majority from 21 to 19 years.

16 The United States and the Soviet Union reopen strategic arms limitation talks (SALT) in Vienna, Austria.

17 Apollo 13 makes a successful splashdown in the Pacific Ocean, 610 miles southeast of American Samoa.

20 President Nixon announces that he plans to withdraw 150,000 more U.S. troops from South Vietnam by spring of 1971.

22 Communities across the United States observe Earth Day as millions of Americans focus on environmental problems.

24 Communist China sends its first satellite into space.

The Gambia, Africa's smallest state, is proclaimed a republic within the Commonwealth of Nations.

30 In a nationwide address, President Nixon announces that he is sending U.S. combat troops into Cambodia to destroy Communist sanctuaries there.

MAY

1 A large allied task force, including 5,000 U.S. infantrymen, moves into Cambodia.

4 Four students are killed at Kent State University, at Kent, Ohio, when National Guardsmen fire into a group of antiwar demonstrators.

The U.S. Supreme Court rules, by a 7–1 vote, that

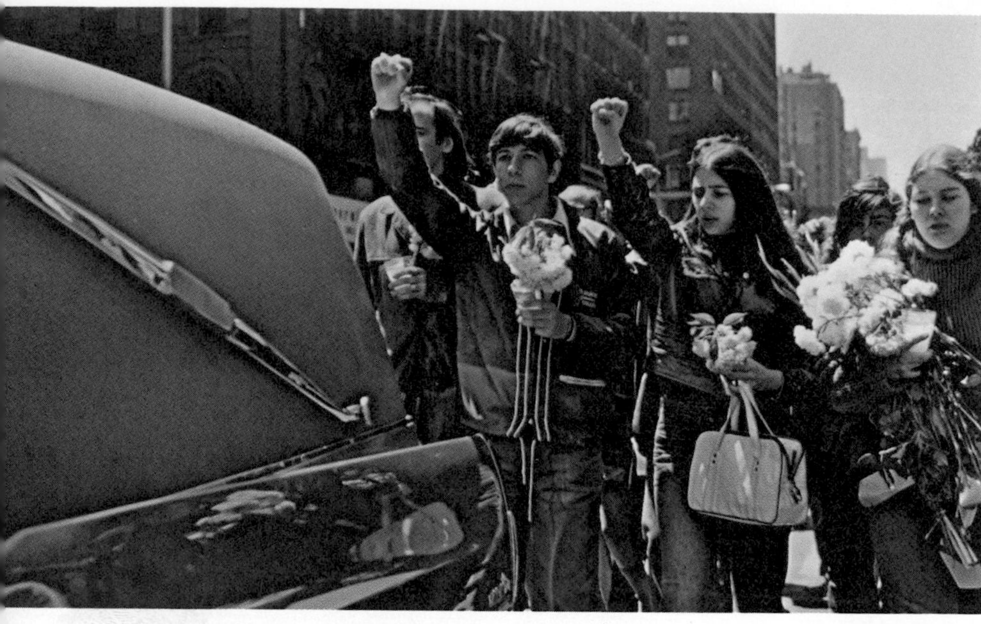

A young girl (below) grieves over the body of one of four students slain by the National Guard at Kent State University in May. Students (left) march in the funeral procession of one of the four.

LEFT: BURK UZZLE FROM MAGNUM
BELOW: JOHN P. FILO, © 1970 ''TARENTUM VALLEY DAILY NEWS''

laws exempting church property from taxation do not violate the U.S. Constitution's provision against state support of religion.

5 The third major assault by a joint force of U.S. and South Vietnamese troops begins against what are believed to be enemy base camps in northeastern Cambodia.

6 North Vietnamese and Viet Cong representatives call off the 66th plenary session of the Paris peace talks on Vietnam.

8 Construction workers break up student antiwar demonstrations on New York City's Wall Street.

9 Between 75,000 and 100,000 antiwar protesters, drawn mostly from U.S. campuses, demonstrate peaceably near the White House.

12 The U.S. Senate confirms, by a 94–0 vote, the nomination of Judge Harry A. Blackmun to be an associate justice of the U.S. Supreme Court.

Six black men are reported killed and 75 other persons wounded during a night of racial violence in Augusta, Ga.

14 Urho K. Kekkonen, president of Finland, appoints a caretaker government, thus ending six weeks of negotiations aimed at forming a cabinet.

15 Two black youths are shot and killed by police during a night of violence on the campus of Jackson State College, at Jackson, Miss.

16 France's President Pompidou calls for public calm after a wave of unexplained bomb and arson attacks in Paris and other parts of France.

18 In a sweeping attack, the Soviet Union charges Communist China with seeking the total domination of Asia, rejecting calls for concerted Communist action in Indochina, and creating an anti-Soviet, warlike atmosphere.

Communist China announces the cancellation of the May 20 session of U.S.-Chinese ambassadorial talks in Warsaw.

19 The UN Security Council approves, by a vote of 11–0, a resolution condemning Israel for its attack on Lebanon the week before.

Cuba's Premier Fidel Castro confirms that his country's massive drive to harvest a record 10-million-ton sugar crop will fall short by about one million tons.

22 Twelve persons are killed and 20 wounded, most of them children, when an Israeli school bus is ambushed by Arab guerrillas about 500 yards from the Lebanese border.

23 Portugal and Spain sign an agreement expanding the provisions of the Iberian pact, a friendship treaty, and extending it for ten years.

24 Communist China pledges to provide North Vietnam with more economic and military aid in 1970.

25 Prices on the New York Stock Exchange record their largest single-day decline since the assassination of President John F. Kennedy on Nov. 22, 1963.

27 Foreign ministers of Cambodia and South Vietnam sign documents in Saigon giving South Vietnam an extensive and open-end mandate for military activity in Cambodia.

31 Canada announces that the Canadian dollar, fixed at 92.5¢ to the U.S. dollar since 1962, will be allowed to float freely in the world exchange market.

A severe earthquake rocked Peru on May 31. At least 10,000 people died, and approximately one million were left homeless. Whole towns disappeared, and thousands of acres of farmland were flooded in the aftermath.

CATHERINE LE ROY FROM NANCY PALMER AGENCY

Edward Heath (right), a Conservative, was elected prime minister of Great Britain in June.

WIDE WORLD

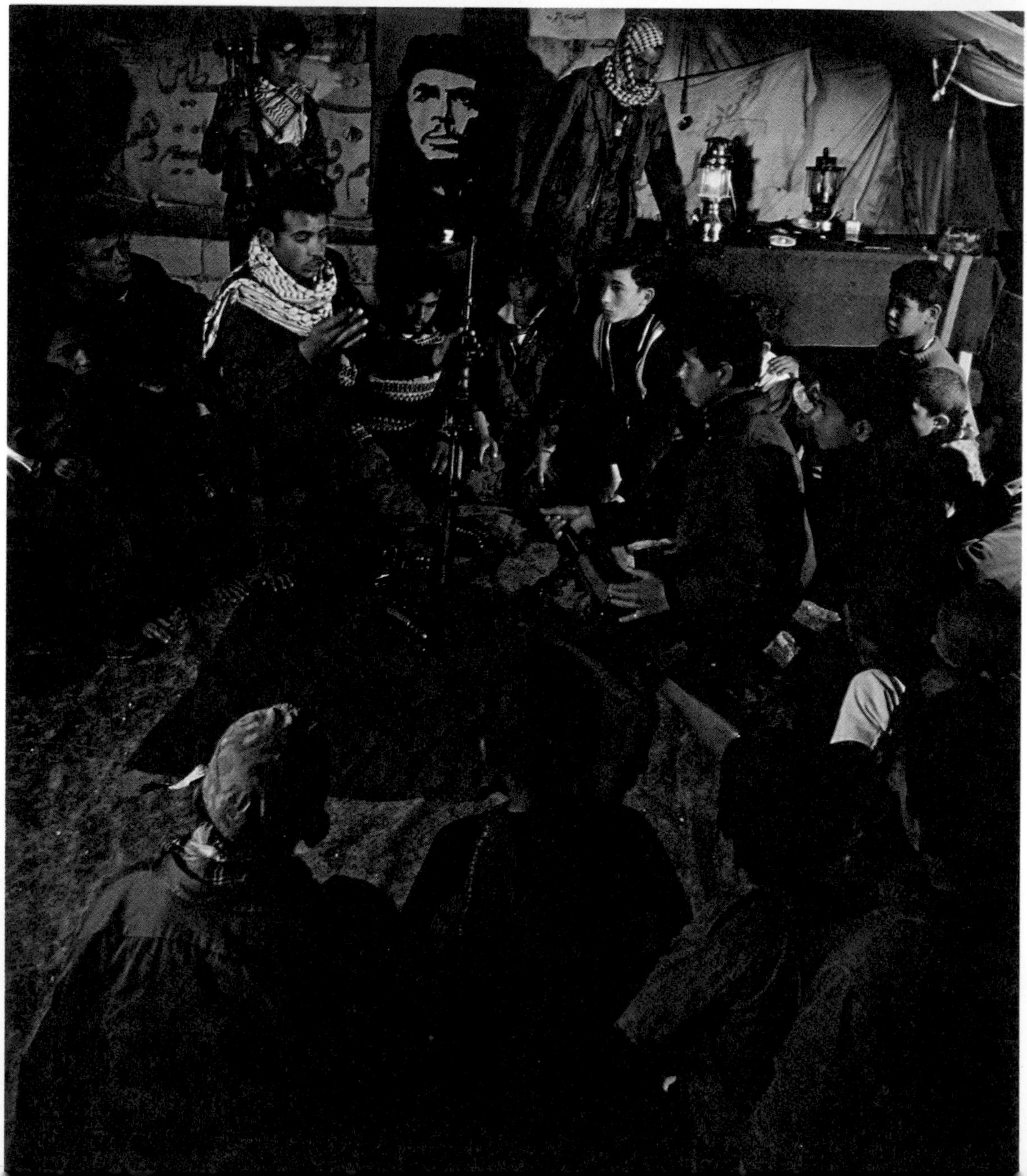

A Palestinian guerrilla (below) speaks to an enraptured audience of young boys.

PIERRE BOULAT, LIFE MAGAZINE © TIME INC.

JUNE

1 The U.S. Supreme Court rules, by a 5–2 vote, that federal judges may prohibit workers from striking if their collective bargaining contracts include no-strike clauses.

4 Tonga, in the South Pacific, is proclaimed an independent kingdom within the Commonwealth of Nations.

El Salvador and Honduras agree to the establishment of a demilitarized zone, 1.8 miles on either side of their border.

7 In a national referendum, an all-male Swiss electorate narrowly defeats a constitutional amendment that would have expelled 300,000 foreign workers from Switzerland.

A U.S. Senate subcommittee discloses that the United States has been paying Thailand $50 million a year to send a combat division to South Vietnam.

8 Argentina's President Juan Carlos Onganía is forced to resign by the commanders in chief of the army, navy, and air force.

10 Major Robert Perry, U.S. military attaché in Amman, Jordan, is shot to death by Palestinian commandos.

11 West Germany's ambassador to Brazil, Ehrenfried von Holleben, is kidnapped by terrorists in Rio de Janeiro.

16 Israeli forces strike deep into Syria to shell a military camp and blow up a highway bridge.

18 The Conservative party wins an upset victory in the British parliamentary elections, taking 330 of the 630 seats in the House of Commons.

Venezuela and Guyana agree to a 12-year moratorium on their border dispute.

19 Conservative leader Edward Heath takes office as Great Britain's prime minister.

The Soviet spacecraft Soyuz 9 returns to earth after a record-breaking 17-day flight.

21 Penn Central Transportation Co., the largest U.S. railroad, is granted authority to reorganize under the bankruptcy laws.

22 President Nixon signs a bill lowering the voting age to 18 years, but he asks for a prompt test of its constitutionality.

President José María Velasco Ibarra of Ecuador assumes dictatorial powers.

25 The Cambodian government orders every citizen between the ages of 18 and 60 to perform military duty or service of national interest.

26 Alexander Dubcek, the former liberal Czechoslovak Communist party first secretary, is expelled from party membership by the Central Committee.

29 The last U.S. ground combat unit in Cambodia withdraws to South Vietnam.

For two weeks in June, five women scientists lived in these quarters under the waters of Lameshur Bay in the Virgin Islands, as part of the Tektite 2 experiments in underwater research.

STAN WAYMAN, LIFE MAGAZINE © TIME INC.

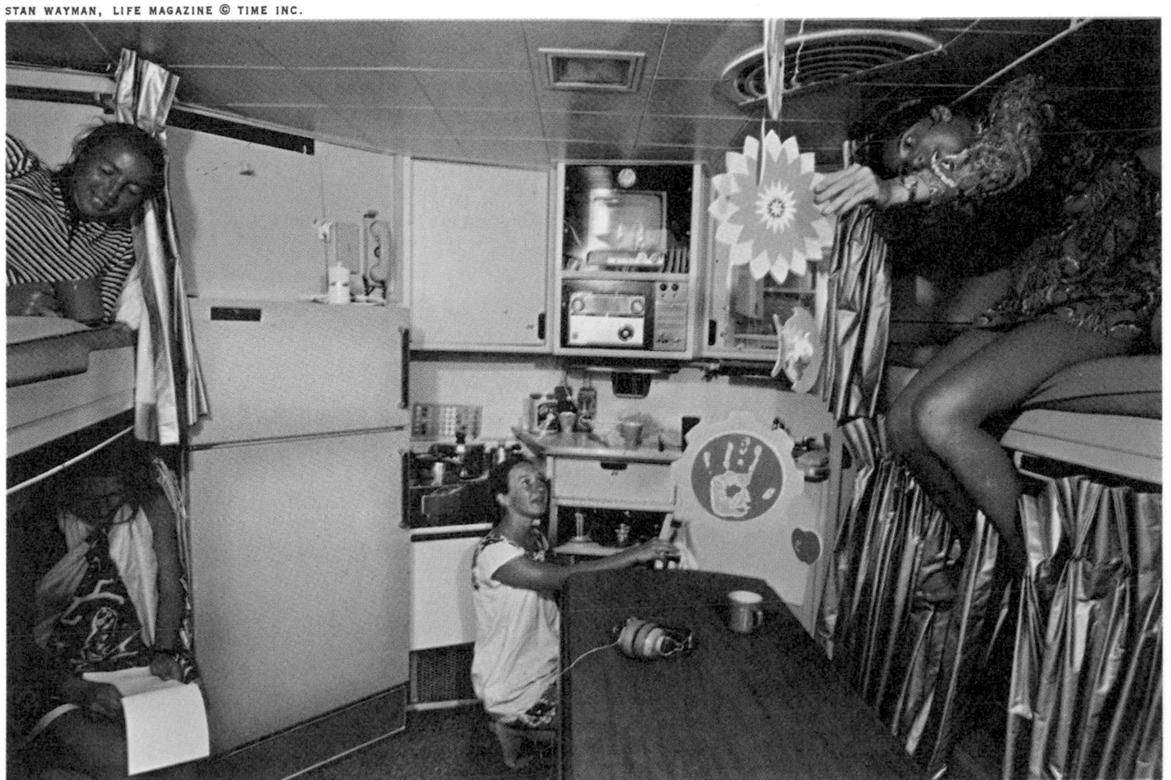

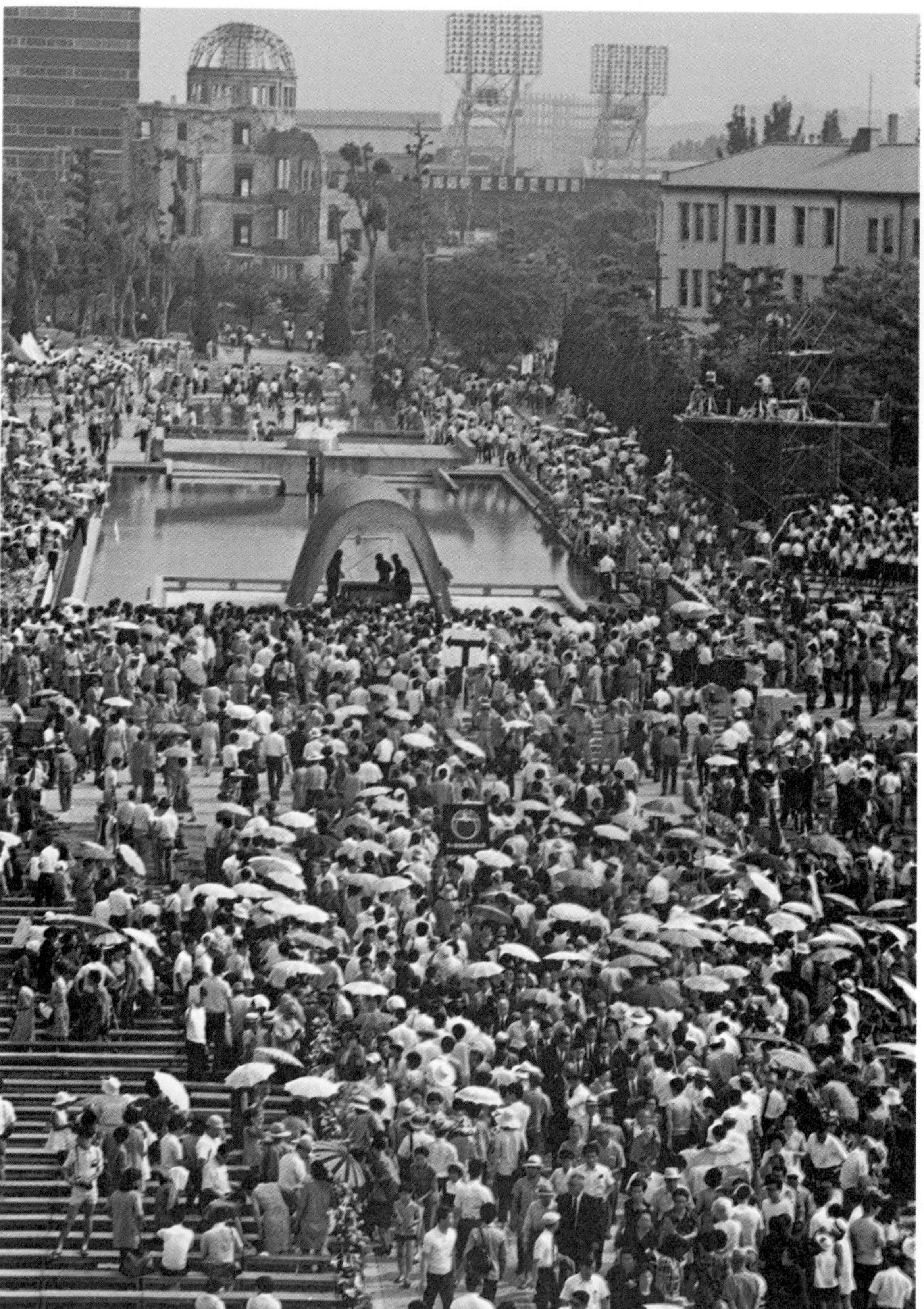

30 The U.S. Senate adopts, by a 58–37 vote, the long-debated Cooper-Church amendment barring the president from spending funds for future military operations in Cambodia without Congressional approval.

JULY

1 President Nixon announces the appointment of David K. E. Bruce to head the U.S. delegation at the Paris peace talks on Vietnam.

Colonel Carlos Araña Osorio is sworn in as president of Guatemala and pledges that he will end terrorism and undertake social reform.

2 Fire bombs hit four Latin American embassies in Washington, D.C.

The British Conservative party, in the traditional speech from the throne at the opening of Parliament, announces a program that gives top priority to tax cuts and labor-union reform.

3 Five persons are killed and about 50 wounded during rioting in Belfast, Northern Ireland.

5 The United States and South Vietnam make a joint plea to their allies in the Indochina war to provide urgent assistance to Cambodia.

Luis Echeverría Alvarez is elected president of Mexico in national elections.

6 Israel's chief of staff, Maj. Gen. Haim Bar-Lev, says that Israeli planes have engaged in intensive combat involving missile sites manned by Soviet personnel.

7 President Nixon invokes emergency powers to halt a strike by railway firemen and their union allies against three of the largest U.S. railroads.

12 Police in Montreal, Que., defuse a 150-pound dynamite bomb set to explode outside the head office of the Bank of Montreal.

14 Finland's political crisis ends with the formation of a new cabinet by Prime Minister Ahti Karjalainen of the Center party.

15 The Supreme Soviet, the Soviet Union's legislative body, reappoints Premier Aleksei N. Kosygin and President Nikolai V. Podgorny, keeping intact the country's collective leadership.

16 A state of emergency is declared in Great Britain as a nationwide dock strike virtually paralyzes the movement of goods through its ports.

21 The South Vietnamese government announces that it has discontinued the use of "tiger cages" at Con Son prison pending improvements.

The Nixon Administration announces that it will present to Congress a new explosives-control bill to combat the sharp rise in nationwide bombings.

23 The government of Northern Ireland bans public parades for six months in an effort to reduce tensions.

24 The U.S. Department of Defense announces that it will withdraw about 6,000 military personnel from the Philippines by July 1, 1971.

26 West Germany's Foreign Minister Walter Scheel arrives in Moscow for negotiations on a West German-Soviet treaty renouncing the use of force in settling disputes.

28 The U.S. government announces a deficit of $2.9 billion in the federal budget for the fiscal year that ended on June 30, 1970.

31 Israel's cabinet decides, by a 17–6 vote, to accept the U.S. formula for a temporary cease-fire and the opening of peace talks with the UAR.

A memorial service (facing page) was held at the Hiroshima Peace Memorial in Japan on August 6, the 25th anniversary of the atomic bomb attack on Hiroshima.

WIDE WORLD

A supporter of Salvador Allende carries his picture on a placard (right). Allende, a Marxist, was elected by popular vote as the president of Chile in September.

FREDERIC OHRINGER FROM NANCY PALMER AGENCY

AUGUST

2 A Pan American World Airways 747 jet, hijacked to Cuba, is met by Premier Castro on its arrival in Havana.

France explodes a nuclear device at its testing site in the South Pacific.

3 The 11th annual conference of Canada's provincial premiers meets aboard a cruiser on Manitoba's Lake Winnipeg.

4 President Nixon declares the Corpus Christi, Tex., region a disaster area after it is severely damaged by Hurricane Celia.

6 The United States and Spain sign an agreement in Washington, D.C., providing for the continuing U.S. use of military bases in Spain.

Italy's new cabinet, headed by President Emilio Colombo, is sworn in.

The U.S. Department of Defense announces that draft calls for the last four months of 1970 will total 39,000, to make the lowest yearly total since 1964.

7 A 90-day cease-fire goes into effect on the Israeli-Egyptian border along the Suez Canal.

Misael Pastrana Borrero is sworn in as president of Colombia.

10 President Nixon signs a bill extending unemployment insurance coverage to an additional 4.7 million workers.

12 Iraq and Syria reaffirm their opposition to UAR efforts to seek a peaceful solution of the Middle East crisis.

The Soviet Union and West Germany sign a treaty in Moscow renouncing the use of force.

13 The U.S. House of Representatives overrides President Nixon's veto of an education appropriations bill but sustains his veto of an appropriations bill for housing, space, and other programs.

14 U.S. television networks are ordered by the Federal Communications Commission (FCC) to provide prime viewing time for the presentation of views on the Indochina war that run contrary to those of President Nixon.

Yugoslavia and the Vatican announce the resumption of diplomatic relations after nearly 18 years.

15 Ceremonies in Japan mark the 25th anniversary of that country's surrender to the Allied powers in World War II.

16 Legal maneuvering collapses in Washington, D.C., after a three-day effort to stop the U.S. Army from sinking 418 concrete vaults of deadly nerve gas into the Atlantic Ocean.

17 The Lebanese Chamber of Deputies elects Suleiman Franjieh to succeed Charles Hélou as president of Lebanon.

Israel's Foreign Minister Abba Eban charges that the UAR and the Soviet Union are continuing to construct missile sites close to the Suez Canal.

18 The U.S. Senate overrides, by a 77–16 vote, President Nixon's veto of the $4.4-billion education appropriations bill, completing enactment of the measure.

19 The United States and Cambodia conclude a military assistance agreement in Phnom Penh, Cambodia.

23 Israel names Foreign Minister Eban as its chief delegate to proposed peace talks on the Middle East.

28 The U.S. Department of Agriculture announces further curbs on the use of DDT.

31 Edward Akufo-Addo is elected president of Ghana by the National Assembly and 24 tribal chiefs.

SEPTEMBER

1 King Hussein I of Jordan escapes an assassination attempt near Amman.

The U.S. Senate defeats, by a 55–39 vote, an amendment to withdraw all U.S. soldiers from Indochina by the end of 1971.

2 Two of the six remaining U.S. lunar landings are canceled by the National Aeronautics and Space Administration in an economy move.

3 Xuan Thuy, North Vietnam's chief negotiator at the Paris peace talks, ends his nine-month boycott of the talks.

4 The Canadian government and postal union negotiators sign a 30-month settlement to end the year-long postal dispute.

5 The UN Security Council adopts, by a 14–0 vote, a resolution demanding complete and immediate withdrawal of Israeli forces from Lebanon.

6 Three jets bound for New York City with more than 400 passengers aboard are hijacked over Europe by members of an Arab guerrilla group; a fourth hijacking attempt fails.

8 International efforts are launched to seek the release of airline passengers and crews held as hostages in Jordan by Arab guerrillas.

9 Arab guerrillas hijack a British commercial jet with 117 aboard and land it in the desert near Amman.

11 President Nixon orders a contingent of federal armed guards to begin flying immediately on domestic and overseas flights of U.S. airlines.

12 Palestinian guerrillas blow up three hijacked airliners in the Jordanian desert, after removing the remaining hostages.

17 Jordanian troops fight Palestinian guerrillas in Amman and in other areas of northern Jordan.

19 Fighting continues in northern Jordan after Palestinian guerrillas reject a call for a cease-fire.

20 The Soviet Union announces that its unmanned spacecraft Luna 16 has made a soft landing on a relatively unexplored area of the moon.

21 President Nixon names Lieut. Gen. Benjamin O. Davis, Jr. (ret.), to head the Administration's new program to deter airline hijackers.

Several major U.S. banks reduce the prime interest rate from 8% to 7.5%.

Gamal Abdel Nasser, president of the United Arab Republic, died in September. His funeral was attended by hundreds of thousands of Arabs demonstrably stricken by the loss.

GORDON CLARK FROM LIAISON AGENCY

25 King Hussein's government and the Arab guerrilla leadership agree on a cease-fire in Jordan.

26 The President's Commission on Campus Unrest issues a report warning of an unparalleled crisis on U.S. college campuses.

28 The death of the UAR's President Gamal Abdel Nasser sends the Arab world into deep mourning; Anwar-el-Sadat is named acting president.

29 Australia's Prime Minister John G. Gorton survives, by a 56–51 vote, a censure motion brought against him in the House of Representatives.

OCTOBER

1 A truce agreement to restore peace in northern Jordan is signed in Ramtha by Jordanian army officers and Arab guerrilla representatives.

2 India's Prime Minister Indira Gandhi suspends the government of Uttar Pradesh.

5 French Canadian separatists kidnap James R. Cross, a British diplomat, in Montreal.

7 Leftist Gen. Juan José Torres Gonzales declares himself president of Bolivia in a countercoup that ousts Gen. Rogélio Miranda, Bolivia's army chief of staff, who seized power on October 6 from President Alfredo Ovando Candía.

Communist China announces its agreement to provide aid to North Vietnam in 1971.

10 Fiji, in the South Pacific, becomes an independent nation within the Commonwealth of Nations.

Pierre Laporte, Quebec's minister of labor and immigration, is kidnapped from his home by French Canadian terrorists.

12 The U.S. Senate passes and clears for the president a controversial bill to curb racketeering and terrorist bombings.

President Nixon vetoes a bill that would have limited television and radio spending in political campaigns, beginning with the 1972 presidential election.

13 Fiji becomes the 127th member of the UN.

Canada and Communist China establish diplomatic relations; Canada breaks off relations with Nationalist China.

14 The UN opens its 25th-anniversary celebration at its headquarters in New York City.

Communist China resumes its nuclear testing program with an explosion in the atmosphere.

15 The Baltimore Orioles defeat the Cincinnati Reds 9–3 in the fifth game, to win the 1970 World Series.

16 Canada's Prime Minister Pierre Elliott Trudeau imposes emergency wartime regulations to suppress what he describes as an insurrection by Quebec terrorists.

17 Anwar el-Sadat is sworn in as president of the UAR.

18 The body of Pierre Laporte is found; he was presumably murdered by Quebec terrorists.

General Charles de Gaulle died in November at Colombey-les-Deux-Églises, France. Young men of the village (below) carry his coffin to his grave after the simple funeral he requested. World leaders flocked to Notre Dame Cathedral (facing page) in Paris for memorial services for France's ex-president.

DOMINIQUE BERRETTY FROM BLACK STAR

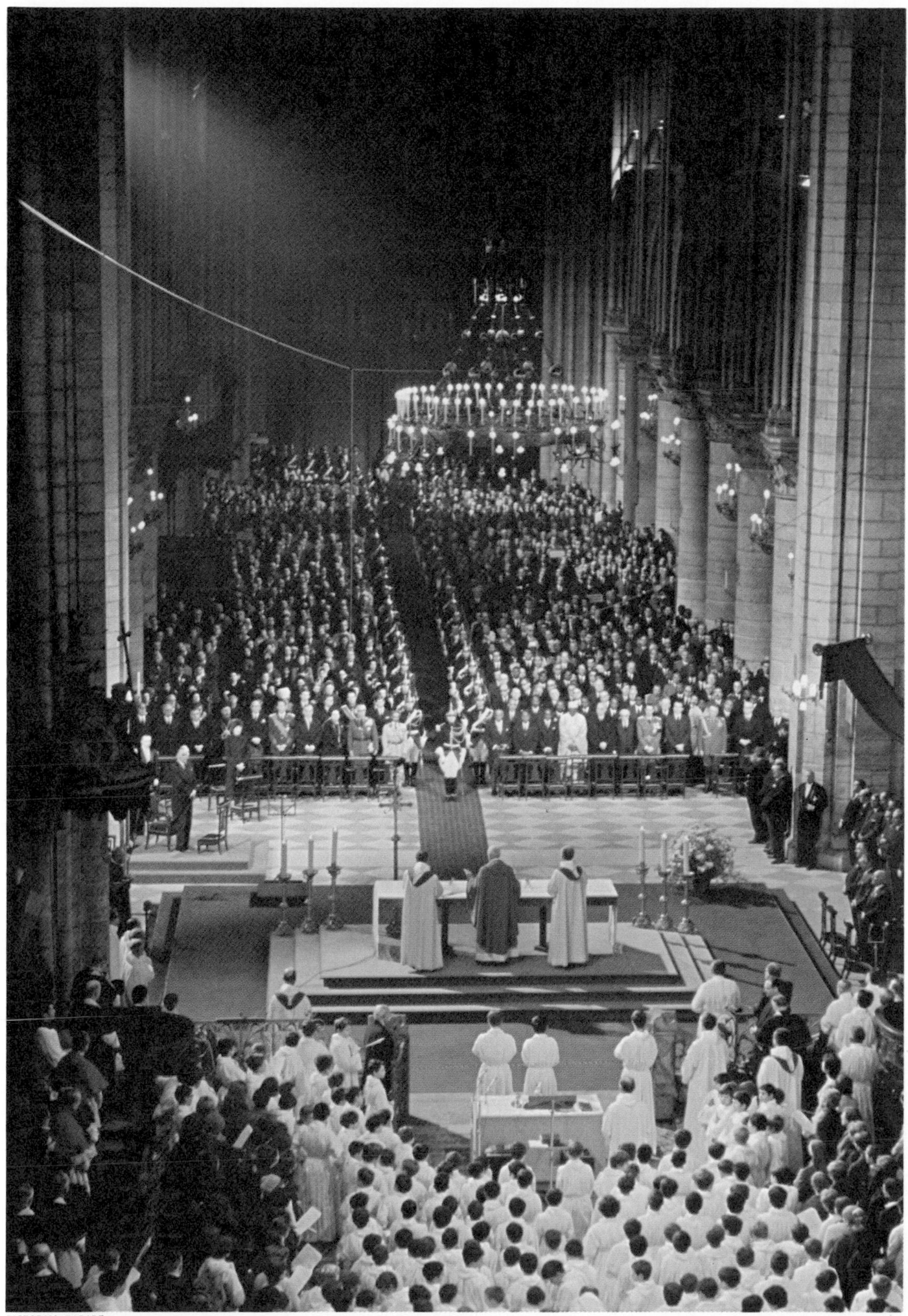

PICTORIAL PARADE

19 Canada's House of Commons approves, by a 190–16 vote, the proclamation by Prime Minister Trudeau invoking wartime measures.

21 The Nobel peace prize for 1970 is awarded to Norman E. Borlaug of the United States.

24 Marxist leader Salvador Allende is elected president of Chile by the national congress.

President Nixon and Japan's Premier Eisaku Sato agree on the resumption of U.S.-Japanese textile negotiations.

26 Paul A. Samuelson of the United States is awarded the 1970 Alfred Nobel memorial prize in economics.

27 The Canadian government announces the sale of 98 million bushels of wheat to Communist China.

28 King Hussein of Jordan appoints a new cabinet under Prime Minister Wasfi el-Tal.

29 It is revealed that the United States and the Soviet Union signed an agreement to develop joint rendezvous and docking systems for space vehicles.

NOVEMBER

2 Strategic arms limitation talks between the United States and the Soviet Union resume in Helsinki, Finland.

3 The Democratic party retains control of the Senate and the House of Representatives and wins key governorships in U.S. elections.

4 The UN General Assembly adopts, by a 57–16 vote, a UAR-backed resolution calling for a three-month extension of the Middle East cease-fire and for the unconditional resumption of Arab-Israeli peace talks.

6 Two bombs explode in the central bus station in Tel Aviv, Israel, killing one person and wounding 24.

7 The Soviet Union marks the 53d anniversary of the Bolshevist Revolution with a display of military equipment and anti-U.S. rhetoric in Moscow's Red Square.

9 The U.S. Supreme Court, in a 6–3 ruling, refuses to hear a suit by the Commonwealth of Massachusetts challenging the constitutionality of the Vietnam war.

11 The UAW and GM agree on tentative terms designed to end the union's eight-week-old strike.

12 Chile's new Marxist government reestablishes diplomatic relations with Cuba.

Memorial services in Paris for France's former President Charles de Gaulle, who died on November 9, are attended by scores of dignitaries, including U.S. President Nixon.

13 The Guatemalan government imposes a state of siege to halt a new wave of terrorist violence.

The left-wing Syrian government is seized by rightist army leaders in a bloodless coup d'etat.

17 The Soviet Union announces that it has landed a self-propelled eight-wheel vehicle, Luna 17, on the moon.

19 Syria's defense minister, Lieut. Gen. Hafez al-Assad, becomes premier of Syria.

In November East Pakistan was struck by a massive and deadly cyclone storm and tidal waves, which swept through the islands and the coastal areas. Communications were knocked out, and it was several weeks before the world knew how many hundreds of thousands of people perished.

GAMMA FROM PHOTOREPORTERS

RAY CRANBOURNE FROM BLACK STAR

Pope Paul VI addresses students in Manila, Philippines, on an Asian tour in December. Though an attempt was made on his life earlier at the Manila airport, he ignored the incident.

20 Communist China wins simple-majority support but fails to receive the required two-thirds vote in its attempt to gain a seat in the UN.

UAW President Leonard Woodcock announces that his union's members have ratified the new three-year contract with GM.

22 President Sékou Touré of Guinea charges that Portuguese forces have invaded his nation.

23 The U.S. Senate fails to override President Nixon's veto of the bill to limit spending for television and radio time in political campaigns.

The United States and Mexico sign a treaty ending border disputes between the two countries.

25 President Nixon dismisses Secretary of the Interior Walter J. Hickel and announces his intention to nominate Representative Rogers C. B. Morton (R, Md.) to the post.

30 The Bureau of the Census reports that the 1970 U.S. census has counted 204,765,770 persons, 24 million more than in 1960.

DECEMBER

1 President Giuseppe Saragat of Italy signs legislation legalizing divorce.

Eugen Beihl, West Germany's consul in San Sebastián, Spain, is kidnapped by Basque separatists.

3 British diplomat James Cross is freed unharmed by Quebec terrorists after his kidnappers are flown to exile in Cuba.

7 Poland and West Germany sign a treaty recognizing Poland's post-World War II acquisition of former German territory.

Giovanni Enrico Bucher, Switzerland's ambassador to Brazil, is kidnapped in Rio de Janeiro.

8 The UN Security Council votes to condemn Portugal for "invasion" of Guinea.

10 The U.S. Congress passes legislation banning a nationwide railroad strike; railroad unions strike for 18 hours before backing down.

11 President Nixon appoints Representative George Bush (R, Tex.) to succeed Charles W. Yost as U.S. ambassador to the UN.

14 Polish workers, protesting the announcement of substantial increases in food prices, riot in Danzig and other Baltic coast cities.

15 The Supreme Court in India rules that a presidential order abolishing royal privileges is unconstitutional.

17 The U.S. Department of Defense issues new antidiscrimination directives following the release of a report of unrest among black troops stationed in West Germany.

19 Guinea's President Touré charges that Portuguese troops are massed at his nation's border and calls for the UN to safeguard Guinea's independence.

Paik Too Chin is named by South Korea's President Park Chung-hee to replace Chung Il Kwon as prime minister.

20 Poland's Communist Party First Secretary Wladyslaw Gomulka and other key members of his 14-year regime resign; Edward Gierek is named first secretary.

24 A Leningrad court sentences to death two Jews charged with planning to hijack a Soviet airliner and gives prison terms to the nine other defendants.

30 Spain's chief of state, Generalissimo Francisco Franco, commutes to 30-year prison terms the death sentences of six Basque separatists found guilty of terrorist acts.

31 A Soviet court commutes the death sentences of two Soviet Jews and reduces the prison terms of nine others charged with planning a plane hijacking.

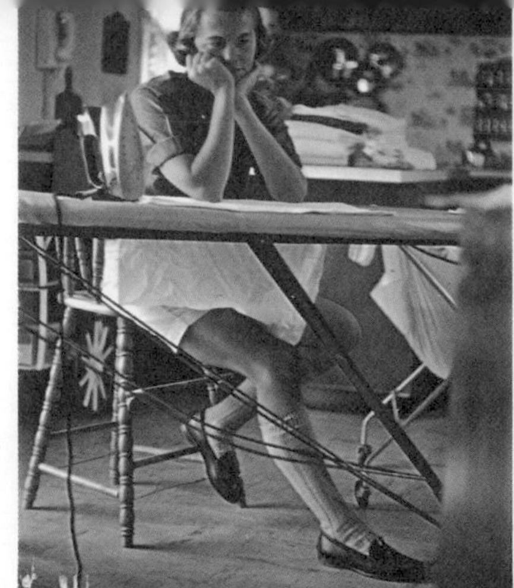

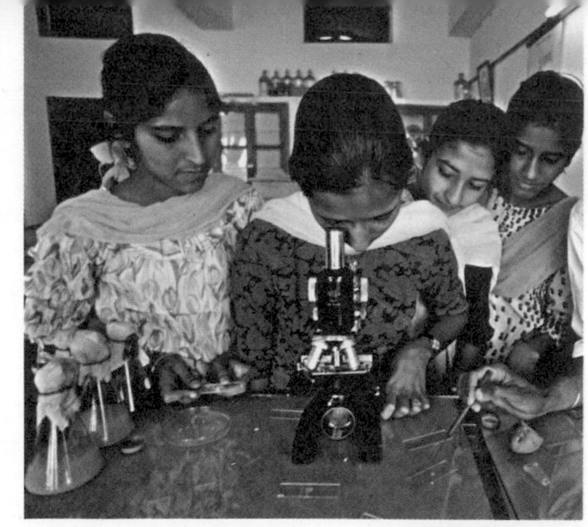

EQUAL JOBS
EDUCATION

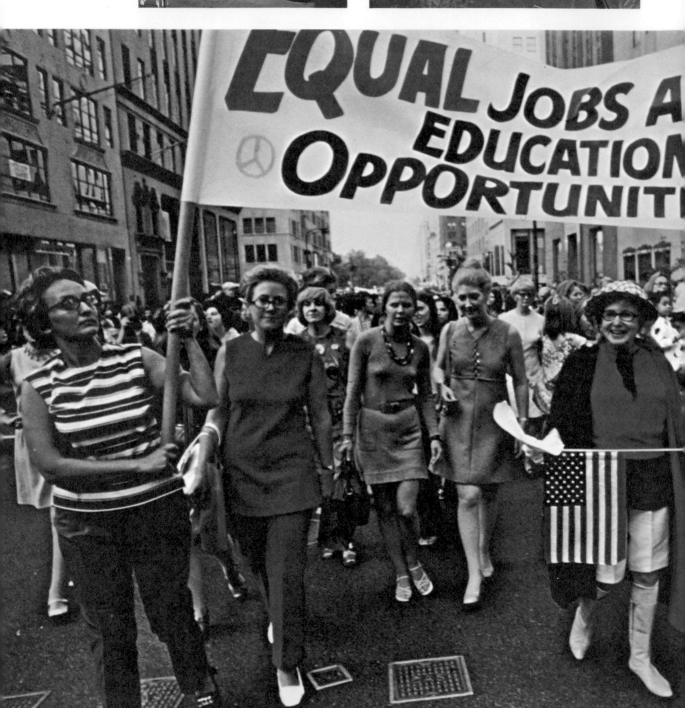

Women in Society:

the Search for "Personhood"

by Jacqueline Wexler

President, Hunter College, City University of New York

A noted college educator, Jacqueline Grennan Wexler, formerly Sister Jacqueline of the Sisters of Loretto, is an outstanding example of a woman who has consistently sought "growth, change, and revolutionary challenge" as her chosen life-style. As president of Webster College, at St. Louis, Mo., she was catapulted to national attention in the mid-1960's when she transformed the small Roman Catholic girls' school into an influential, innovative center of learning. She came to public notice again in 1967 as she successfully sought permission from the Vatican to secularize the school and at the same time to be released from her vows as a nun. Now married to Paul J. Wexler, a New York City recording company executive and a Jewish widower with two college-age children, she is president of Hunter College, part of the City University of New York.

In the following article, Mrs. Wexler examines the "women's liberation movement" and its objectives and offers her view of what steps might be taken to "free" women and to allow them a wider range of personal life-styles.

TOP LEFT: WAYNE MILLER FROM MAGNUM
TOP RIGHT: MARC & EVELYNE BERNHEIM FROM RAPHO GUILLUMETTE
LEFT: LESLIE LEON FROM KEYSTONE

I have long been convinced that the essential freedom being sought, demanded, and battled for by every individual and every group—including the "women's liberation movement"—is for "personhood"—the right to be a person capable of responding and relating to all other persons in honest interaction. I am a person who is a woman, a Roman Catholic, a citizen of the United States, a native Midwesterner, a wife, an adoptive mother, a professional educator. Each of these qualities and many others are innately or environmentally part of my personhood, but I am more than any one of them. Indeed, I believe it is accurate here to say that the whole is greater than the sum of its parts. However, *unless* I am convinced that each quality of my personhood is beautiful in my own eyes, and at least potentially beautiful in the eyes of those with whom I interrelate, my personhood is in jeopardy.

Of course, an obvious trap in such a thesis is that all things are beautiful *in their own place.* We place objects where we want them—where for short or long periods they please us. But objects have no power to share in a mutual relationship. To the degree that elitist power blocs have placed women, blacks, religious and ethnic groups, and the poor to suit their needs and their desires as they perceived them, these groups inevitably responded by asserting their individual dignity, their individual heritage, their individual right to share in determining their own destiny in a world of peers. Any group that has perceived the essential indignity of a lifelong role of saying "Yes, boss" fights for liberation from the world of the bosses and the bossed.

The Pitfall of "Chauvinism"

The basic irony of the fight for liberation is that it almost inevitably causes the liberating elements to look like mirror images of the very authoritarian boorishness they so properly resent. The more militant in the quest for freedom and the search for personhood for women talk and write passionately and often stridently about *male* chauvinism. In their own excessive and blind patriotism to a new cause they themselves are at times perceived by their sisters as 20th-century versions of the much-ridiculed Nicolas Chauvin.

A major editorial in *The New York Times,* dealing with the Aug. 26, 1970, mass demonstration commemorating the 50th anniversary of women's suffrage in the United States, drew a really important potential comparison. Lauding the achievements of the suffragettes of a half century ago, the editorial called attention to the fact that the descendants and beneficiaries of

JOHN ROBATON FROM CAMERA 5

JOHN LAUNOIS FROM BLACK STAR

these prime movers did not become a generation of carbon copies of the prototypes in style.

Thus I find it important to try to separate the aims and causes of this phase of the women's lib movement from the personal styles of some of its leaders. The person who has been most wounded by an oppressor is most likely to summon the energy to fight back if he or she has not already been destroyed by the oppression. But the life-style we are seeking, it seems to me, must transcend the fighting and the fighting back. I am not really free as an adult to respond to parents, husband, colleagues, or authority figures until I no longer need be preoccupied with rejection of their dominance over me. The degree to which protesters and heretics are so often possessed by that which they protest, almost maniacally preoccupied with those they are bent to reject, has always concerned me as a societal and personal pitfall. Each of us is in some way an integration of what we have consciously and unconsciously assimilated from our past and likewise attempted to reject and redress. If the longer-range evolutionary pattern succeeds in compensating for our personal wounds without in another way distorting the freedom of choice for coming generations, women will be genuinely liberated. Then will they be free to espouse an expanding set of personal choices, including the oldest patterns of wife and mother roles and decisions about career possibilities formerly limited to men as well as in areas that the human race has not yet even envisioned.

Wanted: an Honest Range of Choices

Freedom of choice, freedom for the individual to choose within the limits and capacities of his or her own talents and temperament, is the really critical issue. If life categorically closes out to us any potential opportunity because of one of the qualities of our identity, our identity is threatened from without and we are in danger of threatening our own identity, our own personal wholeness, by our resulting preoccupation with that particular quality of our personhood. To the extent that any well-meaning liberation movement restricts this range of freedom by trying to push us all into a mold that may be necessary for one person's freedom but not for another's, the movement is caught in the age-old zealotry that has beset mankind through all of history.

If Betty Friedan, Kate Millett, and Portnoy's mother had all had an honest range of choices, including the psychic freedom to choose without needing the majority of other women to make the same or a similar choice, Millett's 'Sexual Politics' and Philip Roth's 'Portnoy's Complaint'

JOHN LAUNOIS FROM BLACK STAR

The severity of Amish life is accepted by Amish women (right). Many women, however, feel that society has made traditional "women's roles" such as homemaking (far left) and child care (left) restrictive and tedious. Yet there are few other available roles for most women.

would have lacked the subject matter that made them both best sellers. A September 1970 issue of *Look* magazine carried a cover article entitled "The Motherhood Myth." The author's concluding thesis—like my own—is a call for more alternatives for women, meaning, she says, "more selective, better, happier motherhood—and childhood and husbandhood (or manhood) and peoplehood." But the concluding cry for alternatives has little tonal empathy with the total article, which describes women of the 1940's and 1950's in totally judgmental and derogatory terms. "Like heavy-bellied ostriches," Miss Betty Rollin describes them, "they grounded their heads in the sands of motherhood." She later maintains that women (other women, of course) feel they have little else to give anyone other than babies and that producing babies is much easier and faster than producing a painting!

"Personal choice," to many women, includes the right not to have children.

ROBISON FROM BETHEL AGENCY

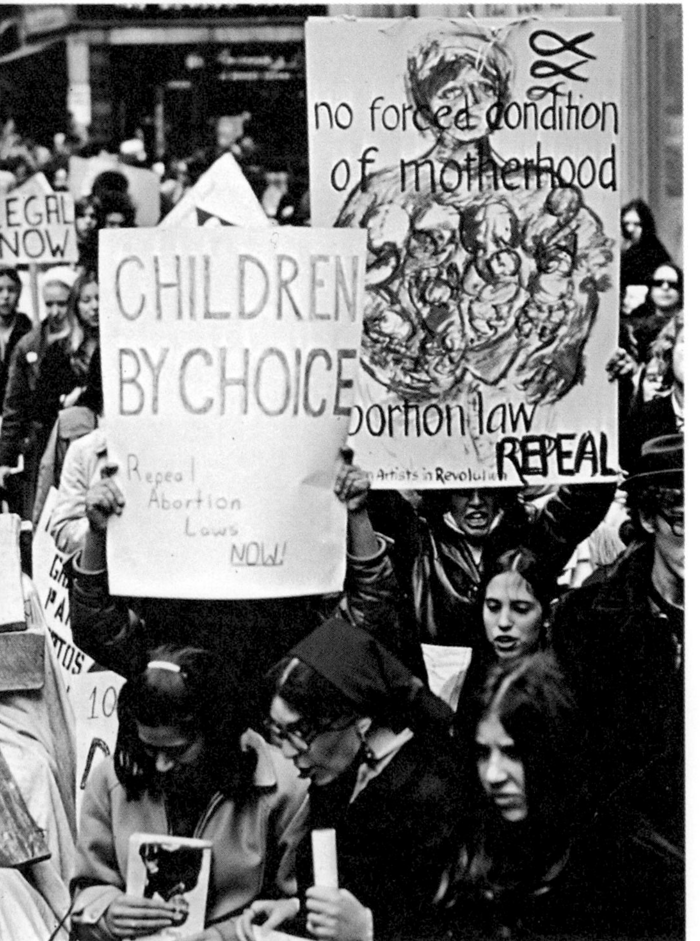

Without placing value judgments on the personal choices of other women within a widening range of opportunities, let us try to examine some of the permissive steps that must continue to be taken in order to allow individual women a wider range of personal choices. As I see them, four such key areas might be:

—expanded opportunity for employment in a wide range of time-commitment patterns;
—expanded opportunity for education, again in a wide range of time-commitment patterns;
—expanded opportunity for child care with a full choice of professional centers, cooperatives, and semicooperatives, and once again, a wide range of time-commitment patterns;
—major innovation in urban planning for city living with a full range of economically feasible unit sizes and effective rapid transit.

I am proposing what I fear many radical feminists will view as regressive: a refocusing on the unique aspects of a woman's role and self-concept as it exists at this moment without necessarily determining the biological or cultural causes that have produced the present situation. Only if the mass of women in our society can *progressively* test out the expansion of their own personal roles without necessarily uprooting their own personal and cultural histories will they, I believe, be able to explore the opportunities available to them and to use their political and social suasion to expand the possibilities still further for themselves and for their sisters.

Expanded Opportunities for Employment

The demand on the part of the liberationists for equal pay for equal work is a sound one yet to be realized in many professional areas. In my own case, there is parity of salary for college presidents and for professors at comparable levels within the City University of New York. Collective bargaining for teachers and professors makes judgment of merit performances difficult indeed; on the other hand, it insures against categorical wage discrimination by mandating a universal scale within the established formulas. Let me suggest, however, that a militant position on equal pay for equal work as the priority objective at this time may well put the concept of equal work in such focus that we close the op-

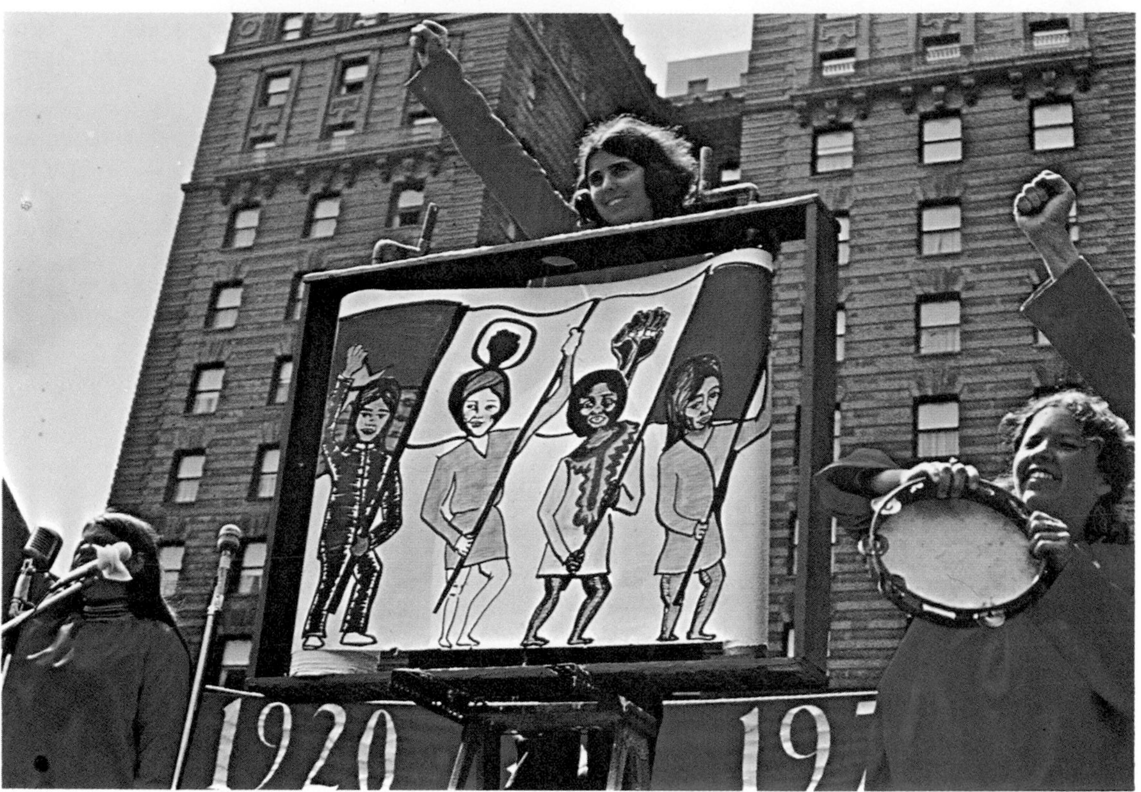

JOY LOCKE

These demonstrators in San Francisco, Calif., showed their support of women's liberation as an international and multiracial movement. Women's liberation groups around the world became increasingly militant in 1970.

portunity door to masses of women because they cannot espouse that degree of opportunity.

I have long believed, for example, that our elementary and secondary schools would benefit immeasurably if they encouraged many teachers to be full-time staff for less than full-week schedules rather than part-time staff on ostensibly full contracts. Many bright, educated, talented women would give fully of themselves on half-time or one-third-time appointments in these schools even while they are choosing to share themselves fully with their families within the time needs of that personal choice. Within our present school organizations, we force teachers into one time-commitment mold and all too often unduly encourage women to enter the teaching field primarily because the hours and the calendar of the school mesh so effectively with the calendars of their own time-demanding children. Women with preschool children are unable to remain in the teaching field unless they are able to secure competent full-time child care *and wish to do so.*

We have ordered almost all of our professions and jobs on a full-time basis dictated by a work-society that demands a heavy concentration of "man"-hours to accomplish the available tasks. Even as we become aware of the need to reverse the trend of full-time employment if we are to have full employment opportunity for all of our citizens, we remain wedded to our old pattern of full-time jobs. Shorter hours for all workers is a universal union demand, and lighter loads for all teachers is at least a universal cry; but a really open system designed for multiple types of employment has at best only token acceptance in our society.

If the movement toward fullness of opportunity for women in this country could use its power and its present developmental status to free employment from its old one-man, one-week work frame, it would be a giant step made by women for all mankind in the future. A doctor should be capable of being a good doctor even while she limits her practice to a reasonable fraction of the case load elected by other doctors. Perhaps even fields like advertising and journalism are capable of slowing down the rat race by redefining work loads for all but those who really choose to live on treadmills.

There remains one very important phenomenon of our complex professional society that some of us must face squarely and clearly. As we find and implement multiple and varied task definitions for more and more of our citizens, the nonnegotiable time demands imposed by such a system on our top levels of administration and management seem to increase too, in almost a direct ratio. As a woman who has voluntarily assumed that kind of demanding role, I am aware of how statistically improbable it is that great numbers of women will be in a position to choose similar roles or to have had the prior life experience to be chosen for them in the immediate future. When we analyze the statistical studies that show the low ratio of women at the top levels of management, we must be aware of the relatively low percentage of women in our time who have gone through the sustained experience that even partially readies one for such tasks. I am convinced that such experience, however, will come for ever-increasing numbers of women.

As one who lived her early middle years in one kind of feminist society—the Roman Catholic sisterhood—I am grateful for the professional growth that life provided for me and for many of my "sisters." At the same time, I am poignantly sensitive to some of the trends within the women's liberation movement that seem to be an attempt to deny sexuality in order to make us all "brothers." To share my husband's children at this point in my life is an enriching experience that restores much of a lost side of my own development. Had they not been away at school, I probably would not have chosen to accept the presidency of Hunter College at this time. Some might call that a regressive step for the liberation of women. I would instead call it a radical step for one woman in search of her own fullness. The fact that there were and are other professional commitments of a less demanding kind available to me is a kind of lyrical protection in continuing to live out this one. Can we not define similar electives for women of all ages, temperaments, and talents?

Expanded Opportunities for Education

Unless we can begin to envision and make available employment opportunities within many different time-commitment scales, universal higher education for women will be largely an intellectualized finishing school and/or an investment in frustration. As an educator, I am becoming increasingly aware that a large measure of the frustration of college students today is due to their inability to focus on any personal/-professional life commitment as a recognizable and important goal of their undergraduate education. Liberal arts education has been largely irrelevant to any such personal/professional commitment. For most of us intellectual life is sparked and developed in conjunction with the realization of a sense of defined purpose for our rational and affective energies.

In the past few decades, great masses of young women have entered our colleges and universities. However, the great majority of them bring no sense of a professional life commitment with them when they enter nor, indeed, possess such a sense when they graduate from these schools.

They have seen professional life at best as a short-term adventure to be tried before the advent of their own young children, perhaps to be returned to, at least in a part-time way, in later life. Unless a continuing involvement in professional life with a wide range of time-commitment patterns can be perceived by young women in colleges and universities, I am convinced that the great majority of them will fail to see and thus fail to choose the areas that could open to them the greatest potential for development of personal and professional life.

Educators—and particularly women educators—have for some time seen the critical need for providing higher education for women in much more flexible time modules than the two-semester, four-year pattern that the colleges assumed as they sustained the high school pattern for young adolescents (and perhaps did much to sustain adolescence itself). Two great women college presidents, Mrs. Mary I. Bunting (currently at Radcliffe College, Cambridge, Mass.) and Mrs. Esther Raushenbush (at Sarah Lawrence College, Bronxville, N.Y., from 1965 to 1969), were among those who pioneered in creating programs for women who by choice or necessity could not attend classes in the old prescribed pattern of time commitment. Colleges and universities are only beginning to relax the stringent and legalistic regulations that made "transfer of credit" from one so-called "learning center" to another an extraordinarily wasteful and demoralizing experience.

Women have been more transient in pursuing higher education than have men. Some of us still choose to follow our husbands when they move on, and I believe the majority of young women will continue to do so at least through the remaining decades of this century. If we can help ourselves and each other open up the

(*continued on page 44*)

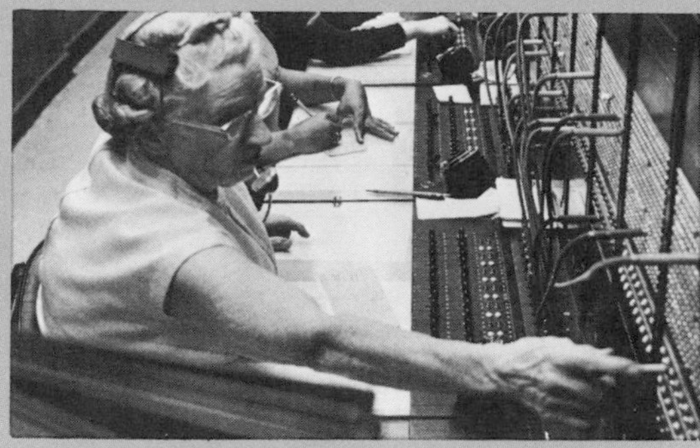

The Unequal Status of U.S. Women in Employment and Education

Jobs for Women–Growing Rapidly

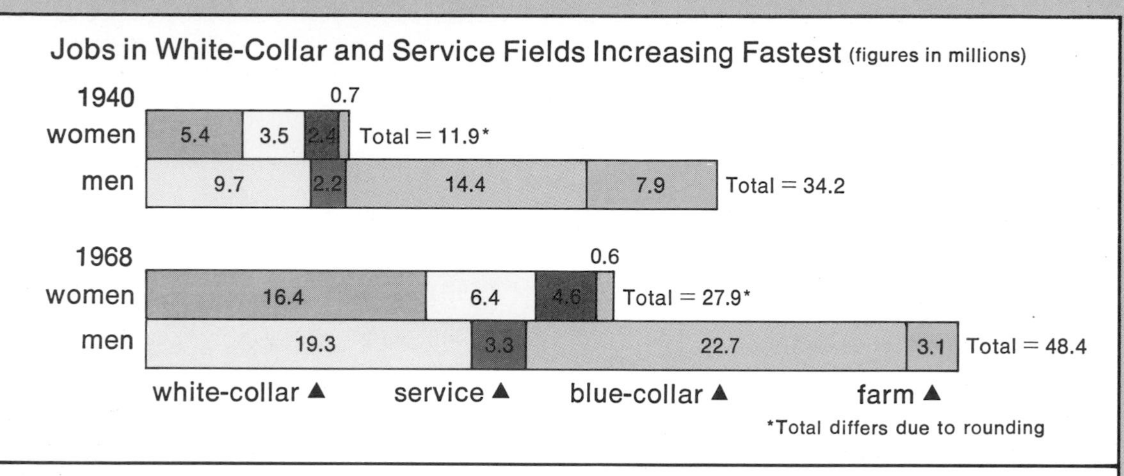

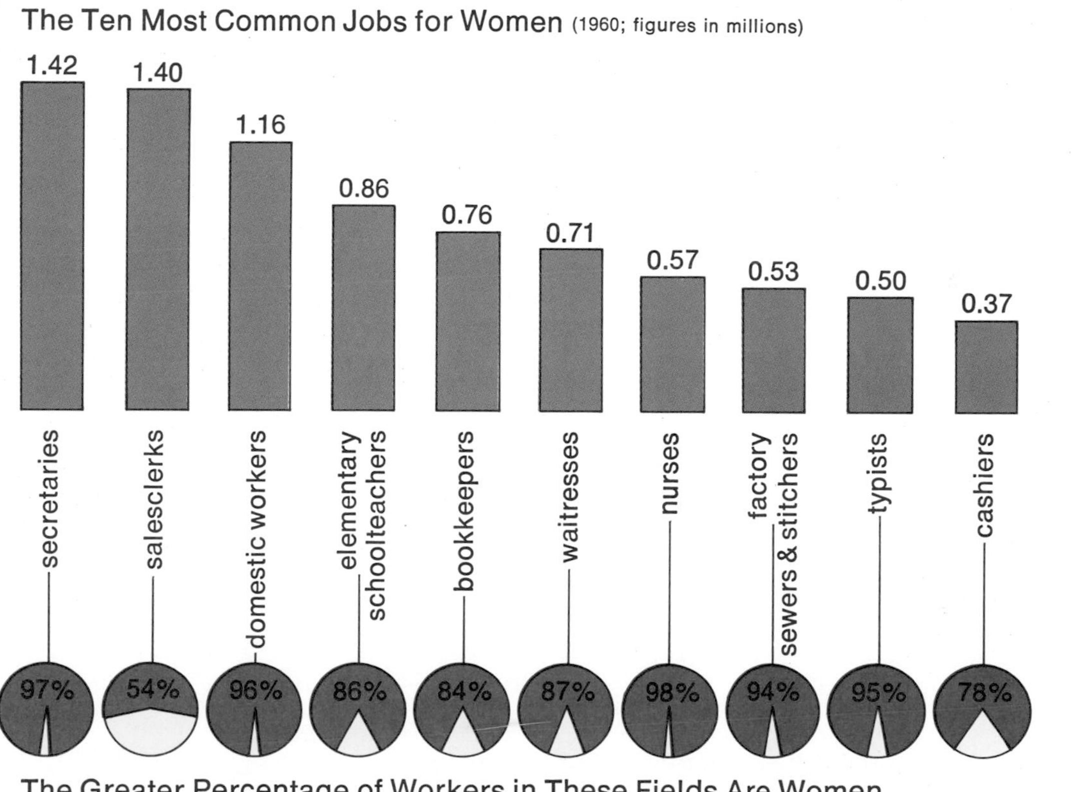

But Women's Income Lags Far Behind Men's

Women Head Higher Proportion of Poverty Families

(% = poor families in each category)

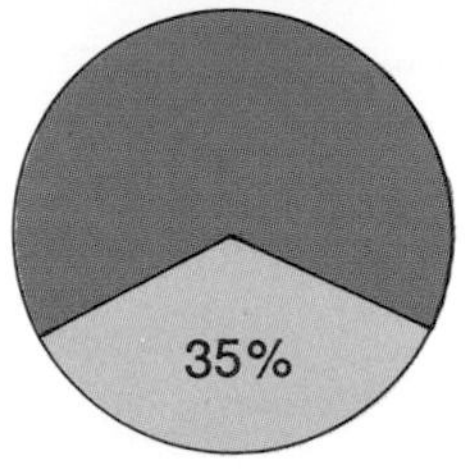

female head

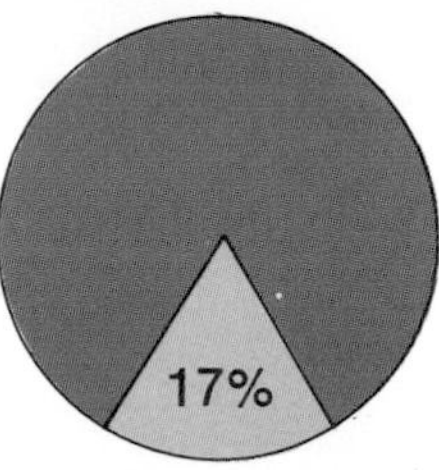

male head without wife

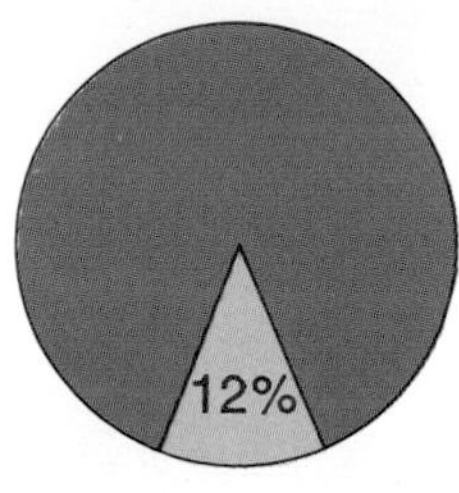

male head wife homemaker

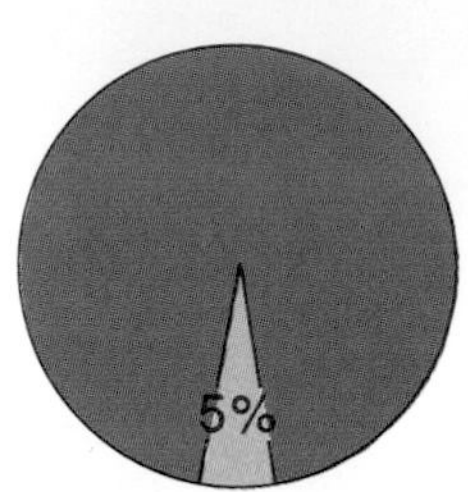

male head wife working

The Earnings Gap Between Women and Men Is Widening

(median earnings of full-time workers)

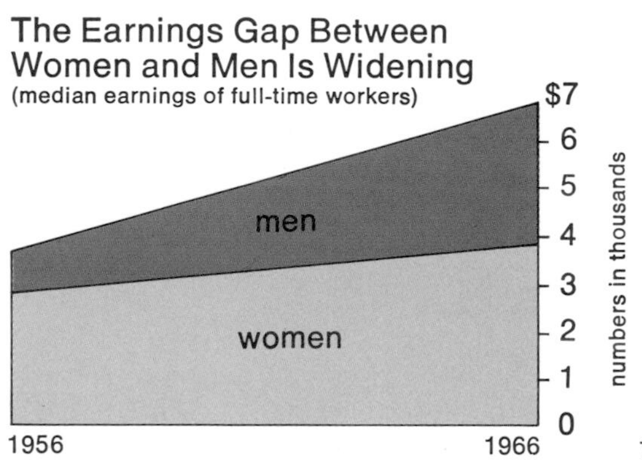

Women Have Higher Unemployment Rate

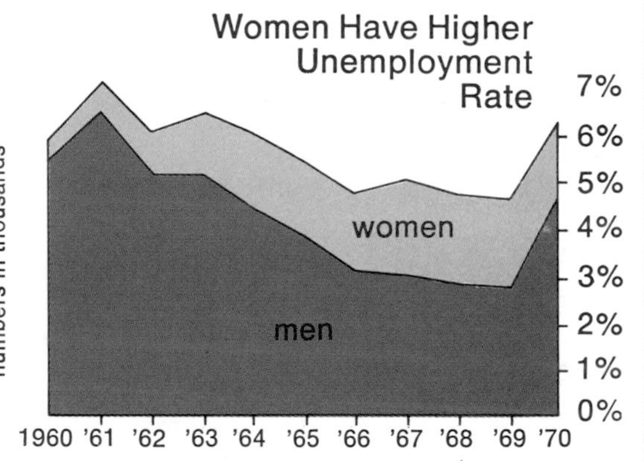

Women Receive Substantially Lower Income Than Men (median wages; 1966)

$6,848

$3,973

men

women

full-time workers

% with annual earnings

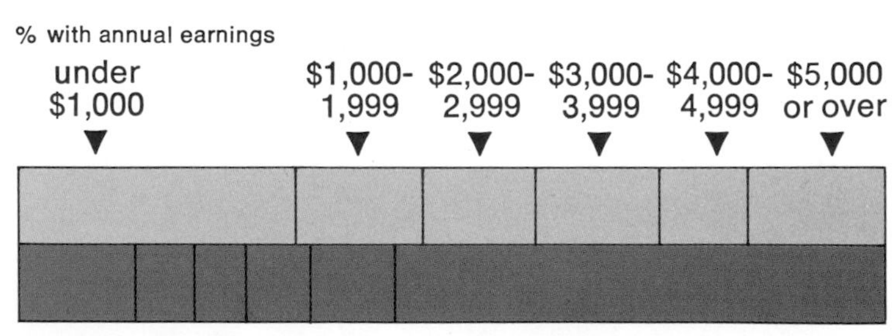

earnings level

Educational Achievements of Women–Increasing But Still Not Equal to Men's

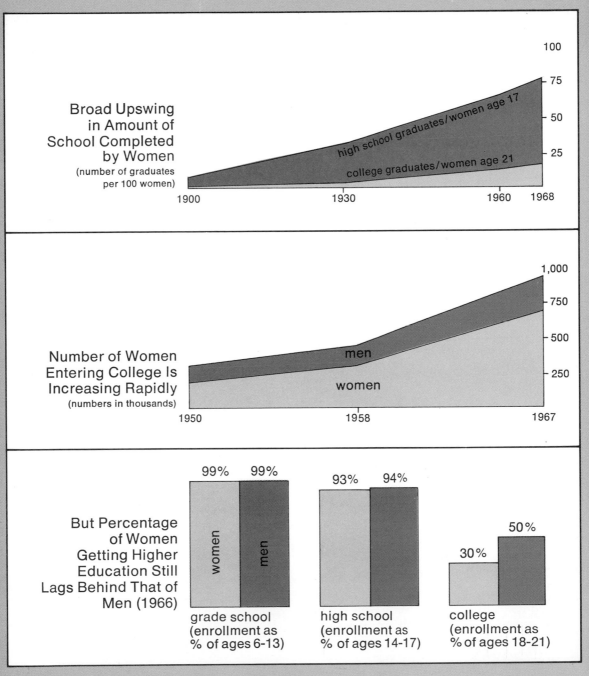

Broad Upswing in Amount of School Completed by Women
(number of graduates per 100 women)

Number of Women Entering College Is Increasing Rapidly
(numbers in thousands)

But Percentage of Women Getting Higher Education Still Lags Behind That of Men (1966)

More Education Leads to Better Jobs, Higher Income for Women

Largest Percentage of College Women Train in Education

(degrees conferred in 1966-67)

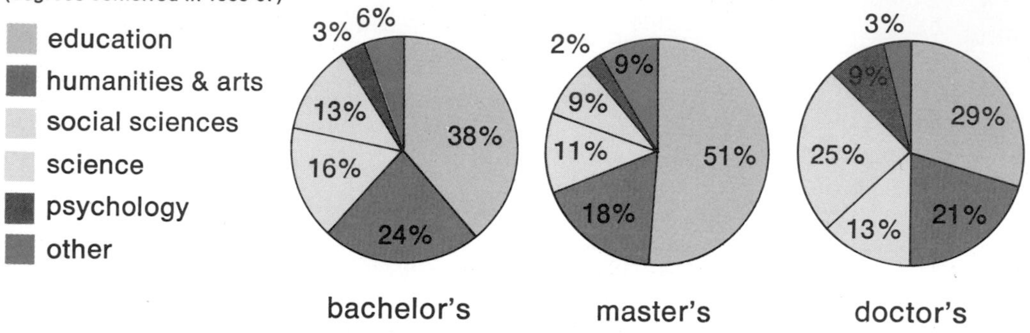

	bachelor's	master's	doctor's
education	38%	51%	29%
humanities & arts	24%	18%	21%
social sciences	16%	11%	13%
science	13%	9%	25%
psychology	3%	2%	9%
other	6%	9%	3%

How Amount of Woman's Education Influences Type of Job Obtained . . .

(percentages in 1968)

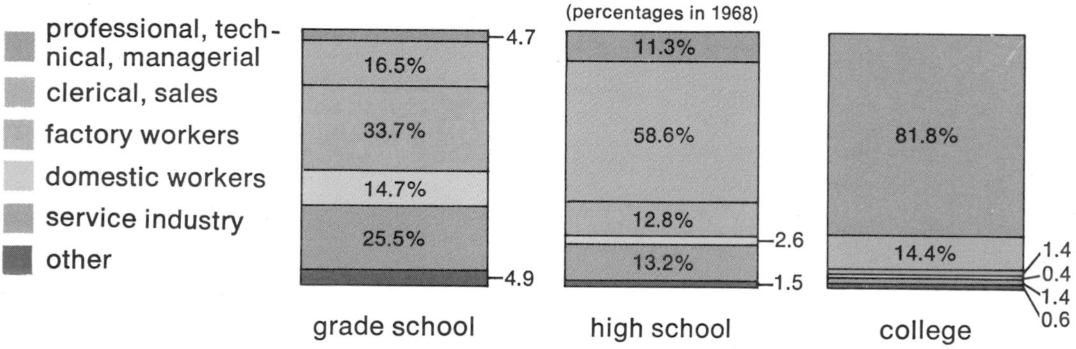

	grade school	high school	college
professional, technical, managerial	4.7	11.3%	81.8%
clerical, sales	16.5%	58.6%	14.4%
factory workers	33.7%	12.8%	1.4
domestic workers	14.7%	2.6	0.4
service industry	25.5%	13.2%	1.4
other	4.9	1.5	0.6

. . . and Her Earnings

(median; 1968)

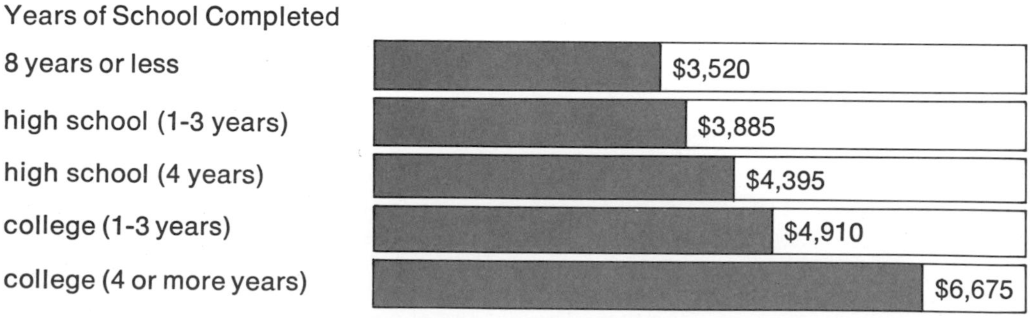

Years of School Completed	
8 years or less	$3,520
high school (1-3 years)	$3,885
high school (4 years)	$4,395
college (1-3 years)	$4,910
college (4 or more years)	$6,675

But Women's Education and Salary Levels Have Not Yet Reached Men's

Women's Share of Higher Education Degrees Has Not Surpassed 1930 Level

(% of degrees earned by women)

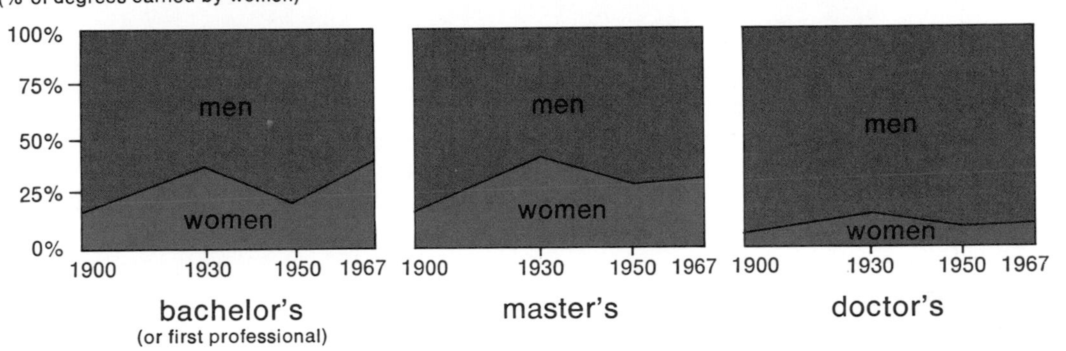

Women Earn Less Than Men with Similar Education

(median income of those who reported some money income in 1966)

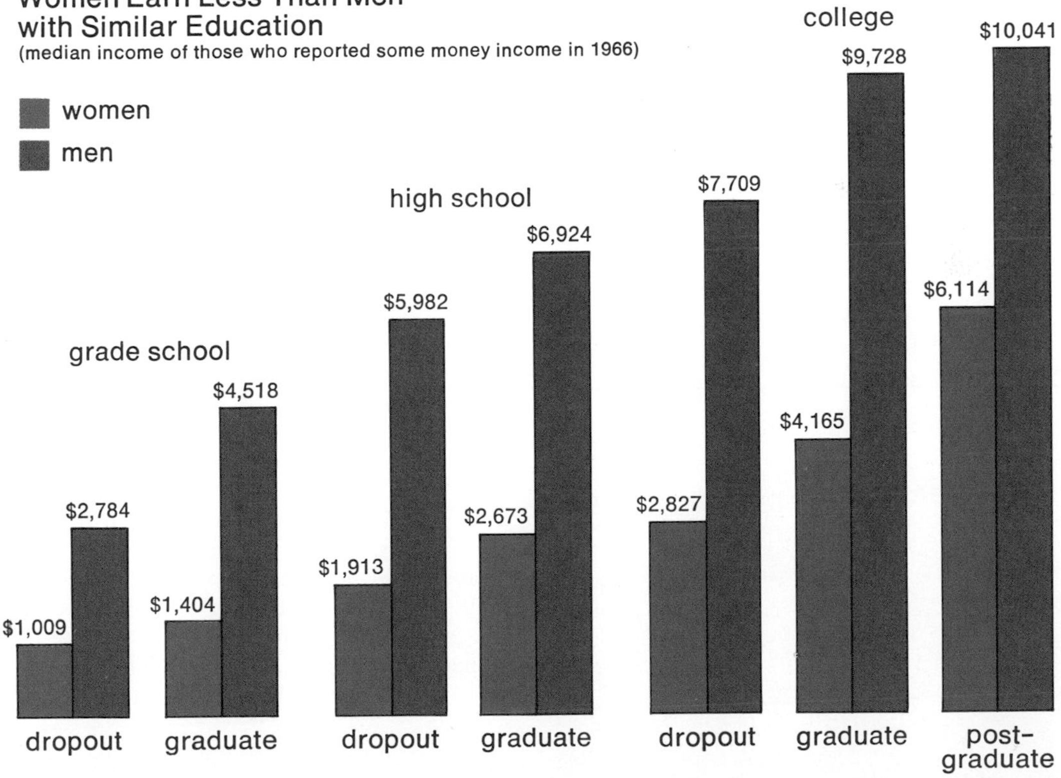

		women	men
grade school	dropout	$1,009	$2,784
grade school	graduate	$1,404	$4,518
high school	dropout	$1,913	$5,982
high school	graduate	$2,673	$6,924
college	dropout	$2,827	$7,709
college	graduate	$4,165	$9,728
college	post-graduate	$6,114	$10,041

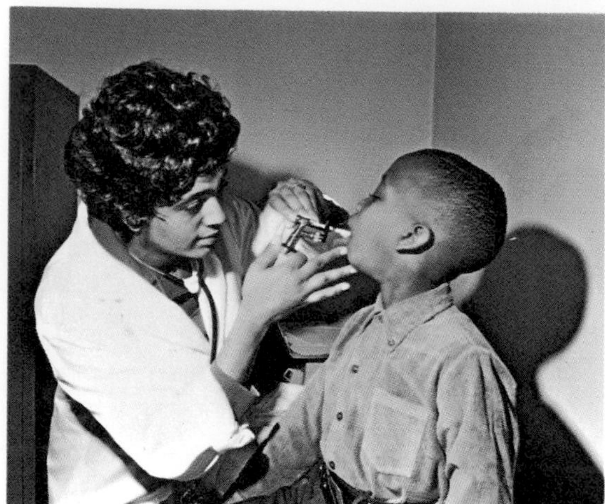

A. HINTON FROM NANCY PALMER AGENCY

Educational and social systems as they are presently structured make it difficult for women to achieve professional status; this Jamaican doctor (above) is an exception in a profession dominated by men. These women in New York City (below), following the example of the suffragettes, are determined to end such inequalities.

KEN REGAN FROM CAMERA 5

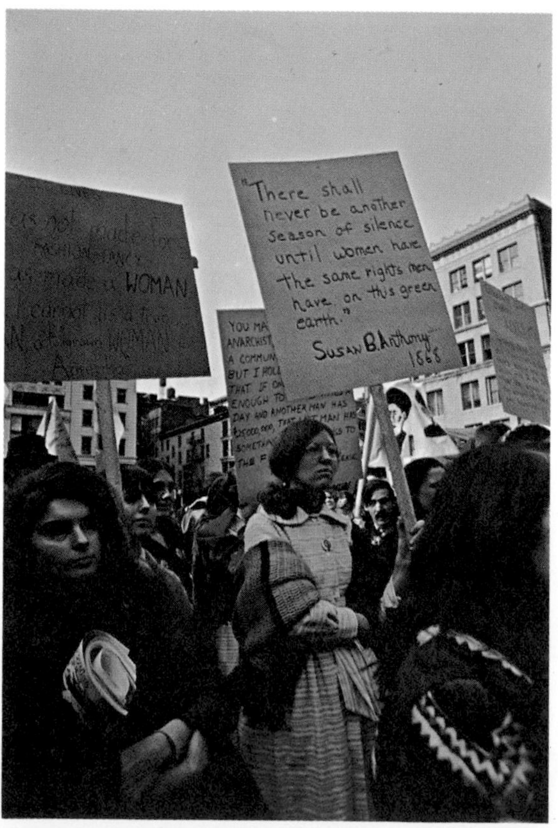

(*continued from page 38*)

personal/professional opportunities within that choice pattern, I am convinced we will do much to gain our integrity precisely because we are refusing to do undue violence to the continuity of our individual and of our collective lives. At the same time, we will be humanizing higher education by prodding it to realize that the individual is the integrating center of his or her own education. A particular college or university may provide more or less of the substance chosen by that person for his or her own pattern of personal integration.

Some good institutions—colleges and other agencies set up to complement them—will provide strong and sensitive advisory services to help persons put together the mosaic of their own educational lives and to recognize and realize the professional opportunities that are available to them within their choice patterns. Independent study and clinical work experiences in business, education, social agencies, and the arts will revitalize women in their hopes and aspirations. Higher education may well be revitalized in the process.

If we are to release the educational process from the umbilical cord that ties it to adolescence, we must release it from teen-age dependence on one's family. Is there hope that women will begin to use political persuasion and their franchise to provoke legislation toward guaranteed income for all our citizens for a period of at least four years or its equivalent?

The human family would simply be recognizing its wholeness and assuming the responsibility now espoused by the majority of U.S. families with resources to do so. We sustain our children for at least four years while they pursue a college education. Again, my concern as an educator is that we are sustaining their adolescence by keeping them in the parent-child economic frame long past the age when our own fathers and mothers saw themselves (and were seen) as adults "earning their own living." A period of guaranteed income for every citizen would give every citizen at least the opportunity to pursue an education in the pattern of his or her own choice—inside and outside the educational establishment, age 18 or 58, in a sustained or in a broken calendar pattern to fit his or her own needs and desires.

Proponents of liberal education have long insisted that man never stops learning, even as they quite arbitrarily define minimum requirements that are supposed to produce an educated person. Let us free the system to reflect our own rhetoric by creating educational patterns and the economic systems to support them that will allow our citizens to go on learning all of their lives. The choice should not be tied to the question of whether father or mother, wife or husband supports the student. The United States is capable of sustaining men and women learners for a period of years as well as—or, please God, instead of—supporting men and women in military service for long periods of years.

Again, what I am trying to stress is that the basic human problems of U.S. society are not different from the basic problems of women in that society. By responding to the situational needs of women as they have evolved from our cultural tradition, I believe we will be charting a future that is more functional and sensitive for all of us and for our descendants.

Expanded Opportunities for Child Care

Much has been said and written of the critical need for child-care facilities in the United States. The need, in my opinion, can no longer be argued. It is obvious that working mothers and student mothers must have available to them some form of a quality child-care service. Discussing the need for quality service for retarded children, Mrs. Rose Kennedy has frequently called attention to her own financial ability to afford supporting help in the years in which she and her husband kept their retarded daughter, Rosemary, within the family circle. The governess and the "nanny" in some form have for centuries been the child-care services for the social and economic aristocracy. Certainly the United States at this period in its history must develop and support systems of child-care service that give the student and the employed mother the same freedom enjoyed by the woman who was "born well" or "married well" by the old elitist standards.

I have already insisted on the critical importance of a wide variety of time-commitment patterns for employment opportunities and for programs in higher education if the mass of women in our society are to *progressively* test out the expansion of their personal roles without necessarily uprooting their personal and cultural histories. The woman who is testing this must have available to her a form of child care that fits the time demands of her work or studies and that satisfies reasonably well her value judgments about her own role in relationship to her children. Some encouraging steps are being taken to develop child-care programs staffed jointly by professionals in that field and by cooperating

WOMEN'S LIBERATION MOVEMENT

On Aug. 26, 1970, thousands of U.S. women took part in a "Women's Strike for Equality," publicly demonstrating in rallies and marches across the country their dissatisfaction with their less-than-equal status with men in U.S. society. The day chosen to signify the inauguration of a new crusade for equality was particularly appropriate. It was the 50th anniversary of the passage of the 19th Amendment to the U.S. Constitution, which gave women the right to vote.

These new female activists were not concerned with suffrage but with achieving full equality for women in employment and educational opportunities, more liberalized abortion laws, and the establishment of government-sponsored child-care clinics. They saw as one of their immediate goals the ratification of an "equal rights" amendment to the Constitution that would end discrimination based on sex and guarantee "equality of rights under the law" to women, but they were unsuccessful in 1970.

Backing the demonstrations was a loose alliance of feminist organizations collectively known as the "women's liberation movement." The largest group was the National Organization for Women (NOW), which took a moderate approach, working for "full equality for women in America in truly equal partnership with men" basically by trying to change social structures through effective lobbying. But also included in "women's lib" were small, radical groups such as New York City's Redstockings and Boston's Bread and Roses, which disdained any cooperation with men and hoped to do nothing less than "revolutionize" the female. It was the radical groups that most frequently seized the headlines through strident "man-hating" statements and such attention-getting devices as bra-burning and karate demonstrations.

Under such leaders as Betty Friedan, author of 'The Feminine Mystique' and founder of NOW, and Kate Millett, author of 'Sexual Politics' and often dubbed the theoretician of the movement, women's lib continued to mushroom in strength. And women's liberation groups also began to appear in Western Europe. While the U.S. movement had not achieved any major victories at year's end, its growing membership and the increasing militancy of that membership served as public notice that women would no longer be content to suffer injustice and discrimination silently.

mothers. In addition to their economic consequences, such centers involve the mother in the life of the center. She does not see the program only as a "dumping ground" for her child while she is busy with other things. There should and will be centers that do not require the personal involvement of the mother at all. Many women will have professional commitments that do not permit this activity. Indeed, many women may not support this kind of involvement.

I am insisting only that our programs respect the situational demands and the personal value systems of the full range of our citizens if they are really to be supportive of the personal evolution of the individual woman and of the evolutionary liberation of women in general. In devising and lobbying for the wide range of child-care programs let us not demean those women who choose to remain their own child-care centers and who wish to integrate their own lives fully as "wife-mother-citizens" in the suburbs, the towns, the farms, or the urban areas. Civil libertarians are, I believe, rightly incensed about recent "no-knock" legislation, which allows law enforcement agencies the right, under certain circumstances, to enter a family home without knocking. Let me only suggest that the new women libertarians have as much respect for the privacy of a personal home and allow each woman the dignity of her own choice.

Major Innovations Needed in Urban Planning

The rising expectation, demand, quest, and hunger of every emerging group in the world today is for recognition as persons within a community of persons. We are often baffled and disheartened by our awareness that economic mobility and cultural growth are not sufficient of themselves to provide for the individual or for the society a matching growth in perception of and satisfaction with our own worth. The causes for our discontent are beyond any attempt at total comprehension. Whatever the list of causes turns out to be, however, I am convinced that physical and psychic space for the individual and for small groups of persons in their interrelationships is perhaps as critical a priority as any other. The old farm-family culture in which I grew up provided this kind of personal and psychic space—space to assemble, space to wander, space to be noisy, space to be quiet, space to be together, space to be alone. In some ways, the much-maligned suburb has created such space, but in so doing it has often cut the suburb and its in-

Satire played a role in some demonstrations for women's rights, as in New York City, where the point was made that women are not robots, chattels, or toys.

MARC AND EVELYNE BERNHEIM FROM RAPHO GUILLUMETTE

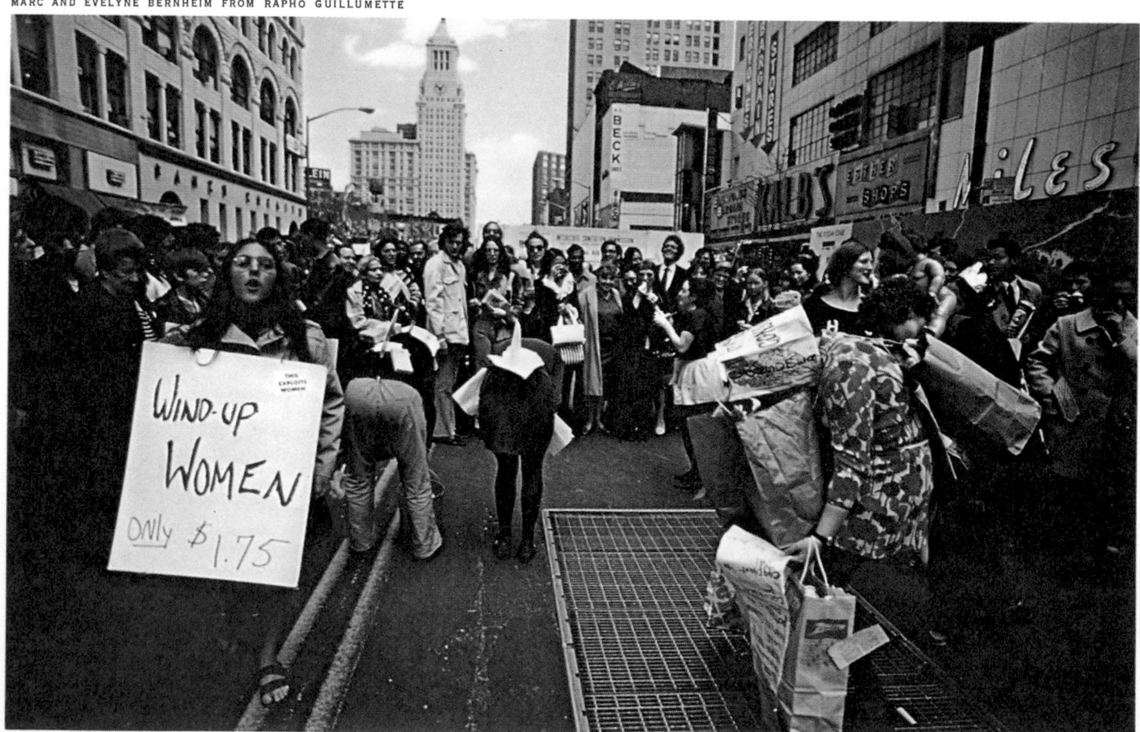

habitants off from the life movements of the larger culture. The common charge is that they are bedroom communities for commuting males and insular traps for women and children. The family farm and the small town kept the major elements of social, economic, and cultural life within easy access of the entire family unit. As we inevitably move more and more toward an urban society, we must design and support housing and transportation that restores to us all the physical and psychic space to wander, to be noisy, to be quiet, to be together, to be alone, as individuals, as families, and as civic, professional, and social groups.

Legislation and taxation to support these developments are as relevant to the woman who lives on a farm in Illinois, in a small town in Montana, or in a suburb in Pennsylvania as they are to the woman who is a government executive in Washington, D.C., or a mother in the Harlem district of New York City. All anyone needs to do is to trace her own family tree back through this century to see the extraordinary mobility in life-styles that has characterized the U.S. family. Unless all of us support legislation that can dignify and humanize the inevitable urban patterns of a highly developed society, we are failing to take out life insurance for our society.

Liberating the Human Family

I have long believed that a woman's concern for her personal family ought to provide the prototype for her concern for the human family. Focus on one's individual family unfortunately can also turn one inward on a short-sighted and narrow acquisitiveness for their individual good. Modern man and woman cannot live in that kind of insularity. The destinies of the mother and child in Harlem—indeed the destinies of the mother and child in North and South Vietnam—are inextricably bound up with our own destinies. Selfish interest and magnanimity are interdependent. We have been led and lured into supporting taxation for massive defense systems to "protect" us from our real and perceived enemies. If the women of the United States can lead the legislators into supporting taxation for massive domestic systems that provide education, professional opportunities, child-care services, and facilities for humanized urban living, they will, I believe, liberate themselves in liberating the human family.

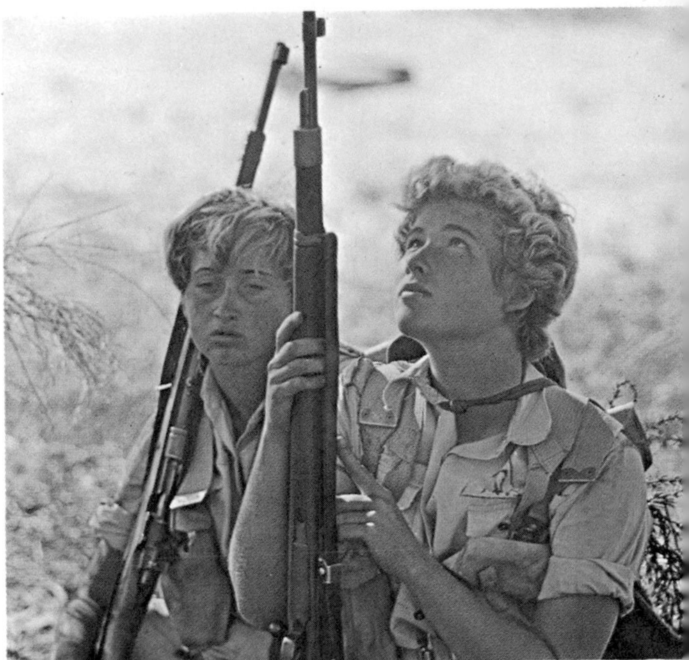

BURT GLINN FROM MAGNUM

In countries where needed skills are in short supply, women fulfill more varied roles. These women are Israeli soldiers.

The areas of family planning and of the male-female relationship inside and outside marriage have been widely discussed and rightly so. I have not elaborated on them here because I am convinced that the personal choices by men and women that determine these two central issues will be modified and enriched largely as a consequence of our coming to terms with the four critical social areas I have offered as priorities in this article.

Each of us will integrate the qualities of our personhood and our life's roles in different ways. Richness of opportunity implies the right to reject as well as to accept elements of the opportunity. My mother, a Midwestern farmer's wife, was and is a rich human person. Her daughters have moved on to professions and families and urban situations. My hope and dedication to expanding opportunities for our own personal and worldwide children are a direct consequence of my reverence for her and her role in opening life for herself by opening it for us and for others. It is our investment in liberating worldwide humanity that will in our lifetime provide liberation and fulfillment for ourselves.

747
Safari Hilton

Let's Travel

by Horace Sutton

Associate Editor, *Saturday Review*

"Your attention, please," a pleasant voice announced over the loudspeaker. "A buffet service is now ready for passengers in tourist class." The travelers filed in front of the platters elegantly arranged with cheese, sliced ham, cold chicken, fruit, and pastries. They selected soft drinks or poured glasses of chilled white Bordeaux or a rich red Burgundy.

The scene took place last summer, not aboard an ocean liner but five miles above the Atlantic Ocean aboard a Boeing 747, the largest commercial plane yet built. While it was surely not the only propellant, the arrival of the 747 early in 1970 ignited another afterburner in the skyrocketing travel business. The novelty of flying for the first time in a new-style aircraft, in unaccustomed comfort, pushed travel on scheduled airlines over the North Atlantic up 18% from January to June.

Travelers flooded the Louvre, crowded into the Tower of London, elbowed one another for a look at the ceilings in the Sistine Chapel, jostled for space on the beaches of the Costa Brava, and spilled over into such lesser-known realms as Romania, Bulgaria, and Hungary—once considered as unviewable as the dark side of the moon.

In its first full year of transatlantic and transpacific travel, the 747, the forerunner of other jumbos to come, proved both popular and controversial. There were passengers who missed the comparative coziness of the 707's and the DC-8's; they felt that the last vestiges of personalized service had flown off into the wild blue

KEYSTONE

Paris (above); Piccadilly Circus in London (below)

KEN REGAN FROM CAMERA 5

yonder as airlines searched for higher profits with larger planes.

The 747 offered roomier seats, especially in economy or tourist class, but meal service at one's seat proved a difficult logistical and engineering feat. The complex trays that arrived were filled with so many foldable, packaged, and containerized foods and condiments—even canned water and wine in plastic bottles—that some passengers felt like astronauts off to explore the cosmos. Yet, with the jumbos, airlines could offer no-smoking sections, an upstairs lounge, and two different movies—one for "general" audiences and one for "mature" audiences —in both first-class and coach sections. The choice of where to sit often left passengers adrift in a major quandary.

The 747, for all its popularity among its partisans, proved less successful on the ground. There was not an airport in the world fully equipped to handle the large loads being ferried by the jumbo airplane. Even Orly Airport in Paris—highly touted as the only major facility to be ready for the big plane—showed some glaring faults. Its waiting rooms were not large enough to seat an entire planeload. In the case of nagging, short delays, dozens of passengers leaned against walls or sat on suitcases. Its long moving sidewalk, only sometimes in working order, served solely to convey passengers between its jumbo facility and the main terminal. Arriving passengers for the 747 were channeled, therefore, through the already strained regular airport facilities, causing discomfort and delays in recovering baggage.

Whatever were the problems in Paris and other world airports, they were nothing compared with the shambles of an arrival at New York City's John F. Kennedy International. With new terminal facilities still in the early stages of construction, with the international arrivals building swamped with the influx of travelers, and with further delays caused by redoubled efforts to find dope smugglers among the arriving tourists, an arrival at Kennedy was often a trying return to the United States. Some experienced travelers making their homes in the East were inspired to return by way of Dulles International Airport in Washington, D.C., or Logan International Airport in Boston, Mass.

Incentives to Fly or to Sail

Despite these discomforts and the added threat of political hijackings, few seemed determined to stay home. The lure of new and roomier planes aside (even with their concomi-

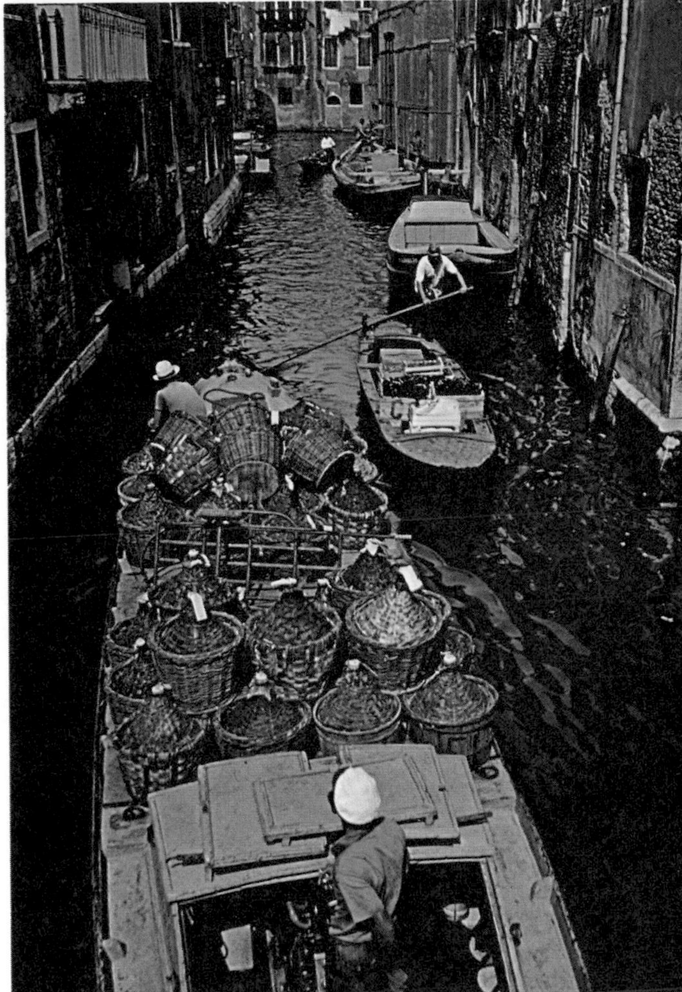

ERICH HARTMANN FROM MAGNUM

Canal in Venice, Italy (above)
The 747 (below)

DEAN BROWN FROM NANCY PALMER AGENCY

AUTHENTICATED NEWS INTERNATIONAL

Carnival in Trinidad (above)
Religious ikon in Greece (below)

COSTA MANOS FROM MAGNUM

tant woes), among the major attractions accounting for the boom were the special rates, the low-cost group tours and the charters. Excursion fares, family fares, and student fares all served to coax a variety of travelers from the hearthside. Group fares, legal and illegal, made trips at low rates irresistible to many.

According to U.S. law, passage on charter flights may be offered only to members of six months' standing in clubs and groups that have not been organized specifically for travel. Some travel agencies, however, have formed instant 'clubs' and, running their own informal airline, have been able to sell tickets from New York to London round trip for about $200 plus a small membership fee. It is estimated that in 1969 a mere 32% of Europe-bound travelers originating on the West coast flew on regularly scheduled airlines. The others went on charter flights. Aircraft for charter flights can be supplied by regular airlines, but more frequently the planes are supplied to charters by nonscheduled, supplemental carriers. The organizing group that charters the airplane buys the use of the plane and flies only when the plane is full. A scheduled airline sells seats, and an airline flying a 747 must fill 40% of the seats in order to break even.

Despite the encroachments of the charter flights, the airlines of the non-Communist countries operating scheduled service carried 287 million passengers some 216 billion passenger miles in 1969, up about 10% in a year. In a world beset by the ague of inflationary prices the airline fare has proved one of the few stable commodities. In 1940, a year after transatlantic service began, the fare from New York City to London was $880. Some crystal-gazers within the travel industry estimate that by 1978 the lowest scheduled service ought to drop to about $138.

As the new decade began to gather momentum, there were winter intervals when no passenger liner steamed across the Atlantic. Those major lines that remained in service—the splendid Dutch, French, Italian, Norwegian, and Swedish ships, as well as the new British *Queen Elizabeth 2*—were all cruising in warm waters. The 1970's would seem, on the face of it, to be the age of air. Yet, oddly, there has been a rustle in the shipping lanes, too, though of a different kind. No longer merely a mode of transport, the passenger ship has become a floating resort, a hotel of the high seas, slipping from one pleasure port to the next, the views from its decks changing daily, sometimes hourly. To encourage

KEYSTONE

AUTHENTICATED NEWS INTERNATIONAL

Bazaar in Marrakesh, Morocco (above)
Native of Ghana (right)
Marketplace in Tashkent, Uzbek, U.S.S.R. (below)
Tourists in Ibiza in Spain (below, right)

C. A. PETERSON FROM RAPHO GUILLUMETTE

J. M. VINCENT FROM CAMERA 5

AUTHENTICATED NEWS INTERNATIONAL

COSTA MANOS FROM MAGNUM

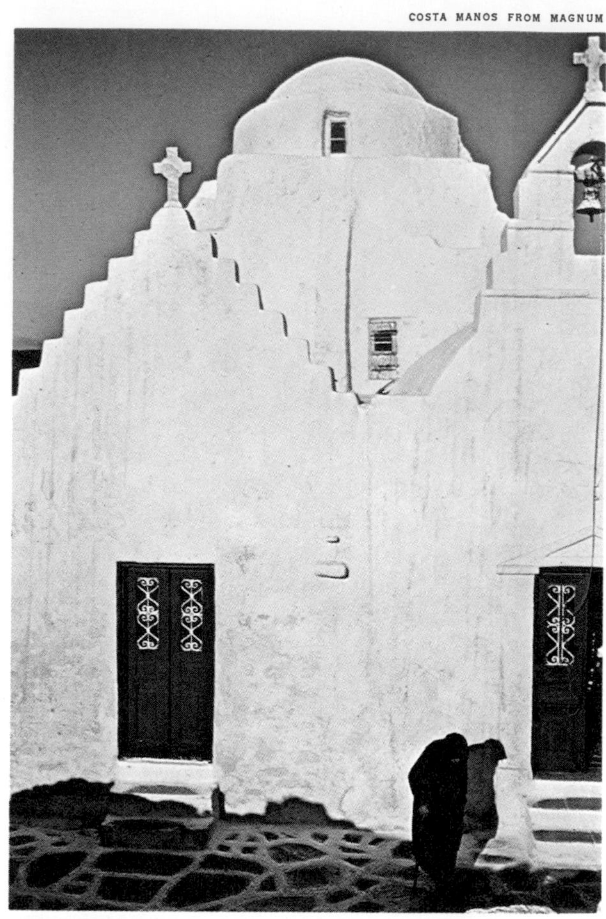

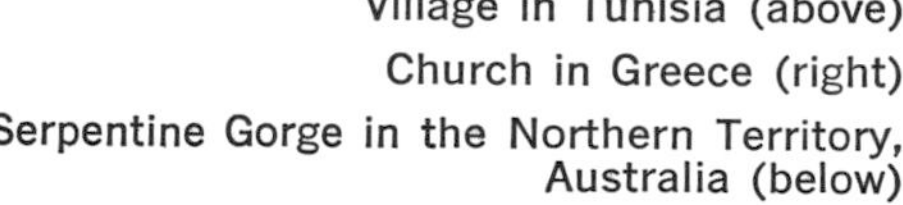

Village in Tunisia (above)
Church in Greece (right)
Serpentine Gorge in the Northern Territory, Australia (below)

AUTHENTICATED NEWS INTERNATIONAL

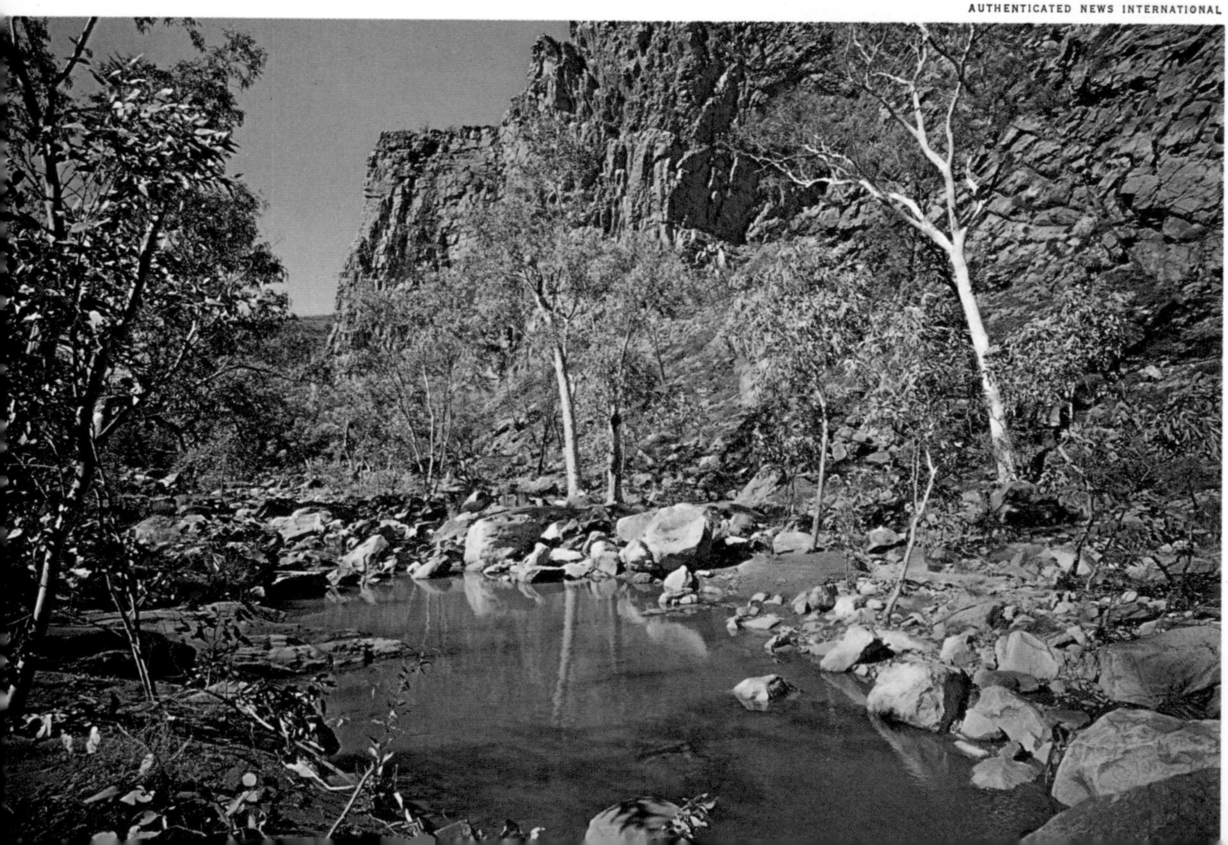

travelers, the airlines themselves have begun to promote cruises that originate in foreign ports, a sort of fly-now, sail-later plan.

More than a score of new cruise ships will be launched early in the decade. There is also evidence that the center—for winter cruising, anyway—is shifting away from the drafty, windblown piers of New York City, a port that is, after all, more than a day's sail away from the warm waters of the West Indies. The entire new $100-million fleet of the Norwegian-Caribbean Lines will sail from the $5-million, 275-acre terminal at Miami, Fla. But even before the arrival of the Vikings in the Sunshine State, cruise business soared 56% in 1969. Cruise ships that sail the Mediterranean in summer migrate across the Atlantic to sail the Caribbean in winter. Cruise ships that in summer sail from Seattle, Wash., to Alaska turn southward to Tahiti in winter. The long-line P and O ships, nominally plying between Australia and England, start from Vancouver, B.C., stop in Mexico, slip the Panama Canal, and in winter gambol among the toasty West Indian isles.

BERNARD SILBERSTEIN FROM RAPHO GUILLUMETTE

Rock castle in Üçhisar, Turkey (above)

Parliament buildings in Kuala Lumpur, Malaysia (below)

DEAN BROWN FROM NANCY PALMER AGENCY

The Lure of Strange Places

While the familiar ports of call, especially in Europe, have been crowded to the rafters in the high season, there seems no place too strange, too far, or too inaccessible to defy the U.S. traveler. It is now fairly common for Americans (notably those who don't mind sitting for eight days) to ride the Trans-Siberian Railroad. They invade the Mongolian People's Republic to visit The Gobi. Both Samarkand and Bukhara in Soviet Central Asia—shades of Genghis Khan and Tamerlane—have become regular hosts to off-trail tourists.

Romania, where the caviar is excellent and the beach resorts at Mamaia on the Black Sea rise like some Marxist Miami, has had a phenomenal increase in visitors. Latin, and somewhat independentist as satellite nations go, Romania had a large increase in tourism during the first six months of 1970. By the end of the year Romania had opened many new hotels, most of them on the Black Sea, an area that already has about a third of all of the country's hotel rooms and that, so the Romanians estimate, will eventually accommodate a million hotel beds. About half of them will be built during the next five-year plan. Romania is also beginning to develop the Carpathian Mountains for the skiing season.

Bulgaria, a little farther off track, requires no visa of any national who stays at least 24

COURTESY, JAPAN NATIONAL TOURIST ORGANIZATION

Takayama Festival in Japan (above)
Red tile rooftops of Copenhagen, Denmark (below)

DENNIS STOCK FROM MAGNUM

hours and less than two months. Air France, Lufthansa, and Royal Dutch (KLM), among others, have service to Varna, which is a few miles from Drouzhba, the oldest Bulgarian resort on the Black Sea. The season lasts from May to October, with the temperature ranging between 60° and 75° F. It has a score of first-class hotels, as well as mineral springs to cure everything from gout to hangover, and, like the resorts of the Romanian Riviera, is popular with West Europeans and a comparatively few enterprising, pioneering Americans. At Zlatni Pyasutsi, or "Golden Sands," the visitor has a choice of 67 hotels, ranging from deluxe-international with indoor swimming pools to spare-and-modest. One can stop by the Wigwams or The Water Mill, a pair of folk-style restaurants, for the *kurban chorba* (mutton soup) and drop by later at the Gypsy Camp or the Masked Dancers, two of the local *boîtes,* for a night of tambourines and violins. On these shores the Age of Aquarius has hardly arrived.

Although the Soviet Union dispenses no figures on the tourists it receives, an estimated 40,000 U.S. citizens visited there during 1970, or about double the number of two years before. North Americans favor tours to Moscow, Leningrad, and Kiev; Yalta, Sochi, and the Soviet Black Sea; and Central Asia. Intourist is building 40 hotels for completion within the next two to three years. Although the Soviet Union can now give shelter to 2 million visitors a year, and more Americans go there than to any other East European country, the Kremlin has not been able to veer from the stiff, proper, and instructional attitudes to the warmer hospitality that one is likely to find in Romania, Hungary, and—if it can be considered a satellite—Yugoslavia (one of the most popular tourist countries in Europe).

Led chiefly by the hotel chains—Hilton (now affiliated with Trans World Airlines), Intercontinental (the hotel arm of Pan American World Airways), and Western International (now part of United Air Lines), to say nothing of Howard Johnson's and Holiday Inns, both still unaffiliated—the U.S. innkeepers have spread across the globe making the world safe, so to speak, for the U.S. traveler. Moving in with their expertise, both Hilton and Intercontinental have arrived in Nairobi, Kenya. Hilton will also operate hunting lodges in Amboseli, off the Nairobi-Mombasa road. Intercontinental, which has long operated the Hotel Ducor in Liberia, now manages an impressive resort complex in Abidjan, Ivory Coast. Its Hôtel Ivoire contains an ice-skating rink (the first in Africa), a bowling alley, a theater, a shopping arcade, and a supermarket. The Ivoire will anchor one end of a 10,000-acre "African Riviera" designed by architect William Pereira of California in association with Thomas Leitersdorf of Tel Aviv, Israel.

Intercontinental has established an outpost in far-off Afghanistan and in 1971 will open in Kinshasa (formerly Léopoldville), in the Democratic Republic of the Congo. Flagship Hotels, the innkeeping branch of American Airlines, has opened in Seoul, South Korea, and has future designs on Fiji, Samoa, New Zealand, and Australia. Sheraton of Boston, Mass., has plans for Tunisia and Turkey; Rio de Janeiro, Brazil; and Buenos Aires, Argentina. Most of the big chains see South America as the continent of the future, a notion that has not as yet captured much of the North American imagination. Perhaps the most startling of all is the Intercontinental's move into Eastern Europe, with U.S.-accented operations in Hungary, Romania, and Czechoslovakia.

Operating from its world headquarters in Memphis, Tenn., Holiday Inns will be extending a Tennessee welcome to any wayfarer who shows up in Marrakesh, Singapore, Bombay, Taipei, Bangkok, and even, one day, Phnom Penh. By the end of 1970, Holiday Inns had accumulated 1,200 inns. By the end of the decade, it hoped to have a roster of 3,000 inns.

But one man's Zlatni Pyasŭtsi is another man's Honolulu. While some travelers are willing to journey by everything short of yak-back to get to distant corners, there are those for whom a faraway place (about 2,400 miles from the U.S. mainland) is Honolulu, Hawaii—with its mixture of cultures, its myriad blossoms, its balmy weather, and its rolling surf. There on that Pacific shore that once resounded to the battle cry of the Hawaiian kings, Sheraton is unveiling the 1,800-room, $60-million Sheraton-Waikiki alongside the Royal Hawaiian.

Will there be people to fill all those rooms? Well, coming are such social improvements as early retirement and, in the United States at least, three-day weekends instead of single-day, midweek national holidays. Eventually, there will be the four-day workweek, holidays or no. Only two or three years away is the first of the SSTs (supersonic transports) that will, by increasing airline speeds to 1,400 miles per hour, shrink the globe by half. It's all just around the corner, but none of it will get here soon enough to satisfy nearly everybody's urge to be somewhere else.

RENÉ BURRI FROM MAGNUM

Church in the Swiss Alps (above)
Lake Scutari in Yugoslavia (below)

EVERTS FROM RAPHO GUILLUMETTE

બેત્રણ બાળકો થાય ... એટલે ઘણાં
ડોકટર કહે તેમ કરો

The Need for Population Control

by Paul R. Ehrlich
Professor of Biology, Stanford University
and Anne H. Ehrlich
Senior Research Assistant

In mid-1970 the earth's human population passed the 3.6-billion mark. If the current growth rate of 2% per year were to continue, the population would double in 35 years, or by the year 2005. Such enormous numbers of people and such a rapid growth rate are completely without precedent in human history. At the time of the agricultural revolution, about 10,000 years ago, there were perhaps 5 million people scattered around the world. More people than that now live in the Chicago metropolitan area alone. In 1925 there were only half as many people in the world as there are today.

The growth rate of a population is the difference between the birthrate and the death rate (ignoring migration). The birthrate is the number of individuals who are born and the death rate is the number who die, per thousand per year in the population. As long as the birthrate exceeds the death rate a population will grow. If the death rate exceeds the birthrate, the population will decline. If they are equal, population size is stable. When the death rate goes down, life expectancy, of course, increases.

Before the agricultural revolution, the human population grew extremely slowly, with numerous local and temporary setbacks. The development of agriculture provided more security than did the previous hunting and food-gathering existence. Food supplies expanded and the establishment of permanent settlements meant that food could be stored against times of shortage. Death rates therefore began to fall, while birthrates remained more or less unchanged, and as a result life expectancies increased. Later improvements in agricultural practices, the industrial revolution in Europe and North America, and particularly the development of modern medicine led to further reductions in death rates. These reductions were especially dramatic in Western countries and

In India, family-planning posters are printed in all of the Indian dialects and posted in all villages and public places.
India's family-planning program began in 1952, and today it is one of the best programs anywhere.
RAGHUBIR SINGH FROM NANCY PALMER AGENCY

were followed by some reduction of birthrates in the West over the last century, largely as a result of changing social and economic conditions following industrialization. This so-called "demographic transition" has partially compensated for the lower death rates and helped slow growth. Today the populations in developed countries are growing at an average rate of about 1% per year, which doubles the population every 70 years.

Following World War II, modern medical technology was introduced to the underdeveloped countries. This was not accompanied by any serious effort at introducing birth control techniques. The result was a spectacular drop in death rates and practically no change in birthrates. Indeed, where there was change, birthrates tended to rise as improved health removed some causes of infertility. The underdeveloped areas of the world—most of Africa, South America, and Asia—are now growing at an average rate of about 2.5% per year. Their populations will double in about 30 years, and in many countries even sooner. There is little hope for a spontaneous drop in the birthrates of these nations, as the socioeconomic conditions that produced a demographic transition in the West are not present.

The stress put on the earth's resources and life-support systems by this burgeoning human population is only beginning to be widely realized. It is becoming clear that this uncontrolled growth cannot be sustained for long. When the population of any other living organism develops the sort of growth pattern humanity is now displaying, biologists call it an "outbreak." A population outbreak is invariably followed by a "crash," brought on by an exhaustion of food resources, a sudden change in climate, an epidemic disease, an increase in predators, other severe environmental changes, social or behavioral disruptions, or by a combination of such factors. Sometimes the outbreak population is completely annihilated; sometimes it is only reduced to a low, supportable level. Many people think that we are safe from all of the above possibilities. But are we?

Food and Other Resources

Perhaps as many as *half* the people in the world today are hungry. They are either undernourished (lacking calories) or, more commonly, malnourished (usually lacking in protein). There already exists an absolute shortage of food. If all the world's food were equally distributed, everyone would have sufficient calories, but everyone would also be protein deficient. Of course, food is not equally distributed. There are severe problems of inequitable distribution of the available food, both within and among nations. There are also massive preventable losses to pests and to spoilage between the harvest and the table. In spite of all this, we still read about "surplus" food. Such food surpluses are economic surpluses—food which no one will buy. These surpluses create a misleading appearance of abundance where, in fact, shortages exist. Destitute people around the world (including the United States) go hungry because they cannot afford to *buy* the food they need.

If the human race is unable to feed itself adequately today, how can we hope to feed additional hundreds of millions a few years from now? The food that is being produced today, particularly in developed countries, is gained at considerable expense to the environment through the use of powerful synthetic pesticides and inorganic fertilizers. Our farming practices may result in lowered soil fertility and less food in the long run. Various schemes have been proposed to raise food production or to supplement protein supplies. The most likely of these to succeed involves the introduction into underdeveloped countries of new high-yield forms of traditional grains, together with more efficient farming methods. This program is known as the "Green Revolution."

The Green Revolution, at best, may enable agricultural production to keep pace with population growth for the next decade or two. However, there are numerous social, economic, and environmental obstacles to its success. Not the least of these is the fact that these new grains require large amounts of fertilizers and irrigation water to grow. Moreover, they may require much more protection from pests than do naturally resistant traditional crops. Thus, agronomists from developed countries are trying to introduce into underdeveloped countries the same fertilizing techniques and wide use of synthetic insecticides that are causing so many environmental problems where they are now used.

In addition to the Green Revolution, other panaceas for solving the food crisis have been proposed. One that is being promoted especially as supplying protein is food from the sea. If sea life were protected and carefully husbanded, its productivity might be doubled toward the end of the century. Since population size will also have doubled by then, ob-

LAURENCE R. LOWRY FROM RAPHO GUILLUMETTE

This photograph of East Bay, Long Island, N.Y., shows the extensive loss of wetlands due to housing, roads, and commercial developments, which also pollute the waters of the bay. Population density is a key feature of this suburb.

viously no improvement in the average diet can be expected from that source. And, unfortunately, far from protecting this vital source of food, we are polluting the oceans with perhaps half a million different substances, including pesticides. Moreover, pollution is worse near continental shores, where sea life is most abundant. Rather than husbanding oceanic food resources, man is grossly overexploiting many fisheries. Some, including several species of whales, have been driven nearly to extinction.

Some other suggestions for food supplements involve unconventional foods, ranging from fish protein concentrate to algae raised on sewage. Promoters of the latter obviously expect someone else to eat these foods. But even if such novel foods can be made acceptable, their potential to aid humanity in the critical decades ahead is small.

Besides food, other resources are running short, particularly nonrenewable ones such as copper and petroleum. The United States and other developed countries consume the overwhelming bulk of these, although increasing amounts of the raw materials are obtained from the underdeveloped countries. Presently known reserves of petroleum and many other important minerals will be exhausted within 50 to 150 years at the current rates of consumption. The technology and way of life of Western countries demand the use of these resources. The underdeveloped world expects to enjoy the blessings of Western-style technology in the future. But it is clear that consumption of these materials in the present wasteful fashion cannot continue much longer in the developed countries alone, and the dream of industrializing the entire world can never be realized. The earth simply does not have the resources.

Humanity is also depleting renewable resources, such as forests, soils, and fresh water. In all three cases, consumption exceeds the rate of replenishment. The United States is now beginning to develop schemes for water projects to utilize Canada's stores of fresh water; the U.S. demand for water is expected to exceed the domestic supply within 20 years.

Environmental Factors

Another factor that can lead to the extinction of a species, with or without an outbreak-crash pattern of growth, is a massive environmental change. There is some evidence that dinosaurs disappeared from the earth as the result of a drastic change in climate. Man could become a latter-day dinosaur with one important difference: the original dinosaurs were not responsible for their own demise.

As a factor in human health and well-being, environmental deterioration is a serious cause for alarm, especially in developed countries where most pollution is generated. Air pollution has led to an increase in respiratory diseases; water pollution can contribute to increases in the incidence of other diseases; the ubiquity of chlorinated hydrocarbon insecticides and industrial compounds represents a dangerous long-term health risk to everyone; incessant noise, crowded urban areas, and ugly surroundings pose unknown dangers to mental health.

It is clear, then, that man's impact on his environment has reached a state where it presents a grave danger to the entire earth. The poisonous substances we are heedlessly releasing into soils, waters, and the atmosphere injure not only ourselves but also the ecological systems on which we depend for oxygen to breathe, for food to eat, and for the recycling of our wastes. The ability of our planet to support mankind is in jeopardy.

Long-lived chlorinated hydrocarbons, such as DDT, are found in living plants and animals around the world, on land and in the sea. The DDT accumulates in organisms because it is easily dissolved in fat, and all plants and animals contain fat. But DDT does not break down readily into harmless substances; rather it is concentrated by ecological systems. Animals get it by eating plants, and then they pass it on to the predators that devour them. Although only about 10% of the food an animal eats is incorporated into its body, almost 100% of the DDT is. That is why the concentration of DDT is greatest in animals such as predatory birds and fishes that feed at the upper end of food chains (a "food chain" is an eating sequence such as cow eats grass, man eats cow, tiger eats man). Most chlorinated hydrocarbons and some other pollutants have similar characteristics. Numerous species of predatory birds and fishes are threatened with extinction today. As the quantity of these poisons increases in the environment, species lower in the food chains will be affected. These organisms, especially tiny marine plants, are often involved in the food chains that produce food for human beings. This is one reason why food from the sea is likely in the future to contribute less rather than more to the average human diet than it does today.

Pesticides are just one of the serious pollutants produced primarily by agricultural activities; inorganic fertilizers and dust are two others. Inorganic fertilizers not only pollute rivers and lakes, killing off useful fishes in the process, but also appear to interfere with the natural processes of the soil that refresh and renew it. Artificially high soil fertility may be achieved temporarily at the cost of lower soil fertility over the long term.

Air pollution damages trees and crops as well as human tissue. Even more disturbing is the potential change in climate it may induce. Air pollution is no longer a local problem; the entire atmosphere is contaminated. A major source of this contamination is dust generated by farming and grazing. Whether the long-term effect of air pollution will be to warm or cool the planet remains uncertain, but at the moment it seems to be causing a cooling trend. To complicate matters, global cooling may cause local warming or vice versa. It is clear, at any rate, that if air pollution continues to build up, there will be an acceleration of climatic change. With such acceleration, agricultural production will be profoundly and adversely affected.

Another increasing human influence on climate is the heat generated by the use of power. This accompanies any power use, whether it is the burning of gasoline in a car, the running of a refrigerator, or the generation of electricity by power plants. If the consumption of power continues to increase at current rates, what is now mainly a local problem of thermal pollution will soon escalate into a worldwide one.

Disease

Medical propaganda has created the impression that man has been almost freed from the ravages of epidemic disease. To some degree this is true. But from time to time new forms of old diseases (such as influenza) appear, or lethal diseases never before seen in man suddenly transfer from animals to humans. Such a disease is Marburg virus, which broke out among laboratory workers in Marburg, West

Germany, in 1967. Of the approximately 30 people who contracted it, 7 died. The source was a shipment of laboratory monkeys that had been in a London airport only two weeks earlier.

The human population today is the largest, weakest, and most densely packed that has ever existed. For the majority of people, medical care is essentially nonexistent. A new virus could be carried around the world by modern transport within hours; an epidemic could spread within days or weeks. Developing vaccines and manufacturing drugs on a mass scale takes time. If, in 1967, Marburg virus had not been contained, or if it had escaped at the London airport, millions of people could ultimately have succumbed to it.

In addition to the chance of a naturally occurring epidemic, biological-warfare laboratories are creating dangerous new disease agents. Accidental escapes of disease agents have been known to occur, and more are inevitable.

War and Disruption

Man has virtually eliminated all of his predators but one: himself. One important factor in most, if not all, modern wars is population pressure. This appears most frequently as pressure on resources—a need for more resources or a need to deny others access to them. The war in Vietnam is no exception. The petroleum, tin, rubber, and other resources of Southeast Asia have been determinants of policy in that area for a long time. As the world's population grows, the potential for conflict will become even greater.

War is always undesirable, but the advent of thermonuclear war has provided humanity with a new means for achieving self-extinction. It would not be necessary to annihilate the entire population directly in order to wipe out mankind. Even a limited nuclear exchange could sufficiently impair the life-support systems of the earth to prevent survival in the long run. At the very least, civilization would be utterly destroyed.

Even if war can be avoided (or better, abolished), what about the internal disturbances that seem to be plaguing so many countries, including the United States? Most of the dissent and disruption in the United States can be traced to obvious social causes such as racial injustice, an exploitive economic system, and a distant, costly, unjust war. Nevertheless, it seems reasonable to suggest that, especially in our malfunctioning cities, the stress of rapid population growth may be contributing to our troubles. It has been shown that crime rates rise as population density rises. It appears that mental disturbance may also be more prevalent in areas of high density.

Many social animals respond to crowded conditions with aberrant behavior. Crowded laboratory rats fight, fail to reproduce, and kill their young. The arctic lemming, whose population goes through regular outbreak-crash cycles, is perhaps the best-known example of such behavior from nature. In 1970, lemmings again migrated from their overcrowded homes, and millions perished in the sea. People, on the other hand, appear to have very high tolerances

No open space is visible in this intensely packed slum area of Hong Kong.

BRIAN BRAKE FROM RAPHO GUILLUMETTE

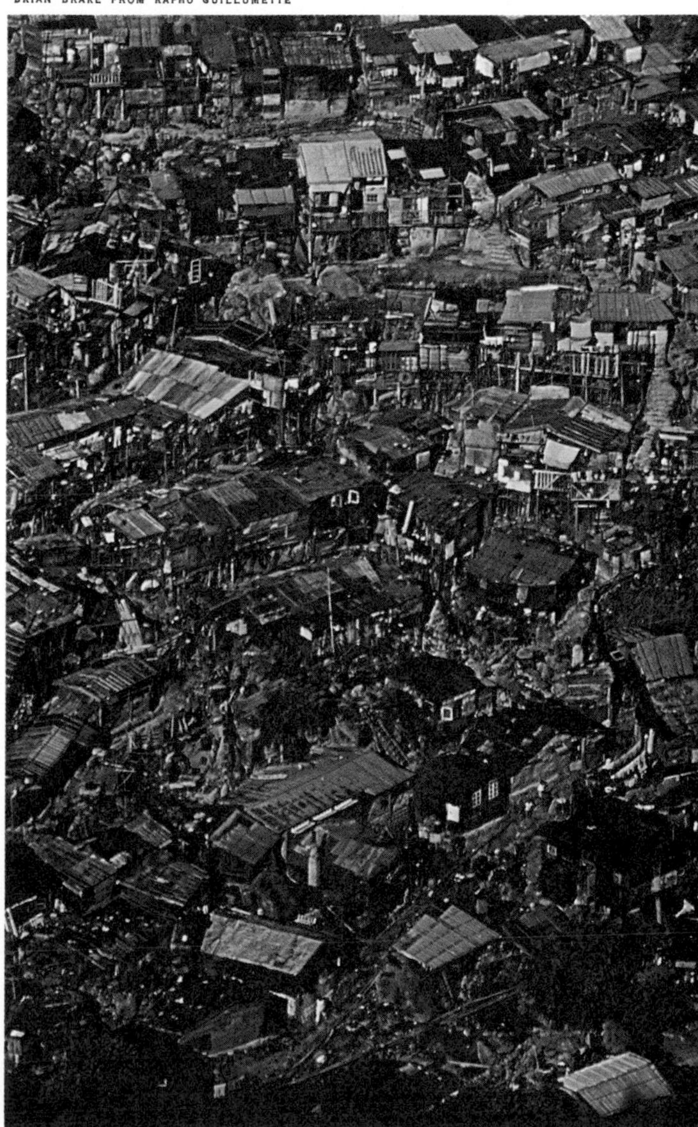

for crowding and great ability to adapt to adverse social conditions. Our adaptability cannot be limitless, however, and the stresses may be beginning to show among the more sensitive individuals.

Determining the Optimum

It is obvious that population growth must soon stop and ultimately be reversed. If humanity fails to regulate its own numbers, nature will do it for us, sooner or later.

How many people can the earth support? This is a complicated question involving numerous factors. First we must decide what the average standard of living should be in terms of food, shelter, clothing, and other material goods. At the average U.S. standard, the world could temporarily support between .5 billion and one billion people ("temporarily" because this does not take into account the depletion of nonrenewable resources—when they are gone the world will be able to support far fewer people). By this optimistic measurement, there are already 3.5 to 7 times too many of us. At a much lower standard of living—perhaps the average that prevails worldwide today—we probably could temporarily support more people than now exist, particularly if food and materials were more equitably distributed and less wastefully used. But we could not support so many for long; the environmental stress, even if we were much more careful in controlling pollution, would be too great.

In addition to the problems of basic support, thought must be given to the ideal number of people needed to keep each society functioning efficiently. It has been suggested, for example, that the United States could function very well with a population of 50 million (one quarter of the present population), or even less. Given the same level of technology, the U.S. pollution problems certainly would be much smaller. Canada might not require so drastic a cut in population; it might need more than 5 million people (one quarter of the present population) in order to keep its society running. Such decisions must be based on the type of society that will prevail locally, regionally, and nationally. A primarily industrial area will naturally require more people than an agrarian one, and some kinds of agriculture demand more people than others. Ideally, an optimum population would permit diverse lifestyles. There should be enough people so that large cities can exist, but few enough so that there can be open space available for everyone, enabling hermits to live undisturbed.

Achieving Population Control

Far more difficult than *determining* the optimum population size will be *achieving* it. The ancient, obsolete idea still prevails that among nations or political groups there is strength in numbers. If that were true, Communist China and India would be the most powerful nations in the world, and Israel would long since have disappeared.

Officials and economists in many underdeveloped countries (and some developed countries) still believe that more people are needed

Unwanted automobiles blight the landscape the world over. Here in the lovely Italian countryside, junked cars destroy the view. As the population grows, the amount of environmental pollution increases.

ROBERT DOISNEAU FROM RAPHO GUILLUMETTE

to carry out development. They cling to this belief, though high birth and population growth rates repeatedly have been shown to hinder economic progress, and though most of these countries are suffering from severe unemployment problems. One of the consequences of a high birthrate is a very young population. In most underdeveloped countries approximately 45% of the population are under 15 years old. This large proportion of dependent children is an economic drag. In a population control program, obviously this is the group that would proportionately be reduced first if fewer children were born, bringing immediate economic benefits. At the same time this huge proportion of young people guarantees that, even with the most effective imaginable program of population control, these populations will continue to grow for *at least* another generation.

People in developed countries also mistakenly believe that they have no population problem because they practice family planning and their populations are growing more slowly than those in underdeveloped countries. However, it is these slowly growing populations that are creating the bulk of the environmental deterioration that is endangering the entire world. They are consuming most of the world's renewable and nonrenewable resources and taking an unfair share of food resources. Since their growth is, therefore, the greater threat to the future of man, it is most imperative that developed countries establish genuine population control. If population control is ever to be achieved, the world's exploiters of resources, especially the United States and the Soviet Union, must lead the way. Otherwise, people in underdeveloped countries will consider population control simply a plot to keep them from gaining their share of the world's goods.

Family planning is not equivalent to population control. Population control is the regulation of population size by a society. Family planning serves only to regulate the sizes of individual families. Unless a society at least attempts to influence the goals of family planning, there is no control of population. As long as people want and have an average of significantly more than two children per couple, a population will grow. In the United States, surveys revealed that people want an average of 3.4 children. In Canada, in 1960, it was 4.2—higher than in many underdeveloped countries, where desired family sizes generally run high.

Governmental programs for family planning have been introduced into numerous underdeveloped countries since 1960. India's program was started in 1952, but it was poorly supported and ineffective for the first decade. Since 1965 it has become one of the most vigorous and one of the few actively promoting small (two-child) families. Most of the programs in other underdeveloped countries operate as the early birth control centers did in the United States and England. They open clinics and provide information and free or low-cost contraceptives—usually intrauterine devices (IUDs) or contraceptive pills. Their propaganda chiefly consists of spelling out the personal advantages of planning and spacing children and of avoiding unwanted children. This is socially valuable, but it has had very little effect on birthrates.

Family size goals are generally associated with such social factors as the parents' education, economic status, and urbanization. This association holds in all countries and among all races. Urbanized, educated, and more affluent people want and have fewer children than their rural, less educated, and poorer fellow countrymen. The populations of underdeveloped countries are on the average poorer, less educated, and less urbanized than those of developed countries. Moreover, people in underdeveloped countries have had a relatively short time to adjust to low death rates. Everything in their tradition emphasizes the value of producing many children.

The idea of population control is resisted almost instinctively by many people. Having only recently (within three generations) accepted the idea that parents have the right to decide how many children they will have, people are now prepared to defend that right against the urgent needs of society. Others still resist the idea of birth control on religious grounds.

Because human beings still exploit and distrust one another around the world, many groups are justifiably suspicious of population control. The far Right calls it a Communist plot, minority militants call it a genocidal plot, and the new Left in developed countries and the radical Left in underdeveloped countries believe that it is a new means of economic imperialism. The advocates of population control must be scrupulously vigilant, as the means of population control could be grievously misused if they fell into the hands of politically motivated extremists from any camp.

Means of Population Control

The first prerequisite of any form of population control is that birth control be readily

MICHAEL ROUGIER, LIFE MAGAZINE © TIME INC.

This ugly street, "The Speedway" in Tucson, Ariz., was once a trail that led to the mountains. The heavy traffic is typical of most U.S. urban areas.

available to all members of each society. At present, birth control information and/or devices are still illegal in many countries, largely because of pressure from the Roman Catholic church, which disapproves of "artificial" birth control. There are various techniques for birth control; some are time-honored methods, such as the practice of withdrawal and use of condoms. More recent developments include a variety of chemicals and mechanical devices to be employed by women as barriers to conception. Since about 1960, the oral contraceptive pill and IUDs have come into widespread use. The pill is the most effective method yet developed, but there can be failure in its use, and both it and the IUD often have serious side effects.

When birth control fails, abortion can be used. Although there is a great deal of controversy about the morality of abortion, the fact remains that it is by far the most commonly employed form of birth control in the world. This is true even though abortion is illegal in the majority of countries. There has recently been a trend to legalize abortion in many countries, and several states in the United States have liberalized or abolished the restrictive clauses in their laws regulating it.

Complete availability of contraceptives and abortion will not alone produce population control, since people still want too many children. Some means must be found to convince individuals of the need to limit their reproduction to an average of two children per family, or less. In fully literate, relatively world-oriented areas such as North America, Europe, and Japan, this might be achieved simply through an educational campaign to convince society of the consequences of continued population growth, and to foster appropriate cultural attitudes. These might include approval of nonmarriage and childlessness, conditions presently viewed with pity or disapproval. Women's roles as wife and mother can be de-emphasized and participation in society outside the family encouraged. The very real advantages to both children and parents of very small families can be stressed. After World War II, in the face of extreme overpopulation, disapproval of large families developed in Japan. Abortion was legalized, and the birthrate was halved within ten years, changing it from a rate typical of an underdeveloped country to one very close to the present U.S. birthrate. Possibly an intensified campaign could reduce it still further, while a similar one might be effective in other developed countries.

If family planning and educational campaigns fail to reduce birthrates to the desired level, socioeconomic measures may be required. Tax laws in the United States and many other countries presently encourage reproduction. These can be changed, preferably in such a way that they do not penalize poor families (in poor families, it is the children, not the parents, who would suffer). There could be special bonuses or tax incentives for childless couples and single people; encouragement of and subsidy for adoption; free or low-cost day care for children, allowing mothers to work; and bonuses for sterilization.

Relatively repressive measures could also be used, such as assigning public housing without regard to family size, discontinuing dependency allowances for servicemen, restricting the years of free schooling per family to enough for the education of two children, and limiting paid maternity leaves. Such measures, however, should be considered only when less coercive programs have clearly failed.

Involuntary birth control, through the use of implanted steroids or sterilizing ingredients in food or water, is often discussed. There is at present no available sterilant that could be utilized. It would be extremely difficult, if not impossible, to find one without untoward side effects, especially on other organisms. It is to be hoped that the United States and the rest of the world will find less socially disruptive ways to control population. But these possibilities should be discussed because they may ultimately be called for if successful voluntary efforts toward population control are not initiated in the near future.

Obviously, population control will not solve all human problems. It will, however, provide us with an *opportunity* to solve them. Without population control, our efforts to solve other problems are ultimately doomed to failure.

What More Can We Do?

Besides controlling human numbers, we must cease our abuse of the environmental systems on which we depend for our lives. We must also halt our greedy consumption of renewable and nonrenewable resources. This means much more than putting smoke filters in smokestacks and improving sewage treatment facilities.

It means nothing less than that the present Western way of life must be changed fundamentally. The emphasis on material goods should be diminished and wasteful methods of production must be abandoned. All materials should be manufactured with a view to durability and recycling. Agriculture should be practiced in cooperation with nature, not as a war against it. Cities and other human habitations should be planned with human beings, not automobiles, in mind. Alternate, less wasteful, and less polluting forms of transportation must be designed. A new economic system must be devised, based on stability and quality goods rather than growth and junk. Societies should be rated on the well-being of their citizens rather than on their gross national products. The ethics that put profit and possessions above humanity must, above all, be abandoned.

The change of basic values that must take place before we can solve our problems must include the rejection of war as a means of settling differences and the ending of racism and the exploitation of poor people and nations. So long as men in insulated groups compete for resources and power with other groups, consuming and destroying both natural and human resources in the process, we can never hope to solve our problems.

The Changes of the Future

The last two or three decades have been witness to a more profound change in human life than was seen in centuries before. This is attributable, in part, to the size of the population and the rapidity of its growth. Another major factor is the growth of technology. This rapid change is doubtless also largely a cause of the generation gap. There is no question that many young people view their world otherwise (and perhaps more clearly) than their elders. What they see frightens and horrifies them; they see the possibility of oblivion.

In generations past, each society had a vision of the future, and it built and planned for that future. Today we seem bent only on continuing to build on past goals, without evaluating their worth or feasibility. Any remaining vision of the future is out of alignment with reality. Resisting change is useless. Our choice now is whether to control and direct the changes of the future toward new goals derived from the hard realities we face, or to continue drifting until the "solutions" find us. It is possible that today's young people can create a new vision for the future that can benefit and inspire all men.

The Art of Photography

by John Szarkowski

Director, Department of Photography, Museum of Modern Art, New York City

The invention of photography required the coexistence of two separate bodies of scientific knowledge—one concerned with optics, the other with chemistry. In addition, it required a frame of mind that could conceive the possibility of a picture's being formed by the energies of nature.

The optical principle of the camera was well understood by the 16th century. It was demonstrated that light passing through a very small hole into a darkened room would form, on the opposite wall, an inverted image of the scene outside. In the following centuries the camera was developed in a number of portable forms and was extensively used by painters and scientists to study the rules of perspective and the behavior of light. The image produced, however, was as fleeting as that in a mirror. If it was to be recorded, it was necessary to draw the image by hand, with the inevitable subjectivity and distortion that human intervention implies.

In the early years of the 19th century, the idea occurred independently to several men that the camera's image might be recorded automatically by the action of light on a material of the proper chemical nature. It had long been known that certain materials change their appearance on exposure to light. Once this principle was linked to that of the camera, the basic concept of photography was complete. Between 1822 (or earlier) and 1839, three men had solved the problem of permanently fixing the camera image; they were Joseph Nicéphore Niepce and Louis Jacques Mandé Daguerre of France and William Henry Fox Talbot of England.

The first of these inventions to be made public was Daguerre's; his camera images—or daguerreotypes—were presented to the French Academy in 1839. The process astonished public and scientists alike. The small silvery pictures were so precise that they seemed almost a substitute for the subject itself.

Photography Spreads Worldwide

Photography spread with incredible speed throughout the world. The U.S. painter and inventor Samuel F. B. Morse exhibited a daguerreotype that he had made a few days after the arrival of the first instruction manual in the fall of 1839. By 1853 it was estimated—perhaps extravagantly—that 3 million daguerreotypes had been made in that year in New York City alone.

Like all truly radical inventions, photography was born into a world that had very little idea of how to use it. Those who had invented photography had been artists and scientists, but those who flocked to its commercial practice were generally neither. It may be assumed that they came primarily from the ranks of artisans and skilled craftsmen: printers, tinkers, jewelers, pharmacists, and so forth. These men had no common training or tradition; in the beginning

'Poet's House (First Version)', 1965, by Jerry Uelsmann

LENT BY PHOTOGRAPHER

they learned the new process from manuals that were at best far from exhaustive. Each man puzzled out the process as best he could and decided according to his own circumstances how photography might be profitably used.

Photography as a Record Maker of People, Places, and Events

In the first quarter century of photography's life, it was used primarily to make portraits and to record those great architectural monuments that had previously been known only to a few travelers. The social significance of the photographic portrait is perhaps more profound than has been generally recognized. Before photography, only the well-to-do had their portraits painted; in a sense, it was only prosperous families who had ancestors. The common man's sense of his own history was limited by the quickly failing memories of his family's living members. By the beginning of the 20th century, however, even the peasant and the proletarian possessed pictures of dead ancestors, and thus a heightened sense of identity.

Photography of the great monuments of past cultures changed men's sense of both time and space. Familiarity with these achievements had previously been the privilege of the scholar or the wealthy traveler. Within the first generation of photography's life, the great monuments of the old Mediterranean cultures and of medieval Europe had been photographed and published. For thousands to whom these works had been scarcely more real than fairy stories, the world was made a richer and a smaller place. Indeed, it is unlikely that the modern comparative studies of archaeology and art history could have flowered without the reproducible visual records that photography offered.

By the time of the U.S. Civil War, photographers had begun to try to deal with events as well as static facts. The photographic record of that war, for its breadth of concept and brilliance of execution, remains one of photography's most impressive achievements. Conceived and funded first by the photographer Mathew B. Brady, the total document was, in fact, produced by several independent units and by perhaps a dozen photographers.

Photography at the time was still a lengthy and painstaking process. Working within the limits that the medium imposed, the photographers recorded the men at rest, the sites of the battles, and the grisly human remains left on the field after the battle. Perhaps no other work of fact or fiction has done so much to destroy the concept of war as an exciting and romantic adventure.

In the latter decades of the 19th century, one of photography's most interesting challenges was the recording of the natural landscape. Large areas of the world's surface were still unmapped and unexplored. The natural wonders and the potential wealth of these areas were described by photographers who accompanied the explorer-scientists on their missions and who brought back to an eagerly receptive public visual evidence of the world's wild places.

Scientific Photography

In the same period, photography became an important tool of the biological and physical sciences. Eadweard Muybridge in the United States and Jules Étienne Marey in France made basic contributions to the study of physiology and animal locomotion. Astronomers fixed cameras to their telescopes and recorded stars too dim to be seen by the eye, even through the most powerful instruments. Physicists and medical researchers used photography to record invisible energy sources: X rays, ultraviolet light, heat, and electron emission.

In these and other cases, photography has increased our vision. It has shown us phenomena that had been invisible because they were too rapid in motion, or too small, or too distant.

The Family Snapshot

Photography was revolutionized in the 1880's by the perfection of dry emulsions and flexible film, which, in turn, allowed the development of small, simple hand cameras. Photography then was brought within the range of anyone who wished to make pictures. George Eastman's *Kodak* became virtually a synonym for *camera* among the millions who made casual snapshots of their families and pets and picnics. These pictures were made simply to provide food for the private pleasures of nostalgic retrospect.

Nevertheless, the best of them survive not only as moving evocations of their time and place, but also as images of surprising graphic and symbolic force. Their virtues are the result partly of accident and partly of the spirit of play—the uninhibited and careless candor—that produced them.

Photography as a Fine Art

Toward the turn of the century, a small but dedicated minority of photographers devoted themselves to the problem of securing for photography full acceptance as a fine art. These photographers felt that photography should be admired as an art form equal—at least in potential—to the arts of painting and sculpture. In the United States, the focal point of this campaign was Alfred Stieglitz and the group called the Photo-Secession that he gathered around him. In addition to being an effective prophet and publicist of photography as an art, Stieglitz was himself among the greatest and most influential of photographers. The force of his aspirations and definitions remains a vital force today, 24 years after his death. Stieglitz demonstrated more clearly than anyone before him the subjectivity of photography; he photographed not what his subjects had been known to mean, but what they meant to his own intuitive and personal vision.

In the 1920's, other photographers, primarily in Europe, defined a different approach to photography. This approach was based less on exploration of the subject and more on exploration of the photographic medium itself. The *photograms* of Man Ray and László Moholy-Nagy, made without a camera by casting the shadows of simple objects directly onto photographic paper, were typical products of this attitude.

The "Artless" Photograph

To a considerable degree, Stieglitz and his followers and allies were successful in achieving recognition for photography as a fine art. Ironically, however, their insistence on the artistic status of the medium came to seem almost a variety of servility to some younger photographers. These people felt that too close an association with the traditional arts might burden the newer medium with values and standards not really relevant to its own problems and potentials. Walker Evans' work of the 1930's epitomized the new attitude. By the conventional standards of pictorial excellence Evans' pictures seemed as artless as newsreels. But their effect was deeply challenging, for in them the anonymous and mundane details of the U.S. environment assumed somehow the role of symbols, speaking of a spiritual condition.

The photographers who reacted against what seemed a too-easy alliance with the accepted art world discovered in photography's past their own precedents and heroes. The Civil War photographers were among them, but perhaps the most revered predecessor was the Frenchman Eugène Atget, who died almost unknown in 1927. These predecessors were often called primitives, meaning that they were innocent of a sense of themselves as fine artists.

Photojournalism

In the late 1920's and 1930's, the sudden rise of popular picture magazines radically changed the nature of professional photography. Advertising illustration offered interesting problems and great rewards to photographers, but probably the most challenging opportunity was the area of photojournalism. A photographer's work in the magazines might reach millions of viewers in a single week.

The price paid by the photographer for this opportunity was a high one, however; he had become one member of a large journalistic team, and his stories were often published in a form that seemed less his work than that of the editors. Nevertheless, magazines like *Life* seemed to many photographers to represent the most exciting potential for photography during the 1940's and 1950's. Once television came into virtually universal use, however, it assumed much of the journalistic function of the magazines and much of their former vigor.

A New Means of Expression in Man's Vocabulary

Increasingly since World War II, photography has been a subject receiving serious attention in U.S. colleges and universities. It has generally been taught in close association with the other arts, and the basic approach in most schools has not been professional but humanistic; photography has been taught less as a specialized skill than as a new dimension in man's common expressive vocabulary.

Considering the continually increasing simplicity of the photographic process, the future of professional photography is probably a diminishing one except in highly specialized areas. Professional photographers in the past have performed a function in some ways comparable to that of the scribes in predominantly illiterate cultures. In the future we can expect instead the achievement of a world in which educated people are visually as well as verbally articulate. These people will make and use photographs as a natural function of their work and their private lives as easily as they now use language.

Edwin H. Land, whose Polaroid process created the most recent of photography's technical revolutions, has defined the future role of photography in these words: "Photography can go beyond amusement and record-making to become a continuous partner of most human beings. As a new eye and a second memory, it will enhance the art of seeing and reinforce recalling."

The Art of Photography

Mr. Szarkowski personally selected the pictures on the following 24 pages to illustrate the development of photography.

THE MUSEUM OF MODERN ART, NEW YORK CITY

'Family Portrait (Daguerreotype)', Unknown (facing page)

'Prof. Michael Faraday', 1859, by Maull & Polyblank (above)

THE MUSEUM OF MODERN ART, NEW YORK CITY

THE MUSEUM OF MODERN ART, NEW YORK CITY

'Home of a Rebel Sharpshooter, Gettysburg', 1863, by Alexander Gardner (top left)

'Karnak from the Southeast', circa 1876, by Sir William Abney (bottom left)

'Niagara Suspension Bridge', 1859, by William England (above)

LIBRARY OF CONGRESS

'Rebel Works in Front of Atlanta, Ga., No. 5', circa 1864, by George N. Barnard (top left)

'Green River near Flaming Gorge', circa 1869, by T. H. O'Sullivan (bottom left)

'Blackfoot Brave Before a Tepee and Pony', after 1873, Unknown (above)

THE MUSEUM OF MODERN ART, NEW YORK CITY

THE MUSEUM OF MODERN ART, NEW YORK CITY

'Winter on Fifth Avenue, New York', 1893, by Alfred Stieglitz (left)

'Gathering Water Lilies', 1886, by P. H. Emerson (above)

'Bird in Flight: Twelve Exposures', 1883–87, by Eadweard Muybridge (below)

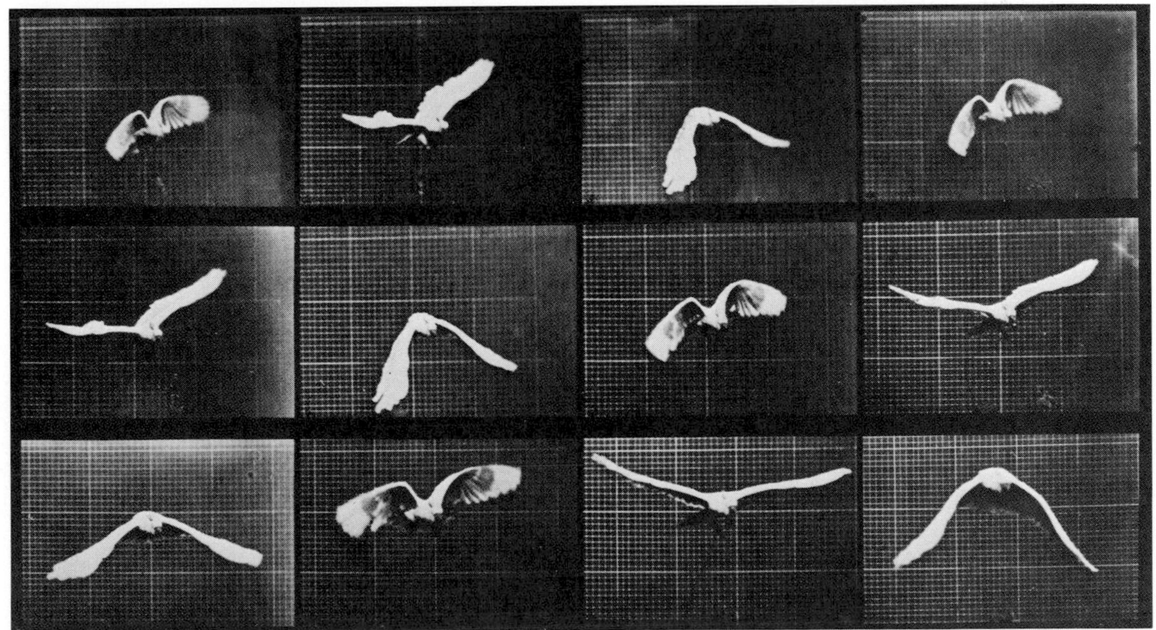

THE MUSEUM OF MODERN ART, NEW YORK CITY

THE MUSEUM OF MODERN ART, NEW YORK CITY, GIFT OF MRS. MERVYN PALMER

THE MUSEUM OF MODERN ART, NEW YORK CITY

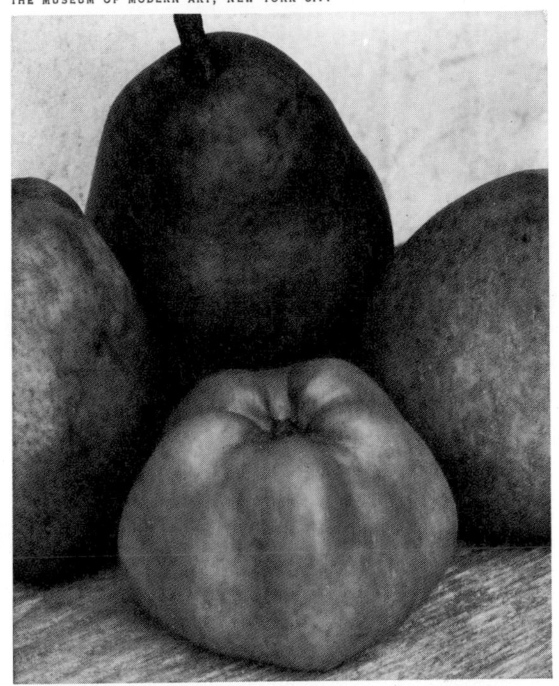

'Miss Grace', 1898, by Clarence H. White (facing page)

'Three Pears and an Apple', circa 1921, by Edward Steichen (left)

'Child in Carolina Cotton Mill', 1908, by Lewis W. Hine (below)

THE MUSEUM OF MODERN ART, NEW YORK CITY

JACQUES-HENRI LARTIGUE FROM RAPHO GUILLUMETTE

'Grand Prix of the Automobile Club of France', 1912, by Jacques-Henri Lartigue (above)

'Rayograph', 1923, by Man Ray (right)

'Avenue des Gobelins', 1907, by Eugène Atget (facing page)

THE MUSEUM OF MODERN ART, NEW YORK CITY, GIFT OF JAMES THRALL SOBY

32
43
22
36
69
79
75
65
55
55
42
28
39
121

THE MUSEUM OF MODERN ART, NEW YORK CITY

LENT BY PHOTOGRAPHER

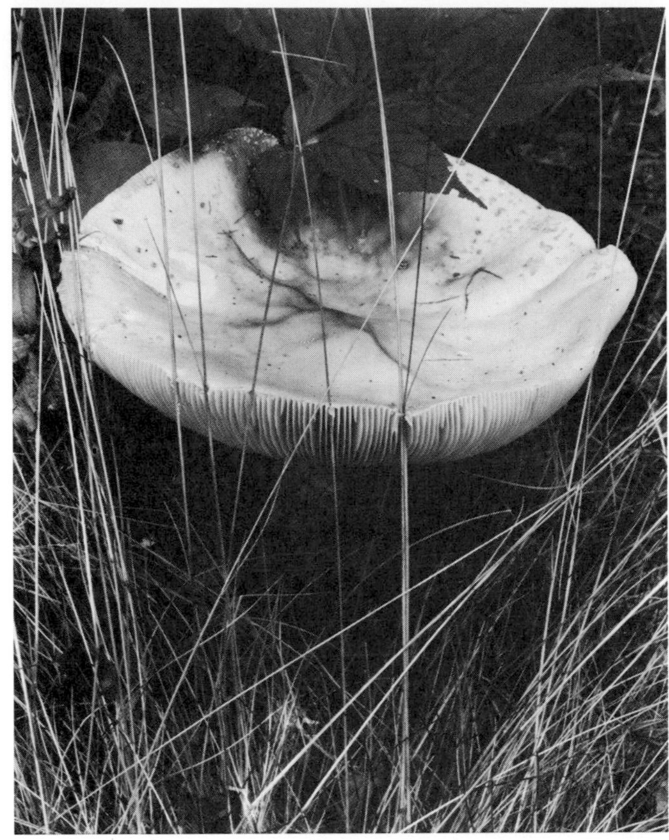

'From the Radio Tower, Berlin', 1928, by László Moholy-Nagy (facing page)

'Toadstool and Grasses', 1928, by Paul Strand (left)

'Seville, Spain, 1933', by Henri Cartier-Bresson (below)

PHOTOGRAPHY BY HENRI CARTIER-BRESSON/MAGNUM

LENT BY PHOTOGRAPHER

LENT BY PHOTOGRAPHER

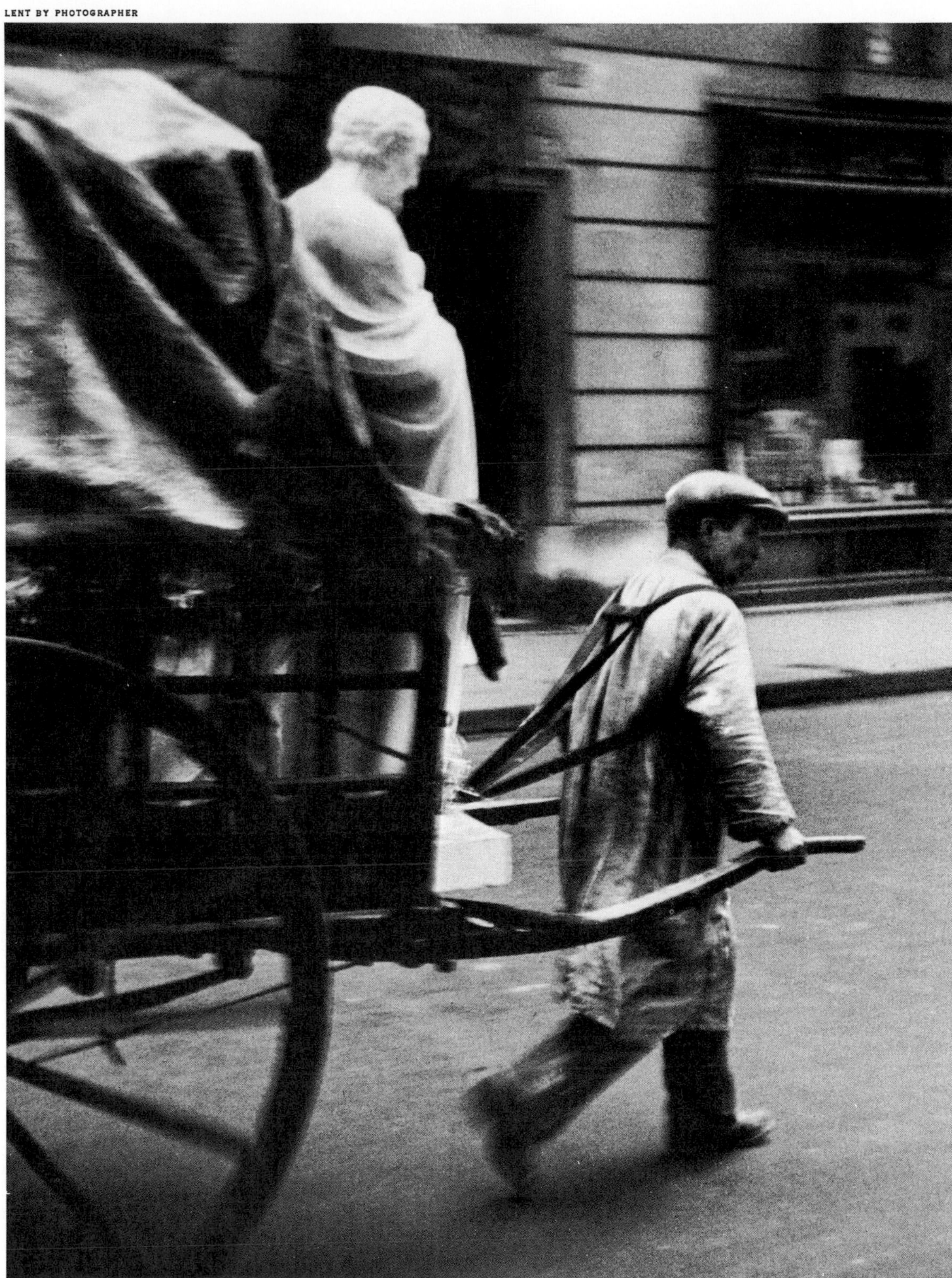

'Lunch Wagon Detail, New York, 1931', by Walker Evans (left)

'Montparnasse, Paris', 1928, by André Kertész (above)

LENT BY PHOTOGRAPHER

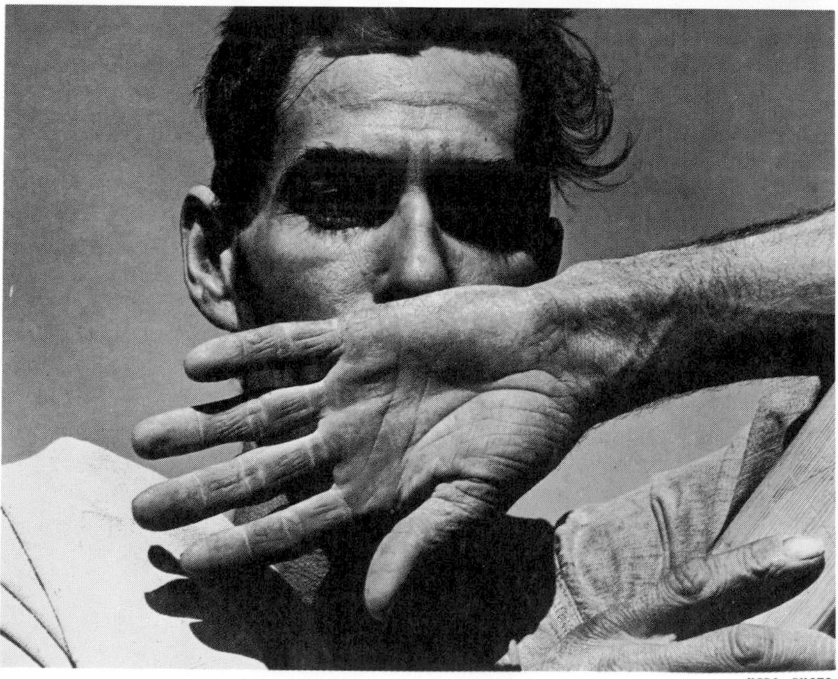

USDA PHOTO

LENT BY PHOTOGRAPHER

'Martha's Vineyard, Massachusetts', 1950, by Aaron Siskind (facing page, top)

'Migratory Cotton Picker, Eloy, Arizona', 1940, by Dorothea Lange (facing page, bottom)

'Brigitte Bardot', 1959, by Richard Avedon (left)

'Chicago About 1950', by Harry Callahan (below)

LENT BY PHOTOGRAPHER

BRASSAÏ FROM RAPHO GUILLUMETTE

'Pimp and Girl', 1933, by Brassaï (right)

'Dunes, Oceano', 1936, by Edward Weston (below)

'Old Faithful Geyser, Late Evening, Yellowstone National Park, Wyoming', 1942, by Ansel Adams (facing page)

THE MUSEUM OF MODERN ART, NEW YORK CITY

ANSEL ADAMS, COURTESY, FIVE ASSOCIATES, INC., REDWOOD CITY, CALIF.

LENT BY PHOTOGRAPHER

COURTESY, NATIONAL ATOMIC ENERGY COMMISSION OF ARGENTINA

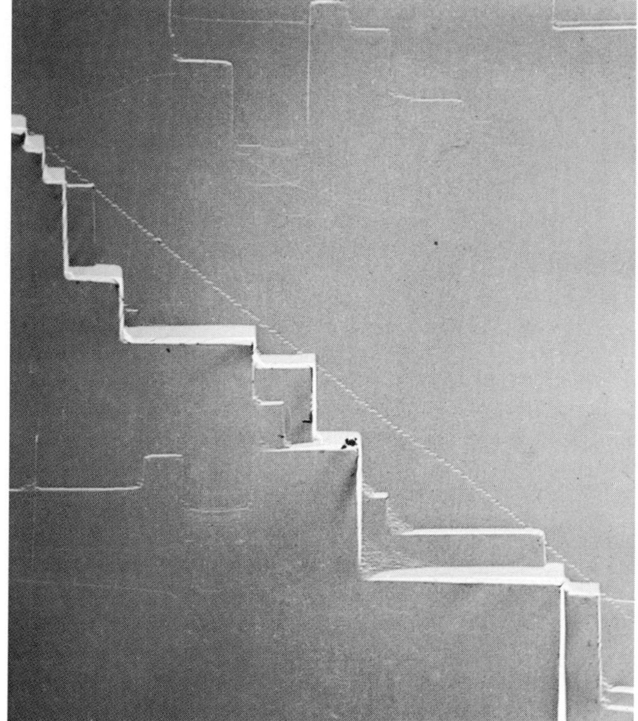

'Sun Spot in Cracked Mud, Capitol Reef, Utah' (from Sequence 17), 1961, by Minor White (facing page)

'Electron Micrograph of Sodium Chloride Crystal', thermally etched by Dr. Maria J. de Abeledo and Lelia de Wainer (left)

'Untitled', 1963, by Garry Winogrand (below)

LENT BY PHOTOGRAPHER

LENT BY PHOTOGRAPHER

'Guardia Civil', 1950, by W. Eugene Smith (above)

'Stroboscopic Photograph of W. E. Fesler Kicking a Football', 1935, by Dr. Harold E. Edgerton (right)

'Chicago—Political Rally' (from 'The Americans'), 1956, by Robert Frank (facing page)

LENT BY PHOTOGRAPHER

LENT BY PHOTOGRAPHER

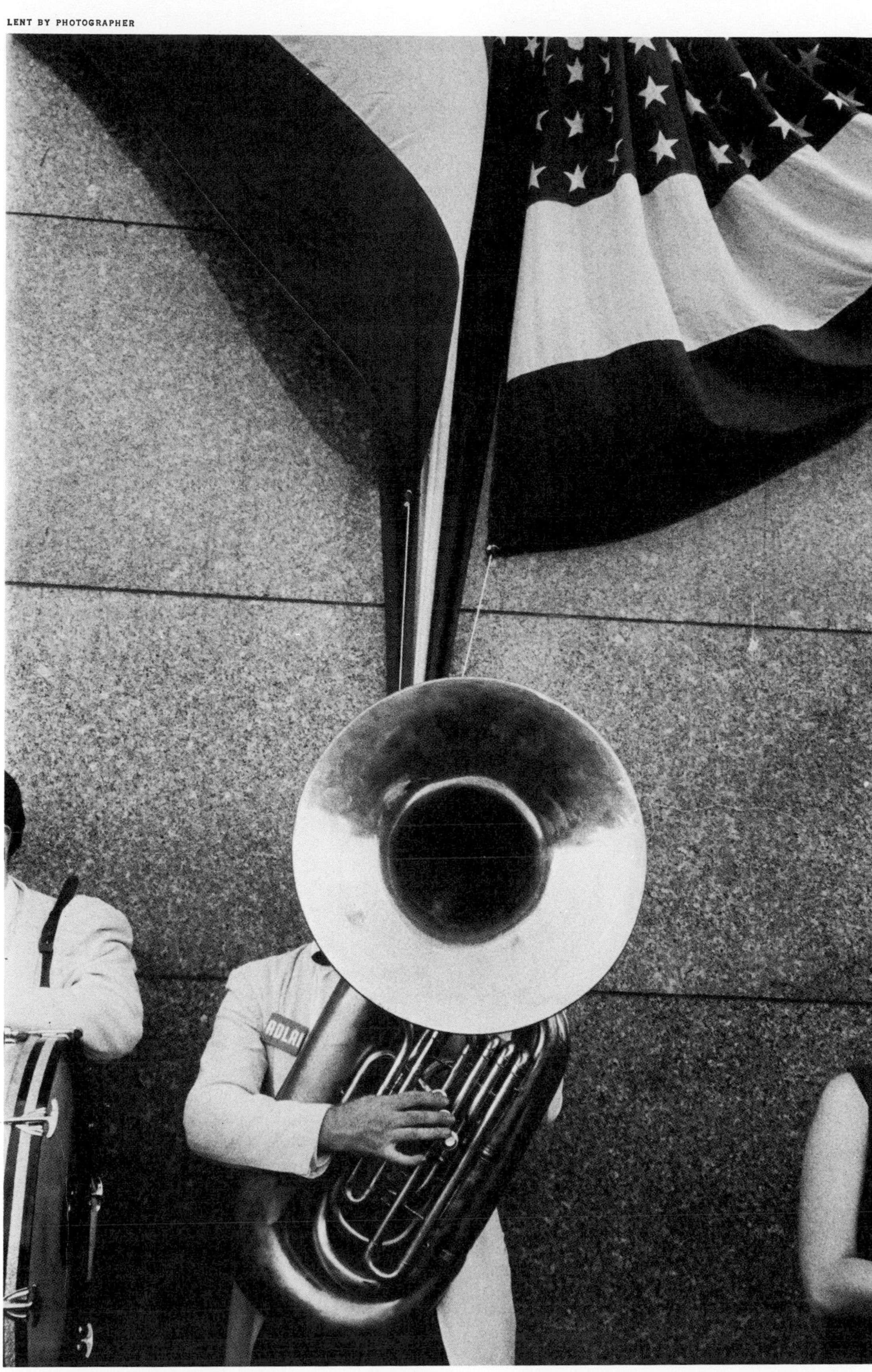

drugs and youth

by Dr. Stanley Fausst Yolles

Assistant Surgeon General, U.S. Public Health Service

One of the most controversial problems of current concern is drug abuse, particularly among young people. In the United States the majority of the country's estimated 8 million to 12 million drug abusers are believed to be young people between the ages of 9 and 25. Marijuana, or "pot," is the most widely used drug among young people, but increasing numbers are also using psychedelic drugs, amphetamines and barbiturates, and "hard narcotics," mostly heroin. Doctor Yolles, one of the nation's foremost experts on drugs, was formerly director of the National Institute of Mental Health. In this article he takes a close look at the U.S. "drug culture" and suggests ways to prevent drugs from becoming the "escape mechanism through which America's most promising generation drops out."

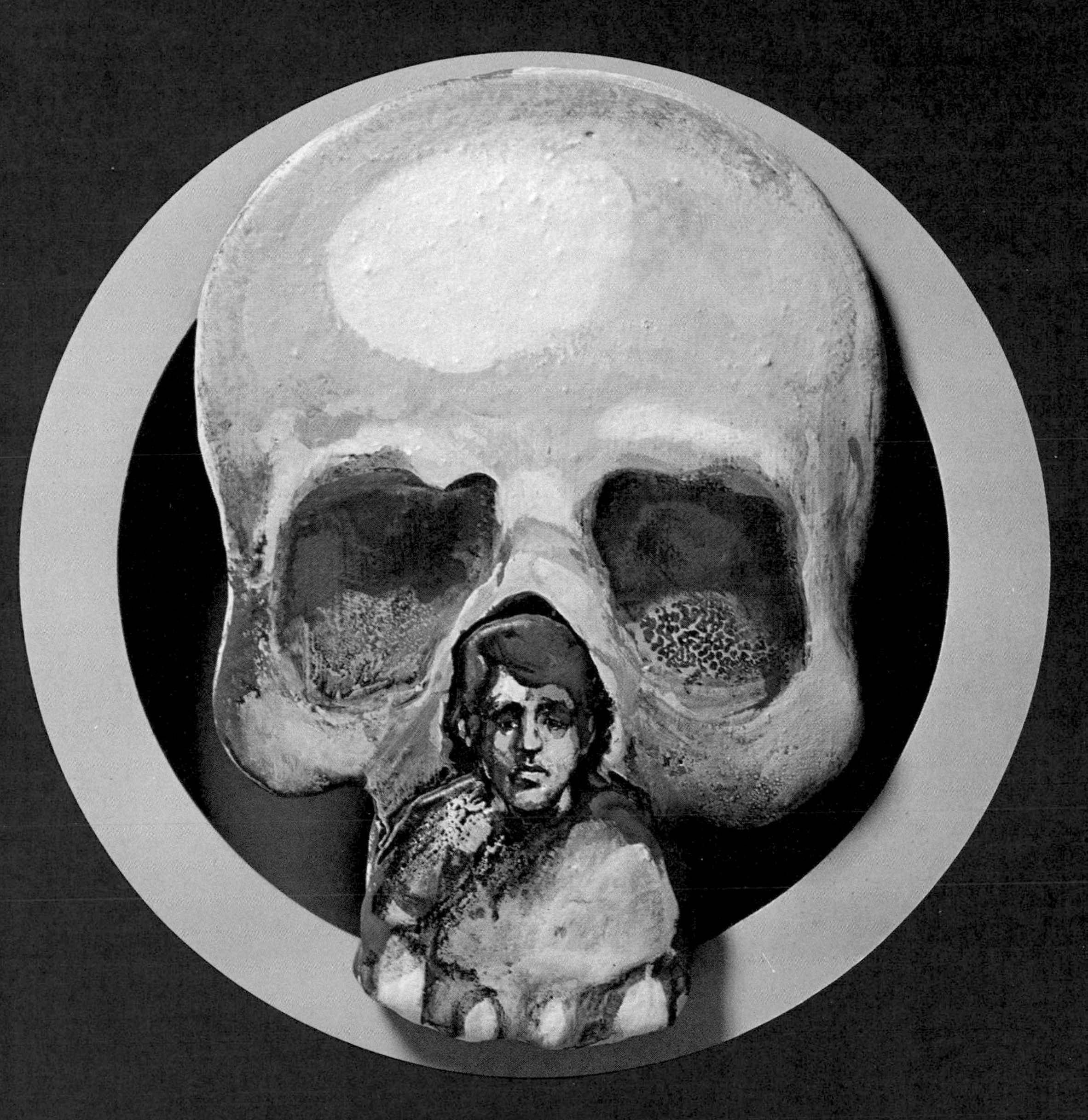

During 1970 the attention of the United States was focused prominently on drug use, particularly among young people. This was evidenced by the increasing numbers of drug users, by the great degree of mass media exposure to the U.S. "drug culture," and by the amount of legislation introduced in an attempt to alleviate the drug problem.

It is currently estimated that between 8 million and 12 million people in the United States—the majority between the ages of 9 and 25—are abusers of drugs; that is, they use drugs for nonmedicinal purposes. The drugs abused cover a wide variety of categories, from the "soft" to the "hard": marijuana (from the hemp plant, *Cannabis sativa*) and hashish (a more potent form of cannabis), LSD (lysergic acid diethylamide) and other hallucinogenic or psychedelic ("mind-manifesting" or "mind-expanding") drugs; stimulants and depressants, primarily amphetamines ("pep pills") and barbiturates (sedatives); and hard narcotics, mainly heroin.

Although we speak about drug abuse by categories for clarity and convenience, it should be noted that many, perhaps most, heavy abusers do not restrict their drug use to one category of drugs. Multiple drug use is a common complicating factor in analyses of drug-using behavior. The drugs used also depend in part on availability. The occasional social user of marijuana, for instance, may switch to the more potent hashish to achieve a higher "high" when the former is not available. Similarly, the heroin user who cannot get his supply may use barbiturates or codeine cough syrups temporarily. Moreover, since the quality, quantity, and composition of drugs sold on the street are quite variable, the user himself may be ignorant of the actual substances consumed.

The abuse of drugs presents a rapidly changing pattern with multiple currents and countercurrents—some disquieting and vexing, and a few hopeful. Since the nonmedical use in the United States of "narcotics and dangerous drugs" (opium and coca products and marijuana) is illegal, users are secretive about their activities. The problem of drug abuse, therefore, partially eludes ordinary techniques for surveying social problems. Furthermore, constant resurveying is necessary because of the rapidly changing scene.

We can delineate the following trends during 1969 and 1970:

1. The misuse of drugs was not limited to the United States. It posed serious problems in such places as Great Britain, Sweden, Japan, France, and Australia.

2. The abuse of narcotics, sedatives, and stimulants continued to increase. In particular, the intravenous injection of methamphetamine (known as "speed," or by its trade name, Methedrine) among thousands of adolescents and young adults became a new cause for concern because of the associated physical and mental hazards.

3. A steep increase in marijuana and hashish use could be discerned. Although most users were experimenters or infrequent indulgers, perhaps 5% to 10% of all who were involved were chronic cannabis smokers.

4. Less LSD was being taken. Apparently, the spectacular increase in LSD consumption from 1961 to 1967 was checked to a degree through a health-oriented educational approach.

5. The rising level of drug abuse in all categories was, in large part, a phenomenon of younger age groups, no doubt to some extent because of the potency of fads in early adolescence. These drug-involved preadolescents and adolescents are to be found mainly in cities and suburbs.

6. During 1969 and 1970 there was a marked increase in the number of young Americans arrested abroad for illegally using or trafficking in drugs. In March 1969 there were 142 young people being detained in 20 countries. By March 1970 this figure had risen to 522.

7. Of greatest concern has been the increasing number of deaths among young drug abusers. In Massachusetts, for example, statistics for 1969 showed a fivefold increase over 1968 in the number of deaths from overdosage. Preliminary statistics for the first five months of 1970 showed an increase of 133% over 1969. Of 32 persons who died reportedly as a result of taking LSD, narcotics, and amphetamines, the largest number were in their mid-twenties.

The most frightening increase in deaths attributed to drugs occurred in New York City—the largest U.S. city. In 1969 there were 950 deaths from narcotic abuse; 224 were teenagers, of whom 55 were under the age of 16. In the first six months of 1970 there were at least 377 deaths attributed to narcotics, mostly heroin.

WHY DRUGS?

Drug abuse can perhaps be best conceptualized as a behavioral pattern through which people try to cope with the stress of overwhelming and uncontrollable change and disruption.

The hopeless despair of chronic poverty and the frustrating alienation of a hostile society send the ghetto dweller as well as the economically affluent to the same drugs. Poverty and alienation breed a common compulsion to "cop out" or "turn off" through drugs.

Drug use is particularly strong in the hippie subculture. In a pilot study of hippies in New York City's East Village, investigators found that all respondents reported prior or current use of marijuana, most having been introduced to marijuana in their late teens. The vast majority of respondents admitted experience with a wide variety of drugs, including LSD, hashish, methamphetamine, peyote, and DMT (dimethyltryptamine).

The data uncovered in this study suggested that the hippie movement is primarily a symptom of alienation. Most hippies in the group studied (the majority of them between the ages of 18 and 25) felt removed from or uncommitted to the dominant values of society. This may stem in part from disenchantment with prior home environment and a discrepancy perceived between society's claims and its actual practices. The prevalence of drug use is no doubt related to these feelings of alienation.

Many of today's vigorous, idealistic youths suffer from the same sort of alienation. They see the world beset with problems and in need of change. For some, the problems are so great and the roadblocks to improvement so high that they have chosen, in anger, despair, or dread, to turn their backs and seek a less distressing world—the world of drugs. It is widely noted that many have decided, since they cannot alter the world or determine the direction in which it will go, they will instead alter their own state of consciousness and perception. They prefer to cop out of here-and-now reality.

Fear of reality, known or unknown, has thus perhaps been the major impetus for seeking escape through drugs. There are undoubtedly other reasons why young people use drugs—to satisfy curiosity, to conform to peer group pressures, and to provide pleasure and "kicks." Some of the prophets of the new drug cults are convinced that modern man needs to think less and feel more, and drug taking is a sensual, not an intellectual, experience. Indeed, a recent psychedelic happening starring a cult leader was appropriately titled "The Death of the Mind."

A NATIONAL HEALTH PROBLEM

It is not possible, however, to talk about young people's use of drugs as though this were an isolated segment of the drug phenomenon. Drug abuse in the United States is not restricted to the young; it is found at all social and economic levels, in the core city and the suburbs. Drug abuse is not only the heroin user injecting his "H," the "speed freak" high on methamphetamine, or the 14-year-old sniffing airplane glue. It is also the suburban housewife using her diet pills for a quick pick-me-up, the driving executive or the long-distance trucker alternating between stimulants by day and sleep-inducing barbiturates at night, the athlete using a pep pill for an extra spurt of energy, or the urbanite needing one or two extra lunch-hour martinis.

The drug dilemma facing the United States has become a national concern. Scientists, physicians, law enforcement officers, the judiciary, and the public have become involved in a debate regarding the pros and cons of a "hard" or "soft" approach to drug control, which, in many cases, is noteworthy more for its emotional content than for its reason. While there are increasing signs of more thoughtful, less panicky societal responses to the problem, public reaction continues to be emotionally charged.

THE "HARD" VERSUS THE "SOFT" APPROACH

The problem of drug abuse has led historically to the development of two polarized points of view regarding its solution—the hard and the soft, or the punitive and the permissive. The hard line is an essentially punitive approach against the drug abuser, putting him away from society for as long as possible. In contrast to this attitude is a softer or more permissive approach that has as its premise the belief that drug abuse is the symptom of an underlying emotional disorder and thus the drug abuser is a sick person in need of treatment.

Laws have been instituted against the drug addict, imposing severe penalties aimed to pressure or compel the addict to make stronger efforts to conquer his need for drugs. For many years the system that operated in the United States was essentially one calling for the application of criminal sanctions for violations of laws governing the nonmedical use of what were termed by law "narcotics and dangerous drugs." To many people, however, it has been clearly demonstrated that threats and the imposition of severe punishment have not been an effective deterrent in the area of drug abuse.

Within recent years, there has been a noticeable shift in U.S. public opinion and in the laws of the federal and state governments toward a

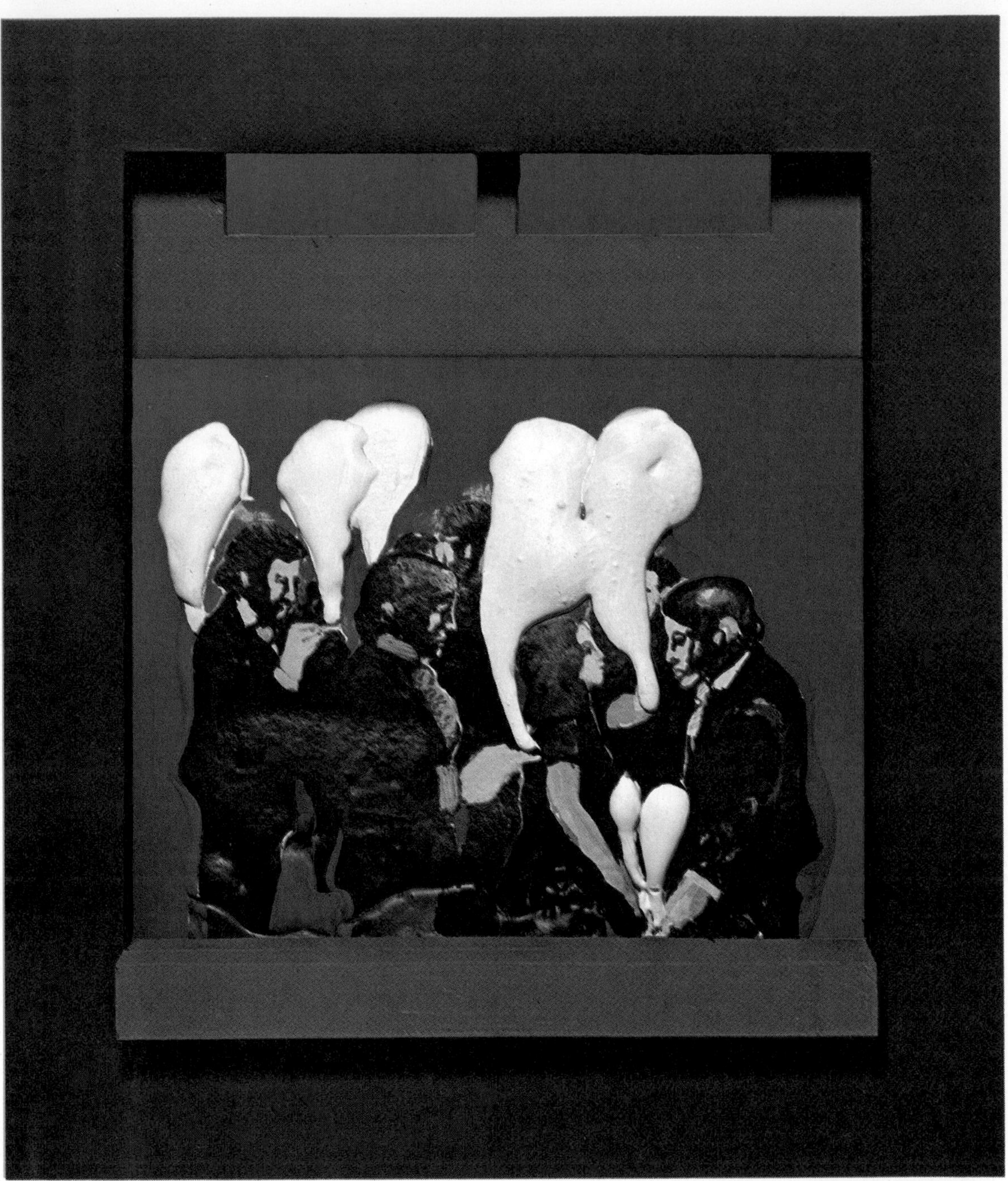

less punitive approach with regard to the hard narcotic addict. The Narcotic Addict Rehabilitation Act of 1966 was a milestone in this development; it viewed addiction as an illness to be treated and recognized the need for a comprehensive approach to the management of the addict.

Public opinion concerning marijuana is uncertain but is tending toward the less punitive. One reason for the uncertainty is the lack of knowledge about the drug's effects. Proponents of "pot" have argued that it is a recreational drug like alcohol and that, in fact, the effects of marijuana are actually less dangerous to society than those of alcohol. In light of this, a protest movement has developed that argues against the injustice of the currently severe legal penalties against marijuana. Recently, in 27 states the drug laws dealing with the possession of marijuana have been revised to reduce the offense for first-time possession of marijuana from a felony to a misdemeanor.

In a Canadian government report released in June 1970, Canada came closer than any other Western nation to a radical revision of its policy toward marijuana. The report was hailed as a social landmark in Canada not only because of its liberal recommendations but also because of its acute sensitivity to youth culture. The report recommended that maximum penalties for simple possession of cannabis be reduced to a $100 fine rather than a jail term. "There is universal agreement," the report states, "that cannabis is not a narcotic and should not be classified legally with opiate narcotics. Such classification is misleading and undermines respect for the rationality of law. . . . We believe that emphasis must shift from a reliance on suppression to a reliance on wise exercise of freedom of choice."

MARIJUANA

Of all the illegal drugs currently in use, marijuana has generated the most popular concern. Next to alcohol, it is the most widely abused drug and its use is on the increase throughout the world. Measured by the criteria available in 1970, there are at least 250 million users of marijuana worldwide.

In the United States, in recent years, there has been a marked increase in the use of marijuana. Based on a number of surveys, it is estimated that, nationwide, 20% to 40% of high school and college students have tried marijuana at least once. In Florida a survey of 5,000 college students indicated that 20% regularly smoked marijuana. In a survey conducted at Columbia University Law School, 69% of the students enrolled admitted using marijuana at least once and, of those, 93% had used it more than once. In the past two to three years, use has begun to spread to junior high school and grade school students. It is also believed that large numbers of middle-class adults are involved in the smoking of marijuana. It is estimated that the number of people in the United States who have smoked marijuana at least once is somewhere between 8 million and 12 million; it may be closer to 20 million.

Of all those who have tried marijuana, about 65% are experimenting, trying the drug from one to ten times and then discontinuing its use. Some 25% are social users, smoking marijuana on occasion when it is available, usually in group context. Perhaps 5% to 10% can be considered chronic users who devote significant portions of their time to using the drug.

A team of research psychiatrists reported recently that they had found large-scale differences in the social adjustment, working capabilities, and level of mental health between casual smokers of marijuana and chronic users of the drug who were matched for age, race, social class, and educational level. Casual users smoked marijuana once a week or less and were generally healthy individuals with good work habits who rarely used other drugs, except for alcohol. They had few problems in the area of sexuality in contrast to the chronic users, who had poor relationships with friends and had many sexual problems. The chronic marijuana users, researchers found, smoked marijuana at least once a day and looked to the drug for enhanced insights and "a sense of harmony" as well as pleasure. The chronic users also experimented widely with other drugs.

There is sharp disagreement among well-informed scientists regarding the degree of threat posed by marijuana. Adequate data, particularly on the implications of long-term, low-dosage social use, are generally lacking. Much of the controversy arises out of overinterpretation or misinterpretation of what few facts are presently available. Studies of cannabis use in foreign societies, for example, lack the controls generally considered essential for reaching valid conclusions.

Physical and Psychological Effects of Marijuana

The effects of marijuana vary with the potency of the agent, the psychological set of the user, and the setting in which use takes place. It has been estimated that half of those who use marijuana the first time experience no effects at all. Marijuana is not physically addicting in that no withdrawal symptoms accompany termination of its use, but it is thought by some to be psychologically habituating.

Over the past several decades scientific observers have noted confused speech, "spurious thinking," and paranoid or catatonic reactions associated with marijuana use. Recent studies have identified a disturbance of immediate memory that induces gaps in the stream of thought and produces aberrations in speech content in marijuana users. One researcher demonstrated an alteration of sequential thought in his marijuana subjects, according to a conference report presented at the Jonas Salk Institute, La Jolla, Calif., in January 1970. Other scientific observers reported a speech impairment caused by the loss of immediate recall and difficulty in retrieval of recently acquired information.

Other psychological reactions have been noted. Research reported late in 1967 indicated that high doses of tetrahydrocannabinol (THC)—the active ingredient of cannabis—could produce delusions, hallucinations, and psychotic reactions similar to those produced by LSD. In December 1968 a paper presented at the American College of Neuropsychopharmacology reported that small doses of THC produced somatic discomfort, dizziness, "weirdness," and dreamlike floating states. The individuals under the influence also felt sleepy and high.

A number of articles have appeared describing adverse reactions to marijuana in U.S. soldiers serving in Vietnam. Most recently, at the National Academy of Sciences and National Research Council meeting in February 1970, researchers reported on 16 marijuana smokers who required psychotherapy for anxiety, paranoid states, depression, rage reactions, inability to concentrate, and psychotic episodes.

The significance of these reports of acute effects of marijuana use needs to be evaluated carefully. In regard to their "real life" significance, however, it seems evident that for some people marijuana is not a "harmless weed."

A Preference for Nonrational Thinking?

There is a broader question of greater concern. Do repeated episodes of bizarre thinking, dreamlike states, self-removal from life situations, interference with recent recall and memory—all in the context of euphoria—result in a sustained disinclination to become involved in logical, rational thinking? Does the constant user come to prefer nonrational thinking to problem solving? Dr. Louis J. West, at the Salk Institute meeting in January 1970, spoke of subtle changes among chronic marijuana users: ". . . decreased drive, apathy, distractibility, poor judgment, introversion, depersonalization, diminished capacity to carry out complex plans or prepare realistically for the future, magical thinking, a peculiar fragmentation of thought, and progressive loss of insight."

One needs to be particularly concerned about the potential effect of a reality-distorting agent on the future psychological development of the adolescent user. We know that normal adolescence is a time of great psychological turmoil. Patterns of coping with reality developed during the teen-age period are significant in determining adult behavior. Persistent use of an agent that serves to ward off reality during this critical developmental period is likely to compromise seriously the future ability of the individual to make an adequate adjustment to a complex and demanding society.

There remains a real need for controlled, in-depth studies of cannabis use. The research should include investigation of the physical effects of varying dosage levels and of the psychological and social consequences of its use. Only when the full physical and psychological effects are known can society make an appropriate judgment about the use of marijuana.

STIMULANTS AND DEPRESSANTS

The number of nonnarcotic drug abusers, including those addicted or habituated to agents such as sedatives, stimulants, and certain tranquilizers, can only be grossly estimated. Probably more than 500,000 people in all age categories are dependent on these agents.

Abuse of amphetamines and barbiturates ranges from the practice of using illicitly obtained drugs to the more hidden forms of abuse represented by inappropriate usage of medically prescribed drugs. Some experts would also include the prescribing of amphetamines in programs of weight reduction as an iatrogenic (physician-induced) form of drug abuse.

What college survey data have been accumulated seem to indicate that the use of amphetamines is limited, most commonly related to cramming for examinations. For example, one survey at a university of high academic standing indicated that about one student in ten had used these drugs nonprescriptively. In another study at a large university, 21% of all students had tried amphetamines, with the family medicine cabinet one important source. Of the 21%, most were infrequent users.

Of particular concern, however, is the recent upsurge in the high doses, usually intravenous, of methamphetamine taken by young people. Increasing numbers of young people have been found to be using up to 100 times the average medical dose in a single injection, and they may repeat such injections a number of times daily. Such "speed freaks" may exhibit impulsive paranoid behavior, becoming a danger to themselves and those around them. When this severe misuse of methamphetamine is prolonged, malnutrition, hepatitis, brain cell damage, and cardiac arrhythmia (irregular heartbeat) become possibilities.

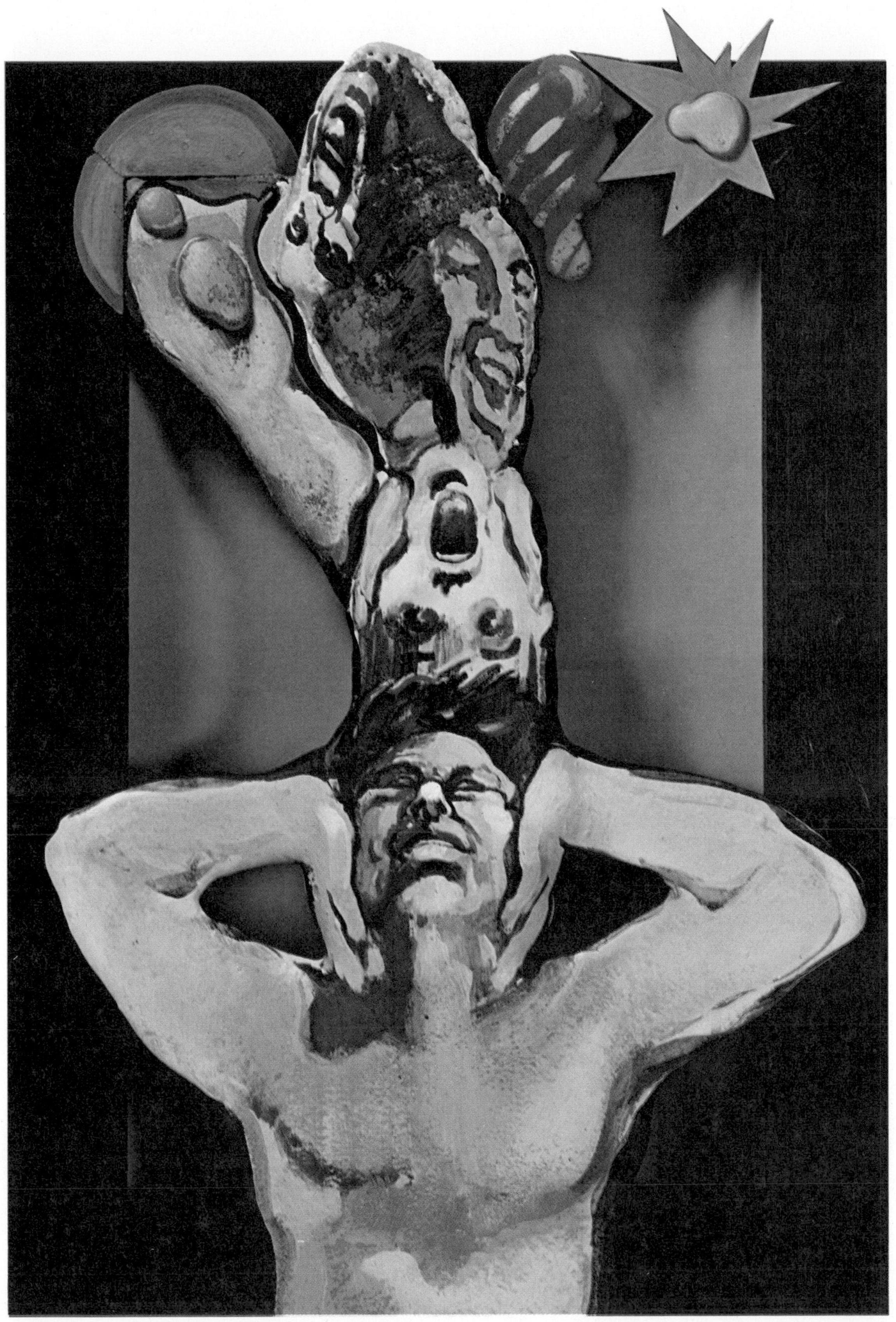

There is some concern that the use of barbiturate and nonbarbiturate sedative and stimulative drugs during pregnancy may cause mental retardation in offspring of the pregnant human user. Research is currently being conducted to see if such a cause-and-effect relationship does exist.

LSD AND OTHER HALLUCINOGENS

Few drugs have had so profound an effect on American culture in so short a time as lysergic acid diethylamide, familiarly known as LSD. Its use, however, has never been great in terms of the percentage of the population who have tried it. While LSD is the most potent and widely publicized of the hallucinogens, it shares its mind-manifesting properties with such other drugs as peyote and mescaline (derived from the peyote cactus), psilocybin (a mushroom derivative), dimethyltryptamine (DMT), and a number of other chemicals.

The best estimates of the extent of use of LSD among college students indicate relatively modest usage. Surveys of selected college populations from 1967 to 1969 show that 2% to 9% of the students in the survey sample had tried LSD. The 1969 Gallup Poll reported 4%. Very few college students who were polled had consumed LSD more than ten times.

There is evidence that since 1967 the use of LSD by college students has been declining. The reasons for this reversal are several, but significant advances in the understanding of the consequences of LSD ingestion are certainly a major factor. Research has demonstrated the possibility that LSD can precipitate prolonged anxiety, depressive states, and chronic psychotic reactions; these findings have been amply confirmed by clinicians. In addition, those who had used the drug extensively were eventually impressed by the "bummers" or "bad trips" and by unpredictable "flashbacks."

Another reason why proponents of LSD have changed their minds in recent years has been the evanescent nature of the enlightenments and the insights that were supposed to accompany the experience. A nonchemical form of meditation and contemplation was found by some to be more genuine and sustaining.

The relationship between the intensive use of LSD and other hallucinogens and chromosome damage and birth defects is still being investigated. Conclusive evidence must be regarded as incomplete at this time.

While college-age youths are abandoning the use of LSD, the situation is not so encouraging among young people in junior and senior high schools. Experimentation with LSD by people in this age group may, in fact, be on the increase, probably the result of mimicking what is believed to be "in" college behavior.

NARCOTICS

Typically, the known narcotic addict is a young ghetto dweller in a densely populated city. He is a member of a racial minority group, and he and his family are poor.

While narcotic addiction appears to be epidemic in urban slums among economically deprived young people, it also exists in other sections of society. There is evidence that narcotic abuse is increasing in middle- and upper-middle-class U.S. populations. In the majority of instances, however, that abuse is experimental rather than addicting. What is alarming is the increasing use of narcotics by grade school and high school pupils that has been recorded during 1969–70. Children as young as 12 years old have been found to be chronic users of heroin.

The U.S. Bureau of Narcotics and Dangerous Drugs statistics for 1969—based on reports from law enforcement agencies—indicated that there were approximately 68,000 narcotic addicts in the United States. It is probable that the actual number of active narcotic abusers is closer to 200,000.

Treatment

Effective treatment of the narcotic addict continues to be a refractory problem. Results in the past, particularly if the criterion of success is total abstinence from drugs, have often been discouraging. At least part of the difficulty with treatment has been that the addict was most often treated in a hospital far from his home community, and upon his release the treatment was not adequately followed up. Hopefully, the new centers for treatment of the addict will effectively cope with this problem.

There are currently two federal treatment centers, at Lexington, Ky., and Fort Worth, Tex., which provide group psychotherapy and education and vocational programs designed to put the former addict back into the community freed from the psychological need for drugs. There are also 16 federally sponsored community drug abuse centers and more than 100 aftercare programs for rehabilitation of the addicts. Several states have facilities emphasizing a medical treatment approach, including Connecticut, New York, and California. Most of these centers use a variety of treatment modalities to rehabilitate the addict, including methadone maintenance.

Methadone Maintenance and Narcotic Antagonists

Perhaps the most widely publicized experimental program for treating drug addicts is methadone maintenance. Methadone is a synthetically manufactured, addicting narcotic that can be used to block the mental effects of heroin for many addicts. In methadone maintenance the addict is given orally administered methadone as a replacement for heroin. The goal of the treatment is to achieve socially acceptable behavior on the part of the addict rather than to require abstinence from drugs per se. This approach is based on the principle that if *any* medication permits a narcotic user to become a law-abiding and productive member of society, it should be acceptable medication. Since methadone maintenance involves the continued use of an addicting narcotic on a long-term basis, it has been the object of some criticism.

The research with the greatest importance for treatment of the addict is the search for new and improved narcotic antagonists—drugs that occupy the sites on the nerve cell ordinarily occupied by heroin. If these sites can be blockaded by safe agents, the heroin high can be prevented. The use of narcotic antagonists such as Cyclazocine has been promising.

All of these drugs suffer the disadvantage of being relatively short acting. Research is currently being conducted on ways to extend the duration of the effects of such drugs.

Other Rehabilitation Methods

Another method that has been successful in rehabilitating addicts is Synanon, a type of group encounter. The treatment consists of confrontation of the addict patient by ex-addicts who are not taken in by the addict's rationalization and fabrication.

A host of other new encounter programs have been developed, modeled on Synanon but with changes in techniques used. These have been variably successful.

MISCELLANEOUS DRUG ABUSE

In addition to those classes of drugs already mentioned, a number of other substances are being abused. Some of this activity reflects a search for a different high; some of it is in the expectation of just a temporary oblivion.

Among such substances are volatile solvents, including model airplane glue, lacquer thinner, gasoline, certain fingernail polish removers, and cigarette lighter fluids. When these solvents are inhaled, or sniffed, the result is a temporary intoxication. Certain chemicals in the solvents will do acute or chronic damage to the body. In the ten years prior to 1970 at least 110 young persons, whose ages ranged from 11 to 23, died because of solvent sniffing. About 75% of the deaths were in youths from suburban middle-income families. The number of such deaths is rising sharply, according to Dr. Millard Bass of Johns Hopkins University, Baltimore, Md., in a survey published in the *Journal of the American Medical Association.*

The deliriants of the belladonna family have been used since ancient times to produce visions, mental distortions, and confusional states. At the present time only two members of this group have come to attention as methods of "blowing one's mind"—jimsonweed, which grows wild in many parts of the United States, and Asthmador, a patent medicine for asthma.

Some cough syrups contain codeine or a chemically related substance. Heroin addicts without a source of heroin supply and young people experimenting for kicks sometimes take one or more bottles of cough syrup at a time in order to achieve a high.

In addition, there remains a vast array of other substances that will intoxicate. Assuredly someone at some time has sampled them in search of a new high.

EDUCATION AND UNDERSTANDING

The years 1969 and 1970 will no doubt be remembered in the United States as the years of the drug debate. As recently as the summer of 1970, proposals introduced in the U.S. Congress to control drug abuse varied widely in respect to penalties and other control procedures; proponents of such legislation expressed fundamentally opposing views about how to cope with the problem of drug abuse. Attitudes have become less polarized, however, as the facts about drug abuse have become more widely known. These changes in attitude were clearly expressed in 1970 by U.S. President Richard M. Nixon when he stated that, though he had once assumed that increasing penalties would solve the drug abuse problem among youths, he now believed a solution would be found through education and understanding.

It is evident that the prevention of drug-taking behavior and the conversion of the drug abuser into an abstinent person are the ideal solutions to the problem of drug dependence. To

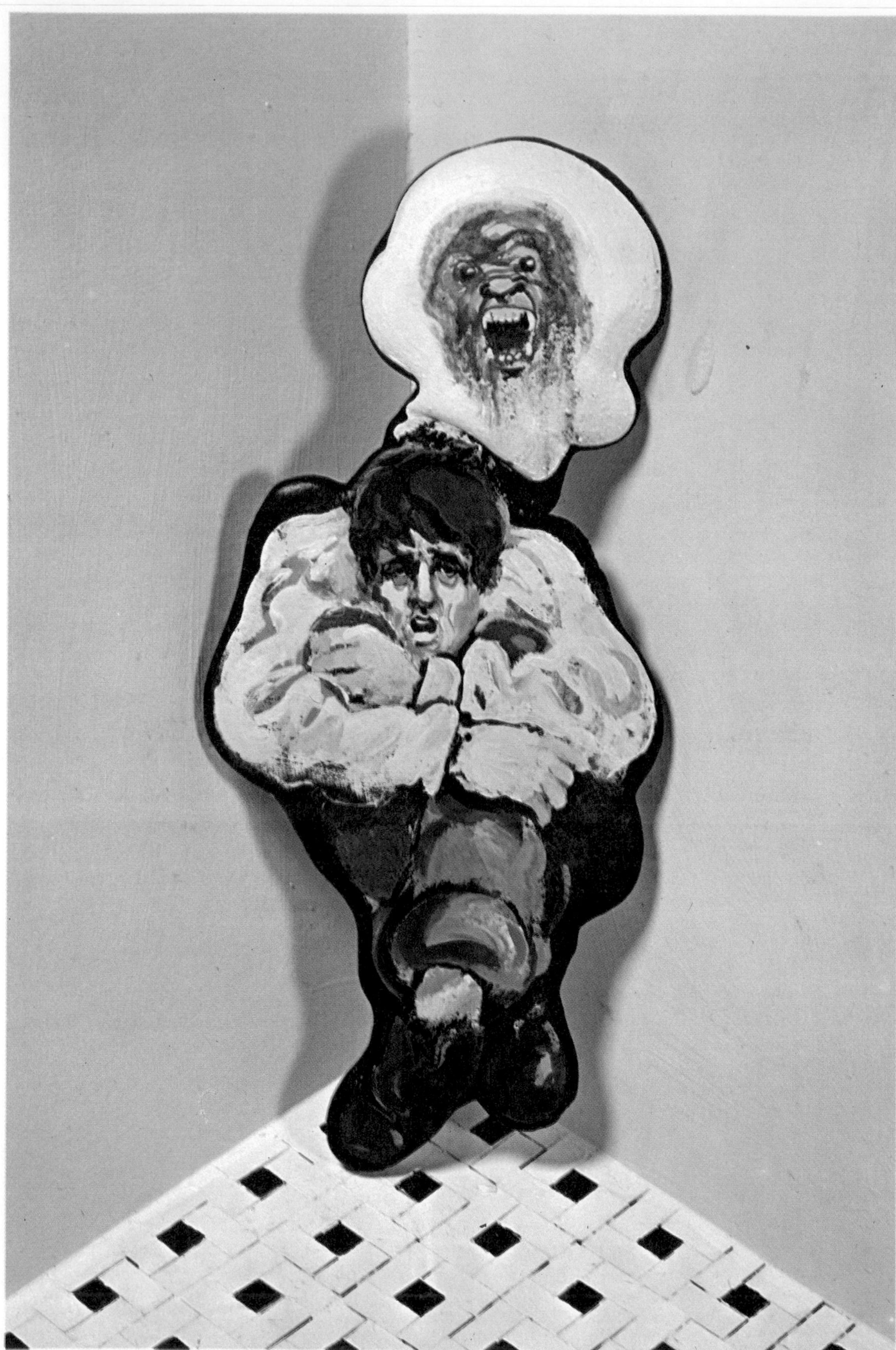

achieve these will require a modification of attitudes and beliefs. This change can best be accomplished by skillfully presenting factual information and by correcting false ideas about the abused drugs. It has been demonstrated that the presentation of unbiased information is sufficiently impressive to deter many potential or actual users. Attempts to sermonize or to scare with inaccurate statements are likely to fail or even to encourage mass drug abuse. This is so because young people are likely to rebel against patently false information.

Educating a Pill-Popping Society

Our society has developed into a magic pill-popping culture. A barrage of appeals and encouragements to use more and more chemicals to relax, to sleep, to be alert, and to assuage minor aches and pains is continuously presented on television and radio and in magazines and newspapers. For many people, drug abuse begins with purchases in the corner drugstore, with prescriptions too casually issued in a doctor's office, and with easy access for all members of the family to the contents of home medicine chests. In these circumstances, hopes for control and prevention lie in the development of ways to inform and educate all levels of society about drugs. Respect for *all* drugs must be taught, but beyond this, people must be motivated to find out for themselves that the world is not changed for the better when individuals retreat from troubles with a magical pill.

Effective education about drugs is a very human and personal thing. It cannot be the sole responsibility of the federal government or of any other governmental level. Government must make resources available commensurate with need, but the medical and health communities, the media, the industries involved, and enforcement agencies have a major responsibility.

Reaching the "Lonely Empties"

It is obvious, of course, that no amount of education can totally solve the problem of drug abuse. Besides education, understanding the conditions that lead to drug abuse and rectifying them are key factors.

To take one example: one of the major reasons for taking drugs is alienation. To cope with this problem, attempts can be made to reduce the polarization that exists between generations and contributes to misunderstanding and tension. Most young people, given the opportunity, want to communicate with adults. Too many of them are what one psychiatrist working in drug abuse rehabilitation describes as the "lonely empties." It is well known that a child is most likely to tell his troubles to—and be influenced by—a friendly, understanding adult who listens without condemning or sermonizing, someone with whom he can talk things over. The effort to communicate, which should become more of a human experience than a task, should involve all professional, educational, and volunteer organizations in each community, as well as parents.

And while they are bridging the generation gap through communication, parents who are concerned about their children's life-style might also take a hard look at their own way of life. If parents are setting a poor example—living irresponsibly, setting superficial goals, and having trivial standards—they can hardly expect to influence their children for the better.

CONCLUSION

Drug abuse is a health, legal, social, economic, and moral problem. It is a complex phenomenon in which the major interacting factors are the characteristics of the drug abused, the characteristics of the person abusing the drug, and the characteristics of the society in which the drug is abused. It is evident that there will be no simple solution to drug abuse. Substantial effort must be devoted to the discovery of new knowledge and to the development and testing of innovative approaches.

It is evident that strict controls over the illicit manufacture, transportation, smuggling, and dealing in large amounts of abusable substances are necessary and desirable. It is also evident that stringent laws and severe penalties for simple possession and use of these same substances have not been effective. Drug abuse is a problem of prevention, education, and treatment, and any comprehensive legislation dealing with such abuse should include concern with research in these areas.

It is the task of all levels of society—government, the mass media, the industries concerned, voluntary organizations, parents—to organize and mount the programs needed to deal flexibly with the many problems of drug abuse. If this is not done, there is serious danger that large numbers of youths will continue to seek a solution to their problems through drug abuse. We should not allow drugs intended to relieve suffering to become the escape mechanism through which this most promising generation drops out.

COVELLO-LAUNOIS FROM BLACK STAR

Earth Day

"Hard hat" demonstration

DAVID MOORE FROM BLACK STAR

The mini vs. the midi

JOHN DOMINIS, LIFE MAGAZINE © TIME INC.

COURTESY, NASA

Apollo 13

Solar eclipse

FRED WARD FROM BLACK STAR

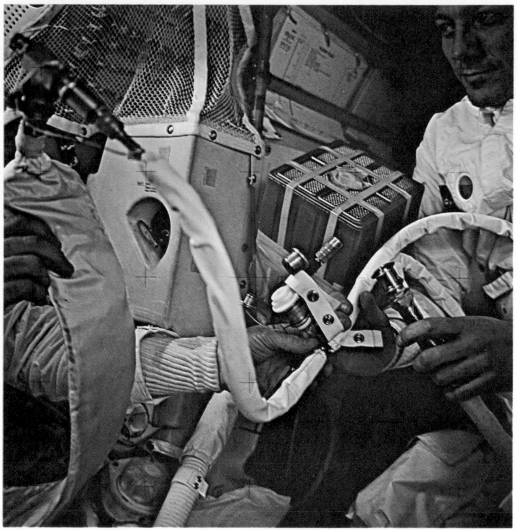

Events of the Year 1970

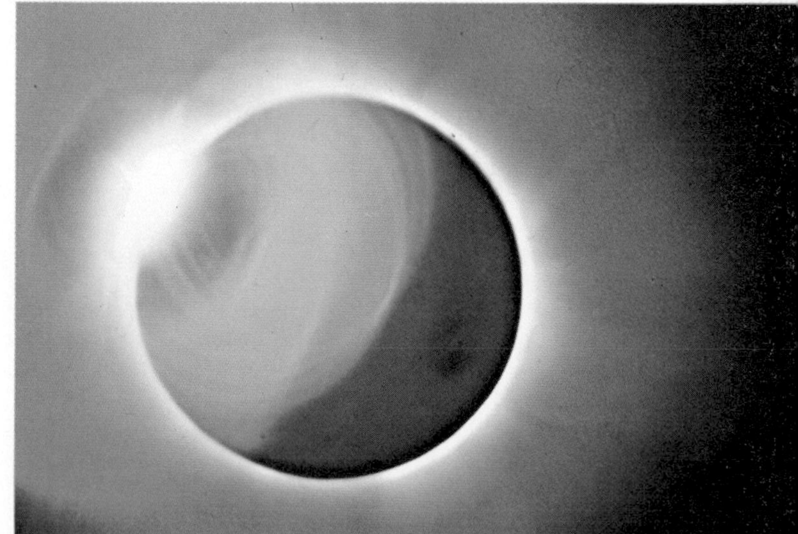

COURTESY, MILES LABORATORIES, INC.

The Alka-Seltzer commercial "The Groom's First Meal" was one of the most popular television ads in 1970. It brought fame to its actors and marked a clear departure from the old familiar hard-sell commercial.

ADVERTISING. As 1970 drew to a close, it seemed certain that it would be the tenth consecutive year in which the volume of U.S. advertising increased over the preceding year. But not even the most optimistic forecaster was predicting a gain of the magnitude of 7.7%, which was how much the ad volume in 1969 exceeded the ad volume of the preceding year. Total dollar volume in 1969 was $20.4 billion; how much greater it might be in 1970 was a question mark in the last few weeks of the year. One substantial dent in ad expenditures in the last quarter was caused by the prolonged strike against General Motors Corp. The strike started just as the new-model year was starting, which is when ad expenditures by car makers are the heaviest. Ad expenditures were off also in other hard-goods lines. Those who kept close tabs on ad expenditures agreed that the 1970 total would be greater than the total posted for 1969; cautious estimates of the gain ranged from 2% to 4%; optimistic estimates, on the other hand, ranged from 4% to 6%.

The year would definitely have to be described as an off-year as far as national advertising volume in the country's major advertising media was concerned. As 1970 drew to a close, all but one of the seven major media—outdoor advertising—were predicting that their dollar volume for the year would be down from the 1969 dollar-volume figures. Moreover, the combined volume for all seven seemed likely to dip from the preceding year's total of $9.95 billion to a 1970 total of about $9.1

The year 1970 saw an increase in public-service advertisements advocating peace. This ad was created by the agency Pesin, Sydney & Bernard, Inc.

COURTESY, HARRY PESIN FROM PESIN, SYDNEY & BERNARD, INC.

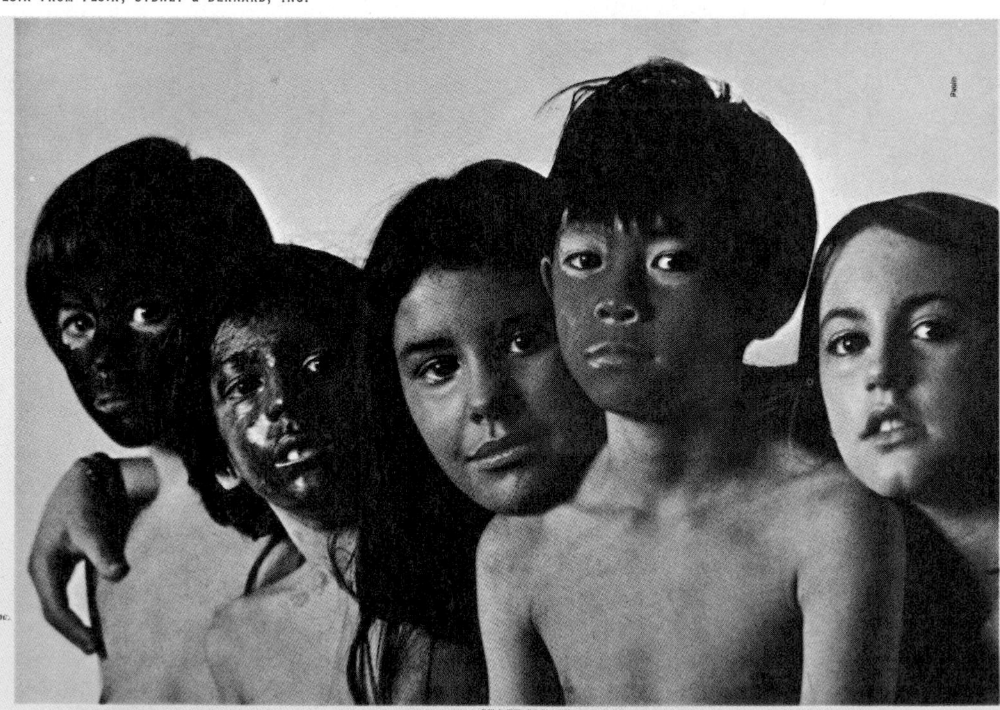

billion in national ad dollars (local advertising dollars were not included in these figures).

The one 1970 event affecting advertising that overshadowed all others was the issuance by the Federal Trade Commission (FTC) of a proposed complaint against Coca-Cola Co. and Standard Oil Co. of California. In the case of Coca-Cola, the company was found guilty of misrepresenting the nutritional value of its Hi-C fruit drink. As for Standard of California, the FTC ruled that it had falsified the antipollution potential of the F-310 additive in its Chevron gasoline.

After a six-year battle between the cigarette forces and the anticigarette forces, the U.S. Congress finally passed a bill in March banning cigarette advertising from the nation's airwaves after Jan. 1, 1971, and requiring manufacturers to beef up health warnings on all cigarette packages. (*See also* Magazines; Newspapers; Television and Radio. *See in* CE: Advertising.)

AFGHANISTAN. There was little change in the composition of Afghanistan's parliament in 1970, following the elections held in 1969 for the House of the People and for one third of the House of Elders. Since political parties were not legalized in time for the elections, most of the candidates were men of local prominence and were again chosen for their personal prestige rather than their political views. Only about 50% of the electorate voted. Except in times of national crisis—when traditional and tribal differences are buried—political life is highly localized, and throughout 1970 the interest in central institutions remained minimal. However, in Kabul, the capital, and its environs, the live broadcasts of proceedings in parliament, during which Prime Minister Noor Ahmad Etemadi and his new cabinet were confirmed, attracted large crowds of listeners in the streets and tea shops.

There is very little industry in Afghanistan. One-man enterprises are common, however.

ROBERT AZZI FROM NANCY PALMER AGENCY

External communications were stimulated by a marked improvement in relations with Pakistan, the traditional gateway to the outside world. The Afghan government showed increasing interest in the economic success of the Regional Cooperation for Development plan that was being vigorously pursued by Pakistan, Iran, and Turkey. Although the country in 1970 remained handicapped by its shortage of capital and dearth of local industries (except carpetmaking), it benefited by good relations with a number of countries in the Communist and non-Communist worlds alike. (*See in* CE: Afghanistan.)

AFRICA. A decade after Africa's momentous year of independence (1960) the continent in 1970 continued to experience the benefits and difficulties of freedom. The year's climax came at the start, with the Nigerian government's military victory over secessionist Biafra on January 12.

In 1960, 17 countries, including Nigeria, the Belgian Congo, the British and Italian Somalilands, and the former French states cut their colonial ties; others followed suit. Ten years later, the exaggerated predictions of utopia or chaos had not been realized. In recent years numerous coups, tribal disputes, border frictions, and economic problems plagued the continent. No state, however, during this era petitioned for a return to colonial status. As in preceding years, Africans displayed both an assertive nationalism and a recognition of their dependence upon outside countries. But while economically tied to foreigners for capital, trade, and skills, they could now maneuver for aid from sources other than their former colonial governors.

Political Events

The breakaway of Biafra, which had begun in July 1967, ended with the capture of the city of Owerri on January 10. Original estimates of deaths by starvation (several hundred thousand) were revised downward to between 20,000 and 50,000. At the peak of operations, in March, more than 2 million people were receiving emergency aid. Although Radio Nigeria broadcasts in 46 languages, Maj. Gen. Yakubu Gowon described the victory as a triumph of Nigerian unity. The war had cost the country approximately $800 million. Yet, in Gowon's words, it had contributed to the objective of asserting "the ability of the black man to build a strong, progressive, and prosperous modern state."

Praise for the federal military victory was given to the Soviet Union. The latter was also studying

The Ashanti tribe of Ghana chose a new king in July 1970. One of the last few remaining African kings, Nana Opoku Ware II, assumed the "golden stool" (the symbol of Ashanti power and tradition) in a long and intricate ceremony in Kumasi, Ghana.

MARION KAPLAN

the feasibility of building an iron and steel complex. Gowon promised that there would be no policy of vindictiveness, but that high-echelon Biafran leaders would be barred from holding office. In September reconciliation was achieved with the four countries which had recognized Biafra: Tanzania, Zambia, Gabon, and the Ivory Coast. Biafra's leader, Gen. Odumegwu Ojukwu, took refuge in the Ivory Coast. One of the social by-products of the war was an increase in crime.

In the People's Republic of the Congo (Brazzaville) four persons received capital sentences for their part in an attempted coup on Nov. 8, 1969, to bring back President Fulbert Youlou, ousted in 1963. On Mar. 24, 1970, 63 persons were reported killed in an attempt to overthrow the government. In Dahomey, after 17 months of rule, the regime of President Emile Derlin Zinsou was superseded on Dec. 10, 1969, by the military rule of the army chief of staff, Lieut. Col. Maurice Kouandete. In the aftermath of violence, the new government (there had been five previous coups) annulled the elections of March 1970.

A constitutional coup occurred in Lesotho subsequent to the electoral defeat on January 27 of Prime Minister Chief Leabua Jonathan. With the words, "I have seized power and I am not ashamed of it. . . . In my conscience I know that the majority of the people are behind me," Chief Jonathan proceeded to imprison at least 30 leaders of the opposition Basutoland Congress party and to drive King Moshoeshoe II into exile; they were accused of conspiring with international Communism. An estimated 150 rebels were killed by police in April.

An unsuccessful plot against the government was reported by Somalia on April 27. In Togo the official newspaper *Togo-Presse* reported on August 10 that 17 people including Ghanaians and Dahomans had been arrested in an abortive coup. Skeptics, however, suggested that the regime had staged the affair for the purposes of propaganda.

Nationalism

Continuing to seek their identities, African states displayed nationalism in a variety of ways in 1970. Kenya, on May 9, proclaimed Swahili to be the official national language, and a plan to adopt a national dress was broached. In Uganda, Ghana, Malawi, and Tanzania, Asian businessmen without secure licenses were to lose their holdings.

Ghana, in its own economic vise, compelled approximately 200,000 African "foreigners" to leave

Nigeria's leader Maj. Gen. Yakubu Gowon addresses a press conference in Lagos, Nigeria. The Nigerian civil war ended in 1970.

UPI COMPIX

the country. Libya saw the British (March 31) and Americans (June 11) leave their military bases.

The Economy

Per capita income for 11 African countries as reported by the United Nations Economic Commission for Africa was between $300 and $400 per year; for 13 countries it was $100 to $200 per year; and in 17 countries it was less than $100 per year. Most Africans still lived in a subsistence economy, but they and their leaders wanted the products of modern industrialism.

Needing external capital and skills, many thought, nonetheless, that they were prisoners of a "neocolonial" economy. Several countries nationalized portions of their industry. In the spring all the banks, insurance companies, and important industries and plantations of Uganda were nationalized; the fishing industry, employing 30,000, was developed through external assistance.

Southern Africa

No major change occurred in the European-dominated southern states. Rhodesia became a republic on March 2 and held its first election on April 10; Prime Minister Ian D. Smith's party won all 50 white seats of the 58 seats in the parliament. Under the new Land Tenure Act, Europeans were allocated one half of the land, despite the 20-to-one population ratio favoring the blacks. Protest came from the Roman Catholic church, which feared that interracial worship would be prevented. Funds for the education of the black population, which to a large degree had been channeled through mission schools, were to be reduced.

In South Africa results from the general elections held on April 22 showed a loss of nine seats to the United party and a gain of four from the ultrarightist Reconstituted Nationalists. Black nations continued to oppose South Africa's regime and received a promise of economic aid from the World Council of Churches in September to help guerrillas in fighting racism. Efforts to isolate the South Africans economically were rebuffed by Japanese interests that negotiated to build a $428 million iron ore export harbor. The new Conservative government of Great Britain decided to resume arms sales to South Africa, ostensibly to protect the sea route around the Cape of Good Hope. Britons, too, were cognizant of their $600 million annual sales to South Africa. Of course, black Africans were also conscious of the fact that Great Britain sold $860 million worth of goods to them. (*See also* individual countries by name; International Relations. *See in* CE: Africa; countries by name.)

STEVE NORTHRUP FROM CAMERA 5

During the rigorous fall campaign schedule, U.S. Vice-President Spiro T. Agnew often took time out to play a hard game of tennis.

AGNEW, SPIRO T.

During 1970 U.S. Vice-President Spiro T. Agnew succeeded in elevating the vice-presidency to a position of importance if not universal respect. Following a pattern he established in 1969 by criticizing both the press and any opposition to the Administration of U.S. President Richard M. Nixon, Agnew threw the force of his rhetoric into Congressional and gubernatorial campaigns throughout the nation.

Beginning the year on a crest of popularity (a Gallup Poll ranked him as the third most admired man in the nation—behind President Nixon and the Rev. Billy Graham), he performed official duties and spoke at successful fund-raising dinners for the Republican party. In both capacities Agnew seasoned his speeches with alliterative epithets branding his critics as "vicars of vacillation" and "hopeless, hysterical hypochondriacs of history." He also assailed a number of Democrats and some Republicans as "radical liberals."

One "radical liberal," Senator Charles Goodell (R, N.Y.), was referred to by Agnew as the "Christine Jorgensen of Republican politics." The reference brought objections from Miss Jorgensen as well as Goodell. Moreover, Goodell lost his Senate seat to Conservative candidate James Buckley.

Overall, however, Agnew's campaigning yielded disappointing results. The Democrats retained control of both houses of Congress and gained a net of 11 governorships. After the results had been tallied, there was talk of replacing Agnew on the presidential ticket in 1972. (*See also* Nixon.)

AGRICULTURE. The world agricultural situation in 1970 could be described as one of renewed but limited progress. During the year some of the developed areas, especially Western Europe and North America, produced somewhat less than in 1969. But, whereas in 1969 almost all of the underdeveloped regions had less food per capita, in 1970 the big increases were in India, the Soviet Union, and perhaps Communist China. Widespread skepticism remained concerning the Green Revolution, which in one form had led quickly to the planting of new varieties of wheat and rice in Asia. It was estimated that an annual expenditure of $11 billion by governments, industry, and private sources would be required to expand the global food supply to meet world needs in 1979.

In the United States, farmers and the general public were reminded in 1970 of the complex and sometimes fragile chain of conditions on which the abundant productivity of modern agriculture depends. In August the Southern corn-leaf blight developed and expectations of a record yield corn crop were lowered. By early autumn, after blight damage to the corn crop was officially confirmed and prices of feed grains climbed higher, farmers began to slow down future production of red meats, poultry, and eggs.

The number of U.S. farms declined at the beginning of the year to 2.9 million; in ten years the number had declined by 28%. The average farm size increased, as did income per farm.

U.S. Crop Production

Crops planted for harvest in 1970 totaled about 300 million acres, and it was expected that 2.7 million acres more than in 1969 would be harvested. Prospects as late as early August nearly equaled the record yield of 1969, but later that month a major crop, corn, was damaged. Continued hot, dry weather in the Great Plains and adjacent parts of the corn belt accounted for a portion of the reduction, but the chief damage occurred after mid-August from a widespread infection of Southern corn-leaf blight, a blackish-brown rot.

Prospects as of July 1 had indicated a corn crop of 4.8 billion bushels (a new record high) as compared with nearly 4.6 billion bushels in 1969; the August report estimated 4.7 billion bushels, and the September report 4.4 billion bushels. A special report released on October 2, tied to conditions as of September 23, reduced the estimate to 4.2 billion bushels, 12.5% less than the July forecast, 393 million bushels (almost 9%) less than in 1969, and about 11% below the record crop of 1967. Yield per acre was indicated at 72.2 bushels, as compared with the record high final figure of 83.9 bushels in 1969.

In September Iowa was the leading corn-producing state with an indicated per-acre yield of 95 bushels, for a total of 957.1 million bushels, followed by Illinois with 871.3 million bushels and Indiana with 417.6 million bushels.

Among other feed grains, sorghum was indicated at 687 million bushels; oat production was estimated at 891.3 million bushels. Barley was estimated at 410.3 million bushels.

The total wheat crop was estimated at 1.4 billion bushels, 7% less than in 1969. Average yields of winter wheat were at a new record high of about 33.6 bushels per acre. Kansas was the leading producer with 295.8 million bushels. Spring wheat, other than durum, was 201 million bushels; durum wheat was 49.9 million bushels.

Hay yields declined to 1.99 tons per acre, and the total crop was indicated at 124.9 million tons. Alfalfa yields came to approximately 72.6 million tons, and clover and timothy totaled 23.9 million tons. Oilseed production was expected to reach 40.7 million tons. The soybean crop for 1970 was estimated at a new record of more than 1.1 billion bushels. Cottonseed was estimated up 7% from 1969, and the prospective peanut crop was up 11% to 2.8 billion pounds.

The cotton crop was estimated at 10.6 million bales, and the production of sugarcane was indicated at 25.3 million tons. The sugar-beet crop was expected to be 25.7 million tons, and maple syrup production was 1.1 million gallons. Production of all types of tobacco was indicated at a total of about 1.9 billion pounds.

Supplies of fresh vegetables from winter and spring crops were somewhat smaller than those of the preceding year, largely because of heavy rains

Farmers in Missouri have quick access to agricultural information via a statewide network established by the Missouri Farmers Association, which has 20 specialists to advise farmers on a variety of matters.
AUTHENTICATED NEWS INTERNATIONAL

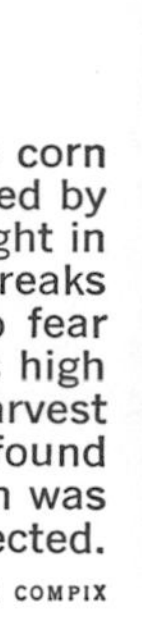

The Midwestern corn crop was threatened by corn-leaf blight in 1970. Early outbreaks led growers to fear crop losses of as high as 30%, but at harvest time damage was found to be less than was expected.
UPI COMPIX

and freezing conditions in Florida. The estimated potato production was 313.8 million hundredweight. Indicated sweet-potato production was 14.2 million hundredweight. Dry field peas totaled 4.4 million hundredweight.

The total crop of seven major deciduous fruits was 13% below 1969. The 151.3 million bushels (6.4 billion pounds) of apples was 4% smaller than the record crop of 1969. The peach crop was 64.5 million bushels (3.1 billion pounds), 16% smaller than in 1969. Pears were forecast at 547,800 tons; the Pacific coast Bartlett type constituted 382,000 tons. The grape harvest was about 3.1 million tons. Plums and prunes, except in California, were down 47% from 1969, but the California crops were up 46% for prunes and 84% for plums. The cranberry crop was expected to reach 1.9 million barrels, and the strawberry crop was estimated at 474.4 million pounds. Apricot production was 169,000 tons; nectarines were at 63,000 tons; sweet cherries amounted to 111,700 tons; the tart cherries were about 147,000 tons.

The first forecast of pecan production was 156.1 million pounds; almonds were put at 130,000 tons; filberts were forecast at 8,600 tons; walnuts were set at 106,800 tons. Early and incomplete reports on the citrus crop indicated a record crop of 174.5 million boxes of Florida oranges for 1970–71.

Livestock, Dairy, and Poultry Production

Unlike the situation with crop production, livestock and their products in 1970 made an increased contribution to the U.S. economy. On Jan. 1, 1970, the cattle inventory was 112.3 million head; the beef herd was 91.1 million head, up from 88.3 million head a year earlier; the dairy herd was 21.2 million, a drop of about 2% or 421,000 head. Texas was the leading cattle state with 12.2 million head (cattle and calves), of which total 11.6 million were beef cattle. Iowa was second with 7.5 million, followed by Nebraska with 6.3 million head. Wisconsin continued as the leading dairy state with 2.1 million milk cows (two years old and over), followed by New York and Minnesota with 1.1 million head. All cattle and calves had an average value of $180, up from $158 over the preceding year, but dairy cows, at an average $302 per head, increased from $269 for the preceding year. The calf crop of 1970 was about 46 million head, up 2% from 1969.

With a slower decline in milk-cow numbers and a larger rise in milk output per cow, milk output for 1970 was estimated to be slightly more than the 116.2 billion pounds of 1969. Consumption of some products such as cheese, low-fat fluid milk, nonfat dry milk, and frozen desserts increased, but per-capita consumption of milk in all dairy products was forecast to continue its decline.

The 56.7 million hogs on farms Dec. 1, 1969, were about 6% less than the number on hand the preceding year. They were valued at $39 per head against $30.50 the preceding year. This followed a 7% reduction in the pig crop of June to November 1969 which, with generally higher hog prices and favorable feeding ratios in 1969, encouraged a 12% increase in the spring pig crop of 1970; early intentions were to increase fall farrowings by 17%. Hog prices were favorable during the earlier part of 1970 but, beginning in July, broke sharply to about $20 per hundredweight. Inventories in September of hog numbers indicated 13% more than the preceding year.

The 20.4 million head of sheep and lambs on farms and ranches at the beginning of 1970 were a reduction of 4% from 1969. The average value of stock sheep was up slightly to $24.70 as compared with $22 in the preceding year. The lamb crop for 1970 totaled 13.4 million head, 2% smaller than the preceding year.

The inventory at the beginning of 1970 showed 431.5 million chickens, 3% more than the preceding year. The laying flock in September totaled

315 million hens, about 2% more than in 1969. Production of 5.8 billion eggs during the first seven months was 1% up from the same months of 1969. Output of broiler meat in federally inspected plants during the January through July period was 14% larger than that of the preceding year. Chick placements for marketing in September and October were 5% larger than for the comparable period in 1969. There were 6.7 million turkeys on farms in January; 3.4 million of them were breeder hens. The turkey crop of 1970 was estimated at 115 million birds, 8% more than in 1969.

Employment, Wages, Income, Land Values

Approximately 5.3 million persons were employed in farming in late September 1970; 3.7 million of them were "family" labor and 1.5 million were "hired." The composite per-hour wage rate was $1.46 on October 1, as compared with $1.37 a year earlier.

Cash receipts from farm marketings during the first half of 1970 were at a seasonally adjusted annual rate of about $49 billion as compared with $47.2 billion in 1969. Farm real-estate values rose 4% during the year ending March 1, 1970, to a national average of $193 per acre, the smallest advance in seven years. (*See in* CE: Agriculture.)

AIRCRAFT. The controversial U.S. supersonic transport (SST) development program suffered an uncertain fate in the U.S. Congress in 1970. Although the House of Representatives narrowly voted to finance construction of the faster-than-sound aircraft, the Senate decisively voted against it. A House-Senate conference committee proposed to continue the program with a lower appropriation. Senator William Proxmire (D, Wis.), one of the chief critics of the SST, threatened a filibuster. A compromise agreement was reached in the Senate in the final days of the lame-duck congressional session. Funds were voted to continue the program until March 1971, when a final decision would be made. The agreement actually represented a major victory for the foes of the SST.

Congressional objections to the SST were primarily based on its environmental dangers, among them the aircraft's noise on takeoff and its sonic boom, and the program's monumental cost. The Boeing Co., which was working on construction of two prototype SST models, had estimated that another $1.5 billion to $2 billion would be needed.

The Concorde SST, a joint Anglo-French venture, received its share of criticism. A former French minister predicted that the eventual cost of the Concorde program would exceed $2.5 billion (the current projected figure was $1.8 billion). He charged that the French aircraft industry, engrossed in the Concorde, would end up with nothing else to sell by 1980, when competing U.S. and Soviet SSTs would be on the market. In its August tests, the British prototype, Concorde 002, reached a speed of over 1,000 mph, equaling the testing record of Concorde 001, the French prototype.

The first of the new wide-bodied commercial airplanes, the Boeing 747, began operational service early in the year. With all its interior space, the plane was a great success with passengers, but it quickly demonstrated that, with the exception of Paris' Orly, no airport was ready to handle the volume of passengers it carried. Passenger, customs, food handling, baggage, and ground transportation facilities were all overloaded. By the end of the year, at least 200 jumbo jets had been ordered by 30 leading airlines. The jumbos were

This is a full-scale mockup of the Boeing supersonic transport.
COURTESY, THE BOEING CO.

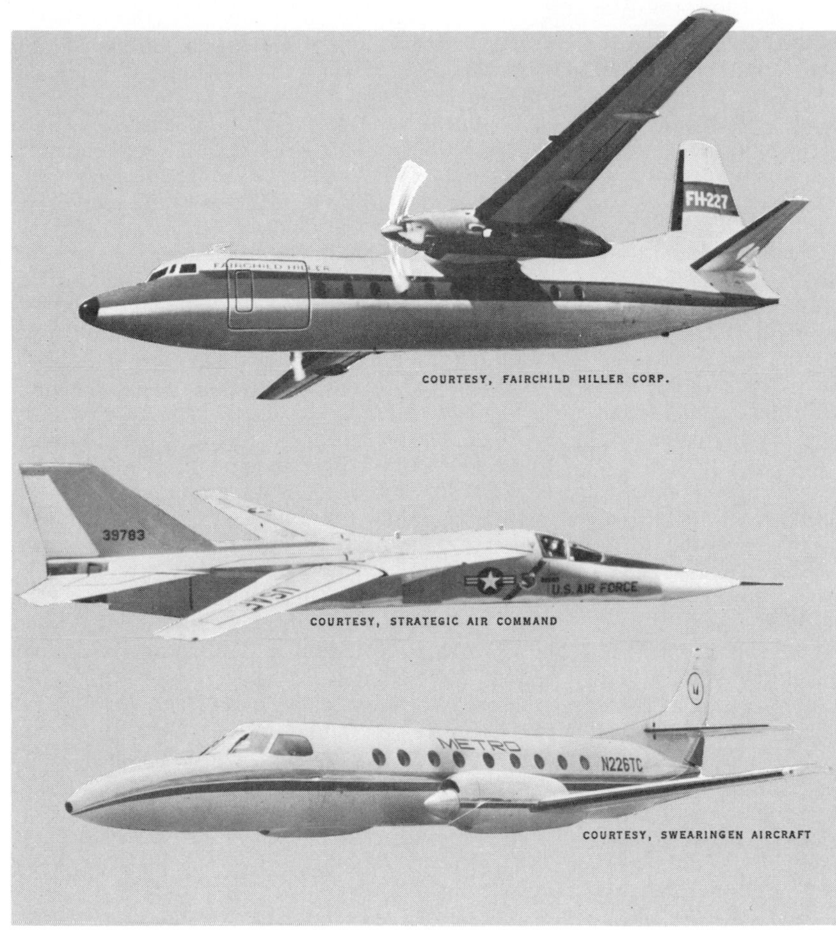

The Fairchild FH-227 (top), designed for both passengers and freight, is a short-range jet transport. The FB-111 Strategic Bomber (center) is a variation of the F-111 Tactical Fighter. Metro (bottom) is the first of a new generation of commuter airliners; it seats 22 passengers.

expected to reduce costs and produce new revenue in the airfreight business, but with about 350 seats to fill per flight, airlines were resigning themselves to empty seats for a time to come.

In a report by *The Armed Forces Journal,* the C-5A, the Air Force's giant cargo plane, was faulted for having a fatigue strength far below contract specifications. An Air Force-appointed panel recommended further testing of the wings for metal fatigue. Air Force Secretary Robert C. Seamans, Jr., suggested that the Air Force should have had more direct control over the program in order to avoid problems such as the cost overruns and wing strength difficulties that plagued the C-5A. In the meantime, Lockheed Aircraft Corp., having produced 15 C-5As, costing some $54 million apiece, requested emergency interim financing of over $400 million from the Pentagon because of the cost of design problems. As a result of C-5A cost overruns, the Defense Department ruled that new aircraft designs bought by the Air Force must be substantially developed before the contractor may begin production.

Engineering and development contracts for the Air Force's replacement for its B-52 strategic bomber were awarded to North American Rockwell Corp., though it had been expected that Boeing would get the contract. The Air Force initiated a new policy by releasing the dollar bids on the contract as well. Named the B-1, the new plane would be smaller, fly higher, lower, and faster, and it would carry more payload than the B-52. A crew of four would operate it, and four turbofan engines would drive it.

Also on the Air Force planning board was a close-support aircraft known as the AX. A twin-engine turboprop, the AX was designed to feature survivability, long loiter time, short takeoff capability, and easy maintenance. Air Force planners expected the AX to be a combination of a number of tactical aircraft, but its primary role would be close air support. The AX would have a small turning radius and carry a 30-mm. gun and all types of conventional bombs. The Air Force asked for $27.9 million to permit development of the AX, which was expected to be in production by the mid-1970's.

In the development and production stage was the F-15 air superiority fighter being built by the McDonnell Douglas Corp. A single-place, twin-engine jet capable of Mach 2, it was expected to make its first flight in 1972. The F-15 would carry both short- and medium-range missiles and an internally mounted rapid-fire gun.

Lockheed demonstrated an exceptionally quiet airplane developed for military use; called the Q-Star, it was described as looking like a stub-nosed glider. It has a 57-foot wingspan and a slow-turning, multibladed wooden propeller mounted on the nose. The propeller is driven through a ten-foot shaft from the engine, which is located behind the cockpit. The engine is a Wankel-type rotary piston engine, the first to be used in an airplane. It was developed by the Curtiss-Wright Corp., holder of U.S. rights to the Wankel design. The engine's design, its low power, and its muffler made the plane the quietest one in the air, according to Lockheed. In tests, the Q-Star flew at a speed of 140 knots and reached an altitude of 14,000 feet; its theoretical ceiling was estimated at 19,000 feet.

Spurred by the nature of the fighting in Vietnam, helicopter development remained one of the busiest segments of the aircraft industry in 1970. The familiar HH-3 "Jolly Green Giant" Sikorsky helicopter was replaced by the HH-53 "Buff" (for "big ugly friendly fellow"). The Jolly Green Giant had been in operation since 1965; its credits included the rescues of 550 downed airmen. The Buff had increased capability and speed and mounted three 7.62-mm. Miniguns for self-defense and protective air cover.

The UH-1N, a versatile new helicopter capable of operation as a ground-support gunship, reconnaissance aircraft, and troop or cargo carrier, came into the Air Force inventory late in the year. Descended from the Bell Huey helicopter family, the new UH-1N was known as the TwinHuey, since its power came from two turboshaft engines, either of which could operate the craft if the other failed or was damaged. The TwinHuey carried 2.75-mm. rockets, 7.62-mm. Miniguns, and 40-mm. grenade launchers when armed as a gunship.

An advanced technology helicopter, the Boeing 347, flew for the first time in June. The 347 model research craft was the result of a Boeing-funded program to explore the capability of a pure helicopter configuration and to investigate the potential of a winged helicopter.

Boeing also announced that it had acquired marketing rights for the five-place, twin-engine BO-105 helicopter, developed by the Messerschmitt-Boelkow-Blohm Co. of Ottobrunn, West Germany. The BO-105, featuring a simplified rigid rotor, was the largest in its class and the only small helicopter in current production with twin engines. It had a maximum speed of 144 knots. (*See in* CE: Airplane articles.)

ALBANIA. In 1970 Albania's Communist Party First Secretary Enver Hoxha continued to make speeches against the United States and the Soviet Union. But, following the appearance of the Soviet navy in the Mediterranean Sea, he held out an olive branch to Yugoslavia and even an olive twig to Greece. At Tropojë, near the Yugoslav border, Hoxha said that, ideological differences notwithstanding, Albania wanted to improve trade and other relations with Yugoslavia and to foster friendship. In May an Albanian trade delegation arrived in Greece to negotiate with the Athens Chamber of Commerce. The first agreement called for $1.5 million in trade in which Albania would send crude petroleum and by-products to Greece in exchange for industrial goods and raw materials.

Albania also turned its attention to Western Europe. In July it established diplomatic relations with Denmark and Switzerland and concluded modest trade agreements with a score of nations.

Communist China, however, remained Albania's best friend. It granted the Albanians a loan of $200 million for the construction of 30 major industrial plants to be built during the fifth five-year plan (1971–75). Included in the group were a metallurgical combine with a yearly processing capacity of 800,000 tons of iron and nickel ore and a hydroelectric power station with a yearly production of 1.7 billion kilowatt-hours. The new five-year plan emphasized the need for decentralization and more initiative and responsibility at all levels of the party cadres.

Great effort was made in 1970 to develop the foreign-tourist trade in Albania. During the year, only one 400-room hotel, in Durazzo, was open to foreigners, but a few more hotels were under construction along the Adriatic coast.

On September 20, a new national assembly of 214 members was elected. The electors voted unanimously for the official candidates of the Democratic Front. (*See in* CE: Albania.)

ALGERIA. Algeria's long-standing dispute with Morocco over their border in the Tindouf region was settled in May 1970. Algeria's President Houari Boumédienne and Morocco's King Hassan II, meeting at Tlemcen in northwestern Algeria, agreed to establish a joint military commission to delineate the border in southeastern Morocco. They also agreed to joint exploitation of the rich iron ore deposits in the Tindouf region, over which the two nations had gone to war in 1963. In September Algeria, Morocco, and Mauritania decided to pursue a common policy calling for Spain to decolonize the Spanish Sahara, which is bordered by the three nations.

Following the Arab-Israeli cease-fire in August, Algeria withdrew its troops from the Suez Canal, where they had been stationed in support of the United Arab Republic, or Egypt, since the 1967 Middle East war. However, Algeria continued to view armed conflict as the only means of settling the Palestinian Arab issue, and it provided training courses for Arab guerrillas at a military school near Algiers, the capital.

In 1970 the Algerian government inaugurated a four-year program to expand the domestic uses of natural resources, develop industries, increase agricultural production, and improve education.

The $5-billion cost of the program was to be financed by Algeria's oil revenue, by foreign credits and investments, and by money sent home by Algerians working in Europe. About half of the total sum was to be invested in industry. A plan for agrarian reform was also issued during the year. Its aims included limiting the size of private estates, banning land ownership by people with other sources of income, and distributing land recovered by these measures to peasant cooperatives.

Algeria took further steps in 1970 to increase its share of revenue from oil, its principal resource, and to obtain control over the oil industry. In June the government nationalized the Algerian subsidiaries of four foreign oil producers, including the U.S.-owned Phillips Petroleum Co., and warned other foreign oil firms of possible nationalization unless they invested in Algerian oil exploration. In July, while Algerian negotiations with France over higher oil prices were temporarily suspended, Algeria unilaterally imposed a new tax base on oil exported from Algeria by French companies. French firms produce about two thirds of Algeria's oil. (*See also* Middle East. *See in* CE: Algeria.)

WIDE WORLD

Walter J. Hickel, U.S. secretary of the interior, was concerned in 1970 about the fate of endangered animal species like the snow leopard. The pelt of a snow leopard brings a high price on the fur market. The jaguar and the cheetah are also in danger.

ANIMALS AND WILDLIFE. Concern for the many species of endangered wildlife increased during 1970 and in some cases turned to outright alarm. In the United States alone, some 130 animals were in danger of extinction, including the alligator, the Southern bald eagle, the peregrine falcon, the sea otter, the bighorn sheep, and the grizzly bear. Around the world, many countries were finding even their most characteristic species threatened: kangaroos in Australia, tigers in India, elephants in Ceylon.

Some of the vanishing animals were hunted for sport, like grizzly bears; some were hunted for their skins, like alligators, or their fur, like tigers. Some were slaughtered for meat, like kangaroos, which are made into canned pet food sold in the United States. Some, particularly birds, were dying as a result of overuse of DDT and other pesticides. A recent case study of the peregrine falcon showed that DDT, absorbed in the bird's diet, weakens the shell of the bird's eggs so that the weight of the nesting mother breaks the eggs.

Among the many endangered species, none received more attention in 1970 than whales, certain kinds of which were in danger of being hunted out of existence. Blue and humpback whales have been hunted so much that they are now protected by international agreement; even so, the number of blue whales declined in the last 30 years from an estimated 100,000 to less than 3,000. Blue whales

Nearly 150 false killer whales swam ashore near Fort Pierce, Fla., to die. Rescue teams hauled them back to deep water, but most of the whales headed back to shore. Conservationists think the whales followed their leader to their deaths.

UPI COMPIX

WIDE WORLD

This young fawn is getting ready to plunge into the deep water of the Florida Everglades to get to another island to search for food. The hard work to find food was killing many fawns there.

are the largest living creatures; some are as long as 100 feet and weigh up to 150 tons.

Whales are hunted for the oil in their bodies. The International Whaling Commission places limits on the number of whales that may be killed each year, but scientists recommended in 1970 that these quotas be reduced. The commission did not reduce them, however, nor could its members agree on any form of inspection to make sure quotas are being kept. In the United States, whales were placed on the list of protected animals in the federal Endangered Species Conservation Act of 1969, which became law in June 1970. This new act makes it illegal to import or to ship interstate any product of a protected animal.

Aiding the whales' cause were the announcement that whales sing and the release of a record of whale songs. Cetologist Roger S. Payne, of the New York Zoological Society, recorded the sounds of humpback whales singing underwater off Bermuda. Whale songs, like bird songs, are considered songs because they have a definite melodic line and a repeated theme, but whale songs are much the more complex and last from 5 to 30 minutes. Payne speculated that the songs may be signals that help the whales find and recognize each other as they migrate. (*See* Fish and Fisheries.)

The Nature Conservancy, a privately financed organization for the preservation of natural areas, continued to purchase wildlife sanctuaries. Wassaw Island, near the mouth of Georgia's Savannah River, was preserved as a federally controlled refuge for egrets, ospreys, and more than 50 other birds. Approximately 15,000 acres in Arizona, including Aravaipa Canyon, became a shelter for rare and endangered species in the area. Cottrell Marsh, a 4,000-year-old estuary in Connecticut, was obtained for its ecological importance as well as for a wildlife haven. On Florida's Gulf coast, St. Vincent Island was purchased and stocked with hundreds of animals, including some species not native to the island. The Nature Conservancy failed in an attempt to save Bald Head Island, the only undeveloped island on the Carolina coast. The island's salt marshes are considered ecologically vital as spawning grounds for marine life.

The Federal Highway Administration began an experiment in which scientists trapped and affixed transmitters to birds, mammals, and fish in order to study travel patterns of the released animals. With the data obtained, it was expected that highways could be planned that would not interfere with natural wildlife areas.

In a new study in animal psychology, controlled experiments with six laboratory rats at the University of California at Los Angeles indicated that the rats preferred food they had worked for to food they received without working. After first allowing the rats to become accustomed to eating free food daily, psychologists Brooks Carder and Kenneth Berkowitz trained the animals to obtain the same kind of food by pressing a lever. When the rats had learned to feed themselves by pressing the lever, they were again given free food. The rats so much preferred to earn their food that, after pressing the lever, they would shove a dish of free food out of the way in order to reach the earned food. However, when the number of lever pressings necessary to obtain food was increased to ten, the rats tended to return to the free food. The researchers concluded that the rats preferred to earn their food as long as the work demands were not too high.

Large movements of animals continued to puzzle mankind. A herd of nearly 150 false killer whales followed their leader onto a beach near Fort Pierce, Fla., in January. State wildlife officials, with the help of the U.S. Coast Guard and local volunteers, tugged and towed the whales back into the water, only to see most of them rush back onto the beach. Only 22 of the whales were saved from this mass suicide.

In March a plague of mice suddenly appeared 200 miles northwest of Melbourne, Australia, and swarmed across the countryside like a moving carpet, devouring crops, infesting orchards and gardens, blocking traffic on highways, and even invading homes and public buildings. Ecologists suspected that poisons set out for the mice had also killed their natural predators, making possible a rapid rise in the mouse population.

In the realm of lesser-known animals, scientists studying Scotland's Loch Ness monster found new evidence indicating that it may be a descendant of giant sea eels trapped in the loch millions of years ago, when the sea that had covered the area receded. Sherpa guides in the Himalayas sighted a baby yeti, or abominable snowman, and British mountain climber Donald Whillans photographed the animal's paw prints.

At the edge of a woodland in Surrey, England, a pair of falcons built a nest and halted a $4-million pipeline-laying project until the fledglings were hatched and ready to fly. They were hobby falcons, a species approaching extinction in Great Britain.

When a farmer in South Africa sold five homing pigeons to a friend some miles distant, he removed the birds' wing feathers so they could not fly back to their old home. A month later the pigeons showed up at their home loft, the bottoms of their feet worn raw from the long walk back.

Nellie, the oldest horse in the world, died of a heart attack in 1970 at the age of 53 at her home near Danville, Mo. Snaggletooth, famed king of the Yellowstone National Park grizzly bears, wandered into the West Yellowstone, Mont., city dump and was shot by two men, who were later arrested and forfeited bonds of $200 each for the illegal killing.

A crow named Blacky was arrested in Ogden, Utah, for snatching parking tickets off automobiles and flying away with them. He was found guilty and sentenced to 30 days in a wire enclosure. (*See also* Conservation.)

ANNIVERSARIES AND CELEBRATIONS.

On July 4, 1970, a special Honor America Day celebration was held in Washington, D.C. The festivities, which included singing, speechmaking, and musical entertainment, were highlighted by the appearance of such notables as the evangelist Billy Graham and entertainers Kate Smith, Bob Hope, and Jack Benny. The celebration attracted an estimated 350,000 people at its peak time, during the evening performances. The day began with religious services in front of the Lincoln Memorial.

During the year the state of South Carolina celebrated its 300th birthday. It was in 1670 that the first permanent English settlement in Carolina was founded on the Ashley River and named Charles Town for England's King Charles II; ten years later it was moved to the present site of Charleston. All of the state's 46 counties staged their own celebrations, and there were special tercentennial events, including the first Charleston performance of the DuBose Heyward and George Gershwin opera 'Porgy and Bess'.

The famous Boardwalk at Atlantic City, N.J., celebrated its centennial birthday during the year with many special events, beginning in January with a 24-foot-high cake. The year also marked the 350th anniversary of the landing of the Pilgrims, and thousands of tourists stopped in Plymouth, Mass., for a look at Plymouth Rock.

In September U.S. President Richard M. Nixon approved the plans drawn up by the American

Ex-prisoners of Nazi Germany march in commemoration of the 25th anniversary of their liberation from a Nazi prison camp located at Compiègne, north of Paris.

A.F.P. FROM PICTORIAL PARADE

KEYSTONE

On June 26 in San Francisco, Calif., ceremonies were held to commemorate the signing of the UN Charter in that city 25 years ago.

Revolution Bicentennial Commission making the city of Philadelphia, Pa., the international exposition site and focal point for the upcoming 200th birthday of the United States in 1976. Washington, D.C.; Boston, Mass.; and Miami, Fla., were also named chief sites for the national celebration.

May 7 was the 25th anniversary of V-E Day, the day on which Nazi Germany surrendered to the Allies; and September 2 was the 25th anniversary of Japan's formal surrender to the Allied powers. Another 25th anniversary occurring in 1970 was that of the first atomic bomb explosion, which was set off in a remote area of New Mexico desert on July 16, 1945. The 25th anniversary of the United Nations (UN) was observed in June and October, with many world leaders attending.

The 100th anniversary of the death of Charles Dickens (on June 9, 1870) was observed in England during the summer. Plays, movies, television programs, readings, and concerts were presented throughout England. In London the British Museum and the Victoria and Albert Museum staged large Dickens exhibits, and at Westminster Abbey (where Dickens is buried) a memorial service was held, attended by the Queen Mother and members of the royal family.

The 200th anniversary of the birth of William Wordsworth drew an increased number of visitors to Grasmere and Rydal Mount in England's Lake District, where the poet spent the last 50 years of his life. Wordsworth was born on April 7, 1770, at Cockermouth.

On May 9 there were celebrations lasting all day in London's Covent Garden, marking the 300th anniversary of the famous market there. The market, which came into existence when the duke of Bedford obtained a charter in 1670 from Charles II, was scheduled to be moved in 1973 to Nine Elms, in the Vauxhall area of London.

At the Kremlin Palace of Congresses, on April 21–22, the 100th anniversary of the birth of Nikolai Lenin was celebrated. All prominent Soviet officials attended, as well as representatives of Communist parties from 66 other nations.

Ludwig van Beethoven's 200th birthday was celebrated in December. (*See also* Fairs and Shows.)

ANTARCTICA. Ten nations occupied 33 stations in the Antarctic Treaty area (south of 60° S. latitude) and nine stations on sub-Antarctic islands during the winter of 1969–70. At almost all stations observations were continued for the purposes of meteorology, ionospheric and auroral studies of the upper atmosphere, and geomagnetic and seismic studies of the earth.

From an Antarctic Treaty meeting on telecommunications emerged proposals aimed at speeding up the transmission of meteorological data both between the Antarctic stations and between the Antarctic and the outside world. Matters discussed at an Antarctic Treaty consultative meeting included the control of Antarctic pelagic sealing, international notification of scientific rocket launchings, the preservation of historic huts in the Antarctic, and the effects of Antarctic tourism upon scientific programs. New Zealand had proposed a hotel for tourists on the Ross Ice Shelf.

The announcement of the discovery by U.S. scientists of *Lystrosaurus,* a sort of fossil "hippopotamus," in the Transantarctic Mountains during the winter of 1969–70 provided startling evidence that Antarctica was once part of the hypothetical land mass that scientists have termed Gondwanaland. Examples of *Lystrosaurus,* an animal that could never have crossed any sea, have also been found in South Africa, India, and China.

A number of cooperative programs continued. Argentine, Norwegian, and U.S. scientists worked aboard the U.S. Coast Guard cutter *Glacier* in the third International Weddell Sea Oceanographic Expedition. Work continued on the study of the formation and extent of Antarctic bottom water. The Scott Polar Research Institute, of Cambridge, England, installed and operated radio-echo ice-sounding instruments in a U.S. Navy C-130 Hercules transport plane. The Scott Institute team flew nearly 100,000 miles from McMurdo Sound in the radar scanning, and a much more detailed picture of the rock surface beneath Antarctica's ice cap was beginning to appear. (*See also* Arctic. *See in* CE: Antarctica; Polar Exploration.)

ANTHROPOLOGY. Norwegian anthropologist/explorer Thor Heyerdahl, who first won fame in 1947 for crossing the Pacific Ocean on a balsa raft, in 1970 succeeded in navigating the Atlantic in a boat built of papyrus reeds. The 57-day passage (May 17–July 12)—from Safi, Morocco, to Bridgetown, Barbados—was intended to support Heyerdahl's theory that early Egyptian explorers might have crossed the ocean to lay the foundation for such advanced New World civilizations as those of the Incas of Peru, the Mayas of Mexico, and the Mound Builders of North America.

Heyerdahl's craft, *Ra II* (*Ra* for the Egyptian sun-god, *II* because it was the successor to a similar craft that had failed when well short of its goal in 1969), was modeled upon vessels pictured on the walls of ancient Egyptian tombs. It was made of Ethiopian papyrus by Indian craftsmen from Bolivia, who still make similar craft for use on Lake Titicaca. Its eight-man crew was multinational.

Significant discoveries in a desert region on the eastern shore of Lake Rudolf in northwestern Kenya were announced in 1970 by 25-year-old Richard E. Leakey, son of the noted anthropologists Louis and Mary Leakey. These included stone artifacts that may be the oldest (2.6 million years) tools ever found, as well as the partial skull of a hominid, not surely identified, who may have been their maker. It was felt that further study of the region might extend knowledge of man's prehistory a million or more years farther into the past than it has previously reached.

In southwestern France, scientists succeeded in stemming further deterioration of the famed prehistoric wall paintings of the Lascaux Cave. The cave, however, remained closed to tourists—who generated the heat and carried the bacteria that had caused the damage. (*See also* Archaeology. *See in* CE: Anthropology.)

ARCHAEOLOGY. Volatile political climates, limited research funds, and rankled feelings in the Near East over the illegal trafficking of antiquities hamstrung much of the archaeological activity in the Eastern Hemisphere. Twice in 1970 it appeared that archaeological fieldwork undertaken in Turkey by U.S. teams would be stopped by the Turkish government because two U.S. museums had accepted gifts of illicitly acquired antiquities reputedly coming from Turkey. In contrast, numerous field expeditions, large and small, were

An anthropologist is sketching findings of prehistoric and early historic remains of Eskimo life at the site of Tukuto Lake in the Brooks Range in northern Alaska.

COURTESY, EDWIN S. HALL, JR., THE OHIO STATE UNIVERSITY

A compound where an early Plains people penned and slaughtered buffalo was discovered on the Wyoming Plains. The site contained postholes and bones in their original positions (right) and decomposed logs and buffalo skulls (below).

COURTESY, GEORGE C. FRISON, UNIVERSITY OF WYOMING

initiated in the Western Hemisphere in 1970. However, they too were plagued by lack of funds.

Discoveries in the Eastern Hemisphere

One of the most significant archaeological finds of 1970 was the unearthing of a series of fine frescoes—said to be the only truly classical Greek wall paintings yet found—in tombs near the Gulf of Salerno in Italy. The tombs, which are adjacent to the temples of Paestum, date from about 300 B.C. They were built by the Lucanians, a tribe that overpowered the Greeks of Poseidonia (later named Paestum) about 400 B.C. Presence of the well-executed frescoes in the Lucanian tombs, however, seemed to authenticate the availability of Greek artists in the region after the conquest.

Not long ago, religious fundamentalists were heartened by a find of wood high on Mount Ararat, the resting place of Noah's Ark, according to the Bible. In 1970 the wood in question was radiocarbon-dated to about A.D. 700, some 3,000 years after Noah's Biblical voyage. However, archaeologists have not yet explained what an estimated 50 tons of ice-encased hewn wood was doing at the 14,000-foot level of the mountain, several thousand feet above the timberline and more than 300 miles from trees large enough to supply the wood. One theory held that the timbers were part of a hermitage built to pay homage to the belief that Noah landed at the site.

On the plain of Marathon in Greece, the scene of an epic battle between Greeks and Persians in 490 B.C., a small burial mound was uncovered near the well-known larger one. It held the skeletal remains of perhaps 20 young men. They were identified as Plataeans, a group who fought alongside the Athenians during the famed battle.

The Stoa of the Basileus, a portico in Athens' ancient marketplace where the philosopher Socrates was tried and condemned to death in 399 B.C., was found in 1970. Archaeologists and other scholars were especially delighted with the discovery because the remains perfectly matched early descriptions of the site.

Further studies of Lepenski Vir, the Neolithic settlement in Yugoslavia, revealed that the dog was the sole domesticated animal in the site's earliest phases, sometime before 5500 B.C. Cattle, sheep, and pigs did not roam the settlement until later.

Recent salvage operations in England turned up traces of a large henge monument at Durrington. The circular structures within the monument were built of timber. Excavation on the largest English henge, at Marden, revealed a circular roofed structure there. With the discovery of larger henges, Stonehenge, on the Salisbury Plain, has been demoted to the status of a "parish church," albeit a royal one because of its sophistication—according to *Current Archaeology* magazine.

Political and military uncertainties in the United Arab Republic, or Egypt, prompted archaeologists to restrict their work to urban sites where security could be assured. Also with a mind toward safety, archaeologists in Israel were most active in the less conflict-torn Mediterranean area of the nation. At Gezer, a city gate dating from the time of Solomon was uncovered.

Iran became the focal point for many archaeologists displaced from trouble-plagued countries of the Near East. For several years an Italian team had been excavating a vast site, Shahr-i-Sokhta, in east-central Iran. It apparently was occupied before 2000 B.C. and seemed to be a center for trade in lapis lazuli, a semiprecious stone much favored by the ancients.

Spirit Cave, in northern Thailand, continued to yield evidence of very early plant domestication—a number of seeds found there and thought to be grown by man have been radiocarbon-dated as about 12,000 years old. If further findings confirm this, Thailand could replace the Fertile Crescent of the Middle East as the cradle of agriculture. In northeastern Thailand, the prehistoric village site of Non Nok Tha produced evidence of rice-growing dating from about 3500 B.C., much earlier than rice was grown in China or India. Implements found at the site, including a bronze ax that could accommodate a handle, suggested that the ancient villagers were as facile in toolmaking as their Middle Eastern contemporaries and were using bronze before the Chinese.

Archaeology in the Western Hemisphere

Archaeologists were reconstructing a marshy area in Long Island, N.Y., to learn what it was like during prehistoric times. They found that the site was once a shallow bay and subsequently broad mud flats abundant with edible soft clams. Prehistoric man made greatest use of the site in the mud-flat stage, but as the open water disappeared, the soft-clam populations decreased significantly, depriving man of his food supply. The prehistoric inhabitants then left for a new site.

A buffalo pound built about A.D. 250 was investigated near Gillette, Wyo. Nearly all man-made, the pound consisted of two fence lines that led to an enclosure where the animals were slaughtered.

A pre-Columbian civilization that flourished some 1,300 years ago in southern Mexico and then suffered a disastrous decline may have done so because its people abused their natural environment. Evidence unearthed on Monte Albán, which overlooks the city of Oaxaca, indicated faulty land management as the cause of the decline. Subjected to erosion because of careless deforestation and one-crop agriculture, the soil could no longer produce the food needed by the populace.

Archaeologists from the University of California at Los Angeles discovered the earliest evidence of man in South America yet reported. Artifacts of human industry—crude unifacial tools, choppers, and a burin—were located beneath a cave floor in Peru. Three occupation zones existed in the cave; the most recent dated from about 12,000 B.C. It seemed probable that older dates would be established for the remaining zones. (*See in* CE: Archaeology; Man.)

ARCHITECTURE. The outstanding architectural event of 1970 was Japan's Expo '70, a world exhibition held on a site in the Senri Hills outside Osaka. It equalled the high architectural standards set by Canada's Expo 67. As has become traditional with such expositions, it was a proving ground for new ideas in architecture, planning, and environmental technology.

Simon Fraser University, at Burnaby, B.C., is a "megastructure" of several interconnected units designed by Erickson, Massey, of Vancouver, B.C.

COURTESY, SIMON FRASER UNIVERSITY

The Central University Research Library at the University of California, at San Diego, designed by William L. Pereira and Associates, rises like a massive tree on the campus.

COURTESY, UNIVERSITY OF CALIFORNIA, AT SAN DIEGO

The central feature was Theme Hall and Festival Plaza, a multilevel circulation area covered by a vast roof designed by the official Expo architect Kenzo Tange and engineer Yoshikatsu Tsuboi. This spectacular structure was hailed by the influential *Architectural Review* as the one astonishing architectural achievement of the show, providing fruitful new ideas for the treatment of central spaces in towns of the future.

Many of the national and commercial pavilions were outstanding examples of exhibition architecture. Canada's pavilion was among the more spectacular constructions, consisting of a vast, mirror-faced, truncated pyramid designed by architects Erickson and Massey. The U.S. pavilion made use of an adventurous form of construction. It was sunk into the ground with a minimum of visible external walling. The vast oval interior was covered with an air-supported roof of translucent vinyl-coated fiber glass. The architects for the pavilion were Davis, Brody, Chermayeff, Geismar, and De Harak Associates.

The Swiss exhibit was not a building at all, but rather a stylized aluminum "tree," 68 feet high, festooned with 35,000 electrical lamps. The structure broadcast electronic music and, in hot weather, emitted cool air. The architect was Willi Walter, who collaborated with Charlotte Schmid and Paul Leber. Among other exciting pavilions were those of Czechoslovakia, Great Britain, and the Netherlands and of several of the Japanese commercial and industrial groups, namely the Fuji, the Takara, and the Sumitomo. The Takara exhibit was one of the most successful architectural fantasies, consisting of a steel-pipe framework in which cubic stainless-steel capsules were inserted to house the exhibits.

School and University Buildings

Once again throughout the world many of the more forward-looking architectural productions were commissioned by schools and universities. In the United States, a new departure in school design was exemplified by the Butler County Community Junior College, El Dorado, Kan., by architects Shaefer, Schirmer, and Eflin. It was to consist of a dozen or more individual buildings, ten of which had been built by 1970, linked by steps, ramps, and landscaped terraces designed to provide informal areas for discussion and relaxation. The campus of the University of California, at San Diego, had a new and magnificent focal point—the Central University Research Library. Designed by William L. Pereira and Associates, it was a vast concrete structure that cantilevered five levels over a narrow podium to create a treelike shape. One feature of the design was that even on the widest horizontal level a student was never more than two minutes away from any other part of the building. Another excellent new library was the Goddard Library at Clark University, Worcester, Mass. Designed by John Johansen, the library was intended to resemble a gigantic "box of books" with myriad shapes protruding from the central core.

The British firm of Howell, Killick, Partridge, and Amis was responsible for no less than three new college buildings at Cambridge University, in England, which helped to uphold the university's reputation as the center for modern architecture in Great Britain. Among the new buildings were combination rooms, kitchens, and offices for Downing College, designed to harmonize with the famous 19th-century Greek Revival exteriors, by William Wilkins.

High-Rise Office Buildings

High-rise office buildings continued to dominate city buildings as urban land values shot up everywhere. The skyline of the City of London, where not so long ago the dome of St. Paul's Cathedral had been the highest point, was taking on a new look with an increasing number of tall office buildings. Among the best of 1970 were the Commercial Union Building and the P & O Building, both by Gollins, Melvin, Ward and Partners. The buildings were square towers that faced one another across a common plaza.

In Boston, Mass., the First National Bank's new headquarters was taking shape. Designed by architects Campbell, Aldrich, and Nulty, its novel design featured the first six stories set back to leave room for a plaza and the next eight stories bulging out to make up the lost space. Above the bulge, the building continued straight up in the normal way. A new addition to the San Francisco, Calif., skyline was the Aetna Life and Casualty Building, by Welton Becket and Associates. This was an octagonal tower of steel, sheathed with dark granite and bronze-tinted windows.

Other Projects and Events

One developing trend in the U.S. architectural community in 1970 was an increasing concern for designing for the poor, particularly in the urban environment. The Acorn housing project, a low-cost design in West Oakland, Calif., exemplified this trend. Designed by Burger and Coplans, it was built by a black contractor and was to have a 50% black population. The dwellings, which were of a timber-frame construction that could be built rapidly and cheaply, consisted of three-story blocks of apartments joining rows of two-story family houses.

In New York City an increasing number of black people were taking advantage of a program of architectural training that was sponsored by the Architects Renewal Committee in Harlem.

"THE NEW YORK TIMES"

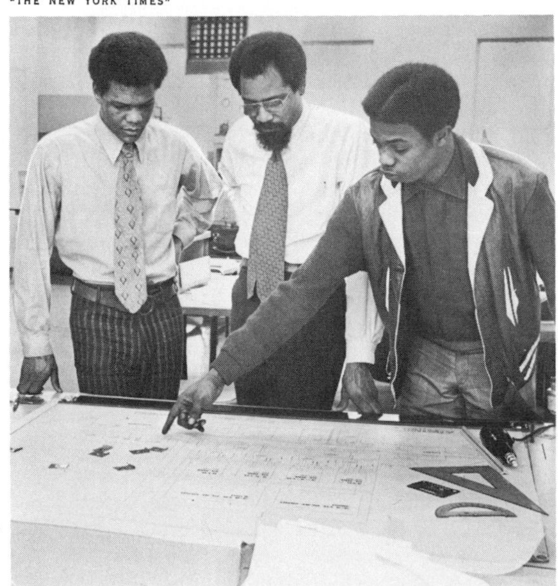

Among the religious centers that aroused architectural interest in 1970 was the new, almost-completed Roman Catholic cathedral by P. Belluschi and P. L. Nervi in San Francisco. The vast cruciform concrete edifice was described by *Architectural Review* as "an extraordinary exercise in enclosing the smallest amount of space with the greatest amount of wall."

The Royal Institute of British Architects (RIBA) awarded its Royal Gold Medal for 1970 to Sir Robert Matthew. The American Institute of Architects similarly honored Buckminster Fuller (recipient of the RIBA medal two years before). Los Angeles lost one of its most significant examples of early modern architecture in 1970 when the Dodge House, built in 1916 and designed by Irving Gill, was finally demolished after a long fight to save it proved unsuccessful. (*See also* Building Construction; Cities and Urban Affairs. *See in* CE: Architecture.)

ARCTIC.

Greater attention was being paid to delicate ecological balances in Arctic regions in 1970. The recent major oil find in Alaska's North Slope, for example, posed the tricky problem of how to transport that oil to markets without damaging Arctic tundra or wildlife. The trans-Alaska pipeline system proposed for moving the oil at a high temperature was bogged in controversy in 1970. A study was under way to assess the environmental effects of the pipeline in the Alaskan Arctic. (*See* Conservation Special Report.)

So precarious was the fate of the grizzly bear that Alaska banned hunting of the animal during the 1970 spring season. Polar-bear hunting was curtailed there when it became apparent that efficient snowmobile-aided and airborne hunting methods were speeding the extinction of that Arctic animal.

Plans for the building of U.S. icebreakers for Arctic service were under consideration in 1970. The Soviet Union disclosed that it would build two nuclear-powered icebreakers by 1975. They would be twice as powerful as the *Lenin,* the pioneer Soviet nuclear-powered icebreaker.

Chartered tours between Alaska and Siberia plus other parts of Soviet Russia, including Moscow, were inaugurated in 1970. Cooperation between Alaska Airlines; Aeroflot, the Russian airline; and Intourist, the Soviet travel agency, made possible the travel operation.

Canada hoped to extend its jurisdiction over Arctic waters up to 100 nautical miles off its northern coast. The Canadian government stressed that such a measure was not an assertion of sovereignty but an attempt to exert an effective form of pollution control over shipping and resource exploitation in those waters.

ULUSCHAK, "EDMONTON JOURNAL," FROM BEN ROTH AGENCY

A Danish scientist working on the Greenland ice cap learned that the Arctic island would soon get colder. Maximum cold was expected to occur well into the 21st century, with perhaps disastrous effects on the Greenland fishing industry. (*See in* CE: Arctic Regions.)

ARGENTINA. The four-year rule of Argentina's president, Lieut. Gen. Juan Carlos Onganía, who came to power after a military coup in 1966, ended on June 8, 1970, when Onganía himself was removed by a three-man junta of the country's top military commanders. He was succeeded by Brig. Gen. Roberto Marcelo Levingston, the former Argentine military attaché in Washington, D.C.

Originally a proponent of democratic rule, Onganía had used increasingly dictatorial means, outlawing political parties and suppressing newspapers, to restore economic and social stability. Public resentment against these policies, combined with Onganía's power struggle with the military, led to his downfall. He was also castigated for his handling of the investigation into the kidnapping and murder of former President Pedro Eugenio Aramburu. President from 1955 to 1958 after the fall of dictator Juan Perón, Aramburu was abducted in late May by Peronistas, who claimed to have executed him in retaliation for the execution of 27 Peronistas by the government in 1956.

As he took office, Levingston announced that he intended to restore democratic government but set no date for elections. One of the new regime's first moves was to devalue the currency, reducing the value of the peso from $.2857 to $.25. Some observers believed that the peso was devalued so that the government could better afford to placate labor with wage increases.

In 1970 Brig. Gen. Roberto Marcelo Levingston seized power in Argentina.
KEYSTONE

However, Levingston announced in the fall that the country's political parties, dissolved in 1966, would not be reinstituted but rather would be replaced by new parties. His statement provoked furious opposition. The national labor organization, the Confederación General del Trabajo (CGT), called for a general strike on October 9. The new government's troubles with labor had already been exacerbated by the August 27 terrorist assassination of labor leader José Varela Alonso.

The national rate of inflation increased from 3.6% for the first eight months of 1969 to 11.2% for the same period of 1970, mainly because of rises in the price of beef and other primary consumer goods. (*See in* CE: Argentina.)

ARMED FORCES, UNITED STATES. In 1970 the armed forces of the United States continued to be engaged throughout the world in helping maintain the security of the non-Communist world. All branches of the armed forces still employed their personnel in Vietnam, but steady cutbacks in the actual fighting forces were maintained. (*See* Defense; Selective Service; Vietnam.)

AIR FORCE

For the U.S. Air Force, 1970 was a year of retrenchment. The Air Force authorization request for fiscal 1970 called for the purchase of only 390 aircraft, compared with 948 in fiscal 1969—thus there was a total operational and combat loss of 470 aircraft in calendar year 1969. This was the smallest number of aircraft procured in any one year in the history of the Air Force, since the days of the Army Air Corps in 1935. The Air Force's personnel strength was reduced by about 100,000; a number of major installations were closed; and the Air Force budget was lowered by more than $1.5 billion. Even so, more than one million active duty Air Force personnel and civilians manned nearly 200 installations around the world, and the Air Force budget slightly exceeded $24 billion.

Even though the Air Force retired its supersonic B-58 bombers from the inventory of active aircraft, it kept about 500 B-52 and FB-111 bombers and 1,000 Minuteman I and II and 54 Titan II intercontinental ballistic missiles, and it introduced the advanced Minuteman III into the inventory. The Minuteman III will have multiple independently targetable reentry vehicle (MIRV) warheads. The MIRV will permit a single missile to deliver warheads to several separate targets and also to carry penetration aids to confuse enemy defenses.

The Air Force's airlift capacity increased in 1970 when the C-5A entered the Air Force inventory. The C-5A possesses a combination of features not

OFFICIAL U.S. AIR FORCE PHOTO

The U.S. Air Force's airlift capacity increased in 1970 when the C-5A heavy transport plane entered the Air Force inventory.

all possessed by any other single aircraft: the ability to operate from semiprepared airstrips as short as 4,000 feet; capacity for outsize cargo; roll-on and roll-off loading and unloading for rapid cargo handling; self-contained avionics and navigational systems; and heavily stressed cargo floors that permit the easy positioning of heavy vehicles inside the airplane.

North American Rockwell Corp. was awarded the contract for development of the airframe for a new strategic bomber, the B-1. Design of the B-1 will take advantage of the many technical advances made during the past decade. Compared to the B-52, the B-1 will have, among other improvements, a higher penetration speed, larger bomb capacity, a better capability to penetrate at lower altitudes, quicker reaction launch, and the ability to operate from austere bases.

McDonnell Douglas Corp. was awarded the contract to develop the airframe for a new air-superiority fighter aircraft, the F-15. It will be a single-place, twin-turbofan, fixed-wing aircraft that will weigh about 40,000 pounds when loaded with missiles and an internal cannon. It will be an extremely agile, highly maneuverable aircraft that will have an extra thrust enabling it to accelerate rapidly in order to cope with any maneuvers made by enemy aircraft. It will be capable of speed in excess of Mach 2 and will have a mix of air-to-air weaponry, including both medium- and short-range missiles and an internal rapid-firing gun. (*See also* Aircraft. *See in* CE: Air Force, U.S.)

ARMY

In 1970 the U.S. Army began its prosecution of the enlisted men and officers accused of being responsible for the alleged 1968 massacre of more than 100 Vietnamese civilians in the My Lai 4 hamlet of the village of Song My. The Army also ascertained during the year that high-ranking officers attempted to cover up the affair. Among those accused of trying to conceal the incident was Maj. Gen. Samuel Koster, superintendent of the U.S. Military Academy at West Point, N.Y. He had been commander of the Americal Division in Vietnam at the time the alleged massacre took place. When this evidence was revealed Koster resigned from his post at West Point. Thirteen other officers were also accused of suppressing information; however, charges against several of the officers were dropped.

The first of 17 men accused in the alleged My Lai massacre to come to trial was Staff Sgt. David Mitchell. The Army prosecutor called only 3 of 14 subpoenaed witnesses to the stand, and Mitchell's attorney argued that certain elements were trying to "undermine and destroy the military." This, the defense contended, was an attempt to destroy the United States. Mitchell was found not guilty on November 20.

Another defendant, Sgt. Esequiel Torres, was granted a delay in the court-martial proceedings against him by a federal judge. The judge granted a restraining order until a civilian panel could rule on the legality of the Vietnam war. Torres' attorney also claimed that U.S. President Richard M. Nixon had prejudiced the case against Torres. In September Torres filed charges against Gen. William C. Westmoreland for dereliction of duty and blamed him for the My Lai deaths.

Captain Ernest L. Medina was charged in March with murdering and maiming Vietnamese civilians at My Lai. In April he was charged with the responsibility for the deaths of at least 175 villagers.

The court-martial of the chief defendant, First Lieut. William L. Calley, Jr., began on November 12. He was charged with the murder of 102 civilians. The court-martial heard testimony that Calley had fired into captive groups of unarmed women, children, and old men, killing them. A witness who had been granted partial amnesty, Paul D. Meadlo, refused to testify. The defense contended that

PICTORIAL PARADE

The first two women were nominated for appointment as generals by U.S. President Richard M. Nixon. Flanked by Secretary of the Army Stanley R. Resor and Army Chief of Staff Gen. William C. Westmoreland, they are Brig. Gen. Anna Mae Hays (left) and Brig. Gen. Elizabeth P. Hoisington.

Calley was only following orders in a "free-fire zone," where all the inhabitants were presumed to be hostile. The court-martial continued into 1971.

In December a lawsuit for $400 million was filed against the U.S. government on behalf of the survivors of My Lai. Along with Calley, Secretary of the Army Stanley Resor and Secretary of Defense Melvin R. Laird were named as defendants in the suit.

In an unrelated incident, First Lieut. James B. Duffy on March 29 was found guilty of the premeditated murder of a Vietnamese. Duffy admitted to ordering the man's execution because he said that he was expected to bring in a body count, not prisoners. Later the court-martial, after learning that the charge carried a sentence of life imprisonment, decided that Duffy was only guilty of involuntary manslaughter. He was sentenced to six months' imprisonment.

Other tales of war atrocities emerged during the year. A discharged Army medic revealed that two officers in 1969 had ordered their men to fire into huts inhabited by Vietnamese civilians. The officers were charged with attempted murder. In April a former Army helicopter pilot told the National Committee for a Citizens Commission of Inquiry on United States War Crimes in Vietnam that a major had killed 33 Vietnamese civilians in 1967.

The investigation into charges of corruption in the operation of U.S. Army service clubs continued in 1970. In March a master sergeant was charged with larceny, bribery, and graft. Also as a result of the investigation, Earl F. Cole, a former brigadier general, was demoted to colonel and retired from the Army.

The year's most notable plea for conscientious-objector status came from Cary E. Donham, a West Point cadet. Donham said that accounts of the My Lai incident had made him realize "what war is," and as a result he became opposed to war. The Army denied his request for an honorable discharge. A West Point graduate, First Lieut. Louis P. Font, refused to fight in Vietnam and asked for discharge as a selective conscientious objector. (*See also* Vietnam.)

COAST GUARD

The U.S. Coast Guard, the nation's oldest seagoing armed service, continued in 1970 to perform a wide variety of duties in areas ranging from Vietnam to Greece. The 180-year-old service also initiated during the year some new means of meeting its varied responsibilities in a changing world. These ranged from oil pollution control studies to a wider use of faster, larger helicopters for search and rescue and other tasks.

At the close of fiscal 1970, the Coast Guard had 38,172 military personnel and 5,841 civilians serving in the United States and 15 other countries throughout the world. The service had 307 floating units and 116 aircraft, 106 of these being helicopters.

Coast Guard operations in South Vietnam over the five preceding years exemplified the service's dual capacities for carrying out wartime and peacetime functions. In 1970, in accordance with the "Vietnamization" program, the Coast Guard turned over the last of its 26 patrol boats in South Vietnam to that country's navy. The 82-foot boats had logged more than 4 million miles in the war and had been involved in more than a quarter million inspections of vessels suspected of carrying enemy supplies or personnel into South Vietnam.

In 1970 the Coast Guard continued its acquisition of the new long-range HH-3F amphibious helicopters. Increasingly, the service was relying on the turbine-powered craft to perform a variety of missions. The big helicopter, which cruises at 150 miles per hour, is capable of flying 345 miles out to sea, hovering for 20 minutes, picking up six survivors, and returning to land.

The Coast Guard, which long has been interested in preventing and dealing with pollution of the waterways, was named by U.S. President Richard M. Nixon in 1970 as the chief enforcer of provisions of the Water Quality Improvement Act of 1970. Also, in May the Coast Guard completed preliminary tests of a system that can be air-dropped to a distressed tanker in order to contain leaking oil in a large inflatable "bladder," which has a capacity of 140,000 gallons. Further tests and evaluation were necessary before such a system could be implemented. In August the Coast Guard announced awards of contracts for feasibility studies on systems to separate and recover oil spillages at sea. (*See also* Conservation.)

Besides its antipollution enforcement duties, the Coast Guard enforced various fisheries conservation laws and treaties. In the 1970 fiscal year, five fishing vessels were seized for violations. A total of 181 violations of fisheries zones and treaties were recorded during the year. Coast Guard aerial and surface units patrolled approximately 20.6 million square miles in enforcing fisheries laws. (*See* Refugees. *See in* CE: Coast Guard, U.S.)

MARINE CORPS

The U.S. Marine Corps met a variety of commitments in 1970. Moving simultaneously on several fronts, it continued to provide its fullest support to Marines still engaged in the Vietnam war; carried out large-scale troop redeployments; and lessened its overall troop levels. At the same time, it was busy realigning its force structure to meet post-Vietnam requirements.

Still in the combat zone as 1970 began were the 1st Marine Division, remaining elements of the 1st Marine Aircraft Wing and Force Logistic Command, and necessary supporting units. Together, they comprised the Third Marine Amphibious Force (III MAF) in Vietnam, numbering approximately 55,000 Marines.

The 1st Division, the Marine Corps's only ground element still in combat, maintained steady pressure against Viet Cong and North Vietnamese army forces in the Da Nang area. The division also continued its defense of Da Nang city and the vital air base there.

The air arm of the Marines, the 1st Wing, was also a potent weapon, though redeployments had cut strength by about one third. The 1st Wing was responsible for almost all tactical air support given allied forces in the I Corps tactical zone of Vietnam. Thousands of fixed-wing sorties were flown, while helicopters remained a vital element in resupply of troops and evacuation of wounded. In addition, 1st Wing pilots flew interdiction missions along the Ho Chi Minh Trail.

Ground Marines continued to fight what was essentially a war of counterinsurgency. While some large-unit operations were conducted, the emphasis was on small-unit and counterguerrilla actions.

By April approximately 12,900 Marines had departed Vietnam under U.S. President Richard M. Nixon's Phase III redeployment, which began in January. In July the Phase IV redeployment began and was to continue into October. Included were several redeploying units of the III MAF which proceeded to the continental United States or Hawaii. Other units moved to the western Pacific area where they formed part of the U.S. strategic reserve. By August 20, there were approximately 36,500 Marines left in Vietnam.

In a U.S. military court in Da Nang on August 15, Pfc. Samuel G. Green, Jr., of Cleveland, Ohio, was sentenced to five years in prison after being found guilty of murdering 15 South Vietnamese women and children in a village southwest of Da Nang on Feb. 19, 1970. Green was the second Marine to be convicted in the case, the first being Pvt. Michael A. Schwarz of Weirton, W.Va., who was sentenced to life imprisonment.

With a total of about 300,000 Marines at the beginning of 1970, the Marine Corps moved gradually toward a projected goal of 204,000, its approximate pre-Vietnam level. By the end of fiscal 1970, there were approximately 24,900 Marine officers and 234,700 enlisted Marines. About 81,000 new Marines completed recruit training; 3,070 new Marine officers were commissioned; and 912 Marine student aviators received their wings.

In 1970 recruit training was increased from eight to nine weeks and individual combat training from three to four weeks. Basic school instruction for newly commissioned officers was increased from 21 to 26 weeks. The Navy continued to train the majority of Marine pilots, aided (since the outbreak of the Vietnam war) by the Air Force and the Army. (*See also* Defense; Vietnam. *See in* CE: Marine Corps, U.S.)

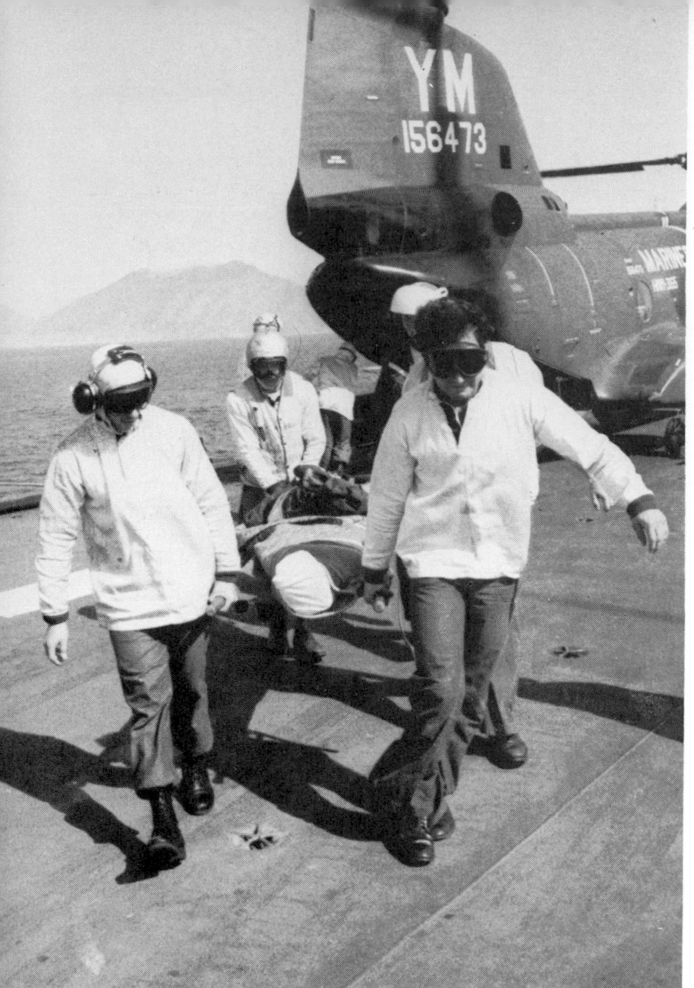

OFFICIAL U.S. NAVY PHOTO BY PH3 N. A. MILLER

A U.S. Marine helicopter brought an injured Peruvian earthquake victim to the USS *Guam* for medical aid in June. Navy men and Marines carry the victim to the ship's hospital below deck.

NAVY

The extensive U.S. Navy cutbacks and decommissionings of the preceding few years continued in 1970. By midyear, naval manpower had declined to about 694,000 men, down almost 80,000 from the year before.

In fiscal 1970, fleet strength dropped by 125 to about 750 vessels. During fiscal 1971 approximately another 100 were scheduled for mothballing, including the attack carrier USS *Bon Homme Richard,* the support carrier USS *Hornet,* and the heavy cruiser USS *St. Paul.* New construction of about 60 ships will bring the average age of the fleet down to about 16 years.

The Navy's second nuclear-powered carrier, USS *Nimitz,* was scheduled for launching late in 1970. (The first, USS *Enterprise,* had been in the fleet for almost a decade.) On August 15, the keel was laid for a third nuclear carrier, USS *Dwight D. Eisenhower,* which was expected to join the fleet in about five years. The new carriers were the best protected and the least vulnerable ever designed. They will be capable of operating for up to 13 years without refueling and of handling any naval tactical aircraft in the air or on the drawing board in 1970.

During the year the Navy also signed a long-term contract with Litton Industries, Inc., for the construction of 30 new destroyers. The new ships will become the backbone of the fleet's antisubmarine warfare capability in the late 1970's.

On July 1, Adm. Elmo R. Zumwalt, Jr., moved into the highest military post in the Navy chain of command, chief of naval operations. At 49 he was the youngest in history to hold the position. Zumwalt had previously commanded naval forces in Vietnam. He relieved Adm. Thomas H. Moorer, who became chairman of the Joint Chiefs of Staff, replacing retiring Army Gen. Earle G. Wheeler. Moorer was the second naval officer to head the Joint Chiefs; Adm. Arthur Radford held the post from 1953 to 1957.

In Vietnam, training became an increasingly important part of the U.S. Navy's "Vietnamization" efforts as the Republic of Vietnam's navy grew in size and strength. In the largest single turnover of the war, 273 river combat boats were transferred to the South Vietnamese navy in June. This brought to 525 the number of riverine and coastal craft turned over to the Vietnamese and made their navy the ninth largest in the world.

The U.S. Navy was scheduled to turn over its last 123 in-country combat craft to the Vietnamese in December 1970 and thus relinquish all surface combatant responsibilities in Vietnam, according to Secretary of the Navy John H. Chafee. However, of 42 naval bases in Vietnam, only one had been completely turned over to the Vietnamese by June. The rest were manned by both U.S. and Vietnamese navy men.

On April 27, a five-officer Navy court in Washington, D.C., ordered a reprimand and a bad-conduct discharge for Apprentice Seaman Roger Lee Priest of Houston, Tex. Priest, arrested in April 1969 for publishing an antiwar newspaper, was found guilty on April 23, 1970, of promoting "disloyalty and disaffection" among armed forces members.

When earthquakes devastated a 600-square-mile area in central Peru on May 31, the carrier USS *Guam* arrived with a fleet of helicopters and medical aid and supplies for some of the estimated 100,000 injured and 800,000 left homeless by the disaster. During the emergency relief operations, helicopters from the ship flew hundreds of mercy missions into remote mountain areas, carrying medical teams and tons of food, fuel, and shelter to villages still cut off from other outside help. (*See in* CE: Navy, U.S.)

ARTS. Inflation, the stock market drop, and the general slowdown in the economy were all factors that worsened the already grave financial crisis in the arts in the United States in 1970. As private contributions fell off, pressure increased on government bodies, particularly at the federal level, to provide support for the nation's orchestras, museums, theaters, dance and opera companies, and other cultural institutions.

Their sad financial plight was dramatically outlined by several world-famous artists in February in testimony before a U.S. House of Representatives subcommittee on education. Choreographer Agnes de Mille, violinist Isaac Stern, dance and drama critic Clive Barnes, and others gave witness to the lagging quality of U.S. intellectual and aesthetic life, sharply criticizing a nation that placed its budget priorities on war, science, and technology. One congressional supporter of federal aid to the arts pointed out that—while Austria spent a yearly sum equal to $5.50 per person on the arts, France spent 20¢, and Great Britain 18¢—the United States, the richest country in the world, budgeted only a paltry 3¢.

In response, Congress, with U.S. President Richard M. Nixon's strong support, passed a bill allotting $40 million to the National Endowment for the Arts for fiscal 1971, more than doubling the previous year's appropriations. This sum, however, was still criticized by many in the U.S. artistic community as a "pittance" that would provide only limited help.

Nancy Hanks, chairman of the National Endowment for the Arts, announced that the greater portion of the newly appropriated funds would be given to groups that had national or regional influence. Among the first major recipients were 34 symphony orchestras, which received an initial grant of $1.68 million.

Other financial support for the arts came from the Ford Foundation, which in May announced grants totaling $2.1 million to 17 organizations, the largest amounts going to the Arena Stage theater in Washington, D.C., and the Dance Theater of Harlem and the Negro Ensemble Company, both in New York City. The New York State Legislature led the states in subsidies by appropriating a year's support of about $20 million for the arts.

Approximately 800 artists, businessmen, teachers, and politicians attended the fifth annual conference of the Associated Council of the Arts in May. The general theme stressed was that the arts should be made a fundamental part of U.S. life, particularly part of "the educational experience for all children. . . ." To that end, U.S. Commissioner of Education James E. Allen, Jr., announced a $900,000 federal grant to be used to sponsor programs of teaching and performances by professional artists in elementary and high schools. (*See also* Dance; Museums; Music; Painting and Sculpture; Theater. *See in* CE: Arts, The.)

ASIA. Events in Southeast Asia, and especially those concerned with the war in Indochina, again held the spotlight in Asia during 1970. In short, the war spread during the year, and peace seemed no closer at hand.

What Indonesia's foreign minister was to call "the most crucial year for Southeast Asia" started with a deceptive calm. On New Year's Day U.S. Vice-President Spiro T. Agnew was visiting Vietnam, and that seemed about the most exciting event in the region at the time. In a way it was also symbolic of what Southeast Asian countries were expecting for most of the year—continuing efforts by the United States to pull out of the region; a sustained Western campaign to reassure Asian allies of future military backing; further maneuvers in the so-called Indian Ocean power vacuum; and a scramble for leverage by Southeast Asian governments themselves in the emerging era of "Asian solutions to Asian problems."

The mood changed with dramatic suddenness following the change of government in Cambodia in

Striking workers of the Filipino-owned U.S. Tobacco Corp. in Manila were joined by leftist Filipino youths at a rally in Miranda Square, where the U.S. flag was burned in May.

REY PALARCA FROM UPI COMPIX

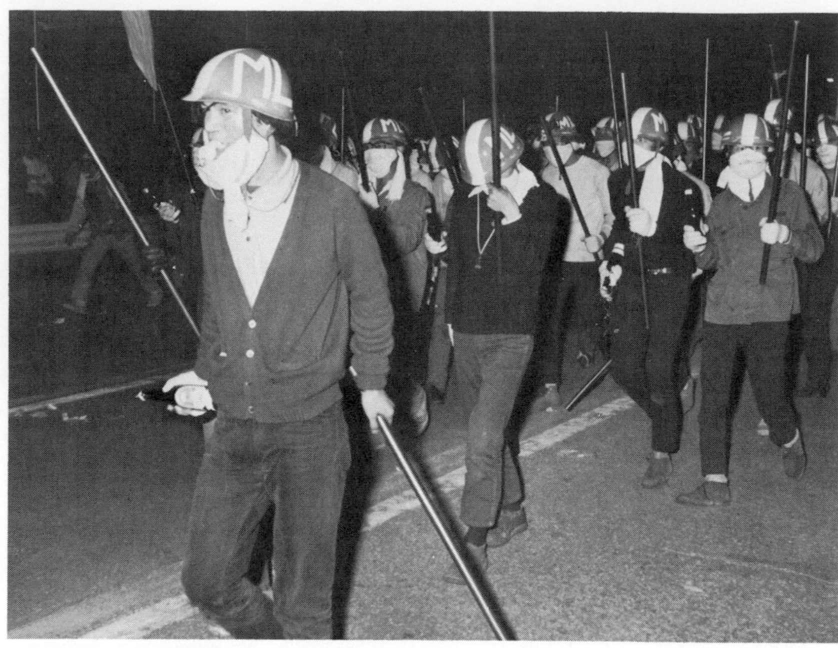

Members of the Marxist-Leninist faction of militant Japanese students, carrying Molotov cocktails and metal pipes, rioted in Tokyo against the Vietnam war and against the U.S.-Japanese security treaty in June.
PICTORIAL PARADE

March. Communist regimes in the region quickly realized that they were faced with an entirely new situation. Anti-Communist governments saw new serious threats to their own security. Nonaligned elements discovered that, instead of subsiding, the Indochina conflagration was now spreading. All of them had the same instinctive reaction: to get more directly into the act and try to influence the situation more effectively than in the past. For most of the year thereafter, the war and peace issues of Indochina were to be a major preoccupation with Southeast Asian governments.

High-Level Conferences

The Communists, already involved in the fighting, were the first to meet for discussions. Their get-together was in the form of a unique Indochinese summit conference on April 24–25. The exact location was never announced; it was believed to have been somewhere in the Communist China-Vietnam-Laos border area. The importance that the Communists attached to the conference was clear from the strength of their delegations' leaders. Communist China did not officially participate, but Premier Chou En-lai was on hand to host a banquet for the leaders.

Perhaps the most important political aspect of the Indochinese summit was the emphasis laid on the responsibility of each country for its own future. The official communiqué said that "the liberation and defense of each country are the business of its people"; one country would go to the help of another only on the basis of "the desire of the party concerned and mutual respect." This was considered a victory for the North Vietnamese position that "volunteers" from outside Indochina should not fight there and that within the peninsula each country should be allowed to develop according to its own light.

In contrast to the smooth Communist summit, the non-Communist governments found both the organization of a conference and the formulation of a common stand difficult. The idea that they should make a unified move for peace in Indochina found its greatest supporter in Adam Malik, Indonesia's foreign minister. For some time past he had been trying to organize a Southeast Asian initiative to bring peace to Vietnam. He and other foreign ministers of the region met in Manila, Philippines, in April to attend the Assembly for One Asia, sponsored by the Press Foundation of Asia. The crisis in Cambodia, which was invaded by U.S. and South Vietnamese troops on April 30, figured prominently in their discussions, and the decision was informally taken to organize a foreign ministers' conference aimed at finding a solution to the conflict.

Dissension began as soon as the invitations from Indonesia went out to 20 countries. The Communist Chinese government, one of the invitees, vehemently denounced the idea and persuaded its allies to boycott the conference. Countries within the Soviet sphere of influence also boycotted it. The crippling blow was the decision of several nonaligned countries—India, Pakistan, Ceylon, Burma—to decline the invitation on the grounds that they would prefer to be associated with an exclusive conference of nonaligned Asian countries. Eventually only 12 countries participated in the Djakarta (Indonesia) conference, on May 16–17, including Japan, Australia, New Zealand, and South Vietnam. Cambodia's foreign minister went to observe.

As soon as it opened, the conference found it necessary to lower its sights, for sharp divisions arose over the question of arms and troop supplies to the Cambodian government. The subsequent shelving of the arms and troop proposal and the decision to "take the road of a negotiated settlement" helped produce a consensus and a communiqué calling for Cambodian neutrality, withdrawal of foreign troops, and reactivation of the International Control Commission. Apart from a spate of headlines, nothing concrete came out of the Djakarta conference as far as Indochina was concerned. It was nevertheless of considerable political interest because it was the first time that members of the Association of Southeast Asian Nations had made a concerted effort to play an active diplomatic role in regional politics.

The other regional alliance, the Southeast Asia Treaty Organization (SEATO), held its 1970 Ministerial Council meeting in Manila in July. Thailand's foreign minister, Thanat Khoman, pledged continued support to the organization but attacked "the weakening resolve in some quarters" to live up to SEATO obligations. Thailand's criticism was indicative of some member states' concern over proposed U.S. military disengagement from the region.

These South Vietnamese soldiers are walking through the rubble of homes that were totally destroyed in Tonle Bet, Cambodia.

WIDE WORLD

They seemed unimpressed by U.S. Secretary of State William P. Rogers' strong reaffirmation at Manila that SEATO was part of the Nixon doctrine for Asia and that the United States stood fully committed to it. The only announcement that produced some enthusiasm came from Great Britain's new Conservative government, which said that it would maintain a military presence in the Malaysia-Singapore area beyond 1971—the time set by the previous Labor government for the withdrawal of British forces from the region.

As SEATO continued its languid existence, there was some new animation in other areas connected with regional defense. In the thick of the Cambodian fighting, South Vietnam projected the idea of an Indochinese anti-Communist defense alliance. In July representatives of South Vietnam and Thailand held talks in Bangkok, Thailand, and agreed that they "might" have to organize a military alliance with Cambodia and Laos for common protection against future Communist aggression. However, in the briefing given to reporters by Thailand's foreign minister, it was significantly emphasized that such an alliance was "a matter for future consideration." The proposal hardly progressed beyond the discussion stage.

There was more action over the so-called power vacuum in the Indian Ocean. Those Asian leaders most concerned welcomed the defeat of the Labor government in Great Britain in June; the Conservatives had pledged themselves to maintaining the British military status quo in the area. After assuming power, the Conservative government adopted the policy of working out new defense arrangements for Southeast Asia while allowing the reduction in British forces to continue.

Other Asian Highlights

Communist China, on April 24, successfully launched its first space satellite into orbit around the earth. During ceremonies celebrating the 21st anniversary of Communist rule in China, new titles were given to two of the top leaders. Communist Party Politburo Chairman Mao Tse-tung was made supreme commander of the whole nation, and Communist Party Vice-Chairman Lin Piao was made deputy commander.

Once again Communist China was refused a seat in the United Nations, but for the first time a simple majority of the countries voting approved admitting China. A two-thirds majority was required. (*See* United Nations.)

Touring Asia in August, U.S. Vice-President Spiro T. Agnew assured South Korea's president, Park Chung-hee, that the Administration of President Richard M. Nixon intended to provide capital to modernize the South Korean armed forces. In October Japan's Premier Eisaku Sato won an unprecedented fourth term as his party, the Liberal-Democrats, continued to dominate Japan's government. (*See also* individual countries by name. *See in* CE: Asia; individual countries by name.)

ASTRONOMY. The total solar eclipse of March 7, 1970, drew a record number of scientific expeditions to Mexico, the southeastern United States, and Nova Scotia. The eclipse was remarkable for the great brilliance of the corona (solar atmosphere) and for the spectacular streamers that radiated outward more than six solar diameters.

Ground-based observations included measurements of the intensity and polarization of the corona, of the deflection of starlight by the sun's gravitational field (a test of general relativity), and of the distribution of temperatures in the corona. The eclipse was also monitored from high altitudes by dozens of instrument-bearing rockets. An experiment devised by astronomers from Canada, Great Britain, and the United States obtained ultraviolet spectra just as the solar disk was covered by the moon, allowing the composition and temperature of specific layers in the sun's atmosphere to be determined. Another team obtained X-ray photographs that permitted identification of coronal features having temperatures in excess of about 1,800,000° F. (1,000,000° Kelvin). Experimenters also found that large sections of the solar atmosphere are interconnected by plasma-filled loops.

Studies of the Moon and Comets

Several important results emerged from the Apollo flights to the moon, though fundamental questions concerning the formation of the lunar surface and the state of the moon's interior remained unanswered. Analysis of the more than

The Stratoscope II telescope, which can photograph stellar objects, is borne aloft by a 660-foot-tall balloon (above). The 36-inch-diameter mirror (left) is the primary optical element in the telescope system.

COURTESY, CORNING GLASS WORKS

WIDE WORLD

Five views of the total solar eclipse in March, as seen in Norfolk, Va., show the progress of the moon across the face of the sun.

250 natural seismic events detected by the seismometer left by the Apollo 12 astronauts permitted scientists to distinguish between those tremors caused by the earth's tidal force and those resulting from meteorite impact. One rock returned by Apollo 12—the oldest yet analyzed—was dated at 4.6 billion years, nearly the age generally accepted for the solar system.

Many bright comets appeared late in 1969 and in 1970, leading to some significant discoveries. On January 14 an Orbiting Astronomical Observatory detected an unanticipated halo of hydrogen gas around Comet Tago-Sato-Kosaka (named after its discoverers). This huge envelope spanned more than a million miles.

During the spring Comet Bennett—the finest in many years—was visible to the unaided eye. Large telescopes revealed an unusual pinwheel formation in its head, as well as other structures not seen in more than a century. Again a giant hydrogen cloud enveloping the comet was present, indicating that this may be a feature of any large comet that comes sufficiently close to the sun.

Deep-Space Discoveries

Microwave observations added more molecules to those already known to exist in interstellar space. The National Radio Astronomy Laboratory announced the detection of carbon monoxide, hydrogen cyanide, and cyanoacetylene. A rocket obtained ultraviolet spectra that revealed for the first time the signature of molecular hydrogen (H_2). At least in the direction of the star Xi Persei, H_2 was found to be a third as abundant as free hydrogen atoms.

While quasars remained little better understood than they were a decade earlier, pulsars yielded some of their secrets. It became practically certain that pulsars are stars composed of neutrons, neutral particles of unit mass. Pulsars are tiny bodies, perhaps only a few tens of miles in diameter, that spin around in as little as $\frac{1}{30}$ of a second. Their matter is packed to fantastic densities of trillions of grams per cubic centimeter, their temperatures exceed 180,000,000° F., and they have powerful magnetic fields. The pulsed radio emission received on earth probably emanates from a single spot on the surface of each neutron star. As the star rotates, its radio beam sweeps across our line of sight.

More than 50 pulsars are now known, making it possible to determine their common properties. All well-observed pulsars, for example, are slowing down. This implies that the most rapid spinners are the youngest, and the rate of deceleration suggests ages between 2,000 and a billion years. Pulsars are now known to be members of our galaxy, most of them being within 10,000 light-years of the sun.

Stratoscope II, a 36-inch balloon-borne telescope, obtained photographs of the galaxy NGC 4151. Its nucleus was found to be less than 13 light-years in diameter and may be packed with 10 billion stars, leading to collisions. These objects may be related to quasars. (*See in* CE: Astronomy.)

AUSTRALIA.

There was a continuing adjustment of Australia's foreign policy during 1970 to fit the nation's new role as an emerging power in the Pacific area. While supporting the United States on issues involving the war in Indochina, the Australian government was nevertheless anxious to align itself with other Pacific nations, such as Indonesia and Japan. The unstable political situation in Papua and the Territory of New Guinea presented major problems for Australian diplomats during the year. Poverty and racial questions presented themselves as causes for domestic concern.

Foreign Affairs

After a four-day delay the Australian government finally voiced its support for the U.S. policy of attacking Communist sanctuaries in Cambodia. On May 16–17, however, Australian representatives attended a conference of Asian and Pacific nations on the Cambodian issue. The purpose of the conference was to find ways of exerting pressure for the removal of foreign troops from Cambodia and the restoration of Cambodia's neutrality (*see* Cambodia; United States).

In April Prime Minister John G. Gorton announced the first withdrawal of Australian troops from South Vietnam. Gorton stated that one of the three Australian battalions would be withdrawn by November. He made it clear, however, that the withdrawal decision was based entirely on the

AUSTRALIAN NEWS AND INFORMATION BUREAU

Construction was expected to begin in 1971 on a 53-story hotel and office building in Melbourne, Australia (scale model shown). When completed, it would be Australia's tallest building.

U.S. policy of troop withdrawal and did not reflect his government's feelings about Australia's commitment to the defense of South Vietnam. Gorton's government did not want Australian troops to be left alone in Vietnam without U.S. support. Gorton defended Australia's involvement in Vietnam and implied concern over the speed at which U.S. troops were being withdrawn.

Approximately 100,000 Australians participated in a moratorium on May 8 to protest the war in Vietnam and to call for immediate Allied troop withdrawals. The demonstrations in Australia's major cities were orderly and there was very little violence. A poll conducted in the spring, however, showed that 50% of the Australians favored a gradual withdrawal of troops (*see* Vietnam).

Papua-New Guinea rivaled Vietnam as the chief problem area for Australian diplomats in 1970. The crucial issue was the date of independence, on which even the territorial population could not agree. Gorton visited the area in July but refused to set a date for independence. He did, however, grant territorial control over many internal affairs.

Domestic Issues

A crisis of confidence in the government was narrowly avoided in May, when Prime Minister Gorton defeated a no-confidence motion in Parliament. The motion accused the government of breaking agreements with the states regarding offshore mineral rights.

During 1970 there was a growing awareness of a racial problem between white Australians and the native aborigines. One aboriginal tribe filed suit

Curious motorists stop to watch the progress of the Indian-Pacific passenger express train on its inaugural run between Sydney and Perth, Australia, in February 1970.

AUSTRALIAN NEWS AND INFORMATION BUREAU

claiming ownership of the rich bauxite deposits on Gove Peninsula. Reports during the year estimated that about a million Australians, many of them aborigines, lived in dire poverty.

In 1969–70 the Australian economy achieved a high rate of growth; the gross national product increased by about 6%. To reduce the possibility of inflation, a precautionary budget was introduced in August. (*See also* Commonwealth of Nations. *See in* CE: Australia.)

AUSTRIA. For the first time in 25 years a Socialist government was elected in Austria in 1970. The Socialists campaigned on a platform calling for improved education, health services, and labor-management relations and strict controls against environmental pollution. This platform had considerable appeal for Austrian youths, and 19-year-olds were allowed to vote for the first time in this election.

The Socialist party won a surprising victory in the March 1 election, receiving 2,193,717 votes to 2,026,100 votes for the People's party. The right-wing Freedom party polled 247,007 votes and the Communist party 46,000 votes. This gave the Socialist party 81 seats in the Austrian parliament and the People's party 79 seats. The Freedom party managed to hold 5 seats, but the Communist party and other splinter groups were unable to win any seats at all.

Bruno Kreisky

LONDON "DAILY EXPRESS" FROM PICTORIAL PARADE

In the new government that was formed Bruno Kreisky replaced Josef Klaus as chancellor. Following the elections Kreisky held talks with the opposing People's party and attempted to set up a coalition government. The two parties could not agree on policy, however, and so Kreisky appointed an all-Socialist cabinet. The new Socialist government was committed to upholding Austria's neutrality and declared itself strongly anti-Communist.

After the election, dissension broke out in the defeated People's party, and Klaus resigned as head of the party. He was replaced by Hermann Withalm. When Withalm and Kreisky found that they could not reach an agreement, Withalm threatened to form a coalition with the Freedom party and bring down the Socialist government.

The new government faced its first crisis in May when it was revealed that Hans Oellinger, the minister of agriculture, was a former Nazi and member of the elite Waffen Schutzstaffel (SS). Kreisky investigated, found that Oellinger had resigned from the SS in 1940 and had not been guilty of any crimes, and lent Oellinger his full support. However, Oellinger resigned after suffering a heart attack. Kreisky, Austria's first post-World War II chancellor of Jewish descent, had been forced to flee to Sweden when the Nazis entered Austria in 1938. (*See in* CE: Austria.)

AUTOMOBILES. While the fashion industry hassled over the length of milady's skirt, the U.S. auto industry unhesitatingly swung to the mini-size car in 1970, confident that the small car was the highway fashion of the future. General Motors (GM), Ford, and American Motors (AM) each presented new mini compacts that they hoped would stem the growth of foreign-car sales in the United States. Among U.S. producers, only Chrysler was without a domestically made entry in the small-car market at year-end.

The first of the minis to be introduced was AM's Gremlin, which debuted in April. In final form it was actually a conversion of the Hornet, AM's compact-size car. It offered the Hornet's six-cylinder, 232-cubic-inch engine (though the standard engine was 199 cubic inches), as well as its transmission, suspension, and basic body components. The Gremlin was built in one body style. Its dimensions—96-inch wheelbase and 161¼-inch overall length—were much shorter than any other car then made in the United States. The two-passenger base car carried a list price of $1,879, just $40 more than the Volkswagen and a full $120 less than Ford's Maverick, up to then the lowest-priced U.S. car. By the end of 1970 an estimated 50,000 Gremlins had been sold.

Ford, GM Enter Mini Market

In August, GM and Ford introduced their minis—the Chevrolet Vega 2300 and the Pinto. Built in four two-door body styles—sedan, coupe, wagon, and delivery truck—the Vega was 169.7 inches long and weighed almost 2,200 pounds. The body was of unit construction.

Vegas were assembled on a new line at Lordstown, Ohio, where a number of innovations in body assembly were introduced. Of particular interest was the automatic door-hanging machine that attached doors to hinge pillars without the aid of human guidance. Chevrolet said the body was formed to such exacting tolerances that the door hinges were welded in place, there being no need for adjustment after the doors were hung. The Vega assembly line was programmed for an eventual 100 cars an hour. (The next fastest Chevrolet assembly line had a speed of 65 cars per hour, the

The U.S. automobile industry went all out to compete with small foreign cars by introducing more mini-size cars. These were (from top) the Ford Pinto, the American Motors Gremlin, and the General Motors Vega 2300.

same rate as Volkswagen's final assembly line.)

A shipping innovation was another Chevrolet effort to cut Vega costs. Vegas destined for the West coast were shipped in new sealed flatcars that carried as many as 30 cars each—12 more than a conventional trilevel railroad auto carrier. Offering protection from vandalism, theft, and air pollution, the new flatcars also lowered insurance costs. Vegas were suspended nose down on the walls of the cars, 15 to a side. The walls swung to the ground to permit the cars to be driven on and off.

Perhaps the most outstanding innovation in the Vega program, however, was the new aluminum engine. The four-cylinder, overhead-cam engine had the first die-cast block built in the United States since the early days of the auto industry. For the first time, iron liners were discarded and bare aluminum cylinder walls employed. The blocks were cast of aluminum with high silicon content; subsequent chemical etching of the cylinders left a hard silicon surface fully compatible with the piston material that would rub against it while the engine was running. The engine was of 140-cubic-inch—or 2,300 cc—displacement (whence the "2300" part of the Vega's name) and was offered in two versions—90 and 110 horsepower. Although the lowest Vega list price was $2,091—more than $200 above that of the Volkswagen—first-year sales of 400,000 to 500,000 Vegas were predicted by competitors as well as by Chevrolet.

Ford's Pinto turned out to be exactly the minicar Detroit watchers had predicted. It was low priced, small—with virtually the same length and wheelbase as the Volkswagen—and available in a single two-door body style. Conventionally engineered, it was available with a standard English-built 97.6-cubic-inch engine or an optional 122-cubic-inch German-built overhead-cam engine. The weight of the basic car was held to 2,013 pounds, permitting fuel economy of 25 miles to the gallon. Sales of 400,000 to 500,000 Pintos were predicted for its first full year of production. Ford touted Pinto's final base price of $1,919 and its ease of owner maintenance.

Mercury announced another line of cars—a new Comet—in 1970. A near duplicate of Ford's Maverick, the Comet was offered in two- and four-door models with V-8 or 6-cylinder engines.

Economics of the Auto Industry

Overall in 1970, the U.S. auto industry—crippled by a strike at GM—sold an estimated 7.6 million cars, down sharply from the 8,464,375 retailed in 1969. Meanwhile, foreign-car sales in the

United States totaled an estimated 1.25 million—or 14% of the domestic market—compared with 1,061,617 registrations, or 11.24% of the market, in 1969.

GM was shut down on September 15 by a strike of hourly workers belonging to the United Automobile Workers (UAW), whose demands included retirement after 30 years' service, a 50¢-an-hour immediate wage boost, and full protection against rises in the cost of living. The strike immediately idled 343,000 UAW workers and, in time, eventually affected the tens of thousands of workers employed by GM suppliers. In November GM and the UAW agreed on a contract providing a 13% pay raise, inflation raises, and early retirement. During the strike GM lost its weekly production of about 105,000 cars and 15,000 trucks. The UAW, however, permitted GM hourly workers involved in safety and emission-control projects to stay on the job, and the union did not strike those GM plants which produced parts, such as steering units, for the other three major U.S. car makers.

Anticipating higher labor costs as a result of the strike, GM, Ford, and Chrysler raised prices and reduced warranty coverage on their models for 1971. Price boosts averaged 5.5% to 6% on both basic cars and optional equipment. Warranties that had encompassed as much as five years or 50,000 miles on power trains and 24 months or 24,000 miles on the rest of the car were reduced to 12 months or 12,000 miles on all components.

Safety and Pollution Control

The auto industry in 1970 continued to receive pressure from government and consumer groups to increase the safety and collision-damage resistance of its products and to improve controls of exhaust emission. The industry replied that crash protection for both occupants and vehicle was receiving high priority.

In May the U.S. Department of Transportation (DOT) held a conference to study the feasibility of installing quick-inflating air bags in cars to protect occupants in collisions. The auto industry argued that the bags were as yet insufficiently developed and that they could cause injuries. DOT postponed the mandatory use of the bags from 1972 to 1973.

The clamor for alternatives to the internal-combustion engine increased during the year. Research continued on electric motors, steam engines, and turbines. Congress passed a law in 1970 requiring that the auto industry eliminate 90% of the polluting fumes from cars by 1977. Hydrocarbons and carbon monoxide must be reduced by Jan. 1, 1975, and nitrogen oxide by Jan. 1, 1976. The Environmental Protection Agency was given discretion to extend those deadlines by one year, and the industry was expected to seek such an extension.

As a result of manufacturers' preoccupation with safety and pollution control, U.S. cars for 1971 offered few new features. However, 95% of the engines were capable of running on low-octane, lead-free gasoline. Buick's Riviera offered the optional "Max Trac," an electronically controlled system that prevented wheelspin during acceleration by automatically reducing engine power. For Pontiacs, GM's Delco Remy division brought out a maintenance-free battery that never requires water. Chrysler's 1971 Imperial became the first automobile to offer—as an option at about $350 extra cost—a four-wheel nonskid braking system. The system prevents the wheels from locking, giving the driver better control and providing reduced stopping distance. (*See also* Business and Industry; Safety. *See in* CE: Automobile articles.)

This 1928 Stutz Black Hawk speedster sold for $15,000 at the Parke-Bernet Galleries. It was the prize purchase at an auction that attracted automobile collectors who spent nearly $150,000 on the purchase of old cars.

"THE NEW YORK TIMES"

AUTO RACING. The 1970 season of Grand Prix auto racing was a tragic one. Three of the sport's premier drivers were killed in track mishaps: Bruce McLaren of New Zealand, while testing a sports racing car in England; Piers Courage of Great Britain, during the Dutch Grand Prix at Zandvoort; and Jochen Rindt of Austria, in a practice run at Monza, Italy. Rindt was driver's world champion posthumously for 1970. Driving a Lotus, he won the Monaco, Dutch, French, British, and German Grand Prix races.

In other Grand Prix races, Jackie Ickx of Belgium won in Austria, Canada, and Mexico in a Ferrari; Clay Regazzoni of Switzerland won in Italy driving a Ferrari; Jackie Stewart of Scotland won in Spain with a March Ford; Pedro Rodriguez of Mexico won in Belgium in a V-12-cylinder BRM; Jack Brabham of Australia won in South Africa, driving a Brabham-Ford. Emerson Fittipaldi of Brazil, with a Lotus-Ford, won the richest of them all—the $250,500 U.S. Grand Prix at Watkins Glen, N.Y.

Porsche of Germany easily captured the world manufacturer's championship for sports cars, winning all but one of the premier endurance races. The exception was the Sebring, Fla., 12-hour race, won by Mario Andretti (U.S.) in a Ferrari.

KEITH COMSTIVE FROM CANADIAN PRESS

Dan Gurney (48), in the car Bruce McLaren was to have driven, finished first in the opening race of the 1970 Can-Am series at the Mosport Park circuit in Ontario, Canada, in June.

Emerson Fittipaldi of Brazil finishes first at the Watkins Glen Grand Prix circuit to win the U.S. Grand Prix in October 1970.

WIDE WORLD

The great Indianapolis 500-mile race, which has been run every Memorial Day in the United States, apart from war years, since 1911, attracted 84 entries in 1970 with elimination trials deciding the qualifiers for the 33 places on the starting grid. The race was won by Al Unser of Albuquerque, N.M., who drove a P. J. Colt-Ford which averaged 155.749 mph for the 200 laps of the semibanked Indianapolis oval. The qualifying speeds had been as high as 170 mph, and the best race lap, by Joe Leonard of San Jose, Calif., in his P. J. Colt-Ford, was turned at 167.785 mph. The winner was followed home by Mark Donohue of Media, Pa., who drove a Lola-Ford. Dan Gurney of Santa Ana, Calif., finished third, and Donnie Allison of Hueytown, Ala., came in fourth.

It was Al Unser's year in the United States Auto Club (USAC) competition. The 31-year-old driver, the youngest of three racing brothers, won ten Championship Trail races (including the Indianapolis 500) and all five dirt-track races to amass winnings of over $400,000. The dirt-track races won were the Hoosier 100 at Indianapolis, Ind., and the races at Sacramento, Calif.; Du Quoin, Ill.; Springfield, Ill.; and Sedalia, Mo. Unser also won races at Trenton, N.J.; Phoenix, Ariz.; and Clermont, Ind.

The other USAC championship triumphs were well spread: Gurney won at Sears Point, Calif.; Lloyd Ruby of Wichita Falls, Tex., came in first at Trenton; Joe Leonard won at Milwaukee, Wis.; Mario Andretti finished first at Castle Rock, Colo.;

Gary Bettenhausen of Tinley Park, Ill., won the Michigan 200; Bobby Unser won at Langhorne, Pa.; and Jimmy McElreath took the race at Ontario, Calif. Roger McCluskey repeated for Plymouth as the USAC stock-car king, and Larry Dickson became the top sprint-division driver of all time as he regained that crown.

Chrysler Corp. dominated the National Association for Stock Car Auto Racing (NASCAR) events for 1970. One of the principal reasons for the domination was the return of Richard Petty to the Plymouth fold. Petty won the Carolina 500 at Rockingham, N.C., the Falstaff 400 at Riverside, Calif., and the Dixie 500 at Atlanta, Ga. He also won at least 15 other races enroute to another season of earnings close to $150,000.

Pete Hamilton of Dedham, Mass., also driving for Plymouth, won the prestigious Daytona 500 at Daytona Beach, Fla., and both races at Talladega, Ala.; in the second, the Talladega 500, he averaged 158.517 mph. Other winners included: A. J. Foyt, who won the Motor Trend 500 at Riverside; Cale Yarborough, the winner of the Motor State 400 in Michigan; Donnie Allison, who took the Firecracker 400 at Daytona Beach; David Pearson of Spartanburg, S.C., winner of the Rebel 400 at Darlington, S.C.; Charlie Glotzbach of Georgetown, Ind., winner of the Yankee 400 in Michigan; and Buddy Baker, who captured the Southern 500 at Darlington.

The Grand American Challenge Cup, contested in small-engine American sporty cars, was a runaway for veteran "Tiny" Lund of Cross, S.C., in his Chevrolet Camaro. Denis Hulme of New Zealand won the Canadian-American Challenge Cup title, the premier series of the Sports Car Club of America. The Trans-American Sedan series was won by Ford Mustang with driver Parnelli Jones winning the major share of the races. (*See in* CE: Automobile Racing).

AWARDS AND PRIZES. Aleksandr I. Solzhenitsyn, widely regarded as the greatest living Soviet writer, won the 1970 Nobel prize for literature. The award caused a great furor in the Soviet Union since Solzhenitsyn was regarded as a literary outcast and his works were banned.

Solzhenitsyn first came to public notice in 1962 when his novel 'One Day in the Life of Ivan Denisovich' was published during Soviet Premier Nikita S. Khrushchev's de-Stalinization campaign. However, when "re-Stalinization" was imposed, Solzhenitsyn became a literary persona non grata, his works were outlawed, and eventually, in 1969, he was expelled from the official Soviet Writers' Union. Texts of his works, including 'The Cancer Ward' and 'The First Circle', were smuggled out of the country and were published in the West.

Solzhenitsyn originally announced that he would like to go to Sweden to accept the award. However, after receiving a round of abuse and criticism in the Soviet press, he changed his mind and decided to accept the Nobel with a minimum of ceremony in Moscow. The episode was reminiscent of that which caused the Soviet writer Boris Pasternak to refuse the Nobel prize for literature in 1958.

A U.S. plant pathologist known for his work in developing hybrid strains of cereal grains that produced enormous yields was the winner of the 1970 Nobel peace prize. Dr. Norman E. Borlaug was honored as a "prime mover of the Green Revolution . . . (who), through his improvement of wheat and rice plants, has created a technological breakthrough which makes it possible to abolish hunger in the developing countries in the course of a few years." Borlaug himself was less optimistic about what the "Green Revolution" meant. "The revolution has simply bought us some time. If the population keeps growing at its current rate, there will be a point at which there will not be enough food."

Paul A. Samuelson, a professor at the Massachusetts Institute of Technology, was awarded the 1970 Alfred Nobel memorial prize in economics.

WIDE WORLD

Another U.S. citizen, Paul A. Samuelson, was awarded the Alfred Nobel memorial prize in economics. Samuelson, a liberal economist and author of the most widely read and influential economics textbook in the modern world, was cited for having "done more than any other contemporary economist to raise the level of scientific analysis in economic theory."

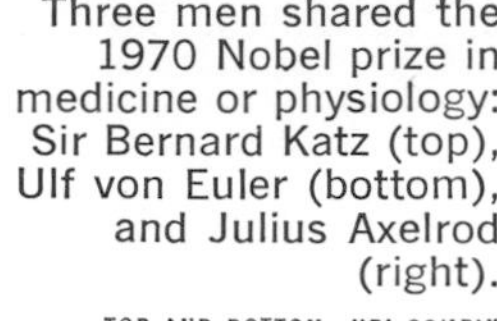

Three men shared the 1970 Nobel prize in medicine or physiology: Sir Bernard Katz (top), Ulf von Euler (bottom), and Julius Axelrod (right).

TOP AND BOTTOM: UPI COMPIX
RIGHT: WIDE WORLD

Three men—Dr. Julius Axelrod, a U.S. pharmacologist; Sir Bernard Katz, a British biophysicist; and Dr. Ulf von Euler, a Swedish physiologist—were jointly awarded the Nobel prize in medicine or physiology. They were honored for their explorations of the chemistry of nerve impulses.

Dr. Luis F. Leloir, an Argentine biochemist, won the 1970 Nobel prize for chemistry. He was recognized for his work concerning the ways that sugars are broken down into carbohydrates.

The 1970 Nobel prize for physics was shared by a Swedish physicist, Dr. Hannes Alfvén, and a French magnetic expert, Dr. Louis Néel. Alfvén was honored for his pioneering work in magnetohydrodynamics—the study of plasmas (a form of matter distinct from solids, liquids, or normal gases) in magnetic fields. Néel was cited for work in the fields of antiferromagnetism and ferrimagnetism.

Pulitzer Prizes

The 54th annual Pulitzer prizes in journalism and arts and letters were awarded in May. In the categories of reporting, prizes went to Seymour M. Hersh (international reporting) for his story of the alleged My Lai massacre of Vietnamese civilians by U.S. troops; to William J. Eaton of the *Chicago Daily News* (national reporting) for his disclosures on Circuit Judge Clement F. Haynsworth, Jr., whose nomination to the U.S. Supreme Court was rejected by the U.S. Senate; to Thomas Fitzpatrick of the *Chicago Sun-Times* (local reporting, general) for his eyewitness account, written in 45 minutes under deadline pressure, of a running street battle between the Weatherman faction of the Students for a Democratic Society and Chicago police; and to Harold Eugene Martin, publisher of the *Montgomery-Alabama Journal,* for his articles revealing the use of state prisoners for drug experimentation (local reporting, special).

Winners in other journalism categories were Thomas F. Darcy of *Newsday* for editorial cartoons, Philip L. Geyelin of the *Washington Post* for editorial writing, Steve Starr of the Associated Press for his photograph of black militant students at Cornell University in Ithaca, N.Y. (spot news photography), and Dallas Kinney of the *Palm Beach Post* for photographs of black migrant workers (feature photography). *Newsday* was given the Pulitzer for meritorious public service for its three-year-long exposé of wrongdoing by public officials in eastern Long Island, N.Y.

In a new Pulitzer category—criticism or commentary—the award was divided. Ada Louise Huxtable, the architecture critic of *The New York Times,* was honored for criticism, and Marquis W. Childs of the *St. Louis Post-Dispatch* received the award for commentary.

In arts and letters, two awards attracted particular interest. Charles W. Wuorinen, a composer of electronic music, received a Pulitzer in music for his electronic composition, 'Time's Encomium', and Charles Gordone, a black playwright, won the award in drama for his play, 'No Place to Be Somebody'—the first off-Broadway play ever to be cited. Other awards went to Jean Stafford (fiction) for her 'Collected Stories'; T. Harry Williams (biography) for 'Huey Long'; Dean G. Acheson (history) for 'Present at The Creation: My Years in the State Department'; Erik H. Erikson (general nonfiction) for 'Gandhi's Truth'; and Richard Howard (poetry) for 'Untitled Subjects'.

Awards in Literature

Three women were among the winners of the National Book Awards, the U.S. publishing industry's most prestigious prizes: Joyce Carol Oates was honored for her novel, 'Them' (fiction); playwright Lillian Hellman (arts and letters) for her memoirs, 'An Unfinished Woman'; and Elizabeth Bishop (poetry) for 'The Complete Poems'. Other winners were Erik H. Erikson (philosophy and religion) for 'Gandhi's Truth'; T. Harry Williams (history and biography) for his biography, 'Huey Long'; Isaac Bashevis Singer (children's literature) for 'A Day of Pleasure: Stories of a Boy Growing Up in Warsaw'; and Ralph Manheim (translation) for his rendition of 'Castle to Castle' by the French writer Louis-Ferdinand Céline. The awards were once again shrouded in controversy. (Two widely discussed books, Philip Roth's 'Portnoy's Complaint' and Vladimir Nabokov's 'Ada', were not included among the nominations.)

Norman E. Borlaug, 1970 Nobel peace prize recipient, gained recognition for his work in developing high-yield wheat, an important contribution to the Green Revolution.

WIDE WORLD

The $4,000 Bancroft prizes for distinguished works in U.S. history, diplomacy, and international affairs published in 1969 went to three authors. Dan T. Carter was honored for 'Scottsboro: a Tragedy of the American South'; Charles Coleman Sellers for his biography, 'Charles Willson Peale'; and Gordon S. Wood for 'The Creation of the American Republic, 1776–1787'.

Awards in Science

The National Medal of Science award, the U.S. government's highest honor for distinguished achievement in the fields of science and engineering, went to six men in 1970, each known for work in a different scientific discipline. In a ceremony at the White House, U.S. President Richard M. Nixon presented the awards. The recipients were: Dr. Herbert C. Brown (chemistry), Dr. William Feller (mathematics), Dr. Ernst Mayr (zoology), Dr. Robert J. Huebner (biology), Dr. Jack S. Kilby (engineering), and Dr. Wolfgang K. H. Panofsky (physics).

A man who headed the Los Alamos Scientific Laboratory for 25 years received the $25,000 Atomic Energy Commission's Enrico Fermi Award for 1970. Dr. Norris E. Bradbury was honored for his important work in nuclear weaponry and in developing peaceful uses for atomic energy.

The 1970 Albert and Mary Lasker Awards for Medicine, considered the American "Nobel" for medicine, went to two men. Dr. Robert A. Good was honored for his pioneering work in immunity and the application of his findings to cure otherwise fatal diseases, and Dr. Earl W. Sutherland was cited for his discovery of cyclic AMP, a chemical that appears to govern hormone action. (*See also* Literature.)

BANKS. There were 14,158 banks in the United States at the beginning of 1970, 21 fewer than at the beginning of 1969. Over the same period, however, the number of branches rose from 19,911 to 21,196. Total deposits held by commercial banks stood at $428.7 billion in August, an increase of $26.9 billion since August 1969. Loans outstanding also rose, with the Federal Reserve Board reporting an August total of $296.5 billion, up $15.8 billion from the August 1969 figure.

Reductions in the prime interest rate—the rate that banks charge their most creditworthy customers—reflected progress in the government's efforts to control inflation. From a historic high of 8.5% at the beginning of the year, it dropped to 8% on March 25, to 7.5% on September 21, to 7.25% on November 12, and to 7% on November 23.

Despite an overall trend toward "tight money," mortgage loans made by commercial banks increased. The Federal Reserve reported a first-quarter total of nearly $71 billion, $3.8 billion above the 1969 first-quarter figure.

Holders of bank credit cards were demonstrating a great deal of responsibility in handling this form of credit, according to the results of a three-month survey by the American Bankers Association (ABA). One third of all accounts had balances outstanding at the end of each of the three months, with an average of just over $200. Average monthly payments on such accounts varied from $41.51 to $54.12. During any one month, 4 of every 100 cardholders used their cards to make purchases. For each $6 of card usage, $5 went for merchandise and $1 for cash advances. Cardholders obtaining cash advances borrowed an average of $125.

The growing popularity of landscape scenes and other designs as background printing on checks caused concern in some banking circles. An industry committee warned that many such checks are difficult to read and cannot be microfilmed successfully. The committee recommended that all checks be tested for readability and "microfilmability" before being put into use. Another industry task force announced that it had completed designing forms to automate the paper work of the securities industry. The suggested forms were readable by both people and machines.

The banking industry's efforts to improve the quality of life for minority groups took two major forms in 1970. In April representatives of the U.S. commercial banking industry announced commitment to a goal of $1 billion in loans to minority-operated businesses in the next five years. In September it was announced that a middle-management training program for black bankers, begun in 1969, would be doubled in size. The program is designed to increase management resources for banks owned by members of minority groups. It is a cooperative effort by the ABA and the National Bankers Association, an organization of black-owned banks.

A 12-month survey of bank-robbery convictions published early in the year revealed that three out of four convicted bank robbers were sentenced to prison terms of ten years or more. About a third of such convicts received sentences ranging from 20 years to life. The most frequently imposed sentence was 15 years.

The median age of those convicted was 28 years, but one in nine was a teen-ager. The youngest was a girl of 15 who feigned possession of a gun while trying—unsuccessfully—to rob a bank in Philadelphia, Pa. (*See also* Economy; Money and International Finance. *See in* CE: Bank.)

BARBADOS. A three-year development plan launched in December 1969 provided a framework for expanding Barbados' economy, which in 1970 continued to depend on sugar (its staple export) and the further growth of a thriving tourist industry. Envisaging a total expenditure of $23 million, the plan apportioned $6.7 million for infrastructure projects (notably a major improvement of the Seawell airport to cost $3.6 million) and $6.3 million for social welfare programs in which education had a high priority. The 1970–71 education program was to receive approximately 20% of the current expenditure totaling $44.8 million in the budget estimates for that period.

Some progress was made with agriculture diversification—to reduce food imports—and with fishery development. In the manufacturing sector the plan allotted $375,000 a year for building industrial estates which, together with increased activity in the construction and service industries, could help to reduce an unemployment rate running in 1970 from 10–13%. The sugar industry, short of manual labor and relying during the sugarcane harvest on migrant workers from other islands, was intent on mechanization and rationalization; its main concern, however, was over the future of Barbadian producers if Great Britain should join the European Economic Community, or Common Market.

The tourist industry grew apace. Latest statistics showed that in 1969 Barbados attracted nearly 138,000 visitors. The gross revenue from tourism was estimated at over $28 million. (*See in* CE: Barbados.)

BASEBALL. The Baltimore Orioles of the American League (AL) followed third baseman Brooks Robinson to baseball's biggest jackpot in 1970. The Orioles eliminated the National League (NL) champion Cincinnati Reds, four games to one, in the World Series. Robinson, voted the series' most valuable player, collected nine hits—including two home runs—and jolted the vaunted Cincinnati offense with superb defensive play.

Baltimore had won the AL pennant by capturing the Eastern Division race, then defeating Western Division champion Minnesota, three games to none, in the play-offs. Similarly, Cincinnati won the NL's Western Division race, then blanked Pittsburgh of the Eastern Division three games to none in the play-offs.

Minor league umpires worked the first game of the Cincinnati-Pittsburgh play-off series after the major league arbiters voted to strike for higher pay. They asked $5,000 per man for the league play-offs, $10,000 per man for the World Series. They settled for $3,000 and $7,000, respectively, before the second play-off game began, pending further negotiations in which any agreement would be retroactive to the postseason games in 1970.

Baltimore won Eastern Division honors in the AL by 15 games over the runner-up New York Yan-

FINAL 1970 MAJOR LEAGUE STANDINGS

AMERICAN LEAGUE

Team	Won	Lost	Pct.	GB
Eastern Division				
Baltimore	108	54	.667	—
New York	93	69	.574	15
Boston	87	75	.537	21
Detroit	79	83	.488	29
Cleveland	76	86	.469	32
Washington	70	92	.432	38
Western Division				
Minnesota	98	64	.605	—
Oakland	89	73	.549	9
California	86	76	.531	12
Kansas City	65	97	.401	33
Milwaukee	65	97	.401	33
Chicago	56	106	.346	42

PLAY-OFFS: Baltimore 3 games, Minnesota 0.

NATIONAL LEAGUE

Team	Won	Lost	Pct.	GB
Eastern Division				
Pittsburgh	89	73	.549	—
Chicago	84	78	.519	5
New York	83	79	.512	6
St. Louis	76	86	.469	13
Philadelphia	73	88	.453	15½
Montreal	73	89	.451	16
Western Division				
Cincinnati	102	60	.630	—
Los Angeles	87	74	.540	14½
San Francisco	86	76	.531	16
Houston	79	83	.488	23
Atlanta	76	86	.469	26
San Diego	63	99	.389	39

PLAY-OFFS: Cincinnati 3 games, Pittsburgh 0.

WORLD SERIES: Baltimore (AL) 4 games, Cincinnati (NL) 1.

kees. The Orioles produced three pitchers who won 20 games: Mike Cuellar (24–8), Dave McNally (24–9), and Jim Palmer (20–10). Minnesota took the Western Division by nine games, with Oakland second.

Cincinnati's margin in the NL's Western Division was 14½ games over Los Angeles. The closest divisional race came in the NL East, where Pittsburgh outlasted the Chicago Cubs by five games and the New York Mets by six in a blistering stretch fight.

Baltimore came from behind to win the opening game of the World Series, 4–3, before a capacity crowd of 51,531 in Cincinnati. Brooks Robinson's seventh-inning home run provided the margin of victory, giving Palmer a five-hit win.

Trailing 4–0 after three innings of the second game, Baltimore rallied again, scoring five runs in the fifth inning and going on to win 6–5. Relief pitcher Tom Phoebus received credit for the win.

Dave McNally pitched and batted the Orioles to victory in game three, 9–3, as the series moved to Baltimore. A crowd of 51,773 saw McNally become the first pitcher to hit a grand-slam home run in a World Series game. It came in the sixth inning and boosted the Orioles' lead to 8–1.

Cincinnati thwarted Baltimore's bid for a four-game sweep in game four when Lee May's three-run homer in the eighth rubbed out a 5–3 deficit and brought the Reds a 6–5 triumph. Clay Carroll earned the win in relief.

The Orioles ended it all in the fifth game, however, rolling over the Reds 9–3. The Orioles collected 15 hits off six Cincinnati pitchers in support of winner Mike Cuellar, who yielded 6 hits.

Baseball Newsmakers

Pitcher Denny McLain of Detroit, a 31-game winner in 1968, made baseball's largest headlines in 1970. He was suspended several different times. On April 1, Commissioner Bowie Kuhn suspended McLain until July 1 for involvement with gamblers. After his return to the Tigers, McLain appeared in 14 games, posting three wins and five losses, then was suspended for seven days by the Detroit management for throwing ice water on two sportswriters. Kuhn then suspended McLain for the rest of the season, charging that McLain had been carrying a gun. Later, Kuhn revealed that McLain had been traded to the Washington Senators.

Refusing to recognize his trade to the Philadelphia Phillies, outfielder Curt Flood filed an antitrust suit against the major leagues.

UPI COMPIX

Brooks Robinson singles for the Baltimore Orioles in the fifth game of the World Series, tying the series record of nine hits in five games.
UPI COMPIX

Another major postseason trade saw the St. Louis Cardinals send celebrated slugger Richie Allen to the Los Angeles Dodgers for infielder Ted Sizemore and minor league catcher-outfielder Bob Stinson. Allen hit 34 home runs and drove in 101 runs in 1970, even though injuries allowed him to play only one game in the final seven weeks of the season.

In October 1969 Allen had gone to the Cardinals in a deal that sent outfielder Curt Flood to the Philadelphia Phillies. Flood, however, elected to test the reserve clause of the players' contract, which binds a player to the team that owns the contract. On August 12 a U.S. district court in New York City ruled against Flood in his antitrust suit, upholding the defense argument that, as a result of U.S. Supreme Court decisions in 1953, 1955, and 1957, the federal antitrust laws do not apply to baseball. Flood's attorneys planned an appeal.

Milwaukee, Wis., rejoined the ranks of major league cities after an absence of four years when the Seattle Pilots became the Milwaukee Brewers. A bankruptcy court approved the transfer of the franchise, which had been financially unsuccessful in Seattle, Wash. The Milwaukee purchasers of the franchise paid $10.8 million.

The NL unveiled two new parks—Riverfront Stadium in Cincinnati, Ohio, and Three Rivers Stadium in Pittsburgh, Pa. The occupants thereof, the Reds and the Pirates, won divisional titles.

Major League Stars

Hank Aaron of the Atlanta Braves and Willie Mays of the San Francisco Giants hit their 3,000th hits in 1970, becoming the ninth and tenth players to reach that career total. Ernie Banks of the Cubs hit his 500th career home run. Only eight others have reached that plateau.

Four major league pitchers registered no-hit, no-run games: Dock Ellis of Pittsburgh, Clyde Wright of the California Angels, Bill Singer of the Dodgers, and rookie Vida Blue of the Oakland Athletics. Tom Seaver of the Mets struck out ten successive San Diego batters on April 22 to set a new major league record. His 19 total strikeouts in the game tied another record.

The NL endurance record owned by Billy Williams of the Cubs came to an end on September 3 as Williams sat one out after playing in 1,117 consecutive games. Hoyt Wilhelm of Atlanta, a much-traveled major league pitcher since 1952, pitched in his record 1,000th game on May 10, two months before his 47th birthday. Vic Davalillo of the Cardinals collected 24 pinch hits in the season to tie the major league record. The National Baseball Hall of Fame, at Cooperstown, N.Y., inducted four new members: Ford C. Frick, Lou Boudreau, Jesse Haines, and Earl Combs. Frick is the former commissioner of baseball.

Rico Carty of Atlanta grabbed the NL batting championship with an average of .366, the highest in the majors since Ted Williams hit .388 in 1957. The AL batting race ended only on the final day of the season, when Alex Johnson of the California Angels got two hits in three times at bat to finish with an average of .3289, edging Boston slugger Carl Yastrzemski, who had completed his season a day earlier with an average of .3286.

Frank Howard of Washington led the AL in home runs, 44, and runs batted in, 126. The league produced seven 20-game winners. In addition to Baltimore's Cuellar, McNally, and Palmer, they were Jim Perry (24–12) of Minnesota, Clyde Wright (22–12) of California, Fritz Peterson (20–11) of the New York Yankees, and Sam McDowell

(20–12) of Cleveland. McDowell also paced the league in strikeouts with 304.

In the NL, Bob Gibson (23–7) of St. Louis turned in his fifth 20-game season. San Francisco's Gaylord Perry, brother of Minnesota's Jim Perry, was 23–13. Ferguson Jenkins of Chicago posted his fourth consecutive 20-game year with a 22–16 mark. Cincinnati's Jim Merrit (20–12) was the NL's fourth 20-game winner. Tom Seaver of the Mets led in strikeouts with 283. Johnny Bench of the Reds captured the home-run title with 45 and also led in runs batted in with 148.

An average of 8.68 runs were scored per game in the major leagues, up from 8.16 in 1969. It was the highest run production since the 8.92 of 1962.

The NL beat the AL 5–4 in 12 innings in the 41st All-Star game, played at Cincinnati's new Riverfront Stadium. Jim Hickman of the Cubs singled home the Reds' Pete Rose for the winning run. The winning pitcher was Claude Osteen of the Dodgers, the loser Clyde Wright of the Angels. It was the NL's eighth straight victory, bringing its All-Star game record to 23 wins, 17 losses, and one tie.

Midseason managerial changes found Bob Lemon replacing Charlie Metro at Kansas City and Charlie Fox taking over for Clyde King at San Francisco. A late-season shift found Chuck Tanner taking the reins of the Chicago White Sox from Don Gutteridge. After the season, Dick Williams took over for John McNamara at Oakland, and Billy Martin moved in for Mayo Smith at Detroit.

WIDE WORLD

Umpires picket the Three Rivers Stadium in Pittsburgh, Pa., before the National League play-offs. They were striking for more money for officiating at play-offs and World Series games.

"Mister Cub," Ernie Banks, hits the 500th homer of his long career in the second inning of a game with the Atlanta Braves.

UPI COMPIX

Amateur Baseball

Southern California ruled the College World Series for the sixth time in 1970. The Trojans won the National Collegiate Athletic Association title by stopping Florida State 2–1 in a 15-inning championship game. Second baseman Frank Alfano's infield single with the bases loaded and none out in the 15th decided the week-long, double-elimination tournament.

Wayne, N.J., returned the Little League World Series championship to the United States in August. Wayne beat Campbell, Calif., 2–0 in the final game at Williamsport, Pa. (*See in* CE: Baseball.)

BASKETBALL. The University of California at Los Angeles (UCLA) in 1970 continued to dominate collegiate basketball, despite the loss by graduation of All-American center Lew Alcindor. With a balanced attack—none of their starters were among the nation's top 60 scorers—the Bruins finished the season with a 28–2 record. For the fourth successive year they won top honors in the National Collegiate Athletic Association (NCAA) tournament, played in College Park, Md.

1970 NCAA BASKETBALL TOURNAMENT

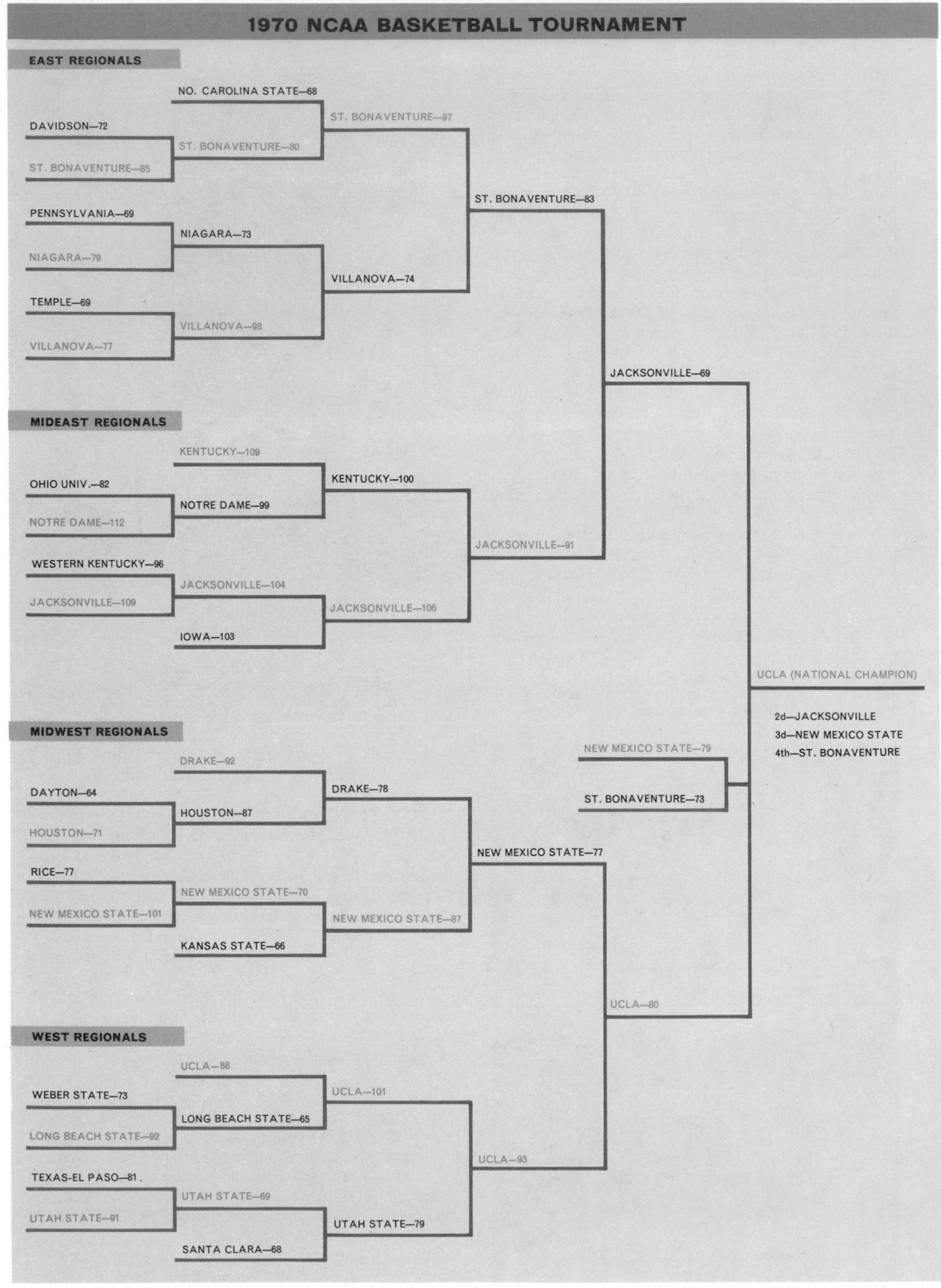
EAST REGIONALS
NO. CAROLINA STATE—68
DAVIDSON—72
ST. BONAVENTURE—85
ST. BONAVENTURE—80
ST. BONAVENTURE—97
PENNSYLVANIA—69
NIAGARA—79
NIAGARA—73
TEMPLE—69
VILLANOVA—77
VILLANOVA—98
VILLANOVA—74
ST. BONAVENTURE—83
JACKSONVILLE—69
MIDEAST REGIONALS
KENTUCKY—109
OHIO UNIV.—82
NOTRE DAME—112
NOTRE DAME—99
KENTUCKY—100
WESTERN KENTUCKY—96
JACKSONVILLE—109
JACKSONVILLE—104
IOWA—103
JACKSONVILLE—106
JACKSONVILLE—91
UCLA (NATIONAL CHAMPION)
2d—JACKSONVILLE
3d—NEW MEXICO STATE
4th—ST. BONAVENTURE
NEW MEXICO STATE—79
ST. BONAVENTURE—73
MIDWEST REGIONALS
DRAKE—92
DAYTON—64
HOUSTON—71
HOUSTON—87
DRAKE—78
RICE—77
NEW MEXICO STATE—101
NEW MEXICO STATE—70
KANSAS STATE—66
NEW MEXICO STATE—87
NEW MEXICO STATE—77
UCLA—80
WEST REGIONALS
UCLA—88
WEBER STATE—73
LONG BEACH STATE—92
LONG BEACH STATE—65
UCLA—101
TEXAS-EL PASO—81
UTAH STATE—91
UTAH STATE—69
SANTA CLARA—68
UTAH STATE—79
UCLA—93

In 1970 the New York Knickerbockers won their first NBA title, while UCLA retained the NCAA championship. Sidney Wicks (left) of UCLA guards his opponent in the championship game. Walt Frazier (below) attempts a lay-up for New York.

LEFT: WIDE WORLD. BELOW: WALTER IOOSS, JR., FOR SPORTS ILLUSTRATED © TIME INC.

Jacksonville University reached the NCAA finals by whipping St. Bonaventure, 91–83. In the meantime, UCLA defeated New Mexico State, 93–77, in their semifinal match. Jacksonville and UCLA then met in the climactic championship game with the Bruins finishing on the long end of an 80–69 score.

Marquette University won the National Invitation Tournament played at New York City's Madison Square Garden Center. The Warriors defeated St. John's University, 65–53, in the finals.

Pete Maravich of Louisiana State University (LSU), a talented and record-breaking shotmaker, was named college basketball's player of the year. He broke his own records while winning the NCAA's major division scoring championship. Maravich set new standards in the two major categories: most points for one season and most points for a college career (3,667). For the season, Maravich scored 1,381 points on 522 field goals (also a record) and 337 free throws. Maravich's sensational play overshadowed the highest-scoring field in NCAA history. Austin Carr of Notre Dame was second to Maravich in scoring with 1,106 points, for a 38.1 average. Rick Mount of Purdue was third with a 35.4 average.

Players chosen on the first-team consensus All-America, as published in the 'Official NCAA Basketball Guide', were Mount, Purdue; Bob Lanier, St. Bonaventure; Calvin Murphy, Niagara; Maravich, LSU; and Dan Issel, Kentucky. The second team consisted of Carr, Notre Dame; Jimmy Collins, New Mexico State; John Roche, South Carolina; Charlie Scott, North Carolina; and Sidney Wicks, UCLA.

Professional Basketball

The New York Knickerbockers, stressing defense and always trying to hit the open man on offense, won their first National Basketball Association (NBA) championship by defeating the Los Angeles Lakers in a memorable seven-game play-off. Tied at three victories each after six games, the Knicks won the seventh and final game 113–99, bringing to an end 24 years of championship frustration.

Coached by William (Red) Holzman, a former court great who emphasized fundamentals, the Knicks finished their regular season with a record of 60 victories and 22 defeats to win the Eastern

Division race. The Atlanta Hawks led the NBA's Western Division with a 48–34 record, finishing two games ahead of the Lakers.

New York then defeated Baltimore in seven games and Milwaukee eliminated Philadelphia in five games in the Eastern Division semifinal playoffs. In the Western Division semifinals, Atlanta eliminated the Chicago Bulls in five games, and Los Angeles rallied to beat the Phoenix Suns. The Lakers, then at the peak of their game, whipped Atlanta in four straight in the Western Division finals. New York, meanwhile, eliminated Milwaukee in five games in the Eastern Division finals. The stage was thus set for the Knicks' championship win over Los Angeles.

Jerry West of Los Angeles, a ten-year NBA veteran, won the league's individual scoring title with a total of 2,309 points, for a 31.2 average. Alcindor of Milwaukee was second, and Elvin Hayes of San Diego was third. Willis Reed of the Knicks was selected the league's most valuable player; Alcindor was chosen as the NBA rookie of the year.

The Indiana Pacers won the championship in the rival American Basketball Association (ABA), defeating the Los Angeles Stars four games to two. Subsequently, there was considerable discussion of the possibility of a merger between the established NBA and the comparatively new ABA, but the leagues were still operating independently of each other when the 1970–71 season began. (*See in* CE: Basketball.)

BELGIUM. Renewed efforts were made during 1970 to establish cultural autonomy for the Dutch-speaking Flemish and the French-speaking Walloon communities in Belgium. In February Premier Gaston Eyskens announced a plan for ending the friction between the two communities by changing the constitution to give some degree of cultural and economic autonomy to each group, without actually making Belgium a federal state. The plan was given approval by the coalition cabinet of Social Christians and Socialists.

When the constitutional changes were brought before the parliament in July, however, the proposal was defeated. The plan called for three separate communities—Flanders, Wallonia, and Brussels, the capital. Although both languages are spoken officially in Brussels, French predominates. In the surrounding suburbs only Dutch is spoken. One of the proposed changes was to place the 19 boroughs of the metropolitan area under the control of a Greater Brussels Council. The Flemish leaders feared that such a bilingual administration would lead to an encroachment of the French culture on the Flemish suburbs. Consequently the constitutional changes were voted down. One bill was passed, however, dividing the task of economic planning between the Flemings and the Walloons.

During the year the Belgian government decided to expand the ports of Antwerp, Ghent, and Zeebrugge to accommodate oil tankers of up to 125,000 tons. A plan for building an island port to

Women demonstrate against U.S. participation in the war in Indochina in front of the U.S. Embassy in Brussels, Belgium.

BELGA FROM PICTORIAL PARADE

berth giant 200,000-ton tankers was abandoned during the year.

Relations between Belgium and the Democratic Republic of the Congo (Kinshasa) grew even friendlier during 1970. In June King Baudouin I and Queen Fabiola visited the Congo to attend ceremonies celebrating its tenth anniversary of independence. They also visited Burundi and Rwanda, which were formerly one United Nations trust territory administered by Belgium. (*See also* Congo, Democratic Republic of the. *See in* CE: Belgium.)

BIOLOGY. A very real and far-reaching attempt to assess the role of biology in man's day-to-day affairs was evident in 1970. As popular interest in ecology grew, it was obvious that the biologist could no longer divorce himself from the social, economic, and political consequences of his research. Despite budgetary restrictions more severe than any since World War II, considerable research was directed against population and environment problems. (*See* Feature Article: "The Need for Population Control.")

DNA → RNA → Protein?

According to modern genetics a cell's genetic information flows in only one direction: deoxyribonucleic acid (DNA) in the genes transfers instructions to ribonucleic acid (RNA), which directs the ribosomes to produce the desired protein (or, in genetics shorthand, DNA → RNA → protein). In 1970, however, almost simultaneously three U.S. research centers reported that the flow of information can be reversed, that RNA can transmit information to DNA.

The discovery grew out of research with viruses that consist of only an RNA core inside a protein coat and that are known to cause cancer in animals they infect. When these viruses enter cells, they appear to produce their own DNA, which becomes incorporated into the cell's reproductive process, undoubtedly with the help of a specific, as yet unidentified, enzyme.

Cellular Studies; Biological Syntheses

It was announced during the year that scientists at the State University of New York at Buffalo had achieved the first artificial synthesis of a living cell. They accomplished this by partly dismembering amoebas (single-celled animals) and then reconstructing them using parts from other amoebas. The reconstructed amoebas continued to live and were also able to reproduce. They were indistinguishable from natural amoebas. The experiments were heralded as a momentous step toward artificial life synthesis.

Work in embryology focused on the theory that a developing cell differentiates, or becomes a specific kind of cell, because it is aware of its position in time and space. Debate concerned whether an initial cell produces a chemical that diffuses in varying concentrations to give the cell positional information or whether the information comes from the periodic pulses of a "pacemaker" cell.

WIDE WORLD

Paul Ehrlich, a biologist at Stanford University, has become a vocal spokesman for population control, advocating government intervention to alleviate the population crisis.

After six years of work Har Gobind Khorana (Nobel prizewinner in 1968) achieved in 1970 the first successful synthesis of a gene—one consisting of 77 units, or nucleotides—that codes for a transfer-RNA in yeast. Commercially available chemical substances were combined to make up short segments that were mated to form double-stranded DNA. The first man-made part of a human cell, a lysosome, was produced by two New York University scientists, Gerald Weissmann and Grazia Sessa, from commercially available enzymes and fatty substances called lipids.

Evolution and Enzymes

Recent research has shown that not all genetic mutations give an organism a selective advantage or disadvantage in the battle for survival of the fittest. Slight variations in the sequence of amino acids, the building blocks of all proteins including enzymes, were found in the enzyme cytochrome *c* in various life forms from microbes to man.

Researchers concluded that the changes were caused by mutations in the genes that code for the enzyme and that the mutations were neutral because they had no effect on the function of the enzyme. (*See in* CE: Biology.)

BIRTHS. Among the births that attracted public notice in 1970 were:

To the Aga Khan IV, Prince Karim, spiritual leader of the world's 20 million Ismaili Muslims, and his wife, the Begum Aga Khan, on September 18, a daughter.

To Johnny Cash and June Carter, popular country singers, on March 3, a son.

To Mia Farrow, actress ('Rosemary's Baby'), and André Previn, conductor and composer, on February 26, twin sons.

To Tisa Farrow, actress and sister of Mia Farrow, and Terry Dene, producer, on July 25, a son.

To Audrey Hepburn, screen star ('Breakfast at Tiffany's', 'Two For the Road'), and Andrea Mario Dotti, Italian psychiatrist, on February 7, a son.

To Dustin Hoffman, actor ('Midnight Cowboy'), and his wife, Anne, on October 15, a daughter.

To Princess Irene of the Netherlands and Prince Carlos Hugo, Carlist pretender to the Spanish throne, on January 27, a son.

To Luci Johnson Nugent, younger daughter of former U.S. President Lyndon B. Johnson, and her husband, Patrick J. Nugent, on January 11, a daughter.

To Mary Quant, British fashion designer whose best-known creation was the miniskirt, and Alexander Plunket-Greene, on November 10, a son.

To Lynda Bird Johnson Robb, elder daughter of former U.S. President Lyndon B. Johnson, and her husband, Marine Corps Maj. Charles S. Robb, on June 5, a daughter.

To Andrés Segovia, classical guitarist, and his wife, Emilia, on May 24, a son.

To Shah Mohammed Reza Pahlavi, ruler of Iran, and his wife, Empress Farah, on March 27, a daughter.

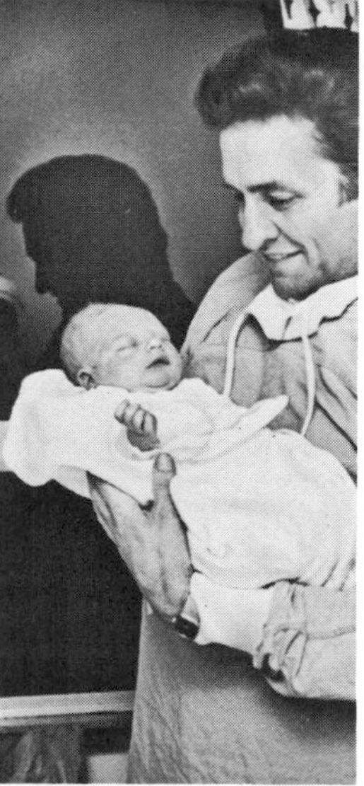

Actress Vanessa Redgrave and actor Franco Nero stroll with their son (above) in the Borghese Garden in Rome. Country-and-Western singer Johnny Cash (left) proudly holds newborn son, John Cash.

ABOVE AND LEFT: UPI COMPIX

Mr. and Mrs. William G. Kienast of Liberty Corner, N.J., leave Babies Hospital in New York City with their quintuplets, Edward, Abigail, William Gordon, Sarah, and Amy, born Feb. 24, 1970.

"THE NEW YORK TIMES"

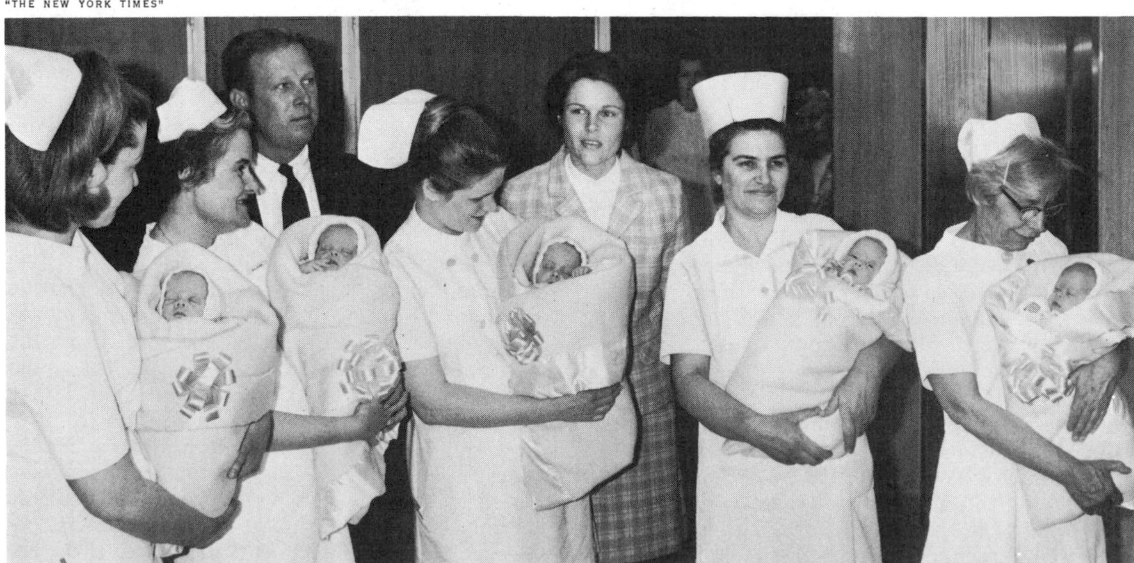

BLACKMUN, HARRY A. Harry A. Blackmun came close to missing the opportunity to become an associate justice of the U.S. Supreme Court. Considered once but passed over by U.S. President Richard M. Nixon in the summer of 1969, Blackmun was not even considered when the president made a second try in January 1970 to fill the seat on the high court vacated by the resignation of Justice Abe Fortas. But after two rejections by the U.S. Senate of Southern nominees (first, U.S. Circuit Judge Clement F. Haynsworth, Jr., of South Carolina and second, U.S. Circuit Judge G. Harrold Carswell of Florida), the president claimed he had no choice but to turn to the North for a nominee.

Harry A. Blackmun of Minnesota became an associate justice of the U.S. Supreme Court in May 1970.

PAUL CONKLIN FROM PIX

Harry Andrew Blackmun of Minnesota was the choice. The Senate, fully satisfied with this third nominee, confirmed the nomination by a vote of 94–0 on May 12.

Blackmun's first written utterance as a member of the court aligned him closely with Chief Justice Warren E. Burger; they both dissented from the majority's reversal of an obscenity conviction. This alignment seemed to follow a pattern between the two Minnesotans. Blackmun and Burger were close friends, and the new justice had obviously come highly recommended by Burger to President Nixon.

A modest man, Blackmun had devoted his adult life to the law, and he had become so preoccupied with it that his closest friends chided him as a legal bookworm. Born in 1908, Blackmun grew up in a financially struggling family in St. Paul, Minn. He graduated *summa cum laude* from Harvard College, at Cambridge, Mass., in 1929 and received his law degree from Harvard Law School in 1932. After a law clerkship, he practiced law in a private firm from 1934 to 1950. He then became the resident counsel of the Mayo Clinic in Rochester, Minn., and held that position until U.S. President Dwight D. Eisenhower appointed him to the U.S. Court of Appeals for the Eighth Circuit in 1959. (*See also* Supreme Court of the United States.)

BOATS AND BOATING. The attention of the entire yachting world was focused upon the Atlantic Ocean, just off Newport, R.I., during the 21st America's Cup Challenge, held in September 1970. The U.S. boat *Intrepid* won the final series, defeating the Australian challenger, *Gretel II,* four races to one in the best-of-seven series.

To reach the finals, the Australians had to defeat a French boat, *France*. The Aussie seamen had given good accounts of themselves with *Gretel* in 1962 and *Dame Pattie* in 1967, and this experience was thought to have given them the edge over the European entry. Britton Chance, Jr., of the United States, had designed a 12-meter "trial horse," *Chancegger,* for the French, but it was not eligible to compete because a challenger must basically be designed and constructed in the country it represents. There is no doubt that much was learned from Chance's work, but Baron Marcel Bich, the French maker of Bic ball-point pens and head of the syndicate that owns the *France,* proved to be no match for the Australian sailors and their *Gretel II*.

In the competition to determine which U.S. boat would defend the cup, a new 12-meter sloop,

During the America's Cup Challenge, Australia's *Gretel II* (foreground) races to escape the U.S. *Intrepid*. However, the *Intrepid* went on to win by one minute and 18 seconds.

WIDE WORLD

The *Delta Queen*, the only surviving steamboat in 1970, was declared a fire hazard by the U.S. Congress. The owners are required to make the boat fireproof in the next three years.

JOHN LOENGARD, LIFE MAGAZINE © TIME INC.

Heritage, was the sentimental favorite, partly because the popular Charles E. Morgan, Jr., was its designer, builder, and skipper. Olin J. Stephens II, the "old master" of America's Cup designing, had a new hull, *Valiant,* which was clearly the real favorite. Stephens had designed *Intrepid* for the successful races in 1967, and Chance had radically redesigned her bottom for the series in 1970. *Intrepid* won the competition and so became the first boat since *Columbia* (in 1899 and 1901) to defend the America's Cup more than once.

Gretel II was not impressive in the lackluster victory over *France,* but when designer Alan Payne and skipper Jim Hardy moved the mast back 5¾ inches, the boat took on new life. Bill Ficker and his finely tuned crew sailed off with the first race in *Intrepid,* while the Australians made tactical errors, fouled sails, and committed the unpardonable sin of losing a crewman overboard. The second race was canceled on the first try because of fog. When the second race was restaged, it was a fiasco, with a collision at the start that was to disqualify *Gretel II* though it crossed the finish line first; the score was thus two to nothing.

On the next outing, *Intrepid* won by one minute and 18 seconds, and many observers were ready to pack up and go home, confident that the U.S. boat would have the necessary four wins on the next race day. The Aussies, however, broke into the win column in the following race, and excitement rose. *Intrepid* then wrapped it up in the final competition, leading at all five marks.

Other Results

American Eagle, owned by Robert E. Turner III, won the Southern Ocean Racing Conference championship series, with first-place finishes in four events: St. Petersburg (Fla.)-to-Venice (Fla.); the Lipton Cup; Miami (Fla.)-to-Nassau (Bahamas); and the Nassau Cup races. Skipper Dick Nye and his *Carina* won the Newport-to-Bermuda run; and the Port Huron (Mich.)-to-Mackinac Island (Mich.) was won by *Charisma,* owned by Jesse Phillips.

In the North American Yacht Racing championship the Mallory Cup was taken by John Jennings of the St. Petersburg (Fla.) Yacht Club. Jan O'Malley, of the Mantoloking (N.J.) Yacht Club, won the Adams Cup for the women's championship; and the Sears Cup for juniors was captured by Dan Williams of the Houston (Tex.) Yacht Club.

Houseboats and sailing boats continued to gain in sales in 1970 but sales of medium-size cruisers were off. (*See also* Sports Champions of 1970. *See in* CE: Boats and Boating; Canoes and Canoeing; Motorboats.)

BOLIVIA. In 1970 the left-wing forces of Bolivian nationalism found firm expression once again when leftist Gen. Juan José Torres took over the presidency in October. It soon became clear that Torres' brand of nationalism was similar to that being expounded by the leftist revolutionary regime in power in Peru and by Chile's Marxist president, Salvador Allende. (*See also* Chile; Peru.) Torres indicated a somewhat moderated nationalist approach, however, with his announcement that he would honor an agreement reached earlier in the year to pay nearly $79 million in compensation to the U.S.-owned Bolivian Gulf Oil Co., which Bolivia had nationalized in 1969.

Torres' leftist take-over came in the wake of two short-lived right-wing coups, the first organized by Gen. Rogélio Miranda, against Bolivia's president, Gen. Alfredo Ovando Candía, who had attempted and failed, during his year in office, to satisfy either left- or right-wing forces with his policies. In late September, President Ovando came under particularly strong pressure from right-wing officers, headed by General Miranda, to resign in favor of a military triumvirate with the declared aim of restoring constitutional rule. On October 4, Miranda attempted a coup, and he eventually forced Ovando to resign. Miranda was then ousted by a three-man military junta. These right-wing coups provoked an outcry from organized forces of the left—mineworkers, peasants, students, and political parties. They rallied around Torres and swept him into power October 7.

Despite general political turmoil, the country's economic position improved in 1970. The world price of tin, Bolivia's economic mainstay, increased greatly. The oil industry's prospects were brightened by the resumption of shipments to the United States and an agreement with Camba (a firm backed by the Spanish government) to market Bolivian oil abroad. (*See in* CE: Bolivia.)

BOTSWANA. The principal issue in Botswana in 1970 was the controversy and confusion surrounding the proposed construction of an international highway that would link Botswana and Zambia, at the narrow point where they adjoin across the Zambezi River. Both nations directly involved were in favor of the project, and the United States offered to finance a hardtop road (including a modern ferry) to run between Nata, in Botswana, and Kazungula, in Zambia. Strong opposition, however, came from South Africa, which claimed that the two countries did not have a common frontier. In reply to this charge, the Botswana government said that there was indeed a common, though undefined, boundary at Kazungula.

Access by ferry between Botswana and Zambia had long been established by the grace of South Africa, but the South Africans have been strongly against any ideas of improving communications there, being fearful that black nationalist guerrillas would use it to infiltrate southward into Rhodesia, South-West Africa (Namibia), and South Africa. Some observers of the situation believed that the case would ultimately have to be resolved by the International Court of Justice at The Hague, Netherlands.

Botswana continued during the year to receive more than half its revenue from foreign aid, remaining largely dependent upon South Africa for transportation, trade, and labor. It also became the first black African state to seek a loan on the Johannesburg Stock Exchange in South Africa.

The opening of the Bamangwato Concessions, Ltd., copper and nickel mines at Selebi-Pikwe (about 55 miles from Francistown), with a contract for $7 million to a South African shaft-sinking company, gave Botswana its biggest single economic boost and a promise of future financial independence. (*See in* CE: Botswana.)

BOWLING. The 67th annual American Bowling Congress (ABC) championships were held in Knoxville, Tenn., with 4,802 teams competing. The prize fund was $587,110. Capturing the classic (professional) division team title was the youthful Merchant Enterprises of New York City, which shot 3,154 in a roll-off composed of the six leading teams in regular competition. In other classic division play, Glenn Allison of Whittier, Calif., won the singles with 730; Dave Soutar, Gilroy, Calif., and Nelson Burton, Jr., St. Louis, Mo., topped the doubles with 1,431; and the all-events championship was captured by Bob Strampe, Detroit, Mich., who fired a nine-game total of 2,043. It was Allison's fourth ABC crown and the third for both Strampe and Burton.

The ABC's regular division champions were: team, Hamm's Beer, Minneapolis, Minn., 3,243; singles, Jake Yoder, Fort Wayne, Ind., 744; doubles, Dick Selgo and Don Bredehoft, Toledo, Ohio, 1,371; and all events, Mike Berlin, Muscatine, Iowa, 2,004. Yoder highlighted his singles series with a 300 game, the 22d perfect game in the history of the tournament. Don Glover, Bakersfield, Calif., won the 20th annual ABC Masters tournament championship, emerging from the loser's bracket to outscore veteran Bob Strampe.

Dick Weber, a new member of bowling's Hall of Fame, gives a fine performance at the 1970 American Bowling Congress tournament.

COURTESY, AMERICAN BOWLING CONGRESS

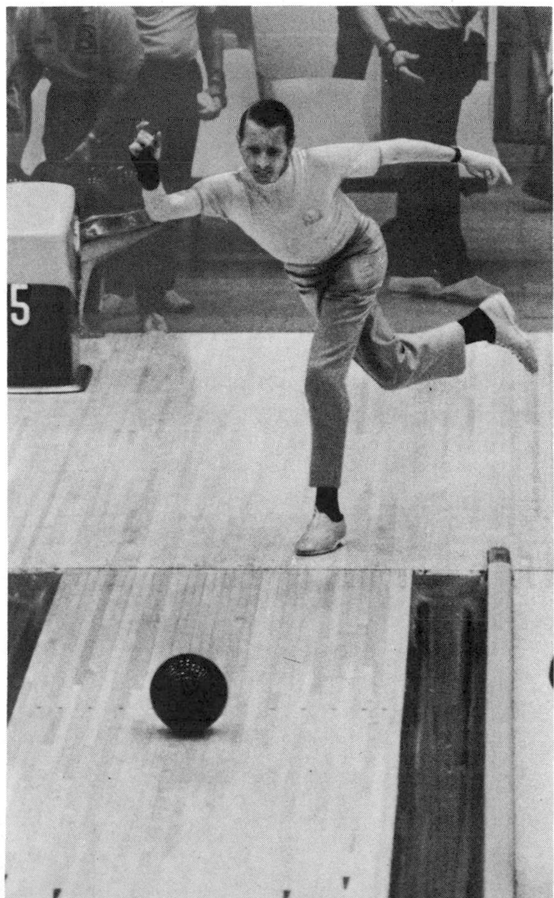

Champions of the 51st annual Woman's International Bowling Congress (WIBC) tournament, conducted in Tulsa, Okla., were: team, Parker-Fothergill Pro Shop, Cranston, R.I., 3,034; singles, Dorothy Fothergill, North Attleboro, Mass., 695; doubles, Gloria Bouvia, Portland, Ore., and Judy Cook, Kansas City, Mo., 1,256; and all events, Dorothy Fothergill, 1,984. Mildred Martorella, Rochester, N.Y., walked off with the WIBC Queens tournament championship, her second first-place finish in the ten-year history of the event.

Bobby Cooper, Houston, Tex., and Mary Baker, Central Islip, N.Y., won the National All-Star tournament. Cooper averaged 234 for 48 games, a tournament record.

Don Carter, Tarzana, Calif., and Dick Weber, St. Louis, Mo., were named to the ABC Hall of Fame. Honored for meritorious service was Sam Weinstein, Chicago.

On the collegiate scene, Harding College of Searcy, Ark., won the National Association of Intercollegiate Athletics tournament, topping the field of eight teams. Charles Burt of Harding captured the singles title, while Al Malone and Steve Poling of Glenville State College (W.Va.) won the doubles. In the Association of College Unions-International championships, Wayne Zmrhal, Northern Illinois University, De Kalb, won the singles with a 659 and also was first in the all events with 2,033.

In February Billy Hardwick of Louisville, Ky., was named the 1969 male bowler of the year by the Bowling Writers Association of America. Hardwick won six Professional Bowlers Association tourneys and earned $64,160. Dick Weber of St. Louis, Mo., was the runner-up in the balloting by the writers. (*See in* CE: Bowling.)

BOXING.

Joe Frazier of Philadelphia, Pa., was widely recognized as the official heavyweight champion of the world in 1970 after he stopped Jimmy Ellis of Louisville, Ky., in four punishing rounds at New York City's Madison Square Garden on February 16. Frazier successfully defended his title in November in Detroit, Mich., against Bob Foster in a bout that lasted only two rounds. The heavyweight situation remained clouded, however, as Cassius Clay (Muhammad Ali) returned to the ring after a forced three-year exile.

Clay had been the official world heavyweight champion, but because of his refusal on conscientious grounds to join the U.S. armed forces in 1967, most states refused to recognize his title. The World Boxing Association eventually accepted Ellis as the new champion; seven U.S. states recognized Frazier. Even after Frazier's victory over Ellis, however, many boxing fans continued to support Clay as the real champion. Clay was finally given permission to fight again in Georgia. On October 26 in Atlanta, Ga., Clay fought an impressive three-round bout with Jerry Quarry, winning by a technical knockout. Clay then went on to defeat Oscar Bonavena in New York City on December 7.

1970 WORLD CHAMPIONSHIP FIGHTS

Division	Boxer *	Date and Place
Flyweight	Chartchai Choinoi Efren Torres †	March 20 Bangkok, Thailand
	Erbito Salavarria Chartchai Choinoi †	December 7 Bangkok, Thailand
Bantamweight	Ruben Olivares † Jesus Castillo	April 18 Inglewood, Calif.
	Jesus Castillo Ruben Olivares †	October 16 Los Angeles
Featherweight	Johnny Famechon † Masahiko Harada	January 6 Tokyo
	Vicente Saldivar Johnny Famechon †	May 9 Rome
	Shozo Saijo ‡ Frankie Crawford	July 5 Sendai, Japan
	Kuniaki Shibata Vicente Saldivar †	December 11 Tijuana, Mexico
Lightweight	Ismael Laguna Mandel Ramos †	March 3 Los Angeles
	Ismael Laguna † Ishimatsu Suzuki	June 6 Panama City, Panama
	Ken Buchanan ‡ Ismael Laguna †	September 26 San Juan, Puerto Rico
Welterweight	José Napoles † Ernie Lopez	February 14 Inglewood, Calif.
	José Napoles † Pete Toro	October 6 New York City
	Billy Backus José Napoles †	December 3 Syracuse, N.Y.
Middleweight	Nino Benvenuti † Tom Bethea	May 23 Umag, Yugoslavia
	Carlos Monzon Nino Benvenuti †	November 7 Rome
Light Heavyweight	Bob Foster † Roger Rouse	April 4 Missoula, Mont.
	Bob Foster † Mark Tessman	June 27 Baltimore, Md.
Heavyweight	Joe Frazier † Jimmy Ellis ‡	February 16 New York City
	Joe Frazier † Bob Foster	November 18 Detroit, Mich.

* Top name in each pair is winner. † Title defender.
‡ As recognized by World Boxing Association.

Other Titles; Honors

Bob Foster continued his domination of the light-heavyweight division, stopping Roger Rouse

SHEEDY & LONG FOR SPORTS ILLUSTRATED © TIME INC.

Ruben Olivares (right) beat Jesus Castillo in this bantamweight title fight. Later, however, Castillo took the crown from him.

after three rounds in April and Mark Tessman in ten rounds in June. Nino Benvenuti of Italy successfully defended his middleweight crown in May by stopping Tom Bethea in eight rounds, but lost it at the hands of Carlos Monzon of Argentina by a 12th-round knockout in November. José Napoles of Mexico lost his welterweight crown to Billy Backus. Mandel Ramos lost his lightweight title to Ismael Laguna of Panama in March by a technical knockout. Laguna retained his honor by stopping Ishimatsu Suzuki of Japan in 13 rounds in June, but he lost his title when he was defeated by Ken Buchanan of Scotland in September.

Johnny Famechon of Australia retained his featherweight title in January by stopping Masahiko Harada of Japan in the 14th round, then lost it four months later to Vicente Saldivar of Mexico. Saldivar in turn lost to Kuniaki Shibata of Japan in December. Shozo Saijo of Japan retained his World Boxing Association version of the title. Ruben Olivares of Mexico reigned as top bantamweight most of 1970 but was beaten by Jesus Castillo, also of Mexico, in October. Chartchai Choinoi of Thailand defeated Efren Torres of Mexico in a title match in Bangkok in March to regain his flyweight crown; however, he lost the title again in December to Erbito Salavarria of the Philippines.

Spain and Italy dominated European boxing, with Spain taking honors in the heavyweight, lightweight, and featherweight divisions; Italy took the light-heavyweight, bantamweight, and flyweight titles. Denmark claimed the middleweight title and Austria claimed the welterweight. In November, Great Britain took the heavyweight title from Spain.

Frazier, recognized heavyweight champion in New York and five other states, was named 1969 Fighter of the Year by the Boxing Writers' Association in February. "Jersey Joe" Walcott, heavyweight titleholder in 1951–52 at the age of 37, and Carmen Basilio, former welterweight and middleweight champion, were elected to the Boxing Hall of Fame in January.

The boxing world was saddened by the death of two former champions during 1970. Early in the year Carlos Teo Cruz, who won the lightweight championship from Carlos Ortiz in 1968, was killed in a plane crash off the coast of the Dominican Republic. Late in May, Manuel Ortiz, world bantamweight champion from 1942 to 1944 and again in 1946, died of cirrhosis at San Diego Naval Hospital at the age of 53.

Amateur Boxing

The national Golden Gloves championships in Las Vegas, Nev., late in March saw William Thompson of Chicago defeat Lawrence Podesta of San Francisco, Calif., for the heavyweight title. Three winners—Tony Moreno, 112 pounds; James Buceme, 125 pounds; and Melvin Dennis, 147 pounds—assured the team championship for Fort Worth, Tex.

In a battle for the Rocky Marciano Trophy in Rome in June, the Italian amateur team beat the U.S. boxers, six matches to five. United States light-heavyweight Nat Jackson of Memphis, Tenn., and heavyweight Ronald Lyle of Denver, Colo., registered first-round knockouts, the only ones scored by either team. (*See in* CE: Boxing.)

Away from the boxing ring for three and a half years because of draft problems, Muhammad Ali (right) returned to defeat Jerry Quarry.

UPI COMPIX

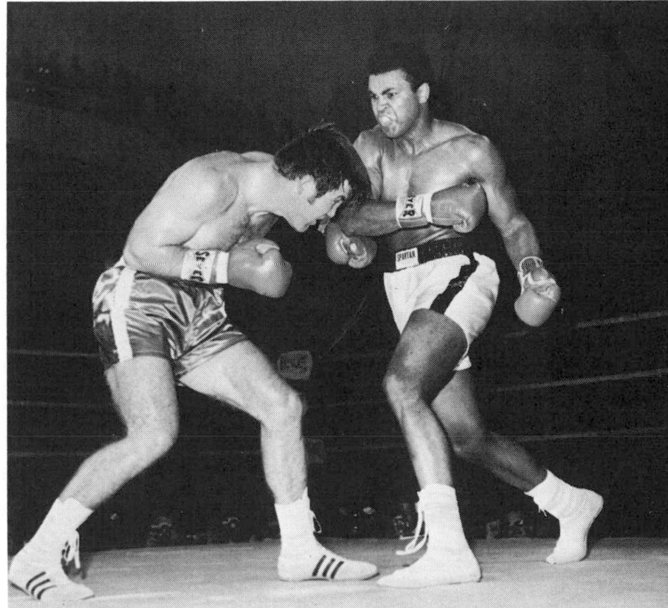

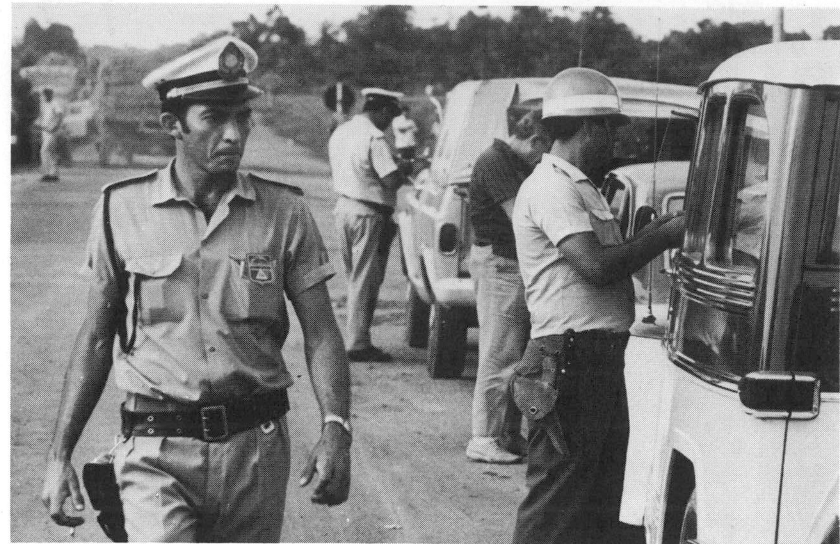

Along Brazil's Route 116, military, air, and police forces halt traffic to conduct a thorough search for guerrilla terrorists.

MANCHETE FROM PICTORIAL PARADE

BRAZIL. In the face of political repression from the ruling military regime and terrorist activities of leftist radicals, Brazil in 1970 enjoyed another year of economic boom. Prospects for the future, however, were dimmed by the continuing depletion of coffee surpluses. During the year left-wing terrorists kidnapped foreign diplomats and held them hostage for the release of Brazilian political prisoners. There were charges from private citizens and organizations that political prisoners in Brazil were subjected to physical torture.

Early in the year Gen. Emílio Garrastazú Médici, president of the military-controlled government of Brazil, cast doubts on the possibility of a rapid return to a democratic system. He emphasized that he had expressed hope for the restoration of democracy when he took office in 1969, but he pointed out that he had not promised democracy would be restored by the end of his term in 1974. The regime actually instituted more repressive policies during the year, exemplified by the censorship law passed in February. The new law required editors and publishers to get the approval of the federal police on all books and periodicals before distribution.

Charges of torture of political prisoners were leveled against the military regime many times during 1970. The charges were made by private citizens, the Brazilian Bar Association, and the International Commission of Jurists. A carefully worded government statement released on May 8 denied the charges. The statement followed expressions of concern from the U.S. State Department and from Pope Paul VI. Roman Catholic bishops in Brazil had expressed disapproval of the practices of the military regime.

The Brazilian government finally acknowledged the existence of "death squads," vigilante groups who murder petty criminals. It was estimated that between 1964 and 1970 there were 500–1,000 victims of the death squads. Médici denounced the squads and promised to investigate.

On March 11 the Japanese consul general in São Paulo was kidnapped by Brazilian revolutionaries. The government released five political prisoners, as the kidnappers had demanded, and the consul general was freed. In April an attempt to kidnap a U.S. consul failed. In June, however, West Germany's ambassador to Brazil was kidnapped. The terrorists demanded the release of 40 prisoners. Again the government met the demands and the ambassador was released.

Brazil's coffee reserves in 1970 dropped to 30 million bags and were expected to be depleted in three years. Further, a leaf rust attacked coffee trees in parts of Brazil, and there were fears that the disease would spread to major coffee-growing areas. The 1970 crop was estimated at 11.5 million bags, but 27.2 million bags were needed to fill the demand. In spite of the coffee problem and a severe drought in the northeast, Brazil's economy continued to grow. (*See also* International Relations; Latin America. *See in* CE: Brazil.)

BUILDING CONSTRUCTION. The construction industry and its influence on the U.S. economy received a large measure of government attention in 1970. In March U.S. President Richard M. Nixon underlined the concern of his Administration in a special statement on construction. In it he outlined a series of long-range measures to reduce the cost of mortgage money, to increase the supply of skilled manpower, and to improve management techniques within the industry. At the same time he announced that $1.5 billion in federal and local construction funds, which had been frozen in September 1969, would be released. The action represented a shift in Administration policy and indicated the belief that earlier actions had begun to bring inflation into check.

However, in August the Council of Economic Advisers issued its first inflation alert. The council reported that wage hikes of "15% per year or more" in the construction industry "are far beyond even a generous estimate of gains in output per man-hour." The report indicated that such wage increases would necessarily lead to inflated costs in producing buildings, highways, and other structures. An earlier study had shown that unionized construction workers received hourly wages averaging 52% higher than those of nonunion workers —a fact that was cited as a result of the unions' ability to effectively limit entry into the industry.

The movement to open more jobs in the construction industry to blacks gained some momentum in 1970. In January a "memorandum of understanding" was propounded by the Black Construction Coalition, representatives of some 15 contractor associations, and the Pittsburgh Building and Construction Trades Council. An agreement to employ 1,250 blacks as journeymen in Allegheny County over the next four years was included in the memorandum. The agreement followed six months of controversy and confrontation between blacks and whites in the Pittsburgh area. In July Secretary of Labor James D. Hodgson announced that 73 cities would be added to the list of urban areas in which federal quotas for racial hiring would be enforced. The areas were to be given time to develop voluntary job plans for construction work before the government would step in.

At the end of the first half of 1970 the total value of all new construction erected was running at an average annual rate of about $88 billion, based on U.S. Bureau of the Census estimates adjusted for seasonal variation. The pace was slightly below the record annual average for 1969, largely due to the influence of earlier restrictive fiscal and monetary measures. In physical terms, construction output in 1970 was down by even more, allowing for the continued rise of construction costs.

Demands for new construction in 1970 followed a general pattern established in 1969. About 30% of all new construction erected during the first six months of the year was for schools, hospitals, sewage disposal plants, waterworks, and other public facilities. Highways and streets accounted for the largest single share of all public construction. In addition, nearly 40% of the total consisted of office buildings, shopping centers, and other private nonresidential facilities.

Responding to both cost pressures and the lure of the economies of scale, builders continued to develop large projects whenever feasible. The most striking example of this trend came with the proposal to erect a 1,450-foot-tall, $100-million building in Chicago. The structure, to be the new headquarters of Sears, Roebuck and Co., will be the world's tallest building and largest private office building. (*See in* CE: Building Construction.)

BULGARIA. The year 1970, the last of Bulgaria's fifth five-year plan of national development, was the occasion for a downpour of speeches in which government leaders emphasized transformation of the national economy since World War II. Industrial production in 1970 was said to be 33 times greater than that of 1939. Between that year and 1969 generation of electric power rose from 266 million to 17.2 billion kilowatt-hours; the extraction of coal from 2.4 million to 34.4 million short tons; the production of steel from 6,600 to 1.6 million tons; and the production of cement from 247,950 to almost 4 million tons. The con-

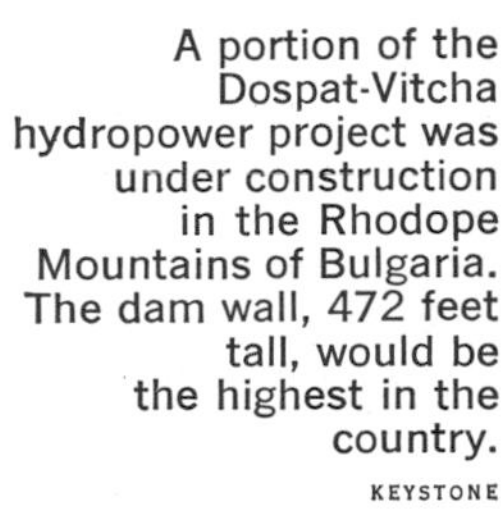

A portion of the Dospat-Vitcha hydropower project was under construction in the Rhodope Mountains of Bulgaria. The dam wall, 472 feet tall, would be the highest in the country.
KEYSTONE

struction of a 373-mile-long pipeline for natural gas from the Soviet Union was expected to begin in 1970; and a 159-mile-long pipeline to carry petroleum products from Burgas to Plovdiv was also being built. The first atomic power station was in construction at Kozlodui, on the Danube River, with a capacity of 880 megawatts.

Collectivization of agriculture was completed in 1959, and by 1969 more than 84,000 tractors and 15,000 combine-harvesters were operated on collective farms. In April 1970, however, the plenary session of the Central Committee of the Bulgarian Communist party decided that a further concentration in agriculture and animal husbandry was necessary. The existing collective farms will merge in huge agrarian-industrial complexes of about 50,000 to 125,000 acres and will specialize in producing one kind of high quality crop or in rearing one kind of livestock.

On September 11 and 12, at Ruse, Bulgaria, and Giurgiu, Romania, Bulgaria's Premier Todor Zhivkov and Nicolae Ceausescu, president of Romania's State Council, discussed the joint building of a power station on the Danube River at Islaz, Romania-Somovit, Bulgaria. They agreed to sign in November a new 20-year treaty of friendship and mutual aid to replace the Bulgarian-Romanian treaty of Jan. 16, 1948. (*See in* CE: Bulgaria.)

BURMA. Throughout 1970 Burma continued to plod along the "Burmese Way to Socialism" with no significant economic or political gains. Some observers even felt that the nation had slid farther backward during the year.

Communist guerrillas continued their activity in 1970, but the situation was within the ability of the Burmese army to handle. Most of the new guerrilla activity was in the northeastern part of Burma along the border with Communist China. Even though government forces captured quantities of Chinese-made rifles and rocket launchers, the Burmese government would not publicly accuse China of supplying and training the insurgents. In March, after a guerrilla attack on the border town of Kyukok, the government announced that it had abandoned the town because defending it would have meant firing into Chinese territory. This statement strongly insinuated that the Burmese government knew guerrillas were allowed to use Chinese territory for the purpose of launching attacks across the border into Burma.

Another threat to Burma's security came from former Prime Minister U Nu, who carried on his campaign from Thailand to instigate a rebellion against Gen. Ne Win, prime minister and chairman of the Revolutionary Council. The armed forces and the people in general, however, accepted the leadership of Ne Win, and the threat from U Nu was not taken seriously. In September Ne Win took the bold step of releasing 900 political prisoners, many of whom were former followers of the exiled U Nu.

Economic conditions in the country were poor during 1970, and the shortage of consumer goods continued. There was further improvement in Burma's relations with India, and the two countries concluded a trade agreement. (*See in* CE: Burma.)

BURUNDI. The Unity and National Progress party, headed by Burundi's President Michel Micombero, was strengthened in July 1970 when the National Political Bureau adopted the party's charter. Micombero thus became party secretary-general, and a five-man executive of the Central Committee was formed to implement party congress directives and Central Committee decisions. The biannual congress consisted of the Central Committee, plus a number of provincial and local representatives.

Although Chinese Communist influence in Burundi, aimed primarily at using the country as a gateway to the Congo and at arming the Tusi refugees against Rwanda, was still present in 1970, there was a general shift toward the Western countries in economic and military affairs. Belgium provided military and technical aid, and France signed a treaty of military assistance in April. President Micombero, in welcoming Belgium's King Baudouin I on his visit to Burundi, emphasized the importance of Belgian aid in every sector of the economy and assured foreign investors of safety and stability for their investments. International aid for 1970 included $380,000 from the International Development Association for transport development and $719,000 from the United Nations (UN) Development Programme to develop fisheries on Lake Tanganyika.

For its six refugee (mostly Tusi) settlements, Burundi received the largest single allocation granted by the UN High Commission for Refugees for 1970. (*See in* CE: Burundi.)

BUSINESS AND INDUSTRY. The year 1970 was a difficult one for business and industry in the United States. Costs soared, profits plummeted, sales declined, taxes increased, and wage demands—fueled by workers' own cost-price squeeze—made bargaining history. It was a year that unseated a clutch of industrial and financial titans and toppled some of the biggest business empires. In fact, by May the consensus among businessmen was that the nation was indeed in a recession.

The recession took its toll. Corporate profits at the end of the second quarter stood at an annual rate of $77.5 billion—$8 billion below the rate for 1969. Near the end of the same period, business investment projections were about 7.8% over 1969—2.8% less than had been predicted at the beginning of the year. At the same time, unemployment continued to rise, reaching 5.1% in August for the first time since 1964.

The three biggest business stories of the year were the collapse of the Penn Central Transporta-

UPI COMPIX

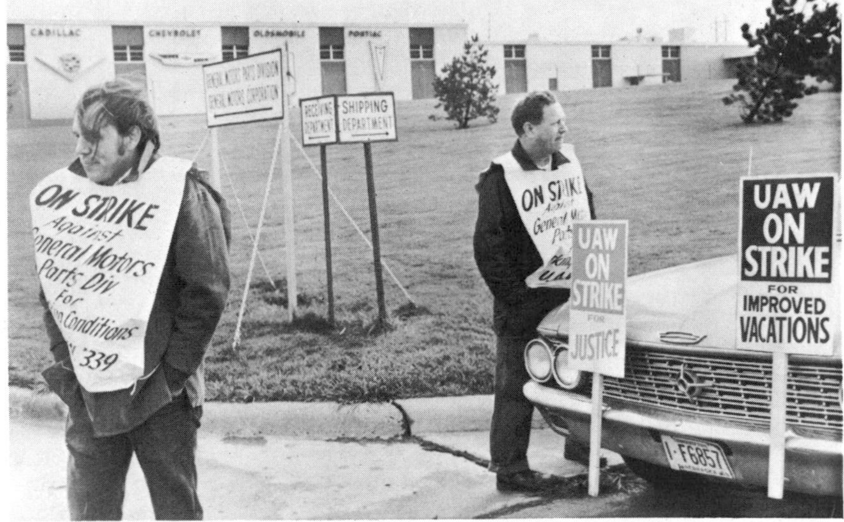

WIDE WORLD

Striking UAW members picket in Omaha, Neb. The strike against General Motors was led by union president Leonard Woodcock (above).

tion Co., the end of the "bear" market on Wall Street, and a strike by the United Automobile Workers (UAW) against General Motors Corp. (GM). The Penn Central went into bankruptcy in June when its credit had dried up, its once promising diversification efforts had faltered, and the U.S. government had refused to insure a $200-million loan that would have sustained it a while longer.

In terms of assets—$4.6 billion in 1969—the Penn Central bankruptcy was the biggest in history. Even more important, it threatened to trigger a rash of bankruptcies among the rest of the nation's financially troubled railroads, many of which were creditors of the Penn Central. Its massive debt threatened the financial fortunes of many creditors, including several of New York's largest banks. Throughout the second half of 1970, these banks worked to shore up some of the railroad's more valuable subsidiaries in order to avoid derailments of their own.

The Penn Central's collapse sent tremors through Wall Street and underscored the liquidity problems of many of the nation's largest companies. However, it did not sidetrack the modest stock market recovery then under way. By late August, the nation's 31 million shareholders felt the faint stirrings of hope for the first time in months, and by early October the Dow-Jones index had risen almost 90 points above its standing on May 13 when it "bottomed out."

However, Wall Street itself was destined to bear the scars of damage wrought by the bear market. Many of its prestigious investment houses were hurt and a large number of firms were forced to merge or go out of business.

In mid-September, the UAW ordered 343,000 members out of the plants of GM. (*See* Automobiles; Labor Unions.) The GM strike kept the auto industry from making a strong start on the 1971 automobile year. From January through August, U.S. companies produced 600,000 fewer automobiles and 6,000 fewer trucks and buses than in the same period of 1969.

Ecology and consumer movements began to have marked effects on business and industry during 1970. Many large companies received public condemnation as polluters. As a result, a survey of 248 major companies reported that expenditures for pollution control rose 23% in 1969 and were expected to increase further during 1970.

Consumer advocates, led by attorney Ralph Nader, persisted as business gadflies. "Nader's Raiders," a force of 200 young lawyers, engineers, doctors, and students, investigated the practices of numerous business and government agencies including the First National City Bank of New York City, GM, The Rand Corp., and the Federal Trade Commission. Protesters also invaded stockholders' meetings, challenging companies such as Honeywell Inc., Gulf Oil Corp., and Commonwealth Edison Co. on issues ranging from defense production to women's rights.

(*continued on page 166*)

Although Bernard Cornfeld lost control of his financial empire when he was fired from his executive position on the Investors Overseas Services, Ltd., conglomerate, he was still the largest single stockholder in the organization.

WIDE WORLD

Special Report: Franchising

by Charles G. Burck,
Associate Editor, *Fortune* Magazine

The year 1970 was one of bursting bubbles on Wall Street, and among the stock market's notable casualties were many franchising companies. Their troubles were a part of generally poor market conditions, but they also reflected the problems of a business suffering from growing pains and overpromotion.

Franchising has been "discovered" during the past few years by entrepreneurs and investors, and new franchising companies have proliferated. It is not a new way of doing business; for instance, for more than half a century, automobile manufacturers have used it for product distribution. What *is* new is its growing popularity. About 90% of the franchise companies now in operation have started since 1954. The best-known enterprises are the fast-service food companies such as Kentucky Fried Chicken and McDonald's. But franchising is spreading into a bewildering array of other fields, ranging from muffler repair shops to income-tax advisory services, tool rental stores, and business colleges.

So many have sprung up recently that firm estimates of their numbers are hard to come by. The best guess is that there are more than 1,200 franchise companies and between 400,000 and 600,000 outlets. Their sales total somewhere near $90 billion, or about 10% of the gross national product.

Why has franchising become so popular? One answer is provided by Ray Kroc, the founder of McDonald's. Kroc was a paper-cup salesman before he started the company. Today McDonald's has annual sales of more than $450 million. Kroc himself is worth well over $100 million, and he says with conviction, "Franchising has become the updated version of the American dream."

The Ray Krocs, of course, are exceptional; not everyone can found a chain. But at its best, franchising can offer a man with no special skills or advantages the opportunity to get ahead by working hard. It combines the proven product and management techniques of the *franchiser,* which is the national chain, with the drive and motivation of the *franchisee,* the man who owns the stand, store, or outlet selling the franchiser's goods or services.

In a typical franchise arrangement, the franchisee pays an initial fee and a monthly percentage of his gross profit to the franchiser. In exchange he gets the right to sell a product or service, along with advice on site location and construction planning. He also gets advertising and marketing help and training in the techniques needed to run the operation successfully. After his business is established, he will usually get continuing services that include advertising and the assistance of company troubleshooters who can help him straighten out operating problems.

The number of services provided and the cost of them vary widely. A company like Snap-On Tools, for instance, uses franchisees as distributors for its line of tools. Snap-On charges neither franchise fees nor royalties, but it provides free advice and some bookkeeping forms. The franchisee sets up his own conditions of doing business. A man who wants to run a McDonald's stand, on the other hand, has to lay out as much as $100,000. The company sets him up in a "turnkey" operation that includes every last piece of equipment, from neon sign to catsup dispenser. It gives him an intensive three-week training course and provides him with a 385-page operating manual that outlines virtually everything he needs to know to run the store.

Because it is "new" and full of promise, franchising has suffered from overpromotion. The classic boom-and-bust example was Performance Systems, Inc., perhaps better known by its original name of Minnie Pearl's Chicken System. Minnie Pearl's organizers sold franchises by the hundreds, and the company's stock rose from an issue price of $20 in early 1968 to a peak of $68. But the promoters found it much harder to run the business and sell chicken. By the end of 1969, Minnie Pearl had sold about 1,600 franchises—but only 263 stores were in operation. Since the company could sell only so many franchises, and since very little money was coming in as operating income, the handsome profits of the first year turned abruptly into a substantial loss. By the middle of 1970, Minnie Pearl stock was selling for less than a dollar a share.

The fate of Minnie Pearl sobered many investors and signaled the beginning of the end for "the-sky-is-the limit" promotion of franchise stocks. It also helped generate pressure for stricter accounting procedures for franchise companies. Like many others, Minnie Pearl counted franchise sales as current income, thus creating vastly overstated profits that could not be matched in subsequent years from operations. By the end of 1970, most reputable franchisers, pressured by the public and by their accountants, had abandoned that practice.

NANCY PALMER AGENCY

Food-service franchising companies have located along U.S. main streets and roads in fierce competition for the nation's drive-in business. The older established companies have sold their franchises in every state; their signs are a familiar sight on crowded thoroughfares and in rural areas.

Stockholders are not the only people to have suffered from overpromotion. Fast-growing, loose, and unregulated, the franchise business has been a natural hunting ground for incompetent or unethical organizers, and many would-be franchisees have been disappointed or defrauded. The burden at present is on the potential franchisee to investigate carefully the reputation and experience of any company he is considering.

The ambitious plans of even the legitimate company are not always in the best interests of its franchisees. The contract between franchiser and franchisee often gives the company the right to "terminate" the franchise, or make the holder relinquish his business. The franchiser needs that power to protect his standards by weeding out the incompetent franchise holder; however, the power is often abused. With termination a threat, the franchisee has little choice but to comply with any company demands. If the franchise is terminated, the franchisee usually loses heavily. Most contracts do not make any provision for the patronage built up by the franchisee's hard work.

Two bills were considered during 1970 that would have regulated these problems at the federal level. One, created by Senator Philip Hart (D, Mich.), would have put the burden on the franchiser to show "good cause" in terminations. Another, sponsored by Senator Harrison Williams (D, N.J.), would have called for disclosure of the officers' background and experience and contract terms of any franchise offering. But the Hart bill died in committee, and the Williams bill seemed doomed to the same fate.

In a number of cases, franchisees have formed protective associations to counter franchise abuses. Some have sued their companies. Pressure is even growing for the legitimate franchisers to take some self-policing action in order—in the words of Thomas H. Murphy, a respected observer and critic of franchising—" . . . to burnish franchising's somewhat tarnished public image."

Ralph Nader continued his crusade for consumer protection, investigating business and government agencies engaged in unfair business practices.
WIDE WORLD

(*continued from page 163*)
Security also became a new concern to business in 1970. Bombings were blamed for damaging two branches of the Bank of America National Trust & Savings Association in Berkeley, Calif.

One former growth industry that foundered badly during 1970 was franchising. Tight money and high interest rates narrowed borrowing opportunities for both franchisers and franchisees. Among the franchise companies retreating into bankruptcy during the year were Four Seasons Nursing Centers of America and Dolly Madison Industries, Inc. (*See* Business and Industry Special Report.)

Very little was heard from those onetime big newsmakers, the conglomerates, in 1970. The decline in stock values and the high cost of money clipped the wings of some of the highest fliers in the group, most of whom had made past acquisitions on borrowed money and stock swaps. One of the largest conglomerates, Ling-Temco-Vought, Inc. (LTV), was hard hit with losses or falling profits in key subsidiaries and was faced with a mountainous long-term debt of about $860 million. The LTV board unseated James J. Ling, the man who engineered the company's dazzling growth during the 1960's.

Thus Ling joined an impressive list of corporate chieftains who were displaced during 1970. The list includes Stuart Saunders of Penn Central, Robert E. Williams of Youngstown Sheet & Tube Co., and Bernard Cornfeld of Investors Overseas Services, Ltd., the massive investment fund that faltered when foreign investors lost confidence in U.S. securities. (*See also* Economy. *See in* CE: Industry, American.)

CAMBODIA. The year 1970 was Cambodia's year of reckoning. The government of Prince Norodom Sihanouk, Cambodia's long-time chief of state, was overthrown, Lieut. Gen. Lon Nol assumed dictatorial control, and the country was invaded by U.S. and South Vietnamese forces, thus plunging it into an economic and political maelstrom in which its very survival as an entity was in question.

Early in the year, Sihanouk left Cambodia for a visit to France. Taking advantage of his long absence, his ministers decided to challenge him. They began in early March by organizing anti-Vietnamese demonstrations in an obvious attempt to arouse popular sentiment in their favor; the Vietnamese are historic enemies of the Cambodians and some 500,000 of them, mostly traders and technicians, were living in Cambodia at the time. On March 11 the embassies of North Vietnam and the Provisional Revolutionary Government of South Vietnam (Viet Cong) in Phnom Penh, the capital of Cambodia, were sacked by crowds led by government soldiers. The next day the cabinet cabled Sihanouk that the demonstrations represented the legitimate indignation of the people over his allegedly pro-Communist policies and that it had now decided on radical changes in the government's foreign and military policies. It then demanded that the North Vietnamese and the Viet Cong authorities withdraw all guerrilla troops from Cambodian territory in two days.

The final blow came on March 18 when the National Assembly met. Its historic decision was later announced by National Assembly President Cheng

Victims of war lie along the road as U.S. troops press deeper into Cambodia. Public outrage against extending the war forced the withdrawal of U.S. troops.
LONDON "DAILY EXPRESS" FROM PICTORIAL PARADE

Heng: ". . . the National Assembly and the Council of the Kingdom, meeting in joint session, have withdrawn, conforming to the constitution, in a unanimous vote, their confidence from Prince Norodom Sihanouk in his position as Chief of State." The Assembly chose Cheng Heng as the new provisional chief of state, a job that was reduced to titular status. Lon Nol continued as premier and Prince Sisowath Sirik Matak (a cousin of Sihanouk), reputedly the strongman of the cabinet and the brain behind the coup, remained first deputy premier (in a July announcement he was named sole deputy premier).

At first the new leadership found considerable support for their action. For all Sihanouk's popularity among the peasants, the urban elites were against him. So were students and teachers, frustrated by the lack of opportunities under a one-man rule. The government's popularity, however, waned as the military situation quickly deteriorated. The Cambodian army, numbering barely 45,000, was ill-trained and ill-equipped and was more often than not defeated in its battles with North Vietnamese and Viet Cong troops, who controlled major parts of Cambodia. The Lon Nol government survived only on the strength of the South Vietnamese army, which had invaded the country shortly after the fall of Sihanouk in order to fight Communist troops in Cambodia. On April 30 U.S. President Richard M. Nixon announced that U.S. troops were, on that day, marching into Cambodia for the limited purpose of destroying Communist sanctuaries along the border. What developed was an all-out allied offensive, though U.S. troops officially stayed within 21.7 miles of the border. The war rapidly enveloped previously unaffected areas of Cambodia as Communist troops, driven out of their border sanctuaries by oncoming allied troops, pushed on to gain control of vast areas in the south and southeast as well as in the north and east of the country. At one point the Lon Nol government was reportedly resigned to conceding half the country to the Communists.

The U.S. troops withdrew from Cambodia by June 30 as scheduled. South Vietnam continued to maintain a large presence in the country, and Thailand became involved in a marginal way. As if in retaliation for the Lon Nol government's bloody repression of the Vietnamese minority in the country, South Vietnamese troops plundered the Cambodian villages they overran, raping and looting. They helped evacuate to South Vietnam part of Cambodia's remaining Vietnamese population, which had been confined to detention camps by the Lon Nol government.

Meanwhile, Prince Sihanouk had traveled from Paris to Moscow with his ouster coming hours before his departure for Peking, People's Republic of China. However, while in Peking, Sihanouk received unexpected strong support from the Chinese government. The Chinese promised full military and economic assistance. International diplomatic circles concluded that China was motivated by both a desire to undercut the Soviet Union and to prop up Sihanouk and Cambodia as an eventual Indochinese counterbalance to the independently minded government of North Vietnam. Keeping Peking as his headquarters, Sihanouk traveled to North Vietnam and North Korea and kept up a barrage of letters and press statements to win support for his cause. (*See also* China, People's Republic of; Communist Movement.)

On May 5 Sihanouk announced the formation of a government-in-exile, with himself as head of state,

Effigies representing the Viet Cong, corruption, and royalty are displayed in Phnom Penh, Cambodia, during mass demonstrations on Oct. 10, 1970.

UPI COMPIX

Samdech Penn Nouth as premier, and Sarim Chhak, Hu Nim, Khieu Samphan, and Hou Yuon as chief ministers. In Cambodia these last three had been leaders of the underground Khmer Rouge (Red Cambodia) movement that Sihanouk had hounded while he was in power. In fact, these men had been reported as killed by Cambodian government troops. The government-in-exile was recognized by a number of countries, but the list did not include the Soviet Union and India. During the summer the government of Lon Nol put Sihanouk and all his men on trial *in absentia,* and the prince and some of his leading ministers were sentenced to death. Sihanouk ridiculed the trial, arguing that the Lon Nol government was unconstitutional and that he alone was the legal head of state.

As premier of Cambodia, Lieut. Gen. Lon Nol was faced with increasing opposition from Communist forces during 1970.

LONDON "DAILY EXPRESS" FROM PICTORIAL PARADE

A direct consequence of the war that finally caught up with Cambodia was the complete shattering of the economy. Tourism and the rubber industry, two principal foreign-exchange earners, were ruined. The big rubber plantations were completely shut down or razed, some by allied bombings. Rice exports were seriously affected as fields turned into battlegrounds and trade movements were disrupted by insecurity in the countryside. The Cambodian riel decreased in value on the open market to more than 55 riels to the U.S. dollar against the official rate of 35 riels to the dollar. The U.S. Agency for International Development estimated that the Cambodian government would need some $200 million in outside support to keep the economy functioning through 1971. The total extent of U.S. assistance was not disclosed. Toward the end of the cataclysmic year the only certainties were that Cambodia had lost all initiative for action and that its fate lay in the hands of outside powers: North Vietnam, South Vietnam, and the United States. In October Cambodia was officially declared a republic. (*See also* Foreign Policy, U.S.; Vietnam. *See in* CE: Cambodia.)

CAMEROON. On March 28, 1970, Ahmadou Ahidjo was reelected president of Cameroon; he ran unopposed. Salomon Tandeng Muna was elected vice-president. Nevertheless, the opposition in Cameroon continued to provide considerable difficulties for the president.

In July, two medical attendants were killed and two others wounded in an armed attack on a clinic at Loum in the northwestern part of the country. Two weeks later, about 30 Nigerian nationals were reported to have been killed by Cameroon customs officials in a pitched battle. The report was immediately denied by the president's office. It was not clear whether this was in fact a straightforward border incident or a political incident.

On August 19, Ernest Ouandie, leader of the illegal opposition party, the Union of the Cameroon Peoples (UPC), was taken prisoner by government forces. On August 27, Monsignor Albert Ndongmo, archbishop of Nkongsamba, was also arrested on his return from Rome and was accused of participating in a plot against the head of state. The case of Ouandie and Ndongmo focused attention not only upon the ten-year-old state of emergency that permitted preventive arrest and detention, but even more upon the persistence of discontent among the Bamileke population. (*See in* CE: Cameroon.)

CAMPING. In the United States the camping boom of the 1960's continued unabated in 1970, but a new factor was added. As public attention focused on pollution and waste, conservation and ecology gained a high ranking among the nation's priorities, and campers were urged to be more heedful of the damage they could do to the land.

Spurred by concern for the dwindling American wilderness, many campers took to the deep woods and the high mountains where they could rough it far from civilization. For these hardy types, more lightweight tents and equipment were available than ever before; some companies produced a disposable paper sleeping bag. But purists preferred to make their own or even to improvise in the woods.

Generally, however, camping in comfort was what appealed to most U.S. campers, whose number in 1970 included one family in every five, according to latest estimate. Many campgrounds provided so many facilities that the average investment ran as high as $1,200 per site in a new campground with 80 to 100 sites. Recreational vehicles were increasingly popular, and campers bought more elaborate and expensive equipment; motor homes, the most extravagant form of camping vehicle, rose in sales from 4% of the market in 1969 to 10% in 1970. At the same time, the total number of vehicles built, including camping trailers, pickup campers, travel trailers, and motor homes, increased from 500,000 to 600,000.

Businesses active in camping included campground franchisers, 12 of which were operating. Also active were some motel chains, which planned to operate campsites in conjunction with their motels; some oil companies, which were developing roadside campsites along major highways; and some lumber companies, which were building campsites in their forests. Several airlines began a fly-in/camp-out program offering vacationers a rental camper or motor home and camping information at their destination.

The number of summer camps remained around 12,000 in 1970, with attendance estimated at 7 million. The American Camping Association received a grant to develop a national program for training camp counselors qualified to instruct summer campers in all facets of ecology. (*See in* CE: Camping.)

CANADA. In late 1970 Canada, normally one of the most stable nations in the Western world, experienced an outbreak of political terrorism. The actions of a few extremists known as the Quebec Liberation Front (FLQ) resulted in the murder of a prominent Quebec provincial Cabinet minister and the temporary suspension of civil liberties in Canada. The crisis provided a severe test for the two-year-old government of Prime Minister Pierre Elliott Trudeau. Trudeau, however, moved swiftly to undercut the menace that had appeared in Quebec, even at the risk of estranging public opinion.

Unaccustomed Terror

The crisis began with a political kidnapping. On October 5 British diplomat James R. Cross was abducted from his home. His kidnappers subsequently revealed that they were members of the FLQ and demanded a substantial ransom for Cross. Their demands included the release of 23 "political prisoners" and the payment of $500,000 in gold. The ultimatum asked for the safe conduct of the prisoners, who had been convicted of crimes of violence carried out for the sake of Quebec independence, to refuge in Cuba or Algeria.

Two weeks of anxiety followed the kidnapping of the British diplomat, and during that time a second

Chief Dave Courchene (right) introduces Queen Elizabeth II to members of the Manitoba Indian Brotherhood during her visit to a reserve at The Pas in Canada.

PETER BREGG FROM CANADIAN PRESS

abduction occurred. On October 10, Pierre Laporte, minister of labor and immigration in Quebec's provincial Cabinet, was seized by a group of armed FLQ members in front of his home. Prior to the kidnapping of Laporte the FLQ had lowered its ransom demands, but with the two men held captive they reverted to their original demands.

The Quebec government attempted to negotiate with the FLQ through Robert Lemieux, a radical lawyer. The government refused to consider the FLQ's original demands but offered to let the kidnappers leave Canada safely if they would surrender Cross and Laporte. At one point the government offered to release 5 of the 23 "political prisoners."

As tensions increased there were rumors of plots to blow up public buildings and to assassinate leading political figures. Early on the morning of October 16 the federal government, acting at the request of the Quebec government, proclaimed a state of emergency in Canada under the War Measures Act. The emergency powers assumed by the federal government outlawed the FLQ and all other violence-oriented organizations. The police were given sweeping authority, including the right to search property and arrest persons without a warrant. At the same time military protection was provided for officials of the federal and Quebec governments, especially in the Montreal area.

CANADA WIDE FROM PICTORIAL PARADE

CANADA WIDE FROM PICTORIAL PARADE

Prime Minister Trudeau (above, center) and Quebec's Premier Bourassa (above, right) attend the funeral of Pierre Laporte. The leftist Front Rassemblement d'Action Politique (left) supported the kidnapping of Cross and Laporte. An armed soldier (below) stands by a helicopter in downtown Montreal.

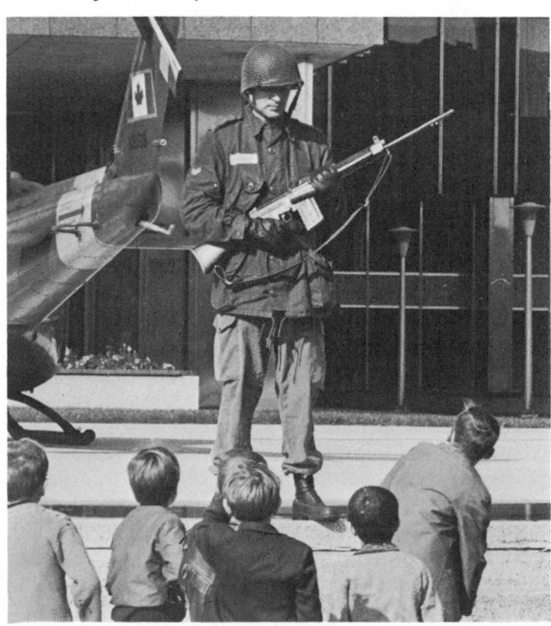

CANADA WIDE FROM PICTORIAL PARADE

Armed soldiers were called out for guard duty in major cities. The next day the FLQ struck back by brutally murdering Laporte and leaving his body in the trunk of a taxi near a Canadian Armed Forces base south of Montreal.

An extensive manhunt was launched to find Laporte's murderers and to rescue Cross. Although over 400 persons were detained by the police, no prime suspects in the case were apprehended. By early November most of the detainees had been released, but over 60 persons were held for trial on various charges of subversion and related activities. Reward money was offered by the federal and provincial governments for information leading to the arrest of the suspected terrorists.

During the intensive search there were charges made against the police of overzealousness and even brutality. On one occasion police entered a university in Montreal and seized an art exhibit entitled "Cubism." Later the police officers explained that they had thought the exhibit was a form of Cuban propaganda.

On December 3 the manhunt produced concrete results. The authorities discovered the house in Montreal where Cross was being held. The house was surrounded, and government officials offered the kidnappers safe passage to Cuba in exchange for the release of Cross. The FLQ members accepted the offer, and Cross was set free.

Legislation specifically drafted to meet the terrorist menace in Quebec was introduced into the House of Commons on November 2. This legislation, the Public Order (Temporary Measures) Act, continued the ban on the FLQ but provided that persons arrested be charged within three days to a week. Rights to counsel and trial by jury were also guaranteed to the accused. The right of the police to search, seize, or make arrests without a warrant was also spelled out in the new legislation. (*See also* Canadian Provinces.)

Foreign Policy

The most noteworthy event in foreign affairs during 1970 was Canada's diplomatic recognition of Communist China. Following 20 months of talks on the subject the Canadian and Chinese governments announced their agreement on October 13. The Canadian government issued a statement saying that it did not consider it "appropriate either to endorse or to challenge the Chinese Government's position on the status of Taiwan." The joint communiqué merely said that Canada "takes note" of the view of the Chinese government that Taiwan is an integral part of Communist Chinese territory. The Nationalist Chinese ambassador left Canada on the day the decision was announced, and shortly afterward a team of officials from the Canadian Department of External Affairs flew to China to begin the task of setting up the Canadian Embassy.

In 1970 the Trudeau government unveiled a comprehensive statement of its views on an appropriate foreign policy for Canada. The statement was presented in the form of six booklets entitled "Foreign Policy for Canadians," and each booklet covered a separate area. Canada's basic national aims were defined as the preservation of an independent political identity, the maintenance of an expanding prosperity, and the making of constructive contributions to the needs of humanity. To achieve these general aims the government concluded that future action should be grouped under six policy areas. Three of these fields—economic growth, social justice, and the "quality of life"—were considered especially important for present-day Canada and were given a high priority in future policy recommendations. Three other areas—safeguarding sovereignty, working for peace and security, and ensuring a harmonious natural environment—were given a lower priority.

The policy statement stressed the need to continue Canada's historic involvement with Europe in spite of increasing interests in the Pacific area and in Latin America. In the United Nations, Canada promised to continue traditional objectives, such as peace-keeping and limiting the arms race, while undertaking new initiatives in such areas as satellite systems, the use of the seabed, and the preservation of the environment.

Canada reacted strongly to the presence of Soviet fishing vessels in the continental-shelf areas off the Canadian Pacific coast in 1970. A series of incidents occurred in which Canadian vessels were sideswiped by Soviet boats, and there was much agitation among west coast fishermen at the alleged depletion of fishery resources by the Russians. Some Canadian fishermen demanded a 200-mile territorial-water limit for Canada. The Canadian government registered a stiff protest against the Soviet Union on July 28 over the sideswiping incidents.

There was friction between Canada and the United States in 1970 over Canada's claims to Arctic territory and over the transfer of natural resources between the two nations. The Canadian Parliament passed a bill containing pollution controls for Arctic waters with fines up to $100,000 for violations. Canada also announced an extension of its territorial-water boundaries from 3 to 12 miles off shore. The United States protested both these moves as interfering with the exercise of the freedom of the seas and representing unilateral assertions of jurisdiction by Canada. Japan also protested the Canadian acts. In what was interpreted as a show of support for the Canadian claim to the Arctic, Great Britain's Queen Elizabeth II toured the Northwest Territories during the summer of 1970.

In March the United States government announced that it would reduce oil imports from Canada from an average of 634,692 to 395,000 barrels a day. This was regarded as a tactic to demonstrate the U.S. desire for a common policy regarding the use of North American energy resources. Such a long-term agreement was resisted by the Canadian government. In September the United States agreed to increase its Canadian natural-gas imports by 6.3 trillion cubic feet over the next 15 to 20 years.

Another energy source, uranium, was in the headlines during 1970. In March the sale of 25.5% of the shares of Denison Mines Ltd., Canada's largest uranium producer, to a U.S. firm was halted by an order of the Canadian Cabinet. Subsequently, amendments to the Atomic Energy Control Act were proposed to set a 33% maximum on the total foreign ownership of Canadian uranium properties of proven productivity. Foreign ownership in a uranium company could be divided among four investors with none holding more than 10% of the shares.

Canada's emerging national spirit even affected television programming in 1970. The Canadian Radio-Television Commission called for the "Canadianization" of broadcasts, cutting out many imported programs from the United States and other countries and substituting Canadian-produced shows.

Other Affairs

The legislative output of Parliament was diverse in 1970. One measure approved was intended to outlaw literature promoting or inciting hatred between groups; however, this raised the issue of free speech. Several strong conservation measures were passed, particularly in the area of water pollution. In May a group of militant women chained themselves to chairs in the House of Commons to demonstrate the need for free abortions.

Canada suffered a nationwide postal strike in 1970. Canada's two postal unions disagreed with the government over wage-increase demands. Postal workers staged 24-hour rotating strikes in major distribution centers, and the government responded by shutting down regional offices.

A report issued by the official commission investigating drug abuse recommended that prison terms be abolished for possession of such drugs as marijuana, LSD, opium, and heroin. The commission also suggested that marijuana and hashish not be grouped with narcotic drugs. (*See also* Commonwealth of Nations; Indians, American; Trudeau. *See in* CE: Canada.)

CABINET

In 1970, a year filled with internal troubles and strife, there were few changes in the Canadian Cabinet. The year's changes in Prime Minister Pierre Elliott Trudeau's Cabinet consisted of a single limited shuffle of five ministers, an indication of the government's stability and of Trudeau's confidence in the men he originally picked in 1968.

The immediate reason for the shuffle, which took place in late September, was the appointment of Minister of National Defense Léo A. J. Cadieux as ambassador to France. Cadieux had been in favor of retaining an impressive Canadian military force both in Canada and in the North Atlantic Treaty Organization (NATO) forces in Europe. His successor, Donald S. Macdonald, 38, was an advocate of Canada's partial withdrawal from NATO commitments. Macdonald became the youngest defense minister in Canadian history.

THE CANADIAN CABINET

Members of the Canadian Cabinet at the close of 1970, listed in order of precedence, were these:

Prime Minister . . . Rt. Hon. Pierre Elliott Trudeau
Leader of the Government in the Senate . . . . Hon. Paul Joseph James Martin
Secretary of State for External Affairs . . . . Hon. Mitchell Sharp
Solicitor General of Canada . . . . . . Hon. George James McIlraith
Minister of Public Works . . . . . Hon. Arthur Laing
President of the Queen's Privy Council for Canada . . . . Hon. Allan Joseph MacEachen
President of the Treasury Board . . . . Hon. Charles Mills Drury
Minister of Finance and Receiver General . . . . Hon. Edgar John Benson
Minister of Industry, Trade, and Commerce . . . Hon. Jean-Luc Pepin
Minister of Regional Economic Expansion . . . . Hon. Jean Marchand
Minister of Energy, Mines, and Resources . . . . Hon. John James Greene
Minister Without Portfolio . . . . . . Joseph Julien Jean-Pierre Côté
Minister of Justice and Attorney General of Canada . . Hon. John Napier Turner
Minister of Indian Affairs and Northern Development . . . . Hon. J. J. Jean Chrétien
Minister of Labor . . Hon. Bryce Stuart Mackasey
Minister of National Defense . . . . . . Hon. Donald Stovel Macdonald
Minister of National Health and Welfare . . . . Hon. John Carr Munro
Secretary of State of Canada . . . . Hon. Gérard Pelletier
Minister of Fisheries and Forestry . . . . Hon. Jack Davis
Minister of Agriculture . . . . Hon. Horace Andrew Olson
Minister of Veterans Affairs . . . . Hon. Jean-Eudes Dubé
Minister of Consumer and Corporate Affairs . . . . Hon. Stanley Ronald Basford
Minister of Transport . . . . Hon. Donald Campbell Jamieson
Minister of Communications . . . Hon. Eric William Kierans
Minister Without Portfolio . . . . Hon. Robert Knight Andras
Minister of Supply and Services . . . . Hon. James Armstrong Richardson
Minister of Manpower and Immigration . . . . Hon. Otto Emil Lang
Minister of National Revenue . . . . Hon. Herb Gray
Minister Without Portfolio . . . . Hon. Robert D. G. Stanbury

TOP LEFT AND RIGHT: CHARLES MITCHELL FROM CANADIAN PRESS

PETER BREGG FROM CANADIAN PRESS

Three distinguished members of the Canadian Cabinet in 1970 were Communications Minister Eric W. Kierans (right), External Affairs Minister Mitchell Sharp (top left), and Transport Minister Donald C. Jamieson (above left).

In Macdonald's place as president of the Queen's Privy Council for Canada and government leader in the House of Commons Trudeau appointed Allan J. MacEachen. MacEachen had served for two years as minister of manpower and immigration after running against Trudeau for the party leadership in 1968.

Other Cabinet changes in 1970 were the promotion of Otto E. Lang, a minister without portfolio, to minister of manpower and immigration and the transfer of Joseph Julien Jean-Pierre Côté from minister of national revenue to a minister without portfolio, but with the responsibility for the operations of Canada's post office. By turning the post office over to Côté, Trudeau left Minister of Communications Eric W. Kierans free to devote his entire attention to a fast-expanding new department concerned with modern information systems, including satellite communications. Kierans had become identified with labor problems.

CANADIAN ECONOMY. In 1970 Canada continued to feel the pain of anti-inflationary measures. During the year the nation's economic growth was almost at a standstill, while unemployment continued to climb and labor leaders resisted the government's attempts to establish wage guidelines.

The restrictive monetary and fiscal policies that had been in force since late in 1968 finally took their toll. The gross national product in real terms grew only 3% between mid-1969 and mid-1970. By June, total output of goods and services had finally flattened to no-growth levels, and it remained approximately the same for the rest of the year. The pallid economic picture did bring about a relaxation of monetary policy, however. In November the Bank of Canada announced that the rate of interest on loans to commercial banks would be reduced to 6%. It was the fourth in a series of interest reductions in 1970 that cut the rate from an all-time high of 8%.

Joblessness became a problem of greater proportions during the year. The unemployment rate reached a seasonally adjusted level of 6.7% in July, the highest figure since 1961. To compound the problem, an increase in the work force of 3% to 3.5% during the year was expected by some to push the jobless level to 9% by year-end. The high level of unemployment, however, did not act as a deterrent to demands for increased wages. Despite government attempts to establish voluntary wage restraints, limiting increases to 6%, most contracts negotiated in industry during the year showed annual wage hikes of 8% to 9%.

In contrast to these gloomy aspects of the Canadian economy, other indicators pointed to brighter days ahead. The consumer price index had risen only 3.2% between mid-1969 and mid-1970, in comparison to a 12-month increase of 6% or more in the United States. In addition, capital spending for the year was expected to reach almost $18 billion, $100 million more than was forecast at the beginning of 1970. The rise in business investment was attributed primarily to greater outlays for mining, manufacturing, and utilities. Although private housing investment fell a little more than 10% during the year, nonresidential construction invest-

"Does that include Western Canada. . . ?"

YARDLEY JONES, "TORONTO TELEGRAM," FROM BEN ROTH AGENCY

ments rose by about 14%, causing a 6% increase in total construction outlays.

Moreover, Canada found itself in the midst of an unexpected export boom. The largest trade surplus in Canadian history developed—reaching over $1.2 billion in the first half of the year, equaling the figure for all of 1968, and doubling the surplus of 1969. Total export sales for the year promised to hit $17 billion, up $2 billion from 1969. At midyear, exports to Great Britain and Japan had risen 26% and 31% respectively. Exports to the United States, Canada's biggest customer, were up 8% during the same period. Enormous growth occurred in shipments of automotive products to the United States, under the Canada-U.S. agreement in which the major auto makers with plants in both countries are allowed to ship autos and parts tariff-free across the border.

The soaring rate of exports, coupled with a flood of U.S. capital into Canada, exerted an upward pressure on the Canadian dollar, which was valued at 92.5¢ to the U.S. dollar. In an attempt to bring the value of Canadian currency into line, Canada's Prime Minister Pierre Elliott Trudeau announced that the dollar would be set free of its peg on June 1 and allowed to float at whatever value supply and demand might set. During the next few months its value vacillated between 96¢ and 98¢. Canada pledged to set a new peg when conditions permit.

Premier Edward Schreyer of Manitoba faced a major crisis in an auto insurance debate in 1970 but managed to regain needed support and to avoid a defeat in the legislature.
"WINNIPEG TRIBUNE"

Robert A. Bourassa became premier of Quebec in April. He was formerly the leader of the official opposition in the national legislature.
"LE SOLEIL" (MONTREAL)

CANADIAN PROVINCES. The year 1970 marked the beginning of a more earnest attempt to remodel Canada's constitution, the British North America Act. The problem of constitutional reform had become particularly acute in recent years. Canada's ten provinces had a firm sense of regional identity and they exercised more power over their own affairs than, for example, did the 50 states of the United States. The provinces controlled education, health, and welfare and had direct jurisdiction over cities. Because these were the vital and developing areas of government concern and expenditures, decisions of the provinces had become more and more important relative to those of the federal government in the last decade.

Federal-provincial discussions on constitutional reform began in earnest under former Prime Minister Lester B. Pearson in 1967 but, in 1969, bogged down in major differences between the two levels of government—and among the provinces themselves—over the cultural and linguistic rights of French-speaking Canadians and the vesting of taxation and spending powers. Debate among government leaders moved off these basic themes in 1970. Their meetings tackled on a pragmatic basis some of the more immediate issues—lagging growth in the poorer regions of the country, the control of pollution, restraints necessary to hold down costs of education and health, jurisdiction over financial institutions, and reform of Canada's income taxes. No breakthroughs occurred but the participants in the debate altered with the election of a new government in French-speaking Quebec. The new government took a more positive constitutional stand toward federalism than had previous Quebec governments.

Quebec

The provincial election that took place in Quebec in April may have been a turning point in that province's search for identity. Four parties—the ruling Union Nationale, the Liberal party, the Parti Québecois, and the Créditiste party—were pitted against one another, and the lines of the contest were sharply defined.

The Union Nationale under Premier Jean-Jacques Bertrand, which held a slim majority in the provincial legislature, was divided on the issue of separation. Some members favored a Quebec-within-Canada federalism; others tended to support separation of the province from the rest of Canada. Thus the party did not come out strongly on either side of the separation issue.

The Liberal party, out of office in the province since 1966, replaced retiring leader Jean Lesage with a young economist, Robert A. Bourassa. He took a strong line in support of retaining federalism and promised to bargain hard with the federal government for payments of various kinds to Quebec that the Union Nationale had failed to claim. Bourassa also promised to encourage investment in the province and to provide 100,000 new jobs by the end of 1971.

The newly formed separatist Parti Québecois under René Lévesque advocated a sovereign Quebec that would be politically independent but still economically linked to Canada. The April election was its first electoral test. The Créditiste party also entered into provincial politics for the first time. Rural-based, it was strongly conservative and federalist.

Bourassa and his Liberals swept the election, capturing 72 of the 108 assembly seats and reducing the Union Nationale share to 17 seats. The Parti Québecois won only seven seats, and the Créditistes 12. The vote was interpreted by some as a "last chance" for federalism. However, the Parti Québecois had actually polled about 24% of the vote, failing to obtain more seats only because its support was in the cities, which had long been underrepresented on Quebec's outdated electoral map.

The separatists stood to capitalize during Premier Bourassa's four-year term of office on any further frustrations Quebecers might experience in attaining the goals summed up by the popular expression *maître chez nous* ("master in our own house"). Bourassa was aided to a great extent by the Liberal government of Prime Minister Pierre Elliott Trudeau, which recognized the need to show that Quebec could benefit most by remaining in Canada. Trudeau thus turned on every possible federal money tap after the election in order to help Bourassa straighten out a budgetary dilemma inherited from Bertrand. Business confidence revived to some degree, though economic conditions were generally depressed for the remainder of the year.

In October, before the effect of Bourassa's policies could be assessed, Quebec and the nation were plunged into a major crisis precipitated by two political kidnappings and the murder of one of the abducted men, the work of a revolutionary Marxist-oriented separatist movement known as the Quebec Liberation Front (FLQ). The events shocked the nation, drew worldwide attention, and caused the federal government to seize sweeping powers of arrest and detention to permit police to deal with the terrorist group.

The FLQ struck first by abducting British diplomat James R. Cross in Montreal, Que. Five days later, Pierre Laporte, Quebec's minister of labor and immigration, was also kidnapped. The FLQ stated demands to be met before the men would be released. These included the freeing of 23 FLQ members convicted or accused of having committed terrorist acts for the underground organization. The provincial government considered the demands impossible.

The federal government reacted by invoking the War Measures Act—never before used in peacetime—to permit wholesale arrests of suspected FLQ members and sympathizers, and federal troops were sent in to aid local police in their search for the kidnappers. The body of Laporte was subsequently found; apparently he had been murdered by his abductors. Late in the year Cross was released in exchange for passage to Cuba for his kidnappers. (*See* Canada; Trudeau.)

Ontario

Ontario, the economic balance wheel of Canada, suffered less than the rest of the country from the general slowdown in business activity. Buoyed by record exports from its manufacturers and resource industries, it held its unemployment rate to less than 5%.

Ontario continued to demonstrate political leadership among the provinces. It led other provinces in criticism of the federal government plans for tax reform and embarked on pattern-setting labor legislation, including outlawing discrimination in employment on the basis of sex.

Two Eskimos play a game of *aqsaaraq*, or tug-of-war, during the opening ceremonies of the First Arctic Winter Games in Yellowknife, N.W.T., in March.

"EDMONTON JOURNAL"

British Columbia and the Prairie Provinces

British Columbia widened its commercial and cultural ties with the United States and with countries in the Far East during 1970. The first stage of the Roberts Bank superport was completed, ending a reliance on the cramped and shallow harbor of Vancouver and signaling the start of a vast trade in coal to supply Japan's steel mills.

In the Manitoba legislature during 1970, the government of Premier Edward R. Schreyer came within a vote of defeat time and time again. A defeat in the legislature, if it had come, would have forced Schreyer to call an election barely a year after his New Democratic party (NDP) had been elected, forming the only avowedly Socialist government in North America. The speaker of the legislature, an NDP member, often cast the deciding vote to save the government. But in a crisis-ridden period at midyear, Premier Schreyer almost lost the support of an independent member who had previously been voting with the government. The crisis arose when Schreyer moved to introduce universal compulsory, government-operated automobile insurance that could have put many private insurance companies out of business. Schreyer finally made changes that ensured passage of the bill. He gave the industry a say in details of the plan and also cushioned its financial loss.

Saskatchewan, more than any other province in the Canadian West, felt the impact of the market slump in agriculture and the twin burdens of rising prices and tight money. Its Liberal government announced its first deficit budget in six years of office. Some pickup in wheat sales late in 1970 promised to lift the province out of its worst agricultural slump since 1955. By and large, however, farmers were moving out of the wheat business and into other grains or livestock, while some had left farming entirely and were seeking work elsewhere. The province's population in April was estimated at 948,000, down from 960,000 a year earlier.

With a potential labor shortage and, consequently, heavy pressure to increase wages looming on the horizon, the provincial government slapped down a 6% guideline for wage increases in the province. Unlike the identical national guidelines established by the federal Prices and Incomes Commission, Saskatchewan made specific moves of enforcement. It threatened to delay a series of provincial construction projects unless the guideline was observed, and it passed legislation at a special midsummer session of the provincial legislature as a general device to prevent strikes and stoppages. Plumbers and electricians struck for two weeks across the province in their struggle with employers and the government.

Alberta was another province obliged to abandon "pay-as-you-go" government financing in 1970. The Social Credit government budgeted for a deficit to provide for its growing commitments in social services and education.

JOE HOURIGAN FROM CANADIAN PRESS

René Lévesque, head of Quebec's nonviolent separatist Parti Quebecois, expresses grave disappointment after losing in the Quebec election.

Atlantic Provinces

Governments in two of the four Atlantic Provinces were turned out in election upsets during 1970. In both cases the results seemed to portray nothing more complicated than a desire for change.

In Nova Scotia, the Progressive Conservative government of Premier G. I. Smith was nudged aside in October by the Liberal party, led by Gerald Regan. The Liberals captured 23 seats of the 46-seat legislature and were assured of an effective majority by the promised support of the Socialists, the New Democratic party, which got two seats.

The defeat of Liberal Premier Louis J. Robichaud in New Brunswick was considered less surprising. The Progressive Conservatives under Richard Hatfield attracted enough votes from the French-speaking population to achieve power, winning 32 of the 58 seats in the legislature.

CENTRAL AFRICAN REPUBLIC. In February, June, and August 1970 President Jean-Bedel Bokassa carried out certain reshuffles in his government, but little was known on the outside about the internal development of the Central African Republic during the year. In foreign affairs, the year was characterized by considerable tension in relations between the Central African Republic and France and by a marked turn toward the East on the part of the nation's leaders.

Relations between France and the Central African Republic, already cool as a result of the expulsion of some 24 French technicians working in the diamond concerns in November 1969, became progressively more bitter. Time and again French technical assistants were accused of subversive activities and expelled from the country. Finally the government asked the French ambassador to leave.

On April 19 Bokassa announced that the Central African Republic had recognized East Germany. In May relations were established with Albania and Czechoslovakia, in February with Hungary. On July 6, an agreement for economic and technical cooperation with the Soviet Union was signed in Moscow. (*See in* CE: Central African Republic.)

CEYLON. The major development in Ceylon during 1970 was the election of a left-wing coalition government headed by former Prime Minister Sirimavo Bandaranaike. Ceylon's three leftist parties had banded together and defeated the ruling United National party (UNP) in a landslide victory on May 27. The UNP managed to win only 19 of the 151 seats in the House of Representatives. Mrs. Bandaranaike, who had been prime minister from 1960 to 1965, replaced Dudley Senanayake as the head of government on May 29.

The new government immediately began to implement the socialist policies it had promised. Diplomatic recognition was extended to the governments of East Germany, North Korea, and North Vietnam. Relations with Israel were broken off, and Mrs. Bandaranaike stated they would not be resumed until Israel withdrew from the Arab territories it had occupied since the June 1967 war. The U.S. Peace Corps program in Ceylon was canceled, and the Peace Corps volunteers were given 90 days to leave the country.

The new government's domestic program could only be described as revolutionary. It promised a new constitution to make Ceylon "a free, sovereign and independent republic," thus ending its status as a sovereign state in the Commonwealth of Nations. The government's aim was to create a socialist republic. Foreign banks and the British-owned companies that managed tea, coconut, and rubber plantations were to be nationalized. As had been promised in the campaign, Mrs. Bandaranaike's government increased the weekly rice ration from two to four pounds per person.

In July the prime minister convened all members of the House of Representatives and announced that a constituent assembly would frame the new constitution. The House duly passed the necessary resolution, and the task of drafting the new constitution was begun. (*See in* CE: Ceylon.)

Sirimavo Bandaranaike, the prime minister of Ceylon, arrived in Paris on a state visit in September.

AGIP FROM PICTORIAL PARADE

POPPERFOTO FROM PICTORIAL PARADE

A rebel suspect, his hands tied behind his back, is questioned by French troops in Chad, where a war is being fought between Moslem tribesmen and the ruling Christian blacks.

CHAD. The killing of 11 French soldiers in an ambush in the northern region of Chad in October 1970 marked the lowest point of a deteriorating situation. The advantages of the French intervention, increasingly unpopular both in France and abroad, seemed clear only to President François Tombalbaye.

French forces in Chad, which had numbered some 2,500 men in 1969, were reduced to 1,900 in 1970. There was talk of repatriating the entire corps by 1971, leaving only some 900 troops to man permanent installations at Fort-Lamy, the capital, and a few dozen French officers and noncommissioned officers attached to the Chad national army as technical aids. However, even this modest plan was put in doubt by the ambush, which aroused a large body of opinion in France hostile to a policing operation carried on for the benefit of an independent African government facing internal opposition. Hostility had been increased, both by the ambiguous attitude of successive French governments and by

Tombalbaye's persistent refusal to acknowledge the extent of the conflict and his constant dismissal of the Chad National Liberation Front as mere "bandits." There was pressure in the French parliament to withdraw from Chad. (*See in* CE: Chad.)

CHEMISTRY. A team of scientists in 1970 made element 105 at the Lawrence Radiation Laboratory of the University of California at Berkeley. Sharing in the experiment were Albert Ghiorso, director of the heavy-ion linear accelerator (HILAC) at Berkeley, Dr. Matti Nurmia, Dr. Kari A. Y. Eskola, Pirkko Eskola, and James A. Harris.

The scientists made element 105 by bombarding californium 249 (element 98) with a narrow beam of 84-million-electron-volts nitrogen 15 in the HILAC. When a californium nucleus absorbed a nitrogen nucleus, four neutrons were emitted as the nucleus became element 105 with an atomic weight of 260. This isotope of element 105 has a half-life of about 1.6 seconds. It was identified by its rate of decay and by the appearance of lawrencium 256 (element 103), into which it decays. The Berkeley scientists also suggested the name rutherfordium for element 104, a subject of dispute.

University of Chicago physicist Albert V. Crewe revealed that he had "seen" single uranium and thorium atoms, magnified a million times with a scanning electron microscope. The key development of Dr. Crewe's modified microscope—capable of detecting a single atom less than two angstroms in diameter—was an ultra-small source of electrons. Crewe had developed the source in six years at a cost of between $750,000 and $1 million, provided by the U.S. Atomic Energy Commission.

Crewe predicted that within two years it should be possible to see atoms as small as those of iron and copper. Although the ability to view atoms and determine their arrangement in molecules would markedly affect all science, Crewe believed that medicine, biochemistry, and genetics would especially benefit.

Whether or not polywater exists remained an unsettled question in 1970. Evidence continued to pile up on both sides of the question of the existence of water in polymeric form.

Polywater, or anomalous water, is made by condensing water in silica or borosilicate capillary tubes with diameters of one to ten microns (thousandths of a millimeter). The material produced is stable to 300° C. and is up to 15 times more viscous than water. It has a density of 1.4 grams per cc, freezes below −10° C., and has a higher refractive index than water.

The discovery of polywater was announced by Soviet scientists in the mid-1960's. Some U.S. scientists followed the Russians' method of preparation. By 1969, infrared and Raman spectroscopic studies of the substance—both in and out of the capillaries in which it had been produced—led them to propose that the material was a true high polymer, consisting of H_2O monomer units.

Those scientists who believe that polywater does not exist think that the properties of the questioned substance stem from impurities in the water. Some workers who analyzed samples found them to contain high concentrations of sulfate, potassium, and chlorine, plus carbonate, nitrate, borates, and silicates. No group, however, had produced more than a few milligrams of polywater—and it was

Agricultural chemists (right) discovered an active synthetic attractant named "grandlure," to trap the boll weevil (above).

COURTESY, U.S. DEPARTMENT OF AGRICULTURE

felt that the question of its existence would be settled only when larger samples became available for analysis.

Scientists at the University of Miami (Fla.) believed they discovered minute quantities of amino acids in lunar material brought back by the Apollo moon mission. The natural occurrence of amino acids on the moon would influence theories of the chemical evolution of life. Other groups studying lunar material, however, either failed to detect amino acids or were unready to announce conclusions. The minute quantities that were involved generated questions of sample contamination. (*See in* CE: Chemistry.)

WIDE WORLD

Soviet grand master Tigran Petrosian (left) and U.S. champion Bobby Fischer play a fourth-round game in the world chess tournament in Belgrade. The Soviet Union won.

CHESS. The greatest chess match of 1970, later termed the match of the century, was played in Belgrade, Yugoslavia, between March 28 and April 5. It set a team of ten of the Soviet Union's best players, led by current world champion Boris Spassky, against ten players from the rest of the world. Spassky played Danish grand master Bent Larsen and withdrew after three of the four rounds, having won one game, lost one, and drawn one. Bobby Fischer of the United States played on the second board against former world champion Tigran Petrosian and scored two wins and two draws. The Soviet Union finally won the match, $20\frac{1}{2}$–$19\frac{1}{2}$.

The Belgrade match marked an apparent end to Fischer's 18-month absence from international chess. After Belgrade, he remained in Yugoslavia to win decisively both the "blitz" tournament at Hercegnovi and the Tournament of Peace at Rovinj and Zagreb. He also won the invitational tournament at Buenos Aires, Argentina, in July and August. Although he had not taken part in the U.S. Zonal Tournament, the International Chess Federation agreed to allow him to play in the Interzonal Tournament at Palma, Spain, in November if one of the U.S. qualifiers would cede his place to Fischer.

Sammy Reshevsky won the U.S. Chess Championship, which was also the U.S. Zonal Tournament, in New York City on Dec. 17, 1969. Larsen won the U.S. Open Chess Championship in Boston, Mass., in August. A U.S. student team took the world team title at Haifa, Israel; the meet was boycotted by the Soviet Union, the winner for the preceding six years, and other Communist nations.

The first chess game to be played in outer space took place aboard Soyuz 9 in June between Soviet cosmonauts A. Nikolayev and V. Sevastyanov. The world's first computer chess tournament was played in New York City. (*See in* CE: Chess.)

CHILE. In 1970 Chile became the first nation in the world to vote a Marxist regime into power by popular election. The Marxist candidate Salvador Allende secured the presidency by a very narrow margin. Allende, running against two other candidates, won 39,000 more votes than the second-place candidate, the conservative Jorge Alessandri Rodriguez. He failed, however, to win an absolute majority. The final choice between Allende and Alessandri was made by the Congress.

On October 24 Allende was elected president by a special session of both houses of Congress. The vote was 153 in favor of Allende, 35 for Alessandri, and 7 abstentions.

The main campaign issues centered around economic and social reform. Allende and the Christian Democratic candidate proposed similar programs, including a more radical agrarian reform,

Salvador Allende, the Marxist candidate, was elected president of Chile in 1970.

FREDERIC OHRINGER FROM NANCY PALMER AGENCY

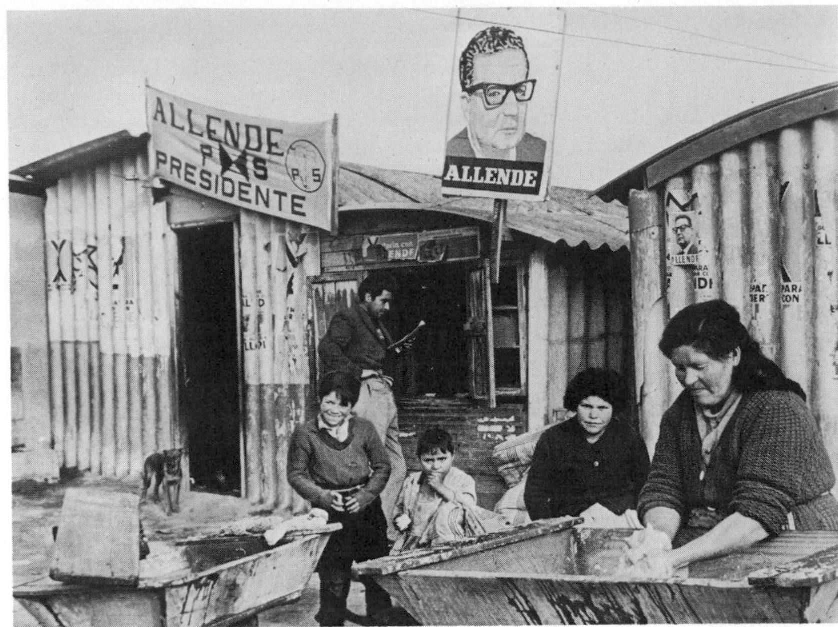

President Allende had his greatest support among the poor of Chile, many of whom papered their houses with his campaign posters.
CAMERA PRESS FROM PIX

nationalization of basic industry, and control over foreign trade. Alessandri's program accepted the reforms already carried out by former President Eduardo Frei Montalva, but did not go beyond them.

Two days before the confirmation of Allende as president an extremist shot the army's commander, Gen. René Schneider Chereau. Martial law was declared and tight security measures imposed. Fear of extensive nationalization of private enterprises and of possible political repression was reflected in the sudden emigration of technicians, professionals, and wealthy persons. Industrial production temporarily fell by 9%, and sales in some industries fell by 80%. The Christian Democrats obtained several modifications in the constitution designed to insure the nation's democratic traditions, including guarantees on the right to vote, freedom of the press, freedom of opinion, and freedom of education. (*See also* Latin America. *See in* CE: Chile.)

CHINA, PEOPLE'S REPUBLIC OF. Less official information from the People's Republic of China was available in 1970 than at any time since the beginning of the devastating "cultural revolution" in 1966. China watchers suggested two explanations for the reduced flow of information: one opinion held that government leaders were using means other than the official press to publicize policy, while the other interpretation claimed that policy and power disputes in Peking, the capital, were slowing the normal executive procedures.

Internal Affairs

The Communist party in China, which had been badly disrupted by the cultural revolution, was still not reorganized in 1970—despite the resolution of the Ninth National Party Congress in April 1969 to rebuild. According to the most recent information available, fewer than 50 out of 2,000 counties had party committees, and there were no provincial committees at all. It was assumed that the rebuilding of the party was going so slowly because of the requirement that every party official be an irreproachable Maoist.

In August and September, the party's Central Committee held its second plenary session since the party congress and concluded by announcing plans to convene the Fourth National People's Congress. The congress was not expected to meet until the party had been substantially rebuilt, however. The Third People's Congress had reelected Liu Shao-chi as chairman of the People's Republic of China in 1965; since Liu was officially purged during the cultural revolution, it was expected that the Fourth Congress would elect a successor to him.

In the meantime, Communist China remained without an official chief of state. However, at the nation's 21st-anniversary celebration on October 1, Politburo Chairman Mao Tse-tung and Vice-Chairman Lin Piao were officially designated "supreme commander and deputy supreme commander of the whole nation and the whole army." This designation caused speculation that Mao and Lin would be chosen chief and deputy chief of state at the upcoming party congress.

In March, a meeting of the State Council, or cabinet, was announced for the first time since 1966. Government ministries in 1970 were repairing the damage of the last four years; some ministries were apparently being merged, and one appointment was announced during the year: Chien Chin-kuang, new minister of light industry. Foreign diplomats in Peking reported that Chen Yi was still officially considered to be foreign minister, though he had not acted as such for two years; ill health was supposedly keeping him from his duties.

From all indications, the army was least disrupted by the cultural revolution and quickest to revive, partly as a result of Lin Piao's position as defense minister. As a result, by 1969 the army had become the dominant force in China, and many state offices listed military men in key posts in 1970. Provincial committee lists showed an increase in local army influence, especially in the provinces near the Soviet border. All former field marshals (except Lin Piao) were absent from the official May Day celebration in Peking, but several regional commanders were present.

Communist China launched its first earth satellite on April 24, a 381-pound orbiting spacecraft broadcasting a song, "The East Is Red." On October 14, China set off another in its series of nuclear blasts at the Lop Nor testing area in Sinkiang region; it was an atmospheric explosion, estimated at three megatons. Coincidentally, both the Soviet Union and the United States also set off nuclear explosions on that day, the first day of the 25th-birthday celebration of the United Nations (UN).

China's universities reopened in September for the first time since the start of the cultural revolution, when all schools were closed down. The new university curriculum was described as Maoist, indicating that studies would incorporate Mao's thought, that students would work in factories or on farms as part of their course of study, and that science and engineering would be emphasized. Liberal arts courses were apparently no longer offered, and the normal study course was shortened from four or more years to two or three.

In order to minimize the prestige of an education and prevent the forming of an intellectual class in society, Mao decreed in 1968 that educated young people should be sent to the rural areas to live. In May 1970 the *People's Daily* newspaper reported that, since December 1968, several million graduates had been moved to the country. Resettlement was praised as the best means to bring education and technology to the peasants.

The Chinese economy during 1970 was reported to be growing at an unprecedented rate, and it was believed in the West that the official government claims of economic progress were truer than they had been for several years. Many industries had supposedly surpassed their yearly quotas by October 1, harvests were said to be well above those of recent years, and domestic petroleum production was claimed to be sufficient to fill all the country's needs.

The year 1970 seemed to be a record year for the Chinese economy, apparently topping previous highs in gross national product, foreign trade, industrial production, and farm yields. Yet these gains were not expected to improve the standard of living much. It was estimated that the population

Several hundred thousand people assembled in Peking to watch a mass display by the armed forces, in celebration of the 21st anniversary of the People's Republic of China in October.

CAMERA PRESS FROM PIX

EASTFOTO

Prince Norodom Sihanouk (left), Cambodia's deposed head of state, attended China's 21st anniversary festival with Politburo Chairman Mao Tse-tung.

was growing by 10 million to 15 million a year and that this increase would nullify economic gains. The government began a new austerity drive at the beginning of the year and continued to stockpile food and strategic materials. These measures were officially explained as preparations for a possible war with the Soviet Union, with which China was continuing its border dispute.

Foreign Affairs

With the subsiding of domestic turmoil, Peking was able to give attention to foreign relations in 1970, in contrast to the isolation of the cultural revolution. The Chinese diplomatic coup of the year was official recognition by Canada, which was granted on October 13 after two years of negotiation. Shortly after, Italy extended diplomatic recognition to Communist China; Belgium was expected to follow suit in the near future. China and Yugoslavia also exchanged ambassadors during the year. During the height of the cultural revolution, all but one of the more than 40 Chinese ambassadors had been recalled to Peking; by October 1970, 28 of China's embassies had ambassadors once again.

China agreed in 1970 to resume its talks with the United States in Warsaw, Poland, after a two-year suspension. Sessions were held on January 20 and February 20; a third session, scheduled for May 20, was canceled by the Chinese because of the U.S. invasion of Cambodia. Instead, on that date Chairman Mao made a rare public statement urging the world to revolt against U.S. imperialism.

However, such statements did not detract from Communist China's interest in trading with the United States, following the U.S. Department of State decree of Dec. 19, 1969, that U.S. companies might sell nonstrategic items to China and buy Chinese products for resale on foreign markets. A Chinese agreement with an Italian firm of truck manu-

The Chinese launched their first oceangoing oil tanker, the *Taching No. 27,* in June 1970. The tanker was designed and built by the Chinese using rolled steel from their own mills.

EASTFOTO

facturers in July specifically asked that the engines of the trucks purchased be made by General Motors. The Chinese further showed willingness to improve relations with the United States when in July they released the Most Rev. James Edward Walsh, a Roman Catholic bishop from Maryland who had been in prison in China for 12 years.

Premier Chou En-lai fulfilled the duties of foreign minister, greeting and talking with foreign visitors and delegations, making diplomatic rounds in Peking, and making state visits to other countries. A long foreign tour, planned for the end of the year, was to take him to Southern Yemen, Romania, and France, as well as Tanzania and Zambia, but did not occur and apparently was postponed. The Chinese had agreed to build a 1,000-mile railroad from the port of Dar es Salaam, Tanzania, to landlocked Zambia. They were also building a naval base for the Tanzanians at Dar es Salaam. The French government sent a delegation headed by André Bettencourt, minister for planning and territorial development, to confer in Peking in July, and Chou gave a rare interview for French television.

Communist China's border dispute with the Soviet Union eased sufficiently in 1970 that the two countries resumed talks over the dispute in January. The two exchanged ideological polemics in connection with the 100th anniversary of the birth of Nikolai Lenin on April 22. Observers believed that the Inner Mongolian region was partitioned during the year to improve the Chinese border defenses, but there were no reports that the fighting had resumed.

In an attempt to strengthen its position as head of the Communist bloc in Asia, Peking resumed relations with North Korea, welcomed Prince Norodom Sihanouk of Cambodia after he was deposed by a military coup in March, and hosted a subsequent conference of Indochinese Communist leaders. The Chinese also helped Sihanouk set up a government-in-exile.

Once again, the Communist Chinese made a bid for admission to the UN as the representatives of the Chinese nation. At the UN's 25th-anniversary session, Tanzania and France supported the bid, and Canada announced it would vote for approval; nevertheless, the proposal was once again defeated. (*See in* CE: China, People's Republic of.)

CITIES AND URBAN AFFAIRS. The problems of the cities continued to grow and multiply in 1970 with no prospect of satisfactory solutions in sight. There was a greatly increased public consciousness of blight and pollution during the year, and some major efforts were made to deal with these problems. Nevertheless, major cities in the United States and the world suffered some of the worst smog-filled days in their history. Added to crime in the streets was the increased activity of the politically motivated left-wing urban guerrillas and right-wing terrorists.

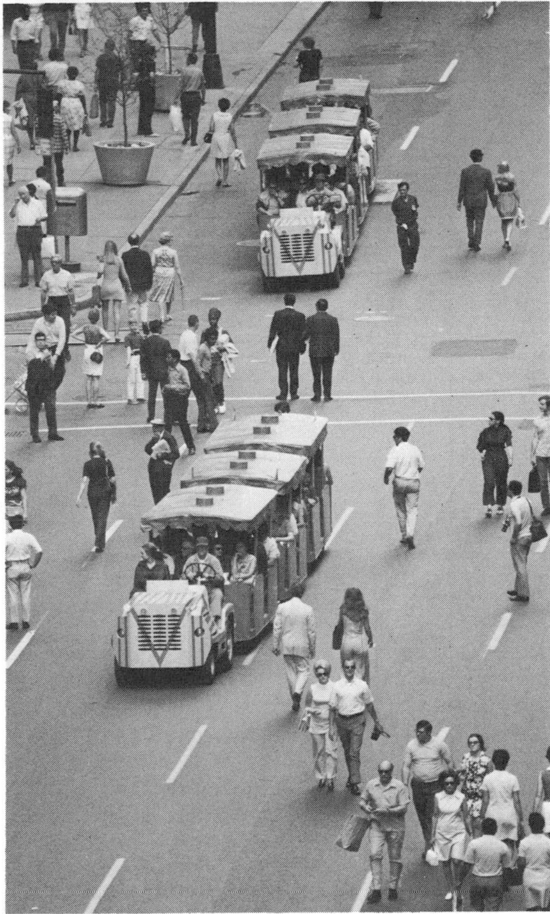

"THE NEW YORK TIMES"

New York City's Mayor Lindsay closed part of Fifth Avenue to auto traffic as an experiment during the year.

Bombs and Banners

Planting bombs and creating bomb scares became a favorite tactic of extremists in the United States during 1970. In the course of the year there were about 3,000 actual bombings and some 50,000 bomb threats. Schools, department stores, skyscrapers, police stations, and civic buildings were favorite targets of the bombers. Some of the worst incidents took place in New York City. A rash of bomb threats occurred there during March after the offices of three large companies were bombed.

Prime suspects in many of the bombing incidents were members of the radical Weatherman faction of the Students for a Democratic Society. Early in March an explosion demolished a town house in New York City's Greenwich Village. An investigation revealed that bombs were being made in the basement of the building and that persons involved in the incident were known to be connected with the Weathermen. A short time later another explosion occurred in a building where

Angry because garbage had not been picked up for days, some residents of Brownsville in New York City started garbage fires and looted stores.
"THE NEW YORK TIMES"

bombs were apparently being made. Black Panther literature was found at the scene. Although in several instances Black Panthers were charged with conspiracy, there was no evidence directly connecting Panthers to any of the bombing incidents during the year.

Two U.S. Congressional subcommittee hearings on bombings were held in July. Officials from New York State and California testified that the planting of bombs was not limited to radical leftists; extremist right-wing groups, such as the Minutemen, were believed responsible for some of the bombing incidents during the year. In Denver, Colo., anti-integrationists blew up 23 school buses. Members of a right-wing group in Texas were convicted of destroying 36 school buses, and rightists were suspected of having bombed a liberal Houston, Tex., radio station.

Kenneth A. Gibson takes the oath of office to become the 34th mayor of Newark, N.J. He is the first black mayor of a large Eastern city.
UPI COMPIX

In addition to the increase in bombings, there was an increase during 1970 in the number of attacks against police officers. By the end of the summer, 15 policemen had been murdered in the United States; by contrast, seven had been killed in unprovoked attacks in all of 1969. One of the cities in which this form of urban guerrilla activity was most evident was Chicago. In a single one-month period three police officers were ambushed and killed. Chicago, however, had been found to have the highest rate of reported instances of police brutality of all the major U.S. cities. (*See* Police.)

The increase in urban terrorism resulted in a flurry of proposals for new laws on the state and national levels alike. A U.S. Bureau of Mines report issued in April showed that 23 states had either poor regulations governing the purchase of dynamite and other explosives or no restrictions at all. The federal government proposed legislation for the licensing of persons engaged in manufacturing and selling explosives and for broader federal law enforcement measures.

Again in 1970, for the second consecutive year, there was a decrease in major urban disorders but an increase in smaller disturbances. A new phenomenon was demonstrations against, and assaults on, antiwar protesters by superpatriots and establishment supporters of the Administration of U.S. President Richard M. Nixon.

On May 8 a mob of construction workers (known as "hard-hats" because of their protective headgear) rampaged through New York City's financial district in a counterdemonstration against antiwar protesters. The construction workers attacked and beat 65 youths and four policemen and also charged the City Hall. The flag at City Hall had been lowered to half-mast in honor of the students who had been killed at Kent State University at Kent, Ohio. (*See* Colleges and Universities.)

New York City's Mayor John V. Lindsay denounced the police for failing to control the construction workers and also called for an investigation. During the following week, white- and blue-collar workers alike, carrying signs with "patriotic" slogans and waving U.S. flags, marched in protest against Mayor Lindsay. The marchers tied up traffic, and some of the more unruly elements stormed buildings and demanded that the flag be displayed.

Racial violence flared in the resort city of Asbury Park, N.J., early in July. About 100 persons were injured, 46 of them from gunshot wounds. No one specific cause was given for the rioting and looting that broke out in the black community, but unemployment and discrimination in employment were thought to be major factors. There were also minor disturbances in several smaller towns near Asbury Park.

After four nights of disorder in New Bedford, Mass., the violence appeared to be over when a car containing white youths reportedly entered the black community, fired a shotgun into a group of people, and killed a black youth. To end the violence, the area had to be evacuated. During the year the unemployment rate in New Bedford became the second highest in the nation.

Severe racial troubles broke out in Miami, Fla., in June, sparked by protest against a white-owned supermarket. Allegedly, spoiled food was being sold and black employees were underpaid.

Growing hostility in the huge Mexican-American area of Los Angeles exploded into violence in August. A riot began during a Mexican-American antiwar protest, and before it was over, 60 persons had been injured and three killed, including the Mexican-American newspaper columnist Ruben Salazar. He was struck by a tear-gas container fired into a café by police. The container was designed to penetrate walls and was not intended for riot-control use.

The virtual race war in Cairo, Ill., continued during 1970. After a series of sniping incidents state troopers equipped with an armored car were sent in to keep the peace. Black and white youths alike rioted in Chicago during a free rock concert. Three persons were shot. (*See also* Race Relations.)

No Calcuttas

The condition of Calcutta, India, was pointed out during the year as an example of the type of situation in which all cities could find themselves if drastic measures were not taken in the areas of pollution and population control. An estimated one million people in Calcutta were without sewers, proper roads, or electricity. It was also estimated that perhaps more than a million people were without any type of housing at all. Per capita income had dropped to $2 a year.

During the summer, cities along the East coast of the United States were trapped under a heavy blanket of smog. The amount of pollution in the air almost reached a level dangerous to health. In New York City air pollution reached a crisis level late in July, and the mayor considered banning automobiles from parts of the city. The pollution problem was accompanied by an acute electrical power shortage. Tokyo was plagued by a dangerously high level of oxidants for two weeks in July, and 9,000 persons were treated for pollution-related ailments.

On April 22 the first Earth Day was observed in cities and towns across the United States, to awaken the public consciousness to the dangers of environmental pollution. (*See* Conservation.)

In September President Nixon gave his approval to the Model Cities program and announced that the program would be a basic element in the Administration's plans for urban aid. The announcement followed a long debate about the value of the program. The Administration was in favor of allowing increased state and local control over federal funds for the project, and this plan was endorsed by the National League of Cities and the U.S. Conference of Mayors. It was announced that three different plans for channeling funds would be tested in a dozen or more cities in the near future.

Earlier in the year urban renewal programs were threatened by cutbacks in federal grants. The Conference of Mayors denounced the budget cuts and urged the federal government to reorder its priorities by diverting funds from such programs as space and highway building to programs designed to aid urban areas. (*See also* Housing; Space Exploration Special Report.)

Sidewalk art on Madison Avenue between 78th and 79th streets in New York City is the work of artist Alexander Calder.

WIDE WORLD

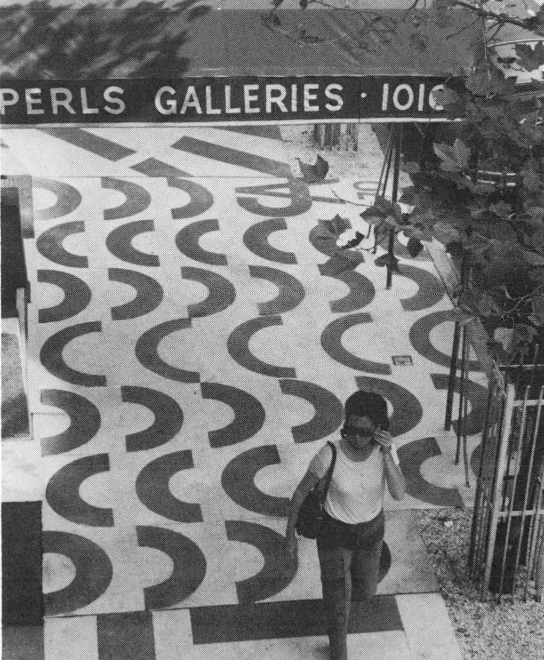

In 1970 New York City experimented with the closing of a section of Madison Avenue to vehicular traffic and turned the street into a shopping mall several times. A parade of 1,000 bicyclists was staged in New York City to dramatize the role that bicycles could play in solving urban traffic problems. Mayor Lindsay said that special bicycle lanes would be considered. Bicyclists also lobbied for their cause in Chicago.

Secretary of the Interior Walter J. Hickel announced in August that his department would promote a program for developing areas within U.S. cities that would be closed to motor vehicles. The proposed landscaped streets would be termed "green belts." Hickel hoped for at least $25 million to carry out the project. In October President Nixon signed a bill authorizing $463 million over a three-year period to aid cities and states in constructing waste disposal systems.

Civic Servants

Revelations of scandal and corruption shocked residents of Newark, N.J., during 1970. Mayor Hugh J. Addonizio, while being tried on charges of extortion and conspiracy, was defeated in the mayoral election by a black candidate, Kenneth A. Gibson. Addonizio was later convicted of the charges. In San Diego, Calif., Mayor Frank Curran and several city officials were indicted on charges of bribery and conspiracy.

Policemen, firemen, and sanitation workers in New York City demanded huge increases in wages and benefits and raised the possibility of a strike if their demands were not met by December 31. Municipal employees in Atlanta, Ga., and San Francisco, Calif., staged strikes during the year. (*See also* Crime; United States. *See in* CE: City; Municipal Government.)

COIN COLLECTING. Director of the Mint Mary Thomas Brooks in August 1970 announced the establishment of a U.S. mint numismatic service department. The mint does not sell coins, except proof and mint sets of the current year, but it does produce various medals for sale to individuals. Information may be obtained from the United States Mint, Numismatic Service, Philadelphia, Pa., 19106.

A silver medal was struck in 1970 to honor the late Senator Everett M. Dirksen.

COURTESY, AMERICAN NUMISMATIC ASSOCIATION

The hobbies of collecting coins, paper money, medals, and tokens attracted many new devotees during the year. Membership in the American Numismatic Association (ANA) increased from 24,837 to 25,751. Although there was some slowdown in commercial activities, prices in the bourse and auction at the 1970 ANA convention were firmer and better than had been expected. Price changes in the 1971 edition of the standard 'A Guide Book of United States Coins' were erratic in practically all series. The prices of colonial coins, pre-1878 silver dollars, and some commemorative coins advanced, but many other coins dropped in value.

Nations issuing commemorative coins in the year included Australia (Captain Cook), Austria (Franz Lehar and Innsbruck University), Canada (Manitoba), Czechoslovakia (Bratislava National Theater), East Germany (Heinrich Hertz and Johann Friedrich Böttger), West Germany (1972 Olympic Games), India (Mahatma Gandhi), Israel (Mikveh Israel), New Zealand (Captain Cook), Norway (liberation from Nazi occupation), Panama (Central American and Caribbean Games), Poland (People's Republic), U.S.S.R. (birth of Nikolai Lenin), and Western Samoa (Robert Louis Stevenson). Among new coins issued for circulation were

This dollar bill with an unusual serial number was spotted by a collector in a small grocery store.

COURTESY, AMERICAN NUMISMATIC ASSOCIATION

the first coinage of the Turks and Caicos Islands and a set of decimal coins by Bermuda. A number of countries issued special coins to promote the war against hunger waged by the Food and Agriculture Organization of the United Nations.

In the United States the issuance of a dollar to honor the late President Dwight D. Eisenhower was held up pending the decision of Congress on whether to use silver in it. The same issue held up the striking of regular-issue half-dollars in 1970, though the mint was authorized to strike 2 million of them for inclusion in mint sets for 1970. During the year the U.S. mint struck coins for Costa Rica, Liberia, and the Philippines.

Pre-1965 silver coins all but disappeared from circulation in 1970. Many, presumably, were being held for speculation in the silver market. Speculators anticipated that a price rise would follow the late-year discontinuance of government silver sales.

The issuance of commemorative and other medals by private concerns increased as techniques for producing them in high quality at a relatively low cost advanced. Such medals appealed largely to collectors interested in art and historical themes.

Continuing a trend of recent years, collectors in growing numbers—impelled by the rising prices of most scarce U.S. coins—turned their interests to paper money, medals, and tokens. National nonprofit organizations represented these specialized fields—the Society of Paper Money Collectors and the Token and Medal Society. Both issued magazines and published books.

Two programs of interest to collectors received concrete impetus in 1970. An authentication service, expected to reduce the manufacture and sale of bogus coins, was formed. Under the sponsorship of the ANA, a $50,000 fund was raised to provide facilities for detecting counterfeit and altered coins made to defraud collectors and, through cooperation with federal agencies, for apprehending the makers. (*See also* Hobbies; Stamps. *See in* CE: Mint, U.S.; Money.)

COLLEGES AND UNIVERSITIES. During 1970, colleges and universities in the United States witnessed a disruption of normal activities that was of greater magnitude than ever before. The turmoil was largely a response to national issues—particularly the war in Southeast Asia and internal repression. Before year-end, campus disturbances had resulted in the deaths of several students as well as a massive destruction of property in universities throughout the nation.

The most shocking confrontation between students and authorities came in May at Kent State University, Kent, Ohio, where four students were shot to death by National Guardsmen. The Guardsmen had been called out by Ohio's Gov. James Rhodes to help quell disturbances in the town of Kent on Saturday, May 2. On Monday, May 4, while breaking up a demonstration protesting U.S.

UPI COMPIX

These students graduating from the University of Massachusetts, at Amherst, wore the symbols of peace and protest with their caps and gowns during graduation exercises on May 30.

involvement in Cambodia, Guardsmen fired into the crowd, killing the four students and injuring ten others. Apparently some of the victims had not been involved in the demonstration.

The following week a similar scene occurred at Jackson State College, Jackson, Miss., resulting in the deaths of 2 students and the wounding of 12 others. At Jackson State, a predominantly black coeducational school, police were called to answer a complaint that a crowd of black students was stoning passing cars. As police neared a women's dormitory, they were met by a crowd of about 100 men throwing rocks and bottles. They fired a volley of about 150 shots into the crowd and dormitory.

Both incidents triggered a nationwide reaction. Students rallies and strikes protesting the expansion of the Vietnam war and the deaths at Kent State and Jackson State were held across the country. The protest culminated in a march and rally in Washington, D.C., late in May.

After months of investigation into the factors precipitating the Kent State and Jackson State shootings, the President's Commission on Campus Unrest, headed by Pennsylvania's former Gov. William Scranton, issued its report in October. The report cited the war in Indochina as the most important cause of campus demonstrations. It also outlined a number of steps that could be taken to alleviate student tensions, among them action by the president to create better channels of communication between students and government officials. The report also stated that the use of deadly force by Guardsmen and police was completely unjustified in both instances. That conclusion had been

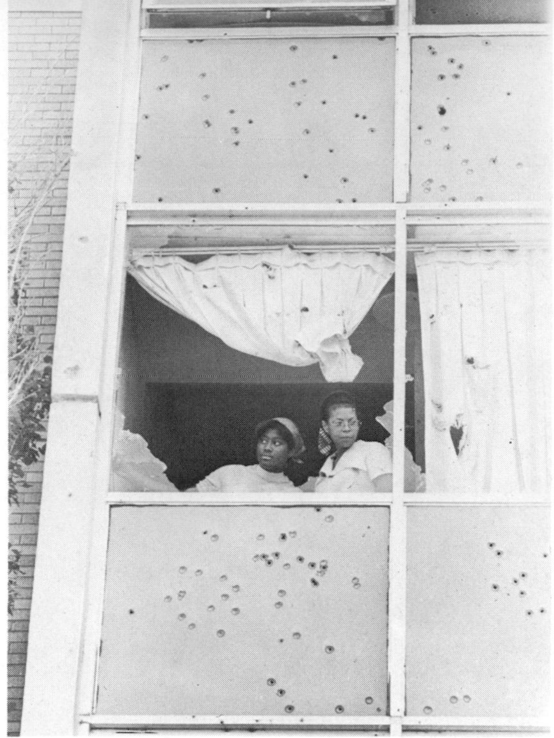

WIDE WORLD

A bullet-riddled window of a girls' dormitory at Jackson State College in Mississippi (above) is examined by two students. Two youths were killed here by police fire. National Guardsmen (below) aim their rifles at approaching students demonstrating on the Kent State campus in Ohio. Four students were killed.

JOHN P. FILO, © "VALLEY DAILY NEWS," TARENTUM, PA.

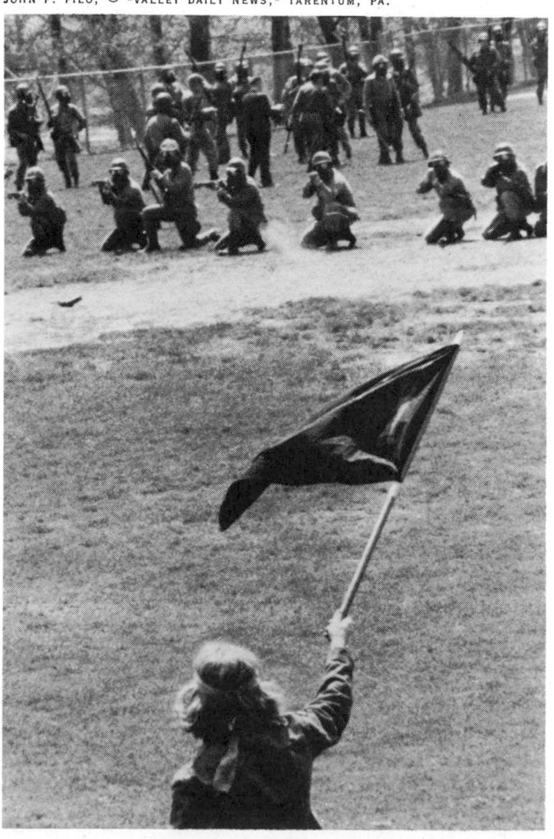

reached earlier by members of the Federal Bureau of Investigation (FBI) who conducted an inquiry into the Kent State incident. The FBI report quoted Guard officers as stating that the lives of the Guardsmen were not in danger and that it was not a shooting situation.

The FBI and Scranton commission reports were in direct contradiction to findings by local grand juries. A Hinds County, Miss., grand jury declared that policemen "were justified" in shooting into the dormitory. Similarly, an Ohio grand jury exonerated the National Guard from any blame in the Kent State killings. To underscore its position, the jury issued an indictment naming 25 persons on various charges, including rioting. Those indicted were students, instructors, and young nonstudents. No National Guardsmen were indicted.

The widening of the war and the Kent and Jackson State killings had a profound effect on young people. A new legion of moderate, previously uninvolved students joined the antiwar movement. Many of these students responded by actively campaigning for "peace candidates" in U.S. senatorial and Congressional elections. To promote student activism within the system, a number of institutions followed the lead of Princeton University and recessed classes for two weeks before the November elections to allow students to campaign.

Concern over the war, repression, and racism affected even the traditional commencement rites of a number of U.S. colleges. While many colleges retained the customary graduation rites, others instituted such changes as abandoning the cap and gown, delivering commencement addresses reflecting the concerns of the campuses, and substituting a moment of silence for a convocation. A number of schools canceled commencement exercises entirely and mailed diplomas to students instead.

Despite the willingness of many students to try to change the system from within, others continued to employ guerrilla tactics. The most dramatic instance of terrorist activity occurred at the University of Wisconsin, where a bomb explosion destroyed the Army Mathematics Research Center in August, killing one student. (*See* Crime.)

In an effort to avoid similar reprisals, other universities were beginning to sever their connections with military-financed research facilities. Massachusetts Institute of Technology announced plans to make Charles Stark Draper Laboratory, where research on guided missiles was carried out, independent of the university. Similar separations had also occurred between Stanford University and the Stanford Research Institute and between Princeton University and the Institute for Defense Analyses.

There was one happy exception to the general rule of violent confrontations on campus during 1970. In May violence was averted by careful planning and cooperation between students, faculty, and administration at Yale University. The campus was selected as the site for a protest over police treatment of the Black Panthers, eight of

Joseph Rhodes, Jr., a student at Harvard University, was named a member of the President's Commission on Campus Unrest by U.S. President Richard M. Nixon. U.S. Vice-President Spiro T. Agnew criticized Rhodes for his views on student unrest.
WIDE WORLD

whom were facing trial for murder and kidnapping in New Haven, Conn. Although 4,000 U.S. Marines and paratroopers and several units of the National Guard were deployed to enforce calm at Yale, the 12,000 protesters who had turned out for the rally and demonstration enjoyed a relatively peaceful weekend.

While most of the nation's colleges and universities were preoccupied with political and social issues during the year, a few academic concerns did make the news. In New York City higher education was opened essentially to all city high school graduates. In September more than 35,000 freshmen enrolled in the City University of New York. Blacks and Puerto Ricans comprised over 33% of the incoming class in comparison to under 20% in 1969.

A three-year study undertaken by the College Entrance Examination Board's Commission on Tests produced findings that may spur an educational revolution. In studying the College Board testing program, which serves as an important admission criterion for 2 million college applicants each year, the commission declared the present test to be "insensitive, narrowly conceived, and inimical to the interests of many youths." It recommended that the examinations be broadened to assess not only verbal and quantitative facility but also abilities in a wide range of areas from art and music to mechanics and social leadership.

In addition to the other woes besetting the campuses during 1970, an acute financial crisis was descending. Higher education felt the strain of rising costs, reduced grants and research funds, and a faltering stock market that diminished endowment funds. (*See also* Education. *See in* CE: Universities and Colleges.)

COLOMBIA. On April 19, 1970, presidential and congressional elections were held in Colombia. Misael Pastrana Borrero, presidential candidate of the National Front coalition of Conservative and Liberal parties, won 1,614,419 votes, as against 1,557,782 cast for Gustavo Rojas Pinilla, representing the National Popular Alliance party (Anapo). Two other contenders, Belisario Betancur and Evaristo Sourdis, polled a total of 805,891 votes between them.

Supporters of the narrowly defeated Rojas Pinilla, alleging electoral fraud, staged demonstrations that threatened to get out of hand, and a state of siege was imposed from April 21 until May 15. President Carlos Lleras Restrepo appealed to all four candidates to restore political harmony. Rojas Pinilla said there could be no dialogue with the National Front unless the government freed political prisoners, accepted Anapo's basic ideology, and recognized that electoral fraud had been widespread. Lleras ordered a recount. Pastrana's victory was officially confirmed shortly before the new Congress assembled on July 20, and he was duly sworn in on August 7. The National Front had an effective majority of 18 in the Senate and 14 in the House of Representatives.

Although sound financial policies and firm coffee prices strengthened the country's economic growth, business confidence was shaken after the April elections. It seemed unlikely that confidence would be fully restored until the Pastrana government demonstrated its ability to win congressional cooperation. (*See in* CE: Colombia.)

COMMONWEALTH OF NATIONS. In 1970 the number of full members of the Commonwealth of Nations rose from 28 to 31 with the accession of three Pacific countries—Tonga on June 4, Western Samoa (the first independent non-Commonwealth state to join) on August 28, and Fiji on October 10. British plans for resuming arms sales to South Africa aroused unusually bitter opposition from several African leaders who threatened either to leave the Commonwealth or to call for Great Britain's expulsion at the Commonwealth Heads of Government Conference to be held in Singapore on Jan. 14–22, 1971.

The choice of Singapore reflected an earlier preoccupation with an area where Great Britain—as reaffirmed at a Southeast Asia Treaty Organization meeting in July—stood committed to partnership with Australia, New Zealand, Singapore, and Malaysia in a five-power Commonwealth defense force. For the Conservative government of Great Britain, elected on June 18, this policy interlocked with that of safeguarding the Cape of Good Hope route to the Far East (by honoring the Simonstown, South Africa, naval agreement) at a time when Soviet naval strength in the Indian Ocean and the growth of ideological divisions in Africa together posed a political challenge to Western interests. For Britain's African critics, however, the real threat to the Commonwealth was racism, not political ideology—a point made very plainly in exchanges over arms sales during the United Nations (UN) 25th-anniversary session in October.

Africa

The ending in mid-January of Nigeria's civil war prefaced a continuing period of rehabilitation in this most densely populated of African states. In the same area, Ghana's civilian government, grappling with the formidable legacy of the country's earlier departure from democratic rule, found that measures to expel aliens and limit foreign enterprise failed to solve its persistent financial problems. The Gambia—which on April 24 became a republic within the Commonwealth—faced the reality of Senegal's retreat from moves toward their political union.

In 1970, however, it became clearer than ever that the continent's ideological fulcrum was on the fringe of the white-dominated southern bloc: South Africa, Portuguese Africa, and Rhodesia (which declared itself a republic on March 2). A Communist Chinese interest-free loan to Tanzania and Zambia of about $403 million for building the Tanzam Railway was announced in July, and this project, scheduled for completion in 1975, was formally inaugurated by Zambia's President Kenneth Kaunda on October 26.

Kenya and Uganda, committed to "Africanization," continued to expel Asians (a process that had badly strained Great Britain's capacity to absorb immigrants). In order to nationalize foreign-owned enterprises, Kenya embarked in July on a so-called "tripartite" system to raise by 10% the proportion of Africans in employment. Kenya obtained an International Monetary Fund loan of $6.1 million to improve farming skills among its 90% rural population, while $60 million of British aid (of which $32.4 million represented the cancellation of previous debts) included $7.2 million for buying out British-owned farms. In Kenya, many of the Asian population were effectively deprived of citizenship. In Uganda, the state acquired a 60% share in private business concerns "to be paid for out of future profits" and simultaneously abolished the right to strike. Conditions in Tanzania (where a treason trial dragged on) were illustrated by Zanzibar's continued subjection to the arbitrary rule of Sheikh Abeid Karume and by the large number of political prisoners held without trial.

During Zambia's six years of independence its imports from South Africa had dropped in proportion to its total imports. By September 1970 Zambia's economy had improved enough to allow the signing of a trade embargo against South Africa, Portugal, and Rhodesia. On June 15, the UN Security Council's sanctions committee reported that Rhodesia's total exports in 1969, valued at about $336 million, were still 30% below the 1965 (pre-rebellion) level but 24% higher than in 1968. The committee also reported that European immigration remained substantial and that recorded cases of suspected sanctions-breaking had increased. On September 2, the Commonwealth committee on sanctions recommended their continuance. Malawi's relationship with the southern bloc was demonstrated in May by the visit of South Africa's Prime Minister Balthazar J. Vorster to President H. Kamuzu Banda (his first to a black African state) and by the opening of a rail link to the Mozambique coast at Nacala for potential exports of Malawi's hitherto untapped bauxite reserves.

Other Countries

From Indian elections in March, Prime Minister Indira Gandhi's government emerged with a greatly reduced majority—suggesting a political trend to the right. In May, however, Ceylon's pro-Western government was routed at the polls by a left-wing coalition led by Mrs. Sirimavo Bandaranaike, pledged to secession from the Commonwealth and closer ties with Communist countries. Malaysia, under its new prime minister, Abdul Razak, remained free from racial outbreaks in 1970. In Pakistan, a trade agreement with the Soviet Union

Thousands of unemployed Africans lined up in Nairobi, Kenya, seeking jobs after President Jomo Kenyatta ordered the government and private companies to increase their work load by 10%.
WIDE WORLD

REX AUDLEY, "LONDON DAILY TELEGRAPH," FROM BEN ROTH AGENCY

"Naturally, we wouldn't expect the little matter of your ejection from the Commonwealth to disrupt your programme of aid for the developing countries!"

demonstrated a mutual interest in curbing Chinese Communist influence. Australia and New Zealand took a more serious interest in their aboriginal and Polynesian minorities and, while strengthening their regional links, remained anxious about the economic impact of Great Britain's potential membership in the European Economic Community, or Common Market.

Canada's Prime Minister Pierre Elliott Trudeau also visited Commonwealth countries in the Pacific, but Canada's strongest economic links (reinforced by its aid program) continued to be with the Caribbean area—where an April revolt by black power extremists in Trinidad and Tobago suggested a new danger to political stability. On February 23, Guyana became the first Commonwealth country in that area to assume republican status—as a "cooperative republic." (*See also* individual countries by name.)

COMMUNIST MOVEMENT. On the whole, 1970 was a year of stabilization within the Communist movement. The dissension within the Communist world caused by the 1968 Soviet-led invasion of Czechoslovakia was in the process of being healed, and Soviet relations with Communist China were slightly improved. The Communist movement, however, was unable to present to the world anything resembling a united front. In Eastern Europe, Romania and Yugoslavia persisted in following policies independent of the Soviet Union. In Indochina, the Soviet Union and China vied with each other for influence over the area.

100 Years After

The Soviet Union and China used the centenary celebrations of Nikolai Lenin's birth as an occasion for hurling invectives at one another. Both nations, contenders for leadership in the international Communist movement, recognized Lenin, along with Karl Marx, as the true architect of the modern Communist state. Each side accused the other of carrying out anti-Leninist policies.

On April 21–22 the Lenin centennial celebrations took place in Moscow. All of the world's Communist parties sent representatives, with the exception of China and Albania. The Soviet Union's Communist Party General Secretary Leonid I. Brezhnev opened the Moscow celebrations with a speech emphasizing the so-called "Brezhnev doctrine" of limited sovereignty for socialist nations. He also denounced the Chinese for their verbal attacks on the Soviet Union and referred to the Chinese as "apostates from the revolutionary Leninist cause."

Speeches were given and celebrations were held in the other Communist nations. Czechoslovakia's Communist Party First Secretary Gustav Husak justified the 1968 Soviet-led invasion of Czechoslovakia by saying that Czechoslovakia had strayed from the path of Leninism and therefore had suffered dire consequences. (*See* Czechoslovakia.)

The Hungarian government joined the Soviet Union in denouncing the Chinese Communists. Romania's Communist Party First Secretary Nicolae Ceausescu, however, stated that Romania would not take sides in the dispute between China and the Soviet Union. Ceausescu also rejected the Brezhnev doctrine of limited sovereignty by saying that each nation had the right to choose its own course independently and without fear of foreign intervention.

Yugoslavia's President Tito also remained aloof from the ideological struggle between the Chinese and Soviet Communists. He stated that Lenin believed each revolutionary movement had to proceed in its own way and that the experience of one Communist nation could not be used as a criterion for judging revolutionary movements in other nations.

The Chinese Communists used the occasion of the celebrations to launch one of their most vicious propaganda attacks against the Soviet Union. An editorial appearing in China's major newspapers denounced the Soviet leadership as a "social Fascist oligarchy." They accused Brezhnev and the other leaders of having betrayed Lenin. The articles warned that the Soviet Union was preparing to make war on China and called on the people of the world to overthrow the Soviet government.

Another incident cast gloom over the Soviet Union's Lenin centennial celebrations. The Soviets had issued the impressive "theses" on Lenin, but some of the quotations attributed to Lenin in the theses had actually been made by the Austrian Social Democrat Otto Bauer. Bauer had been de-

A.F.P. FROM PICTORIAL PARADE

The French Communist party held its 19th Congress in Nanterre, a suburb of Paris, on March 2. A thousand international delegates attended the meeting in the Nanterre Sports Palace; Georges Marchais, a leader of the party, is addressing the delegation.

nounced by Lenin. The error was caught by East Germany's Communist Party First Secretary Walter Ulbricht, but not before the document had fallen into the hands of the Chinese, who used it to heap further ridicule on the Soviets.

Asian Tug-of-War

The ongoing border talks between China and the Soviet Union were endangered as a result of the propaganda war between the two nations. In May the Soviets delivered a resounding tirade against the Chinese, charging that all the power in China lay in the hands of the military. They also sent a radio broadcast into China attacking Politburo Chairman Mao Tse-tung personally and blaming him for the death of his first wife.

To complicate the ideological situation both nations continued to build up their military strength along the Soviet-Chinese border. There was, however, evidence of some improvement in relations later in the year. The border talks did not break down, and in September the Soviets appointed Vasily S. Tolstikov ambassador to China. Until that time there had been no Soviet ambassador to China since 1967.

The U.S. invasion of Cambodia added further complications in relations between the world's Communist nations. The Chinese seized the initiative by inviting Cambodia's overthrown ruler Prince Norodom Sihanouk to set up a government-in-exile in China. The Soviet Union offered Sihanouk their sympathies but did not grant him diplomatic recognition. (*See* Cambodia.)

The Chinese also asserted their growing leadership in Asian Communist affairs by promising to coordinate the activities of the guerrilla movements in South Vietnam, Laos, and Cambodia. The move served to promote closer ties between China and North Vietnam. At the same time the Chinese established better relations with North Korea.

As the Chinese won out over the Soviets in the struggle for influence in Indochina, the Soviet Union issued statements accusing China of interfering in the internal affairs of other Asian nations and of trying to gain total control of Southeast Asia. On the issue of Cambodia, the Russians claimed that Chinese interference had precipitated a right-wing reaction that led to the downfall of the Sihanouk government. They also accused the Chinese of preventing the formation of a united "anti-imperialist" effort for their purpose of restoring Sihanouk to power.

Eastern Europe

In Eastern Europe Romania caused the Soviet Union a great deal of concern during the year.

Romania continued resisting Soviet efforts to increase the military strength of the Warsaw Pact. Also, Romania refused to support the formation of an international investments bank by the Council for Mutual Economic Assistance, the Communist common market. In May Ceausescu was called to Moscow and warned by Brezhnev that Romania could not expect the protection of the Warsaw Pact if Romania did not cooperate with the member nations.

Later in the year Ceausescu further disturbed the Soviets by calling for an international debate among Communists for the purpose of modernizing the concepts of Marxism-Leninism. Nevertheless, Romania and the Soviet Union signed a 20-year friendship treaty in 1970. The government of Czechoslovakia also signed a treaty with the Soviet Union during the year—the first treaty to incorporate the doctrine of limited sovereignty as one of its terms.

In August the Warsaw Pact nations approved the new treaty between West Germany and the Soviet Union, but there was some criticism of the treaty in the East German press. (*See also* Europe; individual countries by name. *See in* CE: Communism.)

COMPUTERS. The most important trend in the computer field during 1970 was the increase in production and application of semiconductor memories. The use of ferrite cores, or tiny rings of ferrite strung on wires, had been standard in computer memories since the early 1950's. The absence or presence of an electric charge in the cores gave the machine its memory. However, in September, International Business Machines Corp. (IBM) surprised the computer industry by announcing that semiconductor circuits would be used exclusively in their new System 370 model 145 computer. The new model uses silicon chips, each containing 1,400 microscopic circuit elements. The chips are less than ⅛ inch square.

In unveiling its 370 series, the first new series since 1964, IBM inaugurated a "fourth generation" of computer technology. The 370 computers are capable of operating with the same programs as the 360 computers and can switch between 370-mode programs and most existing programs without change. The 370's can also call other IBM computers for a diagnosis if they run into problems.

To go with the 370's IBM introduced a line of accessories. Among them were a storage disk capable of holding up to 800 million characters of data and a high-speed printer that can produce 2,000 lines of copy per minute.

On the corporate level, the computer industry expected a record income of about $12.3 billion in 1970. The figure includes $9.2 billion on the sale of computers, $1.2 billion on the sale of data-processing supplies, and $1.9 billion for software and services.

The biggest corporate news of the year was the sale of General Electric Company's computer division and its related operations to Honeywell, Inc. The resultant company, known as Honeywell Information Systems, Inc., became the second largest firm in the computer industry. However, IBM retained control of 70% of the total revenue for the industry.

Computers took on new social and political implications when it was revealed in June that the U.S. government had been compiling computerized files of hundreds of thousands of "suspect" citizens. Individuals listed are those thought likely to incite riots or violence or to "embarrass" or harm the

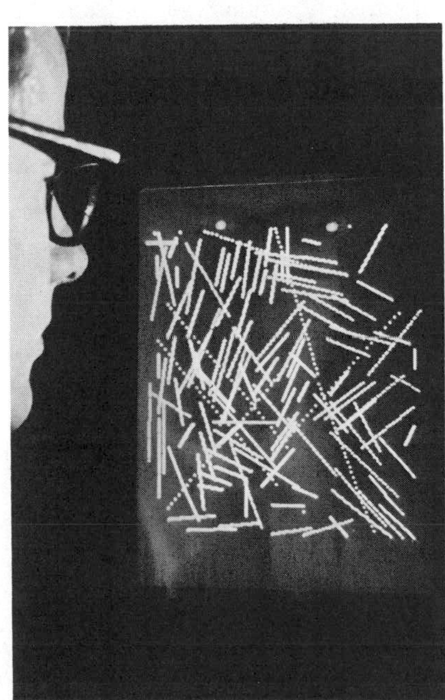

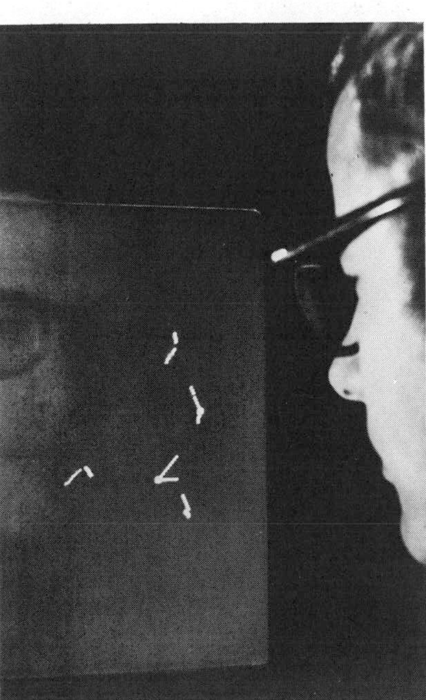

Air controllers could fend off airplane collisions by using the Staran IV computer system developed by Goodyear Aerospace Corp. A radar display screen shows the paths of 128 airplanes (left). Out of this mass of planes, the computer singles out ten (right) headed for collisions and determines the paths the planes should take to avoid disaster.

COURTESY, GOODYEAR AEROSPACE CORP.

nation's leaders. The system had many critics, among them Senator Sam J. Ervin, Jr. (D, N.C.), chairman of the Senate Subcommittee on Constitutional Rights. (*See also* Electronics. *See in* CE: Computers.)

CONGO, DEMOCRATIC REPUBLIC OF THE (Kinshasa). The disappointing diplomatic exchanges between the Democratic Republic of the Congo and its African neighbors during the preceding 12 months took a turn for the better in 1970. There had been a foretaste of this change when President Joseph D. Mobutu met the presidents of Burundi and Rwanda in Rwanda on Dec. 19, 1969. The three leaders adopted a resolution confirming their joint determination to strengthen the mutual understanding among their countries and to achieve integration "in the economic, technical, and cultural spheres." Three weeks later, the celebration of the tenth anniversary of the independence of Cameroon, held on January 10, provided an opportunity for Mobutu to meet the presidents of Chad and the Central African Republic and for the three to announce a reconciliation of their nations, which had been estranged since December 1968. This was followed with an announcement on Jan. 15, 1970, by the foreign ministry of the Central African Republic that diplomatic relations with the Congo would finally be resumed.

KEYSTONE

President Joseph Mobutu (left) of the Democratic Republic of the Congo visits U.S. President Richard M. Nixon in Washington, D.C.

There were indications in April of heightened tension between the Congo and its western neighbor, the People's Republic of the Congo (Brazzaville). However, Mobutu's campaign of reconciliation took a step forward in this quarter also when he met President Marien Ngouabi on June 16 to sign an agreement restoring diplomatic relations, broken off in October 1968, between the two countries. (*See in* CE: Congo, Democratic Republic of the.)

CONGO, PEOPLE'S REPUBLIC OF THE (Brazzaville). The Republic of Congo began 1970 with a new name: the People's Republic of the Congo. A new flag featured a hammer-and-hoe motif. Under the new constitution, the president of the newly created Congolese Workers' party, elected by the Party Congress for a five-year term, would also be chief of state. No national assembly was provided for. The single party comprised a Central Committee of 41 members and an eight-man Political Bureau.

These profound changes proved insufficient to restore stability, and announcements of attempted coups and political trials followed in rapid succession. In March, Maj. Marien Ngouabi, the chief of state, announced the crushing of a coup planned by elements in the army; three military men were executed. In September, a former minister of public works was sentenced to ten years' hard labor. (*See in* CE: Congo, Republic of.)

CONGRESS, UNITED STATES. The second session of the Democratic-controlled 91st Congress was the occasion for increasing clashes with U.S. President Richard M. Nixon, a Republican. Early in the session, the Senate, for a second time, rejected a presidential appointment to the Supreme Court. On April 8, Judge G. Harrold Carswell of Florida was rejected 51–45. Late in 1969, the Senate had rejected appointment of Judge Clement F. Haynsworth, Jr., of South Carolina. During lengthy debate on Carswell, several senators cited charges of racial bias and mediocrity. President Nixon, however, accused Carswell's opponents of anti-Southern bias and hypocrisy. He charged that "while the Senate would not accept a strict constructionist of the Constitution from the South, it would accept a jurist of similar views from the North." The president subsequently nominated Appeals Judge Harry A. Blackmun of Minnesota, a moderate conservative with a record of moderate views on racial issues. The nomination was confirmed without serious difficulty.

Immediately after the rejection of Carswell, the Republican minority leader in the House, Gerald Ford of Michigan, circulated a petition asking for creation of a committee to decide whether liberal Supreme Court Justice William O. Douglas should be impeached. The inquiry, however, was taken over by the Judiciary Committee, which dropped the charges against Douglas after a lengthy subcommittee hearing. Charges against Douglas ranged from writing material that tended to foment rebellion to association with underworld figures and conflict of interest.

Foreign Policy

Congress devoted much attention in 1970 to a searching debate over its power to control actions of the president as commander in chief of the armed forces. Beginning with U.S. ground action in Cambodia, Senate antiwar forces repeatedly sought to

WIDE WORLD

Speaker of the House John W. McCormack (D, Mass.) announced in May that he would retire from Congress at the end of 1970.

curb the president's power to make war in Southeast Asia.

In the end, amendments to foreign-aid bills repealed the Gulf of Tonkin resolution—used by President Lyndon B. Johnson to justify large-scale U.S. intervention in Vietnam—and forbade use of any funds to support U.S. ground troops or military advisers in Cambodia. Administration forces indicated, however, that they doubted the legal effect of the moves. They asserted that the president had the inherent right as commander in chief to take whatever action was necessary for protection of U.S. forces abroad.

Welfare Policy Clash

Congress failed to act on two major proposals of the Nixon Administration for domestic reform. A plan to share tax revenue with the states was never seriously considered. The plan would have allocated $500 million to the states the first year. The amount would have risen gradually to $5 billion.

A vast welfare reform porposal passed the House but failed in the Senate. The House bill would have abolished major portions of the present welfare system and would have established for the first time the principle that the federal government should guarantee every family a minimum annual income, even if one or more of its members was working. (*See* Social Services.)

The bill was stalled in the Senate for the rest of the session by an unusual coalition of conservatives, who felt that the bill was too expensive and would encourage people to stay on welfare, and liberals, who objected that it did not cover enough persons or provide high enough levels of income. At the end of the year, President Nixon obtained assurances from Senate leaders that the plan would receive quick consideration in 1971. All legislation dies at the end of each Congress unless passed, so the bill will have to be redrafted, resubmitted, and passed by both houses to become law.

Crime Control

During the year, Congress passed major Administration proposals relating to organized crime. The 1970 Organized Crime Control Act would allow special grand juries to report on noncriminal ties of appointed officials with organized crime. Federal judges would be allowed to impose additional sentences of up to 25 years on persons convicted of two previous felonies, whose offense was part of a pattern of crime or whose offense was part of a conspiracy to engage in organized crime. The law also would make it a federal offense to bribe state officials in order to engage in illegal gambling business or to use income from organized crime to establish or acquire control of legitimate interstate businesses. Federal licenses were required for manufacturing explosives or carrying them across state lines, and the Federal Bureau of Investigation was authorized to investigate bombings on college campuses. The law authorized detention for up to 18 months for witnesses who defied court orders to testify, and it offered protection to witnesses in organized crime cases.

Another major measure passed was the crime control bill for the District of Columbia. It reorga-

Senator Frank Church (D, Idaho) displays some of the mail he received about his amendment to cut off funds for the Cambodian operation after June 30. Most letters supported the amendment.

UPI COMPIX

nized courts and judicial procedures, creating a public defender system in the process. It authorized the detention of certain suspects before trial and gave "no-knock" authority for police searches and arrests with court orders but without warning in specified types of cases. The bill also gave expanded police wiretapping authority, imposed a mandatory five-year sentence for a person convicted of a second armed crime, and lowered from 18 to 16 the age for trial as adults in serious cases. The bill was regarded by some legislators on both sides of the controversy over passage as a possible model for tougher criminal codes to be passed by the state and federal governments, rather than as simply a regulation for Washington, D.C. The no-knock provision was also included in a narcotics control bill, giving federal agents the right to enter buildings where they believed narcotics were stored—again after the agents obtained court permission. The bill raised criminal penalties for sale and distribution of drugs, while penalties for mere possession were reduced. It authorized $189 million over three years for rehabilitation, treatment, and drug abuse programs.

Concern about the new areas of criminal law explored in the bills resulted in creation, as part of the Organized Crime Control Act, of a commission to determine whether any of the legislation violated individual rights. Commission findings and court tests of the new legislation could be expected to be important influences on future legislation.

UPI COMPIX

Senator Strom Thurmond (R, S.C.) was pelted with marshmallows after a speech he gave to students at Carnegie-Mellon University, at Pittsburgh, Pa., in January.

Postal and Rail Reform; Air Pollution Control

One of the most far-reaching measures passed by Congress was a plan to phase out the Post Office Department within a year and replace it with an independent federal agency, the U.S. Postal Service. The president would select nine members of a board of governors with the consent of the Senate. These appointees in turn would select two other board members, the postmaster general and deputy postmaster general. This board would give orders to the postmaster general on all matters relating to the operation of the service except decisions on rates and mail classifications. These would be made by a separate five-member board appointed by the president. This Postal Rate Commission could be overruled only by a unanimous vote of the governors or by a court decision. Future wages and working conditions would be set by bargaining between the Postal Service and unions chosen by the majority vote of postal employees. Strikes would be barred. The system would be financed by revenues, sale of securities, and Congressional appropriations limited to 10% of 1971 costs, declining to 5% or less of 1971 costs by 1984.

Congress also passed a bill to create a national corporation to take over financially ailing rail passenger systems. The corporation, to be funded by the railroads and private investors, would be authorized to receive $340 million in federal loans and grants to start the service. Another bill bound the government to provide $3.1 billion in loans and grants for financially ailing public mass-transit systems.

A tough antipollution measure was passed during the year. It stipulated that violators of the Federal Clean Air Standards Act can be fined $25,000 a day or imprisoned for one year for a first offense. Fines and prison sentences could be twice as heavy as those for a second offense. Autos sold after Jan. 1, 1975, will have to emit 90% less carbon monoxide and hydrocarbon than current models. A 90% reduction in nitrogen oxide emissions will be required by Jan. 1, 1976. The administrator of the newly created Environmental Protection Agency would be empowered, however, to grant a one-year extension of the auto standards deadline. Congress authorized the spending of $1 billion over the next three years to fight pollution.

Two Vetoes Overridden

Two vetoes were overridden by Congress in 1970. One was President Nixon's veto of an extension of the Hill-Burton hospital construction bill. The $2.8-billion, three-year program of direct grants and federal guarantees on loans was excessive, the president insisted. He also felt more emphasis

(continued on page 201)

MEMBERS OF THE CONGRESS OF THE UNITED STATES

1st Session, 92nd Congress *

THE SENATE

President of the Senate: Spiro T. Agnew

State	Senator	Current Service Began	Current Term Expires
Ala.	John Sparkman (D)	1947	1973
	James B. Allen (D)	1969	1975
Alaska	Theodore F. Stevens (R)	1969	1977
	Mike Gravel (D)	1969	1975
Ariz.	Paul J. Fannin (R)	1965	1977
	Barry M. Goldwater (R)	1969	1975
Ark.	John L. McClellan (D)	1943	1973
	J. W. Fulbright (D)	1945	1975
Calif.	Alan Cranston (D)	1969	1975
	John V. Tunney (D)	1971	1977
Colo.	Gordon Allott (R)	1955	1973
	Peter H. Dominick (R)	1963	1975
Conn.	Abraham Ribicoff (D)	1963	1975
	Lowell P. Weicker, Jr. (R)	1971	1977
Del.	J. Caleb Boggs (R)	1961	1973
	William V. Roth, Jr. (R)	1971	1977
Fla.	Edward J. Gurney (R)	1969	1975
	Lawton Chiles (D)	1971	1977
Ga.	Richard B. Russell (D)	1933	1973
	Herman E. Talmadge (D)	1957	1975
Hawaii	Hiram L. Fong (R)	1959	1977
	Daniel K. Inouye (D)	1963	1975
Idaho	Frank Church (D)	1957	1975
	Len B. Jordan (R)	1962	1973
Ill.	Charles H. Percy (R)	1967	1973
	Adlai E. Stevenson III (D)	1971	1977
Ind.	Vance Hartke (D)	1959	1977
	Birch E. Bayh (D)	1963	1975
Iowa	Jack Miller (R)	1961	1973
	Harold E. Hughes (D)	1969	1975
Kan.	James B. Pearson (R)	1962	1973
	Robert Dole (R)	1969	1975
Ky.	John Sherman Cooper (R)	1957	1973
	Marlow W. Cook (R)	1969	1975
La.	Allen J. Ellender (D)	1937	1973
	Russell B. Long (D)	1948	1975
Maine	Margaret Chase Smith (R)	1949	1973
	Edmund S. Muskie (D)	1959	1977
Md.	Charles McC. Mathias, Jr. (R)	1969	1975
	J. Glenn Beall, Jr. (R)	1971	1977
Mass.	Edward M. Kennedy (D)	1962	1977
	Edward W. Brooke (R)	1967	1973
Mich.	Philip A. Hart (D)	1959	1977
	Robert P. Griffin (R)	1966	1973
Minn.	Walter F. Mondale (D)	1964	1973
	Hubert H. Humphrey (D)	1971	1977
Miss.	James O. Eastland (D)	1943	1973
	John C. Stennis (D)	1947	1977
Mo.	Stuart Symington (D)	1953	1977
	Thomas F. Eagleton (D)	1969	1975
Mont.	Mike Mansfield (D)	1953	1977
	Lee Metcalf (D)	1961	1973
Neb.	Roman L. Hruska (R)	1955	1977
	Carl T. Curtis (R)	1955	1973
Nev.	Alan Bible (D)	1954	1975
	Howard W. Cannon (D)	1959	1977
N.H.	Norris Cotton (R)	1955	1975
	Thomas J. McIntyre (D)	1963	1973
N.J.	Clifford P. Case (R)	1955	1973
	Harrison A. Williams, Jr. (D)	1959	1977
N.M.	Clinton P. Anderson (D)	1949	1973
	Joseph M. Montoya (D)	1965	1977
N.Y.	Jacob K. Javits (R)	1957	1975
	James L. Buckley†	1971	1977
N.C.	Sam J. Ervin, Jr. (D)	1954	1975
	B. Everett Jordan (D)	1958	1973
N.D.	Milton R. Young (R)	1945	1975
	Quentin N. Burdick (D)	1960	1977
Ohio	William B. Saxbe (R)	1969	1975
	Robert Taft, Jr. (R)	1971	1977
Okla.	Fred R. Harris (D)	1964	1973
	Henry Bellmon (R)	1969	1975
Ore.	Mark O. Hatfield (R)	1967	1973
	Robert W. Packwood (R)	1969	1975
Pa.	Hugh Scott (R)	1959	1977
	Richard S. Schweiker (R)	1969	1975
R.I.	John O. Pastore (D)	1950	1977
	Claiborne Pell (D)	1961	1973
S.C.	Strom Thurmond (R)	1955	1973
	Ernest F. Hollings (D)	1966	1975
S.D.	Karl E. Mundt (R)	1949	1973
	George McGovern (D)	1963	1975
Tenn.	Howard H. Baker, Jr. (R)	1967	1973
	William E. Brock III (R)	1971	1977
Tex.	John G. Tower (R)	1961	1973
	Lloyd M. Bentsen (D)	1971	1977
Utah	Wallace F. Bennett (R)	1951	1975
	Frank E. Moss (D)	1959	1977
Vt.	George D. Aiken (R)	1941	1975
	Winston L. Prouty (R)	1959	1977
Va.	Harry F. Byrd, Jr.‡	1965	1977
	William B. Spong, Jr. (D)	1957	1973
Wash.	Warren G. Magnuson (D)	1944	1975
	Henry M. Jackson (D)	1953	1977
W.Va.	Jennings Randolph (D)	1959	1973
	Robert C. Byrd (D)	1959	1977
Wis.	William Proxmire (D)	1957	1977
	Gaylord Nelson (D)	1963	1975
Wyo.	Gale W. McGee (D)	1959	1977
	Clifford P. Hansen (R)	1967	1973

* Convened January 1971.
† Party designation: Conservative Party (of New York).

‡ No party designation (Independent).

THE HOUSE OF REPRESENTATIVES *

Speaker of the House: Carl Albert

Alabama
Jack Edwards, 1 (R)
William L. Dickinson, 2 (R)
George Andrews, 3 (D)
Bill Nichols, 4 (D)
Walter Flowers, 5 (D)
John Buchanan, 6 (R)
Tom Bevill, 7 (D)
Robert E. Jones, 8 (D)

Alaska
Nick Begich (D)

Arizona
John J. Rhodes, 1 (R)
Morris K. Udall, 2 (D)
Sam Steiger, 3 (R)

Arkansas
Bill Alexander, 1 (D)
Wilbur D. Mills, 2 (D)
John Paul Hammerschmidt, 3 (R)
David Pryor, 4 (D)

California
Don H. Clausen, 1 (R)
Harold T. Johnson, 2 (D)
John E. Moss, 3 (D)
Robert L. Leggett, 4 (D)
Phillip Burton, 5 (D)
William S. Mailliard, 6 (R)
Ronald V. Dellums, 7 (D)
George P. Miller, 8 (D)
Don Edwards, 9 (D)
Charles S. Gubser, 10 (R)
Paul N. McCloskey, Jr., 11 (R)
Burt L. Talcott, 12 (R)
Charles M. Teague, 13 (R)
Jerome R. Waldie, 14 (D)
John J. McFall, 15 (D)
B. F. Sisk, 16 (D)
Glenn M. Anderson, 17 (D)
Robert B. Mathias, 18 (R)
Chet Holifield, 19 (D)
H. Allen Smith, 20 (R)
Augustus F. Hawkins, 21 (D)
James C. Corman, 22 (D)
Del Clawson, 23 (R)
John H. Rousselot, 24 (R)
Charles E. Wiggins, 25 (R)
Thomas M. Rees, 26 (D)
Barry M. Goldwater, Jr., 27 (R)
Alphonzo Bell, 28 (R)
George E. Danielson, 29 (D)
Edward R. Roybal, 30 (D)
Charles H. Wilson, 31 (D)
Craig Hosmer, 32 (R)
Jerry L. Pettis, 33 (R)
Richard T. Hanna, 34 (D)
John G. Schmitz, 35 (R)
Bob Wilson, 36 (R)
Lionel Van Deerlin, 37 (D)
Victor V. Veysey, 38 (R)

Colorado
James D. (Mike) McKevitt, 1 (R)
Donald G. Brotzman, 2 (R)
Frank E. Evans, 3 (D)
Wayne N. Aspinall, 4 (D)

Connecticut
William R. Cotter, 1 (D)
Robert W. Steele, Jr., 2 (R)
Robert N. Giaimo, 3 (D)
Stewart McKinney, 4 (R)
John S. Monagan, 5 (D)
Ella T. Grasso, 6 (D)

Delaware
Pierre S. du Pont IV (R)

Florida
Robert L. F. Sikes, 1 (D)
Don Fuqua, 2 (D)
Charles E. Bennett, 3 (D)
Bill Chappell, Jr., 4 (D)
Louis Frey, Jr., 5 (R)
Sam Gibbons, 6 (D)
James A. Haley, 7 (D)
C. W. (Bill) Young, 8 (R)
Paul G. Rogers, 9 (D)
J. Herbert Burke, 10 (R)
Claude Pepper, 11 (D)
Dante B. Fascell, 12 (D)

Georgia
G. Elliott Hagan, 1 (D)
Dawson Mathis, 2 (D)
Jack Brinkley, 3 (D)
Benjamin B. Blackburn, 4 (R)
Fletcher Thompson, 5 (R)
John J. Flynt, Jr., 6 (D)
John W. Davis, 7 (D)
W. S. Stuckey, 8 (D)
Phil M. Landrum, 9 (D)
Robert G. Stephens, Jr., 10 (D)

Hawaii
Spark M. Matsunaga (D)
Patsy T. Mink (D)

Idaho
James A. McClure, 1 (R)
Orval Hansen, 2 (R)

Illinois
Ralph Metcalfe, 1 (D)
Abner J. Mikva, 2 (D)
Morgan Murphy, 3 (D)
Edward J. Derwinski, 4 (R)
John C. Kluczynski, 5 (D)
George Collins, 6 (D)
Frank Annunzio, 7 (D)
Dan Rostenkowski, 8 (D)
Sidney R. Yates, 9 (D)
Harold R. Collier, 10 (R)
Roman C. Pucinski, 11 (D)
Robert McClory, 12 (R)

GRAHAM, "ARKANSAS GAZETTE," LITTLE ROCK, FROM BEN ROTH AGENCY

* Numbers after names indicate Congressional districts; where no number is given, congressman is elected at large.

Philip M. Crane, 13 (R)
John N. Erlenborn, 14 (R)
Charlotte T. Reid, 15 (R)
John B. Anderson, 16 (R)
Leslie C. Arends, 17 (R)
Robert H. Michel, 18 (R)
Tom Railsback, 19 (R)
Paul Findley, 20 (R)
Kenneth J. Gray, 21 (D)
William L. Springer, 22 (R)
George E. Shipley, 23 (D)
Melvin Price, 24 (D)

Indiana

Ray J. Madden, 1 (D)
Earl F. Landgrebe, 2 (R)
John Brademas, 3 (D)
J. Edward Roush, 4 (D)
Elwood Hillis, 5 (R)
William G. Bray, 6 (R)
John T. Myers, 7 (R)
Roger H. Zion, 8 (R)
Lee H. Hamilton, 9 (D)
David W. Dennis, 10 (R)
Andrew Jacobs, Jr., 11 (D)

Iowa

Fred Schwengel, 1 (R)
John C. Culver, 2 (D)
H. R. Gross, 3 (R)
John Kyl, 4 (R)
Neal Smith, 5 (D)
Wiley Mayne, 6 (R)
William J. Scherle, 7 (R)

Kansas

Keith G. Sebelius, 1 (R)
William Roy, 2 (D)
Larry Winn, Jr., 3 (R)
Garner E. Shriver, 4 (R)
Joe Skubitz, 5 (R)

Kentucky

Frank A. Stubblefield, 1 (D)
William H. Natcher, 2 (D)
Romano Mazzoli, 3 (D)
M. G. (Gene) Snyder, 4 (R)
Tim Lee Carter, 5 (R)
John C. Watts, 6 (D)
Carl D. Perkins, 7 (D)

Louisiana

F. Edward Hébert, 1 (D)
Hale Boggs, 2 (D)
Patrick T. Caffery, 3 (D)
Joe D. Waggonner, Jr., 4 (D)
Otto E. Passman, 5 (D)
John R. Rarick, 6 (D)
Edwin W. Edwards, 7 (D)
Speedy O. Long, 8 (D)

Maine

Peter N. Kyros, 1 (D)
William D. Hathaway, 2 (D)

Maryland

Rogers C. B. Morton, 1 (R)
Clarence D. Long, 2 (D)
Edward A. Garmatz, 3 (D)
Paul Sarbanes, 4 (D)
Lawrence J. Hogan, 5 (R)
Goodloe E. Byron, 6 (D)
Parren Mitchell, 7 (D)
Gilbert Gude, 8 (R)

Massachusetts

Silvio O. Conte, 1 (R)
Edward P. Boland, 2 (D)
Robert Drinan, 3 (D)
Harold D. Donohue, 4 (D)
F. Bradford Morse, 5 (R)
Michael Harrington, 6 (D)
Torbert H. Macdonald, 7 (D)
Thomas P. O'Neill, Jr., 8 (D)
Louise Day Hicks, 9 (D)
Margaret M. Heckler, 10 (R)
James A. Burke, 11 (D)
Hastings Keith, 12 (R)

Michigan

John Conyers, Jr., 1 (D)
Marvin L. Esch, 2 (R)
Garry Brown, 3 (R)
Edward Hutchinson, 4 (R)
Gerald R. Ford, 5 (R)
Charles E. Chamberlain, 6 (R)
Donald W. Riegle, Jr., 7 (R)
James Harvey, 8 (R)
Guy Vander Jagt, 9 (R)
Elford A. Cederberg, 10 (R)
Philip E. Ruppe, 11 (R)
James G. O'Hara, 12 (D)
Charles C. Diggs, Jr., 13 (D)
Lucien N. Nedzi, 14 (D)
William D. Ford, 15 (D)
John D. Dingell, 16 (D)
Martha W. Griffiths, 17 (D)
William S. Broomfield, 18 (R)
Jack H. McDonald, 19 (R)

Minnesota

Albert H. Quie, 1 (R)
Ancher Nelsen, 2 (R)
Bill Frenzel, 3 (R)
Joseph E. Karth, 4 (D)
Donald M. Fraser, 5 (D)
John M. Zwach, 6 (R)
Bob Bergland, 7 (D)
John A. Blatnik, 8 (D)

Mississippi

Thomas G. Abernethy, 1 (D)
Jamie L. Whitten, 2 (D)
Charles H. Griffin, 3 (D)
G. V. (Sonny) Montgomery, 4 (D)
William M. Colmer, 5 (D)

Missouri

William Clay, 1 (D)
James W. Symington, 2 (D)
Leonor K. Sullivan, 3 (D)
William J. Randall, 4 (D)
Richard Bolling, 5 (D)
W. R. Hull, Jr., 6 (D)
Durward G. Hall, 7 (R)
Richard H. Ichord, 8 (D)
William L. Hungate, 9 (D)
Bill D. Burlison, 10 (D)

Montana

Rihard G. Shoup, 1 (R)
John Melcher, 2 (D)

Nebraska

Charles Thone, 1 (R)
John Y. McCollister, 2 (R)
Dave Martin, 3 (R)

Nevada

Walter S. Baring (D)

New Hampshire

Louis C. Wyman, 1 (R)
James C. Cleveland, 2 (R)

New Jersey

John E. Hunt, 1 (R)
Charles W. Sandman, Jr., 2 (R)
James J. Howard, 3 (D)
Frank Thompson, Jr., 4 (D)
Peter H. B. Frelinghuysen, 5 (R)
Edwin B. Forsythe, 6 (R)
William B. Widnall, 7 (R)
Robert A. Roe, 8 (D)
Henry Helstoski, 9 (D)
Peter W. Rodino, Jr., 10 (D)
Joseph G. Minish, 11 (D)
Florence P. Dwyer, 12 (R)
Cornelius E. Gallagher, 13 (D)
Dominick V. Daniels, 14 (D)
Edward J. Patten, 15 (D)

New Mexico

Manuel Lujan, Jr., 1 (R)
Harold L. Runnels, 2 (D)

New York

Otis G. Pike, 1 (D)
James R. Grover, Jr., 2 (R)
Lester L. Wolff, 3 (D)
John W. Wydler, 4 (R)
Norman F. Lent, 5 (R)
Seymour Halpern, 6 (R)
Joseph P. Addabbo, 7 (D)
Benjamin S. Rosenthal, 8 (D)
James J. Delaney, 9 (D)
Emanuel Celler, 10 (D)
Frank J. Brasco, 11 (D)
Shirley Chisholm, 12 (D)
Bertram L. Podell, 13 (D)
John J. Rooney, 14 (D)
Hugh L. Carey, 15 (D)
John M. Murphy, 16 (D)
Edward I. Koch, 17 (D)
Charles Rangel, 18 (D)
Bella Abzug, 19 (D)
William F. Ryan, 20 (D)
Herman Badillo, 21 (D)
James H. Scheuer, 22 (D)
Jonathan B. Bingham, 23 (D)
Mario Biaggi, 24 (D)
Peter A. Peyser, 25 (R)
Ogden R. Reid, 26 (R)
John Dow, 27 (D)
Hamilton Fish, Jr., 28 (R)
Samuel S. Stratton, 29 (D)
Carleton J. King, 30 (R)
Robert C. McEwen, 31 (R)
Alexander Pirnie, 32 (R)
Howard W. Robison, 33 (R)
John H. Terry, 34 (R)
James M. Hanley, 35 (D)
Frank Horton, 36 (R)
Barber B. Conable, Jr., 37 (R)
James F. Hastings, 38 (R)
Jack F. Kemp, 39 (R)
Henry P. Smith III, 40 (R)
Thaddeus J. Dulski, 41 (D)

North Carolina

Walter B. Jones, 1 (D)
L. H. Fountain, 2 (D)
David N. Henderson, 3 (D)
Nick Galifianakis, 4 (D)
Wilmer (Vinegar Bend) Mizell, 5 (R)
Richardson Preyer, 6 (D)
Alton Lennon, 7 (D)
Earl B. Ruth, 8 (R)
Charles Raper Jonas, 9 (R)
James T. Broyhill, 10 (R)
Roy A. Taylor, 11 (D)

North Dakota

Mark Andrews, 1 (R)
Arthur A. Link, 2 (D)

Ohio

William J. Keating, 1 (R)
Donald D. Clancy, 2 (R)
Charles W. Whalen, Jr., 3 (R)
William M. McCulloch, 4 (R)
Delbert L. Latta, 5 (R)
William H. Harsha, 6 (R)
Clarence J. Brown, 7 (R)
Jackson E. Betts, 8 (R)
Thomas L. Ashley, 9 (D)
Clarence E. Miller, 10 (R)
J. William Stanton, 11 (R)
Samuel L. Devine, 12 (R)

Charles A. Mosher, 13 (R)
John F. Seiberling, Jr., 14 (D)
Chalmers P. Wylie, 15 (R)
Frank T. Bow, 16 (R)
John M. Ashbrook, 17 (R)
Wayne L. Hays, 18 (D)
Charles J. Carney, 19 (D)
James V. Stanton, 20 (D)
Louis Stokes, 21 (D)
Charles A. Vanik, 22 (D)
William E. Minshall, 23 (R)
Walter E. Powell, 24 (R)

Oklahoma

Page Belcher, 1 (R)
Ed Edmondson, 2 (D)
Carl Albert, 3 (D)
Tom Steed, 4 (D)
John Jarman, 5 (D)
John N. Happy Camp, 6 (R)

Oregon

Wendell Wyatt, 1 (R)
Al Ullman, 2 (D)
Edith Green, 3 (D)
John Dellenback, 4 (R)

Pennsylvania

William A. Barrett, 1 (D)
Robert N. C. Nix, 2 (D)
James A. Byrne, 3 (D)
Joshua Eilberg, 4 (D)
William J. Green, 5 (D)
Gus Yatron, 6 (D)
Lawrence G. Williams, 7 (R)
Edward G. Biester, Jr., 8 (R)
John H. Ware III, 9 (R)
Joseph M. McDade, 10 (R)
Daniel J. Flood, 11 (D)
J. Irving Whalley, 12 (R)
R. Lawrence Coughlin, 13 (R)
William S. Moorhead, 14 (D)
Fred B. Rooney, 15 (D)
Edwin D. Eshleman, 16 (R)
Herman T. Schneebeli, 17 (R)
Robert J. Corbett, 18 (R)
George A. Goodling, 19 (R)
Joseph M. Gaydos, 20 (D)
John H. Dent, 21 (D)
John P. Saylor, 22 (R)
Albert W. Johnson, 23 (R)
Joseph P. Vigorito, 24 (D)
Frank M. Clark, 25 (D)
Thomas E. Morgan, 26 (D)
James G. Fulton, 27 (R)

Rhode Island

Fernand J. St. Germain, 1 (D)
Robert O. Tiernan, 2 (D)

South Carolina

† 1
Floyd Spence, 2 (R)
Wm. Jennings Bryan Dorn, 3 (D)
James R. Mann, 4 (D)
Tom S. Gettys, 5 (D)
John L. McMillan, 6 (D)

South Dakota

Frank E. Denholm, 1 (D)
James Abourezk, 2 (D)

Tennessee

James H. Quillen, 1 (R)
John J. Duncan, 2 (R)
LaMar Baker, 3 (R)
Joe L. Evins, 4 (D)
Richard Fulton, 5 (D)
William R. Anderson, 6 (D)

WETZEL FROM BEN ROTH AGENCY

Ray Blanton, 7 (D)
Ed Jones, 8 (D)
Dan Kuykendall, 9 (R)

Texas

Wright Patman, 1 (D)
John Dowdy, 2 (D)
James M. Collins, 3 (R)
Ray Roberts, 4 (D)
Earle Cabell, 5 (D)
Olin E. Teague, 6 (D)
W. R. Archer, 7 (R)
Bob Eckhardt, 8 (D)
Jack Brooks, 9 (D)
J. J. Pickle, 10 (D)
W. R. Poage, 11 (D)
Jim Wright, 12 (D)
Graham Purcell, 13 (D)
John Young, 14 (D)
Eligio de la Garza, 15 (D)
Richard White, 16 (D)
Omar Burleson, 17 (D)
Robert Price, 18 (R)
George H. Mahon, 19 (D)
Henry B. Gonzalez, 20 (D)
O. C. Fisher, 21 (D)
Bob Casey, 22 (D)
Abraham Kazen, Jr., 23 (D)

Utah

K. Gunn McKay, 1 (D)
Sherman P. Lloyd, 2 (R)

Vermont

Robert T. Stafford (R)

Virginia

Thomas N. Downing, 1 (D)
G. William Whitehurst, 2 (R)
David E. Satterfield III, 3 (D)
Watkins M. Abbitt, 4 (D)
W. C. (Dan) Daniel, 5 (D)
Richard H. Poff, 6 (R)
J. Kenneth Robinson, 7 (R)
William Lloyd Scott, 8 (R)
William C. Wampler, 9 (R)
Joel T. Broyhill, 10 (R)

Washington

Thomas M. Pelly, 1 (R)
Lloyd Meeds, 2 (D)
Julia Butler Hansen, 3 (D)
C. G. (Mike) McCormack, 4 (D)
Thomas S. Foley, 5 (D)
Floyd V. Hicks, 6 (D)
Brock Adams, 7 (D)

West Virginia

Robert H. Mollohan, 1 (D)
Harley O. Staggers, 2 (D)
John M. Slack, 3 (D)
Ken Hechler, 4 (D)
James Kee, 5 (D)

Wisconsin

Les Aspin, 1 (D)
Robert W. Kastenmeier, 2 (D)
Vernon W. Thomson, 3 (R)
Clement J. Zablocki, 4 (D)
Henry S. Reuss, 5 (D)
William A. Steiger, 6 (R)
David R. Obey, 7 (D)
John W. Byrnes, 8 (R)
Glenn R. Davis, 9 (R)
Alvin E. O'Konski, 10 (R)

Wyoming

Teno Roncalio (D)

† Vacancy caused by the death of L. Mendel Rivers (D), Dec. 28, 1970.

UPI COMPIX

Senate Minority Leader Hugh Scott (R, Pa.) reassures the Senate Foreign Relations Committee the Administration will continue to withdraw U.S. troops from Vietnam.

(*continued from page 196*)
should have been placed on loan guarantees and less on grants. He particularly objected to provisions that all of the money appropriated each year had to be spent.

The second measure to become law over the president's veto was a $4.4-billion appropriation for the Office of Education. The bill covered primary and secondary schools, plus some college programs. The president objected to the total amount, particularly the amount appropriated to aid "impacted" schools, which educate large numbers of children of federal workers.

Other Legislation

A five-year extension of the federal Voting Rights Act was passed, including a provision allowing 18-year-olds to vote. The provision was later held by the Supreme Court to apply only to federal elections. A proposal for direct election of presidents, in effect abolishing the electoral college system, passed the House but died in a Senate filibuster. The District of Columbia was given a single, nonvoting delegate in the House. The delegate was to be chosen in March 1971.

Two major issues were put over to the next Congress. A short-term $210-million appropriation was made for the controversial development of a supersonic transport (SST) plane. The measure, expiring March 30, 1971, was a compromise to avoid a filibuster by senators concerned about the expense and the practicality of the project, as well as the noise that would be produced by a mammoth SST. An increase in social security benefits also was deferred. Both houses agreed there should be an increase but could not agree on the amount. Also at issue was the president's proposal to tie future increases to the cost-of-living index.

Changes in Representation

The 1970 census marked a shift of national political power westward. California showed the largest population increase and will have five additional representatives in the House in 1973. Florida gained three seats; Arizona, Colorado, and Texas each gained one. New York and Pennsylvania each lost two seats; Alabama, Iowa, North Dakota, Ohio, Tennessee, West Virginia, and Wisconsin each lost one. (*See in* CE: Congress of the United States.)

CONSERVATION.

Much oratory and considerable action in 1970 was centered on cleaning up the environment and bettering the "quality of life." So important was the need to stem environmental deterioration that U.S. President Richard M. Nixon, on January 1, signed into law the National Environmental Policy Act of 1969. It provided for a permanent three-man Council on Environmental Quality, a Cabinet-level group, which Russell E. Train was selected to head on January 29.

At the urging of Senator Gaylord Nelson (D, Wis.) and others, Earth Day was organized by a number of activist students on April 22. At colleges and in communities throughout the United States, parades, cleanups, and "teach-ins" were undertaken to recruit popular support for antipollution and other ecologically motivated campaigns.

In July President Nixon announced the consolidation of all U.S. environmental agencies—those in the departments of Agriculture, the Interior, and

"We just adore animals, too."

"THE NEW YORK TIMES"

Sandbags are used at Cape Hatteras, N.C., to save the eroding shoreline from the pounding waves. The Cape, which is a National Seashore, is also threatened by overuse in summer. There were some 1.1 million visitors to the shore in 1969.

Health, Education, and Welfare, for example—into two new agencies. One, the Environmental Protection Agency, would concentrate on setting and enforcing pollution-control standards. The other, the National Oceanic and Atmospheric Administration, would deal with sea and air research.

The first report of the Council on Environmental Quality was sent to Congress in August. Although the paper called for sweeping changes in U.S. life in order to conserve the raw materials needed for products and energy, it posed no immediate salves for environmental ills. Instead, it soothed Congress by asserting that government programs and industry incentives would protect the nation's resources without halting economic growth.

After a five-year study, the Public Land Law Review Commission (PLLRC) recommended that most public lands remain in federal hands. Conservationists hailed continuing federal ownership of the lands, some one third of the total acreage in the United States, but lamented PLLRC proposals to increase timber, mining, and grazing uses of public lands. They feared that many hard-fought conservation battles of the past would have to be refought if Congress followed all the commission's recommendations.

Oil Slicks Now Part of the Seascape

Ironically, a year after the disastrous oil spills of January 1969 from offshore wells in the Santa Barbara Channel off southern California, a 40-square-mile oil slick reappeared in the same area, due to an oil leak that began Dec. 16, 1969. After a tanker was wrecked off the coast of Nova Scotia on February 4, it released oil that polluted two harbors and 20 miles of coastline. Local fisheries were forced to curtail activities as a consequence. About a week later, a large tanker ran aground in Tampa Bay, near St. Petersburg, Fla. Oil covered miles of bay water, took a heavy toll of birds, and posed a serious threat to mangrove bayous along the bay. Oyster beds near the affected area were closed to avoid the marketing of tainted shellfish.

Oil spills continued with appalling regularity in 1970. On February 21, a ruptured barge spilled 84,000 gallons of gasoline into Humboldt Bay, off Eureka, Calif. On February 26, an oil-filled barge collided with a freighter in Florida's St. Johns River and dumped a coating of oil along miles of wildlife habitat. In early March a tanker gashed open on a reef in Torres Strait, north of Australia, and spread its cargo over 30 miles of sea. It endangered Australia's vast oyster beds near Thursday Island. At the same time, some 200 miles of Alaska's shoreline was sullied by oil purportedly dumped from tankers. Thousands of dead birds were found along nearby beaches.

The first indications that one of history's worst oil spills was taking place in the Gulf of Mexico were found in late January when beaches were blackened on Louisiana's Grand Isle. Then, in early February, a cluster of offshore oil wells exploded and burst into flames. After raging for a month, the fire was extinguished. But another calamity occurred; a 100-foot-high gusher began raining oil onto the gulf. Three weeks elapsed before the leak was capped. In August Chevron Oil Co., operator of the wells, was fined $1 million for drilling violations that led to the disaster.

While Norwegian explorer and anthropologist Thor Heyerdahl and his crew were sailing a boat made of papyrus reeds across the Atlantic Ocean, they came across vast stretches of ocean that were polluted with lumps of asphaltlike oil and other materials. After completing the journey, in July, Heyerdahl accepted an invitation to testify before a U.S. Senate committee on ocean pollution.

No End in Sight to Dirtied Waters

The Nixon Administration in 1970 intimated that water cleanup costs would be high. The federal government planned to appropriate $10 billion over a five-year period for water treatment. But the ultimate cost for cleansing all U.S. waters was put at a staggering $100 billion. Private industry, smarting under accusations blaming it for the major portion of pollution, committed $2 billion for antipollution efforts in 1970.

The United States and Canada jointly vowed to put an end to pollution of the Great Lakes and the St. Lawrence River. Representatives of both nations agreed on antipollution contingency plans as a first step toward this goal in a June meeting.

HOWARD PETRICK FROM NANCY PALMER AGENCY

In March 1970 folk singer Pete Seeger, an avid conservationist, participated in an antiauto show demonstration in New York City.

Detergent phosphates and fertilizer nitrates finding their way into lakes and slow-running rivers continued to nourish the algae that were threatening to choke those waters. Conservationists called for the banning of all phosphate detergents. Re-

The sloop *Clearwater*, sailing the Hudson River in support of conservation, passes by an enormous junkyard while on its way to Washington, D.C., for Earth Day, April 22.

UPI COMPIX

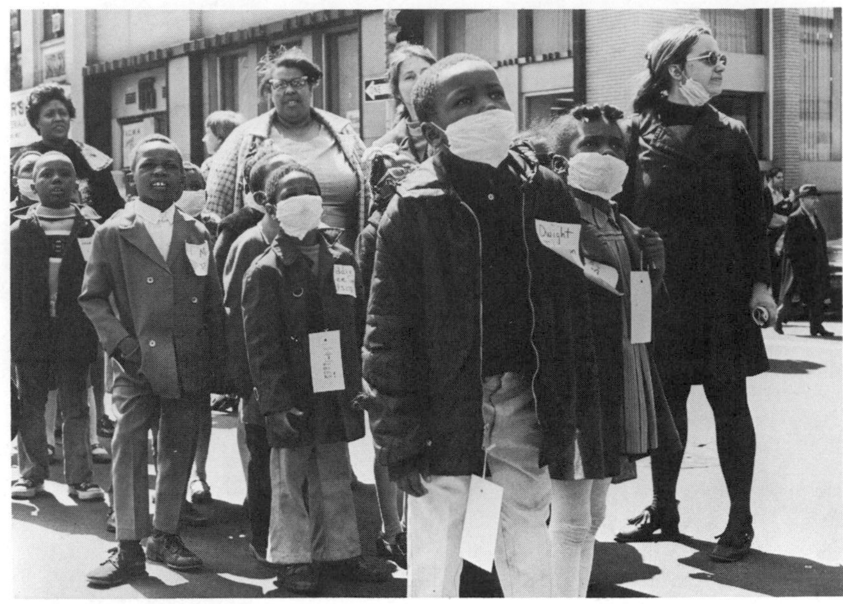

RIGHT: LESLIE LEON FROM KEYSTONE. BELOW: JERRY BRIMACOMBE, LIFE MAGAZINE © TIME INC.

New York City children demonstrate against air pollution on Earth Day (right). At the University of Minnesota, students bury an automobile engine (below) in January.

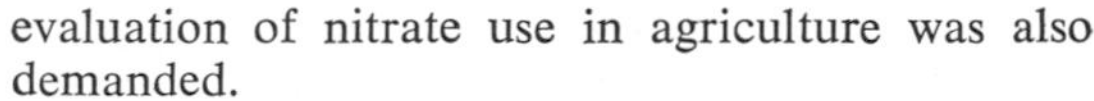

evaluation of nitrate use in agriculture was also demanded.

In September the Department of the Interior issued a list of the phosphate content of nearly 50 popular detergents. The Federal Water Quality Administration was quick to deny that it was suggesting a boycott of those with high-phosphate content. The soap industry sensed that a phosphate ban was in the offing and experimented with nitrilotriacetate (NTA) as a substitute in detergents. In Sweden, where the compound has been used extensively, no evidence was found of ecological damage from NTA use. In December, however, detergents containing NTA were removed from the U.S. market after it was found they could cause death and birth defects in laboratory animals.

Another problem loomed among 1970 water ills —mercury pollution. In April fish taken from waters between Lakes Huron and Erie sometimes contained more than 1.3 parts of mercury per million parts of fish. The maximum safe level of mercury for human consumption, however, had been determined as only 0.5 parts per million. Factories had been dumping mercury wastes into waterways for years, assuming that they would sink harmlessly to the bottom. However, the metallic mercury in the water was being converted to more toxic methylated forms, perhaps by bacteria, and absorbed by fish. Public health officials were especially worried because by the time mercury poisoning in humans could be confidently diagnosed, irreparable brain damage would have occurred. In July the U.S. Department of Justice began to sue mercury polluters under the Refuse Act of 1899.

On August 18, the U.S. Army sank an old Liberty ship loaded with some 12,500 rockets filled with lethal nerve gas about 280 miles off the coast

(continued on page 207)

Special Report: The Alaska Pipeline

by Thomas M. Brown,
Reporter, *Anchorage Daily News*

During 1970 one of the hottest battles on the conservation front in the United States was being fought in the sprawling, sparsely peopled 49th state, Alaska. The conflict involved a choice between two seemingly irreconcilable goals: economic development and preservation of the natural environment.

The conflict began in 1968 when Atlantic Richfield Co. struck oil below the tundra of Alaska's remote northern rim at Prudhoe Bay. The discovery, which quickly proved to be the biggest ever in North America, confronted Alaska with two possibilities: on the one hand, great wealth badly needed by a poor state beset with many problems, and, on the other, the destruction of the wilderness environment that makes Alaska unique. In short, two valuable resources—oil and wilderness—were placed in direct conflict. That conflict did not ease in the intervening three years.

Development Versus Conservation

There is tremendous pressure for rapid development of the Prudhoe Bay oil fields for two reasons. The oil industry is anxious to retrieve its $2-billion investment in the area (known as the North Slope) and to reap the great profits that would follow, and the state government urgently needs the money that oil royalties would bring in.

Many Alaskans favor rapid exploitation of the oil fields—even at the expense of the environment—because of the economic impact it would have on the state, bringing an estimated $4 billion to $6 billion during the life of the field. And Alaska has an abundance of problems to spend the money on. It has little in the way of a domestic economy. There has never been enough money to deal with the appalling poverty that particularly afflicts the state's Indians, Eskimos, and Aleuts. Educational development has lagged. Social services are mediocre. Even the most elementary facilities—sewers, pure drinking water, hospitals, and roads—are lacking more often than not.

There appears, however, to be a growing awareness among Alaskans that their desire to improve living standards through the exploitation of oil is in many ways in direct conflict with the requirements of prudent conservation. This message has been driven home by conservation groups throughout the United States. Wilderness is fast vanishing throughout the world. The last big piece of it in the United States is Alaska, and much of Alaska's remaining true wilderness lies on the North Slope. Because of the scarcity of this nonrenewable resource and the appeal it has for many people, conservationists believe that the Alaskan wilderness will prove far more valuable in the long run than its oil. They have set high priority on preserving as much of it as possible.

The Vulnerable Arctic Environment

The Arctic receives little sunlight and is thus very poor in the production of plant life. Because of poor plant production, there is relatively little food for plant-eating animals and, in turn, for the meat-eating animals, which feed on the plant-eaters. The low production of plant and animal life means that the Arctic has one of the simplest ecosystems and thus one of the most fragile. It cannot withstand much pressure from man.

The low level of solar radiation in the Arctic ensures the existence of permafrost—frozen rock and soil beneath the earth's surface. Some permafrost remains stable when thawed. Permafrost underlying much of the North Slope (and many areas along the route suggested for a proposed trans-Alaska pipeline to transport the oil), however, is of the so-called "ice-rich" variety with a high content of frozen water. When thawed, it becomes an unstable slurry of watery, oozing mud. Normally, the vegetative cover of tundra insulates the ground. But the U.S. Geological Survey reported: "The simple passage of a tracked vehicle that destroys the vegetation mat is enough to upset the delicate (thermal) balance and to cause the top of the permafrost layer to thaw. This thawing can cause differential settlement of the surface of the ground, drainage problems, and severe frost action. Once the equilibrium is upset, the whole process can feed on itself and be practically impossible to reverse."

In addition to these potentially dangerous environmental problems, there is yet another. The Arctic plain is largely flat and featureless. Thus it is a susceptible environment to the visual pollution of litter. There are places where a single oil drum can be visible for miles.

Just how vulnerable this environment is was demonstrated during World War II, when the federal government dispatched oil crews to explore a 23-million-acre area roughly between Prudhoe Bay and Barrow. The crews left a trail of trash and countless miles of bulldozer trails. Unsightly junk

JOSEPH RYCHETNIK FROM VAN CLEVE PHOTOGRAPHY

Fifty miles of pipe are stockpiled awaiting a decision on the controversial Alaska pipeline. Conservationists fear that the pipeline would cause extensive damage to the environment.

heaps still stand, protruding like rusting skyscrapers from the flat tundra. The bulldozer trails exposed the permafrost and eroded into gullies, draining lakes and changing the character of surrounding areas. Thousands of oil drums were left that eventually polluted the shallow lakes where migratory waterfowl molt each summer.

Development of the North Slope oil fields by private enterprise poses the same kinds of environmental threats on a much larger scale. Compared with the abuses of the federal and state governments, the performance of the oil industry has been good. Still, damage has occurred.

Before the historic Prudhoe Bay strike, when there was little public knowledge of what was going on there, some of the worst environmental abuses were occurring. Some abuses were similar to the despoilation that previous oil exploration crews had wrought; others were much more devastating. Geophysical exploration crews, for instance, did much seismic surveying, a technique that involves planting and detonating dynamite charges below the surface of the ground. In some instances, the vegetative cover of the tundra was removed in a straight line for ten miles, leaving trails that later eroded into water-filled ditches. Close behind the seismic crews came the drillers, who often left massive marks on the land with their drilling rigs, exposing the tundra to erosion. As the oil boom intensified, more and more oil companies explored and drilled, multiplying environmental damage.

At the same time, conservation organizations throughout the United States began taking an active interest in what was happening. With conservation pressure on, the major oil companies soon realized that they would have to demonstrate a stronger concern for the environment if they were to be allowed to develop their oil discoveries. They began instituting development practices that were the least harmful environmentally of any ever employed in the American Arctic. Instead of haphazard bulldozer trails, for instance, the oil companies began constructing all-weather gravel roads made five feet thick to adequately insulate the underlying permafrost. Drilling rigs were put on gravel pads so they could be operated in the summer without thawing the permafrost. Pressure was put on the oil crews to clean up after themselves.

Yet even these exemplary practices were not without their environmental drawbacks. Conservationists wondered whether the network of roads, airfields, and drilling pads might not prove to be a monument as enduring—and not nearly so attractive—as the pyramids. They were also concerned that removal of millions of cubic yards of gravel from Alaska's rivers might irreparably damage them.

The Pipeline Controversy

Disturbed as they were about some of the things that were happening on the North Slope, there was little the conservationists could do legally except complain. Therefore, they concentrated on the proposed trans-Alaska pipeline, which for many had become symbolic of the entire question of conservation versus development. Conservationists also felt they had a better chance of exerting influence on the pipeline project since most of the proposed route lay over federal land and its construction required approval of the U.S. secretary of the interior.

The pipeline project worried the environmental protection groups on a number of counts, mainly the permafrost problem, possible oil leaks, and damage to surrounding areas during construction. The oil industry insisted that it could bury 95% of the pipeline, thereby eliminating some of the objections to it as an eyesore and a barrier to caribou migration. The conservationists were skeptical about the practicality of burying a huge pipeline, carrying oil with a temperature of about 160° F., in permafrost. They wanted to know what would happen when the permafrost melted. They also pointed out that a major break in the pipeline could deluge the surrounding countryside with oil. And they were concerned that, though the requested pipeline right-of-way was only 100 feet wide by 800 miles long, or about 15 square miles, a very much larger area would be affected. This was because an access road would have to be constructed so that equipment could get into the area to lay the pipeline, and because an enormous amount of gravel would have to be dug from pits along the way to be used during construction.

The Department of the Interior was similarly concerned. Late in 1970 U.S. Secretary of the Interior Walter J. Hickel announced that the major unanswered issues were how the pipeline would be constructed in permafrost areas and its final design specifications. Only when these questions were dealt with satisfactorily, he said, would a construction permit be issued. He added that he hoped this would not be later than the spring of 1971.

Despite the conservationists' concern, the pipeline appeared to be the lesser of two evils environmentally. The most commonly discussed alternative was the use of giant icebreaking tankers or submarine tankers, which would follow the Northwest Passage from the top of Alaska to East Coast markets. In questioning the advisability of Arctic tanker operations, conservationists cited studies demonstrating the slow decomposition of oil in cold water, thus ensuring that a spill would be more persistent than in warmer waters. Such a spill almost certainly would have disastrous effects on the short, vulnerable Arctic marine food chain.

The pipeline and Arctic tanker operations are not the only threats that oil poses to Alaska. In short, it has become clear that no matter how much care is exercised in developing the Arctic, the face of the land will be changed and there will be some environmental damage. The crucial question is how much damage is acceptable. There is no consensus on that.

(*continued from page 204*)

of Florida. Conservationists made repeated but unsuccessful attempts to stop the action. The Department of Defense, however, promised that it would never again bury nerve gas at sea.

Delicate Ecological Balances Threatened

The defoliation program conducted by U.S. military forces in Vietnam came under investigation after reports that herbicide defoliants were causing harm to Vietnamese and their livestock. The spraying program was in operation for about eight years, but the detrimental effects of such chemicals as 2,4,5-T were undetermined. However, laboratory experiments with 2,4,5-T revealed a high incidence of birth deformities in test mammals.

No action had been taken in 1970 on the planned trans-Alaska pipeline, an 800-mile-long oil line from Alaska's North Slope to the deepwater port of Valdez. Conservationists feared that the heat needed for transportation of the oil would melt the permafrost underlying the pipeline, causing it to sink, break, and spill tons of oil over the delicate Arctic tundra. (*See* Conservation Special Report.)

Florida's Everglades, a unique ecosystem comprised of about 5,000 square miles of freshwater swamp, received a reprieve of sorts from extinction in January when plans for a major airport on its northern fringes were scrapped. The jetport, according to opponents, would interfere with the critical flow of water through the Everglades. Then, Seminole and Miccosukee who claim portions of the Everglades leased exploration rights to some major oil companies. Conservationists feared that oil exploration would pose a new danger to the Everglades if high-quality oil was found there. Thus far, only low-quality oil has been discovered.

Air Pollution Continues Unabated

Once restricted almost solely to urban areas, smog has recently drifted to formerly pristine rural regions. Even the crystal-clear air of the Andes Mountains of South America has been stenched with the pollutants that pour from the automobiles, furnaces, and incinerators of Santiago, Chile. One optimistic report conceded, however, that despite the enormity of air pollution in recent years, the oxygen content of the atmosphere has remained constant during the past 60 years.

The major part played by the automobile engine in air pollution was dramatized in the United States in 1970. In late summer a cross-country race was staged between cars with antipollution devices or with nongasoline propulsion systems. Earlier in the summer the automobile industry said that "impressive emission reductions" would be a feature of 1971 model cars, but it needed more time to produce a "clean" car.

Other Steps to Improve the Environment

The glass industry announced in late June that it would redeem used nonreturnable bottles for ½¢

each or 1¢ per pound. About 11 billion bottles could be thus salvaged annually.

The U.S. aviation industry was advised by the Department of Health, Education, and Welfare to voluntarily eliminate the smoke from its jet engines. The industry agreed to meet government demands for smoke-free operations by the end of 1972.

The supersonic transport (SST) continued to make headlines during the year, even though no U.S. SST had been built. Some scientists asked for the suspension of SST development until a full study was made of the environmental effects of the swift but noisy plane. (*See also* Animals and Wildlife. *See in* CE: Conservation.)

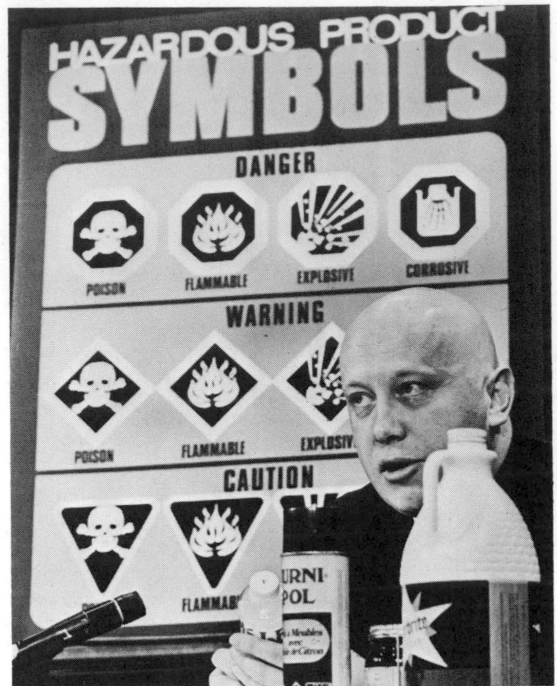

CHARLES MITCHELL FROM CANADIAN PRESS

New regulations governing the labeling of hazardous household chemicals in Canada were explained in March by Consumer and Corporate Affairs Minister Stanley R. Basford in Ottawa.

CONSUMER PROTECTION. A study conducted by the President's Committee on Consumer Interests during 1970 revealed the areas in which U.S. consumers felt they needed the greatest amount of protection. The committee received more complaints about new and used cars than any other consumer product. Following cars on the list were home appliances and food products.

For the most part, it appeared that such consumer complaints were well founded. In October consumer advocate Ralph Nader asked for a U.S. Senate investigation of General Motors Corp. He claimed that the automobile company had deliberately suppressed information indicating that early models of the Chevrolet Corvair were unsafe. Also in October Colston E. Warne, president of Consumers Union of U.S., Inc., urged Ford Motor Co. to recall 4 million cars because of a safety defect on their front wheel systems. His plea followed a warning by the National Highway Safety Bureau that the defect existed in various models of Ford and Mercury cars. Ford denied the existence of a defect and refused to recall the cars. However, Ford did recall 26,000 models of its 1971 Pinto because of an accelerator linkage problem and 26,700 trucks and bus chassis (1968, 1969, and 1970 models) because of brake reservoir problems.

In an important decision in September, a U.S. federal court ruled that a number of state and city governments and private citizens could bring triple-damage suits against the major automobile manufacturers for having allegedly conspired to prevent the development and installation of antismog devices. The ruling cleared the way for trials in many similar antitrust cases throughout the nation. Previously, antitrust cases had been restricted to areas of commercial damage such as overcharging, boycotting, and unfair competition.

During 1970 the Federal Trade Commission undertook a study of "planned obsolescence" in the manufacture of appliances. The investigation was being directed at three practices: the unavailability of replacement parts during the reasonable life of the product, frequent changes in the product not affecting its function, and the inclusion of some components with a shorter life expectancy than that of the product.

One positive response to consumer complaints was taken by several supermarket chains that initiated the practice of unit pricing. Under the system the prices of different brands of the same product are given as the number of cents per ounce, quart, square foot, or other unit, making comparison shopping much easier. Among the chains using unit pricing were Jewel Food Stores of Chicago; Safeway Stores, a nationwide chain; Benner Tea Co. of Burlington, Iowa; and cooperative food stores in Berkeley, Calif., Greenbelt, Md., and Chicago. However, at least in the case of Jewel stores, the system was not bringing benefits to those customers who needed it most. It was being used more by high-income, well-educated shoppers than by those in low-income groups.

Another marking process designed to help the consumer made its way into supermarkets during the year. At least one chain, Jewel Food Stores, showed consumers how to decode some of the markings that indicate when an item was packaged or when it is scheduled to be pulled from the shelf. Consumer groups campaigned for legislation demanding similar "open dating" practices at other stores.

In October the U.S. government released long-awaited test data on the 1.7 million nondefense products it buys each year. The report was a disappointment to consumer groups because it contained comparatively few brand names and

WIDE WORLD

Concrete slabs and debris cover the street in front of a federal office building in Minneapolis, Minn., following an explosion on Aug. 17, 1970. The building houses an armed forces examination center and has been the target for numerous war protests.

van Fine, 18, a former night editor of the university student newspaper *The Daily Cardinal;* and Leo Frederick Burt, 22, a summer student at the university.

In Danbury, Conn., on Feb. 13, 1970, two gunmen set off bombs in a police station, a bank, and a parking lot and made off with $40,000 as the three explosions rocked Main Street. The first bomb exploded in the police station, blowing out its windows and buckling its floors; 26 persons were injured, none critically, by flying glass and falling fixtures. Moments later, two men, armed with a submachine gun and a sawed-off shotgun, entered the Union Savings Bank, herded the bank employees into an anteroom, and robbed the bank. As the bandits departed, they lobbed a bomb into the bank's main room. As broken glass rained on Main Street, the robbers ran to a municipal parking lot where they jumped into a white Chrysler station wagon that had previously been stolen from New York City's John F. Kennedy International Airport. After driving it for two blocks to a shopping-center parking lot, the bandits transferred to another car. As they left, the third bomb was placed in the Chrysler station wagon, which was demolished. On March 7, 1970, 27-year-old John Russell Pardue was arrested in Danbury and charged with bank robbery. On the same day his brother, James Peter Pardue, 23, was arrested in Rockville, Md., on the same charges. Each was held in lieu of $250,000 bail.

On Jan. 5, 1970, the bodies of Joseph A. Yablonski, 59, defeated candidate for president of the United Mine Workers of America (UMW), his wife, Margaret, 57, and daughter, Charlotte, 25, were found in the Yablonski home in Clarksville, Pa. They had been murdered on the night of Dec. 30–31, 1969, three weeks after the bitterly disputed union election of December 9. Yablonski had charged that his defeat for the union presidency by W. A. (Tony) Boyle was based on massive fraud. Prior to the election, Yablonski and his wife had noticed a strange automobile outside their home, and Yablonski began keeping a shotgun near his bed at night as well as compiling a list of license numbers of suspicious automobiles. Following the election, Yablonski reportedly was scheduled to testify before a federal grand jury regarding alleged union election fraud.

In January 1970, a federal grand jury in Cleveland, Ohio, returned a seven-count indictment charging Paul Eugene Gilly, Claude Edward Vealey, and Aubran Wayne Martin with conspiracy to kill Yablonski. Named as coconspirators but not defendants, were James Charles Phillips and Annette Gilly, the wife of Paul Gilly. Another federal indictment was returned in Cleveland on Feb. 25, 1970, against Silous Huddleston, president of Local 3228 of the UMW in La Follette, Tenn., who was accused of "directing" his daughter, Annette Gilly, and her husband in carrying out the slaying with two other men hired in Cleveland by Paul Gilly. Vealey and Martin were described in the indictment as having been hired for $1,700 each. On May 6, 1970, in Washington, Pa., indictments charging first-degree murder were returned against Gilly, Vealey, and Martin. Separate indictments charged them with burglary, larceny, and robbery of the Yablonski home "while armed." Separate indictments also accused Annette Gilly and Silous Huddleston of first-degree murder.

After a 4½-month trial, filled with turmoil and courtroom disruption, a federal court jury in Chicago on Feb. 18, 1970, acquitted seven defendants on charges of conspiring to incite a riot during the 1968 Democratic National Convention in that city. However, five defendants—David T. Dellinger, Rennie C. Davis, Thomas F. Hayden, Abbie Hoffman, and Jerry C. Rubin—were found guilty of crossing state lines with intent to incite a riot and then giving inflammatory speeches for that purpose. Two other defendants—John R. Froines and Lee Weiner—were acquitted on both the conspiracy and individual counts. On Feb. 20, 1970, Judge Julius J. Hoffman, who presided over the trial in Chicago, sentenced each of the five convicted defendants—Dellinger, Davis, Hayden, Hoffman, and Rubin—to serve five years in prison and to pay a fine of $5,000; the defendants were also ordered to pay for the "costs of prosecution." (*See also* Labor Unions; Law; Law Special Report; Police; Prisons. *See in* CE: Prisons and Punishments.)

CUBA. The worst economic conditions since Premier Fidel Castro came to power plagued Cuba in 1970. The steady economic decline was evident in low labor productivity, a severe shortage of consumer goods, high absenteeism in the work force, and a decline in the production of staple foods and in manufactured goods. Although the economic situation produced discontent and disillusionment among the population, the political situation remained stable. Cuban exiles launched raids against Cuba during the year, but they were reportedly brought under control. There were indications that some Latin American nations favored a resumption of diplomatic and economic ties with Cuba.

WIDE WORLD

A brigade of young Americans proceeds toward the fields in Havana province where they will spend the day cutting sugarcane. The young people went to help the Cubans reach the harvest goal set by Premier Castro.

Going for Broke

Even though the 1970 sugar harvest reached a record of 8.5 million tons it fell short of the 10-million-ton goal set by Premier Castro. The importance of reaching the harvest goal had far more than economic significance, for Castro had staked the honor of the revolution on a 10-million-ton harvest. Castro mobilized a huge work force of Cubans from all walks of life—students, professionals, and factory workers—to help with the harvest. Groups of radical young people from the United States and other nations also went to Cuba to help with the harvest. Nevertheless, problems with harvesting, transporting the sugarcane, and processing it in the mills caused the harvest to be 1.5 million tons short of the goal.

In a historic speech on July 26 Castro admitted the failings of his government in not being able to establish a sound economy. He particularly laid the blame on himself and told the people that they could change the Cuban leadership if they so desired. Castro conceded that administrative officials were not competent in the area of economics and stated that the all-out effort to produce 10 million tons of sugar in 1970 had created severe imbalances in the economy. He also acknowledged that there was widespread discontent among Cubans.

In all the speeches made during the year, however, the blame was not entirely laid on government officials. Castro, in his May 31 speech, criticized the irresponsibility, poor discipline, and low labor productivity of Cuban workers. The theme of the failure of the workers was taken up again by Labor Minister Jorge Risquet in a speech published August 3. He criticized the labor force for high absenteeism and low productivity. There appeared to be moves toward revamping the administrative level of the Cuban government. Several ministers were dismissed during the year, including the minister of education and the minister of the sugar industry. Castro also announced the formation of a new cabinet post for coordinating administrative and economic planning.

New Raids—New Rapport

A guerrilla band of exiled Cubans calling themselves Alpha 66, based in Miami, Fla., attempted to invade Cuba in April. After the Cuban government announced that eight of the guerrillas had been captured, Alpha 66 members sank two Cuban fishing boats and held 11 Cuban fishermen as hostages. Castro refused to give up the captives, and after two weeks the fishermen were released by Alpha 66.

There was some evidence of a desire by a number of Latin American governments to restore commercial and diplomatic ties with Cuba. Chile undertook to supply \$3 million worth of agricultural products in 1970 and \$8 million worth in 1971. Several nations, including Colombia and Trinidad and Tobago, pressed the United States to ease its Cuban blockade. Castro sent earthquake-relief supplies to Peru and declared support for its military regime (*see* Peru).

The hijacking of airplanes to Cuba continued throughout 1970. In August a hijacked Boeing 747 jet airliner landed at Havana, the capital, and Castro went out to view the first jumbo jet in Cuba. In another hijacking, the Cuban government, for the first time, returned to the United States a U.S. serviceman who had hijacked a plane on August 24. (*See in* CE: Cuba.)

In May 1970 Premier Castro appeared on nationwide television in Cuba to discuss low productivity and general economic conditions with the Cuban people.

PRENSA LATINA FROM KEYSTONE

CYPRUS. In 1970 negotiations between the Greek and Turkish Cypriots on the administrative structure of a united and independent Cyprus made no headway. A new challenge to the policy of President Archbishop Makarios came from the National Front, a right-wing Greek Cypriot movement that wanted immediate *enosis* (union with Greece). Using terrorist tactics, it created tensions that came to a head early in the year.

On March 8, shots were fired from a rooftop at the president's helicopter as it took off from Nicosia, the capital. Makarios escaped unhurt, but his pilot was wounded. Although those held responsible for trying to kill Makarios were never officially named, there were suggestions that Polycarpos Georgiades might have been involved in the attack, which was widely attributed to the National Front. On March 15 Georgiades was fatally shot near the city. Throughout the preindependence campaign against British rule, Georgiades had been a prominent member of the militant EOKA (National Organization of Cypriot Fighters) resistance movement. He held ministerial posts from 1960 until 1968, when he fell into disfavor with the Greek government, which forced his resignation. The political atmosphere in which the shootings occurred had been building up since the National Front emerged in 1969 to revive the demand for enosis.

Despite the prevailing tension, the island's first elections since independence in 1960 took place without incident. The elections, held on July 5, gave 15 of the 35 Greek Cypriot seats in the House of Representatives to the moderate right-wing Unified party, led by Glafkos Clerides, president of the House and a man committed to broad support of the Makarios policy. All 15 of the parliamentary seats allocated to the Turkish Cypriots were held by adherents of the community's leader, Rauf Denktash. (*See in* CE: Cyprus.)

CZECHOSLOVAKIA. Throughout 1970 the situation in Czechoslovakia could be compared to a tug-of-war between the hard-line enemies of reform on the one hand and Gustav Husak, the Communist party's first secretary, on the other. The issue at stake was not the continuation, or even the salvaging, of the real substance of the reforms proposed in 1968; it was Husak's desire to slow up the purges, which were decimating the country's most competent cadres, and his reluctance to sanction the staging of political show trials. Husak was only partially successful, though he enjoyed the confidence and trust of the Soviet leadership. The Soviet Union, it seemed, wanted in 1970 to play safe in Czechoslovakia. Anything that might arouse the people to demonstrate their discontent was to be avoided, but the reality of control along lines approved by the Soviet Union was to be maintained with a minimum of trouble. As long as Husak seemed able to carry out this policy, there appeared to be no reason why the Soviet Union would withdraw its support from him merely to

KEYSTONE

Soviet and Czechoslovakian troops participate in joint military maneuvers in August 1970 on Czechoslovakian territory.

satisfy a handful of hard-liners in Prague, the Czechoslovak capital.

The old-guard conservatives made a gain at the beginning of the year. In January it was announced that the conduct in 1968 of former Communist Party First Secretary Alexander Dubcek would be investigated. At the same time eight resignations from the Communist party's Central Committee were announced. Oldrich Cernik, a somewhat equivocal survivor from 1968, was replaced as premier by Lubomir Strougal, who had served as minister of the interior in the Antonin Novotny regime (which, in turn, had given way to that of Dubcek in 1968). Strougal was considered the obvious challenger to Husak's authority. On the other hand, his rise coincided with the removal of the Slovak Communist party leader, Stefan Sadovsky, reportedly for his failure to back Husak's policies with sufficient vigor. Yet on January 30 Husak thought it necessary to state that, as long as he was first secretary, there would be no return to the show trials common in the era of Soviet dictator Joseph Stalin.

Dubcek arrived in Ankara, Turkey, on January 26 to take up his post as ambassador to Turkey. On March 21 his suspension from membership in the Communist party was announced. In June he was recalled from Turkey, expelled from the party, and consigned to provincial obscurity in Slovakia. Husak went on record to criticize him for "destroying relations with the Soviet Union and the other allied states."

Dubcek's fate had been decided in 1968 by the Soviet-led invasion of Czechoslovakia. His subsequent tribulations were merely symptomatic of the general line pursued by his successors. The most significant purge occurred within the Communist party itself, beginning in 1969; it had to be cleansed of "unreliable" elements to enable it to function again as the main mechanism of control. Dubcek's colleagues were weeded out systematically from positions of influence, and during the summer of 1970 the new leaders took the purge to the grass roots of the party by calling in party membership cards, interviewing suspect individuals, and denying new cards to some.

Severe restrictions were applied in the cultural sphere. Many of the journalists, writers, academics, and intellectuals who supported the 1968 reform program were removed from their posts and compelled to take up menial jobs in the provinces. Some writers were tried on charges of subversion or of uttering slander about the alliance with the Soviet Union. The Czechoslovak Writers' Union was virtually cut off from official funds, and royalties were paid only to authors who supported the present order. Other professional associations —of journalists, architects, students—were restricted and attacked. The autonomy of the Czechoslovak Academy of Sciences was practically abolished in July.

In the field of foreign policy, both Husak and Strougal gave a cautious welcome in August to the West German–Soviet treaty on the renunciation of force. This was preceded in June by a new trade agreement between Czechoslovakia and West Germany that provided for an extension of trade between the two countries. However, the major exercise in foreign policy was the signing of yet another 20-year Soviet-Czechoslovak treaty of friendship, cooperation, and mutual assistance. The draft was discussed with Andrei A. Gromyko, the Soviet foreign minister, during his visit to Prague in March. In May Soviet Communist Party General Secretary Leonid I. Brezhnev himself went to Prague to sign the treaty, which legitimized the presence of Soviet troops in Czechoslovakia, describing them as necessary for the "defense of the Western frontier of the Socialist community." The treaty also incorporated the essence of the so-called "Brezhnev doctrine," stating that "the support, the strengthening, and the protection of Socialist acquisitions, which were achieved through heroic efforts and sacrifice-filled toil by the people of the two countries, are the joint international duty of the Socialist countries." Husak acclaimed the pact as a guarantee of "a free life" for the people of Czechoslovakia. Significantly, a communiqué issued in Moscow after Brezhnev's return praised Husak's leadership for having successfully eliminated the subversive effect of the right-wing and counterrevolutionary forces on Czechoslovakia's relations with the Soviet Union.

Yet this did not appear to have satisfied the hard-line opposition, which continued to look to Strougal for support. In the second half of October, the dismissal of the Czechoslovak minister of the interior, Josef Groesser, was followed by the removal of Gen. Otakar Rytir, the chief liaison officer with Soviet forces in Czechoslovakia. It was reported that the two were implicated in a move to complain to the Soviet leaders about Husak's alleged liberalism. (*See in* CE: Czechoslovakia.)

After having served more than 30 years, Alexander Dubcek was expelled from the Czechoslovak Communist party on June 26, 1970. The former Communist party first secretary had been in disfavor with the Russians since his attempt to democratize the party in 1968.

WIDE WORLD

DAHOMEY. The presidential election that was to have taken place in Dahomey between March 9 and March 31, 1970, was not completed as a result of numerous violent incidents, particularly around Parakou, electoral stronghold of former President Hubert Maga. On March 28 the ruling military directorate temporarily suspended voting. There was a movement toward secession among Maga's supporters in the north. On April 3 Lieut. Col. Paul Emile de Souza announced the definitive annulment of the election and the formation, within a month, of a government of national unity. The results obtained by the presidential candidates in their respective electoral strongholds—Maga in the north, Justin Ahomadegbe in the southwest, and Sourou Migan Apithy in the southeast—made the crisis particularly difficult to unravel.

Two weeks later, a charter or "fundamental state law" was adopted to rule the country pending a general election and the institution of a constitutional regime. This named the Presidential Council as supreme organ of the state with collegiate responsibility. Maga, president of Dahomey from 1960 to 1963, became the first president of the Council on the basis of a rotation system whereby Ahomadegbe would become president in May 1972 and Apithy in May 1974. (*See in* CE: Dahomey.)

DANCE. The most spectacular event of 1970 in the field of dance was the defection of the Soviet ballerina Natalya Makarova to the West. Makarova, one of the most celebrated dancers of the Kirov Ballet, asked for asylum in Great Britain while she was dancing with the Kirov during its 1970 engagement in London. The reason for her defection was evidently for artistic and not political reasons; she stated that she wanted new challenges as a dancer. Subsequently, Makarova joined the American Ballet Theatre and made her New York City debut with the company in December in the ballet classic 'Giselle'. In New York City she also danced her first 'Coppélia' and the dramatic lead in Antony Tudor's modern ballet 'Lilac Garden', in which she was hailed by press and public. Another Soviet dance defector was Aleksandr Filipov, who also joined the American Ballet Theatre.

Besides adding two defectors to its ranks, the American Ballet Theatre celebrated its 30th anniversary in 1970. The company added to its repertoire a lavish new production of the Michel Fokine-Igor Stravinsky 'Petrouchka'; 'The River', a new work to a Duke Ellington score by black choreographer Alvin Ailey; and two pure modern dance works, 'The Moor's Pavane' and 'The Traitor', by José Limón.

The York City Ballet produced an entirely new George Balanchine-Jerome Robbins-Igor Stravinsky 'Firebird', with settings and costumes executed after designs by the painter Marc Chagall. Robbins also created his second all-Chopin ballet, 'In the Night', based on Chopin nocturnes, for the company. In the summer, at the company's headquar-

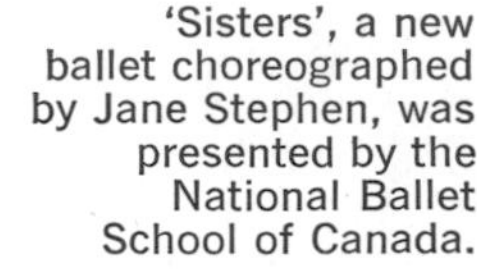

'Sisters', a new ballet choreographed by Jane Stephen, was presented by the National Ballet School of Canada.
COURTESY, NATIONAL ARTS CENTRE

ters at Saratoga Springs, N.Y., a working rehearsal of Robbins' newest pure dance work, 'Goldberg Variations', was shown publicly.

The City Center Joffrey Ballet and Eliot Feld's American Ballet Company had successful New York City seasons. The Joffrey group produced a major new staging of 'Petrouchka' (which was not so well received as the American Ballet Theatre's production), and Joffrey's leading choreographer, Gerald Arpino, created an instant hit with the rock ballet 'Trinity'. The American Ballet Company featured new works by the prolific Feld, among them 'Early Songs', 'A Poem Forgotten', and 'Cortège Parisien'.

Rudolf Nureyev stars in the world premiere of Rudi van Dantzig's 'The Ropes of Time'.
FOX PHOTOS FROM PICTORIAL PARADE

The first all-black classical ballet company ever organized, the Dance Theatre of Harlem, had its first extended engagement during the year, a one-week stand at the world-famous Jacob's Pillow Dance Festival in Lee, Mass. The company had been founded barely two years before by Arthur Mitchell, a principal with the New York City Ballet, and was directed by him and by Karel Shook.

Among the non-New York City ballet troupes active during the year were the Boston Ballet, the San Francisco Ballet, the Atlanta Ballet, Ballet West, the Pennsylvania Ballet, and the National Ballet of Washington, D.C. Ballet's superstar Dame Margot Fonteyn danced with the Boston Ballet (with Richard Cragun as her partner) and with the National Ballet in a new full-length 'Cinderella' choreographed by Ben Stevenson.

In the field of modern dance, U.S. companies continued to predominate, with the Merce Cunningham, Paul Taylor, Alvin Ailey, and Alwin Nikolais groups the most active. The Alvin Ailey group suffered such severe financial difficulties during the year that at one point it had to disband. However, it managed eventually to find backing, reorganize, and go on to extremely successful engagements in the late fall in London and the Soviet Union. Rumors circulated in the dance world during the year that the *grand dame* of modern dance in the United States, 76(?)-year-old Martha Graham, was finally retiring from the stage after a career spanning 50 years.

The most important news in dance in Europe was the retirement of Sir Frederick Ashton as director of Great Britain's Royal Ballet. (He planned to concentrate on his own choreography.) During its New York City tour and in London, the company honored Ashton with special gala performances that included extracts of ballets he had created over the last 35 years. Kenneth MacMillan and John Field succeeded Ashton as joint directors of the Royal Ballet, but later Field resigned.

Prior to Ashton's retirement the Royal Ballet company mounted two new works: Rudi van Dantzig's 'The Ropes of Time' (to Jan Boerman's electronic score), a vehicle for the famed Rudolf Nureyev, and Ashton's 'Lament of the Waves'. The Royal Ballet's touring company was even more active, mounting four new works, including Ashton's 'Creatures of Prometheus', which was performed first in Bonn, West Germany, as part of the Ludwig van Beethoven bicentenary celebrations.

The most important feature of ballet in Britain was the development and growing popularity of companies with a contemporary outlook. Ballet Rambert, for example, had sold-out London seasons and successful tours of Europe and the Middle East. The newest addition to the company's work was a program for children, 'Bertram Batell's Sideshow' (a form of dance revue created by dancers in the company). For more adult audiences Norman Morrice created 'Blind Sight' (to Bob Downes's jazz score) and Christopher Bruce choreographed 'Living Space' (to words by Robert Cockburn).

Gelsey Kirkland performs in the New York City Ballet's revival of 'Firebird'.

WIDE WORLD

London Contemporary Dance Theatre, based on the school and techniques of Martha Graham, was firmly established by 1970 as a vital part of the British dance scene. The company's home, The Place, became a center for avant-garde dance.

In continental Europe the main activity was in the Netherlands (the Netherlands Dance Theater and the Netherlands National Ballet) and in West Germany (the Stuttgart Ballet from the Württemberg State Theater). The Stuttgart company, directed by John Cranko, had become one of the most important European groups. It made a successful U.S. tour in 1969 and planned a return engagement in the near future. (*See in* CE: Ballet; Dance.)

DEFENSE. The shape of U.S. defense policy for 1970 was outlined by Secretary of Defense Melvin R. Laird in a February report to the U.S. Congress. In voicing his primary concern, Laird stated that continued acceleration of the Soviet missile program threatened to place the United States "in a second-rate strategic position" by the middle of the decade. He called for the expansion of the Safeguard antiballistic missile system on the grounds that it would enable the Administration of U.S. President Richard M. Nixon to put off making "hard decisions about adding to our offensive systems." He did, however, indicate the hope that negotiations with the Soviet Union would de-escalate the arms race.

Laird also covered a number of other topics in his annual defense report. He stated that draft calls were expected to fall to 200,000 for the year —down 90,000 from 1969. (*See* Selective Service.) In conjunction, he added that the "Vietnamization" of the war was expected to bring about the withdrawal of additional thousands of U.S. troops during the year. However, he declared that the $350-million ceiling placed by Congress on military assistance might not be adequate if U.S. forces were to be pulled back without abandoning national commitments.

Strategic Arms Development and Control

The Administration met partial defeat in its battle to extend the Safeguard system. In September a conference of the House and Senate Armed Services committees rejected a plan to extend the system to provide an area defense for U.S. population centers against a possible Chinese Communist attack. Instead it authorized only two additional Safeguard sites that were designed to provide defense against a possible Soviet attack.

During the year the United States and the Soviet Union continued to hold strategic arms limitation talks (SALT) in Vienna, Austria. In the meantime, however, both nations were developing multiple independently targetable reentry vehicles (MIRVs). Every MIRV carries a number of warheads, each of which can be fired against a separate

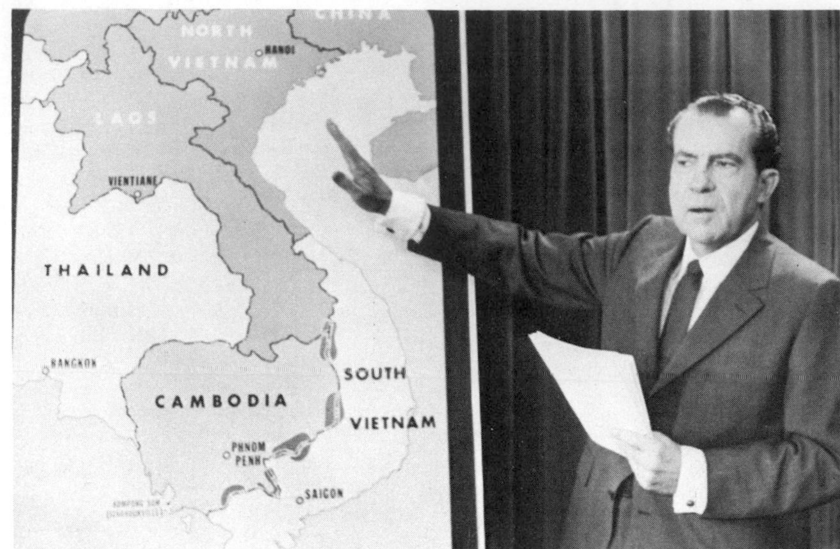

After expanding the war in Southeast Asia by sending troops into Cambodia, U.S. President Nixon explains his position on nationwide television. Unconvinced students led demonstrations throughout the United States.

EARL HICKS FROM PICTORIAL PARADE

target while the missile is in midflight. The construction of the MIRV also makes it very difficult for one power to estimate how many warheads the other has, since spy satellites are capable of counting missiles, but not the number of warheads on each missile. The deployment of the first U.S. MIRVs in June threatened to escalate the arms race, though some Administration officials contended that it would instead furnish greater bargaining power for SALT.

The Cambodian Incursion

In an apparent contradiction of policy, President Nixon ordered U.S. ground troops to make an incursion into Cambodia to destroy North Vietnamese sanctuaries there. Public outcry against the May incursions influenced President Nixon to cease operations in Cambodia on June 30.

After the announcement of the Cambodian invasion, several reports were issued stating that Secretary Laird had advised against substantial U.S. involvement in the area. However, he denied all such reports, stating that he fully supported the decision.

Defense Spending, Procurement, and Personnel

In a January statement Secretary Laird announced a reduction in defense spending during the 1970–71 fiscal year. Budget cuts during that period were expected to result in the loss of 1.25 million jobs within the military establishment and defense-related industries. The defense budget was projected at around $73.6 billion—$5.2 billion below the budget for the previous fiscal year. Administration critics charged that more substantial cuts could have been realized. They implied that the Pentagon had done little more than scale down operations in Vietnam, and that research and the procurement of new weapons were still proceeding at a rapid pace.

In June the Department of Defense issued a broad policy directive aimed at avoiding cost overruns. Prior to the directive, fixed price contracts had been used for military development programs. Under the new system, a cost target and profit margin would be agreed upon by both the contractor and Defense. The contractor is given an incentive to increase profits by keeping costs below the target figure.

By August, Administration forces and Congress were beginning to concentrate on the 1971–72 defense budget. At that time Administration aide Caspar Weinberger stated the view that it would be dangerous to cut the next budget below the $73.6-billion level. However, in October the House of Representatives slashed $2 billion from an Administration request for a $68.75-billion appropriation for Defense. It defeated an amendment to hold defense expenditures to $65 billion.

Proposed Pentagon Reorganization

After a yearlong study a 14-man panel headed by Gilbert W. Fitzhugh, chairman of the board of

Frank Render II was appointed to the position of deputy assistant secretary for civil rights for the U.S. Department of Defense on May 22, 1970. He thus became the highest ranking black civilian in the department.

UPI COMPIX

Metropolitan Life Insurance Co., released its critical report on the state of organization within the Defense Department. The report, which voiced 113 recommendations for changes within the department, criticized the Pentagon for its excessive size and for the cumbersome quality of its bureaucratic machine.

Among its major recommendations were the decentralization of Defense into three branches, each headed by a deputy secretary; the elimination of many major military commands and reorganization of commands along functional rather than geographic lines; the development and testing of prototype weapons prior to production; and the establishment of an agency to evaluate the performance and cost of weapons. The panel also recommended removing the Joint Chiefs of Staff from any operational capacity, limiting their functions to those of military advisers to the president and heads of their own branches of the service.

The Nerve Gas Controversy; NATO

The disposal of obsolete nerve gas rockets brought the U.S. Army and the Defense Department under violent attack on both national and international levels. Despite pleas from members of Congress, the government of Great Britain, and United Nations Secretary-General U Thant, the Army carried out its plan to transport 418 vaults of the deadly gas by train from depots in Alabama and Kentucky to Sunny Point, N.C. After the failure of suits brought by the Environmental Defense Fund and Florida's Gov. Claude R. Kirk, Jr., to prevent its disposal in the Blake Bahamas Basin 280 miles off the coast of Florida, the gas was scuttled at the site in mid-August. Army officials contended that any damage to the ocean environment by the gas would be "temporary" and "minimal."

Early in October President Nixon pledged to maintain U.S. forces assigned to protect the nations of the North Atlantic Treaty Organization. Later in the year, however, the National Security Council was considering the possibility of a long-range withdrawal of U.S. troops and a heavy reliance on nuclear weapons that produce little fallout. The change in strategy was cited as a possible response to the growth in Soviet nuclear power. (*See also* Armed Forces, U.S.; Cambodia; Congress, U.S.; Foreign Policy, U.S.)

DENMARK. In 1970 Denmark continued to undergo a major economic crisis, the result of a severe balance-of-payments deficit and inflation, created by a heavy boom in demand. To cope with the crisis, the government made even greater efforts to cool the overheated economy. A six-month halt in new government construction was ordered in March, the 1971–72 government budget was cut, and taxes were increased. Denmark's Premier Hilmar Baunsgaard also announced plans to introduce an incomes policy, embracing all sections of the community and working in accordance with principles of social justice. A partial price freeze effective until February 1971 was also introduced. In the meantime, it was hoped that agreement could be reached with employers' and employees' organizations on a prices-and-incomes structure.

One government proposal was to abolish the system of automatic wage regulation linked with a consumer price index that had been in force for many years. Trade unions replied that, while they would accept an alternative system that provided compensation to wage earners for price increases, they were unwilling to give up the principle of "inflation insurance." In the early autumn, a system was introduced whereby the government paid a portion of the automatic wage increases directly

Gasoline bombs exploded during a violent demonstration in front of the Royal Theatre in Copenhagen where delegates from the World Bank and the king and queen of Denmark were attending a special ballet performance.

UPI COMPIX

to the employers in order to help prevent a continuation of a wage-price inflationary spiral.

Denmark continued to eagerly seek admission into the European Economic Community (EEC), or Common Market, with the sole reservation that it wished to join the EEC in company with Great Britain. Unlike Britain, Denmark did not ask for a special transitional period for agriculture. Joining the EEC, it was felt, would help solve Denmark's trade imbalance by greatly enlarging its market for exports. Denmark, however, was also anxious to maintain close cooperation with its Nordic neighbors. (*See also* Europe, Great Britain. *See in* CE: Denmark.)

DENTISTRY. Could the pain and discomfort of dental caries (tooth decay) and periodontal disease become just a murky memory by the close of the 1970's? Perhaps, said the National Institute of Dental Research, but only if certain conditions are met. First, maximum use must be made of fluoride-enriched water supplies and fluoride-containing toothpastes. Then, antibacterial chemicals capable of selectively killing the caries-causing bacteria would have to be developed. Lastly, plastic coatings would have to be found effective in sealing teeth against bacterial infection.

In related experiments, Dr. Michael Buonocore of the Eastman Dental Center in Rochester, N.Y., found that a plastic sealer painted on teeth and hardened with ultraviolet light covered the tiny pits and cracks in teeth that evade fluoride treatment. A large-scale test was under way in 1970 to determine the efficacy of the plastic coating.

Sunlight may have a beneficial effect on dental health, according to dental researchers in Boston, Mass. They subjected hamsters to a daily dosage of ultraviolet radiation—in amounts present in sunlight. The animals contracted significantly fewer cavities than hamsters subjected only to the light of conventional bulbs.

The 25th anniversary of fluoridation was celebrated in the United States in 1970. The American Dental Association (ADA) cited fluoridation as the prime factor in the improving oral health in the United States. During the year more than 80 million persons had access to fluoridated U.S. water supplies.

By mid-1971 the ADA hoped to have the findings of a reevaluation of its position on proposed national health-care programs. Unless the reassessment proves otherwise, the ADA will remain against "unreasonable" government controls over personal health care and free care for those who can afford to purchase it. (*See also* Medicine. *See in* CE: Dentistry.)

DISARMAMENT. The strategic arms limitation talks (SALT) between the United States and the Soviet Union were the main focus of arms-control efforts during 1970. Begun in Helsinki, Finland, in 1969, the talks underwent their second phase from April 16 to August 14, in Vienna, Austria. The delegations returned to Helsinki on November 2 for the third phase.

In the closing weeks at Vienna, the United States submitted an outline proposal for numerical limitation of all offensive and defensive strategic weapons. The plan elicited an interested response from the Soviet delegation, which many observers viewed as a sign of real progress. Nevertheless, the only official assessment available at the end of the second phase was that there had been "forward movement" in the talks.

As the talks at Vienna proceeded, the Administration of U.S. President Richard M. Nixon announced plans to go ahead with the expansion of the Safeguard ABM (antiballistic missile) system and the deployment of MIRVs (multiple independently targetable reentry vehicles). This action was taken in the face of strong opposition from United Nations (UN) Secretary-General U Thant, the U.S. Senate, and a special presidential advisory panel—all of whom reportedly urged the president to call for a U.S.-Soviet moratorium on further deployment of strategic weapons. (*See also* Defense; United Nations.)

In other developments, the Treaty on the Non-Proliferation of Nuclear Weapons—considered a "bridge" to SALT—was brought into force on March 5, following ratification by the United States, the Soviet Union, Great Britain, and at least 40 other countries. Two nuclear powers, France and the People's Republic of China, refused to sign, although France did indicate that it would respect the principles of the agreement. India, Israel, and Brazil—each possessing the capacity to become a nuclear power in a short time—were among the other abstaining nations.

"Do you mind!!"

HUFFAKER, "NEWS & OBSERVER," FROM BEN ROTH AGENCY

UPI COMPIX

Celebrating the resumption of the strategic arms limitation talks are delegates Gerard Smith of the United States (second from left), Vaino Leskinen of Finland (center foreground), and Vladimir Semyonov of the Soviet Union (far right).

In September the UN Conference of the Committee on Disarmament (CCD), in Geneva, Switzerland, gave virtually unanimous approval to a joint U.S.-Soviet draft treaty banning the installation of nuclear and other mass-destruction weapons on the ocean floor. The draft was sent to the UN General Assembly for endorsement. The achievement represented two years of negotiations and extensive revision of drafts to accommodate the wishes of other delegations. Notable conflicts had arisen regarding further negotiations to eliminate the arms race from the seabed, verifications procedures, and questions on law of the sea. The finished draft was exclusively an arms-control measure, avoiding such matters as exploration and exploitation of the seabed.

Chemical and biological weapons came in for a large share of attention during the year. Debate in the CCD centered largely on the question of whether there should be joint or separate instruments relating to production and stockpiling of such weapons. Major Western powers favored adoption of a British-sponsored draft convention outlawing the production and stockpiling of biological weapons, along with continued study of the more complex problem of controlling chemical weapons. The Soviet Union and its allies insisted that chemical and biological weapons should be dealt with together in a single treaty.

On August 13 the U.S. Senate received Additional Protocol II of the Treaty for the Prohibition of Nuclear Weapons in Latin America, which in 1967 established a nuclear-free zone in Latin America. The protocol would oblige the United States to respect the special status of the zone. (*See also* International Relations.)

DISASTERS OF 1970.

Among the catastrophes that occurred in the world in 1970 were:

Air Disasters

Feb. 15 Off Santo Domingo, Dominican Republic. While taking off, a Dominican DC-9 jetliner suddenly plunges into the shark-infested waters of the Caribbean, killing all 102 persons aboard.

July 4 Near Arbucias, Spain. The worst air disaster in Spain's history occurs when a British Comet airliner crashes in mountainous terrain as it comes in for a landing at Barcelona Airport; all 112 passengers and crewmen aboard perish.

July 5 Toronto, Ont. A Canadian DC-8 jetliner landing at Toronto International Airport cracks up in a cornfield north of the airport, killing all 109 persons aboard.

Aug. 9 Near Cuzco, Peru. In the worst air disaster in the history of Peru, a Peruvian Lockheed Electra turboprop develops engine trouble soon after takeoff from Cuzco Airport, plunges into a hillside, and explodes, bringing death to 99 passengers (including 51 U.S. teen-age students) and crewmen; the copilot survives.

Nov. 14 Huntington, W.Va. A chartered U.S. DC-9 jet explodes as it approaches the foggy, rainbound Tri-State Airport; all 75 persons aboard perish, including 43 players and coaches of the Marshall University football team.

Fires and Explosions

Jan. 9 Marietta, Ohio. A fire blazes through a nursing home and brings death to 31 elderly patients.

April 8 Osaka, Japan. Explosions set off by leaking gas at a subway construction site erupt into a crowded street tearing a hole 450 feet long and 30 feet wide; about 75 persons are killed and more than 300 others are injured.

May 22 Cairo, United Arab Republic. Brush fires ignited by the 118° F. temperature reached on the hottest day in 60 years bring death to 41 persons and destroy 660 homes.

Sept. 25–30 Southern California. Brush and timber fires of five days' duration ravage more than 200,000 acres; 14 persons die and 1,500 buildings are burned, with damage estimated at $175 million.

Nov. 1 Saint-Laurent-du-Pont, France. Flames caused by a discarded match race through the plastic and papier-mâché interior of a dance hall, driving the occupants toward unopened exits where 142 young revelers perish; 4 of the seriously burned later die to bring the total fatalities to 146.

Dec. 20 Tucson, Ariz. Fire of unknown origin occurs in the 11-story Pioneer International Hotel, trapping many of the 112 guests; 28 persons perish in the flames, and 27 others are injured.

Marine Disasters

March 4 Cape Camaret, France. A French submarine, the 850-ton *Eurydice,* disappears during diving maneuvers, possibly as a result of an inboard explosion; all 57 crewmen are lost.

July 5 Near Masulipatnam, India. A large launch capsizes and sinks; about 150 persons are presumed to have drowned.

Aug. 1 Off Basseterre, St. Kitts island. Overcrowded with more than 200 passengers, the Caribbean ferryboat *Christena* capsizes, plunging the passengers into shark-infested waters; about 125 persons are believed to have perished in the sea.

Dec. 15 Korea Strait. A Korean ferryboat, the 362-ton *Namyung-Ho,* overloaded with cargo, capsizes, flinging its 278 crewmen and passengers into the icy waters; at least 261 persons perish.

Mine Disasters

Sept. 25 Lusaka, Zambia. Millions of tons of sand collapse at the Mufulira copper mine, Zambia's second largest, entrapping 89 mine workers in seas of mud and water; all perish.

Dec. 30 Wooton, Ky. A coal-dust explosion caused by a charge of explosives blasts through a coal mine, entrapping 38 miners; all are killed.

Natural Disasters

March 28–31 Kütahya Province, Turkey. Severe earthquakes occur, centered in Kütahya Province; 1,087 persons die, at least 1,500 are injured, and another 90,000 are left homeless.

April 16 Plateau D'Assy, France. The third major avalanche of the year plunges down an Alpine slope and envelops several buildings housing tubercular children and their nurses; 72 people perish under the tons of snow and debris.

May 14–31 Romania. The worst floods in centuries, triggered by torrential rains and melting snow, inundate 37 of Romania's 39 districts, laying waste to 1,000 villages and about 2 million acres; at least 225 persons die.

May 31 Peru. A devastating earthquake levels towns and cities along the coastal mountain areas; the official toll is 66,794 dead or missing, with 800,000 persons homeless.

The villagers of Saint-Laurent-du-Pont mourn the deaths of more than 140 young people who perished in France's worst fire in 73 years. Trapped in a burning dance hall purposely locked to keep out gate-crashers, only a few persons escaped the fire.

GAMMA FROM PHOTOREPORTERS

Oct. 12 Philippines. Typhoon Joan roars across the islands, killing at least 525 persons; 169 others are missing and 912 injured.

Oct. 19 Philippines. Typhoon Kate, the second typhoon to hit the islands in a week, leaves 501 persons dead, 312 missing, and 76 injured.

Oct. 26–30 South Vietnam. Severe floods sweep five northern provinces; at least 237 persons die and more than 204,000 are made homeless.

Nov. 12 Northern Colombia. Month-long storms and an earthquake take the lives of more than 200 persons, with 460 others reported missing.

Nov. 12–13 East Pakistan. Possibly the greatest catastrophe of the century occurs when gigantic, cyclone-driven tidal waves pound the coast of East Pakistan, affecting 3.3 million persons in a 3,000-square-mile area; the official death toll is close to 200,000 persons, with another 100,000 missing, but it is believed a total of 500,000 may have died.

Railroad Disasters

Feb. 1 General Pacheco Station, Argentina. The worst train crash in Argentine history occurs when an express train rams into a stalled commuter train; 141 persons die, and 179 others are injured.

Feb. 16 Kaduna, Nigeria. A train wreck claims the lives of at least 80 persons; an additional 52 injured passengers are killed when a truck transporting them to a hospital crashes.

Traffic Accidents

July 22 Near Badrinath, India. A flash flood engulfs a cluster of vehicles caught in a narrow gorge; 500 persons are believed dead.

Oct. 14 Near Onyang, South Korea. A bus loaded with junior high school boys is struck by a train and pushed 100 yards before bursting into flames; 52 boys and the driver are killed, and 24 other students are injured.

Miscellaneous Disasters

June 21 Rio de Janeiro, Brazil. A celebration of Brazil's victory over Italy in the World Cup soccer finals ends in death for at least 44 persons, and 1,800 others are injured.

UPI COMPIX

President Balaguer hands out money and shoes to villagers near Santo Domingo during his successful campaign for reelection.

DOMINICAN REPUBLIC.

Events in the Dominican Republic in 1970 were dominated by the May presidential election, which resulted in the reelection of President Joaquín Balaguer to a second term. Balaguer's potentially strongest opponents—two former presidents—did not participate in the election; Héctor García-Godoy died in April and Juan D. Bosch boycotted the election. Nevertheless, Balaguer barely achieved a majority of the votes cast, despite his reported widespread use of bribery and intimidation. The entire campaign was carried out in an atmosphere of terrorism and violence, and more than 50 persons were said to have been killed.

Despite increased political tensions, the Balaguer government became the first democratically elected government to complete a full term of office within 40 years of Dominican history. To its credit were four years of relative stability, marked by some economic progress. Still, Balaguer's conservative policies, aimed at assuring him support from military, business, and landed interests, did little to solve the basic problems of the country: massive unemployment, one of the world's highest birthrates, and social and economic inequities, which meant that the majority of the Dominican people still lived in grinding poverty. Furthermore, Dominicans voiced concern that Balaguer's *continuismo*—his seemingly strong determination to keep himself in office—augured ill for the future. (*See in* CE: Dominican Republic.)

DRUGS.

Rising instances of drug abuse, especially among youth, ranged from use of such "hard" narcotics as heroin to the sniffing of model-airplane glue. The enormity of the problem prompted outcries against the easy availability of drugs subject to abuse, including the amphetamines. In August Dr. Charles C. Edwards, head of the U.S. Food and Drug Administration (FDA), criticized the makers of amphetamines for producing some 8 billion pills a year of a drug with only limited medical use. (*See* Feature Article: "Drugs and Youth.")

Drug Regulation

In June the FDA took final legal steps to ban the sale of 87 drugs containing more than one antibiotic, on grounds that the additional antibiotics

AUTHENTICATED NEWS INTERNATIONAL

As part of a nationwide multimedia campaign against drug abuse, a huge antidrug billboard is displayed in Washington, D.C.

were therapeutically useless. A National Academy of Sciences-National Research Council (NAS-NRC) survey of the usefulness of more than 3,600 drugs on sale from 1938 to 1962 found that the combination antibiotics were either ineffective, dangerous, or both. In another June lawsuit, however, the FDA found itself accused by the American Public Health Association and by the National Council of Senior Citizens for failing to act quickly enough in banning the several thousand drugs and drug combinations that were found ineffective by the NAS-NRC study.

Oral contraceptives, controversial from their inception, were again under clinical and consumer attack. At U.S. Senate hearings the "pill" was held responsible for ills ranging from weight gain to cancer. (*See* Families.) As a result, in September the FDA ordered oral contraceptives to be accompanied by a warning statement, in layman's language, of the possible harmful side effects resulting from their use. It was a step, however, marked with some difficulty. The original warning was drafted in March and revised in April under drug-industry and medical pressure. By June it seemed that the powerful American Medical Association (AMA) would challenge the FDA. The AMA felt that any direct message from the FDA to the consumer was a government intrusion into medical practice.

An oral drug used in treating moderately severe cases of diabetes mellitus was accused of causing cardiovascular and other diseases. Tolbutamide, better known by its trade name Orinase, was sharply attacked, but the FDA did not take the drug off the market. An estimated 800,000 diabetics take daily doses of tolbutamide. The AMA advised physicians to scrutinize diabetics taking the oral drug. However, the American Diabetes Association cautioned diabetics not to become overly distressed by research findings indicting tolbutamide, arguing that the drug was still part of the accepted way of treating milder cases of diabetes.

Proponents of generic-drug marketing—selling drugs by chemical name rather than by proprietary (brand) name—long believed that little difference existed between theirs and proprietary drugs. However, brand-name drug manufacturers disagreed and had been backed by research findings. Although the generic drugs might be chemically the same as their brand-name counterparts, they may not behave similarly in the body; their bioavailability might be different. As a result, the FDA began to insist that any claims of bioavailability equivalency made by the makers of generic drugs be true.

Drug Companies Pay Off

On trial since 1968 for developing and selling thalidomide, the sedative that left many deformed babies in its wake, Chemie Grünenthal offered a $27.3-million settlement to the 2,000 surviving West Germans allegedly deformed by the drug. Thalidomide, on sale in 1957, was withdrawn from the West German market in 1961.

In June five U.S. drug firms on trial since 1961 on price-fixing charges offered $82.5 million in settle-

Twelve-year-old heroin addict Ralph DeJesus testifies at a state legislative hearing in New York City. The boy, accompanied by his doctor, described his experiences to the legislators.

WIDE WORLD

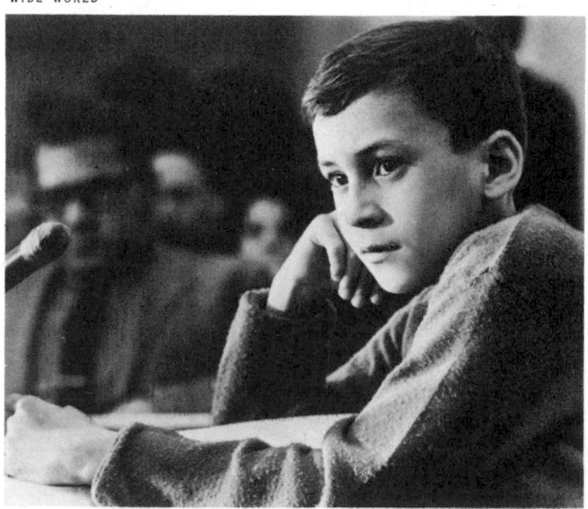

ment—the largest ever in antitrust annals—even though a conviction of three of the companies was overturned by a federal appeals courts. Originally charged with fixing high prices on certain antibiotics, the firms—Chas. Pfizer & Co., Bristol-Myers Co., American Cyanamid Co., Olin Mathieson Chemical Corp., and Upjohn Co.—decided to settle the thousands of claims filed against them, though a trial judge noted that there was no direct evidence of price fixing.

In April a $1-million suit was filed against the J. B. Williams Co., Inc., maker of Geritol, and its advertiser, for violating Federal Trade Commission (FTC) orders. The FTC charged the companies with making deceptive statements about the overall effectiveness of Geritol in restoring vitality to its users. The FTC, however, did not take issue with Geritol's claim of effectiveness against iron-deficiency anemia, or "tired blood."

Drug Development

In June the FDA approved sale of L-dopa (levodihydroxyphenylalanine) for the treatment of Parkinson's disease. The FDA cautioned physicians to use L-dopa carefully and ordered the makers of the drug to continue clinical studies on it, an unusual step for an approved drug. (*See* Medicine.)

Ketamine hydrochloride, a new type of short-acting intravenous anesthetic, was recently made available. It was termed a "dissociative anesthetic" because it dissociated patients from pain and awareness of noise without putting them out in the manner of conventional anesthetics.

The hormonelike prostaglandins were undergoing considerable study in 1970. They might become a new generation of birth-control agents, capable of inducing early abortion of the fertilized egg. (*See also* Chemistry; Medicine. *See in* CE: Drugs.)

EARTH SCIENCES. Results of the continuing study of lunar surface samples collected by the astronauts of Apollo missions 11 and 12 were a focus of interest in the earth sciences in 1970. During the year more was learned about the history of the moon and its geologic processes than had been discovered in all previous lunar research.

Moon's History Unfolds

About half the rock specimens collected from the Apollo 11 landing site were found to be pieces of basalt, the most common kind of volcanic rock on earth. Though generally similar to earth basalt, lunar basalt is richer in titanium and has other distinctive geochemical characteristics. Lunar basalts crystallize at essentially the same temperatures (about 1,150° to 1,200° C., or 2,100° to 2,200° F.) as do earth basalts. It was felt that the findings nearly completed the evidence that the so-called seas, or maria, of the moon are vast plains that have been formed by the outpouring of great floods of basaltic lava from the lunar interior.

Dating by both the rubidium-strontium and the uranium-thorium-lead methods indicated that the lunar basalts ranged from 3.7 billion to 4.2 billion years in age, older than any rocks so far discovered on earth. It became clear that a geological record of events that occurred very early in the history of the solar system is preserved on the face of the moon. The floods of basalt that formed the lunar "seas" occurred fairly late in the sequence of events that could be deciphered. Most of the craters and rocks of the lunar highlands were formed earlier.

Basalts collected from the Ocean of Storms (Apollo 12) were about 300 million years younger than those from the Sea of Tranquillity (Apollo 11). This difference in age was much less than had been expected, however, indicating that the rate at which craters were formed on the moon declined fairly rapidly during the early part of lunar history.

Detailed mineralogic and chemical studies of fine particles of lunar soil produced many surprises. About half of the soil particles turned out to be glass, and several percent were beautiful tiny glass spheres. Glass formed by the shock of meteorite impact was expected to be a constituent of lunar soil, but not in nearly so great a proportion as was observed.

Moonquakes Analyzed

Seismic signals continued to be recorded more than a year after the Apollo 12 astronauts placed a seismograph on the lunar surface in November 1969. One or more moonquakes were occurring every 28.4 days, each time the moon in its orbit came closest to the earth. The quakes appeared to center in the Fra Mauro highland crater, some 50 miles south of the planned landing point of Apollo 14 in February 1971. They usually occurred in pairs, one at perigee and another a few days later when the face of the moon bulges 20 to 30 inches toward the earth. This bulging, caused by the earth's gravitational pull, apparently produces strain within the moon. It was thus indicated that the moon may have some internal heat.

All the recorded natural moonquakes were small. The magnitude of the largest events was between 1 and 2 on the Richter scale—barely perceptible even near the epicenter. The sources of the moonquakes were estimated to be not more than a mile beneath the surface. Moonquakes were believed to be generated much as are earthquakes—by the slippage of opposite faces of faults past one another. A lunar surface structure of very low ability to absorb seismic waves was believed responsible for the very long reverberations that resulted from deliberate crashes of spacecraft components onto the moon.

Deep-Sea Drilling Project

One of the most important sources of new geological information continued to be the National

COLORADO DEPARTMENT OF HIGHWAYS

Edwin McKee of the U.S. Geological Survey suggested to Colorado officials that they make this geological showcase out of Interstate 70 by making cuts in the Rocky Mountains to reveal the geological history of the area.

Science Foundation's Deep Sea Drilling Project, managed by Scripps Institution of Oceanography at La Jolla, Calif. The project, which entered its third year of operation in 1970, involved obtaining samples of sediments and hard rock from the sea floor using a specially constructed research vessel, the *Glomar Challenger*.

One of the project's major discoveries in 1970 was the existence in the sediments of the North Atlantic Ocean of a fairly abundant layer of chert (a rock resembling flint) dating from the Eocene epoch (some 40 million–60 million years ago). The abundant presence of chert gave important evidence concerning the formation of sedimentary rocks from seawater. Evidently the chemistry of the bottom waters of the North Atlantic during the Eocene epoch was favorable to the depositing of opaline skeletons of microorganisms. The silica contained in the skeletons apparently combined with other oceanic sediments over a period of time to form the chert.

Other interesting findings of the drilling project have greatly increased knowledge of the geological development of the Mediterranean Sea. Evidence from drilling samples indicated that during the late Miocene epoch the Mediterranean was cut off from the Atlantic Ocean. During a period of extreme evaporation it evidently desiccated, leaving only salt brines. Later geological movements restored an outlet to the Atlantic, thus replenishing the sea. (*See also* Oceanography.)

Earthquakes; Seismic Studies

The most disastrous earthquake in terms of loss of life in Latin American history occurred on May 31 off the coast of Peru. Centered about 12 miles southwest of Chimbote, the tremor, of 7.8 Richter

An ancient polar ice cap formed this channel in the sandstone of the Sahara. Professor R. W. Fairbridge of Columbia University, who discovered the channel, considers it to be evidence that the crust of the earth has moved.

COURTESY, COLUMBIA UNIVERSITY

magnitude, took 50,000 lives and devastated villages in the Callejón de Huaylas, the valley that parallels Peru's Pacific coast. Although a mud-and-earth slide covered Yungay and a nearby village with tons of debris and took thousands of lives, the principal cause of the high death toll was strong earth vibration that led to the collapse of innumerable poorly designed structures.

Scientists at the University of Washington were generating "miniquakes" to identify and study the characteristics of various soils subjected to seismic impacts. Readings from an instrument capable of simulating earthquake motions at any level indicated what the resonance of ground motion would be in an actual earthquake. The scientists hoped to describe seismic zones, in terms of earthquake destructive capabilities and damage expectations, throughout Washington state, and to formulate requirements for structural design for each of the seismic zones.

Soviet scientists reported that hot water reaching the surface from deep layers of the earth's crust can provide advance notice of impending earthquakes. This was first observed during the Tashkent earthquake of 1966 and verified more recently by Tadzhik S.S.R. seismologists. The weak disturbances of the earth's crust that precede a sharp earthquake are capable of changing the chemical composition of thermal waters as well as their temperature. When crustal rocks shift during an earthquake, the water changes its course to the surface, is enriched by microelements, and becomes hotter or loses heat. Such information will assist seismologists in developing earthquake prediction methods.

After several years of study, California engineers proposed building multistory structures on ball- or roller-bearing foundations in earthquake zones to eliminate the transfer from foundation to superstructure of lateral forces induced by seismic vibrations. A system of ball bearings, neoprene springs, and horizontal controls can isolate the foundation slab from the structural frame. The vertical building loads would be transferred to the foundation through a system of ball bearings sandwiched between steel-bearing plates. Lateral wind loads would be transferred to the foundation through horizontal control rods set between the building's core and the foundation walls. The neoprene springs between the core floor and the foundation slab could safely arrest any motions of the superstructure under lateral loading.

One characteristic of California earthquakes is their shallow depth, no more than 10 to 20 kilometers (6 to 12 miles) below the earth's surface. One reason proposed for this phenomenon is that geological motion in the region is probably occurring on preexisting faults. Although fracturing of new material may be involved, studies indicate that it is probably small in comparison to the total area of the fault. It has been suggested that frictional sliding on fault surfaces may thus be the major cause of the earthquakes. The increase in temperatures at lower depths in the earth might be the reason for the lack of earthquakes at such levels. (*See also* Space Exploration. *See in* CE: Earth; Geology; Maps; Moon.)

BERNIE, "AUX ECOUTES" (PARIS), FROM BEN ROTH AGENCY

ECONOMY. As 1970 drew to a close, the debate on whether the U.S. economy was in a recession finally appeared to have been resolved. By mid-September the National Bureau of Economic Research had come to a preliminary conclusion: "A very mild recession, somewhat different in character from other postwar contractions, began sometime last year." Not only was the nation laboring under the onus of an official recession but it was also engaged in a continuing struggle against inflation.

At the end of the third quarter, major economic indicators seemed to underscore the two-faced quality of the economy. The gross national product—the total measure of the nation's output of goods and services—rose to $985.5 billion. The dollar rise was slightly higher than that in the second quarter; however, the growth rate was less than 1.5% after allowances were made for increased prices. For the same period, unemployment rose, reaching the 5.5% level, as compared to 3.5% at the end of 1969. (The jobless rate for December rose to 6%.)

The industrial production index also showed a marked decline; its September level of 166.1 was down about 2% from the average level of 1969.

The Administration of U.S. President Richard M. Nixon, however, remained confident that it would eventually bring inflation under control. Throughout the first 21 months of his term of office, President Nixon and his economic advisers employed a "game plan" against inflation. The first phase of the plan, which was in effect throughout 1969, was to apply economic restraints. These restraints took the form of cuts in the federal budget and a general tightening of monetary policy. During the second phase of the plan, which began early in 1970, the emphasis was shifted to cushioning the downturn in the economy. Steps taken at that point involved primarily a relaxation of credit and the reduction of prime lending rates. Whatever favorable effects the Nixon game plan might have had on the economy were diminished—if not canceled—by the protracted strike against General Motors Corp. by members of the United Auto Workers (UAW) union in the fall. (*See* Labor Unions.)

Even apart from the UAW strike, the Administration seemed to have fallen short of the goals of its game plan. One particularly embarrassing fact was that there seemed to be no chance of realizing the $1.3-billion budget surplus that President Nixon had forecast for the 1970–71 fiscal year. Instead, economic predictions seemed to indicate the probability of a deficit in the neighborhood of $13 billion. The projected deficit was in line with adjustments in other economic predictions. Originally, corporate profits before taxes had been forecast at $89 billion, but at midyear they were running at an annual rate of only $77 billion.

Administration critics charged that failure to bring about a greater recovery was also due to President Nixon's reluctance to employ more of the economic tools at his disposal. Among the tools was an "incomes policy" propounded by Arthur F. Burns, chairman of the Federal Reserve System's Board of Governors. Such a policy might involve presidential persuasion to hold down wages and prices, the establishment of industry-composed wage guidelines, or the publicizing of statistics that point up exceedingly high wage or price increases. Anti-Administration forces also contended that the president might have called for reduced tariffs, farm and shipping subsidies, and liberalized oil import quotas; he might also have sold more goods from strategic stockpiles.

The Cost of Living

The U.S. Department of Labor's Bureau of Labor Statistics reported that the Consumer Price Index had risen to 136.6 at the end of the third quarter, indicating that the cost of living had risen 36.6% since the base period, 1957–59. The cost of living rose at an annual rate of 5.8% during the first quarter, 6% in the second quarter, and 4.2% in the third quarter. The Consumer Price Index for October 1970 was 5.9% higher than that for October 1969.

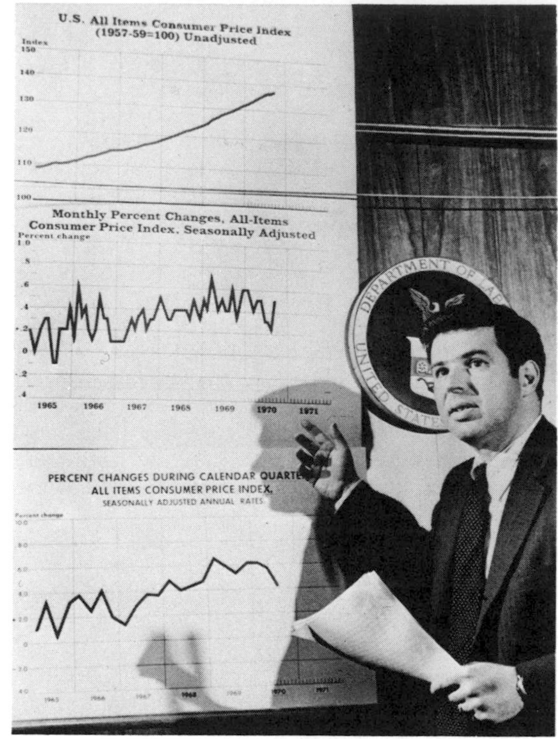

UPI COMPIX

The U.S. Bureau of Labor Statistics released charts to show how the cost of living soared in 1970 despite Administration efforts to curb it.

The largest increase was in the area of medical care. At the end of the third quarter, medical costs were 67.6% above the 1957–59 average and 6.4% above those prevailing in September 1969. The price of food at the end of the third quarter stood at 33.3% above the 1957–59 level—an increase of 4.5% over the corresponding period in 1969. Housing costs had increased 37.8% since the 1957–59 period and had gone up 7.1% since the third quarter of 1969.

Personal Income

Personal income in the United States was at a record seasonally adjusted $811.8 billion at the end of the third quarter. For the same period in 1969 the figure was $763.1 billion; for the whole of 1968, it was $688.7 billion. Of the total, salaries and wages comprised $546.6 billion; income from other labor, $31.1 billion; business and professional income, $51.8 billion; farm income, $16.1 billion; rental income, $22.8 billion; personal interest income, $66.7 billion; and transfer payments, $79.4 billion.

Personal income did not grow steadily throughout the first three quarters. After increasing from $777.8 billion in January to $806 billion in April, it fell to $799.7 billion in May and $798.2 billion in June. From that point it continued to increase steadily, reaching the $811.8 billion figure in September 1970.

Consumer Spending

A survey conducted by the National Industrial Conference Board on consumer spending for the first six months of 1970 revealed that the year was generally a bad one for the retailer. Although spending ran about 2.5% above the rate for the same period in 1969, inflation drove prices up 5%, adding up to a real loss of 2.5%. Several major industries found that the increase in their asking prices had risen above the increase in their dollar volumes. Included in this category were sales of durable goods, food and beverages in restaurants and bars, and home furnishings.

Appliances, in contrast, fared relatively well. Dollar sales increased 4% over the year ending June 30, 1970, while prices climbed only 1.5%. Department stores also managed to hold their own during the period, registering a 5.5% sales increase while holding price increases between 4% and 5%. Gasoline stations actually lowered prices 1.5% while increasing sales by 3%. Automobile sales went in the opposite direction, falling 7% in addition to a 2% price increase.

It appeared as though consumers were reluctant to make purchases while inflation was increasing and unemployment figures rising. Instead, they seemed to be preparing for a rainy day. At the end of the third quarter, personal savings had grown to $52.5 billion from $42 billion during the same period in 1969. During the same period, savings amounted to 7.5% of disposable income as opposed to 6.5% the previous year.

Consumer Credit

Total consumer credit outstanding at the end of September was $123.9 billion, compared to $118 billion at the end of September 1969. Installment loans made up $100.1 billion, and noninstallment credit $23.8 billion of the total.

Automobile loans totaled $36.7 billion in September, up $400 million from the previous year. Home repair and modernization loans totaled $4.1 billion, up about $130 million; personal loans $31.2 billion, up approximately $2 billion; other consumer goods loans $28.1 billion, up $2.3 billion; single payment loans $9.3 billion up $210 million; charge accounts $7.5 billion, up $500 million; and service credit $7 billion, up $380 million.

Monetary Policy

The reduction of the prime interest rate from 8.5% to 8% in March reflected a gradual softening in business conditions and the easing in the Federal Reserve System's credit policy. The rate was lowered several times at the end of the year—to 7.5% in September, to 7.25% and then to 7% in November, and to 6.75% in December.

The first reduction in the lending rate followed the disclosure by Federal Reserve Chairman Burns that the Federal Reserve System would begin to relax its extremely restrictive monetary policy and would permit an increase in the amount of currency and of demand deposits. Until the March announcement there had been virtually no growth in the money supply since June 1969.

Although the Federal Reserve System had intended for the money supply to grow at a fairly quiet rate of 2% to 3% a year, it had reached an annual expansion rate of more than 9% by the end of May 1970. After hovering around the $200-billion mark during the last quarter of 1969 and the first quarter of 1970, the total value of demand deposits and currency fluctuated between $205 billion and $207 billion in October 1970. Financial analysts predicted that such a rapid growth rate would slow down the adjustment of inflation. (*See also* Banks; Business and Industry; Employment; Money and International Finance; World Trade. *See in* CE: Economics.)

ECUADOR. The year 1970 was marked by a worsening of Ecuador's economic and political difficulties. These difficulties finally led Ecuador's President José María Velasco Ibarra to assume dictatorial powers late in June.

Velasco acted when it became obvious, with Congress' adjournment in May, that no legislative action would be taken to solve the government's mounting budget deficits and shrinking revenues, which were effectively emptying the treasury. Velasco attempted to solve the financial crisis himself by promulgating decrees that would abolish major tax exemptions and impose new taxes. The powerful business community, which traditionally has resisted any tax increase, reacted angrily and petitioned the Supreme Court to declare the decrees unconstitutional. On learning of the Supreme Court's intention to veto his measures, Velasco declared himself "supreme leader" (under the constitution of 1946) for the rest of his term, ending in 1972.

Supported by the armed forces, Velasco suspended Congress, reshuffled the Supreme Court, and closed university campuses that had been centers for student disorders during the year. Public uncertainty mounted, and a devastating bank run occurred that caused one major bank to close its doors. The bank's failure played a definitive role in the government decision in August to alter the official exchange rate from 18 to 25 sucres to the U.S. dollar, a devaluation of about 39%. At the same time, sweeping economic reform measures were instituted.

The economy was in desperate need of these reforms. Ecuador's international monetary reserves had steadily declined, and the country had suffered an increasingly adverse balance of trade despite some rise in its major export, bananas. The only bright spot in the economy was the continuing successful development of the country's oil resources. (*See in* CE: Ecuador.)

EDUCATION. In 1970 many of the concerns that characterized the 1960's continued to plague U.S. educators and students alike. The voice of student dissent was heard at all levels of the educational system. A report by the House Internal Security Committee charged that the Students for a Democratic Society (SDS) was focusing on the nation's high schools as a new target for agitation and recruitment. Militant protest against school and society even spread to some elementary schools, where pupils drew inspiration from the example set by older student activists in high schools and colleges alike. (*See* Colleges and Universities.)

Statistics indicated that arson, assault, property destruction, and narcotics offenses were increasing in U.S. schools. In many big-city schools, where racial and ethnic tensions were blamed for much of the violence, police patrolled school corridors and cafeterias. Reports of an alarming rise in drug use among elementary and high school students moved the Administration of U.S. President Richard M. Nixon to launch a $3.5-million program to train teachers in the fundamentals of drug education. (*See* Feature Article: "Drugs and Youth.")

AUTHENTICATED NEWS INTERNATIONAL

Real-life settings illustrate the texts of the Heath Urban Reading Program, "Time to Think," used in Lexington, Mass. A young boy listens to a man who ran away to sea as a youth.

A teacher at Denison House, a bilingual school in Roxbury, a district of Boston, Mass., encourages a pupil to return to the classroom.

"THE NEW YORK TIMES"

Desegregation

In January the U.S. Supreme Court ruled that desegregation in six Deep South states could not wait until the start of the 1970–71 school year. The Court delivered a strict order to the 14 school districts involved, requiring them to desegregate before Feb. 1, 1970. The order affected some 300,000 children, black and white.

Governors of most of the states involved were quick to denounce the Court's action. Among the most outspoken were Mississippi's Gov. John Bell Williams and Georgia's Gov. Lester G. Maddox. Maddox advised children in his state not to board buses that would take them to integrated schools. The most flagrant violation of the order, however, came from Florida's Gov. Claude Kirk, Jr., who declared that forced busing was illegal and intervened to prevent compliance with the Court's ruling. Carrying out his threat to suspend any local board that approved busing plans, Kirk dismissed the Manatee County school board, installed himself as superintendent of schools, and defied federal marshals by barricading himself inside the school district's headquarters. A federal court judge finally cited Kirk for contempt and threatened him with a fine of $10,000 a day. Other Southern leaders, among them South Carolina's Gov. Robert E. Mc-

Nair and Virginia's Gov. Linwood Holton, accepted the order with calm resignation.

The flight of white students to private, all-white schools was accelerated by the Court order. A sudden proliferation of such schools—dubbed "segregation academies"—occurred in areas scheduled for immediate desegregation. Later in the year, decisions by federal courts prohibited state support to all-white, private schools and revoked the tax-exempt status of such discriminatory institutions. These decisions dealt a severe blow to the already weak financial status of the new schools.

As school reopened in the fall of 1970, it appeared—on the surface, at least—that desegregation was being carried out in most districts without incident. Many white students had already transferred to private schools, however, and legal action had been initiated against forced busing. Some schools admitted black pupils, but maintained separate classrooms and lunch hours for blacks and whites.

The Nixon Administration's position regarding desegregation remained ambiguous throughout the year. In March the president delivered an 8,000-word policy statement on the subject. He declared that the federal government would oppose official barriers to desegregation, in line with Supreme Court rulings. At the same time, he indicated that specific measures to achieve racial balance must originate at the local level; busing would not be required by the federal government. Mr. Nixon noted the distinction between *de jure* and *de facto* segregation, stating that federal action would not be taken against the latter. The president also proposed federal funds of $1.5 billion to be used in aiding "racially impacted" school districts.

As expected, there were mixed reactions to the president's words. Southern leaders appreciated the recognition that de facto segregation exists in both the North and South. Civil rights leaders were angered by the Administration's reluctance to take positive action enforcing desegregation.

The subsequent removal of three top U.S. government officials—all advocates of strong federal action against segregation—was interpreted by many observers as a further attempt to appease the South. The three officials were: Robert H. Finch, secretary of the Department of Health, Education and Welfare (HEW); Leon Panetta, director of HEW's Office for Civil Rights; and James E. Allen, Jr., U.S. commissioner of education.

The Financial Crisis

A growing financial crisis in the nation's schools began to overshadow all other problems in 1970. Continual voter rejection of school bond issues, combined with the rising costs of education, resulted in a severe shortage of funds in many dis-

The Parkway Program school in Philadelphia, Pa., treats education as a social activity. The program is so popular that 10,000 students applied for 500 available spaces. Final selection was made by lottery. These students enjoy a guitar session between classes.
WIDE WORLD

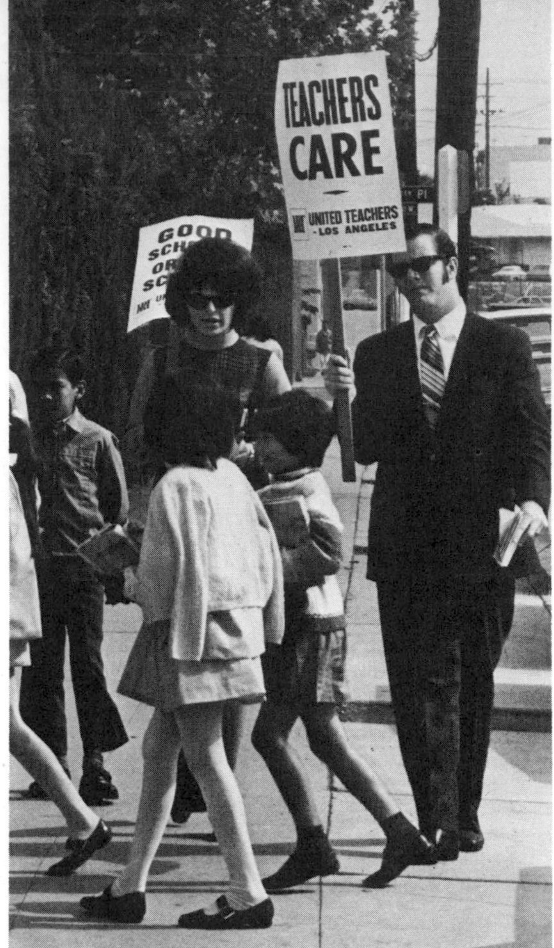

UPI COMPIX

Teacher strikes occurred throughout the United States in 1970. Fourth grade students from the Tenth Street school in Los Angeles gather around their teachers on the picket line.

tricts. Some schools were forced to postpone the beginning of the fall semester for lack of money. In other districts, schools opened in September with only enough money to cover operating expenses for the first few months. The problem was especially critical in Ohio, where many school districts faced bankruptcy, and in Missouri. In Philadelphia, Pa., schools were refused bank loans on the grounds that the school system was a poor credit risk.

To ease this situation, the U.S. Congress passed a record federal education appropriations bill—overriding a presidential veto on the measure. The new legislation provided $4.4 billion for schools.

Teacher Union Developments

The total number of teacher strikes rose to a record high in 1970, leaving few sections of the country unaffected. Teachers became more militant in pressing their demands for better pay and more benefits. Among the major demands articulated by the American Federation of Teachers (AFT) were a four-day workweek and a $10,000 minimum annual salary. The National Education Association (NEA), largest U.S. teacher organization, also favored a shorter workweek.

Prospects for a merger of the two teacher groups looked a bit more hopeful in 1970. Los Angeles teachers approved the first merger of a major urban local of the NEA and the AFT. The newly created organization, called United Teachers of Los Angeles, consolidated 88% of the district's 25,000 teachers into a single union. At the same time, however, a drive to integrate separate black and white affiliates of the NEA caused a substantial loss of membership, especially in the South.

The biggest news for teachers in 1970 was the prediction of a teacher surplus for the 1969–1980 period. Officials did point out that teacher shortages persist in certain fields, including vocational and technical education, mathematics, and science. (*See in* CE: Education.)

ELECTIONS. The 1970 elections in the United States continued to reflect the close division of political opinion that had prevailed for a decade. The Democrats lost two seats in the U.S. Senate but retained control by a comfortable margin. They gained nine seats in the House of Representatives, making the new House 255 Democrats and 180 Republicans. The gain was less than usual for the party opposing a president in an off-year election. Thus U.S. President Richard M. Nixon was faced with a Congress controlled by Democrats during the next two years in office, as in the preceding two years.

Party control of 15 governorships changed hands. Democrats won 13 states previously held by Republicans, and the Republicans won 2 previously held by Democrats. The Democrats also captured at least 7 of 99 state legislative chambers and achieved ties in 3 previously dominated by Republicans.

Both sides claimed victory. President Nixon said he would be able to "speak with a stronger voice . . . in the . . . Senate." The defeat of some opponents and the election of conservatives, he said, would give him a "working majority of four" that would "enormously strengthen our hand at home" and contribute to his moves to "win a full generation of peace." The Republicans were able to see bright spots even in the gubernatorial elections. The President hailed reelection of Republican governors in New York and California.

Democratic National Chairman Lawrence O'Brien said that the change in governorships was "the most politically explosive development." He asserted that his party had recaptured the electoral base that was vital to winning the White House in 1972. But Senator Edmund S. Muskie (D, Me.), the Democratic vice-presidential candidate in 1968 and a leading presidential possibility in 1972, called the results a "mixed bag," and the Republican Ripon Society called them a "major setback for the Republican party."

Campaign Issues

The Republicans, led by President Nixon and Vice-President Spiro T. Agnew, stressed law and order in the campaign. The Democrats stressed economic issues, particularly unemployment, which had risen to well above 5% of the labor force. The issues came into sharp focus the night before the election. President Nixon's car had been stoned by an unruly mob in San Jose, Calif., on October 29. The president made a speech in Phoenix, Ariz., which was telecast by the Republicans on the eve of the elections; he referred to that episode and made a strong plea for voters to "stand up and be counted against the appeasement of the rock throwers and obscenity shouters of America."

Senator Muskie responded on behalf of his party. In a telecast sponsored by a newly created committee of prominent Democrats, he replied that crime was bipartisan by its very nature but that Republicans were seeking political advantage "not by offering better solutions, but with empty threats and malicious slander." Thus, he added, the voters had been deprived of what he called the real issues: inflation, unemployment, war, the plight of the cities, and a generally shabby economy. The results were generally viewed as a test of the appeal of the parties' principal issues.

Senate Races

Thirty-five of the 100 seats in the Senate were at stake in the November elections. Of these, the Republicans won 11, the Democrats 22, the Conservative party one, and an independent one. This was expected to mean that the vote on organizing the Senate would be 55 for the Democrats, 45 for the Republicans.

Republicans seized Democratic seats in four states: Connecticut, Maryland, Ohio, and Tennessee. In Connecticut, Representative Lowell P. Weicker, Jr. (R), defeated Joseph D. Duffey (D) and Thomas J. Dodd (incumbent Democratic senator who was defeated in the primaries and ran as an independent). Weicker benefited from a split in

TOP AND BOTTOM: WIDE WORLD

Winners of U.S. Senate races in 1970 include: Robert Taft, Jr. (top left), whose victory in Ohio meant the resurgence to power for Taft Republicans; Adlai E. Stevenson III (bottom left), a Democrat who won a landslide victory in Illinois against the incumbent Ralph Tyler Smith; Senator Vance Hartke (D, Ind.; top right), who was reelected to the Senate in one of the closest races in recent history; James L. Buckley (bottom right), Conservative party candidate who defeated incumbent Charles E. Goodell and Representative Richard L. Ottinger in a bitterly fought campaign in New York State.

TOP AND BOTTOM: UPI COMPIX

WIDE WORLD

WIDE WORLD

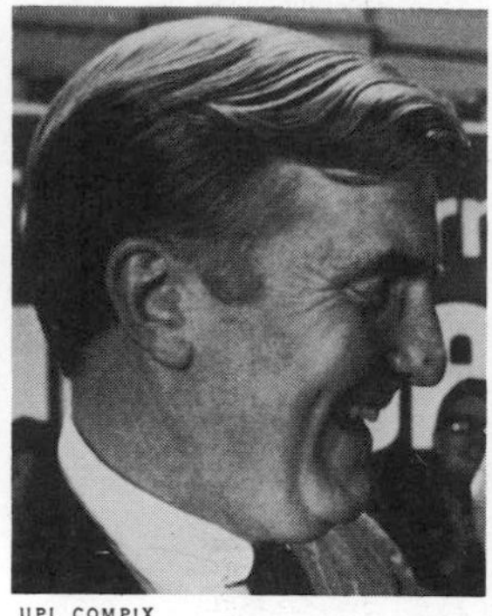
UPI COMPIX

WIDE WORLD

Victorious gubernatorial candidates include (from left): Thomas Meskill, new governor of Connecticut; Gov. William G. Milliken of Michigan, elected to a full term; John Gilligan, new governor of Ohio; and Gov. Nelson Rockefeller of New York, reelected for a fourth term.

the Democratic vote between Dodd and Duffey. Dodd was repudiated by party leaders because of his censure by the Senate for misuse of campaign funds. Despite a certain amount of help from Duffey's staff, the Democrats lost the governorship to Thomas J. Meskill (R).

Representative J. Glenn Beall, Jr. (R), won the Senate seat of the incumbent Joseph D. Tydings in Maryland. Tydings, a prime target of the Nixon campaign, was plagued with charges that he improperly influenced a government agency on behalf of a company in which he had a financial interest. He also was hurt by the opposition of groups that were hostile to gun registration measures he favored. The turnout of voters in Baltimore, a Democratic stronghold, was light, possibly because of the lack of an important racial issue.

Representative Robert Taft, Jr. (R), defeated Howard Metzenbaum (D) for the Ohio Senate seat vacated by the retiring Stephen M. Young (D). Taft ran unexpectedly strong in the northern, Democratic half of the state. It appeared that Metzenbaum was hurt by a racial split in his party. A faction led by Carl Stokes, the black mayor of Cleveland, backed him but repudiated John J. Gilligan (D) for governor. A split vote in normally Democratic white areas, where Stokes was unpopular, aided Taft but provided the margin of victory for Gilligan and a number of other Democratic candidates for major Ohio offices.

In Tennessee, Representative William Brock III (R) defeated three-term incumbent Senator Albert Gore (D) in a major test of liberal and conservative appeal in the mid-South. Brock assailed Gore as a "radical liberal" ally of the Eastern establishment. Gore said that Brock's stands on social and economic issues had injured Tennessee. Gore was a special target of the Nixon Administration because of his antiwar stand and his votes against the president's appointments to the U.S. Supreme Court. Along with Brock, Winfield Dunn (R) was elected, replacing Buford Ellington (D) as governor.

Another important test for the Administration came in New York State. There, the Senate election was won by James L. Buckley of the Conservative party. During the campaign, Vice-President Agnew virtually read incumbent Senator Charles E. Goodell out of the Republican party. He described the senator as a "radical liberal" who had "left his party." In a complicated situation that threatened traditional political patterns, Gov. Nelson A. Rockefeller (R) endorsed Goodell but gave him little campaign support. New York City's Mayor John V. Lindsay backed Goodell but endorsed the bid of Arthur J. Goldberg (D) against Rockefeller. Richard Ottinger, the Democratic senatorial nominee, appealed vainly to Goodell to drop out of the race to prevent Buckley's election. Rockefeller won by a large majority. Buckley said he would line up with Senate Republicans.

The Rev. Robert Drinan of Massachusetts is the first Roman Catholic priest ever elected to the U.S. House of Representatives.
UPI COMPIX

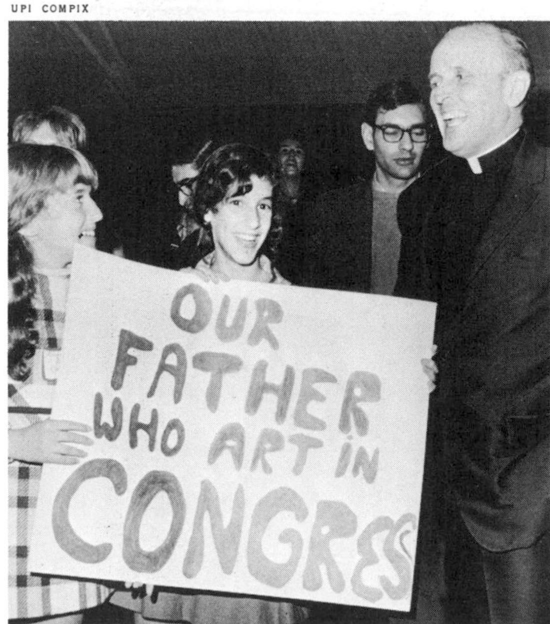

In Illinois, Adlai E. Stevenson III, son of the 1952 and 1956 Democratic presidential candidate, easily defeated incumbent Senator Ralph T. Smith (R). Stevenson led the Democrats to major gains in state offices, including a tie in the previously Republican Illinois Senate.

In California, Representative John V. Tunney (D), son of the former heavyweight boxing champion Gene Tunney, defeated incumbent George Murphy (R) for the Senate seat. In both Illinois and California, the Republicans put heavy stress on the issue of law and order and Democrats hit the slackening of the economy under the Republicans and complained of excessive Republican campaign spending. While Murphy was defeated, his running mate Gov. Ronald Reagan easily won reelection. The controversial California school superintendent, Max Rafferty, a strong opponent of what he described as permissiveness in education, was defeated by his liberal black deputy Wilson Riles.

In Virginia, Senator Harry F. Byrd, Jr., a Democrat who left the party in March 1970 in protest over an expected requirement that Democrats pledge support for the party's 1972 presidential candidate, was reelected as an independent. He was expected to vote with the Democrats on the organization of the Senate but with the Administration in many conservative stands.

Governorships

Republicans captured two governorships previously held by Democrats. They were those in Tennessee and Connecticut, both mentioned above. The Democrats gained 13 previously held by the Republicans. In addition to Ohio, mentioned above, the most significant gain was in Pennsylvania, the third most populous state, where Milton J. Shapp became the first Democratic governor elected there since 1958. At the same time, Pennsylvania voters returned minority leader Hugh Scott to the Senate.

Other governorships captured from Republicans by the Democrats were in Alaska, Florida, Arkansas, Oklahoma, Idaho, Minnesota, Nebraska, Nevada, New Mexico, South Dakota, and Wisconsin. Before the 1970 elections, the Republicans held 32 governorships, and the Democrats 18. Afterward, the margin was 29 Democrats, 21 Republicans.

Youth and the Election

Proposals to lower the voting age were defeated in most of the 15 states where the question was on the ballot. Unofficial returns showed that voters in Maine and Nebraska approved lowering the voting age to 20, Montana and Massachusetts to 19, and Alaska to 18. But proposals to lower the voting age apparently were defeated in Washington, Colorado, Wyoming, South Dakota, New Jersey, Minnesota, Connecticut, Florida, Michigan, and Hawaii. Interest was reduced by a federal law to lower the voting age in all elections to 18. In December the Supreme Court ruled that the law was valid for federal elections only. This meant that 18-year-olds could vote for presidential and Congressional candidates but could not vote in state or local elections unless permitted by state constitutions.

Student efforts, while far from decisive in the elections, had pronounced effects. The Movement for a New Congress (MNC), a Princeton Uni-

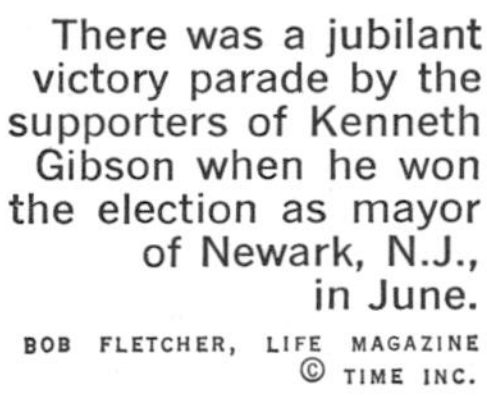

There was a jubilant victory parade by the supporters of Kenneth Gibson when he won the election as mayor of Newark, N.J., in June.

BOB FLETCHER, LIFE MAGAZINE © TIME INC.

The Movement for a New Congress was founded at Princeton University to help elect peace candidates to Congress. In New Jersey, student campaigners worked for their candidate by visiting each family in the district.

BILL EPPRIDGE, LIFE MAGAZINE © TIME INC.

versity-based group working to end the war in Southeast Asia and revise national priorities, reported that 8 of the candidates whom it supported for the Senate and 24 for the House were elected. Six of the candidates whom it endorsed for the Senate and 30 endorsed for the House were defeated. Only 2 of the successful Senate candidates and 5 House candidates defeated incumbents, but several of the unsuccesful candidates supported by the MNC ran significantly better against well-established incumbents than did previous opponents. (*See also* Congress, U.S.; Political Parties.)

ELECTRONICS. Collision avoidance systems continued to receive major attention in the field of avionics (aviation electronics) during 1970. Three major types of systems designed to diminish the chance of collisions in the air were under consideration. In one system, each aircraft would broadcast information about its location at three-second intervals, allowing other planes to make comparisons with their positions and to take steps necessary to avert collisions. However, the incidence of false alarms, especially near airports, was considered quite high. A second system involved a flashing xenon lamp on the tail of the aircraft and a detector on the wing tips. Its capabilities were limited to warnings of dangerously close aircraft. A third system, named SECANT (separation control of aircraft by nonsynchronous techniques), had a lower rate of false alarms than the first system and provided a greater warning period than the second. Although it had only been simulated on paper, the actual system could be made in elaborate models for large airliners as well as for inexpensive models for private planes.

Communications

More companies in 1970 filed with the U.S. Federal Communications Commission for permission to build and operate new private data-communications networks. American Telephone and Telegraph Co. (AT&T) and Western Union joined Data Transmission Co. (Datran) and Microwave Communications, Inc. (MCI), which had filed in 1969.

Nearly all data communications previously had been conducted over Western Union telegraph lines or AT&T lines, both of which had become overcrowded. The Datran plan involved the building of a network on microwave channels for digital transmission only; no voices were to be transmitted. MCI planned to lease channels to subscribers to use for voice communication as well as for digital information. Western Union's system involved a data-transmission satellite 22,000 miles above the equator. AT&T was thought to have filed with the FCC only as a competitive move against the other three firms.

Technological Advances

Metal oxide semiconductor integrated circuits, or MOS circuits, which perform nearly all of the circuit operations of vast arrays of transistors, accounted for a domestic volume of from $50 to $80 million during 1970. The MOS, used in calculators, computers, and small electronic equipment, did not appear to any great extent until 1969.

In 1970 many of the difficulties of mass producing MOS circuits were overcome by new methods. One such method employed an ion accelerator—a low-energy version of a cyclotron—to implant impurity atoms such as boron and phosphorus that make a material semiconducting.

Consumer Electronics

The video playback system was one of the hottest consumer electronics products of the year. Several electronics firms were manufacturing video playback devices designed to enable the viewer to create his own television programming. One model, developed for production by Motorola, Inc., was a unit the size of a briefcase that, when hooked up to any television set, played prerecorded films in either black and white or color. Another model, developed by Cartridge Television, Inc., included a tape deck and a 19-inch color screen. It played video tape cartridges. The retail price of both models was set at about $800 or $900.

A portable, all-electronic consumer calculator called the Pocketronic was unveiled in April. The machine can handle up to 12 digits and can add, subtract, multiply, and divide. (*See also* Computers. *See in* CE: Electrons and Electronics.)

EL SALVADOR. Repercussions from the brief but disruptive open conflict between El Salvador and Honduras in mid-1969 were evident in El Salvador in 1970. Diplomatic and trade relations between the two nations remained severed. However, a series of bilateral peace talks beginning late in January 1970 attempted to restore these relations. The meetings were held in San José, Costa Rica, and mediated by José A. Mora of Uruguay, the former secretary-general of the Organization of American States (OAS). El Salvador and Honduras each sent three delegates. On June 4, El Salvador and Honduras accepted a plan to establish a demilitarized zone (DMZ), 1.8 miles wide on either side of their common border. Military planes of either nation would not be allowed over the DMZ or within three miles of the outer edge of the DMZ.

Costa Rica, Guatemala, and Nicaragua, the other participants in the San José talks, acted as "guarantors" of the agreement, which went into effect on July 16. The OAS supervised the withdrawal of Salvadoran and Honduran forces but allowed each nation to maintain security patrols in certain defined places within the DMZ. The OAS also financed and appointed military observers to see that the June 4 agreement was honored.

Voting was held in March to elect members of the 52-seat Legislative Assembly. The incumbent Party of National Conciliation gained control of 34 seats; the principal opposition party, the Christian Democratic party, won 16 seats. The right-wing Salvadoran Popular party and a new leftist party, the Nationalist Democratic Union, each won one seat. (*See in* CE: Salvador, El.)

EMPLOYMENT. Unemployment rates continued to climb throughout 1970. For December the jobless rate stood at 6%—the highest figure in nearly nine years. In contrast to the preceding year when rising unemployment seemed to catch government officials unaware, the jobless level of 1970 came as a surprise to no one. Earlier in the year, George P. Shultz, then U.S. secretary of labor, predicted that the level of unemployment would continue to climb. Another member of the Administration, Andrew F. Brimmer of the Board of Governors of the Federal Reserve System, went on record as claiming that an unemployment rate of about 5.5% was necessary to check inflation.

While the 6% figure represented a nationwide average, the percentage was considerably higher in several areas. By the end of the third quarter, 38 major labor market areas had been placed on the list of areas with "substantial" unemployment. In these areas the jobless rate was well over 6%. For example, in Seattle, Wash., an unemployment rate of 7.6% for the month of February was attributed to cutbacks in defense spending. This limited production at Boeing Co., forcing a layoff of a projected 25,000 employees during the year. In other cities the increased unemployment was attributed to nationwide trends such as construction slowdowns, labor disruptions, and industrial spending cutbacks.

With a comparatively high rate of unemployment accepted as at least a temporary fact of life, new measures were instituted to soften the blow. In August U.S. President Richard M. Nixon signed a bill extending unemployment insurance coverage to 4.7 million more workers. Those workers given new coverage included employees of concerns having less than four employees. Previously only employees of firms with more than four employees were eligible. The new act also covered agricultural processing workers, employees of nonprofit organizations, county and municipal institutions, and some Americans working abroad. Emergency benefits of up to 13 weeks additional compensation would be applicable when the national unemployment rate reached 4.5% for three months. The provision, which was designed to cushion the move from a wartime to a peacetime economy, was to take effect in January 1972.

The composition of the ranks of unemployed was about the same as it had been in earlier years. Blacks and the young were the hardest hit. At the end of August, the Negro unemployment rate

The president of the Coca-Cola Co., J. Paul Austin, promised to improve the working conditions of migratory workers employed by his company.

UPI COMPIX

WIDE WORLD

In October 1970, when California's unemployment rate was more than 50% higher than it was in the preceding year, some 700 applicants lined up for four job openings as meter readers with the Southern California Gas Co.

of 8.4% was up by about a third from the rate a year earlier. For the same period, the teen-age unemployment rate stood at 15.9%, the highest since April 1965. The high summer unemployment rate among the young was attributed to the lack of summer jobs, which were down 30% to 50% from 1969. The rate of unemployment among whites at the end of August was only 4.8%.

However, a sizable number of well-educated white-collar workers did end up on the unemployment rolls in 1970. Physicists in particular were having difficulty finding permanent jobs, largely because of a great slackening in government demand. The Atomic Energy Commission cut staffs at several of its major laboratories including those at Los Alamos, N.M.; Livermore, Calif.; and Oak Ridge, Tenn. Professional and managerial employees were increasingly becoming victims of joblessness. In July their unemployment rate was up 74% from the same period in 1969, reaching the 394,000 mark.

If the grim employment outlook had one beneficial effect, it was to spawn some creative job-placement programs. In Chicago, The Opportunity Line, a job-placement television show which had been responsible for finding employment for 140,000 men and women since 1967, presented a half-hour special in May. The program was aimed at finding summer jobs for young people. A new profession specializing in relocating executives grew up during the year. Firms called "outplacement agencies" located new jobs for business executives who were about to be fired. The company doing the firing paid the agency's fee.

In June the U.S. Department of Labor's Bureau of Labor Statistics issued projections on the makeup of the U.S. work force during the next decade. It stated that more jobs will arise from replacement needs than from employment growth. It also projected that the number of service workers will increase 40%; managers, officials, and proprietors as a group, more than 20%; clerical workers, about 33%; sales workers, almost 30%; craftsmen, nearly 25%; and semiskilled workers, 10%. (*See also* Economy; Labor Unions.)

A new computer hiring system replaces the old hiring hall for longshoremen who work on a daily basis for the Port of New York.

"THE NEW YORK TIMES"

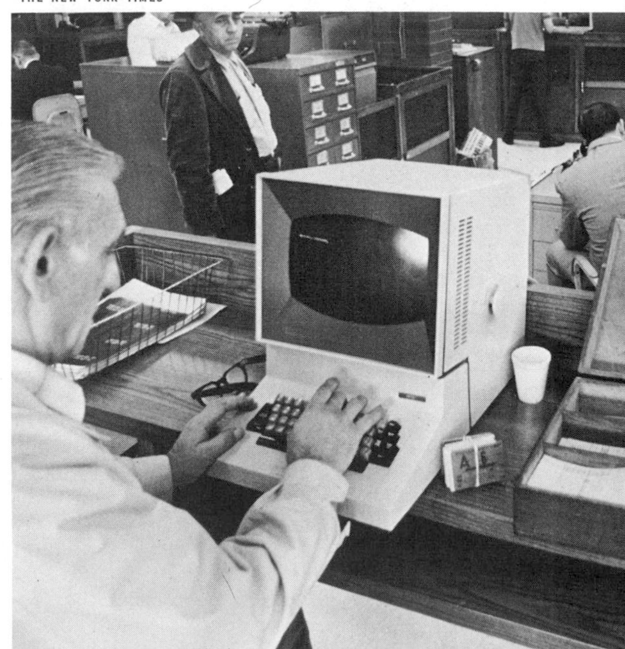

ENGINEERING PROJECTS.

Heavy-construction activity continued at a high level throughout the world in 1970. Mounting public concern over the adverse effects upon the environment of some large construction projects, however, increasingly compelled engineers to consider ecological factors as well as cost and feasibility when planning bridges, dams, roads, and tunnels. It was anticipated that ecologically sound design would increase costs.

BRIDGES

Work began in 1970 on the Eurasia Bridge over the Bosporus Strait, linking Europe and Asia. With a central span of 3,524 feet, it will be the longest suspension bridge in the world outside the United States. Similar in conception to the Severn Bridge in Great Britain, it incorporated a number of original features—among them side spans (758 feet on the European bank, 837 feet on the Asian) that would not be suspended, but carried by steel columns articulated at the top and foot, reducing flexion in the pylons and allowing the cables to join the anchorings at a more abrupt slope.

The Rhinehausen Duisburg-Neunenkamp Bridge across the Rhine River in West Germany, which set a new world record for cable-stayed bridges with a central span of 1,148 feet, had an all-welded deck comprising a triple-webbed caisson and an orthotropic plate. A number of other major bridges of this type were also under construction.

One partially completed cable-stayed bridge, however, was visited by tragedy. In October a side span of the West Gate cable-stayed box-girder bridge over the Yarra River at Melbourne, Australia, collapsed, killing 34 workmen. Construction was delayed while a royal commission investigated the failure. Another orthotropically decked box-girder bridge, this of the inclined-prop type, took four lives when it collapsed while under construction over the West Cleddau River at Milford Haven, Wales. When completed, the Milford Haven Bridge was to have the longest unsupported span (700 feet) in Europe. In the wake of these two disasters, the British government began an independent inquiry into the design and construction of large box-girder bridges.

Other major inclined-prop box-girder bridges under construction included the new viaduct over the Danube River at Vienna, Austria, and a bridge spanning the navigable channel of San Diego Bay in California. Yet another—984 feet long and at a height of 425 feet—spanned a gorge on the Santiago River near Guadalajara, Mexico.

The successive-cantilevering method of construction was being used in a number of large prestressed-concrete bridges. However, in the United States construction of the Three Sisters Bridge over the Potomac River was halted by court order while its piers were being erected because its design, which provided for a 750-foot-long central span, was considered dangerous. The world record for bridges of this type was thus still held by the Bendorf Bridge in West Germany, with a 682-foot-long central span.

KEYSTONE

Traffic moved across the first section of the new London Bridge in February. When completed, the bridge will be 80 feet wide.

Construction employing large prefabricated components was preferred for very long structures. This method was employed, for instance, in the bridge between Rio de Janeiro and Niterói, Brazil; its total length of 8½ miles was made up of caisson girders ranging in depth from 262 feet to 374 feet.

For spans of about 80 to 150 feet, the use of prefabricated, prestressed-concrete girders remained the most economical form of construction. For the erection of continuous structures with spans of between 100 and 200 feet, the use of self-launching centering proved economical where the overall length was sufficient to justify the cost of the equipment. (*See in* CE: Bridge.)

DAMS

In 1970 some 270 dams were under construction in the United States, and about 400 more were projected. Construction of the Auburn double-curvature arch dam on the North Fork River in California was in its early stages. The dam's

AUTHENTICATED NEWS INTERNATIONAL

Renovation of the first span of the Delaware Memorial Bridge was completed in December 1969. The second span of the twin suspension bridge was completed in 1968.

designed height was 680 feet, its arch length 3,500 feet, and its volume 6 million cubic yards. Work continued on the Kentucky rock-fill dam (1,420 feet long, 282 feet high, some 3 million cubic yards in volume) in Laurel County, Ky. Also being built was the Grasshopper Hollow earth-fill dam (350 feet high, $2\frac{1}{2}$ million cubic yards in volume) near Berkeley Springs, W. Va.

Early in the year the U.S. Department of the Interior awarded a contract for the construction of an additional power plant at Grand Coulee Dam on the Columbia River in Washington. When completed a decade or more hence, the plant is expected to bring Grand Coulee's total generating capacity to 9.6 million kilowatts, making it the world's largest single power station. The present record—6.1 million kilowatts—is held by the Soviet dam at Krasnoyarski, in Siberia.

In Canada, construction continued on the Mica earth-and-rock-fill dam (800 feet high, 42 million cubic yards in volume) on the Columbia River. It was scheduled for completion in 1973. The Bighorn earth-fill dam (300 feet high, 3.8 million cubic yards in volume) on the North Saskatchewan River was to be completed in 1972, and the Lower Notch Dam on the Montreal River was also under construction. Work began in 1970 on the Manic 3 earth-fill dam (355 feet high, 12 million cubic yards in volume) on the Manicouagan River.

In South America the Esmeralda rock-fill dam (754 feet high, 14.1 million cubic yards in volume), with an included impervious core, was under construction on the Bata River of Colombia. Another Colombian undertaking was the Alto Anchicayá rock-fill dam (459 feet high, 3 million cubic yards in volume), with an upstream face of concrete, on the Anchicayá River. In Brazil the Ilha Solteira earth-and-concrete gravity dam, being built on the Paraná River, was 262 feet high, 20,300 feet long, and 32.8 million cubic yards in volume. The Mantaro River concrete gravity dam in Peru was under construction. In Argentina the Chocón-Cerros Colorados earth-fill dam (295 feet high, 7,500 feet long, 18 million cubic yards in volume) on the River Limay was also being constructed.

Construction continued in the Soviet Union on the Inguri Dam, near the Black Sea, which is to be the world's highest concrete-arch dam at 892 feet, and on the Nurek Dam on the Vakhsh River, near the border of Afghanistan, planned to be 1,017 feet high, of earth fill. Elsewhere in Europe, major dam-construction projects were under way in Spain, Great Britain, Romania, Bulgaria, and Yugoslavia.

Work progressed in Pakistan on the Tarbela earth-and-rock-fill dam on the Indus River, to be "the world's largest man-made mountain" with a height of 485 feet, a length of 9,000 feet, and a volume of 186 million cubic yards. In Malaysia, the Muda reinforced-concrete buttress dam (105 feet high, 720 feet long) with short-gravity wings neared completion; it was of engineering interest because of an unusual arrangement of post-tensioned steel cables to anchor the dam to its foundations.

Three dams were under construction in Australia. The Ord River rock-fill dam was to provide irrigation for 178,000 acres. (*See in* CE: Dam.)

ROADS

In almost all countries of the world, road-building programs continued to gather momentum in 1970. While the proportion of national resources spent on highways varied from country to country, a worldwide average was about 1% of national income. A number of major highway projects were completed during the year.

It was announced that in the United States in 1968 (the latest year for which complete figures were available) 2,083 miles of highway were built. In South America, work progressed on the Pan American Highway system. In January, with the completion of a 42-mile section of the new road between Valparaiso, Chile, and Mendoza, Argentina, part of it more than 10,000 feet above sea level, the entire Chilean segment of the system was paved. Another part of the system, from Riohacha to Paraguachon, Colombia, was opened in May. The final section (Quitaúna to Chuy) of the first paved connection between Brazil and Uruguay was also opened during the year.

A number of European highway projects were completed in 1970. An important new highway between Corinth and Patras, Greece, was opened to traffic. Major sections of two Swiss national roads were finished, as were several highway sections in West Germany. In France an 8.7-mile length of the highway between Marseilles and Lyon was opened, as was the first carriageway of the Paris-to-Rungis motorway. The latter was intended to relieve Orly Airport traffic congestion.

Westway Road, the first stage of the West Cross route, was opened in London in 1970. The route is part of the Greater London Council's plan to control traffic problems.

FOX PHOTOS FROM PICTORIAL PARADE

Two new sections of the Brenner expressway in Austria and Italy were opened, as were new sections of several other major Italian highways. Britain moved closer to its goal of completing 1,000 miles of expressway by the early 1970's. In 1970 some 630 miles were completed and 350 miles were under construction.

In South-West Africa, highway construction since 1958 reached 1,345 miles in 1970. The work was well ahead of schedule, the 20-year plan envisioning only 1,245 miles by the end of 1978. In South Africa the Chrissiesmeer-to-Oshoek section of the road between Johannesburg and Swaziland was tarred, providing a completely waterproofed surface throughout the length of the road.

Upper Volta completed two main projects in 1970, the road from Bobo-Dioulasso to the Mali border and the road from Ouagadougou to Po, near the Ghana border. The highway authorities of Nigeria built 51 miles of road in the Idoma region.

In Israel, the opening of a new 6.2-mile-long road reduced travel time between Tel Aviv-Jaffa and Lod Airport. The 266-mile-long, four-lane Seoul-to-Pusan expressway in South Korea was completed in 1970. The new expressway replaced an old road and more than halved travel time between the two cities. The economic benefits of the road were expected to outweigh its cost, estimated at more than $150 million.

The Ella-to-Wellawaya road in Ceylon was completed, connecting the northern and southern parts of Uva Province with the central and southern provinces. In New Zealand, the seaward lanes of the first section of the Wellington motorway between Kaiwharawhara and Aotea Quay were opened to traffic. (*See in* CE: Roads and Streets.)

TUNNELS

An indication of the total value of tunneling being carried out in 1970 was given during the Organization for Economic Cooperation and Development conference on tunneling in June in Washington, D.C. The combined annual rate of expenditure on tunneling in the 20 participating countries was about $1 billion ($3 billion including mine tunnels). During the previous decade a total of at least 8,000 miles (270,000 miles including mine tunnels) of tunnels with an excavated volume of at least 390 million cubic yards (5 billion cubic yards including mining) were constructed.

In West Germany, work started at Hamburg on a six-lane, triple-barrelled, two-mile-long tunnel (estimated cost in 1968, $104 million) under the Elbe River. It will form a major link in the E3 highway between Stockholm, Sweden, and Lisbon, Portugal. The central section of the tunnel was being bored through clay and marl by two 36-foot-diameter mechanical shields. Each shield cost $3 million and was driven forward by 40 jacks exerting a combined force of 9,000 tons.

In Japan, increased pressure by political and business groups seemed to indicate that the long-proposed Seikan tunnel between the northern island of Hokkaido and the main island of Honshu might become a reality. The hope was that the national budget would provide sufficient funds for construction to begin during the summer of 1971. Upon completion, the tunnel would extend for 38.6 miles. It would be the world's longest tunnel.

As part of Spain's highway program, a second road tunnel, costing $14.5 million and 2¼ miles long, was being pushed through the Sierra de Guadarrama on the route between Madrid and La Coruña. The completed tunnel would be 40 feet wide, with 15 feet of headroom and a 12-foot space above for ventilation ducts.

In England the Robbins tunneling machine boring the 34-foot-internal-diameter, 7,300-foot-long second Mersey Tunnel holed through in March. Driving began of the 6,606-foot-long pilot bore for the third Mersey Tunnel, to be completed in three years.

In many of the world's large cities in 1970 extensive lengths of tunnel were being constructed for subway systems. Work continued in Toronto, Ont., on the five-mile-long Yonge Street extension scheduled for completion in 1973. In New York City, the chief of an extensive program of improvements was the 63d Street East River tunnel, consisting of two 750-foot lengths of immersed-tube construction connected by a tunnel blasted under Welfare Island. The four 38-foot-by-38-foot concrete tube sections used were 375 feet long, double-decked with two tracks on each level.

In San Francisco, Calif., construction of Bay Area Rapid Transit system subway structures was more than 80% complete. The 75-mile-long system is expected to incorporate some 20 miles of subway.

Extensive tunneling went on in many cities to meet demands for water supply and sewage disposal. For example, in New York City contracts totaling $222.6 million were let for construction of a 13.7-mile-long water-supply tunnel, mostly of 24-foot diameter tunnel in hard rock deep under the city.

The world record for rate of advance of bored and permanently lined tunnel was claimed by Edmund Nuttall, Sons & Co., Ltd., of England, for their construction of 1,426 feet in one week during December 1969. This was achieved while driving the 12-mile-long aqueduct tunnel that is part of the Essex River Authority's Ely-Ouse flood-protection program. The tunnel was 8 feet and 4 inches in internal diameter and was lined with precast concrete segments. It was driven by a tunneling machine made by Robert L. Priestly, Ltd. (*See in* CE: Tunnels.)

EQUATORIAL GUINEA. In January 1970, President Francisco Macías Nguma made his first official visit abroad since Equatorial Guinea became independent in October 1968. He spent several days in Cameroon, during which time he attended that country's independence day celebrations. In August, the president visited Nigeria and voiced the hope that relations between the two countries would become closer and more cordial. Macías discussed a long-standing source of complaints from the Nigerian government—the treatment of the large number of Nigerian workers on the plantations of Fernando Po. He stated that his government would draw up a new contract agreement to replace the harsh labor laws that had previously been in force.

Efforts to establish links with other nations continued during the year. On July 31, it was announced in Prague, Czechoslovakia, that the Czechoslovak government and Equatorial Guinea had agreed to establish diplomatic relations at the ambassadorial level. Relations with Spain improved steadily in 1970, and Equatorial Guinea's economic and financial position was strengthened with Spanish assistance.

ETHIOPIA. Because the Ethiopian economy remained largely dependent on coffee, it benefited to some extent in 1970 from a blight that reduced coffee yields in Brazil. At the same time steps were being taken within the framework of the country's third five-year plan to diversify crops and exports. Agricultural development centered on various regional "package deal" projects—notably in the Awash River valley, Chillalo, and Wolamo districts south of Addis Ababa, the capital, and in the Setit Humera region, northwest of Lake Tana along the Sudan border. Financial backing for the Awash, Wolamo, and Setit Humera projects came from the World Bank, and for the Chillalo project from Sweden.

Other moves to strengthen the economy included proposals to reorganize the financial intermediaries in the government's development banking and investment structure. While a new investment code was being considered, new rates of income tax and land tax were approved to provide support for expanding social services, particularly education. Military aid from the United States amounted to $12 million in 1970, bringing the total since 1953, when the U.S. base at Kagnew, Eritrea, was set up, to $159 million.

In the industrial sector, a metal tool factory was opened in Addis Ababa with Polish assistance; a Greek-financed chemical detergent industry was to become operational in 1971; and, with $323,000 from the United Nations Development Programme, studies were initiated to determine the feasibility of exploiting geothermal power sources in the Great Rift Valley and the Afar Plain. In 1971 work was scheduled to begin on the section from Dilla to Moyale (on the Kenya border) of a continental

MARION KAPLAN

Ethiopia's Emperor Haile Selassie I opens a new session of parliament, Nov. 2, 1970. The year marks the 40th anniversary of his reign.

highway project to link East African countries. Meanwhile, road communications in southwest Ethiopia were greatly improved by the installation of Bailey bridges.

A visit to Ethiopia by President Jean-Bedel Bokassa of the Central African Republic led to mutual agreements on telecommunications links and cultural exchanges. Other distinguished visitors were Prince Bernhard of the Netherlands, who was concerned, as president of the World Wildlife Fund, with the development of Ethiopia's nature reserves; Rose Kennedy, for the inauguration of a John F. Kennedy memorial library in the Haile Selassie I University at Addis Ababa; and Robert S. McNamara, president of the World Bank, to review the bank's projects in Ethiopia. (*See in* CE: Ethiopia.)

EUROPE. The year 1970 will be remembered in the history of Europe as the one in which World War II in effect ended with the signing of a treaty on renunciation of force between West Germany and the Soviet Union. There were also attempts during the year to improve relations between nations in Eastern and in Western Europe, but East-West tensions still existed over the Berlin issue and clouded the prospect of a final resolution of the post-World War II situation in the immediate future.

Getting Together

The Treaty of Moscow was signed on August 12 by West Germany's Chancellor Willy Brandt and Soviet Premier Aleksei N. Kosygin. The ceremony took place in St. Catherine's Hall of the Great Kremlin Palace in Moscow. In addition to renouncing the use of force, by signing the treaty the two leaders agreed to accept the existing boundaries in Europe. The treaty awaited ratification by the West German Bundestag and by the Supreme Soviet before taking effect.

Eastern and Western governments alike praised the signing of the treaty. Some European newspapers, however, expressed reservations and pointed out that earlier German-Soviet nonaggression treaties had not been honored.

On signing the treaty Brandt stated, "This is the end of an epoch but, it seems to me, a very good beginning." Kosygin agreed. In addition to improving diplomatic relations the West Germans and the Soviets hoped to reap economic benefits by establishing closer ties. It was also hoped that an improved East-West economic trend would extend to the nations of Eastern Europe as well. The Soviets made known their desire to establish long-term economic and technological ties with West Germany.

"Security Is Two Blankets"

LIEDERMAN FROM BEN ROTH AGENCY

Brandt signed another renunciation of force treaty on December 7, this one with Poland. The terms of the treaty recognized the Oder-Neisse line as Poland's post-World War II western boundary. The treaty did not legally fix the Oder-Neisse line as the permanent boundary between Poland and East Germany but merely guaranteed that West Germany could not press territorial claims against Poland. Responsibility for fixing boundaries remained with the World War II Allied powers.

Because 6 million Poles had been killed by the Nazis during World War II, Poland harbored great hatred for West Germany. The Treaty of Warsaw was seen as an important step toward mitigating the hostility. In a speech Brandt stated that the 40,000 square miles of German territory taken over by Poland after World War II was a sacrifice for "Hitler's crimes."

In signing these treaties the governments of Poland and the Soviet Union disregarded demands by East Germany's Communist Party First Secretary Walter Ulbricht that diplomatic recognition must be granted to East Germany before any progress could be made in improving East-West relations. The first meeting between the leaders of East and West Germany took place during 1970. On March 19 Brandt met with East Germany's Premier Willi Stoph in East Germany. (*See* Germany Special Report.)

Representatives of France, Great Britain, the Soviet Union, and the United States—the four powers occupying Berlin—met on March 26 for the first time in 11 years to discuss the tensions in that city. The Western powers agreed to allow East Germans travel privileges to North Atlantic Treaty Organization (NATO) nations without special authorization from the occupying powers. Many such meetings were held during the year, but no concessions were made by the Soviets. They insisted that West Berlin was politically separate from West Germany and demanded that West German officials leave the divided city. Late in the year the East Germans closed off routes out of the city to protest a West German Christian Democratic Union meeting held in West Berlin. The West German government indicated that progress toward easing the tensions over Berlin would have to precede ratification of the West German-Soviet treaty.

The Warsaw Pact and NATO

Hopes for a European security conference between NATO and Warsaw Pact nations alternately rose and fell throughout the year. On May 27, NATO ministers invited the Soviet Union and the Warsaw Pact nations to engage in exploratory talks on the issue of balanced troop reductions in Europe. It was hoped that such talks might lead to a major security conference. The Soviet Union's initial response to the invitation was unenthusiastic, but at a Warsaw Pact meeting held in Hungary in June the Communist nations drew up an expanded agenda for a European security conference. The agenda included such topics as the renunciation of force among European nations and the expansion of trade and East-West scientific and cultural ties.

The new Warsaw Pact proposal was treated cautiously by the Western powers. In their proposal for talks on troop cuts the Communist nations did not mention balanced reductions, and this was one of the specific items that the United States insisted must be included in any conference. The United States also wanted to discuss the Soviet Union's

The U.S. secretary of state, William P. Rogers (right), talks with Spain's Generalissimo Francisco Franco (center) and Gregorio Lopez Bravo, Spain's minister of foreign affairs, at the El Prado Palace, on May 29 in Madrid, Spain. Rogers visited Spain to negotiate with Franco on keeping U.S. military bases in Spain for another five years.

UPI COMPIX

KEYSTONE

The Italian Communist party sponsored a massive demonstration in May against the North Atlantic Treaty Organization meeting held in Rome. Exiled Greek composer Mikis Theodorakis attended the demonstration.

"Brezhnev doctrine" of limited sovereignty if a European security conference were held. In December the NATO ministers met and decided to take no further action on the Warsaw Pact proposals until restrictions were lifted on travel to and from West Berlin and the Soviet Union showed good faith by making some concessions on East and West Germany.

European defense was a major NATO concern during 1970, particularly since the nations of Western Europe were faced with the possibility of cutbacks in U.S. troop strength. Early in the year there was Congressional pressure on the Nixon Administration to reduce the number of U.S. troops in Europe after June 1971. The NATO defense planners feared that a smaller ground force in Western Europe would be unable to hold off any invasion from the East, and therefore the chances of massive nuclear warfare would be greatly increased.

In April West Germany's chancellor flew to the United States and asked U.S. President Richard M. Nixon not to withdraw any U.S. troops from the NATO forces in Europe. The Nixon Administration then issued a statement saying it had no immediate plans to reduce U.S. troop commitments after June 1971.

In October the European members of NATO agreed to contribute $300 million annually toward the maintenance of a U.S. military presence in Europe. President Nixon had indicated that he preferred greater European troop commitments, but West Germany opposed the expansion of its military force for political reasons. In December Nixon promised not to reduce the number of troops in Western Europe until the Warsaw Pact nations made similar troop reductions in Eastern Europe.

The British government in March announced that it would return the 4,500 troops withdrawn from Europe in 1968. West Germany agreed to reimburse Great Britain for most of the cost of maintaining the troops.

In December NATO ministers announced plans to strengthen conventional military forces in Western Europe. Improvements were planned in the areas of armored forces, air and antiaircraft forces, naval forces, and communications. The NATO planners also intended to improve ground troop deployment and to strengthen defenses in the north.

A high-level meeting of the Warsaw Pact was held in East Berlin in December. Reportedly the Communist leaders discussed European security and other world problems such as Vietnam and Guinea. Six Warsaw Pact nations participated in military maneuvers held in East Germany during October. Romania sent only military observers to the Warsaw maneuvers.

Economic Alliances

As a prelude to the opening of negotiations with Great Britain, Norway, Denmark, and Ireland, the

UPI COMPIX

Turkish Janizaries march past the official residence of West Germany's President Gustav Heinemann just before the October visit of Turkey's President Cevdet Sunay.

European Common Market in April settled all the details of its plan for financing agriculture. In exchange for continued EEC farm support, the French gave their formal consent to allow consideration of Britain's application for membership.

Ironically, when the Common Market finally agreed to consider Great Britain's application, the British began losing interest in joining. A survey conducted during the year showed that 75% of Britain's citizens opposed entry, and many members of Parliament were withdrawing their support for EEC membership. A British economic report isued during the year concluded that there would be no economic advantages for Britain in joining, and that membership would raise food prices.

The negotiations for an expanded Common Market began on June 30 when the four applicants presented their bargaining positions. Common Market farm prices presented special problems for Great Britain, Norway, and Ireland. Great Britain, by importing food from Commonwealth nations, had lower food prices than EEC nations, but Norway paid higher farm-price supports than EEC nations. Norway also wanted to protect its fishing industry. Denmark was concerned about the free flow of capital. The Common Market members in turn warned the applicants that they would have to accept the provisions of the Treaty of Rome and all subsequent policies decided upon by the EEC.

During the year the Executive Commission of the EEC was reduced from 14 to 9 members. Jean Rey, a Belgian, was replaced as president by an Italian, Franco Maria Malfatti.

There was discussion during the year about possible ways to extend economic cooperation within the Common Market by establishing a monetary union. Provisions for short-term mutual financial assistance were set up in January. The EEC ministers in March agreed also to attempt the establishment of a joint foreign policy.

In February the EEC entered into a three-year trade agreement with Yugoslavia. This was the Common Market's first trade treaty with an East European nation. In 1970 West Germany was the leading EEC nation in trade with Communist countries.

The Soviet Union in 1970 made an energetic attempt to strengthen Comecon, the Communist common market. At a Comecon meeting held in Warsaw, Poland, in May the Soviet Union and six other Comecon nations agreed to set up an investment bank for financing Comecon projects. Western observers saw this as a political move designed to promote the economic dependency of East European nations on the Soviet Union. Romania refused to endorse the agreement.

In March Iceland became a full member of the European Free Trade Association. (*See also* individual countries by name; International Relations. *See in* CE: Europe.)

FADS OF 1970. Fads in the United States in 1970 focused predominantly on what people were wearing. The controversy over the midi—the new below-the-knee to midcalf length—put most U.S. women in a quandary over what to wear during the year. Some bravely stepped out in their new midis, some fiercely held on to their old minis, but most compromised with the pantsuit, which became the year's big seller. In part, no doubt, because of its popularity among men as an alternative to the midi, the pantsuit became accepted office wear for women of any age in 1970. Adding variety to the pants scene were gaucho pants, knickers, and even old-fashioned jeans in every color and fabric. To cinch their pants or midiskirts, women used elaborate belts (the more unusual the better, made of fringed suede or leather, sometimes decorated with hand-painted scenes); hippie-style embroidered cotton sashes; or even a cartridge belt, with or without bullets, in the style of a Mexican revolutionary.

Alternatives to pants for women were more individualized costumelike garb, such as gypsy- and peasant-inspired outfits complete with the ever-present boots. Tie-dyed clothes were popular for both men and women, particularly do-it-yourself versions. Even the lowly T-shirt was elevated to a fashionable status, decorated with pictures of Batman, Superman, or cartoon characters. To complete their outfits, women wore dog collars made in a variety of designs, including simple home-made beads, Edwardian velvet bands, metal collars, and elaborate bejeweled chokers.

Popular hairstyles for women included frizzed hair and a short-in-the-front, long-in-the-back haircut most often called "the Ape." Men continued to wear their hair long, much to the dismay of U.S. barbers, whose business suffered appreciably.

Identifying one's political and philosophic views with visual symbols, mostly in the form of campaign-style buttons, jewelry, car decals, or sew-on clothes patches, was a widespread trend during the year. The most commonly seen symbols were the U.S. flag, the peace symbol, the Black Panthers' clenched fist, the militant-feminist biological symbol, and ecological messages. Another politically inspired fad was the Spiro Agnew watch, which showed on its face a caricature of the U.S. vice-president. (*See also* Fashion.)

The Spiro Agnew watch, designed and marketed by Dirty Time, Inc., was a popular novelty item among both liberals and conservatives.

"Sweatshirt art" was popular in 1970. These three patterns showing Batman, Superman, and Sylvester the Cat were designed by Elaine Post.

JOHN STEMBER, LIFE MAGAZINE © TIME INC.

The Renaissance Pleasure Fair was held September 6–27 at Hidden Wood in San Rafael, Calif. The idea of the fair was conceived by Ron and Phyllis Patterson. It was intended to be a background for a Commedia dell' Arte performance by the Piccolo Playmakers, a children's theater group directed by Phyllis. The fair attracted thousands of people, many in costume, who flocked to see magicians, minstrels, and art and craft exhibitions.

JOY LOCKE

FAIRS AND SHOWS. Despite inflation, environmental crises, and other social and economic problems that affected nearly every nation of the world in 1970, fairs and shows continued their pattern of stability and growth. Attendance and revenues were generally higher in all sectors of this multibillion-dollar industry, with profits considered uniformly good.

The over 14,000 general public fairs around the globe attracted an estimated one billion persons. Some 950 general and specialized trade and commercial fairs accounted for an additional 42 million visitors, a large percentage of whom were registered buyers. More than 2 billion people flocked to over 16,500 amusement and theme parks, aquariums, zoos, and tourist attractions.

The focal event of 1970—and, indeed, of world's fair history—was Japan's Expo '70, held on a site in the Senri Hills northeast of Osaka. The first world's fair in Asia, it drew a record 64,218,770 visitors in its 183 days of operation. On September 5, a one-day world's fair attendance record was set by 835,832 visitors.

Free exhibit space was granted to 77 nations, and more than 115 varied pavilions dotted the 815-acre fair site. Expo's theme building, surrounded by a 64-acre Japanese garden, was a vast rectangular roof of giant aluminum ball-and-joint construction spread over theaters and display halls and covered, but not concealed, by plastic sheathing. Other features of the fair included the 396-foot-high Expo tower, moving sidewalks, and 210 restaurants serving foods from around the world.

During the year Philadelphia, Pa., was selected as the site of a proposed $1.5-billion exposition that would be a part of the celebration in 1976 of the 200th anniversary of the Declaration of Independence. It was proposed that half the cost of the fair be borne by the federal government and that the balance be paid by city, state, and private sources. Major roles in the celebration were assigned to Boston, Mass.; Washington, D.C.; and Miami, Fla.

North American events were, for the most part, well-attended during the peak season. The more than 3,200 U.S. fairs and an estimated 800 in Canada drew more than 115 million people. Of the larger fairs, numbering about 200, 55% reported substantial attendance increases over 1969 while 18% suffered declines. The gross revenues of North American state, county, district, and provincial fairs were estimated to be well over $200 million. The collective plant-and-land value of these fairs was listed at more than $2 billion.

Canadian and U.S. fairs spent an estimated $23 million for live talent and attractions, largely for grandstand shows that were offered free to fair patrons to offset the impact of increased admission prices. Most fairs also raised commercial exhibit space rates in 1970. European fairs, reacting to higher labor and materials costs, also raised admission prices during the year. Asian and Central and South American fairs, however, uniformly held to lower tariffs.

Although it drew fewer people than it had in 1969, the Canadian National Exhibition at Toronto,

Ont., led North American fairs in attendance in 1970 with 3,171,000 visitors. Its closest competitor was the state fair at Dallas, Tex., which reported its biggest year with a grand total of exactly 3,022,495 visitors.

Some 50 million North Americans—buyers and sellers—participated in retail and wholesale industrial shows, exhibits, and conventions that numbered more than 260,000. Boat and automobile shows continued to lead in attendance and consumer sales, followed by sports, camping and recreational equipment, and home-furnishings shows.

More than 75% of the estimated 820 international trade fairs held in 76 countries reported sharp gains in exhibit-space demands and in buyer registrations. The overseas Trade Fair Centers, sponsored by the U.S. Department of Commerce, increased to 300 in number in 1970.

The carnival industry in North America grossed more than $452 million in 1970, but showed a lower profit ratio than in previous years because of higher costs for labor and equipment. Rodeo performers, numbering more than 4,000 in the United States and Canada, competed for over $5 million in prize money at some 3,300 sanctioned and nonsanctioned events in 1970. More than 660 circuses were held throughout the world in 1970, with ranking units reporting their best season with gains ranging from 15% to 19% over 1969. Livestock and horse shows also continued to increase in popularity. (*See also* Anniversaries and Celebrations; Photography Exhibitions. *See in* CE: Fairs and Expositions.)

FAMILIES. A federal government report released in April 1970 revealed some harsh facts about families in the United States. A survey conducted by the U.S. Department of Health, Education, and Welfare showed that from 1964 through 1966 one third of all the firstborn children in the United States were conceived out of wedlock. In most of these cases the parents married before the birth of the child, and more than 37% of these hastily established families had annual incomes of less than $3,000. According to the survey one out of every seven firstborn children was illegitimate.

The divorce rate increased spectacularly in California during 1970. On January 1 California's new liberal divorce law went into effect, requiring only two grounds for divorce: incurable insanity or irreconcilable differences. In the first nine months of 1970 there were 81,912 divorces in California, an increase of 50% over the same period in 1969.

For the first time in the history of modern Italy, divorce became legal in 1970. The Italian parliament passed the divorce law in December in spite of the objections of Pope Paul VI.

Birth Control and Abortion

Birth control pills came under heavy attack during 1970. In January a U.S. Senate subcommittee opened hearings on the subject. Some witnesses testified that the pills may cause blood clots, loss of fertility, or even cancer. In response to this testimony the American College of Obstetricians and Gynecologists issued a statement deploring what it termed the "inaccurate or sensational reports." Other witnesses praised the pill as being the most

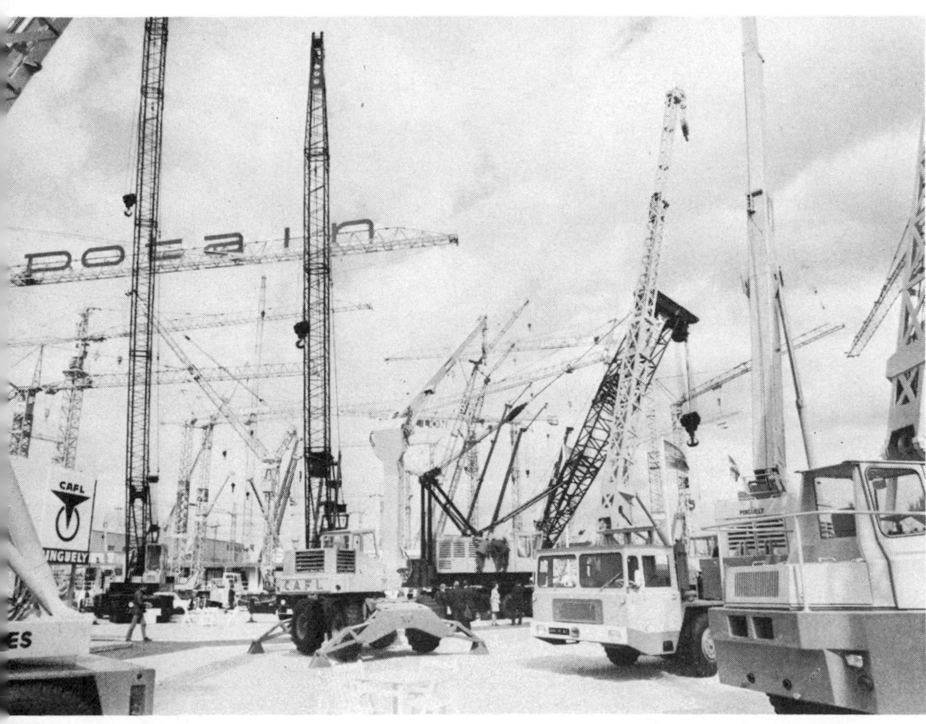

The cranes are part of "Expomat," an international exhibition of public works equipment and housing that opened May 22, 1970, at the Le Bourget Airport near Paris.
A.F.P. FROM PICTORIAL PARADE

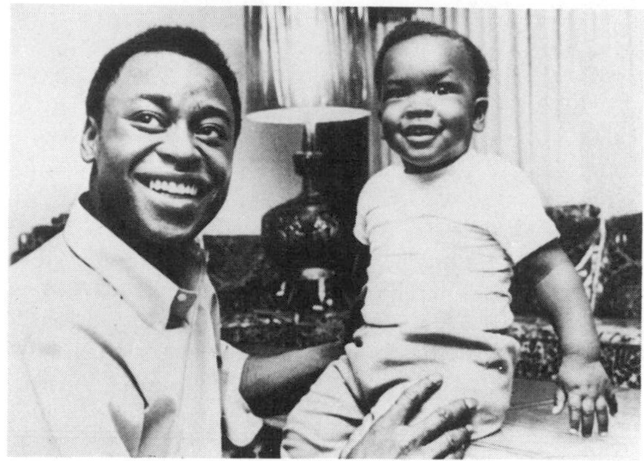

UPI COMPIX

Lepolia West, 29, a Chicago policeman, became a bachelor father in January 1970 when he adopted four-year-old Alan. West first met Alan in a hospital in 1968.

effective method of contraception, claiming that benefits far outweighed any adverse side effects. Nevertheless, the search continued during the year for an intrauterine device that would be as effective as birth control pills. Also, the Association for Voluntary Sterilization reported that every year approximately 100,000 U.S. citizens, today most of them males, undergo sterilization. Requests for sterilization operations greatly increased in 1970.

The New York State Legislature in April passed a bill liberalizing the legal conditions for abortion. According to the new law, which went into effect July 1, abortion became a medical question to be settled between the woman and her doctor up to the 24th week of pregnancy.

In February the Hawaii Legislature passed a bill making abortions available to pregnant women on request. The Maryland General Assembly also passed a liberal abortion measure in 1970, but the bill was vetoed by the governor. The Department of Defense announced in August that abortions and sterilization operations would be available to all active and retired military personnel and their dependents at U.S. military hospitals, regardless of local laws.

Minority Members

A much-abused minority family member, the mother-in-law, showed signs of militancy in 1970. The Mothers-in-Law Club International was organized in New York State for bringing these women together to discuss their problems.

A New Jersey judge during the year ordered a couple living in Illinois to return a child to a New Jersey adoption agency because the couple did not believe in a Supreme Being. In August a white man and a black woman challenged the Mississippi law against interracial marriage and won. Theirs was thought to be the first interracial marriage in Mississippi in more than 100 years. (*See also* Social Services; State Governments, U.S.)

FASHION.

In the world of fashion 1970 is destined to go down as the year of the great midi controversy. During the year designers decreed the most dramatic descent of the hemline since Christian Dior unveiled the New Look in 1947.

The midi—a term loosely applied to any garment length falling from just below the knee to just above the ankle—had appeared in designer collections for a number of seasons but did not become prominent until showings of the spring collections for 1970, when it shared the stage with the shorter skirt. However, in the fall collections the midi was strictly the name of the game; few designers featured any alternative.

The credit—or the blame—for the midi dictatorship was assigned to the editors of *Women's Wear Daily* (*WWD*), the most influential trade publication of the fashion industry. Among its readership *WWD* also listed 20,000 nontrade subscribers, including most of the "Beautiful People" and members of the "best-dressed" list. Reportedly, the paper got its inspiration from the 1930's costumes worn in the motion picture 'The Damned'. Using the term "longuette" to describe the midcalf fashions, it promoted the look almost exclusively.

Retailers were a little more reluctant to introduce the length. In the early months of the year a number of stores, including Peck & Peck and

About 100 women participated in this antimidi demonstration in West Germany in August.

D.P.A. FROM PICTORIAL PARADE

Abraham & Strauss in New York City, tried to reassure their customers that a "wardrobe of lengths" and not exclusively the midi was to be the picture of fashion for the year. However, with the introduction of the fall line, a great number of stores found themselves quite committed to the midi. Bonwit Teller, which in a February advertisement proclaimed, "We don't see any one length this fall . . . ," devoted 95% of its new autumn stock to the below-the-knee length. Other stores taking approximately the same position were Saks, Franklin Simon, Henri Bendel, and Bloomingdale's.

However, in the final analysis, it was up to the consumer to decide the fate of the midi. By mid-September it was still doubtful whether or not the midi would be successful enough to ensure its longevity. A number of women in the public eye had opted for the longer length, among them Great Britain's Princess Margaret; Mme Georges Pompidou, wife of the president of France; and Jacqueline Onassis. A large and vocal antimidi segment of the population protested the look in demonstrations sponsored by such organizations as FADD (Fight Against Dictating Designers), STEMS (Society to Encourage Miniskirts), and POOFF (Preservation of Our Femininity and Finances). In an effort to resolve the question, a Gallup Poll revealed in September that 70% of all women preferred hemlines at the knee, 18% preferred the mini length, and 10% the midi length. Among men polled, 51% preferred the knee length, 33% the mini, and 9% the midi. (The remainder offered no opinions.)

There was little doubt that the midi length had accomplished at least one thing: it had heightened the demand for women's pants. Pants seemed the only way out for a woman who wanted to resist the midi and still feel fashionable in 1970. At the same time the popularity of pants and pantsuits in previous seasons had led to their greater acceptability in offices, restaurants, and formal gatherings. New pants styles often conformed to the midi length, however. Gaucho pants with wide legs falling just below the knees were shown accessorized with wide-brimmed hats, bolero jackets, and high boots. Knickers were also popular.

After the midi, the reptile look was the single distinguishing characteristic of the 1970 fashion scene. Snakeskin patterns were executed in every conceivable fabric from cotton to jersey to vinyl and fashioned into nearly every article of clothing from boots to underwear.

Accessories

Most of the accessories introduced in 1970 were designed as an adjunct to the midiskirt in executing the long, narrow silhouette. Broad belts worn at

New fashions include (from top): knickers, for getting around the hemline problem; a Dior suit trimmed in black snakeskin; a Louis Feraud Ban-Lon jersey midi dress; and Emilio Ungaro's feminine wool jersey jump suit.

WIDE WORLD

Preschoolers are taught how to tie, button, and zip with these fashionable educational clothes. A little girl tries on a dress with a large easy-to-use zipper.

the natural waistline were fastened with heavy buckles or were cinched with laces. Hats were generally one of two shapes—large and wide brimmed or small and close fitting. Among the close-fitting headgear helmets, cloches, and snoods were especially popular.

Boots continued to accelerate in popularity because they were well suited for both the midi look and for pants. The most popular style of 1970 was the laced boot that was almost a prerequisite for the "total look." Higher heels of 2 to 2½ inches were also common. During the year, the boot found its way into evening wear made of satin, peau de soie, lamé, and velvet.

The long, flowing scarf all but disappeared from the scene. It was replaced by a smaller neckerchief knotted cowboy style. Another innovation in neckwear was the choker and its many variations ranging from leather dog collars to velvet ribbons. Curtains of beads suspended from neckbands were highly visible with peasant dresses.

Hairstyles remained simple, with the chignon enjoying a revival. The "nonhairdo" was shown by many stylists. Named "the Ape" for its resemblance to the animal's natural coiffure, the hairdo incorporates short hair on the top of the head with long, shaggy hair at the sides and back. It was worn by many formerly well-coiffed people.

Men's Fashions

The midi also invaded the men's fashion industry, but with considerably less commotion. Designers such as Bill Blass, Oscar de la Renta, and Valentino showed midcalf overcoats exclusively in their fall collections. The designers, all of whom were women's designers originally, and all of whom favored the midi look in their feminine collections, expected less resistance from male clients.

On other fronts the Peacock Revolution continued unabated. The English designer Hardy Amies unveiled an open-neck printed silk shirt to be worn without a tie with dinner jackets. De la Renta came up with short pants. His cuffed trousers stop at the calf and are meant to be worn with boots or with long black stockings and patent leather shoes. Men's underwear appeared in bright prints and lacy crochet work. It was introduced as being "not just for the boys in the band [but] also for the boys in the bank." (*See also* Fads of 1970; Furs. *See in* CE: Fashion; Dress.)

FIJI. After 96 years of British rule, Fiji became an independent nation on Oct. 10, 1970. The new South Pacific state had a population of about 527,000, of whom about 42% were indigenous Fijians of Melanesian and Polynesian ancestry and more than 50% were Indians, descendants of indentured laborers brought over from India to work in the sugarcane fields.

The conflict between the Indian population and the Fijians had at first presented a major stumbling block to the achievement of independence. The Indians had wanted a constitution based on the principle of one man, one vote. Fearing Indian control, the Fijians preferred to maintain a system of communal voting which favored them. A compromise was eventually worked out. Fiji was granted independence by Great Britain as a sovereign, self-governing dominion in the Commonwealth of Nations, but a final decision on the thorny question of electoral representation was postponed.

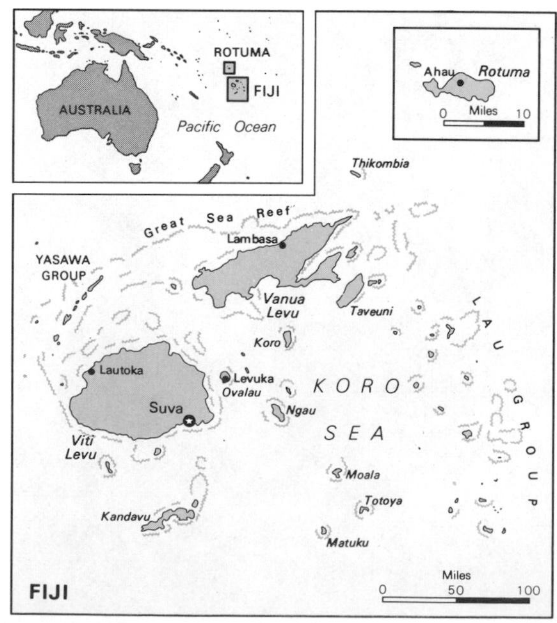

In the interim, a complicated system of communal and cross voting was to be used, which, for example, guaranteed equal representation to Fijians and Indians in the lower house of Parliament.

With its political future settled, Fiji's main concern was its economy. The uncertain future of the sugar industry, the country's economic mainstay, made the development of alternate income-producing sources imperative in the near future. (*See in* CE: Fiji Islands.)

FINLAND. An election victory for Finland's conservative parties in 1970 created a serious crisis of government. In the March 15–16 election Finnish voters gave 87 seats in the Diet to the Communists and Social Democrats; the remaining 113 seats went to members of nonsocialist parties. The single party with the highest percentage of the vote was the Social Democrats. The Communist party suffered the greatest setback. The greatest advance was made by the Small Farmers party, which had held only one seat but in the March election increased its share to 18.

Two months of fruitless negotiations to assemble a new government that would reflect the swing to the right followed the election. On May 14 the government of Prime Minister Mauno Koivisto was succeeded by a caretaker government of civil servants headed by Teuvo Aura, the mayor of Helsinki, the capital. Finally, in July a five-party coalition similar to that of Koivisto's government was formed. Ahti Karjalainen, a member of the Center party, became the new prime minister. His cabinet consisted of five Social Democrats, four members of the Center party, three Communists, two members of the Swedish People's party, one member of the Liberal party, and two nonpolitical ministers.

In March the Finnish prime minister announced that Finland would not enter into an economic and customs union with Denmark, Norway, and Sweden. The treaty establishing such a union was to have been signed on April 3, but the Finnish government felt that such an agreement would jeopardize Finland's neutrality. Finland then declared that it was ready to negotiate a commercial relationship with members of the European Economic Community (EEC), or Common Market, as long as such an agreement would be compatible with Finnish neutrality. Most of Finland's import-export trade in 1970 was with members of the EEC and the European Free Trade Association. (*See in* CE: Finland.)

"VANCOUVER SUN"

The Soviet fishing boat *Suifun* is filled with valuable bottom fish and salmon caught 40 miles off the coast of Vancouver Island—much to the anger of the west Canadian fishermen.

FISH AND FISHERIES. The year 1970 in fish and fisheries appeared to be dominated by shrimp, for which the U.S. market continued to be insatiable. French, Polish, and Spanish shipyards shared large orders for fishing vessels for the Middle East, Cuba, and South America, and expansion of the Mexican and U.S. fleets showed no sign of slackening. With Greenland, Iceland, and Norway also active in the Northern Hemisphere, and Australia and Southeast Asia in the Southern Hemisphere, shrimp catching was worldwide, suggesting the desirability of a close future watch on stocks. A number of farsighted nations, especially Japan, continued to experiment with the cultivation of suitable species in artificial conditions.

It was a boom year for scallops, too, with the discovery of a 200-mile bed of the calico variety off Florida. This was the first commercial bed to be charted by submarine—the U.S. submersible *Aluminaut*. For the first time scallops were shucked and processed on board by mechanized equipment. In northwestern Scotland, the discovery of a 45-mile bed of large scallops and the smaller "queens" (similar to a calico scallop) caused a fleet of 300 boats to be fitted out. A new delicacy was produced—smoked scallops, which enjoyed immediate success—but the greater part of the catch was exported to the United States.

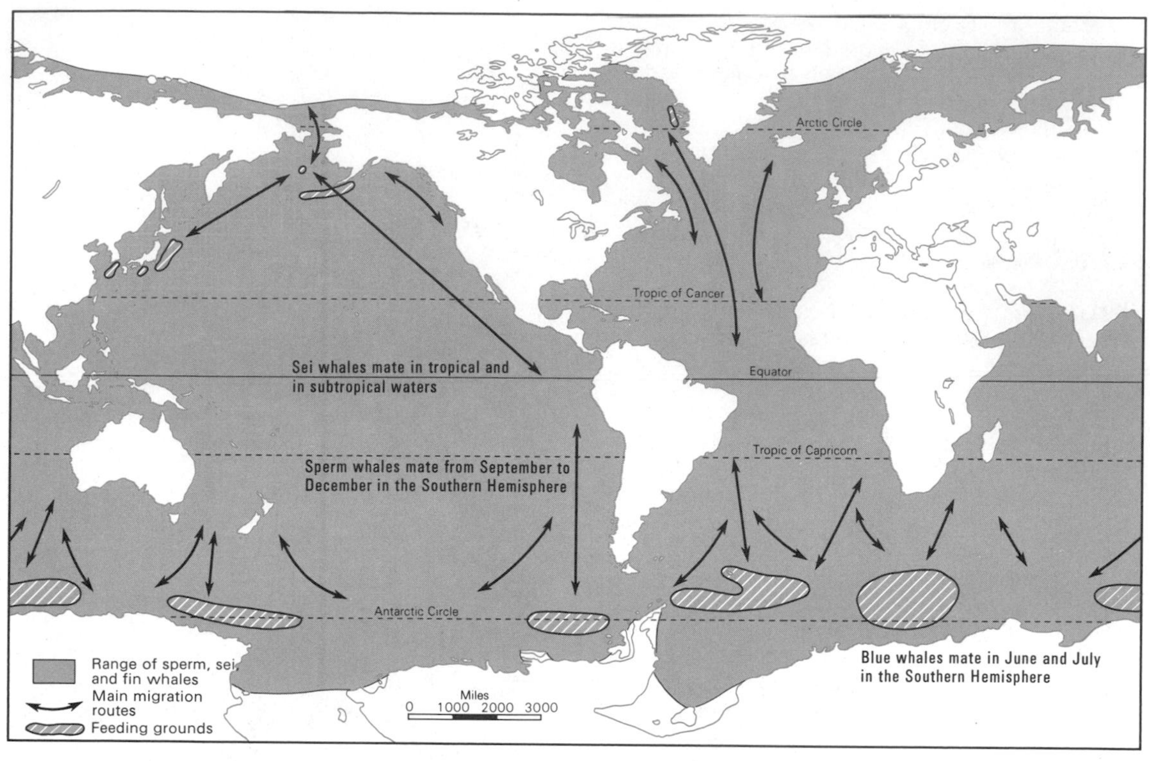

Japan, Norway, and the Soviet Union were the three main whaling countries in 1970. The catch limit for the 1970–71 season was set at 2,700 blue whale units in Antarctica.

Scientists and conservationists continued to be alarmed over the threatened extinction of whales and urged that the catch quotas be substantially reduced. Norway, owner of the world's third largest whaling fleet, appeared willing to abandon its hunting expeditions in the Antarctic; and the United States placed a ban on all imports of whale products.

Canada announced its first alert on mercury contamination during the year. The government was forced to ban commercial fishing in Lake Erie and other waters. The mercury problem, which was first noticed in Canada in the fall of 1969, was also judged a threat in the United States. (*See in* CE: Fisheries.)

FISHING AND HUNTING. Pollution of the water by mercury in 1970 led to the banning or restriction of fishing in Lake Erie, Canada's Lake St. Clair, and the St. Clair and Detroit rivers. The mercury—released into the waters by industries—tends to concentrate in fish. It is highly poisonous. The Canadian government regards fish containing more than one-half part per million of mercury as unfit for human consumption. Fish in the affected waters were found to contain two, three, or even more times as much mercury.

Scientists who studied Chinook salmon in the Columbia River in the state of Washington reported in 1970 that the fish seem unaffected by the warm-

Smelt fishermen ply the Cowlitz River near Kelso, Wash. The smelt are six to seven inches long in this area.

WIDE WORLD

ing of the water that occurs when it is used to cool the hot water discharged by nuclear reactors. Dams on the river, however, have caused the salmon to shift their egg-laying sites from the river proper to its tributaries. The salmon swim undaunted past the nuclear plants and bypass the dams.

The U.S. Fish and Wildlife Service in August announced an easing of some regulations on the hunting of certain migratory birds. The affected birds were band-tailed pigeons, woodcocks, rails, common snipes, gallinules, and doves. Hunting seasons for several of the birds were extended, though daily limits on bagging and possession, in general, remained unchanged.

A New York duck hunter, tired of being cold, wet, and cramped, invented a blind that brings new comfort to hunters of waterfowl. Designed for permanent installation along flyways, it is a four-foot-high, four-foot-diameter tube of reinforced plastic. Watertight and warmed by a heater, it is sunk into the ground to a depth of about 3½ feet. Inside, the hunter sits on a revolving stool, surrounded by shelves for his equipment. (*See in* CE: Fishing; Hunting.)

FLOWERS AND GARDENS. Concern among gardeners about air pollution, water pollution, noise, and harmful effects from the use of some pesticides appeared to increase sharply during 1970. The celebrated Longwood Gardens, near Kennett Square, Pa., reported steadily increasing damage to plant material from air pollutants and forecast that by 1974 the continued pollution buildup would effectively prevent it and similar gardens and arboretums throughout the United States from carrying out their objectives. Research showed that the green leaves of plants serve to some degree as air purifiers, and gardeners were urged to plant more trees and shrubs.

Three new roses were given 1971 All-America awards: Aquarius, a pink grandiflora; Redgold, a bicolor chrome-yellow and red floribunda; and Command Performance, an orange-red hybrid tea rose. Aquarius was the winner of the Gold Medal award for the best large-flowered new rose at the 1970 Annual International Competition for new roses at Geneva, Switzerland; and it was also awarded the grand prize of the city of Geneva.

Four flowers and two vegetables had been chosen as All-America Selections for 1970 introduction. They were Bolero, a dwarf marigold; Madame Butterfly, an F_1 hybrid snapdragon; China Doll, a double *Dianthus chinensis;* a morning glory named Early Call Rose; an F_1 hybrid cherry tomato named Small Fry; and a winter squash named Waltham Butternut.

A Michigan State University researcher, John E. Kauffmann, reported that he may have discovered why bent-grass lawns and putting greens stop growing when surface temperatures go above 95° F. The reason could be an enzyme called nitrate reductase that changes nitrate to nitrite, according to Kauffmann. Studies indicated that selecting grasses with stabilizing levels of the enzyme could lessen problems with lawns and golf greens. At present when the weather gets hot, greenkeepers cool the greens to encourage enough growth to permit recovery from the wear and tear of golfers and golf balls.

COURTESY, ALL-AMERICA SELECTIONS

The giant hibiscus Southern Belle was one of the 1971 All-America selections. The flower received a gold medal.

Lilacs have always required a chilling period during winter in order to break dormancy in the spring. For this reason it has not been possible to grow this popular flowering shrub in warm climates. Now, the Monrovia Nursery Co., a California wholesale nursery, has introduced a lilac named Lavender Lady that will grow and bloom in subtropical as well as cold climates. (*See in* CE: Flower, Fruit, Garden, and Plant articles.)

FOOD. World harvests in 1970 proved more abundant than yields in 1969. Not all major crops posted gains everywhere during the year, however. Grains in Western Europe were less bountiful than the preceding year's crop. But a surplus of grains was registered in the United States and Canada. The wheat yield was especially high in both countries.

A rise in wheat trade and a strong demand for meat, fats, and oils held world food trade at high levels in 1969–70. Rising incomes in many industrial nations, particularly Japan, supported heavy demands for meat.

Green Revolution Cited

The so-called Green Revolution—due in great measure to the widespread adoption of high-yield varieties of wheat and rice in developing areas of the world—played a significant part in the improved outlook for world food supplies. An estimated 40 million acres of land, especially in Asia, were planted in the high-yield grains. The new varieties were also said to be under cultivation in North Vietnam, Communist China, North Korea,

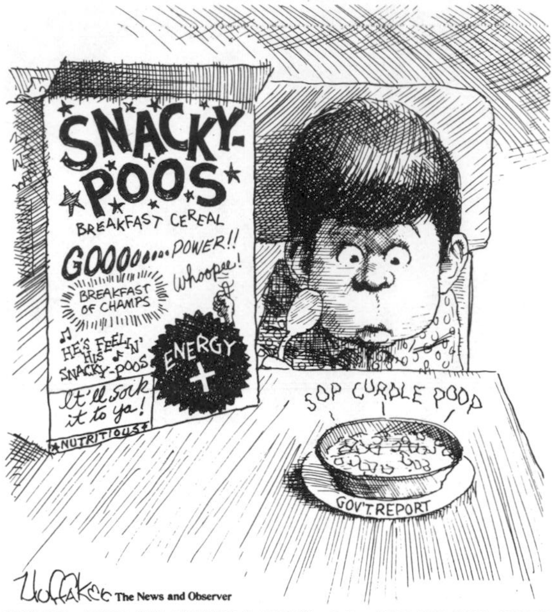

HUFFAKER, "NEWS AND OBSERVER," RALEIGH, N.C., FROM BEN ROTH AGENCY

and Cuba. On the whole, the intensive worldwide farm effort held promise for future generations. Clifford M. Hardin, U.S. secretary of agriculture, predicted that man had the technology in hand or in sight to feed the world's population of A.D. 2000, if it were effectively used by every nation.

Some consumers were less than ecstatic over the new high-yield grains, however. In parts of Asia, where people customarily eat rice with their fingers, the new varieties were considered too gluey to eat with comfort.

Vast Ocean Food Supply Debunked

A prevailing view holds that the seas are virtually limitless reservoirs of enormous quantities of fish; only lack of adequate means of harvest prevents widespread exploitation of ocean food resources. However, a recent study revealed that only about 10% of the ocean contained a rich food supply. Because of limited nutrient resources, the other 90% constituted a biological "desert," according to oceanographers engaged in the study. And the harvestable 10%, in relatively shallow waters near the continental coasts, was already undergoing intensive fishing.

West Germany and Thailand began a joint study in 1970 to determine whether protein-rich one-celled algae could be cultivated and processed as a food in some Thai areas. Experiments have already shown that algae can be dried and reduced to a powder for use as a protein additive to soups, crackers, and desserts.

Cereals and Sweeteners Scrutinized

An independent food researcher, Robert B. Choate, Jr., jolted attitudes about the effectiveness of many popular dry breakfast cereals. According to Choate, two thirds of the leading U.S. cereals held so little nutritional value that they constituted "empty calories." Cereal manufacturers retorted that Choate failed, among other things, to consider the value of the milk ordinarily served with cereal. However, he was defended by a Cornell University nutritionist who claimed that most breakfast cereals lacked the nutritional value of such unglamorous foods as hominy grits and wheat bread.

Cyclamates, the sweeteners banned from diet foods and diet soft drinks in 1969 by the Food and Drug Administration (FDA), were finally barred from all foods and drugs as of Sept. 1, 1970. In addition, some FDA officials felt that saccharin should be regulated, although a panel in July gave this sweetener a clean bill of health. (*See also* Agriculture.)

Robert Dick was head taster of the Federal Board of Tea Tasters until the board was abolished by U.S. President Richard M. Nixon in February. In his large New York City office, Dick samples some tea; he estimated that he tasted 20,000 cups of tea a year while the board was in operation.

WIDE WORLD

FOOTBALL. On Jan. 17, 1971, the fifth annual Super Bowl game was played in Miami, Fla., before 80,035 spectators. The Baltimore Colts, of the National Football League (NFL) American Conference, squeaked by the Dallas Cowboys, of the National Conference, 16–13, in a bizarre game marred by numerous fumbles and sloppy plays. The Colts' Jim O'Brien kicked a 32-yard field goal with five seconds remaining to provide the winning margin. The game was the first Super Bowl contest to be played since the merger of the NFL and the American Football League; the latter became the American Conference under the new setup.

Divisional Races and Play-offs

Baltimore dominated play in the Eastern Division of the American Conference after the equally favored New York Jets lost quarterback Joe Namath because of an early-season injury. The Miami Dolphins, directed by former Baltimore coach Don Shula, gave the Colts their strongest challenge and qualified for the play-offs.

The Oakland Raiders, who were unable to win any of their first three games, rallied behind the game-saving heroics of quarterback George Blanda, who accounted for five consecutive last-quarter victories with his field goal kicking or passing. This streak enabled the Raiders to surge past the Kansas City Chiefs and win the American's Western Division championship. For his efforts, the 43-year-old Blanda was voted the most valuable player in the American Conference and was also named the male athlete of the year.

The Cincinnati Bengals, coached by Paul Brown, won top honors in the American's Central Division. The Bengals won their regular-season opener, beating Oakland, then lost six in a row before executing a dramatic turnabout and finishing with seven successive victories and an 8–6 record.

The Dallas Cowboys, after floundering early in the season, also came on strong at the finish and won their last five games to capture the title in the National's Eastern Division. Duane Thomas, a rookie running back, paced the Dallas offense. Dallas also featured a highly publicized "doomsday defense" that allowed only 15 points in the last four regular-season games. Veterans Bob Lilly, a tackle, and cornerback Mel Renfro were the Dallas defensive stars.

The Minnesota Vikings, who had the league's best defense, led from start to finish in winning the National's Central Division championship. The Vikings' offense was undistinguished but their defense was superb, permitting only 14 touchdowns, the fewest ever scored on a team through a 14-game schedule. The Vikings had a 12–2 record, best in the NFL. Detroit, beaten twice by the Vikings, finished second in this division and won its last five games, four of them against division leaders.

The San Francisco '49ers won their first championship in 25 years of competition, finishing first in the National's Western Division. John Brodie, a 36-year-old quarterback who was picked as the league's most valuable player, was the San Francisco star. Los Angeles, the preseason favorite, finished second in this division with a 9–4–1 record. San Francisco was 10–3–1.

All play-off games were held within each conference, to decide a conference champion. Baltimore shut out Cincinnati 17–0 and Oakland edged Miami 21–14 in the American semifinals. The following week Baltimore won the title by eliminating Oakland 27–17. In the National semifinals, Dallas beat Detroit 5–0 and San Francisco ousted Minnesota 17–14. Dallas then defeated San Francisco 17–10 for the National championship, qualifying as Baltimore's opponent in the Super Bowl.

New Records; Outstanding Players

The most sensational of the new records in 1970 was a 63-yard field goal by Tom Dempsey of the New Orleans Saints. Dempsey's kick came with only two seconds left to play and lifted his team to a 19–17 victory over Detroit. The previous professional field goal record, which stood for 17 years, was 56 yards, set by Bert Rechichar of the Baltimore Colts.

Only two players, Larry Brown of the Washington Redskins and Ron Johnson of the New York Giants, both of the National Conference, were able to rush for more than 1,000 yards. Brown led with 1,125 yards gained from scrimmage, and Johnson was second with 1,027 yards. Floyd Little of Denver led the American Conference rushers with 901 yards.

The leading passers were John Brodie of San Francisco in the National and Daryle Lamonica of Oakland in the American. Dick Gordon of Chicago and Marlin Briscoe of Buffalo led in pass receiving. The top scorers were two field goal kickers—Fred Cox of Minnesota, who led the National Conference with 125 points, and Jan Stenerud of Kansas City, who led the American Conference with 116 points.

College Football

Nebraska's Cornhuskers won the nation's mythical college football championship for the first time. The honor came in the final Associated Press poll, taken in January 1971 after the Bowl games. Nebraska's No. 1 ranking was the result of a sequence of Bowl upsets triggered by Notre Dame, which, aiming for first, finished second in the final voting. Texas was third, Tennessee fourth, and Ohio State fifth.

Notre Dame's Irish defeated Texas 24–11 in the Cotton Bowl at Dallas, Tex. This loss ended the Longhorns' 30-game winning streak. Ohio State, of the Big Ten, lost to Stanford 27–17 in the Rose Bowl at Pasadena, Calif. At the Orange Bowl in Miami, Fla., Nebraska won over Louisiana State University (LSU), 17–12, completing the season with a record of 11 victories, no losses, and one tie.

WIDE WORLD

Nebraska beat Louisiana State in the 1971 Orange Bowl game when Jerry Tagge (14) made the final touchdown from one yard out.

Nebraska also won the Grantland Rice Trophy as the nation's top team in a vote of the Football Writers Association of America. Texas and Ohio State had the consolation of being selected as co-winners of the McArthur Bowl, awarded annually by the National Football Foundation.

In the East, Dartmouth won the Ivy League title with a 7–0 conference record and a 9–0 overall mark. As a reward, Dartmouth won the Lambert Trophy as the outstanding team in the East.

Connecticut won the Yankee Conference title with a conference record of four victories, no losses, and one tie. Navy lost nine games in succession before defeating Army 11–7 in their traditional finale.

Texas won the Southwest Conference championship with a flawless 7–0 conference record. Arkansas was second in the conference with a 6–1 mark, and Texas Tech was third with 5–2. Louisville won top honors in the Missouri Valley Conference.

Featuring an especially strong defense, LSU won the Southeast Conference title with a 5–0 mark. Tennessee, which was not on the LSU schedule, was second and Auburn third. The LSU team allowed an average of 52.2 yards rushing and was led by tailback Art Cantrelle who carried the ball on almost half of the team's running plays, breaking Steve Van Buren's 27-year-old LSU rushing record. The school had not won an undisputed conference title since 1958. Wake Forest won the Atlantic Coast Conference championship, and William and Mary captured top honors in the Southern Conference.

In the Midwest, Ohio State, a perennial power, won the Big Ten title by defeating Michigan 20–9 in the final conference game for both teams. Michigan, undefeated prior to its confrontation with Ohio State, finished in a second-place conference tie with Northwestern, both achieving 6–1 records. Ohio State had one of the nation's leading rushers in John Brockington, who gained 1,041 yards in the Buckeyes' nine regular-season games. Other Ohio State standouts were Tim Anderson, Jack Tatum, and Jim Stillwagon. Notre Dame lost only once, bowing 38–28 to Southern California in its regular-season finale. Quarterback Joe Theismann, who completed 58% of his passes, directed an awesome Irish offense that was extremely well balanced. He averaged 510.5 yards during the regular season, 252.7 passing and 257.8 rushing. Top-ranking Nebraska won the Big Eight Conference title outright by defeating Oklahoma 28–21 in the final quarter of its last conference game. Quarterback Jerry Tagge, kicker Paul Rogers, and pass catchers Johnny Rodgers and Guy Ingles were among the Nebraska stars. Unbeaten and untied Toledo won the title in the Mid-American Conference.

In the Far West, Stanford's Indians, led by All-American quarterback Jim Plunkett, won the Pacific Eight title with a 6–1 record. They lost in the conference only to California, which finished in a four-way tie for second place with Washington, Oregon, and the University of California at Los Angeles (UCLA). Arizona State won the title in the Western Athletic Conference.

College Stars

As usual, there were many outstanding players, but the most honored of the individual stars was Plunkett, a senior quarterback from Stanford. The most prolific passer in college football history, Plunkett won the coveted Heisman Memorial Trophy as the nation's outstanding player. Two other quarterbacks, Theismann of Notre Dame and Archie Manning of Mississippi, finished second and third, respectively. Running back Steve Worster of Texas was fourth in the balloting. Plunkett was the first Stanford player to win the Heisman and set three principal National Collegiate Athletic Association (NCAA) career records: (1) most yards gained in total offense (rushing and passing), 7,887; (2) most yards gained in passing, 7,544; and (3) most yards in total offense, per-game average, 254.4.

Chuck Hixson of Southern Methodist University shattered the NCAA's career record for pass completions with 642. Steve Ramsey, with 491 completions, had been the previous record holder. Elmo Wright of Houston set a career mark of catching 34 touchdown passes; Bob Jacobs of Wyoming established a new career record for the most field goals, 37; Marv Bateman of Utah had a punting average of 45.7 yards, bettering the previous one-season record set by Bobby Joe Green of Florida in 1959; and Don McCauley of North Carolina had 1,720 yards rushing, improving upon the previous record of 1,709 set in 1968 by O. J. Simpson of Southern California. (*See in* CE: Football.)

FOREIGN POLICY, UNITED STATES.

The most important issues of U.S. foreign policy in 1970 were the Vietnam war and the precarious situation in the Middle East. Neither seemed any closer to resolution at the end of the year than it had at the beginning. Another U.S. concern was East-West relations, symbolized in particular by the strategic arms limitation talks (SALT) between the United States and the Soviet Union that went on during the year at Vienna, Austria, and Helsinki, Finland. Europe was undergoing a period of major transition heralded by the policy of *Ostpolitik* of West Germany's Chancellor Willy Brandt—seeking normalization of West Germany's postwar relations with the Soviet Union and Eastern Europe. Perhaps because of preoccupation with these issues, the United States devoted less attention during the year to Latin America, Africa, or, in general, to the Third World of underdeveloped countries.

Vietnam

United States President Richard M. Nixon stated in his 1970 State-of-the-Union message that "the major immediate goal of our foreign policy is to bring an end to the war in Vietnam." Although no progress was made during the year toward a negotiated settlement of the war, the president continued to reduce U.S. involvement in Vietnam by withdrawing additional troops and encouraging the South Vietnamese government to assume a greater share of the fighting. This policy, however, was seemingly reversed when on April 30 Nixon announced that U.S. troops had invaded Cambodia to clear out sanctuaries used by the North Vietnamese and Viet Cong forces. The action, which geographically widened the war, provoked a domestic uproar and international condemnation. To some extent this vociferous reaction died down when U.S. forces were pulled out of Cambodia on June 29, one day before the deadline set by the president.

In October Nixon proposed a new peace plan for Indochina. The plan indicated U.S. readiness "to negotiate an agreed timetable" for total withdrawal of U.S. troops "as part of an overall settlement." It also called for a standstill cease-fire, an expanded peace conference that would seek to end the fighting in Laos and Cambodia as well as in South Vietnam, efforts by both sides to "search for a political settlement that truly meets the needs of all South Vietnamese," and the "immediate and unconditional release of all prisoners of war." North Vietnamese and Viet Cong representatives at the Paris peace talks denounced the Nixon proposal.

Another dramatic development in the Vietnam war came in late November when U.S. planes carried out widespread bombing attacks on North Vietnam. United States Secretary of Defense Melvin R. Laird described the raids as "protective reaction" —in response to the shooting down of an unarmed U.S. reconnaissance plane over North Vietnam the preceding week. The news of the bombing raids was followed by a disclosure that a U.S. task force had landed about 25 miles from Hanoi, the capital of North Vietnam, in an attempt to rescue U.S. prisoners of war believed to be held captive at a camp there, but that no U.S. prisoners were found. The bombing raids were viewed by a number of Congressional critics as a major escalation of the war that would only damage any chances for a negotiated settlement of the war.

The Middle East

The simmering conflict between Israel and its Arab neighbors provided another major concern of U.S. foreign policy in 1970. It prompted President Nixon to comment in July, "I think the Middle

William P. Rogers (left), U.S. secretary of state, and Anatolii F. Dobrynin, Soviet ambassador to the United States, resumed formal talks on the Middle East late in March.
UPI COMPIX

East now is terribly dangerous, . . . where the two superpowers, the United States and the Soviet Union, could be drawn into a confrontation that neither of them wants." The president's remarks came six days after U.S. Secretary of State William P. Rogers announced a new proposal to bring peace to the Middle East. The plan called for a 90-day cease-fire while United Nations mediator Gunnar V. Jarring resumed indirect peace talks with the United Arab Republic (or Egypt), Jordan, and Israel. (*See* Israel.)

The Middle East situation took a dangerous turn in September when civil war broke out in Jordan between Palestinian guerrillas, who were opposed to the cease-fire, and the army of Jordan's King Hussein I. By September 19, Syrian troops were reported to have entered Jordan to come to the guerrillas' aid. President Nixon was quoted as saying that the United States was "prepared to intervene directly in the Jordanian civil war should Syria and Iraq enter the conflict and tip the military balance against the government forces loyal to King Hussein." A direct warning to Syria against intervention in Jordan was issued by the U.S. Department of State on September 20, and pressure was applied on the Soviet Union, Syria's chief mentor, to use its influence to end the crisis. The Syrian troops withdrew shortly after.

Nixon underscored U.S. interest in the Middle East by making an eight-day, five-nation tour of Europe in the fall. A prominent part of the trip—a visit to the U.S. Sixth Fleet—served to highlight the president's statement that a "primary, indispensable" principle of U.S. foreign policy was "to maintain the necessary strength in the Mediterranean to preserve the peace against those who might threaten the peace." At year-end the situation in the Middle East remained uneasy.

Foreign Policy in the 1970's

In what was described as the first presidential State-of-the-World message, Nixon submitted to Congress on February 18 a report entitled "United States Foreign Policy for the 1970's: a New Strategy for Peace." The message stressed that the United States would maintain its global treaty commitments but it would also bring to its commitment appraisals a firm assessment of the U.S. interests involved. It also emphasized a partnership relationship as opposed to one of domination, and negotiation and multinational cooperation as opposed to great-power rivalry or ideological contention.

The general thrust of the message—that the United States was turning away from the activist role it had assumed in the post-World War II period—was widely applauded as in keeping with the new mood of "isolationism" in the nation. It was pointed out, however, by critics of the Nixon Administration, that the actual policies of the Administration were frequently at strong variance with the stated objectives of the "new strategy for peace." (*See also* Africa; Congress, U.S.; Disarmament; International Relations; Middle East; Vietnam.)

FOREST PRODUCTS. The world's output of forest products continued in 1968 the steady rise in volume and value that it has maintained since World War II, according to figures compiled in 1970 by the Food and Agriculture Organization of the United Nations. In constant 1960 dollars, the total value of world forest products output in 1968 was $45.5 billion, compared with $43.1 billion in 1967 and $41 billion in 1965. The comparable figure for 1960 was $33.9 billion; for 1950, $23.9 billion. World trade in forest products also expanded rapidly.

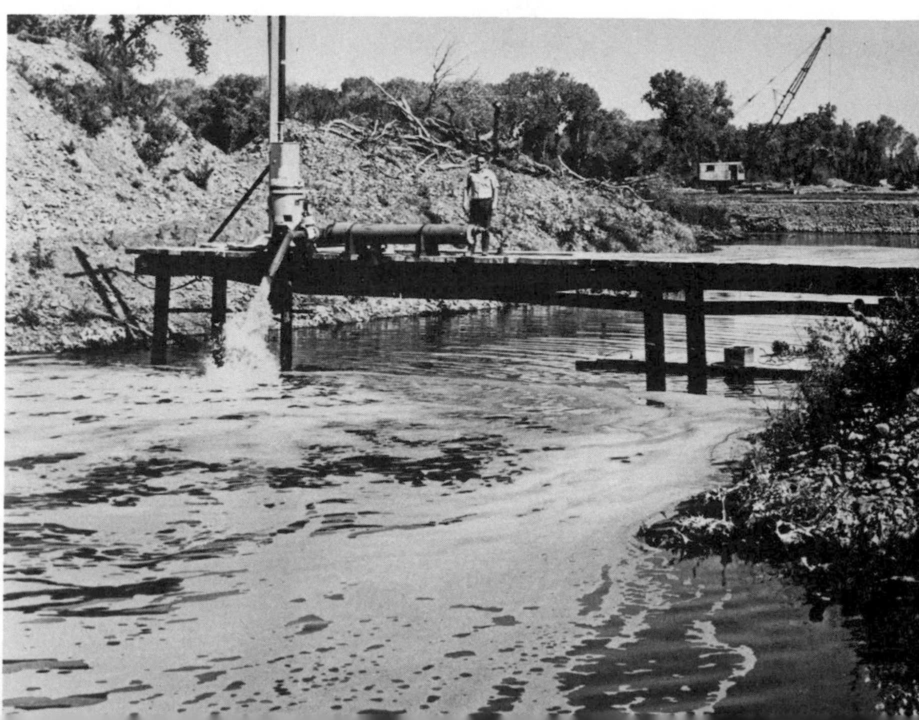

The use of the medieval moat as a protective device was reinstituted in Oroville, Calif., in 1970. This moat, however, was designed to protect the area outside, and not within, its confines. Waste water from a new sawmill is trapped in the moat and is thus prevented from polluting adjacent streams. Much of the trapped water can be reused by the mill after solid wastes are filtered out.
AUTHENTICATED NEWS INTERNATIONAL

The more highly processed products—such as panel and pulp products—showed the greatest gains. Of the 1968 total, lumber represented $15.9 billion, panel products $5.4 billion. Paper and paperboard accounted for $19 billion and other products $5.2 billion.

The Soviet Union again ranked first in lumber production in 1968, its output of 46.7 billion board feet nearly equaling the combined production of the United States (37.1 billion board feet) and Canada (11.1 billion board feet). Japan's output totaled 16.5 billion board feet. According to preliminary estimates by the National Forest Products Association, U.S. lumber production in 1969 exceeded 37.9 billion board feet.

The U.S. Department of Commerce accepted a new standard for softwood lumber. Because lumber shrinks as it dries, the revised standard requires green lumber to be finished to a size sufficiently larger than dry lumber so that both will have the same dimensions after seasoning. (*See in* CE: Lumber; Paper; Plywood; Wood.)

A.F.P. FROM PICTORIAL PARADE

The garbage collectors of Paris went on strike in April 1970 for higher pay and administrative reforms. French soldiers were called in to pick up the accumulating garbage.

FRANCE. The death of Charles de Gaulle on November 9, 1970, a year and a half after his resignation as first president of the Fifth Republic, overshadowed all other events in France in 1970. De Gaulle's death brought testimony from throughout the world of his immense prestige and of the influence he had wielded in international affairs during the post-World War II era.

A requiem Mass at the Cathedral of Notre Dame in Paris, the capital, offered in memory of De Gaulle, was attended by a gathering of world leaders such as could seldom have been equaled in modern times. In contrast, De Gaulle's simple funeral at Colombey-les-Deux-Églises was without state honors. French emotion at the loss of the symbol of France's resurgence after its defeat in 1940, whose life's inspiration had been "a certain idea of France," was put into words by De Gaulle's successor, President Georges Pompidou, in his broadcast announcement to the nation: "General De Gaulle is dead. France is a widow."

A Challenge to the Gaullists

The general consensus was that Pompidou, during his first 18 months of office, had shown himself to be an able successor to De Gaulle. He continued to reaffirm the preeminence of the president in every field and, though aiming lower than his predecessor, he obviously had the same idea of national interest.

One challenge to Gaullist authority during 1970 appeared in the form of Jean-Jacques Servan-Schreiber, an author, former journalist, and dynamic leader of the Radical party. Servan-Schreiber's aim was to unite the non-Communist left against the Gaullist majority in order to provide a more forceful legislative opposition and, in the long run, an alternative government. In June Servan-Schreiber carried off a striking by-election victory in the city of Nancy, winning a seat in the National Assembly with the support of more than 55% of the voters. Three months later in Bordeaux, however, Servan-Schreiber won only slightly more than 16% of the vote in a confrontation with Premier Jacques Chaban-Delmas over the latter's seat in the National Assembly; Chaban-Delmas gained an easy victory, taking somewhat more than 63% of the vote. The premier's personal standing was noticeably enhanced by this success. Undaunted, Servan-Schreiber continued his reformist efforts with a view to 1971 local elections.

The Economy

The French economy improved greatly during the year. Following the devaluation of the franc in August 1969, the government had instituted an austerity program; by April 1970, the program had achieved impressive results. France's trade position improved to such an extent that a trade surplus of $360 million was forecast. Inflation slowed and seemed to be under control. As a result, confidence in the economy was restored, and symbolically, for the first time in years, French savings were being placed in French banks, rather than being sent outside the country.

With the economy in good health, the government turned its attention to future growth. One of President Pompidou's chief aims was to make France a major modern industrial state. Thus the government's sixth economic plan (1971–75) called for increasing industrial production by almost half. In June the National Assembly adopted a bill approving the basic objectives of the sixth plan.

The government also adopted a series of measures affecting industrial relations, in line with its

MARC RIBOUD FROM MAGNUM

A huge photograph of Charles de Gaulle looms behind President Georges Pompidou as he talks.

view that the workers should be brought into the industrialization process. These measures included a profit-sharing plan for workers in the state-owned Renault automobile concern. The profit-sharing principle was to be extended to other nationalized industries in the future.

The climate in labor relations improved during the year. One reason was that the government sanctioned generous wage increases as a means of preventing outbreaks of social unrest like that of May 1968.

In October Premier Chaban-Delmas outlined his government's economic and social policies to make France "a fully modern nation." His program, which put a marked emphasis on social problems—old people, the status of women, the humanization of the urban environment—received an overwhelming vote of confidence from the National Assembly.

Urban Violence

However, not all social unrest was contained. During the year France was troubled by the violent activities of left- and right-wing extremist groups in both Paris and the provinces, particularly at the universities. In May a series of bomb attacks and other acts of sabotage occurred in numerous areas around the country.

The government responded to the violence with a tough "antiwreckers bill" designed to combat "certain new forms of delinquency." After heated debate, the National Assembly finally passed a compromise version of the bill in June.

WIDE WORLD

Maoist students rioted in the Latin Quarter of Paris in May. The disturbance was touched off by the trial of two leaders of a Maoist organization.

Foreign Policy

French foreign relations continued to follow the main lines laid down by De Gaulle—friendly contacts with countries of both the Eastern and Western blocs. The high point of the year was Pompidou's visit to the United States in February and March, the first official visit by a French president in ten years. Private conversations between Pompidou and U.S. President Richard M. Nixon were friendly, though demonstrations by various U.S. Jewish groups showed that Pompidou had not managed to defuse the hostility aroused by the sale of French Mirage jets to Libya and the continuation of its embargo on supplying arms to Israel. (*See also* Middle East.)

Pompidou's concern that France should remain outside the bloc of either of the superpowers was symbolized by his visit to the Soviet Union in October. The protocol and the joint communiqué published at the end of his talks with Soviet leaders included an agreement to "extend and deepen" political consultations on major international problems between the two countries, reflecting a strong desire on the part of both to improve Franco-Soviet relations.

Of major importance during the year was the relaxation of the French position on the opening of negotiations for the enlargement of the European Economic Community, or Common Market, and the possible entry of the main candidates (Great Britain, Denmark, Norway, and Ireland). The crisis between France and its six partners of the Western European Union ended in June when France resumed the seat it had left vacant since February 1969. (*See also* Europe; World Trade. *See in* CE: France.)

FUEL AND POWER. In the United States, 1970 may be remembered as the year of the great energy crisis. As the year drew to its end, supplies of coal, natural gas, and fuel oils had become seriously deficient, electric generating capacity was strained to the limit in some parts of the country, and the efforts of fuel users to line up supplies for 1971 had become desperate.

The impact of efforts to reduce environmental pollution—especially the increasingly severe limitations upon the sulfur content of fuels burned in large metropolitan centers—was the single most important factor in the crisis. Supply problems developed as fuel users turned to low-sulfur coal and oil and to sulfur-free natural gas.

Natural-gas reserves dropped for the second year in a row as producers curtailed exploration, well drilling, and sales offerings while awaiting Federal Power Commission (FPC) action on proposals for price increases. In this situation, many gas distributors began refusing new customers or increased commitments to existing customers.

Coal supplies were affected by a relative lack of low-sulfur coal deposits near major markets, by the temporary closing of many mines as a new federal coal-mine safety act went into effect, by labor shortages and wildcat strikes, by a shortage of railroad coal cars, and by increased export demand for low-sulfur coal. As a result, many electric utilities operated virtually at the edge of coal famine.

Low-sulfur fuel-oil supplies also fell well short of demand. Refineries were unable to install desulfurization equipment rapidly enough as demand rose by about 50%. By year-end many established and potential users of low-sulfur oil had no idea where their next year's supply was coming from—or if it was coming at all.

The fuel shortages added to the woes of electric utilities, already affected by delays in completing nuclear power plants. Nuclear-plant construction had variously been slowed by opposition to the plants on the grounds of environmental protection, by delays in equipment delivery, and by strikes. Shortage of reserve generating capacity brought widespread voltage reductions and some curtailments of service—particularly in the East—during peak-demand summer periods.

Elsewhere in the world, turmoil in the Middle East disrupted oil shipments. The discovery of Europe's largest known oil field—estimated at more than 7 billion barrels—in the North Sea between Norway and Scotland, however, raised hopes that Europe might be able to reduce its dependence upon Middle Eastern and African oil.

COAL

In 1970 the U.S. coal industry expected to exceed its 1969 sales level, the highest in 20 years, mainly because of a 5% increase in demand from electric utilities. Power plants, which had consumed a record 310 million tons of coal in 1969, were expected to burn 325 million tons in 1970.

Overall U.S. consumption and exports of bituminous coal in 1970 was expected to reach 582 million tons, 3% above the 1969 figure and likely to exceed domestic production. In the first half of 1970 U.S. bituminous-coal output rose by 16 million tons from the figure for the first half of 1969.

It appeared that U.S. coal exports in 1970 might be the third highest in history. Exports in the first half totaled 33.2 million tons, more than 42% of which went to Japan.

It was revealed that in 1969 world hard-coal production totaled an estimated 2.29 billion tons, an increase of 22.8 million tons over the 1968 level but less than the record 2.31 billion tons of 1966. The Soviet Union remained the world's leading coal producer with some 660 million tons.

Trends in coal output followed those of 1968, with reductions in major Western countries balanced by increases in Eastern coal-producing areas. Production in Western Europe dropped by 5%, but Eastern European production (including that of Russia) showed an increase of 1.4%. The biggest advance shown in the 1969 estimates was for Communist China, where the serious reversals of 1967 appeared to have been halted, and production increased by an estimated 28 million tons over the 1968 figure, but did not regain the pre-1967 output. Significant production gains were recorded in Australia, due to increased exports to Japan. Elsewhere in the world, coal production followed a pattern similar to that of recent years. (*See in* CE: Coal.)

ELECTRICITY

Production of electricity continued to rise rapidly in most countries during 1970. Generally, the rise exceeded an annual growth rate of 7.2%—a doubling of production every ten years. The latest figures, for 1969, showed these growth rates over the previous year in the major industrial nations: Japan, 12.4%; France, 11.1%; West Germany, 10.2%; Canada, 8.5%; United States, 8.1%; Russia, 7.8%; and the United Kingdom, 6.4%.

Orders for nuclear power stations recovered during 1970. In the United States, for example, 14 reactors with a combined capacity of 14,000 megawatts were ordered during the first nine months of 1970; only eight, totaling 8,060 megawatts, were ordered in the whole of 1969. The cause of the recovery was the increase in fossil-fuel prices—sometimes more than 50% in less than a year—that improved nuclear energy's economic competitiveness.

The first nuclear power reactors in the 1,000-megawatt range are being built by the Tennessee Valley Authority, near Decatur, Ala. Unit 2 of three units is shown here.

COURTESY, TENNESSEE VALLEY AUTHORITY

According to the U.S. Atomic Energy Commission, nuclear power stations under construction or projected in the United States in January 1970 numbered 109, with a total capacity of 81,254 megawatts. Nuclear power in service during 1970 was expected to reach approximately 6,000 megawatts.

Despite the rising cost of fossil fuels, their use increased more rapidly than did that of nuclear energy, which was handicapped by installation costs and construction delays. A conventional power station can be built much more quickly than can a nuclear plant, and the rapidly rising demand for electricity compelled several U.S. utilities to abandon nuclear projects and return to conventional power-generating methods. In the construction of power stations—nuclear and conventional—increasing attention was paid to reducing environmental pollution.

Gas turbines continued to grow in importance as means of providing emergency power supplies during breakdowns and of meeting peak power demands. Their rate of development was in the region of 25% a year, spurred by relatively low installation costs and high levels of safety and availability.

The Soviet Union led the world in the number of hydroelectric projects under way. The tenth—and last—500-megawatt generator group became operative at Krasnoyarsk, the world's most powerful station. The first group in the Djerdap project on the Danube River came into production in July.

In France the Vallabrègues plant on the Rhône River went into operation, raising potential output to 10,700 million kilowatt-hours from the seven dams on the river. Construction of a 600-megawatt station began at Lake Kariba, Zambia. The Aswan High Dam in the United Arab Republic, or Egypt, was inaugurated in July. Brazil received an $80-million loan from the World Bank for construction of a 1,400-megawatt installation at Maribondo Falls on the Rio Grande.

The Tennessee Valley Authority began construction of a pumped-storage station at Raccoon Mountain, six miles west of Chattanooga, Tenn. It was scheduled to go into service in 1974–75, with a capacity of 1,350 megawatts from four groups of reversible turbopumps. Such installations, however, were tending to fall out of favor because it was felt that gas turbines offer a cheaper and more practical method of meeting peak power demands. (*See also* Nuclear Energy. *See in* CE: Electric Power.)

GAS

Demand for natural gas in the United States remained strong in 1970, but exploration for, and development of, new resources lagged as the gas industry awaited FPC decisions upon requested price increases. Meanwhile, a supply pinch developed as states worried about a severe winter and electric utilities sought to switch from coal to gas to reduce atmospheric pollution.

The pricing uncertainty was evident in two FPC cases. After seven years of proceedings, gas producers in the Hugoton-Anadarko area of the Texas Panhandle, Kansas, and western Oklahoma agreed to reduce prices by about $6.1 million annually and to refund $47 million to their pipeline customers. The area produces 19% of the gas sold in interstate commerce. The FPC found that producers in the Permian Basin of southwestern Texas and southeastern New Mexico received as much as 9¢ more per 1,000 cubic feet for gas sold intrastate than for gas sold interstate. Gas producers found that it was relatively easier to get a price increase within a state than to obtain one from the federal government, and that it was thus often more profitable to sell gas within a producing state than without.

At the beginning of 1970, according to the American Gas Association (AGA), U.S. proved reserves were 275.1 trillion cubic feet, down 4.2% in a year, as consumption in 1969 climbed 7% to a record 20.7 trillion cubic feet while gross additions to reserves fell to 8.4 trillion cubic feet, compared with 13.7 trillion cubic feet in 1968. The AGA estimated that 1,227 trillion cubic feet of gas were available in addition to proved reserves. The new gas discoveries in Alaska were largely unproved, and there were also questions of the cost and ecological effects of developing the Alaskan fields.

Canada used 850 billion cubic feet of natural gas in 1969 and estimated an increase to 935 billion cubic feet in 1970. An additional 680 billion cubic feet were slated for export to the United States. Canada's marketable reserves were estimated at nearly 52 trillion cubic feet. (*See in* CE: Gas, Manufactured; Gas, Natural.)

PETROLEUM

In the world petroleum industry two issues were outstanding in 1970. On the North American continent, considerations of conservation and pollution involved delay in the construction of a trans-Alaska pipeline and brought new regulation of offshore drilling. Elsewhere, increasing economic nationalism in some producing countries affected marketing, refinery operations, pricing, and supplies. Political difficulties in the Middle East were reflected in the continued closure of the Suez Canal and in Syria's objections to repair of the Trans-Arabian pipeline damaged in May.

The year's most notable oil discovery was that of the first commercial field in the North Sea, between Norway and Great Britain. Later in the year the prospecting company, Phillips Petroleum Co., reported a second promising field nearby. Production from the first discovery was expected to reach 225,000 barrels a day by 1973.

In 1970 a $75-million oil refinery was under construction in Edmonton, Alta. Pillars of reinforced concrete form the foundations.

Most major oil companies experienced a decline in the rate of return on capital investment and in profits in the first half of 1970 due to higher tanker rates, the Middle Eastern difficulties, and higher operating costs. In the United States, fears of a severe fuel crisis in the mid-1970's led to an easing of oil-import restrictions.

At the beginning of 1970 total world proved and probable oil reserves amounted to 540.6 billion barrels, compared with 509.9 billion barrels a year earlier. Of this, Western Hemisphere reserves totaled 77.5 billion barrels, or 14.3%. The Middle East had the largest share of the total, 332.8 billion barrels. Reserves in Alaska were estimated at about 10 billion barrels.

World crude-oil production in the first half of 1970 rose 7.5% from that of the 1969 first half to 46.65 million barrels a day. The Middle East remained the leading oil-producing area, increasing its first-half production by 8% to 13.4 million barrels a day. United States production in the first five months of the year averaged 11.2 million barrels a day.

It was revealed that total world consumption of petroleum increased by 8.5%—from 39.1 to 42.6 million barrels a day—from 1968 to 1969. The

Men work to repair the Chevron Oil Company's well No. 6 in the Gulf waters off the coast of Louisiana. Six wells were damaged by a month-long fire, which began in February, causing the worst oil slick in U.S. history. Oil poured into the surrounding waters for weeks.
WIDE WORLD

United States remained the largest consumer at 13.8 million barrels a day. In the first half of 1970, world consumption increased by 10%. World refining and tanker capacity increased apace, and petrochemical production continued its rapid growth. (*See in* CE: Fuel; Petroleum articles.)

FURS. Under the pressures of an economic slowdown, radical fashion changes, and the ecology movement, the retail sales of furs in the United States declined in 1970. In the first half of the year, the number of insolvencies among fur merchants was equal to the total number of insolvencies registered in 1969. Moreover, it was expected that the volume of fur sales in 1970 would fall below the $300-million mark that was reached the preceding year.

The monetary situation that prevailed throughout most of the year was a prominent factor in the fur business slump. Because of high interest rates —averaging about 10.5% for fur industry loans— the furriers were unable to discount many of their customers' notes in order to pay off debts.

In August the Furriers Joint Council of New York, a union representing practically all of the fur workers in the United States, reached an agreement with the World Wildlife Fund to discontinue the use of the furs of such endangered species as tigers, leopards, cheetahs, ocelots, and jaguars. Although these spotted furs had accounted for only 1% of annual sales in the fur industry, a wide variety of substitutes had been marketed by year-end. Copies of the outlawed skins were executed in man-made furs or stenciled on mink.

Fashion changes had a two-sided effect on the fur industry. Some furriers blamed the wide-scale move to the midi length as a deterrent to would-be buyers who disliked the new look. However, the use of additional pelts—averaging about 20 extra per coat—helped keep the retail price of coats at the 1969 level. Ordinarily, the lower prices of pelts would have decreased the retail price of coats. Stylistically, the midi length seemed to be the only common denominator for fashions in 1970. Otherwise, coat styles ranged from wide, sweeping tents to skinny zip-up models. Capes enjoyed a new popularity and shawl collars were revived by several designers. (*See also* Fashion. *See in* CE: Furs.)

A brown-and-white ranch-mink coat (left) and a stencil zebra midi coat were new in 1970.
CENTRAL PRESS FROM PICTORIAL PARADE

GABON. In September 1970, Jean Marc Ekoh, minister of state for agriculture, was arrested, charged with the abduction of a Gabonese official and his wife, and sentenced to ten years' imprisonment. Implicated in the attempted coup of February 1964, Ekoh had previously been imprisoned but had returned to favor with the accession of Albert Bernard Bongo to the presidency.

In July, relations with Israel became strained as a result of Mrs. Bongo's visit to Jerusalem. Dissatisfied with her reception there, the government recalled first its ambassador and then Gabonese students and trainees from Israeli territory.

A series of complicated negotiations took place between Gabon and Nigeria on the question of repatriating refugee children from Biafra who had come to Gabon during the Nigerian civil war. Agreement had been reached in June to hasten the children's return to Nigeria, but the matter was still at a standstill in October. (*See in* CE: Gabon.)

A.F.P. FROM PICTORIAL PARADE

President and Mrs. Bongo (center) paid a state visit to France in July.

GAMBIA, THE. In 1970 The Gambia became a republic within the Commonwealth of Nations. Its republican constitution was adopted on April 24 following a referendum that sanctioned this change by more than the required two-thirds majority. Under the new constitution, Sir Dawda Kairaba Jawara, whose governing party had supported the republic proposal, became president. The two opposition parties, which had campaigned against the referendum, found themselves considerably weakened by their inability to organize popular support.

In foreign relations, The Gambia moved closer to Senegal, which geographically almost completely surrounds it. In June The Gambia asked that Senegal look after Gambian interests wherever Senegal was represented (except where only Commonwealth countries were concerned). The two countries also agreed to consult each other before either entered into any international discussions. (*See in* CE: Gambia.)

LEFT AND RIGHT: D.P.A. FROM PICTORIAL PARADE

Foreign Minister Walter Scheel (left) outlined West Germany's foreign policy to the parliament in June. Kurt Kiesinger of the opposition took issue with the government's position on Europe and the East.

GERMANY. A breakthrough in relations between East Germany and West Germany occurred in 1970 when, after long negotiations, direct talks were held by the government leaders of the two states for the first time since the division of Germany. On March 19 East Germany's Premier Willi Stoph was host to West Germany's Chancellor Willy Brandt at Erfurt, East Germany. Brandt was greeted with unexpected and fervant enthusiasm by large crowds in the streets. In contrast, when Stoph held a second meeting with Brandt at Kassel, West Germany, on May 21, street disorders marred the occasion.

East Germany

Early in the year East Germany harassed traffic on the highway linking West Berlin to West Germany as a protest against West German parliamentary activities in Berlin and a visit by Brandt to the city. East Germany maintained a hard line on the Berlin issue in 1970 even though its Warsaw Pact allies pressed for easing tension in the city.

Since East Germany does not recognize West Berlin as part of West Germany, Berlin was excluded from an agreement to expand communications facilities between the two Germanys. East Germany agreed to increase telephone and Telex lines across the iron curtain in exchange for West German payments on postal debts claimed by East Germany.

The signing of a Soviet-West German treaty in August was interpreted by the East Germans as a change in European relations from which diplomatic recognition of East Germany should "logically" follow. Recognition by a number of Western powers, including the United States, was actively sought. During 1970 East Germany established diplomatic relations with the People's Republic of the Congo (Brazzaville), Somalia, the Central African Republic, Algeria, Maldives, Ceylon, and

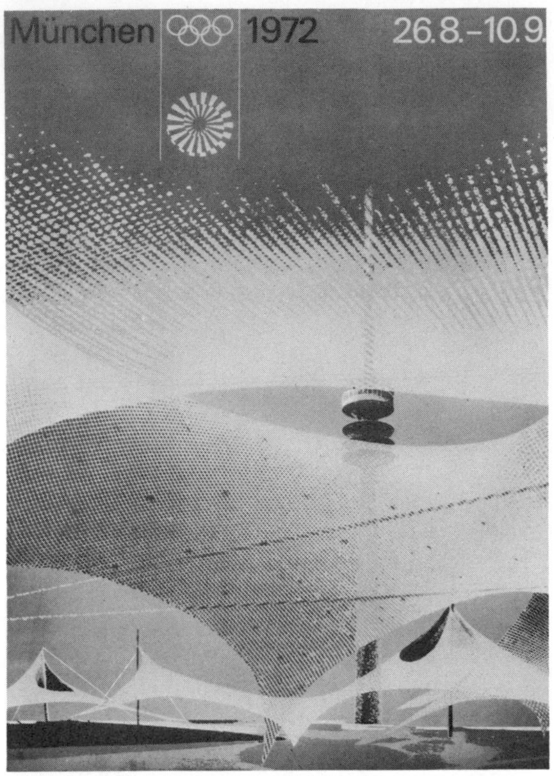

Guinea. France, Austria, and England took steps to expand trade with East Germany.

Because of serious lags in industrial and agricultural production in 1970, East German workers were called on to put in extra workdays, and in July students were put to work at construction sites. Under a new law, effective October 1, East German citizens, male and female, became subject to the draft for "national service" at the age of 16. The East German industrial trademark was changed from "Made in Germany" to "Made in the GDR" (German Democratic Republic).

West Germany

Under the leadership of Chancellor Brandt, the West German coalition government of the Social Democratic party (SPD) and Free Democratic party (FDP) marked its first full year in office in 1970. The government's policy of improving relations with Eastern Europe, known as the *Ostpolitik,* dominated its actions during the year.

After several months of political maneuvering, Chancellor Brandt met with Premier Stoph at Erfurt in March and at Kassel in May. At the meetings, Stoph demanded West German recognition of East Germany by treaty as a basis for further relations; West Germany rejected such a treaty on the grounds that it would legalize a permanent division of Germany. The discussions

ABOVE AND BELOW: AUTHENTICATED NEWS INTERNATIONAL

The 1972 Olympic Games will be held in West Germany. The poster above is one of five that were designed to advertise the games. Käthe Strobel, the federal minister for youth, families, and health, tells some children (below) about a competition for the best Olympic essay or work of art.

WIDE WORLD

In March the big-four powers met for the first time in 11 years to discuss Western access to East Berlin. Demonstrators assembled in the Allied control zone to protest the Berlin wall.

ended inconclusively without provisions for further meetings.

The United States, Great Britain, France, and the Soviet Union—the "big four" powers responsible for Berlin since World War II—began on March 26 a series of talks on easing tensions in Berlin. The aim of the three Western powers was to end East German interference with road and rail traffic between West Berlin and West Germany; to improve communications between East and West Berlin; and to reopen East Berlin to visits by West Berliners. The Soviet aim was to curtail West German political activity in West Berlin. As a conciliatory gesture at the beginning of the talks, the Western powers ceased to require that East Germans obtain special permission to visit NATO (North Atlantic Treaty Organization) countries. The Berlin talks adjourned in December without having made progress.

Treaty negotiations between West Germany and the Soviet Union, begun in February, reached a successful conclusion in August. Under the treaty, both nations renounced the use of force to settle disputes and recognized the existing frontiers of all European states, including the Oder-Neisse river frontier between Poland and East Germany and also, in effect the current frontier between the two Germanys. The treaty was signed by Brandt and Soviet Premier Aleksei N. Kosygin in Moscow on August 12. Brandt told the Soviets that ratification of the treaty would depend on a successful outcome of the four-power talks on Berlin. (*See* Germany Special Report.)

Negotiations between West Germany and Poland took place from February to November 18, when the foreign ministers of the two nations initialed a treaty in Warsaw, Poland. The treaty, signed on December 7, provided for recognition of the Oder-Neisse line as Poland's western boundary and for normalization of relations.

The first tangible results of the West German-Soviet treaty appeared in September, when the West German Scientific Research Society of Bonn and the U.S.S.R. Academy of Sciences signed an agreement for scientific and technological cooperation in many fields. Early in the year the Soviets and West Germans concluded a pact providing for an exchange of 1.2 million tons of German steel pipe for 1.82 trillion cubic feet of Soviet natural gas over a 20-year period.

A five-year agreement for trade and economic cooperation was concluded with Hungary on October 27. The initial steps in setting up negotiations between West Germany and Czechoslovakia were also taken in 1970. As a result of an agreement between Polish and West German travel organizations, Poland admitted tourists from West Germany for the first time since World War II.

In elections for the parliaments of three West German states in June, Brandt's coalition government suffered serious setbacks. The FDP was

(*continued on page 272*)

Germany

Special Report: East Meets West

by Philip Windsor, Reader in International Relations, London School of Economics and Political Science, University of London

D.P.A. FROM PICTORIAL PARADE

A historic meeting occurred in March between West Germany's Chancellor Willy Brandt (right) and East Germany's Premier Willi Stoph.

Throughout much of 1970, West Germany conducted three sets of parallel negotiations: with the Soviet Union, with Poland, and with East Germany. The somewhat generalized attempt to improve relations with Eastern Europe that had been characteristic of the *Ostpolitik* (Eastern policy) of the "grand coalition" government during 1966–69 assumed this more distinct form after Willy Brandt had taken office as chancellor in October 1969.

The early history of the West German government's *Ostpolitik* was characterized by confusion. Equally, both German states were divided domestically over the implications of the new diplomatic moves. Thus it was difficult to discern any real progress in the talks that were going on during the first part of the year. After Brandt's two special envoys, Egon Bahr in Moscow and Georg Ferdinand Duckwitz in Warsaw, Poland, had engaged in discussions for some weeks, the final agreement was made (and clearly under considerable Soviet pressure on East Germany) for a meeting between the two German heads of government at Erfurt, East Germany. What this meeting signified, however, was far from clear. Its real importance lay in the fact that it was a "historic occasion," the first such meeting since the division of Germany in 1945. But the only tangible agreement reached was that the two should meet again. In all other respects, the meeting seems even to have been self-defeating if it was regarded as an attempt on the West German side to draw East Germany into the process of negotiation. The meeting was followed by a sharp downturn in the progress of negotiations in Moscow. Indeed, at the end of March, the Soviet ambassador to East Germany, Pyotr A. Abrasimov, made a speech in which he insisted anew on all the demands that had been quietly dropped over the preceding year—in particular that for full international recognition of East Germany. This was a diplomatic defeat for the Soviet government as much as for the West German government, and it revealed the extent to which the Soviet leaders were vulnerable, not to the threat of East German power but to that of an East German crisis.

This East German demand did not last. It was indicative only of the extent to which the West German insistence and the Soviet demands had made Walter Ulbricht, East Germany's president, vulnerable to domestic revolt, and of the extent to which the Soviet government was anxious to avoid the manifestations of such revolt in the leading circles of East Germany's Socialist Unity party. But although the demand did not continue to affect the direct course of negotiations between the Soviets and the West German government, it did, in effect, let East Germany off the hook. For months thereafter, East Germany made no visible concessions to the imperatives of the Western *Ostpolitik,* and a second meeting in May between the two heads of government, this time in Kassel, West Germany, was so unproductive that not even a date for a subsequent meeting was agreed upon when it came to an end. Thereafter, the East Germans would be able to stall until the approaching success of the Soviet-West German negotiations led again to renewed demands from the Soviet government.

Nonetheless, the points raised by the East German government, and in particular those of the East Berlin officials, continued to make the course of Soviet-West German negotiations difficult. The essence of the proposed treaty was simple—that the two governments should, in renouncing the use of force, provide for recognition of the existing political map of Europe without engaging the West German government in forms of legal recognition which, either for domestic reasons or for reasons of political principle, it was not willing to engage in. However, the question of Berlin immediately made all such attempts more difficult. The finding of formulas was in one sense simple: the West German government could recognize the political reality of East Germany or of the East German-Polish frontier, the Oder-Neisse line. But if the Soviet Union were asked, by the same token, to recognize the political reality of West German links with West Berlin, it refused categorically. At the same time, the West German representative came under heavy domestic attack; by agreeing to the Soviet search for formulas to cover the political map of Europe, he was also recognizing the Soviet right to speak on behalf of what were supposedly fully sovereign states in Eastern Europe. In West Germany, this was denounced as a virtual endorsement of the Soviet Union's "Brezhnev doctrine." Yet the Soviet Union was not only safeguarding its own interests: the complex of difficulties it faced in Eastern Europe made it virtually impossible to risk provoking the East German government into a total boycott of the negotiations by recognizing the West German links with West Berlin. This knot of difficulties held up the outcome of the negotiations for some weeks. It was finally resolved by direct meetings between the West German and Soviet foreign ministers, Walter Scheel and Andrei A. Gromyko. In reaching a conclusion, the Soviet government made two concessions to the West German government. First, by accepting a reordering of the treaty, putting certain proposed articles into an agreed preamble, and allowing each party to make a separate declaration of what it understood by the treaty, it did much to ensure that the West German government would not have to face intolerable domestic criticism and possibly risk a rejection of the treaty. Secondly, it agreed to allow for a delay in the ratification of the treaty until the "big four" discussions over Berlin that were in progress had reached an agreed conclusion.

This saved the West German government from domestic embarrassment; it also gave the Soviet Union a direct incentive to reach agreement with the three Western powers over Berlin. At the same time, however, it increased the risk that ratification of the treaty could be delayed to the point where it was no longer of great political importance, if the Berlin negotiations should prove to be too drawn-out. The treaty was initialed on August 12 but had not been ratified by the end of 1970.

In spite of these concessions and these risks, the Soviet government gained more from the treaty than did West Germany. It secured virtual recognition by a leading Western power that it was competent to negotiate on behalf of other East European governments. It ensured that West German-Soviet negotiations would provide the framework for West German-Polish and perhaps other subsequent bilateral negotiations. And it immediately acquired considerable resources in capital investment by doing so, for West Germany agreed to give the Soviet Union economic aid.

In consequence, the West German-Polish negotiations were partly held up by the progress of the Soviet round, and they made serious substantive progress only after the main Soviet-West German agreements had been reached. But the West German gains were also significant. Relations with the Soviet Union were put on a firmer footing than at any time since World War II.

On Dec. 7, 1970, Chancellor Brandt and Poland's Premier Jozef Cyrankiewicz signed a treaty establishing normal ties between the two countries. The principal item in the pact recognized Poland's occupation of 40,000 square miles of former German territory, thus establishing Poland's western border with East Germany on the line formed by the Oder and Neisse rivers.

The East German government was thus confronted with a situation in which it was—if only because of its own self-interest and the preservation of economic links—likely to make more concessions than before. In July, Ulbricht had suggested that the two German states could exchange ambassadors without full international recognition. It was a measure of how far West German policy had developed in 1970 that this could now be regarded as an East German concession; at the same time, such a concession suggested that the course of relations between the two German states might prove to be one of the most significant elements of international politics in 1971.

West German demonstrators urge Brandt not to sell out during his East German trip.

D.P.A. FROM PICTORIAL PARADE

(*continued from page 269*)
swept out of office in two states and barely managed to retain representation in the third. As a result, the coalition's majority in the lower house of parliament was reduced from 12 to 6. The opposition Christian Democratic Union (CDU) gained in the elections. In elections in Hesse in November, however, the FDP picked up votes.

Following the June elections, right-wing FDP rebels formed a "National Liberal Action" group to protest the party's course. Nonetheless, Walter Scheel, West Germany's foreign minister and vice-chancellor, was reelected to the FDP chairmanship.

West Germany's booming economy continued to be marked by inflation during most of the year, though by October there was evidence of a slowdown. In July parliament passed a bill to curb inflation through a six-month suspension of write-offs on capital investments and a temporary surcharge on personal and corporate taxes. Wages rose faster than prices in 1970, and an acute labor shortage remained.

The government's domestic program included liberalization of the laws against political demonstrators and amnesty for some 4,000 persons previously arrested during political protests. In June parliament lowered the voting age in federal elections to 18. An emergency antipollution program, announced in September, included provisions for water purification plants, the measurement of air pollution, and controls on the lead content in automobile fuels. (*See in* CE: Berlin; Germany, East; Germany, West.)

GHANA. The institutional process of Ghana's return to a democratic system of civilian government culminated on Aug. 31, 1970, in the election by the National Assembly of Edward Akufo-Addo, a former chief justice, as president for a four-year term. Nominated by the ruling Progress party and elected by a substantial majority, Akufo-Addo took over from the interim three-man presidential commission, comprised of Brig. Akwasi A. Afrifa, John W. K. Harlley, and Maj. Gen. A. K. Ocran.

Toward the end of 1969, Ghana's relations with its West African neighbors were badly jolted by the cabinet of Prime Minister Kofi A. Busia, which enforced a deportation order against aliens who had failed to ask for residence permits. The order, issued on Nov. 19, 1969 (in the prime minister's absence), gave those without permits two weeks to apply for them or leave the country. Those involved may have numbered more than a million out of Ghana's 2 million aliens, who made up almost a quarter of the country's total population, with some 700,000 Nigerians, about 500,000 Upper Voltans, and smaller numbers from Dahomey, Togo, Ivory Coast, Niger, and Liberia. Following a practice that had been officially condoned along the West African coast since colonial days, most of these immigrants were engaged in petty trading and many had settled without obtaining permits.

To seek a long-term accommodation that would ease pressures for the repayment of Ghana's external debts, government delegations visited Western and Communist capitals in April and May. A U.S. loan of up to $15 million was negotiated in Washington, D.C. Aided by a credit of $8.5 million from the United Nations International Development Association, Ghana embarked on the first stage of a program to rehabilitate the cocoa industry; by 1982 this project was calculated to increase cocoa production in the Eastern Region by about 19,000 tons. (*See in* CE: Ghana.)

GOLF. Tony Jacklin won the 1970 U.S. Open at Chaska, Minn., by an impressive seven-stroke margin. He was the first British golfer to accomplish this feat since Ted Ray did so in 1920. Runner-up in the classic, which paid Jacklin $30,000 for his efforts, was Dave Hill, whose caustic remarks about the course at the Hazeltine National Golf Club earned him a fine of $150 along with his second-place $15,000 check. After 14 years of frustration, California's Billy Casper won the Masters at Augusta, Ga., in April by a five-stroke margin over Gene Littler. The third major U.S. tournament—the Professional Golfers' Association of America (PGA) championship—went to Dave Stockton, who edged Arnold Palmer at the Southern Hills Country Club at Tulsa, Okla., with a one-under-par 279 in August. Overseas, Jack Nicklaus took the elusive British Open at St. Andrews, Scotland, in July, beating Doug Sanders by a single stroke. Tony Jacklin, the defending champion, finished fifth with a 286.

Winners of other major tournaments in 1970 were Bert Yancey in the Bing Crosby Pro-Am; Pete Brown, the Andy Williams-San Diego Open; Frank Beard (the leading money winner in 1969), the Tournament of Champions; Hugh Royer, the Western Open in Chicago; Jack Nicklaus, the World Series of Golf at Akron, Ohio; Palmer and Nicklaus, the National Four-Ball meet at Ligonier,

Jack Nicklaus won the Byron Nelson Golf Classic in Dallas, Tex., in May. He defeated Arnold Palmer in a sudden-death play-off.
WIDE WORLD

UPI COMPIX

Billy Casper won the 1970 Masters tournament in Augusta, Ga., by beating Gene Littler in an 18-hole play-off.

Pa.; Australia's Bruce Crampton, the Westchester Golf Classic; and Kermit Zarley, the Canadian Open at London, Ont. Bobby Nichols won the $60,000 top prize in the year's richest tournament—the Dow Jones Open—at Clifton, N.J. Roberto de Vicenzo of Argentina took the individual title and Australian's Bruce Devlin and David Graham won the team title in the World Cup.

Early in the year Arnold Palmer, the 40-year-old slugger from Latrobe, Pa., was chosen by a nationwide poll of sportwriters and broadcasters as the athlete of the decade. Top U.S. golf money winner of 1970 was Lee Trevino, with a total of $157,037.

In amateur play, Lanny Wadkins won the 70th U.S. National Amateur championship at Portland, Ore., and Bob Risch took the national public links championship. The University of Houston won both the individual and team National Collegiate Athletic Association university division titles; Jim Smith of St. Petersburg, Fla., the National Junior College individual title; and Miami-Dade North Junior College, the team title.

Feminine fairway play in 1970 was highlighted by a decisive 11½–6½ victory by the U.S. amateurs over the English in Curtis Cup play at Boston, Mass. It was the 13th U.S. victory in 16 competitions. Shirley Englehorn won the Ladies PGA championship at Sutton, Mass., in June; Donna Caponi, her second straight U.S. Women's Open victory, in a $30,000 classic played at Muskogee, Okla. Martha Wilkinson scored an impressive 3 and 2 victory over Cynthia Hill to annex the Women's National Amateur golf championship at Darien, Conn., in August, and Cathy Gaughan of Arizona State upset a fellow student, defending champion Jane Bastanchury, 4 and 2, to win the Women's National Intercollegiate title at El Cajon, Calif.

In the fall a joint committee of the Royal and Ancient Club of St. Andrews and the U.S. Golf Association agreed that a uniform-size golf ball of 1.66-inch diameter should be recommended for use throughout the world. The new ball would be confined to a maximum velocity of 250 feet per second. (*See in* CE: Golf.)

Arnold Palmer grimaces as he misses a putt on the 15th green in the first round of the Greater Greensboro Open Golf tournament. In January Palmer was named Pro Golfer of the Decade.

WIDE WORLD

GREAT BRITAIN AND NORTHERN IRELAND, UNITED KINGDOM OF. In a general election on June 18, 1970, Great Britain's Conservative party turned out the Labor government that had been in office since October 1964. Harold Wilson resigned after having been prime minister for more than five years, and his place was taken by the Conservatives' leader, Edward Heath, Britain's first bachelor prime minister since 1905.

Prior to the general election, the Labor party made substantial local election gains during April and May. In elections for the Greater London Council (GLC) on April 9, Labor gained 16 seats, though the Conservatives retained control with 65 of the 100 GLC members. Elections were held April 6–11 for 59 English and Welsh county councils, but party control remained unchanged. Polling took place on May 7 in 342 English and Welsh boroughs for one third of the seats on the councils. Labor had a net gain of 443 seats and the Conservatives a net loss of 327 seats. In the Scottish burgh council elections on May 5, the Labor party had a

WIDE WORLD

Pietro Annigoni poses beside his new portrait of Queen Elizabeth II. The stark painting has been very controversial.

net gain of 57 seats, largely at the expense of the Scottish National party (SNP).

On May 18, encouraged by local election results and opinion poll findings, Wilson announced that a general election would be held on June 18. Nominations closed on June 8, with a total of 1,819 candidates for the 630 seats in the House of Commons. Despite most of the pollsters' predictions, the Conservatives were returned to power with a majority of 31 seats over all other parties (excluding the speaker) in the House of Commons and of 43 over Labor. Labor gained ten seats but lost 70 of the 347 (including one vacancy) which it had held at the dissolution of the old Parliament.

In the new House of Commons there were 330 Conservative members, 287 Laborites, six Liberals, and seven others (including the speaker). The percentages of the total votes cast were: Conservative 46.4; Labor 43.1; Liberal 7.5. The total Conservative vote increased by about 1,600,000, and the Labor vote fell by about 900,000. Although the Liberal party's vote of over 2,100,000 was only about 10% less than in the previous (1966) election, the party lost more than half its seats. Among former Labor ministers who were defeated was George Brown, who was deputy leader of the party and a former secretary of state for foreign affairs.

The election campaign centered on Britain's economic performance under the Labor government, with Labor supporters arguing that their party had inherited a $1.9-billion balance-of-payments deficit from the Conservatives in 1964 and had turned it into a surplus running at an annual rate of $1.4 billion. Conservative tactics were to concentrate the argument on rising prices and to question the soundness of Labor's economic policy, particularly as the country seemed to be threatened by an outbreak of strikes and inflationary wage increases. The apparent collapse of Labor's income policy in the year preceding the election added force to the argument. Industrial disputes, including a newspaper strike for four days in the middle of the election campaign, gave added point to the Conservative promise of legislation on labor relations.

Heath's new Cabinet included Reginald Maudling (home secretary) and Sir Alec Douglas-Home (secretary of the state for foreign affairs). Anthony Barber became chancellor of the exchequer in July. The total number of ministers in the Cabinet was 17, the smallest since 1957.

Industrial Problems

In Britain, 1970 was the worst year for strikes since 1926, the year of the "general strike." The manufacturing industry was the hardest hit. Nearly two thirds of the 3,491 stoppages in the first ten months of the year arose out of wage disputes (more than three times as many as in 1965).

The automotive industry, in particular, was severely hit by strikes in the component production factories. A strike lasting seven weeks at GKN-Sankey components factories was estimated to have cost the automotive industry $110 million in lost production. A long-drawn-out strike in the Pilkington glass firm also disrupted car production. The Conservative government proposed a tough industrial relations bill to handle the strikes.

The Economy

The balance of payments had been Britain's besetting economic problem ever since the Labor government took office in October 1964, but 1969 produced an estimated surplus of $922 million on current account as the reward for the tough economic policies imposed by the Labor chancellor of the exchequer, Roy Jenkins. To secure a massive switch of resources away from domestic consumption to exports, Jenkins had to clamp down on demand at home at the expense of economic growth. However, the opening months of 1970 brought the best trade figures for many years, and in May Jenkins was able to forecast a surplus of $1.3 billion for the year.

Meanwhile, Britain's currency was strong, foreign funds flowed into London, the capital, and it was possible to pay off more than half of the $7.2 billion that had been borrowed in the deficit years 1964–68. On March 5, the bank rate was reduced from 8% to 7.5%. Yet the trends in the early part of 1970 were not entirely satisfactory. From February to April imports were rising faster than exports, which were up only 1% on the preceding three months. At home, prices and wages were rising, but growth flagged and unemployment remained high at about 2.5%.

Foreign Policy and Defense

A new emphasis on what were regarded as British interests characterized the foreign policy of the new Conservative government. In the opening debate of the new Parliament, Prime Minister Heath said, "The main aim of our foreign policy must be to make a modern and broadly based assessment of where British interests lie." This doctrine was foremost in the controversy over the intention to sell maritime arms to South Africa, which was defended as a necessary countermeasure to the Soviet Union's naval penetration of the Indian Ocean.

The new British government was also determined to keep a small military presence in Southeast Asia. However, the main emphasis of Conservative foreign policy lay in Europe, with a reaffirmation of support for the North Atlantic Treaty Organization (NATO) and the commencement of negotiations for Britain's entry into the European Economic Community, or Common Market.

Northern Ireland

The programs of social reform and economic development initiated in 1969 in Northern Ireland were implemented during the year against a background of continuing violence. A local government review body, established in December 1969, produced its report on June 25, 1970. A five-year economic development program, published on June 23, proposed an increase of $179.3 million in public expenditure with a five-year program for building 73,000 houses, an increase of one third on the housing performance of the preceding five years. With its emphasis on employment and industrial training, the objective was to reduce unemploy-

British troops patrol in Belfast, Northern Ireland (above), after another outbreak of violence.
A rioter is taken into custody (below) by British soldiers in Londonderry.

ABOVE: RALPH ERIC SCHNACKENBERG FROM NANCY PALMER AGENCY. BELOW: LONDON "DAILY EXPRESS" FROM PICTORIAL PARADE

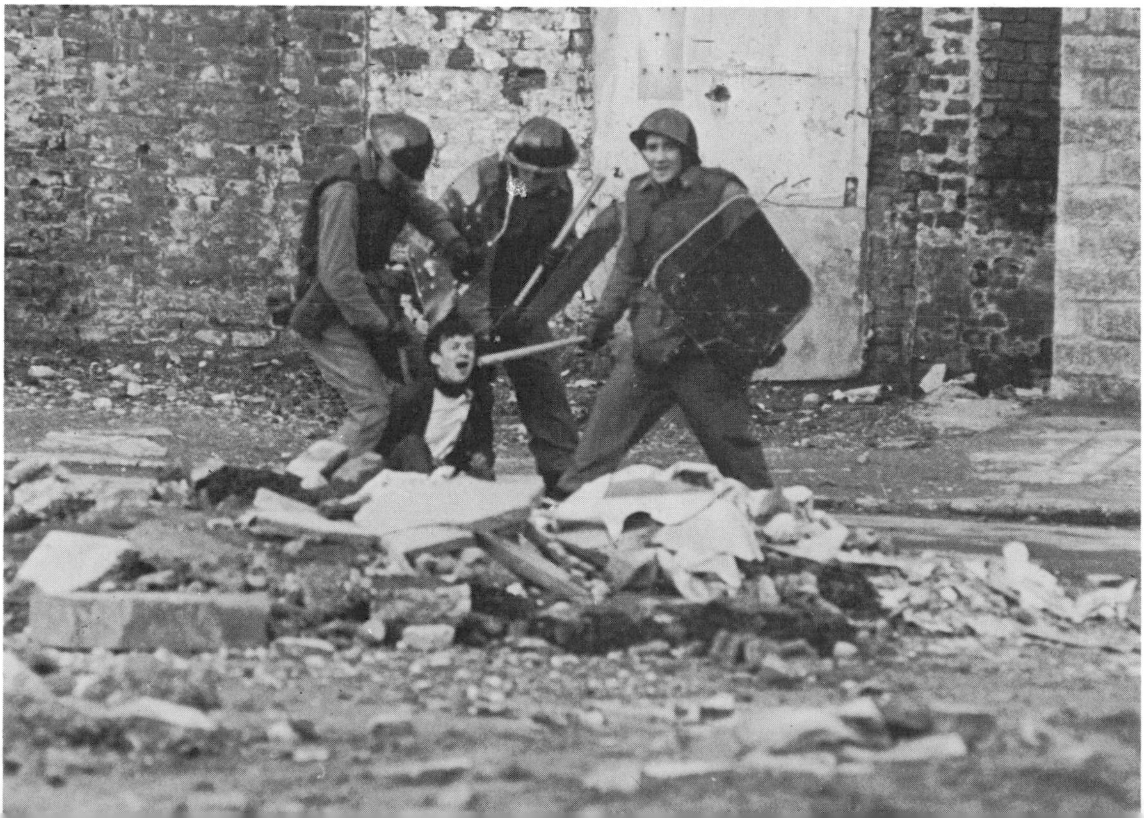

POPPERFOTO FROM PICTORIAL PARADE

Voters crowd into London's Trafalgar Square on June 19, 1970, to view the election results. The Conservatives were victorious in upsetting the Labor government of Prime Minister Wilson.

ment and raise living standards, and so to eradicate some of the root causes of unrest in Northern Ireland.

Unrest persisted, however, both in the provincial parliament at Stormont, near Belfast, the capital, and in the streets. Disagreement over the reorganization of the police led to a revolt by five Ulster Unionist back-bench members, and this feeling was reflected by the victory of the new and extreme Protestant Unionist party at by-elections on April 16, when the Rev. Ian Paisley was elected to the Northern Ireland House of Commons for Bannside and the Rev. William Beattie for South Antrim (in Britain's general election, Paisley also won a seat at Westminster). Nevertheless, Northern Ireland's prime minister, Maj. James Chichester-Clark, retained his hold on the province's government.

After a relatively quiet winter, disturbances broke out again in February and March with demonstrations against the new Public Order Act (passed on February 5), which strengthened regulations to control processions and demonstrations. Three nights of rioting in Belfast (March 31–April 2) showed some evidence of being supported by the underground Irish Republican Army, which threatened attacks against British troops. This drew from the British government an assurance that troops would stay as long as necessary, and from the commander in chief, Lieut. Gen. Ian Freeland, a warning that rioters using gasoline bombs would be shot.

Bernadette Devlin, the militant member of Parliament for mid-Ulster, was imprisoned June 26 on charges of incitement to riot in Londonderry in August 1969. This led to three nights of violent clashes in Londonderry, with more than 200 persons injured, including 100 soldiers. At the same time, the worst riots since 1969 broke out in Belfast, with five persons shot dead, 200 injured (66 with gunshot wounds), and 100 fires started during the nights of June 27 and June 28, when 3,500 troops were engaged and more than 1,000 tear-gas canisters were fired. Reginald Maudling, as the new home secretary, made his first visit to Northern Ireland on June 30–July 1, giving his backing to the reform program and repeating the Labor government's pledge to make British troops available as long as needed. In another violent outbreak in Belfast on July 3, five persons were shot dead and 50 injured with gunshot wounds.

The summer rioting led to the passing of emergency legislation. The Prevention of Incitement of Hatred Act made it an offense "to use threatening, abusive, or insulting language to stir up hatred against, or arouse the fear of, any section of the community on grounds of religion, belief, color, race, or ethnic or national origin." On July 23 a six-month ban on processions was imposed. Nevertheless, sporadic outbreaks of rioting, some of them serious, continued to occur.

Clashes with troops in Belfast on July 31–August 4 led Chichester-Clark to blame "sinister elements" operating in the republican cause rather than for civil rights. On August 10 Maudling hinted that if there were a breakdown in the reform program agreed upon between the two governments, there might have to be direct rule by the British government. In addition to rioting, there were many bombings and explosions—more than 70 between May and September. Miss Devlin was released from Armagh jail on October 20. (*See also* Heath; Ireland Special Report. *See in* CE: Great Britain and Northern Ireland, United Kingdom of.)

GREECE. The resumption of full-scale U.S. military aid to the army-sponsored Greek regime was by far the most significant event in Greece in 1970. It was widely regarded as a major victory for the leaders of the 1967 military coup and their policies. First, by resisting all the pressures for an acceleration of the "democratization" process, they had been able to convince the United States that the heavy arms embargo it had imposed after the coup had been totally ineffective as a political lever. Second, by negotiating purchases of embargoed weapons from France and elsewhere, they had apparently aroused U.S. fears that a continuation of the arms embargo might alienate the regime at a time when a lack of loyal allies in the eastern Mediterranean Sea region was becoming a source of grave concern for the United States.

These developments took place against a background of slow "liberalization" of the regime; it was becoming less repressive as it consolidated its position domestically. Some constitutional safeguards, including those against arbitrary arrest, were restored. The number of political prisoners was reduced from about 1,500 to fewer than 700. One of the most prominent Communist political prisoners, the composer Mikis Theodorakis, was freed and allowed to go abroad. It was an unprecedented gesture made by Premier George Papadopoulos in response to a personal plea from Jean-Jacques Servan-Schreiber, the French writer and political leader.

Despite these moves at leniency, new accusations of torture and alarming descriptions of police brutality came to international notice. Trials conducted by special military courts also continued, and more than 100 regime opponents were convicted, some of them sent to prison for life.

To mark the third anniversary of the coup, Premier Papadopoulos announced a plan to set up a "consultative committee on legislation." This body, or "mini-parliament," as it came to be called, was to be made up of 56 members, most of them selected by the premier from nominations made by trade and professional unions and by local government bodies. Also included in the 56 were 10 members of the premier's own choosing. Its functions, clearly, would be purely academic since the regime, which ruled by decree, would have no obligation to heed the committee's legislative recommendations.

Archbishop Makarios (center), president of Cyprus, meets in Rome with the exiled King Constantine II and Queen Anne Marie of Greece.

UPI COMPIX

The first major crisis within the junta occurred at the end of August. It was precipitated by the gradual creation by Papadopoulos of a staff of junior ministers to act as his brain trust. This buffer zone arrangement was strongly resented by other junta members. Some of them, arguing that the regime had lost its "revolutionary" impetus, called for the premier's resignation, which he agreed to sign. The post was then offered to the chief of the armed forces, who declined, reaffirming his loyalty to the leader of the coup. This crisis subsided as the rebels realized their impotence, and Papadopoulos was thus reconfirmed as premier.

In foreign affairs, Greece remained aloof toward its hostile West European allies, encouraged good relations with France and the Balkan states, and made it a point at all times to underline its loyalty to the North Atlantic Treaty Organization. Its only other foreign interest was Cyprus, where there were poor prospects for a permanent settlement. (*See* Cyprus.)

The economy was characterized in 1970 by a growth rate of approximately 7% and relative monetary stability. The scarcity of foreign capital inflow, however, forced the government to borrow abroad at harsh terms in order to protect its balance of payments. (*See in* CE: Greece.)

GUATEMALA. At midyear 1970, the second legal transfer of executive power in the 150-year history of the republic of Guatemala took place with the assumption of the presidency by Col. Carlos Araña Osorio. An upsurge of urban terrorism that began in December 1969 continued unabated throughout the first half of 1970. A two-month respite after the July inauguration of President Araña was followed by a resumption of terrorist activity beginning in September.

Prior to the inauguration, Guatemala City, the capital, was subjected to seven months of urban terrorism on an unprecedented scale. Between December 1969 and February 1970, a campaign of arson, bombings, and assassinations reportedly inflicted a total of 20 deaths and $10 million in damages. Political candidates, government officials, policemen, and guerrillas were among the victims. A leftist guerrilla group, the Rebel Armed Forces, was generally credited with most of these attacks. Between late February and April a new dimension of terrorism was witnessed in the successive kidnappings of Alberto Fuentes Mohr, Guatemalan foreign minister; Sean M. Holly, U.S. embassy aide; and Count Karl von Spreti, the West German ambassador. Fuentes Mohr and Holly were both

WIDE WORLD

Alberto Fuentes Mohr (above), Guatemala's foreign minister, is released by kidnappers. Col. Carlos Araña Osorio (below) is victorious in the presidential election.

WIDE WORLD

freed in exchange for the release of "political" prisoners. The Guatemalan government, however, refused to negotiate for the release of Von Spreti in exchange for 22 prisoners and $700,000 in ransom. The ensuing assassination of Von Spreti in early April increased tensions between the West German and Guatemalan governments and culminated in the recall of their respective diplomatic missions.

Throughout the autumn terrorism continued unabated, claiming the lives of prominent Guatemalan citizens, both to the left and to the right of the political spectrum. (*See in* CE: Guatemala.)

GUINEA. After 12 years of constant friction, the dialogue between France and the Republic of Guinea was reopened in 1970 on a new footing. Diplomatic relations, broken off in November 1965 after Guinean leaders had accused several former French ministers of plotting to assassinate President Sékou Touré, were being progressively normalized. Although in February President Touré had once again accused France of trying to overthrow his government, in March he invited Edmond Michelet, then France's minister of culture, to attend a festival of African art and culture at Conakry, the capital. In May, speaking on the occasion of the 23d anniversary of the founding of the Democratic party of Guinea, Touré called for "loyal cooperation between France and Guinea."

On November 22 President Touré announced that Portuguese armed forces had invaded Guinea from the sea and that an attack had been made on Conakry. Portugal immediately denied that Portuguese troops were involved; however, there was friction between the two countries because of the guerrillas in Portuguese Guinea, who had found shelter in Guinea. On the following day, the government said that a number of the president's European advisers had been killed in the fighting. After a second invasion attempt was repulsed on November 24, the situation reverted to normal again. On December 4 a United Nations fact-finding group announced that Portuguese troops, led by white officers, were responsible for the invasion attempts on Guinea. (*See in* CE: Guinea.)

GUYANA. On Feb. 23, 1970, Guyana became a "cooperative republic" within the Commonwealth of Nations. The governing party, the People's National Congress, nominated former Supreme Court Judge Raymond Arthur Chung for president, and he was elected on March 17.

Prime Minister Forbes Burnham said in February that the Cooperative Republic of Guyana had two objectives—to eradicate the people's "colonial mentality" and to harness the people into a "self-help program based on a national system of cooperative ventures."

On the industrial front, the government's declared aim was to set up a full partnership with private enterprise and to emphasize the processing of local raw materials inside Guyana. There was also a growing firmness in demands for state participation in the expanding bauxite industry (the country's largest export earner).

In June a Port of Spain (Trinidad) protocol established a 12-year moratorium on Venezuela's claim to more than 57,000 square miles of Guyana, west of the Essequibo River. (*See in* CE: Guyana.)

HAITI. Yet another attempt to overthrow the government of François Duvalier, president of the Republic of Haiti, was made in 1970. On April 24 and 25 three Haitian coast guard cutters shelled the capital, Port-au-Prince, aiming for the presidential palace. Duvalier requested U.S. military planes to put down the disorder, but the U.S. government refused. Duvalier then sent troops into Port-au-Prince, closed down the airport, imposed a curfew, and restricted telephone communications.

After shelling the capital, the Haitian boats, with more than a hundred crew members, sailed to the U.S. naval base at Guantanamo, Cuba. The crews requested political asylum in the United States. The three coast guard cutters and their crews constituted most of Haiti's naval force. The U.S. government granted asylum to the coast guardsmen in June, except for one lieutenant who did not request asylum.

Duvalier stated that the coast guard attack was part of a Communist plot and held that Col. Octave Cayard, the commander of the coast guard, was responsible. A number of persons were then arrested, including a bank president and the minister of justice. Reportedly nine men charged with being implicated in the plot were executed in April.

Former Haitian army Col. René J. Leon, who in 1969 had dropped homemade bombs from an airplane over Port-au-Prince, was in 1970 convicted of having violated neutrality laws by a U.S. district court in Miami, Fla. Another action by a foreign court involving Haiti occurred in France. The French court ruled that Duvalier had been libeled in the motion picture 'The Comedians' and awarded him the equivalent of 18¢ in damages.

Again in 1970 Haiti ranked as the poorest of all Latin American countries. In June the Inter-American Development Bank granted Haiti a $5.1-million loan for the improvement of the water supply in and around Port-au-Prince. (*See in* CE: Haiti.)

UPI COMPIX

Rural Haiti remains poor. Children often must work in the fields to keep from starving.

Members of the Tonton Macoute, Haiti's secret police, march in support of President Duvalier in Port-au-Prince after the city was shelled by rebel Haitian coast guard vessels.

WIDE WORLD

HEADS OF GOVERNMENT

Although not all of those listed were official heads of state, they controlled the government as of Dec. 31, 1970.

CAMERA PRESS FROM PIX

EMILIO COLOMBO

ANWAR EL-SADAT

WIDE WORLD

COUNTRY	LEADER
Afghanistan	Mohammed Zahir Shah
Albania	Communist Party First Secretary Enver Hoxha
Algeria	President Houari Boumédienne
Argentina	Brig. Gen. Roberto Marcelo Levingston
Australia	Prime Minister John G. Gorton
Austria	President Franz Jonas
Barbados	Prime Minister Errol W. Barrow
Belgium	Premier Gaston Eyskens
Bolivia	Gen. Juan José Torres Gonzales
Botswana	President, Sir Seretse Khama
Brazil	Gen. Emílio Garrastazú Médici
Bulgaria	Premier Todor Zhivkov
Burma	Gen. Ne Win
Burundi	President Michel Micombero
Cambodia	Premier Lon Nol
Cameroon	President Ahmadou Ahidjo
Canada	Prime Minister Pierre Elliott Trudeau
Central African Rep.	President Jean-Bedel Bokassa
Ceylon	Prime Minister Sirimavo Bandaranaike
Chad	President François Tombalbaye
Chile	President Salvador Allende
China, People's Rep. of	Politburo Chairman Mao Tse-tung
Colombia	President Misael Pastrana Borrero
Congo, Dem. Rep. of the	President Joseph Mobutu
Congo, People's Rep. of the	President Marien Ngouabi
Costa Rica	President José Figuéres Ferrer
Cuba	Premier Fidel Castro
Cyprus	President Makarios
Czechoslovakia	Communist Party First Secretary Gustav Husak
Dahomey	President Hubert Maga
Denmark	Premier Hilmar Baunsgaard
Dominican Rep.	President Joaquín Balaguer
Ecuador	President José María Velasco Ibarra
El Salvador	President Fidel Sánchez Hernández
Equatorial Guinea	President Francisco Macías Nguma
Ethiopia	Emperor Haile Selassie I
Fiji	Prime Minister, Chief Ratu Sir Kamisese Mara
Finland	Prime Minister Ahti Karjalainen
France	President Georges Pompidou
Gabon	President Albert B. Bongo
Gambia, The	President, Sir Dawda Kairaba Jawara
Germany, East	Communist Party First Secretary Walter Ulbricht
Germany, West	Chancellor Willy Brandt
Ghana	Prime Minister Kofi A. Busia
Great Britain	Prime Minister Edward Heath
Greece	Premier George Papadopoulos
Guatemala	President Carlos Araña Osorio
Guinea	President Sékou Touré
Guyana	Prime Minister Forbes Burnham
Haiti	President François Duvalier
Honduras	President Osvaldo López Arellano
Hungary	Communist Party First Secretary Janos Kadar
Iceland	(Acting) Premier Johann Hafstein
India	Prime Minister Indira Gandhi
Indonesia	President Suharto
Iran	Shah Mohammed Reza Pahlavi
Iraq	President Ahmed Hassan al-Bakr
Ireland	Prime Minister John Lynch
Israel	Prime Minister Golda Meir
Italy	Premier Emilio Colombo
Ivory Coast	President Félix Houphouët-Boigny
Jamaica	Prime Minister Hugh L. Shearer
Japan	Premier Eisaku Sato
Jordan	King Hussein I
Kenya	President Jomo Kenyatta
Korea, North	Premier Kim Il Sung
Korea, South	President Park Chung-hee
Kuwait	Sheikh Sabah al-Salim al-Sabah

Laos	Premier Souvanna Phouma
Lebanon	President Suleiman Franjieh
Lesotho	Prime Minister, Chief Leabua Jonathan
Liberia	President William V. S. Tubman
Libya	Revolutionary Command Council Chairman, Col. Muammar el-Qaddafi
Luxembourg ...	Premier Pierre Werner
Malagasy Rep.	President Philibert Tsiranana
Malawi	President H. Kamuzu Banda
Malaysia	Prime Minister Abdul Razak
Maldives	President Ibrahim Nassir
Mali	Lieut. Moussa Traoré
Malta	Prime Minister George Borg Olivier
Mauritania	President Mokhtar Ould Daddah
Mauritius	Prime Minister, Sir Seewoosagur Ramgoolam
Mexico	President Luis Echeverría Alvarez
Monaco	Prince Rainier III
Mongolia	Communist Party First Secretary Yumzhagiyin Tsedenbal
Morocco	King Hassan II
Nauru	President Hammer de Roburt
Nepal	King Mahendra
Netherlands	Premier Piet J. S. de Jong
New Zealand ...	Prime Minister, Sir Keith J. Holyoake
Nicaragua	President Anastasio Somoza Debayle
Niger	President Hamani Diori
Nigeria	Maj. Gen. Yakubu Gowon
Norway	Premier Per Borten
Oman	Sultan Qabus bin Said
Pakistan	President Agha Mohammed Yahya Khan
Panama	Brig. Gen. Omar Torrijos Herrera
Paraguay	President Alfredo Stroessner
Peru	Gen. Juan Velasco Alvarado
Philippines	President Ferdinand E. Marcos
Poland	Communist Party First Secretary Edward Gierek
Portugal	Premier Marcello José das Neves Alves Caetano
Rhodesia	Prime Minister Ian D. Smith
Romania	Communist Party First Secretary Nicolae Ceausescu
Rwanda	President Grégoire Kayibanda
Saudi Arabia ..	King Faisal
Senegal	President Léopold S. Senghor
Sierra Leone ...	Prime Minister Siaka Stevens
Singapore	Prime Minister Lee Kuan Yew
Somalia	Maj. Gen. Mohammed Siad Barre
South Africa ...	Prime Minister Balthazar J. Vorster
Southern Yemen	Presidential Council Chairman Salem Ali Rubaya
Spain	Generalissimo Francisco Franco
Sudan	Maj. Gen. Gaafar Mohammed al-Nimeiry
Swaziland	Prime Minister, Prince Makhosini Dlamini
Sweden	Prime Minister Olof Palme
Switzerland	President Hans-Peter Tschudi
Syria	Premier Nureddin al-Attassi
Taiwan (China, Rep. of)	President Chiang Kai-shek
Tanzania	President Julius Nyerere
Thailand	Premier Thanom Kittikachorn
Togo	President Étienne Eyadema
Tonga	Premier, Prince Tu'ipelehake
Trinidad and Tobago	Prime Minister Eric Williams
Tunisia	President Habib Bourguiba
Turkey	Prime Minister Suleyman Demirel
Uganda	President Milton Obote
Union of Soviet Socialist Reps.	Communist Party General Secretary Leonid I. Brezhnev
United Arab Rep.	President Anwar el-Sadat
United States ..	President Richard M. Nixon
Upper Volta	President Sangoulé Lamizana
Uruguay	President Jorge Pacheco Areco
Venezuela	President Rafael Caldera Rodriguez
Vietnam, North	Premier Pham Van Dong
Vietnam, South	President Nguyen Van Thieu
Western Samoa	Prime Minister Tupua Tamasese Lealofi IV
Yemen	President Abdul Rahman al-Iryani
Yugoslavia	President Tito
Zambia	President Kenneth Kaunda

WIDE WORLD

LON NOL

SALVADOR ALLENDE

LONDON "DAILY EXPRESS" FROM PICTORIAL PARADE

KEYSTONE

After leading Britain's Conservative party to victory, Edward Heath became prime minister.

HEATH, EDWARD. June 19, 1970, was moving day at No. 10 Downing Street, London, the official residence of Great Britain's prime minister, after Edward Heath and the Conservative party won a surprise victory in the June 18 general election. Before the election, public opinion polls had shown that the Labor party, headed by the incumbent Prime Minister Harold Wilson, would win by a wide margin. Just before the election, however, the polls showed that the Labor party's strength was declining.

There was much speculation about the reasons for the Conservative party's upset victory. Labor party officials preferred to believe that the confident predictions of a Labor victory by the pollsters encouraged Laborite voters to stay home. Heath and other Conservatives believed that their success was due to the policies put forward during the campaign.

While Wilson was relying on his personal image, Heath was bringing basic economic issues before the voters. Heath warned that under Labor a dire economic emergency would occur in the near future. By coincidence an unfavorable trade figure was released just before the election, and the Conservatives used this to illustrate their point and also to warn of possibly another devaluation of the British pound sterling.

During the campaign Heath promised to reduce taxes, to reform labor laws, and to streamline the government. These pledges apparently had great appeal for the voters. After taking office Heath affirmed another campaign promise—to reassert Great Britain's influence in Asia, the Middle East, and Africa. His decision to sell arms to South Africa proved controversial.

Heath, a 54-year-old bachelor, was educated at Oxford University and has had a long political career. He was first elected to Parliament in 1950 and served as minister of labor during 1959–60. From 1960–63, as lord privy seal, he was in charge of Britain's unsuccessful negotiations to join the European Economic Community, or Common Market. (*See also* Great Britain and Northern Ireland, United Kingdom of.)

HOBBIES. One of the fastest-growing hobbies in 1970 was model rocketry. One company announced that it had sold 20 million model rocket engines to boys and men of all ages. In response to the enthusiasm of rocket hobbyists, generated by the Apollo moon flights, the U.S. Marine Corps Helicopter Air Station at Santa Ana, Calif., provided a large manufacturer with a one-mile-square area for research and development work on model rocketry safety. Subsequently, all major manufacturers and the National Association of Rocketry agreed upon a code proposed by the Hobby Industry Association of America covering 14 points of safety for solid-propellant model rockets. The most important standards specify the use of lightweight materials, a gross maximum weight of 16 ounces, and a remotely controlled, electrically operated launching system.

A rock identification computer capable of identifying 127 different kinds of rocks was offered to rock collectors in 1970. Rock collecting was said to rank third among hobbies, after stamps and coins.

Car racing continued to be popular in 1970, one reason being perhaps the development of very fast HO-gauge cars, which achieved 760 scale miles per hour, a speed never recorded before. In car models the dune buggy was an extremely popular kit, along with kits of many late-model cars that enjoyed a resurgence in popularity.

Model railroading continued as a major hobby among many individuals and clubs. One dealer reported that some hobbyists spend up to $200 per month on equipment and that one customer had $450,000 invested in equipment.

In the crafts field, paint-by-number was very popular, as usual, but some dealers complained about rising prices and customer resistance. However, crafts were expanding, and one company president predicted a boom in new crafts plus increased sales in established ones.

In the northern part of the United States, snowmobiling increased in popularity, and there was an accompanying demand for safety and noise regulations. Snowmobile clubs were reported to be on the upswing. (*See in* CE: Hobbies.)

HOME ECONOMICS. Consumer education and protection once again played an important role in the field of home economics during 1970. However, the emphasis in consumer education shifted from attaining the greatest good for the individual to improving the environment for the good of the entire community.

The disclosure that the phosphates used in most laundry detergents were polluting the water supply sparked a number of reactions throughout the year. Housewives were urged to forsake "whiter than white" washes for cleaner lakes and rivers. In June the House Committee on Government Operations issued an 88-page report recommending that the detergent industry be required to discontinue the use of phosphates by 1972. Although phosphates were still on the market at year-end, several phosphate-free detergents had been introduced. One, sold by Sears, Roebuck and Co., was endorsed by former Secretary of the Interior Stewart L. Udall.

Another product inspired by the ecology movement was the Whirlpool Corporation's Trash Masher. The machine, which is the size of a small filing cabinet, is capable of compressing up to 60 gallons of garbage into a 9- by 16- by 17-inch package. The garbage is deodorized before one ton of pressure is applied to compress it.

The "kitchen of tomorrow" was shown in two variations during 1970. One, designed by British art student Ilana Henderson, is centered around a core that contains the sink, stove, refrigerator, and cupboards. Another, the creation of Swiss-Polish designer Luigi Colani, is more sophisticated. Among its features are computer-controlled cooking that utilizes a microwave oven and a television monitor to keep track of the children. In both instances the kitchen of tomorrow will require little space. Colani's model requires a circle eight feet in diameter. (*See in* CE: Home Economics and Management.)

To alleviate the housewife's trash problem, Whirlpool has designed a compactor to reduce the bulk of trash on a four-to-one ratio.

COURTESY, WHIRLPOOL CORP.

HONDURAS. Efforts were made in 1970 to resolve the hostilities between Honduras and El Salvador that erupted briefly but intensely into open warfare in mid-1969 and resulted in the severing of diplomatic relations and the curtailment of trade between the two nations. At the end of January 1970, Honduras and El Salvador each sent three delegates to San José, Costa Rica, for the first of several bilateral peace talks mediated by the former secretary-general of the Organization of American States (OAS), José A. Mora of Uruguay. Finally, at an OAS-sponsored meeting of the Central American foreign ministers in Costa Rica on June 4, Honduras and El Salvador agreed to a plan to establish a demilitarized zone (DMZ), 1.8 miles wide on either side of their common border. Costa Rica, Guatemala, and Nicaragua were designated "guarantors" of the agreement.

On July 16, 1970, one year after the war, the DMZ went into effect, and, under OAS supervision, Honduras and El Salvador withdrew their armed forces except for small security patrols in certain specified locations within the zone. Military aircraft of both nations were barred within three miles of the outer edge of the DMZ. The OAS financed the observer activities attendant to the border zone and appointed at least 30 military advisers to see that the agreement of June 4 was carried out.

The closing of the Honduras-El Salvador border resulted in serious strains on the Honduran economy that remained unresolved. Honduran agricultural exports, which traditionally have a major market in El Salvador, found no alternative buyers among the other Central American countries. Conversely, Honduras was denied access to Salvadoran industrial goods in exchange and had to seek such items elsewhere in Central America at unfavorable rates of exchange. (*See also* El Salvador. *See in* CE: Honduras.)

HOSPITALS. The U.S. Congress overrode a veto by U.S. President Richard M. Nixon in June and extended the Hill-Burton program relating to hospital construction. The program was expected to provide about $2.8 billion for three years of hospital construction or modernization. A provision of the bill directed the president to spend whatever money Congress authorized for health programs through fiscal 1973. President Nixon objected to this provision, calling it "fiscal irresponsibility."

Veterans Administration (VA) hospitals were also slated for more money in fiscal 1971. In mid-1970 a $122-million increase in VA hospital funding was passed. But the increase, 7.5% over fiscal 1970 allocations, was thought adequate only to cover the inflation-linked rise in hospital costs.

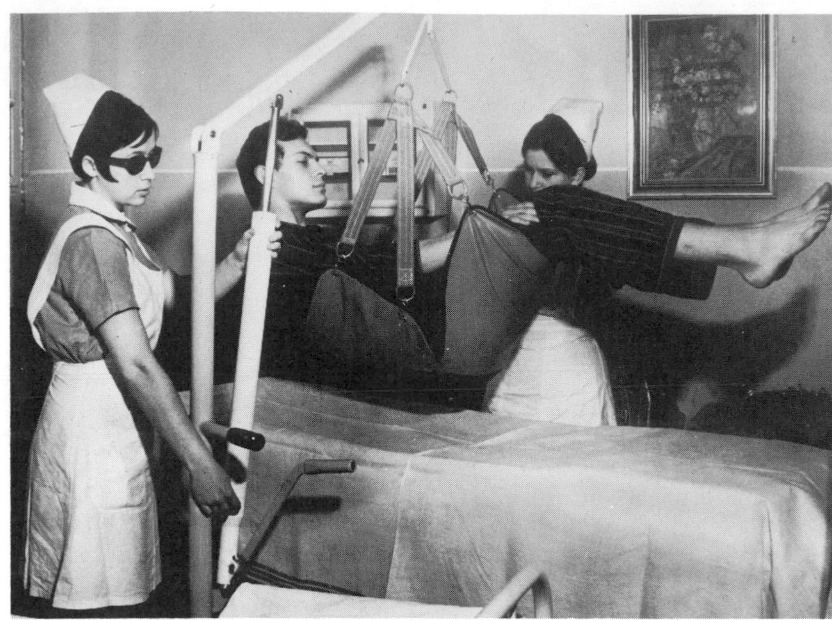

A hospital crane equipped with a hydraulic jack is being tested for transporting patients at the SKODA enterprise hospital in Plzen, Czechoslovakia.
KEYSTONE

Unchecked, hospital expenses continued to soar. By the start of 1970 the cost of an average day's stay in a community (nonfederal, short-term, general, and special) hospital was $70.03, up 10% over similar charges at the onset of 1969. The average length of stay of a patient in any of the 5,820 U.S. community hospitals was 8.1 days as 1970 began. According to the American Hospital Association, medicare patients usually had a longer hospital stay—13 days on the average.

Payrolls continued to be the major factor in skyrocketing hospital expenses. The combined outlay for salaries and for other hospital costs amounted to a total of $16.6 billion at the start of 1970.

In 1970, hospitals were trying to provide more community-directed health aid. Going out to their patients, as it were, hospitals were operating neighborhood health centers in some instances, or mobile units for the care of shut-ins in others. By far the fastest-growing hospital service was ambulatory (outpatient) care. By 1970 six persons were treated as outpatients for every person admitted to a hospital. (*See also* Medicine; Nursing. *See in* CE: Hospitals.)

HOTELS AND MOTELS.

Even though continuing inflation and the credit crunch caused many U.S. citizens in 1970 to cut back on consumer spending for durable goods (such as automobiles, refrigerators, and color television sets), their travel plans remained virtually unscathed, thus ensuring a good year for hotel and motel owners. The introduction of the Boeing 747 "jumbo jet," new bulk fares to Europe, and the lure of the Japan World Exposition, in Osaka, all contributed to a substantial increase in foreign travel.

Despite the high cost of borrowing money, construction of new hotels and motels both in the United States and abroad continued at a generally rapid pace, with chain organizations such as Hilton, Sheraton, and Holiday Inns accounting for the bulk of this activity. According to the American Hotel and Motel Association, the giants of the industry in 1970 were five hotel-motel chains that operated 250 or more lodging establishments each. More than half of the association's 7,500 members were affiliated with a chain.

An innovation in hotel-motel construction was the tri-arc configuration pioneered by TraveLodge International in its $3-million, 212-room property in Atlanta, Ga., which opened in April. Adopted as the key to TraveLodge's expansion program over the next five to seven years, the tri-arc design was to be repeated in 180 nine-story TraveLodge motor hotels planned for construction in the United States and Canada. The tri-arc design permits each room to have a view, and the wedge shape of guest rooms permits each to have an unusually large bath and dressing area. The central core of the tri-arc motor hotel contains elevators, linen rooms, utilities, vending machines, and ice-cube areas.

The completion of a planned addition of 1,250 rooms to the New York Hilton would return the title of the largest (3,400 rooms) hotel in the world to the United States. The honor passed during the year from the Conrad Hilton in Chicago to the 3,128-room Rossiya Hotel in Moscow.

A 38-story, 1,300-room hotel, the Ala Moana, was being built in Honolulu, Hawaii, by the lodging subsidiary of American Airlines. When finished, it would be Hawaii's tallest building.

In Tokyo the new 900-room Imperial Hotel opened its doors on March 10. It replaced the

Frank Lloyd Wright structure of the same name that was razed in 1967.

With demand for lodging accommodations at a record high, Holiday Inns announced a goal of 3,000 motels to be built worldwide in the next ten years; Ramada Inns planned 1,000 properties in the next five years; and Sheraton, Loew's, Western International, Hilton, and Hyatt Corp. planned as many as 100 new hotels each in the United States and overseas in the next few years. Loew's first European hotel, the 489-room, nine-story Churchill in London, was opened in May.

Computerized systems, which make it possible to get immediately confirmed lodging reservations by dialing toll-free telephone numbers, experienced tremendous growth during the year. The largest of these systems maintains availability data on, and confirms bookings for, more than 450,000 rooms in chain and independent hotels and motels in the United States and abroad.

WIDE WORLD

A youth fights eviction of his family. The Chicago police were called to assist the sheriff in serving eviction notices to families of the Contract Buyers League who withheld payments to get renegotiated contracts.

HOUSING. During 1970 the prospects for housing in the United States brightened despite a general slowdown in the economy. Beginning the year at a rate of fewer than 1.1 million units annually, housing starts had risen to a seasonally adjusted annual rate of 1.5 million units by the end of September. Total housing starts for the year were estimated at approximately 1.4 million units.

An office building in New York City has been transformed into Westbeth artists' housing with loft-type living and working units.

LAWRENCE FRIED

The upturn in the number of housing starts was largely attributable to the influence of the federal government. By one estimate, about 43% of new housing units started during 1970 were to be built under some kind of federal program. The fastest-growing type of federal support to housing was in the form of direct subsidies to help low- and middle-income families rent or buy.

The Emergency Home Finance Act of 1970 provided a $250-million appropriation to the Federal Home Loan Bank System to allow member lending institutions to provide homeowners with mortgages at 7%. Similar powers were accorded the Federal National Mortgage Association and the Federal Home Loan Mortgage Corp. The latter two organizations were also enabled to become secondary markets for conventional mortgages.

Another housing bill was passed by the U.S. Senate in September and passed a test vote in the House of Representatives in a compromise version in December. The provisions of the bill included the development of a "new cities" program outside urban centers, expansion of existing housing and urban renewal programs, and the authorization of federal crime insurance, if needed, for areas with a high crime rate.

In February George Romney, secretary of housing and urban development (HUD), unveiled 22 building designs that were chosen as prototypes for

(continued on page 289)

Special Report: Tenants on the Move

by Peter C. Stuart,
Staff Correspondent, Washington, D.C.,
Christian Science Monitor

When an apartment tenant signs his lease, he enters an arrangement that is little different from the kind that once bound feudal serfs to their landlords. The intervening centuries have righted, one by one, many of the historic imbalances between man and woman, employee and employer, black person and white. But the tenant-landlord relationship has somehow withstood the tides of reform. Until now, that is.

In the last several years the time-encrusted laws slanted toward landlords have begun to tumble before an onslaught by local organizers, civil rights activists, and the courts. This is a development of far-reaching significance in the United States, now becoming more a nation of tenants. Today, one citizen in three rents his housing. And as population and land values explode, proportionately more will do so.

Protest Organizations

Beginning in the slums of New York City's Harlem in 1963 and 1964, tenants started to organize and strike—successfully—against exploitive landlords. Their grievances, and those of renters in other ghettos and barrios, were fundamental: peeling plaster, broken plumbing, worn-out furnaces, rat bites, and similar complaints. Before long they were joined by another group of tenants—middle-income residents—with a far different set of complaints: dirty swimming pools, undependable air conditioning, exorbitant rent hikes. More recently, college and university students became the third element in the movement; their tenant activity differs from that of the other two in its radicalism.

Tenants have organized chiefly in urban areas, and particularly in the East and Midwest, where apartment living is most extensive. But tenant organizations have sprung up in virtually all major cities and in most states.

The rapid growth of these organizations is illustrated by the flowering of the National Tenants Organization (NTO). Its roots may be traced to a fund made available for a tenants' rights program by the American Friends Service Committee. A leader of that program was Anthony R. Henry, who also worked for the Southern Christian Leadership Conference and later became director of NTO.

Three hundred tenants turned out for the NTO organizational convention in St. Louis, Mo., in October 1969. One year later each of its four regional conferences attracted at least that many persons.

The growth of the NTO—which counted more than 150 local affiliates at mid-1970—has occurred largely spontaneously. The group supported a staff of only three full-time employees and two volunteers, all in Washington, D.C.

Despite its success, NTO embraced a scant 1% of the nation's tenants. In an effort to reach more, the organization opened its first regional office—in Atlanta, Ga.—in September 1970.

An estimated 60% of the organized tenants lived in public housing. Their poverty and centralized landlord (a local housing authority) seemed to facilitate organization. The remaining 40% who lived in private housing, on the other hand, were economically more secure, and the distribution of their landlords dispersed accountability. Yet private, middle-income apartment buildings in the District of Columbia, for example, were organizing at the rate of one or two a week.

Each individual tenant organization, of course, has its own specific objectives. But all share, in varying degrees, the overall goal of the entire tenants' rights movement. It is a goal borrowed directly from the establishment, as articulated in the Housing Act of 1949: "a decent home and a suitable living environment for every American family." More specifically, the NTO lists seven objectives in its "Tenants Bill of Rights":

1. Rent control
2. Tenant organization, recognition, and bargaining rights over the terms of tenancy
3. Social and economic integration of all housing
4. Notice and the right to a hearing on general rent increases
5. National housing code standards
6. No rent due if those standards are not met
7. All housing should be beautiful

Tenants' rights proponents do not, however, confine themselves strictly to housing issues. They see themselves as part of a larger movement—what used to be called the civil rights movement and what now might be termed the "power to the people" movement.

UPI COMPIX

Jesse Gray, a National Tenants Organization (NTO) leader, addresses a rally in the Harlem district of New York City. In 1970 the NTO confronted public housing authorities in Chicago; St. Louis, Mo.; and New York City with demands for important administrative reforms.

At the local level, tenants' rights groups often are indistinguishable from welfare rights organizations, so closely are the two intertwined. Tenant groups also commonly work with such organizations as the Urban Coalition, the National Urban League, and legal aid societies.

Rent Strikes, Legislation, Court Cases

In pursuing their goals, organized tenants possess weapons of several calibers. The ultimate one remains the rent strike. In the movement's beginnings, when tenant groups had to battle for recognition, the strike was virtually the only weapon. The most sensational—and one of the most successful—convulsed St. Louis for nine bitter months in 1969. It ended when the local public housing authority, nearly bankrupt, consented to roll back rents for 1,000 tenant families.

There has not, however, been a major rent strike since then. Tenant leaders say the strikes have decreased simply because they are so effective—the mere threat of a city-wide strike is sufficient. "Our validity is better now," explained an NTO official. "We can get recognition without striking."

Instead, tenants are turning increasingly to two other approaches: legislation and court cases. The change sweeping the movement is typified by the transformation of Jesse Gray from a leader of the then-revolutionary Harlem rent strikes of 1963 and 1964 into a testifier (as chairman of the NTO) before prestigious congressional committees. "You don't hit home runs in this game," said a Washington, D.C., tenants' rights lawyer, B. Michael Rauh. "You win bits and pieces at a time." Even so, the movement has scored well in the courts.

A major victory has been the erosion of the legal principle—handed down from medieval England—that a tenant owes rent regardless of the physical condition of his housing. A federal court in the District of Columbia ruled in May 1970 that a tenant may withhold part or all of his rent if the state of the dwelling violates the local housing code. The U.S. Supreme Court upheld this ruling in November.

The courts have also charged landlords with another new responsibility in behalf of their tenants: protecting them from criminal intruders. A District of Columbia federal court in August held the owners and management of a Washington luxury apartment building liable for damages sought by a tenant who had been assaulted and robbed in one of the hallways.

Although court victories stir the most drama, organized tenants have won many successes

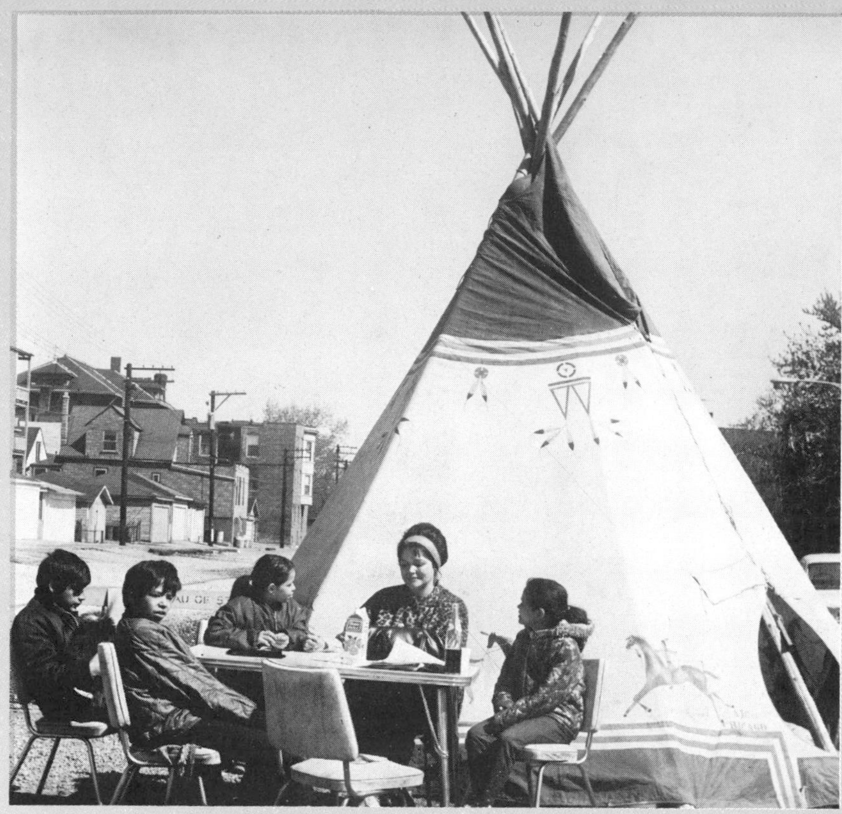

Carol Warrington, a Menominee Indian, camps in a tent in front of her former residence in Chicago. She was evicted from her apartment for refusing to pay rent for inadequate housing.
UPI COMPIX

through quiet consultation. Tenants, as represented by the NTO, sat on an American Bar Association commission drafting a uniform national housing code. If adopted nationwide, as intended, the uniform code would protect tenants from encountering uneven housing standards as they move from one community to another.

The NTO also helped draw up a model lease and grievance procedure for public housing developments supervised by the U.S. Department of Housing and Urban Development (HUD). The model lease would correct many chronic sources of tenant friction:

1. Tenants could no longer be evicted under the blanket term "just cause," but only for failure to pay rent or for interference with other tenants.
2. "Confession of judgment" and "waiver of liability" clauses would be eliminated.
3. Leases would be perpetual, permitting law-abiding tenants to stay as long as they wished.

Tenants also are winning friends—and friendly legislation—in Congress. Senator Edward W. Brooke (R, Mass.) added a provision to the 1969 housing bill to underwrite operating deficits of local housing authorities and limit public housing rents to 25% of a tenant's income (affecting nearly one fourth of all tenants). Implementation of the Brooke provision, however, has disappointed many.

The NTO sued HUD in April for allegedly permitting rents above the new ceiling. Senator Brooke charged in July that the Administration of U.S. President Richard M. Nixon had requested only $33 million of the $75 million authorized for fiscal 1971—while admitting that housing authority deficits alone reached $100 million.

Two congressmen even joined the ranks of rent strikers. Representatives Frank Annunzio (D, Ill.) and Thomas S. Gettys (D, S.C.) were among some 100 striking tenants in a Washington, D.C., luxury apartment building who were served with notices to leave by the landlord in June. Representative Annunzio responded by introducing a series of bills to install rent control in the District of Columbia. The bills languished in committee.

Tenant Involvement in Policy Making

Public housing tenants are increasingly being given the opportunity to try their hands at being "landlords." Commissioners who set policy for most public housing developments have little in common with their tenants. They tend to be older and to be either white businessmen or labor union leaders. A vast "understanding gap" results.

Tenants are beginning to ask—and win permission—to serve on these policy-making commissions. At last count, a dozen cities included tenants on their housing boards. They range from major cities such as Boston, Mass.; Providence, R.I.; New Haven, Conn.; and St. Louis to smaller communities like Catskill, N.Y.; Cumberland, Md.; and Columbia, Mo.

(*continued from page 285*)
housing to be built under Operation Breakthrough. The designs were chosen from a field of 236 entries in a national competition. All employ prefabricated components that can be assembled with a minimum of delay.

The year also saw a number of proposals for alleviating the problem of housing for the poor. In the face of growing pressures to open suburban housing to low-income blacks, the U.S. Department of Justice brought an increasing number of suits against real estate companies, housing developers, and local governments for restrictive housing practices. In the period from October 1969 to July 1970 Justice Department lawyers filed 33 cases, a number of which attacked local zoning ordinances against low-income housing on the grounds that they were used in a discriminatory manner. In a landmark decision in February, the Pennsylvania Supreme Court struck down a local ordinance banning the construction of a high-rise apartment building in Providence Township, Pa.

In November it was announced that HUD was developing a standard lease and grievance procedure for tenants of public housing across the nation. (*See also* Building Construction. *See in* CE: Housing.)

KEYSTONE

Hungary's Minister of Defense Gen. Lajos Czinege inspects flood damage and reassures an aged farmer who was one of many hit hard by the disastrous May–June floods.

HUNGARY. In 1970 Hungarians celebrated the anniversaries of two major events in their nation's history. On April 4, the 25th anniversary of Hungary's liberation from German occupation by the Soviet Army was marked by a massive parade in Budapest, the capital. Warsaw Pact troops, Hungarian workers, athletes, youths, and floats depicting Hungary's progress under Communism were reviewed by the Communist party leaders of Hungary, the Soviet Union, and other Eastern European countries. In addition, Hungary granted amnesty to persons convicted of minor crimes and of leaving the country illegally. A new subway was inaugurated in Budapest.

Secular and religious celebrations marked the 1,000th anniversary of the birth of King Stephen I on August 20. The founder of Hungary, Stephen was also a Roman Catholic saint known for introducing his people to Christianity.

Hungary's economy continued to operate under economic reforms established in 1968. In May the government decreed shorter working hours for persons in jobs holding health hazards. A five-year plan for 1971–75, adopted by the Central Committee of the Hungarian Socialist Workers' party in July, stressed modernization of energy resources, transport, and building methods; the manufacture of aluminum, chemicals, trucks, and buses; increased animal husbandry; the utilization of computers; and modern methods of organization and management.

A government decree of March 3 granted Hungarian citizens the right to have passports. Although numerous exceptions were listed and some restrictions on travel were made, the law was considered unique for an Eastern European country.

During 1970 Hungary established diplomatic relations with the Central African Republic and ended an 18-month diplomatic break with Algeria. Economic agreements were made with Peru and the Soviet Union. Hungary was one of several Eastern European nations struck by floods that began in May. (*See in* CE: Hungary.)

ICE HOCKEY. The Boston Bruins won the National Hockey League (NHL) Stanley Cup in 1970—their first in 29 years. Highlighting the triumph was the brilliant play of Bobby Orr, 22-year-old Bruin defenseman, who won four individual trophies during the 1969–70 season and in the cup play-offs. Orr captured the Art Ross Trophy and $2,000 for his NHL scoring record of 120 points, 33 goals, and 87 assists; the Hart Trophy and $1,500 as the most valuable player in hockey; and the James Norris Memorial Trophy and $1,500 as the best defenseman in the game. He also won the Conn Smythe Trophy and $1,500 for his brilliant performance in the Stanley Cup play-offs.

Boston's cup triumph was achieved by downing the St. Louis Blues in four straight games in the finals. The Bruins gained the finals by besting the New York Rangers (four games to two) and the Chicago Black Hawks (four games to none), while the Blues were sweeping the Western Division with four games to two over both Minnesota and Pittsburgh.

Tony Esposito, Chicago goalkeeper, won the Calder Memorial Trophy as the NHL's outstand-

RIGHT: KEYSTONE. BELOW: WIDE WORLD

Swedish players rejoice after scoring (right) during a match with the Soviet Union in the world ice hockey amateur championships, held in Stockholm, Sweden, in March. Sweden won the match, but for the eighth straight year the U.S.S.R. won the championship. The Boston Bruins (below) won the 1970 Stanley Cup despite a penalty in the first period of the game for the blow their goalie struck at #20 of the St. Louis Blues.

ing freshman and the Vezina Trophy for allowing the fewest goals. Phil Goyette of St. Louis won the Lady Byng Trophy for outstanding play.

Named to the all-star first team by the NHL writers and broadcasters were goalie, Tony Esposito, Chicago; defense, Orr, Boston, and Brad Park, New York; center, Phil Esposito, Boston; right wing, Gordie Howe, Detroit; and left wing, Bobby Hull, Chicago, who was also named hockey's athlete of the 1960 decade.

Other Pro Developments

Two new teams were added to the league during the year for a total of 14—the Vancouver Canucks and the Buffalo Sabres, each admitted for $6 million. Realignments for the coming season included shifting Chicago to the Western Division and adding Vancouver and Buffalo to the Eastern Division. Charles O. Finley, owner of the Oakland Athletics baseball team, became the new owner of the Oakland Seals.

In minor league play, Vancouver beat the Portland Buckaroos 4–1 for the Western League crown, while the Buffalo Bisons shut out the Springfield Kings 4–0 in the American League. The Omaha Knights won the Central League title by downing the Iowa Stars 4–1.

The hockey world was saddened in late May by the death of Terry Sawchuk, a 21-year veteran who was considered by many to be the greatest goalie of all time.

Amateur Ice Hockey

In amateur play-offs held at Stockholm, Sweden, in March, the U.S.S.R. won the world and European titles for the eighth successive year. Sweden finished in the runner-up spot, followed by Czechoslovakia, Finland, East Germany, and Poland. Canada, which had been scheduled to be the host team, dropped out of the competition when the International Olympic Committee ruled in January that national teams that included professionals would be disqualified for the XI Winter Olympic Games in 1972.

The National Collegiate Athletic Association championship, played at Lake Placid, N.Y., in March, was won by Cornell University. (*See in* CE: Ice Hockey.)

ICELAND. The events of 1970 in Iceland were overshadowed by a personal and public tragedy. In the early hours of the morning on July 10 Iceland's Premier Bjarni Benediktsson, his wife, and their four-year-old grandson died in a fire at the official summer residence at Thingvellir. The cause of the fire was not known. Campers nearby spotted the blaze and called the fire department at Reykjavik, the capital. The campers also reported that there had been an explosion. The house was completely destroyed before firemen arrived on the scene. Reportedly the wooden structure, built in 1907, burned to the ground in about 15 minutes.

President Kristjan Eldjarn appointed Johann Hafstein, the minister of justice and industry, acting premier of the Independence party-Social Democratic party coalition government, pending the elections scheduled for the spring of 1971. Benediktsson had led the government since 1963.

On March 1, 1970, Iceland became a member of the European Free Trade Association. The event seemed likely to spur plans for diversifying the economy by encouraging new industries.

Mount Hekla began erupting on May 5 and was active for several weeks but did little damage. Tourism became an increasingly important economic factor. An estimated 55,000 persons visited Iceland during 1970 (not including passengers from cruise liners). (*See in* CE: Iceland.)

ICE SKATING. The world ice-dance and figure-skating championships were held at the Tivoli Sports Hall, Ljubljana, Yugoslavia, on March 3–7, 1970. Fifteen nations were represented by 112 skaters.

Tim Wood of the United States impressively retained his men's title after a crucial tussle with Ondrej Nepela of Czechoslovakia, the European champion, who led after the compulsory figures segment of the competition. In free-style, Wood, from Michigan, included a great triple salchow, an extra-high split lutz, a triple toe-loop jump, and an originally positioned jump-parallel spin.

Gabriele Seyfert of East Germany successfully defended her women's crown, leaving no doubt about her free-style supremacy. She gave a flawless display to overtake with ease the earlier lead established in the figures by Beatrix Schuba of Austria, who was runner-up.

The pairs title was narrowly retained by Alek Ulanov and Irina Rodnina of the Soviet Union. They withstood a spirited challenge from their compatriots Andrei Suraikin and Ludmila Smirnova. The margin would have been more comfortable had Ulanov not fallen during a combination jump.

Aleksandr Gorshkov and Ludmila Pakhomova of the Soviet Union captured the vacant ice-dance title, the first Soviet victory in this event. In the closest finish of the meeting, they scored only one tenth of a point more than James Sladky and Judy Schwomeyer of the United States, the judges voting 5–4 for the winners.

Memories of Donald Jackson's 1962 amateur triumph were revived in the 14th world professional championships, at Wembley, England, on April 17. Jackson, a Canadian, again won the men's title and proved that, at 30, he had lost none of his rare ability to gain spectacular elevation. Hana Maskova of Czechoslovakia scored the first victory for her country in the women's contest. British partnerships—Raymond Wilson with Linda Bernard and Ian Phillips with Yvonne Sudick—won the pairs and ice-dance events respectively.

The year's outstanding speed-skating achievements were dominated by the Netherlands performers. Ard Schenk became overall world men's champion in Oslo, Norway, on February 14–15, and his compatriot Atje Keulen-Deelstra gained the women's title at West Allis, Wis., on February 28–March 1.

Magne Thomassen of Norway won the men's 500-meter sprint. Schenk took the 1,500-meter, and another Dutchman, Jan Bols, was first in both

Gabriele Seyfert (far left) and Ludmila Titova were champion skaters in 1970.

FAR LEFT: "PARIS MATCH" FROM PICTORIAL PARADE. LEFT: WIDE WORLD the 5,000-meter and the 10,000-meter. Although judged the best all-around performer, Mrs. Keulen-Deelstra failed to win any of the four women's events. Ludmila Titova of the Soviet Union won the 500-meter and tied for first place in the 1,000-meter with Sigrid Sundby of Norway. The 1,500-meter and the 3,000-meter were both won by yet another Dutch skater, Johanna (Ans) Schut.

Although the championships themselves produced no new records, previous best world times were lowered during the season, ten times by men and five times by women. Hasse Björjes of Sweden raced the fastest-ever 500-meter in 38.46 seconds, at Inzell, West Germany, on March 8. Valeri Muratov of the Soviet Union lowered the 1,000-meter record to 1 minute 19.25 seconds at Alma-Ata, U.S.S.R., on January 25. Cornelis Verkerk of the Netherlands reduced the best 1,500-meter time to 2 minutes 1.9 seconds at Inzell on March 8, and Bols became the fastest man to cover 3,000 meters, clocking 4 minutes 16.4 seconds at Cortina, Italy, on January 27. (*See in* CE: Skates and Skating.)

IMMIGRATION AND CITIZENSHIP. Efforts to revise the U.S. immigration laws enacted in 1965 gained momentum during 1970. This movement, which received support in the U.S. Congress and from U.S. President Richard M. Nixon, resulted from the unforeseen consequences of the 1965 law. The 1965 statute was a wholesale alteration of the immigration laws that had been in effect since the 1920's. The new system wiped out the old entry quotas based on the country of origin and instead established a system of "preferences" designed to reunite families and to favor needed occupations.

After a gradual introduction, the new system went into full effect on July 1, 1968, and immediately revealed consequences that set in motion the follow-up drive for revision. A clear result of the new law was a shift in the patterns of immigration into the United States away from such countries as Great Britain, Ireland, and West Germany toward a heavier influx from the Philippines, Italy, Greece, Portugal, and other nations which formerly had not been allowed as many entries under the old national-origin quotas. A ceiling of 120,000 placed on entries from the Western Hemisphere for the first time also radically restricted immigration into the United States from that part of the world. As a result of these new laws, heavy backlogs of visa applications occurred for certain countries.

"We're not going to make the same mistake the North American Indians made!"

ULUSCHAK, "EDMONTON JOURNAL," FROM BEN ROTH AGENCY

Such patterns emerged as soon as the 1965 laws went into effect and continued into 1970. According to preliminary figures by the U.S. Department of State, the number of visas issued during fiscal 1970 for non-Western Hemisphere countries showed that the Philippines led the list of countries of origin for immigrants into the United States with 25,425, followed by Italy with 24,481, Greece with 16,542, Nationalist China with 16,297, and Great Britain and Northern Ireland with 13,925. They were followed by Portugal, India, Korea, West Germany, and Yugoslavia. The fiscal 1970 ranking for Western Hemisphere countries was as follows: Mexico, Cuba, Jamaica, Canada, Dominican Republic, Haiti, Colombia, Trinidad and Tobago, Ecuador, and Argentina.

INDIA. In 1970 Indira Gandhi, India's prime minister, continued to stir up controversy with her political moves and methods. The nationalization of the nation's banks ran into a legal snag. The status of former rulers of princely states was contested. The Union cabinet was shaken up and reformed. Three new states were added. Taxes were increased during the year.

Domestic Affairs

In 1970 there was a gradual polarization of the political parties, based not around ideology but around support or opposition to Mrs. Gandhi. The Organization Congress (the faction of the party bosses) drew closer to the Jan Sangh and the Swatantra party and, with the support of the Samyukta Socialist party and the Communist party (Marxist), repeatedly offered battle in Parliament and outside that body to the Ruling Congress of Mrs. Gandhi—which in turn was backed by the Communist party of India, the Dravida Munnetra Kazhagam, the Muslim League, and the Akali Dal. Through a series of swift policy initiatives and political moves, Mrs. Gandhi established greater personal ascendancy on the political scene, arousing intense feeling.

Both factions of the Congress held plenary sessions just before the year opened. The Ruling Congress elected Jagjivan Ram as its president. Its session, held in Bombay, adopted a radical program involving ceilings on urban property, an extension of state trading to more commodities, and a takeover of the sugar industry in Uttar Pradesh.

Two rival groups of Sikhs clash outside the Oberoi Intercontinental Hotel in New Delhi, India, May 18. The short scuffle occurred an hour before Sant Fateh Singh, the top authority of Sikhism, was due to arrive for a reception. The two groups were for and against Sant.

LONDON "DAILY EXPRESS" FROM PICTORIAL PARADE

Nationalization of banks, which lit the fuse for the preceding year's split in the Congress party, was declared invalid by the Supreme Court on Feb. 10, 1970. In a ten-to-one judgment, the court held that while nationalization was within the competence of Parliament, the compensation given to the banks under the 1969 act did not fulfill the provisions of Article 31 of the constitution.

In a speech to the joint session of Parliament on February 20, India's President Varahagiri Venkata Giri declared that the government would introduce a bill to amend the constitution to do away with the privy purses and privileges of former rulers of princely states. These payments and privileges (such as exemption from taxation, gun salutes, and the right to fly a personal flag) had been agreed to when the princely states were integrated with the rest of the country at the time of independence. Their abolition was one of the items in the ten-point program adopted by the undivided Congress.

The home minister, Y. B. Chavan, introduced the 24th Constitution Amendment Bill in the Lok Sabha (House of the People) on May 18 to delete the clauses relating to the princes. The bill was adopted by the Lok Sabha early in September by 339 votes to 154, though it became a rallying point for all groups that opposed the government. But in the Rajya Sabha (Council of States), where the membership of the Ruling Congress was depleted owing to the biennial elections, the voting was 149 for and 75 against, and the measure thus failed to secure the two-thirds majority required for constitutional amendment. This was perhaps the biggest setback so far for Mrs. Gandhi's government.

Within hours, however, the president, on the advice of the cabinet, signed letters withdrawing recognition of the princes. This action was taken on the opinion of the law officers that the president had the power to recognize the princes, and that once the recognition was withdrawn, payments and privileges automatically ceased. The princes filed petitions in the Supreme Court, which ruled in their favor in December. Mrs. Gandhi promised to seek legislative means of removing princely privileges as soon as possible.

Another major event of the year was the reshuffle of the Union cabinet on June 26. Mrs. Gandhi transferred the finance office to Chavan and took over the home office from him. Jagjivan Ram was

Indians plant trees along the banks of the Maithon multipurpose dam, built with funds from a World Bank loan, in the Damodar Valley.

AUTHENTICATED NEWS INTERNATIONAL

made defense minister. Fakhruddin Ali Ahmed was moved to food and agriculture, Swaran Singh to external affairs, and Dinesh Singh to industrial development. Mrs. Gandhi also formed a political affairs committee of five (consisting of herself, Chavan, Ram, Swaran Singh, and Ahmed) to make decisions on domestic and foreign policy matters. The reshuffle was seen as evidence of growing power for the prime minister.

On December 27, President Giri dissolved the Parliament at Mrs. Gandhi's request. New elections were to be held early in 1971. This was the first time since independence in 1947 that an election was called mid-term. Mrs. Gandhi said that she hoped to gain a new mandate for her policies.

There were important developments in the states. In West Bengal, the united front government collapsed in March after a long period of feuding between the dominant Communist party (Marxist) group and the group led by the chief minister, Ajoy Mukerjee. In Punjab, a split in the Akali Dal forced Gurnam Singh out of the chief ministership in March, and a government was formed headed by P. S. Badal. In Kerala, the coalition government headed by Achuta Menon of the Communist party of India resigned in June and advised the governor to hold midterm elections. These led to a significant realignment of forces in the states and perhaps in the country. Polling took place on September 17. The results showed a sharp increase in the number of seats held by the Ruling Congress and a decline in the strength of the Communist party (Marxist). A coalition government, headed again by Achuta Menon, took office on October 4 with the Ruling Congress remaining outside the coalition but offering it support.

The Union government decided to grant statehood to the federally administered territories of Himachal Pradesh, Manipur, and Tripura. In April, the autonomous state of Meghalaya within Assam came into being, and a government headed by Williamson Sangma was sworn in.

In several states, leftist parties launched a "land grab" movement in August to seize large agricultural holdings and redistribute them among the landless. In May, serious Hindu-Muslim riots occurred in the towns of Bhiwandi and Jalgaon in Maharashtra. Naxalites (extreme leftists) continued to create violent incidents in West Bengal and other states.

The Economy

The budget of the Union government, presented by Mrs. Gandhi on February 28, increased excise duties on luxury articles and direct taxes on incomes and wealth, especially urban property. Holding "growth with social justice" to be its aim, it outlined schemes for helping small farmers while letting off the corporate sector lightly.

Agricultural production and prospects during the year were good, despite floods in several states. Grain production in the agricultural year 1969–70 was estimated around 104 million metric tons. Prices of both food articles and industrial raw materials rose. The general index of wholesale prices stood at 184 on September 12, compared to 174.8 on Sept. 13, 1969, a rise of 5.3%.

A number of measures were taken to enlarge the public sector and reduce economic concentration and disparities. These included the appointment of a monopolies commission and a committee to investigate tax evasion, the formation of a cotton corporation to administer the import trade in cotton, and the passage of a long-proposed patents bill, which fixed the royalty payable at 4% and the life of a patent at five years.

The country's first nuclear power station was formally inaugurated at Tarapur, Maharashtra, in January. An important scientific achievement was the success of the Indian Atomic Energy Commission in separating uranium 233 from thorium.

Foreign Affairs

The prime minister participated in the conference of nonaligned countries in Lusaka, Zambia, in September and in the silver-jubilee ceremonies of the United Nations (UN) in New York City in October. It was announced that India would sponsor Bhutan's membership in the UN. The closing of U.S. cultural centers at the demand of the foreign office caused much controversy.

Some progress was made in negotiations with Pakistan to settle the eastern waters dispute. At talks held in July in Delhi, it was agreed that waters from the Ganges River would be supplied to Pakistan at Farakka and that the volume would be decided at a separate meeting to be held within six months. There was considerable anxiety over the steady flow of refugees from East Pakistan, estimated at 200,000 during the first nine months of the year. (*See also* Asia; Pakistan. *See in* CE: India.)

INDIANS, AMERICAN.

Efforts by American Indians to gain settlements for lands taken from them, to protect rights granted them under various treaties, and to improve their standard of living intensified during 1970. There were protests and demonstrations staged by Indians in almost every part of the United States. In addition, U.S. President Richard M. Nixon gave his support to the Indians in their struggle, and some progress was made during the year.

Militant Indians continued their occupation of Alcatraz island, off San Francisco, Calif. Early in the year the Indians announced plans for building a university and turning the island into a cultural center. In March they requested a federal grant of almost $300,000 to help finance the project. The government rejected the proposal and in May announced that the island would be converted into a national park that would emphasize Indian culture. The Indians rejected the government's counterproposal and said they would go ahead with their plan in spite of the government.

In an effort to force the Indians off the island, electricity and water supplies were cut off. Several fires broke out on the island during the year, which the Indians claimed were set by white men. The government accused the Indians of having attacked U.S. Coast Guard boats with bows and arrows and warned that if such incidents continued the Indians would be removed by force.

An attempt to take over Ellis Island in Upper New York Bay in March failed when the motorboat carrying a group of Indians broke down. The Coast Guard was alerted and set up a security zone around the island.

Groups of Indians attempted to take over Fort Lawton and invaded Fort Lewis, military bases near Seattle, Wash. More than 70 persons were arrested by the military police, including the actress Jane Fonda. In June Indians in San Francisco tried to arrest the president of the Pacific Gas and Electric Co. They charged that the company was trespassing on land in northern California that legally belonged to Indians.

The Navajo nation made plans to sue several Western and Southwestern states over water rights. A dispute over fishing rights on the Puyallup River in Washington led to clashes between the police and Indians in September. Protests and demonstrations also occurred in Niagara Falls, N.Y.; in Denver, Colo.; and on reservations in North and South Dakota.

Thanksgiving Day was designated an unofficial day of mourning for American Indians. In Massachusetts about 200 Indians staged a demonstration during which they buried Plymouth Rock under sand and boarded the replica of the Mayflower.

President Nixon in July proposed a new policy toward American Indians. He suggested that Indians assume control over federal aid programs and renounced the government's policy of terminating the special status accorded to Indians. He also urged the U.S. Congress to increase substantially the amounts of money allocated for Indian aid and development programs.

In December the Senate returned 48,000 acres of Kit Carson National Forest in New Mexico to the Taos Pueblo Indians. The land area included Blue Lake, which was considered sacred by the Indians. The return of the Blue Lake area was remarkable

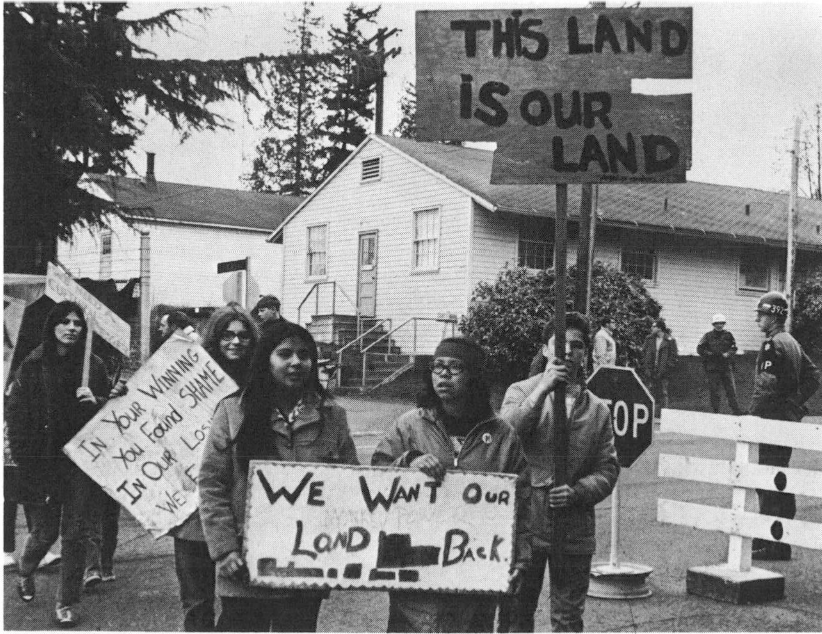

Young Indians picket the U.S. Army's Fort Lawton March 16, in Seattle, Wash., as MPs guard the fort. Earlier, 72 Indians were arrested when they "invaded" the fort.

ABOVE: GRAHAM, "ARKANSAS GAZETTE," FROM BEN ROTH AGENCY.
LEFT: WIDE WORLD

since ordinarily the government's policy was to pay cash for lost lands but not return them.

The government awarded the Seminole Indians more than $12 million for the land taken from them in the 19th century. The land area, however, covered almost all of Florida, and the Seminoles had asked for $47.9 million.

The Osage Indians were awarded more than $13 million for lands in Arkansas, Kansas, Missouri, and Oklahoma. The Indian Claims Commission in June upheld land claims of the Navajo and Hopi Indians, and plans were made to reimburse them.

The Senate in July voted a settlement for Alaskan natives of $1 billion and 10 million acres. A preliminary injunction was granted against the construction of the Alaska pipeline through Indian-claimed lands. Indians in Canada were concerned about a proposed government plan to end the special legal status of Indians. (*See also* Conservation Special Report. *See in* CE: Indians, American.)

Two Seminole Indians enjoy the Florida Everglades. The Indian Claims Commission awarded $12.3 million to the Seminole tribe for land taken from them some 150 years ago.

PICTORIAL PARADE

HARRY VOLK FROM PICTORIAL PARADE

Shirley Garcia, a public relations officer, checks food and clothing sent to her fellow Indians occupying Alcatraz.

INDONESIA. In 1970 Indonesia observed the 25th anniversary of its proclamation of independence, a milestone that found the country remarkably stable and unified. This state of affairs vividly contrasted with the almost uninterrupted series of vest-pocket rebellions, political upheavals, economic chaos, and social disarray that had marked earlier years of independence.

The contrast between the past and the present was symbolized by the death in June of Sukarno, the flamboyant, demagogic former president, who was removed from power following an abortive, Communist-oriented putsch in 1965 to which he was privy. (What exactly his part was in the putsch was never revealed by the government. However, it was obviously regarded as significant since Sukarno was not buried in Indonesia's cemetery for national heroes.) Sukarno's death found his quiet, modest presidential successor, Gen. Suharto, still embroiled in the myriad of problems left from the tumultuous Sukarno era, notably, corruption, army domination of politics, a disorganized bureaucracy, and a sluggish economy.

Domestic Events

In the course of 1970 the honeymoon between Suharto and the country's student and intellectual groups waned, though he still commanded their strong support. The government was strongly criticized for its failure to combat massive corruption. Amid demands for action Suharto finally established an advisory committee to look into the charges. The committee's report, which was not made public, apparently uncovered large-scale corruption in government departments, particularly involving the army.

Suharto was then caught in a dilemma; he was fearful of weakening his position by moving against his fellow army officers and fearful that student discontent would lead to demonstrations of the character that had helped topple Sukarno. Meeting with student leaders, Suharto quieted their clamor and achieved their support with the slogan "Let things proceed slowly, provided they are proceeding and achieve their goal," which in fact characterized Suharto's entire approach to governing. In October, three months after the student conference, Suharto announced a housecleaning of the army; more than 80 officers were pensioned off, though Suharto did not characterize their removal as a purge. Throughout the year preparations for the 1971 general elections, the second in Indonesian history, proceeded smoothly. Through a complicated system of appointed members to parliament and other devices, Suharto and the army would retain effective power probably into 1978, whatever the electoral outcome. However, the elections were considered important since they marked another step forward in Suharto's program to fully restore representative government.

The Economy

A notable achievement in 1970 was holding inflationary forces in check and restoring confidence in the rupiah. This, in turn, permitted the government to concentrate on achieving the goals of the country's five-year plan (1969–74). Foreign investors, attracted by Indonesia's unexploited natural wealth, cheap labor, and political stability, continued to invest heavily in its various development projects.

Despite the high rate of private capital investment and more than $600 million in foreign aid, mostly from Western sources, the economy remained sluggish. Production was almost stagnant, the Green Revolution failed to materialize despite the introduction of "miracle rice" technology (Indonesia actually increased rice imports in 1970), and the estimated gross national product barely kept ahead of population growth.

Foreign Affairs

For the first time in the post-Sukarno era Indonesia adopted an active foreign policy. Suharto made 11 state visits abroad and attended the conference of nonaligned nations at Lusaka, Zambia. Indonesia also sponsored a conference on Cambodia, which was attended by 11 other Asian and Pacific nations.

The chief highlight of Suharto's foreign travel was a visit to the Netherlands, where he was accorded the singular honor of a personal royal welcome. Suharto was the first Indonesian head of state to visit the Netherlands since Indonesia proclaimed its independence from Dutch rule in 1945.

Another highlight was Suharto's first visit to the United States. The visit coincided with the political furor accompanying the U.S. attack on Viet Cong sanctuaries in Cambodia. While in the United States, Suharto publicly held that the Indochina war should not be widened, that all nations should respect Cambodia's sovereignty and neutrality, and that *all* foreign forces should withdraw from Cambodian soil. His views mirrored the final communiqué drawn up in May at the Indonesian-sponsored conference on Cambodia. Beyond such rhetoric, however, the conference achieved little.

Having restored good relations with the West, Indonesia moved to patch up its relations with the Communist powers. Indonesia reached a favorable agreement with the Soviet Union on the repayment of Indonesia's $1.2-billion debt (a legacy of the Sukarno era) to the U.S.S.R. and Eastern Europe. The U.S.S.R. acceded to Indonesian requests to delay debt repayment only after Indonesia's Japanese and Western creditors had voluntarily reached a similar accord on repayment of another $1.2 billion of the "Sukarno debt." Indonesia also made a bid to reopen diplomatic relations with Communist China but did not receive a positive response. (*See in* CE: Indonesia, Republic of.)

President Suharto of Indonesia is welcomed to Washington, D.C., by U.S. President and Mrs. Richard M. Nixon.

AUTHENTICATED NEWS INTERNATIONAL

INSECTS AND PESTICIDES. An important step in the control of pesticides was taken in June by U.S. Secretary of the Interior Walter J. Hickel. Hickel ordered 16 pesticides to be withdrawn from use on more than 500 million acres of public lands controlled by his department. The discontinued pesticides included DDT, aldrin, 2,4,5-T, dieldrin, endrin, and DDD. At the same time 32 other chemicals and classes of chemicals were placed on a restricted list by Hickel; their use was to be tightly controlled.

United States Secretary of Agriculture Clifford M. Hardin, on the other hand, declared in June that he did not intend to outlaw sales of DDT, the pesticide which had become the most notorious for possibly harmful effects on other forms of life. In defending his refusal to ban DDT, Hardin stated that there was no conclusive evidence that DDT "constitutes an imminent hazard to human health" or that it poses an imminent threat to fish, wildlife, or the environment. He also stated that DDT has beneficial uses in agriculture that cannot be duplicated by any other known chemical. He did admit, however, that DDT can harm some animals.

In July, 15 European nations agreed on a plan to protect the European environment against pesticide misuse. All but two nations of the Council of Europe endorsed the program. Switzerland and the Netherlands, which both have large chemical industries, were the dissenters.

While controls on pesticide use were becoming more restrictive in 1970, headway was being made in the development of biological control of insect pests. The U.S. Department of Agriculture reported that a type of small European wasp was being used successfully against the highly destructive alfalfa weevil. A three-year study showed a 90% reduction in weevils where the wasps had been applied. Alfalfa weevils in any form—eggs, larvae, pupae, and adults—were eaten by the wasps.

In Australia, the Commonwealth Scientific and Industrial Research Organization reported another effective use of one insect against another. In certain areas, the Australians found, a serious pest of cattle, the buffalo fly, had been brought under control by the introduction of the dung beetle. The buffalo fly, which lives on the blood of cattle, is eaten by the beetle.

A gypsy moth eats away at a leaf (below). The moths have stripped thousands of acres of trees, leaving barren landscapes like this one (right) in the northeastern United States.

BELOW AND RIGHT: UPI COMPIX

The male field cricket has a repertory of melodies in his "song bag," reported University of Florida entomologist Thomas J. Walker in 1970. Two songs, according to Walker, are mating calls. One of these calls attracts the attention of a female cricket, another call arouses her deeper interest once she has been attracted. The third call, discovered Walker, is to warn other male crickets to stay away. (*See also* Conservation. *See in* CE: Insecticides; Insects.)

INSURANCE. The total amount of life insurance in effect was expected to have reached a new record once again in 1970. During the year U.S. citizens were insured for more than $1.5 billion dollars, with the average sum held by a family amounting to more than $20,000 in private life insurance protection. Benefits paid during the year exceeded $17 billion.

Assets of U.S. life insurance companies also reached a new record of almost $200 billion at midyear. Of the total, approximately 5.5% was invested in government securities, 36% in bonds, 6.5% in stocks, 36.5% in mortgages, 3% in real estate, 7.5% in policy loans, and 5% in miscellaneous assets.

One of the major company changes of the year came in May with the announcement by the Prudential Insurance Co. of America that it would expand into the property-liability field. Through a management-consulting contract with the Kemper Insurance Co. group, Prudential, the largest life insurer in the world, was expected to enter the auto and homeowner insurance business in the spring of 1971.

Property and liability insurance also reached new highs during 1970. Sales grew at an approximate annual rate of 10% to more than $30 billion. However, underwriting losses were also expected to result for the year as they had during the two preceding years. Major factors in the increasing loss trend were rising losses in automobile insurance, windstorms (particularly Hurricane Celia), serious losses from brush fires in residential sections of California, and losses in aviation insurance caused by airplane hijackings.

Automobile insurance, accounting for more than 40% of total property and liability income, came in for stronger governmental scrutiny during the year. Massachusetts became the first state to pass compulsory "no fault" legislation, effective in 1971. Under the "no fault" system, all policyholders involved in automobile accidents would be reimbursed by their own companies for medical bills and most lost wages up to $2,000. This represented a marked deviation from the former liability system in which the injured person had to collect his losses from the negligent driver. The new system was developed to alleviate the growing costs and problems of automobile liability insurance.

Public health insurance continued to be a highly debated topic during 1970. In August, 15 U.S. senators introduced a bill that would set up a health security program to combine all existing federal plans for health care under one administration. The program would pay three quarters of the health-care expenses of all U.S. citizens and would cost the government about $40 billion annually. (*See in* CE: Insurance.)

INTELLIGENCE OPERATIONS. There was a noticeable lack of spectacular international intelligence operations during 1970. News of the quiet underworld of spies was eclipsed by such activities of various guerrilla groups as kidnappings and airplane hijackings. Most of the intelligence operations revealed during the year took place in West Germany, and the usual number of Soviet diplomats were expelled from foreign countries on charges of spying. There was a certain amount of upheaval in the United States, however, over the activities of its own Army.

Up-to-Date Army

The largest intelligence operation revealed in the United States during the year did not involve foreign spies, but the U.S. Army. Christopher Pyle, a former Army captain, revealed that the Army had set up an elaborate system for watching U.S. civilians and keeping a record of their political activities. The story was printed by *The Washington Monthly* magazine in January.

According to Pyle and the article the Army used undercover agents to infiltrate various groups and kept files on individuals and organizations covering a wide range of U.S. society from militant leftist groups, such as the Students for a Democratic Society, to extreme right-wing organizations, such as the Minutemen—and even the Young Democrats. Reportedly, the Army had gone as far as to infiltrate local church groups. This revelation brought a quick response from the American Civil Liberties Union (ACLU), which filed suit against the Army in an attempt to block the collecting of information regarding civilian political activities. The ACLU itself was included in the clandestine surveillance program.

The ACLU in its suit contended that the collection of such information served no military purpose and was therefore not within the province of military authorities. The ACLU saw the Army's activities as a threat to the constitutional rights of all U.S. citizens. On April 22, however, a federal judge dismissed the case and stated that if newspapers had the right to keep records on political protests, so did the Army. The ACLU announced that it would appeal the case.

Immediately following the publication of the magazine article there were protests against the Army by members of the U.S. Congress. To calm Congressional fears the Army sent a letter to the House of Representatives' subcommittee on the invasion of privacy giving assurance that all copies of the so-called "blacklist" had been withdrawn.

In regular military intelligence-gathering activities the Army did not fare well during the year. The unsuccessful raid on a U.S. prisoner of war camp in North Vietnam in November was blamed on poor intelligence. According to U.S. Secretary of Defense Melvin R. Laird there had been intelligence reports of U.S. prisoners being held at the site of the raid months before the raid actually took place. (*See* Armed Forces, U.S.: Army; Computers; Vietnam.)

The International Routine

In March the West German government disclosed that three members of a major East German spy ring had been arrested in West Germany. One was a 43-year-old woman psychologist who had "escaped" from East Germany and was working in a West German publishing house. She was described as a lieutenant colonel in the East German State Security Service. The second woman, a 51-year-old widow, was the chief secretary in the office of the West German minister of scientific research. The third person was an 80-year-old former judge and one-time member of the Nazi party.

The fantastic story of the theft of a Sidewinder missile from a North Atlantic Treaty Organization base in West Germany and its subsequent shipment by airfreight to the Soviet Union in 1967 had its epilogue in October 1970 before a West German court. The three men accused of that theft—an architect, a mechanic, and a former jet-fighter pilot—were sentenced to prison terms of up to four years.

The Canadian government expelled a Hungarian diplomat in January for attempting to organize a spy ring in Canada. In February a Soviet translator for the United Nations was charged with espionage and expelled from the United States. In the spring the Belgian government expelled a Soviet sales representative, and the government of the Netherlands expelled two members of the Soviet embassy staff. On the Communist side the Czechoslovak, Hungarian, Polish, Soviet, and Yugoslavian governments all arrested various persons during the year and charged them with having spied for Western nations.

William Owen and his wife are relieved to hear that he was acquitted of charges that he sold British secrets to Czechoslovak spies. He is a former member of Parliament.
POPPERFOTO FROM PICTORIAL PARADE

INTERIOR DECORATION.

Spatial simplicity, flexibility, and a renewed interest in shape and form determined the direction of interior decoration in 1970. For the first time, it appeared that modern styling was making definite inroads in the furniture markets. Contemporary styles were in the forefront at the Southern Furniture Market in High Point, N.C., where traditional designs had long held a monopoly. The trend toward Mediterranean furnishings, which had been dominant throughout the 1960's, also seemed to be on the wane as the 1970's opened.

The preoccupation with shape was especially evident in contemporary seating units introduced during the year. Materials such as fiber glass and polyurethane foam were used to form units that could be defined neither as chairs nor as couches. Examples were the long seating unit designed by Max Clendinning of Great Britain and the smaller seating shapes designed by Tobia and Afra Scarpa of Italy.

A similar concept was employed by Robert J. Olsen, a student at Parsons School of Design in New York City, who developed a four-foot cube with puzzlelike pieces that can be used in 28 different ways. The seven pieces of abstract furniture that form the cube are made of polyurethane foam covered with purple jersey. Singly or in combination, the components of the cube can be rearranged to form chairs, a bench, an ottoman, a chaise, and a bed.

Foam was employed in a number of other notable new pieces of furniture during 1970. One of the most novel was the expandable chair which, when removed from its flat rectangular storage box, swells up to become a standard-sized chair. Other foam constructions that were seemingly unusable were actually quite comfortable. Ranging in such unlikely shapes as triangles, spirals, and boulder-like lumps, the chairs have cushions that plump down as soon as they are sat upon. Among designers showing "squooshable" furniture were Charles Eames and Piero Gilardi.

A French designer, Maria Pergay, took a harder view of materials and fashioned a collection of

"THE NEW YORK TIMES"

A delightful mushroom table-and-chair set for children, at $165, comes in different colors and is made to order by William Schlademan and Howard Hampton of New York City's The Tickle Tree.

home and office furniture from stainless steel. The collection included a chaise called the "flying carpet," which is a wide ribbon of steel resting on a rectangular steel platform. It comes with a foam mattress covered in fur or leather. An unpadded "target chair" consists simply of a bull's-eye encircled by two bands that form both the back and the seat. The chair is supported by a four-pronged pedestal. All pieces in the collection are polished to a platinumlike finish and have no visible joints or seams.

Another material that came into prominence in the fabrication of furniture during the year was water. It was used to fill the mattress of the aptly named "water bed." The water bed consists of a molded plastic frame containing a heating unit for warming the water to above room temperature. The plastic mattress, filled by garden hose to the desired degree of firmness, can be covered with standard-sized sheets and bedding. The bed conforms to the shape of the sleeper's body and lulls him with a floating sensation. When filled, the bed weighs more than 1,000 pounds; when empty, 75 pounds.

Another innovation that portended a change in the look and feel of the bedroom was the "environment bed." One model shown during the year consisted of a mattress covered in a black plastic fabric that is bounded on four sides by a white Formica box frame. Storage compartments in the frame hold extra bedding, a radio, and books. Another model was similar in conception; however, its white fiber-glass frame opens out to form a vanity, a storage unit, and a television table.

One of the most imaginative approaches to lighting a room was presented by Josef Head. His lighting wall was constructed of acrylic sheeting and shelves. Supporting the shelves are 20 boxes through which light shines. The lighting wall will light a room without other lamps.

Other designers were displaying lamps that were more recognizable. Joe Colombo created a lamp

The Cuddle Chaise was one of many new items at Chicago's annual January furniture show.

WIDE WORLD

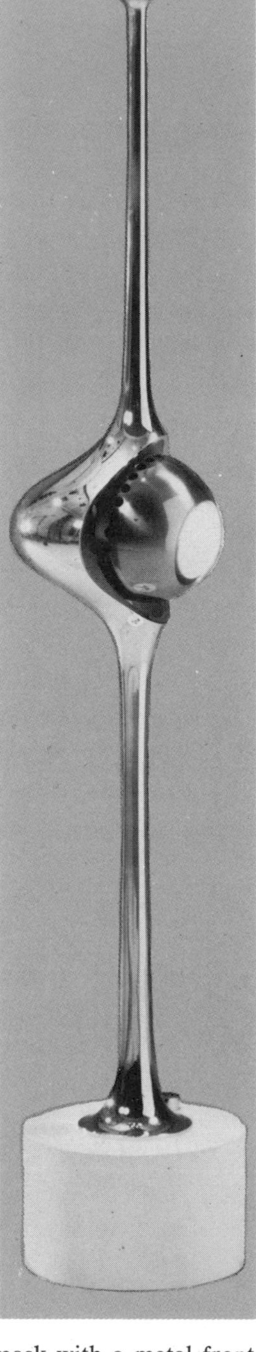

The Cobra, a 24-inch-tall high intensity lamp, was designed by Angelo Lelii of Italy. Its chrome body contains a magnetized metal ball with a light in it that swivels to illuminate paintings and sculpture.
COURTESY, GEORGE KOVACS

that looks like a welder's mask with a metal front that flips up to emit a beam of light. Another Italian-designed lamp consisted of a canisterlike container holding four spotlights. Each light is attached by the type of cord usually used to connect a telephone receiver. The cord allows each light to be removed from its container and placed in another area of the room. One of the prettiest lamps shown during the year was a simple blue glass cylinder topped by three rings of dull chrome and a chrome cap. When the lamp is on, the rings form concentric shadows on the tabletop.

Lamps created by U.S. firms and designers during the year often seemed to be disguised as other objects. One floor lamp appeared to be a tank with several varisized periscopes emerging from the top, each giving off a beam of light. Another, which came disguised as a camera, was actually a multidirectional light mounted on a telescoping tripod. A glowing apple named "Forbidden Fruit" housed a tiny neon lamp.

During 1970 a number of designers continued to concentrate not just on creating furniture but rather on developing an entire environment. English designer John Wright's answer was a terraced rubber space that he titled "Monotone One Space Living Amphitheater." It was constructed of geometric forms covered with brown velvet that could be rearranged to form different pieces of furniture. Robin Moore Ede chose to create an environment within a limited area of space. Although he also chose cushions that could be joined together for seating or bedding, his cushions were covered in very bright colors. A hanging steel table in the center of the room could retreat to the ceiling when not in use.

Perhaps the most private environment displayed in 1970 was a creation by two brothers, Martin and Roger Dean. Their Retreat Pod is a large anthead shape constructed of plastic. Once inside, the occupant is removed from all external stimuli. The walls of the pod are lined with polyurethane covered with purple synthetic fur. It is lighted by hundreds of tiny orange lightbulbs. (*See in* CE: Interior Decoration.)

INTERNATIONAL RELATIONS. In 1970 international relations continued to be dominated by the two superpowers, the United States and the Soviet Union. Their relations appeared to seesaw precariously between confrontation and détente during the year.

The chief stage for U.S.-Soviet conflict was the Middle East, where both powers acutely felt their prestige and influence at stake. The presence of large Soviet and U.S. military forces in the Mediterranean particularly emphasized the threat of a direct clash between the two superpowers.

The United States and the Soviet Union, however, appeared to work in concert—the Soviets applying pressure on the Arab states and the United States pressuring the Israelis—to achieve a 90-day cease-fire agreement beginning August 7 between the main belligerents. The accord, however, did not lead to the start of meaningful peace negotiations. Shortly after the agreement took effect, Israel charged that the United Arab Republic (UAR), or Egypt, had violated it by continuing to install Soviet missiles. Israel refused to negotiate until the missiles were removed. The Soviet Union and the UAR refused to concede that the Israeli charges were true, despite overwhelming evidence to the

HUFFAKER, "NEWS AND OBSERVER," RALEIGH, N.C., FROM BEN ROTH AGENCY

contrary. Speculation arose that the Soviet Union purposely allowed the UAR to violate the cease-fire agreement in order to maintain an uncertain situation that afforded it a position of maximum influence in Middle East affairs.

Chances for a resolution of the Middle East crisis were further complicated by the outbreak of war between Palestinian guerrilla groups, who were strongly opposed to the cease-fire, and the army of Jordan's King Hussein I. The crisis reached a critical point when Syrian troops invaded Jordan to aid the Palestinians. The threat of the use of U.S. force to keep Hussein in power, however, evidently persuaded the Soviets to pressure the Syrians to withdraw. President Gamal Abdel Nasser of the UAR then arranged a truce between the guerrillas and King Hussein, and tension abated. However, Nasser's death in September postponed any possibility of peace negotiations.

The situation became quiescent but precarious, and the United States continued its efforts to bring about peace negotiations. The cease-fire agreement was extended after the November deadline until February 1971. (*See also* Israel; Jordan; Middle East.)

Disarmament Talks

While the Middle East crisis dominated the headlines, the United States and the Soviet Union quietly continued their strategic arms limitation talks (SALT) in Helsinki, Finland. The U.S. position was to limit the agreement to strategic weapons systems, but the Soviets were reported to be insistent on including the issue of U.S. tactical air units in Western Europe.

The talks moved more slowly than had been anticipated. It was thought that no accord would be reached until at least 1971. (*See* Disarmament.)

Anatolii F. Dobrynin (right), Soviet Ambassador to the United States, presents the Soviet Union's ratification of the Treaty on the Non-Proliferation of Nuclear Weapons to Charles I. Bevans, U.S. State Department Assistant Legal Adviser, in Washington, D.C., in March.

WIDE WORLD

Grim Jewish young people picketed the Soviet Embassy in London in February, protesting the Soviet Union's increasing harassment of its Jewish population.

"THE TIMES," LONDON, FROM PICTORIAL PARADE

Europe

The most hopeful changes in the East-West situation occurred in Europe in 1970. A new era seemed to be dawning, primarily as West Germany's Chancellor Willy Brandt pursued a policy of *Ostpolitik*—seeking an accommodation with Eastern Europe and the Soviet Union. The most tangible results of Brandt's policy in 1970 were a nonaggression treaty between West Germany and the Soviet Union and a "normalization" treaty with Poland recognizing the latter's post-World War II western boundary.

The touchy question of settling the permanent status of Berlin remained. Talks were carried out on the issue between the four Allied victors responsible for Berlin—the Soviet Union, France, the United States, and Great Britain—but no solution was reached during the year. (*See* Germany Special Report. *See also* Europe.)

Asia

The war in Vietnam continued, but at a somewhat slower pace. In general, the U.S. policy was to withdraw U.S. troops and at the same time to strengthen the armed forces of South Vietnam. This policy of "winding down" the war underwent a temporary reversal on April 30 when the United States invaded Cambodia for the stated purpose of wiping out North Vietnamese and Viet Cong sanctuaries. The action precipitated a domestic uproar in the United States and international condemnation for the widening of the Vietnam war into an Indochina war. In late November the United States instituted a series of retaliatory bombing raids on North Vietnam, which were felt by some to represent a "major escalation" of the war and to threaten the continuation of the already deadlocked Paris peace talks. (*See* Cambodia; Foreign Policy, U.S.; Vietnam.)

Communist China continued to emerge as a legitimate force in international relations in 1970. After several years of self-imposed isolation, China began to pursue a more vigorous diplomatic offensive in 1970 to extend its influence in many parts of the world. Conversely, the number of nations extending diplomatic recognition to China also increased. (*See* China, People's Republic of.)

Africa and Latin America

With the war between Nigeria and the breakaway state of Biafra ending in January 1970, Africa's main problem during the year was the conflict between independent black African states and the white-dominated governments of South Africa, Rhodesia, and the Portuguese colonies. The new Conservative government of Great Britain was strongly attacked by numerous African leaders for its decision to send arms to South Africa. The guerrilla movements in the Portuguese colonies continued to receive support from a number of African countries. In fact, Guinea was attacked in November (ostensibly because of its sympathetic policy toward anti-Portuguese guerrillas) by a group of mercenaries who it claimed were under Portuguese leadership.

The general social and economic unrest in Latin America was reflected by the emergence of two more "leftist nationalist" governments in 1970—by coup in Bolivia and by the election of an avowed Marxist in Chile. These governments were characterized by their interest in genuine social and economic progress and their nationalist sentiments. Elsewhere, agitation for social and economic reform resulted in a general increase in right-wing military control over civilian governments.

Another trend in Latin America was the rash of diplomatic kidnappings perpetrated by dissident minority groups to achieve political goals. The technique spread rapidly through Latin America and was also used in Canada and in Spain. The political kidnapping thus joined with the aerial hijacking in 1970 as a potent new tool in international affairs for which no government had found a satisfactory response. (*See* Canada; Latin America; Spain. *See in* CE: International Relations.)

IRAN. Throughout the first quarter of 1970, Iran's main problems involved foreign affairs. Its relations with Iraq, already soured by their dispute over navigational rights on the Shatt-al-'Arab, worsened with Iraqi allegations of Iranian support for Kurdish insurgents. Iran denied these charges, but there were border skirmishes and large-scale expulsions of Iranians from Iraq.

On January 21 Iraq announced that it had put down a "right-wing plot" against its government and accused Iran of helping to arm and finance the conspirators. Iraq expelled its neighbor's ambassador with four of his staff. They were followed home by the Iranian chargé d'affaires, whose account of his treatment in Baghdad, the capital of Iraq, inflamed public resentment.

In reply, Prime Minister Amir Abbas Hoveida asked Iraq's ambassador to leave and massed troops on the frontier. These moves prompted Iraqi requests to the United Nations secretary-general and to Iran's close friend Turkey to use their good offices in the interests of peace. However, when Iran's budget for 1970 was presented to the Majlis (the lower chamber of the parliament) on February 8, it included a big increase in defense estimates to protect the country against Iraqi hostility. In March the settlement of the Kurdish demands in Iraq induced a calmer mood in Baghdad, and Iranian feelings, though still running high, were sensibly restrained by Shah Mohammed Reza Pahlavi and his government.

Maintaining its traditional friendship with Communist and non-Communist powers, Iran obtained useful aid from both sides. In 1970 a ten-year agreement (signed in September 1969) came into effect for supplying Romania with crude oil to the value of $100 million in exchange for industrial equipment, including 20,000 tractors, 500 railroad cars, a modern dairy farm, and a timber plant. In March, during a six-day visit to Iran by Soviet Chief of State Nikolai V. Podgorny, plans were disclosed for the further increase of Soviet-Iranian trade exchanges, as well as for the simultaneous inauguration of an oil pipeline to the Soviet Union and a hydroelectric plant at the border on the Araks River. (*See also* Iraq. *See in* CE: Iran.)

Northeast Iran was devastated by an earthquake on July 30, 1970. A young survivor searches for recognizable belongings in the wreckage of her home.

UPI COMPIX

IRAQ. For the regime of Iraq's President Ahmed Hassan al-Bakr, 1970 was a year of venturesome diplomacy and growing internal strain. A peace settlement in March with the Kurds, whose demands for autonomy had kept Iraq in a state of intermittent civil war for nearly a decade, left the government free not only to step up its territorial claims in the Persian Gulf but also to transfer troops from the Kurdish north to Jordan. As the

After negotiations with Kurdish General al-Barzani (left), Iraq granted autonomy to the Kurds on March 11, ending over eight years of sporadic warfare.

WIDE WORLD

year wore on, however, the U.S. plan for Arab-Israeli peace talks revealed divisions within the Arab world that tempted the Iraqi government to challenge the leadership of the United Arab Republic (UAR) and side with the Palestinian guerrillas against a negotiated settlement.

In September, when the guerrillas plunged Jordan into civil war, no help was forthcoming from the 12,000 Iraqi troops in the area. Iraq's pretensions to Arab leadership thus lost credibility, with repercussions that (compounded by the death of UAR's President Gamal Abdel Nasser on September 28) caused the dismissal of Air Marshal Hardan Takriti, one of Iraq's two vice-presidents. The al-Bakr administration continued but was reportedly split by a power struggle.

The Kurdish settlement (strongly urged by the Soviet Union) was the outcome of negotiations opened in January with the Kurdish leader Mullah Mustafa al-Barzani. On March 11, these negotiations produced a 15-point agreement that ended the fighting, declared a general amnesty for all insurgents, gave the Kurdish language equal status with Arabic in Kurdish majority areas (which were to have Kurdish administrators), and stipulated the appointment of a Kurdish vice-president in the Iraqi government. On March 29 al-Bakr formed a new cabinet whose 24 members included five Kurds.

Iraq's announcement on January 21 of an attempted right-wing coup, allegedly with Iranian and U.S. backing, led to the execution of 44 people, including 7 Iraqis convicted earlier of spying for the U.S. Central Intelligence Agency. This development brought relations with Iran close to rupture. (*See also* Iran. *See in* CE: Iraq.)

IRELAND. Two ministers in the cabinet of Ireland's Prime Minister John Lynch were removed from their posts in 1970 after charges of gunrunning were brought against them. On May 5 Lynch dismissed Neil T. Blaney, the minister of agriculture, and Charles J. Haughey, the minister of finance. A third minister, Kevin Boland, the minister for local government and social welfare, resigned in protest. The action precipitated a major government crisis.

The following day in an emergency session of the *Dail Eireann,* Ireland's house of representatives, Lynch accused the two ministers of having been involved in an illegal attempt to import arms into Ireland with the intention of passing them on to Roman Catholic rebels in Northern Ireland. Later in the week he announced that the matter was in the hands of the attorney general. In spite of the crisis, one of the most serious that the government has had to face, Lynch won the unanimous support of his own party and carried a confidence motion in the Dail.

On May 28 Blaney and Haughey were arrested and formally charged. Three other men were arrested on the same charge. After a preliminary court hearing in which the judge ruled that there was insufficient evidence against Blaney, he was released. The other four were brought to trial in September.

The trial ended on October 23 when Haughey and the three other men were all acquitted of the charges of conspiring to illegally import arms and ammunition into Ireland. This marked the beginning, however, of a new crisis for Lynch's government and made the explosive problem of uniting Northern Ireland with the Republic of Ireland an active issue in Irish politics once again.

Lynch held firmly to his policy of moderation in dealing with Northern Ireland; he felt reunification could come about only through peaceful means. Extremists such as Blaney and Haughey called for reunification by force and favored sending arms to the Catholics in Northern Ireland for purposes of self-defense. Through his trial and acquittal Haughey gained a great deal of emotional support and announced that he would try to have Lynch removed as prime minister. There were other calls for Lynch's resignation from within his own party,

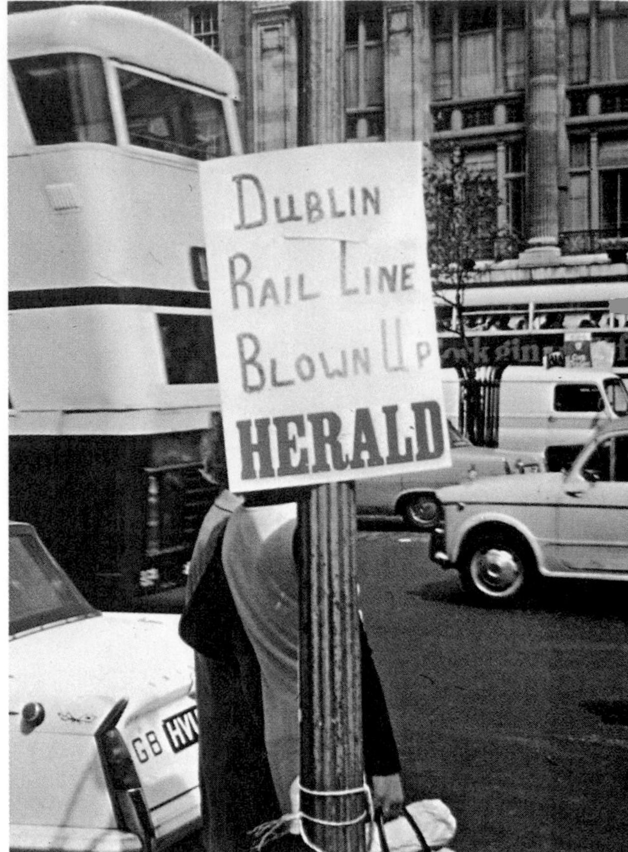

AUTHENTICATED NEWS INTERNATIONAL

An advertisement for the "Herald" on a street corner in Dublin, Ireland, announces that the Dublin Rail Line has been demolished by terrorists.

the Fianna Fail, and from the opposition. The government barely survived from day to day.

In December Lynch's government suddenly announced it was assuming emergency powers because of the existence of a "secret armed conspiracy" to kidnap political leaders. Although the move (evidently aimed at extremists) was strongly criticized, Lynch appeared to have enough political support to sustain his "get tough" approach.

The economic situation in Ireland steadily worsened during 1970. A serious inflation problem coupled with strikes in important industries put a heavy strain on Ireland's already weak economy. The government was eventually forced to introduce a strict 6% wage increase ceiling and other stringent controls over inflationary factors.

A strike by bank employees closed Ireland's banks for 22 weeks during 1970. A strike of cement workers disrupted the whole construction industry in Ireland in the early part of the year. In April the government announced that it would seek membership in the European Economic Community, or Common Market. (*See also* Ireland Special Report; Great Britain. *See in* CE: Ireland.)

Ireland

Special Report: The Two Irelands

by Bruce Arnold, Free-Lance Journalist and Writer

In the half century encompassing rebellion, civil war, and the emergence of the 26-county Republic of Ireland it had seemed that maturity, rational government, self-confidence, and a firm belief in the future had come to Ireland, north and south. Bitterness remained beneath the surface, however, and finally exploded in riots in Northern Ireland and political unrest in the republic as the 1960's drew to a close. The situation grew even more complicated in 1970.

The rioting that broke out in Northern Ireland during 1968 and 1969 and the sufferings of the Roman Catholics in the north rekindled the zeal of such extremists as the outlawed Irish Republican Army and aroused the sympathies of the general population in the republic. Further, in 1970, extremist elements were found in the highest levels of Ireland's government. Two cabinet ministers were dismissed for allegedly plotting to ship arms to the Catholics in the north.

In addition to precipitating a major government crisis in the republic, the rumored plans for gunrunning added coals to the verbal fire of Protestant extremists in Ulster, particularly a self-styled minister, the Rev. Ian Paisley. Ulster Protestants pointed to the gunrunning story as evidence of the treachery of the Catholics across the border. Some Catholics and militant republicans in the south held to their position that arms should be sent north for the self-defense of the Catholic minority in Ulster. As the year drew to a close, positions seemed to be hardening on both sides.

In the Beginning

Ireland has experienced only two successful conquests: the evangelization of the country by the church of Rome in the 5th century and the plantation of Ulster in the 17th century. To these two conquests can be traced the trouble that erupted in Northern Ireland in 1968 and the resulting di-

British soldiers guard barricades in the Catholic Falls Road area in Belfast, Northern Ireland. The area has been plagued with outbreaks of violence between Catholics and Protestants.

DAVID LOMAX FROM PIX

Protestant Orangemen parade through Ulster on July 13, 1970, to celebrate the victory of William III, a Protestant, over the troops of the exiled Roman Catholic King James II at the battle of the Boyne in 1690.
KEYSTONE

vision and unrest that prevailed in the republic during 1970.

The religious conquest of Ireland, begun by St. Patrick, was successful because its object was the conquest of souls—not of people, land, or wealth. The plantation of Ulster was quite different. Unlike all other intrusions into Ireland, this one was total. Protestant English landowners came and brought with them artisans, laborers, and craftsmen—in short, a whole society. The result was that the native Irish were pushed out of the mainstream of national life. In this manner the foundation for a separate state within Ireland was laid down long before separation from England was ever considered.

Before independence, the structure of society throughout Ireland was quite blatantly one of first- and second-class citizenship. The nation was ruled by a Protestant ascendancy, and the inevitable social hierarchy had its roots in the religious distinction between the masses, who were Catholic, and the predominantly Protestant ruling class. After independence this changed in the republic. In Northern Ireland, however, the old order of Protestant domination continued and was backed by a substantial majority of the population.

The struggle for Irish independence in the early part of the 20th century was a heroic failure. It produced martyrs, but not independence. Following the 1916 Easter Monday rebellion and the ensuing war for independence from Great Britain a compromise was reached. Under the Government of Ireland Act of 1920, Ireland was partitioned into the predominantly Protestant north and the predominantly Catholic south, with separate parliaments for each. Most of Northern Ireland was happy to retain its ties to Great Britain, but southern Ireland (having achieved the status of Irish Free State) continued to struggle for complete independence and in 1949 succeeded in breaking all ties with the Commonwealth of Nations and became the Republic of Ireland. In one of those strange parallels that history occasionally throws up, Ireland in 1970 seemed to be reaping the sad fruits of that compromise in the troubles in Northern Ireland and the crisis in the republic provoked by those troubles.

Old Wounds Reopened

The attitudes of the plantation ancestors of the 20th-century Protestant majority in Ulster had been formalized by the end of the 18th century with the formation of the Orange Order. The Orange Order preserved up to the present day the religious separateness and much of the bigotry that exist in Northern Ireland. Its divisive and openly unfair intrusion into jobs, housing, and local government and the Catholic reaction to this intrusion produced the marches, riots, and deaths that shocked the world in 1968 and 1969.

The unique comprehensiveness of the plantation of Ulster at the beginning of the 17th century gave to Northern Ireland as a whole a large Protestant working class. They suffer, as do the Catholics, from the high level of unemployment and from the fact that economically Northern Ireland has lagged behind the rest of the United Kingdom. If the Protestant working class fears poverty, however, it fears the Catholics and their traditional republicanism far more. Its fierce loyalty to the British Crown and to Protestantism has been sustained by the Orange Order, and this loyalty is expressed in the form of support for the ultraconservative Unionist party—however contradictory this must seem.

When the Catholic civil rights movement began to grow in strength after 1968, the poverty-ridden Protestant working class became fiercely determined to preserve for itself the marginal advantages derived from the inequality of opportunity. The result was violent confrontations between the two working classes, Protestant and Catholic.

Old Ambitions Reawakened

The events in Northern Ireland challenged with increasing penetration the moderate policies of the ruling Fianna Fail party in the Republic of Ireland. Originally the Fianna Fail was formed with two chief objectives, both of which became increasingly hollow with the passing of years. One of these was the restoration of the Irish language; the other was the reuniting of the two parts of Ireland into a single independent republic. Under Prime Minister John Lynch, however, the government of Ireland held the position that reunification could not take place until Northern Ireland and the republic both voluntarily agreed to such unity.

During the disturbances in Northern Ireland Prime Minister Lynch made emotional speeches, sent his foreign minister to the United Nations to ask for a peace-keeping force, mobilized the army reserve, and set up border hospitals. All of his actions, however, were thought out in terms of internal considerations, national and political. He had to cope with a dissident, extremist element within his own party led by the minister of agriculture, Neil T. Blaney, and with the general feeling among the population of powerless sympathy for the Catholic victims in the north.

The very real fact remained, however, that Catholics in Northern Ireland were being beaten and shot, and there was the threat of pogroms. Refugees were crossing the border into the republic and demands were being made for help, including requests for guns. The cabinet in the republic was divided, and there was no really strong hand controlling the individual members. Although the differences between the militants in Fianna Fail and the prime minister were becoming increasingly public, and there appeared to be cause for alarm about possible extremist actions, Lynch declined to dismiss anyone.

Then the cabinet crisis in the republic broke on May 5, 1970. Lynch dismissed Blaney and Finance Minister Charles J. Haughey, accusing them of having been involved in an alleged conspiracy to import guns illegally into Ireland with the intention of passing them on to Catholics in Northern Ireland. The minister of local government, Kevin Boland, resigned in protest, stating that Lynch used gestapo tactics to keep his ministers under surveillance.

Later in the month Blaney, Haughey, and several others were arrested on the gunrunning charge. Blaney was released after a judge found there was insufficient evidence against him. In the autumn the others were tried and found not guilty.

Soft on Belfast

The trial and acquittal of Haughey brought the dissension within Fianna Fail out into the open with a direct challenge to Lynch's leadership. It was a challenge made more bitter by Lynch's own espousal of "realistic attitudes" toward the situation in Northern Ireland. The growing sympathy in the republic's attitude toward Northern Ireland and the uncertainty of Lynch's handling of the problem—even during the rioting—did not raise the fundamental issue of the aims of Fianna Fail. The results of the trial, however, did.

The original aim of Fianna Fail, the reunification of Ireland, once again became a political issue. Militants within Fianna Fail rejected Lynch's moderate policy and rallied behind the emotional appeal of Haughey. Once again the idea of reunification at any price—even civil war—appeared to many Irishmen as the way to a viable solution. There seemed to be a possibility that Lynch would be forced out of office and replaced by someone far more militant.

The trial itself was regarded by some Irish politicians as a political device for getting rid of difficult cabinet ministers. Instead of being in a position of prestige from which he and his country could look forward to gradually increasing efforts to bring Ireland together, Lynch in the autumn of 1970 was faced with a complicated power struggle within his own party and a somewhat damaged reputation abroad.

It is easy to say of Ireland that what was done a half century ago is there and must be lived with, and that self-determination is the only valid principle. Such a view, however, seems to be at the root of the continued pessimism felt by Irishmen north and south of the border about the future of their country as a whole. Even a moderate such as Lynch has publicly admitted that the division of Ireland into north and south is responsible for the trouble. Yet the majority of people in the republic, while they give their spiritual support to the idea of reunification, are not anxious for any immediate moves in that direction. Reunification in the near future would mean a significant drop in the standard of living for all Irishmen.

ISRAEL. By the end of 1970 it was evident that the year would go down in Israel's history as one of an emergent new political leadership and as the beginning of the first major change in Israeli foreign policy. The central factor in both was Defense Minister Moshe Dayan. At the beginning of 1970 Dayan's influence in the cabinet council and in the country at large was still overshadowed by the number of ministers—including Prime Minister Golda Meir—arrayed against him. It was against Dayan's advice that the cabinet majority had supported the decision to embark on deep-penetration air attacks against the United Arab Republic (UAR), or Egypt. These attacks continued until mid-April, and the targets included positions in the suburbs of Cairo, Egypt, and industrial objectives in the Nile Delta. The principal military objective, however, was the radar system serving the UAR air force, and this was progressively and effectively destroyed during the first ten weeks of the year.

Meanwhile, Israeli casualties on the Suez Canal had been considerably reduced as a result of the more intensive air attacks on Arab positions. In December 1969, Israel had suffered 113 dead and 330 wounded on the canal front; that figure had dropped to 60 dead and 137 wounded in May 1970. Meanwhile, the event predicted by Dayan when the government embarked on the deep-penetration raids had materialized. On April 29 an Israeli government communiqué said that Soviet pilots had been flying operational missions near Cairo and Alexandria, Egypt, for some time. In order not to clash with them the Israelis had halted their attacks on targets outside the immediate Suez Canal zone. The extent of this Soviet help was emphasized by President Gamal Abdel Nasser of the UAR in his May Day speech, when he said, "Without Soviet help [to the UAR], Moshe Dayan would now be sitting in Cairo."

WIDE WORLD

In an address to her parliament, Golda Meir responds to the latest U.S. peace proposal.

These military events had been accompanied by a seeming deterioration in Israel's relations with the Administration of U.S. President Richard M. Nixon. It had begun with the formal presentation of a peace initiative by U.S. Secretary of State William P. Rogers on Dec. 9, 1969, which set out the political terms and suggested a geographical basis for a possible settlement between Israel, the UAR, and Jordan. The Israeli government flatly rejected the "Rogers Plan."

This critical Israeli position was further confirmed by the hostile notes sent by the Soviet government to the U.S., British, and French governments on February 3, and by President Nixon's reply four days later. Nixon called for a total em-

Israeli soldiers examine a bus that was bombed in an ambush by terrorists near the border with Lebanon. A number of children were killed in the incident.

WIDE WORLD

bargo of arms to the Middle East and said that the United States would halt deliveries to Israel if the Soviet Union would stop its supplies to the Arab countries. Israel's worst fears were further reinforced by Secretary of State Rogers' statement on March 23 which indicated that Israel's request to purchase another 25 Phantom and 100 Skyhawk planes would temporarily remain "in abeyance."

Meanwhile, the Israeli air attacks on the UAR had been pressed with increasing intensity. It became known that President Nasser was under great pressure because of them and had paid a three-day secret visit to Moscow on January 28 to seek more direct Soviet aid. By mid-April the implications of the new Soviet commitment were becoming apparent in the United States and Israel. On April 14 the State Department's assistant secretary for Near Eastern and South Asian affairs, Joseph J. Sisco, considered to be President Nixon's principal adviser on the Arab-Israeli conflict, arrived in Israel after having had somewhat fruitless talks with President Nasser in Cairo. On April 15 Sisco met privately with Defense Minister Dayan. The next day Dayan declared that henceforth the main problem would be with Soviet involvement in the Middle East conflict.

The Israeli air force intensified its assault on Arab artillery, missile, and army positions along the Suez Canal. In the course of three months (May, June, and July) it virtually destroyed all effective UAR air defense and radar installations and virtually neutralized the UAR air force. The introduction of the latest Soviet air-defense missile, the SAM-3, limited the Israeli success somewhat and led to the loss of five Israeli Phantom planes during the attacks, but it served to emphasize at the same time that only direct Soviet intervention could turn the tables on the canal front. Meanwhile, the most reliable neutral estimates put UAR military casualties as a result of these Israeli air attacks at not fewer than 10,000 dead during these three months. The pressure on President Nasser to seek an alternative way out was therefore considerable. The Israelis were also becoming anxious to find an alternative to war. The sheer cost of war and the drain on resources proved to be very great.

With this general situation in mind—and in light of the private conversations that Sisco had with Dayan in April—Secretary Rogers addressed another initiative to the UAR and Israeli governments on June 19. This was framed in much more general terms but specifically suggested a cease-fire. President Nasser formally accepted the proposals made by Rogers on July 23, and the Israeli government followed suit on August 4. The cease-fire, which was to last for 90 days, came into effect at midnight on August 7; it was renewed for another 90 days on November 5.

A critical development concerning the future of Israel and its relations with the superpowers took place during the cease-fire. The Israelis charged that the Arabs, with Soviet help, had utilized the cease-fire standstill agreement in order to situate a considerable number of missiles and heavy guns along the canal front and had thus changed the military status quo in favor of the UAR. After some initial confusion and doubt the United States accepted the charge; and President Nixon, once convinced that there had been, as he put it, "a breach of faith" on the part of the UAR and the Soviet Union, reacted with great vigor. Israel received more Phantom planes and a wide range of the most sophisticated electronic equipment and arms to counter the UAR buildup. By the time the cease-fire was up for renewal, Israel's military superiority was probably greater than ever.

These changes in foreign-policy approaches and the significant part played in them by Defense Minister Dayan were also reflected in domestic affairs. The most dramatic form was the emergence of Dayan as the spokesman for a more flexible foreign policy—for not insisting on direct negotiations and a peace settlement as the basic Israeli diplomatic objective. Instead, Dayan proposed a more pragmatic approach in order to reach at first a partial settlement with the UAR. To this end, he suggested that Israel would be prepared to withdraw some 20 miles from the canal to allow it to be reopened and to seek a general demilitarization of the Suez front as a first step. Despite initial opposition from Foreign Minister Abba Eban, Deputy Premier Yigal Allon, and the majority of the cabi-

Israelis opposed to the U.S. peace plan picket the Knesset as parliament meets.
STEVE EAGLE FROM NANCY PALMER AGENCY

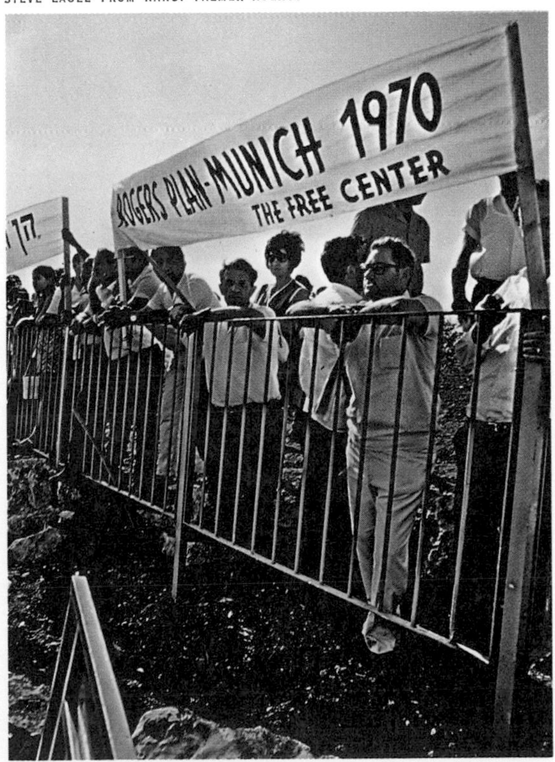

net, Dayan won the support of the prime minister and the cabinet's approval on November 29. He was authorized to discuss his ideas with Administration leaders and with President Nixon in Washington, D.C., on behalf of the cabinet. (*See also* Middle East. *See in* CE: Israel.)

ITALY. In 1970 Italy was beset by difficulties. Two government crises and fears of economic setbacks mingled with social unrest to give a dramatic overtone to all major events. On February 7 Premier Mariano Rumor offered the resignation of his Christian Democratic government, unable to continue in office without direct participation by the three parties of the previous center-left coalition, the Socialists, Social Democrats, and Republicans. Although talks had begun with the leaders of those parties in an effort to restore the previous coalition, the crisis dragged on and every solution presented great difficulties. On February 28 Rumor gave up the attempt to form a center-left coalition. On March 3 President Giuseppe Saragat asked former Premier Aldo Moro to form a new government, but he also failed; Rumor was again called in and was successful on March 27. The new government consisted of 17 Christian Democrats, 6 Socialists, 3 Social Democrats, and one Republican. On April 10 the Senate endorsed it by 167 to 117, and on April 17 the Chamber of Deputies accepted it by 348 votes to 239.

A second government crisis followed on July 6, when Rumor resigned due to difficulties in bringing the four coalition parties to agree upon a common policy. On July 11 Christian Democrat Giulio Andreotti was asked to form a new coalition government, but the refusal of the Social Democrats to accept a "policy of intent" forced him to give up. The finance minister in the previous government, Emilio Colombo, formed a government on August 6. Its first decisions were aimed at strengthening the economy by arresting inflation, improving the balance of payments, and controlling private expenditure in order to free larger sums for investment.

Controversy occurred between church and state when the parliament discussed a bill to legalize divorce. The bill, accepted by the Chamber of Deputies, just survived the Senate with changes, and a compromise was reached. It was returned to the Chamber as amended. The articles were approved by parliament, and although the Roman Catholic church condemned the measure, the strong lobby in favor of divorce prevailed.

Foreign Affairs

The main aims of Italian policy in 1970 were to achieve domestic peace, to carry on a more flexible relationship with East European countries, and to attempt a realistic contribution to pacification in the Middle and Far East. The Alto Adige problem, a South Tyrol dispute that had troubled the country in preceding years, seemed finally solved with the presentation early in the year of a new bill aimed at modifying the special statute of the Trentino-Alto Adige region. Wider autonomy for the provinces of Bolzano and Trento, a direct financial relationship between the Italian government and the two provinces, and new regulations guaranteeing the welfare of the Italian- and German-speaking communities in the region were the main points. Hopes grew that there would be an end to terrorism by minority groups.

Restraint was shown in face of action by the Libyan government of Col. Muammar el-Qaddafi, who on July 21 announced the confiscation of Italian property and the freezing of savings deposited in both Italian and Libyan banks in Tripoli. Foreign Minister Aldo Moro met his Libyan coun-

Police attempt to extinguish a flaming car outside the police station in Reggio di Calabria, Italy. The fire, set by protesters with Molotov cocktails on July 22, 1970, also damaged the police station.

WIDE WORLD

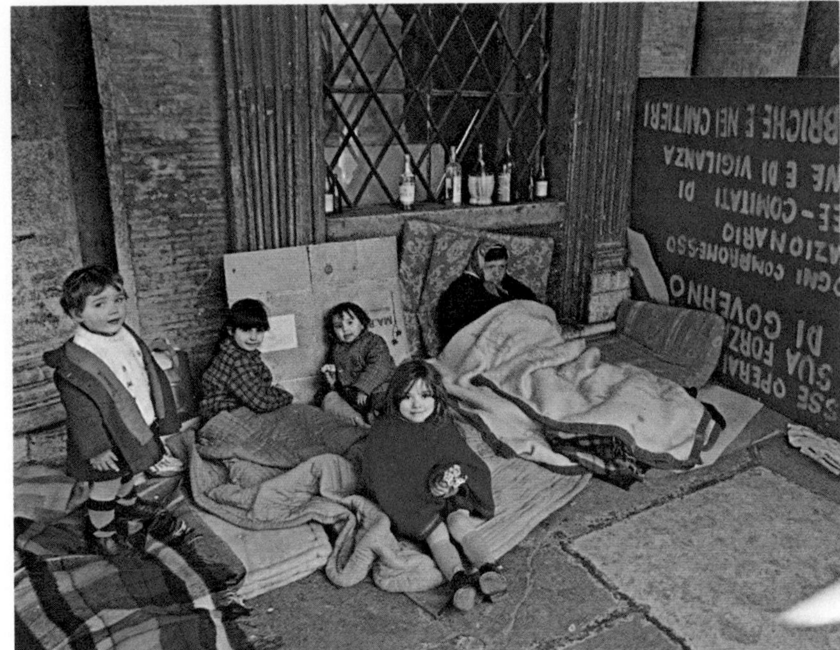

A homeless Italian family rests after having spent the night in an outdoor demonstration on March 16, 1970. The demonstration was held to draw attention to the urgent need for new housing programs in Rome.

WIDE WORLD

terpart, Saleh Buessir, in Beirut, Lebanon, without definite results. By the end of October almost all the remaining 19,000 Italians of an original 25,000 in Libya had left.

The Economy

On August 27 the government approved a series of measures aimed at averting an economic crisis. These consisted mainly in reducing pressure on home demand, balancing the public accounts while assuring the necessary bases for urgent reforms, and giving new incentives for production and investment through rearranged credits and taxation.

Following a series of strikes that hit all major Italian manufacturers, the car industry showed signs of stress that were reflected in the production figures for the first six months of the year. In that period 918,312 units were produced, a reduction of 1.9% over the figure for the first six months of 1969. Exports were seriously hit, decreasing by 9.1% from 372,274 to 338,239 units. Fiat, Italy's principal car manufacturer (which during the year increased its interest in the French company Citroën to 49%), was particularly hard hit by strikes. In the first six months of the year it was estimated that the company lost production of more than 98,000 cars; 777,000 were produced, a reduction of 63,000 from the first six months of 1969. (*See also* Europe. *See in* CE: Italy.)

IVORY COAST. In May 1970 Ghana's Prime Minister Kofi A. Busia visited the Ivory Coast. The two countries signed a treaty of friendship and agreed to establish a joint commission for mutual cooperation. Ghana and the Ivory Coast later reached an agreement to end border disputes.

In October, the Democratic Party of the Ivory Coast (the ruling party) reaffirmed its main objectives: rehabilitation of former political prisoners, speedier promotion of the young intellectual elite to governmental responsibility, and adherence to the principles of a liberal economy. President Félix Houphouët-Boigny also stressed the need to temporize with the states of southern Africa—particularly the Republic of South Africa—adopting a position similar to that of Malawi. Reports in November that French troops had helped to quell a tribal rising at Gagnoa were denied by President Houphouët-Boigny and the French government. (*See also* Africa; Ghana; Malawi; South Africa. *See in* CE: Ivory Coast.)

JAMAICA. There was considerable concentration in 1970 on finding the finance for development in Jamaica. Emphasis was laid on creating an interlocking system of financial institutions, both public and private, to provide capital from at home and abroad. At home, vigorous efforts were made to close the loopholes that over the years have made possible a fairly substantial amount of tax avoidance and to stimulate savings through the introduction of unit trusts.

Jamaica was admitted to membership of the Inter-American Development Bank on Dec. 30, 1969, and thereafter received a large loan for farm improvement. With the announcement in October of an agreement to make available Canadian Aid funds up to $30 million, lines of credit were established with Jamaica's chief trading partners, Canada, Great Britain, and the United States. Jamaica also became a member of the Caribbean Regional Development Bank. (*See in* CE: Jamaica.)

LARRY BURROWS, LIFE MAGAZINE © TIME INC.

British Columbia showed films about the province at Expo '70 in a timber tower (above). The U.S. pavilion featured moon exploration with exhibits including a moon rock, models of astronauts on the moon, and the Apollo 8 space capsule (below).

DEAN BROWN FROM NANCY PALMER AGENCY

JAPAN. In 1970, exactly 25 years after its defeat and surrender in World War II, Japan was once again on its way to becoming a major world political power. Japan's remarkable economic growth was celebrated in the first world's fair to be held in Asia, Expo '70. Even though Japan's new power was based on economics rather than on armaments, there was some concern expressed during the year over the rise of right-wing militarism. On the left, radical students repeatedly staged demonstrations protesting policies toward the United States, and one group staged a spectacular airplane hijacking.

Another Sunrise

In his first speech of the year to the Diet, Japan's Premier Eisaku Sato predicted that Japan "will carry unprecedented weight in world affairs" during the 1970's. Sato also called for a substantial increase of some 17% in military spending. He pledged, however, that Japan's wealth and power would be used to promote world peace.

Evidence of Japan's growing political influence among Asian nations appeared during the conference on Cambodia held at Djakarta, Indonesia, on May 16–17. The Asian and Pacific nations attending adopted Japan's resolution calling for reactivation of the International Control Commission and the withdrawal of all foreign troops from Cambodia (*see* Cambodia; Vietnam).

Reports issued in January 1970 showed that Japan's balance of payments had reached a record surplus of $2.28 billion. The gross national product for fiscal year 1969 (April 1, 1969–March 31, 1970) was more than $174 billion, and per capita income stood at $1,335.

In April Japan and Communist China renewed their semiofficial trade agreement. Japanese trade with Communist China was 78% more in the first half of 1970 than it had been in the first six months of 1969. Trade with Nationalist China increased only 19% for the same period.

Serious disagreement arose between the United States and Japan over textile imports. Talks broke down in June when the two nations failed to agree on voluntary restrictions on Japanese textile imports to the United States.

Liberalization of Japan's trade was accelerated in 1970. Nine import quotas were lifted in the first quarter, and it was announced that quotas on all but 30 items would be removed by 1973. In August the government said that 323 types of businesses would be opened to foreign investment.

Japan's rapid economic growth precipitated two severe problems, inflation and pollution. The antiquated food-distribution system caused prices on staples to rise by as much as 60% in the first six months of 1970. There were public protests against the pollution of Tagonoura Harbor by the paper mills at Fuji. In August $3.6 million was appropriated to fight air pollution in Tokyo, the capital.

In the glitter of lights displayed at night, the impressive Soviet pavilion towers above the other structures at Expo '70.

PAOLO KOCH FROM BLACK STAR

Okinawa, Treaties, and Trouble

Preparations were begun during the year for the transfer of Okinawa and the other Ryukyu Islands from U.S. to Japanese control by 1972. In March a joint commission was set up on Okinawa to coordinate reversion activities.

Okinawan workers on U.S. military bases went on strike in January to protest the dismissal of almost 1,200 workers. The military workers union demanded an increase in severance pay and longer advance notice of dismissal. The strike ended after five days without resolution of the issues.

Crimes committed by U.S. servicemen against Okinawan civilians prompted demands for law enforcement and judicial powers to be turned over to Okinawan authorities. In the first five months of 1970, reportedly 345 such crimes had been committed.

Another cause for complaint was the storage of nerve gas and chemical weapons on the island. The gas had been scheduled for shipment to Oregon early in the year, but the proposed transfer was called off when state officials objected. The U.S. government took a step toward relieving tensions on Okinawa in September when it announced that the B-52 bombers would soon be removed.

In the first half of 1970 leftist Japanese students staged demonstrations against the U.S.-Japanese security treaty and pledged to bring about a revolution in Japan. The demonstrations were relatively peaceful, unlike those of 1969. When 1970 began, 22 institutions of higher education were still entirely or partially closed because of the disturbances of the preceding year.

As the date for the extension of the security treaty neared, elaborate precautions were taken and the police made many preventive arrests. The treaty was automatically extended for an indefinite period on June 23, and though there were some strikes and protests the disturbances quickly died down.

In August the U.S. government announced that the responsibility for defending Japan against conventional attack had been turned over to the Japanese. It was also announced that the Japanese government would share control of many U.S. military bases in Japan. The new U.S. policy toward Japan was in line with the so-called "Nixon doctrine" of encouraging Asian nations to carry more of the burden of defending themselves.

Nine Japanese youths belonging to a radical group called the Red Army hijacked a Japan Air Lines plane on March 31 and demanded to be taken to North Korea. After a refueling stopover at Fukuoka the pilot landed at Seoul, the capital of South Korea. Officials disguised Seoul's airport to resemble the one at Pyongyang, the capital of North Korea, but the hijackers were not deceived. After two days of negotiations Shinjiro Yamamura, Japan's vice-minister of transport, was exchanged for the passengers as hostage, and the jet was flown to North Korea. On April 5 the plane and Yamamura were returned to Tokyo.

After four failures, Japan successfully launched its first satellite into orbit on February 11. (*See also* Fairs and Shows. *See in* CE: Japan.)

ABOVE AND BELOW: ROBERT TROSTLE FROM BLACK STAR

Two hijacked planes (above) remain on a desert airstrip in Jordan in September as Palestinian commandos negotiate for the return of Arab terrorists held in jail. When negotiations faltered, the commandos destroyed the planes. The hostages from the planes were released later.

JORDAN. Events in Jordan in 1970 were dominated by mounting conflicts between the army of King Hussein I and Palestinian guerrillas operating against Israel from Jordan. Armed clashes between the army and the guerrillas erupted on February 11, a day after the king decreed enforcement of measures to control guerrilla activities within Jordan. Fighting ended on February 13 when the king agreed to "freeze" the control measures; the guerrillas undertook to enforce controls among themselves. In the meantime, ten guerrilla factions formed a unified command. They ranged from the moderate *al Fatah,* headed by Yasir Arafat, to the extremist Popular Front for the Liberation of Palestine (PFLP).

Between June 9 and 16 the army and the guerrillas clashed again over government restrictions. Hussein removed two senior army officers to meet guerrilla demands and formed a new cabinet with a proguerrilla majority on June 27.

On July 26 Jordan's acceptance of a U.S. plan for Arab-Israeli negotiations was seen by the guerrillas as a betrayal. Anti-U.S. riots broke out in Amman, the capital, and the guerrillas vowed to undermine the negotiations. Under the plan an Arab-Israeli cease-fire went into effect on August 8. Jordan and Israel had clashed earlier in the year.

Early in September fighting between the army and the guerrillas broke out once more, and the PFLP hijacked to Jordan three foreign airliners and their passengers, creating an international incident. On September 16 King Hussein established a military government and declared martial law. The next day civil war erupted. Heavy fighting occurred in Amman and in northwest Jordan, where guerrillas held key cities.

Following a cease-fire arranged by an inter-Arab mission on September 25, Hussein and Yasir Arafat signed a truce. Under its provisions Jordanian sovereignty and guerrilla freedoms were both pledged, and a withdrawal of forces of both sides from towns was to be supervised by an Arab observer team. After a second agreement, on October 13, Hussein restored civilian rule. In spite of the truce some fighting continued, and the withdrawal of forces was only partial. Passengers of the hijacked planes, held as PFLP hostages, were freed in September. During the year several attempts were made to assassinate King Hussein. (*See also* Middle East. *See in* CE: Jordan.)

King Hussein, who was faced with increased opposition during 1970, reviews his troops.

ROBERT AZZI FROM NANCY PALMER AGENCY

KENYA. Opening the first session of Kenya's newly elected National Assembly on Feb. 6, 1970, against a background of recent unrest in the Kisumu area, President Jomo Kenyatta stressed the need for a national outlook and declared that the National Assembly should act as a bridge between government and the people. He announced that the government would concentrate upon making the country self-sufficient as far as basic food stuffs were concerned. One of the most important factors contributing to the achievement of this aim was the land reform program, and the minister for lands and settlement made an effort in January to explain to the rural population the method of registering titles to land and the importance of doing so.

Early in March, Vice-President Daniel Arap Moi announced that a more rigorous attitude would be adopted towards Asians holding British passports who became unemployed in Kenya. Hitherto, the government had not pressed its policy of deporting British Asians who had no work permit, but this was now to be enforced. At the same time Britain resisted pressure to increase the annual admissions quota of Asians holding British passports, and a number of British Asians found themselves shuttling between airports in an endeavor to find a country willing to accept them.

In October, Kenya saw the other side of the picture when many thousands of Kenyan subjects were expelled from Uganda as part of President Milton Obote's plan to find employment for the citizens of his own country. A visit to Uganda by President Kenyatta failed to alleviate the trouble. The Kenya National Chamber of Commerce felt constrained to oppose a proposal by the central organization of trade unions to organize a boycott of goods bound for Uganda from Mombasa, Kenya, on the grounds that this would have an adverse effect upon Kenya's economy. (*See also* Africa; Commonwealth of Nations; Uganda. *See in* CE: Kenya.)

KOREA. In 1970 North Korea chose the 20th anniversary of the outbreak of the Korean War to offer a nonaggression pact with South Korea, contingent on total U.S. withdrawal from South Korea. For the first time, the government in Seoul, South Korea's capital, gave a favorable, if guarded, reply to a Northern proposal of steps toward reunification. South Korea's President Park Chung-hee offered to work toward reunification if the North would renounce the use of force. His offer was rejected by the North Koreans, who claimed it lacked practical suggestions; they countered by proposing a confederation of South and North, again contingent on U.S. withdrawal.

Otherwise, border clashes and incidents continued. Early in June North Korea claimed to have sunk a U.S. spy ship, implying another *Pueblo* incident; but the craft turned out to be a South Korean patrol boat. Later that month the South Korean coast guard captured a North Korean spy boat off the west coast, south of Inch'ŏn.

South Korea

The U.S. intent to reduce the number of its troops in South Korea from approximately 60,000 to 40,000 caused trepidation in Seoul, and Prime Minister Chung Il Kwon threatened to resign with his whole cabinet if the plan were carried out. By August, however, the government was willing to discuss the reduction in force. Later that month, when U.S. Vice-President Spiro T. Agnew visited Seoul, he reiterated the U.S. offer of funds to modernize the South Korean army and promised the transfer of a wing of F-4 Phantom jet fighters to South Korea from Japan. However, U.S. Congressional resistance to further defense spending—and, in particular, the U.S. Senate vote to stop paying subsidies to South Korean soldiers in South Vietnam—made the Administration reluctant to accede to Seoul's request for $3 billion in defense aid over the next five years.

The South Korean government decided to slow the economy in 1970 by reducing the gross national product (GNP) growth rate to an 11% increase, among other measures. The rapid growth of the South Korean economy, which had a 15% GNP increase in 1969, caused problems such as inflation (6% to 10% in 1969) and a widening disparity between the nation's industrial development and agricultural growth.

PETER FEBBRORIELLO FROM NANCY PALMER AGENCY

South Koreans harvest the 1970 rice crop. The crop yield should exceed the 1969 record crop, which reached 5.6 million tons.

North Korea

North Korea's relations with Communist China improved in 1970 for the first time since the "cultural revolution" in China, apparently as a result of a mutual concern over the growing strength of Japan. In April Communist China's Premier Chou En-lai made a three-day friendship visit to North Korea. Other visitors included the deposed ruler of Cambodia, Prince Norodom Sihanouk.

In April Finance Minister Choe Yun Su reported a $105-million budget surplus for 1969 and a notable increase in railway transport capacity. He also said that priority in government spending would go to capital construction, mining, power, chemicals, and building industries. North Korean defectors reported that basic food was still closely rationed, that the standard of living was not much improved, and that the society was rigorously controlled by the government. (*See in* CE: Korea.)

KUWAIT. During 1970 Kuwait experienced an economic recession in spite of the continued growth of its oil revenues, which exceeded $700 million. Many factors contributed to the recession, including a shortage of credit; a ceiling on interest rates that led Kuwaitis to invest their money abroad; a lack of prospects for development in Kuwait; and government restrictions on immigration and on the entry of foreigners, which reduced consumer demand. Real estate prices fell by 20%, and several domestic enterprises, including the Kuwait National Petroleum Co., showed financial losses. Kuwait's long-term economic prospects remained good.

Early in the year the National Assembly increased Kuwait's annual monetary contributions to the United Arab Republic, or Egypt, and the Palestinian Liberation Organization. Tunisia and Yemen received loans from the Kuwait Fund for Arab Development.

The future of the Persian Gulf region was Kuwait's primary concern in foreign affairs in 1970. In May the minister of defense and the interior declared that Kuwait would defend the security of the Arab emirates in the area. Kuwait rejected an Iraqi proposal for an Arab military alliance in the region following the withdrawal of British forces in 1971. A number of Kuwaiti military men serving with Arab Legion forces in the Suez area were killed by Israeli attacks in 1970. (*See in* CE: Kuwait.)

LABOR UNIONS. Organized labor in the United States was responsible for a number of major news stories during 1970. Among them were the deaths of two labor leaders, strikes and their settlements, and the changing political alignment of the labor unions.

The death of Walter P. Reuther, president of the United Automobile Workers for 24 years, came on May 9 in an aircraft accident shortly after he was reelected to another term of office. The death of the controversial labor leader was cited by U.S. President Richard M. Nixon as "a deep loss not only for organized labor but also for the cause of collective bargaining and the entire American process." Reuther was succeeded by a former aide, Leonard Woodcock, who stated that he would pursue the same causes that Reuther had.

Another union leader, Joseph A. (Jock) Yablonski, met a violent death the night of Dec. 30–31, 1969. On Jan. 5, 1970, a few weeks after he was defeated by incumbent W. A. (Tony) Boyle for the presidency of the United Mine Workers of America (UMW), Yablonski, his wife, and daughter were found slain in their home. Five suspects were arrested, but none had been brought to trial by year-end. However, the U.S. Department of Labor challenged the Boyle reelection and brought the whole structure of the UMW under investigation. (*See* Crime.)

Collective Bargaining

Midyear statistics for 1970 showed that major collective-bargaining settlements during the first six months of the year resulted in average wage increases of about 8% a year in salaries alone under the terms of the new contracts. Fringe benefits brought these increases to around 8.6% over a two- or three-year period. In money terms, raises during the first half of the year averaged about 25¢ an hour, or 4.4¢ higher than those during the same period of 1969. Examples of wage hikes agreed upon in 1970 included a 53.5% increase in wages and fringe benefits for New York City tug crew members over three years and a 21.3% pay increase for ladies' garment workers over the same time period.

Strikes and Settlements

Strikes continued to take a heavy toll in 1970. Idleness resulting from strikes was estimated at 41.5 million man-days for the first nine months of the year, or 0.30% of the total work time for that period. A strike by more than 340,000 auto workers against General Motors (GM) Corp. began September 15 and continued to mid-November, when GM and the United Auto Workers settled for increases totaling 25% to 30%. This estimate includes raises under an unlimited cost-of-living clause that links wages to prices.

As the year began, a coalition of the International Union of Electrical Workers, the United Electrical Workers, and ten smaller unions was still striking against General Electric Co. (GE). The walkout, which began in October 1969, continued until the end of January 1970 when GE settled for what it termed as "inflationary but not super-inflationary" terms. Unions estimated their gains at an average of $1.05 per hour, or about 25% over 40 months.

The strike was particularly significant because the unions, formerly jealous rivals, were able to mass their bargaining strength and to develop their

Construction workers in New York City march to city hall, waving flags and carrying placards to demonstrate their massive support for U.S. President Richard M. Nixon.

WIDE WORLD

unity to a degree that made coalition bargaining a more popular method of negotiating. It was thought that coalition bargaining would be employed increasingly in future disputes.

The boycott proved to be a fairly effective weapon in the hands of the United Farmworkers Organizing Committee. The farm workers gained recognition for their union, led by César Chavez, after four and a half years of striking and grape boycotts. They were also able to bring one of the largest California lettuce growers into an agreement after a strike lasting a week.

The United Rubber Workers struck two major companies, the Goodyear Tire & Rubber Co. and B. F. Goodrich Co., and won settlements valued at \$1.30 and \$1.39 an hour in wages and fringe benefits over three years. Other rubber companies negotiated similar settlements to prevent strikes.

In December four railroad unions staged an 18-hour nationwide strike. One union was threatened with a fine of \$200,000 a day for each day of the strike. Congress passed a bill giving the unions a retroactive 13.5% pay increase, but the issue of work rules remained to be negotiated by March 1, 1971.

The two-million-member International Brotherhood of Teamsters (IBT) put the greatest pressure on wages during the year and set a pattern that was observed by the UAW and the United Steelworkers of America. Frank E. Fitzsimmons, general vice-president of the IBT, acting for the union's jailed president, James R. Hoffa, led the IBT to a settlement of about \$1.10 per hour over 39 months in national negotiations with Trucking Employers, Inc. (TEI), the trucking firms' bargaining agent. The settlement was less than the union's rank and file had expected; wildcat strikes broke out. Meanwhile, IBT locals and a strong independent union engaged in separate bargaining in Chicago. When they struck selected firms in a demand for a bigger settlement, the whole industry shut down in Chicago, at a cost of hundreds of millions of dollars to the local economy. When the settlement came, the Chicago unions had won a \$1.65-per-hour raise over 36 months. The national union and TEI reopened their agreement to raise the settlement to a similar \$1.85 per hour over 39 months.

The trucking agreement is estimated at about a 41.3% increase over 39 months. It is thought that it would result in a trend away from national trucking negotiations to regional bargaining in 1973.

Union leader César Chavez (far left) is about to address his followers in Guadalupe, Calif. He announced another successful contract.

EMIL FRAY FROM PIX

Labor and Government

Organized labor and the Nixon Administration were often at odds during the year, although toward the end of 1970 the Republicans were seriously trying to woo unions and their blue-collar members away from the Democratic party.

President Nixon disregarded union recommendations in designating Edward B. Miller, a Chicago management attorney, as chairman of the National Labor Relations Board (NLRB). The unions also opposed the later proposal of Ralph Kennedy, an NLRB regional director from Los Angeles, to fill another opening on the five-member board. Both men were thought to have possible biases against labor causes.

The labor movement was also firm in its opposition to the Nixon Administration's economic policies and objected to many of the government's domestic priorities. It remained deeply divided on the issue of Vietnam, with unions participating in both antiwar movements and prowar rallies. After construction workers and longshoremen in New York City marched in the Wall Street area to show support of the Administration's war policy, President Nixon invited their "hard-hat" leaders to Washington, D.C., and personally thanked them.

President Nixon also invited many of the nation's top union leaders to a White House dinner on Labor Day and an additional several thousand labor union employees to a celebration afterward on the White House lawn. The unprecedented invitation was significant because most of those who were invited accepted their bids to the dinner party and military show. At the dinner George L. Meany, president of the American Federation of Labor-Congress of Industrial Organizations (AFL-CIO), made remarks that indicated displeasure with the Democratic party. However, attendance by AFL-CIO leaders at the celebration led to some criticism within union ranks for the apparent friendliness toward a Republican administration.

President Nixon surprised organized labor on June 10 when he designated Secretary of Labor George P. Shultz as director of the newly created Office of Management and Budget. The president named Undersecretary of Labor James D. Hodgson to succeed Shultz. Hodgson had previously been chief labor negotiator for the Lockheed Corp. He was praised by the International Association of Machinists as "a straight-shooting management man," and Meany assured him of the same degree of cooperation that his predecessor had received. (*See also* Business and Industry; Economy; Employment. *See in* CE: Labor.)

LEONARD FREED FROM MAGNUM

The carving on Stone Mountain in Georgia was dedicated as a Confederate memorial in 1970. The carving, the world's largest, covers an area the size of a football field.

LANDMARKS AND MONUMENTS.

In 1970, New York City was just one of many cities devoting time and energy to the preservation of its landmarks and monuments. A project for an 11-block, 38-acre area along the waterfront was sponsored by the South Street Seaport Museum to include the former Fulton Fish Market, old houses, commercial buildings, and warehouses. The plans called for the rehabilitation of some of the historic structures and for the revival of commerce in the area, with new shops and restaurants to recall the 19th century. A major maritime museum was planned and had already acquired several exhibits. Privately financed office and apartment buildings were called for, to be built in keeping with the surroundings. Full taxes would be paid on these developments, thus increasing neighboring real estate values while providing a low-density recreational and cultural area for tourists and residents of the city.

Another example of the trend to preserve historically interesting residential zones of New York City while ensuring low-density occupation was the move to rehabilitate 19th-century residences initiated by the Brownstone Revival Committee. (The term "brownstone" is used loosely to refer to 19th-century residential buildings built of brick, limestone, or masonry.) Privately financed neighborhood restoration was economically feasible, avoiding the high budgets required for publicly financed urban-renewal projects. However, the success of the project depended upon zoning regulations forbidding high-rise structures in those areas and imposing lower real estate taxes. The committee published a guide identifying 25 brownstone neighborhoods, and there were waiting lists of prospective purchasers.

Two significant events took place in Texas during the year. On June 13, in Johnson City, the U.S. government acquired the titles to both the restored birthplace and the boyhood home of former President Lyndon B. Johnson. And, on June 24, in

Dallas, a cenotaph was dedicated to the memory of the late President John F. Kennedy; the empty tomb was placed approximately 200 yards from the spot where the assassination took place on Nov. 22, 1963.

In Great Britain, a campaign was launched to raise $1,200,000 to restore and preserve the Albert Hall in London, and work on the exterior was completed in 1970. The interior was to be redecorated before the building's centenary in 1971. Projects to adapt historically interesting buildings for new purposes also continued. One was the conversion of old malthouses at Bishop's Stortford, Hertford, into a major concert hall and arts complex. The project was estimated to cost $600,000 and was scheduled for completion in 1972.

An outstanding example of the restoration of an historic quarter was the project for the Marais in Paris, sparked by the restoration of the Place des Vosges and legislation to aid public and private restoration projects. The coach house of the Hôtel de St. Aignan was restored and adapted for the use of the International Council of Monuments and Sites and as an international documentation center. The hotel itself was cleared of unwanted later additions; reconstruction and adaptation for the Archives of the City of Paris were scheduled to begin in 1971. As a result of this work, it was gradually becoming fashionable to live in the Marais, and middle- and upper-class residents were returning. (*See also* National Park Service.)

At the Kalong outpost in Laos government soldiers guard fortified bunkers and connecting trenches 20 miles from the Ho Chi Minh Trail.

WIDE WORLD

LAOS. The search for a political solution to bring peace to Laos through mutual concessions prevailed in 1970 over the military escalation that had been the central fact of the preceding year. The governments of the United States and North Vietnam, the parties most responsible for this escalation, accepted the idea that their Laotian allies—the pro-U.S. premier, Prince Souvanna Phouma, and the pro-Communist Prince Souphanouvong, leader of the Neo Lao Hak Sat (Laotian Patriotic Front), the political arm of the Pathet Lao—should enter publicly into discussions that could lead to a cease-fire in 1971.

Prince Souphanouvong (second from right), leader of the Neo Lao Hak Sat, holds a meeting at headquarters.

PIX

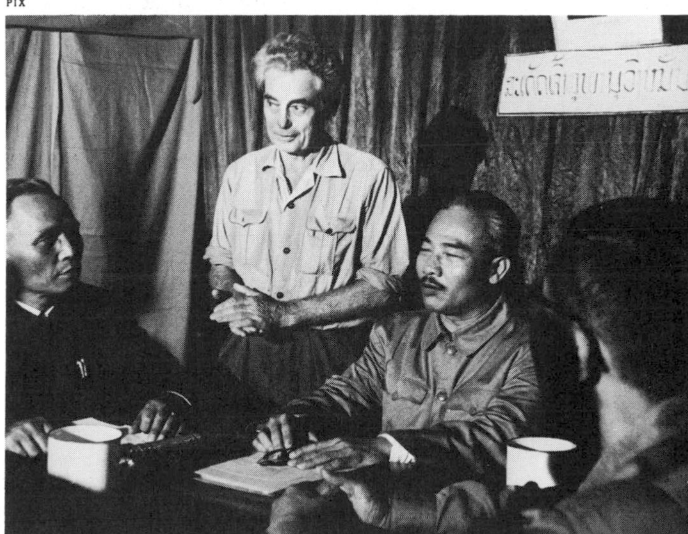

Late in January, while the Laotian government was preparing the evacuation of the Plain of Jars—which had been taken from its adversaries in the preceding year by a secret army controlled by the U.S. Central Intelligence Agency—the premier suggested that the Plain of Jars should be neutralized. This plan was rejected by the Neo Lao Hak Sat later in the week; but as soon as its forces and those of North Vietnam had reoccupied the Plain of Jars, it published, early in March, a five-point "plan for a political solution to the Laotian problem," proposing the ending of U.S. bombing, the withdrawal of all U.S. forces and weapons from certain regions, and the formation of a provisional coalition government.

A still more significant fact was that Prince Souphanouvong sent a colonel from his "liberation army" to Vientiane, the capital, to hand over the plan directly to Prince Souvanna Phouma, together with a personal letter from him, two weeks later. The overthrow of Prince Norodom Sihanouk in Cambodia a few days earlier and the intervention in that country of North Vietnamese forces, Viet

Cong, and then U.S. and South Vietnamese troops impeded the rapprochement that was being worked out in Laos. Prince Souphanouvong's messenger went back to the "liberated zone" empty-handed, while the Vientiane government engaged in delaying tactics to hold up its reply, delivered early in April.

The pro-Communist forces suddenly relaxed their position in late July, when they sent a new messenger, Prince Tiao Souk Vongsak, a member of the Neo Lao Hak Sat Central Committee, to the Laotian capital. He immediately met with the Laotian premier and, less than two weeks later, an agreement was made for talks to begin officially between a representative of Prince Souvanna Phouma and one of Prince Souphanouvong at Khang Khai, an area controlled by the Neo Lao Hak Sat. The latter gave up its precondition of an end to U.S. bombing—though its representative raised the matter again during the talks.

The initial contact that had been made between Souvanna Phouma and Tiao Souk Vongsak became bogged down in procedural difficulties and was then interrupted for a long period because of a tour of Western capitals by Prince Souvanna Phouma in September and October. Nonetheless the level of military operation remained—except on the Ho Chi Minh Trail—lower than in preceding years. There was a minor offensive by the government forces, who in September recaptured the former neutralist base of Muong Soui, situated on the northern edge of the Plain of Jars.

Shortly after the return of Prince Souvanna Phouma to Vientiane, Prince Tiao Souk Vongsak also went back there, late in October. The general feeling was thus strengthened in the Laotian capital that the efforts undertaken by both sides in an attempt to find a political solution were far from being abandoned. (*See also* Cambodia; Vietnam. *See in* CE: Laos.)

LATIN AMERICA. Events in Latin America in 1970 combined to suggest that a new phase in the Western Hemisphere's internal relations was beginning. In the United States, President Richard M. Nixon introduced a cooler approach to Latin America and its problems, while the Latin Americans showed a more general disenchantment over the failure of their relations with the United States to help solve their difficulties.

Among the Latin American nations themselves certain trends that had been discernible in 1969 became clearer in 1970. The emergence of more decidedly defined nationalist trends was evident as the governments of Brazil and Peru completed another year in office, Chile elected a Marxist to the presidency, and Bolivia made another change of government. In the Latin American context, the concepts of the cold war and of hemisphere solidarity ceased to have much significance.

Regional and Subregional Integration

The Latin American Free Trade Association (LAFTA) made no more than slow progress in 1970 toward its ultimate goal of complete trade liberalization and an eventual common market. At the ninth annual meeting, held in Caracas, Venezuela, toward the end of 1969, the members found it impossible to reach agreement on the expansion of the "common list" of liberalized items, and the date by which liberalization should be completed was postponed from 1973 to 1980. The goal of a common market, originally foreseen for 1985, was deferred indefinitely.

It was widely recognized that formal intergovernment trade concessions had been carried as far as was feasible for the time being. It seemed that further general liberalization, especially since it would increasingly involve industrial goods, would depend on major economic changes, including the

Political prisoners in the Dominican Republic were ransomed in exchange for the life of a kidnapped U.S. air attaché. The prisoners are boarding a bus to the airport, where they will be flown to exile in Mexico.
WIDE WORLD

This anti-American poster appeared at a rally for Salvador Allende, who was campaigning for the presidency of Chile. It reads "Homage to the Yankee Culture."

FREDERIC OHRINGER FROM NANCY PALMER AGENCY

nationalization of industrial structures, within the individual countries. At a less formal level, however, there was a continued and appreciable expansion of intra-LAFTA trade in manufactures derived from complementation agreements in individual private sectors such as the motor vehicle industry, in which there had been a notable growth in the interchange of components. Another promising long-term project, launched in April, was a study of food prices and availability and of national consumption habits, with a view to improving trade in, and supply of, food products in the region.

The Central American Common Market (CACM), the progress of which was halted in mid-1969 by the war between El Salvador and Honduras, began to show signs of a slow recovery; there was a limited resumption of the movement of goods and an improvement in official relations. Notwithstanding the political difficulties, however, the five CACM central banks agreed on the formation of a monetary stabilization fund, from which member banks could make short-term borrowings to ease temporary balance-of-payments difficulties.

The subregional group that has made the greatest impact, both on its component members and on the rest of the Western Hemisphere, is the Andean Group, or Andean Common Market, consisting of Bolivia, Chile, Colombia, Ecuador, and Peru. The group acquired formal existence with the ratification by all five countries of the Agreement of Cartagena, which came into force in October 1969. It acquired legal and operational identity on Nov. 24, 1969, with the adoption of the Andean Subregional Integration Agreement and the setting up of an administrative board with headquarters in Lima, Peru. The Andean Development Corporation held its first meeting in June 1970, and there were discussions on the establishment of a regional investment bank. A round of tariff reductions on intraregional trade, in accordance with LAFTA principles, was concluded later in the year.

On the Atlantic side, some progress was made in developing the concept of the Río de la Plata Basin group. The countries involved—Argentina, Bolivia, Brazil, Paraguay, and Uruguay—pursued their studies of the basin's major natural resources.

THE ORGANIZATION OF AMERICAN STATES

Changes were made in the charter of the Organization of American States (OAS) in February 1970, giving the Inter-American Economic and Social Council (CIES, from the initials of its name in Spanish) and the recently established Inter-American Council for Education, Science, and Culture the same permanent status and importance as the political Permanent Council (formerly OAS Council). The first annual meeting of the General Assembly—which replaced the Inter-American Conference as the supreme authority of the OAS—was held in June 1970. After the changes in the charter were adopted, attention was centered on the problems of kidnapping, sabotage, hijacking, and other forms of terrorism and on the question of restoring relations with Cuba. Although violence in its many forms was recognized as having political consequences and might fall in the jurisdiction of the Permanent Council, it was widely seen as having economic and social origins.

The ministers in the General Assembly generally believed that terrorism and violence were spontaneous domestic problems, the product of frustration and lack of opportunity. Few representatives at the General Assembly believed that terrorism was inspired by Cuban designs, or indeed those of any other foreign state. The consensus on the real origins of violence, as being engendered by social and economic conditions in each country, gave the CIES outstanding importance as a body whose deliberations must be, at the very least, highly relevant to this disturbing problem.

The restoration of relations with Cuba and, by inference, the readmission of Cuba into the OAS, or into a similar organization that might be formed without U.S. participation, were ideas that rapidly gained wider acceptance in 1970, and not only in countries with markedly left-wing governments. With Chile in the lead, the South American republics were increasingly coming around to the view, unwaveringly held in Mexico, that Cuba was a Latin American state first and that a truly independent foreign policy called for a difference of opinion with the United States over relations with Cuba.

The OAS was quick to respond to the plight of Peru, which on May 31 suffered an earthquake described as the worst disaster of the century in the Americas. Immediately following the quake, a $250,000 fund for relief was authorized by the OAS Permanent Council, and the member countries, in addition to their individual contributions, pledged hundreds of thousands of dollars to aid Peru.

Central America's foreign ministers signed an agreement in June to guarantee peace between Honduras and El Salvador, which were involved in an undeclared "hundred hours' war" in 1969. The two countries accepted a plan of pacification under the sponsorship of the OAS, with a guarantee by the other Central American governments. Military observers from the OAS were designated to carry out the peace plan. (*See also* articles on individual countries. *See in* CE: Articles on individual countries; Latin America; South America.)

WIDE WORLD

William Kunstler, attorney for black militant H. Rap Brown and for seven of the Conspiracy 8 defendants, gives the clenched-fist salute as he leaves court in Bel Air, Md.

LAW. Fundamental questions regarding the fairness of jury trials and the basic U.S. judicial process were raised in law circles during 1970. A legal furor was created over the actions of judges in two important trials, and there was much debate over how to maintain order in the courtroom.

At the close of the so-called "Conspiracy Eight" trial in Chicago in February, Judge Julius J. Hoffman began handing out contempt sentences moments after the jury left the courtroom to begin deliberations. The seven defendants—one defendant was severed from the case in November 1969—were sentenced to prison terms ranging from more than 2 months to almost 2½ years. Hoffman went even further and sentenced the defense attorneys. William Kunstler was sentenced to 4 years and 13 days in prison; Leonard Weinglass, to 1 year, 8 months, and 3 days for contempt of court.

The harsh sentences brought a sharp response from members of the legal community. The American Civil Liberties Union accused Hoffman of exercising an unconstitutional use of power. Various other groups of lawyers denounced Hoffman's conduct of the trial as well as the contempt sentences.

Judge Hoffman imposed the contempt citations because of disruptions in the courtroom during the trial. During the year this became a major issue in other trials. The pretrial hearings in New York City of 13 Black Panthers accused of conspiracy were disrupted by outbursts from the defendants. State Supreme Court Justice John M. Murtagh recessed the hearings on February 25, sent the defendants back to jail, and refused to release them on bail until they signed a good-behavior pledge. Many suggestions for maintaining order in the court were made in 1970, including the confinement of defendants in soundproof plastic cages or keeping defendants in separate rooms equipped with closed-circuit television. During the year the U.S. Supreme Court ruled that unruly defendants waive their right to be present at their trial.

One reason for courtroom disruptions was the belief by some litigants—especially blacks—that they could not receive justice under the existing system. In Michigan, three suspended white De-

(*continued on page 327*)

Representative H. James Shea, Jr., of the Massachusetts legislature, sponsored a bill providing that citizens of his state could not be forced to fight in a foreign war that had not been officially declared by the U.S. Congress. The bill passed the legislature and was signed by the governor but was invalidated by the courts.

UPI COMPIX

Special Report: Chicago Conspiracy Trial

by J. Anthony Lukas, Staff Writer, *The New York Times;*
Author of 'The Barnyard Epithet and Other Obscenities'

In the Chicago "Conspiracy" trial, the defendants—Tom Hayden, Rennie Davis, David Dellinger, Abbie Hoffman, Jerry Rubin, John Froines, Lee Weiner, and Bobby Seale—were tried under the antiriot provisions of the Civil Rights Act of 1968. These provisions originated with Southern congressmen determined to prosecute the "outside agitators" whom they held responsible for racial unrest. Federal laws did not prohibit rioting or even incitement to riot, for those were state offenses and most states already had ample legislation against them. The new law gave the federal government a legal hook to snag the agitators: their "intent" to incite a riot as they moved from state to state.

The U.S. Department of Justice did not want that hook. The then U.S. attorney general, Ramsey Clark, felt that riots were properly the responsibility of the states and localities. Moreover, he feared that prosecutions for intent might infringe upon constitutionally protected rights to freedom of speech, assembly, and movement.

Even after the U.S. Congress passed the provisions, Clark was reluctant to use them. After the violence during the 1968 Democratic National Convention, he called U.S. attorney Thomas Foran and ordered him to proceed cautiously through a "lawyer's investigation" rather than with a grand jury. When word of this got to Chicago's Mayor Richard J. Daley, he was outraged. Stung by widespread criticism of his hard-line tactics during the convention, he wanted vindication and revenge on the radicals who had dared to challenge him.

So the Daley machine ground smoothly into operation. Chief Federal District Judge William Campbell, long a close friend of the mayor, summoned a grand jury and instructed it to look for violations of the antiriot law. Foran, who owed his appointment directly to the mayor, came up with supporting evidence, and on March 20, 1969, the jury returned indictments against the eight demonstrators, both for conspiring and acting individually to cross state lines with an intent to incite a riot during the Democratic convention.

By this time, the Administration of U.S. President Richard M. Nixon was in power in Washington, D.C. The reluctant Ramsey Clark had been replaced by John Mitchell, who was publicly proclaiming his eagerness to go after the radicals with every instrument at his disposal. Seeing that his interests neatly coincided with Mayor Daley's in this case, he gave the final go-ahead for prosecution. Everything else that followed, I would contend, stemmed from that decision by the Justice Department to carry a political battle into court. Once a political prosecution was launched, it was probably inevitable that it should be met by an aggressive political defense and presided over by an openly political judge.

WIDE WORLD

A courtroom sketch of the Conspiracy trial shows five defendants hearing their sentences. Cameras were barred from the courtroom.

The most unpredictable element of the trial proved to be Judge Julius J. Hoffman. Through it all, the judge looked down from the bench with an air of professorial distaste. At times, he reminded me of a spinster schoolteacher in a classroom of unruly children, forever rapping his ruler for order and sending children to stand in the corner, but stirring more trouble with each new act of discipline. Yet, as the trial wore on, I felt he was more than an eccentric old curmudgeon. I began to see a pattern in his vocal theatrics and lapses of memory. Invariably his inflections helped to underline a government point or to ridicule the defense—and best of all, they would never show up in the stenographic appellate record.

Roughly, one could divide the trial into five phases:

Phase One—or "Jelly Beans," as the defendants called it—lasted from the trial's start on Sept. 24 through Oct. 13, 1969. During that period, the defendants took a gently mocking stance toward the trial, symbolized by their distribution of jelly beans to the press and spectators. It was so uneventful that the judge found only six contempts during the three weeks—one of them was Abbie Hoffman's blowing a kiss to the jury.

Phase Two—which I suppose could be called "Gags and Shackles"—lasted from October 14 through November 5. Some of the increased tension during this period may have stemmed from the defendants' feeling that their mockery had misfired and that too many potential sympathizers regarded the trial as a joke. But most of the contempts stemmed directly from Seale's continuing demand that he either be permitted counsel of his choice or the right to defend himself. The counsel of his choice was Charles R. Garry, a white Californian who had defended many Black Panthers and won their respect. But in August, Garry came down with a gall bladder condition that his doctors said required an immediate operation, and the defense asked a two-month postponement of the trial to permit him to recover. Judge Hoffman refused. When Seale was brought to Chicago from California and held in Cook County Jail, defense lawyer William Kunstler signed an "appearance" (normally signifying an intention to represent a client) so he could get in to see him. On September 26, when Seale rose to insist he was being denied his constitutional right to counsel, the judge seized on the appearance as evidence that he was adequately represented by Kunstler. Whatever technical points the judge had, the right to be represented by a lawyer you trust or, alternatively, to speak in your own behalf seemed to me so fundamental that I came to admire Seale's dogged persistence. But he and the judge were locked into an increasingly bitter conflict that resulted in Seale being bound and gagged on October 29 and then on November 5 severed from the case, convicted on 16 counts of contempt, and sentenced to four years in prison.

Phase Three—call it "The Government's Day in Court"—lasted from November 6 until December 10. As Professor Harry Kalven, Jr., of the University of Chicago noted, there were only nine contempt citations during this period. This reflected, in part, natural decompression after the pressure-cooker tensions of the Seale period; probably an element of caution once the judge had shown how tough he could be; and perhaps a growing recognition of just how weak the government's case was and a feeling that if they "cooled it" they just might squeak through with a hung jury.

Phase Four—"Sing Along with Phil and Judy"—was the early portion of the defense case, from Dec. 11, 1969, to Jan. 22, 1970. After a lengthy wrangle about whether to present a defense at all (some defendants felt they already had a hung jury and could gain nothing more), they decided to put on an elaborate political-cultural defense aimed largely at the "big jury out there." The defendants sought to explain and demonstrate their "identity"—through such witnesses as Timothy Leary, the "high priest" of the drug culture, and Jacques Levy, director of the play 'Oh! Calcutta!', as well as through the songs of Phil Ochs, Judy Collins, Arlo Guthrie, "Country Joe" McDonald, and Pete Seeger. There were relatively few contempts during this period.

Phase Five—"The Barnyard Epithet"—lasted from January 23 to February 7 when testimony was completed. This was a time of gradually building tension, culminating in the epithet (Dellinger's use of the word "b_____t" in describing a government witness' testimony) and the revocation of Dellinger's bail. The judge was massively overreacting now, often impulsively and even irrationally. Convinced they had him on the verge of some apocalyptic step, Abbie Hoffman and Rubin shrugged off all restraints and cut loose with a barrage of grotesque Yippie raillery ("You're a disgrace to the Jews, runt." "Tell him to stick it up his bowling ball."). This period produced 48 contempts.

When the verdict was in—all seven defendants were acquitted of conspiracy, but five of them (Hayden, Davis, Dellinger, Hoffman, and Rubin) were convicted on the individual counts—most liberal editorial pages and columnists praised the jury for performing its task well. Time and again the jurors were singled out for their discrimination and dedication in reaching a just decision.

And then the jurors began talking about how they had reached their decisions. Those who talked agree that the jury had divided into two camps long before they sat down to deliberate. One group of eight believed all the defendants were guilty on both counts. The other four favored acquittal for all on both charges. The deadlock that lasted almost four days was broken by Kay Richards, a young computer operator, who later described her own role as follows: "I acted as mediator. . . . I went back and forth between the two camps, insisting on a verdict. In the end they agreed to compromise, and it was hard for them to do it. Their beliefs hadn't changed as far as guilt or innocence went, and after the verdict there were some of them who wept in anger and frustration. One was almost ill. . . . I hardly realized it, but I think I am probably the only one of the 12 jurors who is really happy or satisfied with our decision."

Miss Richards sold her story of the trial to the *Chicago Sun-Times* for several thousand dollars. And she deserved it. Mayor Daley could not have pulled off a niftier compromise. Just as the mayor splits the difference between two warring ward bosses, Katie split the difference between the government and the defense. Thanks to her, the verdict was perfectly appropriate: a political end to a political trial.

(*continued from page 324*)
troit policemen and a Negro guard were acquitted of charges of conspiring to violate the civil rights of persons in a motel during the 1967 riots. The fact that the trial was held in Flint, Mich., and heard by an all-white jury raised doubts about the fairness of the trial. Two jurors in the Chicago conspiracy trial later stated that the jury had twice announced that it was deadlocked but that Judge Hoffman made them continue deliberating. (*See also* Law Special Report; Race Relations.)

During the year the Office of Economic Opportunity (OEO) announced a plan for decentralizing the Legal Services program, which provides counsel for the poor. Opponents of the new plan claimed that it would weaken the program and make it prey to local and state politics. They pointed out that the ten regional directors of OEO are all political appointees. The existing program was not immune, however, from national politics. In November the national director of Legal Services, Terry F. Lenzner, and the deputy director were removed from their posts. The decentralization plan was abandoned in December. (*See* Social Services.)

Judicial ethics came under review during 1970. The American Bar Association began revising its Canons of Judicial Ethics, and Chief Justice Warren E. Burger appointed a panel to set up guidelines for federal judges. Judges were advised to limit their business connections and to be circumspect in accepting travel expenses.

In March Palestinian commandos stepped up their guerrilla warfare in Lebanon. On the streets of Beirut, Lebanese soldiers (below) locate a sniper and prepare to return fire.

KEYSTONE

LEBANON. The activities of Palestinian guerrillas continued to cause unrest in Lebanon in 1970. Guerrilla attacks on Israel from southern Lebanon led to severe Israeli reprisals, including armed incursions in May, August, and September. Government attempts to restrain the guerrillas in order to protect the south were unsuccessful.

Lebanon's right-wing Christians pressed for the guerrillas' expulsion from the country. In March fighting erupted in Beirut, the capital, between the guerrillas and a Christian paramilitary group, and in August the guerrillas fought in Saida with supporters of President Gamal Abdel Nasser of the United Arab Republic, or Egypt, who had accepted a U.S. formula for Arab-Israeli peace talks.

In May shops, banks, schools, and transportation facilities were closed down by a general strike in support of demands by southern Lebanese for government assistance and border defenses. The government voted relief funds for refugees from the south and said that starting June 15 guerrillas were banned from firing rockets into Israel.

On August 17 the Chamber of Deputies elected Economy Minister Suleiman Franjieh to succeed Charles Hélou as Lebanon's president. After Franjieh took office on September 23, guerrilla leaders took steps to smooth relations with the government. Individual guerrilla groups agreed to centralized control by the Palestine Liberation Organization. (*See in* CE: Lebanon.)

LESOTHO. On Jan. 27, 1970, Lesotho held its first general election since 1966. The basic issue was relations with South Africa, which surrounds Lesotho. Prime Minister Chief Leabua Jonathan's Basuto National party (BNP), favoring close ties with South Africa, was opposed mainly by Ntsu Mokhehle's Basutoland Congress party, which sought fewer South African ties.

The Congress party won. Chief Jonathan, however, refused to accept his loss of power and suspended the constitution, invalidated the election, and arrested Mokhehle and other opposition members. He also forced King Moshoeshoe II into exile.

On April 1 the British government, refusing to recognize Chief Jonathan's coup, suspended aid to Lesotho. Faced by economic crises and by violent rebellions, Chief Jonathan began negotiations with the opposition on a new constitution. King Moshoeshoe returned to Lesotho in December; he accepted his loss of power. (*See in* CE: Lesotho.)

LIBERIA. Liberia's austere economy continued to show improvement in 1970 even though foreign debts absorbed about a third of the government's revenue. Both the gross national product and the production of major natural resources rose during the year. Iron ore production was expected to exceed 21.4 million tons, a record amount reached in 1969. The production of natural rubber and timber increased significantly. A $7.4-million loan was granted to Liberia by the World Bank for the expansion of the nation's electric power facilities.

In August Liberia sealed its border with Guinea to prevent the spread of a cholera epidemic into Liberia. This was the first time cholera had been reported in Africa south of the Sahara.

In February U.S. Secretary of State William P. Rogers visited Liberia during the course of an African tour. A month later Liberia deposited its ratification of the nuclear nonproliferation treaty with the United Nations. (*See in* CE: Liberia.)

LIBRARIES. Legislation creating a National Commission on Libraries and Information Services was signed on July 20, 1970, by U.S. President Richard M. Nixon. The commission will serve as an independent agency within the executive branch. It consists of the Librarian of Congress and 14 members appointed by the president, with the consent of the U.S. Senate. Its role is to advise the president and the U.S. Congress on the needs of libraries and to oversee library operations.

During the summer, a portion of the collected papers of the late U.S. President John F. Kennedy was made available to qualified scholars and researchers. The Kennedy library, housed temporarily at the Federal Records Center in Waltham, Mass., contains 15 million pages of documents and manuscripts—among them are 300 oral-history interviews of world-famous figures, including one made by former Soviet Premier Nikita S. Khrushchev.

On October 14, at the English-Speaking Union, in London, a new library was opened as a memorial to Adlai E. Stevenson, the former U.S. ambassador to the United Nations and a two-time Democratic party presidential nominee. The library was stocked with books donated by 250 of Stevenson's friends, including Great Britain's Prime Minister Edward Heath and his four predecessors.

The American Library Association (ALA) continued to play an important part in international library work. It administered grants from the Ford Foundation to rehabilitate the university library at Algiers, Algeria, and to develop the collections of the University at Addis Ababa, Ethiopia, and of Brasília University, in Brazil.

In the international field, libraries were involved with International Education Year 1970, designated by the United Nations Educational, Scientific, and Cultural Organization (UNESCO). The work of the International Federation of Library Associations (IFLA), a nongovernmental organization in consultative relations with UNESCO, reached its annual climax at the General Council, held in Moscow from August 28 to September 7. This was followed by two days of sessions and visits to libraries in Leningrad, U.S.S.R., and further tours to other parts of the Soviet Union. The main theme of the session in Moscow was "Libraries as a Force in Education," chosen for International Education Year. At a special plenary session on that theme in the House of Unions, the audience of over 700 participants from approximately 40 countries was addressed by N. I. Mokhov, deputy minister of culture of the Soviet Union, and by Malcolm Adiseshiah, deputy director-general of UNESCO. The remainder of the week's session was devoted to specialized meetings on library techniques and cooperation.

During the year, UNESCO gave subsidies of $10,000 and $20,000 respectively to the two international organizations in the library field, FID and IFLA. In cooperation with them, UNESCO initiated research projects on the national structure of library services, library statistics, a national bibliography of English-speaking countries of Africa, and a manual of document preservation. UNESCO financially supported the following meetings in 1970: a seminar on automation of libraries at Regensburg, West Germany, in April; a symposium on national systems of libraries at Prague, Czechoslovakia, in April; a symposium on planning national structures of scientific and technical information at Madrid, Spain, in October; and an experts' meeting on national planning of documentation and library services at Kampala, Uganda, in September. (*See in* CE: Library articles.)

LIBYA. The new Libyan regime, instituted in September 1969, became increasingly army-dominated in 1970, and by September the cabinet had only five civilian members. The trials of former members of the Revolutionary Command Council alleged to have attempted a countercoup in December 1969 continued throughout the year. Another attempted coup was thwarted in July.

The head of the military government, Col. Muammar el-Qaddafi, took a leading part in Mid-

In June Libyan children wearing guerrilla uniforms marched in a parade celebrating the departure of U.S. troops from their country.

WIDE WORLD

dle Eastern affairs, organizing a number of high-level meetings of Arab leaders, including the summit meeting in Tripoli, one of two capitals of Libya, in June. He was given strong personal support by President Gamal Abdel Nasser of the United Arab Republic (UAR), or Egypt, and there were many reciprocal visits before Nasser's death in September. Ideas of economic union between Libya, the UAR, and Sudan were explored, and the cooperation between these countries was evident in the number of Egyptian, and to a lesser extent Sudanese, advisers and contractors entering Libya in 1970.

The British and U.S. air bases were closed down in March and in June respectively. Following general hostility to the international oil companies, the marketing of petroleum products was nationalized in July. That month also brought a ban on the ownership of land by Italian excolonists, accompanied by strong expressions of resentment against the former Italian colonial administration (1911–42). Oil exports rose again in 1970 but not in line with the 29.5% average annual rate of increase of the 1964–69 period. (*See in* CE: Libya.)

LITERATURE. Despite a general sense among publishers in the United States that the days of large-scale mergers might be at an end, in 1970 one big house, Atheneum Publishers, followed the pattern that has become so common. It became a subsidiary of Raytheon Education Co., an electronics firm that in 1966 had purchased D. C. Heath and Co. A second publisher, Simon and Schuster, Inc., announced first that it would merge into Norton Simon Inc. and then that it would not. Simon owns McCall Publishing Co. as well as Canada Dry and Hunt Foods. An indication that a new area of mergers might lie in distribution was given when Time-Life Books acquired both the Book Find Club and the Seven Arts Book Society. Already complaints of impersonality were being raised as editors were wooed and replaced, firms were reorganized, and writers and their works were suddenly treated as chattel in new corporate structures. At Harper and Row, Publishers, where reorganization and general business slowdown led to wholesale reductions in the number of new titles, there were also troubles with the upsurging women's liberation movement. The company was struck when three female junior editors were excluded from a projected sales meeting in Virginia.

The insistence by editors that these new conglomerates would not directly affect the industry was mirrored in the large number of new writers who appeared. Nevertheless, the telltale pressure for quick sales to justify large initial expenses was apparent in the topicality of and massive television campaigns attendant to many books. Women's liberation made it into the best-seller lists with Kate Millett's 'Sexual Politics'. The 1920's and 1930's were evoked in such books as 'Zelda', Nancy Mil-

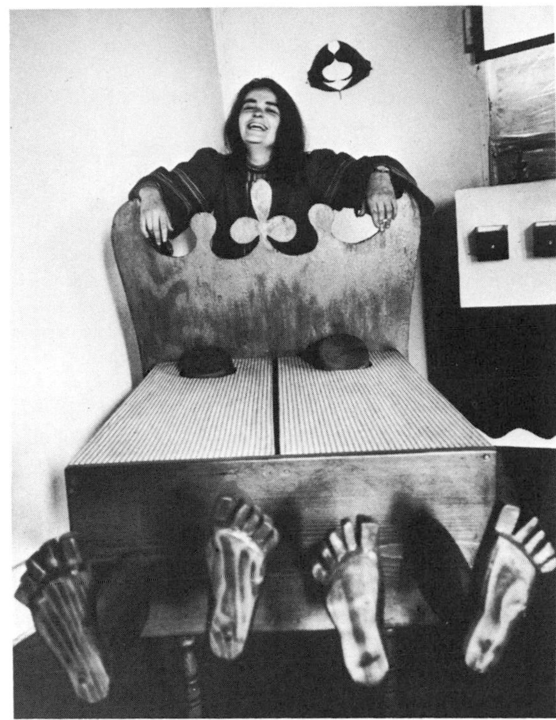

Kate Millett, author of 'Sexual Politics', which went through five printings in two months, poses with her sculpture of a double bed.

ford's best-selling account of the girl who became the wife of novelist F. Scott Fitzgerald. Erich Segal and James Dickey, both authors of best-selling novels, made a great number of national television appearances, and celebrities continued to take up larger segments of the publishers' lists. Baseball pitcher Jim Bouton penned a best seller, 'Ball Four', recounting the escapades of his former teammates.

History and Biography

Recent history was reexamined by two women in Mrs. Lyndon Johnson's 'A White House Diary' and Pearl S. Buck's 'The Kennedy Women: a Personal Appraisal'. Prizewinning novelist James A. Michener thoughtfully surveyed current problems in 'The Quality of Life', and Michael Crichton, who in the preceding year contributed the best-selling novel 'The Andromeda Strain', explored the problems of hospital care in 'Five Patients'. Robert Townsend's 'Up the Organization' offered wryly useful advice on running a business sensibly, humanly, and, above all, profitably, and Helen Leavitt attacked the destruction accompanying much recent road building in 'Superhighway—Superhoax'. Former Attorney General Ramsey Clark took a look at 'Crime in America', while Richard Harris in 'Justice' recorded some of the shortcomings of the Justice Department under Clark and his successor. Robert Sherrill was even more outraged, in 'Military Justice Is to Justice as Military Music Is to Music', at the way the military penal system handled protesters; and Tom Hayden, who was tried in Chicago for conspiracy, wrote of that bizarre experience in 'Trial'. John Aldridge's 'In the Country of the Young' took a close look at adolescents, and prolonged childhood was the subject of A. D. Jonas' and Doris Klein's 'Man-Child'. Internationally, two recollections of Nazi Germany appeared: Albert Speer's 'Inside the Third Reich' and Joachim C. Fest's 'The Face of the Third Reich'. In 'Lost Names', Richard E. Kim wrote a moving novelistic account of his growing up in Korea under Japanese occupation.

More traditional historical and biographical perspectives appeared in such books as Angus Wilson's 'The World of Charles Dickens', Hiller B. Zobel's 'The Boston Massacre', Martin Cooper's 'Beethoven', Elizabeth Longford's 'Wellington', Dumas Malone's 'Jefferson the President', Joseph Wall's 'Andrew Carnegie', William Manners' 'TR and Will', and James MacGregor Burns's 'Roosevelt: the Soldier of Freedom'. As in 'Zelda', the special world of the 1920's and 1930's was chronicled in John Keats's biography of Dorothy Parker, 'You Might as Well Live'; in Studs Terkel's 'Hard Times'; in Michael J. Arlen's recollection of his parents' wanderings, 'Exiles'; in Jay Martin's 'Nathanael West'; and in Lawrance Thompson's second volume on Robert Frost. This last book proved unequal to the task of depicting the poet who once confessed, "When I am too full of joy, I think how little good my health did anyone near me." 'The Collected Essays and Occasional Writings of Katherine Anne Porter' was issued, and 'Enid Bagnold's Autobiography' recalled the varied stages of her career. Noel Stock's 'The Life of Ezra Pound' provided a valuable account of the man whose energy helped direct that era.

Fiction

The year's biggest fiction book was Segal's 'Love Story', a brief, sentimental novel about a rich Harvard boy's learning to face life, thanks to a poor Radcliffe College girl. Segal, a personable classics professor at Yale University, was able to weave these ingredients into a moving tale. Dickey, a poet by nature, provided a second of the year's best-selling novels, 'Deliverance', which tells of violence and cruelty during a hunting trip. The year also saw the appearance of 'Last Things', the 11th and final volume of C. P. Snow's 'Strangers and Brothers' sequence, as well as Iris Murdoch's 'A Fairly Honourable Defeat'. Eudora Welty's longest effort to date, 'Losing Battles', set the year's general tone and mood. The novels all seemed losing battles with readers whose interests were increasingly toward nonfiction. Pearl S. Buck traveled into India for 'Mandala', Ira Levin into science fiction for 'This Perfect Day', and Gore Vidal into sex again for 'Two Sisters'. John Updike furnished a fresh but unimportant book in 'Bech: a Book'. Peter DeVries proved again his skill at sentimental comedy in 'Mrs. Wallop', and Eleanor Clark provided a very readable 'Baldur's Gate'. Donald Barthelme's experiments did not bring off 'City Life' nor did Irwin Shaw's sociological bias work for 'Rich Man, Poor Man'. Occasional flashes of excellence characterized Vance Bourjaily's 'Brill Among the Ruins' and Harvey Swados' 'Standing Fast'.

Soviet author Aleksandr I. Solzhenitsyn, whose works include 'The First Circle' and 'The Cancer Ward', received the 1970 Nobel prize for literature. The award was heavily criticized within the Soviet Union as being political, and a few weeks before the Nobel ceremonies Solzhenitsyn announced that he would not attend.
WIDE WORLD

Donald Barthelme wrote 'City Life', a satirical book with clever drawings that are an extension of his prose.
COURTESY, FARRAR, STRAUS & GIROUX, INC.

The most important novels of the year were posthumous—Malcolm Lowry's 'October Ferry to Gabriola' and Ernest Hemingway's 'Islands in the Stream'. Lowry's book was marred for most readers by the editing and rewriting that Mrs. Lowry did to the unfinished manuscript. Still, the book has moments of intensity and the poetic skill that marked 'Under the Volcano', the 'Inferno' of this once projected trilogy which was to rival Dante's 'Divine Comedy'. Far more faithful is the Hemingway volume. Again part of a projected trilogy, 'Islands in the Stream' was completed before the writer's death.

Heading the list of short-story collections was 'The Wheel of Love and Other Stories', by Joyce Carol Oates. The collection, like the author, had far more than the usual number of prizes. Moreover, the prizes were deserved. Also interesting were the Chekhovian explorations into small private pains that marked Frank Tuohy's 'Fingers in the Door' and the studies in selfishness which Mary Lavin's 'Happiness and Other Stories' traded on.

Poetry; Mark Twain's Manuscript

The year in poetry was generally as lackluster as that in fiction. John Berryman contributed an important new volume, 'Love and Fame', and Robert Lowell added more than 90 new poems to an expanded version of 'Notebook'. Irving Feldman's 'Magic Papers and Other Poems' showed his increasing range, but both Denise Levertov's 'Relearning the Alphabet' and William Stafford's 'Allegiances' failed to break new ground.

Second books by poets proved far more significant. Richard Emil Braun offered a savagely funny look at U.S. culture in 'Bad Land', paling the gentler, more whimsical attacks of Michael Benedikt's 'Sky' and James Tate's 'The Oblivion Ha-Ha'. Miss Oates reaffirmed the talent for poetry she displayed in 'Anonymous Sins' with her new collection 'Love and Its Derangements'. 'Depth of Field' introduced a new and promising poet in William Heyen. A previously unknown Mark Twain manuscript was acquired by the New York Public Library's Berg Collection—a 400-page letter written, but apparently never sent, to William Dean Howells six months before Twain's death. It recounts how for two years Twain had been cheated by his business manager, Ralph W. Ashcroft, and by his secretary.

Recent Developments in the Soviet Union

The release in September of Yuli M. Daniel from prison highlighted an equally amorphous year for Soviet writers. Daniel was convicted in 1966 for publishing the satirical 'This Is Moscow Speaking' under the name of Nikolai Arzhak. In 1969 he led a hunger strike at Potma, the secret prison camp 250 miles east of Moscow where he was being held. The release culminated a long effort by writers both within and outside of the Soviet Union to have his original five-year sentence set aside. Among the writers most outspoken in their support and in condemnations of censorship in general were Aleksandr T. Tvardovsky and Aleksandr I. Solzhenitsyn, who in 1970 spent part of their energies in obtaining the release of Zhores A. Medvedev, a biologist and outspoken critic of the government. Medvedev had been imprisoned in a mental hospital for political reasons. The release came after 19 days.

That the release of Daniel was not a softening of the government toward its critics was underscored earlier with the arrest in May of Andrei A. Amalrik. Amalrik's 'Will the Soviet Union Survive Until 1984?' had been published abroad. He was accused of spreading "deliberate false fabrications, defaming the Soviet state and public order," a charge punishable by as much as three years in prison. The book predicted that the Soviet Union would be torn apart by rivalries among its ethnic communities, inertia and bureaucracy in its central administration, and an inevitable war with Communist China.

A play by Solzhenitsyn, whose works are banned in the Soviet Union, was premiered at the Tyrone Guthrie Theatre in Minneapolis, Minn. The play, published as 'The Love-Girl and the Innocent', is set in 1945 in a Stalinist slave-labor camp similar to the one where Solzhenitsyn spent eight years.

Solzhenitsyn was awarded the Nobel prize for literature in 1970. The award was criticized as an anti-Soviet political act by representatives of the Soviet literary establishment.

In Moscow, for three nights before it was closed for ideological reasons, 'Watch Your Faces' played to large crowds. The revue was a collage of poetry by Andrei Voznesensky, imaginative pantomime, topical humor, and mild social comment. The members of the audience were shown themselves in two large mirrors and told that they must look to themselves to build a future. Voznesensky was also one of the principal writers attacked by Ivan Shevtsov in his anti-West, anti-Zionist, and anti-intellectual novel 'In the Name of the Father and of the Son'. The novel was attacked in turn by *Komsomolskaya Pravda,* the Communist youth organization paper, as a harmful book.

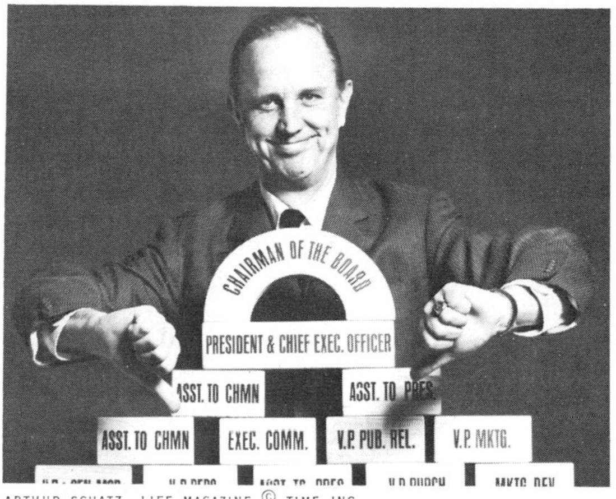

ARTHUR SCHATZ, LIFE MAGAZINE © TIME INC.

Robert Townsend turns thumbs down on the structure of big business, as he did on paper in his best-selling 'Up the Organization'.

Lively and warm reflections on Anna Akhmatova and Boris Pasternak appeared in the memoirs of Osip Mandelshtam's widow. The book covers a period from 1934 to 1937, just before Mandelshtam's death in 1938. Critics felt that the publication of the memoirs might be part of a long-awaited restoration of the works of the poet, considered a leader of Soviet classical style.

The Year in Other Countries

Equally unpredictable was the year in other East European countries. In Yugoslavia, Mihajlo Mihajlov, sentenced in 1967 for his criticism of

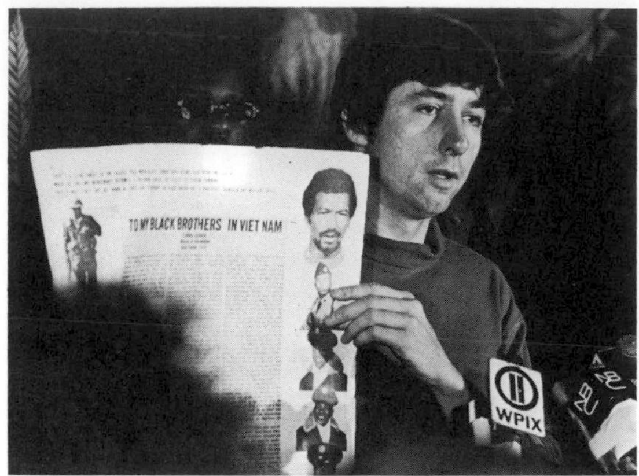

JIM ANDERSON FROM NANCY PALMER AGENCY

Tom Hayden speaks about the Black Panthers in New Haven, Conn., in May. He is the author of 'Trial', an account of the experiences of the Chicago Conspiracy defendants.

the Soviet Union, was released in March 1970. The release stipulated that he was not to write or speak publicly for four years. This tied up the announced publication of 'Pensées', a book written while Mihajlov was in prison. Mihajlov's U.S. publisher decided to adhere to the Yugoslav ruling.

In Czechoslovakia, Minister of Culture Miloslav Bruzek kept his promise made in November 1969 that only those artists and intellectuals who had proved total commitment to the present party line would be allowed to go abroad. He prevented the author and playwright Pavel Kohout from going to Lucerne, Switzerland, for a talk. Kohout, who supported the drive for reform in 1968, was accused of being an "advocate of Israeli aggression." He and two other liberal writers had already been expelled from the Czechoslovak Communist party. By midyear, the government had seized the publishing house and recreation center of the Czechoslovak Writers' Union, making it nearly impossible for a nonconformist writer to be printed.

But not all the censorship was limited to Eastern Europe. Brazil imposed strict controls on pornography; and a judge in Sydney, Australia, upheld that nation's customs ban on 'Myra Breckinridge', calling the Vidal novel "filthy, bawdy, lewd, and disgusting." The South Korean government indicted three journalists and a politician accused of publishing a defamatory poem, 'Five Thieves'. The poem, written by Kim Chi Ha, charged government leaders, generals, politicians, and businessmen with corruption. The four were arrested for having violated an anti-Communist law. In Japan the militant Buddhist political party, Komeito, came under fire for its efforts to block the publication of 'Slashing the Soka Gakkai', an exposé of the opportunism of that fast-growing Buddhist sect and its president, Daisaku Ikeda. The book was written by Professor Hirotatsu Fujiwara.

Simone de Beauvoir, whose 'The Second Sex' still produced heated controversy in France, brought out 'La Vieillesse', a sociological treatment of how the lives of old men and women are conditioned by the class structure of capitalism. In Italy, Alberto Moravia collected 30 of his stories into 'Il Paradiso'. The stories are all first-person narratives told by women. Almost half of Guido Piovene's existential novel 'Le Stelle Fredde' was given over to the return of the Russian novelist Fedor Dostoevski from the dead to tell all (in French). Other interesting Italian fiction included Arrigo Benedetti's 'Gli Occhi' and Goffredo Parise's 'Il Crematorio di Vienne'. Antonio Papisca arrived on the scene with a fine little collection of poems, 'Fellowship'.

Two works seemed to dominate the West German literary world. Herbert Rosendorfer, an official of the Department of Justice in Munich, contributed the best-selling 'Der Ruinenbaumeister', a collection of ironic tales. 'Zettels Traum' by Arno Schmidt proved to be not only one of the largest German novels ever printed but a serious one as well. (*See also* Awards and Prizes.)

LITERATURE, CANADIAN. In 1970 Canadian fiction reflected the major socioeconomic and political disparities in the country, including the problems of Canada's native Indian and Eskimo minorities and the gulf between the language cultures of French and English. In her short novella 'Windflower', Gabrielle Roy produced a compassionate study of a simple Eskimo girl and her blond, blue-eyed, American-fathered son, who fled his primitive heritage in the North. Mort Forer's 'The Humback' is a chilling picture of a métis settlement in Manitoba which has an environment and an economy that are both out of step with the 20th century. The cultural gulf separating Canada's founding peoples is exemplified in 'La Guerre, Yes Sir!', a translation of Roch Carrier's book of 1968. Disparity is equally evident in the sordid poverty and brutalized childhood described in 'The Manuscripts of Pauline Archange', by Marie-Claire Blais. In a lighter vein, Robert Kroetsch's 'The Studhorse Man' is about a ribald safari across Alberta of a man and his stallion, each looking for the perfect mate. Mavis Gallant's 'A Fairly Good Time' presents an openhearted Canadian girl living in Paris who attracts problem people while her own personal life remains an emotional shambles. Richard Wright wrote a funny first novel, 'The Weekend Man', which displays vigorous imagination. 'The Honeyman Festival', by Marian Engel, is set in Toronto, Ont.; Europe; and a small Ontario town. Hugh Hood's 'A Game of Touch' takes place in Montreal, Que.

Noteworthy volumes of poetry published in 1970 included Joan Finnigan's 'It Was Warm and Sunny When We Set Out', Gail Fox's 'In Dangerous Season', and R. A. D. Ford's 'The Solitary City'. John Glassco brought out 'The Poetry of French Canada in Translation', an anthology of French Canadian poems translated by English-speaking poets.

Harry Howith's 'Fragments of the Dance', published in 1969, also appeared.

Among the leading nonfiction books were John Glassco's 'Memoirs of Montparnasse', describing Paris as experienced by a young man, and Robert Speaight's 'Vanier: Soldier, Diplomat and Governor General', written in great detail and interspersing much of Canada's recent history in a thoroughly readable account of Canada's first French Canadian governor-general. Pierre Berton's 'The National Dream, the Great Railway 1871–1881' is a lively look at the conception and building of the Canadian Pacific Railway. Donald Waterfield's 'Continental Waterboy' is an articulate and sad chronicle of the events preceding and following the signing of the Columbia River Treaty. Jim Lotz wrote "Northern Realities', an intensely interesting account of Canada's Yukon Territory, its problems of climate, its delicate ecology, and the difficulties of administration in this multiracial, sparsely populated area. Other outstanding nonfiction works were Farley Mowat's 'Sibir: My Discovery of Siberia', Peter Mellen's 'The Group of Seven', Moshe Safdie's 'Beyond Habitat', Donald Creighton's 'Canada's First Century, 1867–1967', and George Woodcock's 'Canada and the Canadians'.

Important novels in the French language included 'Kamouraska', by Anne Hébert; 'La Séparation', by Jean Simard; 'La Rivière sans repos', by Gabrielle Roy; 'Le Feu sacré', by Pierre Dagenais; 'Le Dernier havre', by Yves Thériault; 'Les Apparences', by Marie-Claire Blais; 'Les Voyages d'Irkoutsk', by Jean Basile; and 'L'Amélanchier', by Jacques Ferron. The best of the volumes of French poetry were probably 'L'Homme Rapaillé', by Gaston Miron; 'Débâcle' and 'A l'Orée des travaux', by Yves Préfontaine; and 'Parler de septembre', by Fernand Dumont. (*See also* Literature. *See in* CE: Canadian Literature.)

LITERATURE, CHILDREN'S. Among the developments of 1970 in the field of children's literature was the appearance of a number of books about the moon landing, books reflecting the growing concern about pollution and ecology, and books for and about black people. There was a noticeable relaxation of taboos in language and in subject, exemplified by the appearance of a number of books dealing with drugs and sex.

For Younger Children

Quite a few picture books without texts were published during the year for the youngest group. One of the most noteworthy was Martha Alexander's 'Bobo's Dream', about a small and devoted dog who dreams of protecting his young master's property. Another wordless book was Edward Ardizzone's 'The Wrong Side of the Bed', in which a grumpy child stalks through a long day to find peace and security in an understanding mother's hug.

Two very different alphabet books were published: 'Still Another Alphabet Book', by Seymour Chwast and Martin S. Moskof, and 'The Marcel Marceau Alphabet Book', illustrated with photographs of the famous mime. 'I Write It', by Ruth Krauss, celebrates the joy of being able to write one's own name.

Among the general books for small children was Lore Segal's 'Tell Me a Mitzi'. Humorous yet informative was the photographically illustrated 'A Dog's Guide to Tokyo', by Betty Jean Lifton.

Another book with a contemporary Japanese setting was 'Sumi & the Goat & the Tokyo Express', by Yoshiko Uchida. 'Sara Somebody', by Florence and Louis Slobodkin, describes a Polish-American community at the turn of the century.

A biographical offering was the simply written 'The One Bad Thing About Father', by F. N.

LEFT: DONALD E. JOHNSON, COURTESY HARPER & ROW. BELOW: ILLUSTRATION BY EDWARD FRASCINO, HARPER & ROW PUBLISHERS

Author E. B. White (left) wrote 'The Trumpet of the Swan', a children's book about a swan (below) that had no voice.

Monjo, describing Theodore Roosevelt from his small son's viewpoint. Among the ever-popular animal stories was Gladys Conklin's 'Little Apes', about a day in the lives of a baby gorilla, chimpanzee, gibbon, and orangutan. Marjorie Weinman Sharmat's 'Gladys Told Me to Meet Her Here' depicts a small boy who waits anxiously at the zoo for a tardy friend.

During the year five books based on the children's television show Sesame Street were published, covering subjects from letters and numbers to people and things. 'Journey to the Moon', by Erich Fuchs, gives an easy-to-understand description of the flight of Apollo 11.

The 8-to-12 Group

In the area of fantasy and general fiction for older children was a new book by E. B. White, 'The Trumpet of the Swan'. Another outstanding fanciful story was 'Jason's Quest', by Margaret Laurence. In 'Grover', by Vera and Bill Cleaver, a boy faces his mother's death and the isolation of his father's grief. A touching and impressive picture of a black family is presented in John Shearer's 'I Wish I Had an Afro'.

Several legendary tales were remade and published in 1970. Among the best of these were 'The Seventh Mandarin', by Jane Yolen, illustrated by Ed Young, and 'Sundiata: the Epic of the Lion King', retold by Roland Bertol. Some very good poetry appeared in such volumes as 'Here I Am', edited by Virginia Olsen Baron, and 'Black Out Loud', an anthology of poems by black authors, edited by Arnold Adoff.

Two excellent biographies were 'Jeanne d'Arc', by Aileen Fisher, and 'Malcolm X', by Arnold Adoff. A fine collective biography was Hope Stoddard's 'Famous American Women'.

Pictures of other cultures and peoples were presented in 'The Moscow Circus School', by Leon Harris, and in Peter Spier's story about the Netherlands' struggle against the sea, 'Of Dikes and Windmills'. In a historical vein, the tragedy of atomic war was poignantly evident in Betty Jean Lifton's 'Return to Hiroshima'. Human relations as well as facts about reproduction were covered in 'Love and Sex and Growing Up', by Eric W. Johnson and Corinne B. Johnson.

For Adolescents

A sign of the times and interests of adolescents was exhibited in such titles as 'America and the Cold War', by Richard J. Walton, and 'The Making of Urban America', by Barbara Habenstreit. The

Kali Grosvenor, age 9, wrote a book called 'Poems by Kali'. Most of her poems are about black power. She had in mind black militant H. Rap Brown when she wrote:
"Lady Bird, Lady Bird
Fly away Home
Your house is on fire
And Rap's on the phone." *
The book is dedicated to the four black girls killed in 1963 in the bombing of a church in Birmingham, Ala.

ROBERT FLETCHER, COURTESY, DOUBLEDAY & CO., INC., PUBLISHERS drug problem was taken up in 'What You Should Know About Drugs and Drug Addiction', by Harvey R. Greenberg, M.D., and 'What You Should Know About Drugs', by Charles W. Gorodetzky and Samuel T. Christian. Science fiction echoing an ecological concern was the basis for Audrey Coppard's 'Who Has Poisoned the Sea?'

The best of the general fiction for teen-agers included 'Fireweed', by Jill Paton Walsh; 'Amanda's Choice', by Isabelle Holland; and 'Dave's Song', by Robert McKay. The biography of black leader W. E. B. Du Bois was presented in 'Cheer the Lonesome Traveler', by Leslie Alexander Lacy.

Awards

The National Book Award for children's literature went to Isaac Bashevis Singer for 'A Day of Pleasure: Stories of a Boy Growing Up in Warsaw'. William H. Armstrong won the John Newbery Medal for 'Sounder'. The Caldecott Medal was presented to William Steig for 'Sylvester and the Magic Pebble'. The Laura Ingalls Wilder Award, given every five years to an author whose books have made a lasting contribution, was presented to E. B. White.

The Canadian Books of the Year for Children Awards in 1970 went to Edith Fowke for 'Sally Go Round the Sun' and to Lionel Gendron for 'La Merveilleuse Histoire de la Naissance'. The Carnegie Medal of the Library Association of the United Kingdom went to "K. M." (Kathleen and Michael) Peyton for 'Flambards in Summer'; its Kate Greenaway Medal, to Helen Oxenbury for her illustrations in 'The Quangle-Wangle's Hat' and 'The Dragon of an Ordinary Family'. The Hans Christian Andersen Awards Illustrator's Medal was given to Maurice Sendak. (*See in* CE: Literature, Children's; Literary Awards.)

LUXEMBOURG.

On March 20, 1970, Luxembourg joined with representatives of 20 other French-language nations of Europe, Africa, Asia, and North America to form an agency for cultural and technical cooperation. The French-speaking states chose Paris as the headquarters for the agency and Jean-Marc Léger, a Canadian, as its director.

Colette Flesch, a 32-year-old graduate of Wellesley College in Massachusetts, was elected mayor of Luxembourg, the capital city—the youngest and only female mayor in its recent history. Miss Flesch, an active athlete, represented Luxembourg in fencing at the Olympic Games held in Rome, Tokyo, and Mexico City, Mex. She had also had an active career in Luxembourg's diplomatic service as well as in politics.

On April 8, 1970, Prince Felix of Luxembourg and Nassau, the Austrian-born consort of Grand Duchess Charlotte and the father of Grand Duke Jean, died at the age of 77. Prince Felix was the sixth child of Prince Robert of Bourbon and Princess Maria Antonia of Braganza, infanta of Portugal. (*See in* CE: Luxemburg.)

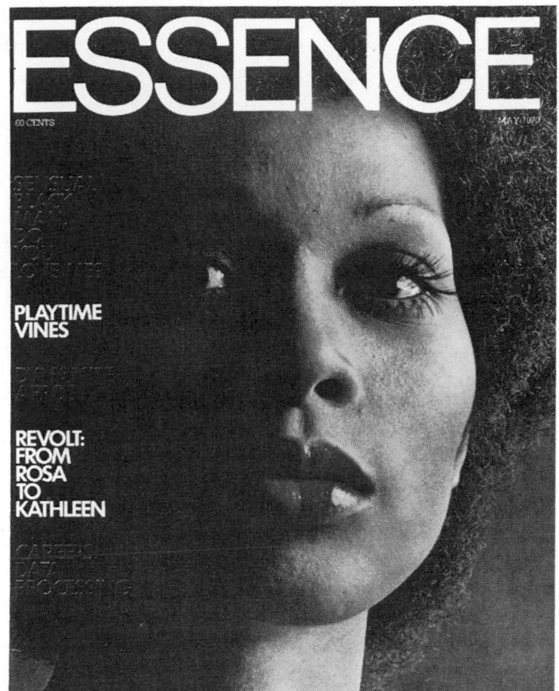

COURTESY, ESSENCE MAGAZINE

Recognizing a market long ignored, four young black businessmen in spring 1970 launched a new magazine, *Essence*, devoted to the black woman.

MAGAZINES.

Angry women and advertising losses dominated the 1970 magazine scene. Members of the women's liberation movement stormed into the offices of the *Ladies' Home Journal* on March 18. More than 100 vocal members demanded a chance to put out a "liberated issue" of what they considered "one of the most demeaning magazines towards women." While failing to concede the militants' charges, editor in chief John M. Carter agreed to an eight-page August supplement. After publication, the women called it a political victory. Carter thought it something less, doubted whether readers would identify with the movement, and suggested it would have no lasting effect on editorial policy. The publishers of *McCall's,* delighted in the uprising, pointed out that they feared little from the rebels. Why? Because they alone of the three major women's magazines (the other being *Good Housekeeping*) boasted a woman editor, Shana Alexander.

Despite the optimism of both *McCall's* and *Ladies' Home Journal,* a staff reporter writing in the *Wall Street Journal* (Aug. 3, 1970) indicated that the magazines were simply out of touch, not only with the women's liberation movement but also with the younger generation. "Half the women who read the two magazines are over 41 years old," he reported, "and only one in eight has finished college." Publishers of other magazines, from *Newsweek* to *Playboy,* felt the wrath of the

WIDE WORLD

A group of more than 100 women invaded the office of *Ladies' Home Journal* editor John M. Carter and asked him to resign in favor of a woman. He heard them out, but he did not resign.

Rags, a new magazine aimed at young people, was released in June.

COURTESY, ROSY CHEEKS PUBLISHERS, INC.

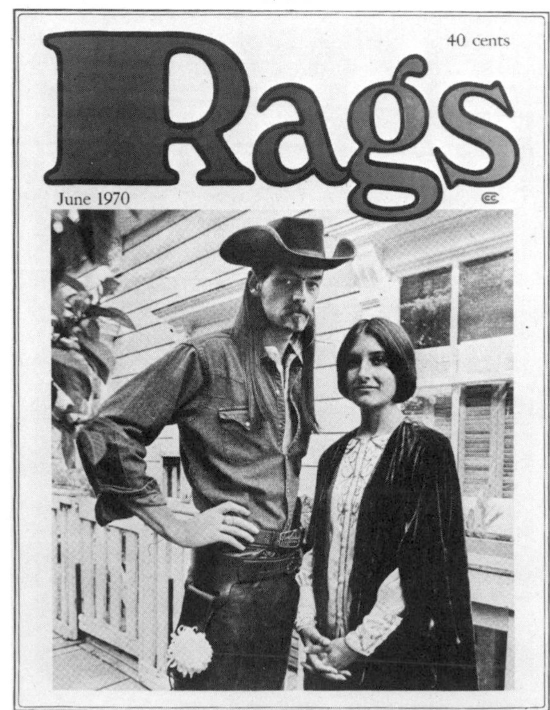

distaff side. At *Newsweek* 46 women staffers charged the magazine with discrimination against women in editorial jobs. Editors denied it, as they did at *Time*, where 94 women filed similar complaints.

The blues, if not the death chant, sounded up and down the land among commercial magazines. In keeping with a less than cheerful economic year generally, publishers were dolefully calculating how much their advertising revenue was likely to be off in 1970. While advertising revenues for major magazines had reached a record $1.25 billion in 1969, approximately 4.4% more than in 1968, the experts saw a decline in 1970. American Business Press, Inc., representing some 2,400 publications, forecast an 8% loss in advertising pages for 1970. *Life, Look, McCall's*, and *Time* all reported losses in the first half of 1970. Gardner Cowles, chairman of the corporation that publishes *Look*, attributed the cutback to "advertisers retrenched in anticipation of diminished profit margins," and he met the crisis by lowering advertising rates and chopping back circulation. (*See also* Newspapers; Television and Radio. *See in* CE: Magazines.)

MALAGASY REPUBLIC. In January 1970, the Malagasy Republic's President Philibert Tsiranana was taken to a Paris hospital, suffering from a stroke, and he remained under medical treatment there until May. Vice-President Calvin

Tsiebo took over the president's duties during this lengthy absence.

Legislative elections took place on September 6. The government Social Democratic party (PSD) gained 104 of the 107 seats in the National Assembly, the three remaining seats going to the main opposition party, the Congress Party for the Independence of Madagascar (AKFM).

On November 20, Foreign Affairs Minister Jacques Rabemananjara and South Africa's Foreign Minister Hilgard Muller signed four economic agreements between the two countries, under which the Malagasy Republic would receive loans amounting to $3.24 million. (*See in* CE: Malagasy Republic.)

MALAWI. As in the preceding year, President H. Kamuzu Banda began 1970 with a number of new ministers. One of them, however, G. E. Ndema, minister of local government, did not hold office for long and was expelled from the government and the Malawi Congress party on April 30.

In November 1969, Malawi's four British high-court judges announced that they were to relinquish their appointments. The international commission of jurists shared their disquiet, but the minister of finance, Aleke Banda, stated in London that the judges, accustomed to the British system of justice, had failed to understand the significance of superstition in Malawi which could only be dealt with by other methods.

In May, South Africa's Prime Minister John Vorster visited Malawi, accompanied by his foreign minister, Hilgard Muller. This was the prime minister's first visit to an independent black African state. (*See in* CE: Malawi.)

Malawi's President Banda explains that he favors coexistence with South Africa.

MOHAMED AMIN FROM KEYSTONE

MALAYSIA. In 1970 Malaysia largely recovered from the tragic setbacks of the May 1969 racial disturbances. The ban on politics and on publications of political parties was lifted in September 1970. After the May 1969 clashes Parliament was suspended along with constitutional government following the proclamation of a state of emergency throughout the country. Parliament was scheduled to resume in February 1971. The remaining nationwide curfew was lifted on September 21.

King Abdul Halim Muazzam was installed as Malaysia's fifth supreme chief of state on September 21. Abdul Rahman stepped down as prime minister on the same date, after 15 years in office, and his longtime deputy and heir, Abdul Razak, was sworn in as Malaysia's second prime minister the next day.

The remaining elections in Sabah and Sarawak, suspended because of the May 1969 disturbances, were held in July 1970 with the Alliance party winning 27 of the 48 seats in Sarawak and 31 of the 32 seats in Sabah. The Alliance party, made up of a coalition of the United Malays National Organization, the Malaysian Chinese Association, and the Malaysian Indian Congress, achieved a grand total of 93 seats in the 144-member House of Representatives.

One threat to Malaysia's stability was posed by armed Communist terrorists on the Malaysian-Thai border and in Sarawak. It was necessary in 1970 to mobilize all efforts and resources to face this threat, which continued throughout the year.

From April to June, five nations participated in war exercises held off the east coast of West Malaysia. Taking part were units from Great Britain, Malaysia, Singapore, New Zealand, and Australia. The event was designed in part to train and exercise the combined forces of the five nations under conditions that would prevail after the reduction of British military forces in the area. (*See in* CE: Malaysia, Federation of.)

MALDIVES. The republic of Maldives signed an agreement with the East German government on May 23, 1970, in Colombo, Ceylon, to establish diplomatic relations. It was later announced that the East German ambassador to Ceylon was to be ambassador to Maldives also. After the leftist victory in the May 27 elections in Ceylon, Maldives followed that country's lead in establishing diplomatic relations with North Korea.

During the year, Maldives closed down both its embassy to the United States and its mission to the United Nations. Maldives' only other diplomatic representation abroad was in Ceylon.

The islands were threatened in 1970 by a mass increase in noxious crown-of-thorns starfish, which spread from the Pacific to the Indian Ocean. The Maldivians were aided in their efforts to control the starfish menace by divers from the British Royal Air Force base on Gan Island in Addu Atoll. (*See in* CE: Maldive Islands.)

MALI. In 1970, two years after the takeover of power in Mali by the army, political unrest persisted in Bamako, the capital. In March, seven intellectuals were sentenced to imprisonment for offenses against Lieut. Moussa Traoré, the head of the military government, and for defamation of certain ministers.

In September an important cabinet reshuffle took place. Three civilian members of the government, including Louis Nègre, principal engineer of Franco-Malian financial agreements, were replaced by army officers. In the shuffle, Lieut. Baba Diarra was given the post of finance minister; Capt. Yoro Diakité became minister of state in charge of defense, interior, and security; and Lieut. Joseph Mara was appointed minister of justice. All three new ministers were members of the ruling Military Committee of National Liberation. These measures were designed to strengthen the army's hold on the government. (*See in* CE: Mali.)

WIDE WORLD

Sammy Davis, Jr., and Altavise Gore

MALTA. The change of government in Great Britain in June 1970 broke the deadlock existing between the British and Maltese governments on financial aid. Discussions were resumed shortly after the Conservative party assumed power, and in October agreement was reached on whether the $54.4 million remaining from the ten-year financial agreement of 1964 was to be considered a grant or a loan. Of this amount, the British government agreed to make available to Malta as a gift $2.4 million for the restoration of historic buildings and $7.2 million for dockyard development, plus 75% of the balance. The other 25% was a loan.

In 1967 Malta had approached the European Economic Community (EEC), or Common Market, with the idea of establishing an association with it. In July 1970 an agreement was reached on the creation of a customs union that would, over a period of ten years, lead to the elimination of tariffs, quotas, and other restrictions between the EEC and Malta and to the adoption by Malta of the Community's common external tariff.

The Maltese government passed legislation to raise a regular armed force in anticipation of the responsibility of taking over the Royal Malta Artillery. To attract new residents, the law was changed to exempt estates from the payment of double death duties. In July the government opened an area of the continental shelf for the granting of petroleum production licenses. A license to erect and operate a relay broadcasting station in Malta was granted to a West German corporation. (*See in* CE: Malta.)

Albert Finney and Anouk Aimée (below); Douglas Langston Rogers and Nancy Ann Hardin (right)

WIDE WORLD

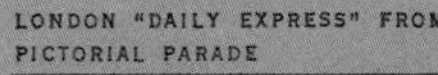

LONDON "DAILY EXPRESS" FROM PICTORIAL PARADE

Dr. Christiaan N. Barnard and Barbara Zoellner

WIDE WORLD

MARRIAGES. Among the well-known public figures who were married in 1970 were:

Svetlana Alliluyeva, 44, Joseph Stalin's daughter who defected to the United States in 1967, to William Wesley Peters, 57, architect and vice-president of the Frank Lloyd Wright Foundation; April 7, in Scottsdale, Ariz.

"THE SUN," LONDON, FROM PICTORIAL PARADE
Judy Carne and Bob Bergmann

Dr. Jonas E. Salk and Françoise Gilot
WIDE WORLD

Svetlana Alliluyeva and William Wesley Peters
UPI COMPIX

Dr. Christiaan N. Barnard, 47, South African physician who pioneered in heart-transplant surgery, to Barbara Zoellner, 19, daughter of a South African millionaire industrialist; February 14, in Johannesburg, South Africa.

Judy Carne, 31, actress ('The Boy Friend'), to Bob Bergmann, 23, free-lance film producer; May 3, in New York City.

Sammy Davis, Jr., 44, entertainer, to Altavise Gore, dancer; May 11, in Philadelphia, Pa.

Birendra Bir Bikram Shah Deva, crown prince of Nepal, 24, to Aishwarya Rajya Laxmi Devi Rana, 20; in two-day rites February 27–28, in Katmandu, Nepal.

Mia Farrow, 25, actress, to André Previn, 40, conductor and composer; September 10, in London.

Albert Finney, 34, British actor, to Anouk Aimée, 38, French actress ('A Man and a Woman'); August 7, in London.

Peggy Fleming, 21, ice-skating star and 1968 Olympic gold medalist, to Gregory Jenkins, 24; June 13, in Los Angeles.

Katharine Hawes Lindsay, 19, eldest daughter of New York City Mayor John V. Lindsay, to Richard Lance Schaffer, 23; June 6, in New York City.

Lee Marvin, 46, actor ('Cat Ballou'), to Pamela Feeley, 39; October 18, in Las Vegas, Nev.

Marguerite (Trenny) Trenholm Robb, 22, former fashion model and sister-in-law of Lynda Bird Johnson Robb (former U.S. President Lyndon B. Johnson's elder daughter), to Robert Pforzheimer, 21; August 23, in Rio, N.Y.

Douglas Langston Rogers, 23, son of U.S. Secretary of State William P. Rogers, to Nancy Ann Hardin, 21, daughter of U.S. Secretary of Agriculture Clifford M. Hardin; January 31, in Washington, D.C.

Franklin Delano Roosevelt, Jr., 55, son of the former U.S. president, to Felicia Schiff Warburg Sarnoff, 42, heiress to the Warburg banking fortune; July 1, in New York City.

Dr. Jonas E. Salk, 55, physician who developed the Salk polio vaccine, to Françoise Gilot, 48, artist and mistress to Pablo Picasso for 11 years; June 29, near Paris.

MAURITANIA. The reconciliation between Mauritania and Morocco, achieved the preceding year, began to assume a positive form when the first agreements were concluded in February 1970. Shortly before this, the two governments had agreed to exchange ambassadors.

In June Morocco's King Hassan II received Mauritania's President Mokhtar Ould Daddah in Rabat, Morocco. The political future of the Spanish Sahara was discussed and a treaty of solidarity and cooperation was signed. In July commercial agreements were signed at Rabat between Mauritania and Morocco, and shortly afterward a common intergovernmental committee was set up. On his return, Ould Daddah received Spain's minister of foreign affairs, Gregorio Lopez Bravo.

A meeting in September between President Houari Boumédienne of Algeria, King Hassan, and President Ould Daddah resulted in only the expression of a hope "to hasten the decolonization of the Spanish Sahara." (*See in* CE: Mauritania.)

CAMERA PRESS FROM PIX

The Soviet ship *Priboj* (Surf) docks at a harbor in Mauritius. Soviet-Mauritian relations were increasingly friendly in 1970.

MAURITIUS. The strategic position of Mauritius in the Indian Ocean, in the line of Soviet naval expansion, was emphasized by the visit of India's Prime Minister Indira Gandhi, in June 1970. A joint communiqué expressed alarm at the buildup of foreign navies in the area. A fishing agreement with the Soviet Union in 1969 was expanded to a trawler landing rights agreement in July 1970, but no naval rights were included.

Following Mrs. Gandhi's visit, agreements were made for Indian industry and irrigation expertise to be put at the island's disposal. Neither Africa nor India was able to help solve the population problem by emigration. The Mauritian government expressed the economic hope of turning Mauritius into a free port and trade center. To this end, the Indian government agreed to help improve a civil airport, develop industrial estates for small-scale enterprise, and to make Mauritius an Indian port of call. (*See in* CE: Mauritius.)

MEDICINE. Almost anyone needing medical care in 1970 was caught in the crunch of soaring health costs, boosted in some part by economic inflation. Dr. Roger O. Egeberg, U.S. assistant secretary for health and scientific affairs, linked higher medical bills with supply-and-demand factors. In September Egeberg said the "health care crisis" may have spawned "demands which exceed our ability to deliver. When demand exceeds supply, the cost of the product goes up."

National Health Insurance the Answer?

Some government and labor leaders wondered just how high that cost would go. A national health insurance (NHI) program covering all age groups in the United States had been proposed as a means of lessening individual medical expenses. Exhaustive Congressional hearings took place in 1970 on the worth of several introduced NHI plans.

Observers felt that NHI would spark considerable controversy in 1971 and might even become an election issue by 1972. The Administration of U.S. President Richard M. Nixon had little fondness for a NHI that would provide sweeping health care for all, explaining that the "inconceivable cost" of such a program would impose on each U.S. household a federal health tax equivalent to $1,000 each year. Instead, the Nixon Administration proposed a more modest "catastrophe" insurance plan providing benefits after a person stricken with a costly illness first incurred and paid a significant portion of his bill.

A Booster Shot Needed for Health-Care Delivery

The "health-care crisis" cited by Egeberg was painfully real to the estimated 30 million persons in the United States who lacked adequate care. In November Dr. Walter C. Bornemeier, president of the American Medical Association (AMA), urged the medical establishment to encourage ghetto medical practice. Removal of AMA opposition to federal funds for group medical practice in ghetto areas would hasten expanded health care for disadvantaged persons, according to Bornemeier.

A federal program for retraining military medical corpsmen for physician-assisting civilian duties saw slight success in 1970. Called Medex, the program was another of the attempts to shore up a health-delivery system sadly lacking physicians.

Dr. William Feinbloom examines the "bioptic telescope system" he developed. The patient, Russel Strayer, 11, was born legally blind but has about 50% vision with the system.

UPI COMPIX

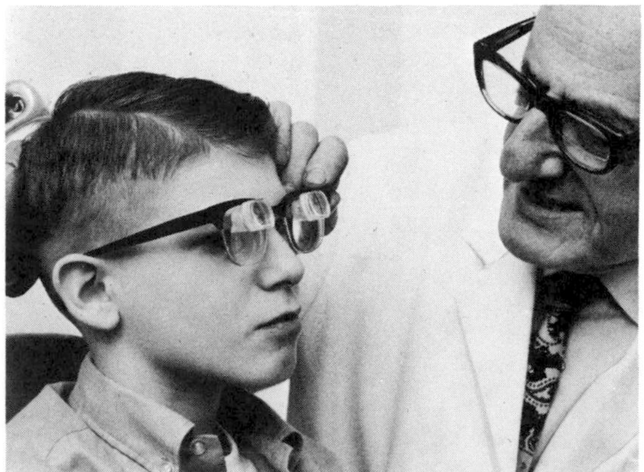

Although many medical schools were on the verge of bankruptcy, their total enrollment increased on the whole in 1970, according to a November report of the Association of American Medical Colleges (AAMC). The AAMC endorsed a program through which there would be 175 physicians per 100,000 population by the mid-1980's, if funds held out. In 1970 only about 130 physicians served an average 100,000 population.

In October the Carnegie Commission on Higher Education called for a revamping of the medical curriculum. The commission recommended a cut in a physician's medical training from eight years to six. Furthermore, it pressed for more women and minority-group members in the medical field, nine additional medical schools (101 medical schools were operating in 1970), and the establishment of a national health manpower commission to evaluate the needs of all medical personnel.

The AMA held its annual convention in Chicago in June. Hoping to escape the turmoil of the 1969 convention when militant physicians and medical students charged the AMA with lack of social action in medicine, the AMA House of Delegates met behind guarded doors. However, at the opening day's public forum, conducted by the AMA to hear complaints from consumer groups, all decorum collapsed when militants denounced the staid medical organization on a variety of social issues.

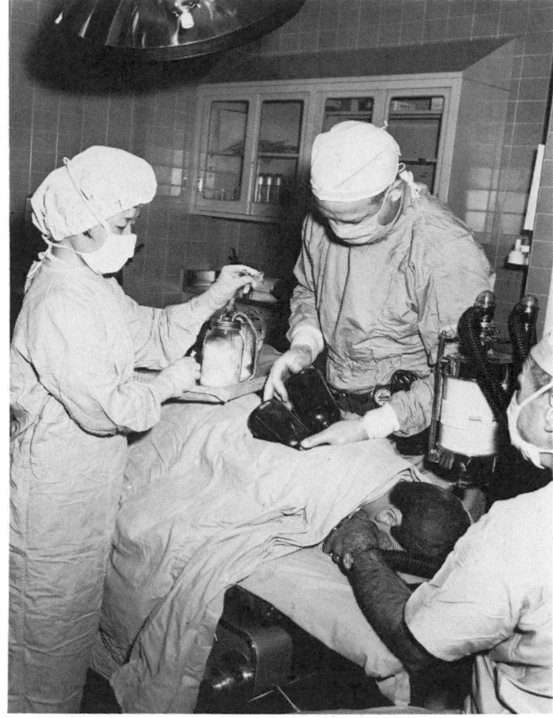

UPI COMPIX

Smoking Sam, a dummy used in a hospital's antismoking program, gets a "lung" transplant. Tar deposits blocked the glass tubing that leads to his spun-glass lungs.

More Study on Genetic Diseases

A national task force on genetics research was recommended by Dr. Joshua Lederberg, a Nobel laureate in genetics. Lederberg stressed that a new era in medicine would begin when hereditary diseases could be prevented or treated by altering the biochemical abnormalities underlying them.

A finding at Johns Hopkins University, at Baltimore, Md., reinforced the urgency of discovering more about genetic diseases. Records showed that 20% of the children admitted to the pediatric section of Johns Hopkins Hospital suffered from hereditary ailments.

About 100 genetic diseases had been uncovered by 1970, and the number was growing. In February a five-center network was established at U.S. and Canadian sites to treat persons with genetic ills and to counsel their families. The centers were located at Cornell University medical school at Ithaca, N.Y., the Johns Hopkins University medical school, the University of California (San Diego) medical school at La Jolla, McGill University medical school at Montreal, Que., and the City of Hope Medical Center at Duarte, Calif.

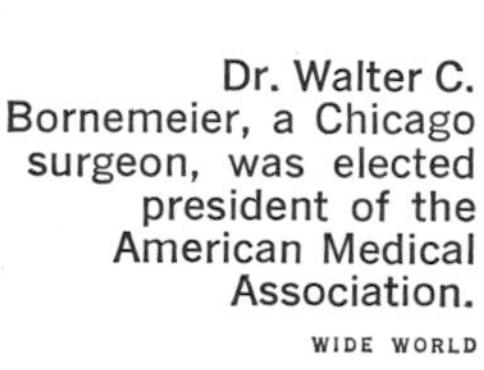

Dr. Walter C. Bornemeier, a Chicago surgeon, was elected president of the American Medical Association.

WIDE WORLD

New Drugs and Recent Clinical Findings

In 1970 L-dopa, a drug that controls tremors in a number of cases of Parkinson's disease, was licensed for prescription use. Rifampin, a semisynthetic antibiotic, was used in the treatment of meningitis and advanced tuberculosis.

A vaccine effective against type C meningitis was developed by the U.S. Army. It had been safely tested on Army recruits and on some children. About nine of every ten meningitis infections occur in children.

A viruslike protein particle called the Australian antigen was discovered in the blood of many known carriers and past victims of serum hepatitis. This disease is transmitted through blood transfusions and dirty syringes and hypodermic needles. Now that the antigen was known, hopes were that it could be pinpointed in the blood of a hepatitis victim by a standard test. Furthermore, should the

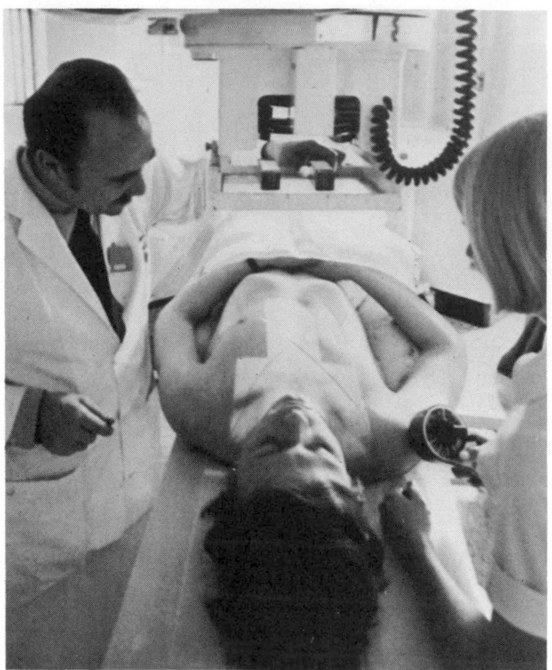

WIDE WORLD

A patient undergoes complex treatment for cancer in the outpatient clinic of a Los Angeles medical center.

antigen be a virus, production of an antihepatitis vaccine became plausible.

CANCER

Scientists were sure that great strides would take place in the 1970's toward conquering cancer. In its many forms the disease strikes more than 600,000 persons in the United States every year. More than half of all cancer cases are fatal. Nonetheless, medical researchers investigating cancer were still in a quandary over the cause or causes of the disease in 1970.

Theories of carcinogenesis continued to draw debate. Some scientists believed cancer was a virus disease. Indeed, researchers at the National Institutes of Health at Bethesda, Md., in June reported finding a whole virus associated with breast cancer. It was like a virus that unquestionably caused mammary tumors in mice. Other workers, however, felt that chemical agents, including those in polluted air or in tobacco smoke, triggered the uncontrolled multiplication of cells characterizing cancer. At the tenth International Cancer Congress in Houston, Tex., in May, scientists gathered to share research findings in hope of piecing together the elusive cancer puzzle in the foreseeable future.

Chemical Found with Cancer

A substance called OSF (overgrowth stimulating factor) was discovered emanating from cancer cells by Dr. Harry Rubin of the University of California at Berkeley. Ordinarily, normal cells slow their reproduction rate when a peak number of cells fill a given area, a biological phenomenon called "density dependent inhibition." However, it seemed that OSF somehow cancels this inhibition, perhaps explaining why cancer cells continue to divide in densely packed tissue.

Analysis of OSF indicates it may have a protein makeup. Should OSF prove a prime factor in cancer cell proliferation, formulation of a chemical "antidote" then becomes possible to stymie the OSF action.

The battle against cigarette smoking seems to be gaining momentum. Pharmacist Isidore Farber stands before a window display that explains why he stopped selling cigarettes.

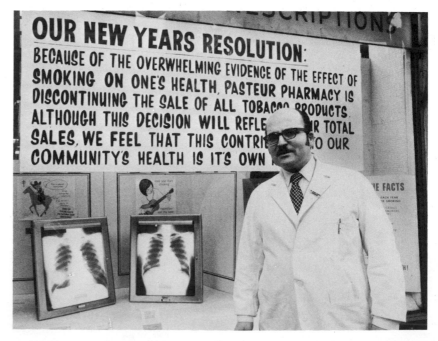

"THE NEW YORK TIMES"

Smoking Dogs Get Cancer

A scientist who helped amass the statistics indicting cigarette smoke as a cause of lung cancer reinforced these findings with experimental evidence. Dr. Oscar Auerbach, at the Veterans Administration (VA) Hospital in East Orange, N.J., subjected 86 dogs to varying amounts of inhaled cigarette smoke each day. Thirty-eight of them constituted the heavy-smoker group, inhaling the smoke of seven nonfilter cigarettes daily. By the time of the February report, 12 of the dogs were dead of cancer after more than two years of smoking. Eight nonsmoking dogs used as a control group did not develop any lung disease. Sixteen of the 48 dogs subjected to varying degrees of daily smoke inhalation also died by the time of the report. Twelve of them died of lung diseases, including cancer, emphysema, and bronchopneumonia.

Anticancer Drugs Sought

A plant protein called Con A could stem the rampant growth of cancer cells without killing them. Workers at Princeton University at Princeton, N.J., said in November that Con A had restored the cancer cells to their normal state during a six-day period of test-tube culture.

An obscure drug called BCNU promised to be a fairly effective anticancer agent, according to the National Cancer Institute (NCI). The drug seemed particularly adept at attacking malignant brain tumors. However, the NCI emphasized that BCNU offered only temporary tumor control.

An experimental drug called Laetrile, purported to treat and prevent cancer, was denied an investigational use permit by the Food and Drug Administration (FDA) in May. The FDA charged that the animal test data submitted with the investigational drug application for Laetrile was insufficient to warrant its use with humans. However, Laetrile is a legal drug in several countries, including Mexico and Japan, where physicians report its effectiveness as an anticancer drug.

HEART

Cardiovascular diseases continued to take a high toll of life, more than a million deaths in 1970. Furthermore, an estimated 27 million or more persons in the United States suffered from some type of heart or blood-vessel disease. In addition to the human suffering, the economic cost of the diseases was staggering: more than $6 billion in estimated wages lost yearly.

Drive Against Heart Disease

An intensive move against cardiovascular disease was in the planning stage by the Inter-Society Commission for Heart Disease Resources in 1970. The commission was a joint undertaking by the Regional Medical Programs Service and the American Heart Association to establish a sweeping medical program for the treatment and prevention of all heart and blood-vessel disorders, particularly atherosclerosis (hardening of the arteries). The more than 100-member commission said atherosclerosis was the greatest health threat in the developed countries of Europe and the Western Hemisphere.

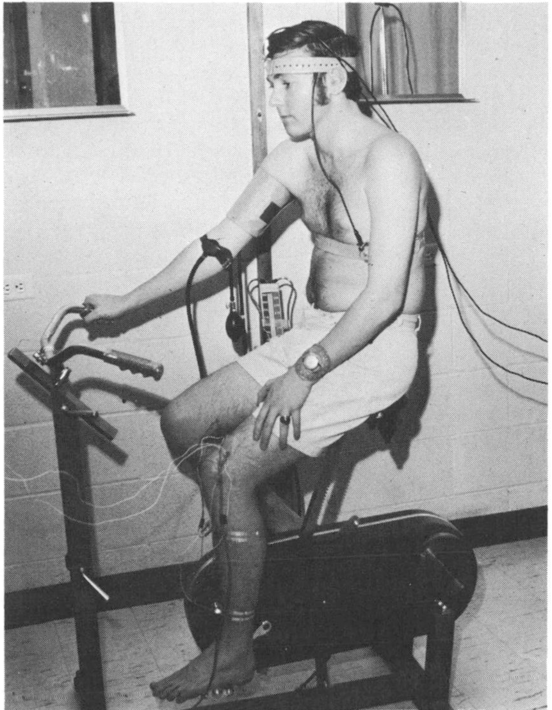

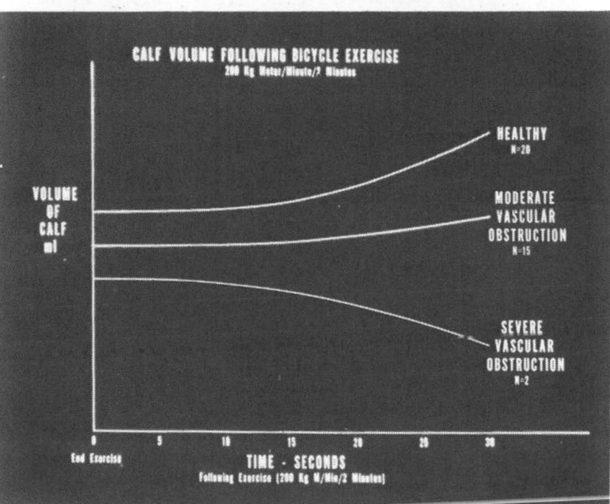

COURTESY, DR. ROBERT D. ALLISON

An improved, painless bicycle test has been developed to assess vascular obstruction. Data is recorded on curves that indicate the extent of the blockage.

Meanwhile, the National Heart and Lung Institute (NHLI) planned a ten-year research study of atherosclerosis. A 13-member NHLI task force was assigned the research effort.

Cigarette smoking had been implicated as a cause of cardiovascular as well as lung diseases. According to the National Clearinghouse for Smoking and Health, an agency of the U.S. Public Health Service (USPHS), some 20% of the 50 million persons in the United States who smoked regularly in 1966 had kicked the habit by 1970. The decline in cigarette consumption was expected to be speeded considerably by the Public Health Cigarette Smoking Act passed by Congress in 1970. The new law banned cigarette commercials from television and radio beginning in January 1971.

In 1970 the NHLI championed a new system of classifying potentially dangerous levels of blood fat. According to the NHLI system, blood fat levels are ranked from I to V. Types II and IV, indicating high levels of cholesterol and triglyceride respectively, and type III, in which both substances are about equally elevated, represent the highest risk of coronary heart disease.

Nuclear Pacemakers; Unsuspected Heart Attacks

In April a team of French cardiologists and scientists reported the historic implantation of a nuclear-powered heart pacemaker by a French surgeon. Enclosed in a plastic container about the size of a 35-mm. film cassette, the pacemaker was powered by plutonium 238. Australian scientists in 1970 were developing a similar pacemaker, except that it would be powered by the fairly inexpensive promethium 147. (*See also* Nuclear Energy.)

A long-term medical survey by the NHLI disclosed that a surprising number of persons had experienced heart attacks without knowing it. The study, based on routine medical checkups on more than 5,000 residents of Framingham, Mass., over a period of more than 14 years, showed that of 232 persons who had heart attacks, 44 of them were not aware of it. Only when an electroencephalogram examination revealed damage to heart tissue were the heart attacks detected.

As of August Louis B. Russell, Jr., of Indianapolis, Ind., became the longest-lived heart transplant patient. At that time Russell had survived for two years with a new heart.

Dr. Jefrey Arlen (left) runs St. Mark's Clinic, a free medical center for young people in New York City's East Village area.

"THE NEW YORK TIMES"

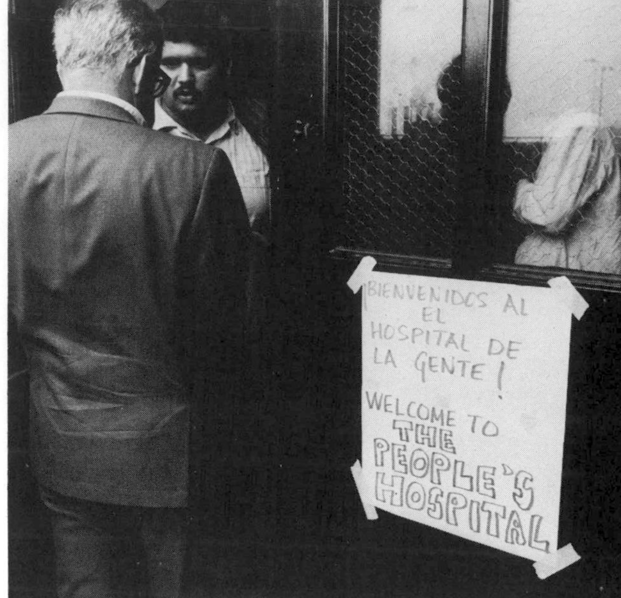

UPI COMPIX

A militant group took over a building of the Lincoln Hospital in the Bronx, New York City, to protest inadequate medical care.

PUBLIC HEALTH

Epidemics struck portions of the world in 1970. The severest was a widespread cholera epidemic. In the United States the incidence of venereal disease (VD) had risen to alarming heights.

Cholera Sweeps a Wide Area

The seventh cholera pandemic since 1817 had by 1970 moved from Indonesia, where it had started in 1961, to West Africa. The current rampage of the deadly disease was caused by the El Tor strain of the cholera bacilli. Cholera is a disease that kills by dehydrating its victims. Its severe diarrhea drains the body of vital fluids and electrolytes. Cholera is most often spread through water supplies contaminated with feces of the victims. The epidemic tragically showed the woefully substandard state of the water supply and sanitation systems in many regions.

In May the World Health Organization (WHO) began a campaign to uproot yellow fever from its African strongholds. Yellow-fever epidemics in Ghana, Upper Volta, Mali, Nigeria, and Togo in 1969 posed a serious threat to world health. The

United States offered a $400,000 contribution to WHO's anti-yellow-fever effort, if the other 127 member states would donate $600,000.

Epidemics Hit the United States

Diphtheria struck the Mexican-American and Negro section of San Antonio, Tex., in August. The city of 648,000 residents was largely unprotected when the epidemic hit. Public health officials there began a massive inoculation program to quell the outbreak. At least 116 cases of diphtheria were recorded before the epidemic finally subsided.

The American Social Health Association (ASHA) disclosed figures in 1970 showing that VD, long thought on the wane, was staging an awesome comeback, especially among U.S. youth. Gonorrhea was responsible for the greatest upswing in cases. About 495,000 cases of the disease were reported. Moreover, ASHA officials believed the actual number of gonorrhea cases was four times the reported figure. They voiced regret over the failure of private physicians to report more than one in nine of the VD cases they treat.

Malaria was also on the rise in the United States but in an indirect manner. Its incidence was almost solely restricted to servicemen returning from Vietnam, some 3,800 cases by the start of 1970. Malaria had not spread to the civilian populace of the U.S. areas where the malaria-carrying *Anopheles* mosquito thrives, but USPHS workers kept a close watch over the imported cases.

Measles, considered pacified by the vaccine licensed in 1963, staged a comeback. During the first 32 weeks of 1970 nearly 39,000 cases of measles were reported, compared to nearly 19,000 cases for the same period of 1968. When the Vaccination Assistance Act expired in mid-1969, funds for measles vaccination stopped, making it hard for some children to receive free vaccinations.

Environmental health and antipollution measures relating to it were front-page news throughout 1970. In one case, a New York study showed that there was a close bond between polluted air and asthma and eczema in children under 15 years of age.

Some concern was expressed over the efficacy of the rubella (German measles) vaccine. Originally believed to confer lifelong immunity, the vaccine has now been found to offer such immunity to only about half of the recipients. Nevertheless, in 1970, plans for extensive rubella vaccination went on unabated. It was hoped that so many persons would become immune that any epidemic threat would be minimized. Rubella takes a harsh toll in death or disfigurement of newborn children whose mothers contracted the disease in early pregnancy.

SURGERY

In 1970, surgeons showed less enthusiasm for organ transplantation, particularly of hearts, than in preceding years. The problem of organ rejection remained to be solved. However, because of better surgical techniques, transplant recipients stood a greater chance of survival for longer periods of time than ever.

Liver transplantation still ranked among the most difficult of transplant operations. So many key blood vessels are linked with the organ that blood loss during surgery is a major problem. Also, the liver regulates the levels of blood sugar and other substances, so the body is jeopardized greatly when the liver is dissociated from the body—even during the fairly short time involved in transplant surgery. Close scrutiny of the patient's circulation and metabolism by the anesthetist during the transplant, however, markedly improves the patient's survival chance. At the VA Hospital in Denver, Colo., where Dr. J. Antonio Aldrete had developed anesthesiological methods for liver transplant surgery, the success rate for the first month after surgery was about 80%, compared with about 25% elsewhere.

Removal and replacement of diseased hip joints with artificial parts posed annoying surgical problems. The stainless steel ball replacing the head of the femur, the upper leg bone, is usually screwed into the bone. But the steel part sometimes works loose, forcing another operation. A surgeon in England announced great success in fixing the steel ball into the femur with a cementlike plastic commonly used in dentistry, methyl methacrylate. Orthopedic surgeons in the United States began experimenting with the bone cement in 1970. They also tried to minimize the excessive infection in hip surgery by performing it in an air-filtered operating room while costumed from head to foot in space suits.

Siamese twin girls born joined at the abdomen, who were separated in November 1969, wait for their parents, Mr. and Mrs. John Kobierski, to take them home from the hospital in January.

UPI COMPIX

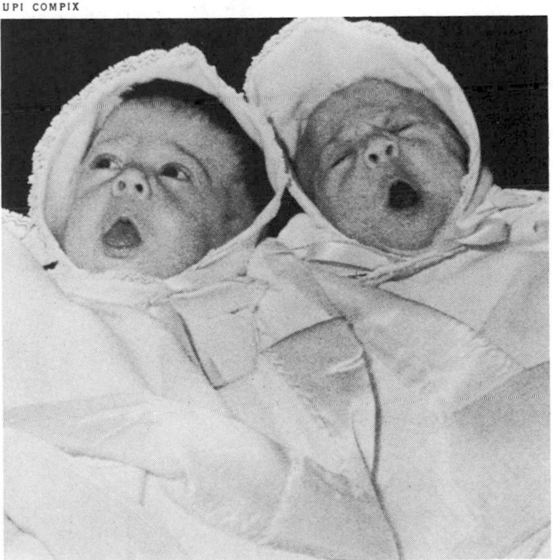

Soviet surgeons used high-frequency sound in 1970 to weld together broken bones. The ultrasonic technique also functioned as a pain-killer. A day after surgery, patients reported they experienced no pain.

A British subsidiary of the American Cyanamid Co. announced development of a synthetic suture called Dexon. It could be absorbed by the body and was also compatible with human tissue. In a still unknown way the body absorbs Dexon and expels it as water in the urine and carbon dioxide in the breath.

Heart-lung machines have a new experimental use. They have been removing massive blood clots in the blood vessels leading to the lungs. The clots are drawn from the pulmonary arteries through a catheter inserted into them through the right external jugular vein. The catheter is connected to a heart-lung machine that provides the suction. (*See also* Dentistry; Drugs; Hospitals. *See in* CE: Diseases, Infectious; Diseases, Noninfectious; Medicine; Surgery.)

MENTAL HEALTH. The community mental health center program suffered a disappointing setback in 1970 when cutbacks in the federal budget forced more than 60 of the centers to be without operating funds. Even so, the proposed number of new centers jumped from 376 to 420, of which 245 were in operation during 1970. These centers were instrumental in reducing the number of persons confined to mental hospitals—about 367,000 patients in 1969 compared with slightly more than 700,000 in 1945.

Massachusetts General Hospital in Boston began operation of long-distance, two-way television psychiatric sessions in 1970. The closed-circuit TV hookup, which was linked with the Veterans Administration Hospital in Bedford, Mass., 25 miles away, permitted psychiatrists at Massachusetts General to conduct face-to-face interviews with distant patients from a "teleconsultation" room.

In a scene from the film 'Other Voices', Dr. Albert M. Honig holds a psychotic patient. The film portrays his treatment technique, which emphasizes strong human contact.

COURTESY, DOROWITE CORP.

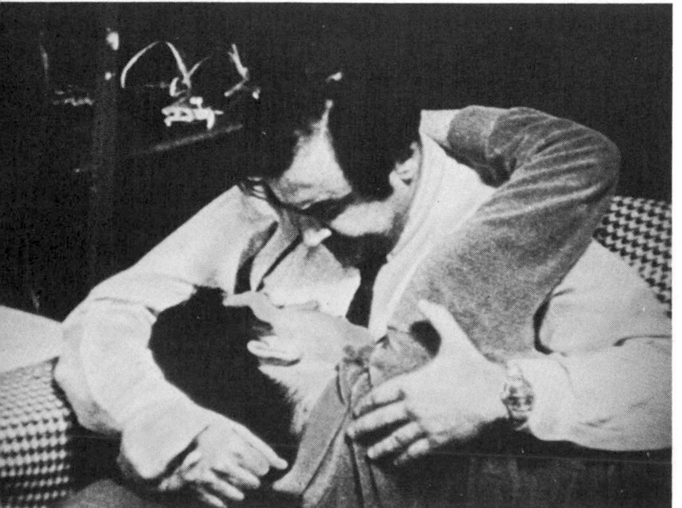

The American Psychiatric Association (APA) took note of protest voiced by black psychiatrists at the 1969 APA meeting and in 1970 appointed a black psychiatrist, Dr. Charles Prudhomme, as an APA vice-president. In Washington, D.C., the National Institute of Mental Health (NIMH) planned to form a unit that would handle only the mental problems of minority groups. Proposal of the new unit came shortly after Dr. Stanley F. Yolles resigned as head of the NIMH, complaining that the Administration of U.S. President Richard M. Nixon showed little enthusiasm for supporting mental health programs.

Amid continuing improvement of mental health care in the United States, a government study group —the Joint Commission on Mental Health of Children—reported that the nation woefully lacked acceptable services for its 10 million children believed to be mentally disturbed. Commission recommendations to correct the situation included: creation by each state of a child-development agency and the establishment of a presidential advisory council on children. (*See also* Psychology.)

METALS. In the United States the two metals that figured most prominently in the news during 1970 were steel and copper, largely because of changes in their pricing. Other metals received adverse attention as water pollutants or atmospheric pollutants.

It was at best a lackluster year for the steel industry. Earnings for the first quarter were more than 25% below those for the same quarter in 1969. In an effort to improve an anemic profit-and-earnings picture, the major steel companies initiated price hikes during the second quarter. By the end of June, prices on about 70% of industry shipments had been elevated. The average price increase was approximately 4%.

However, the price hikes did not compensate for the increase in costs, and steelmakers became caught in a cost-price squeeze. The result was that for the first three quarters of 1970, while total industry production increased 1% over 1969, earnings dropped to $430.8 million, 30% below the 1969 level. The poor profits picture made it inevitable that steel prices would be increased again in 1971.

Copper producers had also had a dismal year. In May a special subcommittee of the Cabinet Committee on Economic Policy issued a report following a four-month study of the copper market. The report recommended either action by the U.S. Department of Justice or legislation to abolish copper's two-tiered price structure. Under that system, established customers are charged less than the open-market price.

In June two of the largest copper smelting companies in the Western states announced that air-pollution control rules would cause them to curtail production seriously. Other metals were tentatively named as pollutants by six federal agencies in 1970. The metals—in addition to mercury which had been labeled harmful to drinking water earlier—were copper, zinc, lead, molybdenum, arsenic, vanadium, boron, iron, aluminum, tellurium, cadmium, chromium, and nickel. (*See also* Conservation; Mines and Mining. *See in* CE: Metals.)

MEXICO. Luis Echeverría Alvarez took office on Dec. 1, 1970, as president of Mexico, succeeding Gustavo Díaz Ordaz. Echeverría, interior minister since 1964 under Díaz Ordaz, was elected on July 5, with 86% of the total vote. His party, the Institutional Revolutionary party (PRI), which had won every national election for 40 years, emerged with all 60 Senate seats and with 178 of the 213 seats in the Chamber of Deputies. Although being nominated as his party's candidate had practically ensured his election, Echeverría had campaigned strenuously throughout Mexico, building faith in his party, listening to dissent and complaints, and wooing young voters, whose number was much increased by a 1970 constitutional amendment lowering the voting age from 21 to 18. Young voters had been notably cool toward the otherwise broad-based PRI and in particular toward Echeverría, who as interior minister had been blamed for the police shooting of several hundred students during demonstrations in Mexico City, the capital, before the 1968 Olympics.

A national census was taken in January and February; it showed a 38.3% population increase during the 1960's to 48.3 million. The illiteracy rate was reported to be 22%, down from 35% in 1960. The census also indicated a rapid population increase in the area around the capital, where 40% of the country's industrial facilities were concentrated. This concentration had caused a large influx of landless unemployed from depressed agricultural regions. Transport and pollution problems increased in the area. As a result, the government announced in midyear that no new manufacturing plants would be allowed in the Federal District after 1975 or in the area around the district after 1980.

Minimum wage rates were increased starting Jan. 1, 1970, by 14.5% and 13.7% a day for urban and rural workers respectively. A subsequent unusual rise in the cost-of-living index, together with fears that the U.S. economic recession might spread across the border, resulted in careful government attempts to regulate the economy. The government tightened credit and held spending on public works at a moderate level. Generally, the economy remained stable, and the peso was still considered one of the world's soundest currencies. Mexico's trade imbalance, much lessened in 1969, increased again in 1970; the import-export deficit for the first six months of 1970 was $119 million greater than for the same period of 1969. Much of the deficit was made up by income from tourism.

In September, Robert H. McBridge, U.S. ambassador to Mexico, announced an increase in U.S. investment in Mexico to help relieve the trade imbalance between the two countries. Earlier in the year, however, the influential Mexican newspaper *Excelsior* noted that U.S. interests, which own or control much of Mexican industry, had taken out more than three times their Latin American investments over the last 30 years and that short-term help became long-term drain. Echeverría's opponent in the presidential election, Efraín González Morfín, was demanding mandatory national reinvestment of profits.

Mexico's relations with the United States improved during 1970, following U.S. apologies for not consulting the Mexicans before beginning a massive attempt to close the U.S.-Mexico border to narcotics traffic late in 1969. Outgoing President Díaz Ordaz met with U.S. President Richard M. Nixon at Puerto Vallarta, Jalisco, for two days in August; they settled boundary disputes involving the shifting of the Rio Grande, which forms over half the border between the two countries. President Nixon hosted Díaz Ordaz at a state dinner in Coronado, Calif., in September. In November President-elect Echeverría paid an informal visit to Washington, D.C. (*See in* CE: Mexico.)

MIDDLE EAST. A peaceful settlement in the Middle East between the Arabs and the Israelis still appeared distant at the end of 1970, but some progress was made toward that goal. A U.S. "peace initiative," which became known as the "Rogers Plan" (for Secretary of State William P. Rogers), was accepted in principle by the Soviet Union, Jordan, Israel, and the United Arab Republic (UAR), or Egypt. However, each country placed its own interpretation on its acceptance. This made possible the relaunching of the mission of Gunnar V. Jarring, the United Nations special representative in the Middle East. A cease-fire in the Suez Canal area was declared on August 7 and remained effective despite Israeli accusations of UAR violations of the military standstill agreement accompanying the cease-fire; the charge was that the UAR had installed new surface-to-air missile sites near the canal. On this ground, Israel withdrew its delegate from the indirect negotiations soon after they had started. However, there was "big four" agreement that the talks should be resumed, and the United States showed its anxiety that its initiative should not be allowed to lapse. The death of UAR President Gamal Abdel Nasser on September 28, however, ended any immediate hopes for the start of direct peace negotiations. (*See also* Foreign Policy, U.S.; International Relations.)

All Middle Eastern states continued to devote an extraordinarily high proportion of their national income and budget to military expenditure. Only

An Israeli soldier questions a local citizen in southern Lebanon. The soldiers were looking for *al Fatah* guerrilla camps.

NEWSPHOT FROM PICTORIAL PARADE

the ending of the civil war in Yemen and of the war with the Kurdish nationalists in Iraq offered some prospect of reducing arms spending in these two countries.

The U.S. peace initiative made progress when President Nasser announced his acceptance of the Rogers proposals on July 23, on his return from a 19-day visit to the Soviet Union. He later told the Arab Socialist Union in Cairo, Egypt, that his government's acceptance was "unconditional." On July 26 Jordan also announced its acceptance but absolved itself from responsibility for Palestinian guerrilla action against Israel. The Palestinian organizations strongly denounced the U.S. initiative, which they unequivocally rejected. On August 4, Israel announced its acceptance of the Rogers proposals after receiving assurances from the U.S. government that the cease-fire would not be used by the UAR to consolidate its position along the Suez Canal. The cease-fire came into force on August 7, and on the same day the 11-member organization of the Central Committee for Palestinian Resistance announced that it would not abide by it.

Hijackings and the Jordan Civil War

On September 6, members of the Popular Front for the Liberation of Palestine carried out four hijackings of jet passenger planes over Western Europe. Of these, an attempt to seize a New York City-bound El Al plane failed, but a Pan American plane was taken to Beirut, Lebanon, and then to Cairo, and Swissair and Trans World Airlines planes were taken to a former Royal Air Force airstrip in the Jordanian desert near the Iraqi border. The guerrillas released most of the women, children, and elderly among the passengers but demanded the release of Palestinians held in Israel, Switzerland, West Germany, and Great Britain in return for the release of the rest of the passengers, whom they held as hostages. On September 9, a British airliner also was hijacked and flown to the same airstrip. The hijackers released all but 56 passengers, including 16 Israelis and Jewish Americans with dual nationality. Following the release of the last of the hijacked hostages, Great Britain, Switzerland, and West Germany released seven Palestinian guerrillas being held in detention.

On September 17 the international crisis caused by the hijackings was overshadowed by the outbreak of civil war in Jordan between the Palestinian organizations and the Jordanian army after King Hussein I had appointed a new military government and the Palestinians had responded by calling a general strike. Intervention by Syrian armored units in northern Jordan caused fears that the conflict might spread, and U.S. Secretary of State Rogers asked the Soviet Union to restrain the Syrians. On September 21 Hussein appealed to the "big four" to take joint action against the Syrian invasion. The U.S. Sixth Fleet was ordered into the eastern Mediterranean. The Soviet Union issued a stern warning against the possibility of U.S. intervention.

A hastily summoned Arab summit conference in Cairo failed to end the civil war because neither Hussein nor the principal Palestinian leader, Yasir Arafat, attended. But the Arab heads of state sent a mission to Amman, Jordan, headed by Sudan's president, Maj. Gen. Gaafar Mohammed al-Nimeiry, on September 22. The mission presided over a cease-fire agreement between Hussein and four leading Palestinian guerrillas who had been captured by the Jordanian army. The Nimeiry mission, however, returned to Cairo without having met Arafat, who denounced the agreement. Fighting continued, and Nimeiry accused the Jordanian army of breaking the cease-fire. The mission returned to Amman, and on September 25 a more effective agreement was reached between Nimeiry, Arafat, and Hussein.

The cease-fire agreement was broken on several occasions, and sporadic fighting continued, though it tended to die out in the following days. In a message on September 26, President Nasser angrily accused King Hussein of violating the cease-fire and denounced the existence of a plot aimed at liquidating the Palestinian resistance. Meanwhile, Hussein and Arafat attended a meeting in Cairo with eight Arab heads of state and their representatives. As a result of this, on September 27 a 14-point agreement was signed providing for the withdrawal of all Jordanian army and Palestinian guerrilla forces from every city in Jordan.

Nasser's death threw the whole Arab world into confusion as it mourned the loss of the only Arab leader of world stature—and the only one who could moderate between conservative and radical Arabs. His death postponed the possibility of direct peace negotiations, and there was a lull in the situation. The United States continued its efforts to bring about negotiations but also agreed to strengthen the Israeli position with more arms. Soviet Premier Aleksei N. Kosygin reaffirmed Soviet desires for a peaceful settlement but said that his nation would continue to supply "defensive" aid to the Arab states. In November the cease-fire agreement was renewed for 90 days.

An Israeli soldier advances on Shadwan Island lighthouse. The Israeli raid on the Egyptian island netted an Egyptian radar system.

UPI COMPIX

Inter-Arab Relations

The underlying division between conservative pro-Western Arab regimes and the radical republican camp persisted but remained latent during 1970. On the conservative side, Jordan's King Hussein aligned his foreign policy closely with that of the UAR, while King Faisal of Saudi Arabia undertook no diplomatic initiatives and finally recognized the republican regime in Yemen.

During the year it became clear that pro-Western regimes were hampered by what the Arabs regarded as unstinted U.S. support of Israel, while the radical camp was strengthened by the adherence of the new regimes in Sudan and Libya—especially Libya with its $1.2 billion a year in oil revenues. (*See also* individual countries by name.)

MINES AND MINING.

The upward trend in U.S. mineral development and production of recent years was slowed somewhat in 1970 by lower industrial, construction, and defense activity. Demand climbed, however, for the energy minerals—coal, oil, and gas. The market for minerals was remarkably steady, though metals prices drifted downward in the second half of the year. (*See* Metals.)

Two copper projects in Arizona were the year's mining highlights in the United States. In April the Anaconda Co. reached a full daily ore-production rate of 30,000 tons at its Twin Buttes Mine south of Tucson. A few miles west, the Duval Corp. achieved capacity output of 72,000 tons of ore a day at its Sierrita copper-molybdenum mine. Arizona was also the scene of several other major mine-plant projects and of intensive exploration for new copper-ore bodies.

Mineral exploration was widespread and intensive throughout the United States. Investigation revealed promising copper-nickel occurrences in south-central Montana. The already productive Southwest copper province, the Eastern zinc area, and mid-continental lead-zinc areas were other scenes of prospecting and test drilling.

Elsewhere, the industry-nationalization policies of some developing nations and political conditions unfavorable for business in large areas of Africa, Asia, and the Middle East combined to produce a concentration of ore-research in countries—such as Australia and Canada—that had stable, free-enterprise economies. In Australia, the year saw intensive development of nickel, iron ore, lead-zinc-silver, bauxite-alumina, and manganese deposits. In Canada, there were major developments in copper-molybdenum, nickel, lead-zinc-silver, and iron ore.

Mining technology advanced in 1970 largely through the introduction of larger and more efficient equipment. Concern for the environment had a growing influence upon mining and mineral-processing technology, and there was new emphasis upon health and safety research. In the United States, enforcement of federal health and safety regulations for metal and nonmetal mines began on July 31. More than 1,000 standards—about half of them mandatory—were applied to ventilation, drilling, blasting, and other mining procedures.

Manganese nodules were mined experimentally from a seabed depth of 3,000 feet 150 miles off the coast of Florida. A deep-sea dredge raised 1,600 tons of the nodules a day. The success of the trials led to plans for commercial mining, probably off the California coast, by 1975. (*See also* Disasters. *See in* CE: Mines and Mining.)

MONACO. The problems involved in the modernization of Monaco's tourist facilities and its general appeal continued into 1970. A report stated, "Monaco is full of memories but needs fewer memories and more tourists." In the pre-World War II period, the principality boasted more than 70 hotels with nearly 4,000 rooms. By 1970 the number had fallen to less than half that of hotels and to 1,600 in the number of rooms. Tourists, and in particular U.S. citizens, flocked to southern France, Italy, and Spain during the year, but the numbers visiting Monaco increased only slightly. In an effort to increase the flow, reclamation projects along the Mediterranean shore continued. The decade-long work was estimated to require an additional five years before completion. The total area of the principality will be increased by nearly 20% as a result of the fill operations, providing new harbors and beaches.

The Austrian driver Jochen Rindt won the 28th annual Monaco Grand Prix on May 10, 1970, at Monte Carlo. Driving his Lotus 49-C, Rindt's winning time for the 155.99-mile-long course was 1 hour, 54 minutes, 36.6 seconds, for an average speed of 81.83 miles per hour. (*See in* CE: Monte Carlo.)

MONEY AND INTERNATIONAL FINANCE. For the first time in more than two years, the international monetary and financial picture was one of relative calm in 1970. However, this newfound stability was not without flaws. Protracted domestic inflation in the United States had brought about extensive borrowing by U.S. banks in the Eurodollar market and had contributed to growing worldwide inflation.

The problem of inflation was cited by the executive directors of the International Monetary Fund (IMF) in their analysis of the world economy in September. They admitted, however, that inflation control had been "particularly difficult" because wage settlements far in excess of increases in productivity were becoming commonplace. The IMF directors offered a number of remedies for inflationary ailments. Among them were the use of more flexible national policies and the strengthening of fiscal policies.

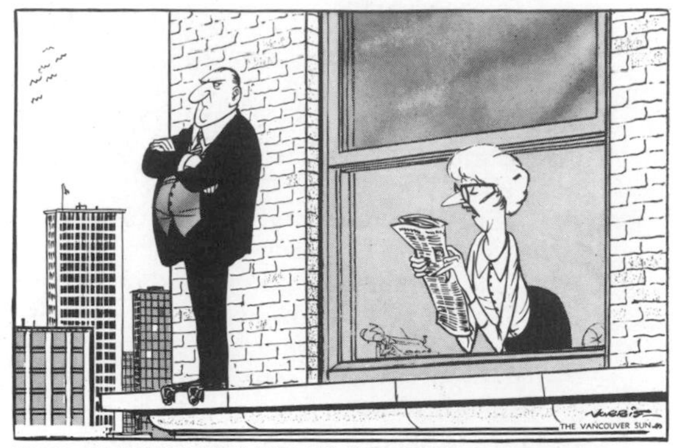

NORRIS, "VANCOUVER SUN," FROM BEN ROTH AGENCY

" . . . on the other hand, some business analysts see the current market slump as a natural leveling process and look to renewed bullish activity as large investors buy in . . . "

The other major problem confronting IMF members at their annual meeting in September was a chronic one—the adjustment of currencies between nations. Under the existing system, the values of currencies are fixed by the IMF and are allowed to fluctuate only within 1% of their pegged values. Two measures to give the system increased flexibility were proposed. One was that nations be allowed to make frequent small adjustments in the exchange rates of their currencies. The other was that the value of a currency be allowed to float temporarily until a new value is established. West Germany used a temporary float of its mark in 1969 before officially revaluing its currency. A third—and more radical—proposal under consideration was that nations be permitted to widen the "band" around the values of their currency from 1% to 2% or 3%. All three plans were rejected in favor of the status quo. However, some governments continued to operate in technical violation of IMF regulations during the year. Canada allowed its currency to float with no firm deadline for a return to a fixed parity. Brazil and Chile habitually employed the system of using small periodic changes in valuation.

Special Drawing Rights Given Out

On January 1, the IMF distributed $3.4 billion in special drawing rights (SDRs) to its members for the first time. The new reserve assets, which are also referred to as "paper gold," will be used to settle accounts on the books of the IMF. The use of SDRs was settled upon as a solution to the scarcity in the supply of monetary gold, which had failed to grow in proportion to the volume of world trade and international transactions. The SDRs will be used for essentially the same purpose that gold had served: in payment from countries with balance-of-payments deficits.

The largest allocation of SDRs went to the United States, which received almost $867 million. Great Britain received approximately $410 million; West Germany, approximately $202 million; India,

$126 million; Japan, approximately $122 million; Canada, approximately $124 million; France, approximately $165 million; and Italy, $105 million.

Before issuing SDRs, the IMF made a special agreement with South Africa concerning the purchase of gold. Under the agreement South Africa will be able to sell newly mined gold to the IMF when the market price of gold drops below $35 an ounce. South Africa will also be able to exchange gold for foreign currencies when they are needed to finance a deficit in international commercial transactions.

The major effect of the agreement was to ease pressure on the U.S. dollar. In earlier years, countries wanting to increase their gold reserves were likely to convert their holdings of U.S. dollars to gold, thus draining U.S. gold reserves and reducing the value of the dollar in relation to the value of gold. Another approach often used was to buy gold from South Africa on the private market, which also helped increase the price of gold and exert downward pressure on the dollar. Under the agreement, major nations agreed not to buy monetary gold on the private market. The agreement in effect replaced the U.S. Treasury with the IMF as the world's major source of monetary gold.

U.S. Economic Interventionism

Throughout 1970 a number of European nations expressed displeasure at the degree to which the United States had penetrated or influenced their economies. A primary source of discontent was that U.S. domestic "stagflation"—a mixture of economic stagnation and inflation—would drag their own economies down. Some European nations visualized themselves caught up in a vicious circle of U.S. economic opportunism. For several years, the United States had incurred balance-of-payments deficits which it settled with dollars. However, U.S. firms had taken over European companies and implanted U.S. banking and business subsidiaries on European soil. Through these businesses, the U.S. was able to regain many of the dollars used to settle its balance-of-payments deficits.

During the annual meeting of the World Bank in Copenhagen, Denmark, Jordan's seat remains empty while an Israeli delegate speaks. A demonstrator against the meeting is arrested (left).

ABOVE AND LEFT: NORDISK PRESSEFOTO FROM PICTORIAL PARADE

In an effort to insulate their economies from U.S. intervention, the nations of the European Economic Community (EEC), or Common Market, tentatively agreed to allow their central banks to intervene in foreign-exchange markets each day. By using U.S. dollars to buy and sell on the market, the banks would be better able to regulate the variance in currency values. By about 1980 the EEC nations planned to eliminate differences in values entirely and to develop a common currency. They would have a common "Federal Reserve Board" and pooled reserves.

Eurodollar and Eurobond Markets

The moderate relaxation of U.S. monetary policy contributed to a substantial slowdown in the growth of the Eurodollar (dollars held in banks outside of the United States) market in 1970. The U.S. banks' Eurodollar borrowing, which reached a peak of $14.5 billion in November 1969, fell to $9.4 billion. This sharp decline in the demand for Eurodollars by U.S. banks was reflected shortly thereafter in a pronounced easing of market conditions in the United States.

On the Eurobond market activity in new issues continued to decline in the first half of the year but began to pick up again in the third quarter. At the end of the first nine months of the year the volume of marketable U.S. government bonds and notes held in foreign countries stood at about $1.03 billion. After beginning the year at the $962-million level, Eurobond holdings fell to $906 million in March before beginning to climb.

Net purchases of U.S. corporate bonds abroad followed a contradictory pattern during the year. After rising to the $161-million level in March, they dropped to a low of $13 million in June, vacillated throughout the summer, and stood at $106 million in September. (*See also* Banks; Economy; World Trade. *See in* CE: Money.)

MONGOLIAN PEOPLE'S REPUBLIC.

As rivalry for influence in the Communist world continued between the Soviet Union and the People's Republic of China, Mongolia's two powerful neighbors, Mongolia remained allied to the Soviets in 1970. Mongolia's position was indicated in a communiqué issued by Mongolia's chief of state, Zhamsarangibin Sambuu, and Czechoslovakia's President Ludvig Svoboda during a visit of the Czechoslovak president to Mongolia in March. The communiqué said the policies of China were inimical to the interests of socialist nations.

Soviet armed forces continued to be stationed in Mongolia. In September a Soviet delegation, led by Defense Minister Andrei A. Grechko, paid an official visit to Mongolia and inspected Mongolian and Soviet troops.

A Mongolian man adheres to traditional building methods as he constructs the latticework for the family tent. The women of the family use modern sewing machines on the tent fabric.

CAMERA PRESS FROM PIX

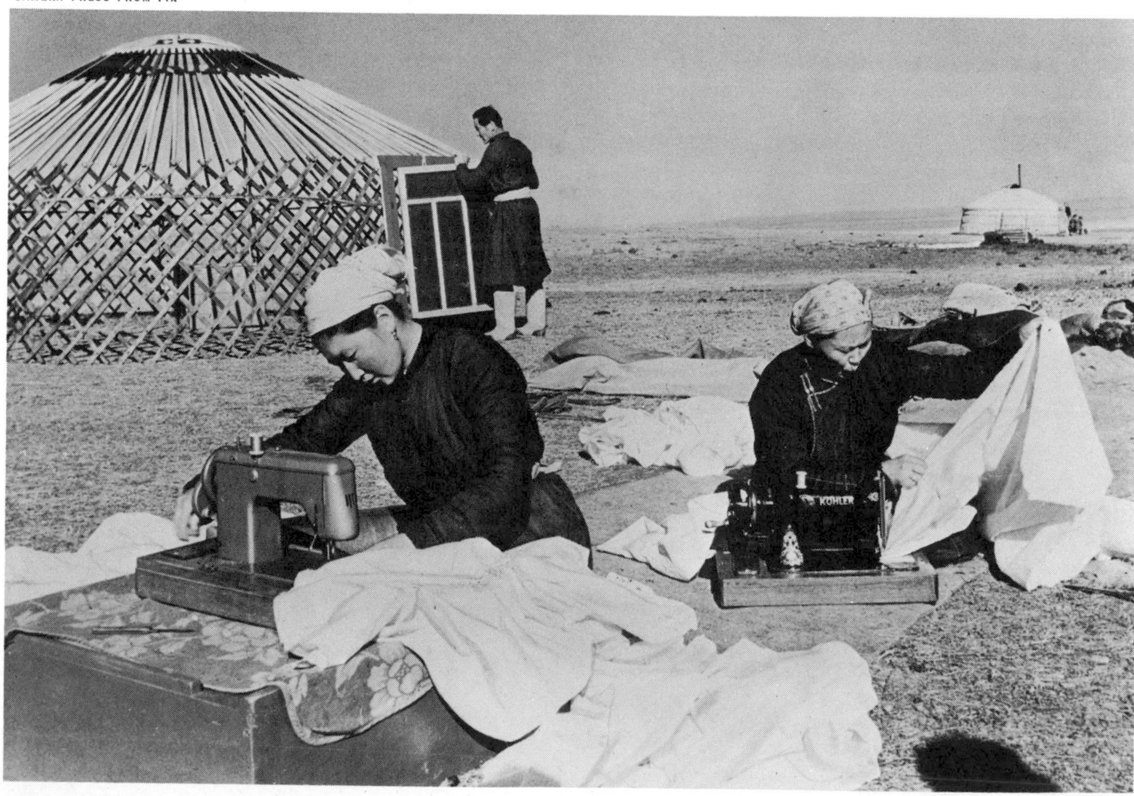

Early in the year Mongolia published figures indicating increases in the national income and in industrial production over the preceding year. Economic agreements with the Soviet Union and with five Eastern European nations assured Mongolia of support for a new five-year development program to be inaugurated in 1971.

With Soviet and Eastern European help, the new industrial city of Darkhan continued to develop. Situated about 80 miles north of the capital city of Ulan Bator, its main industries in 1970 were a power plant, a coal mine, and a cement factory. Ulan Bator was the site of an international Buddhist conference in June. (*See also* Asia. *See in* CE: Mongolia.)

MOROCCO. In 1970 Morocco returned to parliamentary government after five years of direct rule by King Hassan II. A national referendum on a new constitution, announced by the king on July 8, was overwhelmingly approved by voters on July 25. The vote ended the state of emergency decreed by Hassan in 1965 when he dissolved a deeply split parliament. Morocco's chief opposition parties—the leftist National Union of Popular Forces and the middle-class Istiqlal—voted against the referendum because of the powers it gave the king. On July 27 they formed a united National Front.

The new constitution strengthened the king's authority by giving him emergency powers and the use of the referendum as a means of deciding issues. It also reduced parliament to a single Chamber of Representatives of 240 members, to be elected for six-year terms. On August 21, 150 representatives were chosen by electors representing local assemblies and professional and trade organizations. The remaining representatives were elected by universal suffrage on August 28. Because the parties of the National Front boycotted the elections, a large majority of the new representatives were supporters of the king.

In foreign affairs King Hassan strengthened his ties with Mauritania and Algeria. Diplomatic relations with Mauritania were established in January, and in June the two nations signed a treaty of cooperation. Long-standing disputes with Algeria over borders and the Tindouf iron-mining region were resolved in meetings between Hassan and Algeria's President Houari Boumédienne.

A strike by University of Rabat students and faculty demanding a settlement of grievances against the university administration spread throughout the university and secondary school systems in February. Although a promise of educational reforms appeared to have defused the crisis in March, another strike movement was begun in May.

Early in 1970 floods in northern Morocco severely damaged the cereal crop, but good harvests elsewhere made up for the losses. (*See in* CE: Morocco.)

A.F.P. FROM PICTORIAL PARADE

A Moroccan telecommunications center for artificial satellites, inaugurated by King Hassan II, became operational in 1970.

MOTION PICTURES. In the world of motion pictures 1970 was the year of the so-called youth film, emphasizing revolution and campus revolt. It was also another year of decline for the once great Hollywood studios. Independent film producers established themselves more firmly as the new money-makers, and most of the year's awards went to independently produced films. The film industry's self-censoring system of film classification was called into question, and minor changes were made in the rating code.

The Decline of Hollywood

By 1970 almost all of the great old Hollywood studios had been taken over by large financial groups, such as Gulf & Western Industries, Inc., and the Transamerica Corp. The glitter and multimillion-dollar glamour of the old film operations were being replaced by modern business practices, and this called for drastic cuts in budgets for films. In the past, at the industry's peak, about 50 films were made by each major studio each year; in 1970 the average number of films made by each studio had dropped to about 15. As a symbol of the fall of the old empires, the properties of Metro-Goldwyn-Mayer, Inc.—furnishings, costumes, scenery, and other items representing half a century of U.S. movies—were sold at auction.

It was evident during the year that a new generation of film makers was replacing the old producers of commercial motion pictures. Noncommercial productions of low-budget films were sporadic but

LEFT: COURTESY, 20TH CENTURY FOX. RIGHT: COURTESY, PARAMOUNT PICTURES CORP.

In 'M*A*S*H' (above, left), Elliott Gould and Donald Sutherland (with umbrella) portrayed U.S. Army surgeons in Korea. 'Catch-22' featured many film stars, including Orson Welles (left) and Martin Balsam (center) as U.S. Air Force officers during World War II. Both films used tragicomedy to point out the absurdities of militarism and the horrors of war.

determined, and perhaps indicated the future of the medium. These noncommercial films used the medium as a direct and vital means of communication for social, political, and aesthetic ideas.

The year's main technical advance that promised a further change in the economics of the U.S. film industry was the development of the video cassette. Video cassette equipment would allow viewers to build up film libraries in their own homes. Another technical advance was the hologram film production process with its three-dimensional effect. A license for the first hologram film was granted to the Laser Film Corp. of New York during the year.

In January the Motion Picture Association of America (MPAA) announced changes in its voluntary rating system. The M classification was changed to GP (general patronage), but parental guidance was suggested. The age limit for films rated R and X was raised from 16 to 17 years.

Joseph Strick, the producer-director of 'Tropic of Cancer', filed suit in March against the MPAA, Paramount Pictures Corp., and the Paramount Distributing Corp. His film had received an X rating, and Strick charged that the cooperation between organizations in the film industry regarding the rating system was in violation of federal antitrust laws. He claimed that X-rated films were discriminated against by theater owners and that it was difficult to obtain adequate advertising for such films. In May the National Catholic Office for Motion Pictures and the Broadcasting and Film Commission of the National Council of the Churches of Christ in the U.S.A. charged that the rating system did not provide sufficient information and protection for the public.

Awards and Festivals

At the 42d annual awards presentation of the Academy of Motion Picture Arts and Sciences held in April, 'Midnight Cowboy' was named best film of 1969. The award for best actor went to John Wayne for his role in 'True Grit', and the award

In the notable British film 'Kes' a child is enlightened by his experiences with a hawk.

COURTESY, UNITED ARTISTS

for best actress was given to Maggie Smith of Great Britain for her role in 'The Prime of Miss Jean Brodie'. Gig Young in 'They Shoot Horses, Don't They?' was named best supporting actor. Goldie Hawn, formerly of the television show Laugh-In, was chosen as best supporting actress for her role in 'Cactus Flower'.

'Midnight Cowboy' took two other awards, including best director, John Schlesinger. 'Butch Cassidy and the Sundance Kid' won the award for best song, 'Raindrops Keep Fallin' on My Head', and three other Oscars.

The Oscar for best foreign-language film was awarded to 'Z', a French-language film that attacked the military regime in Greece. 'Z' had also been nominated in the general category of best film of the year. Other motion pictures that won Oscars were 'Anne of the Thousand Days', 'Hello, Dolly!', and 'Marooned'. A special award "for sheer brilliance" was presented to the actor Cary Grant.

The New York Film Critics' awards were announced in December. The critics named George C. Scott and Glenda Jackson the best actor and actress of 1970. Chief Dan George and Karen Black were cited for giving the best supporting performances. The critics chose 'Five Easy Pieces' as the best film of 1970.

'M*A*S*H' in 1970 became the third U.S. film to win first prize at the Cannes Film Festival in France. Japan's first International Film Festival was held at Osaka during April.

New Releases

"Youth appeal" was the watchword in the U.S. film industry during 1970. Following the example set by the low budgeted but highly successful 'Easy Rider', film executives cut down on capital outlays and turned to revolutionary film subjects.

'Zabriskie Point', the first film made in the United States by the Italian director Michelangelo Antonioni, was set in Los Angeles and in Death Valley, Calif. The film was criticized for its shallow treatment of the problems and conflicts facing U.S. youth.

Jon Voight starred in 'The Revolutionary,' which traced the development of a student radical from a political liberal to a violent revolutionary. The film concentrated on personal motivations.

The situation on U.S. college campuses was explored in the film 'Getting Straight', with Elliott Gould playing the role of a graduate student. The film's climactic scene centered around an oral examination for a master's degree while troops patrolled the campus.

Two other films about the young were criticized for their youth-exploiting nature. Both of these films, 'R.P.M.' (revolutions per minute) and 'The Strawberry Statement', were set on college campuses. The latter film dealt with events surrounding the demonstrations in 1968 at Columbia University in New York City. The film was criticized for its overdone photographic effects.

A new breed of war movie appeared in 1970. The long-awaited film version of Joseph Heller's World War II novel 'Catch-22', directed by Mike Nichols, received critical praise. Alan Arkin gave a brilliant performance as a panic-stricken bombardier who was convinced that all the world was conspiring toward his death. The elaborate production was arranged in a series of flashbacks within one flashback.

'M*A*S*H', the first-prize winner at Cannes, was a comedy about the Korean War. The antiheroes were surgeons in a field hospital, and the film featured gory operating-room scenes and an absurd football game between the field hospital unit and an evacuation unit. The U.S. Army and Air Force Motion Picture Service would not allow

COURTESY, CANNON RELEASING CORP.

Peter Boyle starred in the motion picture 'Joe', a commentary on violence.

the film to be shown on military bases because they felt it would create fears among enlisted men regarding the medical care they would receive.

A realistic picture of World War II was presented in the film 'Patton: a Salute to a Rebel'. George C. Scott played the role of Gen. George Smith Patton, Jr.

Some films released in 1970 purported to explore the social divisions within the United States. 'Joe' was a film about murder, the relationship between an executive and a "hard-hat" type of worker, hippies, and drugs. 'WUSA' was the title of a film and the call letters of a New Orleans, La., radio station that dispensed right-wing hate propaganda

COURTESY, COLUMBIA PICTURES INDUSTRIES, INC.

In 'Five Easy Pieces' Jack Nicholson gave an outstanding performance as a man trying to escape his past. Karen Black also starred.

under the guise of patriotism. A view of working-class life in the United States, contrasted with upper-middle-class life, was presented in the film 'Five Easy Pieces'.

The phenomenal rock festival held at Bethel, N.Y., in 1969 was immortalized on film in 'Woodstock'. The three-hour-long film covered the highlights of the three-day-long festival, including shots of the spectators as well as uniquely photographed scenes of the performers. Loudspeakers were arranged in motion-picture theaters to create the illusion that the audience was surrounded by the Woodstock crowd.

Another motion picture dedicated to rock music was the Beatles' 'Let It Be'. The film was a documentary of the English rock group's rehearsal and recording sessions.

There were very few Hollywood-style musicals made during the year. A musical motion picture called 'Scrooge' was based on Charles Dickens' story 'A Christmas Carol'. It starred Albert Finney. The successful musical play 'On a Clear Day You Can See Forever' was made into a motion picture featuring Barbra Streisand. In 1970 Miss Streisand played her first nonsinging role, in the comedy motion picture 'The Owl and the Pussycat'.

In the year's offering of Western motion pictures there was more concentration on the American Indian point of view in such films as 'A Man Called Horse' and 'Tell Them Willie Boy Is Here'. One outstanding Western was 'The Ballad of Cable Hogue'.

Among the best films of the year treating so-called taboo subjects was 'The Boys in the Band', a motion picture about male homosexuality. 'Women in Love', based on D. H. Lawrence's novel, showed total male nudity. Various X-rated films did not fare well in the eyes of film critics. Three films criticized for their extraordinarily poor taste were 'Myra Breckinridge' (in which Mae West attempted to make a comeback as a sex symbol), 'Performance' (starring Mick Jagger of the Rolling Stones), and 'Beyond the Valley of the Dolls'.

Costa-Gavras, the director of 'Z', made a motion picture dealing with Communist repression in Czechoslovakia, 'The Confession'. Several outstanding films by other great foreign directors were released during the year. Spanish director Luis Buñuel's 'Tristana' explored the cause and effect of physical desire. Set in late 18th-century France, 'The Wild Child', directed by François Truffaut, was based on the true story of a boy found living wild in the woods. Swedish director Ingmar Bergman's 1970 contribution to the cinematic art was 'The Passion of Anna'. (*See in* CE: Motion Pictures.)

The hilarious spoof 'Cotton Comes to Harlem' proved to be a box-office smash in 1970. It was a wild detective comedy featuring a large cast of blacks.

COURTESY, UNITED ARTISTS

Mountain climbers Dean Caldwell (left) and Warren Harding pause as photographers approach in a helicopter. The two were the first to climb the southeast face of El Capitan mountain, a distance of 3,604 feet. The mountain is in Yosemite National Park.

WIDE WORLD

MOUNTAIN CLIMBING. The successful 27-day-long struggle of two climbers to ascend by a new route the 3,604-foot-high vertical and overhanging face of El Capitan in California's Yosemite National Park captured wide attention in the United States in November 1970. Warren Harding, 46, of West Sacramento, Calif.—who in 1958 had led the first ascent of El Capitan—and Dean Caldwell, 27, of Portland, Ore., had anticipated a 12-day climb. They were slowed, however, by the difficulties of the rock and the unfavorable weather.

A week before they reached the top, the climbers spurned a rescue attempt organized by the National Park Service. At the top, they were greeted by friends, newsmen, and television cameramen who had ascended by an easier route—and by park officials who threatened to bill them for the cost of the rescue expedition.

A number of expeditions visited the Himalayas during the year. Two two-man teams of a Japanese expedition—Neomi Uemura and Teruo Matsura, and Katasutossi Hirabayashi and his Sherpa guide Chot Tare—in May reached the summit of Mount Everest on successive days. One Japanese climber and one Sherpa guide were killed during the expedition.

Members of three expeditions—two British and one French—reached the top of famous Annapurna I. Yugoslavs scaled Annapurna II and IV; Annapurna III yielded to a Japanese women's expedition, and other Japanese climbers ascended Annapurna IV. German climbers surmounted Nanga Parbat. Six lives were lost in the unsuccessful attempt by Austrians to climb Dhaulagiri IV.

In Alaska a U.S. women's expedition reached the summit of Mount McKinley, North America's loftiest peak. A Czechoslovak expedition met disaster in the high and treacherous Andes of Peru. The bodies of 14 Czechoslovak climbers and one Chilean mountaineer were found buried in snow; the men had set out from Yungay the day before the May 31 earthquake. Elsewhere in South America, U.S. and New Zealand parties were among the more successful of several expeditions.

In the Alps the most striking feature of the climbing season was the increasing number of one-man ascents of very hard routes. Foul weather plagued climbers in the Alps during the summer of 1970, and climbing accidents were numerous.

MUSEUMS. The formerly august world of U.S. museums was disturbed in 1970 by the loosely organized but widely publicized protests of various groups of artists. These protests, which occurred in New York City, the U.S. art center, focused on achieving greater artists' rights with regard to museum and gallery policy making; extending the traditional roles of museums and galleries into more socially active community concerns; and protesting various U.S. political issues, mainly the Vietnam war.

Numerous episodes during the year gave evidence of broad support for these goals in the artistic community, though not always for the methods chosen to achieve them. On May 22, in the aftermath generated by the U.S. invasion of Cambodia, a New York artists' strike against "racism, sexism, repression, and war" was held ". . . as an expression of shame and outrage at our government's policies." About 50 galleries and some of New York City's art museums were closed. When New York City's Metropolitan Museum of Art remained open, some strike members held a "sit-out" on the museum steps. In June a group of strike members disrupted the annual convention of the American Association of Museums (AAM) and succeeded in having it consider a resolution on the responsibilities of museums to society. In September an "Art for Peace" exhibition took place in which about 40 galleries participated.

One group vigorously pursuing reform goals was the Art Workers' Coalition (AWC). The AWC

The John F. Kennedy Center for the Performing Arts in Washington, D.C., was scheduled for completion in 1971. The cultural center is an official memorial to the late president.

WIDE WORLD

achieved one victory when New York City's Museum of Modern Art (MOMA) began an experimental program in which admission fees would not be charged on Mondays. Following this success, the AWC presented a number of demands to art galleries concerning artists' rights and the need for "equitable representation" of women, black, and Puerto Rican artists. Along with other groups the AWC also mounted an attack on the controversial expansion plan of the Metropolitan Museum of Art, arguing that instead of extending its present quarters the museum should decentralize into culturally deprived neighborhoods.

To some degree, museums responded to these growing demands that they become relevant to the needs of their communities. The AAM undertook a survey project in order to eventually assist U.S. museums in setting up neighborhood museums and community art centers. The Brooklyn Museum, in New York City, and the Museum of Fine Arts, in Boston, Mass., established projects to exhibit and collect art by black artists. Following the lead of MOMA, New York City's Metropolitan began its own discretionary admission program, which allowed each museum visitor to decide how little or how much he would pay for certain exhibits.

Other Problems

Adding to general museum and gallery problems in 1970 were the rising costs of operation. As shipping and insurance costs rose, museums became loath to lend their works of art for exhibition.

Another problem affecting museums was the origin of their acquisitions. A group of gold objects owned by Boston's Museum of Fine Arts became the center of international controversy in 1970 when the government of Turkey announced that the objects had been illegally exported from that country. The general problem of "stolen" art treasures was serious enough that a committee of the United Nations Educational, Scientific, and Cultural Organization (UNESCO) drew up a code concerning the problem. A special panel of UNESCO members was studying the implementation of their recommendations. The code pledged importing countries to prevent the acquisition by museums of illegally exported materials. (*See also* Painting and Sculpture.)

MUSIC. The celebration of the 200th anniversary of the birth of the composer Ludwig van Beethoven dominated the world of music throughout 1970. In Europe the Beethoven festivities got under way in earnest in May. At that time the International Beethoven Festival opened in Bonn, West Germany, the composer's birthplace; the Vienna Festival in Austria began a far-reaching conspectus of his music; and conductor Otto Klemperer began a complete cycle of the symphonies in London with the New Philharmonia Orchestra. Beethoven was also featured in the programs of the Edinburgh Festival in Scotland. And at the Pablo Casals Festival in Puerto Rico, the 93-year-old cellist proved that he was still in rare form as he conducted an overwhelming performance of Beethoven's 'Ninth Symphony'. Among the major bicentenary events in New York City was a series of concerts, inaugurated in November, given by Eugene Istomin, Isaac Stern, and Leonard Rose, featuring Beethoven's important piano chamber music.

Premieres

During the 1969–70 musical season a number of interesting works had their first performances. One of the more unusual was Peter Maxwell Davies' 'Vesalii Icones', given by the Pierrot Players in London. The piece was "scored" for dancer, cello, and instrumental ensemble. Each of the 14 dances had as its starting point an anatomical engraving from Andreas Vesalius' famous anatomy book of 1543.

In January 1970 the Philadelphia Orchestra under Eugene Ormandy gave the first U.S. performance of Dmitri Shostakovich's 'Symphony No. 13'. In February the New York Philharmonic Orchestra under Leonard Bernstein gave the premiere of Elliott Carter's 'Concerto for Orchestra', considered a superbly organized and well-integrated work. During the same month in New York City, Luciano Berio's work 'This Means That . . .', involving a lecture, folk songs, Gregorian chant, a perfect fifth played continuously on a viola, and electronic sounds, had its premiere. At the Aldeburgh Festival in England, Shostakovich's 14th symphony had its first performance outside the Soviet Union, conducted by its dedicatee, Benjamin Britten. Also at Aldeburgh, Hans Werner Henze's 'El Cimarrón' was premiered. In April in London Pierre Boulez gave the first British performance of the rediscovered 'Waldmärchen', the first part of Gustav Mahler's 'Das klagende Lied', which won acclaim as a fascinating work. One of the season's more novel performances was that of excerpts from Frank Zappa's '200 Motels', given by the Los Angeles Phil-

Conductor Leonard Bernstein (above) visited Vienna, Austria, to conduct a series of concerts for Beethoven's bicentenary. Cellist Pablo Casals (below) conducts one of his own works in New York City.

ABOVE: LONDON "DAILY EXPRESS" FROM PICTORIAL PARADE. BELOW: WIDE WORLD harmonic Orchestra and the popular rock group the Mothers of Invention.

Other Musical Events

Two outstanding European orchestras—the Santa Cecilia from Rome under Fernando Previtali and the Royal Philharmonic from London under Rudolf Kempe—had very successful visits to the United States during the 1969–70 season. In London, one of the season's major events was the visit of Maxim Shostakovich, son of Dmitri Shostakovich, to conduct the London Philharmonic Orchestra in his father's 'Eighth Symphony' and 'Ninth Symphony'.

Two major musicians died in 1970—Sir John Barbirolli and George Szell. Szell had been conductor of the Cleveland Orchestra for 24 years and in that time had built it into one of the world's finest symphony orchestras. Barbirolli had conducted the New York Philharmonic from 1937 to 1943 and, from then until his death, the respected Hallé Orchestra in Manchester, England. (*See also* Opera; Popular Music. *See in* CE: Music.)

NATIONAL PARK SERVICE. For the U.S. Department of the Interior's National Park Service, 1970 was largely a year of adjustment to the stresses of the new decade. First, there was the threat to Everglades National Park, in Florida, posed by the establishment of a major jet airport near the park's northern boundary. Extensive facilities had been completed and training jets were using a runway when the White House suddenly announced on January 15 that the jetport would not be completed. The Department of the Interior had reached an agreement with the state of Florida and the local authorities, under which another jetport site would be found. As soon as it is practicable the training jetport will be closed. Secretary of the Interior Walter J. Hickel and Secretary of Transportation John A. Volpe had earlier completed the agreement with Florida's Gov. Claude R. Kirk, Jr., after a Department of the Interior study showed that the ecological disruption caused by the jetport would destroy the country's only mainland subtropical park.

Threatened also by lack of sufficient freshwater flow, Everglades National Park received further protection. The U.S. Congress approved an act virtually assuring the park of the 315,000 acre-feet of freshwater flow per year that ecologists say is the minimum it needs to exist. The act requires the U.S. Army Corps of Engineers to open the gates of its storage lakes north of the park and to provide the park with water as needed.

Congress also passed the Endangered Species Act, which, it was hoped, would prevent the extirpation of the alligator. By prohibiting the transportation of alligator hides across interstate lines if the hides were taken illegally, the act clamped down sharply on the hunting that had threatened to wipe out the Florida alligator.

The struggle to maintain Everglades National Park continued. During 1970 laws were passed to provide the park with an adequate freshwater supply and to protect the alligator.

COURTESY, NATIONAL PARK SERVICE

Thermal pollution of Biscayne National Monument, 50 miles northeast of Everglades National Park, brought swift action from the Department of the Interior. At Secretary Hickel's request the U.S. Department of Justice brought suit against the Florida Power and Light Co. on the grounds that heated water from the operation of the company's two fossil-fueled power plants would destroy the marine microlife and general ecology of Biscayne Bay. The Bay was popular for its sport fishing and was also a recreation area for a metropolitan population expected to reach 2.7 million by 1980.

At Yosemite National Park, in California, the National Park Service banned automobiles from the eastern end of Yosemite Valley to reduce overcrowded conditions. The rest of the valley road network was converted to a one-way scenic and circulatory road pattern. Visitors could still drive to and from the campgrounds and concession lodgings but most in-valley trips were made on free shuttle buses operated 24 hours a day. The result was a more rewarding park experience through the elimination of the noise, pollution, traffic, and hazards of unlimited operation of private cars.

One of the most significant actions of 1970 was Secretary Hickel's proposal on September 14 to provide 14 national recreation areas in or near some of the nation's largest urban centers. He announced the start of a series of studies to test the feasibility of the plan. It would implement the secretary's "Parks to People" program announced in 1969. Because millions of inner-city people cannot afford trips to distant national parks, Hickel said, the parks must be brought to the people.

The National Park Service, which in 1970 administered 13 national recreation areas among its 278 areas, would also administer the proposed 20,000-acre Gateway National Recreation Area, in New York and New Jersey, to be located at the entrance to New York Harbor. The National Park Service already administered another area under study—the Chesapeake and Ohio Canal National Monument, in West Virginia and Maryland, which a bill in Congress would raise to the status of a national historical park.

The 18-month study program also included a proposed Anacostia National Recreation Area, in Washington, D.C., and Maryland, and a Connecticut River National Recreation Area, in Connecticut, Massachusetts, New Hampshire, and Vermont. In addition to the Washington, D.C., and the New York City-Newark, N.J., complex, metropolitan areas involved include Hartford, Conn.-Springfield, Mass.; San Francisco, Calif.; Los Angeles; St. Louis, Mo.; Houston, Tex.; Atlanta, Ga.; Denver, Colo.; Minneapolis-St. Paul, Minn.; Chicago-Milwaukee, Wis.; Detroit, Mich.-Toledo, Ohio; and Memphis, Tenn. Much of the land and water under study was federally owned.

The year also brought a noteworthy research report from the National Park Service scientists at Hawaii Volcanoes National Park describing the return of visible animal life to barren lava rock newly erupted from Kilauea Crater. Scientists observed orb-weaver spiders colonizing the warm lava less than a week after its eruption.

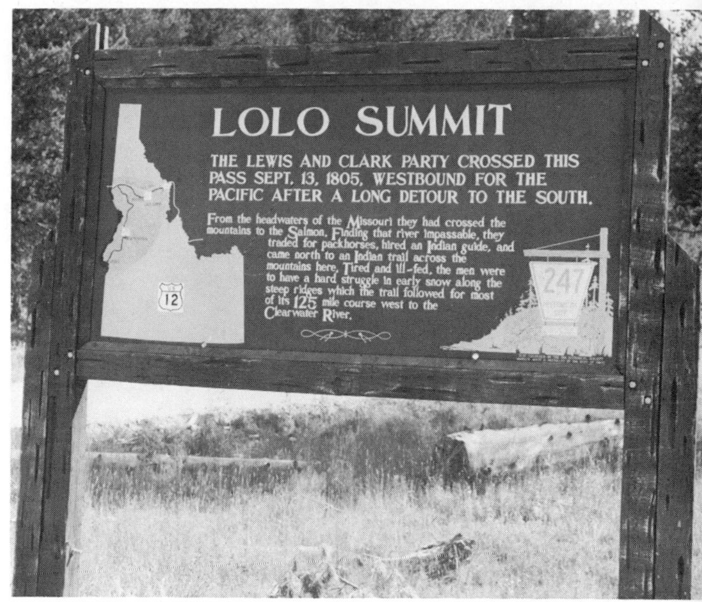

AUTHENTICATED NEWS INTERNATIONAL

During 1970 Lolo Summit Historical Site in Idaho was incorporated into the Nez Perce National Historical Park.

A bill to establish Apostle Islands National Lakeshore, in Wisconsin, passed Congress in September. Legislation was also passed at the end of the year establishing Gulf Islands National Seashore, in Florida and Mississippi, and Voyageurs National Park, near International Falls, Minn.

By October 1, the year had brought an increase of 88 historic landmarks, for a total of 894; 5 natural landmarks, for a total of 147; and 767 additions to the National Register of Historic Places, for a total of 1,960. The national landmarks are sites of national significance and are either publicly or privately owned. The national register contains privately or publicly owned sites nominated by the states for their local and national significance.

Attendance in the U.S. national park system continued to increase in 1970. By August 1, 100.4 million visits had been recorded, compared to 97.1 million for the first seven months of 1969. A total 1970 attendance of 173.6 million appeared likely.

Education Programs

The National Park Service expanded its two environmental education programs, National Environmental Education Development (NEED) and National Environmental Study Area (NESA), in 1970. The NEED program—designed to make the nation's children, from kindergarten through the 12th grade, knowledgeable of their environment—completed the testing of 5th- and 6th-grade materials by approximately 20,000 children. There were

1,200 participants in the first large testing of 3d- and 4th-grade and 7th- and 8th-grade materials.

The NEED program introduced the youngsters to outdoor experiences close to nature in local, state, federal, or private parklands. The objective was to let the children experience the natural environment and note what man does to it.

Paralleling NEED is the NESA program. The National Park Service set aside 64 NESAs in the national park system, and 25 more "outdoor classrooms" were in the planning stage. The schools can use the areas for the NEED program or for other environmental teaching efforts. By the end of 1970 about 85,000 students were to have used the NESAs in 28 states and the Commonwealth of Puerto Rico. (*See also* Conservation. *See in* CE: National Parks articles.)

NAURU. Transportation and communication between Nauru and the rest of the Pacific became a task of high priority in 1970. The American Telephone and Telegraph Co. opened a link between Nauru and Guam. In February, Air Nauru, the smallest international airline in the world, carried out its inaugural flight between the island and Brisbane, Australia.

The Nauru Local Government Council purchased the *Prinses Margriet* from the Holland-America Line. This ship of 9,336 tons had luxury accommodations for 111 people and was to be used to supplement Nauruan services on the Australia-New Guinea-Fiji route.

In an attempt to facilitate tourism, the government of Nauru put up for sale a half-completed modern hotel, formerly owned by Pacific Sporting Pools Ltd. and Central Pacific Hotels Ltd. The unfinished hotel, overlooking Anibare Bay, was well placed to take advantage of Nauru's tourist potential. The number of new Australian companies incorporated or registered in Nauru since independence continued to rise during the year.

NEPAL. Nepal asserted its neutral independence in 1970 by loosening some traditional ties with India and establishing closer relations with its other neighbor, Communist China. At the request of Nepal's King Mahendra, India withdrew its military liaison group from Nepal. Relations deteriorated during the year between the two countries as no agreement was reached on the terms for a new trade and transit treaty.

At the end of February, the crown prince, Birendra Bir Bikram Shah Deva, married Aishwarya Rajya Laxmi Devi Rana, amid rich pomp and pageantry. The bride belonged to the family which ruled as hereditary Nepalese prime ministers before 1951.

Prime Minister Kirti Nidhi Bista resigned on April 12 in order to run for reelection in the parliamentary election scheduled for May. King Mahendra assumed the function of prime minister and appointed a new council of ministers. Elections held on May 28 filled 30 vacated seats in the legislature; Bista was defeated in his bid for reelection, and the king continued to act as prime minister. The speaker of the legislature was reelected. (*See in* CE: Nepal.)

NETHERLANDS. Compared with preceding years, the Netherlands government underwent only minor change in 1970. The minister of economic affairs, Leo de Block, resigned because of the cabinet's refusal to interfere in labor contracts in the metal industry. He was succeeded by Roelf J. Nelissen. The government continued to consist of six members of the Catholic People's party, three members of the People's Party for Freedom and Democracy (Liberals), three members of the Antirevolutionary party, and two members of the Christian Historical Union.

On March 18 and June 3, respectively, the Dutch voters elected representatives to the provincial councils (roughly equivalent to county councils) and to the municipal councils. It was the first time in Dutch political history that voting was not compulsory. The outcome disappointed most politicians. The turnouts of voters were 68.9% (county councils) and 66.6% (municipal councils). Apart from a modest gain by the Communist party in both elections and a successful start of the

Amsterdam policemen prepare to evacuate one of about 30 houses illegally occupied by young people needing a place to live.

KEYSTONE

KEYSTONE

A warning sign erected near the Neerdzee Canal demonstrates the growing problem of water pollution in the Netherlands.

Kabouter ("Gnome") party—a new political movement, supported mainly by young laborers and students—in the elections for the municipal councils, no big changes occurred.

Queen Juliana opened the new session of parliament on September 15. The queen's speech, prepared by the government, began with a reference to the increasing tensions and conflicts in society. Under such conditions, she said, tolerance and the willingness to cooperate and to respect the opinion of others were of great importance. But she promised that, if necessary, the government would take action against groups that abused freedom. The speech concluded with a warning against the pollution of air, water, and soil.

On January 7 the Pastoral Council of the Dutch Roman Catholic church, the only national Roman Catholic pastoral assembly in the world, recommended in a report that celibacy for priests no longer be required. The Dutch bishops later endorsed the recommendation, in spite of a letter from Pope Paul VI urging them to support mandatory priestly celibacy. (*See in* CE: Netherlands.)

NEWSPAPERS. Freedom of the press became one of the most widely discussed issues in newspapers in the United States during 1970. Concern over possible government censorship of the press was kindled by U.S. Vice-President Spiro T. Agnew's repeated criticism of the handling of news in the press. In addition, the U.S. Department of Justice issued a number of subpoenas to newsmen for their notes, film, tapes, and personal testimony in a wide variety of cases throughout the year. Among those served subpoenas by federal or state authorities were *The New York Times* and all four of the daily papers in Chicago. Most of the subpoenas concerned information about militant groups such as the Black Panthers.

The controversy was partially resolved in August when U.S. Attorney General John N. Mitchell announced guidelines to be followed by his department in using the subpoena power against the press. Mitchell did not back off from what he considered the "constitutional and statutory power . . . where, in our opinion, the fair administration of justice requires it." He did, however, recognize the possible limiting effect on 1st Amendment rights that the use of the subpoena would have and promised that "all reasonable attempts should be made to obtain information from nonpress sources before . . . subpoenaing the press."

An important legal victory was achieved for one segment of the newspaper industry in the United States during 1970 when U.S. President Richard M. Nixon signed into law the Newspaper Preservation Act in July. The law offers exemption from antitrust prosecution to newspapers involved in a joint operating arrangement whereby production, circulation, and advertising sales of a failing newspaper and a successful newspaper are handled jointly but with each newspaper operating an independent news staff.

In the area of newspaper ownership, the Times Mirror Co. of Los Angeles expanded its holdings into the Southwest and the East Coast. The owners of the *Los Angeles Times* completed a merger with the *Dallas Times Herald* and bought controlling interest in *Newsday*, a Long Island, N.Y., paper. Cowles Communications, Inc., sold a portion of its media holdings to the New York Times Co. Under a $50-million agreement, Cowles acquired a 23% interest in the New York Times Co., which took, in return, three Florida newspapers; a Memphis, Tenn., television station; a book company; and *Family Circle* magazine.

Two newspapers with directly opposed philosophies were founded in 1970. *The Aquarian Times*, a Sacramento, Calif., weekly, pledged to report only good news. *The Unsatisfied Man* is a critical review of journalism in Colorado.

Underground newspapers continued to thrive in cities and on campuses across the nation. The papers, few of which operate on budgets high enough to pay their staffs living wages, increased in number from about 200 to between 250 and 300 be-

PIEROTTI FROM BEN ROTH AGENCY
"Big Brother"

tween April 1969 and April 1970. Most of the papers emphasized coverage of radical politics.

Two Pulitzer prizes each were won in 1970 by *Newsday* and the Newspaper Division of Field Enterprises, Inc., of Chicago. *Newsday* took honors for public service and for cartoons (Thomas F. Darcy). Thomas Fitzpatrick of the *Chicago Sun-Times* and William J. Eaton of the *Chicago Daily News* were awarded prizes for local and national reporting, respectively. The international reporting award went to Seymour M. Hersh for his disclosure of the My Lai incident in Vietnam. (*See in* CE: Newspapers.)

NEW ZEALAND. In 1970 New Zealand's major problem was its inflationary economy. The economy underwent a wage-price spiral, caused primarily by a shortage of labor, which drove up wages. To cope with the inflation, the government introduced emergency measures, including increased taxes and credit curbs. To help solve the labor shortage, the government initiated a major policy change, vastly expanding its subsidized immigration program to include recruitment of immigrants from the United States and Western Europe. Previously, New Zealand had sought immigrants mainly from Great Britain. Apart from the economic benefits, the new immigration policy was seen as a positive aid in New Zealand's negotiations with the European Economic Community (EEC). In the past, EEC countries had criticized New Zealand's immigration policy as discriminatory.

The negotiations undertaken with EEC during the year were of immense importance to New Zealand. The chief threat to the country's economy was that Britain, its main trading partner, might be admitted to the Common Market without a provision for a transitional period giving New Zealand continued access to British markets. New Zealand, however, also continued to diversify its economy and to find new trading partners, particularly increasing its contacts with Japan.

The country had a number of important visitors during the year, including Great Britain's Queen Elizabeth II, Canada's Prime Minister Pierre Elliott Trudeau, and U.S. Vice-President Spiro T. Agnew. Following the example of the United States, New Zealand announced that some of its troops would be withdrawn from South Vietnam by the end of the year. (*See in* CE: New Zealand.)

NICARAGUA. The economic recession in Nicaragua that characterized the second year of President Anastasio Somoza Debayle's administration continued into the third year, 1970. Again cotton, the chief export crop and indicator of the health of the economy, was responsible for the depressed conditions. In response to a lower price for the crop on the world market, increasing costs of machinery and insecticides, higher interest rates, and tighter credit, the acreage planted to cotton was greatly reduced.

In 1969 the rapidly growing beef industry for the first time surpassed coffee as the nation's second foreign-exchange earner; but the potential for this industry was, in 1970, limited by a restriction of exports to the United States, its principal market. High prices on the world market, an increase in the International Coffee Organization quota, and good weather conditions coincided to make it a good year for coffee growers. Sugar maintained its fourth-place position as a major export crop. The new shrimp and lobster industry grew rapidly during the year. However, these expanding exports combined were unable to compensate for cotton's decline, which in 1969 had resulted in a 2.2% drop in total export earnings over the 1968 figure.

The 54-year-old Bryan-Chamorro Treaty, which gave the United States exclusive rights to construct and operate an interoceanic canal across Nicaragua, was terminated during the year. Also canceled were the lease of the Little and Great Corn islands and the option for the United States to build and maintain a naval base in Nicaraguan territory on the Gulf of Fonseca. (*See in* CE: Nicaragua.)

NIGER. The only event of importance in Niger's internal political development in 1970 was the presidential election in the fall. In July, the political bureau of the ruling Progressive Party of Niger agreed to appoint President Hamani Diori as the sole candidate, and on October 1 he was duly reelected with 98.5% of the vote. Legislative elections were held on October 22.

In the sphere of internal economic development, the participation of Italian and West German interests in the SOMAIR (Société des Mines de l'Air) mining company marked a new stage in the exploitation of uranium deposits at Arhli. An agreement was also signed in Paris regarding the prospecting and exploiting of deposits at Akokane, some 12 miles south of the Arhli deposits already being mined by SOMAIR. The agreement was signed by a representative of the Niger government, by the president of a Japanese industrial consortium, and by a French official. (*See in* CE: Niger.)

NIGERIA. In the Nigerian civil war, the fall of Owerri, headquarters of the Biafran secessionist regime, on Jan. 10, 1970, was followed by the final defeat of the rebels through the federal military government strategy of blockade, bombardment, and land-force advance. On January 11 Gen. C. Odumegwu Ojukwu left the last Biafran enclave and was later granted asylum in the Ivory Coast, one of the few states to have recognized Biafra, leaving Major Gen. Philip Effiong to sue for peace on January 12. Formal surrender took place on January 15, the Biafran leaders accepting the existing political and administrative structure of a united Nigeria and whatever constitutional arrangements representatives of the Nigerian people as a whole should work out.

Immediately after the cease-fire, the federal government set about its proclaimed policies of reconciliation, rehabilitation, reconstruction, and reabsorption, starting with relief operations. Predictions of vengeance and genocide proved unwarranted. While accepting offers of aid from many friendly countries (though not from those that supported Biafra, notably France and Portugal), the government kept the administration of relief firmly in its own hands. The British government's offer of emergency funds was accepted, and a special emissary was sent to Nigeria to discuss the most effective use of relief aid.

Relations between the Ibo and the rest of the community appeared to be improving. However, some dissension in the three states making up the former Eastern Region remained between those who had and those who had not supported secession. On August 15 the government published a decree permitting the dismissal of those civil servants and other public officials who had been actively engaged in hostile acts or rebellion against the federation between 1966 and 1970 and the cancellation of their retirement benefits. The decree also covered those who counseled such acts or any officer whose conduct during this period was such that it would not now be in the public interest to employ him. No court action was permitted, and the only appeal allowed was to the head of the government.

On October 1, eight months after the end of civil war, Nigeria celebrated the tenth anniversary of its independence, and it was evident that the policy of reconciliation had repaid the country in strength and unity, despite the division into 12 states and the differences in tribe, religion, education, and economic potential. In his Independence Day speech, Maj. Gen. Yakubu Gowon, head of state, promised a return to elected civilian rule by 1976. The Nigerian army, still 200,000 strong, needed time for reorganization to a peacetime basis and was temporarily required to aid the police against the severe crime wave, especially of robbery with violence, that swept the country as an aftermath of war. A nine-point program of national reorganization and development was outlined, including measures to eradicate corruption, the preparation of a new constitution, the organization of political parties, the taking of a census in 1973, a settlement regard-

After a costly civil war, Nigerians resumed peacetime activities. Here customers inspect yams, a major product, in the Onitsha marketplace.
UPI COMPIX

ing the number of states, and the adoption of a nonaligned foreign policy.

Nigeria showed signs of rapid economic recovery. Only a relatively small area had been physically devastated, and valuable oil installations were not completely wrecked. Production of oil was back to one million barrels a day by June, and exports were put at 4 million barrels a month. Losses were largely in overseas markets for agriculture and in foreign exchange, to some extent balanced by the development of local industry, and an internal market. It was estimated that, with normal financial prudence, all 12 states would be economically viable by 1971. However, the problems of the East Central State, the heart of Ibo land and the area most ravaged by war, were far from settled. The rehabilitation commission was dissolved because, according to the East Central State commissioner for economic development, S. G. Ikoku, it was plagued by decay and corruption. It was replaced by an interim agency controlled by the military governors of the three eastern states. The agency faced the difficulty that, while the need for aid was greater than in the other states, allocation of more than proportionate revenue brought complaints elsewhere.

In a speech on October 1, General Gowon stated that priority would be given to restoring interrupted and essential services, to be followed by a four-year development program with primary emphasis on agricultural cash crops. "Nigerianization" of industry would proceed as fast as possible, and Nigerian businessmen would get import license preference. Brigadier Robert A. Adebayo, governor of the Western State, demanded of expatriate industrialists a faster intake of senior Nigerian employees, and Nigerian students were limited to flights abroad on Nigeria Airways. (*See also* Africa. *See in* CE: Nigeria.)

NIXON, RICHARD M. United States President Richard M. Nixon reached the midway point of his four-year term of office at the end of 1970, failing to have solved the country's two major problems. He had not ended the war in Vietnam, and he had not solved the country's economic problems, characterized by continuing inflation and sharply rising unemployment. Nevertheless, Nixon vigorously appealed to the "silent majority of Americans," which he had assiduously courted during the first half of his term, to provide a mark of approval for his Administration by voting for Republican candidates in the November elections. The election results were a disappointment for the president and, in the opinion of many observers, foreshadowed a period of reassessment and change in his approach.

Foreign Affairs

In January 1970, President Nixon asserted that "the major immediate goal of our foreign policy is to bring an end to the war in Vietnam." To this end, he continued to follow a policy of troop withdrawals and "Vietnamization"—turning over the conduct of the war to South Vietnamese forces. On April 30, however, Nixon seemed to have suddenly reversed his policy of de-escalation when he dramatically announced that he had ordered U.S. forces into Cambodia to clear out sanctuaries used by the North Vietnamese and Viet Cong. The U.S. invasion of Cambodia, which geographically widened the war, touched off a strong wave of domestic protest. Students in many of the nation's colleges went on strike and demonstrations were also held in major U.S. cities. At one campus, Kent State University in Kent, Ohio, National Guardsmen fired into a protesting group of students, killing four, and thus setting off further domestic demonstrations. (*See* Colleges and Universities; United States.)

WIDE WORLD

President Nixon signs his State-of-the-World message in February in which he emphasizes a "new strategy for peace."

Criticism of the president abated somewhat when he announced on June 30 that all U.S. ground forces had been removed from Cambodia and that the operation had been a success in that it effectively "bought time" in which to make his Vietnamization policy work. (*See* Cambodia.)

In October, Nixon announced what was termed a "new peace initiative." He asked North Vietnam and the Viet Cong to agree to a standstill cease-fire throughout Indochina. In addition, he proposed an international peace conference to negotiate an end to the fighting in Laos and Cambodia as well as in South Vietnam. His initiative, which was applauded by both Republicans and Democrats, was rejected by the North Vietnamese and Viet Cong representatives at the Paris peace talks as merely a ploy designed to impress U.S. voters before the election. (*See* Vietnam.)

The explosive situation in the Middle East was another area of concern for President Nixon in 1970. The United States worked quietly behind the scenes during the year to arrange a cease-fire agreement between Israel (which received strong military assistance from the United States) and the Arab nations, mainly Jordan and the United Arab Republic (UAR), or Egypt; such an agreement was finally achieved in August. However, the outbreak of virtual civil war in Jordan and the invasion of that country by troops from Syria (which received heavy Soviet military assistance) provoked a dangerous new international crisis. On September 27 Nixon began a five-nation European tour to demonstrate, as he said, that a "primary, indispensable" principle of U.S. policy was "to maintain the necessary strength in the Mediterranean to preserve the peace against those who might threaten the peace." The unexpected death of UAR President Gamal Abdel Nasser during the president's trip, however, caused him to cancel an elaborate planned "show of strength" by the U.S. Sixth Fleet, stationed in the Mediterranean. However, Syrian troops withdrew from Jordan, King Hussein I managed to reassert control over the country, and general tension lessened somewhat. It was felt by some observers that President Nixon's firm approach during the crisis, designed to impress the Soviets that the United States would not hesitate to take strong action when the situation required it, had been a major factor in stabilizing the Middle East situation. (*See* Foreign Policy, U.S.; Middle East.)

Domestic Affairs

On the domestic front, Nixon's major problem was the economy. The Administration's "game plan" for coping with inflation resulted in a high rate of unemployment as well as a continuation of rising prices. The Nixon Administration countered criticism by saying that it was too early to tell whether or not the plan was working. Although Nixon had categorically rejected the idea of an "incomes policy"—some sort of policy to officially regulate wage increases—a number of leading economists were arguing at year's end that it had become a necessity. (*See* Economy; Employment.)

Strained relations with the U.S. Congress was another major problem for Nixon. Its effect was to stymie the president's legislative program. The president suffered his most humiliating defeat of the year when the Senate rejected his nomination of Circuit Judge G. Harrold Carswell for associate justice of the Supreme Court. However, Nixon did achieve passage of two key measures before the elections: the District of Columbia crime-control bill and a bill to replace the U.S. Post Office Department with an independent federal agency. (*See* Congress, U.S.; Post Office, U.S.; Supreme Court of the United States.)

It was partially, no doubt, because of Nixon's difficulties with Congress that he decided to pursue a vigorous campaign policy to elect Republican candidates for Congress who would strongly support his program. Vice-President Spiro T. Agnew was the spearhead in the campaign strategy; he toured the country in support of Republican candidates and lashed out strongly against Administration critics in a shower of vitriolic rhetoric. Nixon himself hit the campaign trail in the last few weeks, visiting 22 states in a forceful attempt to win support for his candidates. The Republican strategy was to stress the "social issue"—a rubric embracing the problems of campus unrest, pornography, drugs, "permissiveness," and crime—which they felt the silent majority of Americans feared most. The Democrats in turn stressed the economic issue—the high rate of unemployment and inflation. (*See* Agnew.)

The election results left neither party with a clearcut victory. Some of the Nixon Administration's major targets—liberal Senators Charles E. Goodell (R, N.Y.), Albert Gore (D, Tenn.), and Joseph D. Tydings (D, Md.)—lost their seats, but the numerical party balance in the Senate and House actually changed very little. The Democrats captured an impressive number of governorships and also turned back a concerted Republican effort to increase its support among blue-collar labor groups and in the South. Despite Nixon's claim that he had achieved a working "ideological" majority in the Senate, the general feeling of observers was that Nixon's engagement in the divisive partisan politics and rhetoric of the election might further diminish his ability to work with Congress and to end the deep polarization of the country. (*See* Elections; Political Parties. *See in* CE: Nixon.)

NORWAY. The major economic and political issue in Norway during 1970 was the question of membership in the European Economic Community (EEC), or Common Market. Not all the members of Norway's coalition government were enthusiastic about membership in the EEC. Premier Per Borten, while he was committed to the government's policy of seeking full membership, expressed doubts about the wisdom of joining the Common Market.

The first formal negotiating meeting on Norway's application for full membership in an extended EEC took place on September 22 at Brussels, Belgium. The Norwegian representatives made it clear that Norway accepted the political as well as the economic implications of the Treaty of Rome, but they stated that Norway could not accept the existing EEC fisheries policy. The Norwegians argued that the problems relating to the fisheries policy would not be the same in an expanded Common Market and that with the entry of Norway the EEC would have a surplus of fish rather than a deficit. There was also concern about agricultural policies, since Norway supports farm prices about 15% higher than those of the EEC. (*See* Europe.)

On June 2 the U.S.-owned Phillips Petroleum Co. confirmed the discovery of a large oil field in the Norwegian sector of the North Sea. The Norwegian government, expecting to find even larger fields, made plans for oil prospecting farther north in the Norwegian sector. (*See in* CE: Norway.)

NUCLEAR ENERGY. By 1970 there were about 100 nuclear-powered electricity-generating plants either installed or on order in the United States. When the plants are installed they will bring the nuclear-electric power potential of the nation to 85–90 million kilowatts. By 1980, if the planned number of nuclear plants materialize, this potential should reach 150 million kilowatts, a figure long forecast by the Atomic Energy Commission (AEC). In August the Tennessee Valley Authority announced plans for the 1977 operation of its third nuclear plant, to be constructed near Spring City, Tenn.

Nuclear energy was under continued criticism in 1970. Some conservationists opposed the installation of nuclear plants as an environmental danger. They said that the nuclear facilities posed an ecological hazard to the atmosphere through the radioactive effluents ordinarily emitted by the plants and to nearby bodies of water through pollution. These waters are used to cool the steam condensers in nuclear power plants. Their arguments in part were bolstered by charges made by California scientists Arthur R. Tamplin and John W. Gofman, who said that a rising number of deaths caused by cancer could be expected from "allowable" radiation under AEC standards. The AEC quickly denied any such possibility.

Soviet nuclear engineers continued to direct their efforts toward a sodium-cooled fast-neutron breeder reactor, the "fast breeder" that generates more nuclear fuel than it consumes. However, U.S. plans to build a fast breeder faltered by 1970. Federal budget restrictions lessened the chance of even building a single U.S. fast-breeder prototype in the foreseeable future.

Project Plowshare, the AEC's study of peaceful applications of nuclear explosions, slowed noticeably in 1970, mainly because of public sensitivity to the radioactivity vented from subsurface detonations. Data accumulated in 1970 revealed the great success of the AEC's private-industry-sponsored nuclear test in 1969, which was devised to free underground natural gas in Colorado. However, it was unclear whether the large amounts of gas freed could be fed into a pipeline. Regulations guiding the use of nuclear-detonated natural gas were nonexistent.

In 1970 a French surgeon implanted a nuclear-powered heart pacemaker in a patient. The new pacemakers are designed to last for ten years. Battery-powered pacemakers, by contrast, must be surgically replaced about every 18 months. (*See also* Fuel and Power. *See in* CE: Atomic Energy and Structure.)

NURSING. By 1970 a slight upswing was noted in the number of registered nurses (R.N.s) in the United States. About 700,000 R.N.s were in active practice, some 20,000 more than in the preceding year but still 150,000 short of the number recommended by the U.S. Public Health Service (USPHS) for effective nursing care. The USPHS

Scientists inspect the 10-million-volt terminal in one of two new accelerators at Brookhaven National Laboratory. The paired tandem generators make up the most powerful Van de Graaff accelerator system in the world.

COURTESY, BROOKHAVEN NATIONAL LABORATORY

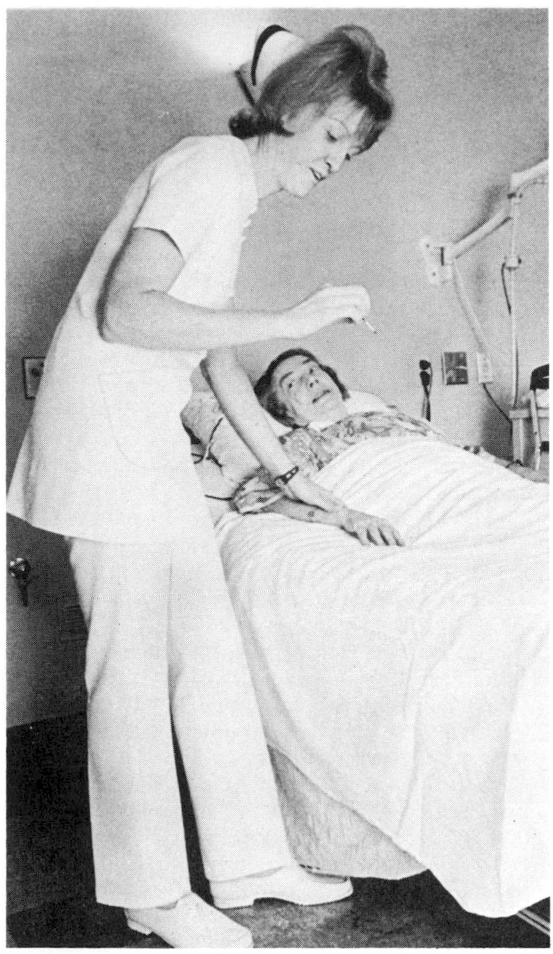

UPI COMPIX

A nurse at the Montreal General Hospital wears a pantsuit, a new development in uniforms.

felt that by 1975 a million nurses would be needed. In 1970 there were 345 nurses per 100,000 population, a slight improvement over the 1969 ratio.

At the biennial convention of the American Nurses' Association (ANA) in 1970, concern was voiced over the need for expanding delivery of health care, improving environmental quality, ending racial bias, and stemming drug abuse. Assuming an increasingly activist role, the ANA conducted a nationwide search for the "most involved" nurse. Audra Pambrun, a nurse working among Indians in Montana, was accorded this title in 1970.

More R.N.s were holding advanced academic degrees than ever. Almost 18,000 held master's degrees, and 600 possessed doctorates. Nursing boasted of some 65,000 students in the 1968–69 school year, the latest year for available statistics. This was in large part due to the proliferation of two-year degree programs in community colleges.

A majority of practicing R.N.s, some 450,000 of them, worked in hospitals and other health institutions in 1970. Nurses pressed for higher wages and a stronger voice in bettering the system of delivering health services. In several states they opted for utilizing labor union techniques of collective bargaining to achieve these ends.

Change was in the wind for the traditional nursing garb in 1970. In several hospitals in the nation nurses appeared in appropriately white pantsuits. Wearers believed them to be more sensible and functional than the skirt, which had long been traditional. (*See also* Hospitals; Medicine. *See in* CE: Nursing.)

OBITUARIES. Among the notable people who died in 1970 were:

S. Y. Agnon, Polish-born Jewish writer, winner of the 1966 Nobel prize for literature (with Nelly Sachs); February 17, Rehovot, Israel, age 81.

Sir John Barbirolli, internationally renowned conductor who led the highly respected Hallé Orchestra of Manchester, England, from 1943 until his death; July 29, London, age 70.

Ed Begley, character actor whose acting honors included an Academy Award in 1963 for his supporting role in the movie 'Sweet Bird of Youth'; April 28, Hollywood, Calif., age 69.

Stanley Benham, bobsled champion who represented the United States in more international sledding events than any other bobsledder; April 22, Miami, Fla., age 57.

Louise Bogan, poet and poetry critic ('Collected Poems, 1923–43'); February 5, New York City, age 72.

Dr. Max Born, German-born nuclear physicist, co-winner of the 1954 Nobel prize in physics; January 5, Göttingen, West Germany, age 87.

Billie Burke, actress whose career spanned half a century and included leading roles in many Broadway musicals and motion pictures ('Topper', 'The Man Who Came to Dinner'); May 14, Los Angeles, age 84.

Richard Cardinal Cushing, retired prelate of the Roman Catholic church and longtime friend of the Kennedy family; November 2, Boston, Mass., age 75.

Brig. Gen. Benjamin O. Davis, Sr., the first Negro to achieve the rank of general in the U.S. armed forces; November 26, North Chicago, age 93.

Charles de Gaulle. (*See* box, page 370.)

Marie Dionne (Mrs. Florian Houle), one of the Dionne quintuplets of Canada; February 27, Montreal, Que., age 35.

John Dos Passos, novelist best known for his trilogy 'U.S.A.'; September 28, Baltimore, Md., age 74.

William Feller, mathematician whose specialty was the theory of probability, winner of a 1969 National Medal of Science; January 14, Princeton, N.J., age 63.

E. M. Forster, influential English novelist and essayist ('A Passage to India'); June 7, Coventry, England, age 91.

CHARLES DE GAULLE

WIDE WORLD

Charles de Gaulle died in Colombey-les-Deux-Églises, France, on November 9 at the age of 79, some 18 months after his resignation as president of the Fifth Republic. The world mourned the death of a prestigious statesman who wielded great influence in international affairs during the post-World War II era. Frenchmen mourned the death of the "man of destiny" who twice at critical moments in French history had stepped in to rescue the nation from grave crisis.

The first such instance came at the time of the humiliating French defeat in 1940 when De Gaulle, an almost unknown brigadier general, broadcast from London his famous appeal to the French people not to give up but to continue the fight. He assumed control of a new "Free French" movement and at once became the symbol of French resistance to German occupation and an ally of the Western powers. After the liberation of Paris in 1944, De Gaulle formed a provisional government and was instrumental in establishing a postwar non-communist government. Eventually the vagaries of French politics disillusioned him, however, and he retired to private life.

The second great crisis came in 1958 when France was threatened with civil war because of the Algerian conflict. The general again emerged as the only figure in French national life capable of inspiring confidence. First as premier, then as president, De Gaulle firmly set about ending the Algerian war, decolonizing the French empire, reforming France's weak political system, and pursuing a foreign policy based on one principle—restoring France to its former grandeur. To a great extent his policies succeeded, particularly in foreign affairs. France assumed a more independent international role, achieving a counterweight status to U.S. hegemony by developing its own nuclear force, withdrawing from the North Atlantic Treaty Organization, and cultivating a détente with the Soviet Union and Eastern Europe.

De Gaulle's domestic policies had less success. His last departure from public life resulted indirectly from the domestic dissatisfaction brought to the surface by the student-worker riots of May 1968. Although De Gaulle weathered the immediate crisis, a year later voters rejected a referendum on a minor reform issue on which he had staked his prestige. The general resigned immediately.

Erle Stanley Gardner, author best known for his 80 mystery novels featuring the lawyer Perry Mason; July 17, Temecula, Calif., age 80.

Rube Goldberg, cartoonist who satirized U.S. folkways, particularly through his depictions of the zany, ingenious contraptions he "invented"; winner of a 1948 Pulitzer prize for political cartooning; December 7, New York City, age 87.

Alfred O. Gross, ornithologist, wildlife authority, and early conservationist who was instrumental in saving the prairie chicken from extinction in the 1930's; May 9, Greenwich, Conn., age 77.

John Gunther, journalist and author of the best-selling "Inside" books ('Inside Europe', 'Inside Latin America'); May 29, New York City, age 68.

Jimi Hendrix, leading U.S. rock performer known for his wild, flamboyant performances; September 18, London, age 27.

Johnny Hodges, jazz great who starred as an alto saxophonist for nearly 40 years with Duke Ellington's orchestra; May 11, New York City, age 63.

Richard Hofstadter, leading U.S. historian, twice winner of the Pulitzer prize (1955, 1964) for his historical works; October 24, New York City, age 54.

William Hopper, actor best known for his role of Paul Drake, the detective in the Perry Mason TV series; March 6, Palm Springs, Calif., age 54.

Edward Everett Horton, character actor most famed for his comic roles in a career that spanned 60 years; September 29, Encino, Calif., age 83.

Hirsch Jacobs, horse trainer who saddled 3,569 winners in his lifetime and whose horses earned more than $12 million in prize money; February 13, Miami, age 65.

Janis Joplin, popular rock singer famed for her loud, haunting blues renditions; October 4, Hollywood, age 27.

Alexander Kerensky, prominent figure in Russian history as head of the provisional government of Russia for four months in 1917 after the fall of Czar Nicholas II; June 11, New York City, age 89.

Frances Parkinson Keyes, prolific U.S. novelist ('The River Road', 'Joy Street'); July 3, New Orleans, La., age 84.

Joseph Wood Krutch, naturalist, conservationist, and author, whose book 'The Measure of Man' won a 1954 National Book Award; May 22, Tucson, Ariz., age 76.

Gypsy Rose Lee (Rose Louise Hovick), entertainer known as the "Queen of Burlesque" who was, in her long career, a striptease artist, actress, and writer; April 26, Los Angeles, age 56.

Louis E. Lomax, noted black author, social critic and university professor; July 30, near Santa Rosa, N.M., age 47.

Vince Lombardi, one of football's most outstanding coaches, with the Green Bay Packers and the Washington Redskins; September 3, Washington, D.C., age 57.

Anita Louise (Anita Louise Fremault), stage, motion picture, and television actress who appeared in more than 70 motion pictures; April 25, Los Angeles, age 53.

Robert S. Lynd, one of the pioneers in the field of U.S. sociology, best known for his penetrating studies ('Middletown', 'Middletown in Transition') of a typical U.S. city (Muncie, Ind.), which he coauthored with his wife, Helen; November 1, Warren, Conn., age 78.

David O. McKay, Mormon religious leader who served as president of the 2.3-million-member Church of Jesus Christ of Latter-day Saints from 1951 until his death; January 18, Salt Lake City, Utah; age 96.

Hal March, television personality (master of ceremonies for The $64,000 Question, a television quiz show that ran from 1955–58) and actor; January 19, Los Angeles, age 49.

Dr. Abraham Harold Maslow, psychologist who is considered the founder of humanistic psychology; June 8, Menlo Park, Calif., age 62.

François Mauriac, French writer, winner of the 1952 Nobel prize for literature, known for his novels as well as for his journalistic writings; September 1, Paris, age 84.

Richard King Mellon, financier and philanthropist, scion of one of the wealthiest families in the United States; June 3, Pittsburgh, Pa., age 70.

Artem I. Mikoyan, Soviet aircraft designer who, with Mikhail I. Gurevich, designed the MiG jet plane; December 9, Moscow, age 65.

Gamal Abdel Nasser. (*See* box.)

Richard Joseph Neutra, Austrian-born architect who was a leading influence in the development of modern architecture; April 17, Wuppertal, West Germany, age 78.

Alfred Newman, composer-conductor who won eight Academy Awards for his motion-picture background scores (among them, 'Call Me Madam'); February 17, Hollywood, age 68.

Barnett Newman, painter and sculptor, an early abstract expressionist; July 3, New York City, age 65.

John O'Hara, writer who portrayed the lives of the U.S. small-town rich in his best-selling novels ('Butterfield 8'), also a prolific short-story writer; April 11, Princeton, N.J., age 65.

William Thomas Piper, aircraft pioneer who founded the giant Piper Aircraft Corp. and developed the versatile Piper Cub; January 15, Lock Haven, Pa., age 89.

Joe Pyne, television personality noted for aggressive confrontations with guests on his show, March 23, Hollywood, Calif., age 44.

Erich Maria Remarque, German-born novelist best known for his classic antiwar work 'All Quiet on the Western Front'; September 25, Locarno, Switzerland, age 72.

Walter P. Reuther, prominent figure in the U.S. labor movement, president of the United Automobile Workers (1946–70), particularly noted for his

GAMAL ABDEL NASSER

LIAISON AGENCY

Gamal Abdel Nasser, president of the United Arab Republic (UAR, or Egypt), died in Cairo on September 28, at the age of 52. His death left a vacuum no other leader in the Middle East could hope to fill. Not only was Nasser an outstanding leader of his people; he was also the driving force behind the Pan-Arab movement. Millions of Arabs personally looked to his charismatic leadership, and at his death they mourned him in a vast outpouring of grief.

Nasser first came to public view in 1952 when he and other junior Egyptian army officers conspired in a successful coup that replaced the Egyptian monarchy with a revolutionary government. Nasser eventually emerged as the national leader. He became prime minister in 1954 and president in 1956.

In domestic affairs Nasser adopted a modernizing program, introducing land reforms and embarking on an ambitious plan to create vast new land for agricultural development through the Aswan High Dam project. But he was most successful in the conduct of foreign affairs. His guiding principle was Pan-Arabism, for which he used Israel as a convenient foil.

To pursue his aims, Nasser often effectively played off the great powers against each other. His greatest opportunity came when the United States and Great Britain withdrew their offers of financial support for the Aswan High Dam project. Nasser retaliated by nationalizing the Suez Canal. The fiasco created by the subsequent Anglo-French and Israeli invasion left Nasser in control of the canal and greatly enhanced his prestige in the Arab world. He then sought and received aid from the Soviet Union to complete the Aswan project. He came to rely increasingly on the Soviets for economic and military aid to bolster the UAR's sagging economy.

Nasser's nadir was the devastating defeat suffered by the UAR, Jordan, and Syria in the June 1967 war with Israel, a war provoked by Nasser. Nasser eventually took the responsibility for defeat and offered to resign but was reinstated by a show of frenzied popular support. Nasser's last major acts—his agreement to a Middle East cease-fire and the truce he helped arrange to end the Jordanian civil war—raised hope that he would help bring an end to the Arab-Israeli conflict. His death, however, removed any possibility for immediate peace negotiations.

© KARSH, OTTAWA FROM RAPHO GUILLUMETTE

WIDE WORLD

WIDE WORLD

Bertrand Russell (left); Jimi Hendrix (below, left); Janis Joplin (below, right)

BELOW, LEFT AND RIGHT: RICHARD BALAGUR FROM NANCY PALMER AGENCY

Richard Cardinal Cushing (above); Vince Lombardi (above, right); Gypsy Rose Lee (right)

WIDE WORLD

leadership of the liberal wing of the labor movement; May 9, near Pellston, Mich., age 62.

U.S. Representative L. Mendel Rivers (D, S.C.), who, during his 29-year Congressional career, was one of the House's most powerful advocates of U.S. military superiority; December 28, Birmingham, Ala., age 65.

Mark Rothko, Russian-born U.S. painter, a pioneer in abstract expressionism; February 25, New York City, age 66.

Dr. Francis Peyton Rous, pathologist and bacteriologist, co-winner of the 1966 Nobel prize for medicine; February 16, New York City, age 90.

Bertrand Arthur William Russell (3rd Earl Russell), English philosopher, considered the most distinguished philosopher of his age, whose major works included 'The Principles of Mathematics' (coauthored with Alfred North Whitehead), a seminal work in mathematics, and the monumental 'History of Western Philosophy', as well as numerous writings on such topics as education, marriage, and morals; winner of the 1950 Nobel prize for literature; and, in his later years, an outspoken advocate for nuclear disarmament and world peace; February 2, Penrhyndeudraeth, Merionethshire, Wales, age 97.

Nelly Sachs, German-born Jewish poet, winner of the 1966 Nobel prize for literature (with S. Y. Agnon); May 12, Stockholm, Sweden, age 78.

António de Oliveira Salazar, Portuguese premier and virtual dictator of his country from 1932 until he suffered an incapacitating stroke in 1968 (and, unknown to him, was replaced by Marcello Caetano); July 27, Lisbon, Portugal, age 81.

Terry (Terrence Gordon) Sawchuk, hockey player for the New York Rangers who won four Vezina trophies as the outstanding goaltender in professional ice hockey; May 31, New York City, age 40.

John T. Scopes, Tennessee schoolteacher whose teaching of Charles Darwin's theory of evolution resulted in the famous "monkey trial" of 1925; October 21, Shreveport, La., age 70.

Dr. Samuel H. Sheppard, osteopath who was the defendant in a sensational murder trial of the mid-1950's, was convicted and imprisoned but eventually granted a new trial and, in 1966, was acquitted of the murder charges; April 6, Columbus, Ohio, age 46.

Herb Shriner, humorist and television star of the 1950's; April 24, Delray Beach, Fla., age 51.

Merriman Smith, longtime White House correspondent for United Press International, winner of a 1964 Pulitzer prize in journalism; April 13, Washington, D.C., age 57.

Inger Stevens, actress in motion pictures ('A Dream of Kings'), stage, and television (The Farmer's Daughter); April 30, Hollywood, age 35.

Anna Louise Strong, U.S. leftist writer who devoted much of her life to writing books and articles extolling Communism; March 29, Peking, Communist China, age 84.

Dr. Alfred Henry Sturtevant, geneticist who was the first to chart the location of chromosomes of

WIDE WORLD

Sukarno

Walter Reuther

WIDE WORLD

the genes governing particular inherited traits; April 5, Pasadena, Calif., age 78.

Sukarno, Indonesian statesman who was instrumental in achieving his country's independence and also served as its first president from 1949 until 1966, when he was ousted after an attempted Communist putsch; June 21, Djakarta, Indonesia, age 69.

George Szell, conductor who led the Cleveland Orchestra for almost a quarter of a century and made it into one of the world's most outstanding symphony orchestras, July 30, Cleveland, Ohio, age 73.

Marshal Semyon Konstantinovich Timoshenko, Soviet military leader whose chief accomplishment was halting the German drive on Moscow during World War II; March 31, Moscow, age 75.

Charles Tobias, songwriter who composed many popular favorites ('Don't Sit Under the Apple Tree'); July 7, Manhasset, N.Y., age 72.

Harold Stirling Vanderbilt, financier, yachtsman (three times successful defender of the America's Cup), and originator of the game of contract bridge; July 4, Newport, R.I., age 85.

Dr. Otto Warburg, German biochemist, winner of the 1931 Nobel prize for medicine, known particularly for his pioneering cancer research; August 1, West Berlin, age 86.

Harry MacGregor Woods, composer who wrote more than 350 popular songs ('I'm Looking Over a Four-Leaf Clover'); January 13, Phoenix, Ariz., age 73.

OCEANOGRAPHY.

The U.S. drilling vessel *Glomar Challenger* in 1970 continued to make important contributions to man's knowledge of the ocean floors and the structure of the earth. The vessel's voyages were sponsored by the National Science Foundation.

Work aboard the vessel revealed that the ocean basins are relatively young, perhaps a tenth to a twentieth the 3.5-billion-year age of some continental rocks. In addition, the concept of sea-floor spreading and of the drifting apart of the continents of North and South America, Europe, and Africa was almost certainly proved: molten rock appears to come up in midocean to form new sub-ocean crust, and the continents are moved apart as this crust spreads out from midocean. The crust spreads at about 3 centimeters per year in the North Atlantic, 4 centimeters per year in the South Atlantic, and 12 centimeters per year in the South Pacific and in the equatorial Pacific.

It was found that much of the deep Gulf of Mexico is underlain by salt, some of which had

An aquanaut peers inside the Project Tektite 2 habitat, an underwater research laboratory inaugurated in April in the Virgin Islands.

COURTESY, GENERAL ELECTRIC CO.

COURTESY, SCRIPPS INSTITUTION OF OCEANOGRAPHY

The ship *Glomar Challenger* embarks on one of a series of ocean voyages, as part of the Deep Sea Drilling Project operated by the Scripps Institution of Oceanography. The ship was to drill 40 to 60 holes in the ocean bottom, in water depths of 5,000 to 20,000 feet.

squeezed up into salt domes that contained oil and gas. This was the first demonstration that hydrocarbons can form and accumulate under deep seas.

A remarkable technological development of the year was the ability to reenter already drilled holes in the ocean floor. Previously, depth of penetration was limited by the endurance of one bit. From the *Glomar Challenger* a 16-foot-diameter "funnel" was placed on the ocean floor over the drilling site. With this large a "target," the string of drilling tools could be withdrawn from the hole, the worn bit replaced, and the string reinserted in the hole with the guidance of acoustical sensors and the aid of water jets on the tool string. The first successful reentry was made in June at a depth of 10,000 feet.

In the United States, a number of federal bodies engaged in studies of the oceans and the atmosphere were merged in 1970 into a new National Oceanic and Atmospheric Administration (NOAA), a division of the U.S. Department of Commerce. The new administration incorporated the Environmental Science Services Administration and elements from the Department of the Interior, the Army, the Navy, and the National Science Foundation.

Concern over pollution of the oceans continued to mount during the year. An agency of the NOAA began studies that it was hoped would lead to more precise understanding of the behavior of substances artificially introduced into the oceans. Enforcement of rules designed to prevent leakage from undersea oil wells was tightened—one company was fined $1 million for spillage in the Gulf of Mexico—and increased attention was given to study of the effects of oil deposited in the open ocean through the normal operations of tankers. Canada, fearing the effects of possible spillage by tankers passing from the Atlantic to northern Alaska, considered special regulations for ships entering the Canadian Arctic archipelago. Public outcry against the disposal of obsolete nerve gas in the Atlantic led the U.S. Army to agree that in the future it would deactivate and dispose of unwanted chemical-warfare agents ashore.

United States President Richard M. Nixon—guided by a report of the Council on Environmental Quality—asked the U.S. Congress to ban the disposal of toxic materials in the ocean and to place strict controls upon the dumping of trash and wastes at sea. Although the proposed legislation would affect only people and organizations controlled by U.S. law, the president hoped it might lead to international agreements. (*See also* Arctic; Conservation; Weather. *See in* CE: Oceanography.)

OMAN. During 1970, the situation of Muscat and Oman (which became Oman August 9) was radically transformed by a coup that replaced Sultan Said bin Taimur with his son Qabus bin Said. Sultan Said had kept his country in a state of medieval backwardness insulated from Western influences; his son undertook to introduce "modern and forceful" government.

Sultan Said had long confined himself to Salala, in the western part of his territory, though it was there that a revolutionary movement with Marxist overtones and Chinese Communist support, known as the Dhofar Liberation Front, was active and had gained control of substantial areas of territory. In March, the air base at Salala was strengthened by 100 men from a Royal Air Force (RAF) regiment. The British government, which had a treaty of friendship with the sultan, denied that RAF planes were being used against the rebels.

On July 23, Sultan Said was deposed in a coup at Salala, organized by his son Qabus. The new sultan announced the removal of his father's ban on travel, public smoking, singing, and the wearing of Western dress and permitted the entry of foreign journalists. On August 9, his uncle Sayyid Tariq bin Taimur, who had returned from exile, formed a new government in which a British officer, Col. H. R. D. Oldman, remained as defense secretary. The new sultan announced that in the future the country would be known as the Sultanate of Oman.

OPERA. Superb singing and innovative productions marked the 1970–71 opera season. New York City's Metropolitan Opera opened on September 14 with an outstanding cast in Giuseppe Verdi's 'Ernani'. Other revivals in the fall season included Gaetano Donizetti's 'Lucia di Lammermoor' and the historic 'Orfeo ed Euridice' of Christoph Willibald Gluck with mezzo-soprano Grace Bumbry. A new staging of Richard Wagner's 'Parsifal' introduced tenor Helge Brilioth.

Highlights of the Met's spring 1970 season were the new productions of Vincenzo Bellini's 'Norma', featuring Joan Sutherland and Marilyn Horne, and of 'Cavalleria Rusticana' and 'I Pagliacci', directed by Franco Zeffirelli. Renata Tebaldi sang the title role in Giacomo Puccini's 'La Fanciulla del West'.

The New York City Opera opened the fall 1970 season with its striking version of 'Mefistofele', by Arrigo Boito. The operatic hit of the year, though, was its revival of Donizetti's 'Roberto Devereux', with Beverly Sills's vivid dramatic and vocal portrayal of Queen Elizabeth I, and Placido Domingo as Essex. Director Frank Corsaro's staging of 'The Makropoulos Affair', by Leos Janácek, aroused interest by its use of mixed media.

Multimedia effects were also used strikingly in the Boston production of Robert Kurka's 'Good Soldier Schweik'. Chicago's Lyric Opera presented the U.S. stage premiere of Benjamin Britten's 'Billy Budd', with Theodor Uppman re-creating the title role. Chicago audiences also heard Montserrat Caballé in 'La Traviata'. At San Francisco, Sir Geraint Evans made his directing debut with a new version of Verdi's 'Falstaff' and sang the title rôle.

Of the U.S. operas that premiered in the 1969–70 season, Carlisle Floyd's 'Of Mice and Men' (Seattle) and Gian-Carlo Menotti's 'Help, Help, the Globolinks!' (Santa Fe) were the most memorable. In August 1970, Santa Fe introduced Luciano Berio's 'Opera'. Malcolm Williamson's 'The Growing Castle' had its first U.S. performance at the

UPI COMPIX

Mezzo-soprano Shirley Verrett (above) made her La Scala debut in 'Samson et Dalila' in January. Soprano Joan Sutherland (below, right) and mezzo-soprano Marilyn Horne performed 'Norma' at the Metropolitan Opera House in New York City.

HENRY GROSSMAN, LIFE MAGAZINE © TIME INC.

Caramoor Festival in Katonah, N.Y., in July. The Who, a British rock group, performed their rock opera 'Tommy' at the Metropolitan Opera House in June.

'Victory', a new work by Richard Rodney Bennett, premiered at Covent Garden, London, in April. The Royal Opera, under music director Georg Solti, also gave a new 'Salome', by Richard Strauss, and introduced 'The Knot Garden', by Sir Michael Tippett. A gala performance in June honored Sir David Webster, retiring as administrator of Covent Garden; John Tooley succeeded him.

The Sadler's Wells summer production of 'Carmen' starred Grace Bumbry, while a bright new 'Tales of Hoffmann', by Jacques Offenbach, opened the company's fall season. English mezzo-soprano Janet Baker was widely praised for her roles in Benjamin Britten's 'The Rape of Lucretia' at Aldeburgh and in the Glyndebourne Festival revival of Francesco Cavalli's 1651 comedy 'La Calisto'.

At Salzburg, conductor Herbert von Karajan presented Wagner's 'Götterdämmerung' at Easter and later produced an effective 'Otello', by Verdi, at the Salzburg Festspielhaus. Like many European and U.S. companies, Salzburg observed the Ludwig van Beethoven bicentennial with a production of 'Fidelio'. The Vienna Staatsoper opened its 1970–71 season with a new 'Don Carlo', by Verdi, and Strauss's 'Die ägyptische Helena'.

Hamburg continued its tradition of world premieres with Ernst Krenek's 'Sardakai' and Carl Orff's 'Kluge'. Two new works also premiered at Sweden's Royal Opera—Hilding Rosenberg's 'House with Two Entrances' and Sven-Eric Bäck's 'Bird'. (*See also* Music. *See in* CE: Opera.)

PAINTING AND SCULPTURE. Art exhibitions proliferated everywhere in 1970. The days of the enormous loan retrospectives seemed to be numbered as the insurance costs and transportation risks involved in lending made many museums reluctant to send works of art long distances. But this difficulty gave new impetus to the organization of smaller exhibitions concentrating on single aspects of artists or small groups of artists. More galleries also experimented with mixed-media exhibitions that made use of such wonders of modern technology as laser beams.

One of the largest and most magnificent exhibitions of the year, "19th Century America," was held at the Metropolitan Museum of Art in New York City. It was the third of the Metropolitan's centenary exhibitions. (Others were the New York school show, held in the fall of 1969, and, in 1970, "The Year 1200," devoted to art of the period 1175–1220.) The American exhibit included painting, sculpture, furniture, the decorative arts, and a subsidiary section on architecture.

The latter section, entitled "The Rise of an American Architecture, 1815–1915," was particularly remarkable. Rather than trying to cover the whole history of this rich period, the organizers concentrated on important happenings, choosing a few significant buildings as illustrations. These included D. H. Burnham and Company's Flatiron Building in New York City; the classical structures for the World's Columbian Exposition of 1893 on Chicago's lakefront, by Daniel H. Burnham, with architectural landscaping by Frederick Law Olmsted; and the Providence Arcade, Providence, R.I., by Russell Warren and James Bucklin. Works by the seminal architects Henry Hobson Richardson, Louis H. Sullivan, and Frank Lloyd Wright were also illustrated.

AUTHENTICATED NEWS INTERNATIONAL

'Two Children at the Seashore', an oil painting by Mary Cassatt, was included in an exhibition of her work at the National Gallery of Art.

The painting and sculpture section of the exhibition resembled a history of American art, with works by Gilbert Stuart, John Singleton Copley, Winslow Homer, Thomas Eakins, Hiram Powers, and John Rogers. The furniture section ranged from the utilitarian everyday furniture of the early American settlers to pieces from the Federal period and items designed by pioneers of the modern movement. Some of the more impressive decorative pieces were the elaborately fashioned glass objects by Louis Comfort Tiffany.

Running concurrently at the Metropolitan was an exhibition of 100 paintings from the Museum of Fine Arts, Boston, Mass. The exhibition was part of the joint centennial celebrations of these two major museums.

Another of the more exciting shows of the year was the long-awaited exhibition of the work of Hector Guimard, the French *art nouveau* architect famous for designing the Paris subway station entrances. The show, sponsored by New York City's Museum of Modern Art, brought together his furniture, drawings, photographs, and decorative objects. It was at the museum from March to May and then went to San Francisco, Calif., and Toronto, Ont.

Two major exhibitions of African art were seen in the United States in 1970. The International Exhibitions Foundation circulated a large show of African sculpture sponsored by the ambassadors of 34 African nations, which traveled to several U.S. cities. It included the famous Tada bronze seated figure believed to represent one of the kings of Ife, in Nigeria, and described as "perhaps the most remarkable work of art discovered in Africa south of the Sahara." In January the Museum of Art of the Carnegie Institute, Pittsburgh, Pa., held a show drawn from the Jay C. Leff collection of black African art. Most of the pieces were made for religious or ritual purposes.

"Selections from the Nathan Cummings Collection" was on view at the National Gallery of Art, Washington, D.C., in the summer and was to move on to New York City's Metropolitan Museum of Art in the summer of 1971. This outstanding modern collection includes works by Honoré Daumier, Édouard Manet, Camille Pissarro, Edgar Degas, Claude Monet, and Vasili Kandinski. Other modern art exhibitions included a retrospective of the work of the Romanian sculptor Constantin Brancusi at The Art Institute of Chicago and two Vincent van Gogh exhibitions, one at Philadelphia, Pa., and another at Columbus, Ohio.

The "Morton D. May Collection of 20th-Century German Masters" was on view at the Marlborough-Gerson Gallery in New York City in the winter and later in the year at the City Art Museum, in St. Louis, Mo. It is considered one of the best private collections devoted to German expressionism, including works by Max Beckmann, Max Pechstein, Erich Heckel, and Ernst Ludwig Kirchner. Some of the same German artists were included in the first museum exhibition in the United States devoted to the work of *Die Brücke,* the pioneering group of 20th-century German expressionists. The exhibition was assembled and mounted at the Andrew Dickson White Museum of Art, Cornell University, in Ithaca, N.Y., and was also shown at Rochester, N.Y.

In a very contemporary spirit was the show "N Dimensional Space: an exhibition of holograms, made with the use of laser beams, with an historical examination of this incredible new technology," held at the Finch College Museum of Art, New York City, in the spring. The show included holograms—three-dimensional photographs made by laser beams—by Robert Indiana, Bruce Nauman, and George Ortman.

The work of U.S. pop artists attracted renewed attention everywhere, and attempts were made to evaluate their contribution to modern art. The Pasadena Art Museum in Pasadena, Calif., organized a major exhibition of the work of Andy Warhol, concentrating on the serial aspect of his production: multiple flower images, soup cans, etc. The show traveled to Chicago, Paris, London, and Eindhoven, Netherlands.

Exhibits in London

In May the Tate Gallery in London featured the work of "Three Los Angeles Artists"—Larry Bell, Robert Irwin, and Doug Wheeler. The show consisted of three complete environments, dealing with the limits of perception and illusion. In the summer the Tate held a retrospective of the work of U.S. pop artist Claes Oldenburg, organized by the Museum of Modern Art in New York City. Two

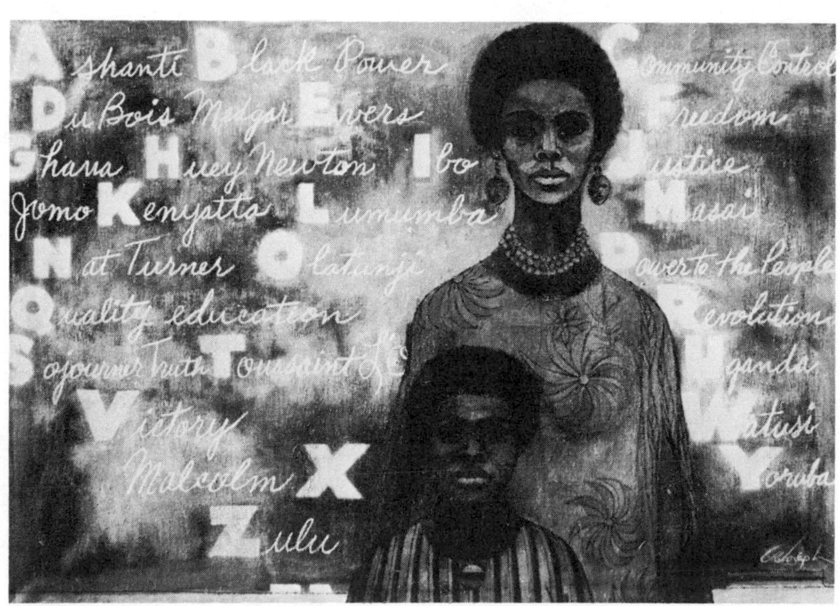

The oil painting 'Blackboard' by Cliff Joseph was included in the Museum of Fine Arts' exhibition "Afro-American Artists: New York and Boston."

DOUG HARRIS, COURTESY, MUSEUM OF FINE ARTS, BOSTON, MASS.

Claes Oldenburg's soft sculpture, 'Sirloin and Hamburger', appeared in an exhibition of his work at the Tate Gallery in London.

"THE TIMES," LONDON, FROM PICTORIAL PARADE

London shows dealt with English pop art: a David Hockney show at the Whitechapel Art Gallery and a Richard Hamilton retrospective at the Tate, which covered 20 years of his work. Hamilton described one of his works as "a sieved reflection of the adman's paraphrase of the consumers' dream." His retrospective was also shown in the Netherlands and in Switzerland. The Hayward Gallery in London held a Frank Stella show in July and August. Sponsored by the Arts Council, the exhibition consisted of 38 large paintings covering the last 12 years of Stella's output. They were all antiabstract expressionist, showing Stella's interest in flat patternmaking and acid high-keyed color.

In the autumn the Arts Council exhibited an "International Survey of Kinetic Art" at the Hayward Gallery. The Institute of Contemporary Arts in London continued to put on shows that excited comment. In the spring the institute exhibited 347 erotic engravings done by Pablo Picasso in 1968 that illustrated his supreme technical mastery of the medium. "Legible City," an exhibition devoted to the exploration of printed words in the urban environment, was mounted at the institute in the fall. It was "designed to take a searching and thoroughly irreverent look at London, Britain's largest and wordiest urban specimen."

Major Shows Elsewhere in Europe

Two important exhibitions honoring Marc Chagall were held in Paris during the year. The Grand Palais paid tribute to the 82-year-old artist with a large exhibition of his work, concentrating on the familiar subjects repeated in his paintings. At the same time the Galerie Vision Nouvelle showed the 105 poetic engravings of the Bible on which Chagall worked from 1931 to 1956.

One of the major exhibits of modern art held in Italy in 1970 was the large show devoted to Giorgio de Chirico in the Palazzo Reale in Milan. De Chirico's personal surrealistic vision was represented by paintings, drawings, etchings, and some pieces of sculpture. In West Germany, one of the year's more impressive shows was "Late Gothic in Cologne and on the Lower Rhine," mounted at the Kunsthalle in Cologne. The show covered the range of Rhenish art at the end of the Middle Ages and included many works from churches in the Rhineland.

In Spain an exhibit of 17th-century Italian painting was held at the Casón del Buen Retiro, Madrid, in April and May that included some 200 canvases. In Czechoslovakia, the National Gallery in Prague celebrated the centenary of Henri Matisse's birth with an exhibition of 14 paintings and 7 drawings. Works were borrowed from the collections of the State Hermitage Museum in Leningrad, U.S.S.R., and the State Pushkin Museum of Fine Arts in Moscow.

Art Sales

The steady rise in salesroom prices of the last few years was not maintained in 1970. In spite of the general trend, however, huge prices were paid for some celebrated works. The London auction house of Christie's received a world-record price of $5,544,000 for Diego Rodríguez de Silva y Velásquez's portrait of his assistant, Juan de Pareja (traditionally titled 'The Slave of Velásquez'). Artemis, an art investment company based in Luxembourg, paid about $1,033,000 for a painting by Georges Seurat, 'Les Poseuses' (smaller version). New world-record prices were set at Parke-Bernet Galleries in New York City for works by Degas,

Van Gogh, Matisse, Kees van Dongen, and Jean Dubuffet. Other modern works reached new values: $150,000 was paid for a bronze by Alberto Giacometti, 'Femme de Venise I' (Woman of Venice I), and $60,000 for a large painting by Warhol, 'Campbell Soup Can with Peeling Label'.

A new rush for well-known watercolors was notable. Silver suffered a severe drop in value, except for certain celebrated English 18th-century pieces. Silver prices had risen dramatically in 1968–69. Unusual French glass paperweights continued to change hands at high prices in London. A world-record price was made in March when a Clichy lily-of-the-valley paperweight was sold for more than $20,000. The fashion for Tiffany glass objects also continued to grow. Parke-Bernet's sold a Tiffany wisteria lamp for $16,000.

Despite the startling top prices, hundreds of items were sold for reasonable sums even at the largest auction houses. Parke-Bernet's, for instance, reported that about 60% of its items were sold for less than $250 in 1970. Thus the small collector with some special knowledge could still participate. (*See also* Museums. *See in* CE: Painting; Sculpture.)

PAKISTAN. An enormous tragedy provided the major news event in Pakistan during 1970. On the night of November 12–13, a massive 20-foot-high tidal wave, driven by a 120-mph cyclone, swept in from the Bay of Bengal and smashed the coastal lowlands and offshore islands of East Pakistan. At the end of the year, the death toll was placed at close to 500,000; at least 2.5 million persons were rendered homeless. The rice crop was wiped out, livestock were drowned, and dwellings leveled. More than 100 offshore islands were hit; it was reported that on 13 islands near the city of Chittagong, not one person survived.

Relief efforts were complicated by transportation problems: there was a lack of helicopters to drop needed supplies to areas made inaccessible to land vehicles. More than 20 countries sent aid, which included medicine, food, vitamins, clothing, blankets, tents, and water-purifying equipment; the United States also sent helicopters as well as relief supplies. The World Bank allocated $185 million for reconstruction.

Although Pakistan's central government participated in the relief effort, it did so, nevertheless, only after a sluggish start. In fact, political leaders in East Pakistan accused the central government—located in West Pakistan, about 1,000 miles across India—of being indifferent to the plight of the survivors of the storm. President Agha Mohammed Yahya Khan was singled out for condemnation in a telegram that said, in part, "You yourself left the province after a cursory glance" at the first flash of news of the tragedy. Yahya Khan denied the charges. After an investigation, it was generally determined that the region's storm-warning system was not put to its most efficient use, though the best of all warnings would not have sufficed.

On December 7, in Pakistan's first general election, a national assembly was elected to draft a constitution in order to return the nation to representative civilian rule, absent since 1958 when martial law was declared. Results showed that the Awami League, with headquarters in East Pakistan, won an absolute majority of the 300 directly elected seats in the new National Assembly. The party, headed by Sheikk Mujibur Rahman, advocated full regional autonomy for East Pakistan. The major winner in West Pakistan was the Pakistan People's party, led by former Foreign Minister Zulfikar Ali Bhutto; it won 82 seats. The provincial assembly elections on December 17 turned up similar results. (*See in* CE: Pakistan.)

WIDE WORLD

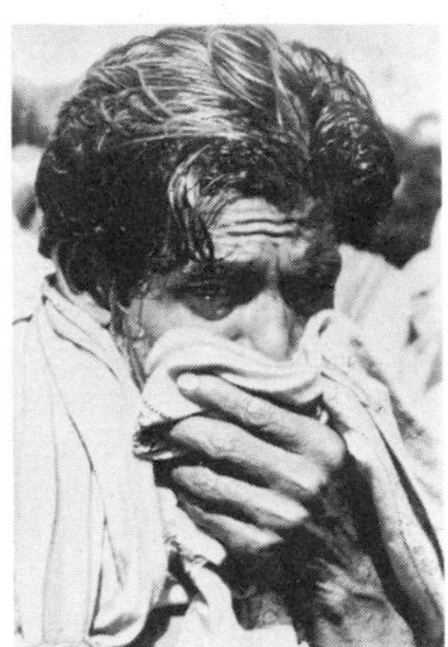

WIDE WORLD

East Pakistan villagers mourn their dead after a cyclone and tidal waves hit the country in November, killing hundreds of thousands.

PANAMA. Brigadier General Omar Torrijos Herrera continued to pursue his program of economic development and political and social reform for Panama in 1970. He showed no interest in replacing his stable if somewhat ruthless military regime with civilian rule.

The year began on an uneasy note. In December 1969, an attempt had been made by disgruntled colonels of the National Guard, the country's only military force, to overthrow Torrijos, who was on a trip to Mexico. However, Torrijos made a triumphant return to Panama, and members of the National Guard loyal to him arrested the rebellious colonels. The figurehead leaders of the governing junta, who had sided with the rebellious colonels, were jailed and civilians were named to replace them. Demetrio Lakas Bahas became the new figurehead president. Torrijos announced that he would not seek revenge.

Torrijos' strength and popularity were attributed, in part, to his positive development program for the country. He sought to curb corruption and to institute more rigid and efficient enforcement of the tax laws.

Relations with the United States remained strained. In September, the Panamanian government, reflecting popular nationalist sentiment, formally rejected draft treaties with the United States on a new status for the Panama Canal. Neither Panama nor the United States indicated much interest in resuming discussions concerning them. Earlier in the year the Panamanian government had reached an agreement with a consortium of European companies to build an oil pipeline across the Isthmus of Panama. The pipeline was to be owned by Panama and built and staffed by Panamanians. (*See in* CE: Panama.)

PARAGUAY. The conflict between the Roman Catholic church in Paraguay and the government of President Alfredo Stroessner continued during 1970. The church's opposition, which began with demands for social, economic, and political reforms in 1969, was met with increasingly harsh repression, including beatings and deportations of priests. Late in 1969, the church retaliated by refusing to celebrate the feast of the Immaculate Conception in the capital city of Asunción.

In January Stroessner banned all social welfare services of the Roman Catholic church in Paraguay. He also required that the $5.5 million worth of aid supplied annually by the Catholic Relief Services in the United States be turned over to the government for distribution.

An attempt to reduce the budget deficit by introducing an income tax for the first time in Paraguay met an unusual display of resistance in the parliament. The balance-of-trade deficit, another of the country's economic problems, reached $31 million in 1969, prompting a recommendation from the International Monetary Fund that the guarani, Paraguay's currency, be devalued. Stroessner refused as a matter of national pride, choosing instead remedies that included reducing export duties. His measures, combined with a rise in world prices for Paraguay's export goods, especially meat, reduced the trade deficit to $9 million for the first half of 1970, compared to $24 million for the same period of 1969. (*See in* CE: Paraguay.)

PEACE CORPS. The Peace Corps completed its ninth year of existence in 1970 beset with a number of pressing problems involving its relationship with the countries it served, with the U.S. Congress, and with its volunteers. Under the leadership of Joseph H. Blatchford, who had been appointed to head the agency by U.S. President Richard M. Nixon in 1969, the corps attempted to solve these problems. It was not clear at year's end, however, how much success had been achieved.

Perhaps the most pressing problem faced by the Peace Corps was that it had lost its popularity among many young people. This was evidenced by the sharp decline in applications to the organization and in its total membership. In 1970 Peace Corps strength dropped to about 8,000 volunteers, half the number in the corps in 1966. This wane in popularity was attributed to the fact that young people viewed the Peace Corps no longer as an organization of idealistic "young people eager to serve the cause of peace" as its founder, U.S. President John F. Kennedy, had conceived it, but as a conservative organization serving the needs of the establishment. Two surveys of former Peace Corps volunteers (publicized in 1970) supported this argument. The surveys reflected a basic disaffection with the agency and general criticism of its approach.

At the same time, the agency's relations with Congress were strained, reflected by Congress' vote to reduce the Peace Corps budget for fiscal 1971 by 10%. Peace Corps Director Blatchford was also personally criticized by Senator J. W. Fulbright (D, Ark.) for having injected politics into

In 1970 Joseph H. Blatchford completed his first full year of service as director of the Peace Corps.

SUSAN BIDDLE, COURTESY, PEACE CORPS

Peace Corps volunteer Ada Haratani teaches English at a school in the Galapagos Islands, Ecuador. Ada, her husband, Joe, former Peace Corps director of Ecuador, and their three sons are the first Corps staff family to become volunteers.

JOAN LARSON, COURTESY, PEACE CORPS

the corps by sending volunteers copies of a speech Blatchford had given at a Republican party fund-raising function.

Peace Corps problems with its host countries revolved around the agency's difficulty or inability to meet their real needs. The requests made by host countries had become more specific and technically oriented than they had been in the past. The Philippines, for example, asked the agency to provide 18 primary schoolteachers whose major field had been education and whose minor had been either chemistry, physics, or mathematics. It became clear that the Peace Corps could no longer rely solely on college liberal arts graduates, who had previously made up the bulk of volunteers, if it was to be most effective.

To cope with these problems, Director Blatchford embarked on a program of "new directions" for the agency. Its major thrust was a change in emphasis from providing large numbers of volunteers with generalized skills to small numbers with specific skills—farmers, soil scientists, craftsmen, and vocational education specialists. The agency also made stronger attempts to diversify its membership by recruiting more blacks and Puerto Ricans (in the past the corps had been about 99% white) and to get older, more experienced people into the corps, in part by reversing an earlier policy and deciding to accept married volunteers with young children. In line with this change, a pilot program was announced that involved placing 200 families in various Peace Corps projects overseas.

As another step in improving its effectiveness the agency made a decision to work in closer partnership with the host countries in planning and executing projects. The first major realization of this was a conference sponsored by U.S. Peace Corps officials in November in Niamey, Niger, to which representatives of 24 African countries that had Peace Corps contingents were invited. The agency also attempted to create local advisory councils in the host country and to fill 50% of its overseas staff with local citizens. (*See in* CE: Peace Corps.)

PEOPLE OF THE YEAR. During 1970 laudable or questionable accomplishment brought the following people before the public eye. For other notable persons of 1970 see individual biographies by name.

Undoubtedly the most popular educators for preschool children in 1970 were **Big Bird, the Cookie Monster,** and **Oscar the Grouch,** stars of the educational television program Sesame Street.

Kingman Brewster, Jr., president of Yale University, expressed his personal view that he was "skeptical of the ability of black revolutionaries to achieve a fair trial anywhere in the United States." Thereafter **U.S. Vice-President Spiro T. Agnew** called for Brewster's removal.

Michael James Brody, Jr., heir to the Jelke oleomargarine fortune, announced that he would give away part of his inheritance (which he claimed was in the range of $25 million) to any deserving person. Besieged with thousands of requests, Brody finally stopped writing checks and dropped out of sight.

British art historian **Kenneth Clark** (Lord Clark of Saltwood) became well known to U.S. television viewers who watched Civilisation, A Personal View, a program that Clark wrote and narrated.

Former Attorney General **Ramsey Clark,** in his book 'Crime in America', revealed his view that the Federal Bureau of Investigation (FBI) placed a higher value on its personal glory than on effective crime fighting and that this "petty" characteristic resulted from the "excessive domination" of **J. Edgar Hoover.** Hoover responded by calling Clark "a worse attorney general" than Robert F. Kennedy, a "jellyfish," and a "softie." Hoover also made news when he claimed that two Roman Catholic priests—**the Rev. Philip F. Berrigan** and his brother **the Rev. Daniel J. Berrigan**—were leaders of a radical antiwar group that planned to kidnap a U.S. public official. Lawyers for the Berrigans, who were serving prison sentences for having destroyed selective service records, denounced Hoover's claim as "a farfetched spy story."

Lammot du Pont Copeland, Jr., scion of one of the wealthiest and oldest families in the United

WIDE WORLD

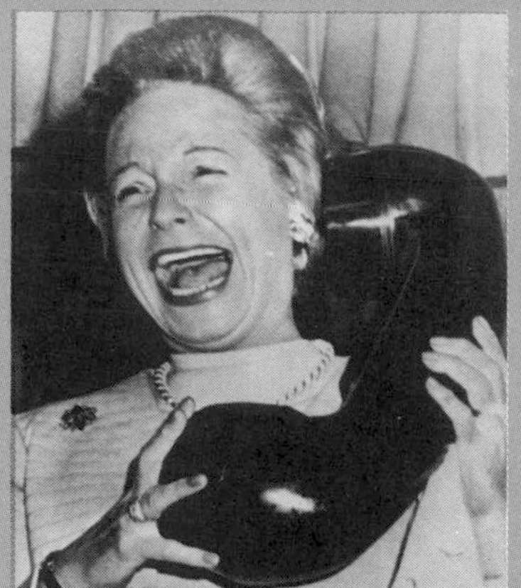

JULIAN H. FISHER FROM PIX

Big Bird (left), Martha Mitchell (above), Kingman Brewster, Jr. (above, right), Virginia Johnson and Dr. William Masters (below), and Chet Huntley (right).

COURTESY, CHILDREN'S TELEVISION WORKSHOP

UPI COMPIX

JUDITH GEFTER FROM PIX

States, filed for bankruptcy, claiming assets of $24 million and liabilities of $55 million.

One of the most publicized young black radicals in 1970 was **Angela Davis.** In June the Regents of the University of California finally succeeded in having her ousted as an assistant philosophy professor at the university's Los Angeles campus because of her Marxist views and her radical protest activities. Her support of one particular cause, that of the "Soledad brothers," led to an even more notorious incident. The weapons used in a violent courthouse raid undertaken in part to publicize the Soledad case (but in which she apparently did not take part) were found to be registered in her name. Consequently, she was charged with murder under California law. She fled, was eventually arrested in New York, and at year's end was extradited to California.

A move to impeach **U.S. Supreme Court Justice William O. Douglas** ended when a special Congressional subcommittee investigating his off-the-bench activities found no grounds for such action.

Folksinger-composer **Bob Dylan,** an anti-establishment hero of the younger generation, was awarded an honorary doctorate from Princeton University.

In the book 'Amelia Earhart Lives', author **Joe Klaas** advanced the thesis that **Mrs. Guy Bolam** of New Jersey was really **Amelia Earhart,** the U.S. flier who had mysteriously disappeared while on a round-the-world flight in 1937.

Actress **Jane Fonda** often made the headlines in 1970 with her public activities in support of American Indians, the Black Panthers, and GI rights.

Betty Friedan became the spokeswoman for the moderate wing of the women's liberation movement, striving for improvement of U.S. women's opportunities in education and employment through legal processes. Among "women's lib" spokeswomen championing a more radical approach was **Kate Millett,** author of 'Sexual Politics', a 1970 best seller.

John W. Gardner, former U.S. secretary of health, education, and welfare, organized a new vehicle for "revitalizing" politics and government, a national citizens' group called Common Cause.

Radio and television personality **Arthur Godfrey,** a strong supporter of conservation, refused to make any further commercials for the enzyme detergent Axion after he learned that it was a water pollutant. Later, in a compromise arrangement, he agreed to make the commercials but insisted that they include the fact that the detergent was a pollutant.

Multimillionaire **Howard Hughes,** well known for his obsession for privacy, attracted a great deal of publicity when a management fight broke out among two factions of his subordinates, each of which claimed his support. The incident set off an

UPI COMPIX

Daniel P. Moynihan (left), Princess Anne (below, left), Prince Charles (below), and Jane Fonda (right).

RUSSELL REIF FROM PICTORIAL PARADE

CAMERA PRESS FROM PIX

POPPERFOTO FROM PICTORIAL PARADE

investigation by Nevada officials to determine if Hughes, who had not been seen publicly for 15 years, was still alive. Hughes suddenly was reported to be in the Bahamas, alive and well and as enigmatic as ever.

Television newscaster **Chet Huntley** retired from broadcasting to become chairman of a new resort development group in Montana.

Kathy Huppe, Miss Montana of 1970, was not allowed to participate in the Miss America contest because of her political views; **Phyllis George** of Texas won the contest. **Stephanie M. Clark** was named Miss Black America.

In November a London newspaper printed a story claiming that the famous 19th-century murderer **Jack the Ripper** may have been Queen Victoria's grandson **Edward,** duke of Clarence. This suspicion was based on an article written by a physician who professed to know the killer's identity but refused to name him openly.

The "skyjacker" of the year was **Leila Khaled,** 24, a Palestinian guerrilla who was arrested in London for attempting to hijack an airplane. To obtain her release, the Palestinian guerrillas hijacked several jets and held the passengers hostage.

Life magazine printed what it claimed to be the authentic memoirs of former **Soviet Premier Nikita S. Khrushchev.** He issued a statement saying he had not cooperated in the publication.

Timothy Leary, a proponent of the drug culture, escaped from a prison in California and fled to Algeria, where he joined Black Panther leader **Eldridge Cleaver.** It was thought that **Bernardine Dohrn,** a member of the revolutionary Weathermen who was wanted by the FBI, was also there.

A book about World War II by the pioneer pilot **Charles A. Lindbergh** caused a stir during the year. He maintained that the United States should not have entered the war and that the Allied powers had in a sense lost the war.

Four armed men forced their way into the New York City apartment of **Sophia Loren.** The robbers escaped with $700,000 worth of jewels.

Natalya Makarova, a ballerina, defected from the Soviet Union in September. She received political asylum in Great Britain.

Frank and practical books about sex were popular in 1970. Among the best-selling authors on the subject were **Dr. William Masters** and **Virginia Johnson** ('Human Sexual Inadequacy'), **Dr. David Reuben** ('Everything You Always Wanted to Know About Sex—But Were Afraid to Ask') and **"J"** ('The Sensuous Woman').

The violinist **Yehudi Menuhin** had his U.S. citizenship revoked because he accepted honorary Swiss citizenship. Later the U.S. State Department said he had not lost his citizenship and apologized for the mistake.

UPI COMPIX

UPI COMPIX

WIDE WORLD

UPI COMPIX

Michael Brody, Jr. (far left, top), H. Ross Perot (far left, bottom), Leila Khaled (left), and the Berrigan brothers (above) Daniel (left) and Philip (center).

During the year **Martha Mitchell,** the voluble wife of the U.S. attorney general, made news by requesting that an Arkansas newspaper "crucify" **U.S. Senator J. W. Fulbright.** She also hired a press secretary whose husband, **William Woestendiek,** a television news editor, was fired for being so closely connected with a controversial public figure.

Daniel Patrick Moynihan, a counselor to **U.S. President Richard M. Nixon,** was offered the post of ambassador to the United Nations. He turned down the offer, choosing to return to Harvard University in 1971. **William D. Ruckelshaus** was made head of the new Environmental Protection Agency. There were other changes in the Administration: **James Farmer,** assistant secretary of health, education, and welfare, resigned, as did **Leon F. Panetta,** the director of the department's Office for Civil Rights. Commissioner of Education **James E. Allen, Jr.,** was removed from his post.

General Motors (GM) Corp. settled an invasion-of-privacy suit out of court by paying **Ralph Nader** $425,000. The consumer-affairs champion intended to use the money for watching over GM in the areas of safety, pollution, and consumer affairs.

The Greek shipping magnate **Stavros S. Niarchos** was under suspicion of having murdered his wife, **Eugenie,** who died mysteriously in May.

Linus Pauling, the Nobel-prizewinning chemist, suggested that large doses of vitamin C may prevent the common cold. Previous studies on this method, he said, had not dealt with large enough doses.

A U.S. billionaire, **H. Ross Perot,** made trips to Southeast Asia in a private effort to send supplies to U.S. prisoners of war in North Vietnam. All his attempts failed.

After England's **Prince Charles** graduated from Cambridge University, he and **Princess Anne** visited the United States. He was the first heir to the British throne to earn a college degree.

By accident a U.S. Army plane carrying **Maj. Gen. Edward C. D. Scherrer,** two U.S. Army officers, and a Turkish officer landed in the Soviet Union near the Turkish border. After being detained for three weeks they were released by the Soviets.

Black Panther leader **Bobby Seale** was extradited from California to Connecticut to stand trial for murder. The charges against him of conspiracy during the 1968 Democratic National Convention were dropped.

As she was being presented with a public service award, 19-year-old **Debra Jean Sweet** startled President Nixon by saying, "I find it hard to believe in your sincerity in giving the awards until you get us out of Vietnam."

An exhibit of the paintings of **Andrew Wyeth** was shown at the White House. It was thought to have been the first such exhibit by a living artist.

PERU. On May 31, 1970, Peru suffered the worst disaster in its history when an earthquake, measuring 7.75 on the Richter scale, shook half the country, leaving more than a million people dead, injured, or homeless. Aid came from all over the world, but rescuers were hampered by bad weather and floods; and the inaccessibility of the disaster areas, most of which were in the high Andes, greatly slowed the distribution of relief supplies.

During 1970, Peru's military regime, led by Gen. Juan Velasco Alvarado, began to both nationalize and socialize industry in Peru. Under the new industrial law, the state started buying control of all basic industries, such as iron and steel, chemicals, and fish meal, Peru's main export. Other foreign-owned industries must be sold to Peruvians or to the state. Finally, each company was to form a cooperative of all the company's employees and contribute 15% of net profits every year toward buying control of the company for the cooperative.

The law also required certain concerns to move their plants away from the central industrial areas to ease the enormous population pressure in urban areas. As a result of these and other new regulations, several firms, including Ford and General Motors, announced that they would shut their plants in Peru by the end of the year.

The new law did not apply to mining and oil companies. However, in April the state announced that it would take over the sale and refining of all minerals in 18 months.

Earlier in the year, the state also took greater control of banking and finance. In May the government declared a monopoly on foreign-exchange dealings and required all Peruvians to convert their foreign currency and investments. By the end of August, the state had acquired control of three of the nation's largest banks and planned to merge them into one.

Two opposition newspapers were seized by the government on March 4. Ownership of each paper was turned over to its employees' cooperative, which was expected to repay the previous owner.

Two leading U.S. construction companies building a major highway in the northern Andes of Peru with U.S. foreign-aid funds were accused by the Peruvian government in August of fraud and conspiracy. The state filed lawsuits totaling more than $23 million against Brown & Root, Inc., and Morrison-Knudsen Co., Inc. (*See in* CE: Peru.)

PETS. The cats and dogs that rule innumerable U.S. households ate better—or at least more expensively—than ever in 1970. Sales of prepared dog foods climbed to an estimated $825 million for the year, some $74 million above the 1969 figure. Cat-food sales rose to some $300 million, about $25 million more than in 1969.

Cat Shows Increase

A record 207 cat shows in the United States in 1970 drew a total of 43,625 entries. The largest was that of the Westminster Cat Club, an affiliate of the Cat Fanciers' Association (CFA), at White Plains, N.Y., in September. Entries numbered 619.

The All-American Cat of the Year was a black Persian female, Walhall's Isolde, a daughter of 1969's Cat of the Year, Conalan's Miss Prettee of Walhall. Both cats are owned by Theodore Napolski of Redondo Beach, Calif. The CFA's Best Cat was Karnak Zapata, a seal-point Siamese male owned by Dr. and Mrs. Steven Karr of New York City.

Two Peruvian women seem helpless amid the ruins of their homes, after the disastrous earthquake that hit the country on May 31.
KEYSTONE

The Sphynx, a new breed of hairless cat; the Bombay, a Burmese-domestic crossbreed; and the Egyptian Mau, thought to be a reconstitution of the original domesticated cat of Egypt, were accepted for registration by most associations. In some, they were given championship status.

More than 55,000 cats were registered in 1970, bringing the total of living registered cats to about 240,000. It was estimated that there were also more than 2 million unregistered purebred cats, plus about 20 million that were household pets and some 10 million farm and feral cats.

In the Year of the Dog

According to the Chinese calendar, 1970 was the Year of the Dog—and, in the United States, it might also be called the year of the poodle, the Shih Tzu, and the boxer. The poodle was revealed to have led new American Kennel Club (AKC) registrations for a tenth consecutive year; the Shih Tzu became the 116th breed to receive AKC recognition; and a boxer won the Westminster Kennel Club's prestigious best-in-show award.

New AKC registrations in 1969—announced early in 1970—totaled 973,100, of which 274,145 were poodles. Other dogs of the "top ten," in order of decreasing popularity, were the German shepherd, the dachshund, the beagle, the miniature schnauzer, the Chihuahua, the Pekingese, the collie, the Labrador retriever, and the cocker spaniel. The St. Bernard, the Great Dane, and the Newfoundland rose rapidly in popularity.

The newly recognized Shih Tzu is a small, silky coated dog that originated centuries ago in China. It is classified as a toy dog.

The boxer that captured top honors in the Westminster show in New York City in February was Champion Arriba's Prima Donna. The female is owned by Dr. and Mrs. P. J. Pagano of Pelham Manor, N.Y., and Dr. Theodore S. Fickes of Marblehead, Mass. (*See in* CE: Cat; Dogs; Pets.)

UPI COMPIX

This Filipino family survives by begging in Manila's slum section. About 80% of the Philippine people live in poverty.

PHILIPPINES. The Philippines faced two momentous problems in 1970—a troubled economy and deep social unrest. At year-end, it was unclear whether the country's president, Ferdinand E. Marcos, had effectively coped with them.

In January Marcos referred to the Philippines' balance-of-payments difficulty (caused chiefly by a rise in imports and a drop in exports during 1969) as having placed the economy "in a strait-jacket." To solve this crisis, the government announced a floating exchange rate for the peso and an "austerity program" of higher taxes and lower government spending.

The brunt of the economic difficulties fell on the people who were faced with rising prices for food, clothing, and transportation. The result was a growing degree of social unrest as significant parts of the population aired their grievances through public demonstrations, which by late March had mushroomed into almost daily riots. The major complaints were government overspending (which was partly to blame for the economic situation), widespread government corruption, and a fear that a constitutional convention scheduled for 1971 would be dominated by Marcos' political allies to such an extent as to ensure his continuance in power. A final grievance was the presence of U.S. military bases in the country.

President Marcos responded to the situation by blaming "Maoist revolutionaries" for instigating the riots. However, he later announced a more aggressive program of land reform and gave assurances that he would not run for a third term. He attempted to counter the alleged Communist Chinese influence and to help the ailing economy by resuming a policy of "opening windows" to European Communist countries, mainly through trade. In July the United States announced that it would withdraw about 6,000 U.S. military personnel by July 1971 from its estimated 26,900-man contingent. (*See in* CE: Philippines, The.)

PHOTOGRAPHY. Western photographic equipment manufacturers in 1970 continued to be attracted by the relatively low labor costs of the Far East. For some time, U.S. companies had been licensing production in Japan. In 1970, for the first time, the West German photographic industry also turned to the Orient. Agfa had some cameras made by Minolta in Japan, and even conservative Rollei broke with tradition and began manufacture in Singapore. It was expected that Singapore—offering labor costs one sixth of those of Europe and one half of those of Japan—might well attract still other photographic firms to contract for production in Asia.

New photographic equipment followed the trends of 1969. More roll-film cameras were produced, mostly in the expensive class for professionals and advanced amateurs. Examples were the Fujica G-690, a range-finder camera with interchangeable lenses that produced 6- by 9-cm. negatives, and the Mamiya single-lens reflex (SLR) that produced 6- by 7-cm. negatives and had a revolving back to permit pictures in horizontal or vertical format.

Many more cartridge-loading cameras, for 126 or "Instamatic" film, were introduced. Most were of the box camera type, with single-element plastic lenses and simple shutters. Some, however, offered automatic exposure control through electronic shutters coupled to cadmium sulfide light sensors. Top-priced SLRs for 126 film were also made by such famous firms as Zeiss and Rollei. Even with good lenses, 126-film picture definition continued to be thought limited by the cartridge's lack of a pressure plate to ensure film flatness and position.

Increasing numbers of compact cameras for 35-mm. film were also produced. Cameras in all-black "professional" finish continued to grow in popularity. Generally, camera systems tended to become more complex with the introduction of wider ranges of accessories and lenses.

Lens design continued to progress. Additional firms produced mirror lenses, which provide long focal length with minimum bulk. Zoom lenses became more compact and improved in optical quality. Wide-angle lenses were also improved. A number of lens makers adopted multiple-layer coating, which increased light transmission.

The Magicube, a four-bulb flashcube fired mechanically instead of electrically, was introduced in June. Other kinds of bulbs could not be used with cameras designed to take Magicubes, which were developed in answer to the reputedly high rate of failure of ordinary flashcubes with three-volt batteries.

In motion-picture photography, standard-8 film became virtually eclipsed by the more modern super-8 size. Several amateur movie cameras became smaller and more portable. Commercial movie-film processing methods became more automated.

Worldwide, trade in photographic goods continued to expand at about the same rate as in 1969. The long-standing rivalry between West Germany and Japan in the areas of manufacture and sale of photographic goods continued and expanded, with neither nation gaining a clear advantage. (*See in* CE: Photography articles.)

PHOTOGRAPHY EXHIBITIONS. One of the most widely viewed photography exhibits in the United States in 1970 was "USSR Photo '70," a collection of some 1,200 prints depicting various aspects of Soviet life and culture. The impressive show was arranged around some two dozen themes including childern, dance, music, sports, architecture, technology, and history. It was the first exhibit of Soviet photography ever held in the United States. After its opening in Washington, D.C., the show traveled around the country.

The Department of Photography at the Museum of Modern Art in New York City continued to produce photography exhibitions of major impor-

Dennis Gabor, a pioneer in holography, displays his new three-dimensional photography system, called sonography. Sound waves instead of light produced the photograph (above) of Abraham Lincoln.

COURTESY, CBS LABORATORIES

ELLIOTT ERWITT FROM MAGNUM

HENRI CARTIER-BRESSON, COURTESY, IBM WORLD TRADE CORP.

A beach scene (above) appears in "Photographs and Anti-Photographs," an exhibition of the work of Elliott Erwitt at the Smithsonian Institution. 'Wall Paintings' (left) is part of the Henri Cartier-Bresson exhibition "Man and Machine" at the IBM Gallery.

tance. Undoubtedly the most socially significant of its exhibits in 1970 was Bruce Davidson's "East 100th Street," which depicted residents of a block in New York City's East Harlem ghetto. The 43 prints in the show were selected from the large body of work produced by Davidson in the two-year period he spent photographing the people who lived in the urban squalor of East 100th Street.

In the summer the Museum of Modern Art had a large exhibition called "Photo Eye of the 20s," which included the work of such major luminaries in the history of photography as Eugène Atget, Edward Weston, Walker Evans, Edward Steichen, and László Moholy-Nagy, as well as lesser-known figures, all of whom were active during the photographically creative period of the 1920's. The exhibit, which was organized by Beaumont Newhall, director of the George Eastman House in Rochester, N.Y., later toured the United States. Of a more avant-garde nature was the museum's show "Photography Into Sculpture," an unusual display of three-dimensional photographic objects. One of the more impressive works was Lyn Wells's "photosensitized contour-molded cloth sculpture," a life-size form made of stuffed cloth imprinted with photographic images showing the front and back views of a man.

Other unusual exhibits of note included two that featured holograms, three-dimensional photographs made by lasers: the show "N Dimensional Space" at Finch College Museum of Art in New York City and "Holograms and Lasers" at Chicago's Museum of Contemporary Art. Another unique photography show was "One-Eyed Dicks," a 14-minute film created by splicing together still shots made by automatic cameras during bank robberies. It was shown at the Musuem of Modern Art in New York City and at the Museum of Contemporary Art in Chicago.

Among the one-man shows held during the year was "Thomas Eakins: His Photographic Works" at the New York Cultural Center in New York City. Included in it were some 200 photographs, most made by Eakins but also including photographs relating to him made by others. The exhibit revealed the photographic talents of the American artist primarily known for his paintings. The Minneapolis Institute of Arts in Minnesota featured Richard Avedon's works in a show that included his celebrity and fashion photos as well as some social commentary—photos he had taken of the seven defendants of the 1969–70 Chicago Conspiracy trial. Henri Cartier-Bresson was the subject of a major photographic exhibit at New York City's IBM Gallery. Titled "Man and Machine," the show consisted of works commissioned by IBM World Trade Corp. from the famed photographer dealing with the theme of man and his relationship to the machines of his environment. (*See also* Museums; Painting and Sculpture. *See in* CE: Photography articles.)

PHYSICS. Significant new discoveries in nuclear physics and in solid-state physics were made in 1970. In elementary-particle physics, research on controlled thermonuclear fusion, and the study of gravitation, much effort went into extending advances made in 1969.

In the summer a Swiss laboratory announced the discovery of antiprotonic atoms. In such an atom, antiprotons—particles with the mass of protons but carrying the negative charge of electrons—orbit the nucleus instead of electrons. Antiprotonic atoms were the latest in a series of exotic atoms—those in which various particles, including pi- and mu-mesons, are made to play the part of electrons. From the radiation emitted by exotic atoms, physicists can learn things about the structure of atomic nuclei that they cannot learn from atoms that have electrons.

Experiments conducted in 1969 and 1970 indicated that both protons and neutrons are made of a number of subparticles. Little was discovered, however, about the nature of the subparticles. They were tentatively named "partons" to avoid identification with the ultraelementary "quark" particles predicted by theory but not yet surely discovered despite eight years of search.

Early in 1970 a group of U.S. scientists announced that they had found a niobium-aluminum-germanium alloy that would remain superconducting at magnetic field strengths far in excess of those that other superconductors can withstand. Superconductors are alloys that, when cooled to temperatures near absolute zero (−460° F.), offer virtually no resistance to the passage of electric current. Electromagnets made from superconductors use very little power and generate almost no heat; the

This photograph is from the exhibition "East 100th Street" by Bruce Davidson at the Museum of Modern Art in New York City. The exhibition prints and the book from which they were taken are the result of Davidson's two-year photographic study of the residents of a single block in East Harlem.
BRUCE DAVIDSON FROM MAGNUM

WIDE WORLD

Albert Ghiorso of the University of California reported the discovery of a new element—number 105 in the periodic table.

strength of superconductor magnets is limited, however, because when the magnetic field reaches a certain strength, it destroys the superconductivity and makes the metal an ordinary conductor. The new alloy remains superconductive until the strength of the magnetic field reaches 410,000 gauss.

Scientists in California announced the successful fabrication of element 105. They proposed that it be named hahnium, after Otto Hahn, the discoverer of nuclear fission. (*See* Chemistry.)

During the year more and more physicists appeared to accept the 1969 announcement by Dr. Joseph Weber of the University of Maryland that he had observed the gravitational waves predicted by Albert Einstein. Scientists in the United States, Great Britain, and the Soviet Union were building equipment to observe the waves themselves. They sought to discover what in the universe produced the waves. It was theorized that they might emanate either from supernovas (exploding stars) or from the (also theoretical) "black holes" that result from the collapse of stars into objects only a few miles in diameter from which neither matter nor energy can escape. Dr. Weber reported that his equipment records about one burst of gravitational waves a month and that most of them seem to come from the center of our galaxy (the Milky Way).

Continuing the search for a means of controlling thermonuclear reactions, U.S. scientists in 1970 duplicated—and apparently improved upon—a successful 1969 Soviet experiment in which an 18,000,000° F plasma was contained by a magnetic field for several thousandths of a second. A plasma is a hot, dense gas composed of dissociated atomic nuclei and electrons. To achieve controlled fusion—the joining of nuclei with consequent great release of energy—it would be necessary to contain a 180,000,000° F. plasma. (*See in* CE: Physics.)

POLAND. The year 1970 ended dramatically for Poland. In foreign relations an era of reconciliation with West Germany was foreshadowed. At home, major cities of the Baltic coast witnessed a violent eruption of popular discontent similar to that of Poznan in 1956. Both revolts had far-reaching political consequences: that of 1956 brought about Communist Party First Secretary Wladyslaw Gomulka's return to power; that of 1970 swept him away as a leader who had lost touch with the people.

The establishment of normal and friendly relations with West Germany on the basis of an existing territorial status quo was one of the chief and constant aims of Poland's foreign policy, but until 1969 the response from the West German government was always negative. The Christian Democratic chancellors seemed to believe that there existed some way of recovering the eastern borders established by the Treaty of Versailles. A radical change in this unrealistic attitude took place in October 1969 when a coalition of Social Democrats and liberals (Free Democrats) assumed power in West Germany. Chancellor Willy Brandt declared that the new West German government was ready to open negotiations with Poland on issues suggested by Gomulka in May 1969, and the Polish government acquiesced in this proposal. On February 5, 1970, Polish-West German talks began in Warsaw, the capital. There were several preparatory meetings held in Warsaw and in Bonn, the West German capital, before the final negotiations started in the Polish capital on November 3 between the two foreign ministers, Stefan Jedrychowski and Walter Scheel. Initialed on November 18, the Polish-West German treaty was signed in Warsaw on December 7 by Chancellor Brandt and Poland's premier, Jozef Cyrankiewicz. In this historic document the West German government declared that the existing border line—determined at Potsdam, Germany, on Aug. 2, 1945, by the governments of the United States, Great Britain, and the Soviet Union, and running from the Baltic Sea to Czechoslovakia along the Oder and Neisse rivers—"forms the western state frontier of Poland", and also that West Germany "affirms the inviolability of this frontier now and in the future."

An unfortunate price regulation was announced by the government on December 12, when 46 items of basic foodstuffs, fuel, and clothing went up in price from 10% to 30%, while 40 other items—household goods, television sets, and automobiles—became cheaper. Economically sensible, this measure of deflation was deeply resented by the majority of the Polish people, especially as it happened 12 days before Christmas. On December 14, at another plenary session of the Central Committee, Gomulka justified the new prices, but at the same time bloody riots were starting in Danzig, Gdynia, and Szczecin, where large Polish shipyards are located. Three days later Premier Cyrankiewicz told the Polish people by radio and television that rioters had been setting fire to public buildings (mainly party headquarters) and looting shops. Police and army units had been authorized to use arms to restore order. There were 10 to 20 persons killed and hundreds injured—both policemen and civilians.

On December 20, Gomulka resigned and was succeeded by Edward Gierek, first secretary of the party organization in the country's richest province since 1957, and a Politburo member since 1959. On December 23, Cyrankiewicz resigned as premier. Broadcasting to the Polish people, Gierek said that he would get rid of the "ill-considered economic policies" of the past and revise the 1971–75 plan in consultation with the workers. He added that there would be no cancellation of the price decree of December 12, but that small wage increases to the lowest-paid workers would partly offset the higher prices. Gierek said there would be no change in Poland's foreign policy. (*See also* Germany. *See in* CE: Poland.)

POLICE. In 1970 U.S. police personnel strength continued to increase. The Federal Bureau of Investigation's Uniform Crime Reports revealed that as of Dec. 31, 1969, cities in the United States had an average of 2.2 police employees per 1,000 inhabitants, which represented an increase of 5% over the 2.1 rate in 1968.

The recruitment of qualified men continued to present a major problem to many police departments. In New York City, in July 1970, it was revealed that the average IQ scores of police recruits the preceding year were the lowest in recent years. Of 2,075 men brought into the New York City Police Department in 1969, the average IQ score was 98.20, with one class of 358 men averaging only 93.19. These average IQ scores compared with 107.7 for recruits in 1962, 107.28 in 1964, and 105.75 in 1967. Some departments, such as the one in Los Angeles, were not appointing men with IQ's under 110. The decline of average IQ scores for recruits in New York City was believed to be related to the rapid increase in the size of the police department and the subsequent easing of standards in the scoring of entrance tests given by the New York City Personnel Department.

Violence against policemen, including sniper attacks, terrorist bombings, and assaults, increased in 1970. By midsummer, 56 officers in just 40 states had been killed in line of duty. Officials in Chicago; Detroit, Mich.; Los Angeles; San Francisco, Calif.; and New York City reported in August that violence against police officers had increased significantly, while attacks on policemen had risen to a lesser degree in Pittsburgh, Pa.; Cleveland, Ohio; and Houston, Tex. The leaders of local patrolmen's benevolent and fraternal associations in Los Angeles, Detroit, and San Francisco reported that older men were retiring promptly at the end of 20 years service because of the rising danger involved in the policeman's job. Carl Parsell, presi-

Georgia's Gov. Lester G. Maddox assigned state police to provide 24-hour protection for this billboard, which warns tourists of a local speed trap.

WIDE WORLD

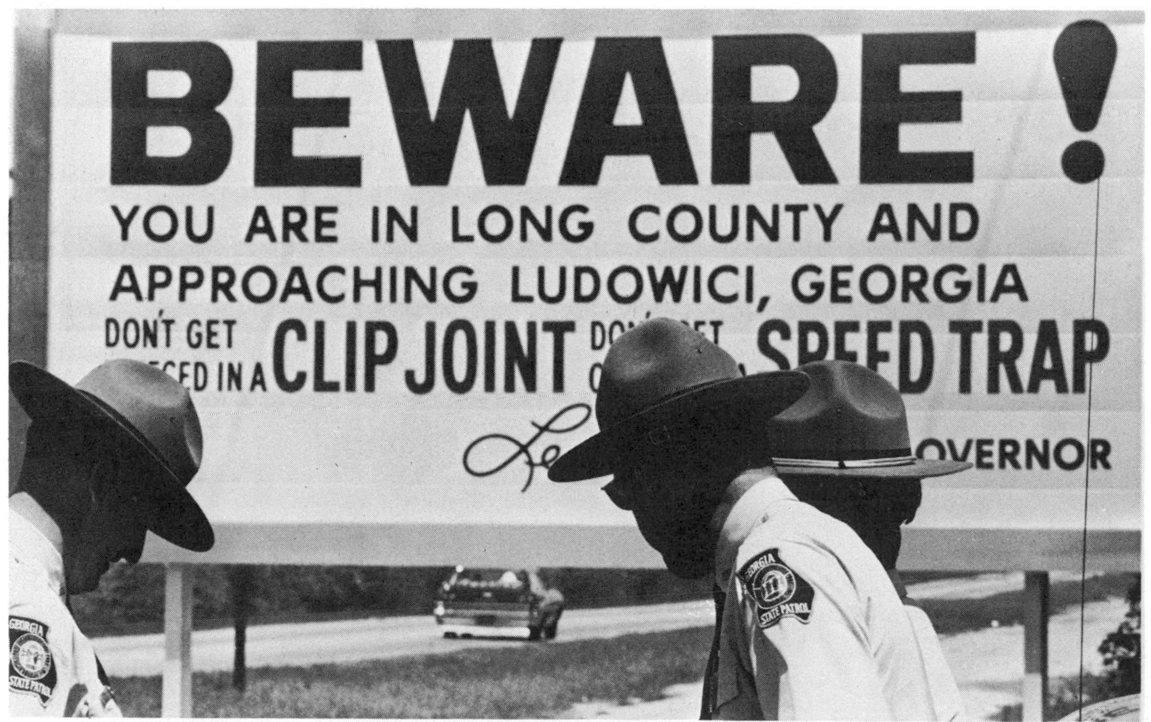

dent of the International Conference of Police Associations, stated that sniper attacks and bombings resulted in the intimidation of police and that calls for assistance were handled more slowly because of the fear of an ambush. (*See also* Crime. *See in* CE: Police.)

POLITICAL PARTIES. For both major political parties in the United States, 1970 was a year of transition. For the Republicans, there was the challenge of developing a unified stand in support of programs of the Administration of U.S. President Richard M. Nixon. For the Democrats, the challenge was recovery from the electoral defeat of 1968, when their party lost the presidency and five governorships.

There were signs of shifts in the balance of political power. A widely circulated Louis Harris opinion poll in February found that while the Democratic party was still the largest in the United States, it had ceased to be a majority party. The poll found that 48% of the persons it sampled regarded themselves as Democrats, 33% as Republicans, and 19% as independents. This represented a four-percentage-point decline for the Democrats in two years. Republicans and independents each gained two.

Republican Party

The Republicans were faced with the problem of capturing most of the independent vote and some disaffected Democrats in the 1970 Congressional election. While the campaign, like most U.S. political contests, was a loosely related array of debates over issues and personalities, something like an overall strategy appeared in the Republican campaign. The strategy was expressed in a book titled 'The Real Majority', by Richard M. Scammon and Ben J. Wattenberg. The authors held that there is a long-range tide of unrest in the United States over the "social issue." The real majority of the population, the authors held, is deeply concerned about crime, racial unrest, campus disorder, drug abuse, and the breakdown of sexual codes. This majority was described as the 70% of the nation that is "un-young, un-poor, and un-black." In the middle of the array, the authors asserted, is "a middle-aged, middle-income, high-school-educated white Protestant, who works with his hands," or "a 47-year-old housewife from the outskirts of Dayton, Ohio, whose husband is a machinist." The way to win a political campaign, they insisted, was to build a program that would appeal to this real majority. The argument had considerable effect on Republican strategists.

The task of implementing Republican strategy for the capture of the middle fell primarily to Vice-President Spiro T. Agnew, who emerged as the spokesman for the party. By the end of the 1970 Congressional campaign, he was by far its best known and most colorful figure. Agnew appealed to the workingmen who are no longer poor, but prosperous, stable members of U.S. society—the type he dubbed "the forgotten man of American politics." He assailed the Administration's opponents as "radical liberals." These people, he indicated, stood for "isolationism in foreign policy, obstructionism on domestic reform, permissiveness on law and order, drugs and pornography."

His attacks grew progressively more vehement. In two speeches on September 30, he described a Republican senator, Charles E. Goodell of New York, as a "radical liberal" who had "left the party." Despite the endorsement by Republican National

WIDE WORLD

WIDE WORLD

Hubert H. Humphrey (far left) holds the hand of Lawrence F. O'Brien, who became chairman of the Democratic National Committee in March. He succeeded Senator Fred R. Harris (above).

ALPHA BLAIR FROM PICTORIAL PARADE

New York City's Mayor John V. Lindsay declined to support fellow Republican Nelson Rockefeller, running for reelection as governor of New York. Instead, Lindsay supported Rockefeller's opponent, Democrat Arthur Goldberg.

Chairman Rogers C. B. Morton and a show of support by Republican liberal senators, Goodell finished last in a three-way election. The episode underscored a division in the Republican party that could conceivably prove damaging in the future. Voter reaction to the Republican campaign strategy was mixed and inconclusive.

In late November, President Nixon appointed National Chairman Morton as secretary of the interior, to replace Walter J. Hickel, whom he had just dismissed. Selection of a new Republican chairman was expected early in 1971.

Democratic Party

The Democrats began and ended 1970 with a large deficit left over from the 1968 presidential campaign. Early in the year, the amount was estimated as over $8 million. However, Chairman Lawrence F. O'Brien said at year's end that it actually had been $9.3 million throughout the year.

Early in February, Senator Fred R. Harris of Oklahoma resigned as national chairman, a post he had held since Jan. 1, 1969. At first O'Brien declined the post but later he reconsidered.

Early in the year, the Democrats moved toward a stronger stand for ending the war in Vietnam. A position paper issued by the Democratic Policy Council on February 9 asked for a firm and definite timetable for withdrawing troops and declared, "We see no reason why this withdrawal should not be completed within 18 months." The council also adopted a sweeping but somewhat equivocal statement on national goals. It declared that poor schools, costly health care, racial injustice, pollution, and a housing crisis might require deep cuts in military spending, "further redistribution of our wealth," and even "restructuring of our instruments of government."

Third Parties

One of the most striking features of the elections in 1970 was the emergence of New York's Conservative party as a significant political force. The party was founded in 1962 by Republicans who feared that the Eastern wing of their party was becoming too liberal. The Conservatives, it was reasoned, could slate opposition candidates who would attract enough votes to make election of liberal Republicans unlikely. The result, it was hoped, would be a greater willingness of Republicans to slate conservatives. The party failed in its objectives in the New York City mayoral election in 1965 and the senatorial election in 1968. In 1970, however, James L. Buckley, the Conservative candidate, was elected senator from New York in a three-way contest.

An analysis of the vote showed that Buckley gained support not only in traditionally Republican areas but also in districts where Democrats were supported by a significant percentage of white middle-class voters. Buckley emphasized that he expected the Conservative party to continue working toward influencing the major parties.

The Democrats were threatened with the development of splinter parties on both the right and

Senator Edmund S. Muskie (D, Me.), though evasive about his plans, was considered a leading candidate for the U.S. presidency in 1972.

WIDE WORLD

the left. George C. Wallace of Alabama, who polled nearly 10 million votes as the presidential candidate of his American Independent party in 1968, won a complex, hard-fought Democratic primary in 1970 and then went on to election as governor of Alabama. Wallace's campaign was based largely on exploiting white fears of an emerging Negro bloc as a power in Alabama politics. The victory raised the possibility that he might again run for president in 1972. He said during the campaign that he would not enter the race if President Nixon kept what Wallace said were campaign promises to "stop bussings and school closings and reestablish freedom of choice as the law of the land in public education." Nonetheless, Wallace kept open his national campaign headquarters and continued to publish a nationally distributed monthly newsletter. Aides said that the American Independent party remained alive in three fourths of the states, so it would be less difficult for Wallace to get on the ballot in all 50 states than it was in 1968.

POPULAR MUSIC. In 1970 the state of popular music seemed to be suffering from a letdown after the Woodstock Music and Art Fair of 1969. The deaths of two rock "superstars," the disbanding of the Beatles, and the failure of a number of festivals contributed to the depression.

Jimi Hendrix, the black guitarist-singer who was noted for his mastery of electronic effects, was found dead in a London hotel room in mid-September. Hendrix, 27, died following an overdose of sleeping pills. His death was followed by that of Janis Joplin, also 27, the white blues-rock singer who had been compared to such legendary figures as Bessie Smith and Billie Holiday. Janis, who first

UPI COMPIX

Benny Goodman, the "king of swing," plays to a sold-out audience in Bucharest, Romania, during a 14-city European tour. He took along a band of 17 British musicians.

The Ike and Tina Turner Revue, a rhythm-and-blues group, appeared at the Newport Jazz Festival in July. Tina (right) is the featured singer, and Ike (rear, right) plays guitar.

RICHARD BALAGUR FROM NANCY PALMER AGENCY

came into fame with Big Brother and the Holding Company, had assembled a new band of her own, the Janis Joplin Full Tilt Boogie Band. Her death was attributed to an overdose of heroin.

The release of the album 'McCartney' in April signaled the demise of the Beatles. A week before the release of the record, on which he played all the instruments and handled the arranging, Paul McCartney issued a statement saying that the Beatles would no longer record as a group. In effect, the Beatles had become defunct months earlier. Their final album, 'Let It Be', released in May, had actually been recorded before their 'Abbey Road' record, which was released in 1969. However, each of the Beatles remained active—all had released solo albums by year-end.

Shortly after the announcement of the Beatles' breakup, a poll taken in London reported that after eight years in the number-one position, they were no longer Great Britain's favorite pop group. First place was taken by Led Zeppelin.

Attempts to re-create Woodstock during the year were disappointing at best. Many festival promoters met with opposition from law enforcement agencies, and court injunctions prevented several festivals from taking place. Among these was the Middlefield, Conn., festival, which proceeded despite a court order that prevented the appearance of most of the scheduled bands. The Kickapoo Creek Rock Music Festival in Heyworth, Ill., drew about 30,000 persons and featured a number of bands even though it had been forbidden by a court injunction. The most successful festival of the year was held in August on the Isle of Wight, which lies off Portsmouth, England. More than 80,000 listened to such diverse pop performers as Joan Baez, Jimi Hendrix, Richie Havens, Sly and the Family Stone, Joni Mitchell, Miles Davis, John Sebastian, and The Who.

A number of new performers emerged as pop stars during 1970. Among them were country-blues singer James Taylor; former backup man Leon Russell; Melanie, a young singer-composer; and Elton John, an English performer whose records were released in the United States for the first time. New groups rising in prominence during the year included the Jackson 5, a family group whose lead singer was only nine years old. The Jackson 5 played music based in rhythm and blues with simple melodies that was known as "soul bubble gum." Other groups tended to follow the jam session techniques characteristic of jazz music in which musicians play together informally. 'Delaney and Bonnie and Friends on Tour with Eric Clapton' and 'John B. Sebastian' were records resulting from such jam sessions.

Among the most successful new albums released during the year were 'Stage Fright', by the Band; 'Bridge over Troubled Water', by Simon and Garfunkel; and 'Self Portrait', by Bob Dylan. Dylan also received an honorary doctorate from Princeton University in June. (*See also* Music.)

POPULATION. As of April 1, 1970, when the 19th decennial census of the United States took place, the nation's population stood at 204,765,770. This figure included U.S. servicemen stationed overseas. Every state but three experienced a rise in population. The exceptions were North Dakota, South Dakota, and West Virginia.

It came as no surprise that population rose in most of the 233 Standard Metropolitan Statistical Areas (SMSAs), each of which consists of a central city containing at least 50,000 persons plus one or more surrounding counties. Sixty-six SMSAs had 500,000 or more persons living in them as of 1970. With 11.4 million inhabitants, the New York City SMSA was still the nation's largest.

"Megalopolis," that 150-mile-wide strip from Boston, Mass., to Washington, D.C., held the greatest concentration of population. It contained 36.2 million persons, 18% of the populace of the United States.

"THE NEW YORK TIMES"

A census taker had to hike to the remote town of Supai, Ariz., to survey the Havasupai Indians.

By preliminary census counts, California was now the most populous state, a distinction long held by New York. The 1970 census also showed that 91% of California's 19.7 million people lived in counties that lay wholly or in part just 50 miles from the Pacific Ocean.

In 1970 there were 150 cities with 100,000 or more inhabitants. According to preliminary reports, New York led with 7,771,730, followed by Chicago with 3,325,263; Los Angeles with 2,782,400; Philadelphia, Pa., with 1,926,529; Detroit, Mich., with 1,492,914; and Houston, Tex., with 1,213,064. These figures were somewhat deceptive, however, because the population in many central cities dropped. About 75% of the national gain, moreover, occurred in suburban areas. For the first time in U.S. history, suburban population was greater than that of the central cities.

Meanwhile, the U.S. farm population continued its decline. As of 1970, it constituted only about 10 million persons, 5 million fewer than the farm population of 1960. In addition, about 50% of all U.S. counties lost population in the decade. In 25% of the other counties, growth was slight.

Los Angeles County remained the nation's largest, with 6,970,733 persons. Cook County in Illinois stood again as the second largest, with 5,430,075 inhabitants. Mohave County in Arizona staged the most impressive percentage gain in population, jumping 224.6% in the decade from 7,736 persons in 1960 to 25,110 in 1970.

The census also revealed that for the first time since the 1870's, more people moved into the South than out of it. The 16 states (and Washington, D.C.) that make up the South contained 61.5 million persons as of April 1, 1970.

The soaring population throughout the world was the concern of various groups in 1970. According to one estimate, the total world population was increasing at the rate of two persons per second. At the First National Congress on Optimum Population and Environment, held in Chicago in June, scientists, government officials, and social workers were among the persons calling for population curbs. It was felt that by limiting the number of births throughout the world, the mounting pressures on the environment would be relieved. Those pressures included environmental pollution and resource exploitation for increasing energy needs and goods. (*See* Feature Article: "The Need for Population Control"; Census Section, page 507. *See in* CE: Census; Population.)

PORTUGAL. António de Oliveira Salazar, leader of Portugal for 40 years, died on July 27, 1970. Salazar's successor as premier, Marcello José das Neves Alves Caetano, actually took office in 1968, when Salazar suffered a stroke. However, Salazar died without knowing he had been replaced; his doctors had feared that the shock might kill him.

Caetano reorganized his cabinet in January, merging several ministries and appointing Rui Manuel Patricio as foreign minister, an office Caetano had tended since October 1969. The post of minister of state, which had amounted to the vice-premiership, was abolished as Alfredo Vaz Pinto retired from it.

Late in February, Portugal's only legal political organization, the National Union, held its first congress in 14 years and changed its name to National Popular Action (ANP). Caetano was elected president of the ANP; his speech to the party congress indicated that the government intended to follow policies established under Salazar and to remain in its African colonies.

Caetano paid a state visit to Madrid, Spain, in May to renew the Iberian pact—the friendship treaty between Spain and Portugal—and to improve relations, particularly economic, with Spain. The Portuguese and Spanish governments were reportedly concerned about Great Britain's possible entry into the European Economic Community (EEC), or Common Market, and the result on the European Free Trade Association.

The Portuguese government set up a commission in July to study the possibility of closer ties with the EEC after France's Foreign Minister Maurice Schumann had promised French support in the EEC. Caetano said in a September speech that Portugal would accept economic but not political ties with the EEC. Portuguese opponents of association with the EEC, led by former Foreign Minister Franco Nogueira, claimed that the country's economic future lay with the African colonies rather than with Europe.

The Portuguese government recalled its ambassador to the Vatican early in July after Pope Paul VI received three leaders of liberation movements in Portugal's African territories. Relations were restored when the Vatican explained that there was nothing political about their discussions. (*See in* CE: Portugal.)

POST OFFICE, UNITED STATES. Postal operations in the United States in 1970 were marked by two historic events: the first national postal strike and the passage of a massive reorganization act which, for the first time since the American Revolution, took the post office out of politics and made it an independent government agency. The two were closely interconnected. The wildcat strike, which led to the largest walkout ever against the federal government, climaxed months of growing resentment among postal employees over low wages and the failure of the U.S. Congress to come through with promised pay increases. When the walkout began in New York City on March 18, top scale for a veteran letter carrier was $8,442 a year; according to government estimates, a family of four required $11,236 to maintain even a modest standard of living there.

While postal union leaders were pushing for pay increases, they were also opposing various aspects of the legislation supported by U.S. President Richard M. Nixon that would radically restructure the postal system. The union leaders feared the loss of civil service status and union recognition, as well as their traditional bargaining influence over Congress, which historically has set both rates

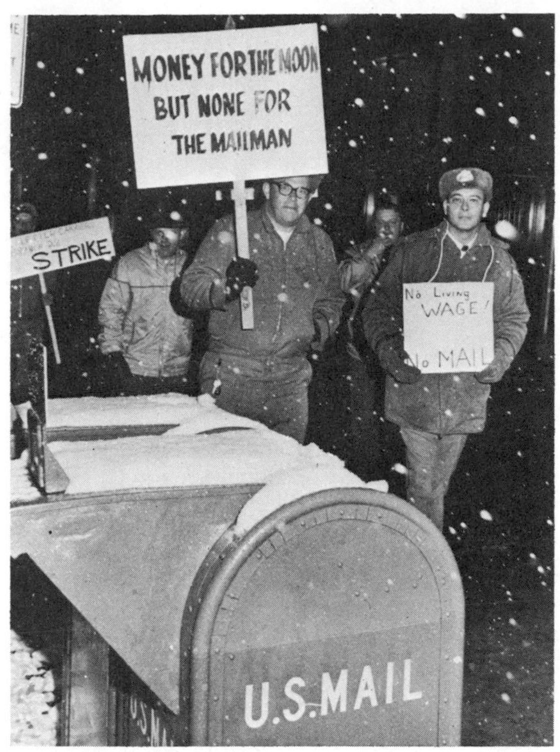

WIDE WORLD

Employees of the U.S. Post Office went on strike in March. Letter carriers in St. Paul, Minn., (above) picket for higher wages.

and wages. However, President Nixon repeatedly insisted that he would veto any pay-raise bill that was not tied to the reorganization he had first requested in 1969. The strike erupted in New York City. The president, union officials, and Congressional leaders began trying to work out a compromise as the walkout spread swiftly to New England and westward, hitting dozens of major cities from coast to coast.

The strike forced a virtual halt to the average daily flow of 270 million pieces of mail the postal system was handling. It also drastically affected the economy, as checks, bills, and other legal documents were caught in the logjam. The walkout lasted as little as a day in some places, over a week in others. Before it was over in New York City, some 25,000 military personnel were mobilized to help move the mail there.

After months of haggling and political maneuvering, Congress on August 6 finally approved the historic legislation creating the U.S. Postal Service as an independent agency of the federal government, empowered to make its own budget and bargain directly with employees. The service will be headed by a board of governors and a postmaster general who, unlike his predecessors for the preceding 141 years, will not be a member of the president's Cabinet. Nine members of the board will be appointed by the president, with the advice and consent of the Senate, to serve staggered terms of nine years each. The 9 will appoint the postmaster general who will serve, at their pleasure, as the chief operating officer of the nation's postal system. The 10 together will select a deputy postmaster general, and all 11 will constitute the board of governors. The relationship will be much like the officers and board of directors of a major corporation which, in effect, the U.S. postal system became in 1970.

Along with the reorganization, Congress granted the nation's postal workers an 8% pay raise effective April 16, in addition to a 6% boost that was allotted to most other federal employees as of July 1, 1970. The House of Representatives and Senate versions of the bill differed chiefly over union-employee relations, the subsidy, and the extent of continuing Congressional influence in the new system.

The new postal corporation, which President Nixon signed into existence on August 12, climaxed years of effort to streamline the department. Former U.S. President Lyndon B. Johnson gave it the first big push when he appointed a special commission which, after extensive study, recommended in 1968 that the government quit the postal service. Until that time, efforts to modernize and mechanize operations had run into staunch opposition from unions fearful that jobs would be lost and from congressmen sensitive to the votes cast by the members of those unions. (*See in* CE: Postal Services articles.)

PRISONS. The conditions in prisons throughout the United States led to some explosive incidents in 1970. However, events during the year also led to increased investigation and evaluation of the nation's penal systems.

In February, U.S. Chief Justice Warren E. Burger urged the state governments to develop a simple method for hearing the grievances of prisoners. During the early months of the year Chief Justice Burger had been visiting prisons in the Washington, D.C., area to inspect conditions. He also conferred with members of the American Bar Association who were developing proposals for overhauling the correctional institutions.

At least one state, Arkansas, was ordered to overhaul its prisons. In February Judge J. Smith Henley ruled that the conditions in the Arkansas State Penitentiary were unconstitutional and that the two prison farms would have to be closed unless conditions were improved. The ruling came after a hearing in January in which 23 prisoners protested living conditions and brutality by prison personnel. In another hearing, Judge Henley fined a former superintendent $1,000 and handed down a one-year suspended sentence after the defendant had pleaded "no contest" to a charge of brutality against inmates.

A prison riot that was called the worst in the history of Philadelphia, Pa., broke out in Holmesburg Prison in July. Approximately 400 prisoners

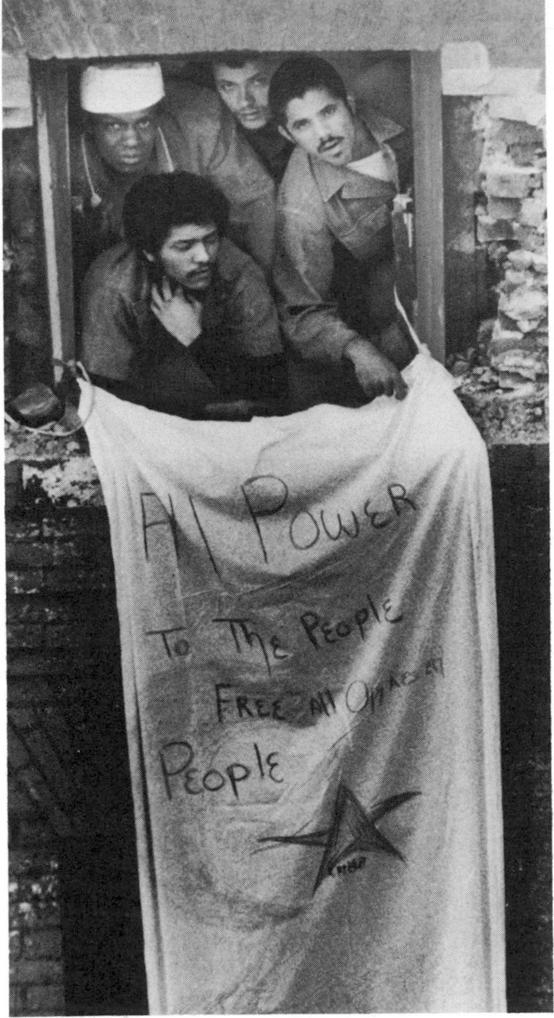

WIDE WORLD

In October inmates of the Queens House of Detention in New York City took over the prison and seized seven hostages. The men were demanding major prison reforms.

rioted for three hours; 82 inmates, 34 guards, and a civilian employee were injured. The causes of the riot were a matter of controversy. Prison officials maintained that the uprising was a result of racial tensions between black and white inmates. However, penologists attributed the riot to overcrowding, a shortage of guards, and generally oppressive conditions. At the time of the riot, nearly 1,200 prisoners were quartered in 680 cells.

Overcrowding was also the prime cause of the nation's most spectacular prison riot of 1970. In August prisoners of New York City's Manhattan House of Detention for Men rioted twice in one week, breaking windows, throwing furniture onto the street below, and holding guards as hostages. During the second day of rioting, prisoners controlled 4 of the 15 floors in the prison, popularly known as the "Tombs," and held three guards hostage for seven hours before city officials agreed to investigate jail conditions.

In a statement of complaint, Tombs inmates protested overcrowded conditions, brutality by the guards, and poor food. They also raised questions concerning the legality of their imprisonment. Nearly all of the inmates had been awaiting trial, some for as long as a year. Commissioner of Correction George F. McGrath acknowledged the validity of many of the complaints. The jail, built to house 932 inmates, held 1,815 prisoners at the time of the riots. In response to a request by New York City Mayor John V. Lindsay, New York's Gov. Nelson A. Rockefeller agreed to have 300 convicted prisoners moved from the Tombs to state prisons to alleviate conditions. An investigation of conditions in the jail and hearings by the New York State Senate Subcommittee on Crime and Correction also followed the riots.

Political prisoners were the subject of a report issued by Amnesty International, a private organization based in Great Britain. The report entitled "The Face of Persecution, 1970" stated that throughout the world there were as many as 250,000 persons imprisoned for their political views. The organization has gained the release of over 2,000 political prisoners since its founding in 1961. (*See also* Crime. *See in* CE: Prisons and Punishments.)

PSYCHOLOGY. During 1970, when the quality of the environment was a pressing concern, psychologists were urged to assist in planning for "livable" cities of the future. It was felt that the size, density of population, and heterogeneity of the existing cities forced urbanites into psychologically "overloaded" situations, caused in part by the sheer number of people they confronted daily in varying social contexts. To compensate, urbanites would cut to a minimum the time spent with others, discourage new acquaintanceships, and interpose institutions between themselves and society.

In 1970 some headway was made toward better understanding and treating of manic depression, a severe psychiatric disorder in which sufferers exhibit a wide shift in moods. Recent studies indicated it might be a sex-linked genetic malady. One investigator found manic-depressive fathers rarely had sons with the disorder, but manic-depressive mothers stood a 40% chance of having similarly affected sons. The gene for manic depression was assumed to be linked to the maternally contributed X chromosome.

In April the U.S. Food and Drug Administration sanctioned the use of lithium carbonate for treatment of the manic state of manic depression. The drug provided marked success with few side effects.

Perspiration analysis has been added to the diagnostic arsenal of psychotherapy. Researchers have isolated a chemical from the sweat of schizophrenics so distinctive that when added to "normal" sweat it produces an odor characteristic of schizophrenics. Other studies indicated that there was a high incidence of schizophrenia among relatives of sufferers. This suggested a genetic basis for schizophrenia, a view doubted by some psychologists.

Minimal brain dysfunction, a poorly understood neurological disorder that affects the learning capabilities of some children, has been almost miraculously alleviated in some cases by drug therapy. Although usually possessing normal or even high intelligence, children afflicted with the disorder exhibit poor muscular coordination, brief attention spans, and, sometimes, physical inability to perceive letters and words in the proper sequence on the printed page. As a result, they are often so frustrated at school that they become aggressive and hostile. However, the drugs that reduce minimal brain dysfunction—the amphetamines—have also been involved in many cases of drug abuse and therefore were viewed with some trepidation by parents of the afflicted children.

Children of mentally retarded mothers are very capable learners under proper conditions, according to a report from the University of Wisconsin at Madison presented in August. When subjected to intensive training programs, these children proved able to begin reading by the age of three. Since only 20% of the 6 million mentally retarded persons in the United States had recognizable disorders of the central nervous system, it was suspected that mental retardation often has social and other environmental causes.

Science has long sought to uncover centers in the brain where such abstract properties as shape and number are discerned. Recently, cells have been found in the cortex of the cat brain that appeared to respond to a numerically based stimulus—such as the second impulse of a series—no matter how intense or irregularly timed was the stimulus.

Electrical stimulation of the brain has been pursued with much interest in recent years. In one reported case, a man suffering from narcolepsy could overcome a strong desire for sleep by activating an electrode that had been implanted in his brain. (*See in* CE: Psychology.)

PUBLISHING, BOOK. The number of corporate mergers and acquisitions in the book publishing world dropped off sharply in 1970. There were, however, at least two major developments: Atheneum Publishers merged with D. C. Heath & Co., a Boston, Mass., textbook house owned by Raytheon Co.; and Simon & Schuster, Inc., was sold to Kinney National Service, Inc., a company involved in many varied enterprises. Also during the year, Harcourt, Brace & World, Inc., became Harcourt Brace Jovanovich, Inc.

In 1969 a total of 29,579 books were published in the United States, according to *Publishers' Weekly*. This showed a slight drop from the 30,387 books published in 1968 and probably indicated a general leveling-off in U.S. book production. Of the 1969 total, 21,787 were new books and 7,792 were new editions. Except for the category of juvenile books, no subject area showed a major drop or rise, and the juvenile discrepancy was probably due to underreporting. The 1969 juvenile total was 1,406 as compared to 2,482 in 1968.

Paperback title production reflected the overall trend, decreasing from 7,241 in 1968 to 7,068 in 1969. Of this total, mass market paperbacks dropped from 2,072 in 1968 to 1,837 in 1969, while those other than mass market increased slightly from 5,169 to 5,231.

Hardcover textbooks increased from 2,210 in 1968 to 2,641 in 1969. Of the total, high school and college textbooks decreased slightly while elementary textbooks rose from 313 to 1,028. Imports dropped from 4,307 to 4,103. The average price of hardcover trade-technical books, as tabulated for a selection of 17,838 books by *Publishers' Weekly*, was $9.37 in 1969 as compared to $8.47 in 1968, a 10% increase.

A distinct change occurred in the comparative sales totals of the ten best-selling hardcover fiction and the ten best-selling nonfiction books in 1969. For the preceding 20 years, nonfiction had outsold fiction by about two to one. In 1969 the ten books on the nonfiction list outsold the ten books on the fiction list by only a little more than 2% as compared with the usual 100%. The top fiction title, 'Portnoy's Complaint', by Philip Roth, sold 418,000

A folio of 31 prints by Samuel Rozin, a Jewish artist living in Soviet Lithuania, was published in 1970. The unusual publication depicts Jewish life in Lithuania and Israel.

COURTESY, YIVO INSTITUTE FOR JEWISH RESEARCH

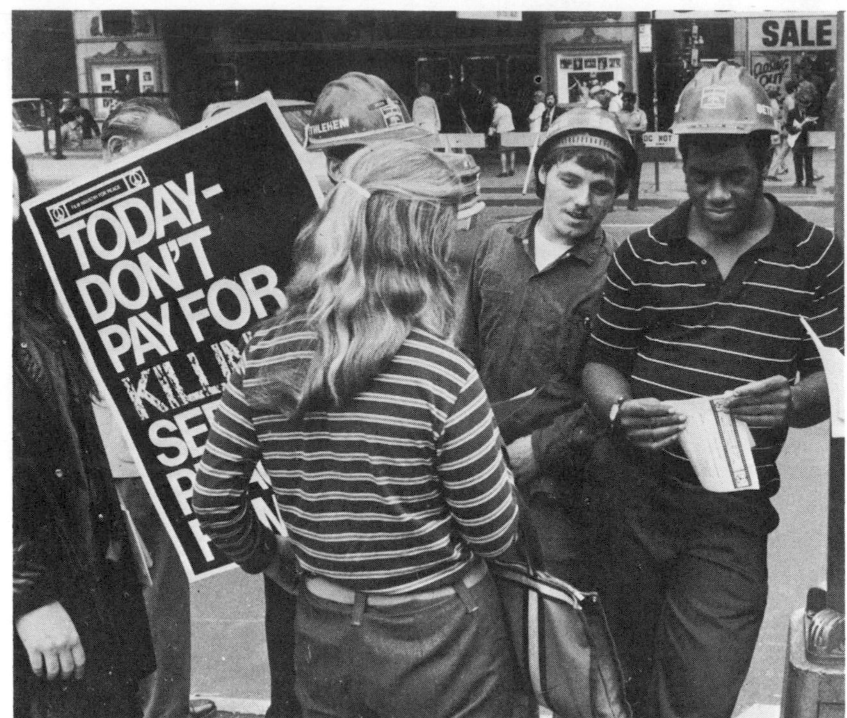

Thousands of people in the book publishing and film industries in New York City stopped work for one day in June to campaign for peace candidates and to distribute books and leaflets against the Indochina war.
"THE NEW YORK TIMES"

copies while 'The American Heritage Dictionary of the English Language', which led the nonfiction list, sold 440,000.

Leading the hardcover fiction list following 'Portnoy's Complaint' were 'The Godfather', by Mario Puzo; 'The Love Machine', by Jacqueline Susann; 'The Inheritors', by Harold Robbins; 'The Andromeda Strain', by Michael Crichton; 'The Seven Minutes', by Irving Wallace; and 'Naked Came the Stranger', by Penelope Ashe.

The top hardcover nonfiction titles after 'The American Heritage Dictionary of the English Language' were 'In Someone's Shadow', by Rod McKuen; 'The Peter Principle', by Laurence P. Peter and Raymond Hull; 'Between Parent and Teenager', by Dr. Haim G. Ginott; 'The Graham Kerr Cookbook', by the Galloping Gourmet; 'The Selling of the President 1968', by Joe McGinniss; and 'Miss Craig's 21-Day Shape-Up Program for Men and Women', by Marjorie Craig.

The paperback best sellers in 1969 followed general trends. Books that sold well in hardcover did even better in paper, an example being 'Couples', by John Updike. The demand for publication of black history, culture, and literature paid off with several best sellers, including books by such black writers as LeRoi Jones, Malcolm X, and Eldridge Cleaver. In June it was announced that James Parton would leave his job as president of American Heritage Publishing Co., Inc., to take a new position as president of Encyclopædia Britannica Educational Corp., an affiliate of Encyclopædia Britannica, Inc. (*See also* Literature. *See in* CE: Books and Bookmaking.)

PUERTO RICO. There was considerable controversy in Puerto Rico in 1970 over the future status of the island. Although the majority of citizens appeared to be satisfied with the commonwealth relationship with the United States, Gov. Luis A. Ferré and his New Progressive party advocated full statehood. Some radical groups resorted to burnings, bombings, and hotly worded propaganda to draw attention to their pro-independence movement. Moreover, the national status issue was a prime topic of dispute at the University of Puerto Rico, and student demonstrations on occasion disrupted the academic routine.

Governor Ferré, a personal friend of U.S. President Richard M. Nixon, continued to advocate the possibility of gaining the presidential vote for his countrymen. His political opponents saw this measure as a move that would ultimately lead to statehood, and they made preparations to resist.

During the year the citizens of the island of Culebra (population 887), a municipality of Puerto Rico 22 miles to the east of the main island, reaffirmed their commitment to fight the U.S. Navy's scheme to take over an additional one third of the land holdings there. The Navy, which uses Culebra for training facilities, had been trying, without success, to buy the entire island for the past 15 years.

In August the Ferré government approved a plan to expropriate approximately 12,000 acres of sugarcane fields and a mill belonging to the Aguirre Co. The move was justified by the government as a necessary step to cut unemployment and bolster the economy. (*See in* CE: Puerto Rico.)

RACE RELATIONS. Progress in U.S. race relations suffered in 1970 because of the black community's loss of confidence in the Administration of U.S. President Richard M. Nixon. In particular, the Department of Health, Education, and Welfare (HEW) and the Department of Justice were criticized during the year.

In February, Leon E. Panetta, chief civil rights officer for HEW, resigned his post, charging that political pressures had been influencing the enforcement of civil rights laws and had forced him to resign. Two weeks later, two more high officials of the same office resigned, while 125 other staff members sent a letter of protest to President Nixon. Their protest was echoed by 2,000 HEW employees, who presented a petition to HEW Secretary Robert H. Finch demanding he explain the department's position on civil rights enforcement and on Panetta.

A legal suit sponsored by the National Association for the Advancement of Colored People (NAACP) was filed against HEW in federal district court in Washington, D.C., in October. The suit charged HEW with general and calculated default in its enforcement of federal school desegregation guidelines.

Presidential adviser Daniel P. Moynihan sent a memo to President Nixon in January suggesting that the issue of race might benefit from a period of "benign neglect." The idea angered civil rights leaders, who called Moynihan's suggestion "symptomatic of a calculated, aggressive, and systematic" effort by the Nixon Administration to "wipe out" nearly two decades of civil rights gains. Moynihan insisted he had merely meant that a "lowering of voices" on the race issue might be a good idea.

Just before President Nixon was to issue a statement on school desegregation in March, John D. Ehrlichman, assistant to the president for domestic affairs, said that he opposed integration that served the social purpose of mixing races without improving educational standards. The president's policy statement on school desegregation was dismissed by many civil rights advocates as rhetorical and lacking in substance or determination to end segregation. The U.S. Commission on Civil Rights, an independent federal agency, said Nixon's statement was inadequate and overcautious and might even signal a major retreat.

Delivering the keynote address to the annual convention of the NAACP in June, Bishop Stephen G. Spottswood, chairman of the board, denounced the Nixon Administration as anti-Negro and refused to retract his charge in the face of Administration remonstrance. His charge and public reaction to it were taken as signs that black moderates as well as black radicals had lost faith in the Administration.

In October, the U.S. Commission on Civil Rights issued a report of a six-month study in which it found that there had been a "major breakdown" in enforcement of federal laws and executive orders against racial discrimination. The commission noted progress in extending civil rights in the areas of public accommodations (restaurants, hotels, etc.), voting, and education in the South, but it found civil rights enforcement lacking in employment, housing, and federally assisted programs.

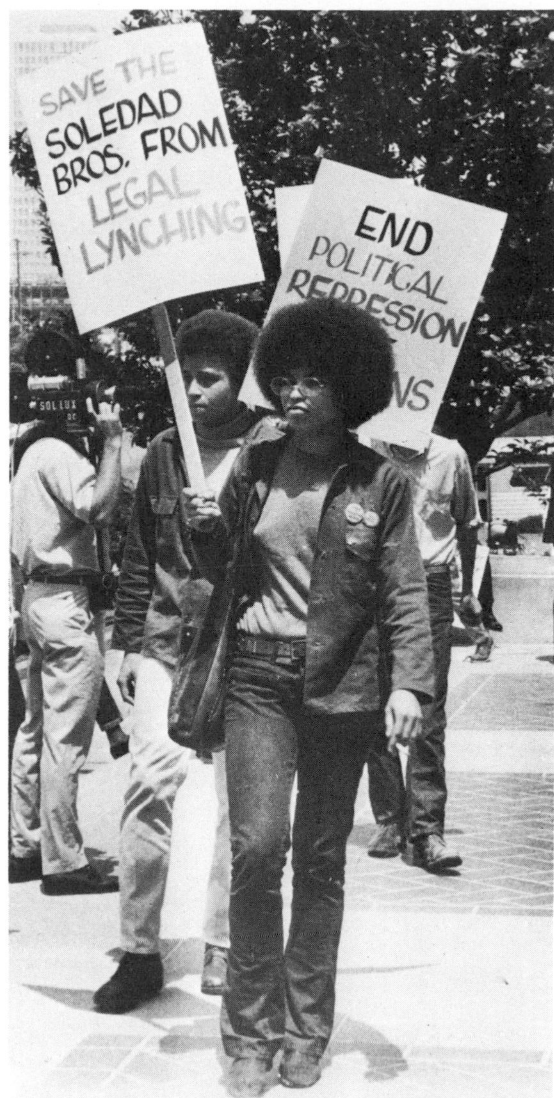

WIDE WORLD

Angela Davis pickets to support the imprisoned "Soledad brothers." Later in the year she was arrested on charges of murder and kidnapping stemming from the deaths of four persons in the San Rafael, Calif., courthouse. Allegedly she supplied guns to Jonathan Jackson, who was killed attempting to help prisoners escape.

Blacks and civil rights advocates were further disheartened by President Nixon's nomination of Judge G. Harrold Carswell to the U.S. Supreme Court in January. During Senate debate on his confirmation, it was found that Carswell had championed segregation during his 1948 political campaign and had been instrumental in incorporating a recreation area into a private club for whites only, after the club had been ordered to desegregate its facilities. Carswell's rejection by the Senate was considered a victory for the cause of civil rights and a repudiation of Administration policy, but the president's support of Carswell in the face of Carswell's record on segregation increased black mistrust of the president.

Other Education News

The issue of school desegregation remained a major matter of contention in 1970. In February Senator Abraham A. Ribicoff (D, Conn.) made a Senate speech indicting *de facto* school segregation in the North as well as *de jure* segregation in the South. Senator Ribicoff pointed out that in Northern cities, ghetto children attend poor schools in the center of the city while suburban children attend good schools, and thus the effect is the same as if the schools were segregated by law. A nationwide survey of recently integrated school systems in smaller cities reported in October that black children's achievement had improved, that white children's achievement was unimpaired, and that racial attitudes and relations had improved in the schools surveyed.

In May, however, the Justice Department advocated allowing tax-exempt status for the segregated private schools recently instituted in the South to avoid federal desegregation orders. After a series of critics, including former Attorney General Ramsey Clark, had denounced Nixon Administration school desegregation policies in testimony before the Senate's Select Committee on Equal Educational Opportunity, Attorney General John N. Mitchell assured the committee in August that federal school desegregation rules would be decisively enforced in the fall. Meanwhile, the Internal Revenue Service announced that the disputed exemptions would be revoked and that contributions to segregated private schools, on which the schools generally depended, would no longer be deductible from federal income tax.

President Nixon asked Congress for $1.5 billion over a period of two years to help pay the costs of school desegregation. He originally announced that the $500 million considered necessary for the first year would be diverted from other domestic programs but later said that only $150 million could be provided in that way, leaving Congress to find the rest.

White opposition to school desegregation was still strong enough to provoke riot. In Lamar, S.C., three buses carrying black children to a newly inte-

Ralph Abernathy (wearing cross), president of the Southern Christian Leadership Conference, and Leonard Woodcock, president of the United Automobile Workers, join hands to help carry coffins in remembrance of the deaths of black people at Augusta, Ga., and at Jackson State University.

UPI COMPIX

ILKA HARTMANN FROM B.B.M. ASSOCIATES

A rally was held in February in San Francisco, Calif., on behalf of Black Panther leaders Huey P. Newton, then in prison, and Eldridge Cleaver, who continued his exile in Algeria. Newton was freed from prison later in the year but faced a second trial on murder charges.

grated school in March were attacked by a mob of whites with baseball bats. State police rescued the children; then the mob overturned two of the buses before it was dispersed. In Trenton, N.J., experimental bussing in the fall of black children to previously all-white schools resulted in the familiar scene of white parents trying forcibly to stop black children from entering a school.

Discrimination in the Military

The military services, particularly the U.S. Army, previously considered less discriminatory than civilian society, were reported in 1970 to be having serious and widespread race problems. An Army survey on racial tensions conducted in 1969 was released in January; it suggested that black soldiers were losing faith in the Army's intent or ability to be fair and unprejudiced. In the Seventh Army in Europe, many company officers reported their biggest problem to be race relations. General James H. Polk, commander in chief of the U.S. Army in Europe, authorized special squads to make spot checks throughout the command to ensure that there was no discrimination. But especially among first-term enlisted men who brought their black pride and white hostility into the Army, incidents that otherwise would have been considered personal often ended up as racial confrontations.

Black and white GIs fought each other and rioted at a barracks in West Berlin, Germany, in August. Throughout West Germany, military police escorting black prisoners to the stockade for various offenses were often attacked by groups of black soldiers and the prisoners freed.

San Rafael, Soledad, and Angela Davis

Jonathan Jackson, 17, a black, attempted a daring escape for three convicts in the San Rafael, Calif., courthouse. Jackson and three other persons were shot and killed during the incident. Black militant Angela Davis was arrested and charged with murder and kidnapping for allegedly supplying Jackson with guns. The authorities attempted to make a connection between this incident and the case of the "Soledad brothers."

George Jackson (brother of Jonathan), Fleeta Drumgo, and John Clutchette were three black inmates of Soledad prison in California. They had been charged with the murder of a white guard—who was killed after three black inmates were found slain—and placed in solitary confinement incommunicado. They claimed that witnesses could affirm their innocence, and the case of the Soledad brothers became important in the black community and in radical political circles. Because Jonathan and George Jackson were brothers, the authorities speculated that Jonathan's actions in the courthouse were designed to gain hostages to exchange for the Soledad brothers. Miss Davis was a vocal supporter of the three "brothers."

Racial Disturbances

Early in May, a march protesting the fatal beating of a black youth in a county jail in Augusta, Ga., resulted in a race riot in that city in which six blacks were shot and killed. Autopsies showed that all six had been shot in the back, and eyewitnesses reported that at least three had been bystanders and that none had been armed. Two white policemen were indicted by a federal grand jury as a result.

Two black students were killed by state police at Jackson State College, Jackson, Miss., during a demonstration on the night of May 14–15. Police claimed they opened fire on a women's dormitory because of sniper fire, but neither witnesses, nor an FBI report, nor a tape recording of the police radio transmissions during the critical time substantiated their story. Black leaders noted with dismay that public indignation was scant compared to the outcry over the killing of four white students at Kent State University in Ohio ten days earlier.

Major U.S. cities were generally free from racial violence in 1970; small cities and towns were not. New Bedford, Mass.; Lima, Ohio; Fort Lauderdale, Fla.; Asbury Park, N.J.; Cairo, Ill.; and many other smaller cities had riots and confrontations during the year.

Black Panthers

Black militants and radicals charged that local and national police authorities were waging a campaign to exterminate them in 1970. Militants fought police in Houston, Tex., and in Detroit, Mich., and police raided Black Panther party centers in Philadelphia, Pa. Meanwhile, a federal grand jury found that Chicago police had grossly exaggerated the resistance of the Black Panthers in the Dec. 4, 1969, raid in which Fred Hampton and Mark Clark were killed. The jury said it did not have enough evidence to indict because the other Panthers in the raid refused to testify.

Eight Black Panthers, including Bobby Seale, the national chairman, were indicted and being tried separately in New Haven, Conn., for the murder of a black informer. As the trial of the first defendant, Lonnie McLucas, opened, Kingman Brewster, Jr., president of Yale University in New Haven, stated that he was "skeptical of the ability of black revolutionaries to achieve a fair trial anywhere in the United States." However, when McLucas' trial was over, McLucas himself called it fair.

In February a pretrial hearing began in New York City for 13 Black Panthers accused of conspiring to bomb public buildings. The judge halted the hearing because of unruly behavior by some of the defendants, but the hearing resumed in April despite the defendants' refusal to sign a pledge that they would abide by standard U.S. courtroom procedure. (*See also* Indians, American.)

WIDE WORLD

The Rollerslide is one of many interesting pieces of play equipment at Flamingo Park in Miami Beach, Fla.

RECREATION. In what must have been the most unusual recreational event of 1970, 18 skydivers bailed out of three small airplanes over the San Francisco Bay area in July. Starting at 13,500 feet, they made contact with one another at 4,500 feet to lock hands in a huge circle, holding this position for a drop of 1,000 feet. They claimed, justifiably, the world's record for formation jumping. A photographer, Ray Cottingham, jumped too and caught the scene with a camera mounted on his helmet. All landed safely.

Three balloonists who set off from a field near East Hampton, L.I., N.Y., on September 20 to cross the Atlantic Ocean, hoping to set a distance record (3,000 miles), were not so fortunate. On departure the three were toasted with champagne by well-wishers, who watched as a northeasterly wind carried them aloft in their 80-foot-high, class 8 balloon, named *The Free Life*. The following day a final radio dispatch from the balloonists said that they were at 600 feet and descending into the ocean in a rainstorm. The Coast Guard failed to find any of them. The balloon was said to be carrying 4,500 pounds of emergency gear (including a gallon jug of 30-year-old cognac), and the balloon's gondola was supposed to have been able to float in the event that the balloon went down at sea.

Other recreationists were taking to the air in more conventional ways. The number of people who were amateur pilots flying for fun was conservatively estimated at 200,000. Campers and skiers who wanted to get away from the crowds often found that the only way to get to an isolated mountaintop was by plane. Because of the number of golfers who fly private planes, many country clubs were forced to build landing strips adjacent to the golf courses.

Snowmobiles were increasingly involved in accidents in 1970. A selling point about the snowmobiles—and they continued to be the fastest-selling recreational vehicle (500,000 were sold during the 1969–70 winter season)—was their speed and maneuverability. The original models went only 30 mph, but 1970 models went 50 to 60 mph, an "improvement" that did not make for safety. (*See also* Camping; Hobbies; Travel; other sports articles.)

REFUGEES. During 1970, a steady increase of refugees in many areas led to a further intensification and broadening of the efforts of the United Nations High Commissioner for Refugees (UNHCR). At the same time, projects negotiated or actually started in preceding years were being implemented. Once again, the major part of the refugee problem of concern to the UNHCR was centered on Africa; the UNHCR's activities covered well over one million refugees on that continent.

In Asia the UNHCR's concern continued to be essentially with some 60,000 Tibetans in India and Nepal and some 80,000 Chinese in Macao. Moreover, the governments of Cambodia and South Vietnam also turned to the UNHCR in their attempts to solve the plight of some recently uprooted groups, some of whom came within the UNHCR's scope.

A highly publicized international incident involving a would-be defector occurred on November

Heavy fighting in Cambodia in the spring created a refugee problem of epidemic proportions for the new Cambodian regime. Villagers displaced by the fighting fled their homes and took shelter wherever they could. These people have taken refuge in a pagoda.

"THE NEW YORK TIMES"

23 off Gay Head, Mass., a town on the island of Martha's Vineyard. A Soviet seaman, Simas Kudirka, was denied political asylum by the officers of the U.S. Coast Guard cutter *Vigilant* after he jumped onto that ship from a Soviet fishing vessel. The sailor, a Lithuanian radioman, was instead handed over to Soviet guards who were permitted to board the cutter and seize him. The two ships were moored alongside each other while talks were going on pertaining to the Cape Cod fishing trade. Three Coast Guard officers involved in the decision to deny political asylum to Kudirka were later relieved of their duties pending an investigation of the incident. Lithuanian Americans protested the U.S. actions. A Coast Guard board of inquiry recommended court-martial for two of the officers, but Secretary of Transportation John A. Volpe overruled the board and allowed the two men to retire. The third man, the commander of the cutter, was transferred to another post.

PICTORIAL PARADE

The Rev. Carl McIntire, a fundamentalist preacher, leads a parade in Washington, D.C., in April to support the Vietnam war.

RELIGION. In 1970 there was a general decline of interest and participation in organized religion in the United States. Church attendance was down, and nearly all of the major denominations reported losses in membership. Statistical reports revealed that for the first time in history Roman Catholics and Lutherans showed slight losses. The Mormons and the Baptists, however, had slight membership gains, and studies indicated that evangelical and fundamentalist groups were growing.

Grace is said before dinner at the Riverside, Calif., home of the Rev. and Mrs. Sean Longacre. They have made their house a refuge for young people needing help.

WIDE WORLD

Another index of the health of the institutional church is the record of individual religious contributions. In its annual report, *Giving—USA*, the American Association of Fund-Raising Counsel, Inc., said that despite the decline in church attendance, religious contributions had increased "because the person who goes to church offers more [than in the past]." Local Protestant church bodies were getting more of this money, but the national organizations were not benefiting. Such interdenominational groups as the National Council of the Churches of Christ in the U.S.A. and the World Council of Churches showed deteriorating financial pictures. Budget cuts were common.

The decline in institutional loyalties was also reflected in the religious press. The Catholic Press Association, which compiles figures for Catholic newspapers and magazines, reported a circulation decline of 7.3%, while the Associated Church Press, which has a largely Protestant and Orthodox membership, reported a circulation loss of 5.6%.

A study by the U.S. Department of Commerce indicated that the amount of money spent on general church and synagogue construction had decreased steadily during the last five years. High interest rates were cited as a major reason. Not mentioned by the Commerce Department was the decision of many churches that they should not sink large sums of money into buildings, but rather expend money on social programs of various kinds.

Ecumenism

The general feeling among many theologians, scholars, and others interested in the unity of all

Christendom has been that ecumenical progress has slowed considerably. Nevertheless, the usual number of interdenominational meetings and discussions took place in 1970. Catholic and Baptist scholars met to consider their differences and emerged from the discussions with an "optimistic consensus" recommending further cooperation, especially on social questions. In May participants in the Episcopal-Catholic dialogue said they had uncovered no theological reason why the two traditions cannot eventually reach "full communion and organic union." Dialogue groups involving Catholics, Lutherans, and Orthodox Christians have reached agreement in many areas of doctrine and theological belief.

The outstanding move for church unity occurred in March when representatives of nine Protestant denominations met in St. Louis, Mo., to draft plans for their proposed merger. The new church of more than 25 million members would bear the name Church of Christ Uniting. All the churches must first study over a two-year period the proposed Plan of Union prepared by the Consultation on Church Union (COCU) study group. The document will then go back for necessary redrafting, after which the nine church bodies must vote on whether or not to accept the Plan of Union. If action is favorable on the part of any two of the nine churches, the Church of Christ Uniting will officially come into being by the latter part of the decade.

Despite the enthusiasm of the delegates to the COCU, many observers felt that this type of church unity through denominational merger had passed its day. There was a widespread feeling among younger churchmen that the attempt to reform archaic structures was energy wasted. These younger, antiestablishment leaders are creating new ecumenical patterns that do not conform to official lines.

The year 1970 was one of crisis for the National Council of Churches. The council, largest U.S. ecumenical agency, represents 33 church bodies, with more than 42 million members. It is now engaged in drafting plans for major reform to meet the criticisms of liberals and conservatives alike. Social activists believe that the Council leadership does not reflect local theological perspectives, which tend to be less ecumenical and less liberal. The crisis was reflected in a severe budget deficit in 1970. Many churchmen thought that the council in its present form would not survive through 1971.

Social and Political Concerns

Several developments on the national scene caused deep concern among religious leaders. The abortion reform bills passed by many states raised strong criticism from Catholic leaders, notably Terence Cardinal Cooke of New York and Patrick Cardinal O'Boyle of Washington, D.C. Orthodox rabbis also condemned the new legislation.

Compulsory chapel attendance at the nation's three military academies came under judicial scrutiny when the American Civil Liberties Union filed a suit in behalf of undergraduates who maintained that their 1st Amendment guarantees were being violated. Top military officials, including Adm. Thomas H. Moorer, chairman of the Joint Chiefs of Staff, testified that compulsory attendance was part of the military's leadership training for future officers. The court ruled in favor of the academies, despite strenuous objections on the part of several church bodies.

In another highly significant court decision, the U.S. Supreme Court voted 7–1 to uphold the tax exemption on church property used for religious purposes. Critics of the exemption had held that it violated the 1st Amendment by indirectly constituting state support of religion. Since the new ruling applied only to property used for religious purposes, there was still some question about other income-producing church holdings. Several suits challenging these tax-sheltered enterprises were in the lower courts at the end of the year. (*See also* Supreme Court of the U.S.)

Rabbi Abel Respes, one of the few blacks to become rabbis, speaks in his New Jersey synagogue to a small congregation of blacks of the Jewish faith.
WIDE WORLD

JUDAISM

Jewish identity, particularly among Orthodox Jews, began to reassert itself in 1970. There was speculation among religious and lay leaders of the Jewish community that the decade of the 1970's may witness great strides in this direction.

In the early part of the year, debate arose on the question of how to define a Jew. The controversy was sparked by a decision made in January by the Israeli High Court. The court held that anyone could claim Jewish identity, even if he rejected Judaism as a religion. The decision, which broadened the traditional religion-based definition, drew protest from Jewish leaders. The Rabbinical Council of America, largest U.S. Orthodox rabbinic body, objected on the grounds that the ruling defined Jewish identity in nationalistic rather than religious terms. Almost immediately, the Israeli cabinet acted to reverse the controversial decision. The cabinet voted to accept an amendment declaring that only the child of a Jewish mother or a convert to the Jewish religion could be registered as a Jew in the population register. In later court action, a dispute arose over the acceptance of conversions performed in Israel by non-Orthodox rabbis.

In the United States, several advances were made against laws discriminatory to members of the Jewish faith. In New York City an Orthodox employee was denied permission to wear a skullcap while on the floor of the stock exchange. After a complaint to the city's Commission on Human Rights, the exchange relented and issued a memorandum allowing the wearing of skullcaps for religious purposes.

Jewish observance of the sabbath was another subject of dispute. The National Jewish Commission on Law and Public Affairs won a judgment against a New York company that had discriminated against a sabbath observer. The commission was also instrumental in getting the New York State Unemployment Bureau to continue payments to persons who would not accept jobs requiring work on the sabbath and other Jewish holy days.

As in previous years, there was widespread public concern over reports of repression and ill-treatment of Jews living in the Soviet Union. In a Passover observance in New York City, some 20,000 persons staged a march on the Soviet Mission to the United Nations. A spokesman for the marchers read a statement calling for restoration of the cultural, religious, and educational rights of Soviet Jewry. In May, faculty members from more than 100 U.S. colleges and universities joined to issue a "declaration of solidarity with Soviet Jews." At the same time a display of reputedly anti-Semitic Soviet newspaper cartoons drew wide attention at a New York City exhibit.

PROTESTANTISM

During 1970, perhaps the biggest news for U.S. Protestants was the number of clergymen seeking elective office. Among the most prominent was Episcopal clergyman John C. Danforth, Republican attorney general of Missouri, who was defeated in his bid for the U.S. Senate by Stuart Symington, the incumbent Democrat. In Connecticut, Joseph Duffey, United Church of Christ clergyman and a Democratic nominee, lost in a three-way race for the Senate. However, not all clerical candidates were defeated.

New church leaders were chosen by several Protestant denominations. The Southern Baptists elected as president the Rev. Carl Bates, pastor of the First Baptist Church of Charlotte, N.C. Although considered more moderate than his predecessor, Bates was not expected to lead the denomination in overcoming the traditional policies of segregation practiced by local congregations.

David O. McKay, 96, prophet, revelator, and president of the Church of Jesus Christ of Latter-day Saints (Mormons) for 19 years, died in January. During McKay's tenure, church membership nearly tripled and the first sacred Mormon temples were established in Europe. The quorum of the 12 apostles, governing body of the church, elected Joseph Fielding Smith, 93, to be the denomination's tenth president. Smith, a strict theologian, was known throughout the Mormon world for his writings justifying the tradition that bars blacks from the Mormon priesthood. Church liberals, hopeful that the ban might soon be lifted, were not encouraged by Smith's election.

One of the most notable meetings of the year was the 20th biennial congress of the Greek Orthodox Church of North and South America. Gathered in New York City were 1,000 lay and clerical delegates, representing 500 parishes throughout the Western Hemisphere. Addressing the group, Archbishop Iakovos, primate of North and South America, called for a series of reforms to make the church more relevant to its American setting. Among the major reforms approved was a resolution permitting the substitution of English and other vernacular languages for Greek in the liturgies. Iakovos also called on the American churches to seek greater autonomy from the ecumenical patriarchate in Istanbul, Turkey.

Many denominations and their local congregations were beginning to feel pressure from the women's liberation movement. Women's caucuses were formed in nearly all the major Protestant churches. Episcopal women won a major battle in securing voting rights in the House of Deputies, the clergy-lay assembly of the church's General Convention.

Most traditional Protestant churches were also under attack to admit women to the ministry, though several—including the United Methodist church, the United Presbyterian church, and the United Church of Christ—already do so. To these growing ranks were added the Lutheran Church in America and the American Lutheran church, which approved measures allowing women to be ordained as ministers. The Episcopal church defeated a similar measure during the year, but voted to permit women to become deacons.

ROMAN CATHOLICISM

Bitter division on the subject of clerical celibacy threatened the unity of the church during 1970. In February the pope strongly affirmed his position, stating that celibacy was a fundamental principle of the church, and one that could neither be abandoned nor even be "put to discussion." One month before, the Dutch Pastoral Council had voted for the abolition of compulsory celibacy for priests. The pope rejected the Dutch proposals, though he reluctantly aired the possibility of ordaining men already married, but only in very special circumstances. The question was still scheduled to be on the agenda for the synod of the church, to meet in Rome in the fall of 1971.

While remaining adamant on the celibacy issue, the pope did amend the traditional church position on marriages of mixed faiths. In a 2,400-word statement, Pope Paul VI eliminated the requirement that the non-Catholic partner of the marriage promise orally to raise the offspring in the Catholic faith. Regulations for authority to grant dispensations for mixed marriages were also eased.

Dissidence within the church continued in 1970. In France, 44 priests left the ministry, declaring that they could "no longer in conscience accept a great many of the present structures of the church." An international meeting of dissident priests took place in Amsterdam, Netherlands, in September–October. Participants voted overwhelmingly in favor of ending compulsory celibacy for priests. There was talk of modifying or abolishing the concordat in Portugal and Spain, where many priests involved in the Basque nationalist movement had been arrested.

Roman Catholic churchmen of many nations entered even more deeply into political activities during the year. In Latin America there was much discussion of "the theology of revolution." Conflicts were particularly harsh in Paraguay and Argentina. Two priests, Fernando Carbone and Fulgencio Alberto Rojas, were arrested and charged with being accomplices in the murder of a former president of Argentina, Gen. Pedro Eugenio Aramburu. In Brazil there were reports that priests and nuns were among political prisoners subjected to torture. Another church-state clash occurred in Rhodesia where the bishops protested vigorously against the Land Tenure Act passed by the government of Prime Minister Ian D. Smith.

There was continuing polarization among U.S. Catholics, who were found on all sides in social and political debates. Daniel and Philip Berrigan, two priests well known in the antiwar movement, were arrested during the year and sentenced to prison for destroying draft records. After a dramatic escape from a rally at Cornell University, Daniel Berrigan managed to elude federal authorities for four months, during which time he was sheltered in the homes of friends and sympathizers.

(*continued on page 412*)

WIDE WORLD

The Most Rev. James E. Walsh (right) arrives in New York City on August 31 after his release from Communist China. The Roman Catholic bishop was in prison in China for 12 years.

Benjamín Mendoza y Amor (far right) is restrained from attacking Pope Paul VI with a dagger. The assailant wore a priest's cassock in order to approach the papal party. The attack took place shortly after the pope landed at the airport in Manila, Philippines. The assailant stepped out of a massive crowd of Filipinos who had broken through police lines to get closer to the pope.

UPI COMPIX

Special Report: The New English Bible

by Basil Willey,
Professor Emeritus of English Literature,
Cambridge University, England

COOKSON, "LONDON DAILY MAIL," FROM BEN ROTH AGENCY

"In the beginning it was real cool, man, and there was no action at the scene . . . !"

On March 16, 1970, 'The New English Bible' (with the Apocrypha) was published jointly by the Oxford and Cambridge university presses. Sponsored by the major Protestant churches of Great Britain, the book is an entirely new translation of the Bible from the original Hebrew, Aramaic, and Greek texts, and the project took 24 years to complete. The New Testament section first appeared in 1961 and had sold approximately 7 million copies (more than 2.7 million in the United States) by early 1970.

Translating the Bible into English raises all the issues involved in the translation of any ancient text, but it raises them in a special form. This is because of the special, the unique, part played by Holy Scripture in the spiritual and cultural history of Western civilization. However hard we may try to treat the Bible—in Benjamin Jowett's phrase—"like any other book," this can be done only within strict limits. No "other book" has been to Christendom what the Bible has been, namely the "word of God"; the purveyor of saving truth; the rule of faith; the supreme authority in doctrine; a means of grace; and a source of comfort, guidance, or admonition. Indeed, it is precisely because the Bible has been all these things, because it has been held to be (or to contain) God's revelation of truths beyond the reach of human reason, that it is considered worthwhile (or indeed essential) to put it into contemporary language. Otherwise, it might just as well be preserved as a historic monument, a masterpiece of Tudor-Elizabethan prose.

Already, in what has just been said, the main problem underlying the whole project has been indicated. Was the enterprise necessary, or justifiable? We already had, in the 1611, or King James, version, a translation whose superlative qualities were universally acknowledged and whose words, phrases, and rhythms have long enriched the very bloodstream of English language and literature. Of the extraordinary hold exerted by this numinous book over the hearts and minds of Englishmen and (later) of all English-speaking peoples, the excellence of its literary quality is one chief cause. For this excellence we are indebted to the translators in 1611 themselves; to their most notable predecessors, William Tyndale and Miles Coverdale; and to the youthful vigor of the English language, of which as yet "custom had not bedimmed the lustre nor dried up the sparkle and the dewdrops." Moreover, the old translators achieved literary distinction largely because they were not self-consciously aiming at it. Convinced that they were dealing with the undoubted word of God, they concentrated upon rendering it faithfully and reverently, and the reward and outcome of their purity of intention was a style that reflected their own nobility. Like all good style, theirs was a by-product; aiming at truth, they achieved beauty without effort or contrivance. Never straining after effect, but imbued with a sense of the momentousness of their task, the translators worked humbly and self-effacingly; and the result is a style that, whether simple or elevated, is as genuine as seasoned timber, free from all that is tawdry or meretricious. To all this must be added the good fortune the English translators enjoyed in working when the language had not yet staled into jargon and cliché.

If, then, the old translation is so admirable, and if it has been so dear and so sacred to the hearts of many generations, what need was there for a modern version? The onus of demonstrating the need rested heavily upon those who promoted 'The New English Bible', and they, therefore, devoted most careful thought to the principle underlying it. They knew it was not likely that any version in 20th-century English, however "timeless," however scholarly, and however free from colloquialism or cliché, would have anything like the literary merit of the King James Version; should they not, then, by reducing its style to the level of contemporary speech or writing, reduce its spiritual influence as well? Granted that the Bible has a unique importance for the spiritual life, should they, by modernizing it, enhance that value, make it more attractive to more people? Or should they, in fact, cheapen and enervate it by robbing it of its antique patina? Misgivings of this kind, which as expected were voiced when the New Testament part appeared in 1961 (as they were even in 1611), were expressed in an able article in *The New Yorker* (Nov. 14, 1953) by Dwight Macdonald criticizing the American Revised Standard Version of 1952. The new version, he said, may make the Bible more "accessible" to the modern reader or listener; it may "slip more smoothly into the modern ear, but it also slides out more easily; the very strangeness and antique ceremony of the old forms made them linger in the mind." Macdonald illustrated his point with some examples: "Thus saith the Lord," for instance, is more impressive and "lordly" than "Thus says the Lord"; "Thou shalt not" is more awesome than "Do not"; and "Hast thou given the horse strength? hast thou clothed his neck with thunder? . . . the glory of his nostrils is terrible. . . . "—this is wilder, more passionate, more poetic than "Do you give the horse his might? Do you clothe his neck with strength? . . . His majestic snorting is terrible" (Job xxxix, 19–20). Macdonald compares reading the Revised Standard Version with walking through the streets of a bombed city: "Is this gone? Does that still survive? Surely they might have spared *that*?"

This line of thought leads logically, if followed right on through, to the position that it does not much matter what is being said, or whether the translation is accurate, as long as the requisite numinous rumble is maintained. The effect, liturgically speaking, might be almost as good if the language were in fact entirely, instead of partially, unintelligible—indeed, not translated at all (I am thinking, naturally, of the uninstructed listener in saying this). It may be said—indeed, something like it has been said—that in the King James Version it sounds as if God were speaking, whereas in 'The New English Bible' the accents are those of English gentlemen, and dons at that. Such is the prestige of the King James Version that an extraordinarily large number of people seem to think, or unconsciously feel, that it *is* "The Bible," and that God himself spoke in Tudor English. This explains the many complaints that 'The New English Bible' translators have "altered" or "tampered with" "The Bible." As a matter of fact, of course, the whole translation was made directly from the best ancient texts into modern English, without dependence on the King James Version at all.

In any process of translation the aim may be primarily to translate the actual *words* of the original, or it may be to translate its *meanings*. The former method may yield what is called a faithful translation, and it was the one that the old translators, imbued as they were with rabbinical notions about the inspiration and sanctity of each Hebrew or Greek construction, word, letter, and even squiggle in the holy text, were inclined to follow. Its disadvantage is that the results may not be English at all, and may be unintelligible. The latter method, the one that must be adopted if the text is to read like something written in English, is the one followed by 'The New English Bible' translators who, free at last from fundamentalist presuppositions, saw it as their "most sacred duty to render [the ancient expressions] into their real modern equivalents," to borrow C. F. Moule's phrase.

One main hope behind 'The New English Bible' project was, then, that the new translation might reach a new reading public, most of whom (it was supposed) were repelled or baffled by the archaic style of the old. It was hoped that, finding that the Bible was no mere special preserve for parsons and pious highbrows but spoke to the public in their own language about things that mattered to them, they might be encouraged to read it.

(Adapted from 'Essays and Studies 1970', published by John Murray Ltd. for the English Association)

The Old Testament panel meets to work on its translation for 'The New English Bible', published jointly by the Cambridge and Oxford university presses.

AUTHENTICATED NEWS INTERNATIONAL

(*continued from page 409*)
While in flight, Berrigan gave interviews to journalists, wrote articles, and even made two public speeches.

In November the Roman Catholic world mourned the passing of Richard Cardinal Cushing, 75. He had served as archbishop of Boston from 1944 until his resignation in October 1970.

RETAIL TRADE. Despite a generally sluggish economy and continuing inflation, retail trade in the United States promised to show an increase in volume in 1970. The year began slowly as traditional January clearance sales failed to draw the expected response despite larger-than-usual markdowns. Sales climbed through the spring and summer, however, and in the month of July rose to a seasonally adjusted record of $30.74 billion, 6% above the figure for July 1969. For the first eight months of the year, chain stores and mail-order companies reported sales gains of more than 8% as their dollar volume for the period reached $19.9 billion. Consumer installment debt showed a parallel increase, reaching $99.3 billion at the end of July.

Retailers reported that late-summer sales of "back-to-school" merchandise were slower than in recent years, with boys' and men's wear moving marginally better than girls' and women's fashions. Sales of women's clothes were affected by slow acceptance of midi-length fashions. Some retailers, indeed, were heard to predict that the midi would prove to be "the Edsel of the fashion industry." (*See also* Fashion.)

Economic conditions—including "tight" money, high interest rates, and rising land, construction, and operating costs—led to a decrease in the rate of construction of new shopping centers, in recent years among the fastest-growing of retail outlets. About 600 new shopping centers were built in the United States and Canada in 1969, some 400 fewer than in 1968, and the International Council of Shopping Centers foresaw construction of about the same number in 1970. It expected construction to decline in 1971 and 1972.

During the year retailers in the United States voiced mounting concern over startling increases in shoplifting and in theft by employees. Many stores reported that shoplifting losses had risen to 4% or 5% of their total sales volume.

Surveys by a New York City-based security firm revealed astonishingly high percentages of sticky-fingered customers. One of every 12 customers in one New York City department store stole something; for a Boston, Mass., store the figure was one in 20, and for a Philadelphia, Pa., store, one in 10. It appeared that a preponderance of shoplifters were youths, though adult thieves tended to pilfer merchandise of greater value. As the use of drugs increased, it also appeared that a growing number of shoplifters—adults and youths alike—employed their gains to support their costly habits.

In self-defense, store operators stepped up anti-theft campaigns. Guards—uniformed ones to provide a deterrent to thieves, plainclothesmen to apprehend shoplifters—were hired in increasing number. Employees were trained and encouraged to be alert for potential shoplifters; and employees, since they account for a substantial portion of store thefts, were themselves kept under closer watch. Electronic theft-detection devices—such as special tags which set off alarms if merchandise bearing them was removed from a store—were increasingly employed. One large chain-store operator made available to stores its 250,000-name list of confessed shoplifters and light-fingered employees. Stores also prosecuted more shoplifters—though operators felt that, with few exceptions, the sentences given convicted shoplifters were too light to be an effective deterrent. (*See also* Consumer Protection; Economy; Food. *See in* CE: Trade.)

RHODESIA. On Jan. 1, 1970, Prime Minister Ian D. Smith claimed that in spite of United Nations economic sanctions Rhodesia was expected to have achieved a favorable balance of trade for the year 1969 and that a surge of economic expansion could be anticipated. Accurate figures on Rhodesia's economic position were hard to come by, however. Great Britain's foreign secretary, Michael Stewart, challenged Smith's optimistic view, stating that Rhodesia's declaration of a republic, on March 2, with Clifford Dupont as president, was illegal. The United States also announced that it would not recognize the Rhodesian government under any circumstances and after a brief hesitation submitted to British pressure and closed the consulate in Salisbury, the capital. A number of other countries closed their consulates, while still others reduced their staff or appointed honorary consuls. Only Portugal and South Africa retained their career representation at its former level.

The council of ministers of the Organization of African Unity, meanwhile, called on the powers to be prepared to use force to achieve a democratic solution in Rhodesia. At a press conference immediately after the declaration of the republic, Smith said he could not understand why the United

Clifford Dupont was sworn in as the first president of Rhodesia in a ceremony held April 16 at Government House in Salisbury.

WIDE WORLD

The making of sculpture is a successful commercial operation on this farm in Rhodesia. The figures had been produced on the farm for years, often by unemployed migrant laborers. An overseas market for their work provided employment and raised their standard of living.

UPI COMPIX

States and Great Britain wanted to destroy Rhodesia. He maintained that, though he considered the black and white races far apart in the process of civilization, Africans had been given 16 seats in the parliament, which in time might increase to 50.

The Rhodesian government judged from the results of the Conservative party conference, in October, that the new British government did not intend to be stampeded by those members of the party who were pressing for an immediate resumption of relations with Rhodesia. However, Britain's new foreign secretary, Sir Alec Douglas-Home, stated that another attempt would be made in due course to reopen negotiations.

Within Rhodesia itself, the multiracial Center party offered its loyalty to the sovereign independent state of Rhodesia. However, in the elections for parliament, held in April, the party failed to win even one of the British seats. All of these seats were captured by Smith's Rhodesian Front, which did not bother to contest the African seats.

Earlier, in January, guerrilla forces carried out raids across the Zambezi River involving attacks on the Victoria Falls airport and on a South African police detachment. Smith warned the Zambian government that essential power and transport services might be withheld if Zambia continued to harbor and assist terrorists and infiltrators. Although the raid caused consternation in Rhodesia, it seemed as if it might mark the end rather than the revival of military activity against Smith's government. Within the Zimbabwe African Peoples' Union (ZAPU), which had organized the attacks from across the Zambian border, divisions were already noticeable when the raid took place. In March James Chikerema, vice-president of ZAPU and the party's effective leader, in the absence of Joshua Nkomo, the detained president, admitted that the defections from his party were numerous and that the army was in disorder. Later in March Chikerema seized power and replaced the military command with a new command structure responsible to himself. As a result of the intervention of Zambia's President Kenneth Kaunda the dismissed war council was reinstated, but in April a number of violent clashes took place among the members of ZAPU.

In early October the government admitted that there was a serious shortage of foreign-exchange earnings. This meant that Rhodesia had difficulty in paying for the internal industrial expansion that the country so badly needed. Tobacco earnings abroad had been reduced virtually to nil as a result of sanctions, and mineral exports also were producing less foreign exchange than had been hoped. (*See also* Africa; Zambia. *See in* CE: Rhodesia.)

ROMANIA. The most significant event of 1970 in Romania was the severe spring flooding—the most devastating in the nation's history. From May 12–25, half of the country received between 21 and 27 gallons of rainfall per square yard, while in the other half the downpour averaged from 9 to 21 gallons. For nearly two months, Romania was ravaged by five successive waves of floods that caused at least 225 casualties and great material damage. By the end of May, farm output on some 2.1 million acres had been affected and 38,600 cattle drowned; production in about 390 industrial enterprises had been halted for weeks; in towns and villages almost 70,000 dwellings had been destroyed as well as nearly 2,300 bridges, large and small.

During this catastrophe Nicolae Ceausescu, Romania's Communist party first secretary, was called to Moscow May 18–19 to a lecture on the virtues of "proletarian internationalism." A week before,

WIDE WORLD

Debris is cleared during the flood in Galati, Romania. At least 225 persons were killed in the disaster, which began in May.

at the Warsaw, Poland, meeting of the Comecon, Romania refused to join the newly created International Investments Bank. For more than two years Romania argued with the Soviet Union about the terms of a new alliance treaty (the previous one, concluded for 20 years, was signed on Feb. 4, 1948). Ceausescu stood his ground, refusing to incorporate into the new treaty a formula with a smack of "Brezhnev doctrine," which says in effect that the Soviet Union has the right to intervene in the affairs of another Warsaw Pact country if socialism seems threatened—as in Czechoslovakia in 1968.

Both sides made concessions. In the preamble to the Soviet-Romanian treaty the principles of "socialist internationalism" are described with some vagueness; there is, for instance, no mention of the "international duty" to intervene in order to "protect the socialist gains," as is the case in the Soviet-Czechoslovak treaty of May 6, 1970. But the main pledge taken by Romania is expressed in terms almost identical to those of the Soviet-Czechoslovak treaty. In Article 7 of the 20-year Soviet-Romanian treaty (signed in Bucharest, the capital, on July 7 by the two premiers, Aleksei N. Kosygin and Ion Gheorghe Maurer), Romania expressed its firm determination to take jointly with other states of the Warsaw Treaty "all the measures necessary to prevent aggression . . . , to ensure the inviolability of the frontiers of the Warsaw Treaty member-states, and to repel an aggressor." Soviet Communist Party General Secretary Leonid I. Brezhnev, irritated by Ceausescu's hard bargaining, canceled his plan to go to Bucharest to personally sign the new Soviet-Romanian alliance.

Two other similar treaties were renewed by Romania: with Poland on November 12, on the occasion of a visit of Poland's Communist Party First Secretary Wladyslaw Gomulka and Premier Jozef Cyrankiewicz in Bucharest, and with Bulgaria on

Romania's Communist Party First Secretary Nicolae Ceausescu (right) and France's President Georges Pompidou review the troops during Ceausescu's visit to Paris in June.

AGIP FROM PICTORIAL PARADE

November 19 when Ceausescu visited Sofia, the Bulgarian capital. Ceausescu spent two weeks on a private visit to the United States; on October 19 he addressed the United Nations General Assembly, and on October 26 he was received by U.S. President Richard M. Nixon. (*See in* CE: Rumania.)

RUBBER. Figures were released in 1970 which disclosed that the world production of natural rubber in 1969 had risen to approximately 3.2 million tons, an increase of over 250,000 from 1968. Production for the first six months of 1970 was estimated at 1.5 million tons, up 39,000 tons from the corresponding period in 1969.

During the year Firestone Tire & Rubber Co. announced developments in both the creation and the destruction of the tire. By manufacturing a tire entirely by an injection process, the company created a revolutionary new tire. The tire carries the regular wire beads to hold it to the wheel rim but does not require carbon black in the tread and can, therefore, be colored. Firestone also piloted the operation of a plant to process scrap auto tires. Shredded tires are fed into a closed reactor and heated to boil off various components. The chemicals, gases, and oils are then collected for reuse.

The tire industry in the United States also felt the pressure of inflationary settlements during the year. Following a wage-hike settlement that was expected to cost the company $70 million over three years, the B. F. Goodrich Tire Co. announced an increase in its tire prices beginning in July. Passenger tire prices were increased by 5% and truck tires by 6%. Goodyear Tire & Rubber Co. also announced similar increases.

The rubber-footwear industry asserted that it was being greatly harmed by imports during 1970. The industry asked for quotas on imports, which took about 24% of the domestic market for footwear in 1969.

Worldwide, the total consumption of rubber was estimated at 3.3 million tons of natural rubber and 5.5 million tons of synthetic rubber in 1970. In 1969 around 77% of the total amount of rubber consumed in the United States was synthetic. (*See in* CE: Rubber.)

RWANDA. President Grégoire Kayibanda of Rwanda signed a treaty of friendship with King Baudouin I of Belgium during the latter's state visit to Rwanda during July 1970. The two also discussed Belgian aid to Rwanda, which in 1970 included not only $4 million but also 261 technicians, to be established at Murumbi, and 2,500 tons of wheat to relieve hunger in the densely populated areas.

A conference was set for late in 1970 to inaugurate the Common Organization for Economic Cooperation in Central Africa. Its members, Rwanda, Burundi, and the Democratic Republic of the Congo, had initiated the forming of the organization at a summit conference at Gisenyi, Rwanda, in December 1969, when the heads of the three states also adopted a resolution to establish greater unity.

International aid to Rwanda during 1970 included $2.4 million from the United Nations (UN) Industrial Development Organization for a pilot pyrethrum plant at Ruhengeri. The UN International Development Association gave $9.3 million for a road between Kigali (the capital) and Uganda.

Rwanda also joined 20 of the world's French-speaking nations in agreeing to form an agency for cultural and technical cooperation among the members. The 21 nations met at Niamey, Niger, in March. (*See in* CE: Rwanda.)

SAFETY. Automobile accidents were once again the biggest safety hazard in 1970, and auto manufacturers worked on further development of cars designed to allow occupants to survive a crash. The newest safety device for cars was the air bag.

Silent Sam, the mechanical flagman, stands on New York City's George Washington Bridge to warn motorists of highway construction sites.

"THE NEW YORK TIMES"

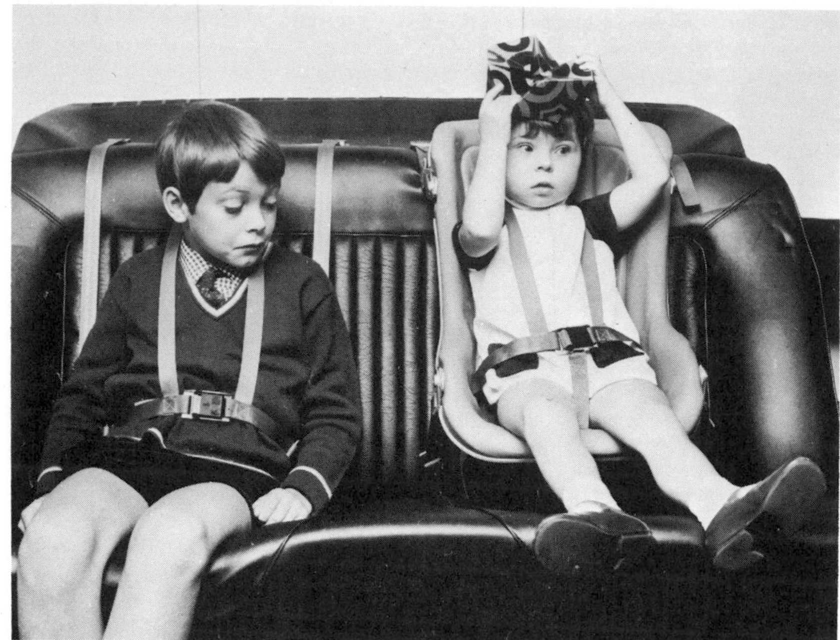

Two new safety devices to restrain children in the back seat of a car were marketed in England in August. One is a molded synthetic seat for young children (right); the other is a harness for children who have outgrown the seat.
KEYSTONE

Mounted inside the dashboard and in the steering column, the bag would automatically inflate during a car crash, catch the rider, and collapse after absorbing the rider's impact. Air bags, which are said to be as safe as wearing a lap and shoulder safety harness, must be installed in all cars sold in the United States starting July 1, 1973, by order of the U.S. Department of Transportation.

Another auto safety device displayed in 1970 was an electronic tester that flashes a series of numbers when the car's ignition key is turned on. If after three tries the driver cannot repeat the sequence of numbers by punching them in order on a row of buttons, the machine assumes the driver is too drunk to drive and will not allow the car to start for a half hour.

The National Safety Council reported that auto accidents caused 56,400 deaths in 1969. Traffic deaths claimed 475,000 lives during the period 1960–69, an increase of more than 25% over the preceding ten-year period. Cost of accidents for the 1960–69 period reached $89.6 billion, nearly twice what they cost for the preceding ten-year period. Disabling injuries during the year 1969 numbered 2 million; deaths increased 2% over 1968 to a total of 56,400 but declined 2% during the first six months of 1970 to 25,320. The death rate per 100,000 persons during 1969 was 27.9, and the death rate per 100 million vehicle miles was 5.3, compared to a rate of 7.59 in 1950.

The crash of a chartered bus near Allentown, Pa., in July, resulting in the deaths of seven schoolchildren from Long Island, N.Y., caused public concern about the safety of charter buses. It was found that some companies were operating buses without Interstate Commerce Commission certification and did not meet safety regulations. Charter buses carried more than 20 million passengers in 1969, and the business was estimated to be growing more than 10% annually.

Job safety was an important issue in 1970. The most recent estimates show that over 14,000 workers are killed and over 2 million injured every year in job-related accidents. The U.S. Congress considered alternate job-safety bills in response to U.S. President Richard M. Nixon's occupational health and safety message of August 1969. Unions advocated giving the U.S. Secretary of Labor the power to set and enforce safety standards, while industry preferred that this power be given to an independent board of experts.

The federal government implemented or considered other safety regulations in 1970. The Federal Coal Mine Health and Safety Act of 1969, which extended federal jurisdiction to surface mines and established safety standards and methods for their enforcement, became effective April 1; a Department of Commerce standard requiring testing of rugs and carpets for flammability was set to go into effect in April 1971; and a boat-safety act was studied by Congress. The National Commission on Product Safety presented a report of its two-year study and urged Congress to authorize mandatory federal safety standards for household products.

Deaths from accidents in the home continued to show a slight decline; the number dropped from 28,500 in 1968 to 27,000 in 1969, a decrease of 5%. Total for the first six months of 1970 was 13,500, down 2% from the same period in 1969.

The National Safety Council also reported that accidents in general claimed 1.05 million lives during the period 1960–69, an increase of more than 12% over the preceding ten-year period. Disabling injuries for the same two periods totaled 100 million and 93 million respectively. However, the accidental death rate declined steadily since 1950, except for an upswing during the middle 1960's. (*See in* CE: Safety.)

SAUDI ARABIA. During 1970 Saudi Arabia maintained its position as leader of the conservative forces in the Arab world. King Faisal continued to be strongly opposed to radical left-wing Arab factions and channeled his support for the Palestinian Arabs through Yasir Arafat's *al Fatah* organization.

Relations with Syria's leftist government, never friendly, were further strained in May when Syria refused to permit the repair of a pipeline used to carry oil from Saudi Arabia across Syria to Mediterranean ports. The pipeline was damaged by a bulldozer in Syrian territory. In retaliation, Saudi Arabia banned the entry of Syrian goods and vehicles and threatened to cut off aid to Jordan, the United Arab Republic (Egypt), and the Palestinian Arabs. Syria responded with a similar ban on Saudi goods and vehicles and raised tariffs on goods destined for Saudi Arabia. Syria foiled Saudi attempts to fly goods in from Lebanon by barring Saudi planes from flying over Syrian territory. Syria eased some of its restrictions in June.

During a revival of civil war in Yemen in February, Saudi Arabia aided the royalist side by supplying arms. However, following the reconciliation between Yemen's royalist and republican factions in May, Saudi Arabia recognized the republic and agreed to exchange ambassadors. The Saudis subsequently granted Yemen $20 million in aid.

The first conference of the foreign ministers of Islamic nations was opened by King Faisal in Jidda in March. The main business of the conference was the establishment of a permanent Islamic secretariat. The conference was attended by representatives of 22 nations and observers for the Palestinian Arabs, the Arab League, and some African states; Syria, Iraq, and Southern Yemen boycotted the meeting. The conference ended with a split between socialist and conservative forces over policies toward Israel. (*See also* Middle East. *See in* CE: Saudi Arabia.)

SCIENCE. Basic science research in the United States was suffering from lack of money in 1970. One science official after another bemoaned the tight science budgets, darkly hinting that the United States had or would soon become second best in some areas of science, particularly astronomy. Indeed, science project slowdowns or cutoffs were forcing many foreign scientists who contributed to the "brain drain" of some countries a few years before to look to their homelands again for jobs.

In the idyllic years of science before the present funding curtailment, jobs for scientists were abundant, especially in defense industries. By 1970, hard times had come to some recently graduated physics Ph.D.s. Jobs for them were so scarce that many had to take on postgraduate work at universities for subsistence.

Science too was losing its appeal among students. A growing number of them felt that scientists, by creating an awesome technology, bore some responsibility for environmental pollution, the threat of nuclear holocaust, and other societal plagues.

In February a new organization called the Council for Biology in Human Affairs was formed by 25 scientists, including 5 Nobel prizewinners. The purpose of the group is to promote consciousness among scientists, particularly biologists, of the political and social consequences of their endeavors. The council is under the sponsorship of the Salk Institute in La Jolla, Calif. It will focus on issues like biological warfare.

In August Lee A. DuBridge retired as science adviser to U.S. President Richard M. Nixon. DuBridge was replaced by Edward E. David, Jr., a Bell Telephone Laboratories computer specialist. The 45-year-old new presidential science adviser set an immediate goal of minimizing complaints among scientists over the recent de-emphasis on science in the federal budget.

More and more scientists were calling for a national science policy to establish priorities of research funding. The National Academy of Sciences (NAS) appeared willing to shoulder the task of establishing an overall science plan even though it had shunned activism in the past. In 1970 the influential Committee on Science and Public Policy of the NAS began to consider national scientific guidelines and goals. (*See in* CE: Science articles.)

SELECTIVE SERVICE. Curtis W. Tarr, assistant secretary of the U.S. Air Force for manpower and reserve affairs and former president of Lawrence University, at Appleton, Wis., became the director of the U.S. Selective Service System in

Curtis W. Tarr (right) became director of the Selective Service System, replacing Lieut. Gen. Lewis B. Hershey (left).

UPI COMPIX

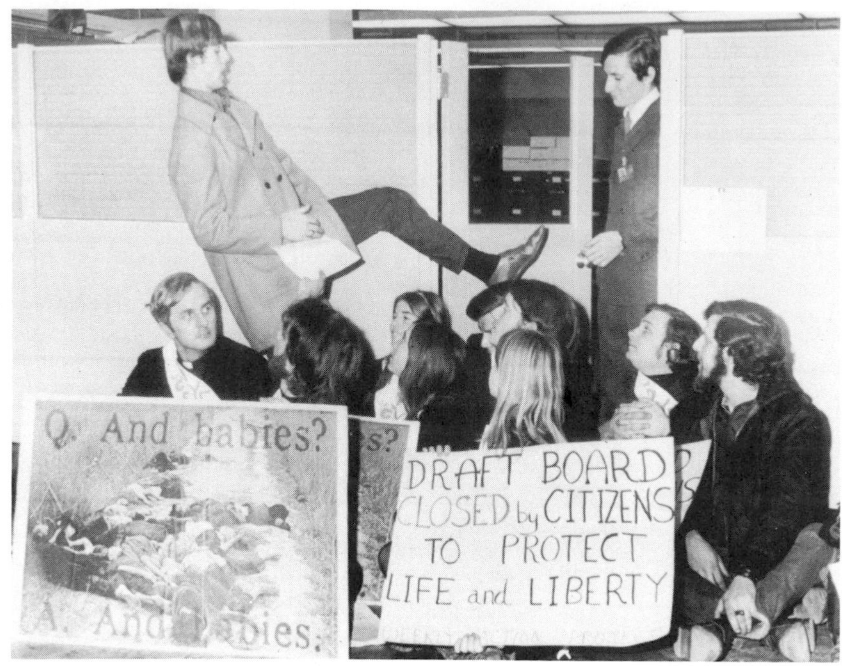

Demonstrators block the entrance to a draft board office in the Federal Building in Philadelphia, Pa., in February. A young man climbs over them to keep his appointment with the board.

UPI COMPIX

April 1970. He succeeded retiring Lieut. Gen. Lewis B. Hershey. In his new post, Tarr faced increasing opposition to the draft.

A national day of demonstration against the draft was held on March 19. The number of federal prosecutions for draft evasion increased from 369 in fiscal 1965 to 2,069 for the first nine months of fiscal 1970, and draft resisters continued to flee the country, notably to Canada, where the number of resisters and deserters from the United States was estimated at 20,000 in May.

In order to correct some of the inequities of the draft, U.S. President Richard M. Nixon abolished occupational and fatherhood deferments on April 23. Both the Administration and congressional critics of the draft favored elimination of undergraduate deferments. The president also affirmed his support of the idea of an all-volunteer army to replace the draft.

On June 15 the U.S. Supreme Court upheld the 1965 ruling in the case United States *vs.* Seeger that moral and ethical objections to military service were valid grounds for draft exemption as a conscientious objector (CO). Previously, only objections based on religious belief qualified a man for CO status. The court also ruled that men who disregard the law requiring them to register for the draft at age 18 cannot be prosecuted after a five-year statute of limitations period has elapsed. In two other decisions, the court further established that draft boards may not reclassify or speed up inductions as punishment for violations of draft law or procedure.

The second draft lottery of the Vietnam war period was held on July 1. Precautions were taken to ensure that the selection of numbers and dates,

A draft protest took place outside a Los Angeles induction center in January.

UPI COMPIX

which determined the order of call during 1971 of men born in 1951, would be as random as possible, since observers had claimed that the selection under the 1969 draft lottery was not as random as it should have been.

The draft call for 1970 was the lowest since 1964, the last year before the Vietnam buildup. In August it was estimated that total conscription for the year would be 163,500.

SENEGAL. On Feb. 22, 1970, an important constitutional reform was submitted to a national referendum in Senegal and approved by 99.7% of votes cast. The text provided for the appointment of a prime minister for the first time since 1962. Although freeing himself of a certain amount of work, President Léopold S. Senghor sacrificed very little of his power. He would still decide national policy and would also appoint the prime minister. A few days later, Abdou Diouf, former minister of planning and industry, became prime minister. In February, a new government was formed.

Foreign policy continued to be dominated by the conflict between Portuguese troops and nationalists in neighboring Portuguese Guinea. In January Senghor issued a solemn warning to the Portuguese government after a series of border clashes, and in June the United Nations (UN) held an inquiry into various incidents. Shortly afterward, Senegalese villages in the Casamance region were shelled by Portuguese artillery. In early July, attacks on three villages resulted in several civilian deaths. (*See in* CE: Senegal.)

SHIPS AND SHIPPING. Piracy on the high seas made newspaper headlines in 1970. The U.S. munitions ship *Columbia Eagle*, bound for the port of Sattahip, Thailand, was hijacked on March 13 by two crewmen and taken instead to a Cambodian port. The cargo of the *Columbia Eagle* was napalm bombs, presumably destined for military use in Vietnam.

The hijackers, Clyde W. McKay, Jr., and Alvin L. Glatkowski, said their action was an expression of protest against the Vietnam war. The two men obtained asylum in Cambodia. On April 8 the government of that country returned custody of the ship, with its cargo intact, to Capt. Donald A. Swann, commander of the hijacked ship. In December Glatowski voluntarily turned himself in to U.S. embassy officials in Cambodia.

The new owners of two former luxury liners, the *Queen Mary* and the *Queen Elizabeth*, had their share of money problems in 1970. Both ships, formerly owned by Cunard Steam-Ship Co. Ltd., a British firm, had been sold to U.S. investors to be developed as hotels.

The city of Long Beach, Calif., revised its estimate for conversion costs of its ship *Queen Mary*, from an original $13.5 million to $57 million. The date for completion of the conversion was advanced from summer 1970 to summer 1971. Diners' Club, one of the project's backers, withdrew after investing $5.5 million.

The investment group that had purchased the *Queen Elizabeth* went into bankruptcy, and the former liner, berthed in Port Everglades, Fort Lauderdale, Fla., was auctioned in September for $3.2 million. To make matters more difficult for the owners of the *Queen Elizabeth*, a tax of $5.7 million was assessed the vessel in 1970, on the ruling that the ship was technically a building.

Shipbuilding at New High

In June, for the first time in shipbuilding history, the tonnage of ships under construction in the world's shipyards (excluding those of the Soviet Union and Communist China) exceeded 20 million. The total number of vessels then being built was 2,019. Orders had been placed for an additional 1,910 ships, with a total additional tonnage of more than 44 million tons. These were not yet being built.

UPI COMPIX

Two ice-breaking ships, Humble Oil's SS *Manhattan* (left) and the Canadian government's *Louis S. St. Laurent*, broke a northwest passage through Baffin Bay in May.

Japan, with more than 22.5 million tons of ships on order, was the busiest shipbuilding nation. Sweden ranked second with almost 5.8 million tons. Great Britain was third with 5 million. France, with 4.9 million tons, was fourth, followed by West Germany, fifth, with 4.3 million tons of ships on order. Spain, Denmark, Italy, and Yugoslavia followed, in that order. The United States, with about 1.8 million tons, ranked 11th.

Giant Buoys Installed

An 84-ton automated navigational buoy was put into operation off the English coast early in 1970. Officials of Trinity House, the British agency for

UPI COMPIX

The Soviet freighter *Sergei Esenin* (left) and the Canadian ferry *Queen of Victoria* collided in Active Pass, just west of Vancouver, British Columbia, on August 2. At least three persons were killed and many others were injured in the accident.

lighthouse operation, believed that the giant buoy and others like it could replace some of the 32 lightships anchored in British waters. According to its manufacturer, Hawker Siddeley Dynamics Ltd., the construction cost of the buoy was about half that of a lightship, and its operation cost 90% less than that of a lightship.

A similiar buoy, but one designed primarily to relay weather data to shore stations, was put into operation at the same time by the U.S. Coast Guard about 180 miles south of Nantucket, Mass. (*See in* CE: Ship and Shipping.)

SIERRA LEONE. In 1970 Sierra Leone was marked by increasing political instability and violence. Although the state of emergency that followed the military regime of the National Reformation Council (NRC) in 1967–68 had long been lifted, the aftermath included a number of trials for treason, resulting in some death sentences that were under appeal in late 1970. On April 18, after treason trials lasting a year, ten defendants—including the leader of the 1967 coup, Brig. David Lansana, former chief of staff of the armed forces—were sentenced to death.

On September 14 Prime Minister Siaka Stevens declared a new state of emergency. Six army officers were arrested and paraded before him in Freetown, the capital, on October 14, following what army circles described as the second attempted coup in one week. Stevens also ordered the expulsion of Mark Colby, political attaché of the U.S. embassy, allegedly linked with the coup plot, though any such involvement was denied by U.S. embassy officials. (*See in* CE: Sierra Leone.)

The foundation for the Central Provident Fund Board building in Singapore takes shape in the shadow of another new building already completed.

UPI COMPIX

SINGAPORE. On Nov. 23, 1970, Singapore's President Inche Yusof bin Ishak died of a heart attack. Yusof was a pioneer of Malay nationalism and a crusading journalist before he was installed as Singapore's first local-born chief of state in 1959 when Singapore attained full self-rule in the Commonwealth of Nations. Later he became president when Singapore became independent in 1965 after breaking away from Malaysia. He was reelected for another five-year term by parliament in 1967. Yeoh Ghim Seng took over as acting president.

Singapore continued to make progress on all fronts. Economically, it had another very successful year, which could be described as a period of transformation from a highly commercialized center to an industrial base. Unemployment was at an all-time low, and Singapore was able to give work permits more freely to foreign workers.

Prime Minister Lee Kuan Yew made a ten-week tour of the Soviet Union, France, West Germany, Great Britain, and the United States. While he discussed world problems with the heads of the respective governments, he also talked about the possibility of foreign investment. He was selective, however, and made it clear that the industrial capital and equipment that Singapore wanted must fit in with the new phase of industralization in the country. He was interested primarily in skills of which there was a shortage in Singapore. (*See in* CE: Singapore.)

SKIING. The expansion of skiing as a holiday recreation was accompanied in 1970 by the development of a revolutionary foam-filled ski boot, intended to achieve a closer fit, lighter weight, and improved insulation. Increasing amenities at mountain resorts were augmented by more artificial training facilities in lowland towns.

Alpine Racing

The 21st World Alpine Ski championships took place in the Dolomites, at Val Gardena, Italy, on Feb. 7–15, 1970. Approximately 250 competitors represented 31 nations. The eight gold medals went to skiers from France (three), Switzerland (two), Austria, Canada, and the United States.

Without winning any of the three events—slalom, giant slalom, and downhill—Billy Kidd of the United States gained the men's combined title by turning in the best total score. Patrick Russel of France was overall runner-up, with Andrzej Bachleda of Poland third. It was the first time that the United States had had a world champion in Alpine combination.

Jean Noël Augert of France won the closest finish, in the slalom. His aggregate for the two runs was only 0.04 second faster than that of Russel, his compatriot. The Austrians took revenge in the giant slalom when veteran Karl Schranz dominated both descents to end 0.39 second better than his fellow countryman Werner Bleiner. The downhill was won by Bernhard Russi of Switzerland, 0.22 second quicker than Karl Cordin of Austria; but a spectacular sensation was Malcolm Milne, whose third-best time gained Australia's first medal in the world championships. Michèle Jacot won the women's combined title for France, ahead of her compatriot Florence Steurer and the U.S. sisters Marilyn and Barbara Cochran, in that order.

In a class of their own in the downhill, Anneroesli Zryd of Switzerland beat the favorite, Isabelle Mir of France, by 0.50 second. Ingrid Lafforgue of France was superior in the slalom with an aggregate of 1.31 seconds better than Barbara Cochran. Youth succeeded in the single-run giant slalom when Betsy Clifford of Canada, only 16 years old,

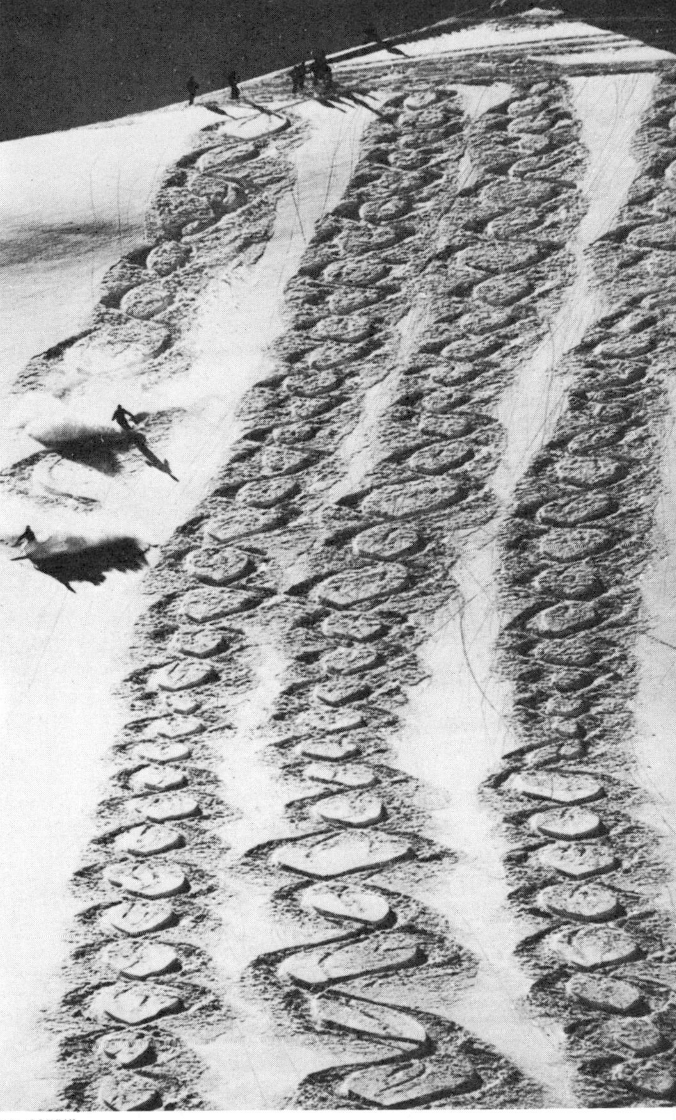

UPI COMPIX

The first annual figure-eight skiing competition was held in Jackson Hole, Wyo., in March. A total of 22 skiers took part in the meet.

outpaced the much more experienced French trio of Mlles Lafforgue, Françoise Macchi, and Jacot, who took the next three places.

Nordic Events

The 28th World Nordic Ski championships were held at the village of Strbske Pleso, near Vysoke Tatry, Czechoslovakia, on February 14–22. Approximately 500 participants represented 18 nations; the ten gold medals were won by the Soviet Union (seven), Czechoslovakia, Finland, and Sweden.

The most successful jumper was Gari Napalkov of the Soviet Union, who won both jumping events. On the smaller 70-meter hill, a great second jump took him from tenth to first, with runner-up Yukio Kasaya of Japan emphasizing his country's escalating strength. On the big 90-meter hill, Napalkov was only 13th in his first effort but his second leap of 359 feet 5 inches gained him his second gold medal, with the Olympic champion Jiri Raska of Czechoslovakia taking the silver.

The 30-kilometer was won by Vyacheslav Vedenin of the Soviet Union with second-place Gerhard Grimmer of East Germany achieving his country's best performance ever in a men's world cross-country championship. Lars Aslund of Sweden dominated the 15-kilometer, finishing with 34.8 seconds in hand over the next man, Odd Martinsen of Norway. The energy-sapping 50-kilometer found Kalevi Oikarainen of Finland the best stayer, overtaking Vedenin in a dramatic final spurt. (*See in* CE: Skiing.)

Greg Swor of Duluth, Minn., a member of the U.S. men's ski jumping team, set a North American record with a jump of 340 feet.
WIDE WORLD

SOCCER. The World Cup finals became the focal point of the soccer world in 1970. Brazil performed brilliantly to win the Jules Rimet trophy for the third time and thus become outright holders of the trophy. Held at five stadiums in Mexico—Mexico City, Toluca, Puebla, Guadalajara, and León—the finals followed the usual pattern of being played on a league system in which the 16 finalists were divided into four groups of four teams, the winner and runner-up of each group providing the eight quarterfinalists. The competition then continued on a knockout basis, and the two beaten semi-finalists met for third place just before the finals. Brazil was certainly not favored by an easy draw; England, Romania, and Czechoslovakia were its opponents in Group 3 at Guadalajara. The other finalists were (Group 1) Mexico, Belgium, El Salvador, and U.S.S.R.; (Group 2) Uruguay, Israel, Italy, and Sweden; and (Group 4) Peru, West Germany, Morocco, and Bulgaria.

The Brazilians defeated Uruguay in their semifinal match, 3–1. While Brazil swung into their familiar offensive rhythm, the Uruguayans played it hard and tough.

Brazil had to wait until the last quarter hour of a tactically absorbing duel for the flying Jairzinho (Jair Ventura Filho) to shoot home their second goal, and then in the final seconds Pelé (Edson Arantes do Nascimento) slipped a pass to Rihle Rivelino to send Brazil into the championship finals.

The other semi-final, at Mexico City, was a titantic struggle between West Germany and Italy and was rated by most observers as the best game of the tournament. Italy won, 4–3.

The World Cup final was played in the Aztec Stadium, Mexico City, on Sunday, June 21, before 112,504 fans. Italy's defense could not hold Brazil's forwards. Brazil proved to be a worthy winner, 4–1. The magnificent Brazilians were matched by the Italians for the first 30 minutes or so of the game with their good defense. Brazil opened its scoring through Pelé after 18 minutes, with a perfectly timed "header" from a Rivelino pass.

Feyenoord of Rotterdam, Netherlands, became the first Dutch team to win a major European competition when they beat Celtic of Glasgow, Scotland, 2-1, for the European Cup. The game, played in the San Siro Stadium, Milan, Italy, on May 6, was decided in an extra time period.

In other results, Manchester City, England, became the third English club to bring home the European Cup-Winners' Cup when they beat Gornik Zabrze of Poland 2–1 in the finals in

TOP AND BOTTOM: UPI COMPIX

Brazil (top, light jerseys) defeated Italy in the World Cup soccer finals in June. The first country to win the Jules Rimet trophy in the competition three times, Brazil gained permanent possession of the cup. Its star player Pelé (bottom) brandishes the trophy.

Vienna, Austria, on April 29. Arsenal captured the Inter-Cities' Fairs' Cup in April when, at their Highbury ground, northern London, they defeated the Belgian team Anderlecht 3–0, to win the two-game final 4–3 on aggregate.

SOCIAL SERVICES. With an inflationary economy the cost of providing social services to those in need in the United States soared in 1970; at the same time high unemployment and more liberalized welfare requirements vastly increased the number of people eligible for help. The result was a fiscal crisis in the nation's public welfare system. According to the U.S. Department of Health, Education, and Welfare the number of U.S. citizens receiving public assistance increased to 12.2 million in June 1970, an overwhelming 20% increase over the previous year. All levels of government were hard pressed to find funds to provide for the vastly expanded welfare rolls.

It was against this background that U.S. President Richard M. Nixon pressured Congress for passage of his family assistance plan (FAP). The plan would provide a guaranteed minimum annual income for poor families—for example, giving a family of four $1,600 a year. The FAP was widely praised as an innovative proposal that would reform the worst deficiencies of the public welfare system. While the House of Representatives passed the program, however, the Senate proved unreceptive and the bill eventually died. President Nixon indicated that he would make the plan a priority item in his legislative agenda for Congress in 1971. (*See also* Congress, U.S.)

Congress did pass a law renewing the food stamp program. Under the program some 9 million people were able to buy food at discount prices. The bill appropriated $1.75 billion for the program for the 1971 fiscal year and included a controversial new "must work" provision requiring able-bodied adults (except students enrolled in school and mothers with dependent children) to accept a job if offered before their families would be eligible to receive food stamps.

"THE NEW YORK TIMES"

Welfare recipients are among the clients of this mental health community center in the Borough Park neighborhood of Brooklyn, N.Y. A group discusses the rearing of children.

The Nixon Administration appeared to have little enthusiasm for the "war on proverty" programs inherited from the Democratic Administration of President Lyndon B. Johnson. Under the leadership of Donald Rumsfeld, a former Republican congressman, the Office of Economic Opportunity (OEO) assumed a "low profile" in accordance with Nixon's view that it should be a small organization primarily occupied with research. In line with this, proposals were considered to slash OEO's next budget by 23% and to eliminate VISTA (Volunteers in Service to America), the domestic version of the Peace Corps (although the proposal to eliminate VISTA was later officially abandoned).

The OEO's Legal Services Program, which provided legal aid for the poor, was also in trouble. The program had been so successful in helping the poor assert their legal rights—frequently against violation by local government agencies—that it had often aroused the ire of local politicians and bureaucrats. Pressure was placed on the Nixon Administration to tone down the organization's activities. In November, two executives of the program were abruptly dismissed. The firings prompted a storm of protest and the White House was charged with allowing political considerations to overrule the needs of the poor. Other protests occurred when OEO Director Rumsfeld twice introduced plans to regionalize the legal program and give nonlawyers control over its activities. Strong public and Congressional criticism caused Rumsfeld to permanently drop the plan. In December Rumsfeld left the OEO to assume the post of presidential adviser, and the president nominated Frank C. Carlucci III to replace him.

Congress considered amendments to the social security program in 1970, but the Senate and the House passed different social security bills. The Senate bill was more generous, providing, for example, a 10% increase in the monthly cash benefits whereas the House bill provided for only a 5% increase, but both versions included provisions for automatic cost-of-living adjustments in benefits in the future. A compromise bill was not worked out before the end of the 91st Congress, but action on it was scheduled for early 1971. (*See in* CE: Social Security.)

SOMALIA. In 1970 the Supreme Revolutionary Council (SRC) remained in control of Somalia and no date was fixed for the promised elections. On April 27, it was announced that a "counterrevolutionary plot" had been foiled. Among those arrested was the first vice-chairman of the SRC, Maj. Gen. Jama Ali Qorshel, minister of the interior, who was dismissed from the government and charged with treason. The announcement alleged that the plotters intended to provoke an attack from Ethiopia and to use this as a pretext for calling in foreign forces.

Following a visit to Somalia on April 6–9 by Otto Winzer, East Germany's minister for foreign affairs, it was announced on April 11 that the Somali government had decided to establish diplomatic relations with East Germany. On May 7, Maj. Gen. Mohammed Siad Barre, chairman of the SRC, gave notice that certain large foreign-owned firms, including banks and oil companies, would be nationalized. On June 2, he announced that the U.S. government had suspended all aid to Somalia because of the SRC's trade relations with North Vietnam.

During 1970 the SRC concentrated on "crash programs" to improve agriculture and animal husbandry and relieve unemployment. In September reductions in the salaries of public and private employees were made known, and rents and prices of essential commodities were fixed by law.

On October 8, the National Security Court in Mogadishu, the capital, passed a death sentence on Yusuf Ismail, accused of assassinating President Abdirashid Ali Shermarke on Oct. 15, 1969. (*See in* CE: Somali Republic.)

SOUTH AFRICA. A parliamentary general election was held in South Africa on April 22, 1970. It was called a year early by Prime Minister Balthazar J. Vorster, who was anxious to stifle the influence of the right-wing Herstigte Nasionale party (HNP, literally Reconstituted National party), formed by a dissident nationalist group under the leadership of Albert Hertzog, a former cabinet minister who was expelled from the ruling party in 1969. The result of the election was: National party, 112 seats; United party, 47; Progressive party, one. The National party lost nine seats to the United party, and the 78 HNP candidates were defeated in all the constituencies they contested. The Progressives retained their one seat in Johannesburg, where Helen Suzman was reelected. In South-West Africa (Namibia) the six seats in the House of Assembly at Cape Town, legislative capital of South Africa, were retained by the National party.

On October 28, elections took place for the provincial councils in all four provinces. In the overall results, the United party gained nine seats from the Nationalists, who remained in control of the councils in the Cape of Good Hope, the Transvaal, and the Orange Free State (where they retained all 25 seats). In Natal, the United party increased its majority. Neither the Progressive party nor the HNP was represented in the provincial councils. A new Senate was also elected, in which the United party achieved increased strength.

In July the minister of transport, B. J. Schoeman, announced plans for a new harbor, to be built by the Iron and Steel Corp. (Iscor) at Saldanha Bay, Cape of Good Hope Province, for the export of iron ore. A railway was also planned for that purpose. Negotiations began with Japan for long-term iron ore sales. The minister also said that a new international airport would be constructed near Durban.

Race Relations

Measures for expediting the development of the Bantu homelands were announced by the minister of Bantu administration and development, M. C. Botha. These measures included further special concessions for the establishment of factories on an agency basis, agricultural development, facilities in the white areas bordering the homelands for training Bantu to work in their own areas, and more responsibility for homelands authorities in economic development. Towns were to be laid out as growth points and transport services instituted, enabling Bantu workers in white areas to visit their families frequently.

In February the Supreme Court acquitted 22 Bantu, charged under the Suppression of Communism Act, but they were immediately placed under indefinite detention. This led to a series of protests and demonstrations. Most of the detainees were later brought to trial under the Terrorism Act but were discharged on the grounds that the charges against them were similar to those heard in the earlier trial. Shortly after their second acquittal,

The tenth anniversary of the massacre at Sharpeville, South Africa, was observed in Trafalgar Square in London, near South Africa House, with a reenactment of the event. A black man carrying a childlike doll approaches a man representing a police chief, who spits on the ground.

LONDON "DAILY EXPRESS" FROM PICTORIAL PARADE

LONDON "DAILY EXPRESS" FROM PICTORIAL PARADE

South African athlete Benoni Malaka lights the torch at Orlando Sports Stadium in Soweto in May to open the nation's Non-White Games.

and while an appeal by the state was pending, restrictive banning orders were served on them. Two were placed under house arrest, including Winifred Mandela, whose husband, Nelson, a former African National Congress leader, was serving a life sentence under the Suppression of Communism Act. B. Ramotse, who had been tried with the others, was found guilty under the Terrorism Act and sentenced to 15 years' imprisonment.

Foreign Affairs

The United Nations (UN) Security Council in 1970 decided to seek the World Court's opinion on the legal consequences of South Africa's continued presence in South-West Africa (Namibia). The South African government announced its intention to defend its case. The United States declared its intention to withdraw support for U.S. investment and trade with South-West Africa. The UN General Assembly, at its 1969 and 1970 sessions, called on member states to end relations with South Africa and Rhodesia. A Security Council resolution also requested member states to bar unconditionally the sale of arms to the republic. In July the newly elected Conservative government in Great Britain stated that it would consider resuming the sale of arms to South Africa for defense of the Cape sea route under the Simonstown Agreement, in view of the growing Soviet naval presence in the Indian Ocean. (*See* Commonwealth of Nations.)

By a decision of the International Olympic Committee, in May, South Africa was excluded from future Olympic Games activities. During the year it was also excluded from various other international sports organizations.

The Economy

The budget, presented on August 20 by the minister of finance, N. J. Diederichs, was designed to rectify the imbalance in fixed investment and encourage investment in private manufacturing industries and exports. Domestic consumption had increased rapidly, and personal savings had fallen.

Inflation continued to be a problem and there were stresses and strains in the banking and monetary systems. Inflationary pressures increased in the second half of the year, with a high degree of consumer spending and of imports. Measures were taken to encourage savings, and the banks and other financial institutions were freed from ceiling restrictions on interest rates. These moves were balanced by a government subsidy on certain categories of mortgage bonds to relieve the burden on smaller house owners. (*See in* CE: South Africa.)

Ben Dekker, a bearded young man in hippie garb, ran for Parliament in South Africa's Rondebosch constituency.

WIDE WORLD

SOUTHERN YEMEN. Continued internal dissension and economic difficulties plagued Southern Yemen in 1970. In January and February it was estimated that at least 1,000 persons were arrested for involvement in a conspiracy of the right-wing Muslim Brotherhood to seize power. The government claimed in March to have uncovered plans for a coup allegedly supported by Saudi Arabia and the United States. Many army officers and civilians, arrested for treason, were tried by the newly established People's Court; a number of the accused were executed.

A purge of the ruling National Liberation Front (NLF) party began in January. The party expelled Qahtan al-Shaabi, one of its founders and the nation's first president, and former Premier Faisal Abdul Latif, who was later reported to have been shot during an attempted escape from detention. In November a clandestine radio station began urging the people to overthrow the regime.

Southern Yemen avoided economic disaster in 1970 only through loans from the Soviet Union, Iraq, and Libya and technical aid from the Soviet Union and Communist China. A joint Algerian-Southern Yemeni oil company, SYAPCO, was formed in January; Algeria agreed to prospect for oil in Southern Yemen.

Friendship with Communist countries and hostility toward the United States and Saudi Arabia continued to mark Southern Yemen's foreign policy. Southern Yemen boycotted the Islamic foreign ministers' conference in Saudi Arabia in March and rejected the U.S. plan for peace negotiations in the Middle East.

The draft of a constitution, approved by the NLF and published in August, described Southern Yemen as a "popular democratic republic" with Islam as its religion. It provided for a 101-member People's Supreme Council to elect the premier and cabinet members. (*See in CE:* Aden; Yemen.)

SPACE EXPLORATION. After the Apollo 11 and 12 lunar landing triumphs of 1969, the year 1970 witnessed retrenchment and disappointment in the area of space exploration. In the United States, a single attempt at landing another Apollo on the moon failed, the budget of the National Aeronautics and Space Administration (NASA) was reduced to a seven-year low, and a general feeling of apathy toward space exploration grew as the country became increasingly concerned with the unpopular war in Indochina and with mounting internal problems.

During the year the Soviet Union launched only a single manned spacecraft, Soyuz 9. It set a new endurance record but did not appear to mark a major advance or turning point in the Soviet space program. The successful retrieval of lunar rock and soil samples by the unmanned Luna 16 spacecraft in September, an important technological feat, may have indicated that the Soviet Union does not plan early manned flights to the moon or planets.

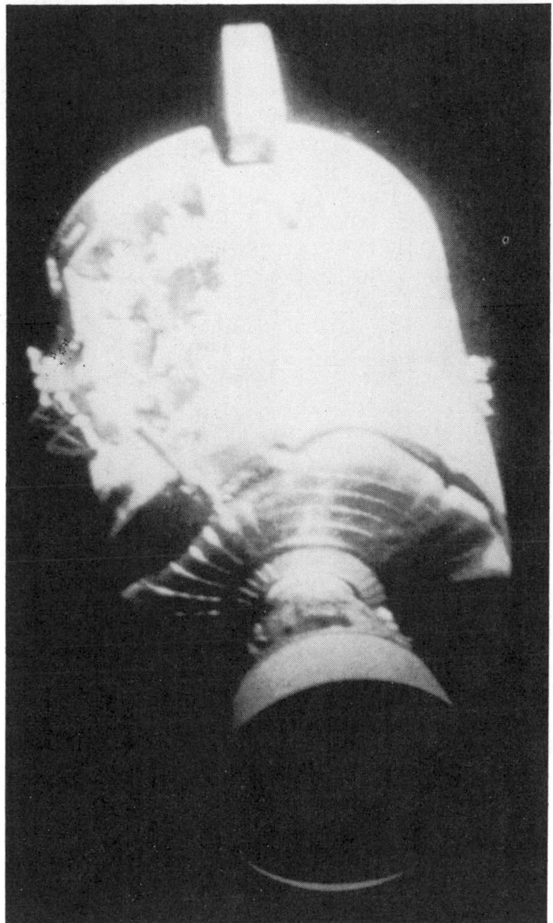

WIDE WORLD

The Apollo 13 service module, with debris in the hole in its side, was jettisoned from the command module and lunar lander. Recovery of the Apollo 13 command module was one of the great space feats of 1970.

In the United States, reduction of the NASA budget to less than $3.3 billion combined with cutbacks in defense and commercial aviation expenditures to cause sharp reductions in employment in the aerospace industry. The Soviet Union, too, announced that because of budget restrictions its relatively cautious space program would continue at a modest pace, and that in lunar exploration "prime emphasis . . . will go to unmanned spacecraft." Among major nations, only West Germany announced plans to increase space expenditures—to $422.4 million in the five years ending Dec. 31, 1974, $104 million more than in the preceding five years. The general fund shortage led to increased consideration of expanded international cooperation.

Apollo 13 in Near Disaster; Other NASA News

The only U.S. manned space flight of the year, the lunar mission of Apollo 13, nearly ended in tragedy. A power failure partially disabled the spacecraft's command module ("Odyssey") as it neared the moon. However, the astronauts—spacecraft commander James A. Lovell, Jr., lunar module pilot Fred W. Haise, Jr., and command module pilot John L. Swigert, Jr.—were able to employ their lunar module ("Aquarius") as a "lifeboat" and accomplish a safe return to earth.

The huge Saturn V launch vehicle of Apollo 13 had lifted away from Cape Kennedy, Fla., at 2:13 P.M. EST April 11. The spacecraft was first inserted into earth orbit, then—at 4:48 P.M.—boosted into lunar trajectory by its still-attached S-IVB third stage. Transposition and docking of Odyssey and Aquarius were carried out, and by 6:14 P.M. Apollo 13 was coasting toward the moon on a path so accurate that the first planned course adjustment was canceled. Later, the craft was transferred to a "non-free-return" trajectory to facilitate the planned landing in the difficult Fra Mauro region of the moon. The transfer meant that, should no further propulsive maneuver be made during the flight, Apollo 13 would not swing around the moon and return directly to earth; it would instead miss our planet by 2,950 miles.

Sunday, April 12, passed without incident, and early Monday evening Lovell and Haise entered Aquarius and began checking systems. Suddenly a loud bang was heard, and electrical power failed in Odyssey. Subsequently, the bang was discovered to have been an oxygen-tank explosion in Odyssey's service module. It disabled the three fuel cells that normally provide electricity and drinking water for the command module.

The astronauts transferred into Aquarius, which had sufficient power, oxygen, and water to sustain them while the crippled spacecraft swung around the moon and returned to earth. The systems of Odyssey—the only module that could reenter the earth's atmosphere—were shut down to conserve its emergency battery power. Early Tuesday morning, as the spacecraft neared the moon, Aquarius' engine was fired to put it back into a free-return trajectory. In the evening Apollo 13 passed behind the moon and, at 7:49 P.M., emerged on its path home. Some 20 minutes later, as planned, the long-discarded S-IVB third stage crashed into the moon, providing an artificial moonquake for study by scientists.

Some two hours later, Aquarius' engine was fired again to increase the spacecraft's velocity, reduce its flight time by ten hours, and assure a splashdown in the Pacific Ocean south of Samoa. A further course correction was made Wednesday morning. Preparing to reenter the earth's atmosphere, the astronauts first discarded the service module, taking valuable photographs of the damaged section as it separated. They then transferred into the command module and discarded the lifesaving Aquarius, which could not return to earth. The command module entered the atmosphere and splashed down on target, 142 hours, 54 minutes, and 41 seconds after the mission began.

After some three months of study, the cause of the explosion was traced to two inadequate thermostatic switches in an oxygen-tank heater assembly. Dysfunction of the switches under load caused overheating that led to an insulation fire and the subsequent blast that tore a side panel from the service module and disabled the fuel cells. Other defects in manufacture and in testing procedures were also found. Further Apollo flights were delayed into 1971 so that modifications could be made to prevent similar incidents.

Its reduced budget forced NASA to scale down its manned space flight program. Early in September, Apollo missions 15 and 19 were canceled. It was planned to employ the Apollo components thus freed in a mid-1970's manned orbital laboratory program. (*See* Space Exploration Special Report.) Work continued, however, on the 75-mile-range lunar roving vehicle that will be carried on later Apollo moon-landing missions.

Several astronauts either left NASA or did not remain on flight status. Frank Borman became a vice-president of Eastern Air Lines. L. Gordon Cooper, Jr., became president of a convention exhibit company. Neil A. Armstrong became deputy associate administrator for aeronautics at NASA's Office of Advanced Research and Technology, while Donn F. Eisele moved to the Langley Research Center in Virginia as technical assistant for manned flight in the Space Systems Research Division. Wernher von Braun was transferred from his post as director of the George C. Marshall Space Flight Center in Alabama to NASA headquarters as deputy associate administrator.

Cosmonauts Set Endurance Mark

On June 2 the Soviet Union resumed manned orbital flight after eight months of inactivity. In the spacecraft Soyuz 9, Andrian G. Nikolayev and Vitaly I. Sevastyanov remained in orbit 17 days, 16 hours, and 59 minutes, breaking the previous endurance mark of 13 days, 18 hours, and 35 minutes set by Gemini 7 of the United States in 1965. The flight was made primarily to test man's ability to endure weightlessness for prolonged periods, though geological and meteorological observations were also made.

Although their health generally remained good, the cosmonauts experienced some difficulties. They developed an inability to perceive colors accurately—especially purple, light blue, and green—and their eye coordination muscles were also affected. After their flight they complained of a "heavy body" feeling and expressed a craving for "earth food." Postflight examinations revealed that they had lost weight and had developed cardiovascular "instability."

Toward the Reusable Spacecraft

Development was begun by NASA of a "space shuttle"—a craft capable of delivering into earth orbit up to 50,000 pounds of men and cargo, then

The world space-endurance record was broken June 15 by Soviet cosmonauts Andrian Nikolayev (in foreground) and Vitaly Sevastyanov. On that date they had been in their craft Soyuz 9 for 14 days.

CENTRAL PRESS FROM PICTORIAL PARADE

returning to earth for reuse. It was thought that the shuttle could reduce the cost of orbiting a pound of cargo from $1,000 with the expendable Saturn V to perhaps $20 to $50.

Potential uses of the space shuttle include the support of space stations and the orbiting, maintenance, and recovery of unmanned satellites. It could also conduct short-duration orbital missions.

Unmanned Satellites and Probes

The Soviet Union scored a technological triumph with Luna 16, an unmanned spacecraft. Launched on September 12, it landed on the moon in the Sea of Fertility on September 20. Directed from earth by scientists who watched its operations on television, it collected rock and soil samples. On September 21 its ascent stage began a successful return to earth. The descent stage remained on the moon, telemetering radiation and temperature data from sensors it carried.

In November the U.S.S.R. achieved an even more impressive triumph when Luna 17 landed on the moon and deployed Lunokhod 1, the first self-propelled vehicle to move across the lunar surface. Luna 17 was launched on November 11 and soft-landed in the Sea of Rains on November 17. Three hours after the landing, the Lunokhod 1, which resembled an eight-wheeled bathtub with a top that opened like a clamshell, rolled off the spacecraft and began its operations. According to Soviet scientists it took pictures and measured "the mechanical properties of the lunar soil." Neither Luna 17 nor Lunokhod 1 was designed to return to the earth.

The Soviet launch of twin Venus probes, however, was only half successful. Venera 7 was successfully placed on a trajectory to Venus on August 17, but Venera 8, launched on August 22, failed to achieve escape velocity and remained in earth orbit, redubbed Cosmos 359.

During the year both the Soviet Union and the United States launched a variety of communications, meteorological, reconnaissance, and scientific satellites. Explorer 1, the first U.S. satellite, decayed from orbit and burned as a meteor south of Easter Island on March 31. It had been launched on Jan. 31, 1958.

Two probes intended to investigate the planet Jupiter were under construction in the United States. It was proposed to launch Pioneers F and G in 1972 and 1973 with Atlas/Centaur boosters. Each of the 550-pound probes will carry some 60 pounds of instruments and, if all goes well, will pass within 100,000 miles of Jupiter.

On February 11 Japan became the fourth nation to orbit a satellite with its own booster. Launched from the Kagoshima Space Center, Japan's Lambda-4S5 rocket placed into orbit the 50.8-pound satellite Ohsumi, which transmitted data for about 12 hours. It was Japan's fifth attempt to orbit a satellite; the first was made in 1966. Japan also planned to launch, beginning in 1975, communications, meteorological, and navigational satellites.

Communist China launched its first satellite on April 24. The 380-pound spacecraft was orbited from a site some 1,000 miles west of Peking by a launch vehicle derived from the Russian SS-4 ballistic missile. It transmitted data on the performance of its components and bursts of the Chinese revolutionary song "The East Is Red" until it went silent in May.

Several other nations announced plans to launch satellites in the future. Brazil revealed that it would develop a communications satellite for

(*continued on page 433*)

Special Report: After Apollo

by Rudy P. Abramson,
Science and Technology Correspondent,
Washington, D.C., Bureau, *Los Angeles Times*

During the 1960's the widely publicized national commitment to put a U.S. astronaut on the moon before the end of the decade gave the space program such urgency and purpose that the U.S. Congress was moved to appropriate, in peak years, more than $5 billion for the National Aeronautics and Space Administration (NASA). But as the manned space effort entered the 1970's, it was under relentless reassessment. The question was where to put space exploration in the scheme of national priorities. The answer seemed clear: space exploration, as a national activity, was deemed far less important than it had been in the preceding years.

By the time of Apollo 11's spectacular fulfillment of the goal of a lunar landing, social problems in the United States were being pressed upon the public conscience as never before; there was a nationwide quest to improve the quality of life. Inflation had become the country's most persistent headache, aside from the Vietnam war, and there was a seemingly sudden public conviction that environmental pollution was a national disgrace.

Space Spending Cut

In this new atmosphere, it was seriously questioned whether the manned space program—the country's most celebrated single undertaking of the 1960's—was squandering limited technological talent and resources. Reduction of space spending came about almost by national consensus.

Congress, exerting its authority more than it had in many years, began taking a tougher attitude toward nearly all high-cost engineering development programs—even those said to be vital to the national defense. Instead of justifying manned space flight as an unavoidable area of competition with the Soviet Union, public officials talked more seriously of substantive cooperation, endorsing the logic of making space exploration an international pursuit. The phrase "cold war," an important one when U.S. President John F. Kennedy proposed the manned lunar landing, was seldom heard anymore. The prime reason for starting the Apollo race to the moon had been to show the world that the United States, not the Soviet Union, was the world's leading power in the new space technology.

By fiscal 1971—beginning July 1, 1970—NASA's budget had been reduced to a little more than $3 billion. Project Apollo was nearing its end; unmanned space projects were being postponed; both government and industry payrolls associated with space projects were being reduced. The once-held dream of some officials to follow up the Apollo moon program with a similar commitment to land men on Mars had long since evaporated.

A new blueprint, altogether different from the space plan of the 1960's, had solidified a year after the first moon landing. There would be no single objective like the deadline for a moon landing. The new approach is to develop a broad capability that can be used for practical returns, scientific research in earth orbit, and continued exploration of the moon and beyond. There is still disagreement over how fast the manned space program should progress and how much the country can afford to spend, but the general direction for the 1970's is now charted.

What is now envisioned is a new family of space transportation vehicles, designed for repeated use. These include a shuttle craft to operate routinely between the ground and low earth orbit; a so-called "space tug" to move heavy objects like space stations or scientific observatories from one orbit to another or to haul cargo between the surface of the moon and a space station in lunar orbit; and a nuclear-powered shuttle for long-distance moving, such as sending a space station from earth orbit to lunar orbit, or starting a scientific payload on its way to neighboring planets from earth orbit.

Development of the earth-to-orbit shuttle—which will also be used by the U.S. Air Force—emerged in 1970 as the first key step in developing the new post-Apollo manned space program. Close behind the shuttle in NASA's plans is a permanent space station capable of supporting a dozen or more scientists in earth orbit.

Skylab

The slowdown in space spending, however, produced a gap between the end of the Apollo moon flights and the first orbital missions of the shuttle. An attempt to bridge the two is a program called Skylab. For this program the third stage of a Saturn V moon rocket is converted into an earth-orbital workshop where teams of three astronauts will work for periods of up to 56 days. It is a forerunner of the permanent space station. Skylab, scheduled for launching late in 1972, carries scientific experiments in the fields of astronomy, space physics, biology, oceanography, water manage-

AUTHENTICATED NEWS INTERNATIONAL

A designer for the Lockheed Corp. submitted these ideas for a nuclear shuttle. An earth-to-orbit space shuttle ejects a fuel tank toward the open nuclear shuttle during a refueling operation. An orbiting space station (left) was also included in the design.

ment, agriculture, forestry, geology, geography, and ecology.

The workshop, equivalent in volume to an average-size three-bedroom house, is divided into two stories, with living quarters and recreational facilities for the astronauts apart from the laboratory work area. Mounted outside the vehicle is a solar telescope that the astronauts will use to study portions of the sun's electromagnetic spectrum not visible to earthbound observatories.

With the workshop, telescope equipment, and docking hardware, Skylab stretches 118.5 feet in length and has a wingspan of 90 feet after its massive solar panels unfold to convert the sun's energy into electricity for the station. During a lifetime of about eight months, Skylab will be used by three different astronaut teams.

The day after a Saturn V lofts the workshop into a 235-mile-high orbit, three astronauts, in an Apollo command module, will be launched by a smaller Saturn I booster. Afterward, they will rendezvous and dock with the station. In a comfortable shirt-sleeve environment, these first visitors will live in Skylab for 28 days before returning to earth. About two months later, a second team will fly to the laboratory for a mission lasting 56 days. A 56-day visit by the third crew will begin about a month after the second team has descended in its Apollo spacecraft.

A prime objective of the three flights is to discover whether there are still unsuspected hazards in prolonged exposure to weightlessness. Through Skylab, the information will be available soon enough to use in the design of the permanent space station. If there are surprising physiological problems from long-term weightlessness, then it might be necessary to design a permanent station so that it is in constant rotation to produce artificial gravity.

Medical and physiological experiments will be assigned top priority on the first Skylab visit. The second crew will have solar astronomy as its foremost assignment, and the third will emphasize earth resources. The latter will use instruments aboard the laboratory—mainly cameras—to see how well orbital observatories, manned or unmanned, can detect natural resources, identify crop diseases, and aid planners in land management.

Skylab will be launched at a greater inclination to the equator than any U.S. manned space vehicle to date. As a result, its cameras will be able to cover any area of the United States and most of the earth's heavily populated regions. Previously, astronauts have passed over the United States along a path cutting across southern California, Texas, the Gulf of Mexico, and Florida.

Because a backup Skylab is being assembled against the possibility of losing the first in a launch failure, NASA has a chance to orbit a second workshop. The first—including the cost of the backup—will cost approximately $2 billion. Depending on how many changes are made, a second Skylab could be flown at a relatively low cost. A decision whether to plan on flying the second workshop is expected in the summer or fall of 1971.

Whether or not a second Skylab is launched, the interim program will not be able to span the gap between Apollo and the new programs. As the budget pinch began, the space agency had already dropped one of its planned moon landings. It decided instead to convert a Saturn V third stage into a Skylab before the launch, rather than use the Saturn I, and to outfit an expended upper stage as a sort of crude workshop after it had reached orbit.

As the pressure became more intense to slash expenses, NASA decided to cut further into the Apollo program in order to keep the plans for the shuttle and space station alive. It speeded the layoff of employees of space contractors and decided to mothball its rocket test facilities in Mississippi and to suspend production of the Saturn V workhorse itself. At Cape Kennedy, Fla., the launch pad where the first manned Apollo mission was launched in 1968 was taken out of service. Later in 1970, two additional Apollo flights were cancelled, so that the program would terminate in mid-1972.

The Shuttle Concept

The shuttle program that NASA hoped to get approved by Congress in 1971 could cost, by the agency's own estimates, upwards of $6 billion. Some skeptics put the figure much higher than that. But the prime motive behind the shuttle concept is to reduce for all time the cost of sending men and equipment into orbit. It may be able to reduce Saturn V's freight rate of $1,000 per pound to about $100 per pound; moreover, it will be able to haul cargo from space down to earth, which conventional rockets cannot do because they are lost on the way up.

Designers are aiming for a shuttle that will operate much in the fashion of a commercial airliner. It must be capable of being readied for launch within two hours and must be able to make at least 100 round trips from earth to orbit without major refurbishment. In reality, the shuttle that NASA wants to build is two vehicles—a booster and an orbiter. Launched vertically like other rockets, the booster will carry the smaller orbiter piggyback style to an altitude of about 200,000 feet, where they will separate. The booster will then descend and, powered by jet engines, fly back to the launch base under control of a two-man crew. The orbiter will continue to an altitude of 100 miles or more and maintain orbital speed—roughly 17,500 miles per hour.

Although the orbiter will be much smaller than the powerful booster that pushes it off the ground, it will be about the size of a Boeing 707 jetliner. The contractors working on preliminary design were instructed by NASA that the shuttle must have a cargo compartment 15 feet in diameter and 60 feet in length. A shuttle of these dimensions will be able to carry as many as a dozen passengers and make the transit to and from orbit gently enough so that middle-aged passengers in reasonably good health can travel as comfortably as professional test pilots. Returning from orbit, it will land at the same base where it took off, touching down on an ordinary runway. Capable of operating at altitudes up to 800 miles, the shuttle will have a payload capacity of 25,000 pounds.

The Skylab program will send aloft this cluster of components. The command and service modules are attached at left. Skylab carries instruments that will make observations in space.

COURTESY, NASA

(*continued from page 429*)
launch into synchronous orbit by a U.S. booster in 1976. The Netherlands announced plans for the launch of a satellite—also by U.S. booster—in 1974. India envisioned a 2,640-pound communications satellite to be orbited by 1980. During the year West German satellites were launched by both the United States and France.

Sounding rockets continued to play an important role in near-earth space research. In mid-January reddish-orange clouds were visible for hundreds of miles along the U.S. East coast after sounding rockets released chemicals to aid in studies of high-altitude winds. Carrying instruments to aid in studies of the March 7 solar eclipse, a barrage of sounding rockets rose from Wallops Island, Va., and Eglin Air Force Base, Fla. (*See in* CE: Space Travel.)

WIDE WORLD

Construction workers in Granada gathered to press for wage hikes in July. Barraged by bricks, police opened fire when their captain was struck. Three demonstrators were killed.

SPAIN. Probably the most obvious change in Spanish public life during 1970 was the growing outspokenness of dissenters, in many instances former supporters of the regime. Generalissimo Francisco Franco remained the undisputed leader, but the nation began to question the validity of his plans to institutionalize a political system notoriously ill suited to present-day world trends. The bill on the reform of the syndicates, in particular, met with fierce criticism throughout the nation, including the normally pliant Cortes, the national legislative body. Whether or not the bill might eventually embody a recognition of the workers' right to strike, strikes were in fact a prominent feature of the national life in 1970, beginning with a virtual paralysis of the Asturias coal mines early in the year and culminating in two strikes that caused considerable disturbance in the summer.

Prince Juan Carlos (left) and Generalissimo Franco review a military parade in May, for the 31st anniversary of the end of the Civil War.

UPI COMPIX

In Granada, the police, while trying to disperse a demonstration by construction workers asking for higher wages, shot and killed three demonstrators. This action angered the nation and brought general sympathy for the workers' plight, as well as explicit support from the Roman Catholic church, which in recent years had begun to dissociate itself from the regime and to take a growing interest in social justice. This incident was followed a few days later by a strike of subway workers in Madrid, the capital. The authorities were particularly anxious to end this strike because of the international attention it received at the peak of the tourist season. The workers were forced to return to work under threat of being drafted into the army.

The most important incident during the year, however, was the court-martial of 15 Basque guerrillas in Burgos, which became an international cause célèbre and severely threatened the longtime stability of the Franco regime. The 15 were charged with belonging to the Basque separatist group ETA (*Euskadi ta Azkatasuna,* meaning "Basque Nation and Liberty"), and six were specifically accused of murdering a police inspector. The defendants admitted their membership in ETA, but the six denied any involvement in the murder.

The trial brought on numerous demonstrations, particularly in the Basque region, and achieved international proportions when ETA guerrillas kidnapped Eugen Beihl, an honorary West German consul to Spain, as a hostage. A day before the verdict was to be announced, Beihl was released by the ETA in a gesture of leniency. Nevertheless, the military court handed down a harsh verdict of death sentences for the six and long prison terms for the rest. Pleas for clemency poured in to Franco from Pope Paul VI, European governments, and countless private groups. Franco was thus placed in the position of having to choose between offending either the military faction, which wanted him to take a severe stand, or the more leniently inclined cabinet, composed mainly of technocrats who wished to avoid tarnishing Spain's reputation with such a repressive action and thus retarding its integration into the European community. Franco finally chose to commute the death sentences to 30-year jail terms.

Franco's cabinet was particularly active in the field of foreign relations. The protracted discussions on the future of the U.S. military bases in Spain came to a conclusion on August 6 when an agreement was reached extending the use of the military installations for five years. Also of importance was the development of commercial and consular relations with East European countries. On the economic front, a major event was the trade agreement signed in June with the European Economic Community, or Common Market, which provided for a gradual rise in preferential treatment on many agricultural and industrial products Spain imported. (*See in* CE: Spain.)

SPORTS CHAMPIONS OF 1970.

Archery. World champions (field): men's barebow—Elmer Moore (Newport News, Va.); men's freestyle—Stephen Lieberman (Reading, Pa.); women's barebow—Sonja Johansson (Sweden); women's freestyle—Eunice Schewe (Rockford, Ill.).

Badminton. All-England open championship (unofficial world champions): men's singles—Rudy Hartono (Indonesia); women's singles—Etsuko Takenaka (Japan); men's doubles—Tom Bacher–Paul Petersen (Denmark); women's doubles—Margaret Boxall–Susan Whetnall (England); mixed doubles—Per Walsoe–Pernille Molgaard-Hansen (Denmark), Thomas Cup (men's world team championship): Indonesia.

Billiards (Pocket). World professional snooker: R. Reardon (Great Britain).

Bobsledding. World champions: 2-man—Horst Floth-Josef Bader (West Germany); 4-man—N. de Zordo, R. Zandonella, M. Armano, L. de Paolis (Italy).

Canoeing. World champions: kayak singles, 500 meters—I. Tichenko (U.S.S.R.), 1,000 meters—A. Shaparenko (U.S.S.R.), 10,000 meters—Y. Tsarev (U.S.S.R.); kayak pairs, 500 meters—L. Andersson-R. Peterson (Sweden), 1,000 meters—G. Pfaff-G. Siebold (Austria), 10,000 meters—A. Kostyenko-V. Konyonov (U.S.S.R.); kayak fours, 1,000 meters—U.S.S.R., 10,000 meters—Norway. Canadian singles, 1,000 meters—T. Tatai (Hungary), 10,000 meters—T. Wichmann (Hungary); Canadian pairs, 1,000 meters—S. Covaliov-I. Patzaichin (Romania), 10,000 meters—C. Maxim-S. Simionov (Romania).

WIDE WORLD

Englishman Len Smith won the World Marbles Championship tournament at Tinsley Green, England, for the 11th time in March.

Cross-Country. International senior champions: individual—M. Tagg (Great Britain); team—Great Britain.

Curling. World champion: Canada.

Cycling. World champions: professional—sprint, G. Johnson (Australia); pursuit, H. Porter (Great Britain); motor-paced, E. Rudolph (West Germany); road, J. P. Monseré (Belgium). Amateur—sprint, D. Morelon (France); pursuit, X. Kurmann (Switzerland); motor-paced, C. Stam (Netherlands); road, J. Schmidt (Denmark).

Fencing. World champions: men—foil, F. Wessel (West Germany); épée, A. Nikanchikov (U.S.S.R.); saber, T. Pesza (Hungary); team—foil, U.S.S.R.; épée, Hungary; saber, U.S.S.R.; women—foil, G. Gorokhova (U.S.S.R.); team foil, U.S.S.R.

Gymnastics. National AAU champions (men): all-round—Yoshiaki Takei (Georgia Southern University); floor exercises—Toby Towson (Michigan State University); side horse—Charles Morse (Michigan State); still rings—Takei; parallel bars—Takei; horizontal bar—Takei; long horse—John Crosby (New York Athletic Club); team—New York. Women's AAU champions: all-around—Linda Metheny (McKinley Memorial YMCA, Champaign, Ill.); floor exercises—Metheny; balance beam—Metheny; uneven bars—Metheny; side horse—

Adele Gleaves (Louisville YMCA); team—Southern California Acrobatic Teams (Scats). NCAA champions: all-around—Yoshi Hayasaki (Washington University); team—Michigan.

Handball. World champion (indoor): Romania. U.S. Handball Association 4-wall champions: singles—Paul Haber (Chicago); doubles—Carl and Ruby Obert (New York City); masters singles—Tim Ciasulli (Scotch Plains, N.J.); masters doubles—Bob Brady-Bill Keays (San Francisco, Calif.). National AAU one-wall champions: singles—Mark Levine (Brooklyn, N.Y.); doubles—Marty Decatur-Artie Reyer (New York City); masters doubles—Sal Chiovari-Jules Stack (Brooklyn).

Horse Racing. Thoroughbred winners: Kentucky Derby, Churchill Downs—Dust Commander (M. Manganello); Preakness Stakes, Pimlico, Md.—Personality (E. Belmonte); Belmont Stakes, Belmont Park, N.Y.—High Echelon (J. Rotz); Santa Anita Handicap, California—Quicken Tree (Alvarez); American Derby, Arlington Park, Ill.—The Pruner (Baeza); Flamingo Stakes, Hialeah, Fla.—My Dad George (Broussard); California Stakes, Hollywood Park—Baffle (Lambert); Hollywood Gold Cup, Hollywood Park—Pleasure Seeker (Pincay); Epsom Derby, England—Nijinsky (Piggott); Grand National Steeplechase, England—Gay Trip (Taaffe); Grand Prix de Paris—Roll of Honor (Piggott); Irish Sweeps Derby, The Curragh—Nijinsky (Ward); French Derby (Prix du Jockey Club)—Sassafras (Saint-Martin); Prix de l'Arc de Triomphe, Paris—Sassafras (Saint-Martin). Harness winners: The Hambletonian, Du Quoin, Ill.—Timothy T. (J. Simpson); Yonkers Futurity Trot, New York—Victory Star (V. Dancer); Roosevelt International Trot, New York—Fresh Yankee (O'Brien); Little Brown Jug, Delaware, Ohio—Most Happy Fella (S. Dancer).

Dwayne Keller (left) wrestles Randy Payne in the 126-pound finals to win the NCAA championship in March.

WIDE WORLD

Horseshoe Pitching. World champions: men—Dan Kuchcinski (Erie, Pa.); women—Ruth Hangen (Buffalo, N.Y.); senior—John Paxton (Ottumwa, Iowa); junior—Bill Holland (Indianapolis, Ind.).

Lacrosse. U.S. champions: intercollegiate—Navy, Johns Hopkins, and University of Virginia (tie); club—Long Island Athletic Association; Collegiate All-Stars—South 11, North 10.

Jean Wadoux of France won the International Cross Country of Chartres in January.

A.F.P. FROM PICTORIAL PARADE

Motorcycling. World champions: 50-cc Class—A. Nieto (Spain); 125-cc—D. Braun (West Germany); 250-cc—R. Gould (Great Britain); 350-cc—G. Agostini (Italy); 500-cc—Agostini; sidecar—K. Enders (West Germany); U.S. Grand National champion—Gene Romero (San Luis Obispo, Calif.).

Polo. U.S. champions: 20-goal—Oak Brook Polo Club (Illinois); 16-goal—Cloudy Clime Farm (San Antonio, Tex.); intercollegiate (indoor)—Yale.

Roller Skating. World speed champions: 500 meters—G. Cantarella (Italy); 1,000 meters—Cantarella; 5,000 meters—D. Hayes (New Zealand); 10,000 meters—J. Folley (Great Britain); 20,000 meters—Hayes; team—Great Britain. World figure champions: men—Michael Obrecht (West Germany); women—Christine Kreutzfeldt (West Germany); dance pairs—Richard Horne-Jane Panky (Detroit, Mich.).

POPPERFOTO FROM PICTORIAL PARADE

The world's first Sand Yachting Championship was held in Lancashire, England, in August. Requiring a wind of at least ten knots, these yachts are waiting for the wind to increase.

Rowing. World champions: single sculls—Alberto Demiddi (Argentina); double sculls—J. Engelbrecht-N. Secher (Denmark); pairs—W. Klatt-P. Gorny (East Germany); fours—East Germany; fours (with coxswain)—West Germany; eights—East Germany.

Sailboat Racing. America's Cup challenge—*Intrepid* (W. P. Ficker, U.S.). San Pedro–Tahiti—*Widgeon* (G. N. Bacon, Santa Barbara, Calif.). Miami–Nassau—*American Eagle* (Ted Turner, Atlanta, Ga.). Sydney–Hobart—*Morning Cloud* (E. Heath, Great Britain). Victoria–Maui—*Greybeard* (L. Killam, Vancouver, B.C.). Newport–Bermuda—*Carina* (R. S. Nye, Greenwich, Conn.). Chicago–Mackinac—*Dora* (L. Williams, Chicago). Mallory Cup (men)—John Jennings (St. Petersburg, Fla.). Adams Cup (women)—Jan O'Malley, (Mantoloking, N.J.).

Shooting. U.S. International champions: 50-meter air rifle and free rifle—Maj. Lones Wigger (Carter, Mont.); 300-meter air rifle and free rifle—Wigger; clay bird—Sgt. Larry Stafford (Thornton, Colo.). U.S. high-powered rifle—Ronald G. Troyer (Andover, Ohio); individual rifle—Sgt. Myles G. Brown (Honolulu, Hawaii); smallbore rifle—Capt. David Ross. U.S. skeet all-around—men, Tony Rosetti (Biloxi, Miss.); women, Karla Roberts (Bridgeton, Mo.). U.S. trapshooting, Grand American Handicap—men, Charles Harvey (Oskaloosa, Iowa); women, Carol Harmon (Roanoke, Tex.).

Speedboat Racing. Unlimited hydroplanes: U.S. champion driver—Dean Chenoweth (Toledo, Ohio); Gold Cup—*Miss Budweiser* (Chenoweth); high-point champion—*Miss Budweiser*. Distance races: Gold Coast Invitation (Miami, Fla., 225 mi.)—Jim Merten (Oshkosh, Wis.); Sam Griffith Memorial (Miami, 200 mi.)—Bill Wishnick (New York City); Hennessey Grand Prix (Point Pleasant, N.J., 197.7 mi.)—Robert Magoon (Miami Beach, Fla.).

Squash Racquets. U.S. champions: men's singles—Anil Nayar (Bombay, India); doubles—Ralph Howe (New York City)-Sam Howe (Philadelphia, Pa.); veterans—H. Salaun (Boston, Mass.); team—Ontario; intercollegiate team—Harvard. British Open champion: J. Barrington (Great Britain).

Surfing. World champions: men—Rolf Arness (California); women—Sharon Weber (Hawaii).

Table Tennis. U.S. champions: men's singles—Dal Joon Lee (Cleveland, Ohio); doubles—Glen Cowan (Los Angeles)-Dal Joon Lee; women's singles—Violetta Nesukaitis (Toronto, Ont.); doubles—Wendy Hicks (Santa Barbara)-Patty Martinez (La Mesa, Calif.); mixed doubles—Dell and Connie Sweeris (Grand Rapids, Mich.). European champions: men's singles—H. Alser (Sweden); women's singles—Z. Rudnova (U.S.S.R.); men's team—Sweden; women's team—U.S.S.R.

Volleyball. National AAU: men—Chart House (San Diego, Calif.); women—Renegades Green (Los Angeles). U.S. Volleyball Association: men—Chart House; women—Shamrocks 1 (Long Beach, Calif.); collegiate—UCLA. Canadian Volleyball Association: men—Hamilton YMCA; women—Calonas (Vancouver).

Water Polo. National outdoor—De Anza Aquatic Club (Cupertino, Calif.); national indoor—New York; national YMCA—Macomb, Ill.

Water Skiing. Women's world speed mark: Sally Younger (Hacienda Heights, Calif.), 105.14 mph. and 103.68 mph. U.S. champions: men—overall, Mike Suyderhoud (San Anselmo, Calif.); slalom, Suyderhoud; jumping, Suyderhoud; tricks, Ricky McCormick (Independence, Mo.); women—overall, Elizabeth Allan (Winter Park, Fla.); slalom, Allan; jumping, Allan; tricks, Christy Lynn Weir (McQueeney, Tex.). European champions: men—overall, R. Zucchi (Italy).

Weight Lifting. World champions: flyweight—S. del Rosario (Philippines), 710½ lbs.; bantamweight—M. Nassiri (Iran), 798¾ lbs.; featherweight—J. Benedek (Hungary), 843 lbs.; lightweight—Z. Kaczmarek (Poland), 969¾ lbs.; middleweight—V. Kurentsov (U.S.S.R.), 1,019¾ lbs.; light heavyweight—G. Ivanchenko (U.S.S.R.), 1,113 lbs.; middle heavyweight—V. Kolotov (U.S.S.R.), 1,184½ lbs.; heavyweight—J. Talts (U.S.S.R.), 1,245 lbs.; super-heavyweight—V. Alekseyev (U.S.S.R.), 1,375 lbs.

STAMPS. Exciting news in 1970 to all philatelists was the March 24 sale of the world's most valuable stamp, the 1856 British Guiana 1¢ black-on-magenta. The stamp, the only one of its kind known to exist, brought $280,000 at a sale conducted by the Robert A. Siegel Auction Galleries, Inc., in New York City. The purchaser was a syndicate of business and professional men that included one philatelist. The previous owner, whose identity had remained a secret since he acquired the stamp for a reported $40,000 in 1940, was revealed to have been Frederick T. Small of Fort Lauderdale, Fla. He had purchased the stamp as an investment and had seen it only once.

Other stamps of major interest auctioned in 1970 included three specimens of the United States 1918 airmail stamp with airplane upside down. They brought, respectively, $29,000, $33,000, and $34,000. The continuing auctions of the extensive Dale-Lichtenstein collection brought its total sales to $2,667,941.

The speculative aspects of philately were noted in the financial press in the year. *The Wall Street Journal* of February 4 headlined one article, "As Other Investments Sour, More Americans Turn to Rare Stamps." The July 1 issue of *Forbes* magazine pointed out that the prices of rare stamps have increased each year, never dropping as stocks often do in periods of tight money, increasing taxes, and high interest rates.

In August a postal reorganization bill became law in the United States, making the former Post Office Department an independent federal agency called the United States Postal Service. Symbolically, the pony-express emblem of the Post Office was replaced by a stylized eagle. Practically, postage rates were expected to increase. In another change, the United States discontinued the sale of savings stamps on June 30. Postmaster General Winton M. Blount appointed William D. Dunlap as his deputy special assistant for philatelic affairs and special projects. (*See also* Post Office, U.S.)

Early in the year the U.S. Post Office revealed that the Apollo 11 moon-landing stamp—issued in September 1969—generated a record demand for first-day covers. Orders totaling 8,743,070 were received from more than 100 nations. The previous record of some 3 million was set by the Project Mercury stamp issued in 1962 after the successful orbital flight of John H. Glenn, Jr.

A new 6¢ definitive stamp bearing the likeness of former President Dwight D. Eisenhower was issued by the United States in August. It replaced the Franklin D. Roosevelt stamp that had been in use since 1966. The discovery of another flawed sheet of the Walt Disney 6¢ commemorative stamp issued in 1968 was announced in March. Eight of the stamps had been used for postage before the absence of the brown color was noticed, leaving a block of 42. A similarly flawed complete pane of 50 of the stamps had earlier sold at auction for $17,000.

On the first day of issue, June 26, the 6¢ value of the United Nations (UN) 25th-anniversary issue sold out, setting a new speed record for UN stamp sales. The anniversary stamps were issued in three values, plus a souvenir sheet.

Anticipating the 1971 introduction of decimal currency in Great Britain, 10-, 20-, and 50-pence

Auctioneer Andrew Levitt holds the British Guiana 1¢ stamp that was sold for $280,000 in March.

RALPH MORSE, LIFE MAGAZINE © TIME INC.

UPI COMPIX

France issued these two stamps on which a small tax was added to benefit the Red Cross.

WIDE WORLD

The United States honored the bald eagle on a stamp in 1970, while New Zealand commemorated sea life.

AUTHENTICATED NEWS INTERNATIONAL

Great Britain received an international award for its stamp honoring Mohandas K. Gandhi.

COURTESY, BRITISH POST OFFICE

stamps were issued there in mid-June. They were modifications of the current Queen Elizabeth II definitive series. "Decimalization day" in Britain was to be Feb. 15, 1971; all pound-shilling-pence stamps issued since 1911 will become invalid for postage 18 months after that date.

The Netherlands issued stamps with totally abstract, nonrepresentational designs. They were probably the world's first computer-designed stamps. Papua and New Guinea began using humidity-resistant gum on their stamps.

In April, Scott Publications, Inc., which publishes 'Scott's Standard Postage Stamp Catalog' and other philatelic materials, was purchased by Harmer, Rooke & Co., Inc., of New York City and the Graphics Publishing Co. of Omaha, Neb. Scott was previously owned by Esquire, Inc., which had acquired it in 1960. The purchase price was approximately $2.25 million.

The Ryukyu Islands issue of folk-opera stamps and souvenir sheets was condemned by many philatelists, including the American Philatelic Society, on the grounds that the stamps had little postal use and were evidently intended primarily to make money from collectors. Many felt that the islands' administration had spoiled its record of philatelic integrity by issuing overpriced and unnecessary stamps during its remaining months under U.S. control. (*See also* Coin Collecting. *See in* CE: Stamp and Stamp Collecting.)

STATE GOVERNMENTS, UNITED STATES.

High on the priority lists of state governments in 1970 were the issues of cleaning up the environment, fighting the drug menace, and coping with campus unrest. The mounting costs of services, together with a declining economy, tended to lower state revenues. In response, U.S. President Richard M. Nixon proposed a plan that would share federal tax revenues with state and local governments. The need for more funds to meet public welfare costs and to finance pollution control systems took on new urgency. In states with heavily populated urban areas the push for highway construction aid expanded to include public transportation systems. Legislative and executive reorganization was undertaken in many states in efforts to achieve more efficient government functioning. Concern for consumer protection increased during the year, and there was a great deal of debate on the issue of state aid to parochial schools.

Notable New Laws

During the year at least 43 state legislatures met in regular, special, or adjourned sessions. Several legislatures moved to increase state revenues by raising tax rates or expanding the tax base. Various business taxes were increased in Arizona, Colorado, Iowa, Kansas, New Hampshire, and New York. Corporate income taxes were raised in Pennsylvania and Rhode Island. The personal income tax was increased in West Virginia by 37.5%.

UPI COMPIX

In 1970 Fred Gray, an attorney, became the first black man to be elected to the Alabama House of Representatives since Reconstruction.

New Hampshire placed a 4% commuters' income tax on the income of nonresidents working in the state.

The sales tax was increased in three states. Louisiana's legislature raised the sales tax by adding a 1% levy to the existing 2% tax. New Jersey increased its sales tax rate from 3% to 5%; Nebraska, from 2% to 2.5%.

The most frequent tax increase was on cigarettes. The legislatures of eight states raised cigarette taxes —Arkansas, Kansas, Kentucky, Louisiana, Michigan, New Hampshire, Pennsylvania, and West Virginia. The increases ranged from ½¢ to 5¢ a pack.

Efforts to liberalize abortion laws were made in several state legislatures during 1970. Among the most liberal new abortion laws passed were those of Hawaii and New York. The legislatures of those states voted to make abortion a medical rather than a legal concern.

Virginia's legislature voted to permit abortions if the mental or physical health of the mother or child were in danger or if pregnancies resulted from rape or incest. Wisconsin's abortion law was ruled unconstitutional by a panel of three federal judges. The Alaska legislature overrode the governor's veto on an almost unrestricted abortion bill, making it law. A governor's veto, however, succeeded in blocking abortion reform in Maryland.

There was an unprecedented amount of state action in 1970 to combat pollution and protect the environment. Legislatures, state officials, and voters all contributed to this activity. Many antipollution measures were adopted in the face of strong industrial and commercial opposition.

One of the broadest antipollution programs was that passed by the legislature of Washington State, which set up a Department of Ecology. The new law imposed unlimited economic liability on oil companies and shipowners discharging oil in state waters, required reclamation of strip-mined areas, and established procedures to evaluate and certify proposed sites for thermal power plants.

GOVERNORS OF THE STATES

(With Party Affiliations and Current Terms)

State	Governor	Party	Term
Ala.	George C. Wallace	(D)	1971–74
Alaska	William A. Egan	(D)	1971–72
Ariz.	Jack Williams	(R)	1971–73
Ark.	Dale Bumpers	(D)	1971–73
Calif.	Ronald Reagan	(R)	1971–75
Colo.	John A. Love	(R)	1971–75
Conn.	Thomas J. Meskill	(R)	1971–75
Del.	Russell W. Peterson	(R)	1969–73
Fla.	Reubin Askew	(D)	1971–75
Ga.	Jimmy Carter	(D)	1971–75
Hawaii	John A. Burns	(D)	1970–74
Idaho	Cecil Andrus	(D)	1971–75
Ill.	Richard B. Ogilvie	(R)	1969–73
Ind.	Edgar D. Whitcomb	(R)	1969–73
Iowa	Robert Ray	(R)	1971–73
Kan.	Robert Docking	(D)	1971–73
Ky.	Louie B. Nunn	(R)	1967–71
La.	John J. McKeithen	(D)	1968–72
Me.	Kenneth M. Curtis	(D)	1971–75
Md.	Marvin Mandel	(D)	1971–73
Mass.	Francis W. Sargent	(R)	1971–73
Mich.	William G. Milliken	(R)	1971–73
Minn.	Wendell R. Anderson	(D)	1971–75
Miss.	John B. Williams	(D)	1968–72
Mo.	Warren E. Hearnes	(D)	1969–73
Mont.	Forrest H. Anderson	(D)	1969–73
Neb.	James Exon	(D)	1971–75
Nev.	D. N. O'Callaghan	(D)	1971–75
N.H.	Walter R. Peterson	(R)	1971–73
N.J.	William T. Cahill	(R)	1970–74
N.M.	Bruce King	(D)	1971–73
N.Y.	Nelson A. Rockefeller	(R)	1971–75
N.C.	Robert W. Scott	(D)	1969–73
N.D.	William L. Guy	(D)	1967–71
Ohio	John J. Gilligan	(D)	1971–75
Okla.	David Hall	(D)	1971–75
Ore.	Tom McCall	(R)	1971–75
Pa.	Milton J. Shapp	(D)	1971–75
R.I.	Frank Licht	(D)	1971–73
S.C.	John C. West	(D)	1971–75
S.D.	Richard S. Kneip	(D)	1971–73
Tenn.	Winfield Dunn	(R)	1971–75
Tex.	Preston E. Smith	(D)	1971–73
Utah	Calvin L. Rampton	(D)	1969–73
Vt.	Deane C. Davis	(R)	1971–73
Va.	Linwood Holton	(R)	1970–74
Wash.	Daniel J. Evans	(R)	1969–73
W.Va.	Arch A. Moore, Jr.	(R)	1969–73
Wis.	Patrick J. Lucey	(D)	1971–73
Wyo.	Stanley K. Hathaway	(R)	1971–75

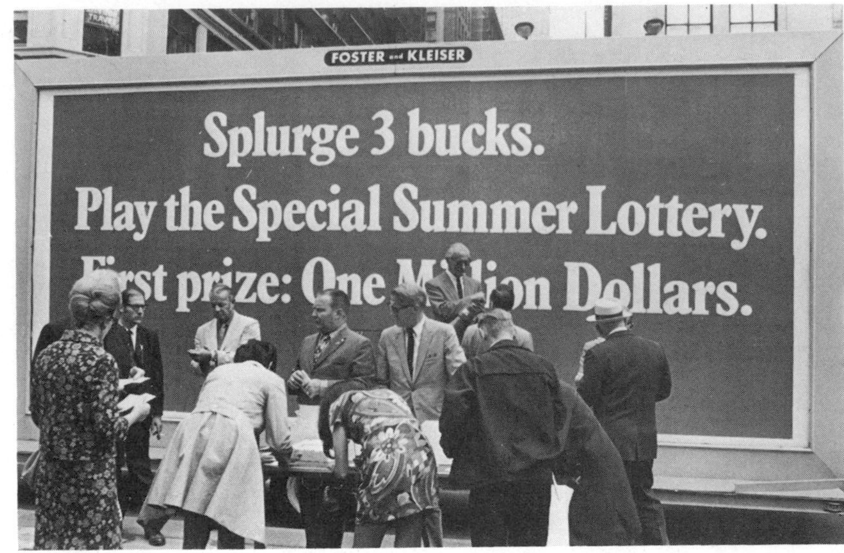

Millions of New Yorkers participated in the summer lottery of 1970 in New York State. The first prize was $1 million. The winner will be paid at the rate of $50,000 per year for the next 20 years, to reduce the income tax rate.

RUSSELL REIF FROM PICTORIAL PARADE

The Maine legislature gave its Environmental Improvement Commission veto power over industrial and commercial development, provided controls over the shipment of oil along the coast of Maine, set up grants for regional planning to control pollution, and allocated bond funds for pollution abatement construction. An impressive set of laws in Vermont included a "scenic easements" act permitting state or municipal governments to purchase land for the purpose of keeping the land open. The package also provided for the protection of lake shorelines from pollution and the setting up of environmental commissions that would have to approve any development project affecting more than ten acres.

New Jersey's legislature gave the state large power to regulate the further development of its coastal wetlands. In Illinois several state pollution control agencies were brought together under the new Environmental Protection Agency. A board was established to set pollution standards, and broader enforcement powers were accorded to the state attorney general.

Attention in legislatures and state agencies centered on disturbances at colleges and universities. Many states adopted laws concerning campus unrest. Among these were provisions to withdraw state scholarship funds from students convicted of participating in illegal demonstrations, dismissal of faculty members for certain types of protests, the strengthening of antitrespass laws, and increased powers for campus police.

California's legislature provided that any student be ineligible for state aid for two years after conviction for participating in campus violence. A Louisiana antiriot law authorized the governor to declare a state of emergency in the event of campus trouble. An Ohio enactment called for the dismissal of a student or faculty member convicted of participating in campus disorders. Wisconsin made it a misdemeanor to refuse to withdraw from an illegal assembly on a public campus or adjacent highways. New Jersey's legislature gave campus police expanded powers to make arrests. A statute on student expulsion was adopted in Kansas, and an Arizona act made violations of rules at colleges and universities a misdemeanor.

There were many measures to increase effective action against drug abuses and to distinguish between types of offenses. In Kansas, Nebraska, and Wisconsin first-conviction possession of marijuana was reduced from a felony to a misdemeanor. In Kentucky marijuana was reclassified as a dangerous drug instead of a narcotic; the legislature increased the penalty for selling dangerous drugs to minors.

The Massachusetts legislature in April passed a law designed to test the constitutionality of U.S. involvement in Vietnam. According to the act, servicemen from Massachusetts could refuse to serve in any foreign conflict unless war had been declared by the U.S. Congress. The law was made invalid by the U.S. Supreme Court. A similar measure was defeated in the Alaska legislature.

Governors and Governments

Seldom have federal-state relations been under such careful examination as in 1970. President Nixon in January renewed his call for a "New Federalism." Prominent among the programs to aid the states was the Administration's proposal for sharing of federal tax revenue with state and local governments. According to the plan $1 billion would flow back to the states in the first year of the program and increase in five annual steps until a total of about $5 billion a year was reached. The other major Administration proposal was for a guaranteed annual income of $1,600 for a family of four persons.

In general the New Federalism received an enthusiastic welcome from state officials, though there were differences on specifics. The National Governors Conference and other interstate bodies strongly backed the sharing of revenue. The governors' conference for the second year in succession called for full federal assumption of public welfare costs, with the administration of welfare programs remaining in the hands of the states.

The movement toward modernizing state governments continued in 1970. The voters of Illinois and Virginia accepted proposed new constitutions during the year. Proposed constitutions were rejected in Arkansas and Idaho. In the November 3 elections, 17 of 28 states proposing constitutional amendments related to the structure and function of legislatures adopted some or all of these amendments. Earlier in the year the voters of California, Oklahoma, and Oregon defeated proposed constitutional amendments.

Proposals to reduce the voting age were on the ballot in 15 states in the November 3 election. They carried in five states—Alaska, Maine, Massachusetts, Montana, and Nebraska. Proposals for lowering the voting age failed in ten states—Colorado, Connecticut, Florida, Hawaii, Michigan, Minnesota, New Jersey, South Dakota, Washington, and Wyoming. In December Illinois voters also rejected a proposed lowering of the voting age.

Forty-five states elected legislators in 1970. The Democrats won overall gains in the state legislatures. (*See* Elections; Political Parties. *See in* CE: State Governments.)

UPI COMPIX

The stock market was plagued with fluctuations in 1970, as prices generally moved downward. Many Americans were concerned by the situation.

STOCKS AND BONDS. The stock market was rather evenly divided between the bears (falling prices) and the bulls (rising prices) during 1970. The first half of the year saw a general drop in stock prices, with an eight-year low on May 26 of 631.16 in the Dow-Jones industrial averages, the most closely followed stock market indicator. In the second half of the year there was a general increase in stock prices, culminating in a Dow-Jones high of 842 on December 29. At year's end the industrial average closed at 838.92. This terminated an upswing of more than 200 points from the year's low point. It was also an increase of more than 38 points from the year's opening average of 800.36 on January 2.

The number of shares traded on the New York Stock Exchange (NYSE) during 1970 was the greatest in history. A total of 2.937 billion shares were traded, compared to 2.850 billion in 1969. The previous record for most shares traded was for 1968, with 2.931 billion.

The plunge in stock prices that finally came to a halt in late May was blamed by analysts on a number of causes. The most important single influence on the stock market, observed Robert W. Haack, president of the NYSE, was the war in Indochina.

A general fear prevailed among investors that the nation's economy was slumping into a deep recession. Investors were also worried by the possibility of a serious confrontation in the Middle East between the United States and the Soviet Union and by continuing campus and racial unrest.

Dale L. Bumpers won election as the governor of Arkansas on November 3. He defeated the incumbent Republican, Winthrop Rockefeller.

UPI COMPIX

The largest transfer of stocks and bonds in the history of Wall Street was made in February. Security guards survey the movement of $3 billion worth of certificates to the new location of the brokerage house Bache & Co.

UPI COMPIX

Many brokerage houses were hard hit by the business decline. In March, McDonnell and Co., one of the nation's major brokers, disclosed that it was no longer able to stay in business and would be forced to liquidate. In May, Bache & Co., the nation's second largest broker, announced plans to acquire Stein Brothers and Boyce. Francis I. du Pont and Co., a major firm, merged in July with Glore, Forgan Staats, Inc., an investment banking house, and with Hirsch and Co., a brokerage house. In December, Merrill Lynch, Pierce, Fenner and Smith, Inc., the nation's largest brokerage firm, acquired Goodbody and Co. as a subsidiary.

Leon T. Kendall, president of the Association of Stock Exchange Firms, observed in September that 80 member firms of the NYSE had merged, dissolved, or liquidated in the previous 18 months. This was a greater number, he said, than all those lost from 1929, when the nation's worst depression began, to 1940. Kendall suggested that changes in federal tax policy with respect to the securities industry could help relieve the adverse effects of business cycles on brokerage firms. The U.S. securities and exchange commissioner, James J. Needham, stated that the failure of some brokerage houses might have been prevented had federal regulation of their operations been more strictly enforced.

Joseph L. Searles III, 30, became the first Negro to hold a seat on the NYSE when he was elected in February. To accept the seat, Searles resigned as director of local business development for the New York City Economic Development Administration. At the exchange he represented Newburger, Loeb, and Co., which appointed him as a general partner as well as broker. (*See also* Business and Industry; Economy; Money and International Finance. *See in* CE: Stocks and Bonds.)

SUDAN. Sudan's increasing involvement in Arab affairs reached a new stage in November 1970 when Sudan, the United Arab Republic (UAR, or Egypt), and Libya agreed to eventual federation of the three nations. Tripartite cooperation was explored by committees throughout the year. Sudan agreed to provide air bases for the UAR.

Internal discord was rife during the year. In March an insurrection against the government of Maj. Gen. Gaafar Mohammed al-Nimeiry was begun by the Muslim Ansar sect. Suppression of the rebellion by armed force was followed by widespread arrests and the passage of measures outlawing opposition to the regime. The Ansar leader, Imam al-Hadi Ahmed al-Mahdi, was killed. Amnesty for some rebels was subsequently granted.

A ministry for southern affairs was created to bring peace to southern Equatoria Province, where separatist black rebels continued to resist the government. An offensive against the rebels was launched in October.

Sudan nationalized all banks, many foreign businesses, and the cotton and grain trades in 1970. Late in the year three leading members of the regime were ousted in the third major cabinet shake-up. (*See in* CE: Sudan.)

SUPREME COURT OF THE UNITED STATES. The term of the U.S. Supreme Court that opened in October 1969 and closed in late June 1970 was noteworthy in that the court had only eight members for almost the entire session. After the resignation of Justice Abe Fortas in May 1969, U.S. President Richard M. Nixon had named two men to fill the vacancy—U.S. Circuit Judges Clement F. Haynsworth, Jr., and G. Harrold Carswell—and the Senate had rejected both (something it had done only once before, in President Grover Cleveland's second term). President Nixon's third nomination for the seat was approved. On June 9, 1970, Harry A. Blackmun of Minnesota, a member of the U.S. Court of Appeals for the Eighth Circuit, took the oath, and the court once more had its full complement of nine justices. Not since 1862 had the court gone for a year or more without a full bench. (*See also* Blackmun.)

In spite of being shorthanded the court disposed of more cases than ever before in its history—a total of 3,409 cases. There were fewer dissenting opinions during this term than in the preceding term, with Justices William O. Douglas and Hugo L. Black filing more dissents (40 dissents) than all of the other justices combined (27 dissents).

Major Court Decisions Involving Criminal Trials, Religion, and Due Process of Law for Juveniles

One of the more important cases decided during the 1969–70 term was Illinois *vs.* Allen. The conduct in court of obstreperous defendants had plagued the trial courts for some time. In recent years repeated interference with court proceedings and the use of vile and abusive language had become almost commonplace. In its decision the Supreme Court held that "flagrant disregard in the courtroom of elementary standards of proper conduct should not and cannot be tolerated." Justice Black said, "We think there are at least three constitutionally permissible ways for a trial judge to handle an obstreperous defendant. . . . (1) bind and gag him, thereby keeping him present; (2) cite him for contempt; (3) take him out of the courtroom until he promises to conduct himself properly."

In another case involving criminal trials, the court upheld the use by a state of a trial jury of fewer than 12 persons in noncapital cases. In Williams *vs.* Florida, Justice Byron R. White noted that the real purpose of a jury—"the interposition between the accused and his accuser of the commonsense judgment of a group of laymen"—has no relation to the number on a jury.

Harry A. Blackmun (right) was sworn in as an associate justice of the U.S. Supreme Court by Chief Justice Warren E. Burger in June.

WIDE WORLD

The only case during the 1969–70 term concerning religion was Walz *vs.* Tax Commission of the City of New York, which upheld a state tax exemption for church property against the charge that such an exemption violated the 1st Amendment's prohibition of laws respecting the establishment of religion. The opinion noted that the exemption actually sets up a situation of "neutrality" rather than of involvement in "establishment."

Due process of law for juveniles has been a concern of the court in recent decisions. In one case of this sort there was a question of whether proof beyond a reasonable doubt was among the essentials of due process and fair treatment required when a juvenile was charged with an act that would be a crime if committed by an adult. In an opinion by Justice William J. Brennan, Jr.—Matter of Winship—the court said the same considerations that protect the adult should apply to the child.

The Draft and the Military Uniform

Judicial interest in the military draft reached a peak in the 1969–70 term. Several cases aroused particular notice. In Welsh *vs.* United States the court held that one could qualify as a conscientious objector on the basis of moral, as distinguished from religious, beliefs. In Toussie *vs.* United States the court held that, for a male failing to register for the draft on the occasion of his 18th birthday, the five-year statute of limitations begins to run at that point rather than at his 26th birthday when his draft registration requirement expires. In Gutknecht *vs.* United States the court held that it was improper for a selective service board to accelerate the induction of a young man because he had left his draft card and notice of classification on the steps of a federal building in protest of the Vietnam war.

Another case involving the military that aroused interest was Schacht *vs.* United States. As part of an antiwar demonstration, U.S. Army apparel had been worn in a street skit. A federal statute prohibited the wearing of the uniform of the armed forces or a distinctive part thereof by unauthorized persons except in a theatrical production "if the portrayal does not tend to discredit the armed forces." In an opinion written by Justice Black, the court unanimously held that this statutory provision—that such dramatic portrayal not discredit the military—was a violation of the guarantee of freedom of speech.

Equal Protection, Race, Libel, and Privacy

Equal protection has in recent years been a continuing problem for the court. In a case that arose in Maryland, Dandridge *vs.* Williams, the court held that equal protection had not been violated

In April the House Judiciary Committee created a special panel to investigate charges that Justice William O. Douglas (right) should be impeached. The panel, headed by Representative Emanuel Celler, found in December that there were no grounds for impeachment.

UPI COMPIX

by the state by an arrangement that imposed an upper limit on the total amount of welfare money any one family unit might receive regardless of the size of the family. Justice Potter Stewart's opinion noted that, if a classification has some reasonable basis, it does not offend the U.S. Constitution simply because the classification is not made with mathematical nicety or because in practice it results in some inequality. He added, "By combining a limit on the recipient's grant with permission to retain money earned, without reduction in the amount of the grant, Maryland provides an incentive to seek gainful employment."

A racial matter was again before the court in Carter *vs.* Jury Commission of Greene County. Here several Negro citizens alleged that they were qualified to serve as jurors and desired to serve but had never been summoned. Under Alabama law, jury commissioners are to select for jury service those persons who are "generally reputed to be honest and intelligent and . . . esteemed in the community for their integrity, good character, and sound judgment." The point was made that, for the past 12 years, the state governor had appointed white jury commissioners and that, though the population of the county as of 1967 was about 65% blacks, the percentage of blacks on the jury roll was only 32%. The opinion by Justice Stewart held that there was no *prima facie* showing of discriminatory exclusion of Negroes from the jury commission or evidence that the statute regulating the choice of jurors was void on its face. He added, "The appellants are no more entitled to proportional representation by race on the jury commission than on any particular grand or petit jury."

The extent to which a private citizen can criticize a "public official" or a "public figure" without risking legal liability was again before the court in Greenbelt Cooperative Publishing Association, Inc., *vs.* Bresler. The unanimous opinion, as written by Justice Stewart, held that in order for there to be a holding of libel involving a public figure, it must be established that there was "knowing or reckless falsehood."

Some years ago the court "discovered" the right of privacy in the "penumbras" of the Bill of Rights as well as implied in the 9th Amendment. This right of privacy was cited by the Supreme Court to uphold a federal law under which a householder may require the U.S. Post Office to prevent mailings to the householder of materials that he considers to be obscene. The court noted in Rowan *vs.* U.S. Post Office Department, with an opinion by Chief Justice Warren E. Burger, that the right of those receiving the mail overbalances the right of the mailer "to communicate." There is no constitutional right to send unwanted materials into a person's home since "no one has a right to press even 'good' ideas on an unwilling recipient." (*See also* Congress, U.S.; Law. *See in* CE: Supreme Court of the U.S.)

WIDE WORLD

Judge G. Harrold Carswell poses with friendly senators before his nomination to the Supreme Court was turned down by the full Senate.

SWAZILAND. Well endowed and racially harmonious, Swaziland in 1970 continued its nearly unique African course of political stability and economic development, attracting large overseas investment and reducing unemployment. The 1970–71 recurrent budget balanced without external aid for the first time since independence. This was due to increased revenue from the revised terms of the South African Customs Union and export returns.

Economic prospects continued to lie in agricultural development, buttressed by mineral resources and manufacturing diversification. South Africa remained the closest partner, supplying 91% of the imports (though trade agreements with Kenya, Uganda, Tanzania, Zambia, and Malawi diverted export trade) and supplying capital and technical aid. Anglo-American Corp. of South Africa reached record iron ore production at Ngwenya and undertook a mineral survey of the whole country by agreement with King Sobhuza II, in whom all mineral rights are vested. The Commonwealth Development Corp. remained Swaziland's biggest investor. The record mineral production enabled the government to finance needed agricultural development. (*See in* CE: Swaziland.)

SWEDEN. At the general election in September 1970, Sweden's Social Democratic government remained in office, but its grip was severely shaken. The election, the first for a new one-chamber parliament, wiped out the government's majority and left it with 45.3% of the vote, a loss of 4.8% from the 1968 election. The nonsocialist opposition parties actually came through with seven seats more than the government. However, the government could rely on the support of the Communists, who unexpectedly gained 17 seats. Gunnar Hedlund, leader of the Center party, emerged as the "winning loser": his party's share of the vote showed the largest increase. The government survived against tough odds, including a deteriorating economy, factory shutdowns, unemployment fears, and crumbling labor relations. In addition, Prime Minister Olof Palme was a sharp contrast to his venerated predecessor, Tage Erlander, a reassuring father figure with a strong personal following.

On the industrial front, Sweden's long-stable labor relations began to show some cracks. Between December 1969 and February 1970, miners at the state-owned iron mines in Swedish Lapland were on strike. Ostensibly about higher pay, the dispute appeared to have other, deeper-lying causes

LONDON "DAILY EXPRESS" FROM PICTORIAL PARADE

Cars producing more than 5.5% carbon monoxide in the exhaust cannot be driven in Sweden. Autos are examined at state testing centers.

—not least, perhaps, a feeling that the union had fallen into the hands of officials estranged from the rank and file. The strike had much significance for a country increasingly concerned with the concept of industrial democracy. The miners protested, among other things, a lack of communication between employer, union official, and worker, and there was a strong feeling that the government could ignore these complaints only at its peril.

Relations between Sweden and the United States,

Cyclists in Stockholm wear face masks as they ride through the city streets in protest against the pollution caused by auto fumes.

KEYSTONE

somewhat cool in recent years, improved slightly with the arrival in April of Jerome Holland as U.S. ambassador to Sweden. The post had been vacant since his predecessor's departure in January 1969. (*See also* Europe. *See in* CE: Sweden.)

SWIMMING. Numerous world swimming marks were shattered in 1970 as aquatic athletes of the United States, Europe, and Australia set their sights on the Olympic Games in Munich, West Germany, for 1972. Major international quadrennial games included the British Commonwealth meet at Edinburgh, Scotland; the World Student Games at Turin, Italy; and the European Championships at Barcelona, Spain. The United States sharpened its swimmers by sending them into summer meets at Bratislava, Czechoslovakia, and Vienna, Austria, and later to Japan and the Philippines. United States swimmers and divers also competed in the World Student Games, August 26–September 6.

Although U.S. swimmers were generally unbeatable, the Europeans surpassed them on several occasions. Swimmers from East Germany and teenagers from Australia were particularly impressive. The former headlined the championships at Barcelona; the latter, the Commonwealth meet.

Dominant Men Swimmers

Particularly impressive during the 1970 season was 18-year-old John Kinsella, a rugged performer from Hinsdale, Ill., who set two world marks—15:57.105 in the 1,500-meter freestyle and 4:02.818 in the 400-meter freestyle—only to have the latter mark erased by Sweden's Gunnar Larsson. Fully as brilliant was Gary Hall, an Indiana University freshman, who negotiated the 200-meter butterfly course in 2:05.019 and the 400-meter individual medley in 4:31.038, both new world standards. Other world record breakers for the United States were Mark Spitz, an Indiana University junior, who established a new mark of 51.941 seconds in the 100-meter freestyle, and Brian Job, a Stanford University freshman, who snatched the world crown from the Soviet Union in the 200-meter breaststroke with a time of 2:23.465.

Among the divers, Jim Henry, a 22-year-old senior from Indiana University, continued unbeatable indoors from the one-meter and three-meter

WIDE WORLD

John Kinsella, a powerful swimmer, relaxes after winning the AAU 1,500-meter freestyle finals.

Mike Burton (right) was the only swimmer to win three gold medals at the NCAA championship meet at the University of Utah. José Fiolo (below, right) broke his own previous record in the 100-meter breaststroke. Mark Spitz (below) swims his way to victory in the 100-meter butterfly at the Santa Clara invitational swim meet in July.

UPI COMPIX

UPI COMPIX

WIDE WORLD

WORLD SWIMMING RECORDS SET IN 1970 (through September 15)

	Event	Name	Country	Time	
MEN	100-meter freestyle	Mark Spitz	United States		51.941 seconds
	400-meter freestyle	Gunnar Larsson	Sweden	4 minutes	2.6 seconds
	1,500-meter freestyle	John Kinsella	United States	15 minutes	57.105 seconds
	200-meter breaststroke	Brian Job	United States	2 minutes	23.465 seconds
	200-meter butterfly	Gary Hall	United States	2 minutes	5.019 seconds
	100-meter backstroke	Roland Matthes	East Germany		56.9 seconds
	200-meter backstroke	Roland Matthes	East Germany	2 minutes	6.1 seconds
	200-meter individual medley	Gunnar Larsson	Sweden	2 minutes	9.3 seconds
	400-meter individual medley	Gary Hall	United States	4 minutes	31.038 seconds
	400-meter freestyle relay	Los Angeles Athletic Club	United States	3 minutes	28.78 seconds
WOMEN	400-meter freestyle	Debbie Meyer	United States	4 minutes	24.343 seconds
	800-meter freestyle	Karen Moras	Australia	9 minutes	2.45 seconds
	100-meter butterfly	Alice Jones	United States	1 minute	4.117 seconds
	200-meter butterfly	Alice Jones	United States	2 minutes	19.324 seconds
	400-meter freestyle relay	National Team	East Germany	4 minutes	0.8 seconds
	400-meter medley relay	National Team	United States	4 minutes	27.4 seconds

springboards, winning both the National Collegiate Athletic Association (NCAA) and the Amateur Athletic Union (AAU) crowns. In the outdoor season, he annexed the AAU one-meter title and was runner-up to Rick Early in platform diving.

Outstanding among European performers was Roland Matthes of East Germany, who dominated the 100-meter backstroke in world record timing of 56.9 seconds and the 200-meter backstroke in 2:6.1, also a new world mark. Sweden's Larsson not only became the world's finest swimmer in the 400-meter freestyle but also established a new world mark of 2:9.3 in the 200-meter individual medley. The Soviet swimmers suffered the worst slump in a decade.

Sparkling Feminine Swimmers

Among the distaff swimmers, 18-year-old Debbie Meyer proved to be the best of the middle-distance performers by setting a new world mark of 4:24.343 in the 400-meter freestyle. Alice Jones, a University of Cincinnati co-ed, shattered two world marks, covering the 100-meter butterfly course in 1:04.117 and the 200-meter butterfly in 2:19.324. The U.S. National Team also set a new world standard of 4:27.4 in the 400-meter medley relay.

Cynthia Potter, a diminutive (5 feet 1 inch) 19-year-old sophomore at Indiana University, overcame illness and bad breaks to retain her ranking as the top woman diver. Of the six AAU titles being contested, she won four (indoor one- and three-meter and outdoor one-meter springboard and tower). She also distinguished herself in the U.S.A.-Europe matches (along with Debbie Lippman) at Fort Lauderdale, Fla., in the springboard and platform events and won in the springboard at the World Student Games.

In the European Championships East Germany's Heidi Becker and Marina Janicke (who did not compete in the Europe-U.S.A. matches) placed one-two in springboard. Miss Janicke was runner-up to Czechoslovakia's Olympic champion Milena Duchkova in the platform event.

Major Meets of 1970

At the NCAA indoor championships at Salt Lake City, Utah, late in March, Mike Burton of the University of California at Los Angeles outshone the field by taking three gold medals, but the Indiana Hoosiers again won the team title. The AAU indoor meet at Cincinnati, Ohio, in April was dominated by Job, Hall, and Kinsella, with Santa Clara Swim Club taking the team title. The AAU outdoor meet at Los Angeles in late August saw 12 world records established. Phillips 66 won the men's team title. (*See in* CE: Swimming.)

SWITZERLAND.

Leisurely discussion of the total revision of Switzerland's federal constitution continued in 1970. An increasingly important consideration was the effect that possible closer association with the European Economic Community, or Common Market, might have on the federative structure.

Around midyear, no fewer than 15 "popular initiatives" (each of which required 50,000 signatures to become effective) calling for partial constitutional revisions or legislative changes had been submitted. The proposals included a "right to housing" (rejected in September), protection of water resources, federal coordination of the cantonal school systems, expansion of social security benefits, intensified control of arms exports, protection against supersonic aircraft noise, introduction of the legislative (in addition to the popular) initiative, cantonal and popular rights in fiscal matters, introduction of a civilian service (to match or replace, in some cases, compulsory military service), a system of financing university studies independent of parents, and more aid for developing countries.

The Swiss policy of neutrality was put to a seri-

KEYSTONE

Male citizens of the Swiss cantons of Appenzell and Unterwalden met in a traditional open-air assembly in April and again denied women of their cantons the vote.

India's President Varahagiri Venkata Giri (right) and Switzerland's President Hans-Peter Tschudi inspect Swiss troops at Kehrsatz.

LONDON "DAILY EXPRESS" FROM PICTORIAL PARADE

ous test by an explosion over Swiss territory of a Swissair plane bound for Tel Aviv, Israel; 47 people were killed. Sabotage by members of the Popular Front for the Liberation of Palestine (PFLP) was suspected but could not be proved. There was no possible doubt, however, of the identity of the authors of the hijacking of a New York City-bound Swissair craft to Ez Zarqa', in Jordan territory occupied by the PFLP. In exchange for the plane the PFLP sought to secure the release of a number of their members held for alleged terrorist acts. The Swiss government released three persons imprisoned after their attack in 1969 on an El Al plane at Zurich's Kloten Airport. (*See in* CE: Switzerland.)

SYNTHETICS. Throughout the world, synthetic materials continued to grow in importance in 1970. Production of plastics rose to nearly 31 million tons from the 27.5 million tons of 1969. The rate of increase in production declined somewhat during the year, however, largely because of the near recession in the United States in the first six months. For the year, U.S. plastics output was thought unlikely to exceed 11 million tons.

Japan's plastics industry, on the other hand, had another year of rapid growth (20% or more) and turned out an estimated 5.4 million tons. This confirmed its position as the world's second producer (after the United States), a title it wrested from West Germany in 1969. West Germany's 1970 production of plastics was an estimated 5.2 million tons. The plastics industries of other European nations also increased their output during the year. In most Western countries, however, the rate of increase in production of man-made textile fibers fell somewhat below expectations.

Chemical modification of existing plastics provided the year's major improvements of materials. Among more sophisticated plastics were a polyethylene with better high-temperature performance; more rigid structural foams; and resins that could be burned without producing toxic gases and were suitable for bottling carbonated drinks. Typically, plastics-making machinery became "bigger and faster" in 1970. (*See in* CE: Fibers, Man-Made; Plastics.)

SYRIA. Under the domination of the extreme leftist Ba'athist regime, Syria remained the most militant of the Arab states in 1970. Late in the year a coup within the Ba'athist party brought to power Syria's defense minister, Lieut. Gen. Hafez al-Assad. Following talks between Assad and President Anwar el-Sadat of the United Arab Republic (UAR, or Egypt), a communiqué announced that Syria would join a proposed union of the UAR, Libya, and Sudan.

During the first six months of the year fighting increased sharply along the Syrian-Israeli front, which had been relatively quiet since the 1967 war. Syrian attacks resulted in Israeli retaliatory raids deep in Syrian territory; the Syrian provocation was aimed at reducing pressure on the UAR's Suez Canal forces. Although Syria rejected a U.S. plan for Arab-Israeli negotiations in June, the Syrian front was finally quiet after a cease-fire went into effect on the Jordanian and Egyptian fronts in August.

Syria's poor relations with Iraq remained an obstacle to a stronger eastern front against Israel. In June a number of pro-Iraqi Ba'athists were arrested; action was also taken against Communists after a leading Syrian Communist indicated support for a peaceful settlement of Arab-Israeli issues. The Syrian press and radio accused the Iraqi regime of betraying the Ba'athist and Arab cause.

Syrian relations with Jordan and Saudi Arabia deteriorated further in 1970. Syria refused to allow repairs to be made to a ruptured pipeline carrying oil from Saudi Arabia across Syrian land; Saudi retaliatory moves incurred Syrian reprisals. When Palestinian guerrillas clashed with Jordanian authorities in June, Syria supported the guerrillas. With the outbreak of civil war in Jordan in September, Syrian forces crossed into Jordan to aid the guerrillas; they were withdrawn after suffering severe casualties.

The action in Jordan contributed to a power struggle within the Ba'athist party. General Assad, head of the party's military faction, was accused by the political faction of refusing to provide air support for Syria's forces in Jordan; Assad criticized political leaders for committing Syrian forces to the war. Following a party congress in November, Assad led the military faction in a take-over of the government. President Nureddin al-Attassi and other political leaders were arrested. A provisional government was formed with Assad as premier and a former teacher, Ahmed al-Khatib, as head of state. The new regime promised to create a national assembly and to draft a permanent constitution. Realignment of the Syrian Ba'athist party was also planned. (*See also* International Relations; Jordan; Middle East; Saudi Arabia. *See in* CE: Syria.)

Hundreds of refugee Palestinians live in tents near the new airport in Damascus. They will not move into houses because they believe that their refugee status is temporary, and that the Israeli occupation of their former homeland is short-lived.

KEYSTONE

TAIWAN. Even though economic growth and social advancement continued in 1970 in Taiwan (seat of the Republic of China, or Nationalist China), the posture and position of the Nationalist government as the sole and legitimate government of all China greatly deteriorated. Factors in this deterioration were Canada's move to shift diplomatic recognition from Nationalist to Communist China; Communist China's renewed interest in bidding for China's seat in the United Nations; the decisions of the United States to reduce its military presence in Asia and to resume Sino-U.S. talks at the ambassadorial level in Warsaw, Poland; and, particularly, the reiteration of U.S. policy to conciliate Communist China with the removal of the regular U.S. Navy patrol in the Taiwan Strait and to allow U.S. tourists to purchase Communist Chinese goods as well as to permit U.S. companies operating abroad to trade directly with the Chinese Communists.

On his goodwill tour of Asia, U.S. Vice-President Spiro T. Agnew visited Taipei, the capital, on January 2–3, and held talks with President Chiang Kai-shek and other high officials on matters of mutual interest and concern.

Deputy Premier Chiang Ching-kuo, in turn, visited the United States April 18–28 and conferred with President Richard M. Nixon, Vice-President Agnew, and the secretaries of state and defense. In New York City, on April 24, Chiang escaped without injury when a student from Taiwan attempted to assassinate him. (*See also* China, People's Republic of. *See in* CE: Formosa.)

TANZANIA. Seven people, including Miss Bibi Titi Muhammad, one of the founders of the Tanganyika African National Union (TANU), were charged in May 1970 with plotting to overthrow the government and to assassinate Tanzania's President Julius Nyerere and the second vice-president, Rashidi Kawawa. They had been under arrest since October 1969. Oscar Kambona, the former foreign minister, also was charged in his absence with directing the plot. The accused were brought to trial in June, with the exception of Kambona, who under Tanzanian law could not be tried in absentia.

In a speech on February 5, marking the third anniversary of the Arusha Declaration proclaiming a socialist policy, Nyerere announced that the government would take over the country's entire wholesaling system during the course of the year. This decision followed the government's take-over on the preceding day of the last surviving privately owned English-language daily newspaper, *The Standard,* and the weekly *Sunday News*.

In July, Kawawa announced that during 1971 he would present to the National Assembly the completed plans for a Tanzanian air force. He gave no indication as to the source of any assistance in the project, but observers believed that Communist China, which was already constructing a naval base for Tanzania at Dar es Salaam, the capital, was likely to be involved. In July, too, final discussions took place in Peking, China, between members of the Communist Chinese government and ministers and bank governors from Tanzania and Zambia to

Kov Lu (right), railway minister of Communist China, tours the East African Railways workshop in Dar es Salaam. He is followed closely by Job Luninde, Tanzania's minister of communications, power, and labor. Hundreds of Chinese railway experts arrived in Tanzania in 1970 to start work on the 1,000-mile-long railroad line between Dar es Salaam and Lusaka, Zambia.

MOHAMED AMIN FROM KEYSTONE

arrange an interest-free loan of just over $400 million to finance the 1,000-mile-long Tanzam railway that would link the two African countries.

In September Nyerere was unanimously nominated as the sole candidate for the presidential election on October 30, when he was reelected by an overwhelming majority. At the same time, parliamentary elections were held on the mainland, but not in Zanzibar. Most of the incumbents were reelected, though two ministers lost their seats. (*See in* CE: Tanzania.)

TELEPHONES. In 1970, telephone companies in the United States continued to have difficulty in meeting the burgeoning demand for their services. Complaints of poor service abounded as customers experienced delays in getting telephones installed or repaired and in obtaining dial tones or reaching an operator. Early in the year, a survey conducted by the Federal Communications Commission revealed that New York City had the nation's poorest telephone service—though other cities were not much better off.

The American Telephone and Telegraph Co. (AT&T), which with its affiliates provides 85% of U.S. telephone service, during the year spent nearly $7 billion to improve and expand its domestic facilities. In the year ending August 31, AT&T's profits rose to $2,177,978,000 on revenues of $16,607,406,000, compared with $2,175,576,000 on $15,142,132,000 in the previous year. In the third quarter of the year, however, the firm's net profits dipped slightly.

On March 22 the highest-capacity communications cable ever to be laid across the Atlantic Ocean went into service between Rhode Island and Spain. Jointly owned by several firms—U.S. and foreign—the cable made possible a series of international rate reductions, including the reduction of rates from the United States to Spain, Portugal, Italy, and Germany by as much as 25%.

The Cybernetics Research Institute of Washington, D.C., announced the development of a device that permits the deaf and the mute to "talk" by telephone among themselves or with others. Messages typed on a keyboard are transmitted by conventional telephone receivers and reproduced by flashing lights, typed out, or tape-recorded for playback.

Professor Raphael A. Kazarian of the Soviet Union reported in March the first "operational" use of laser beams to transmit telephone messages. His 24-channel system operated over a range of 15 miles. (*See in* CE: Telephone.)

TELEVISION AND RADIO. Television had become so firmly established in small as well as large countries by 1970 that there was little room for major expansion. The most dramatic growth occurred in sparsely populated countries such as Liberia, Mauritania, and Sudan, where set ownership increased by big percentages but was still only a fraction of that of the average U.S. city, and in a few of the more densely populated nations such as Spain, Czechoslovakia, the United Arab Republic, Yugoslavia, and Hungary, where set ownership had been increasing for years.

STEPHEN HALE, COURTESY, WTTW-TV

Black students confront their school principal with demands in an episode of Bird of the Iron Feather on WTTW-TV in Chicago.

In 1970, according to figures compiled by *Broadcasting* magazine and *Broadcasting Yearbook*, there were an estimated 231 million television sets and 620 million radio receivers in use in the world. Approximately 85 million of the television sets, or 37%, were in the United States. The Soviet Union had more than 25 million, Japan 22.3 million, and Great Britain 20 million. About 320.7 million, or a little more than half, of the world's radio sets—AM (amplitude modulation) and FM (frequency modulation)—were in the United States.

Approximately 6,360 television stations were on the air or under construction around the world in 1970. No area had gained significantly. There were about 2,000 stations in Western Europe, 2,100 in the Far East, 1,034 in the United States, 905 in Eastern Europe, 170 in South America, 76 in Canada, and 35 in Africa. Radio stations on the air or under construction in the world numbered approximately 12,900. Most were AM, but FM was gaining in both number and proportion. More than half of the stations—7,134—were in the United States, and about one third of these were FM.

Color television expanded. In the United States most transmissions were in color, and 26.2 million homes—43.2% of all TV homes—had color receivers. In Canada 11% of all homes had color TV.

Efforts to reorganize the administration of the

The CBC-TV production of 'Cinderella' with the National Ballet of Canada won an Emmy award as the outstanding classical program shown on U.S. television. Veronica Tennant (kneeling) played Cinderella and Jeremy Blanton (right) played the prince.

COURTESY, CANADIAN BROADCASTING CORP.

International Telecommunications Satellite Consortium, managed since 1964 by the U.S. Communications Satellite Corp., bogged down, but the world's nations were outstandingly successful in organizing around-the-world distribution of special programs. In one of the most massive coverage efforts in history, an estimated 800 million to 900 million people in 40 countries witnessed live TV coverage, via satellite, of the World Cup soccer games in Mexico City. Between May 31 and June 21, more than 470 hours of satellite time were used to distribute the game telecasts—at least 135 more hours than were used in coverage of the first "moon walk" in July 1969. Satellites were also used to relay around-the-world coverage of such events as the splashdown of the crippled Apollo 13 spacecraft and the funeral of Charles de Gaulle of France.

In Canada a satellite system providing six TV channels to serve the entire nation was to be completed by 1972. The Soviet Union continued to use satellites to relay programs from Moscow to remote areas, and the U.S. government invited and received applications from companies seeking to operate domestic satellite services.

Television Feels Pressures

In the United States, pressures—political, social, and economic—upon broadcasters intensified in 1970. With the hope of encouraging new program sources, the Federal Communications Commission (FCC) ordered that, beginning Sept. 1, 1971, network-affiliated stations in the 50 largest markets could carry no more than three hours of network programming between 7 and 11 P.M. EST on any night. The stations already produced a half hour of nonnetwork time, and it was estimated that, in a normal year, loss of the additional half hour would cost the networks $70 million in revenue. Two networks—CBS (Columbia Broadcasting System) and NBC (National Broadcasting Co.) appealed the ruling. The FCC also ruled that the networks must get out of the program syndication business in the United States and severely limit their syndication activities overseas. The networks were further ordered to cease acquiring financial interests in new programs in return for financing their development by independent producers. These rules, too, were being appealed.

In an effort to promote diversification of ownership, the FCC prohibited the owner of a full-time station—radio or TV—from acquiring any other full-time station in the same market. It held that networks could not own community antenna television (CATV) systems anywhere in the United States and that TV stations could not own CATV systems within their own markets.

After much debate, the U.S. Congress in 1970 enacted a ban on the broadcast advertising of cigarettes, effective Jan. 2, 1971. It was estimated that the law would cost broadcasters $215 million in annual revenues. The FCC increased by $20 million the annual fees paid to it by broadcasters and others subject to its regulation.

Broadcasters faced the threat of yet further losses. The FCC had under consideration a petition from a women's organization—Action for Children's Television—to ban commercial sponsorship of children's TV programs and to require broadcasters to carry at least 14 hours of such programming each week, during specified time periods. Another group, the Foundation to Improve Television, sued a station and a program sponsor in an effort to further its goal of outlawing violence in TV programs during hours when large numbers of children are watching.

Spurred by the success of similar efforts in 1969, local citizens' groups in growing number sought to win concessions from some stations and to hold up license renewals for others by filing competing applications at license renewal time. Broadcasters were also disappointed when, after 18 years of consideration, the FCC in 1970 approved the Zenith Radio Corporation's "Phonevision" system of pay TV, the first to win FCC approval. They were also concerned by CATV, which, after growing at an annual rate of 20% for five years, was by mid-1970 serving 3.7 million U.S. households, more than 6% of the total.

Programming Trends

News and sports continued to be the basic services of television and radio broadcasters throughout the world in 1970. In September a nationwide survey in the United States indicated that, for most people, television had increased its lead as both the primary and most credible source of news. Television news operations, however, continued to hear criticism of their handling of "controversial" events, and they felt economic pressures as well. (*See* Television and Radio Special Report.) Reduced advertising revenue led a number of stations to curtail news operations.

Sports continued to attract big audiences and bigger prices. *Broadcasting* reported that payments in 1970 for radio-TV rights for professional and college football came to almost $66.3 million, up $13 million from 1969; baseball commanded more than $38 million, about a $1-million increase; basketball brought $5.5 million; ice hockey required a commitment of more than $1 million; and lesser but increasing sums were being paid for golf and other sports.

Overseas sales of U.S. entertainment programs were expected to reach $100 million for the first time in 1970. They totaled $94 million in 1969.

In U.S. noncommercial broadcasting, Sesame Street, produced by the Children's Television Workshop and broadcast over most of the 200-plus noncommercial stations and some commercial outlets, was easily the most highly acclaimed children's TV program of the year. While Sesame continued in 1970–71, a sequel for older children—seven to ten years old—was planned by the producer to start in October 1971 on a daily basis.

A long-expected reorganization of noncommercial television occurred in mid-1970 when National

(*continued on page 456*)

Tricia Nixon, eldest daughter of U.S. President Richard M. Nixon, shows the "first family's" private dining room to CBS-TV news correspondents. Miss Nixon was hostess for a televised tour of the presidential living quarters on the second floor of the White House. The tour included many rooms never before seen on television.

PICTORIAL PARADE

Special Report: News and Views

by M. Dallas Burnett,
Associate Professor of Communications,
Brigham Young University, Provo, Utah

Television journalism has been practiced in the United States for less than 25 years. It has little history, and no real traditions or folklore. And it does not even enjoy all of the constitutional protection of the print media. Yet television journalism reaches more people with greater impact than any other news form.

As we move another year into the decade of the 1970's, that simple truth also has a great irony attached to it. Television shares with other media a wave of resentment and distrust. One national study made late in 1969 showed that 42% of the television audience believed that the networks favored one side over the other in the presentation of news. Another study completed just a few weeks later found that 52% of those interviewed agreed with U.S. Vice-President Spiro T. Agnew's charge that television journalists distorted the news.

AL SATTERWHITE FROM CAMERA 5

U.S. Vice-President Spiro T. Agnew stimulated a national controversy about TV news coverage.

Public Mistrust and Criticism

During the past three decades the federal government, under Democratic and Republican administrations alike, has been storing in the minds of citizens a vast reservoir of distrust. Whether the phenomenon is called secrecy, news management, or the credibility gap, the results are the same—people are less and less sure that the government is telling the truth or even telling what ought to be told. The presidential campaign of Richard M. Nixon in 1968 made a minor issue of the point that there would be more openness in government and that the chasm of disbelief would be bridged. There was little evidence to show in 1970, however, that the country as a whole had any greater faith in the honesty of government than it did two years before. And from the standpoint of the professional journalist, there was rather solid evidence to suggest that the Nixon Administration would like to control the press just as much as any preceding Administration.

But the real difference today, as contrasted with earlier situations, is that there are many people prepared to support government action against the media. Frustration with media performance, fanned particularly by Vice-President Agnew, has apparently reached the point where 1st Amendment protections of free press and free speech are not so important to many people as order and security. It should be noted also that this reaction against the media is probably due in part to a backlash against violent dissent in the streets and on the campuses. The media have carried the unpleasant news and therefore, in the minds of some, share part of the blame. In fact, there is increasingly serious discussion over the issue of whether the coverage of violent events, particularly by television, actually energizes those events to produce further violence and provide a stimulus for additional lawlessness.

One of the loudest and possibly most valid criticisms of television news is that it thrives on conflict, focuses on violence, and thus grossly distorts many events. Television journalists are quick to point out that the medium did not create the conditions in black ghettos, or on the campuses, or in Vietnam that have led to the radical dissent in this country. The fact remains, though, that many of those who take to the streets, whether peacefully or as lawbreakers, are highly sensitive to the potential value of television to their cause. Television journalists are probably more subtly manipulated by the people in the street than by corporate public relations directors. This is a terrible dilemma for the electronic journalist. How can he decide when an event is real or merely the concoction of a radical public relations expert?

It is not difficult to forgive the honest errors, but it is another matter when television newsmen are caught doing the stage-managing themselves.

No one really knows the magnitude of this particular problem, but the performance of television news coverage during the Democratic National Convention in 1968 and in other situations, such as the staging of a pot party by one network-owned station, has given rise to a healthy suspicion of other events.

One can look at television as basically a recording device. It measures the temperature of a situation. The question being raised here, of course, is whether the mere introduction of the measuring device into the situation increases the temperature. Does a peaceful demonstration turn into a riot because television news is there to cover the scene? Are there occasions when those who intend to riot fail to do so because of the lack of television coverage?

Scientifically established answers to the above questions are not available. Critics and defenders have impressions and can cite an instance here and an instance there, but for the honest observer the issue is still in doubt. The same thing can also be said for the overall problem of the effect of violence in the media on children and adults, despite the opinions of the National Commission on the Causes and Prevention of Violence.

Recapturing Viewers' Confidence

As one looks at television journalism in the United States today, the point needs to be made, as trite as it may sound, that the beast is neither as bad nor as good as some would make out. Television news can and has stimulated intense interest in public affairs. No news form can equal television when it comes to the coverage of live events such as the drama of a walk on the moon or of a presidential funeral. But with this strength comes a built-in weakness. Television deals best with visual events and has its greatest difficulty with ideas. Visualization is the key to television, but many ideas are not told best on film.

This is not to say that television does not deal with ideas and that the pure spoken word is not frequently used in television news broadcasts, but the balance weighs in favor of action and conflict. Vice-President Agnew's implication that a liberal *conspiracy* pervades the network news teams is hardly worthy of comment. The fact remains, however, that most of those selecting and reporting the news would be identified with the liberal end of the political spectrum. Unfortunately, these men do not always rise above their prejudices.

As strange as it may sound, there are grounds for believing that 1970 may have been a good year for broadcast journalism. True, it was a year of mounting criticism from all quarters, especially from government. It was a year in which the government may have been testing to see how far it could go in an attempt to intimidate the media. But on the positive side, it was a year in which broadcast journalists made a quiet assessment of their own performance, despite their vocal defense against the attacks of the vice-president. Furthermore, it was a year when many thoughtful people showed an increasing concern for freedom of expression, even though there was some sentiment in the opposite direction. And it is to be hoped that the Nixon Administration recognized the imprudence of allowing its second-in-command to mount such a vitriolic and continuous attack on the television news effort. The real measure of 1970 will come if and when television newsmen succeed in recapturing the confidence of those millions of disaffected viewers.

A South Vietnamese soldier stabbed to death a North Vietnamese prisoner in an edited film report aired on CBS-TV in November 1969. Rumors were spread that the death scene had been staged, however, and in order to verify its authenticity CBS-TV aired the entire film, including an interview with the soldier who had done the killing, in May 1970.

COURTESY, CBS NEWS

(*continued from page 453*)
Educational Television, the principal programming source for noncommercial stations, was consolidated with WNDT-TV of New York City, a noncommercial station, to form the Educational Broadcasting Corp. The corporation would provide "the most comprehensive and best-financed public television center in the United States" for all noncommercial stations. It was to concentrate upon programming, with distribution to be handled by the Public Broadcasting Service, set up for that purpose late in 1969. (*See in* CE: Radio; Television.)

TENNIS. Top-level tennis competition was highlighted in 1970 by increased prize money and greater emphasis on commercial sponsorship. The U.S. Open championships, played at Forest Hills, N.Y., offered a record $160,000 in prizes. Rod Laver, Australia's outstanding player, with 1969 earnings totaling $123,855, increased his take by about 50% in the first nine months of 1970. Laver, however, failed to dominate the four major championships as in 1969, but shared honors with three other Australians—John Newcombe, Tony Roche, and Ken Rosewall. In women's play, Margaret Court of Australia became the first winner of a "grand slam" since the late Maureen Connolly achieved the honor in 1953.

Other major developments of the year included the suspension of South Africa from Davis Cup play because of its racial policy and the withdrawal of Rhodesia from the same competition. In September Arthur Ashe, Charles Pasarell, and Bob Lutz, the second-, fifth-, and sixth-ranking U.S. players, signed five-year contracts, effective in 1971, to join the World Championship Tennis (WCT) tour of Texas sportsman Lamar Hunt. Late in the year the WCT announced a series of 20 tournaments for 32 men players, with prizes totaling more than $1 million. The International Lawn Tennis Federation (ILTF) also announced at least 31 tournaments for men and women in 1971, with more than $1.5 million in prize money. At the same time, ILTF stressed that these meets would be "open" to every class of player.

WIDE WORLD

Charles Diggs (right), chairman of the House foreign affairs subcommittee on Africa, tells tennis star Arthur Ashe that he will investigate South Africa's refusal to give Ashe a visa.

Davis Cup Competition

In Davis Cup play, the United States retained possession of the trophy at Cleveland, Ohio, in August, beating West Germany, the challenger, 5–0. Arthur Ashe and Cliff Richey swept their singles matches with Germany's two-man team of Wilhelm Bungert and Christian Kuhnke, with Stan Smith and Bob Lutz easily winning the doubles. It was the 22d Davis Cup success for the United

John Newcombe (left) of Australia won the men's singles championship at Wimbledon in 1970; he had also taken the title in 1967. He defeated Ken Rosewall in the finals. Margaret Court (right) of Australia beat Billie Jean King to win the women's singles title at Wimbledon.

LEFT: "THE TIMES," LONDON, FROM PICTORIAL PARADE. RIGHT: KEYSTONE

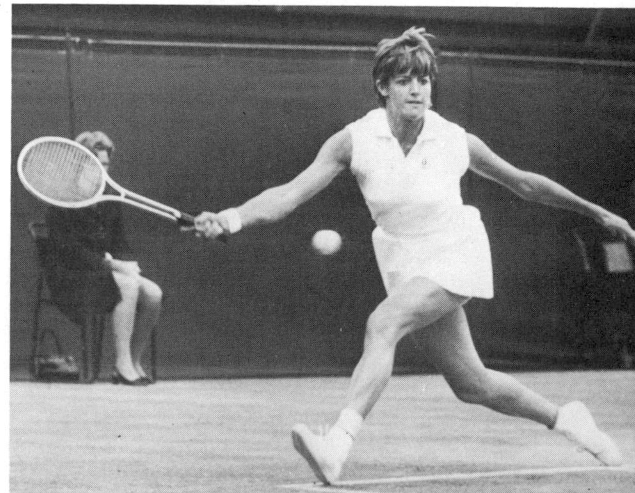

States, tying Australia's record. In zone play, Brazil won the American Zone, Spain the Section A European Zone, and Germany the Section B European Zone. Spain then beat Brazil 4–1, and West Germany blanked India, the Eastern Zone winner, 5–0. Spain lost to West Germany, 4–1, in the finals at Düsseldorf.

Other Major Tournaments

The Australian national championship went to Arthur Ashe in three straight sets over Australia's Dick Crealy, with Bob Lutz and Stan Smith of the United States taking the doubles. Rod Laver of Australia won the South African Open singles for men, John Newcombe defeated fellow Australian Ken Rosewall in five sets for the Wimbledon title, and Tom Okker of the Netherlands won the West German singles title. Rosewall won the U.S. Open singles in a four-set final from Tony Roche.

Mrs. Court scored her grand slam by winning not only the Australian, French, Wimbledon, and U.S. Open championships, but the South African title as well. The United States again beat Great Britain to keep the Wightman Cup, winning 4–3 at Wimbledon. Britain held a 3–2 lead until the last match, but lost the decisive doubles as Billie Jean King and Jane (Peaches) Bartkowicz beat Virginia Wade and Winnie Shaw 7–5, 3–6, 6–2.

Tony Roche won the U.S. professional tennis championship at Brookline, Mass., by beating his countryman Rod Laver in five sets for the top prize of $12,000. The University of California at Los Angeles captured the National Collegiate Athletic Association championships at Salt Lake City, Utah, amassing 26 points against 22 each for runners-up Rice University and Trinity University. (*See in* CE: Tennis.)

TEXTILES. The greatest concern of the U.S. textile industry in 1970 was whether or not import quotas would be leveled against Japanese textile manufacturers. After debating the issue for over a year Representative Wilbur D. Mills (D, Ark.) introduced a bill in the House of Representatives that would "roll back" Japanese imports to the 1967–68 levels. The bill was designed to punish the Japanese for failing to impose voluntary limits on textile imports to the United States.

In June U.S. Secretary of Commerce Maurice H. Stans met with Kiichi Miyazawa, Japan's trade and industry minister in Washington, D.C., to discuss the issue. Talks ended in failure when Stans rejected the Japanese proposal for voluntary control as inadequate. However, in October the textile committee of Japan's majority party passed a resolution asking for a voluntary-quota agreement. The textile talks then reopened but no agreement was reached between the United States and Japan by year-end. The Mills trade bill was passed by the House but eventually died in the Senate.

Nowhere in the U.S. textile industry was the picture particularly rosy in 1970. Representatives of the textile manufacturers as well as textile workers speaking before the House Ways and Means Committee in May stated that some 59,000 jobs had been lost in the industry during the previous year. The increased unemployment was attributed to competition from imported textiles. The economic slowdown was blamed for the drop in wool prices, which had fallen to their lowest level in 30 years by June. In addition, the stock prices of major synthetic-fiber producers plummeted dramatically. In November, Du Pont stock had fallen from 165 in 1969 to 122½; Monsanto, from 56 to 31½; and Celanese, from 73 to 56. (*See in* CE: Textiles.)

THAILAND. Changes in the U.S. Southeast Asian strategy and enlargement of the Indochina war made 1970 a particularly difficult year for the government of Thailand. On the one hand, it found the country's security situation deteriorating. On the other, it was hard put to find the money required to meet rising public expenditures for defense.

Toward the end of 1969 the United States announced that it would soon withdraw 6,000 troops from Thailand. In early 1970, U.S. Vice-President Spiro T. Agnew visited Thailand and reiterated the U.S. commitment to that country. However, the economic effects of the U.S. forces' pullback were already being felt in the country. (Even more troops were withdrawn later in the year.) Thereafter, it became part of Thai government policy to press the United States for increased financial assistance. When the war spilled over into Cambodia, Thailand's leaders recognized the need to collaborate with the new Cambodian government of Lon Nol, but firmly adhered to the view that unless the United States rushed substantial financial aid, Thailand would not play any significant role in Cambodia.

Even before the events in Cambodia, Thailand had indicated that a resurgence of terrorist activities had occurred in the north, in the northeast, and in the south. After the start of the war in Cambodia, there were more serious incidents. Thus by midyear the government found it necessary to adopt what looked like desperate measures to raise revenue to finance an increase in security spending. On June 30 import duties and sales tax on some 200 items were drastically increased. So steep was the threatened increase in the cost of living that massive protests broke out. The prime minister went on television to paint a grim picture of the security situation and to explain how it made the new taxes imperative. The tax decree was approved by the National Assembly by a majority of a single vote, but the repercussions of the crisis were felt within the government's own ranks.

Sixty members of the ruling United Thai People's party demanded a reorganization of the cabinet, dismissal of the ministers for national development and finance, and a constitutional amendment to enable Assembly members to become ministers. The prime minister refused to accept these demands, and by September the uproar had substantially subsided. However, the government suffered a major reverse that month when the budget scrutiny committee slashed several items in the 1971 budget.

In August, while the cabinet crisis was still raging, the government published a new press bill that raised another uproar. The entire press rebelled against what were described as extremely severe measures, which, for example, would authorize government press officers to close newspapers whenever they deemed it necessary to maintain peace and order. In protest, the majority of Thai newspapers jointly boycotted news of Vice-President Agnew's second visit to Thailand in August. Evidently surprised by the press protest, the government shelved consideration of the new bill and promised to change some of its more objectionable clauses.

The economy showed some signs of strain during the year, though the general outlook continued to be bright. Export earnings tended to decline because of fluctuations in world prices for rice and rubber, the country's main exports. (*See also* Asia; Cambodia; Foreign Policy, U.S. *See in* CE: Thailand.)

THEATER. Some of the brightest moments in U.S. theater in 1970 were to be found on the avant-garde front, in particular, with what was sometimes referred to as "performance theater." In this new kind of work, productions were evolved cooperatively by a company of actors, who either improvised without a written text, or freely adapted an old (dramatic or nondramatic) text, or had a text written to suit their needs by a playwright who worked with them as a member of the company.

The last method was extensively employed by the Open Theater, under the leadership of Joseph Chaikin, which during 1970 offered in New York City and elsewhere two greatly admired collaborative works: 'The Serpent: a Ceremony' ("created by the Open Theater Ensemble; words and structure by Jean-Claude van Itallie, under the direction of Joseph Chaikin") and 'Terminal' ("a collective work created by the Open Theater Ensemble, co-directed by Joseph Chaikin and Roberta Sklar, with text by Susan Yankowitz"). One of the great successes of the New York City fall season of 1970 was a performance theater version of 'Alice in Wonderland', created and performed by the Manhattan Project under André Gregory's direction. Perhaps the most promising manifestation of performance theater, however, was "Story Theatre," a technique for staging nondramatic texts that used dialogue, narration, mime, and music. Story Theatre was developed in Chicago by Paul Sills, an important pioneer in improvisational theater. Under the title of 'Paul Sills' Story Theatre', some of the Grimm brothers' folk tales, adapted and directed by Sills, arrived on Broadway in October after a successful engagement in Los Angeles.

MARTHA SWOPE

'The Rothschilds', a musical by Jerry Bock, Sheldon Harnick, and Sherman Yellen, opened on Broadway in October.

Broadway

Qualitatively and quantitatively, it was a barren season on Broadway. According to *The New York Times,* there were 34 new shows during the 1969–70 season as against 42 in 1968–69; and the 1970–71 season was noticeably slow in getting under way. The Broadway theater, once a center of creativity as well as commerce, seemed more and more given over to the production of bland and superficial entertainments, carefully tailored to the requirements of an ever-shrinking middle-aged, middle-class audience.

In recent years Broadway had largely relied on Great Britain to provide it with serious drama, and the fall season of 1970 proved to be no exception. Barry England's ripely old-fashioned thriller 'Conduct Unbecoming'; David Storey's 'Home' (starring Sir John Gielgud and Sir Ralph Richardson), dealing with a group of old people in a mental home; and Anthony Shaffer's 'Sleuth', a mystery play: all were British imports. The leading Broadway import of the 1969–70 season, however, actually came from Ireland: 'Borstal Boy', Frank McMahon's dramatization of Brendan Behan's reform-school reminiscences. It won the New York Drama Critics' Circle Award as the best play of the season.

Among the new U.S. plays that did originate on Broadway was a success by producer David Merrick: 'Child's Play', a thriller about mysterious evil in a Roman Catholic boys' school, by Robert Marasco. Among the comedies, the most successful was 'Last of the Red Hot Lovers', by Neil Simon.

When commerce and creativity did join forces successfully, the result was usually a musical. In 1970 the prime example of this union was 'Company', an acrid, intelligent, and well-crafted musical examination of the liabilities of marriage and bachelorhood in New York City. It was directed by Harold Prince, the music and lyrics were by Stephen Sondheim, and the book was by a newcomer, George Furth. On a more conventional level were the hugely successful 'Applause', a musical version of the movie 'All About Eve', made over to fit Lauren Bacall, and 'Coco', based on the life of the celebrated fashion designer Coco Chanel. 'Coco' was notable chiefly for bringing Katharine Hepburn to Broadway in her first musical comedy role.

There was one positive development on the generally gloomy Broadway scene. With the help of a grant from the National Endowment for the Arts (an arm of the federal government) one Broadway theater was taken over for use as a showcase for the work of various noncommercial companies. Its only successes, however, were two revivals of popular plays, both produced by New York City-based managements: Thornton Wilder's 'Our Town', with Henry Fonda, and Mary Chase's 'Harvey', with James Stewart and Helen Hayes. The revival fad was also in evidence elsewhere on Broadway. David Merrick presented a successful production of Noel Coward's 'Private Lives', with Tammy Grimes and Brian Bedford, that had originally been mounted by the APA (Association of Producing Artists) Repertory Company at the University of Michigan at Ann Arbor.

'The Me Nobody Knows' was a new musical based on a collection of writings by ghetto children in New York City.

BERT ANDREWS

Off-Broadway

Off-Broadway was in a somewhat healthier state than its uptown neighbor, mainly because it was considerably cheaper to put on productions there. In 1969–70 the most successful of the serious off-Broadway plays was a grimly compassionate drama of family life, 'The Effect of Gamma Rays on Man-in-the-Moon Marigolds', by Paul Zindel. It starred Sada Thompson in a much-admired performance as a neurotic mother. Two other family dramas of note were 'A Whistle in the Dark' by Thomas Murphy and 'Lemon Sky' by Lanford Wilson. All three of these plays had been performed in regional resident theaters before they appeared in New York City.

'Slave Ship', by LeRoi Jones, was a ferocious evocation of the black experience, produced by the Chelsea Theater Center in Brooklyn, N.Y., and transferred to Greenwich Village. There were two plays by the South African dramatist Athol Fugard: 'Hello and Goodbye' in the fall of 1969 and 'Boesman and Lena', with James Earl Jones and Ruby Dee, in the early summer of 1970.

Among off-Broadway comedies, the most notable were 'The White House Murder Case', by Jules Feiffer, a bitter, satirical attack on governmental lying; 'Steambath', by Bruce Jay Friedman, in which God was represented as a Puerto Rican steambath attendant; and, in the fall of 1970, 'Happy Birthday, Wanda June', a first play by the novelist Kurt Vonnegut, Jr. The late British playwright Joe Orton, who specialized in a peculiarly original sort of farce, was represented by two productions: a double bill called 'Crimes of Passion', which had a short run toward the end of 1969, and 'What the Butler Saw', produced in the spring of 1970, which was Orton's first important success in the United States. Some musicals fared well, notably 'The Me Nobody Knows' (based on the writings of ghetto children) and 'The Last Sweet Days of Isaac', both of which had modified-rock scores, and the rock musical 'Golden Bat', imported from Japan.

Repertory Theater

The Repertory Theater of Lincoln Center in New York City offered a season of U.S. plays during 1969–70, including the world premiere of Sam Shepard's 'Operation Sidewinder', which was not very successful, and 'Landscape' and 'Silence', a

Striking a rather wooden attitude is the Royal Court, whose master of ceremonies is the Proper Degree of Decorum, seen peeping from behind the protection of a lady's massive headdress. They are all from the show 'The Emergence', which is part of the repertoire of the Company Theatre in Los Angeles.

LES BLANK

bill of two very austere short plays by Harold Pinter. Joseph Papp's New York Shakespeare Festival once again survived its yearly financial crisis. The festival's Public Theater offered a season of rock musicals during the season of 1969–70, of which the most successful was 'Stomp'. At the Delacorte Theater the festival offered, in repertory, William Shakespeare's rarely performed plays about Henry VI, under the title of 'The Wars of the Roses, Parts I and II', and their sequel, 'Richard III'.

Outside New York City, many repertory theaters seemed more willing than ever to present new or unconventional plays. In Providence, R.I., the Trinity Square Repertory Theatre company presented (during its 1969–70 season) the world premieres of 'Wilson in the Promise Land', by Roland Van Zandt, and 'Lovecraft's Follies', by James Schevill, both written for the company in a rather unique style. The Trinity company seemed to be the only regional theater that was developing its own style of playwriting. The company at the Charles Playhouse in Boston, Mass., offered the U.S. premiere of 'Narrow Road to the Deep North', an enigmatic, Zen-permeated drama by the British playwright Edward Bond. The Tyrone Guthrie Theatre in Minneapolis, Minn., scored a major coup when its resident company offered the world premiere of what was billed simply as 'A Play by Aleksandr Solzhenitsyn'. The play had been published as 'The Love-Girl and the Innocent'.

The Stratford Festival Company, also called the Stratford National Theatre of Canada, presented classical repertory (including 'Hedda Gabler' with Irene Worth) at the Festival Theatre and devoted its second house, the Avon Theatre, to a season of contemporary plays, which was not a success. (*See in* CE: Drama.)

TOBACCO. Production of all types of tobacco in the United States in 1970 was estimated at slightly more than 1.8 billion pounds, about the same amount that was harvested in 1969. The average yield of 1,997 pounds per acre, however, was an improvement upon the 1969 figure.

Figures compiled in 1970 indicated that total world production of tobacco in 1969 was about 9.9 billion pounds, almost the same as in 1968 but 4.4% below the record high attained in 1967. Production of American-type cigarette leaves, flue-cured and burley, continued to rise, increasing by 3% to balance a proportional fall in production of oriental and semioriental tobaccos. Production in North America improved by about 6.6%, and South America showed an increase of some 8.1%. In Europe, Asia, and Africa, respectively, production declined by 5.4%, 4%, and 0.8%. In Australia and New Zealand production was expected to be up by about one third to some 5 million pounds more than the 1960–64 average.

Attacks on smoking on health grounds continued to intensify throughout the world in 1970, finding international expression as the United Nations World Health Organization called for antismoking campaigns in every member country. As anxieties about governmental reactions to these pressures grew among tobacco manufacturers, increased attention was given to the development of possible smoking materials other than tobacco.

Work on synthetic smoking materials had been in progress for several years; it was believed that such research was further advanced in Great Britain than elsewhere. This view was strengthened when, in its 1970 budget, the British government introduced legislation allowing the manufacture of tobacco substitutes and their use in smoking products. The new regulations cleared the way for intensified research, but it was estimated that a marketable product would not be ready for at least two or three years.

Similar research was under way in Europe, Japan, and the United States. It was probable that any practical new smoking material that emerged would be mixed with natural tobacco.

It was believed that tobacco substitutes might blunt antismoking propaganda and also reduce manufacturing costs. *(See in* CE: Tobacco.)

TOGO. In August 1970 the Togolese authorities announced the discovery of a plot to overthrow President Étienne Eyadema's government. Clément Kolor, a former deputy, was killed as he attempted to escape, as was the police officer at whose house the conspirators met. Seventeen people were arrested. It was reported that only three of these were in fact Togolese; a number of ex-soldiers from Ghana and Dahomey were implicated.

The presumed instigator of the conspiracy, Noé Kutuklui, a Togolese lawyer in exile, was placed under house arrest by the authorities in Dahomey. Kutuklui, who had been a member of the committee of former President Sylvanus Olympio's United Togolese party, had sought political asylum in Dahomey after the failure of a previous plot in November 1966. However, President Eyadema asked the Dahoman authorities to release Kutuklui, stating that the conspiracy had no popular foundation. *(See in* CE: Togo, Republic of.)

TONGA. On June 4, 1970, the kingdom of Tonga became the third completely independent South Pacific microstate. Membership in the United Nations was too expensive a luxury for it to afford, but full membership in the Commonwealth of Nations was accepted. Although the four-day independence celebrations were the most lavish ever seen in the islands, actual constitutional changes were few. Revisions of the 1900 Treaty of Friendship and Protection with Great Britain had gradually extended the kingdom's power to conduct its own external affairs, and since World War II it had looked to New Zealand for assistance in defense.

King Tupou IV of Tonga inspects the honor guard during lavish independence ceremonies held June 4 in Nukualofa.

WIDE WORLD

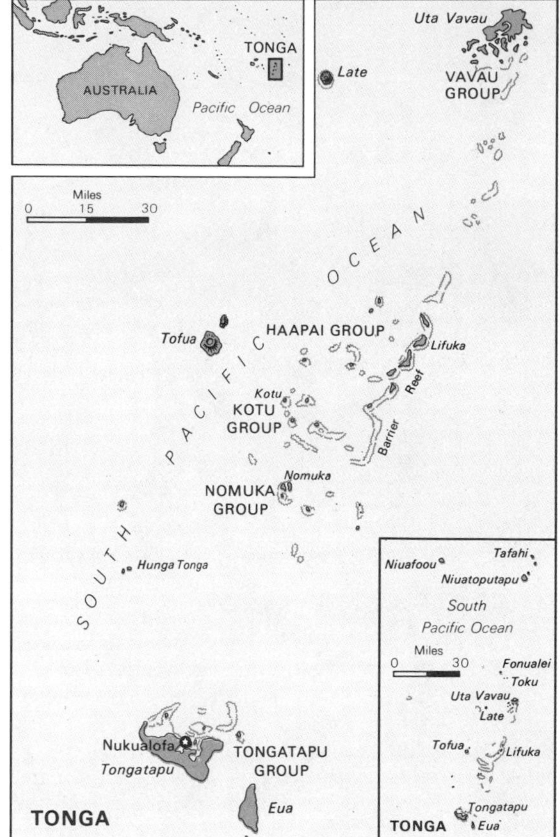

A rigidly stratified society, a narrowly based agricultural economy, a growing population, and a serious land shortage created massive problems. Unemployment was considerable, and likely to grow, because 61% of the population were under 21, and the majority faced a landless future. Moreover, the country's small size and lack of markets provided limited scope for industrial development. The educational system, in which church schools catered to about 40% of the primary and 90% of the secondary pupils, had an academic bias; indeed, about 80% of the students left at $12\frac{1}{2}$ years with no vocational training. To mark the state visit of Tonga's King Tupou IV in August, the New Zealand government announced a pilot scheme to recruit 100 Tongans for six months to work in industry.

TOYS AND GAMES. Dolls traditionally dominate the toys and games market, and 1970 was no exception. Innovations in doll accessories included wigs of synthetic hair similar to adult wigs. The wigs come in complete sets, with a revolving styrofoam head, rollers, clips, and a professional styling brush. Jumpsy was a new performing doll, said to

TRENDON LTD.

Playplax is a building toy designed in England. Slotted rings and squares can be put together to form three-dimensional models.

be the first to jump rope; a battery-operated mechanism is timed so Jumpsy never misses. One of the biggest sellers in 1970 was 19-inch-tall Peggy Pen-Pal. Seated at her desk, Peggy can copy anything the child draws, traces, or sketches on her side of the desk. Eleven-inch-tall Baby Walk 'n' Play can bounce a Yo-Yo, walk, wave a hankie, and paddle a ball.

Space toys enjoyed a great popularity, indicated by an increase in the number of manufacturers; in 1968, the market was supplied by 27 manufacturers, but the number had increased to 78 by mid-1970. There was a change from "to-the-moon" to "on-the-moon" emphasis. Some popular space toys were Golden Astronaut, Interplanetary Patrol, Moon Exploration, Launch, and Space Probe. Orbitoy includes a simulated earth and a space satellite in which a magnetized spinning unit orbits around metal disks. Mission Control Orbiting Spaceway has a mission mechanism that allows the child to speed up or slow down each of the 12 spaceships that orbit a spinning earth and space station.

This bird is a bath toy made of white plastic. The toy is weighted so that it will always right itself in the bath water.

TRENDON LTD.

Scientific toys offered a zoom telescope and a "force finder," a magnetic pendulum that traces a field set up by arrangements of magnets on the base. A feature of educational toys was the Kiddie Typer, which helps the child recognize letters and relate words to pictured objects. Letters change with each press of the key, forming words to match pictures. A separate key changes the picture.

The increase in scientific toys was accompanied by a number of pseudoscientific toys and games, reflecting interest in such occult fads as astrology, phrenology, palmistry, and witchcraft. In the Which Witch game, players try to avoid spells and whammies. In Prediction Rod, 40 disks represent planets, messages, and months. One grasps the rod, asks a question, and allows the rod to move around the board; suddenly it dips down and touches a disk with an answer. The Mystery Zodiac game reveals the player's future through a wizard fortune-teller equipped with a magic wand, a zodiac spinner, and decks of horoscope cards. There was a proliferation of mechanical, electronic, and computerized football, basketball, and hockey games in 1970.

COURTESY, REMCO INDUSTRIES, INC.

Young and old enjoy Remco's new Mystery Zodiac game, which reflects the growing interest in such occult fads as astrology.

The value of manufacturers' shipments of toys and games was expected to surpass $2 billion in 1970, which would result in $3.5 billion in retail sales. The percentage of games in total manufacturers' sales of toys and games increased from 6% of $838 million in sales in 1960 to an estimated 11% of $2.04 billion in 1969. (*See in* CE: Toys.)

UPI COMPIX

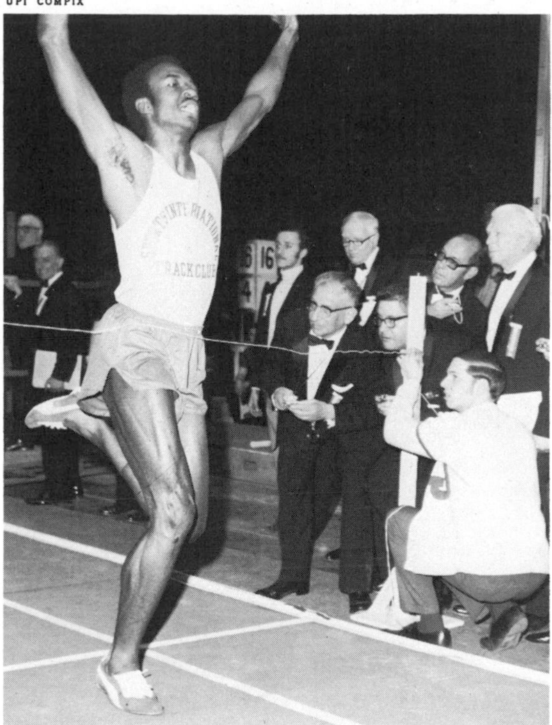

Marty McGrady (above) beat his own previous record in the 600-yard run at the AAU indoor track championship meet in February. Curtis Mills (below) led Texas A & M to victory in the 880-yard event at the Drake Relays.

UPI COMPIX

TRACK AND FIELD. Production of world records during the 1970 U.S. track-and-field season fell far below normal. One hurdler topped the international standard, a relay team shattered a three-year-old world mark, and a second hurdler matched the world record in his event. Ralph Mann, a Brigham Young University junior, ran the 440-yard intermediate hurdles in the National Collegiate Athletic Association (NCAA) championships at Des Moines, Iowa, in 48.8 seconds, erasing the 49.3 standard established by Gert Potgeiter of South Africa in 1960. The second world mark was set at the Drake Relays by a Texas A & M University relay team with a 1:21.7 clocking in the 880-yard event, 0.4 under the record established in 1967 by San Jose State College. Tom Hill, of Arkansas State University, tied the 13.2-second mark in the 120-yard high hurdles at the U.S. Track and Field Federation (USTFF) championships, the mark established by Martin Lauer of West Germany in 1959 and later shared by Lee Calhoun, Earl McCullouch, Erv Hall, and Willie Davenport (all U.S. hurdlers).

Five U.S. records also tumbled. Mark Murro, Arizona State University junior, hurled the javelin an even 300 feet, topping his own national mark by more than 7 feet. Ken Swenson, hard-driving senior from Kansas State University (KSU), set a new U.S. mark of 1:44.8 in the 800-meter event against the West German team at Stuttgart. Earlier he had anchored KSU's two-mile relay team to a record 7:16.4 clocking. Veteran Tom Von Ruden set new U.S. marks in two seldom-run events—2:6.2 in the 1,000 yards and 2:19.0 in the 1,000 meters.

Foreign tracksters fared somewhat better. Ricky Wilde of Great Britain posted a new standard of 7:47 in the 3,000-meter run at Vienna, Austria, in March, and Victor Saneev of the U.S.S.R. established a new record for the triple jump of 55 feet 7¼ inches at the same meet. At an international meet in London in September Jim Alder of Great Britain cut 55 seconds from the world 30-kilometer mark with a time of one hour, 31 minutes and 30.4 seconds, and a Kenya two-mile relay team set a new mark of 7:11.6 for their event. Late in October, Christos Papanicolaou, a 28-year-old Greek, became the first pole vaulter to top 18 feet with a mark of 18 ft. ¼ in. at a meet between Athens, Greece, and Belgrade, Yugoslavia, breaking the mark of 17 ft. 11 in. set by Wolfgang Nordwig of East Germany a month earlier.

Indoor Track and Field

Regular indoor competition resulted in a number of best all-time marks, but only two were notable improvements. Outstanding was Martin McGrady, a veteran runner, who lowered the 600-yard mark three times. A standard distance indoors, the course was covered by McGrady in 1:8.7, then 1:8.5, and finally in a sensational 1:7.6. Another standard event, the 1,000-yard race, was taken by

WIDE WORLD

Chi Cheng of Taiwan set a new world record in the women's 200-meter sprint at an international meet in West Germany.

Ralph Doubell of Australia at Albuquerque, N.M. It was his second successful U.S. trip in two years.

Several indoor "records" were tied, the 60-yard dash alone accounting for six record-equaling performances of 5.9 seconds. John Carlos, San Diego, Calif., accomplished the feat twice, and four other sprinters once each. Willie Davenport of the Houston Striders matched the 60-yard high-hurdles mark of 6.8 seconds and the 45-yard record of 5.3 seconds. Larry Highbaugh of Indiana and Jim Green of Kentucky tied the record indoor time of 6.8 seconds in the 70-yard dash.

Kansas retained the NCAA indoor team title at Detroit, Mich., March 13–14. The Southern California Striders won the Amateur Athletic Union (AAU) team honors on February 27.

Outdoor Championships of 1970

The NCAA national meet was held at Des Moines June 18–20. The University of California won, but in January 1971 the NCAA ruled that the team had used an ineligible runner. The title was awarded to runners-up Kansas, Oregon, and Brigham Young. One world, one U.S., one collegiate, and five meet records were broken. In addition to Mann's mark (also a U.S. record), Bob Bertelson of Ohio University set a collegiate and meet mark of 27:57.5 in the six-mile run. Steve Prefontaine of Oregon set a new meet mark of 13:22 in the three-mile run, and Sid Sink of Bowling Green ran 8:40.9 in the 3,000-meter steeplechase. Rick Wanamaker, Drake University, won the first national decathlon with 7,406 points.

In the AAU outdoor championships at Bakersfield, Calif., late in June, the Southern California Striders repeated their indoor triumph with a team total of 85 points. A feature of the meet was the photo-finish 100-yard dash, with the five first-place finishers all being timed in 9.3 seconds. After studying pictures, a photo jury ruled that Ivory Crockett, Southern Illinois, had retained his title by a fraction of an inch.

A barnstorming tour of Europe in midsummer saw the U.S. tracksters take the opening meet from France, 117–94, after trailing by 6 points the first day. This was followed by a 182–175 loss to West Germany and a 200–173 defeat at the hands of the Soviet Union in Leningrad. In early August, the U.S. athletes took seven firsts in an international meet at Cologne, West Germany, and 10 of 15 events in a similar meet at Malmö, Sweden.

California Polytechnic won the NCAA college division honors, and Eastern Michigan the National Association of Intercollegiate Athletics title. Kansas was the USTFF winner.

Women's Competition; Other Developments

In 1970, U.S. women had an unproductive year for world records. Chi Cheng of Nationalist China dominated the world track scene by breaking world sprint records in both the United States and Europe. She equaled the 100-yard sprint mark of 10.3 seconds on March 28, set an American All-Comers record of 13.3 in the 100 meters in May, and barely missed the 440-yard record of 52.4 in mid-June. But her best day came on June 13 at Portland, Ore.,

Ralph Mann (right) of Brigham Young University won the 440-yard intermediate-hurdles event in the NCAA meet held at Drake University on June 20, 1970.

WIDE WORLD

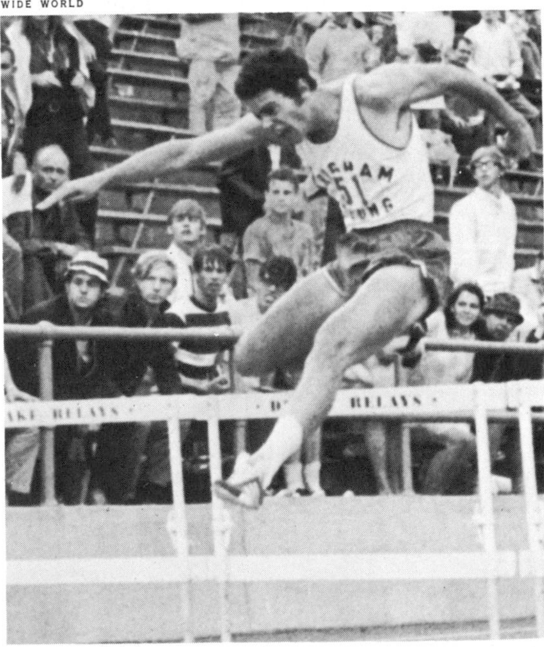

when she clocked 10.1 seconds in the 100 yards (.2 second under the record); cut .2 from the 200-yard record, running 22.7 seconds; and set an American All-Comers mark of 13.2 in the hurdles. Three weeks later she sliced her 220-yard time to 22.6. Indoors, she set new records of 6.5 seconds in the 50 yards and 6.9 in the 50-meter hurdles and won three events in the AAU championships. The Mayor Daley Youth Foundation of Chicago won both the indoor and outdoor AAU championships. A highlight of the latter meet was a new world mark of 3:41.3 in the one-mile relay, set by the Atoms Track Club of Brooklyn, N.Y.

Decathlon king Bill Toomey late in January was named winner of the Sullivan Trophy as the outstanding amateur U.S. athlete in 1969. The International Amateur Athletic Federation ruling requiring the wearing of all-white shoes by track-and-field athletes was relaxed in late April, when the effective date was postponed from May 1 to October 1. (*See in* CE: Track and Field Sports.)

TRANSPORTATION. The transportation industry in 1970 continued to seek means of moving larger units at greater speeds. "Jumbo jets" entered airline service and, despite "teething troubles," flew on a growing number of routes. On test flights, both prototypes of the Anglo-French Concorde supersonic passenger plane reached twice the speed of sound. Civil aviation was increasingly harassed by hijacking and sabotage—four planes were destroyed on the ground and one in the air by the end of September. International action began in the hope of containing this form of piracy.

At sea the trend toward larger vessels, especially tankers, continued. Container and roll-on/roll-off services also continued to increase. The world's major ports planned new facilities to accommodate the new ships. (*See* Ships and Shipping.)

Railroads made headway in their fight against highway competition. Higher speeds on scheduled services attracted additional passengers, and the development of container and other unit-load services, combined with improved terminal facilities and coordination with road and water transportation, improved freight volume.

In highway transport, the major development of 1970 was the rapid expansion of container and roll-on/roll-off freight services. Except for the long-established piggyback truck/train services in the United States, the new services were largely to facilitate the transfer of cargo from ships to trucks. Overall, it was estimated that during the year 85% of all cargo left its point of origin, and reached its destination, by truck.

The extension of natural-gas pipelines accelerated during 1970, far outpacing pipeline construction for crude oil and petroleum products. In Western Europe 473 miles of crude-oil lines were under construction and another 507 miles were planned or under study, while 2,240 miles of natural-gas lines were being built and 692 miles were planned or being considered. The Soviet Union continued to lead in both types of pipeline; its gas lines reached more than 39,000 miles in 1970 and carried some 1.6 billion cubic feet of gas in the first quarter of the year alone.

The largest U.S. pipeline project—a proposed 800-mile-long oil line between Prudhoe Bay and Valdez, Alaska—was still held up in the fall by the Department of the Interior, which required satisfaction that it could be built without threatening the fragile ecology of Alaska's Arctic. Construction was planned to begin in 1971 on the first section of Canada's proposed 1,550-mile-long natural-gas line from Alaska's North Slope to U.S. markets. (*See* Conservation Special Report.)

In the United States, interest in hovercraft, or surface-effect vehicles, increased. In competition with Aerojet-General Corp., Bell Aerospace won U.S. Navy contracts to build two sizes of assault landing craft. Both firms were also working on prototype 100-ton hovercraft that were expected to begin trials in 1971. They also felt that hovercraft might be employed on Alaska's North Slope, where vehicles that press upon the ground heavily enough to break birds' eggs in their nests are forbidden. Great Britain retained its monopoly on regularly scheduled hovercraft services. Those operating between Britain and France carried nearly a million passengers and 100,000 automobiles during the year.

AIRLINES

The faltering traffic growth and rising costs that plagued U.S. airlines in 1969 continued in 1970. Overall load factors continued to decline as only cargo service showed a healthy growth rate. Profits—never very high in the airline industry—dropped sharply, or became losses, for many U.S. carriers. Among the giants, for example, Pan American World Airways reported losses in 1969 of about $20 million, and United Air Lines—the world's biggest carrier apart from the Soviet Union's Aeroflot—reported fairly heavy losses for the first half of 1970.

Consequently, airlines were seriously wondering how they were going to meet the cost—about $10 billion in the next four years—of the vast program of reequipment with Boeing 747's and wide-bodied, high-capacity McDonnell Douglas and Lockheed trijets. A trend toward airline mergers—such as that proposed between Northwest and Northeast—was foreseen if revenues did not improve.

The Problem of Hijacking

Hijacking became an increasingly serious problem for the world's airlines in 1970. Hijacking reached the crisis level when, during a six-day period in September, Palestinian guerrillas hijacked, then destroyed on the ground, four airliners, including a Boeing 747, valued at a total of about $50 million.

Bomb-detection devices such as this one at a London airport have helped somewhat to protect passengers from would-be hijackers.

LONDON "DAILY EXPRESS" FROM PICTORIAL PARADE

Previously, the installation of antihijacking devices—including weapons detectors—had begun at major airports. In the wake of the September incidents, some U.S. and other airlines adopted Israel's practice of stationing armed guards aboard their aircraft. International agreements on the treatment of hijackers were sought.

New Aircraft; Antipollution Efforts

Transport aircraft and engine manufacturers experienced a combination of technical success and financial difficulty in 1970. The huge Boeing 747 entered service early in the year, and both big trijets—the McDonnell Douglas DC-10 and the Lockheed 1011 TriStar—were test-flown later in the year. Initially, the 747's were frequently off schedule, due largely to minor engine ailments. By mid-July, however, they were operating smoothly; the more than 50 then in service with 11 airlines had already carried a million passengers.

Fifteen airlines—five in Europe—had placed firm orders for a total of 119 DC-10's and taken options on 122 more. TriStar orders and options, which had lagged through 1969, totaled 78. These airliners, designed to carry from 250 to 365 passengers on medium and long routes, were scheduled to enter service in 1971.

In Europe, testing of the prototypes of two supersonic transports (SSTs) continued. Both the Soviet Tu-144 and the British-French Concorde reached speeds in excess of Mach 2. Meanwhile, the future of the proposed U.S. SST—larger and faster than the European versions—was in doubt. The SST project was strongly attacked by environmentalist groups. Although the House approved the SST development program, the Senate voted not to appropriate further funds to the project. In the last hours of the 91st Congress a temporary compromise was reached whereby the SST would be funded until March 1971. (*See* Aircraft.)

Plane-Mate is a wheeled passenger lounge developed by the Budd Co. of Philadelphia, Pa., as a partial answer to the rising costs of new terminal buildings. It is part bus and part elevator and will be introduced in 1971 at John F. Kennedy International and La Guardia airports by American Airlines and Pan American World Airways.

COURTESY, THE BUDD CO.

The airlines' safety record was good in 1970. In fact, U.S. scheduled airlines set a safety record, with no fatalities on U.S. domestic flights and only one fatal crash that killed two persons on an overseas flight during the year. Worldwide, jet airliners continued to have a fatality rate only about a tenth of that for propeller aircraft.

New, virtually smoke-free engines were introduced on the Boeing 747 and were to be used on the smaller trijets as part of a continuing effort to reduce air pollution. Plans were advanced to install smoke-reducing devices on older airliners. British and U.S. laws also required that newer airliners meet noise limitations. (*See in* CE: Airlines.)

RAILROADS

A strike by four unions that represent some 80% of U.S. railroad workers halted rail traffic throughout the nation for 18 hours on December 10. The unions sought increased fringe benefits; pay increases of 40% to 45% over three years for their members, whose wages then averaged $3.45 to $3.60 an hour; and retention of work rules that railroad management said compelled the railroads to retain thousands of unnecessary workers at an annual cost of millions of dollars. Management had offered the unions a 37% wage increase but had insisted upon modification of the work rules.

Little more than two hours after the strike began, a federal court—acting under legislation hastily passed by Congress—issued an injunction to halt the strike. The workers did not return to their jobs, however, until the court threatened to fine the principal union—the Brotherhood of Railway Clerks—$200,000 for each day the workers remained on strike. The measure that was passed by Congress forbade any new strike before March 1, 1971; granted the workers an immediate 13.5% wage increase, retroactive to Jan. 1, 1970; and required labor and management to resume negotiations.

In August the railroads, financially hard pressed, were granted a 6% freight rate increase by the Interstate Commerce Commission (ICC), which also approved a further 5% interim increase. In September the railroads were allowed to petition for additional increases.

Railroad earnings declined sharply and, by midyear, 22 Class I railroads were failing to return a profit. The industry's return on investment fell to 1.88% in the year ending June 30, and four Class I railroads—including the Penn Central, the world's largest railroad—were in reorganization or receivership.

Several railroad mergers were approved in 1970. The largest one joined the Great Northern, the Northern Pacific, the Chicago, Burlington and Quincy, the Spokane, Portland and Seattle, and the Pacific Coast Railroad Co. to form the Burlington Northern system. The ICC also approved the merger of the Monon and the Louisville and Nashville. The Kansas, Oklahoma and Gulf was merged with its parent, the Texas and Pacific. The merger of the Chicago and North Western with the Chicago, Milwaukee, St. Paul and Pacific was denied, however, as was the control of the Detroit and Toledo Shore Line by the Grand Trunk Western.

Freight traffic on U.S. railroads in 1970 increased at about the same rate that it did in 1969, totaling an estimated 770 billion ton-miles—a new record. The railroads continued to haul more than half of the automobiles shipped from factories and accounted for about 40% of all intercity freight ton-miles.

Intercity rail passenger traffic continued to decline, while commuter traffic continued to increase. Passenger-miles totaled an estimated 11.5 billion during the year—half the total of ten years before.

By the close of 1970, nearly every freight car in the United States bore a set of "service stripes"—colored strips indicating the car's identification number, owner, weight and capacity, and other information. Scanners were being installed at strategic points along main lines. They will periodically pick up data from the code strips and relay the information to computers, which will store it for quick retrieval. The system, expected to be in operation by early 1971, will greatly aid in keeping track of freight cars. (*See in* CE: Railroads.)

KEYSTONE

The biggest heavy-equipment carrier in the world was developed in West Germany. It consists of two carriages, each with four eight-wheel trucks.

TRUCKS AND TRUCKING

The trucking industry in the United States grew at a slower pace in 1970 than it did in the preceding year. The Interstate Commerce Commission (ICC)-regulated trucking companies, numbering about 15,000, reported that their combined revenues rose to more than $13 billion. Trucking continued to be the foremost common carrier, accounting for more than half of the revenues of all ICC-regulated transportation.

A very difficult transport problem is solved with the use of a 75-foot-long trailer van. McDonnell Douglas Astronautics Co. uses the van to haul the Long Tank Thor, the 66-foot-long first stage of the Delta rocket, to launching pads in Florida and in California. The Thor is lowered by crane into the van (top); the unique top of the van is put into position (center); and the two sections of the van are fastened together (bottom).
AUTHENTICATED NEWS INTERNATIONAL

The number of trucks on U.S. highways rose again. The total number of commercial, farm, and private trucks in operation in 1970 reached a record of well over 17 million. The highway-use taxes paid by the trucking industry increased proportionately: trucking companies paid a total of more than $5 billion in federal, state, and local road-user taxes.

As trucking use increased, so, too, did the demand for new trucks. The year saw near-record sales of all types of trucks, including diesel-powered models. Similarly, truck-trailer sales were high, nearing the record level in 1969.

Containerization of cargo—particularly of goods moved internationally—continued to grow during the year. Containerization eases and reduces the cost of transferring cargo from one mode of transportation—land, sea, or air—to another. Container sizes remained unstandardized, but the trucking industry was hopeful that uniformity could be achieved by manufacturers and shippers. In addition, international accords—intended to facilitate customs clearance—were being drafted.

Government permission to use larger equipment was sought by the transportation industry as a whole during the year. Motor carriers sought allowance to operate larger and heavier trucks on interstate highways to match the enlarged aircraft and railroad cars in use. Size and weight increases would permit, in the view of trucking company officers, improved coordination of truck, rail, and air transport facilities.

The International Brotherhood of the Teamsters and the trucking industry negotiated a new 39-month contract. The final agreement called for an increase of $1.85, or 41.3%, and generated inflationary pressure on U.S. wages in general. (*See* Labor Unions.)

Other trucking industry developments of 1970 included efforts to further computerize billings, tariffs, scheduling, and terminal operations. Emerging federal safety and pollution standards were leading to revised equipment designs. (*See in* CE: Transportation; Truck.)

TRAVEL. In 1970 the shadow of a U.S. recession made some impact upon tourism in the Americas, with the U.S. government's anti-inflation policies affecting consumer spending and borrowing. Early in the year, however, the travel industry had reason to view the prospects optimistically. From November 1969, lower-than-ever air fares on the North Atlantic route drew increasing numbers of U.S. tourists to Europe. The U.S. Passport Office reported that by the end of May the number of passport applications from Europe-bound travelers was up 19% over the same period in 1969. Nevertheless, the lower fares often meant reduced revenues for the airlines, which were faced with rising costs.

Of the estimated 700,000 Americans who visited Europe in the summer of 1970, 40% were under 30. The young tourists and their life-style had become something of a phenomenon on the Continent. In contrast to the Americans traveling abroad in earlier decades, these tourists were for the most part traveling on very limited budgets, living in youth hostels, and hitchhiking across the countryside. The young Americans abroad who sported long hair, beards, shabby clothing, or any trappings of the "hippie" culture, faced some difficulties, however. Some nations, such as the Netherlands and Afghanistan, required that long-haired entrants have sufficient funds to support themselves during their stay.

Charter flights and travel agency tours emerged as the biggest headaches in the travel industry during the year. During the summer around 3,500 U.S. students were stranded in Europe when the agency that booked their tours, World Academy, Inc., of Cincinnati, Ohio, collapsed. Fortunately charter airline passage had been paid in advance, enabling the students to return home. The case brought about a demand for legislation requiring that travel agencies be licensed, and a bill to that effect was introduced in the U.S. House of Representatives. Under the bill, agencies would be required to be bonded to prevent such customer losses.

Young U.S. citizens were often inventive in their low-budget travel plans. These young people are on their way to Europe.

JOAN SYDLOW

WIDE WORLD

Antarctica does not appeal to most tourists. However, a hardy few have visited areas like Paradise Bay on Antarctic Peninsula.

Meanwhile, illegal charter flights were thriving across the United States. The flights, which accounted for as much as 70% of the West coast's European-bound travel during the peak 1969 summer season, offered fares as low as half the price of normal rates. The existing regulations set by the Civil Aeronautics Board (CAB) required that persons on a charter flight be members of an organization not formed primarily for travel and that they should have been members for at least six months. These regulations had been virtually impossible to enforce. In May the CAB proposed new regulations that would limit the number of seats an organization could charter in one year to 2,000 and would establish a variety of criteria on the election of officers and on membership requirements. The new regulations were opposed by a number of organizations and airlines. *(See also* Feature Article: "Let's Travel.")

Canada's Prime Minister Trudeau entertains a group of Eskimo children with a drum dance during his 1970 tour of the Arctic. The dance is an old Eskimo ritual.

PETER BREGG FROM CANADIAN PRESS

TRUDEAU, PIERRE ELLIOTT. Canada's Prime Minister Pierre Elliott Trudeau responded firmly and unequivocally to a crisis that threatened the very core of stable and democratic government in Canada in October 1970—the kidnapping of two men, British diplomat James R. Cross and Quebec's minister of labor and immigration, Pierre Laporte, by an underground terrorist separatist movement, the Quebec Liberation Front (FLQ). After a week of negotiations with representatives of the FLQ to free the men proved fruitless, Trudeau took strong action to deal with the crisis, invoking the War Measures Act for the first time in peacetime. The act suspended many civil liberties and gave the government sweeping powers, allowing the arrest without charge of hundreds of FLQ members and sympathizers. Shortly afterwards, Laporte's body was found; his abductors apparently had killed him in retaliation for Trudeau's hard-line reaction to their demands. Cross was freed in December.

Trudeau asked for a vote of confidence from Parliament and appealed for support to Canadians, arguing that the special powers were necessary to meet the threat to Canada's unity and freedom. Although Trudeau received overwhelming support for his actions, some members of Parliament criticized the government for having assumed powers that were too "harsh" and "broad" to deal with the situation. Trudeau assuaged his opposition by introducing specific legislation to deal with the terrorism. Once it was passed, the Trudeau government planned to lift the War Measures Act.

Trudeau's tough-minded approach was characteristic. In economic matters, Trudeau's government followed harsh, anti-inflationary policies that were generally unpopular though they met with some success. In foreign policy, the government took a major initiative, establishing diplomatic relations with Communist China in a treaty likely to form a model for other Western nations. (*See also* Canada; Canadian Economy; Canadian Provinces.)

TUNISIA. The main political event of 1970 in Tunisia was the trial of Ahmed Ben Salah, former secretary of state for economy and planning and a partisan of economic socialization. He was accused of high treason and abuse of authority. The case came before the High Court in Tunis, the capital, on May 19. He was sentenced to ten years at hard labor.

In June, President Habib Bourguiba returned to Tunisia after six months' medical treatment abroad. Shortly afterward, Prime Minister Bahi Ladgham formed a government of national unity. This included Mohammed Masmoudi, who was formerly Tunisia's ambassador to France, in charge of foreign affairs; Ahmed Mestiri, who had not been a member of the preceding government, now fully reconciled with the Neo-Destour Socialist party and in charge of the interior; and Hedi Nouira, who was previously governor of the Central Bank, in charge of the economy. Following Ladgham's appointment as head of the Arab Cease-Fire Observer Mission in Jordan, Nouira became prime minister in the autumn.

The work of the joint military commission engaged in solving frontier problems between Tunisia and Algeria was brought to a satisfactory conclusion with the signing on May 17 of a 20-year treaty on the delineation of the frontier. (*See in* CE: Tunisia.)

TURKEY. During 1970 Turkey's Prime Minister Suleyman Demirel was assailed within his Justice party, in the parliament, and by the enemies of parliamentary rule. He did, however, succeed in reconstituting his administration and went on to carry out major economic and social reforms.

The enemies of the Justice party and of the parliament were given an opening by the dissatisfaction felt by Prime Minister Demirel's right-wing colleagues at their exclusion from the new government. On January 17, 72 Justice party members signed a memorandum demanding that dissidents not be expelled. When, nevertheless, four deputies and two senators were expelled, seven members of the party executive resigned. On February 11, 41 Justice party deputies voted against the budget, securing its rejection by the National Assembly by 224–214. Demirel thereupon resigned on February 14, but he was asked by President Cevdet Sunay to form a new government. After an interval, during which he split the dissidents and recruited another nine deputies into his party, Demirel presented an unchanged cabinet to the assembly and, on March 15, won a vote of confidence, 232–172. The budget was passed on May

Tents are improvised (left) in the area devastated by the earthquake in Turkey in March. Villagers (below) wander through the ruins that were left by the quake.

LEFT: A.F.P. FROM PICTORIAL PARADE. BELOW: LONDON "DAILY EXPRESS" FROM PICTORIAL PARADE

30, and on June 25 another 26 dissidents were expelled from the Justice party.

The assault on Prime Minister Demirel in the parliament was taken up by the opposition, which demanded an investigation into press allegations that the prime minister had abused his official position to the financial benefit of his brothers. Outside the parliament the democratic regime came under fire from student and worker militants.

Foreign policy continued to be nicely balanced. By July 1 all U.S. bases and facilities in Turkey, with the exception of the air base at Incirlik, near Adana, had been handed back to the Turkish authorities. On August 21 an agreement was signed under which the Soviet Union would lend Turkey $113.7 million for industrial development, in addition to the $200 million already promised. (*See in* CE: Turkey.)

UGANDA. The would-be assassins of Uganda's President Milton Obote were brought to trial, convicted, and on May 6, 1970, were sentenced to life imprisonment. The assassination attempt took place in December 1969. An attempt on the life of another official succeeded in 1970. In January Brig. Gen. Pierino Yere Okoya and his wife were fatally shot at their home.

Information released in January indicated that reaction to the Obote assassination attempt was severe. The government claimed that only seven deaths occurred as the result of the military's search for the assassins, but unofficial reports estimated that as many as 50 persons may have been killed.

The Ugandan Immigration Act, which went into effect May 1, caused concern about the future among the Asian population. The implementation of the act was followed by the disappearance of a British diplomat, Brian Lea. Two days later Lea reappeared and said that he had been kidnapped by four Asians. An inquiry into the incident found that Lea had planned the "kidnapping" to dramatize the plight of Asians holding British citizenship but not being allowed to emigrate to Great Britain because of the British government's quota on Asian immigration.

Relations between Kenya and Uganda became strained when it was announced that thousands of Kenyan workers in Uganda would be replaced with

Ugandan nationals. On May 1, Obote announced the nationalization of the import and export trade, with the exception of imported petroleum products. The government also acquired 60% interest in all banks, public transport, manufacturing industries, mines, and plantations. (*See in* CE: Uganda.)

UNION OF SOVIET SOCIALIST REPUBLICS (U.S.S.R.).

The struggle of attrition between the Soviet establishment and a small and heterogeneous group of dissident intellectuals continued throughout 1970. It was difficult to make any exact estimate of the extent and nature of the situation, as most reports originated from unconfirmed sources and the clandestine newssheets and pamphlets circulating in the Soviet Union. Perhaps the most interesting of these unconfirmed reports concerned an alleged movement for reform on true Communist lines among officers of the Baltic fleet, culminating in the summary execution of a naval officer in Estonia in June. Criticism of the system from writers and poets caused less concern to the Soviet authorities than that voiced by some scientists, in particular by the eminent physicist Andrei D. Sakharov, who coauthored an "open letter" to the Soviet leaders that reached the West in early 1970. Sakharov, who had first stated his views in 1968, argued again that the Soviet Union was falling behind the West economically and technologically because its "antidemocratic traditions" restricted the free circulation of information.

Soviet Jewry increasingly came under attack by the regime. At some risk to themselves, 39 Jewish intellectuals from Moscow, the capital, and 21 from Leningrad addressed letters to the United Nations in March, asking for their "human rights" to be allowed to leave for Israel. The official daily *Izvestia* simply denounced them as "anti-Soviet renegades." Vague reports in June connecting Jewish groups in the Soviet Union with plans to hijack aircraft were followed by more credible reports of fairly widespread arrests among Jews in Leningrad. On December 24, 11 defendants, 9 of them Jewish, were found guilty of attempting to hijack a Soviet airliner. Two of the group were sentenced to be shot by a firing squad, and the others were given stiff prison-camp terms. The Jews had been planning to emigrate to Israel. The sentences set off protest demonstrations in the United States and elsewhere. An appeals court commuted the death sentences to 15 years in prison and reduced the prison terms for three of the other defendants.

The first successful pirating of a Soviet aircraft occurred in October when two Lithuanian dissidents hijacked an Aeroflot AN-24 airliner that was on an internal flight and forced it to land in Turkey. They were allowed to claim political asylum, even though a Soviet air hostess, Nadezhda Kurchenko, had been killed in the struggle for control of the aircraft. Shortly afterward, a light plane carrying three U.S. Army officers and a senior Turkish officer was made to land in Soviet Armenia, having been forced across the Turkish-Soviet border by adverse weather conditions; the officers were released in November.

The Soviet authorities did not by any means ignore the activities of writers in 1970 and took steps to assert the official line on the literary front.

The traditionally militaristic tone of May Day celebrations in Moscow was clearly lacking in 1970. The only military units in the parade through Red Square represented the armed forces academies in the Moscow area.

UPI COMPIX

In February Aleksandr Tvardovsky lost his post as editor of *Novy Mir,* the only literary journal of quality in the Soviet Union. Tvardovsky had always stood for high literary standards and never regarded Communist party orthodoxy as the yardstick for assessing literary values. His dismissal was rightly regarded as a considerable victory for the supporters of strict party control over the arts. This was strongly emphasized by the writers' congress of the Russian Federation held in Moscow in March and attended by both Communist Party General Secretary Leonid I. Brezhnev and Premier Aleksei N. Kosygin; the occasion was used to denounce "ideological laxity" in all its forms and to call for more "popular" literature.

On the whole, however, the official attitude toward intellectual dissent remained firm, and the award of the Nobel prize for literature to Aleksandr I. Solzhenitsyn was officially regarded as an act of provocation in view of his uncompromising criticism of the less attractive aspects of Soviet society. Because of the uproar, Solzhenitsyn withdrew his application to be allowed to go to Stockholm, Sweden, in December to receive his prize. When attacks on Solzhenitsyn were renewed, recalling his expulsion from the Union of Soviet Writers in November 1969, the famous Soviet cellist Mstislav Rostropovich defended the maligned writer in an open letter to Soviet newspapers and recalled in this context the cultural terror practiced in Joseph Stalin's day. Indeed, the tone of domestic policy in 1970 was typified by the appearance in June of a portrait-bust of Stalin on his grave in Moscow's Red Square.

The literary *cause célèbre* of the year was that of the young writer Andrei Amalrik, whose book 'Will the Soviet Union Survive Until 1984?' had predicted the collapse of what he regarded as the corrupted and inefficient Soviet system and forecast its extinction at the hands of Communist China. Amalrik was arrested in May and brought to trial in the remote city of Sverdlovsk, in the Ural Mountains, in November; he was sentenced to three years at hard labor.

The Economy

Pravda reported early in 1970 that industrial production had risen by 7% in 1969 (the economic plan had stipulated an increase of 7.4%). The party paper criticized a number of industrial ministries for "lethargy" and hinted that the Soviet Union was not immune from the worldwide phenomenon of wage inflation, as in some sections of the economy wages had increased at a faster rate than productivity. The five Central Asian Union Republics all failed to fulfill their industrial production targets.

Agricultural production stood at 3% below the 1968 total, a disappointing result attributed to poor weather conditions. However, the decline in the actual production total of milk and meat was alarming, as was the failure to meet housing construction targets. The agricultural problems were ventilated at a collective farm congress that met in Moscow at the end of November 1969—the first since 1935. There an important innovation was announced: a central social insurance fund for collective farmers was set up, thus establishing systematic social insurance for rural workers and extending to them the benefits that their comrades in industry had enjoyed virtually since the October Revolution in 1917. New directives for agriculture were issued in July, providing for immediate cash incentives to increase the production of meat and also calling for improvements in the supply of fruit and vegetables.

Foreign Affairs

Perhaps the most important development in foreign policy was the signing of the Soviet-West German Renunciation of Force Treaty in August. This was the result of new initiatives toward Eastern Europe undertaken by the West German government, beginning with a series of exploratory talks conducted in Moscow by West Germany's special envoy Egon Bahr early in the year. The first sign that the two sides were coming closer together was the conclusion of an agreement in March to exchange consuls general in Leningrad and in Hamburg, West Germany.

On August 12, West Germany's Chancellor Willy Brandt signed the treaty in Moscow, expressing the determination of the two countries to "improve and extend cooperation between them, including economic relations as well as scientific, technological, and cultural contacts." Both parties undertook to refrain from the threat or use of force and agreed to accept the "actual situation" existing in Europe, with particular reference to the present frontiers. In effect, this amounted to recognition of Poland's western border, and though the treaty was subject to ratification (and this in turn depended on agreement in the four-power talks on Berlin), it made an important contribution toward underpinning the status quo. Economic cooperation between the U.S.S.R. and West Germany was expected to be of benefit to the Soviet economy. Early in the year an agreement was concluded for the sale of West German steel pipe to be paid for ultimately by supplies of natural gas from the Soviet Union; the bridging finance for the deal was provided by West German banks. Following the signing of the Renunciation of Force Treaty, there were reports of negotiations on the possible development of a new truck plant in the Soviet Union by a West German firm. (*See* World Trade.) In November Hans Leussink, the West German minister of education and science, visited Moscow at the head of a group of experts for talks on scientific and technological cooperation.

The status quo in Eastern Europe was further strengthened by the cooperation between Moscow and the regime of Gustav Husak in Czechoslovakia. In May Brezhnev went to Prague to sign yet an-

WIDE WORLD

A bust of the late Soviet dictator Joseph Stalin was placed on his tomb in Red Square in Moscow, signifying his return to favor.

other Soviet-Czechoslovak treaty of friendship, cooperation, and mutual assistance. The treaty formally obliged Czechoslovakia to accept the so-called Brezhnev doctrine of limited sovereignty, justifying the intervention of one socialist country in the affairs of another to safeguard the established socialist order.

The Soviet-U.S. dialogue was, of course, the most important concern of Soviet foreign policy during the year. The recognition that relations between the two superpowers had to be improved, despite the frequent ritual references to ideological incompatibilities, had become one of the fundamental facts of international life. During his visit to Washington, D.C., in October, Soviet Foreign Minister Andrei A. Gromyko cleared up the tension that had arisen earlier over the reported preparations for the building of a Soviet missile submarine base in Cuba. Firm U.S. reaction had caused the immediate withdrawal of a Soviet submarine tender and a tug. Following talks at the White House, it was agreed that the Soviets would not construct a base, while the United States would not object to Soviet ships' using Cuba as an occasional port of call. (*See also* Disarmament.)

Soviet diplomacy was presented with a difficult problem in the Middle East. It had to avoid a direct confrontation with the United States while consolidating Soviet relations with the Arab governments. The extremists among the Palestinian guerrillas attempted to upset this balance, and the Soviet attitude toward their hijacking incidents was less than enthusiastic. The Middle East crisis illustrated some of the differences between Communist China and the Soviet Union. The Chinese denounced the peace plan of U.S. Secretary of State William P. Rogers as an attempt by the United States and the Soviet Union to inflict a "new Munich" on the Arabs. (*See in* CE: Russia.)

UNITED ARAB REPUBLIC (UAR). All other events in the UAR, or Egypt, in 1970 were dwarfed by the sudden death of Gamal Abdel Nasser, the nation's president and the Arab world's most popular leader, on September 28. Both before and after Nasser's death, however, the conflict with Israel played a dominant role in shaping government policies.

Early in the year morale in the UAR suffered as a result of Israeli air strikes deep within UAR territory, including the suburbs of Cairo, and Israel's 32-hour occupation of Shadwan Island in the Gulf of Suez. Israeli attacks on nonmilitary installations, allegedly inadvertent, resulted in heavy civilian casualties, including the deaths of 46 children in a delta village. Israel's striking power was curtailed, however, when the Soviet Union significantly stepped up its aid to the UAR in April. Soviet SAM-3 antiaircraft missiles were installed to protect UAR cities and military bases, Soviet airmen began piloting UAR-marked interceptor planes, and the number of Soviet military advisers in the UAR rose from about 3,000 to at least 8,000.

With the UAR's interior more adequately protected, fighting during the late spring and early summer intensified along the Suez Canal front. Land and air attacks were launched by both the UAR and Israel; Israel conducted saturation bombings of SAM-3 sites under construction near the canal.

Although Nasser publicly blamed U.S. support of Israel for the Middle Eastern situation and undertook a diplomatic campaign against the United States, he remained in contact with U.S. officials. Following the opening of a U.S. peace initiative in June, Nasser visited the Soviet Union for consultations with Soviet leaders and for medical treatment. On July 23, a few days after his return, he accepted the U.S. proposals for a three-month cease-fire and indirect Arab-Israeli negotiations. Nasser's acceptance, supported by many Arab states, drew criticism from Syria, Iraq, and others and divided the Palestinian guerrilla movement; two critical Palestinian radio programs transmitted from Cairo were suspended from the air.

The 90-day cease-fire went into effect on the Suez front on August 7. Within a month Israel accused the UAR of violating the agreement by moving missiles into the canal zone; the U.S. supported the charges, while Cairo denied them. In November the UAR accepted a United Nations recommendation for a three-month extension of the cease-fire.

During 1970 the UAR's position in the Arab

world was strengthened by the cooperation and support of new revolutionary regimes in Sudan and Libya. Both nations offered the UAR air bases secure from Israeli attack. Plans to integrate the economies of the three nations were announced in April. At a tripartite conference after Nasser's death, agreement was reached on steps to be taken toward the eventual political federation of the UAR, Libya, and Sudan.

President Nasser, supported by Libya and Sudan, took a leading role in efforts to settle a civil war between Jordanian authorities and Palestinian guerrillas in September. Following an Arab summit meeting in Cairo, at which the dispute was successfully mediated, Nasser was stricken with a fatal heart attack.

Nasser was buried in Cairo on October 1 after millions of mourning Egyptians had followed his funeral cortege through the city streets. Leadership of the UAR passed to Vice-President Anwar el-Sadat, who became acting president. On October 3 the Arab Socialist Union, the UAR's only legal political party, recommended that Sadat succeed Nasser as president. The National Assembly nominated Sadat for the office, and voters overwhelmingly confirmed his election in a national referendum on October 15. Sadat was sworn into office as president on October 17.

Sadat began the formation of a new cabinet almost immediately, with the appointment of Mahmoud Fawzi, an expert on foreign affairs, as premier. The new government moved quickly to

Weeping mourners (below) surround the funeral cortege for the UAR's President Nasser. One man weeps alone (right). Anwar el-Sadat (left) was Nasser's successor as president.

LEFT: WIDE WORLD. RIGHT: JACK BURLOT FROM LIAISON AGENCY. BELOW: CAMERA PRESS FROM PIX

improve living conditions for the people. Prices were cut on a broad range of foods and consumer goods, and the construction of 400 health centers was ordered. Funds were increased for the improvement of city water supplies, telephone service, and educational and employment opportunities. In foreign affairs the Sadat government obtained a pledge of increased support from the Soviet Union and agreed to continue the Middle Eastern policies worked out by Nasser and the Soviets.

On July 21 the Aswan High Dam, built over a ten-year period, was officially commissioned. The University of Asyût was renamed Nasser University after the late president. (*See also* Israel; Jordan; Libya; Middle East; Obituaries; Sudan. *See in* CE: Egypt.)

UNITED NATIONS (UN). Member nations marked the 25th anniversary of the UN in 1970 by paying considerable lip service to its purposes and principles, but at the same time they made no greater effort than in recent years to live up to their pledges. In fact, both the United States and the Soviet Union exploded nuclear test devices at the start of the anniversary celebrations in October.

Anniversary

Most of the lofty language was heard at UN sessions commemorating both the signing of the UN Charter in San Francisco, Calif. (June 26, 1945), and its coming into force (Oct. 24, 1945). On the 25th anniversary of the first occasion, Secretary-General U Thant gave the principal address in San Francisco's Opera House. He reminded delegates of the "sense of dedication and urgency, tempered with realism and a vivid awareness of the horrors of war, which inspired the authors of the Charter"; of the "crisis of confidence" that the UN faces today; and of the need for nations, "especially the great nations," to "improve and change the quality and performance of the United Nations and the way it is used." The alternative, he warned, was international suicide.

United Nations officials watch a tally board like the one at left as the General Assembly votes on admittance of Communist China. For the first time a simple majority voted to admit China, but a two-thirds majority was needed.

WIDE WORLD

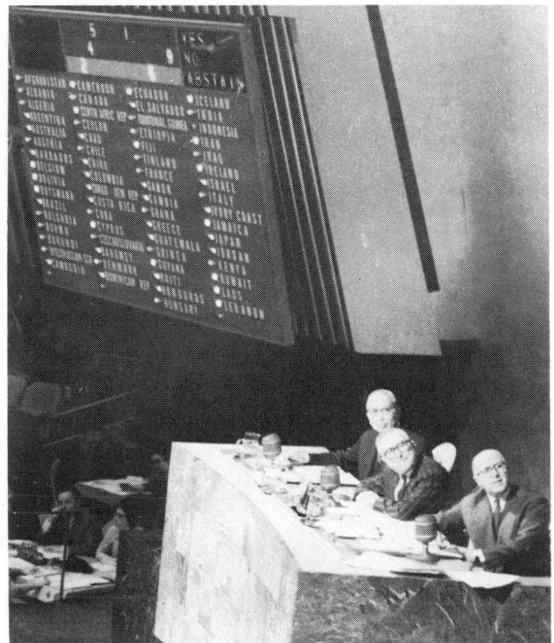

U Thant called on governments to make "a radical change from present power politics to a policy of collective responsibility towards mankind"; he urged again that the UN admit the People's Republic of China and the "divided countries," whose absence gave the UN "a great deal of artificiality"; he asked states to tolerate conflicting beliefs and to recognize that "systems and ideologies are perfect only in theory"; he proposed making economic aid "a matter of international justice and progress and not . . . an appendix of divisive power politics and influence"; and he stressed the need to "diagnose, monitor, and face together the new collective challenges and dangers which arise from a rapidly mushrooming scientific and technological civilization"—problems such as the population explosion, peaceful uses of the seabed and outer space, and preservation of the environment. Finally, he commended to individuals the need to supplement national loyalties with a "second allegiance" to the international community that the UN represents.

The Middle East

Private discussions among the "big four" powers—the United States, Soviet Union, Great Britain, and France—on possible ways of settling the Middle East crisis continued throughout the year and included proposals for reconstituting a UN force and stationing it in the area. Public efforts to deal with the problem resulted, for a short time after August 25, in talks among three parties to the conflict—Israel, Jordan, and the United Arab Republic (UAR, or Egypt). The talks were conducted by Ambassador Gunnar V. Jarring, the secretary-general's special representative to the Middle East. He began his work under the sheltering umbrella of a cease-fire arranged largely by the United States, which lasted from August 7 to November 5 and was then extended until Feb. 5, 1971. Talks had hardly begun, however, when Israel charged that the UAR, with the help of the Soviet Union, had violated the cease-fire terms by moving some surface-to-air missile sites closer to the Suez Canal. Israel declined to participate in the talks until the truce violations were rectified.

With peace talks suspended, Middle East tensions rose in September after Palestinian guerrillas carried out several spectacular airplane hijackings and plunged Jordan into virtual civil war. Earlier hijackings had already commanded the attention of

Secretary-General U Thant began his tenth year as head of the UN in November 1970. He indicated in 1970 that he would retire at the end of his current term in 1971.
WIDE WORLD

the assembly of the International Civil Aviation Organization (ICAO), which had gone on record at an extraordinary session (June 16–30) in Montreal, Que., with recommendations designed to discourage unlawful interference with aircraft and to protect air travelers, crew, and employees. The ICAO assembly recommended special security measures and called on states to prepare an international treaty on unlawful interference with civil aviation. Delegates also called for states to sign the draft treaty on unlawful seizure when it came before a diplomatic conference at The Hague, Netherlands, in December.

On September 9 the Security Council appealed to "all parties concerned" to release "all passengers and crews, without exception, held as a result of hijackings and other interference in international travel." U Thant proposed on September 14 that all governments pledge themselves to extradite hijackers, regardless of nationality or political affiliation, and bring them before a specially created international tribunal. At the request of U.S. President Richard M. Nixon, the 27-nation Council of the ICAO held a special meeting on September 18 to consider a worldwide aviation boycott against states that harbor hijackers and do not themselves prosecute or extradite them. On October 1, by a vote of 14–3–10 (the third figure indicating abstentions), the council approved the U.S. proposal. It was the first occasion on which the ICAO had authorized a penalty for any offense.

South Africa and Rhodesia

Events in southern Africa, as usual, occupied the attention of the General Assembly, the Security Council, the Committee of 24 on decolonization, and other UN bodies. The General Assembly, on October 13, voted 98–2–9 to call on states to implement the complete arms ban that the Security Council had imposed on South Africa on July 23. Only South Africa and Portugal opposed the General Assembly resolution, but Canada, France, Great Britain, and the United States were among those that abstained. The General Assembly asked the secretary-general to follow closely how states implemented the arms ban.

The Security Council, in tightening its arms embargo in July, called on states to strengthen the existing arms embargo by withholding from South African armed forces and paramilitary organizations all vehicles and equipment and their spare parts. The Security Council asked all UN members also to revoke all licenses and military patents granted South Africa for manufacturing arms and munitions, aircraft, naval craft, or other military vehicles; to prohibit investments in, or technical assistance for, manufacturing military hardware; and not to provide military training for any South African military personnel.

Israel's Prime Minister Golda Meir meets with UN General Assembly President Edvard Isak Hambro (below). Conferring at the UN (right) are (from left) UAR Foreign Minister Mahmoud Riad, Soviet Ambassador to the United States Anatolii F. Dobrynin, and Soviet Foreign Minister Andrei A. Gromyko.

WIDE WORLD

WIDE WORLD

On July 29 the Security Council adopted a resolution on Namibia, formerly South-West Africa, in which it asked states to refuse by various means to recognize South Africa's authority in the area. The resolution, adopted 13–0–2 (France and Great Britain), asked states not maintaining relations with South Africa to refrain from any connections, diplomatic, consular, or other, that seemed to acknowledge South Africa's authority over Namibia; it requested states maintaining relations to declare formally that they did not recognize South Africa's authority over Namibia and considered its presence there illegal. States were also asked to cut any commercial and diplomatic relations with South Africa that might extend to Namibia.

The General Assembly took its most direct action against South Africa on November 13, when the black African states challenged the right of the South African delegation to represent its indigenous black population. They introduced a resolution, which the General Assembly adopted by a vote of 60–42–12, declining to accept the credentials of the South African delegation. General Assembly President Edvard Hambro said before the resolution passed that it would be a "very strong condemnation of the policies" of South Africa and a warning, as solemn as any that could be given, but would not unseat the state or deny it the right to participate in the General Assembly.

As regards Rhodesia, the Security Council took the first of the year's several actions on March 18, when it condemned by 14–1 (Spain) the "illegal proclamation of republican status" by Prime Minister Ian D. Smith's regime. The Security Council decided that states should sever all relations with Rhodesia and interrupt all transport links with it. On July 13 the Security Council's sanctions committee reported that measures against Rhodesia had "not been fully effective and . . . not led to the desired results." The report noted that though agricultural exports from Rhodesia had declined, military exports had increased. The committee pointed a finger at South Africa and Portugal for defying Security Council resolutions by continuing to trade with Rhodesia, thereby considerably reducing the effectiveness of sanctions.

On November 17 the Security Council unanimously reaffirmed its "condemnation of the illegal declaration of independence" by the Smith regime and urged all states to continue withholding recognition. Great Britain was again urged to try to end the "illegal rebellion" and enable the people of Rhodesia to exercise their right to self-determination.

Organizational Matters

Membership in the UN rose to 127 on October 13, when the General Assembly admitted Fiji on recommendation (October 10) of the Security Council. (*See* Fiji.)

On November 20 the Assembly took up the question of Communist Chinese membership and for the first time produced a majority in favor of seating China. The vote was 51–49 with 27 abstentions. Because the Assembly had earlier voted 66–52 to require a two-thirds vote to decide the question, the simple majority did not suffice. (*See also* Disarmament. *See in* CE: United Nations.)

UNITED STATES. The divisions among the people of the United States grew wider during 1970, encouraged by the inflammatory rhetoric of left-wing radicals and Administration officials alike. The "politics of fear" grew to such proportions during the year that opinion polls showed that the majority of U.S. citizens were willing to sacrifice their fundamental freedoms guaranteed by the Bill of Rights in favor of "law and order." The economic situation worsened as prices continued to rise and unemployment grew more widespread. Demands for wage increases for automobile, postal, and railroad workers resulted in crippling strikes. The year ended without any substantial progress toward a conclusion of the Vietnam war or toward dealing with the nation's economic and social ills. (*See* Employment; Labor Unions; Post Office, U.S.)

Terrorist tactics, such as airplane hijackings and bombings, contributed to the climate of fear. The number of terrorist bombings increased dramatically during the year. The most widely discussed bombing incident occurred on March 6, when a series of dynamite explosions demolished a New York City townhouse, killing three persons. Investigators said that revolutionaries had operated a bomb factory in the building.

Bombings took place in all sections of the nation and appeared to follow no pattern. The most ex-

GRAHAM, "ARKANSAS GAZETTE," FROM BEN ROTH AGENCY

"Here's Some Civilian Who Thinks the U.S. Is A Democracy--Check Him Out on Our Subversive List!"
PENTAGON
SURVEILLANCE
FILE
GRAHAM

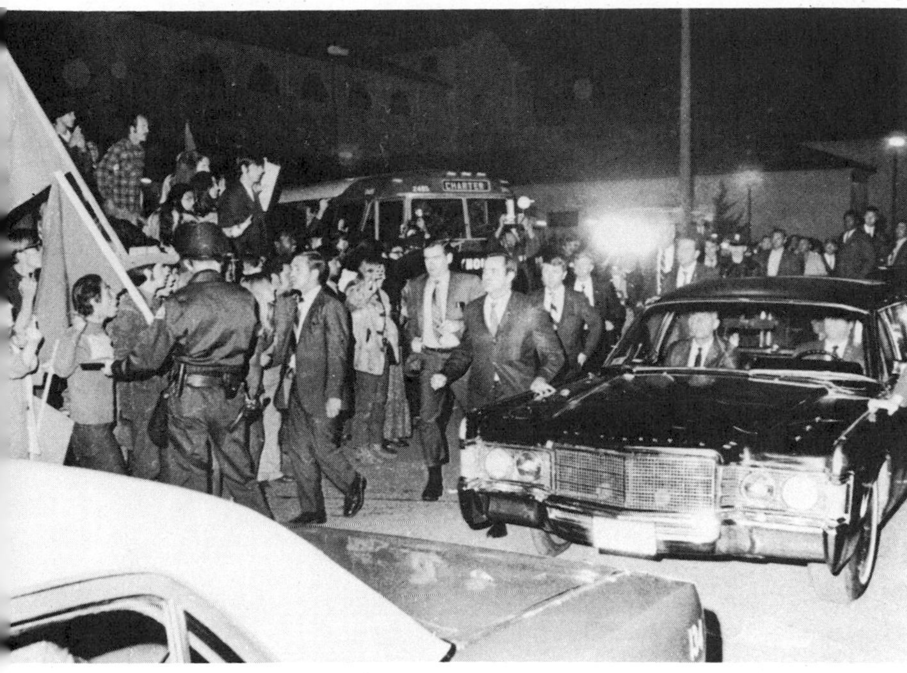

President Nixon's car leaves a Republican rally in San Jose, Calif. On his way from the rally he stood on the hood of his car surrounded by hostile demonstrators. It was reported that eggs were thrown at the president, and the incident received much publicity.

UPI COMPIX

tensive damage from an explosion, amounting to millions of dollars, was suffered by the Humble Oil and Refining Co. at Linden, N.J. A massive explosion occurred at the refinery two hours after police had received a telephoned warning that it would "burn, baby, burn."

Many of the racial incidents of 1970 involved members of black militant groups. In August an armed black youth broke into a San Rafael, Calif., courtroom during a trial in an attempt to free two prisoners and kidnap the judge. During the ensuing gun battle with police the youth, the prisoners, and the judge were all killed. Subsequently, charges of kidnapping and murder were filed against black militant Angela Davis. Police said that she had purchased the guns brought into the courtroom. After remaining at large for two months she was arrested in New York City on October 13.

Two much-publicized court cases involving Black Panthers were still in progress at the close of the year. In New York City 13 Black Panthers were tried on charges of conspiring to bomb public places. In New Haven, Conn., eight Panthers, including the national chairman of the Black Panther party, Bobby Seale, faced charges of conspiracy and murder. The New Haven trials prompted a demonstration at Yale University, and Yale's president, Kingman Brewster, Jr., stirred nationwide controversy by saying that he was "skeptical of the ability of black revolutionaries to achieve a fair trial anywhere in the United States." (*See* Race Relations.)

Tragedy and Crisis

Unrest on the nation's campuses reached unprecedented levels in the spring of 1970. One contributing factor was a remark made by U.S. President Richard M. Nixon, referring to dissenting college students as "bums." The president's remark was made the day after he had announced that U.S. troops had moved into Cambodia to clear out enemy sanctuaries.

News of the Cambodia venture caused a storm of protest on U.S. campuses, and there was a call for a nationwide student strike. An antiwar protest at Kent State University, Kent, Ohio, ended in tragedy on May 4 when four students, two of them women, were killed when National Guardsmen fired their semiautomatic rifles into a crowd of demonstrators.

The Kent State killings gave impetus to a previously planned demonstration in Washington, D.C. A crowd estimated at between 50,000 and 100,000 persons gathered in the nation's capital on May 10 for what turned out to be a peaceful protest against the Cambodian offensive. Then, on May 15, two black students were killed and at least nine others

Walter J. Hickel, secretary of the interior, was fired from his post by U.S. President Nixon in November.

WIDE WORLD

THE 12 EXECUTIVE DEPARTMENTS

(December 1970)

Secretary of State	William P. Rogers
Secretary of the Treasury	John B. Connally*
Secretary of Defense	Melvin R. Laird
Attorney General	John N. Mitchell
Postmaster General	Winton M. Blount
Secretary of the Interior	Rogers C. B. Morton
Secretary of Agriculture	Clifford M. Hardin
Secretary of Commerce	Maurice H. Stans
Secretary of Labor	James D. Hodgson
Secretary of Health, Education, and Welfare	Elliot L. Richardson
Secretary of Housing and Urban Development	George Romney
Secretary of Transportation	John A. Volpe

* Nominated in 1970 to take office February 1971.

wounded at Jackson State College, Jackson, Miss., when police opened fire into a crowd gathered outside a women's dormitory. The nationwide student strike spread rapidly after the Kent State and Jackson State shootings. As a result more than 400 colleges and universities were completely or partially closed. (*See* Colleges and Universities.)

Reaction to the killing of students and the invasion of Cambodia was swift and severe. In Congress Senator J. W. Fulbright (D, Ark.) accused Nixon of subverting the U.S. Constitution by usurping the war-making powers of Congress. Senators John Sherman Cooper (R, Ky.) and Frank Church (D, Idaho) introduced a measure in the Senate to cut off all funds for U.S. troops in Cambodia. Late in the year Congress approved a rider to the defense appropriations bill that prohibited the funding of ground troops in Cambodia. Antiwar protests were voiced by various establishment groups—business executives, government employees, and lawyers.

Among supporters of the Administration's policies were mobs of construction workers in New York City, who attacked young antiwar demonstrators and stormed City Hall. A Gallup Poll survey in May showed that 57% of the people supported the Cambodian action. A poll taken in June, however, showed that most people felt U.S. involvement in Vietnam was a mistake, and 61% of those polled in November favored total withdrawal from Vietnam by the end of 1971. (*See also* Cambodia; Vietnam.)

Immediately following the Kent State killings, the Administration responded rather coldly, with President Nixon saying that violent protest invites tragedy and Vice-President Spiro T. Agnew calling the event "predictable and avoidable." The Administration later softened its tone, and Nixon called for an investigation; Agnew asserted that the National Guard had overreacted. Attorney General John N. Mitchell ordered a federal grand jury investigation into the Jackson State incident. A team of young White House staff members, who toured college campuses at the request of the president, reported that the harsh rhetoric of the Administration had alienated even nonpolitical middle-class students. (*See* Agnew.)

In June Nixon formed the Presidential Commission on Campus Unrest headed by William W. Scranton, former governor of Pennsylvania, to investigate the causes of student violence. The commission's report, issued in September, stated that a "crisis of understanding" was the cause of student unrest. It recommended an end to the Indochina war, urged colleges to be more responsive to student needs, and called on government officials to stop making inflammatory statements.

In response to the report Nixon stated that student protesters alone were responsible for campus violence. Agnew charged that the commission was trying to make a scapegoat of Nixon by calling on the moral leadership of the presidency to unite the nation.

Nixon was in disagreement with another report issued during the year—that of the Federal Commission on Obscenity and Pornography. The majority of the panel members concluded that pornography does not cause adverse social or psychological effects and recommended that laws regulating pornographic material be repealed. Nixon called the report "morally bankrupt" and urged a stronger stand against "smut."

Cabinet Changes; Other Developments

Nixon's difficulties with youth precipitated a split within his Cabinet. Secretary of the Interior Walter J. Hickel stated in a letter to the president that "youth in its protest must be heard." He warned that the Administration was "embracing a philosophy which appears to lack appropriate concern" for youth, and that young people felt they had no means of communicating with the government other than violent confrontation. Hickel ended his letter with an appeal to Nixon to meet more often with individual members of the Cabinet. Hickel reportedly had talked with the president only twice since the inauguration. George Romney, secretary of housing and urban development, supported Hickel's views. One concession to youth made during 1970 was the lowering of the voting age to 18 for federal elections.

Publication of the Hickel letter was embarrassing to Nixon, so it came as no surprise when Hickel was fired late in the year. Republican National Chairman Rogers C. B. Morton replaced him.

Robert H. Finch was replaced as secretary of health, education, and welfare by Elliot L. Richardson in June. Finch was transferred to the president's staff of advisers.

In another Cabinet change, Secretary of Labor George P. Shultz became director of the newly formed Office of Management and Budget. This was part of an extensive reorganization of the president's staff, which included the formation of a Domestic Council. James D. Hodgson was appointed secretary of labor.

In December Secretary of the Treasury David M. Kennedy was replaced by former Gov. John B. Connally of Texas, a Democrat. Nixon promised to promote better relations with his Cabinet by meeting with them every two weeks.

President Nixon experienced several major defeats in Congress during 1970. His family assistance plan was not approved, and he suffered his second Senate rejection of a Supreme Court nominee. Nixon charged that the Senate had acted in a malicious way by rejecting Judge G. Harrold Carswell, a Southerner. (*See* Nixon; Supreme Court of the U.S.)

Later in the year Agnew attacked certain senators who favored a complete troop withdrawal from Vietnam by the end of 1971. He called these senators, among other things, defeatists. At the close of the year Nixon pledged to work more harmoniously with the next session of Congress.

The bitterly contested midterm elections produced mixed results, with Republicans and Democrats alike claiming victory. The Democrats scored a net gain of 11 state governorships. The Administration was pleased by the defeat of three senators—Charles E. Goodell (R, N.Y.), Albert A. Gore (D, Tenn.), and Joseph D. Tydings (D, Md.). (*See* Elections.)

In December the gross national product passed the trillion-dollar mark, with inflation still out of control. Nixon indicated that the policy of slowing the economy would be reversed to check the increase in unemployment. (*See* Economy.)

Chanting "Say it loud, gay is proud!" thousands of young people marched for Gay Liberation on June 28 in New York City. They were led by the Gay Activist Alliance and other homosexual groups.

RUSSELL REIF FROM PICTORIAL PARADE

In the South the federally ordered integration of more than 200 school districts proceeded calmly. (*See* Cities and Urban Affairs; Congress, U.S.; Foreign Policy, U.S.; Law; Middle East; Women. *See also* Census Summary. *See in* CE: United States.)

UPPER VOLTA. In a referendum in mid-June 1970, 98.4% of the electorate in Upper Volta accepted the new draft constitution submitted for their approval. Under its terms, for a transitional period of four years the president of the republic would be the senior army officer of the highest rank. One third of the government would be military men. The government would have a prime minister at its head and could not number more than 15 ministers.

After the transitional period, the president would normally be elected for five years by direct universal suffrage, but no president could have more than two consecutive mandates. The president could preside over the Council of Ministers, but only when exceptional circumstances required this. All acts of the president were to be countersigned by the prime minister and the relevant ministers. He would also be commander in chief of the army and president of the Higher Council of Defense. All the major political parties in Upper Volta had recommended acceptance of the new constitution to their supporters. (*See in* CE: Upper Volta.)

URUGUAY. In 1970 President Jorge Pacheco Areco's popularity with both of Uruguay's political factions and the population as a whole was damaged by the terrorist activities of Tupamaro National Liberation Front—the country's Marxist guerrillas. The Tupamaros continually flouted the authority of the government, army, and police. In May the government was shaken by a dramatic raid on a naval training center in Montevideo, the capital, by guerrillas who carried off a large quantity of arms. It seemed that some agreement was likely between the Tupamaros and the government in June, but toward the end of the month hopes of reconciliation dissipated with renewed guerrilla attacks on banks. The July kidnapping of Judge Daniel Pereira Manelli, who had tried most of the captured Tupamaros, further embarrassed the Pacheco regime even though the judge was subsequently released.

This incident, however, became insignificant in comparison to the kidnappings in late July of Dan A. Mitrione, a U.S. Agency for International Development adviser to the police; Brazilian diplomat Aloysio Mares Dias Gomide; and, soon afterward, Claude Fly, a U.S. agronomist. The government took a firm line against the Tupamaros, who demanded that captured guerrillas be released in exchange for the lives of the three men. Before long, the body of Mitrione was found and pressure on the Pacheco government was redoubled to accept the guerrillas' demands, to no avail. The legislature approved the enactment of Article 31 of the constitution, which, in effect, suspended individual rights and imposed a state of emergency, giving the president greater powers than those that had been in force almost continually for two years.

A combined operation involving 14,000 members of the police and army failed to locate the remaining hostages but did lead to the capture of Raúl Sendic, the most important member of the Tupamaro hierarchy. However, guerrilla activities continued throughout the rest of the year. (*See in* CE: Uruguay.)

VENEZUELA. During a state visit to Washington, D.C., in June 1970, President Rafael Caldera Rodriguez secured a promise from the United States that it would increase Venezuela's share of the U.S. oil market. He had warned that failure to do so would be seen as a refusal to help Latin America. The Venezuelan economy, almost entirely dependent on the export of oil, had suffered from recent changes in the oil market: demand for low-sulfur oil (which Venezuela does not produce), new finds in Alaska, and cheaper transport of Arabian and African oil.

Three major oil companies signed service contracts with the Venezuelan government in November to develop new oil fields in Lake Maracaibo. The contracts, a new type replacing the old concession contracts, gave the state far more control of production than before and raised state earnings from 70% to almost 85% of profits. The new oil fields were the first to be opened since 1957.

Late in August, the government announced that it lacked money to open primary and secondary schools in September and that the opening would have to be delayed until January. More than 300 new schools and 6,000 new teachers were needed for the 300,000 children old enough to start the first grade.

In January a bill was proposed giving the government control of Venezuela's traditionally autonomous universities. Students at National University in Caracas, the capital, rioted at the news, and the campus was occupied by troops. The bill was passed in September and riots broke out at the country's other universities.

Venezuela and Guyana agreed in June to shelve their border dispute for the next 12 years. Venezuela also resumed diplomatic relations with the Soviet Union in 1970; relations had been broken in 1952. (*See in* CE: Venezuela.)

The mainstay of Venezuela's economy is oil. These rigs are situated in Lake Maracaibo in the western part of the country.

WIDE WORLD

VETERINARY MEDICINE. The world animal disease situation in 1970 remained about as it had been since the eradication in 1968 of a foot-and-mouth disease epidemic among cattle in Great Britain. Governments of the developing nations, in conjunction with specialists from the Food and Agriculture Organization of the United Nations, continued to make progress in controlling the more widespread diseases of food-producing animals through vaccination and the development of disease-resistant livestock.

The U.S. hog cholera (swine fever) eradication program advanced. By the fall of 1970, half of the states either had been declared free of the disease or were in the final stages of the campaign, and the remaining states had made substantial progress toward total eradication.

The discovery of a rapid and simple blood test for equine infectious anemia (swamp fever) by veterinarians at Cornell University promised to make control of this disease—which has been a serious threat to the racing industry—an economic possibility. Previous methods of identifying carriers of the disease had been too costly and time-consuming for widespread use.

Scientists at the University of Delaware announced the apparent discovery of an effective vaccine for immunizing poultry against avian leukosis, a form of leukemia that had become a serious problem in most nations that have highly developed poultry industries. Veterinarians at Cornell and the University of California dispelled fears that the virus of feline lymphosarcoma, another form of animal leukemia, could be transmitted from cats to man. Unguarded "popularized" reports of experiments by British and Soviet scientists had suggested

LONDON "DAILY EXPRESS" FROM PICTORIAL PARADE

Delilah, a giraffe residing in London's Chessington Zoo, takes her medicine of warm oil and maize to ward off the flu.

that such passage was possible, and the reports had caused alarm among cat owners. The virus can be passed from animal to animal only under highly artificial "laboratory" conditions.

In an effort to eliminate the possibility of the development of antibiotic-resistant bacteria that could cause disease in man, Great Britain banned—beginning in March 1971—the use in animal feeds of certain antibiotics commonly used in human medicine. No similar action was taken in the United States, though studies of feed additives and veterinary drugs continued. (*See also* Agriculture; Animals and Wildlife. *See in* CE: Diseases, Plant and Animal; Zoos.)

VIETNAM. There was less hard fighting in the Vietnam war in 1970 than at any other time since the first major U.S. buildup of the war in 1965. Both sides avoided real battles. As a result, most of the action during the year was again guerrilla-type warfare, and the United States continued to withdraw troops from Vietnam.

In January, four North Vietnamese regiments were reported to have moved into the Mekong Delta, which for a time had been considered as well pacified as any region in the South. No major action resulted, however. Sharp fighting did occur just below the demilitarized zone (DMZ) early in April; South Vietnamese troops bore the brunt of the attacks. After six days, the fighting subsided without ever having become intense or widespread enough to be called an offensive.

On April 27, U.S. President Richard M. Nixon approved a plan to send U.S. forces into Cambodia to clear out enemy bases and supply depots there. It had been reported that the North Vietnamese seemed to be massing in Cambodia near the border with South Vietnam, and it was feared that they might be preparing a major operation similar to the 1968 Tet offensive. Violent U.S. opposition to what was called an illegal invasion of Cambodia and a widening of the war led Nixon to decree that all U.S. troops would be out of Cambodia by June 30, 1970.

At the same time, the United States resumed bombing raids on North Vietnam. These raids were said to be the first since the official halt to the bombing was called in November 1968, though smaller raids had sometimes been made in purported retaliation for North Vietnamese missile attacks on U.S. reconnaissance planes flying over the North.

After the U.S. forces had pulled out of Cambodia, numerous search-and-destroy missions were mounted in large areas of South Vietnam, but allied initiatives waned as the year wore on. North Vietnamese regulars and Viet Cong maintained a policy of harassment and skirmishing.

Heavy bombing of the North was reported on November 20 and 21. The North Vietnamese claimed that the raids had struck Haiphong and Hanoi, the capital, as well as the provinces between the DMZ and the 19th parallel; although the United States claimed that it had restricted the bombing to

This flamethrower, nicknamed "Zippo" by U.S. troops, uses napalm to defoliate the South Vietnamese countryside of hiding places.

WIDE WORLD

WIDE WORLD

Students from the University of Saigon demonstrated May 7 in downtown Saigon against U.S. involvement in Cambodia and against the killing of Vietnamese civilians by Cambodians.

the latter area, the French press agency in Hanoi confirmed the North Vietnamese claim. The U.S. secretary of defense, Melvin R. Laird, defended the bombing by claiming that it was again retaliatory, but analysts speculated that the U.S. command was trying to scare off a possible Communist buildup in the South.

Several days later, it was revealed that simultaneously with the raids, a U.S. commando contingent had landed from helicopters at a prisoner-of-war camp at Son Tay, about 25 miles from Hanoi, in an attempt to free the U.S. soldiers held there. However, the camp had been evacuated earlier. A week after the bombing raids, the U.S. Defense Department admitted that the bombing raids had indeed struck at Hanoi to cover the commandos.

"Vietnamization" of the war continued during 1970. South Vietnamese forces numbered 420,000 regulars and 593,000 militiamen, and U.S. officials estimated that about half of South Vietnam's 12 army and marine divisions had been brought up to effective combat quality level. The Nha Trang air base was turned over to the South Vietnamese for an air training center, and more than 3,500 pilots and aircraft mechanics were trained in the United States during the year. The large U.S. Marine base at An Hoa and the U.S. Army helicopter base at Soc Trang, an important base in the Mekong Delta, were also turned over to the South Vietnamese.

By the end of the year, foreign observers in South Vietnam saw signs of an important change in the war. The Viet Cong were reported to have been driven out of most of the villages and hamlets in the South into small base areas, and the North Vietnamese regulars, no longer able to depend on the Viet Cong for supplies, were being driven into the mountainous areas along the western border. The operations in Cambodia, which had eliminated the Communist bases and supply lines there, were seen as having an important and continuing effect, since the Communists could no longer seek sanctuary there.

Strength of U.S. troops was reported in October at 390,200, with 40,000 scheduled to leave by Christmas. At that time, the overall U.S. death total since Jan. 1, 1961, was 43,775, with 289,800 wounded and 1,424 missing or captured. One out of every two soldiers who died in combat was a draftee. Viet Cong mines and booby traps took a large percentage of the death and injury toll.

At the peace negotiations in Paris, both the chief North Vietnamese delegate, Xuan Thuy, and the chief Viet Cong delegate, Mrs. Nguyen Thi Binh, boycotted the talks until late summer, after protesting that the United States was "downgrading" the talks. Their complaint was apparently that the post of chief negotiator for the United States was not filled after Henry Cabot Lodge resigned. Shortly thereafter, the Soviet ambassador to France, Valerian Zorin, warned that the North Vietnamese might break off the peace talks altogether unless the United States showed more willingness to negotiate. President Nixon had publicly avowed that the United States would make no new proposals in Paris unless the Communists made further concessions.

After the resumption of bombing raids over North Vietnam in May, Communist negotiators in Paris canceled the 66th plenary session of the peace talks in protest. On July 1, Nixon appointed David K. E. Bruce, former U.S. ambassador to Britain, France, and West Germany, to head the U.S. delegation in Paris. The appointment was thought to have been delayed until all U.S. troops had left Cambodia in order to improve the U.S. bargaining position.

On September 17 the Viet Cong delegation presented an eight-point peace proposal in Paris; all four chief negotiators were present at that day's session for the first time since December 1969. The offer, the first new proposal of any substance in 16 months, stipulated U.S. withdrawal from Vietnam by June 30, 1971; replacement of South Vietnam's President Nguyen Van Thieu, Vice-President Nguyen Cao Ky, and Premier Tran Thien Khiem by an interim coalition government, followed by free elections; gradual reunification of North and South; and a cease-fire. The Viet Cong also offered to assure the safety of the withdrawing troops and to begin negotiations for the release of prisoners; these two offers, as well as the demand for the removal of Thieu, Ky, and Khiem and the offer of a cease-fire, were considered shifts in the Viet Cong position in Paris. Chief U.S. negotiator Bruce called the offer "old wine in new bottles."

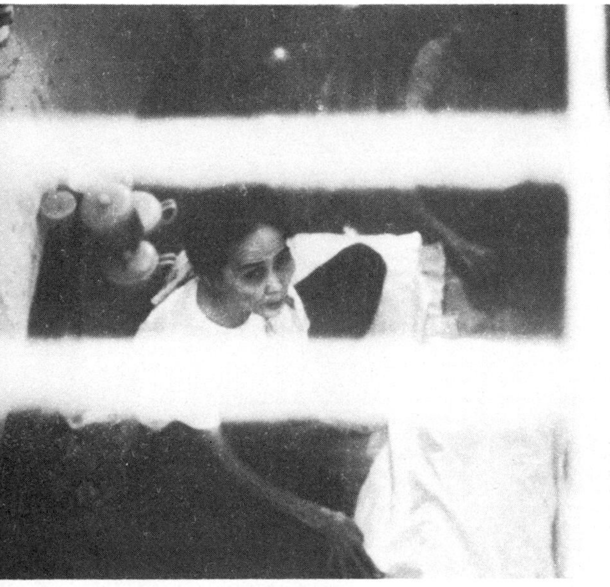

ABOVE AND BELOW: THOMAS R. HARKIN

U.S. Congressional observers were shocked to find the South Vietnamese government confining prisoners in "tiger cage" cells on Con Son island. Prisoners, chained in their cells, said they had to eat lizards and insects.

On October 7 President Nixon, on U.S. television, presented his own peace proposal, including an offer of an immediate cease-fire throughout Indochina, negotiation for withdrawal of U.S. forces, immediate release of all prisoners, and a "fair political solution" in Vietnam. His offer was totally rejected by the Communist delegations; chief North Vietnamese negotiator Xuan Thuy termed the offer "a gift certificate for the votes of the American electorate."

South Vietnam

The economy of South Vietnam was in an increasingly bad state during 1970. Prices rose 50% between the fall of 1969 and the fall of 1970, and it was calculated in October that purchasing power in South Vietnam had been reduced 93% by inflation in the preceding 21 months. Subsidies on U.S. imports had raised the trade deficit to $685 million, and military and civil service pay raises, though necessary, added to the inflation.

According to the Agency for International Development, U.S. economic aid to South Vietnam during fiscal 1970 was estimated to be $365 million, an increase of $60 million over the 1969 figure. Congressional leaders warned that aid might be reduced unless the South Vietnamese economy improved.

In October, President Thieu initiated a dual official exchange rate for the piaster, which had been quoted at 118 to the U.S. dollar. The value was kept at 118 for "necessity" import items but lowered to 275 to the dollar for luxury imported items. The black-market exchange rate, which had been 420 to the dollar, then rose to 450. Austerity taxes raised still further the price of imported items, including rice, the country's food staple, which was still in short supply.

Economic difficulties caused many South Vietnamese to protest government policies during the year; among them were large numbers of disabled South Vietnamese army veterans living on government pensions. Several demonstrations were held in Saigon, the capital, and hundreds of homeless disabled veterans took to building shacks on the streets of Saigon for lack of other housing.

Political protest also increased during 1970. Saigon University's 32,000 students held a general strike, and several hundred Buddhist monks and nuns of the antigovernment An Quang faction held a hunger strike at the end of May. Fifteen members of the South Vietnamese Senate formed an opposition bloc led by Senator Tran Van Don in January, shortly after the House of Representatives had refused President Thieu's demand to strip three deputies of their parliamentary immunity from prosecution for pro-Communist activities.

Elections were held in August for 30 of the 60 seats in the Senate, with 65% of eligible voters casting ballots. The An Quang Buddhist faction's opposition slate (each slate carried the names of ten candidates) polled the heaviest vote. Only one of the three slates endorsed by President Thieu was elected.

In February, opposition deputy Tran Ngoc Chau was convicted by a military court of having damaged national security by having had dealings with his brother, a North Vietnamese intelligence agent. Chau was sentenced to 20 years at hard labor, later changed to 10 years. Chau claimed to have met with his brother with the knowledge and approval of the U.S. Central Intelligence Agency in Saigon and even to have given an early warning of the Communist Tet offensive in 1968, but U.S. officials had disregarded the warning. The United States made no public confirmation or denial of his claim, though an independent source in Washington, D.C., later said that the U.S. State Department had privately intimated that it was true.

Two U.S. Congressmen visiting the South Vietnamese prison on the island of Con Son termed the underground maximum security cells, or "tiger cages," shocking. The subsequent uproar over the tiger cages and alleged inhumane treatment of the criminals and political prisoners held there resulted in some penal reforms.

On January 2 U.S. Vice-President Spiro T. Agnew paid an official call to South Vietnam and visited U.S. military hospitals, in addition to meeting with President Thieu and touring two forward artillery sites. In February, U.S. Secretary of Defense Laird visited Saigon to see how well Vietnamization was progressing; he called it adequate but noted that the United States was looking for ways to speed it up.

South Vietnamese agriculture was aided by a land reform program instituted on March 26, when President Thieu signed into law the so-called Land to the Tiller plan. The new law authorized the government to buy up land from the landlords, who owned over 70% of the farmland in South Vietnam and leased it to tenant farmers. The land would then be distributed free among the peasants farming it.

North Vietnam

The Democratic Republic of Vietnam received military aid from both Communist China and the Soviet Union during 1970. In May, while U.S. forces were capturing supply depots in Cambodia, China announced a gift of economic and military supplies to Hanoi. The Soviet Union signed a new military aid agreement with North Vietnam in June. The North Vietnamese still maintained strict neutrality in the disputes between the two major Communist powers.

WIDE WORLD

The memory of Ho Chi Minh, the late president of North Vietnam, was strong one year after his death. This statue of Ho stands in Hanoi.

In May the National Assembly met for the first time since the death of President Ho Chi Minh in 1969 and formalized the new leadership. Acting President Ton Duc Thang seemed to be a figurehead, while party secretary Le Duan was thought to be the real head of government. National Assembly Chairman Truong Chinh ranked third in the government hierarchy, followed by Premier Pham Van Dong, National Assembly Vice-Chairman Hoang Van Hoan, and the defense minister, Gen. Vo Nguyen Giap.

In a speech marking the 40th anniversary of the Vietnamese Workers (Communist) Party on February 1, Le Duan warned that the North Vietnamese must be prepared to fight many years more before the United States left Vietnam. His speech also emphasized the need for collective leadership, the right of all party members to discuss issues freely, and the importance of opening the party to mass criticism.

His speech also included an economic report in which he stated that his priorities were production, technology, and ideology, in that order. Regional administrations were given charge of light industry and agriculture, while the central government was to oversee heavy industry. The country's greatest problem, he said, was its lack of experience in all but small-scale production.

Marking the 25th anniversary of the revolution, Hanoi issued a progress report in August. According to the report, illiteracy no longer existed; polio, cholera, and smallpox were eradicated; and infant mortality had dropped from 30% under French rule to 2.6% in 1968. The report also mentioned that the United States and allies had dropped more than one million tons of bombs and shells on the North, twice the amount dropped on the entire Pacific theater of operations during World War II. (*See in* CE: Vietnam; Vietnam Conflict.)

WEATHER. A century of weather service was marked by the meteorological services of the United States in 1970. It was on Feb. 9, 1870, that U.S. President Ulysses S. Grant gave his approval to a resolution providing for weather observations and storm warnings.

In October U.S. weather services were significantly affected by the formation of the National Oceanic and Atmospheric Administration (NOAA) in the Department of Commerce. The NOAA combined the functions of the Environmental Science Services Administration (ESSA), the Bureau of Commercial Fisheries, and several other ocean-oriented federal bureaus. In its new home, the ESSA Weather Bureau became NOAA's National Weather Service, and its weather reporting and forecasting activities were broadened to include certain elements of marine environment.

Weather modification experiments conducted in 1970 included the continuing "lake effect" snowstorm project near Lake Erie, precipitation augmentation and suppression experiments in the Western United States, tests in lightning suppression, and seedings of cumulus clouds over the Florida Everglades. Project Stormfury, an effort at hurricane modification, had no suitable targets in 1970.

The 1970 Atlantic Ocean hurricane season was distinctive mainly for its early start. Alma, which reached hurricane force on May 20, was only the third North Atlantic hurricane to occur in May in the 20th century; the last was in 1951. In August the U.S. Gulf coast around Corpus Christi, Tex., was battered by Hurricane Celia. Tropical storm Dorothy, also in August, killed perhaps 50 persons in the Lesser Antilles.

In the Pacific, Typhoon Olga struck Japan's main island of Honshu in July, causing 20 deaths and much damage near Tokyo; storm remnants subsequently caused disastrous flooding and 39 deaths in South Korea. Typhoon Anita killed 20 persons when it struck a Japanese island in August, and Billie killed 15 in the southwestern portion of Korea. Typhoon Georgia killed a reported 300 persons in the Philippines when it struck Luzon early in September.

One of the worst weather disasters in history took place on Nov. 13, 1970. A cyclone and tidal waves hit East Pakistan, killing as many as 500,000 persons. (*See* Pakistan.)

In Lubbock, Tex., on May 11, a massive tornado ripped an eight-mile-long path through the city, killing 23 persons, injuring about 1,000, and causing property damage of some $150 million. An early warning and a tornado-conscious citizenry were credited with keeping the death toll down. Tornadoes in the Texas Panhandle killed 26 on April 17 and 18, and significant tornadoes were reported in and around Oklahoma City, Okla., on April 30 and near Zapata, Tex., on May 23 and 24. Severe thunderstorms in the Arizona-southeastern Utah region brought lethal flash floods on Septem-

A tornado struck Lubbock, Tex., on May 11, killing 23 persons and leaving many homeless. The trail of damage from the twister was about one mile wide and eight miles long.

AUTHENTICATED NEWS INTERNATIONAL

ber 5. On the whole, however, deaths due to severe storms during the first half of 1970 were about 30% below the 1969 toll for the same period.

Heat waves distinguished the U.S. summer and early autumn. In late September, record-breaking temperatures over much of the country east of the Mississippi made power brownouts a daily crisis in some Eastern cities. A dry summer in the Pacific Northwest set the stage for unusually destructive forest fires set by lightning, and brush dried to tinder by persistent Santa Ana winds caused disastrous fires in the San Diego and Los Angeles areas of California. (*See also* Disasters of 1970. *See in* CE: Weather.)

WESTERN SAMOA. The successful adaptation of British parliamentary democracy to Samoan custom was demonstrated by the change of government in Western Samoa that followed the general elections in February 1970. Tupua Tamasese Lealofi IV was elected prime minister in a secret parliamentary ballot, and he selected a new cabinet of eight ministers. A royal son like his predecessor, Fiame Mata'afa, who had held office since 1959, Tamasese had previously been content to pursue a professional career in medicine and to be a member of the Council of Deputies. His entry into politics and the defeat of Mata'afa may have signified the beginning of party politics.

The new cabinet consisted of younger, more progressive, well-educated and titled individuals, several of whom had held responsible positions in the public service. The new deputy speaker was the first woman member of Parliament. More dynamic leadership, rather than radical change, was forecast. Membership in the Commonwealth of Nations was obtained in August. (*See in* CE: Samoa.)

WEST INDIES. Unprecedented expressions of racial feeling reached their peak in the black-power demonstrations that took place in several West Indies countries during 1970. Trinidad and Tobago was particularly hard hit from February 26 to April 21. The often violent disturbances were perpetuated mostly by young people protesting a white-dominated economy, unemployment, and poverty. Following an alleged mutiny in which about 200 of the 800-man army rebelled and seized the military base and arsenal at Teteron, the government proclaimed a state of emergency, to extend to November 20. It sought also reinforcements from other Commonwealth countries in the Caribbean and from Venezuela.

Arms shipments from the United States and Venezuela, destined for the police, and the presence of British and U.S. warships helped to end the crisis, at least on the surface. On November 19, just hours before the end of the state of emergency period, the Trinidad and Tobago government released all political prisoners taken into custody during the disturbances. The prisoners, released by an order from Prime Minister Eric Williams, included black-power, labor, and student leaders, five of whom were scheduled to face sedition charges.

There was considerable irritation in the Bahamas over the U.S. action of dumping 66 tons of nerve gas in the Atlantic Ocean, less than 150 miles from the northeastern tip of Abaco. The big worry was that it would hurt the tourist business, already in a slump due to the recession in the United States.

In another development during the year, Bermuda made a change in its monetary policy by switching from pounds and pence to the decimal system. It was announced in February that the dollar in Bermuda would be pegged to the pound sterling. (*See in* CE: West Indies.)

WOMEN. On Aug. 26, 1970, the 50th anniversary of the granting of the vote to U.S. women, a second generation of feminists took part in a symbolic nationwide "strike for equality," participating in rallies and demonstrations across the country to emphasize their dissatisfaction with the secondary status accorded to women in U.S. society. Their demands centered on three major issues: equality with men in employment and educational opportunities, more liberalized abortion laws, and government-sponsored child-care clinics.

The strike reflected the new feminist consciousness resulting from the growth of the women's liberation movement, or "women's lib," which hit its

Lorne Nystrom and his wife, Gayle, demonstrate in favor of abortion in Ottawa, Ont., in May. He is a member of Canada's Parliament.

PETER BREGG FROM CANADIAN PRESS

LEFT: WIDE WORLD. RIGHT: JIM ANDERSON FROM NANCY PALMER AGENCY

Betty Friedan (left), former president of the National Organization for Women, was a leader of women's strike day, August 26. Gloria Steinem (right), a writer, is another spokeswoman for women's liberation.

full stride in 1970. The movement was actually a loosely coordinated grouping of feminist organizations that ranged widely in their approach—from the moderate National Organization for Women (NOW), which stressed legal action to achieve equal rights for women, to the more radically oriented groups such as Boston's Bread and Roses and New York City's Redstockings, which sought nothing less than a total restructuring of society and woman's role within it. Although these groups found most of their support among the older professional or younger college-educated women, they did much to arouse public awareness of the problems of all females. Not all women, however, supported the movement. Some did not recognize discrimination as a problem or felt that woman's primary role should be in the home as a wife and mother. Many men were also among those opposed to women's lib, particularly as a reaction to the man-hating statements of the more radical feminists.

Nevertheless, women's lib was credited with a number of victories during the year, chiefly in the area of job bias. The federal government issued guidelines barring sexual discrimination in employment among government contractors and also began actively investigating complaints of job bias, which had risen substantially, according to a government spokesman, "mostly as a result of women's liberation and the publicity they have gotten."

The major goal of the moderate wing of the women's lib movement, however—the adoption of an "equal rights" amendment to the U.S. Constitution prohibiting discrimination under the law on the basis of sex—was not achieved. Lack of Congressional support eventually removed any chance of passage for the amendment, at least for 1970. Undoubtedly, it would be reintroduced in the future. (*See also* Feature Article: "Women in Society: the Search for 'Personhood'.")

WORLD TRADE. At the end of the third quarter of 1970 world trade showed a strong annual rate of expansion. The world export total stood at an annual rate of $267 billion, 11% higher than the rate during the third quarter of 1969. Exports of industrial countries during the same period were at an annual rate of $199.1 billion, up 12% from the corresponding period of 1969. Exports of the less developed countries rose 10%.

Some of the increased trade volume was attributable to inflation, however. In a report made in December, the International Monetary Fund noted that the industrial countries were suffering a rise in consumer prices in 1970 that had been exceeded only during the Korean War years. Some of the industrial nations did fare better than others. West Germany showed a smaller price increase than nearly all other European countries.

Throughout the year, the rapidly rising rate of inflation was a cause of concern to economic and trade organizations. In late September the National Institute of Economic and Social Research, an independent nonprofit British research organization, noted that almost all of the current increase in world trade could be attributed to higher prices, resulting mainly from big wage increases. It stated that the volume of world trade was actually showing little expansion and might even be slowing. Both the Organization for Economic Cooperation and Development and the European Economic Community (EEC), or Common Market, reported rising rates of inflation within their member nations. Within the EEC, price increases ranged from a low of 3.3% in Belgium to a high of 5.8% in France for the year's duration.

Trade Practices and Policies in the Industrial Nations

During 1970 the industrial nations of the non-Communist world seemed to be on the brink of a trade war. The imminent threat of a trade conflict was posed by the consideration of a restrictive trade bill by the U.S. Congress. The bill, sponsored by Representative Wilbur D. Mills (D, Ark.), chairman of the House Ways and Means Committee, was designed to combat the refusal of the Japanese government to place voluntary quotas on textile exports to the United States. The trade bill, which was passed by the House of Representatives in the fall, would impose new quotas on the imports of textiles and shoes. It would also enable many other industries to battle foreign competition through the imposition of new quotas or higher tariffs.

The bill was attacked by economists, import and export organizations, and bankers in the United States. Its supporters were limited primarily to members of the textile- and shoe-manufacturing industries. Abroad, however, the opposition to the bill was almost unanimous. The EEC served notice that the passage of the Mills bill would be grounds for limiting the sales of U.S. soybeans in Europe. The EEC nations were joined in November by industrialists from Austria, Great Britain, Denmark, Finland, Norway, Portugal, Sweden, and Switzerland, who warned that the United States would be faced with reprisals by their nations if the provisions of the bill were put into effect. The Senate failed to vote on the measure by year-end, thus killing it for that session of Congress.

European Economic Community

During 1970 Britain appeared to be closer to success in its continuing effort to gain admission into the EEC. The British cause benefited considerably from France's lifting the veto imposed by former President Charles de Gaulle against the nation's membership. The major obstacle to British admission seemed to be its inability to comply easily with requirements to eliminate all industrial tariff walls between itself and other EEC nations within a five-year transition period. Britain had asked for six years to adjust to the EEC agricultural policy, which was expected to bring about a steep rise in British food prices. At year-end representatives of the government of Britain were negotiating with the EEC Commission over a compromise arrangement, with the hope of reaching an agreement by the end of 1971. Under that timetable Britain could become a transitional member of the EEC by Jan. 1, 1973.

Other nations seeking membership or affiliation with the EEC during the year were Ireland, Denmark, Norway, Finland, and Sweden. The latter two nations wanted only economic association with the EEC while retaining complete political independence. Each of the others sought to become full members for different reasons, and each brought special problems to the membership negotiations. Ireland wanted to protect its agriculture and its infant industries; Denmark conveyed a concern over the free flow of capital; Norway wanted to ensure safeguards for its big fisheries industry.

The EEC finance ministers also took the first step toward the creation of a common currency among member nations in 1970. In May the ministers agreed to hold the fluctuation rates of their national currencies to the existing .75% above or below parity. They also agreed to try to realize common tax and budget policies, a common exchange rate between their currencies, and freer capital movements within nine years. During that month the EEC completed the final phase in the adoption of a common commercial policy by adopting a common system for imports from third countries and a common procedure for handling quotas. Member nations agreed in November to work toward coordinating their foreign policies as much as possible in the future.

In the culmination of negotiations dating back to October 1966, the EEC and Israel signed a five-year preferential trade agreement in June. The pact provides for mutual tariff reductions covering more than 70% of the commerce between Israel and the EEC nations. The EEC had been the single most important customer and supplier to Israel. The bloc also signed a trade agreement with Spain.

The General Agreement on Tariffs and Trade

The annual meeting of the General Agreement on Tariffs and Trade (GATT) ended on a some-

A Japanese ship loads logs at Port Angeles, Wash. Trade between Japan and the United States was endangered by a restrictive bill proposed, but not passed, by the U.S. Congress.
MONROE PINCKARD FROM RAPHO GUILLUMETTE

KEYSTONE

Valéry Giscard d'Estaing (right), France's minister of finance, and Vladimir Kirillin, Soviet deputy premier, signed an agreement providing French aid for Soviet industry.

what unhappy note in February. In the GATT session Director General Olivier Long called upon the 76 member nations to prepare for large-scale negotiations to lower trade barriers in 1971. However, the GATT general assembly refused to commit itself to launching another extensive series of negotiations similar to the "Kennedy round" of discussions, which were successfully completed in 1967. Instead GATT nations agreed to consider what "appropriate actions" might be taken to liberalize trade further in agricultural and industrial products. One major obstacle to scheduling such talks was Britain's negotiation with the EEC for membership. Both Britain and the EEC nations expressed doubt on their ability to conduct the membership negotiations while participating in a major GATT conference.

In September GATT released a report that raised the agency's predictions on the expansion in world trade during 1970 from the 4%–8% level to the 8%–10% level. However, much of the increase was attributed to a "sharp upturn" in prices, which were projected at 3% to 4% higher than those prevailing in 1969.

United Nations Conference on Trade and Development

A pact reached between the developing and industrialized members of the United Nations Conference on Trade and Development (UNCTAD) was heralded as the start of a new era in international trade relations. The agreement, concluded in October, followed a six-year search for preferential treatment for exports from developing countries to the industrialized nations. Under the terms of the UNCTAD accord, the Western industrial nations and Japan submitted lists of primarily manufactured and semimanufactured items on which they would undertake to lower or remove tariffs when the items are imported from developing nations.

The developing nations were urged by the United States to eliminate within a "reasonable period of time" any special trade concessions made to other industrialized nations. The industrialized nations all attached escape clauses to their concessions to enable them to be able to rescind or limit concessions if a flood of cheap imports occurred or for other economic or political reasons.

The Coffee Trade Controversy

Throughout the summer, exporting and importing member nations of the International Coffee Agreement wrangled over differences on the amount of coffee to be released on the world market during 1970 and 1971. The controversy grew up after a crippling frost destroyed half of the coffee crop in Brazil in 1969. In the International Coffee Agreement of 1962, export quotas on coffee were fixed for each of the producing countries. Under this system the Brazilian coffee shortage brought about higher prices during 1970 at the established quotas and brought about a demand for larger quotas and thus lower prices by the coffee-consuming nations. Several coffee-producing nations, especially Brazil, countered by asking for the retention of existing quotas and higher prices.

The agreement eventually reached in early September proved to be a victory for some consuming nations and some producing nations. After world quotas were increased by 8 million bags, the price of coffee was expected to be held to a wholesale price range of 46¢ to 52¢. While Brazil would be unable to meet its own export quotas, African nations, which were previously held to small quotas, would gain a greater share of the world market.

Soviet Trade with Non-Communist Nations

Figures released in mid-1970 indicated that trade between the Soviet Union and non-Communist nations in 1969 increased much more rapidly than trade between the Soviet Union and other Communist countries. Trade with industrialized capitalist countries jumped 15%, while trade with developing countries rose 25%. During the same period Soviet trade with Communist China and Cuba declined.

The general softening in attitude toward trading with capitalist nations was evidenced in the extension of an invitation to U.S. industrialist Henry Ford II to help build a Soviet truck plant. However, Ford bowed to pressure exerted by U.S. Secretary of Defense Melvin R. Laird and refused the invitation. Laird objected because the Soviet Union provided trucks to North Vietnam.

In April Japan signed a $26-million contract to supply equipment for a chemical plant in the Soviet Union. (*See also* Economy; Money and International Finance; Textiles. *See in* CE: International Trade.)

YEMEN. During the first months of 1970 civil war continued in Yemen between royalist followers of the Imam Muhammad al-Badr, aided by Saudi Arabia, and the republicans who ousted him in 1962. The royalist forces scored some military gains early in the year.

On February 1, republican Premier Abdullah al-Kirshimi resigned in a budgetary dispute with the armed forces. A new republican government was formed by ex-Premier Mohsin al-Aini, who made conciliatory gestures toward Saudi Arabia. In March he became the first Yemeni republican official to visit Saudi Arabia when he led a delegation to a conference of Islamic foreign ministers at Jidda. During the visit an agreement was reached with the Saudis on conditions for ending the long civil war.

By mid-April, fighting was reported to have ceased, and Saudi aid to the royalists was cut off. Former royalist leaders began returning to San'a, the republican-held capital, on May 23. The republican Presidential Council was expanded from three to five members to include the former royalist foreign minister, Ahmed al-Shami, and a moderate republican, Ahmed Muhammad Noman, who had long advocated reconciliation with the royalists. In addition, 12 royalists were appointed members of the National Assembly, and four other royalists were named to posts in a reshuffled cabinet. The imam and his family, however, were not permitted to return to Yemen from Saudi Arabia.

The Yemeni republican government was officially recognized by Saudi Arabia in July. Recognition by France, Great Britain, and Turkey followed quickly.

Air traffic between Yemen and Saudi Arabia, broken off in 1962, was resumed in September. Earlier in the year an agreement was reached with West Germany for the rebuilding of San'a's international airport. Yemen joined the World Bank and the International Monetary Fund in May.

Three years of severe drought brought famine to parts of Yemen during 1970. In June the government appealed to the United Nations for food supplies; a number of countries, including Saudi Arabia and the United States, responded to the appeal. Two months later the heaviest rains in ten years fell in Yemen, but the rainfall was too late to help farmers. (*See also* Saudi Arabia. *See in* CE: Yemen.)

YOUTH ORGANIZATIONS. If there was a recognizable trend at work within the youth organizations of the United States during 1970, it was an effort to break down racial and religious prejudices where they still existed. There were also determined efforts made by most organizations to enroll young people of lower-income groups.

Boys' Clubs of America

Plans for a five-year, $25-million "Drive For Decency" campaign to reach an estimated 3 million additional boys were revealed during a historic White House meeting of the national board of directors of the Boys' Clubs of America, hosted by U.S. President Richard M. Nixon. Locating and identifying areas of greatest need were essential parts of the campaign.

JOHN R. BURKHART, COURTESY, YMCA

Donald M. Payne, the first black president of the National Council of YMCAs, addresses an international meeting in St. Paul, Minn.

During the year, Boys' Clubs of America grew to 880 clubs, serving more than 875,000 boys. Years of experience have taught the national Boys' Clubs organization that needs will vary widely by region, area, and circumstances.

President Nixon installed James Heath of the Catskill Boys' Club in New York as boy of the year and the "nation's leading example of juvenile decency." Heath received a $4,000 scholarship.

Boy Scouts of America

At the Boy Scouts of America National Council's 60th annual meeting, held in Denver, Colo., in May, Irving Feist, a realtor from Newark, N.J., was re-elected president. Edwin H. Gott, chairman of the board of U.S. Steel Corp., was named a vice-president, and Bryan S. Reid, Jr., board chairman of Cherry-Burrell Corp., was elected treasurer.

Six young people were given Young American awards for outstanding contributions to the nation. They were Rodney Earl Donaldson, San Antonio, Tex.; Paul Douglas Ring, Phoenix, Ariz.; John Parker Stewart, Brighton, Colo.; Rex Kern, Columbus, Ohio; Madeline Manning, Cleveland, Ohio; and Jennifer Sue Inskeep, Cawker City, Kan.

In November, an unusual event took place when James Clark, 16, a scout from Foster, R.I., was denied a promotion to the rank of Eagle Scout; the reason given was that he was an admitted atheist. Later, a Boy Scout review board reversed that decision. (*See in* CE: Boy Scouts of America.)

4-H Clubs

The enlarging of the National 4-H Center on the edge of Washington, D.C.—to handle the ever-growing number of 4-H youths using it—started in April during the 40th National 4-H Conference. Tricia Nixon, elder daughter of President Nixon, led the ground-breaking ceremonies. Sharing the occasion were many notables and either four or five 4-Hers from each of the 50 states, the District of Columbia, and Puerto Rico.

About one in every ten members of 4–H Clubs received special recognition—local, state, regional, or national—for exceptional achievement or progress during the year. Some 1,600, for example, went to Chicago on expense-paid trips to attend the National 4-H Congress in the fall; 286 received a total of $166,700 in national 4-H college scholarships. (*See in* CE: 4-H Clubs.)

Future Farmers of America

The introduction of a community action program and the revision of ongoing awards programs were highlights of the year for the national organization of the Future Farmers of America (FFA). More than 430,000 students of vocational agriculture in 8,200 chapters took part in FFA activities.

In international activities, the FFA continued its "Work Experience Abroad" program. In 1970, 25 participants spent three months living and working on farms in nine countries. In addition, the FFA aided Vietnamese educators in establishing a Future Farmers of Vietnam (FFVN). David Dietz of Canby, Ore., FFA Pacific Region vice-president, traveled for three weeks in Vietnam to meet personally and work with FFVN members, helping them establish a strong organization.

More than 15,000 FFA members and guests attended the 43d National FFA Convention in Kansas City, Mo., setting a new attendance record for the annual event. Merrill Kelsay, a 21-year-old dairy and crop farmer from Whiteland, Ind., was named the star farmer of America, and Earl Weaver, 21, of Middletown, Pa., was named star agri-businessman of America. (*See in* CE: Future Farmers of America.)

Future Homemakers of America

The 1970 national meeting of the Future Homemakers of America (FHA), held in New York City in July, marked the organization's 25th anniversary and was attended by 1,350 youth delegates

Approximately 2,500 women attended the 25th National Convention of the YWCA of the U.S.A. held in Houston, Tex., in April. Some delegates made banners to express their needs and concerns.

COURTESY, YWCA

UPI COMPIX

James Heath, who received the Boy of the Year award from the Boys' Clubs of America, receives a plaque from U.S. President Richard M. Nixon in a White House ceremony in March.

and 350 adult advisers. The meeting focused on the year's objective: to promote communication for the enrichment of human relationships. Ruth Ann Hockenbroch, a high school senior from Richfield, Pa., was elected president for 1970.

Girls Clubs of America

The Girls Clubs of America, Inc., observed its 25th anniversary in 1970 by launching a campaign to increase the number of club centers, especially in low-income areas. Fifteen new clubs were organized during the year and accepted for membership, and additional new clubs were being organized in 50 cities across the country. A total of 172 club centers in the United States and Canada were affiliated with Girls Clubs of America.

Girl Scouts of the United States of America

Efforts to help stop environmental pollution and to combat prejudice were major objectives of most Girl Scout activities during 1970. Always conservation-minded, Girl Scouts united in Eco-Action, a nationwide ecological endeavor, for the decade. Girl Scout-initiated projects involving cleanup, beautification, and antipollution activities began across the country, with emphasis on such areas of special environmental need as the nation's waterways. Two such projects—the cleaning of the Clinton River in Michigan and the cleaning of a seven-mile stretch of the Hackensack River in New Jersey—gained nationwide publicity.

Another nationwide Girl Scout effort—to become more aware of prejudices and to take action to build better relationships among persons of all ages, religions, races, and nationalities—was called Action 70. (*See in* CE: Girl Scouts.)

Young Men's Christian Association

In 1970, the National Council of the 1,700 Young Men's Christian Associations (YMCAs) in the United States, for the first time in its 125-year history, elected a black president, Donald M. Payne of Newark, N.J. The election followed a trend in the organization toward more influential positions for minority members and workers, persons under 30 years of age, and women, who make up 28% of the 5,650,610 members.

There was a general expansion of programs for inner-city youth, highlighted by the formation of the National Training Center for Youth Outreach Workers. Also to be added was a special Drugs Training Component for outreach workers concerned with drug abuse among youths. Draft counseling services were begun to supply draft-age youths with information about their rights. (*See in* CE: Young Men's Christian Association.)

Young Women's Christian Association

At the 25th triennial National YWCA Convention in Houston, Tex., in the spring of 1970, more than 2,500 participants unequivocally adopted one imperative—the elimination of racism—as a focus for the association's 1970–73 program for action. In attendance were delegates representing community and student YWCAs and visiting YWCA leaders from 11 foreign countries.

As a result of convention action, the YWCA established a National YWCA Resource Center on Women. Research-oriented and activist in approach, its function was to prompt women to raise their level of consciousness about restrictions upon them, such as discrimination and exploitation, and to bring about social change envisaged by the YWCA. (*See in* CE: Juvenile Organizations; Young Women's Christian Association.)

YUGOSLAVIA.

The decision to set up a collective presidency of Yugoslavia and to reshape the country's federal system was the main political event there in 1970. The year was characterized in the economic sphere by galloping inflation and a dramatic widening of the foreign-trade gap. In 1970 Yugoslavia moved perceptibly closer to the West.

Domestic Affairs

In January the Central Committee of the Croatian republic decided by an overwhelming majority to replace Milos Zanko as one of Croatia's delegates on the League of Communists' federal standing conference in Belgrade, the capital. Zanko had alleged in November 1969 that nationalist forces were making dramatic progress in Croatia and implied that Croatian leaders were not doing enough to stop them. The leaders interpreted Zanko's challenge as part of a plot to overthrow them by conservative party circles opposed to decentralization advocated by Croat leaders. In April, Zanko

WIDE WORLD

Yugoslav author Mihajlo Mihajlov (left) is accompanied by his lawyer as he leaves prison. He served three and a half years for spreading "hostile propaganda" about his country.

was deprived of his post as a vice-president of the Federal Assembly. Also in April, the League's Presidium adopted a resolution that affirmed the republics' sovereignty and stressed their need for greater autonomy. The Presidium also agreed that top priority in the allocation of development aid in the 1971–75 period must be given to the economically backward province of Kosovo-Mitohiyan, which had been Yugoslavia's politically most troubled region in recent years.

Many clashes took place in the Federal Assembly in the spring and summer between advocates of the speedy adoption of the 1971–75 plan and others (mainly from Croatia and Slovenia) who insisted that major changes in the country's economic and political system must come first. Among other things they demanded radical changes in the system of allocating foreign currency (claimed to be grossly unfair to Croatia and Slovenia as major foreign-currency earners). No agreement was reached on any of the major economic issues, and the passing of the economic plan was postponed until 1971. But agreement was reached on an important political issue. On September 21 President Tito put forward a plan for a collective presidency that would eventually take over the running of the country from him. This presidency, composed of representatives from the six republics and two autonomous provinces and from labor and political organizations, would also take over some of the functions of the federal government and the Federal Assembly and would hand over other powers to the governments of the republics. The federal "center" would retain only the responsibility for defense, foreign policy, and the economic system.

Trailers in Banja Luka, Yugoslavia, house people whose homes were destroyed in an earthquake in October 1969. At least 60,000 were left homeless by the disaster.

KEYSTONE

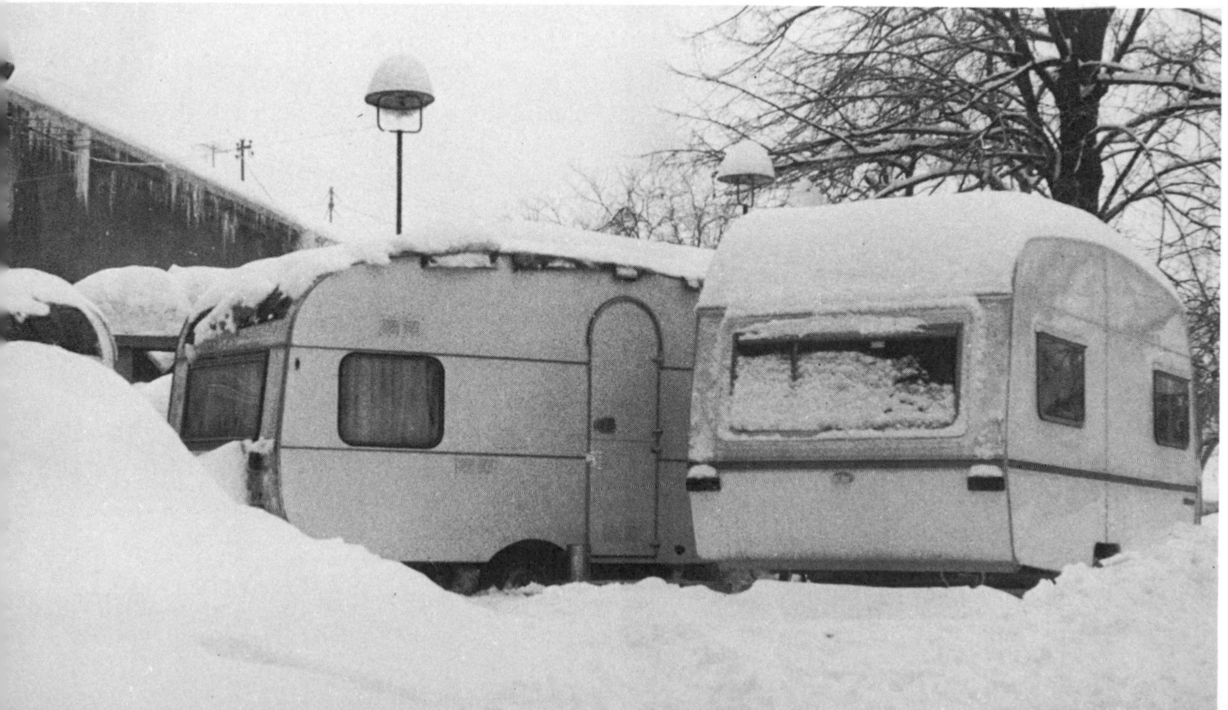

Critics of decentralization greeted the plan with open hostility, but it was eventually adopted unanimously at the end of October by the national conference of the League of Communists.

Throughout the year the authorities continued to clash with left-wing Belgrade students. One of the leaders of this opposition group, Vlada Mijanovic, was sentenced on October 20 to 20 months' imprisonment for "antistate activities." His sentence sparked a strike at Belgrade University and the temporary occupation of some university buildings by the strikers.

Economic Affairs

Foreign investment continued to reach Yugoslavia in 1970. The most important agreement was the $6.5-million contract in July between the West German firm Daimler-Benz and the Yugoslav firm FAP-Famos for the joint production and marketing of commercial vehicles.

In February 1970, Yugoslavia concluded a three-year economic agreement with the European Economic Community (EEC), or Common Market, the first Communist country to do so. This agreement provided for preferential treatment for Yugoslav beef exports to EEC countries.

Foreign Affairs

At the end of January, President Tito visited eight African countries on a one-month tour, in the course of which he vigorously compaigned in favor of holding another nonaligned summit conference. In September, he attended the 54-nation nonaligned summit conference in Lusaka, Zambia, of which Yugoslavia had been one of the main organizers.

President Tito paid state visits to Belgium, the Netherlands, and Luxembourg in October. En route, he had meetings with President Georges Pompidou of France and Chancellor Willy Brandt of West Germany. On September 30, U.S. President Richard M. Nixon began a two-day visit to Yugoslavia. The visit, a great popular success in Yugoslavia, was interpreted as an expression of renewed U.S. interest in Yugoslavia's independence and a subtle warning to the U.S.S.R.

In October, delegations from the Supreme Soviet of the U.S.S.R. and the Komsomol, the Communist youth organization, visited Yugoslavia. These visits and the moderate tone of the Soviet press about Yugoslavia suggested that the Soviet Union as well as Yugoslavia wanted to prevent their mutual relations from deteriorating. (*See in* CE: Yugoslavia.)

ZAMBIA. The mining industries of Zambia, the world's third largest copper producer, were nationalized on Jan. 1, 1970. The state assumed a 51% holding in the country's two giant mining companies, retaining the company management to operate the mines as before. In November it was announced that the state was also assuming a controlling interest in banks and insurance companies.

Kenneth Kaunda, Zambia's president, stopped in London to visit Britain's Prime Minister Edward Heath in October. Kaunda was on his way to visit the United Nations in New York City.

UPI COMPIX

Several foreign mining concerns accepted the Zambian government's invitation to prospect for new mineral deposits in 1970, and in July a large copper find was reported north of Lusaka, the capital. In September a mudslide in Zambia's second largest copper mine at Mufulira, which had been producing more than 20% of the country's total exports, killed 89 men and stopped production for a projected nine months.

Having built a conference hall and delegates' housing facilities in 17 weeks at a cost of more than $14 million, Zambia hosted the third summit conference of nonaligned nations in Lusaka in September, attended by leaders of 54 states. Zambia's President Kenneth Kaunda was delegated as the representative of both the nonaligned nations and the Organization of African Unity to lead a mission in October to the United Nations (UN) and the major Western capitals to seek sanctions against South Africa, Rhodesia, and the Portuguese territories. Zambian-U.S. relations were improved by the state visit to Lusaka of U.S. Secretary of State William P. Rogers in February, but relations suffered when Kaunda, after addressing the UN General Assembly, had to leave the United States without getting an appointment to see U.S. President Richard M. Nixon, who was busy campaigning in Tennessee.

Communist China contracted in July to build a 1,000-mile railroad linking the present Zambian railway system with the Tanzanian port of Dar es Salaam. The railroad, begun in October, would end Zambia's dependence on Rhodesia and the Portuguese territories for transportation of exports, mainly copper, and imports to and from the coast. (*See also* Africa; Rhodesia. *See in* CE: Zambia.)

ZOOS. In 1970 the world's zoos continued to breed more species of animals that were in danger of extinction. A world first was the birth of a white rhinoceros at Pretoria, South Africa. In September New York City's Bronx Zoo reported the first known hatching in captivity of a tufted puffin. The Brookfield Zoo in Illinois recorded the first known breeding in captivity of green-crested basilisks. The Jersey Zoo of England's Channel Islands bred the Szechwan white-eared pheasant, which previously had been successfully bred only in the United States, and at year-end had the largest group of the birds outside of China. In England the Chester Zoo recorded a first with a Louisiade lorikeet; the zoo at Frankfurt, West Germany, had another with the hatching of a pygmy kingfisher.

The San Diego Zoo in California received a grant to make possible the study of a group of ten cheetahs. These large cats were becoming increasingly scarce, and efforts to breed them in captivity had met only limited success.

In order to keep an accurate record of the number of various rare animals in zoos, studbooks listing all individuals were being compiled. In 1970 the latest was an orangutan studbook kept by the Yerkes Primate Center of the United States.

As animal-keeping methods improved, many species were living far longer than they would in the wild state, and therefore they often required more sophisticated veterinary care. An example was the oldest gorilla in captivity, a 38-year-old male at Philadelphia, Pa., which underwent an operation for chronic sinusitis and the removal of bad teeth. Philadelphia zoo officials also reported increased lung-cancer rates among their animals; their studies led them to suspect that air pollution was at least a partial cause.

Zoos in increasing number exchanged animals for breeding. As an example, during the year a black rhinoceros bred in Chester was sent to Moscow for this purpose.

Seeking to improve their educational services, more and more zoos provided recorded talks about their animals. The most ambitious project in 1970 was at the Los Angeles Zoo, where visitors could tune in on any one of 94 different talks.

Zoo architecture continued to move toward more spacious and natural-looking enclosures. Many zoos turned to ditches, rather than wire mesh, to confine animals. The Bronx Zoo announced a $10-million plan to build a 30-acre "natural" display area for Asian animals. Construction of barless enclosures continued at Chicago's Lincoln Park Zoo. In Naples, Fla., Caribbean Gardens announced a $1-million project that would include safari trails through Everglades, Amazonian, Asian, and African exhibits.

Overseas, new lion and tiger enclosures, a large flight aviary, a parrot house with modernistic inside and outside aviaries, and a number of antelope enclosures with ditches were constructed at the Chester zoo. West Berlin completed new zebra enclosures and eight barless dry-moat paddocks. At Kolmarden, Sweden, the first Scandinavian dolphinarium was opened, and at Natal, South Africa, a 243-acre site was purchased for conversion into a modern ditched zoo. East Berlin opened a barless wolf enclosure.

Evidence that zoos continued to be popular in the United States was the report that visitors totaled 100 million annually. In Japan, too, zoos experienced a great upsurge in popularity. (*See also* Animals and Wildlife. *See in* CE: Zoo.)

Ziggy, age 53, is the oldest and largest pachyderm in the United States. He lives in the Brookfield Zoo in Illinois. Ziggy attacked his keeper in 1941 and has been under restraints ever since. Funds were being raised in 1970 to build a new enclosure for Ziggy so that he can enjoy the outdoors.

CHICAGO ZOOLOGICAL SOCIETY

CALENDAR FOR 1971

JANUARY

1 Friday. New Year's Day. Major football bowl games. National Burglar and Fire Alarm Protection Month begins.
3 Sunday. Save the Pun Week begins.
5 Tuesday. Twelfth Night.
6 Wednesday. Twelfth Day, or Epiphany.
9 Saturday. Richard M. Nixon's birthday.
13 Wednesday. Stephen Foster Memorial Week begins.
15 Friday. Birthday of Martin Luther King, Jr.
17 Sunday. Super Bowl football game. Benjamin Franklin's birthday. Jaycee Week begins.
19 Tuesday. Robert E. Lee's birthday.
27 Wednesday. Chinese New Year celebrations begin. Wolfgang Amadeus Mozart's birthday.
29 Friday. William McKinley's birthday.
30 Saturday. Franklin D. Roosevelt's birthday.
31 Sunday. International Clergy Week begins.

FEBRUARY

1 Monday. National Freedom Day. American Heart Month, Boy Scouts of America Anniversary Celebration, and National Pay Your Bills Week begin.
2 Tuesday. Candlemas. Groundhog Day.
7 Sunday. National Children's Dental Health Week and National Crime Prevention Week begin.
10 Wednesday. Total eclipse of the moon.
12 Friday. Abraham Lincoln's birthday. Brotherhood Week begins.
14 Sunday. Saint Valentine's Day. National Negro History Week begins.
15 Monday. George Washington's birthday celebrated.
20 Saturday. Future Farmers of America Week begins.
23 Tuesday. Shrove Tuesday. International Pancake Race. Mardi Gras.
24 Wednesday. Ash Wednesday. Lent begins.

MARCH

1 Monday. National Housing for Handicapped Week National Procrastination Week, and Return the Borrowed Book Week begin.
2 Tuesday. Texas Independence Day.
3 Wednesday. National Peanut Week begins.
7 Sunday. Girl Scout Week begins. Luther Burbank's birthday.
15 Monday. Andrew Jackson's birthday.
17 Wednesday. Saint Patrick's Day.
19 Friday. Swallows return to San Juan Capistrano.
21 Sunday. Camp Fire Girls Birthday Week, National Wildlife Week, and National Poison Prevention Week begin. First day of spring.
25 Thursday. Feast of the Annunciation.
28 Sunday. National Boys' Club Week and National Foreign Language Week begin.
30 Tuesday. National Cherry Blossom Festival.

APRIL

1 Thursday. April Fools' Day. Cancer Control Month and National Laugh Week begin.
4 Sunday. Palm Sunday. Holy Week begins.
8 Thursday. Maundy Thursday. National Panic Week begins. Buddha's birthday.
9 Friday. Good Friday. Sir Winston Churchill Day.
10 Saturday. Passover begins.
11 Sunday. Easter Sunday. Pan American Week and Harmony Week begin.
13 Tuesday. Thomas Jefferson's birthday.
18 Sunday. National Library Week, National Coin Week, National YWCA Week, and Secretaries Week begin.
25 Sunday. Daylight saving time begins.
26 Monday. Confederate Memorial Day.
27 Tuesday. Ulysses Simpson Grant's birthday.

MAY

1 Saturday. May Day. Law Day. Loyalty Day. Senior Citizens Month, Steelmark Month, National Tavern Month, and Mental Health Week begin.
2 Sunday. Humane Sunday. Mother-in-Law Day. National Be Kind to Animals Week begins.
8 Saturday. Harry S Truman's birthday.
9 Sunday. Mother's Day. National Hospital Week and Police Week begin.
10 Monday. National Salvation Army Week begins.
15 Saturday. Armed Forces Day and Peace Officers Memorial Day.
16 Sunday. National Transportation Week and World Trade Week begin.
20 Thursday. International Pickle Week begins.
21 Friday. National Defense Transportation Day.
22 Saturday. National Maritime Day.
29 Saturday. John F. Kennedy's birthday. Indianapolis 500-mile race.
30 Sunday. Whitsunday, or Pentecost.
31 Monday. Memorial Day.

JUNE

1 Tuesday. Fight the Filthy Fly Month, Model Rocketry Month, National Postal Reform Month, National Ragweed Control Month, National Rose Month, and National Seat Belt Month begin.
3 Thursday. Jefferson Davis' birthday.
6 Sunday. National Humor Week begins.
7 Monday. Freedom of the Press Day.
11 Friday. Kamehameha Day, Hawaii.
12 Saturday. The Queen's Official Birthday, England.
13 Sunday. National Flag Week begins.
14 Monday. Flag Day. National Little League Baseball Week begins. Birthday of U.S. Army.
17 Thursday. U.S. Open golf tournament begins.
19 Saturday. National Hollerin Contest.
20 Sunday. Father's Day. Amateur Radio Week begins.
21 Monday. First day of summer. Wimbledon Lawn Tennis Championships begin, England.
30 Wednesday. Old Milwaukee Days begin.

JULY

1 Thursday. Dominion Day, Canada. National Barbecue Month and National Hot Dog Month begin.
3 Saturday. International Frisbee Tournament.
4 Sunday. Independence Day. Calvin Coolidge's birthday. National Safe Boating Week begins.
6 Tuesday. John Paul Jones's birthday.
11 Sunday. John Quincy Adams' birthday.
12 Monday. Orangeman's Day, Northern Ireland. National Cherry Festival begins.
14 Wednesday. Bastille Day, France.
15 Thursday. Saint Swithin's Day.
16 Friday. Captive Nations Week begins.
17 Saturday. Luis Muñoz-Rivera's birthday.
18 Sunday. International Railway Day.
20 Tuesday. Moon Day.
21 Wednesday. Liberation Day, Guam.
22 Thursday. Partial eclipse of the sun.
24 Saturday. Simón Bolívar's birthday.
25 Sunday. National Farm Safety Week begins.
27 Tuesday. Atlantic Telegraph Cable Anniversary.

AUGUST

1 Sunday. Tishah b'Ab, or Fast of Ab. Beauty Queen Week begins.
2 Monday. National Smile Week begins.
4 Wednesday. Coast Guard Day.
5 Thursday. Maine Seafoods Festival begins.
8 Sunday. Family Reunion Day. International Character Day. Better Water for Americans Week begins.
10 Tuesday. Herbert C. Hoover's birthday.
14 Saturday. Victory Day. Atlantic Charter Day.
15 Sunday. Assumption of the Virgin Mary. Sir Walter Scott's birthday. National Allergy Month begins.
19 Thursday. National Aviation Day.
20 Friday. Benjamin Harrison's birthday.
26 Thursday. Shape-Up-With-Pickles Time begins.
27 Friday. Lyndon B. Johnson's birthday. Theodore Dreiser's birthday.
29 Sunday. Freedom of Enterprise Week begins.
30 Monday. Huey P. Long Day, Louisiana.

SEPTEMBER

1 Wednesday. American Youth Month, National Better Breakfast Month, National Pancake Month, and Bourbon Month begin.
2 Thursday. Mustache Day.
6 Monday. Labor Day. Be Late for Something Day.
12 Sunday. National Hispanic Heritage Week and National Home Week begin.
15 Wednesday. William Howard Taft's birthday.
17 Friday. Citizenship Day. Constitution Week begins.
18 Saturday. National Tie Week begins.
19 Sunday. World Peace Day. National Dog Week begins.
20 Monday. Rosh Hashanah, or Jewish New Year.
23 Thursday. Autumn begins.
24 Friday. American Indian Day.
25 Saturday. Kiwanis Kids' Day.
26 Sunday. Gold Star Mothers' Day.
29 Wednesday. Michaelmas. Yom Kippur, or Day of Atonement.

OCTOBER

1 Friday. March Against Muscular Dystrophy and National Restaurant Month begin.
3 Sunday. Fire Prevention Week, National Employ the Physically Handicapped Week, and National 4-H Week begin.
4 Monday. Rutherford B. Hayes's birthday. Child Health Week begins.
5 Tuesday. Chester A. Arthur's birthday.
9 Saturday. Leif Erikson Day.
10 Sunday. National School Lunch Week begins.
11 Monday. Columbus Day.
14 Thursday. Dwight D. Eisenhower's birthday.
17 Sunday. National Forest Products Week begins.
22 Friday. National Day of Prayer.
24 Sunday. United Nations Day. American Education Week and National Cleaner Air Week begin.
25 Monday. Veterans Day.
27 Wednesday. Theodore Roosevelt's birthday.
30 Saturday. John Adams' birthday.
31 Sunday. Halloween. Standard time begins.

NOVEMBER

1 Monday. All Saints' Day. White House Conference on Aging begins.
2 Tuesday. All Souls' Day. Warren G. Harding's birthday.
5 Friday. Guy Fawkes Day, Great Britain.
7 Sunday. International Cat Week begins.
10 Wednesday. Christmas Seal campaign begins.
14 Sunday. National Children's Book Week and Diabetes Week begin.
15 Monday. National Stamp Collecting Week begins.
19 Friday. James A. Garfield's birthday. National Farm-City Week begins.
21 Sunday. International Aviation Month and Bible Week begin.
23 Tuesday. Franklin Pierce's birthday.
24 Wednesday. Zachary Taylor's birthday.
25 Thursday. Thanksgiving Day.
26 Friday. National Indigestion Season begins.
27 Saturday. Army-Navy football game.
28 Sunday. First Sunday in Advent.

DECEMBER

1 Wednesday. Model Railroading Month begins.
2 Thursday. Pan American Health Day. World Community Day.
5 Sunday. Martin Van Buren's birthday. National Mimicry Week begins.
7 Tuesday. Pearl Harbor Day.
8 Wednesday. Feast of the Immaculate Conception.
10 Friday. Human Rights Day. Nobel peace pnze presentation.
13 Monday. Hanukkah, or Feast of Lights, begins.
17 Friday. Pan American Aviation Day. Wright Brothers Day.
21 Tuesday. Forefathers' Day.
22 Wednesday. International Arbor Day. Winter begins.
25 Saturday. Christmas Day.
26 Sunday. Boxing Day, Great Britain.
28 Tuesday. Woodrow Wilson's birthday.
29 Wednesday. Andrew Johnson's birthday.
31 Friday. New Year's Eve.

New Words

This New Words section consists of two parts. The first part is a list of new words officially accepted for use in Merriam-Webster dictionaries. The second part is an essay on new words of recent years and their origins.

New Words from

The list of new words and new meanings on the following pages has been prepared by the permanent editorial staff of G. & C. Merriam Company of Springfield, Massachusetts, publishers of *Webster's Third New International Dictionary* and *Webster's Seventh New Collegiate Dictionary* and other dictionaries in the Merriam-Webster Series.

A

AC/DC *adj* : BISEXUAL

airtel *n* : a hotel situated at or near an airport

anomalous water *n* : POLYWATER

antiversity *n* : an educational institution that offers courses which are outside the traditional disciplines and that emphasizes student involvement

apple *n, specif* : an American Indian who ingratiates himself with white society—called also *Uncle Tomahawk*

aquaspaceman *n* : a scuba diver who lives beneath the surface for an extended period and carries on activities both inside and outside an underwater shelter : OCEANAUT

aquathenics *n pl* : exercises performed in a swimming pool

ashcan *n, specif* : a firecracker that is powerful enough to rip metal

astromonk *n* : a monkey sent into orbit about the earth in a spacecraft for experimental purposes

B

bells *n pl* : bell-bottom trousers

bioelectronics *n* **1** : a branch of science that deals with electronic control of physiological function especially to compensate for defects of the nervous system **2** : a branch of science that deals with the role of electron transfer in biological processes

blahs *n pl* : low spirits : BLUES

blue meanie *n* **1 blue meanies** *pl* : POLICE **2** : one in authority who discriminates against those who do not follow conventional norms (as of dress or hair style)

bottomless *adj, specif* **1** : NUDE ⟨*bottomless* dancers⟩ **2** : featuring nude entertainers ⟨a *bottomless* nightclub⟩

brush shoe *n* : a shoe with many small spikes on the sole worn especially by athletes in running events

bubble gum *n, specif* : rock music characterized by simple repetitive phrasings and intended especially for young teen-agers

bump jumper *n* : a stool mounted on a short ski and ridden on a ski slope

burn artist *n* : a narcotics seller who cheats his customers

C

charity walk *n, Brit* : a long-distance walk made by a large group to publicize or elicit contributions for a charity

chib *vb, chiefly Scot* : to slash with a straight razor

chickendog *n* : a frankfurter containing chicken

chopper-copper *n* : a policeman on patrol in a helicopter

cirsoss *n, Brit* : a completely round sausage

club football *n* : intercollegiate football organized and administered by students

communiversity *n* : a conglomerate of educational and cultural institutions (as schools, museums, theaters, and libraries) designed to serve the needs of the residents of a community

computernik *n* : a specialist in the theory and operation of computers

conglomerateur *n* : one who organizes or manages a conglomerate

coop *n, specif* : a place (as a park) used for cooping

cooping *n* : sleeping while on police duty

cop-frontation *n* : a confrontation between demonstrators and the police

corny dog *n* : a hot dog dipped in corn fat

D

dartchery *n* : a sports event that combines archery and dart throwing

dewat *vb* : to make a deactivated war trophy of a military rifle by irreparably damaging its firing mechanism

dial-in *n* : a barrage of phone calls (as to a telephone company) made as a form of organized protest (as against higher rates)

diamante *n, specif* : a diamond-shaped poem consisting of seven lines and sixteen words

door buster *n* : a widely advertised article designed to attract customers to a store

E

earthathon *n* : a television program lasting several hours that reports on various events (as teach-ins and demonstrations) relating to the condition and the improvement of the natural environment

ecomanagement *n* : the application of ecological principles to the management of environment and natural resources

ecomodel *n* : a model for the management of environment and natural resources according to ecological principles

ecopolicy *n* : a policy for the management of environment and natural resources according to ecological principles

ecumunity *n* : interchurch cooperation in community projects (as adult education)

elint *adj* : fitted out with electronic intelligence-gathering equipment ⟨fleets of *elint* ships⟩

F

fast-food *adj* : specializing in the rapid preparation and service of food (as hamburgers or fried chicken) ⟨a *fast-food* restaurant chain⟩

flop *vb, specif* : to reassign (a policeman) to a less desirable position—**flopping** *n*

folker *n* : FOLK SINGER

Friedmanite *n* : an adherent of the economist Milton Friedman's theory that a nation's money supply is the main determinant of economic growth —**Friedmanism** *n*

frosted *n, specif* : NAILFROST

frozen rope *n* : a line drive in baseball

G

George *n, specif* : PONYTAIL

ghettologist *n* : one who studies ghetto life

graymail *n* : the act or practice of threatening to avenge an injury received

guerrilla theater *n* : an informal dramatic presentation that usually depicts episodes of social injustice and is performed in parks and streets by amateurs who are often joined by spectators—called also *street theater*

H

head shop *n* : a shop that specializes in psychedelic accessories (as hashish pipes, incense, posters, and beads)

hinterurbia *n* : a remote suburb in which city workers reside

hype *n, specif* : ADVERTISEMENT, BLURB ⟨*hypes* on the dust jacket of a novel⟩

I

impansion *n* : a reduction in size, extent of operation, or personnel

infrared astronomy *n* : a branch of astronomy dealing with investigations of celestial bodies by means of the infrared radiation they emit

J

jawboning *n* : a strong appeal by a chief of state to national business and labor leaders for price and wage restraints

jay *n, specif* : a marijuana cigarette : JOINT

jockette *n* : a female jockey

juice head *n* : a frequent or heavy drinker of alcoholic beverages

K

kicker *n, specif* : something (as a share in profits or ownership) demanded in addition to interest by mortgage lenders on commercial real estate

kidvid *n* : television programs for children

L

L-dopa *n* : a compound that consists of levorotatory dopamine, that occurs especially in broad beans and can be prepared synthetically, and that is used in the treatment of Parkinson's disease

loading bridge *n* : a covered walkway from an airline terminal to a plane

longuette *adj* : of, relating to, or being a woman's garment (as a skirt or dress) that extends to the mid-calf—**longuette** *n*

M

maplaza *n* : a roadside plaza having signs for aiding tourists in locating points of interest and service

marathon *n, specif* : a group session in which members remain together for an extended period (as 24 hours) and interact openly and responsively so as to increase self-understanding

maxicoat *n* : an ankle-length coat for outer wear

meat packer *n, specif* : a subway worker who is assigned to cram as many passengers as possible into each car during a rush period

megafamily *n* : a group of unrelated adults of both sexes and their children living together communally

Metroamerican *n* : a relatively young, well-educated, and affluent American living in a suburb

metrophobe *n* : one who dislikes and avoids living in a large city

middlemanitis *n* : a condition of confinement experienced by the occupant of a middle seat (as on a plane)

minithon *n* : a group session that resembles but is several hours shorter than a marathon

minnow skirt *n* : a thigh-length dress or skirt usually worn over shorts

N

nailfrost *n* : a lacquer or enamel that forms an ornamental lusterless covering over the fingernails and toenails

noncountry *n* : a country whose size, location, and economic resources are inadequate for economic self-sufficiency and development

no-no *n* : something that is not acceptable

O

Oreo *n* : a black who ingratiates himself with white society

orthowater *n* : POLYWATER

P

parochiaid *n* : tax support for nonpublic schools

pavement coat *n* : MAXICOAT

photoserigraph *n* : a serigraph made from a photograph

pigmentocracy *n* : a ruling class made up of individuals of one color

plastic credit *n* : credit obtainable through credit cards

polylogue *n* : a dialogue involving more than two people

polywater *n* : a stable viscous compound that results when water is condensed into a glass or quartz capillary tube and that is denser than, freezes at a lower temperature than, and boils at a higher temperature than ordinary water

psycholog *n* : a written record of one's own mental workings (as images, associations, or feelings)

psyops *n pl* : psychological operations planned and carried out by psywarriors

psywarrior *n* : one who wages psychological warfare

pubbie *n* : a graduate of a public high school

pudendicity *n* : OBSCENITY; *esp* : an obscenity relating to the sexual organs

R

rip-off *n* **1** : ROBBERY **2** : SWINDLE

rip off *vt* : ROB, STEAL

rockomastics *n* : the study of the names of rock 'n' roll performers

S

saunaphile *n* : an habitual user of a sauna

sex-egration *n* : discrimination against women in employment

sexploitation *n* : the exploitation of sex especially in motion pictures—**sexploitationist** *n*

shamburger *n* : a hamburger with a high cereal content

sicknik *n* : one who is emotionally disturbed

sick-out *n* : an unofficial strike in which workers call in sick instead of directly refusing to work

skinhead *n, specif, chiefly Brit* : a member of a group of young working-class men who militantly hold to conservative views and mores and are distinguishable by their very short haircuts

skytel *n* : a small hotel for passengers of chartered or privately owned planes

slam *n, specif* : PRISON, JAIL

sleep-in *n* : the occupation of a designated area in which protesters sleep en masse as a means of calling attention to their grievances

slug squad *n* : a squad of plainclothesmen assigned to apprehend individuals who use (as in a subway turnstile) a slug instead of a token

smack head *n* : a user of heroin

snob zoning *n* : the zoning of parcels especially of suburban land so as to prevent ownership by the economically or culturally deprived

soul *n, specif* : BLACK; *esp* : a fellow black

soulist *n* : a black singer of soul music

Sovangliski *n* : Russian marked by numerous borrowings from English

splashup *n* : the return (as by an aquanaut) to the surface

sporterize *vb* : to make a military rifle into a hunting rifle by replacing the stock and barrel

street theater *n* : GUERRILLA THEATER

sunshine *n, specif* : an orange-colored pill containing LSD

superwater *n* : POLYWATER

sweaterpant *n* : women's pants made of a rib-stitch knit

T

taxmobile *n* : a vehicle that serves as an itinerant tax-consultant facility

televiolence *n* : the depiction of violence on television

toke *n* : a drag on a marijuana cigarette —**toke** *vb*

torpedo *n, specif* : a ballplayer who is specifically assigned to injure a member of the opposing team

U

Uncle Tomahawk *n* : APPLE

undercity *n* : the disadvantaged segment of an urban population

uniwear *adj* : designed to be worn by either sex ⟨*uniwear* clothes⟩

W

walking catfish *n* : an Asiatic catfish that is able to scramble overland for considerable distances and that has been inadvertently introduced into waters of the southern states of the U.S.

weekend father *n* : a divorced man who sees his children only on weekends

whitemail *n* : the act or practice of seeking a favor by the promise of a reciprocal favor

Z

zorse *n* : a hybrid between a male horse and a female zebra

Special Essay: Words for Today

by Simeon Potter, Professor Emeritus
of the English Language and Philology,
University of Liverpool, England

The European Conservation Year, beginning in 1970, and Earth Day in the United States focused attention on the ecological system or *ecosystem.* Dirt particles, carriers of sulfur dioxide and other *pollutants,* were dubbed *particulates* when they produced *emphysema* and other respiratory diseases. *Environmentalists* deplored what they called *biodegradation* or prolonged spoliation of the natural environment, whereas the self-styled *biocrats* (Gerald Heard, Arthur Koestler, Jacob Bronowski), sustaining the traditions of Aldous Huxley, declaimed against the deterioration and misuse of our *living space* (echoing the German *Lebensraum*). Clearly *biocides* (blanket term to cover all pesticides, insecticides, and such) were threatening to exterminate far too many forms of terrestrial life.

Urbanology, the study of town planning and rehabilitation at a high level of abstraction, was pursued intensively by *urbanologists,* who bewailed, among other things, the new *brutalism* evinced by architects in their misguided endeavors to make buildings banausic and functional. Was the northeastern seaboard from Boston, Mass., to New York City destined to become one sprawling *megalopolis* (a better formation than *megapolis* since Greek *polis* is of feminine gender)? Indeed, was more than one large area of the inhabited world destined to become a huge *ecumenopolis?*

The aerospace industry made rapid strides. *Space probes* were launched toward the nearer planets, and the hypothesis was confirmed that most *pulsars* are the remnants of exploded *supernovas.* The *steady state* prevailed over the *big bang* theory on the origin of the universe. There was talk of *space shuttles* to transport passengers to and from *space stations* or manned artificial satellites. Contrivances were developed whereby Apollo 14 astronauts could thrust *Geophones,* or vibration detectors, into the moon's surface.

In the field of cytogenetics *purines* and *pyrimidines* were postulated to be chemical precursors of the raw materials of life. *Sporopollenin* was the name given to one of the most durable of biological materials. Was its suspected presence in meteorites a sign of extraterrestrial life? This fundamental question remained unanswered. In Sweden the important new drug *alprenolol* was employed successfully in slowing down the pulse rate. In Africa paleozoologists unearthed the *stegotetrabeledon,* or proto-elephant, which flourished some 6 million years ago. Elsewhere, psychologists extended the term *dysrhythmia* to include "the mental fatigue one suffers when making long easterly and westerly flights in which discord arises between external time and the body's biological clock." *Psychedelic* (an unfortunate malformation for psychodelic) declined in use in favor of the more comprehensive term *psychotropic,* embracing not only "mind-blowing" or "mind-expanding" narcotics but also all drugs affecting man's mental state. *Liminality* took abstraction one stage further in describing the limen or threshold of consciousness.

Datamation was the new computer term used to cover all forms of data processing. *Cobol,* or *Com*mon *b*usiness *o*riented *l*anguage, and *Fortran,* or *For*mula *tran*slation, spread into almost daily speech. *Videotape cassettes* made a television library a possible reality in every home, whereas the *dex one,* or *d*ecision *ex*pediter, promised to speed up business communication by transmitting replicas of documents by telephone to any destination. During the year it was found necessary to institute two additional safeguards against crime, involving the *TV scanner* or *photoscan eye* and the *magnetometer.* In supermarkets and department stores a thief engaged in shoplifting was photographed by the scanner and the picture was transmitted by closed-circuit television to a monitor screen in the security manager's office. In airports, hijacking was forestalled by subjecting passengers to both corporeal frisking and magnetometer screening.

Partly, no doubt, under the influence of Lord Robens' book of that name, *human engineering* tended to oust *ergonomics* and *psychotechnology* as terms denoting close connections between humans and machines in the presently highly charged field of industrial relations. On the other hand, *terotechnology* was actually invented by Anthony Wedgwood Benn (minister of technology in the British Labor government) to indicate all possible forms of maintenance engineering. The fifth British maintenance-engineering conference, which met in the London Hilton toward the end of the year, was officially renamed the Terotechnologic Conference.

Drift toward the invariable word—that inherent tendency of the English language for a thousand years and more—was partially counterbalanced by an increasing liveliness in the creation of all kinds of derivatives and blends. For instance, new nouns were formed in *-ist, -ant, -ee,* and *-eer: audiotypist,* "one typing direct from tape or other recording," and *trialist,* "football player on probation." *Comprehensivist* acquired two distinct meanings: (a) nonspecialist and (b) advocate of all-in schools called "comprehensive" in Great Britain and "composite" in Canada. Among other such derivatives were *discussant,* "one taking part in a formal (often public) discussion or symposium"; *adaptee,* in the fine arts "one lacking in originality"; *appointee,* "person appointed"; *evictee,* "person evicted or displaced"; and *sloganeer,* "one who creates and uses slogans all too frequently." Derivatives with the prefix *de-* and the suffix *-ization* became well established: *demonetization* (of gold), *depoliticization* (of judges), *detribalization* (of native races), and *desalinization* (of seawater). In this last instance there was regrettable vacillation between *desalinization* (better formed) and *desalination* (shorter and therefore often preferred). There was similar vacillation between *fluoridization* and *fluoridation* (introduction of fluorides into public water supplies in order to reduce the incidence of dental decay); between *eutrophicization* and *eutrophication* (pathological overfeeding, especially in the plant world); and between *metricization* and *metrication.* Usage has decided quite definitely in favor of *metrication* as applied to weights and measures, however inconsistent this formation may be when compared with *decimalization* (never *decimalation* or *decimation!*) of money.

Among the more notable portmanteau words or blends that showed signs of survival were *slurbs* for slum suburbs and *dormobiles* for dormitory automobiles. Computer booking offices issued *computickets.* Proletarian culture (or rather subculture) was labeled *prolecult.* Top executives saved time and energy by availing themselves of the unprecedented facilities provided by television confrontation or *confravision.*

Dropouts were referred to, less bluntly, as *disaffiliates.* The world's underdeveloped countries were called, more hopefully and futuristically, the *developing countries,* or, collectively and to avoid any hint of patronizing, the *Third World. Multinational,* suggesting overtones of an evolving supranational unity based on world authority, tended to supersede the slightly tarnished epithet *international.* Instead of *paperback* and *hardback* the book trade adopted the simpler descriptions *paper* and *cased.*

A remarkable semantic twist was given to the vogue word *credibility* in the political world. It came to mean not merely "believability" but also "trustworthiness; confidence; esteem," and then even "plain honesty." It became associated in a somewhat muddled way (though it would be difficult to prove this) with etymologically related *creditability.* The *credibility gap* came to mean little more than the discrepancy between image and reality. *Sophisticated,* signifying formerly "deprived of primitive simplicity; falsified; not straightforward," was slowly losing that pejorative connotation and was coming to signify little more than "intricate; highly complicated" when applied, for instance, to a computerized control system. *Encapsulated,* literally "placed inside a capsule," caught on as a fashionable term for "shut in; enclosed"—Shakespearean "cabin'd; cribb'd; confined." Moreover, *prestigious,* originally "practicing juggling or legerdemain; cheating; deceptive; illusory," suddenly became very popular in the sense of "reputable; esteemed; enjoying prestige."

There were clear signs that differentiating suffixes were sorting themselves out through usage rather than by any kind of lexicographical edict. Thus *arbiter* and *arbitrator* ceased to be convertible terms (at least in most parts of the English-speaking world). An arbiter judged in his own right and was answerable to no one. A Parisian stylist, for example, was an arbiter of fashion. An arbitrator was an *ombudsman* deciding a particular issue referred to him by disputants. *Instinctive* meant "determined by natural impulse or innate propensity," whereas *instinctual* meant merely "relating to instinct." *Distributive* meant "engaged in the actual process of sharing out," but *distributional* meant "relating generally to distribution." *Normality* signified broadly "the state of being normal; conformity to the norm," whereas *normalcy* signified more narrowly "regularity in economic, political, and social conditions" and so came to mean something like "absence of tension" in popular usage.

In some quarters *amenity* was so overworked that it lost its earlier abstract meaning of "natural pleasantness" and came to denote (especially in the plural) any kind of artificial facility or convenience. *Motivation* moved into daily speech from the technical jargon of psychology and came to mean any kind of urge, drive, inducement, or incentive. *Serendipity,* that faculty of making lucky discoveries by accident, ceased to denote "looking for one thing and finding another" and came to signify more loosely any happy chance. A *spectrum,* technically the gradation of the seven colors of refracted light, came to be applied to any series of interrelated ideas or objects that appear to overlap and form a continuous sequence. *Insights,* perhaps influenced by the German *Einsichten,* became an impressive vogue word denoting deep mental penetration (often by intuition) into underlying truths. *Synergistic* was frequently used as a stylistic variant of *cooperative,* and *monolithic* as an impressive epithet describing something solidly uniform. In an increasingly technological world it became more important daily that a person should be *numerate* as well as literate.

Occasionally, however, Anglo-Saxon simplicity was preferred. Dress materials were described as *see-through,* instead of transparent. The predicative phrase *all about* was done to death by broadcasters. "That is what education is all about," they said, instead of "That is education's main purpose and concern." Instead of the latest maximum or minimum, economists and statisticians talked about an *all-time high* or an *all-time low.*

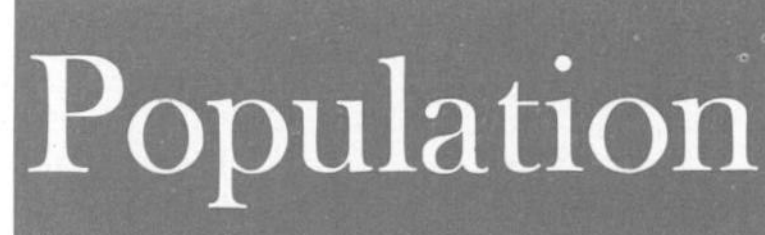

Total population of the United States in 1970 was 204,765,770, an increase of 13.3% over the 1960 total population of 180,697,596.

U.S. Census Data

final 1970 population counts
for urban places of 4,200 or more

Place	POPULATION 1970	POPULATION 1960
Alabama	**3,444,165**	**3,266,740**
Albertville	9,963	8,250
Alexander City	12,358	13,140
Andalusia	10,092	10,263
Anniston	31,533	33,657
Anniston Northwest (U)	6,609	—
Arab	4,399	2,989
Athens	14,360	9,330
Atmore	8,293	8,173
Attalla	7,510	8,257
Auburn	22,767	16,261
Bay Minette	6,727	5,197
Bessemer	33,428	33,054
Birmingham	300,910	340,887
Bluff Park (U)	12,372	—
Boaz	5,621	4,654
Brewton	6,747	6,309
Center Point (U)	15,675	—
Chickasaw	8,447	10,002
Childersburg	4,831	4,884
Clanton	5,868	5,683
Cullman	12,601	10,883
Daleville	5,182	693
Decatur	38,044	29,217
Demopolis	7,651	7,377
Dothan	36,733	31,440
Elba	4,634	4,321
Enterprise	15,591	11,410
Eufaula	9,102	8,357
Fairfield	14,369	15,816
Fairhope	5,720	4,858
Fayette	4,568	4,227
Florence	34,031	31,649
Forestdale (U)	6,091	—
Fort McClellan (U)	5,334	—
Fort Payne	8,435	7,029
Fort Rucker (U)	14,242	—
Fultondale	5,163	2,001
Gadsden	53,928	58,088
Gardendale	6,502	4,712
Geneva	4,398	3,840
Greenville	8,033	6,894
Guntersville	6,491	6,592
Hartselle	7,355	5,000
Homewood	21,245	20,289
Hueytown	7,095	5,997
Huntsville	137,802	72,365
Jackson	5,957	4,959
Jacksonville	7,715	5,678
Jasper	10,798	10,799
Lanett	6,908	7,674
Leeds	6,991	6,162
Marion	4,289	3,807
Midfield	6,399	3,556
Mobile	190,026	194,856
Monroeville	4,846	3,632
Montgomery	133,386	134,393
Mountain Brook	19,474	12,680
Muscle Shoals	6,907	4,084
Northport	9,435	5,245
Oneonta	4,390	4,136
Opelika	19,027	15,678
Opp	6,493	5,535
Oxford	4,361	3,603
Ozark	13,555	9,534
Pell City	5,381	4,165
Phenix City	25,281	27,630
Piedmont	5,063	4,794
Pleasant Grove	5,090	3,097
Prattville	13,116	6,616
Prichard	41,578	47,371
Roanoke	5,251	5,288
Russellville	7,814	6,628
Saraland	7,840	4,595
Scottsboro	9,324	6,449
Selma	27,379	28,385
Sheffield	13,115	13,491
Sylacauga	12,255	12,857
Talladega	17,662	17,742
Tallassee	4,809	4,934
Tarrant City	6,835	7,810
Troy	11,482	10,234
Tuscaloosa	65,773	63,370
Tuscumbia	8,828	8,994
Tuskegee	11,028	7,240
Union Springs	4,324	3,704
Vestavia Hills	8,311	4,029
West End-Cobb Town (U)	5,515	—
Alaska	**302,173**	**226,167**
Anchorage	48,029	44,237
Eielson (U)	6,149	—
Elmendorf (U)	6,018	—
Fairbanks	14,771	13,311
Fort Richardson (U)	8,960	—
Fort Wainwright (U)	9,097	—
Juneau	6,050	6,797
Ketchikan	6,994	6,483
Spenard (U)	18,089	9,074
Arizona	**1,772,482**	**1,302,161**
Ajo (U)	5,881	7,049
Avondale	6,304	6,151
Bisbee	8,328	9,914
Casa Grande	10,536	8,311
Chandler	13,763	9,531
Clifton	5,087	4,191
Coolidge	4,651	4,990
Douglas	12,462	11,925
Eloy	5,381	4,899
Flagstaff	26,117	18,214
Fort Huachuca (U)	6,659	—
Glendale	36,228	15,893
Globe	7,333	6,217
Holbrook	4,759	3,438
Kingman	7,312	4,525
Luke (U)	5,047	—
Mesa	62,853	33,772
Nogales	8,946	7,286
Paradise Valley	7,155	—
Peoria	4,792	2,593
Phoenix	581,562	439,170
Prescott	13,030	12,861
Safford	5,333	4,648
San Manuel (U)	4,332	4,524
Scottsdale	67,823	10,026
Sierra Vista	6,689	3,121
South Tucson	6,220	7,004
Sun City (U)	13,670	—
Superior (U)	4,975	4,875
Tempe	62,907	24,897
Tucson	262,933	212,892
West Yuma (U)	5,552	2,781
Winslow	8,066	8,862
Yuma	29,007	23,974
Arkansas	**1,923,295**	**1,786,272**
Arkadelphia	9,841	8,069
Batesville	7,209	6,207
Benton	16,499	10,399
Bentonville	5,508	3,649
Blytheville	24,752	20,797
Brinkley	5,275	4,636
Camden	15,147	15,823
Clarksville	4,616	3,919
Conway	15,510	9,791
Crossett	6,191	5,370
Dermott	4,250	3,665
Dumas	4,600	3,540
El Dorado	25,283	25,292
Fayetteville	30,729	20,274
Fordyce	4,837	3,890
Forrest City	12,521	10,544
Fort Smith	62,802	52,991
Harrison	7,239	6,580
Helena	10,415	11,500
Hope	8,810	8,399
Hot Springs	35,631	28,337
Jacksonville	19,832	14,488
Jonesboro	27,050	21,418
Little Rock	132,483	107,813
McGehee	4,683	4,448
Magnolia	11,303	10,651
Malvern	8,739	9,566
Marianna	6,196	5,134
Mena	4,530	4,388
Monticello	5,085	4,412
Morrilton	6,814	5,997
Newport	7,725	7,007
North Little Rock	60,040	58,032
Osceola	7,204	6,189
Paragould	10,639	9,947
Pine Bluff	57,389	44,037
Pocahontas	4,544	3,665
Rogers	11,050	5,700
Russellville	11,750	8,921
Searcy	9,040	7,272
Siloam Springs	6,009	3,953
Southwest Little Rock (U)	13,231	—
Springdale	16,783	10,076
Stuttgart	10,477	9,661
Texarkana	21,682	19,788
Trumann	5,938	4,511
Van Buren	8,373	6,787
Warren	6,433	6,752
West Helena	11,007	8,385
West Memphis	25,892	19,374
Wynne	6,696	4,922
California	**19,953,134**	**15,717,204**
Alameda	70,968	63,855
Alamo-Danville (U)	14,059	—
Albany	14,674	14,804
Alhambra	62,125	54,807
Alondra Park (U)	12,193	—
Altadena (U)	42,380	40,568
Alum Rock (U)	18,355	18,942
Anaheim	166,701	104,184
Anderson	5,492	4,492
Antioch	28,060	17,305
Apple Valley (U)	6,702	—
Aptos (U)	8,704	—
Arcadia	42,868	41,005
Arcata	8,985	5,235
Arden-Arcade (U)	82,492	73,352
Arroyo Grande	7,454	3,291
Artesia	14,757	9,993
Arvin	5,090	—
Ashland (U)	14,810	—
Atascadero (U)	10,290	5,983
Atherton	8,085	7,717
Atwater	11,640	7,318
Auburn	6,570	5,586
August School Area (U)	6,293	—
Avocado Heights (U)	9,810	—
Azusa	25,217	20,497
Bakersfield	69,515	56,848
Baldwin Park	47,285	33,951
Banning	12,034	10,250
Barstow	17,442	11,644
Beale East (U)	7,029	—
Beaumont	5,484	4,288
Bell	21,836	19,450
Bellflower	51,454	45,909
Bell Gardens	29,308	—
Belmont	23,667	15,996
Benicia	8,783	6,070
Berkeley	116,716	111,268
Beverly Hills	33,416	30,817
Big Bear (U)	5,268	1,562
Bloomington (U)	11,957	—
Blythe	7,047	6,023
Bonnyview (U)	4,882	4,686
Brawley	13,746	12,703
Brea	18,447	8,487
Broderick-Bryte (U)	12,782	—
Buena Park	63,646	46,401
Burbank	88,871	90,155
Burlingame	27,320	24,036
Calexico	10,625	7,992
Calwa (U)	5,191	—
Camarillo	19,219	—
Camarillo Heights (U)	5,892	1,704
Cambrian Park (U)	5,316	—
Campbell	24,770	11,863
Capitola	5,080	2,021
Cardiff-By-The-Sea (U)	5,724	3,149
Carlsbad	14,944	9,253
Carmel-By-The-Sea	4,525	4,580
Carmichael (U)	37,625	20,455
Carpinteria	6,982	—
Carson	71,150	—
Castro Valley (U)	44,760	37,120
Ceres	6,029	4,406
Cerritos	15,856	3,508
Cherryland (U)	9,969	—
Chico	19,580	14,757
Chico North (U)	6,656	—
Chico West (U)	4,787	—
China Lake (U)	11,105	—
Chino	20,411	10,305
Chowchilla	4,349	4,525
Chula Vista	67,901	42,034
Citrus Heights (U)	21,760	—
Claremont	23,464	12,633

Place	POPULATION 1970	POPULATION 1960
California (continued)		
Clovis	13,856	5,546
Coachella	8,353	4,854
Coalinga	6,161	5,965
Colton	19,974	18,666
Commerce	10,536	9,555
Compton	78,611	71,812
Concord	85,164	36,000
Corcoran	5,249	4,976
Corona	27,519	13,336
Coronado	20,910	18,039
Corte Madera	8,464	5,962
Costa Mesa	72,660	37,550
Covina	30,380	20,124
Cucamonga (U)	5,796	—
Cudahy	16,998	—
Culver City	31,035	32,163
Cupertino	18,216	3,664
Cypress	31,026	1,753
Daly City	66,922	44,791
Dana Point (U)	4,745	1,186
Davis	23,488	8,910
Del Aire (U)	11,930	—
Delano	14,559	11,913
Diamond Bar (U)	12,234	—
Dinuba	7,917	6,103
Dixon	4,432	2,970
Dominguez (U)	5,980	—
Downey	88,445	82,505
East Compton (U)	5,853	—
East La Mirada (U)	12,339	—
East Los Angeles (U)	105,033	104,270
East Palo Alto (U)	17,837	—
Edwards (U)	10,331	—
El Cajon	52,273	37,618
El Centro	19,272	16,811
El Cerrito	25,190	25,437
El Encanto Heights (U)	6,225	—
El Monte	69,837	13,163
El Paso de Robles	7,168	6,677
El Rio (U)	6,173	6,966
El Segundo	15,620	14,219
El Toro (U)	8,654	—
El Toro Station (U)	6,970	—
Encinitas (U)	5,375	2,786
Enterprise (U)	11,486	4,946
Escondido	36,792	16,377
Eureka	24,337	28,137
Exeter	4,475	4,264
Fairfax	7,661	5,813
Fairfield	44,146	14,968
Fair Oaks (U)	11,256	—
Fallbrook (U)	6,945	4,814
Fillmore	6,285	4,808
Florence-Graham (U)	42,895	38,164
Florin (U)	9,646	—
Folsom	5,810	3,925
Fontana	20,673	14,659
Fort Bragg	4,455	4,433
Fortuna	4,203	3,523
Foster City (U)	9,327	—
Fountain Valley	31,826	2,068
Freedom (U)	5,563	4,206
Fremont	100,869	43,790
Fresno	165,972	133,929
Fullerton	85,826	56,180
Gardena	41,021	35,943
Garden Acres (U)	7,870	—
Garden Grove	122,524	84,238
George (U)	7,404	—
Gilroy	12,665	7,348
Glen Avon (U)	5,759	3,416
Glendale	132,752	119,442
Glendora	31,349	20,752
Grand Terrace (U)	5,901	—
Grass Valley	5,149	4,876
Grossmont-Mt. Helix (U)	8,723	—
Grover City	5,939	5,210
Hacienda Heights (U)	35,969	—
Hanford	15,179	10,133
Hawaiian Gardens	8,811	—
Hawthorne	53,304	33,035
Hayward	93,058	72,700
Healdsburg	5,438	4,816
Hemet	12,252	5,416
Hemet East (U)	8,598	1,936
Hermosa Beach	17,412	16,115
Hesperia (U)	4,592	—
Highland (U)	12,669	—
Hillsborough	8,753	7,554
Hollister	7,663	6,071
Home Gardens (U)	5,116	1,541
Huntington Beach	115,960	11,492
Huntington Park	33,744	29,920
Imperial Beach	20,244	17,773
Indio	14,459	9,745
Inglewood	89,985	63,390
Isla Vista (U)	13,441	—
Kensington (U)	5,823	—
La Canada-Flintridge (U)	20,652	18,338
La Crescenta-Montrose (U)	19,594	—
Ladera Heights (U)	6,079	—
Lafayette	20,484	—
Laguna Beach	14,550	9,288
Laguna Hills (U)	13,676	—
Laguna Niguel (U)	4,644	—
La Habra	41,350	25,136
Lakeside (U)	11,991	—
Lakewood	82,973	67,126
La Mesa	39,178	30,441
La Mirada	30,808	22,444
Lamont (U)	7,007	6,177
Lancaster (U)	30,948	26,012
La Palma	9,687	622
La Puente	31,092	24,723
Larkspur	10,487	5,710
La Verne	12,965	6,516
Lawndale	24,825	21,740
Lemon Grove (U)	19,690	19,348
Lemoore	4,219	2,561
Lemoore Station (U)	8,512	—
Lennox (U)	16,121	31,224
Lincoln Village (U)	6,722	—
Linda (U)	7,731	6,129
Lindsay	5,206	5,397
Live Oak (U)	6,443	3,518
Livermore	37,703	16,058
Lodi	28,691	22,229
Loma Linda (U)	9,797	—
Lomita	19,784	—
Lompoc	25,284	14,415
Lompoc Northwest (U)	4,874	—
Long Beach	358,633	344,168
Los Alamitos	11,346	4,312
Los Altos	24,956	19,696
Los Altos Hills	6,865	3,412
Los Angeles	2,816,061	2,479,015
Los Banos	9,188	5,272
Los Gatos	23,735	9,036
Lynwood	43,353	31,614
Madera	16,044	14,430
Manhattan Beach	35,352	33,934
Manteca	13,845	8,242
Marina (U)	8,343	3,310
Martinez	16,506	9,604
Marysville	9,353	9,553
Mather (U)	7,027	—
Maywood	16,996	14,588
Meiners Oaks-Mira Monte (U)	7,025	—
Menlo Park	26,734	26,957
Merced	22,670	20,068
Millbrae	20,781	15,873
Mill Valley	12,942	10,411
Milpitas	27,149	6,572
Mira Loma (U)	8,482	3,982
Mission Viejo (U)	11,933	—
Modesto	61,712	36,585
Monrovia	30,015	27,079
Montclair	22,546	13,546
Montebello	42,807	32,097
Monterey	26,302	22,618
Monterey Park	49,166	37,821
Moraga (U)	14,205	—
Morgan Hill	6,485	3,151
Morro Bay	7,109	—
Mountain View	51,092	30,889
Muscoy (U)	7,091	—
Napa	35,978	22,170
National City	43,184	32,771
Newark	27,153	9,884
Newhall (U)	9,651	4,705
Newport Beach	49,422	26,564
Norco	14,511	—
North Fair Oaks (U)	9,740	—
North Highlands (U)	31,854	21,271
North Island (U)	6,002	—
Norwalk	91,827	88,739
Novato	31,006	17,881
Oakdale	6,594	4,980
Oakland	361,561	367,548
Oak View (U)	4,872	2,448
Oceanside	40,494	24,971
Oildale (U)	20,879	—
Ojai	5,591	4,495
Olivehurst (U)	8,100	4,835
Ontario	64,118	46,617
Opal Cliffs (U)	5,425	3,825
Orange	77,374	26,444
Orangevale (U)	16,493	—
Orcutt (U)	8,500	1,414
Orinda Village (U)	6,790	5,568
Oroville	7,536	6,115
Otay-Castle Park (U)	15,445	—
Oxnard	71,225	40,265
Pacifica	36,020	20,995
Pacific Grove	13,505	12,121
Palmdale	8,511	—
Palm Desert (U)	6,171	1,295
Palm Springs	20,936	13,468
Palo Alto	55,966	52,287
Palos Verdes Estates	13,641	9,564
Palos Verdes Peninsula (U)	39,616	—
Paradise (U)	14,539	8,268
Paramount	34,734	27,249
Parkway-Sacramento South (U)	28,574	—
Pasadena	113,327	116,407
Pendleton North (U)	11,803	—
Pendleton South (U)	13,692	—
Perris	4,228	2,950
Petaluma	24,870	14,035
Pico Rivera	54,170	49,150
Piedmont	10,917	11,117
Pinole	15,850	6,064
Pittsburg	20,651	19,062
Placentia	21,948	5,861
Placerville	5,416	4,439
Pleasant Hill	24,610	—
Pleasanton	18,328	4,203
Pomona	87,384	67,157
Porterville	12,602	7,991
Porterville West (U)	6,200	—
Port Hueneme	14,295	11,067
Portola Valley	4,999	—
Poway (U)	9,422	1,921
Quartz Hill (U)	4,935	3,325
Rancho Cordova (U)	30,451	7,429
Rancho Rinconada (U)	5,149	—
Rancho Santa Clarita (U)	4,860	—
Red Bluff	7,676	7,202
Redding	16,659	12,773
Redlands	36,355	26,829
Redondo Beach	56,075	46,986
Redwood City	55,686	46,290
Reedley	8,131	5,850
Rialto	28,370	18,567
Richmond	79,043	71,854
Ridgecrest	7,629	—
Rio Linda (U)	7,524	2,189
Riverside	140,089	84,332
Rodeo (U)	5,356	—
Rohnert Park	6,133	—
Rolling Hills Estates	6,027	3,941
Roseland (U)	5,105	4,510
Rosemead	40,972	15,476
Roseville	17,895	13,421
Rossmoor (U)	12,922	—
Rowland Heights (U)	16,881	—
Rubidoux (U)	13,969	—
Sacramento	254,413	191,667
Salinas	58,896	28,957
San Anselmo	13,031	11,584
San Bernardino	104,251	91,922
San Bruno	36,254	29,063
San Carlos	25,924	21,370
San Clemente	17,063	8,527
San Diego	696,769	573,224
San Dimas	15,692	—
San Fernando	16,571	16,093
San Francisco	715,674	740,316
San Gabriel	29,176	22,561
Sanger	10,088	8,072
San Jacinto	4,385	2,553
San Jose	445,779	204,196
San Leandro	68,698	65,962
San Lorenzo (U)	24,633	23,773
San Luis Obispo	28,036	20,437
San Marino	14,177	13,658
San Mateo	78,991	69,870
San Pablo	21,461	19,687
San Rafael	38,977	20,460
Santa Ana	156,601	100,350
Santa Barbara	70,215	58,768
Santa Clara	87,717	58,880
Santa Cruz	32,076	25,596
Santa Fe Springs	14,750	16,342
Santa Maria	32,749	20,027
Santa Maria South (U)	7,129	—
Santa Monica	88,289	83,249
Santa Paula	18,001	13,279
Santa Rosa	50,006	31,027
Santee (U)	21,107	—
Saratoga	27,110	14,861
Sausalito	6,158	5,331
Seal Beach	24,441	6,994
Seaside	35,935	19,353
Selma	7,459	6,934
Shafter	5,327	4,576
Sierra Madre	12,140	9,732
Signal Hill	5,582	4,627
Simi Valley	56,464	—
Solana Beach (U)	5,023	—
Soledad	6,843	2,837
Soquel (U)	5,795	—
South El Monte	13,443	4,850
South Gate	56,909	53,831
South Lake Tahoe	12,921	—
South Modesto (U)	7,889	5,465
South Pasadena	22,979	19,706
South San Francisco	46,646	39,418
South San Gabriel (U)	5,051	—
South San Jose Hills (U)	12,386	—
South Whittier (U)	46,641	—
South Yuba City (U)	5,352	3,200
Spring Valley (U)	29,742	—
Stanford (U)	8,691	—
Stanton	17,947	11,163
Stockton	107,644	86,321
Sun City (U)	5,519	—

Place	POPULATION 1970	1960
California (continued)		
Sunnymead (U)	6,708	3,404
Sunnyvale	95,408	52,898
Susanville	6,608	5,598
Taft	4,285	3,822
Tehachapi	4,211	3,161
Temple City	29,673	—
Thermalito (U)	4,217	—
Thousand Oaks	36,334	—
Tiburon	6,209	—
Torrance	134,584	100,991
Tracy	14,724	11,289
Tulare	16,235	13,824
Turlock	13,992	9,116
Tustin	21,178	2,006
Tustin-Foothills (U)	26,598	—
Twentynine Palms (U)	5,667	—
Twentynine Palms Base (U)	5,647	—
Ukiah	10,095	9,900
Union City	14,724	6,618
Upland	32,551	15,918
Vacaville	21,690	10,898
Valencia (U)	4,243	—
Valinda (U)	18,837	—
Vallejo	66,733	60,877
Vandenburg (U)	13,193	—
Ventura (San Buenaventura)	55,797	29,114
Victorville	10,845	—
View Park-Windsor Hills (U)	12,268	—
Visalia	27,268	15,791
Vista	24,688	—
Walnut	5,992	934
Walnut Creek	39,844	9,903
Walnut Creek West (U)	8,330	—
Walnut Park (U)	8,925	—
Wasco	8,269	6,841
Watsonville	14,569	13,293
West Athens (U)	13,286	—
West Carson (U)	15,501	—
West Compton (U)	5,748	—
West Covina	68,034	50,645
West Hollywood (U)	29,448	28,870
Westminster	59,865	25,750
West Modesto (U)	6,135	1,897
Westmont (U)	29,310	—
West Pittsburg (U)	5,969	5,188
West Puente Valley (U)	20,733	—
West Sacramento (U)	12,002	—
West Whittier-Los Nietos (U)	20,845	—
Whittier	72,863	33,663
Willowbrook (U)	28,705	—
Woodland	20,677	13,524
Woodside	4,731	3,592
Yorba Linda	11,856	—
Yreka City	5,394	4,759
Yuba City	13,986	11,507
Yucaipa (U)	19,284	—
Colorado	**2,207,259**	**1,753,947**
Alamosa	6,985	6,205
Applewood (U)	8,214	—
Arvada	46,814	19,242
Aurora	74,974	48,548
Boulder	66,870	37,718
Brighton	8,309	7,055
Broomfield	7,261	—
Canon City	9,206	8,973
Cherry Hills Village	4,605	1,931
Colorado Springs	135,060	70,194
Commerce City	17,407	8,970
Cortez	6,032	6,764
Craig	4,205	3,984
Denver	514,678	493,887
Derby (U)	10,206	10,124
Durango	10,333	10,530
Edgewater	4,866	4,314
Englewood	33,695	33,398
Fort Carson (U)	19,399	—
Fort Collins	43,337	25,027
Fort Morgan	7,594	7,379
Golden	9,817	7,118
Grand Junction	20,170	18,694
Greeley	38,902	26,314
Gunnison	4,613	3,477
La Junta	7,938	8,026
Lakewood	92,787	—
Lamar	7,797	7,369
Leadville	4,314	4,008
Littleton	26,466	13,670
Littleton Southeast (U)	22,899	—
Longmont	23,209	11,489
Loveland	16,220	9,734
Manitou Springs	4,278	3,626
Montrose	6,496	5,044
North Glenn	27,937	—
Orchard Mesa (U)	5,824	4,956
Pueblo	97,453	91,181
Rocky Ford	4,859	4,929
Salida	4,355	4,560
Security-Widefield (U)	15,297	—
Sheridan	4,787	3,559

Place	POPULATION 1970	1960
Sherrelwood (U)	18,868	—
Sterling	10,636	10,751
Stratton Meadows (U)	6,223	—
Thornton	13,326	11,353
Trinidad	9,901	10,691
Walsenburg	4,329	5,071
Welby (U)	6,875	—
Westminster	19,432	13,850
Westminster East (U)	7,576	—
Wheat Ridge	29,795	—
Connecticut	**3,032,217**	**2,535,234**
Ansonia	21,160	19,819
Bethel*	10,945	8,200
Bridgeport	156,542	156,748
Bristol	55,487	45,499
Clinton (U)	5,957	2,693
Conning Towers-Nautilus Park (U)	9,791	3,457
Cromwell*	7,400	6,780
Danbury	50,781	22,928
Danielson	4,580	4,642
Darien*	20,411	18,437
Derby	12,599	12,132
East Hartford*	57,583	43,977
East Haven*	25,120	21,388
Enfield*	46,189	31,464
Fairfield*	56,487	46,183
Greenwich*	59,755	53,793
Groton	8,933	10,111
Hamden*	49,357	41,056
Hartford	158,017	162,178
Madison (U)	4,310	1,416
Manchester*	47,994	42,102
Meriden	55,959	51,850
Middletown	36,924	33,250
Milford	50,858	41,662
Naugatuck	23,034	19,511
New Britain	83,441	82,201
New Canaan*	17,455	13,466
New Haven	137,707	152,048
Newington*	26,037	17,664
New London	31,630	34,182
New Milford (U)	4,606	3,023
North Haven*	22,194	15,935
Norwalk	79,113	67,775
Norwich	41,433	38,506
Orange*	13,524	8,547
Pawcatuck (U)	5,255	4,389
Plainville*	16,733	13,149
Portland*	8,812	7,496
Prospect*	6,543	4,367
Putnam	6,918	6,952
Ridgefield (U)	5,878	2,954
Rocky Hill*	11,103	7,404
Seymour*	12,776	10,100
Shelton	27,165	18,190
Simsbury (U)	4,994	2,745
Stamford	108,798	92,713
Storrs (U)	10,691	6,054
Stratford*	49,775	45,012
Torrington	31,952	30,045
Trumbull*	31,394	20,379
Wallingford*	35,714	29,920
Waterbury	108,033	107,130
West Hartford*	68,031	62,382
West Haven	52,851	—
Westport*	27,414	20,955
Wethersfield*	26,662	20,561
Willimantic	14,402	13,881
Windsor Locks*	15,080	11,411
Winsted	8,954	8,136
Woodbridge*	7,673	5,182
Delaware	**548,104**	**446,292**
Brookside Park (U)	7,856	—
Claymont (U)	6,584	—
Dover	17,488	7,250
Dover Base (U)	8,106	—
Elsmere	8,415	7,319
Milford	5,314	5,795
Newark	20,757	11,404
New Castle	4,814	4,469
Seaford	5,537	4,430
Smyrna	4,243	3,241
Wilmington	80,386	95,827
Wilmington Manor-Chelsea-Leedom (U)	10,134	—
District of Columbia	**756,510**	**763,956**
Florida	**6,789,443**	**4,951,560**
Altamonte Springs	4,391	1,212
Arcadia	5,658	5,889
Auburndale	5,386	5,595
Avon Park	6,712	6,073
Azalea Park (U)	7,367	—
Bartow	12,891	12,849
Bay Harbor Islands	4,619	3,249
Bayshore Gardens (U)	9,255	2,297
Belle Glade	15,949	11,273
Boca Raton	28,506	6,961
Boynton Beach	18,115	10,467

Place	POPULATION 1970	1960
Bradenton	21,040	19,380
Brandon (U)	12,749	1,665
Broadview Park-Rock Hill (U)	6,049	—
Browardale (U)	17,444	—
Browns Village (U)	23,442	—
Bunche Park (U)	5,773	—
Cape Canaveral	4,258	—
Cape Coral (U)	10,193	—
Carol City (U)	27,361	21,749
Carver Ranch Estates (U)	5,515	—
Casselberry	9,438	2,463
Cedar Hammock-Bradenton South (U)	10,820	—
Chattahoochee	7,944	9,699
Clearwater	52,074	34,653
Cocoa	16,110	12,294
Cocoa Beach	9,952	3,475
Cocoa West (U)	5,779	3,975
Collier Manor-Cresthaven (U)	7,202	—
Combee Settlement (U)	4,963	2,697
Conway (U)	8,642	—
Coral Gables	42,494	34,793
Crestview	7,952	7,467
Cutler Ridge (U)	17,441	7,005
Dade City	4,241	4,759
Dania	9,013	7,065
Daytona Beach	45,327	37,395
Deerfield Beach	17,130	9,573
De Funiak Springs	4,966	5,282
De Land	11,641	10,775
Delray Beach	19,366	12,230
Deltona (U)	4,868	—
Dunedin	17,639	8,444
East Lake-Orient Park (U)	5,697	—
East Naples (U)	6,152	—
Eglin (U)	7,769	—
Egypt Lake (U)	7,556	—
Englewood (U)	5,182	2,877
Eustis	6,722	6,189
Fernandina Beach	6,955	7,276
Florida City	5,133	4,114
Fort Lauderdale	139,590	83,648
Fort Meade	4,374	4,014
Fort Myers	27,351	22,523
Fort Myers Beach (U)	4,305	2,463
Fort Myers Southwest (U)	5,086	—
Fort Pierce	29,721	25,256
Fort Walton Beach	19,994	12,147
Gainesville	64,510	29,701
Gifford (U)	5,772	3,509
Goulds (U)	6,690	5,121
Gulf Gate Estates (U)	5,874	—
Gulfport	9,730	9,730
Haines City	8,956	9,135
Hallandale	23,849	10,483
Hialeah	102,297	66,972
Holden Heights (U)	6,206	—
Holly Hill	8,191	4,182
Hollywood	106,873	35,237
Homestead	13,674	9,152
Homestead Base (U)	8,257	—
Indian Harbour Beach	5,371	—
Jacksonville	528,865	201,030
Kendall (U)	35,497	—
Key West	27,563	33,956
Kissimmee	7,119	6,845
Lake Carroll (U)	5,577	—
Lake City	10,575	9,465
Lake Forest (U)	5,216	—
Lake Holloway (U)	6,227	3,172
Lakeland	41,550	41,350
Lake Magdalene (U)	9,266	—
Lake Park	6,993	3,589
Lake Wales	8,240	8,346
Lake Worth	23,714	20,758
Lantana	7,126	5,021
Largo	22,031	5,302
Lauderdale Lakes	10,577	—
Lauderhill	8,465	132
Leesburg	11,869	11,172
Lehigh Acres (U)	4,394	—
Leto (U)	8,458	—
Lighthouse Point	9,071	2,453
Live Oak	6,830	6,544
Lockhart (U)	5,809	—
Maitland	7,157	3,570
Marathon (U)	4,397	—
Margate	8,867	2,646
Marianna	6,741	7,152
Melbourne	40,236	11,982
Melrose Park (U)	6,111	—
Merritt Island (U)	29,233	3,554
Miami	334,859	291,688
Miami Beach	87,072	63,145
Miami Shores	9,425	8,865
Miami Springs	13,279	11,229
Milton	5,360	4,108
Mims (U)	8,309	1,307
Miramar	23,973	5,485
Mount Dora	4,543	3,756
Myrtle Grove (U)	16,186	—
Naples	12,042	4,655
New Port Richey	6,098	3,520

Place	POPULATION 1970	1960
Florida (continued)		
New Smyrna Beach	10,580	8,781
North Andrews Terrace (U)	7,082	—
North Bay	4,831	2,006
North Fort Myers (U)	8,798	—
North Miami	34,767	28,708
North Miami Beach	30,723	21,405
North Palm Beach	9,035	2,684
Norwood (U)	14,973	—
Oakland Park	16,261	5,331
Ocala	22,583	13,598
Ocean City (U)	5,267	—
Opa-Locka	11,902	9,810
Orange Park	7,619	2,624
Orlando	99,006	88,135
Ormond Beach	14,063	8,658
Ormond By-The-Sea	6,002	3,476
Pahokee	5,663	4,709
Palatka	9,310	11,028
Palm Bay	6,927	2,808
Palm Beach	9,086	6,055
Palm Beach Gardens	6,102	1
Palmetto	7,422	5,556
Palm River-Clair Mel (U)	8,536	—
Palm Springs	4,340	2,503
Panama City	32,096	33,275
Parker	4,212	—
Pembroke Pines	15,520	1,429
Pensacola	59,507	56,752
Perrine (U)	10,257	6,424
Perry	7,701	8,030
Pine Hills (U)	13,882	—
Pinellas Park	22,287	10,848
Plantation	23,523	4,772
Plant City	15,451	15,711
Pompano Beach	37,724	15,992
Pompano Beach Highlands (U)	5,014	—
Port Charlotte (U)	10,769	3,197
Port St. Joe	4,401	4,217
Quincy	8,334	8,874
Richmond Heights (U)	6,663	4,311
Riverland Village-Lauderdale Isles (U)	5,512	—
Riviera Beach	21,401	13,046
Rockledge	10,523	3,481
St. Augustine	12,352	14,734
St. Cloud	5,041	4,353
St. Petersburg	216,232	181,298
St. Petersburg Beach	8,024	6,268
Sanford	17,393	19,175
Sarasota	40,237	34,083
Sarasota Southeast (U)	6,885	—
Sarasota Springs (U)	4,405	—
Satellite Beach	6,558	825
Sebring	7,223	6,939
Siesta Key (U)	4,460	—
South Daytona	4,979	1,954
South Miami	19,571	9,846
South Miami Heights (U)	10,395	—
South Patrick Shores (U)	10,313	—
Springfield	5,949	4,628
Starke	4,848	4,806
Stuart	4,820	4,791
Sunrise Golf Village	7,403	—
Sweetwater Creek (U)	19,453	—
Tallahassee	71,897	48,174
Tamarac	5,078	—
Tampa	277,767	274,970
Tarpon Springs	7,118	6,768
Temple Terrace	7,347	3,812
Tice (U)	7,254	4,377
Titusville	30,515	6,410
Treasure Island	6,120	3,506
Tyndall (U)	4,248	—
University (U)	10,039	—
Valparaiso	6,504	5,975
Venice	6,648	3,444
Venice South (U)	4,680	—
Vero Beach	11,908	8,849
Vero Beach South (U)	7,330	—
Warrington (U)	15,848	16,752
West Bradenton (U)	6,162	—
West End (U)	5,289	3,124
West Miami	5,494	5,296
West Palm Beach	57,375	56,208
West Pensacola (U)	20,924	—
West Winter Haven (U)	7,716	5,050
Westwood Lakes (U)	12,811	22,517
Wilton Manors	10,948	8,257
Winston (U)	4,505	3,323
Winter Garden	5,153	5,513
Winter Haven	16,136	16,277
Winter Park	21,895	17,162
Georgia	**4,589,575**	**3,943,116**
Adel	4,972	4,321
Albany	72,623	55,890
Americus	16,091	13,472
Ashburn	4,209	3,291
Athens	44,342	31,355
Atlanta	496,973	487,455
Augusta	59,864	70,626

Place	POPULATION 1970	1960
Bainbridge	10,887	12,714
Barnesville	4,935	4,919
Blakely	5,267	3,580
Brunswick	19,585	21,703
Buford	4,640	4,168
Cairo	8,061	7,427
Calhoun	4,748	3,587
Camilla	4,987	4,753
Carrollton	13,520	10,973
Cartersville	9,929	8,668
Cedartown	9,253	9,340
Chamblee	9,127	6,635
Cochran	5,161	4,714
College Park	18,203	23,469
Columbus	154,168	116,779
Conyers	4,890	2,881
Cordele	10,733	10,609
Covington	10,267	8,167
Dalton	18,872	17,868
Dawson	5,383	5,062
Decatur	21,943	22,026
Dock Junction (U)	6,009	5,417
Doraville	9,039	4,437
Douglas	10,195	8,736
Douglasville	5,472	4,462
Dublin	15,143	13,814
Eastman	5,416	5,118
East Point	39,315	35,633
Elberton	6,438	7,107
Fitzgerald	8,015	8,781
Forest Park	19,994	14,201
Fort Benning (U)	27,495	—
Fort Gordon (U)	15,589	—
Fort Stewart (U)	4,467	—
Fort Valley	9,251	8,310
Gainesville	15,459	16,523
Garden City	5,741	5,451
Griffin	22,734	21,735
Hapeville	9,567	10,082
Hartwell	4,865	4,599
Jesup	9,091	7,304
La Fayette	6,044	5,588
La Grange	23,301	23,632
Lawrenceville	5,115	3,804
Macon	122,423	69,764
Manchester	4,779	4,115
Marietta	27,216	25,565
Midway-Hardwick (U)	14,047	16,909
Milledgeville	11,601	11,117
Monroe	8,071	6,826
Moultrie	14,302	15,764
Nashville	4,323	4,070
Newnan	11,205	12,169
Pelham	4,539	4,609
Perry	7,771	6,032
Quitman	4,818	5,071
Rome	30,759	32,226
Roswell	5,430	2,983
St. Simons (U)	5,346	3,199
Sandersville	5,546	5,425
Savannah	118,349	149,245
Smyrna	19,157	10,157
Statesboro	14,616	8,356
Summerville	5,043	4,706
Swainsboro	7,325	5,943
Sylvester	4,226	3,610
Thomaston	10,024	9,336
Thomasville	18,155	18,246
Thomson	6,503	4,522
Tifton	12,179	9,903
Toccoa	6,971	7,303
Valdosta	32,303	30,652
Vidalia	9,507	7,569
Warner Robins	33,491	18,633
Waycross	18,996	20,944
Waynesboro	5,530	5,359
West Point	4,232	4,610
Winder	6,605	5,555
Windsor Forest (U)	7,288	—
Hawaii	**768,561**	**632,772**
Aiea	12,560	11,826
Ewa Beach	7,765	4,627
Halawa Heights	5,809	—
Hickam Housing	7,352	—
Hilo	26,353	25,966
Honolulu	324,871	294,194
Iroquois Point	4,572	—
Kahului	8,280	4,223
Kailua	33,783	—
Kaneohe	29,903	14,414
Maili	4,397	—
Makaha	4,644	—
Maunawili	5,303	—
Mokapu	7,860	—
Nanakuli	6,506	2,745
Pacific Palisades	7,846	—
Pearl City	19,552	—
Schofield Barracks	13,516	—
Wahiawa	17,598	15,512
Wailuku	7,979	6,969
Waipahu	22,798	—

Place	POPULATION 1970	1960
Idaho	**712,567**	**667,191**
Blackfoot	8,716	7,378
Boise City	74,990	34,481
Burley	8,279	7,508
Caldwell	14,219	12,230
Coeur d'Alene	16,228	14,291
Idaho Falls	35,776	33,161
Lewiston	26,068	12,691
Moscow	14,146	11,183
Mountain Home	6,451	5,984
Mountain Home Base (U)	6,038	—
Nampa	20,768	18,897
Payette	4,521	4,451
Pocatello	40,036	28,534
Rexburg	8,272	4,767
Rupert	4,563	4,153
Twin Falls	21,914	20,126
Illinois	**11,113,976**	**10,081,158**
Addison	24,482	6,741
Alsip	11,141	3,770
Alton	39,700	43,047
Anna	4,766	4,280
Arlington Heights	64,884	27,878
Aurora	74,182	63,715
Barrington	7,701	5,434
Bartonville	7,221	7,253
Batavia	8,994	7,496
Beardstown	6,222	6,294
Belleville	41,699	37,264
Bellwood	22,096	20,729
Belvidere	14,061	11,223
Bensenville	12,833	9,141
Benton	6,833	7,023
Berkeley	6,152	5,792
Berwyn	52,502	54,224
Bethalto	7,074	3,235
Bloomington	39,992	36,271
Blue Island	22,958	19,618
Bolingbrook	7,275	—
Bourbonnais	5,909	3,336
Bradley	9,881	8,082
Bridge View	12,522	7,334
Broadview	9,307	8,588
Brookfield	20,284	20,429
Buffalo Grove	11,799	1,492
Cahokia	20,649	15,829
Cairo	6,277	9,348
Calumet City	32,956	25,000
Calumet Park	10,069	8,448
Canton	14,217	13,588
Carbondale	22,816	14,670
Carlinville	5,675	5,440
Carmi	6,033	6,152
Carol Stream	4,434	836
Carpentersville	24,059	17,424
Cary	4,358	2,530
Centralia	15,217	13,904
Centreville	11,378	12,769
Champaign	56,532	49,583
Charleston	16,421	10,505
Chester	5,310	4,460
Chicago	3,366,957	3,550,404
Chicago Heights	40,900	34,331
Chicago Ridge	9,187	5,748
Chillicothe	6,052	3,054
Cicero	67,058	69,130
Clarendon Hills	6,750	5,885
Clinton	7,570	7,355
Collinsville	17,773	14,217
Country Club Hills	6,920	3,421
Crest Hill	7,460	5,887
Crestwood	5,543	1,213
Crete	4,656	3,463
Creve Coeur	6,440	6,684
Crystal Lake	14,541	8,314
Danville	42,570	41,856
Darien	8,077	—
Decatur	90,397	78,004
Deerfield	18,949	11,786
De Kalb	32,949	18,486
Des Plaines	57,239	34,886
Dixmoor	4,735	3,076
Dixon	18,147	19,565
Dolton	25,937	18,746
Downers Grove	32,751	21,154
Du Quoin	6,691	6,558
East Alton	7,309	7,630
East Chicago Heights	5,000	3,270
East Moline	20,832	16,732
East Peoria	18,455	12,310
East St. Louis	69,996	81,712
Edwardsville	11,070	9,996
Effingham	9,458	8,172
Elgin	55,691	49,447
Elk Grove Village	24,516	6,608
Elmhurst	50,547	36,991
Elmwood Park	26,160	23,866
Evanston	79,808	79,283
Evergreen Park	25,487	24,178
Fairfield	5,897	6,362
Fairview Heights	8,625	—
Flora	5,283	5,331

Place	Population 1970	Population 1960
Illinois (continued)		
Flossmoor	7,846	4,624
Forest Park	15,472	14,452
Fox Lake	4,511	3,700
Franklin Park	20,497	18,322
Freeport	27,736	26,628
Gages Lake-Wildwood (U)	5,337	—
Galesburg	36,290	37,243
Geneseo	5,840	5,169
Geneva	9,115	7,646
Glencoe	10,542	10,472
Glendale Heights	11,406	173
Glen Ellyn	21,909	15,972
Glenview	24,880	18,132
Glenwood	7,416	882
Granite City	40,440	40,073
Grayslake	4,907	3,762
Greenville	4,631	4,569
Hanover Park	11,916	451
Harrisburg	9,535	9,171
Harvard	5,177	4,248
Harvey	34,636	29,071
Harwood Heights	9,060	5,688
Havana	4,376	4,363
Hazel Crest	10,329	6,205
Herrin	9,623	9,474
Hickory Hills	13,176	2,707
Highland	5,981	4,943
Highland Park	32,263	25,532
Highwood	4,973	4,499
Hillsboro	4,267	4,232
Hillside	8,888	7,794
Hinsdale	15,918	12,859
Hoffman Estates	22,238	8,296
Hometown	6,729	7,479
Homewood	18,871	13,371
Hoopeston	6,461	6,606
Itasca	4,638	3,564
Jacksonville	20,553	21,690
Jerseyville	7,446	7,420
Joliet	80,378	66,780
Justice	9,473	2,803
Kankakee	30,944	27,666
Ken Rock (U)	5,945	—
Kewanee	15,762	16,324
La Grange	16,773	15,285
La Grange Highlands (U)	6,920	—
La Grange Park	15,626	13,793
Lake Bluff	4,979	3,494
Lake Forest	15,642	10,687
Lansing	25,805	18,098
La Salle	10,736	11,897
Lawrenceville	5,863	5,492
Lemont	5,080	3,397
Libertyville	11,684	8,560
Lincoln	17,582	16,890
Lincolnwood	12,929	11,744
Lisle	5,329	4,219
Litchfield	7,190	7,330
Lockport	9,985	7,560
Lombard	35,977	22,561
Loves Park	12,390	9,086
Lyons	11,124	9,936
McHenry	6,772	3,336
Macomb	19,643	12,135
Madison	7,042	6,861
Marengo	4,235	3,568
Marion	11,724	11,274
Markham	15,987	11,704
Marseilles	4,320	4,347
Mascoutah	5,045	3,625
Matteson	4,741	3,225
Mattoon	19,681	19,088
Maywood	30,036	27,330
Melrose Park	22,706	22,291
Mendota	6,902	6,154
Metropolis	6,940	7,339
Midlothian	15,939	6,605
Milan	4,873	3,065
Moline	46,237	42,705
Monmouth	11,022	10,372
Morris	8,194	7,935
Morrison	4,387	4,159
Morton	10,419	5,325
Morton Grove	26,369	20,533
Mount Carmel	8,096	8,594
Mount Prospect	34,995	18,906
Mount Vernon	15,980	15,566
Mundelein	16,128	10,526
Murphysboro	10,013	8,673
Naperville	23,885	12,933
Niles	31,432	20,393
Normal	26,396	13,357
Norridge	16,880	14,087
North Aurora	4,833	2,088
Northbrook	27,297	11,635
North Chicago	47,275	22,938
Northfield	5,010	4,005
Northlake	14,212	12,318
North Park (U)	15,679	—
North Riverside	8,097	7,989
Oak Forest	17,870	3,724
Oak Lawn	60,305	27,471
Oak Park	62,511	61,093
O'Fallon	7,268	4,018
Olney	8,974	8,780
Orland Park	6,391	2,592
Ottawa	18,716	19,408
Palatine	25,904	11,504
Palos Heights	9,915	3,775
Palos Hills	6,629	3,766
Pana	6,326	6,432
Paris	9,971	9,823
Park Forest	30,638	29,993
Park Ridge	42,466	32,659
Paxton	4,373	4,370
Pekin	31,375	28,146
Peoria	126,963	103,162
Peoria Heights	7,943	7,064
Peru	11,772	10,460
Pittsfield	4,244	4,089
Plano	4,664	3,343
Pontiac	9,031	8,435
Posen	5,498	4,517
Princeton	6,959	6,250
Prospect Heights (U)	13,333	—
Quincy	45,288	43,793
Rantoul	25,562	22,116
Riverdale	15,806	12,008
River Forest	13,402	12,695
River Grove	11,465	8,464
Riverside	10,432	9,750
Robbins	9,641	7,511
Robinson	7,178	7,226
Rochelle	8,594	7,008
Rock Falls	10,287	10,261
Rockford	147,370	126,706
Rock Island	50,166	51,863
Rolling Meadows	19,178	10,879
Romeoville	12,674	3,574
Roselle	4,583	3,581
Rosemont	4,360	978
Round Lake Beach	5,717	5,011
St. Charles	12,928	9,269
Salem	6,187	6,165
Sandwich	5,056	3,842
Sauk	7,479	4,687
Savanna	4,942	4,950
Schaumburg	18,730	986
Schiller Park	12,712	5,687
Scott (U)	7,871	—
Shelbyville	4,597	4,821
Silvis	5,907	3,973
Skokie	68,627	59,364
South Chicago Heights	4,923	4,043
South Elgin	4,289	2,624
South Holland	23,931	10,412
South Stickney (U)	29,900	—
Sparta	4,307	3,452
Springfield	91,753	83,271
Spring Valley	5,605	5,371
Staunton	4,396	4,228
Steger	8,104	6,432
Sterling	16,113	15,688
Stickney	6,601	6,239
Stone Park	4,451	3,038
Streamwood	18,176	4,821
Streator	15,600	16,868
Summit	11,569	10,374
Swansea	5,432	3,018
Sycamore	7,843	6,961
Taylorville	10,644	8,801
Tinley Park	12,382	6,392
Urbana	32,800	27,294
Vandalia	5,160	5,537
Venice	4,680	5,380
Villa Park	25,891	20,391
Washington	6,790	5,919
Washington Park	9,524	6,601
Waterloo	4,546	3,739
Watseka	5,294	5,219
Wauconda	5,460	3,227
Waukegan	65,269	55,719
Westchester	20,033	18,092
West Chicago	10,111	6,854
West End (U)	7,554	—
Western Springs	12,147	10,838
West Frankfort	8,836	9,027
Westmont	8,482	5,997
West Peoria (U)	6,873	—
Wheaton	31,138	24,312
Wheeling	14,746	7,169
Wilmette	32,134	28,268
Wilmington	4,335	4,210
Winfield	4,285	1,575
Winnetka	14,131	13,368
Winthrop Harbor	4,794	3,848
Wonder Lake (U)	4,806	3,543
Wood Dale	8,831	3,071
Woodridge	11,028	542
Wood River	13,186	11,694
Woodstock	10,226	8,897
Worth	11,999	8,196
Zion	17,268	11,941
Indiana	**5,193,669**	**4,662,498**
Alexandria	5,097	5,582
Anderson	70,787	49,061
Angola	5,117	4,746
Attica	4,262	4,341
Auburn	7,337	6,350
Aurora	4,293	4,119
Austin	4,902	—
Bedford	13,087	13,024
Beech Grove	13,468	10,973
Black Oak (U)	9,624	—
Bloomington	42,890	31,357
Bluffton	8,297	6,238
Boonville	5,736	4,801
Brazil	8,163	8,853
Brownsburg	5,186	4,478
Carmel	6,568	1,442
Cedar Lake	7,589	—
Charlestown	5,890	5,726
Chesterton	6,177	4,335
Clarksville	13,806	8,088
Clinton	5,340	5,843
Columbia City	4,911	4,803
Columbus	27,141	20,778
Connersville	17,604	17,698
Crawfordsville	13,842	14,231
Crown Point	10,931	8,443
Decatur	8,445	8,327
Dyer	4,906	3,993
East Chicago	46,982	57,669
East Gary	9,858	9,309
Edinburg	4,906	3,664
Elkhart	43,152	40,274
Elwood	11,196	11,793
Evansville	138,764	141,543
Fort Wayne	177,671	161,776
Frankfort	14,956	15,302
Franklin	11,477	9,453
Garrett	4,715	4,364
Gary	175,415	178,320
Gas City	5,742	4,469
Goshen	17,171	13,718
Greencastle	8,852	8,506
Greenfield	9,986	9,049
Greensburg	8,620	7,492
Greenwood	11,408	7,169
Griffith	18,168	9,483
Grissom (U)	4,963	—
Hammond	107,790	111,698
Hartford City	8,207	8,053
Highland	24,947	16,284
Hobart	21,485	18,680
Huntingburg	4,794	4,146
Huntington	16,217	16,185
Indianapolis	744,624	476,258
Jasper	8,641	6,737
Jeffersonville	20,008	19,522
Kendallville	6,838	6,765
Kokomo	44,042	47,197
Lafayette	44,955	42,330
La Porte	22,140	21,157
Lawrence	16,646	10,103
Lawrenceburg	4,636	5,004
Lebanon	9,766	9,523
Linton	5,450	5,736
Logansport	19,255	21,106
Madison	13,081	10,488
Marion	39,607	37,854
Martinsville	9,723	7,525
Merrillville-Lottaville-Rexville (U)	15,918	—
Michigan City	39,369	36,653
Mishawaka	35,517	33,361
Monticello	4,869	4,035
Mooresville	5,800	3,856
Mount Vernon	6,770	5,970
Muncie	69,080	68,603
Munster	16,514	10,313
New Albany	38,402	37,812
New Castle	21,215	20,349
New Haven	5,728	3,396
New Whiteland	4,200	3,488
Noblesville	7,548	7,664
North Manchester	5,791	4,377
North Vernon	4,582	4,307
Peru	14,139	14,453
Plainfield	8,211	5,460
Plymouth	7,661	7,558
Portage	19,127	11,822
Portland	7,115	6,999
Princeton	7,431	7,906
Rensselaer	4,688	4,740
Richmond	43,999	44,149
Rochester	4,631	4,883
Rushville	6,686	7,264
Salem	5,041	4,546
Scottsburg	4,791	3,810
Seymour	13,352	11,629
Shelbyville	15,094	14,317
South Bend	125,580	132,445
Speedway	15,056	9,624
Sullivan	4,683	4,979
Tell City	7,933	6,609

Place	POPULATION 1970	1960
Indiana (continued)		
Terre Haute	70,286	72,500
Tipton	5,176	5,604
Valparaiso	20,020	15,227
Vincennes	19,867	18,046
Wabash	13,379	12,621
Warsaw	7,506	7,234
Washington	11,358	10,846
West Glen Park (U)	6,602	—
West Lafayette	19,157	12,680
Whiting	7,247	8,137
Winchester	5,493	5,742
Iowa	**2,825,041**	**2,757,537**
Algona	6,032	5,702
Ames	39,505	27,003
Anamosa	4,389	4,616
Ankeny	9,151	2,964
Atlantic	7,306	6,890
Bettendorf	22,126	11,534
Boone	12,468	12,468
Burlington	32,366	32,430
Carroll	8,716	7,682
Cedar Falls	29,597	21,195
Cedar Rapids	110,642	92,035
Centerville	6,531	6,629
Chariton	5,009	5,042
Charles City	9,268	9,964
Cherokee	7,272	7,724
Clarinda	5,420	5,901
Clear Lake City	6,430	6,158
Clinton	34,719	33,589
Coralville	6,130	2,357
Council Bluffs	60,348	55,641
Creston	8,234	7,667
Davenport	98,469	88,981
Decorah	7,458	6,435
Denison	5,882	4,930
Des Moines	200,587	208,982
Dubuque	62,309	56,606
Eagle Grove	4,489	4,381
Estherville	8,108	7,927
Evansdale	5,038	5,738
Fairfield	8,715	8,054
Fort Dodge	31,263	28,399
Fort Madison	13,996	15,247
Grinnell	8,402	7,367
Hampton	4,376	4,501
Harlan	5,049	4,350
Humboldt	4,665	4,031
Independence	5,910	5,498
Indianola	8,852	7,062
Iowa City	46,850	33,443
Iowa Falls	6,454	5,565
Jefferson	4,735	4,570
Keokuk	14,631	16,316
Knoxville	7,755	7,817
Le Mars	8,159	6,767
Manchester	4,641	4,402
Maquoketa	5,677	5,909
Marion	18,028	10,882
Marshalltown	26,219	22,521
Mason City	30,491	30,642
Mount Pleasant	7,007	7,339
Muscatine	22,405	20,997
Nevada	4,952	4,227
Newton	15,619	15,381
Oelwein	7,735	8,282
Oskaloosa	11,224	11,053
Ottumwa	29,610	33,871
Pella	6,668	5,198
Perry	6,906	6,442
Red Oak	6,210	6,421
Sheldon	4,535	4,251
Shenandoah	5,968	6,567
Sioux City	85,925	89,159
Spencer	10,278	8,864
Storm Lake	8,591	7,728
Urbandale	14,434	5,821
Vinton	4,845	4,781
Washington	6,317	6,037
Waterloo	75,533	71,755
Waverly	7,205	6,357
Webster City	8,488	8,520
West Des Moines	16,441	11,949
Windsor Heights	6,303	4,715
Kansas	**2,249,071**	**2,178,611**
Abilene	6,661	6,746
Arkansas City	13,216	14,262
Atchison	12,565	12,529
Augusta	5,977	6,434
Baxter Springs	4,489	4,498
Chanute	10,341	10,849
Clay Center	4,963	4,613
Coffeyville	15,116	17,382
Colby	4,658	4,210
Concordia	7,221	7,022
Derby	7,947	6,458
Dodge City	14,127	13,520
El Dorado	12,308	12,523
Emporia	23,327	18,190
Fairway	5,133	5,398
Fort Leavenworth (U)	8,060	—
Fort Scott	8,967	9,410
Garden City	14,708	11,811
Goodland	5,510	4,459
Great Bend	16,133	16,670
Hays	15,396	11,947
Haysville	6,483	5,836
Hutchinson	36,885	37,574
Independence	10,347	11,222
Iola	6,493	6,885
Junction City	19,018	18,700
Kansas City	168,213	121,901
Larned	4,567	5,001
Lawrence	45,698	32,858
Leavenworth	25,147	22,052
Leawood	10,349	7,466
Lenexa	5,242	2,487
Liberal	13,471	13,813
Lyons	4,355	4,592
McPherson	10,851	9,996
Manhattan	27,575	22,993
Merriam	10,851	5,084
Mission	8,376	4,626
Newton	15,439	14,877
North Fort Riley (U)	12,469	—
Olathe	17,917	10,987
Osawatomie	4,294	4,622
Ottawa	11,036	10,673
Overland Park	76,623	—
Paola	4,622	4,784
Parsons	13,015	13,929
Pittsburg	20,171	18,678
Prairie Village	28,138	25,356
Pratt	6,736	8,156
Roeland Park	9,974	8,949
Russell	5,371	6,113
Salina	37,714	43,202
Shawnee	20,482	9,072
Topeka	125,011	119,484
Wellington	8,072	8,809
Wichita	276,554	254,698
Winfield	11,405	11,117
Kentucky	**3,219,311**	**3,038,156**
Ashland	29,245	31,283
Bardstown	5,816	4,798
Bellevue	8,847	9,336
Berea	6,956	4,302
Bowling Green	36,253	28,338
Buechel (U)	5,359	—
Campbellsville	7,598	6,966
Cold Spring	5,348	1,095
Corbin	7,317	7,119
Covington	52,535	60,376
Cynthiana	6,356	5,641
Danville	11,542	9,010
Dayton	8,691	9,050
Elizabethtown	11,748	9,641
Elsmere	5,161	4,607
Erlanger	12,676	7,072
Flatwoods	7,380	3,741
Florence	11,457	5,837
Fort Campbell North (U)	13,616	—
Fort Knox (U)	37,608	—
Fort Mitchell	6,982	525
Fort Thomas	16,338	14,896
Fort Wright-Lookout Heights	4,819	—
Frankfort	21,356	18,365
Franklin	6,553	5,319
Georgetown	8,629	6,986
Glasgow	11,301	10,069
Harrodsburg	6,741	6,061
Hazard	5,459	5,958
Henderson	22,976	16,892
Hopkinsville	21,250	19,465
Jeffersontown	9,701	3,431
Lebanon	5,528	4,813
Lexington	108,137	62,810
London	4,337	4,035
Louisville	361,472	390,639
Ludlow	5,815	6,233
Madisonville	15,332	13,110
Mayfield	10,724	10,762
Maysville	7,411	8,484
Middlesborough	11,844	12,607
Morehead	7,191	4,170
Mount Sterling	5,083	5,370
Murray	13,537	9,303
Newport	25,998	30,070
Nicholasville	5,829	4,275
Okolona (U)	17,643	—
Owensboro	50,329	42,471
Paducah	31,627	34,479
Paris	7,823	7,791
Pikeville	4,576	4,754
Pleasure Ridge Park (U)	28,566	10,612
Princeton	6,292	5,618
Providence	4,270	3,771
Radcliff	7,881	3,384
Richmond	16,861	12,168
Russellville	6,456	5,861
St. Matthews	13,152	8,738
Shively	19,223	15,155
Somerset	10,436	7,112
Valley Station (U)	24,471	10,553
Versailles	5,679	4,060
Winchester	13,402	10,187
Louisiana	**3,643,180**	**3,257,022**
Abbeville	10,996	10,414
Alexandria	41,557	40,279
Baker	8,281	4,823
Bastrop	14,713	15,193
Baton Rouge	165,963	152,419
Bayou Cane (U)	9,077	3,173
Bayou Vista (U)	5,121	—
Bogalusa	18,412	21,423
Bossier City	41,595	32,776
Breaux Bridge	4,942	3,303
Bunkie	5,395	5,188
Cooper Road (U)	9,034	—
Covington	7,170	6,754
Crowley	16,104	15,617
Denham Springs	6,752	5,991
De Ridder	8,030	7,188
Donaldsonville	7,367	6,082
Eunice	11,390	11,326
Ferriday	5,239	4,563
Franklin	9,325	8,673
Gonzales	4,512	3,252
Grambling	4,407	3,144
Gretna	24,875	21,967
Hammond	12,487	10,563
Harahan	13,037	9,275
Harvey (U)	6,347	—
Homer	4,483	4,665
Houma	30,922	22,561
Jackson	4,697	1,824
Jeanerette	6,322	5,568
Jefferson Heights (U)	16,489	19,353
Jennings	11,783	11,887
Jonesboro	5,072	3,848
Kaplan	5,540	5,267
Kenner	29,858	17,037
Lafayette	68,908	40,400
Lake Charles	77,998	63,392
Lake Providence	6,183	5,781
Laplace (U)	5,953	3,541
Larose (U)	4,267	2,796
Leesville	8,928	4,689
Little Farms (U)	15,713	—
Mansfield	6,432	5,839
Marksville	4,519	4,257
Marrero (U)	29,015	—
Metairie (U)	135,816	—
Minden	13,996	12,785
Monroe	56,374	52,219
Morgan City	16,586	13,540
Natchitoches	15,974	13,924
New Iberia	30,147	29,062
New Orleans	593,471	627,525
Norco (U)	4,773	4,682
North Fort Polk	7,955	—
Oakdale	7,301	6,618
Opelousas	20,121	17,417
Patterson	4,409	2,923
Pineville	8,951	8,636
Plaquemine	7,739	7,689
Ponchatoula	4,545	4,727
Port Allen	5,728	5,026
Raceland (U)	4,880	3,666
Rayne	9,510	8,634
Reserve (U)	6,381	5,297
Ruston	17,365	13,991
St. Martinville	7,153	6,468
Samtown (U)	4,210	4,008
Scotlandville (U)	22,557	—
Shreveport	182,064	164,372
Slidell	16,101	6,356
South Fort Polk (U)	15,600	—
Springhill	6,496	6,437
Sulphur	13,551	11,429
Tallulah	9,643	9,413
Terry Town (U)	13,832	—
Thibodaux	14,925	13,403
Vidalia	5,538	4,313
Ville Platte	9,692	7,512
West Monroe	14,868	15,215
Westwego	11,402	9,815
Winnfield	7,142	7,022
Winnsboro	5,349	4,437
Zachary	4,964	3,268
Maine	**992,048**	**969,265**
Auburn	24,151	24,449
Augusta	21,945	21,680
Bangor	33,168	38,912
Bath	9,679	10,717
Belfast	5,957	6,140
Biddeford	19,983	19,255
Brewer	9,300	9,009
Brunswick (U)	10,867	9,444
Cape Elizabeth*	7,873	5,505
Caribou	10,419	—
Ellsworth	4,603	4,444
Falmouth*	6,291	5,976

Place	POPULATION 1970	1960
Maine (continued)		
Gardiner	6,685	6,897
Houlton (U)	6,760	5,976
Kittery (U)	7,363	8,051
Lewiston	41,779	40,804
Loring (U)	6,266	—
Madawaska (U)	4,452	4,035
Millinocket (U)	7,558	7,318
Old Orchard Beach (U)	5,273	4,431
Old Town	9,057	8,626
Orono (U)	9,146	3,234
Portland	65,116	72,566
Presque Isle	11,452	12,886
Rockland	8,505	8,769
Rumford (U)	6,198	7,233
Saco	11,678	10,515
Sanford (U)	10,457	10,936
Skowhegan (U)	6,571	6,667
South Portland	23,267	22,788
Waterville	18,192	19,001
Westbrook	14,444	13,820
Winslow (U)	5,389	3,640
Maryland	**3,922,399**	**3,100,689**
Aberdeen	12,375	9,679
Aberdeen Proving Ground (U)	7,403	—
Andrews (U)	6,418	—
Annapolis	29,592	23,385
Arbutus (U)	22,745	22,402
Aspen Hill (U)	16,799	—
Avenel-Hillandale (U)	19,520	—
Bainbridge Center (U)	5,257	—
Baltimore	905,759	939,024
Bel Air	6,307	4,300
Beltsville (U)	8,912	—
Bethesda (U)	71,621	56,527
Birchwood City (U)	9,558	—
Bladensburg	7,488	3,103
Bowie	35,028	1,072
Brooklyn (U)	13,896	—
Calverton (U)	6,543	—
Cambridge	11,595	12,239
Camp Springs (U)	22,776	—
Carmody Hills-Pepper Mill Village (U)	6,245	—
Catonsville (U)	54,812	37,372
Chapel Oaks-Cedar Heights (U)	6,049	—
Cheverly	6,696	5,223
Chevy Chase (U)	16,424	—
Chillum (U)	35,656	—
Colesville (U)	9,455	—
College Park	26,156	18,482
Columbia (U)	8,815	—
Coral Hills (U)	7,105	—
Crofton (U)	4,478	—
Cumberland	29,724	33,415
Defense Heights (U)	6,775	—
District Heights	8,424	7,524
Dundalk (U)	85,377	82,428
Easton	6,809	6,337
Edgemere (U)	10,352	11,775
Edgewood (U)	8,551	1,670
Elkton	5,362	5,989
Ellicott City (U)	9,506	—
Essex (U)	38,193	35,205
Ferndale (U)	9,929	—
Forestville (U)	16,152	—
Fort Meade (U)	16,699	—
Frederick	23,641	21,744
Frostburg	7,327	6,722
Gaithersburg	8,344	3,847
Glenarden	4,502	1,336
Glen Burnie (U)	38,608	—
Good Luck (U)	10,584	—
Greenbelt	18,199	7,479
Hagerstown	35,862	36,660
Halfway (U)	6,106	4,256
Halpine (U)	5,912	—
Havre De Grace	9,791	8,510
Hillcrest Heights (U)	24,037	15,295
Hyattsville	14,998	15,168
Joppatowne (U)	9,092	—
Kemp Mill (U)	10,037	—
Kentland (U)	9,649	—
Landover (U)	5,597	—
Langley Park (U)	11,564	11,510
Lanham-Seabrook (U)	13,244	—
Lansdowne-Baltimore Highlands (U)	16,976	13,134
Laurel	10,525	8,503
Lexington Park-Patuxent River (U)	9,136	—
Linthicum (U)	9,830	—
Lutherville-Timonium (U)	24,055	12,265
Maryland City (U)	7,102	—
Middle River (U)	19,935	10,825
Montrose (U)	6,140	—
Mount Rainier	8,180	9,855
New Carrollton	13,395	3,385
North Potomac (U)	12,546	—
North Takoma Park (U)	7,373	—
Odenton (U)	5,989	1,914
Overlea (U)	13,086	10,795
Owings Mills (U)	7,360	3,810
Oxon Hill (U)	11,974	—
Palmer Park (U)	8,172	—
Parkville (U)	33,897	27,236
Perry Hall (U)	5,446	—
Pikesville (U)	25,395	18,737
Potomac Valley (U)	5,094	—
Pumphrey (U)	6,370	—
Randallstown (U)	33,683	—
Randolph (U)	13,233	—
Reisterstown (U)	14,037	4,216
Riverdale	5,724	4,389
Riverdale Heights-East Pines (U)	8,941	—
Riviera Beach (U)	7,464	4,902
Rockville	41,564	26,090
Rosedale (U)	19,417	—
Salisbury	15,252	16,302
Seat Pleasant	7,217	5,365
Severna Park (U)	16,358	—
Silver Spring (U)	77,496	66,348
South Gate (U)	9,356	—
South Kensington (U)	10,289	—
South Laurel (U)	13,345	—
Suitland-Silver Hill (U)	30,355	10,300
Takoma Park	18,455	16,799
Towson (U)	77,809	19,090
Waldorf (U)	7,368	1,048
Walker Mill (U)	6,322	—
West Laurel (U)	4,478	—
Westminster	7,207	6,123
Wheaton (U)	66,247	54,635
White Oak (U)	19,769	—
Woodlawn-Woodmoor (U)	28,811	—
Massachusetts	**5,689,170**	**5,148,578**
Adams (U)	11,256	11,949
Amesbury (U)	10,088	9,625
Amherst (U)	17,926	10,306
Andover*	23,695	17,134
Arlington*	53,524	49,953
Ashland*	8,882	7,779
Athol (U)	9,723	10,161
Attleboro	32,907	27,118
Auburn*	15,347	14,047
Avon*	5,295	4,301
Ayer*	7,393	14,927
Bedford*	13,513	10,969
Bellingham (U)	4,228	—
Belmont*	28,285	28,715
Beverly	38,348	36,108
Boston	641,071	697,197
Braintree*	35,050	31,069
Brockton	89,040	72,813
Brookline*	58,886	54,044
Burlington*	21,980	12,852
Cambridge	100,361	107,716
Canton*	17,100	12,771
Chelsea	30,625	33,749
Chicopee	66,676	61,553
Clinton*	13,383	12,848
Concord*	16,148	12,517
Dalton*	7,505	6,436
Danvers*	26,151	21,926
Dedham*	26,938	23,869
Easthampton*	13,012	12,326
East Longmeadow*	13,029	10,294
Everett	42,485	43,544
Fairhaven*	16,332	14,339
Fall River	96,898	99,942
Falmouth (U)	5,806	3,308
Fitchburg	43,343	43,021
Fort Devens (U)	12,951	—
Framingham*	64,048	44,526
Franklin (U)	8,863	6,391
Gardner	19,748	19,038
Gloucester	27,941	25,789
Greenfield (U)	14,642	14,389
Haverhill	46,120	46,346
Holyoke	50,112	52,689
Hopedale*	4,292	3,987
Hudson (U)	14,283	7,897
Hull*	9,961	7,055
Hyannis (U)	6,847	5,139
Ipswich (U)	5,022	4,617
Lawrence	66,915	70,933
Leominster	32,939	27,929
Lexington*	31,886	27,691
Longmeadow*	15,630	10,565
Lowell	94,239	92,107
Lynn	90,294	94,478
Lynnfield*	10,826	8,398
Malden	56,127	57,676
Manchester*	5,151	3,932
Mansfield (U)	4,778	4,674
Marblehead*	21,295	18,521
Marlborough	27,936	18,819
Maynard*	9,710	7,695
Medford	64,397	64,971
Melrose	33,180	29,619
Methuen*	35,456	28,114
Middleborough (U)	6,259	6,003
Milford (U)	13,740	13,722
Milton*	27,190	26,375
Natick*	31,057	28,831
Needham*	29,748	25,793
New Bedford	101,777	102,477
Newburyport	15,807	14,004
Newton	91,066	92,384
North Adams	19,195	19,905
Northampton	29,664	30,058
North Andover*	16,284	10,908
North Attleborough*	18,665	14,777
North Reading*	11,264	8,331
North Scituate (U)	5,507	3,421
Norwood*	30,815	24,898
Otis (U)	5,596	—
Oxford (U)	6,109	6,985
Peabody	48,080	32,202
Pinehurst (U)	5,681	1,991
Pittsfield	57,020	57,879
Plainville*	4,953	3,810
Plymouth (U)	6,940	6,488
Quincy	87,966	87,409
Randolph*	27,035	18,900
Reading*	22,539	19,259
Revere	43,159	40,080
Rockland*	15,674	13,119
Salem	40,556	39,211
Saugus*	25,110	20,666
Seekonk*	11,116	8,399
Sharon*	12,367	10,070
Shrewsbury*	19,196	16,622
Somerset*	18,088	12,196
Somerville	88,779	94,697
Southbridge (U)	14,261	15,889
South Yarmouth (U)	5,380	2,029
Spencer (U)	5,895	5,593
Springfield	163,905	174,463
Stoneham*	20,725	17,821
Stoughton*	23,459	16,328
Swampscott*	13,578	13,294
Taunton	43,756	41,132
Turners Falls (U)	5,168	4,917
Wakefield*	25,402	24,295
Waltham	61,582	55,413
Ware (U)	6,509	6,650
Watertown*	39,307	39,092
Webster (U)	12,432	12,072
Wellesley*	28,051	26,071
Westborough (U)	4,474	4,011
Westfield	31,433	26,302
Weston*	10,870	8,261
West Springfield*	28,461	24,924
Weymouth*	54,610	48,177
Whitinsville (U)	5,210	5,102
Whitman*	13,059	10,485
Williamstown (U)	4,285	5,428
Winchester*	22,269	19,376
Winthrop*	20,335	20,303
Woburn	37,406	31,214
Worcester	176,572	186,587
Michigan	**8,875,083**	**7,823,194**
Adrian	20,382	20,347
Albion	12,112	12,749
Allegan	4,516	4,822
Allen Park	40,747	37,494
Alma	9,790	8,978
Alpena	13,805	14,682
Ann Arbor	99,797	67,340
Battle Creek	38,931	44,169
Bay City	49,449	53,604
Belding	5,121	4,887
Benton Central (U)	8,067	—
Benton Harbor	16,481	19,136
Benton South (U)	4,496	—
Berkley	22,618	23,275
Beverly Hills	13,598	8,633
Big Rapids	11,995	8,686
Birmingham	26,170	25,525
Buchanan	4,645	5,341
Cadillac	9,990	10,112
Carrollton (U)	7,300	—
Center Line	10,379	10,164
Charlotte	8,244	7,657
Cheboygan	5,553	5,859
Clawson	17,617	14,795
Coldwater	9,099	8,880
Comstock (U)	5,003	—
Comstock Park (U)	5,766	—
Cutlerville (U)	6,267	—
Davison	5,259	3,761
Dearborn	104,199	112,007
Dearborn Heights	80,069	—
Detroit	1,511,482	1,670,144
Dowagiac	6,583	7,208
Drayton Plains (U)	16,462	—
East Detroit	45,920	45,756
East Grand Rapids	12,565	10,924
East Lansing	47,540	30,198
Eastwood (U)	9,682	—
Eaton Rapids	4,494	4,052
Ecorse	17,515	17,328
Escanaba	15,368	15,391
Essexville	4,990	4,590
Farmington	13,337	6,881

Place	POPULATION 1970	POPULATION 1960
Michigan (continued)		
Fenton	8,284	6,142
Ferndale	30,850	31,347
Flat Rock	5,643	4,696
Flint	193,317	196,940
Flushing	7,190	3,761
Fraser	11,868	7,027
Garden City	41,864	38,017
Gladstone	5,237	5,267
Grand Blanc	5,132	1,565
Grand Haven	11,844	11,066
Grand Ledge	6,032	5,165
Grand Rapids	197,649	177,313
Grandville	10,764	7,975
Greenville	7,493	7,440
Grosse Ile (U)	7,799	—
Grosse Pointe	6,637	6,631
Grosse Pointe Farms	11,701	12,172
Grosse Pointe Park	15,585	15,457
Grosse Pointe Woods	21,878	18,580
Hamtramck	27,245	34,137
Hancock	4,820	5,022
Harper Woods	20,186	19,995
Hastings	6,501	6,375
Hazel Park	23,784	25,631
Highland Park	35,444	38,063
Hillsdale	7,728	7,629
Holland	26,337	24,777
Holly	4,355	3,269
Holt (U)	6,980	4,818
Houghton	6,067	3,393
Howell	5,224	4,861
Huntington Woods	8,536	8,746
Inkster	38,595	39,097
Ionia	6,361	6,754
Iron Mountain	8,702	9,299
Ironwood	8,711	10,265
Ishpeming	8,245	8,857
Jackson	45,484	50,720
Jenison (U)	11,266	—
Kalamazoo	85,555	82,089
Kentwood	20,310	—
Kincheloe (U)	6,331	—
Kingsford	5,276	5,084
K. I. Sawyer (U)	6,679	—
Lakeview (U)	11,391	10,384
Lambertville (U)	5,721	1,168
Lansing	131,546	107,807
Lapeer	6,270	6,160
Lapeer Heights (U)	7,130	—
Lincoln Park	52,984	53,933
Livonia	110,109	66,702
Ludington	9,021	9,421
Madison Heights	38,599	33,343
Manistee	7,723	8,324
Manistique	4,324	4,875
Marine City	4,567	4,404
Marquette	21,967	19,824
Marshall	7,253	6,736
Marysville	5,610	4,065
Mason	5,468	4,522
Melvindale	13,862	13,089
Menominee	10,748	11,289
Midland	35,176	27,779
Milan	4,533	3,616
Milford	4,699	4,323
Monroe	23,894	22,968
Mount Clemens	20,476	21,016
Mount Pleasant	20,504	14,875
Muskegon	44,631	46,485
Muskegon Heights	17,304	19,552
Negaunee	5,248	6,126
Niles	12,988	13,842
North Muskegon	4,243	3,855
Northville	5,400	3,967
Norton Shores	22,271	—
Novi	9,668	6,390
Oak Park	36,762	36,632
Okemos (U)	7,770	—
Owosso	17,179	17,006
Petoskey	6,342	6,138
Plymouth	11,758	8,766
Pontiac	85,279	82,233
Portage	33,590	—
Port Huron	35,794	36,084
Quakertown North (U)	7,101	—
River Rouge	15,947	18,147
Riverview	11,342	7,237
Rochester	7,054	5,431
Rogers City	4,275	4,722
Roseville	60,529	50,195
Royal Oak	85,499	80,612
Saginaw	91,849	98,265
St. Clair	4,770	4,538
St. Clair Shores	88,093	76,657
St. Johns	6,672	5,629
St. Joseph	11,042	11,755
Saline	4,811	2,334
Sault Ste Marie	15,136	18,722
Southfield	69,285	31,501
Southgate	33,909	29,404
South Haven	6,471	6,149
Springfield Place (U)	4,831	5,136
Sterling Heights	61,365	—
Sturgis	9,295	8,915
Swartz Creek	4,928	3,006
Taylor	70,020	—
Tecumseh	7,120	7,045
Three Rivers	7,355	7,092
Traverse City	18,048	18,432
Trenton	24,127	18,439
Troy	39,419	19,402
Walker	11,492	—
Warren	179,260	89,246
Wayne	21,054	16,034
Westland	86,749	—
Westwood (U)	9,143	—
White Lake-Seven Harbors (U)	4,504	2,748
Wolverine Lake	4,301	2,404
Wurtsmith (U)	6,932	—
Wyandotte	41,061	43,519
Wyoming	56,560	45,829
Ypsilanti	29,538	20,957
Zeeland	4,734	3,702
Minnesota	**3,805,069**	**3,413,864**
Albert Lea	19,418	17,108
Alexandria	6,973	6,713
Anoka	13,489	10,562
Apple Valley	8,502	—
Arden Hills	5,628	3,930
Austin	25,074	27,908
Bemidji	11,490	9,958
Blaine	20,640	7,570
Bloomington	81,970	50,498
Brainerd	11,667	12,898
Breckenridge	4,200	4,335
Brooklyn Center	35,173	24,356
Brooklyn Park	26,230	10,197
Burnsville	19,940	—
Chanhassen	4,879	244
Chaska	4,352	2,501
Chisholm	5,913	7,144
Cloquet	8,699	9,013
Columbia Heights	23,997	17,533
Coon Rapids	30,505	14,931
Cottage Grove	13,419	—
Crookston	8,312	8,546
Crystal	30,925	24,283
Detroit Lakes	5,797	5,633
Duluth	100,578	106,884
East Grand Forks	7,607	6,998
Eden Prairie	6,938	—
Edina	44,046	28,501
Ely	4,904	5,438
Eveleth	4,721	5,721
Fairmont	10,751	9,745
Falcon Heights	5,507	5,927
Faribault	16,595	16,926
Fergus Falls	12,443	13,733
Fridley	29,233	15,173
Glencoe	4,217	3,216
Golden Valley	24,246	14,559
Grand Rapids	7,247	7,265
Hastings	12,195	8,965
Hibbing	16,104	17,731
Hopkins	13,428	11,370
Hutchinson	8,031	6,207
International Falls	6,439	6,778
Inver Grove Heights	12,148	—
Lakeville	7,556	924
Litchfield	5,262	5,078
Little Falls	7,467	7,551
Luverne	4,703	4,249
Mankato	30,895	23,797
Maple Grove	6,275	2,213
Maplewood	25,222	18,519
Marshall	9,886	6,681
Mendota Heights	6,165	5,028
Minneapolis	434,400	482,872
Minnetonka	35,776	25,037
Montevideo	5,661	5,693
Moorhead	29,687	22,934
Morris	5,366	4,199
Mound	7,572	5,440
Mounds View	9,988	6,416
New Brighton	19,507	6,448
New Hope	23,180	3,552
New Ulm	13,051	11,114
Northfield	10,235	8,707
North Mankato	7,347	5,927
North St. Paul	11,950	8,520
Oakdale	7,304	—
Orono	6,787	5,643
Owatonna	15,341	13,409
Pipestone	5,328	5,324
Plymouth	17,593	9,576
Red Wing	10,441	10,528
Redwood Falls	4,774	4,285
Richfield	47,231	42,523
Robbinsdale	16,845	16,381
Rochester	53,766	40,663
Roseville	34,518	23,997
St. Anthony	9,239	5,084
St. Cloud	39,691	33,815
St. Louis Park	48,883	43,310
St. Paul	309,980	313,411
St. Paul Park	5,587	3,267
St. Peter	8,339	8,484
Sauk Rapids	5,051	4,038
Shakopee	6,876	5,201
Shoreview	11,034	7,157
Shorewood	4,223	3,197
South St. Paul	25,016	22,032
Spring Lake Park	6,417	3,260
Stillwater	10,191	8,310
Thief River Falls	8,618	7,151
Two Harbors	4,437	4,695
Virginia	12,450	14,034
Wadena	4,640	4,381
Waseca	6,789	5,898
West St. Paul	18,799	13,101
White Bear Lake	23,313	12,849
Willmar	12,869	10,417
Winona	26,438	24,895
Woodbury	6,184	—
Worthington	9,825	9,015
Mississippi	**2,216,912**	**2,178,141**
Aberdeen	6,157	6,450
Amory	7,236	6,474
Bay St. Louis	6,752	5,073
Biloxi	48,486	44,053
Booneville	5,895	3,480
Brookhaven	10,700	9,885
Canton	10,503	9,707
Clarksdale	21,673	21,105
Cleveland	13,327	10,172
Clinton	7,246	3,438
Columbia	7,587	7,117
Columbus	25,795	24,771
Corinth	11,581	11,453
D'Iberville (U)	7,288	3,005
Ellisville	4,643	4,592
Greenville	39,648	41,502
Greenwood	22,400	20,436
Grenada	9,944	7,914
Gulfport	40,791	30,204
Hattiesburg	38,277	34,989
Hazlehurst	4,577	3,400
Holly Springs	5,728	5,621
Indianola	8,947	6,714
Jackson	153,968	144,422
Kosciusko	7,266	6,800
Laurel	24,145	27,889
Leland	6,000	6,295
Long Beach	6,170	4,770
Louisville	6,626	5,066
McComb	11,969	12,020
Meridian	45,083	49,374
Moss Point	19,321	6,631
Natchez	19,704	23,791
New Albany	6,426	5,151
Ocean Springs	9,580	5,025
Oxford	13,846	5,283
Pascagoula	27,264	17,155
Pearl (U)	9,623	5,081
Petal (U)	6,986	4,007
Philadelphia	6,274	5,017
Picayune	10,467	7,834
Senatobia	4,247	3,259
Southaven (U)	8,931	—
Starkville	11,369	9,041
State College (U)	4,595	—
Tupelo	20,471	17,221
Vicksburg	25,478	29,143
Waynesboro	4,368	3,892
West Gulfport (U)	6,996	3,323
West Point	8,714	8,550
Winona	5,521	4,282
Yazoo City	10,796	11,236
Missouri	**4,677,399**	**4,319,813**
Afton (U)	24,067	—
Aurora	5,359	4,683
Ballwin	10,656	5,710
Bellefontaine Neighbors	13,987	13,650
Bel-Ridge	5,561	4,395
Belton	9,783	4,897
Berkeley	19,743	18,676
Blue Springs	6,779	2,555
Bolivar	4,769	3,512
Boonville	7,514	7,090
Breckenridge Hills	7,011	6,299
Brentwood	11,248	12,250
Bridgeton	19,992	7,820
Brookfield	5,491	5,694
Cape Girardeau	31,282	24,947
Carrollton	4,847	4,554
Carthage	11,035	11,264
Caruthersville	7,350	8,643
Charleston	5,131	5,911
Chillicothe	9,519	9,236
Clayton	16,222	15,245
Clinton	7,504	6,925
Columbia	58,804	36,650
Concord (U)	21,217	—

Place	POPULATION 1970	POPULATION 1960
Missouri (continued)		
Crestwood	15,398	11,106
Creve Coeur	8,967	5,122
Dellwood	7,137	4,720
De Soto	5,984	5,804
Des Peres	5,333	4,362
Dexter	6,024	5,519
Ellisville	4,681	2,732
Excelsior Springs	9,411	6,473
Farmington	6,590	5,618
Ferguson	28,915	22,149
Festus	7,530	7,021
Flat River	4,550	4,515
Florissant	65,908	38,166
Fort Leonard Wood (U)	33,799	—
Fulton	12,148	11,131
Gladstone	23,128	14,502
Glendale	6,891	7,048
Grandview	17,456	6,027
Hannibal	18,609	20,028
Harrisonville	4,928	3,510
Hazelwood	14,082	6,045
Higginsville	4,318	4,003
Independence	111,662	62,328
Jackson	5,896	4,875
Jefferson City	32,407	28,228
Jennings	19,379	19,965
Joplin	39,256	38,958
Kansas City	507,087	475,539
Kennett	9,852	9,098
Kinloch	5,629	6,501
Kirksville	15,560	13,123
Kirkwood	31,890	29,421
Ladue	10,491	9,466
Lebanon	8,616	8,220
Lee's Summit	16,230	8,267
Lemay (U)	40,115	—
Lexington	5,388	4,845
Liberty	13,679	8,909
Louisiana	4,533	4,286
Macon	5,301	4,547
Malden	5,374	5,007
Manchester	5,031	2,021
Maplewood	12,785	12,552
Marshall	11,847	9,572
Maryland Heights (U)	8,805	—
Maryville	9,970	7,807
Mexico	11,807	12,889
Moberly	12,988	13,170
Monett	5,937	5,359
Neosho	7,517	7,452
Nevada	9,736	8,416
Normandy	6,306	4,452
North Kansas City	5,183	5,657
Northwoods	4,611	4,701
O'Fallon	7,018	3,770
Olivette	9,341	8,257
Overland	24,949	22,763
Pagedale	5,571	5,106
Perryville	5,149	5,117
Pine Lawn	5,773	5,943
Poplar Bluff	16,653	15,926
Raytown	33,632	17,083
Richmond	4,948	4,604
Richmond Heights	13,802	15,622
Rock Hill	7,275	6,523
Rolla	13,245	11,132
St. Ann	18,215	12,155
St. Charles	31,834	21,189
Ste. Genevieve	4,468	4,443
St. John	8,960	7,342
St. Joseph	72,691	79,673
St. Louis	622,236	750,026
Salem	4,363	3,870
Sappington (U)	10,603	—
Sedalia	22,847	23,874
Shrewsbury	5,896	4,730
Sikeston	14,699	13,765
Spanish Lake (U)	15,647	—
Springfield	120,096	95,865
Sugar Creek	4,755	2,663
Sullivan	5,100	4,098
Trenton	6,063	6,262
Union	5,183	3,937
University City	46,309	51,249
Warrensburg	13,125	9,689
Washington	8,499	7,961
Webb City	6,811	6,740
Webster Groves	26,995	28,990
Wellston	7,050	7,979
West Plains	6,893	5,836
Whiteman (U)	5,040	—
Woodson Terrace	5,936	6,048
Montana	**694,409**	**674,767**
Anaconda	9,771	12,054
Billings	61,581	52,851
Bozeman	18,670	13,361
Butte	23,368	27,877
Deer Lodge	4,306	4,681
Dillon	4,548	3,690

Place	POPULATION 1970	POPULATION 1960
Floral Park (U)	5,113	4,079
Glasgow	4,700	6,398
Glendive	6,305	7,058
Great Falls	60,091	55,244
Havre	10,558	10,740
Helena	22,730	20,227
Kalispell	10,526	10,151
Laurel	4,454	4,601
Lewistown	6,437	7,408
Livingston	6,883	8,229
Malmstrom (U)	8,374	—
Miles City	9,023	9,665
Missoula	29,497	27,090
Missoula South (U)	4,886	—
Missoula West (U)	9,148	—
Sidney	4,543	4,564
Silver Bow Park (U)	5,524	4,798
Nebraska	**1,483,791**	**1,411,330**
Alliance	6,862	7,845
Beatrice	12,389	12,132
Bellevue	19,449	8,831
Blair	6,106	4,931
Chadron	5,853	5,079
Columbus	15,471	12,476
Cozad	4,219	3,184
Crete	4,444	3,546
Fairbury	5,265	5,572
Falls City	5,444	5,598
Fremont	22,962	19,698
Gering	5,639	4,585
Grand Island	31,269	25,742
Hastings	23,580	21,412
Holdrege	5,635	5,226
Kearney	19,181	14,210
La Vista	4,807	—
Lexington	5,618	5,572
Lincoln	149,518	128,521
McCook	8,285	8,301
Millard	7,460	1,014
Nebraska City	7,441	7,252
Norfolk	16,607	13,640
North Platte	19,447	17,184
Offutt East (U)	5,195	—
Offutt West (U)	8,445	—
Ogallala	4,976	4,250
Omaha	347,328	301,598
Papillion	5,606	2,235
Plattsmouth	6,371	6,244
Ralston	4,265	2,977
Scottsbluff	14,507	13,377
Seward	5,294	4,208
Sidney	6,403	8,004
South Sioux City	7,920	7,200
Wayne	5,379	4,217
Nevada	**488,738**	**285,278**
Boulder City	5,223	4,059
Carson City	15,468	5,163
East Las Vegas (U)	6,501	—
Elko	7,621	6,298
Henderson	16,395	12,525
Las Vegas	125,787	64,405
Nellis (U)	6,449	—
North Las Vegas	36,216	18,422
Paradise (U)	24,477	—
Reno	72,863	51,470
Sparks	24,187	16,618
Sunrise Manor (U)	10,886	—
Vegas Creek (U)	8,970	—
Winchester (U)	13,981	—
New Hampshire	**737,681**	**606,921**
Berlin	15,256	17,821
Claremont	14,221	13,563
Concord	30,022	28,991
Derry (U)	6,090	—
Dover	20,850	19,131
Durham (U)	7,221	4,688
Exeter (U)	6,439	5,896
Franklin	7,292	6,742
Hampton (U)	5,407	3,281
Hanover (U)	6,147	5,649
Keene	20,467	17,562
Laconia	14,888	15,288
Lebanon	9,725	9,299
Manchester	87,754	88,282
Milford (U)	4,997	3,916
Nashua	55,820	39,096
Portsmouth	25,717	26,900
Rochester	17,938	15,927
Somersworth	9,026	8,529
Suncook (U)	4,280	2,318
New Jersey	**7,168,164**	**6,066,782**
Absecon	6,094	4,320
Allendale	6,240	4,092
Asbury Park	16,533	17,366
Atlantic City	47,859	59,544
Atlantic Highlands	5,102	4,119
Audubon	10,802	10,440
Barrington	8,409	7,943
Bayonne	72,743	74,215

Place	POPULATION 1970	POPULATION 1960
Beachwood	4,390	2,765
Belleville	34,643	35,005
Bellmawr	15,618	11,853
Belmar	5,782	5,190
Bergenfield	33,131	27,203
Berlin	4,997	3,578
Bernardsville	6,652	5,515
Bloomfield	52,029	51,867
Bloomingdale	7,797	5,293
Bogota	8,125	7,965
Boonton	9,261	7,981
Bordentown	4,490	4,974
Bound Brook	10,450	10,263
Bridgeton	20,435	20,966
Brigantine	6,741	4,201
Browns Mills (U)	7,144	—
Burlington	11,991	12,687
Butler	7,051	5,414
Caldwell	8,719	6,942
Camden	102,551	117,159
Candlewood (U)	5,629	—
Cape May	4,392	4,477
Carlstadt	7,947	6,042
Carteret	23,137	20,502
Chatham	9,566	9,517
Clayton	5,193	4,711
Clementon	4,492	3,766
Cliffside Park	14,387	17,642
Cliffwood-Cliffwood Beach (U)	7,056	—
Clifton	82,437	82,084
Closter	8,604	7,767
Collingswood	17,422	17,370
Cresskill	7,164	7,290
Demarest	6,262	4,231
Dover	15,039	13,034
Dumont	17,534	18,882
Dunellen	7,072	6,840
East Orange	75,471	77,259
East Paterson	22,749	19,344
East Rutherford	8,536	7,769
Eatontown	14,619	10,334
Edgewater	4,849	4,113
Egg Harbor City	4,304	4,416
Elizabeth	112,654	107,698
Emerson	8,428	6,849
Englewood	24,985	26,057
Englewood Cliffs	5,938	2,913
Fairfield	6,731	—
Fair Haven	6,142	5,678
Fair Lawn	37,975	36,421
Fairview	10,698	9,399
Fanwood	8,920	7,963
Florence-Roebling (U)	7,551	—
Florham Park	8,094	7,222
Fort Dix (U)	26,290	—
Fort Lee	30,631	21,815
Franklin	4,236	3,624
Franklin Lakes	7,550	3,316
Freehold	10,545	9,140
Garfield	30,722	29,253
Garwood	5,260	5,426
Gilford Park (U)	4,007	1,560
Glassboro	12,938	10,253
Glen Ridge	8,518	8,322
Glen Rock	13,011	12,896
Gloucester City	14,707	15,511
Guttenberg	5,754	5,118
Hackensack	35,911	30,521
Hackettstown	9,472	5,276
Haddonfield	13,118	13,201
Haddon Heights	9,365	9,260
Haledon	6,767	6,161
Hammonton	11,464	9,854
Harrington Park	4,841	3,581
Harrison	11,811	11,743
Hasbrouck Heights	13,651	13,046
Hawthorne	19,173	17,735
Highland Park	14,385	11,049
Hightstown	5,431	4,317
Hillsdale	11,768	8,734
Hoboken	45,380	48,441
Hohokus	4,348	3,988
Hopatcong	9,052	3,391
Irvington	59,743	59,379
Jamesburg	4,584	2,853
Jersey City	260,545	276,101
Keansburg	9,720	6,854
Kearny	37,585	37,472
Kendall Park (U)	7,412	—
Kenilworth	9,165	8,379
Keyport	7,205	6,440
Kinnelon	7,600	4,431
Lake Hiawatha (U)	11,389	—
Lake Mohawk (U)	6,262	4,647
Lake Parsippany (U)	7,488	—
Lakewood (U)	17,874	13,004
Lambertville	4,359	4,269
Laurence Harbor (U)	6,715	—
Leonia	8,847	8,384
Lincoln Park	9,034	6,048
Linden	41,409	39,931
Lindenwold	12,199	7,335
Linwood	6,159	3,847

Place	POPULATION 1970	1960
New Jersey (continued)		
Little Ferry	9,042	6,175
Little Silver	6,010	5,202
Lodi	25,213	23,502
Long Branch	31,774	26,228
McGuire (U)	10,933	—
Madison	16,710	15,122
Magnolia	5,893	4,199
Manasquan	4,971	4,022
Manville	13,029	10,995
Margate City	10,576	9,474
Marlton (U)	10,180	—
Matawan	9,136	5,097
Maywood	11,087	11,460
Medford Lakes	4,792	2,876
Mercerville-Hamilton Square (U)	24,465	—
Merchantville	4,425	4,075
Metuchen	16,031	14,041
Middlesex	15,038	10,520
Midland Park	8,159	7,543
Milltown	6,470	5,435
Millville	21,366	19,096
Montclair	44,043	43,129
Montvale	7,327	3,699
Moorestown-Lenola (U)	14,179	—
Morris Plains	5,540	4,703
Morristown	17,662	17,712
Mountain Lakes	4,739	4,037
Mountainside	7,520	6,325
Mount Ephraim	5,625	5,447
Neptune City	5,502	4,013
Newark	382,417	405,220
New Brunswick	41,885	40,139
New Milford	20,201	18,810
New Providence	13,796	10,243
New Shrewsbury	5,925	7,313
Newton	7,297	6,563
North Arlington	18,096	17,477
North Caldwell	6,425	4,163
Northfield	8,875	5,849
North Haledon	7,614	6,026
North Plainfield	21,796	16,993
Northvale	5,177	2,892
Norwood	4,398	2,852
Nutley	32,099	29,513
Oakhurst (U)	5,558	4,374
Oakland	14,420	9,446
Oaklyn	4,626	4,778
Ocean City	10,575	7,618
Oceanport	7,503	4,937
Old Bridge (U)	25,176	—
Oradell	8,903	7,487
Orange	32,566	35,789
Palisades Park	13,351	11,943
Palmyra	6,969	7,036
Paramus	29,495	23,238
Park Ridge	8,709	6,389
Passaic	55,124	53,963
Paterson	144,824	143,663
Paulsboro	8,084	8,121
Penns Grove	5,727	6,176
Pennsville (U)	11,014	—
Perth Amboy	38,798	38,007
Phillipsburg	17,849	18,502
Pine Hill	5,132	3,939
Pitman	10,257	8,644
Plainfield	46,862	45,330
Pleasantville	13,778	15,172
Point Pleasant	15,968	10,182
Point Pleasant Beach	4,882	3,873
Pompton Lakes	11,397	9,445
Princeton	12,311	11,890
Princeton North (U)	5,488	4,506
Prospect Park	5,176	5,201
Rahway	29,114	27,699
Ramblewood (U)	5,556	—
Ramsey	12,571	9,527
Raritan	6,691	6,137
Red Bank	12,847	12,482
Ridgefield	11,308	10,788
Ridgefield Park	14,453	12,701
Ridgewood	27,547	25,391
Ringwood	10,393	4,182
River Edge	12,850	13,264
Rockaway	6,383	5,413
Roseland	4,453	2,804
Roselle	22,585	21,032
Roselle Park	14,277	12,546
Rumson	7,421	6,405
Runnemede	10,475	8,396
Rutherford	20,802	20,473
Salem	7,648	8,941
Sayreville	32,508	22,553
Secaucus	13,228	12,154
Somerdale	6,510	4,839
Somers Point	7,919	4,504
Somerville	13,652	12,458
South Amboy	9,338	8,422
South Bound Brook	4,525	3,626
South Orange	16,971	16,175
South Plainfield	21,142	17,879
South River	15,428	13,397

Place	POPULATION 1970	1960
Spotswood	7,891	5,788
Spring Lake Heights	4,602	3,309
Stratford	9,801	4,308
Strathmore (U)	7,674	—
Summit	23,620	23,677
Tenafly	14,827	14,264
Toms River (U)	7,303	6,062
Totowa	11,580	10,897
Trenton	104,638	114,167
Union Beach	6,472	5,862
Union City	58,537	52,180
Upper Saddle River	7,949	3,570
Ventnor City	10,385	8,688
Verona	15,067	13,782
Vineland	47,399	37,685
Waldwick	12,313	10,495
Wallington	10,284	9,261
Wanaque	8,636	7,126
Washington	5,943	5,723
Watchung	4,750	3,312
West Caldwell	11,887	8,314
Westfield	33,720	31,447
West Long Branch	6,845	5,337
West New York	40,627	35,547
West Orange	43,715	39,895
West Paterson	11,692	7,602
Westville	5,170	4,951
Westwood	11,105	9,046
Wharton	5,535	5,006
White Horse-Yardville (U)	18,680	—
White Meadow Lake (U)	8,499	—
Woodbury	12,408	12,453
Woodcliff Lake	5,506	2,742
Wood-Ridge	8,311	7,964
New Mexico	**1,016,000**	**951,023**
Alamogordo	23,035	21,723
Albuquerque	243,751	201,189
Artesia	10,315	12,000
Belen	4,823	5,031
Cannon (U)	5,461	—
Carlsbad	21,297	25,541
Clovis	28,495	23,713
Deming	8,343	6,764
Espanola	4,528	1,976
Farmington	21,979	23,786
Gallup	14,596	14,089
Grants	8,768	10,274
Hobbs	26,025	26,275
Holloman (U)	8,001	—
Las Cruces	37,857	29,367
Las Vegas city	7,528	7,790
Las Vegas town	6,307	6,028
Los Alamos (U)	11,310	12,584
Lovington	8,915	9,660
North Valley (U)	10,366	—
Portales	10,554	9,695
Raton	6,962	8,146
Roswell	33,908	39,593
Sandia (U)	6,867	—
Santa Fe	41,167	33,394
Silver City	7,751	6,972
Socorro	4,687	5,271
South Valley (U)	29,389	—
Truth or Consequences	4,656	4,269
Tucumcari	7,189	8,143
New York	**18,190,740**	**16,782,304**
Albany	114,873	129,726
Albertson (U)	6,792	—
Albion	5,122	5,182
Amityville	9,857	8,318
Amsterdam	25,524	28,772
Ardsley	4,470	3,991
Arlington (U)	11,203	8,317
Auburn	34,599	35,249
Babylon	12,588	11,062
Baldwin (U)	34,525	30,204
Baldwinsville	6,298	5,985
Ballston Spa	4,968	4,991
Batavia	17,338	18,210
Bath	6,053	6,166
Bayport (U)	7,995	—
Bay Shore (U)	11,119	—
Bayville	6,147	3,962
Beacon	13,255	13,922
Bellmore (U)	18,431	12,784
Bethpage (U)	18,555	20,515
Binghamton	64,123	75,941
Blauvelt (U)	5,426	—
Bohemia (U)	8,718	—
Brentwood (U)	27,868	15,387
Briarcliff Manor	6,521	5,105
Brockport	7,878	5,256
Bronxville	6,674	6,744
Buffalo	462,768	532,759
Canandaigua	10,488	9,370
Canastota	5,033	4,896
Canton	6,398	5,046
Carle Place (U)	6,326	—
Catskill	5,317	5,825
Cedarhurst	6,941	6,954
Centereach (U)	9,427	8,524

Place	POPULATION 1970	1960
Central Islip (U)	36,369	—
Clifton Knolls (U)	5,771	—
Cobleskill	4,368	3,471
Cohoes	18,613	20,129
Cold Spring Harbor (U)	5,498	1,705
Colonie	8,701	6,992
Commack (U)	22,507	9,613
Congers (U)	5,928	—
Copiague (U)	19,578	14,081
Corning	15,792	17,085
Cortland	19,621	19,181
Croton-on-Hudson	7,523	6,812
Dansville	5,436	5,460
Deer Park (U)	31,120	16,726
Depew	22,158	13,580
De Witt (U)	10,032	—
Dix Hills (U)	9,840	—
Dobbs Ferry	10,353	9,260
Dunkirk	16,855	18,205
East Aurora	7,033	6,791
Eastchester (U)	21,330	—
East Glenville (U)	5,898	—
East Half Hollow Hills (U)	9,691	—
East Hills	8,675	7,184
East Islip (U)	6,819	—
East Massapequa (U)	15,926	14,779
East Meadow (U)	46,252	46,036
East Neck (U)	5,144	3,789
East Northport (U)	12,392	8,381
East Patchogue (U)	8,092	—
East Rochester	8,347	8,152
East Rockaway	10,323	10,721
East Syracuse	4,333	4,708
East Vestal (U)	10,472	—
Ellenville	4,482	5,003
Elmira	39,945	46,517
Elmira Heights	4,906	5,157
Elmont (U)	29,363	30,138
Elwood (U)	15,031	—
Endicott	16,556	18,775
Endwell (U)	15,999	—
Fairmount (U)	15,317	—
Fairport	6,474	5,507
Fairview (U)	8,517	8,626
Farmingdale	9,297	6,128
Fayetteville	4,996	4,311
Floral Park	18,422	17,499
Flower Hill	4,236	4,594
Franklin Square (U)	32,156	32,483
Fredonia	10,326	8,477
Freeport	40,374	34,419
Fulton	14,003	14,261
Garden City	25,373	23,948
Garden City Park (U)	7,488	—
Gardnertown (U)	4,614	—
Geneseo	5,714	3,284
Geneva	16,793	17,286
Glen Cove	25,770	23,817
Glens Falls	17,222	18,580
Gloversville	19,677	21,741
Goshen	4,342	3,906
Gouverneur	4,574	4,946
Great Neck	10,724	10,171
Great Neck Plaza	5,921	4,948
Greenlawn (U)	8,178	5,422
Half Hollow Hills (U)	12,055	—
Hamburg	10,215	9,145
Hartsdale (U)	12,226	—
Hastings-on-Hudson	9,479	8,979
Hauppauge (U)	13,957	—
Haverstraw	8,198	5,771
Hempstead	39,411	34,641
Herkimer	8,960	9,396
Herricks (U)	9,112	—
Hewlett (U)	6,796	—
Hicksville (U)	48,075	50,405
Highland Falls	4,638	4,469
Hillcrest (U)	5,357	—
Holbrook-Holtsville (U)	12,103	—
Hornell	12,144	13,907
Horseheads	7,989	7,207
Hudson	8,940	11,075
Hudson Falls	7,917	7,752
Huntington (U)	12,130	11,255
Huntington Station (U)	28,817	23,438
Ilion	9,808	10,199
Inwood (U)	8,433	10,362
Irvington	5,878	5,494
Island Park	5,396	3,846
Islip (U)	7,692	—
Ithaca	26,226	28,799
Jamestown	39,795	41,818
Jefferson Valley-Yorktown (U)	9,008	—
Jericho (U)	14,010	10,795
Johnson City	18,025	19,118
Johnstown	10,045	10,390
Kenmore	20,980	21,261
Kings Park (U)	5,555	4,949
Kings Point	5,525	5,410
Kingston	25,544	29,260
Lackawanna	28,657	29,564
Lake Carmel (U)	4,796	2,735
Lake Grove	8,133	—

Place	POPULATION 1970	1960
New York (continued)		
Lakeview (U)	5,471	—
Lancaster	13,365	12,254
Larchmont	7,203	6,789
Latham (U)	9,661	—
Lawrence	6,566	5,907
Le Roy	5,118	4,662
Levittown (U)	65,440	65,276
Liberty	4,293	4,704
Lindenhurst	28,338	20,905
Little Falls	7,629	8,935
Lockport	25,399	26,443
Locust Grove (U)	11,626	11,558
Long Beach	33,127	26,473
Loudonville (U)	9,299	—
Lynbrook	23,776	19,881
Lyons	4,496	4,673
Mahopac (U)	5,265	1,337
Malone	8,048	8,737
Malverne	10,036	9,968
Mamaroneck	18,909	17,673
Manhasset (U)	8,541	—
Manlius	4,295	1,997
Manorhaven	5,710	3,566
Massapequa (U)	26,951	32,900
Massapequa Park	22,112	19,904
Massena	14,042	15,478
Mastic Beach (U)	4,870	3,035
Mattydale (U)	8,292	—
Mechanicville	6,247	6,831
Medina	6,415	6,681
Melville (U)	5,999	—
Merrick (U)	25,904	18,789
Middletown	22,607	23,475
Mineola	21,845	20,519
Monroe	4,439	3,323
Monsey (U)	8,797	—
Monticello	5,991	5,222
Mount Kisco	8,172	6,805
Mount Vernon	72,778	76,010
Nanuet (U)	10,447	—
Nesconset (U)	10,048	1,964
Newark	11,644	12,868
Newburgh	26,219	30,979
New Cassel (U)	8,554	—
New City (U)	27,344	—
New Hyde Park	10,116	10,808
New Paltz	6,058	3,041
New Rochelle	75,385	76,812
New Windsor Center (U)	8,803	4,041
New York	7,867,760	7,781,984
Niagara Falls	85,615	102,394
Nimmonsburg-Chenango Bridge (U)	5,059	—
Niskayuna (U)	6,186	—
North Amityville (U)	11,905	—
North Babylon (U)	39,556	—
North Bellmore (U)	22,893	19,639
North Bellport (U)	5,903	—
North Great River (U)	12,080	—
North Lindenhurst (U)	11,205	—
North Massapequa (U)	23,101	—
North Merrick (U)	13,650	12,976
North New Hyde Park (U)	17,945	17,929
North Patchogue (U)	6,383	—
North Pelham	5,184	5,326
Northport	7,440	5,972
North Syracuse	8,687	7,412
North Tarrytown	8,334	8,818
North Tonawanda	36,012	34,757
North Valley Stream (U)	14,881	17,239
North Wantagh (U)	15,053	—
Norwich	8,843	9,175
Nyack	6,659	6,062
Oakdale (U)	7,334	—
Oceanside (U)	35,028	30,488
Ogdensburg	14,554	16,122
Old Bethpage (U)	7,084	—
Olean	19,169	21,868
Oneida	11,658	11,677
Oneonta	16,030	13,412
Orange Lake (U)	4,348	—
Ossining	21,659	18,662
Oswego	23,844	22,155
Owego	5,152	5,417
Patchogue	11,582	8,838
Pearl River (U)	17,146	—
Peekskill	18,881	18,737
Pelham Manor	6,673	6,114
Penn Yan	5,168	5,770
Perry	4,538	4,629
Plainedge (U)	10,759	21,973
Plainview (U)	32,195	27,710
Plattsburgh	18,715	20,172
Plattsburgh Base (U)	7,078	—
Pleasantville	7,110	5,877
Port Chester	25,803	24,960
Port Jefferson	5,515	—
Port Jefferson Station (U)	7,403	1,041
Port Jervis	8,852	9,268
Port Washington (U)	15,923	15,657
Potsdam	9,985	7,765
Poughkeepsie	32,029	38,330
Rensselaer	10,136	10,506
Riverhead (U)	7,585	5,830
Rochester	296,233	318,611
Rockville Centre	27,444	26,355
Roessleville (U)	5,476	—
Rome	50,148	51,646
Ronkonkoma (U)	7,284	4,220
Roosevelt (U)	15,008	12,883
Roslyn Heights (U)	7,140	—
Rotterdam (U)	25,153	16,871
Rye	15,869	14,225
St. James (U)	10,818	3,524
Salamanca	7,877	8,480
San Remo (U)	8,302	3,160
Saranac Lake	6,086	6,421
Saratoga Springs	18,845	16,630
Sayville (U)	11,680	—
Scarsdale	19,229	17,968
Schenectady	77,859	81,682
Scotia	8,224	7,625
Sea Cliff	5,890	5,669
Seaford (U)	17,379	14,718
Selden (U)	11,613	1,604
Seneca Falls	7,794	7,439
Setauket-South Setauket (U)	6,857	—
Shirley (U)	6,280	—
Sidney	4,789	5,157
Sloan	5,216	5,803
Solvay	8,280	8,732
Southampton	4,904	4,582
South Farmingdale (U)	20,464	16,318
South Holbrook (U)	6,700	—
South Huntington (U)	8,946	7,084
Southport (U)	8,685	—
South Stony Brook (U)	15,329	—
South Valley Stream (U)	6,595	—
South Westbury (U)	10,978	11,977
Spring Valley	18,112	6,538
Springville	4,350	3,852
Stony Brook (U)	6,391	3,548
Stony Point (U)	8,270	3,330
Suffern	8,273	5,094
Syosset (U)	9,970	—
Syracuse	197,208	216,038
Tappan (U)	7,424	—
Tarrytown	11,115	11,109
Thornwood (U)	6,874	—
Tonawanda	21,898	21,561
Troy	62,918	67,492
Tuckahoe	6,236	6,423
Tupper Lake	4,854	5,200
Uniondale (U)	22,077	20,041
Utica	91,611	100,410
Valley Cottage (U)	6,007	—
Valley Stream	40,413	38,629
Vernon Valley (U)	7,925	5,998
Vestal-Twin Orchards (U)	8,303	—
Viola (U)	5,136	—
Walden	5,277	4,851
Wantagh (U)	21,873	34,172
Wappingers Falls	5,607	4,447
Waterloo	5,418	5,098
Watertown	30,787	33,306
Watervliet	12,404	13,917
Waverly	5,261	5,950
Webster	5,037	3,060
Wellsville	5,815	5,967
West Amityville (U)	6,393	—
West Babylon (U)	12,788	—
Westbury	15,362	14,757
West Elmira (U)	5,901	5,763
West Haverstraw	8,558	5,020
West Hempstead (U)	20,375	—
West Islip (U)	16,711	—
Westmere (U)	6,364	—
West Nyack (U)	5,510	—
West Sayville (U)	7,386	—
Westvale (U)	7,253	—
White Plains	50,220	50,485
Whitesboro	4,805	4,784
Williamsville	6,835	6,316
Williston Park	9,154	8,255
Woodmere (U)	19,831	14,011
Wyandanch (U)	14,906	—
Yaphank (U)	5,460	—
Yonkers	204,370	190,634
Yorktown Heights (U)	6,805	2,478
North Carolina	**5,082,059**	**4,556,155**
Ahoskie	5,105	4,583
Albemarle	11,126	12,261
Archdale	6,103	1,520
Asheboro	10,797	9,449
Asheville	57,681	60,192
Balfours (U)	4,836	3,805
Belmont	4,814	5,007
Bessemer City	5,217	4,017
Boone	8,754	3,686
Brevard	5,243	4,857
Burlington	35,930	33,199
Camp Lejeune (U)	34,549	—
Canton	5,158	5,068
Cary	7,430	3,356
Chapel Hill	25,537	12,573
Charlotte	241,178	201,564
Cherry Point (U)	12,029	—
Cherryville	5,258	3,607
Clinton	7,157	7,461
Concord	18,464	17,799
Dunn	8,302	7,566
Durham	95,438	78,302
Eden	15,871	—
Edenton	4,766	4,458
Elizabeth City	14,069	14,062
Farmville	4,424	3,997
Fayetteville	53,510	47,106
Forest City	7,179	6,556
Fort Bragg (U)	46,995	—
Garner	4,923	3,451
Gastonia	47,142	37,276
Goldsboro	26,810	28,873
Graham	8,172	7,723
Greensboro	144,076	119,574
Greenville	29,063	22,860
Hamlet	4,627	4,460
Havelock	5,283	2,433
Henderson	13,896	12,740
Hendersonville	6,443	5,911
Hickory	20,569	19,328
High Point	63,204	60,685
Jacksonville	16,021	13,491
Kannapolis (U)	36,293	34,647
Kernersville	4,815	2,942
Kings Mountain	8,465	8,008
Kinston	22,309	24,819
Laurinburg	8,859	8,242
Lenoir	14,705	10,257
Lexington	17,205	16,093
Lincolnton	5,293	5,699
Lumberton	16,961	15,305
Monroe	11,282	10,882
Mooresville	8,808	6,918
Morehead City	5,233	5,583
Morganton	13,625	9,186
Mount Airy	7,325	7,055
Mount Holly	5,107	4,037
Mount Olive	4,914	4,673
New Bern	14,660	15,717
New River-Gieger (U)	8,699	—
Newton	7,857	6,658
North Belmont (U)	10,759	8,328
Oxford	7,178	6,978
Plymouth	4,774	4,666
Raleigh	121,577	93,931
Reidsville	13,636	14,267
Roanoke Rapids	13,508	13,320
Rockingham	5,852	5,512
Rocky Mount	34,284	32,147
Roxboro	5,370	5,147
Salisbury	22,515	21,297
Sanford	11,716	12,253
Selma	4,356	3,102
Seymour-Johnson (U)	8,172	—
Shelby	16,328	17,698
Siler City	4,689	4,455
Smithfield	6,677	6,117
Southern Pines	5,937	5,198
Statesville	19,996	19,844
Tarboro	9,425	8,411
Thomasville	15,230	15,190
Washington	8,961	9,939
Waynesville	6,488	6,159
West Concord (U)	5,347	5,510
Williamston	6,570	6,924
Wilmington	46,169	44,013
Wilson	29,347	28,753
Winston-Salem	132,913	111,135
North Dakota	**617,761**	**632,446**
Bismarck	34,703	27,670
Devils Lake	7,078	6,299
Dickinson	12,405	9,971
Fargo	53,365	46,662
Grafton	5,946	5,885
Grand Forks	39,008	34,451
Grand Forks Base (U)	10,474	—
Jamestown	15,385	15,163
Mandan	11,093	10,525
Minot	32,290	30,604
Minot Base (U)	12,077	—
Valley City	7,843	7,809
Wahpeton	7,076	5,876
West Fargo	5,161	3,328
Williston	11,280	11,866
Ohio	**10,652,017**	**9,706,397**
Ada	5,309	3,918
Akron	275,425	290,351
Alliance	26,547	28,362
Amberley	5,574	2,951
Amherst	9,902	6,750
Ashland	19,872	17,419
Ashtabula	24,313	24,559
Athens	23,310	16,470
Aurora	6,549	4,049
Austintown (U)	29,393	—

Place	POPULATION 1970	1960
Ohio (continued)		
Avon	7,214	6,002
Avondale (U)	5,195	—
Avon Lake	12,261	9,403
Barberton	33,052	33,805
Barnesville	4,292	4,425
Bay Village	18,163	14,489
Beachwood	9,631	6,089
Bedford	17,552	15,223
Bedford Heights	13,063	5,275
Bellaire	9,655	11,502
Bellefontaine	11,255	11,424
Bellevue	8,604	8,286
Belpre	7,189	5,418
Berea	22,396	16,592
Bexley	14,888	14,319
Blacklick Estates (U)	8,351	—
Blue Ash	8,324	8,341
Boardman (U)	30,852	—
Bowling Green	21,760	13,574
Brecksville	9,137	5,435
Bridgetown (U)	13,352	—
Broadview Heights	11,463	6,209
Brooklyn	13,142	10,733
Brook Park	30,774	12,856
Brookville	4,403	3,184
Brunswick	15,852	11,725
Bryan	7,008	7,361
Bucyrus	13,111	12,276
Cambridge	13,656	14,562
Campbell	12,577	13,406
Canfield	4,997	3,252
Canton	110,053	113,631
Celina	7,779	7,659
Centerville	10,333	3,490
Chagrin Falls	4,848	3,458
Cheviot	11,135	10,701
Chillicothe	24,842	24,957
Churchill (U)	7,457	—
Cincinnati	452,524	502,550
Circleville	11,687	11,059
Cleveland	750,903	876,050
Cleveland Heights	60,767	61,813
Clyde	5,503	4,826
Columbiana	4,959	4,164
Columbus	539,677	471,316
Conneaut	14,552	10,557
Coshocton	13,747	13,106
Covedale (U)	6,639	—
Crestline	5,947	5,521
Crystal Lakes (U)	5,851	1,569
Cuyahoga Falls	49,678	47,922
Dayton	243,601	262,332
Deer Park	7,415	8,423
Defiance	16,281	14,553
Delaware	15,008	13,282
Delphos	7,608	6,961
Dover	11,516	11,300
East Cleveland	39,600	37,991
Eastlake	19,690	12,467
East Liverpool	20,020	22,306
East Liverpool North (U)	6,223	—
East Palestine	5,604	5,232
Eaton	6,020	5,034
Elyria	53,427	43,782
Englewood	7,885	1,515
Euclid	71,552	62,998
Fairborn	32,267	19,453
Fairfield	14,680	9,734
Fairlawn	6,102	—
Fairview Park	21,681	14,624
Findlay	35,800	30,344
Forest Park	15,139	—
Fort McKinley (U)	11,536	—
Fostoria	16,037	15,732
Franklin	10,075	7,917
Fremont	18,490	18,767
Gahanna	12,400	2,717
Galion	13,123	12,650
Gallipolis	7,490	8,775
Garfield Heights	41,417	38,455
Geneva	6,449	5,677
Girard	14,119	12,997
Golf Manor	5,170	4,648
Grandview Heights	8,460	8,270
Greenfield	4,780	5,422
Greenhills	6,092	5,407
Greenville	12,380	10,585
Grove City	13,911	8,107
Hamilton	67,865	72,354
Harrison	4,408	3,878
Heath	6,768	2,426
Highland Heights	5,926	2,929
Hilliard	8,369	5,633
Hillsboro	5,584	5,474
Hubbard	8,583	7,137
Huber Heights (U)	18,943	—
Huron	6,896	5,197
Independence	7,034	6,868
Indian Hill	5,651	4,526
Ironton	15,030	15,745
Jackson	6,843	6,980
Kent	28,183	17,836

Place	POPULATION 1970	1960
Kenton	8,315	8,747
Kenwood (U)	15,789	—
Kettering	69,599	54,462
Kirtland	5,530	—
Knollwood (U)	5,513	—
Lakewood	70,173	66,154
Lancaster	32,911	29,916
Lebanon	7,934	5,993
Lima	53,734	51,037
Lincoln Heights	6,099	7,798
Lincoln Village (U)	11,215	—
Lockbourne Base (U)	5,623	—
Lockland	5,288	5,292
Logan	6,269	6,417
London	6,481	6,379
Lorain	78,185	68,932
Louisville	6,298	5,116
Loveland	7,144	5,008
Lyndhurst	19,749	16,805
Macedonia	6,375	—
Madeira	6,713	6,744
Madison North (U)	6,882	—
Mansfield	55,047	47,325
Maple Heights	34,093	31,667
Mariemont	4,540	4,120
Marietta	16,861	16,847
Marion	38,646	37,079
Martins Ferry	10,757	11,919
Marysville	5,744	4,952
Mason	5,677	4,727
Massillon	32,539	31,236
Maumee	15,937	12,063
Mayfield Heights	22,139	13,478
Medina	10,913	8,235
Mentor	36,912	4,354
Mentor-on-the-Lake	6,517	3,290
Miamisburg	14,797	9,893
Middleburg Heights	12,367	7,282
Middletown	48,767	42,115
Milford	4,828	4,131
Minerva	4,359	3,833
Mingo Junction	5,278	4,987
Montgomery	5,683	3,075
Moraine	4,898	2,262
Mount Healthy	7,446	6,553
Mount Vernon	13,373	13,284
Napoleon	7,791	6,739
Nelsonville	4,812	4,834
Newark	41,836	41,790
New Carlisle	6,112	4,107
New Lebanon	4,248	1,459
New Lexington	4,921	4,514
New Philadelphia	15,184	14,241
Newton Falls	5,378	5,038
Niles	21,581	19,545
North Canton	15,228	7,727
North College Hill	12,363	12,035
North Olmsted	34,861	16,290
Northridge (U)	10,084	—
North Ridgeville	13,152	8,057
North Royalton	12,807	9,290
Northwood	4,222	—
Norton	12,308	—
Norwalk	13,386	12,900
Norwood	30,420	34,580
Oakwood	10,095	10,493
Oberlin	8,761	8,198
Ontario	4,345	3,049
Oregon	16,563	13,319
Orrville	7,408	6,511
Ottawa Hills	4,270	3,870
Overlook-Page Manor (U)	19,596	—
Oxford	15,868	7,828
Painesville	16,536	16,116
Painesville Southwest (U)	5,461	—
Parma	100,216	82,845
Parma Heights	27,192	18,100
Pepper Pike	5,933	3,217
Perrysburg	7,693	5,519
Piqua	20,741	19,219
Port Clinton	7,202	6,870
Portsmouth	27,633	33,637
Ravenna	11,780	10,918
Reading	14,303	12,832
Reynoldsburg	13,921	7,793
Richmond Heights	9,220	5,068
Rittman	6,308	5,410
Rocky River	22,958	18,097
Rossford	5,302	4,406
St. Bernard	6,080	6,778
St. Clairsville	4,754	3,865
St. Marys	7,699	7,737
Salem	14,186	13,854
Sandusky	32,674	31,989
Sandusky South (U)	8,501	4,724
Sebring	4,954	4,439
Seven Hills	12,700	5,708
Shadyside	5,070	5,028
Shaker Heights	36,306	36,460
Sharonville	10,985	3,890
Sheffield Lake	8,734	6,884
Shelby	9,847	9,106
Shiloh (U)	11,368	—

Place	POPULATION 1970	1960
Sidney	16,332	14,663
Silverton	6,588	6,682
Solon	11,519	6,333
South Euclid	29,579	27,569
Springdale	8,127	3,556
Springfield	81,926	82,723
Steubenville	30,771	32,495
Stow	19,847	12,194
Streetsboro	7,966	—
Strongsville	15,182	8,504
Struthers	15,343	15,631
Sylvania	12,031	5,187
Tallmadge	15,274	10,246
Tiffin	21,596	21,478
Tipp City	5,090	4,267
Toledo	383,818	318,003
Toronto	7,705	7,780
Trenton	5,278	3,064
Trotwood	6,997	4,992
Troy	17,186	13,685
Twinsburg	6,432	4,098
Uhrichsville	5,731	6,201
University Heights	17,055	16,641
Upper Arlington	38,630	28,486
Upper Sandusky	5,645	4,941
Urbana	11,237	10,461
Vandalia	10,796	6,342
Van Wert	11,320	11,323
Vermilion	9,872	4,785
Wadsworth	13,142	10,635
Wapakoneta	7,324	6,756
Warren	63,494	59,648
Warrensville Heights	18,925	10,609
Washington	12,495	12,388
Wauseon	4,932	4,311
Waverly	4,858	3,830
Wellston	5,410	5,728
Wellsville	5,891	7,117
West Carrollton	10,748	4,749
Westerville	12,530	7,011
Westlake	15,689	12,906
Whitehall	25,263	20,818
Wickliffe	21,354	15,760
Willard	5,510	5,457
Willoughby	18,634	15,058
Willoughby Hills	5,247	4,241
Willowick	21,237	18,749
Wilmington	10,051	8,915
Wintersville	4,921	3,597
Wooster	18,703	17,046
Worthington	15,326	9,239
Wright-Patterson (U)	10,151	—
Wyoming	9,089	7,736
Xenia	25,373	20,445
Yellow Springs	4,624	4,167
Youngstown	139,788	166,689
Zanesville	33,045	39,077
Oklahoma	**2,559,253**	**2,328,284**
Ada	14,859	14,347
Altus	23,302	21,225
Alva	7,440	6,258
Anadarko	6,682	6,299
Ardmore	20,881	20,184
Bartlesville	29,683	27,893
Bethany	21,785	12,342
Blackwell	8,645	9,588
Bristow	4,653	4,795
Broken Arrow	11,787	5,928
Chickasha	14,194	14,866
Choctaw	4,750	623
Claremore	9,084	6,639
Clinton	8,513	9,617
Cushing	7,529	8,619
Del City	27,133	12,934
Duncan	19,718	20,009
Durant	11,118	10,467
Edmond	16,633	8,577
Elk City	7,323	8,196
El Reno	14,510	11,015
Enid	44,008	38,859
Fort Sill (U)	21,217	—
Frederick	6,132	5,879
Guthrie	9,575	9,502
Guymon	7,674	5,760
Henryetta	6,430	6,551
Hobart	4,638	5,132
Holdenville	5,181	5,712
Hugo	6,585	6,287
Idabel	5,946	4,967
Lawton	74,470	61,697
McAlester	18,802	17,419
Miami	13,880	12,869
Midwest City	48,114	36,058
Moore	18,761	1,783
Muskogee	37,331	38,059
Nichols Hills	4,478	4,897
Norman	52,117	33,412
Oklahoma City	366,481	324,253
Okmulgee	15,180	15,951
Pauls Valley	5,769	6,856
Pawhuska	4,238	5,414
Perry	5,341	5,210

Place	POPULATION 1970	1960
Oklahoma (continued)		
Ponca City	25,940	24,411
Poteau	5,500	4,428
Pryor	7,057	6,476
Purcell	4,076	3,729
Sallisaw	4,888	3,351
Sand Springs	11,519	7,754
Sapulpa	15,159	14,282
Seminole	7,878	11,464
Shawnee	25,075	24,326
Stillwater	31,126	23,965
Sulphur	5,158	4,737
Tahlequah	9,254	5,840
Tecumseh	4,451	2,630
The Village	13,695	12,118
Tulsa	331,638	261,685
Vinita	5,847	6,027
Wagoner	4,959	4,469
Warr Acres	9,887	7,135
Weatherford	7,959	4,499
Wewoka	5,284	5,954
Woodward	8,710	7,747
Yukon	8,411	3,076
Oregon	**2,091,385**	**1,768,687**
Albany	18,181	12,926
Altamont (U)	15,746	10,811
Ashland	12,342	9,119
Astoria	10,244	11,239
Baker	9,354	9,986
Beaverton	18,577	5,937
Bend	13,710	11,936
City of the Dalles	10,423	10,493
Coos Bay	13,466	7,084
Coquille	4,437	4,730
Corvallis	35,153	20,669
Cottage Grove	6,004	3,895
Dallas	6,361	5,072
Eugene	76,346	50,977
Forest Grove	8,275	5,628
Four Corners (U)	6,199	4,743
Gladstone	6,237	3,854
Grants Pass	12,455	10,118
Gresham	9,875	3,944
Hayesville (U)	5,518	4,568
Hermiston	4,893	4,402
Hillsboro	14,675	8,232
Keizer (U)	11,405	5,288
Klamath Falls	15,775	16,949
La Grande	9,645	9,014
Lake Oswego	14,573	8,906
Lebanon	6,636	5,858
McMinnville	10,125	7,656
Medford	28,454	24,425
Milwaukie	16,379	9,099
Monmouth	5,237	2,229
Newberg	6,507	4,204
Newport	5,188	5,344
North Bend	8,553	7,512
Ontario	6,523	5,101
Oregon City	9,176	7,996
Pendleton	13,197	14,434
Portland	382,619	372,676
Roseburg	14,461	11,467
St. Helens	6,212	5,022
Salem	68,296	49,142
Seaside	4,402	3,877
Silverton	4,301	3,081
Springfield	27,047	19,616
Tigard	5,302	—
West Linn	7,091	3,933
Woodburn	7,495	3,120
Pennsylvania	**11,793,909**	**11,319,366**
Abington (U)	8,594	—
Aldan	5,001	4,324
Aliquippa	22,277	26,369
Allentown	109,527	108,347
Altoona	62,900	69,407
Ambler	7,800	6,765
Ambridge	11,324	13,865
Annville (U)	4,704	—
Archbald	6,118	5,642
Ardmore (U)	5,801	—
Arnold	8,174	9,437
Ashland	4,737	5,237
Avalon	7,065	6,859
Baden	5,536	6,109
Bala Cynwyd (U)	6,483	—
Baldwin	26,729	24,489
Bangor	5,425	5,766
Beaver	6,100	6,160
Beaver Falls	14,375	16,240
Bellefonte	6,828	6,088
Bellevue	11,586	11,412
Berwick	12,274	13,353
Bethel Park	34,791	23,650
Bethlehem	72,686	75,408
Blairsville	4,411	4,930
Blakely	6,391	6,374
Bloomsburg	11,652	10,655
Boyertown	4,428	4,067
Brackenridge	4,796	5,697

Place	POPULATION 1970	1960
Braddock	8,682	12,337
Bradford	12,672	15,061
Brandywine Village (U)	11,411	—
Brentwood	13,732	13,706
Bridgeport	5,630	5,306
Bridgeville	6,717	7,112
Bristol	12,085	12,364
Brookhaven	7,370	5,280
Brookville	4,314	4,620
Brownsville	4,856	6,055
Bryn Mawr (U)	5,737	—
Butler	18,691	20,975
California	6,635	5,978
Camp Hill	9,931	8,559
Canonsburg	11,439	11,877
Carbondale	12,808	13,595
Carlisle	18,079	16,623
Carlisle Barracks (U)	4,358	—
Carnegie	10,864	11,887
Carnot-Moon (U)	13,093	—
Castle Shannon	11,899	11,836
Catasauqua	5,702	5,062
Cedarbrook-Melrose Park (U)	9,980	—
Cedar Heights (U)	6,303	—
Chambersburg	17,315	17,670
Charleroi	6,723	8,148
Chatwood (U)	7,168	3,621
Chester	56,331	63,658
Churchill	4,690	3,428
Clairton	15,051	18,389
Clarion	6,095	4,958
Clarks Summit	5,376	3,693
Clearfield	8,176	9,270
Clifton Heights	8,348	8,005
Coatesville	12,331	12,971
Collingdale	10,605	10,268
Columbia	11,237	12,075
Connellsville	11,643	12,814
Conshohocken	10,195	10,259
Coraopolis	8,435	9,643
Corry	7,435	7,744
Crafton	8,233	8,418
Danville	6,176	6,889
Darby	13,729	14,059
Dickson City	7,698	7,738
Donora	8,825	11,131
Dormont	12,856	13,098
Downingtown	7,437	5,598
Doylestown	8,270	5,917
Du Bois	10,112	10,667
Dunmore	17,300	18,917
Duquesne	11,410	15,019
Duryea	5,264	5,626
Easton	30,256	31,955
East Stroudsburg	7,894	7,674
Ebensburg	4,318	4,111
Economy	7,176	5,925
Edgewood	5,101	5,124
Edinboro	4,871	1,703
Edwardsville	5,633	5,711
Elizabethtown	8,072	6,780
Ellwood City	10,857	12,413
Emmaus	11,511	10,262
Ephrata	9,662	7,688
Erie	129,231	138,440
Etna	5,819	5,519
Exeter	4,670	4,747
Farrell	11,022	13,793
Flourtown (U)	9,149	—
Folcroft	9,610	7,013
Ford City	4,749	5,440
Forest Hills	9,561	8,796
Forty Fort	6,114	6,431
Fountain Hill	5,384	5,428
Fox Chapel	4,684	3,302
Frackville	5,445	5,654
Franklin	8,629	9,586
Franklin Park	5,310	—
Freeland	4,784	5,068
Fullerton (U)	7,908	—
General Wayne (U)	5,368	—
Gettysburg	7,275	7,960
Glassport	7,450	8,418
Glenolden	8,697	7,249
Glenside (U)	17,353	—
Greensburg	15,870	17,383
Green Tree	6,441	5,226
Greenville	8,704	8,765
Grove City	8,312	8,368
Hanover	15,623	15,538
Harrisburg	68,061	79,697
Hatboro	8,880	7,315
Hatboro West (U)	13,542	—
Hazleton	30,426	32,056
Hellertown	6,613	6,716
Hershey (U)	7,407	6,851
Highland Park (U)	5,500	—
Hollidaysburg	6,262	6,475
Homeacre-Lyndora (U)	8,415	—
Homestead	6,309	7,502
Honesdale	5,224	5,569
Hummelstown	4,723	4,474
Huntingdon	6,987	7,234

Place	POPULATION 1970	1960
Indiana	16,100	13,005
Ingram	4,902	4,730
Jeannette	15,209	16,565
Jefferson	8,512	8,280
Jefferson-Trooper (U)	13,022	—
Jenkintown	5,990	5,017
Jersey Shore	5,322	5,613
Jessup	4,948	5,456
Jim Thorpe	5,456	5,945
Johnsonburg	4,304	4,966
Johnstown	42,476	53,949
Kane	5,001	5,380
Kennett Square	4,876	4,355
Kingston	18,325	20,261
Kittanning	6,231	6,793
Kutztown	6,017	3,312
Lafayette Hills-Plymouth Meeting (U)	8,263	—
Lancaster	57,690	61,055
Lansdale	18,451	12,612
Lansdowne	14,090	12,601
Lansford	5,168	5,958
Latrobe	11,749	11,932
Laureldale	4,519	4,051
Lebanon	28,572	30,045
Lehighton	6,095	6,318
Lemoyne	4,625	4,662
Lewisburg	6,376	5,523
Lewistown	11,098	12,640
Lititz	7,072	5,987
Lock Haven	11,427	11,748
Lower Burrell	13,654	11,952
Luzerne	4,504	5,118
McChesneytown-Loyalhanna (U)	4,283	3,138
McKeesport	37,977	45,489
McKees Rocks	11,901	13,185
Mahanoy City	7,257	8,536
Manheim	5,434	4,790
Masontown	4,226	4,730
Meadville	16,573	16,671
Mechanicsburg	9,385	8,123
Media	6,444	5,803
Merion (U)	5,686	—
Middletown	9,080	11,182
Midland	5,271	6,425
Millersville	6,396	3,883
Millvale	5,815	6,624
Milton	7,723	7,972
Minersville	6,012	6,606
Monaca	7,486	8,394
Monessen	15,216	18,424
Monongahela	7,113	8,388
Monroeville	29,011	22,446
Montoursville	5,985	5,211
Moosic	4,273	4,243
Morrisville	11,309	7,790
Mount Carmel	9,317	10,760
Mount Joy	5,041	3,292
Mount Oliver	5,487	5,980
Mount Pleasant	5,895	6,107
Munhall	16,674	17,312
Nanticoke	14,632	15,601
Nanty-Glo	4,298	4,608
Narberth	5,151	5,109
Nazareth	5,815	6,209
New Brighton	7,637	8,397
New Castle	38,559	44,790
New Cumberland	9,803	9,257
New Kensington	20,312	23,485
Norristown	38,169	38,925
Northampton	8,389	8,866
North Ardmore (U)	5,856	—
North Braddock	10,838	13,204
North Hills-Ardsley (U)	13,173	—
Norwood	7,229	6,729
Oak Lane (U)	6,192	—
Oakmont	7,550	7,504
Ogontz (U)	5,463	2,254
Oil City	15,033	17,692
Old Forge	9,522	8,928
Olyphant	5,422	5,864
Oreland (U)	9,114	—
Palmerton	5,620	5,942
Palmyra	7,615	6,999
Paoli (U)	5,835	—
Parkville (U)	5,120	4,516
Pencoyd (U)	6,650	—
Penn Square-Plymouth Valley (U)	20,238	—
Penn Wynne (U)	6,038	—
Perkasie	5,451	4,650
Philadelphia	1,948,609	2,002,512
Phoenixville	14,823	13,797
Pitcairn	4,741	5,383
Pittsburgh	520,117	604,332
Pittston	11,113	12,407
Plains (U)	6,606	—
Pleasant Hills	10,409	8,573
Plum	21,932	10,241
Plymouth	9,536	10,401
Port Vue	5,862	6,635
Pottstown	25,355	26,144

Place	POPULATION 1970	1960
Pennsylvania (continued)		
Pottsville	19,715	21,659
Prospect Park	7,250	6,596
Punxsutawney	7,792	8,805
Quakertown	7,276	6,305
Reading	87,643	98,177
Red Lion	5,645	5,594
Ridgway	6,022	6,387
Ridley Park	9,025	7,387
Rochester	4,819	5,952
Roslyn (U)	18,317	—
Royersford	4,235	3,969
Rydal (U)	5,083	—
St. Clair	4,576	5,159
St. Marys	7,470	8,065
Sayre	7,473	7,917
Schuylkill Haven	6,125	6,470
Scottdale	5,818	6,244
Scranton	103,564	111,443
Selinsgrove	5,116	3,948
Sewickley	5,660	6,157
Shamokin	11,719	13,674
Sharon	22,653	25,267
Sharon Hill	7,464	7,123
Sharpsburg	5,499	6,096
Sharpsville	6,126	6,061
Shenandoah	8,287	11,073
Shillington	6,249	5,639
Shippensburg	6,536	6,138
Slatington	4,687	4,316
Slippery Rock	4,949	2,563
Somerset	6,269	6,347
Souderton	6,366	5,381
South Williamsport	7,153	6,972
Springdale	5,202	5,602
State College	33,778	22,409
Steelton	8,556	11,266
Stroudsburg	5,451	6,070
Sugar Creek	5,944	—
Sunbury	13,025	13,687
Swarthmore	6,156	5,753
Swissvale	13,821	15,089
Swoyersville	6,786	6,751
Tamaqua	9,246	10,173
Tarentum	7,379	8,232
Taylor	6,977	6,148
Throop	4,307	4,732
Titusville	7,331	8,356
Towanda	4,224	4,293
Trafford	4,383	4,330
Turtle Creek	8,308	10,607
Tyrone	7,072	7,792
Uniontown	16,282	17,942
Vandergrift	7,873	8,742
Warren	12,998	14,505
Washington	19,827	23,545
Waynesboro	10,011	10,427
Waynesburg	5,152	5,188
West Chester	19,301	15,705
West Hazleton	6,059	6,278
West Mifflin	28,070	27,289
Westmont	6,673	6,573
West Pittston	7,074	6,998
West Reading	4,578	4,938
West View	8,312	8,079
West York	5,314	5,526
Whitehall	16,551	16,075
White Oak	9,304	9,047
Wilkes-Barre	58,856	63,551
Wilkinsburg	26,780	30,066
Williamsport	37,918	41,967
Willow Grove (U)	16,494	—
Wilson	8,482	8,465
Windber	6,332	6,994
Wyomissing	7,136	5,044
Yeadon	12,136	11,610
York	50,335	54,504
Rhode Island	**949,723**	**859,488**
Barrington*	17,554	13,826
Bristol*	17,860	14,570
Central Falls	18,716	19,858
Cranston	73,037	66,766
East Greenwich*	9,577	6,100
East Providence	48,151	41,955
Johnston*	22,037	17,160
Kingston (U)	5,601	2,616
Newport	34,562	47,049
Newport East (U)	10,285	2,643
North Providence*	24,337	18,220
Pawtucket	76,984	81,001
Providence	179,213	207,498
Wakefield-Peacedale (U)	6,331	5,569
Warren*	10,523	8,750
Warwick	83,694	68,504
Westerly (U)	13,654	9,698
West Warwick*	24,323	21,414
Woonsocket	46,820	47,080
South Carolina	**2,590,516**	**2,382,594**
Abbeville	5,515	5,436
Aiken	13,436	11,243
Anderson	27,556	41,316

Place	POPULATION 1970	1960
Avondale-Moorland (U)	5,236	—
Barnwell	4,439	4,568
Beaufort	9,434	6,298
Belton	5,257	5,106
Bennettsville	7,468	6,963
Berea (U)	7,186	—
Camden	8,532	6,842
Capehart (U)	4,490	—
Cayce	9,967	8,517
Charleston	66,945	65,925
Charleston Base (U)	6,238	—
Charleston Yard (U)	13,565	—
Cheraw	5,627	5,171
Chester	7,045	6,906
Clemson	5,578	1,587
Clinton	8,138	7,937
Columbia	113,542	97,433
Conway	8,151	8,563
Darlington	6,990	6,710
Dillon	5,991	6,173
Easley	11,175	8,283
Florence	25,997	24,722
Forest Acres	6,808	3,842
Fort Mill	4,505	3,315
Gaffney	13,253	10,435
Gantt (U)	11,386	—
Georgetown	10,449	12,261
Greenville	61,208	66,188
Greenwood	21,069	16,644
Greer	10,642	8,967
Hanahan (U)	8,376	—
Hartsville	8,017	6,392
Lake City	6,247	6,059
Lancaster	9,186	7,999
Laurens	10,298	9,598
Marion	7,435	7,174
Mount Pleasant	6,155	5,116
Mullins	6,006	6,229
Myrtle Beach	8,536	7,834
Newberry	9,218	8,208
North Augusta	12,883	10,348
Orangeburg	13,252	13,852
Parris Island (U)	8,868	—
Rock Hill	33,846	29,404
St. Andrews (U)	9,202	—
Saxon (U)	4,807	3,917
Seneca	6,027	5,227
Shannontown (U)	7,491	7,064
Shaw (U)	5,819	—
Spartanburg	44,546	44,352
Sumter	24,435	23,062
Taylors (U)	6,831	1,071
Union	10,775	10,191
Wade-Hampton (U)	17,152	—
Walterboro	6,257	5,417
West Columbia	7,838	6,410
Woodruff	4,576	3,679
York	5,081	4,758
South Dakota	**665,507**	**680,514**
Aberdeen	26,476	23,073
Belle Fourche	4,236	4,087
Brookings	13,717	10,558
Ellsworth (U)	5,805	—
Hot Springs	4,434	4,943
Huron	14,299	14,180
Lead	5,420	6,211
Madison	6,315	5,420
Mitchell	13,425	12,555
Mobridge	4,545	4,391
Pierre	9,699	10,088
Rapid City	43,836	42,399
Sioux Falls	72,488	65,466
Spearfish	4,661	3,682
Sturgis	4,536	4,639
Vermillion	9,128	6,102
Watertown	13,388	14,077
Yankton	11,919	9,279
Tennessee	**3,924,164**	**3,567,089**
Alcoa	7,739	6,395
Athens	11,790	12,103
Bolivar	6,674	3,338
Bristol	20,064	17,582
Brownsville	7,011	5,424
Chattanooga	119,082	130,009
Clarksville	31,719	22,021
Cleveland	20,651	16,196
Clinton	4,794	4,943
Columbia	21,471	17,624
Cookeville	14,270	7,805
Covington	5,801	5,298
Crossville	5,381	4,668
Dayton	4,361	3,500
Dickson	5,665	5,028
Dyersburg	14,523	12,499
Eagleton Village (U)	5,345	5,068
East Ridge	21,799	19,570
Elizabethton	12,269	10,896
Erwin	4,715	3,210
Fayetteville	7,030	6,804
Fort Campbell South (U)	9,279	—
Franklin	9,404	6,977

Place	POPULATION 1970	1960
Gallatin	13,093	7,901
Greater Hendersonville (U)	11,996	—
Greeneville	13,722	11,759
Harriman	8,734	5,931
Hixson (U)	6,188	—
Humboldt	10,066	8,482
Jackson	39,996	34,376
Jefferson City	5,124	4,550
Johnson City	33,770	31,187
Kingsport	31,938	26,314
Kingsport North (U)	13,118	—
Knoxville	174,587	111,827
La Follette	6,902	6,204
Lake Hills-Murray Hills (U)	7,806	—
Lawrenceburg	8,889	8,042
Lebanon	12,492	10,512
Lenoir City	5,324	4,979
Lewisburg	7,207	6,338
Lexington	4,955	3,943
McKenzie	4,873	3,780
McMinnville	10,662	9,013
Manchester	6,208	3,930
Martin	7,781	4,750
Maryville	13,808	10,348
Memphis	623,530	497,524
Milan	7,313	5,208
Millington	21,106	6,059
Morristown	20,318	21,267
Murfreesboro	26,360	18,991
Nashville-Davidson	447,877	170,874
Newport	7,328	6,448
Oak Ridge	28,319	27,169
Paris	9,892	9,325
Pulaski	6,989	6,616
Red Bank	12,715	10,777
Ripley	4,794	3,782
Rockwood	5,259	5,345
Savannah	5,576	4,315
Shelbyville	12,262	10,466
Signal Mountain	4,839	3,413
Smyrna	5,698	3,612
Soddy-Daisy	7,569	—
South Cleveland (U)	5,070	1,512
Sparta	4,930	4,510
Springfield	9,720	9,221
Sweetwater	4,340	4,145
Trenton	4,226	4,225
Tullahoma	15,311	12,242
Union City	11,925	8,837
Winchester	5,211	4,760
Texas	**11,196,730**	**9,579,677**
Abilene	89,653	90,368
Alamo	4,291	4,121
Alamo Heights	6,933	7,552
Alice	20,121	20,861
Alpine	5,971	4,740
Alvin	10,671	5,643
Amarillo	127,010	137,969
Andrews	8,625	11,135
Angleton	9,770	7,312
Aransas Pass	5,813	6,956
Arlington	90,643	44,775
Athens	9,582	7,086
Atlanta	5,007	4,076
Austin	251,808	186,545
Azle	4,493	2,969
Balch Springs	10,464	6,821
Ballinger	4,203	5,043
Bay City	11,733	11,656
Baytown	43,980	28,159
Beaumont	115,919	119,175
Bedford	10,049	2,706
Beeville	13,506	13,811
Bellaire	19,009	19,872
Bellmead	7,698	5,127
Belton	8,696	8,163
Benbrook	8,169	3,254
Biggs (U)	4,226	—
Big Spring	28,735	31,230
Bonham	7,698	7,357
Borger	14,195	20,911
Bowie	5,185	4,566
Brady	5,557	5,338
Breckenridge	5,944	6,273
Brenham	8,922	7,740
Bridge City (U)	8,164	4,677
Brownfield	9,647	10,286
Brownsville	52,522	48,040
Brownwood	17,368	16,974
Bryan	33,719	27,542
Burkburnett	9,230	7,621
Burleson	7,713	2,345
Cameron	5,546	5,640
Canyon	8,333	5,864
Carrizo Springs	5,374	5,699
Carrollton	13,855	4,242
Carthage	5,392	5,262
Castle Hills	5,311	2,622
Center	4,989	4,510
Childress	5,408	6,399
Cleburne	16,015	15,381
Cleveland	5,627	5,838

Place	POPULATION 1970	POPULATION 1960
Texas (continued)		
Clute City	6,023	4,501
Coleman	5,608	6,371
College Station	17,676	11,396
Colorado City	5,227	6,457
Commerce	9,534	5,789
Conroe	11,969	9,192
Copperas Cove	10,818	4,567
Corpus Christi	204,525	167,690
Corsicana	19,972	20,344
Crockett	6,616	5,356
Crystal City	8,104	9,101
Cuero	6,956	7,338
Dalhart	5,705	5,160
Dallas	844,401	679,684
Deer Park	12,773	4,865
Del Rio	21,330	18,612
Denison	24,923	22,748
Denton	39,874	26,844
De Soto	6,617	1,969
Dickinson (U)	10,776	4,715
Dimmitt	4,327	2,935
Donna	7,365	7,522
Dumas	9,771	8,477
Duncanville	14,105	3,774
Eagle Pass	15,364	12,094
Edinburg	17,163	18,706
Edna	5,332	5,038
El Campo	8,563	7,700
El Paso	322,261	276,687
Elsa	4,400	3,847
Ennis	11,046	9,347
Euless	19,316	4,263
Everman	4,570	1,076
Falfurrias	6,355	6,515
Farmers Branch	27,492	13,441
Forest Hill	8,236	3,221
Fort Bliss (U)	13,288	—
Fort Hood (U)	32,597	—
Fort Sam Houston (U)	10,553	—
Fort Stockton	8,283	6,373
Fort Worth	393,476	356,268
Fredericksburg	5,326	4,629
Freeport	11,997	11,619
Friendswood	5,675	—
Gainesville	13,830	13,083
Galena Park	10,479	10,852
Galveston	61,809	67,175
Garland	81,437	38,501
Gatesville	4,683	4,626
Georgetown	6,395	5,218
Gladewater	5,574	5,742
Gonzales	5,854	5,829
Graham	7,477	8,505
Grand Prairie	50,904	30,386
Grapevine	7,023	2,821
Greenville	22,043	19,087
Groves	18,067	17,304
Haltom City	28,127	23,133
Harker Heights	4,216	—
Harlingen	33,503	41,207
Hearne	4,982	5,072
Henderson	10,187	9,666
Hereford	13,414	7,652
Highland Park	10,133	10,411
Hillsboro	7,224	7,402
Hitchcock	5,565	5,216
Hondo	5,487	4,992
Houston	1,232,802	938,219
Huntsville	17,610	11,999
Hurst	27,215	10,165
Iowa Park	5,796	3,295
Irving	97,260	45,985
Jacinto City	9,563	9,547
Jacksonville	9,734	9,590
Jasper	6,251	4,889
Kermit	7,884	10,465
Kerrville	12,672	8,901
Kilgore	9,495	10,092
Killeen	35,507	23,377
Kingsville	28,711	25,297
Kleberg	4,768	3,572
Lackland (U)	19,141	—
Lake Jackson	13,376	9,651
Lake Worth Village	4,958	3,833
La Marque	16,131	13,969
Lamesa	11,559	12,438
Lampasas	5,922	5,061
Lancaster	10,522	7,501
La Porte	7,149	4,512
Laredo	69,024	60,678
League City	10,818	—
Levelland	11,445	10,153
Lewisville	9,264	3,956
Liberty	5,591	6,127
Littlefield	6,738	7,236
Lockhart	6,489	6,084
Longview	45,547	40,050
Lubbock	149,101	128,691
Lufkin	23,049	17,641
Luling	4,719	4,412
McAllen	37,636	32,728
McGregor	4,365	4,642
McKinney	15,193	13,763
Marlin	6,351	6,918
Marshall	22,937	23,846
Mathis	5,351	6,075
Mercedes	9,355	10,943
Mesquite	55,131	27,526
Mexia	5,943	6,121
Midland	59,463	62,625
Mineral Wells	18,411	11,053
Mission	13,043	14,081
Monahans	8,333	8,567
Mount Pleasant	8,877	8,027
Muleshoe	4,525	3,871
Nacogdoches	22,544	12,674
Navasota	5,111	4,937
Nederland	16,810	12,036
New Braunfels	17,859	15,631
North Richland Hills	16,514	8,662
Odessa	78,380	80,338
Orange	24,457	25,605
Palestine	14,525	13,974
Pampa	21,726	24,664
Paris	23,441	20,977
Pasadena	89,277	58,737
Pearland	6,444	1,497
Pearsall	5,545	4,957
Pecos	12,682	12,728
Perryton	7,810	7,903
Pharr	15,829	14,106
Plainview	19,096	18,735
Plano	17,872	3,695
Pleasanton	5,407	3,467
Port Arthur	57,371	66,676
Portland	7,302	2,538
Port Lavaca	10,491	8,864
Port Neches	10,894	8,696
Randolph (U)	5,329	—
Raymondville	7,987	9,385
Refugio	4,340	4,944
Richardson	48,582	16,810
Richland Hills	8,865	7,804
Richmond	5,777	3,668
Rio Grande City (U)	5,676	5,835
River Oaks	8,193	8,444
Robstown	11,217	10,266
Rockdale	4,655	4,481
Rosenberg	12,098	9,698
Rusk	4,914	4,900
San Angelo	63,884	58,815
San Antonio	654,153	587,718
San Benito	15,176	16,422
San Diego	4,490	4,351
San Juan	5,070	4,371
San Marcos	18,860	12,713
Sansom Park Village	4,771	4,175
Seagoville	4,390	3,745
Seguin	15,934	14,299
Seminole	5,007	5,737
Sherman	29,061	24,988
Silsbee	7,271	6,277
Sinton	5,563	6,008
Slaton	6,583	6,568
Snyder	11,171	13,850
South Houston	11,527	7,523
Stamford	4,558	5,259
Stephenville	9,277	7,359
Sulphur Springs	10,642	9,160
Sweetwater	12,020	13,914
Taylor	9,616	9,434
Temple	33,431	30,419
Terrell	14,182	13,803
Terrell Hills	5,225	5,572
Texarkana	30,497	30,218
Texas City	38,908	32,065
Tulia	5,294	4,410
Tyler	57,770	51,230
Universal City	7,613	—
University Park	23,498	23,202
Uvalde	10,764	10,293
Vernon	11,454	12,141
Victoria	41,349	33,047
Vidor	9,738	—
Waco	95,326	97,808
Waxahachie	13,452	12,749
Weatherford	11,750	9,759
Weslaco	15,313	15,649
West Orange	4,787	4,848
West University Place	13,317	14,628
Westworth	4,578	3,321
Wharton	7,881	5,734
White Settlement	13,449	11,513
Wichita Falls	97,564	101,724
Woodway	4,819	1,244
Yoakum	5,755	5,761
Utah	**1,059,273**	**890,627**
American Fork	7,713	6,373
Bountiful	27,853	17,039
Brigham City	14,007	11,728
Cedar City	8,946	7,543
Clearfield	13,316	8,833
Cottonwood (U)	8,431	—
East Millcreek (U)	26,579	—
Granger-Hunter (U)	9,029	—
Granite Park (U)	9,573	—
Holladay (U)	23,014	—
Kaysville	6,192	3,608
Kearns (U)	17,071	17,172
Layton	13,603	9,027
Lehi	4,659	4,377
Logan	22,333	18,731
Magna (U)	5,509	6,442
Midvale	7,840	5,802
Moab	4,793	4,682
Mount Olympus (U)	5,909	—
Murray	21,206	16,806
North Ogden	5,257	2,621
Ogden	69,478	70,197
Orem	25,729	18,394
Payson	4,501	4,237
Pleasant Grove	5,327	4,772
Price	6,218	6,802
Provo	53,131	36,047
Richfield	4,471	4,412
Roy	14,356	9,239
St. George	7,097	5,130
Salt Lake City	175,885	189,454
Sandy City	6,438	3,322
South Ogden	9,991	7,405
South Salt Lake	7,810	9,520
Spanish Fork	7,284	6,472
Springville	8,790	7,913
Sunset	6,268	4,235
Tooele	12,539	9,133
Washington Terrace	7,241	6,441
West Jordan	4,221	3,009
White City (U)	6,402	—
Vermont	**444,330**	**389,881**
Barre	10,209	10,387
Bennington	7,950	8,023
Brattleboro (U)	9,055	9,315
Burlington	38,633	35,531
Essex Junction	6,511	5,340
Montpelier	8,609	8,782
Newport	4,664	5,019
Rutland	19,293	18,325
St. Albans	8,082	8,806
Springfield (U)	5,632	6,600
Williston Road Section (U)	5,376	3,259
Winooski	7,309	7,420
Virginia	**4,648,494**	**3,966,949**
Abingdon	4,376	4,758
Alexandria	110,938	91,023
Annandale (U)	27,428	—
Arlington (U)	174,284	—
Bailey's Crossroads (U)	7,295	—
Bedford	6,011	5,921
Belleview (U)	8,299	—
Blacksburg	9,384	7,070
Bluefield	5,286	4,235
Bon Air (U)	10,562	—
Bristol	14,857	17,144
Buena Vista	6,425	6,300
Charlottesville	38,880	29,427
Chesapeake	89,580	—
Chester (U)	5,556	1,290
Christiansburg	7,857	3,653
Clifton Forge	5,501	5,268
Collinsville (U)	6,015	3,586
Colonial Heights	15,097	9,587
Covington	10,060	11,062
Culpeper	6,056	2,412
Dale City (U)	13,857	—
Danville	46,391	46,577
Emporia	5,300	5,535
Fairfax	21,970	13,585
Falls Church	10,772	10,192
Farmville	4,331	4,293
Fort Belvoir (U)	14,591	—
Fort Hunt (U)	10,415	—
Fort Lee (U)	12,435	—
Franklin	6,880	7,264
Fredericksburg	14,450	13,639
Front Royal	8,211	7,949
Galax	6,278	5,254
Groveton (U)	11,750	—
Hampton	120,779	89,258
Harrisonburg	14,605	11,916
Herndon	4,301	1,960
Highland Springs (U)	7,345	—
Hopewell	23,471	17,895
Huntington (U)	5,559	—
Jefferson (U)	25,432	—
Lake Barcroft (U)	11,605	—
Lakeside (U)	11,137	—
Leesburg	4,821	2,869
Lexington	7,597	7,537
Lincolnia (U)	10,355	—
Long Branch (U)	21,634	—
Lynchburg	54,083	54,790
McLean (U)	17,698	—
Manassas	9,164	3,555
Manassas Park	6,844	5,342

Place	POPULATION 1970	1960
Virginia (continued)		
Mantua (U)	6,911	—
Marion	8,158	8,385
Martinsville	19,653	18,798
Mechanicsville (U)	5,189	—
Newport News	138,177	113,662
Norfolk	307,951	304,869
North Springfield (U)	8,631	—
Petersburg	36,103	36,750
Poquoson	5,441	4,278
Portsmouth	110,963	114,773
Pulaski	10,279	10,469
Quantico Station (U)	6,213	—
Radford	11,596	9,371
Reston (U)	5,723	—
Richlands	4,843	4,963
Richmond	249,621	219,958
Roanoke	92,115	97,110
Rose Hill (U)	14,692	—
Salem	21,982	16,058
Seven Corners (U)	5,590	10,783
South Boston	6,889	5,974
Springfield (U)	11,613	10,783
Staunton	24,504	22,232
Sterling Park (U)	8,321	—
Suffolk	9,858	12,609
Vienna	17,152	11,440
Vinton	6,347	3,432
Virginia Beach	172,106	8,091
Waynesboro	16,707	15,694
West Springfield (U)	14,248	—
Williamsburg	9,069	6,832
Winchester	14,643	15,110
Woodbridge-Marumsco (U)	25,412	—
Wytheville	6,069	5,634
Yorkshire (U)	4,649	—
Washington	**3,409,169**	**2,853,214**
Aberdeen	18,489	18,741
Anacortes	7,701	8,414
Auburn	21,817	11,933
Bellevue	61,102	12,809
Bellingham	39,375	34,688
Bothell	4,883	2,237
Bremerton	35,307	28,922
Camas	5,790	5,666
Centralia	10,054	8,586
Chehalis	5,727	5,199
Cheney	6,358	3,173
Clarkston	6,312	6,209
College Place	4,510	4,031
Dishman (U)	9,079	—
Edmonds	23,998	8,016
Ellensburg	13,568	8,625
Enumclaw	4,703	3,269
Ephrata	5,255	6,548
Everett	53,622	40,304
Fairchild (U)	6,754	—
Fircrest	5,651	3,565
Fort Lewis (U)	38,054	—
Hoquiam	10,466	10,762
Issaquah	4,313	1,870
Kelso	10,296	8,379
Kennewick	15,212	14,244
Kent	21,510	9,017
Kirkland	15,249	6,025
Lacey	9,696	—
Lakes District (U)	48,195	—
Longview	28,373	23,349
Lynnwood	16,919	7,207
McChord (U)	6,515	—
Marysville	4,343	3,117
Mercer Island	19,047	—
Moses Lake	10,310	11,299
Mountlake Terrace	16,600	9,122
Mount Vernon	8,804	7,921
Normandy Park	4,208	3,224
Oak Harbor	9,167	3,942
Olympia	23,111	18,273
Opportunity (U)	16,604	12,465
Parkland (U)	21,012	—
Pasco	13,920	14,522
Port Angeles	16,367	12,653
Port Townsend	5,241	5,074
Pullman	20,509	12,957
Puyallup	14,742	12,063
Redmond	11,031	1,426
Renton	25,258	18,453
Richland	26,290	23,548
Seattle	530,831	557,087
Sedro-Woolley	4,598	3,705
Shelton	6,515	5,651
Shoultes (U)	4,754	3,159
Snohomish	5,174	3,894
Spanaway (U)	5,768	—
Spokane	170,516	181,608
Sumner	4,325	3,156
Sunnyside	6,751	6,208
Tacoma	154,581	147,979
Toppenish	5,744	5,667
Town and Country (U)	6,484	—
Tumwater	5,373	3,885
University Place (U)	13,230	—
Vancouver	42,493	32,464
Walla Walla	23,619	24,536
Wenatchee	16,912	16,726
Yakima	45,588	43,284
West Virginia	**1,744,237**	**1,860,421**
Beckley	19,884	18,642
Bluefield	15,921	19,256
Bridgeport	4,777	4,199
Buckhannon	7,261	6,386
Charleston	71,505	85,796
Clarksburg	24,864	28,112
Dunbar	9,151	11,006
Elkins	8,287	8,307
Fairmont	26,093	27,477
Grafton	6,433	5,791
Hinton	4,503	5,197
Huntington	74,315	83,627
Kenova	4,860	4,577
Keyser	6,586	6,192
Martinsburg	14,626	15,179
Morgantown	29,431	22,487
Moundsville	13,560	15,163
New Martinsville	6,528	5,607
Nitro	8,019	6,894
Oak Hill	4,738	4,711
Parkersburg	44,208	44,797
Point Pleasant	6,122	5,785
Princeton	7,253	8,393
Ravenswood	4,240	3,410
St. Albans	14,356	15,103
South Charleston	16,333	19,180
Vienna	11,549	9,381
Weirton	27,131	28,201
Wellsburg	4,600	5,514
Weston	7,323	8,754
Westover	5,086	4,749
Wheeling	48,188	53,400
Williamson	5,831	6,746
Wisconsin	**4,417,933**	**3,951,777**
Allouez (U)	13,753	—
Antigo	9,005	9,691
Appleton	57,143	48,411
Ashland	9,615	10,132
Ashwaubenon (U)	9,323	—
Baraboo	7,931	7,660
Bayside	4,461	3,181
Beaver Dam	14,265	13,118
Beloit	35,729	32,846
Berlin	5,338	4,838
Brookfield	32,140	19,812
Brown Deer	12,622	11,280
Burlington	7,479	5,856
Cedarburg	7,697	5,191
Chippewa Falls	12,351	11,708
Clintonville	4,600	4,778
Cudahy	22,078	17,975
Delavan	5,526	4,846
De Pere	13,309	10,045
Eau Claire	44,619	37,987
Elm Grove	7,201	4,994
Fond Du Lac	35,515	32,719
Fort Atkinson	9,164	7,908
Fox Point	7,937	7,315
Franklin	12,247	10,006
Germantown	6,974	622
Glendale	13,436	9,537
Grafton	5,998	3,748
Green Bay	87,809	62,888
Greendale	15,089	6,843
Greenfield	24,424	17,636
Hales Corners	7,771	5,549
Hartford	6,499	5,627
Howard	4,911	3,485
Hudson	5,049	4,325
Janesville	46,426	35,164
Jefferson	5,429	4,548
Kaukauna	11,292	10,096
Kenosha	78,805	67,899
Kimberly	6,131	5,322
La Crosse	51,153	47,575
Lake Geneva	4,890	4,929
Little Chute	5,365	5,099
Madison	173,258	126,706
Manitowoc	33,430	32,275
Marinette	12,696	13,329
Marshfield	15,619	14,153
Menasha	14,905	14,647
Menomonee Falls	31,697	18,276
Menomonie	11,275	8,624
Mequon	12,110	8,543
Merrill	9,502	9,451
Middleton	8,286	4,410
Milwaukee	717,099	741,324
Monona	10,420	8,178
Monroe	8,654	8,050
Muskego	11,573	—
Neenah	22,892	18,057
New Berlin	26,937	15,788
New London	5,801	5,288
Oak Creek	13,901	9,372
Oconomowoc	8,741	6,682
Oconto	4,667	4,805
Onalaska	4,909	3,161
Oshkosh	53,221	45,110
Perry Go Place (U)	5,912	4,475
Platteville	9,599	6,957
Plymouth	5,810	5,128
Portage	7,821	7,822
Port Washington	8,752	5,984
Prairie du Chien	5,540	5,649
Racine	95,162	89,144
Reedsburg	4,585	4,371
Rhinelander	8,218	8,790
Rice Lake	7,278	7,303
Richland Center	5,086	4,746
Ripon	7,053	6,163
River Falls	7,238	4,857
St. Francis	10,489	10,065
Shawano	6,488	6,103
Sheboygan	48,484	45,747
Sheboygan Falls	4,771	4,061
Shorewood	15,576	15,990
South Milwaukee	23,297	20,307
Sparta	6,258	6,080
Stevens Point	23,479	17,837
Stoughton	6,081	5,555
Sturgeon Bay	6,776	7,353
Sun Prairie	9,935	4,008
Superior	32,237	33,563
Tomah	5,647	5,321
Two Rivers	13,553	12,393
Watertown	15,683	13,943
Waukesha	40,258	30,004
Waupaca	4,342	3,984
Waupun	7,946	7,935
Wausau	32,806	31,943
Wausau West (U)	6,399	4,105
Wauwatosa	58,676	56,923
West Allis	71,723	68,157
West Bend	16,555	9,969
West Milwaukee	4,405	5,043
Whitefish Bay	17,394	18,390
Whitewater	12,038	6,380
Wisconsin Rapids	18,587	15,042
Wyoming	**332,416**	**330,066**
Casper	39,361	38,930
Cheyenne	40,914	43,505
Cody	5,161	4,838
Evanston	4,462	4,901
Gillette	7,194	3,580
Lander	7,125	4,182
Laramie	23,143	17,520
Powell	4,807	4,740
Rawlins	7,855	8,968
Riverton	7,995	6,845
Rock Springs	11,657	10,371
Sheridan	10,856	11,651
Torrington	4,237	4,188
Warren (U)	4,527	—
Worland	5,055	5,806

*Town (township) population.
Dash (—) indicates place did not exist at time of the 1960 Census, or data not available.
(U) indicates unincorporated urban place.
Source: U.S. Department of Commerce publications PC(V1)-2 through PC(V1)-52 (Advance Reports of Final Population Counts).

Reprints from the 1971 Compton's

This section consists of two new or fully revised articles from the 1971 edition of Compton's Encyclopedia. The articles are reprinted here to help the reader keep his home reference library complete and up-to-date.

Reprinted are the following:

ECOLOGY—The Study of Life in Its Environment

ECOLOGY. The science that deals with the ways in which plants and animals depend upon one another and upon the physical settings in which they live is called ecology. Ecologists investigate the interactions of organisms in various kinds of environments. In this way they learn how nature establishes orderly patterns among a great variety of living things. The word "ecology" was coined in 1869. It comes from the Greek *oikos*, which means "household." Economics is derived from the same word. However, economics deals with human "housekeeping," while ecology concerns the "housekeeping" of nature.

Interdependence in Nature

Ecology emphasizes the dependence of every form of life on other living things and on the natural resources in its environment, such as air, soil, and water. Before there was a science of ecology, the great English biologist Charles Darwin noted this interdependence when he wrote: "It is interesting to contemplate a tangled bank, clothed with plants of many kinds, with birds singing on the bushes, with various insects flitting about, and with worms crawling through the damp earth, and to reflect that these elaborately constructed forms, so different from each other, and so dependent upon each other in so complex a manner, have all been produced by laws acting around us."

Ecology shows that man cannot regard nature as separate and detached—something to look at on a visit to a forest preserve or a drive through the country. Any change man makes in his environment affects all the organisms in it. When his vehicles and factories hurl pollutants into the air, animals and plants as well as man himself are harmed. The water he fouls with wastes and silt threatens remote streams and lakes. Even ocean fisheries may experience reduced catches because of pollution. (*See also* Conservation; Pollution, Environmental.)

The Balance of Nature

Each kind of life is suited to the physical conditions of its habitat—the type of soil, the amount of moisture and light, the quality of air, the annual variations in temperature. Each survives because it can hold its own with its neighbors. However, the continued existence of the whole group, or *life community*, involves a shifting balance among its members, a "dynamic equilibrium." The balance teeters with the seasons and in years of extreme weather. So long as the climate does not change, however, these fluctuations pose no threat to the continued existence of the community.

Natural balances are disrupted when crops are planted, since ordinarily the crops are not native to the areas in which they are grown. Such disturbances of natural balances make it necessary for man to impose artificial balances that will maintain or increase crop production. For the effective manipulation of these new equilibriums, information on nature's checks and balances is absolutely essential, and often only a specialist is able to provide it. For example, if a farmer were told that he could increase the red clover in his pasture with the help of domestic cats, he might ridicule the suggestion. Yet the relationship between cats and red clover has been clearly

TROPICAL DECIDUOUS FOREST
Light penetrates the treetops of the tropical deciduous forest, thus permitting dense plant life at the surface. Vegetation is especially lush during the hot, rainy seasons.

STRETCHES OF GRASSLAND
Grasslands are found in varying middle-latitude climates. Some grasses are adapted to moist settings, others to dry ones. Grazing animals and other herbivores thrive in grasslands.

established. Cats kill field mice, thus preventing them from destroying the nests and larvae of bumblebees. As a result, more bumblebees are available to pollinate clover blossoms—a task for which they are especially adapted. The more thoroughly the blossoms are pollinated, the more seed will be produced and the richer the clover crop will be. This cat-mouse-bee-clover relationship is typical of the cause-and-effect chains that ecologists study.

The Wide Scope of Ecology

Long before a separate science of ecology arose, men in all sorts of occupations were guided by what are now regarded as ecological considerations. The primitive hunter who knew that deer had to stop at a salt lick for salt was a practical ecologist. So too was the early fisherman who realized that gulls hovering over the water marked the position of a school of fish. In the absence of calendars, men used ecological facts to guide their seasonal endeavors. They planted corn when oak leaves were the size of a squirrel's ear. They regarded the noise of geese flying south as a warning to prepare for winter.

Until about 1850, the scientific study of such phenomena was called natural history, and the student of the great outdoors was called a naturalist. Afterward, natural history became subdivided into special fields, such as geology, zoology, and botany, and the naturalist moved indoors. There he performed laboratory work with the aid of scientific equipment.

While the scientists were at work in their laboratories, other men were continuing to cope with living things in their natural settings—on timberlands, on rangelands, on croplands, in streams and seas. Although these men often needed help, many of their problems could not be solved in the laboratory.

The forester, for example, wanted to know why trees do not thrive on the prairie, the desert, and the mountaintop. The rancher wanted to know how to manage his pastures so that his cattle would flourish, and how such creatures as coyotes, hawks, rabbits, gophers, and grasshoppers would affect his efforts.

As for the farmer, almost every part of his work posed problems for which scientific answers were needed. The game manager came to realize that his duties entailed much more than the regulation of hunting. To preserve the animals for which he was responsible, he had to make sure they had the right kinds of food in all seasons, suitable places to live and raise their young, and appropriate cover.

The fisherman learned that most aquatic life fares poorly in muddy and polluted waters. He became interested in land management and waste disposal when he discovered that the silt he found so troublesome came from rural areas where timber, rangeland, and cropland were mishandled and that the waters he fished were polluted by urban wastes. The ocean fisherman wanted to know why fish were abundant in one place and scarce in another. He needed information on the breeding habits of his catches and of the tiny animals and plants upon which they fed.

These are all ecological problems. To solve them the ecologist must draw upon many sciences. He must understand biology—the science of living things—including botany and zoology. He must also understand the sciences that deal with weather, climate, rocks, earth, soil, and water.

An ecologist is concerned with both the past and the future. The present and potential condition of a field, stream, or forest cannot be understood without knowing its earlier history. For example, great stretches of light-green aspen trees may grow in parts

HUMID MIDDLE-LATITUDE LAND

Many of the deciduous forests that once flourished in the middle latitudes were cleared for crops. Some famous civilizations have flourished in these warm, moist regions.

THE DESERT

Even the parched desert can support life. Since water is scarce in arid regions, desert plants store it in their tissues. Desert animals are specially adapted to conserve water.

of the Rocky Mountains while nearby slopes are covered with dark-green fir and spruce trees. This indicates that a forest fire once destroyed stands of evergreens. Aspens are the first trees capable of growing on the fire-scarred land. After about 40 years spruce and fir seeds begin to germinate in the shade of the aspens. In the course of time the evergreens can be expected to regain their lost territory. Thus, by means of ecology it is possible to look both backward and forward in time.

SOME PRINCIPLES OF ECOLOGY

Ecology is a relatively young science. Its laws are still being developed. Nevertheless, some of its principles have already won wide acceptance.

The Special Environmental Needs of Living Things

One of these principles can be stated as follows: life patterns reflect the patterns of the physical environment. In land communities vegetation patterns are influenced by climate and soil (*see* Climate; Soil). Climate has a marked effect on the height of dominant native plants. For instance, the humid climate of the Eastern United States supports tall forest trees. Westward from Minnesota and Texas the climate changes from subhumid to semiarid. At first the land has squatty, scattered trees and tall grasses or thickets. As the climate becomes drier, tall-grass prairies dominate (*see* Grasslands). Finally, on the dry plains at the eastern base of the Rockies, short-grass steppe appears. (*See also* Plants, Distribution of.)

Climates and plant varieties change quickly at the various elevations of mountain range. At very high altitudes in the Rockies, alpine rangelands exist above the timberline. Here, the climatic factor of cold outweighs that of moisture, and short-lived tundra vegetation identical with that of the Arctic regions is nurtured. West of the Rockies, however, in basins between other mountains, the desert scrub vegetation of arid climates prevails. Then, near the northern Pacific coast, may be found lush rain forests typical of extremely humid temperate climates.

Though moisture and temperature determine the overall pattern of a region's vegetation, unusual soil conditions may promote the growth of untypical plant species. Thus, even in arid climates cattails grow near ponds and forests rise along streams or from rocky outcrops where runoff water collects in cracks.

In short, every kind of plant and animal flourishes only when certain physical conditions are present. In the absence of such conditions, plants and animals cannot survive without artificial help. Domestic plants and animals ordinarily die out within a few generations without the continued protection of man. Of all the forms of life, man seems least bound by environmental limitations. He can create livable conditions nearly everywhere on the planet by means of fire, shelters, clothing, and tools. Without these aids, man would be as restricted in his choice of habitat as are, for example, such species as the polar bear, the camel, and the beech tree. However, given his capacity to develop artificial environments, man is able to range not only over the entire earth but also in the heights of outer space and the depths of the ocean bottom. (*See also* Animals, Distribution of.)

Communities of Plants and Animals

Closely related to the life patterns principle is the principle of biotic communities. According to this principle, the plants and animals of a given area—its biota—tend to group themselves into loosely organized units known as *communities*. The com-

PRIMARY SUCCESSION

The primary succession of plants illustrated below begins in a pond and ends in either a grassland or a forest. Many plants play a part in succession; those diagramed are merely typical examples. At the submerged stage, such plants as eelgrass and elodea are rooted in the muddy bottom. As humus accumulates, the water becomes shallower. Floating plants such as water lilies take hold. At the water's edge, the soil supports cattails and reeds. Away from the pond, rushes begin to form a meadow. In the drier soil, even further from the pond, dogwoods and cottonwoods develop. This mixed forest is finally succeeded by a climax forest of oaks and hickories or of the more dominant beeches and maples.

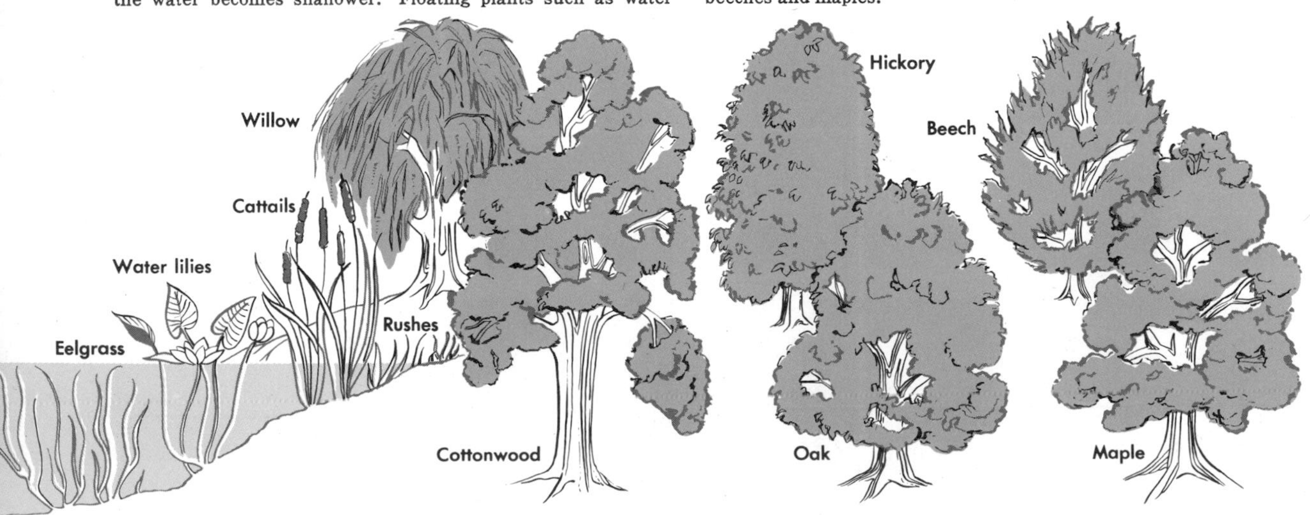

munity is the natural home of each member-species.

This means that certain types of plants and animals live together in readily identified communities. Pronghorn antelope are associated with dry steppe grasslands; moose inhabit northern spruce forests; and such trees as oak and hickory or beech and maple are found together in forests. By contrast, certain living things never share the same natural environment. Cattail and cactus, for example, are never found together. (For a color "transvision" of a typical plant and animal community, *see* Nature Study.)

Large communities contain smaller ones, each with its characteristic biota. Bison, coyotes, and jackrabbits are part of the grasslands community. Fox squirrels, wood pigeons, and black bears are part of the forest community. By means of computers, ecologists have simulated communities containing various plants and animals. In this way they have been able to determine optimum populations for each of the species in a community.

Competition is a characteristic of all communities. Plant roots in dry rangelands compete for water. The trees of a rain forest compete for light. Crops compete for growing space. Competition is unusually keen in *ecotones*, or areas that separate one type of community from another. For example, an ecotone between a shrub community and a marsh contains some aspects of both communities. Animals and plants trying to establish a foothold in the ecotone are compelled to cope with difficulties that are often nonexistent in a stable community. Shrubs moving toward the marshy area must compete with other pioneer shrubs and reeds for light and nutrients. Similarly, reeds attempting to invade the shrubby area must compete with shrubs and other reeds. This shows that competition may often be greatest among living things that have the same needs. For the same reason, competition may be extremely harsh within a species—among wolves for meat or among cattle for grass, for example.

On the other hand, competition is sometimes modified through behavioral adjustments—even *cooperation*—among the members of a community. Shrubs are spaced widely on deserts. Birds nest in patterns that prevent overcrowding. Bees live together in a hive. Man can make similar adjustments, and unlike other species he can achieve cooperation by rational means. Yet human competition sometimes ends in wars, and wars frequently destroy the very things which the belligerents are striving to take away from one another.

Should it become necessary to control an undesirable species in a community, this can best be done by modifying the community. A rancher, for example, may discover that weedy annual plants are invading his native perennial pastures. His initial reaction might be to attack the weeds with chemical herbicides. This approach would be self-defeating since nature would provide the resultant bare soil with an unlimited supply of weed seed. To solve the problem ecologically, the rancher should manage the degree

ECOLOGICAL LAND RECLAMATION

The West once had millions of acres of prairie where bison ranged. Cattlemen discovered that, covered with hardy natural grass, the land was ideal for cattle grazing.

The range eventually became overstocked. The grass was cropped by cattle and sheep, and the underlying sod dried up.

Settlers were mistakenly encouraged to farm this land. When the plow broke the sod, wind and water eroded good topsoil.

Ecology helped reclaim the desert. Furrows were cut across slopes to hold water. Oats, sorghum, and Sudan grass, with a scattering of shrubs and trees, were planted to hold soil.

In less than a year, the desert had been reclaimed. Later, the land was seeded to grass again and restocked with cattle.

ECOLOGY USED IN FORESTRY
Man can modify the environment of some species for his own needs without unduly upsetting natural balances. Young pines (left) are bunched so closely that they cannot grow into tall marketable trees. When a portion of the stand is removed, the remaining trees (right) flourish because competition for water, light, and nutrients is greatly eased.

and time of cattle grazing to permit normal growth of the native plant community, which would then crowd out the undesirable weeds.

Succession in Communities

A third major principle of ecology is that an orderly, predictable sequence of development takes place in any area. This sequence is called *ecological succession.* The successive changes produce increasingly mature communities from a barren or nearly barren start. Succession usually culminates in a *climax,* a fairly stable community in equilibrium with, and limited by, climate and soil.

At one time or another virtually all land surfaces have undergone basic climatic changes and been occupied by types of plants and animals which they may no longer be able to sustain. This, however, is not what is meant by ecological succession. It is known as biotic history, extends over the vast scale of geologic time, and is deduced from fossil remains. The future communities of an area cannot be predicted from its biotic history. Such prediction can be based only on a knowledge of ecological succession.

As soon as the first patches of soil are formed in barren areas, a series of events takes place that eventually terminates in the establishment of a climax community. This process is called *primary succession.* Because soil formation requires the slow weathering of rock, primary succession ordinarily spans hundreds of years. Once it begins, however, the sequence of events rarely alters. As soil formation proceeds, a succession of plants and animals appear. The last stage in this progression is the climax community.

A disturbance at any point during primary succession or even at the climax can destroy the vegetation of a primary succession in whole or in part. The vegetation that follows a disturbance of this kind is called a *disclimax.* The disturbance can be caused by plowing, logging, or overgrazing. When such a disturbance takes place, climate and soil are no longer the principal determinants of vegetation. The further natural growth of plants at the site of a disclimax, as contrasted with the raising of crops, is called *secondary succession.* This can be completed in a few years or, at most, in decades because soil has already been formed. After secondary succession restores a balance between eroded soil and vegetation, the further development of both again becomes dependent on primary succession. Wise landowners use secondary succession to restore overgrazed rangelands, cutover timberlands, and abandoned croplands. They need only protect the land from further disturbances while secondary succession heals the scars of abuse.

Changes in the community during secondary succession are rapid, because every living thing contributes to its alteration. For instance, the weeds that grow on a vacant lot produce shade and increase the soil's ability to absorb and store water. They also attract insects and birds and enrich the soil when they die and decay. The bare ground of the vacant lot is the best possible place for the pioneer sun-loving weeds to grow. Later the weeds are replaced by tree seedlings if the lot is in a forest climate, by native grasses if it is in a grasslands climate. Such changes occur until plants and animals that can make maximum use of the soil and climate are established.

The Ecosystem

A fourth key principle of ecology asserts that a community and its environment—the living and the nonliving—constitute an ecological system, or *ecosystem.* Every natural community draws vital materials from its surroundings and transfers materials to it. Raw materials and decay products are exchanged continuously. Thus, in an undisturbed area basic resources are sustained, never exhausted.

Ecosystems exist on many kinds of lands, in lakes, in streams, and in oceans. They are found wherever soil, air, and water support communities. The combined ecosystems of the earth constitute the *biosphere.*

Ecosystems generally contain many kinds of life. A cornfield, for example, contains more than just corn. Also present are smaller plant species, insects, earthworms, and a host of soil microbes. Each of these organisms fills a specific *niche*—each performs an essential function in the ecosystem.

The inhabitants of an ecosystem are classified as *producers*, *consumers*, and *decomposers*. Green plants of any kind, whether stately oaks or tiny algae, are producers because they make their own food through photosynthesis (*see* Plants, Physiology of). Animals, including man, feed on plants or on other animals and are therefore classed as consumers. Organisms that cause decay—bacteria and fungi—are decomposers.

The sequences in which the organisms within an ecosystem feed on one another are called *food chains*. Usually organisms of higher biological rank feed on those of lower rank. Ecologists group the members of any food chain into a *pyramid of numbers*. At the base of such a pyramid are the green plants, which are the most numerous organisms in the chain. The next level might contain first-order consumers, such as the sheep that eat the green plants. At the peak of the pyramid might be second-order consumers, such as the herdsmen who feed on the sheep. When the producers and consumers of an ecosystem die, their bodies are broken down by the decomposers into nutrients used by new plants for growth. In this manner, the food chain is perpetuated.

The biosphere seems capable of sustaining life even in the absence of consumers. Without consumers, the rate of plant growth would eventually strike a balance with the rate of decay caused by the decomposers. Hence, even if all herbivores, or plant-eaters, were absent from the biosphere, plant growth could be expected to stabilize at certain levels.

Through plant growth and decay, water and carbon, nitrogen, and other elements are circulated in endless cycles. The driving force behind these cycles is the sun. Solar energy becomes converted into food through the photosynthesis of green plants and into heat through the respiration of plants and animals. (*See also* Carbon; Nitrogen; Respiration; Water.)

APPLICATIONS OF ECOLOGY

Ecologists are often employed to solve serious environmental problems. Early in this century, for example, southern Ohio was ravaged by a terrible flood. The inhabitants of the area, determined to prevent a repetition of the disaster, constructed large earthen dams across the valleys north of Dayton to contain future floodwaters. Since the slopes of these dams consisted of gravel with an admixture of clay, they washed away easily. It was necessary to stabilize the steep slopes quickly with plant cover. Knowing which plants would grow best in such places, an ecologist recommended the scattering of alfalfa and clover seed, followed by bromegrass and Japanese honeysuckle. His recommendations were followed, and dam slopes were soon covered with a fine cohesive turf. Many of the hills on neighboring farms lacked such cover and were quickly eroded.

INTERDEPENDENCY IN NATURE

The alligator (left) fills an important niche in the Florida Everglades. Females build their nests by ponds commonly called 'gator holes (right, top). Succeeding generations of female alligators improve the holes, making them wider and deeper. Other kinds of Everglades wildlife feed and take water at the holes (right, bottom), particularly during dry weather.

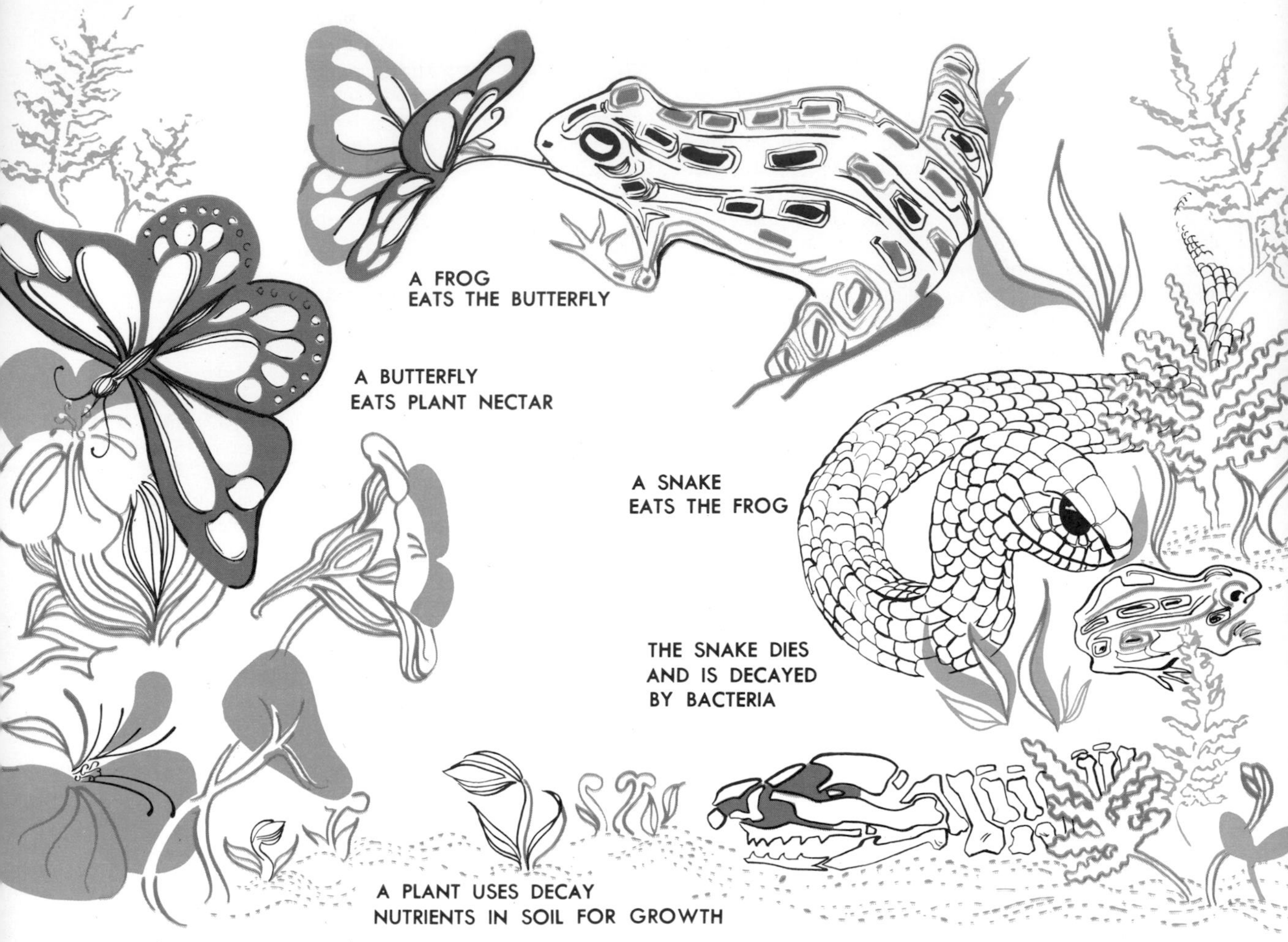
A FROG
EATS THE BUTTERFLY
A BUTTERFLY
EATS PLANT NECTAR
A SNAKE
EATS THE FROG
THE SNAKE DIES
AND IS DECAYED
BY BACTERIA
A PLANT USES DECAY
NUTRIENTS IN SOIL FOR GROWTH

LAND-BASED FOOD CHAIN
Plants are the producers in a food chain. They make their own food. Animals in the chain are the consumers. They derive energy from plant matter, whether they eat plants or plant-eating animals. When members of the food chain die, decomposers—microorganisms—chemically break down their bodies into nutrients, minerals used by plants for growth.

In the Dust Bowl region of Texas, sandy soil in dry areas blew into great dunes after the land was plowed for wheat. Bulldozing these dunes was thought too expensive. However, an ecologist recommended that certain plants be raised near the shifting dunes. The plants in front of the dunes caught and held the soil, while those behind them kept the rear from blowing deeper. In a remarkably short time, wind had leveled off the high dune tops and vegetation had anchored the soil in place.

Ecology and Wildlife Conservation

Measures for the preservation of ducks and other migratory wild fowl are examples of ecological work with animals. When these birds grew scarce, state and federal agencies sought ways to protect them and help them reproduce. At first, laws were recommended that forbade shooting the birds in the spring when they were flying north to nest. Every female killed in the spring could mean one brood less returning in the fall. Further studies showed that many of the birds' breeding places were being destroyed when the land was drained for other uses. Some of these sites were not well-suited for the sustained growth of crops; others, where marshes and potholes once released stored water slowly, now contributed to downstream floods. Draining thus had a doubly harmful effect. Ecologists captured the endangered birds and put aluminum bands on their legs to trace their breeding places and movements. In this way it was discovered that the problem was international. As a result, the United States began to work in close cooperation with Canada and Mexico for the protection of migratory birds.

Ecologists also investigated the food habits of birds. They recognized that if proper food was unavailable, the birds would disappear even if hunting was regulated.

Experts examined the stomach contents of thousands of birds from many different areas. This work led to the finding that bird food consists mainly of plant materials that thrive under natural conditions. To ensure the availability of these materials, man had to cease altering many natural communities and to stop polluting them with his wastes.

By the 1970's ecologists had accumulated considerable evidence demonstrating that the widely used pesticide DDT and its metabolites, principally DDE, altered the calcium metabolism of certain birds. The birds laid eggs with such thin shells that they were crushed during incubation. This discovery was one of many that led to the imposition of legal restraints on the use of some agricultural pesticides. (*See also* Birds; Pollution, Environmental.)

Ecologists know that the well-being of a biotic community may require the preservation of a key member-species. For example, the alligator performs a valuable service in the Florida Everglades by digging "'gator holes." These are ponds created by female alligators when they dig up grass and mud for their nests. During extremely dry spells, these holes often retain enough water to meet the needs of such animals as the bobcat and the raccoon. They also provide a haven for fish until the arrival of rainy weather. Many birds use the holes for watering. Willow seeds take root along the edges, and fallen willow leaves later add substance to the soil. Thus, many forms of life are sustained by 'gator holes. But poachers have been hunting the alligators almost to extinction for their valuable hides. As a result, the number of 'gator holes can be expected to dwindle, and various forms of Everglades wildlife may be deprived of these refuges. Such ecological findings strengthen the case for the protection of alligators. (*See also* Conservation, subhead "Wildlife Conservation.")

Another ecological threat to the Everglades arose in the late 1960's, when plans were made to build a jet airport near the northern end of the national park. The airport would have wiped out part of a large swamp that furnishes the Everglades with much of its surface water. Ecologists and conservationists opposed the project, arguing that it would hamper the flow of surface water through the park and thus endanger the biota of the unique Everglades ecosystem. Their arguments aroused public concern, and in 1970 plans for the airport were dropped.

AQUATIC ECOSYSTEM

An ecosystem contains interdependent plants and animals and their environment. In an aquatic ecosystem, producers (phytoplankton) supply energy to consumers (zooplankton and fish). Oxygen and carbon dioxide are exchanged between phytoplankton (which need carbon dioxide for photosynthesis) and aquatic animals (which need oxygen for respiration).

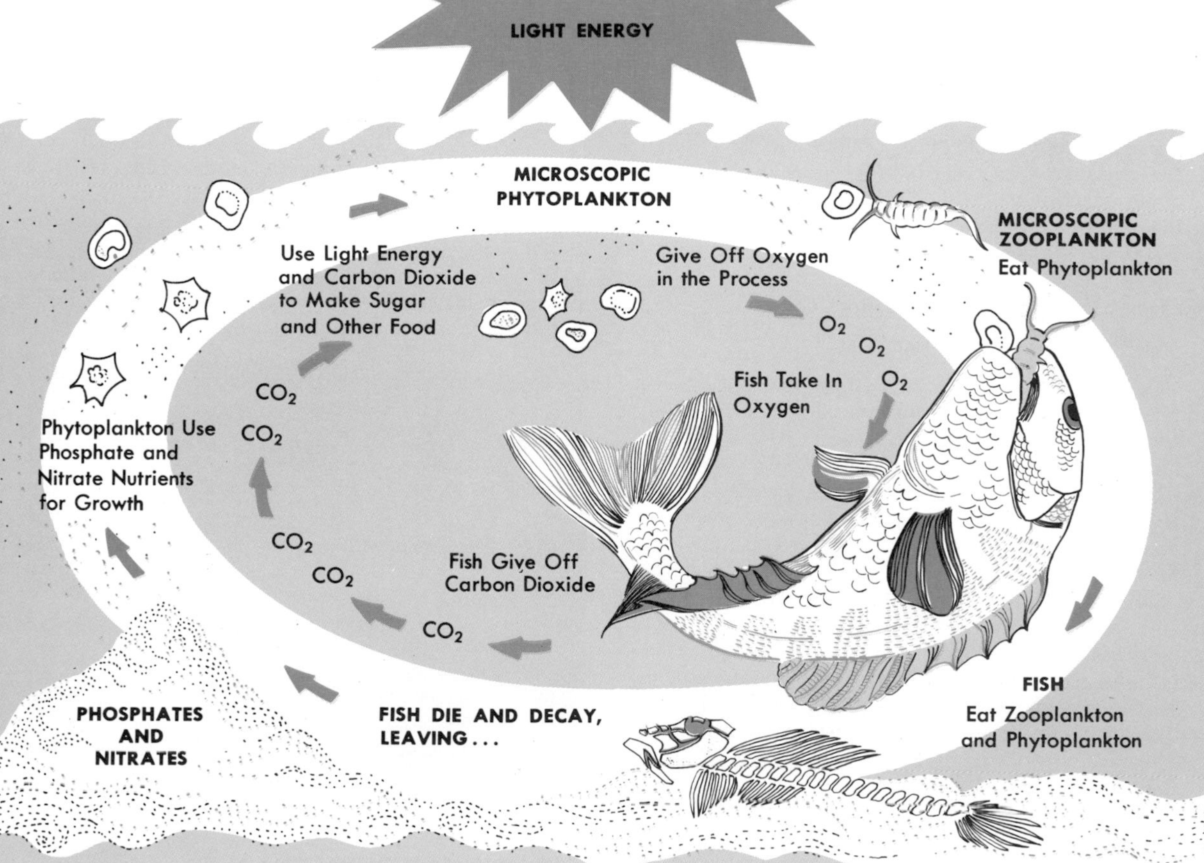
LIGHT ENERGY
MICROSCOPIC PHYTOPLANKTON
Use Light Energy and Carbon Dioxide to Make Sugar and Other Food
Give Off Oxygen in the Process
MICROSCOPIC ZOOPLANKTON
Eat Phytoplankton
O_2
O_2
O_2
Fish Take In Oxygen
CO_2
CO_2
Phytoplankton Use Phosphate and Nitrate Nutrients for Growth
CO_2
CO_2
Fish Give Off Carbon Dioxide
CO_2
FISH
Eat Zooplankton and Phytoplankton
PHOSPHATES AND NITRATES
FISH DIE AND DECAY, LEAVING . . .

HOW DDT KILLED THE ROBINS

Dutch elm disease threatened to destroy most of the majestic elms that once flourished along residential streets. To eliminate the beetles that carry this fungus disease, many communities sprayed their elms with massive doses of DDT. The pesticide stuck to the leaves even after they fell in the autumn. Earthworms then fed on the leaves and accumulated DDT in their bodies. When spring came, robins returned to the communities to nest. They ate the earthworms and began to die in alarming numbers. Of the females that survived, some took in enough DDT to hamper the production or hatching of eggs. Robin populations were so seriously affected by DDT poisoning that the very survival of the songbird seemed in jeopardy. This experience was a vivid example of the far-ranging effects that flow from upsets in the delicate balances of nature. Ironically, the DDT did little to prevent the spread of Dutch elm disease.

An Ecological Mistake

At times, seemingly practical conservation efforts turn out to be mistakes. Cougars, or mountain lions, and deer were once abundant in Grand Canyon National Park and Kaibab National Forest. Because the cougars preyed on the deer, hunters were allowed to shoot the cougars until only a few were left.

With their chief enemy gone, the deer of the area increased so rapidly that they consumed more forage than the Kaibab could produce. The deer stripped the forest of every leaf and twig they could reach and destroyed large areas of forage in the Grand Canyon National Park as well. The famished deer grew feeble, and many defective fawns were born. Finally, deer hunting in the Kaibab was permitted, in the hope that the size of the deer herd would drop until the range could accommodate it. In addition, the few surviving cougars were protected to allow them to multiply. They could then resume their ecological niche of keeping the herd down and of killing those deer not vigorous enough to be good breeding stock.

The Ecological Control of Pests

Many of the insects and other pests that have plagued North America originated in other parts of the world. There these pests were held in check by natural enemies, and the plants and animals they infested had developed a measure of tolerance toward them. However, when they were placed in an environment free of these restraints, the pests often multiplied uncontrollably.

At first, farmers fought the pests with toxic sprays and other powerful chemicals. However, these methods were expensive, sometimes proved unsuccessful, and were often dangerous. After decades of use, some pesticides were banned. In certain instances, the ill-conceived use of pesticides gave way to an ecological approach.

Research showed that severe damage from certain pests—the Mexican beetle and the European corn borer, for example—is confined to crops grown on particular types of soil or under certain conditions of moisture. Changes in land use helped control some pests. Others were controlled biologically by importing parasites or predators from their native lands. This important form of pest control proved successful in limiting damage by scale insects (*see* Scale Insects).

By destroying the breeding places of birds and other animals, man loses valuable allies in his constant war with insects. Once, when the sportsmen of Ohio supported a proposal to permit quail hunting, the farmers of the state objected. They knew that a single quail killed enough insects to make it worth at least as much to them as a dozen chickens.

In some 3,000 locally organized Resource Conservation Districts ecological principles are being used to guide land use and community maintenance practices. These districts encompass the federal lands of the United States and more than 95 percent of its privately owned farmlands.

GOALS OF ECOLOGY

Throughout the world man-made communities have been replacing the communities of nature. However, the principles that govern the life of natural communities must be observed if these man-made communities are to thrive. Man must think less about "conquering nature" and more about learning to work with nature.

In addition, each person must realize his interdependence with the rest of nature, including his fellowmen. To safeguard life on earth, men must learn to control and adjust the balances in nature that are altered by their activities.

Maintenance of the Environment

Climate cannot be changed except locally and sporadically by cloud seeding, inadvertently by air pollution, and on a small scale by making windbreaks or greenhouses. However, human activities can be adapted to the prevailing climatic patterns. Plants and animals should be raised in the climates best suited to them, and particular attention should be

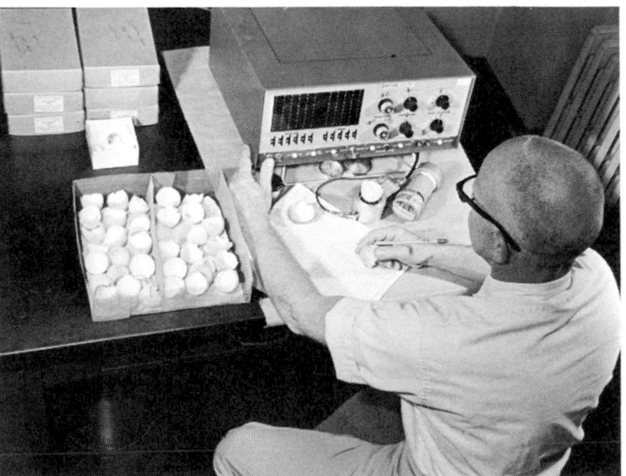

DUCK EGGS DAMAGED BY PESTICIDE
A research biologist uses a radioactive source to determine the thickness of mallard eggs containing DDE, a metabolite of DDT that reduces the hatchability of eggs.

BIOLOGICAL CONTROL OF PESTS
Weevils were damaging alfalfa fields. To eliminate the pests without the use of chemicals, ecologists introduced several species of predator wasps. One is shown attacking a weevil.

SPREADING THE EGGS OF A PEST PREDATOR
Eggs of green lacewings, insects that prey on destructive worms, are being spread among tomato plants. When the eggs hatch, the larvae begin to destroy the tomato pests.

paid to the cold and dry years rather than to average years or exceptionally productive years. In the United States the serious dust storms of the 1930's occurred because land that was plowed up in wet years to grow wheat blew away in dry years. Much of that land should have been kept as rangeland.

Soil is a measure of an environment's capacity to support life. It forms very slowly but can be lost very quickly—an inch in a rainstorm (*see* Soil). Wise land use ensures its retention and improvement.

For agricultural purposes, land is used principally as timberland, rangeland, or cropland. Timberland and rangeland are natural communities. Cropland is formed when what was originally timberland or rangeland is cultivated. To ensure the best possible use of land, it is classified according to its ability to sustain the production of timber, pasture, or crops. (For information on land classifications, *see* Conservation, subhead "Soil Conservation.")

Water, like soil, is a measure of the abundance of life. Usable water depends on the amount and retention of rainfall. However, human activities have often caused excessive runoff of rainwater. Such activities include the building of roads and drainage ditches; the construction of extensive parking areas and shopping centers; the unwise harvesting of timber; year-round grazing of ranges; and the cultivation of easily eroded lands. Excessive runoff may cause floods. It may also lead to drought, which can occur when too little water is stored underground. Moreover, runoff strips soil from the land. This is deposited in reservoirs, ship channels, and other bodies of water. These silt-laden bodies must then be either dredged or abandoned. Water movements in and out of the soil must be controlled in such a way as to minimize damage and maximize benefits. (*See also* Flood; Flood Control; Drought; Land Use.)

The Conservation of Natural Communities

The communities of plants and animals established by man usually consist of only a few varieties, often managed in a way that harms the environment. By contrast, natural communities usually enhance the environment and still yield many products and sources of pleasure to man.

Land once cultivated but now lying idle should be restored to the natural communities that formerly occupied it. In addition, man should use the findings of ecology to improve his artificial communities, such as fields, gardens, orchards, and pastures. For example, few man-made agents for the control of pests can outperform the insect-eating birds that breed in uncut patches of trees or bushes on a farm.

Competition and cooperation are a part of the life of all communities. War and business are well-known spheres of human competition. However, a variety of techniques for cooperation exist within many species of animals and plants, and perhaps these should be used as models for similar efforts among men.

The Curtailment of Waste

Modern machines and weapons and the harmful wastes of technology can be used to destroy the environment. At the same time, the wise use of machinery can also enable man to conserve his surroundings. Negotiation rather than warfare can be employed to resolve international disputes. Means can be devised to curtail the destructive wastes of factories and vehicles. True, an ever-growing demand for goods and services, nurtured by a rapidly increasing human population, is placing more and more pressure on the environment. However, an understanding of the causes and consequences of environmental deterioration may bring about a change in the goals that men pursue and the means they use to achieve them. (*See also* Pollution, Environmental.)

Many ecologists believe that there must be a revamping of the definition of progress. In the past, increases in man's material possessions have been accompanied by a potentially dangerous worsening of the natural environment. A central function of ecology is to study the interactions of man and the natural environment. Since man's physical and mental welfare depends in large measure on the maintenance of a well-functioning natural setting, ecological criteria must become a factor in all the political and technical decisions that affect the environment.

BIBLIOGRAPHY FOR ECOLOGY

Books for Younger Readers

Billington, Elizabeth T. Understanding Ecology (Warne, 1968).
Darling, Lois. A Place in the Sun (Morrow, 1968).
Raskin, Edith. The Pyramid of Living Things (McGraw, 1967).
Shuttlesworth, Dorothy Edwards. Natural Partnerships (Doubleday, 1969).
Silverstein, Alvin. Unusual Partners (McGraw, 1968).
Storer, J. H. Web of Life: a First Book of Ecology (Devin-Adair, 1953).
Wong, H. H. and Vessel, M. F. Our Tree (Addison, 1969).

Books and Films for Advanced Students and Teachers

Brown, Vinson. Reading the Woods (Stackpole, 1969).
Life (periodical). Ecology (Time, 1963).
Milne, L. J. Patterns of Survival (Prentice, 1967).
Nickelsburg, Janet. Ecology: Habitats, Niches, and Food Chains (Lippincott, 1969).
A Strand Breaks, film (Encyclopaedia Britannica Films).
The Strands Grow, film (Encyclopaedia Britannica Films).

ONCE-THREATENED SPECIES FLOURISHES

Trumpeter swans, forced to the edge of extinction by man's desire for feather-filled pillows and quilts and quill pens, are beginning to flourish again because of careful conservation efforts. From a low of 69 in 1932, the number of such swans in the United States was gradually increased to approximately 5,000 by 1968.

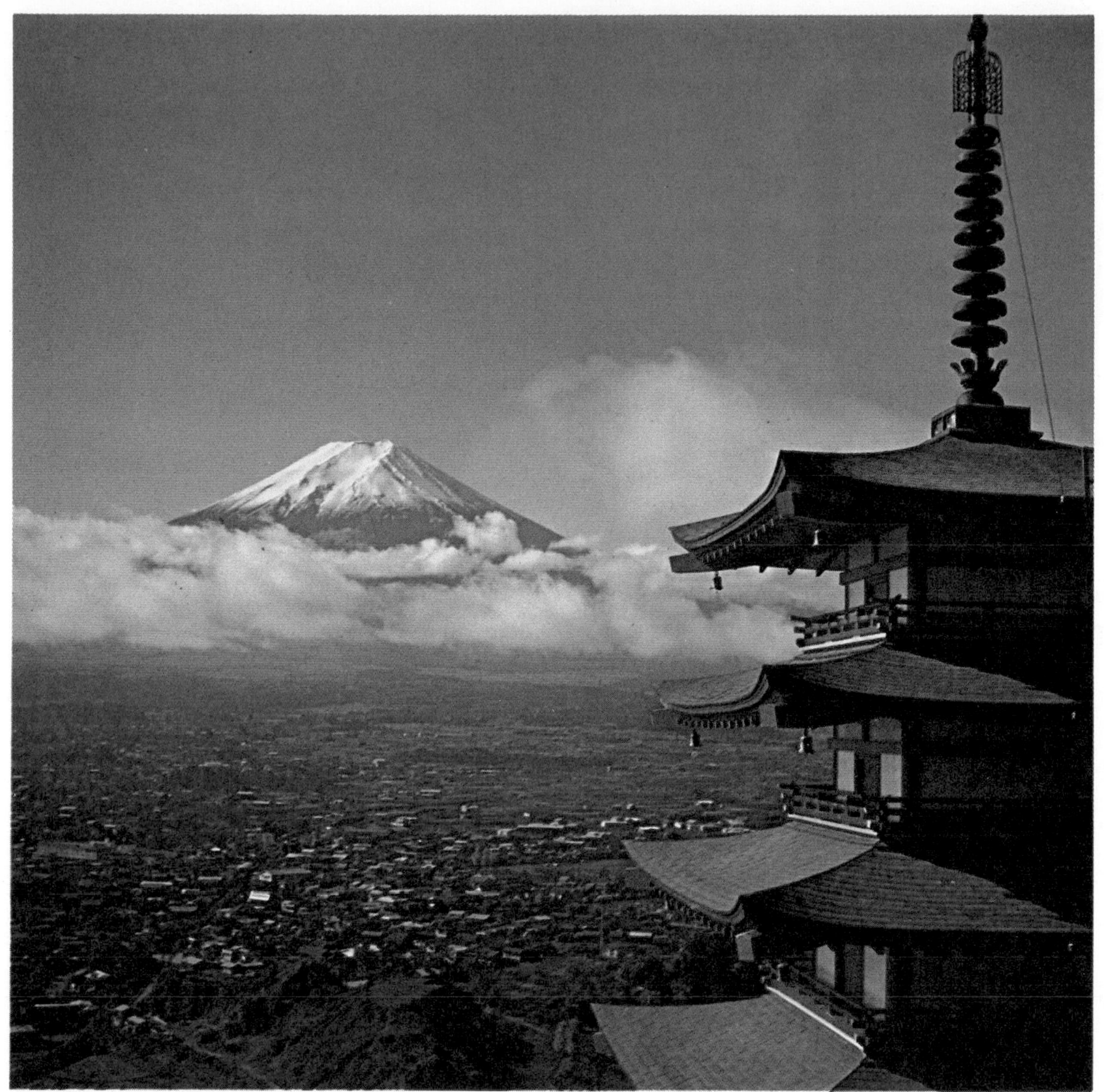

Before the snow-clad summit of Mount Fuji, the eternal symbol of Japan, a classic pagoda overlooks a bustling modern city.

JAPAN

JAPAN. The leading industrial nation of the Orient and the non-Western world, Japan also rivals the most advanced economic powers of the West. It rose rapidly from a crushing military defeat in World War II to achieve the fastest-growing economy of any major nation in the 1960's. Today only the United States and the Soviet Union outproduce it.

A century ago the Meiji Restoration launched Japan onto the road of modernization. The Japanese skillfully developed the technological base for modern industry and built their nation into a leading world power. Set back temporarily by wartime destruction and the consequences of military defeat, Japan has again become a world power. This time, however, its reputation is based not on armed might but on the productivity of its peacetime industry.

The Japanese people are enjoying an unprecedented flow of goods, though their living standards still lag behind those of the United States and Western Europe. Their swelling cities, paced by the giant

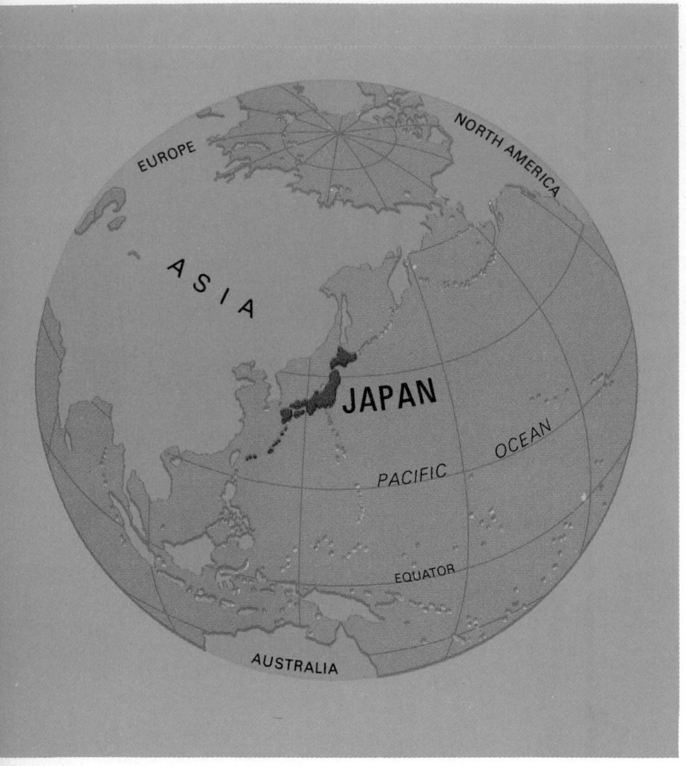

metropolis of Tokyo, are as modern as urban centers anywhere in the world. And they face the problems of great cities everywhere—overcrowded housing, inadequate waste-disposal facilities, air and water pollution, and traffic congestion.

In few other places in the world do the values and traditions of the past continue to flourish so strongly alongside the ideas and practices of the present. The persisting contrast between the new and the old, the modern and the traditional, is one of the most characteristic features of present-day Japan.

Urbanization, industrialization, and modern transportation and communication are rapidly changing the Japanese way of life. The impact of these developments is being keenly felt not only in the cities but in the countryside as well. However, beneath Japan's "new look" lie the deep-seated customs and institutions of traditional Japanese culture—in religion, in politics, and especially in family life. The people of Japan continue to respect and honor their past. They continue to adhere to the concepts of personal loyalty and obligation. Their hearts and minds remain Japanese.

Japan comprises a chain of islands along the east coast of the Asian mainland. The four main islands—Hokkaido, Honshu, Shikoku, Kyushu—stretch some 1,200 miles from northeast to southwest. With the hundreds of smaller islands, Japan is about 1,500 miles long. Its maximum width is about 200 miles.

Japan has no land border with any other nation. Across the Sea of Japan to the west is Korea; across the Sea of Japan to the northwest and the Sea of Okhotsk to the north is the Soviet Union; across the East China Sea to the west is China; along the Ryukyu Islands of Japan to the southwest are Formosa and the Philippines. The open waters of the vast Pacific Ocean wash Japan's eastern and southeastern shores. Across the Pacific, more than 4,000 miles away, are Washington and Oregon.

Japan is 143,000 square miles in area, about the size of Montana. Its largest island by far is Honshu, with about three fifths of the total area. On Honshu are most of Japan's principal cities and about three fourths of its more than 100 million people. Japan ranks high in population density and seventh in population among the world's nations. Its capital, Tokyo, is the world's largest city.

Preview

The article Japan is divided into the following sections:

Included in the article are the following special features:

At the end of the sections "People," "Government," "Economy," "Culture," "Natural Features," and "History" are two study aids—"Words to Remember" and "Questions to Think About."

The following contributors and consultants assisted in the preparation of this article: Michael Berger, Correspondent, *Stars and Stripes* (Tokyo); Peter Duus, Associate Professor of History, Claremont Graduate School; Earle Ernst, Senior Professor and Chairman, Department of Drama and Theatre, University of Hawaii; John D. Eyre, Professor of Geography, University of North Carolina; Yoshio Hiyama, former Professor, Faculty of Agriculture, Graduate School Division of Agricultural Science, University of Tokyo; Yoshiyuki Noda, Professor, Faculty of Law and the Graduate School Division of Law and Politics, University of Tokyo; Kazuo Okochi, former President, University of Tokyo; John Roderick, Foreign Correspondent; Jack Sewell, Curator of Oriental Art, The Art Institute of Chicago.

Facts About Japan

Official Name: Nihon or Nippon.
Capital and Largest City: Tokyo.
Population (1969 estimate): 102,000,000.
Area (in square miles): 142,726 (Honshu, 87,805; Hokkaido, 30,144; Kyushu, 14,114; Shikoku, 7,049).
Population Density (1969): 714 persons per square mile.
Form of Government: Constitutional monarchy (head of state—emperor; head of government—prime minister).
Flag: *See* Flags of the World.
Major Political Subdivisions: Prefectures (47, including Okinawa).
Extent: Point Soya (Hokkaido) to Cape Sata (Kyushu), 1,170 miles.
Highest Elevation: Mount Fuji, 12,389 feet.
Climate: In the north—short, cool summers and long, cold, snowy winters; in the southwest—warm, humid summers and mild, humid winters.
National Anthem: *Kimigayo.*
Monetary Unit: Yen ($.0028, or 360 to the dollar).
Major Language: Japanese.
Major Religions: Shintoism, Buddhism.
Chief Products: Buses, trucks, automobiles, merchant vessels, radios, television sets, caustic soda, synthetic fibers, plastics, sulfuric acid, fertilizer, steel, zinc, aluminum, cement, newsprint, cotton yarn, lumber, whales, fish, eggs, rice, tea.

Everyday Expressions in Japanese

Yes. *Hai.*
No. *Iie.*
Please. *Dozo.*
Thank you. *Arigato.*
You're welcome. *Do itashi-mashite.*
Excuse me. *Gomen kudasai.*
Hello. *Konnichi-wa.*
Good-bye. *Sayonara.*
I understand. *Wakari-masu.*
I don't understand. *Wakari-masen.*
What's your name? *Anata-no namae-wa nan desu ka?*
My name is Kenneth. *Watakushi no namae wa* Kenneth *desu.*
What time is it? *Nan-ji desu ka?*
What's this? *Kore-wa nan desu ka?*
This is ______. *Kore-wa* ______ *desu.*
Where is it? *Doko desu ka?*
It's here. *Koko desu.*
It's over there. *Soko desu.*
How are you? *Gokigen ikaga desu ka?*
I am well. *Watakushi-wa genki desu.*
To the left. *Hidari e.*
To the right. *Migi e.*
Straight ahead. *Massu gu.*

PREFECTURES AND DISTRICTS OF JAPAN

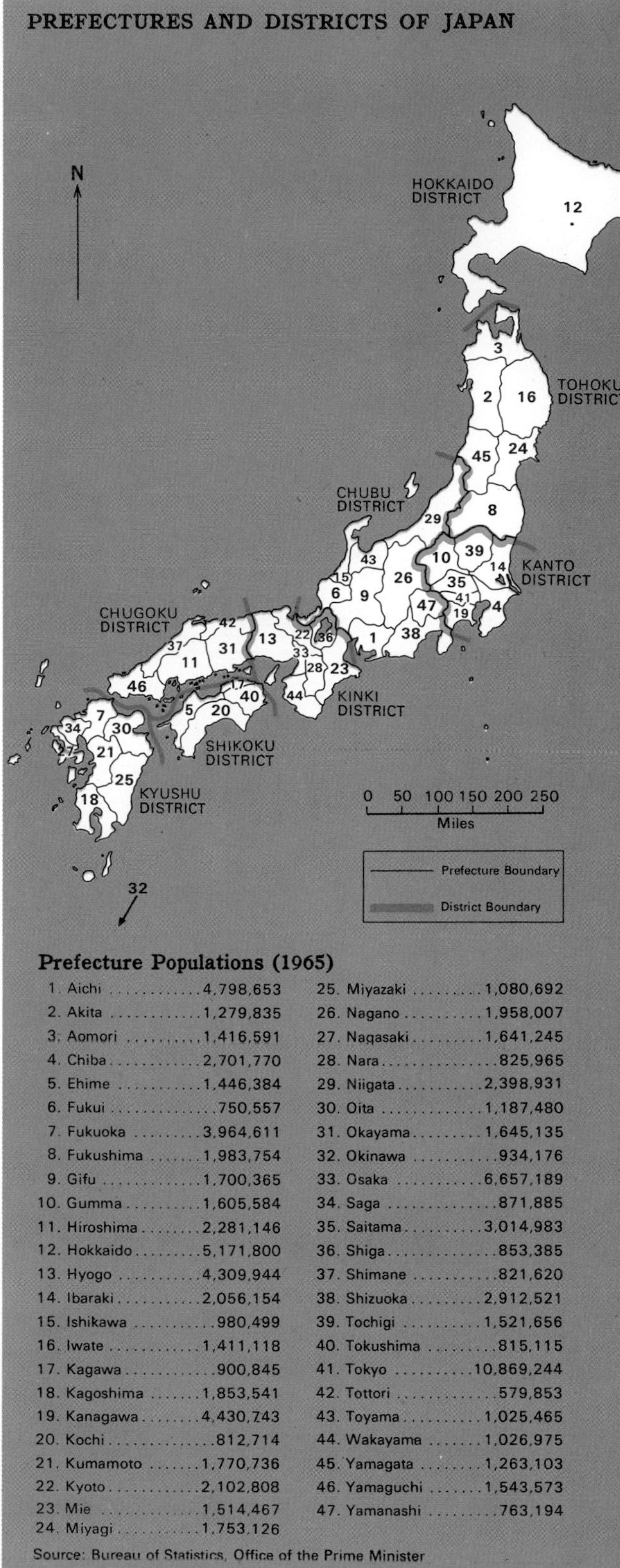

Prefecture Populations (1965)

1. Aichi	4,798,653	25. Miyazaki	1,080,692
2. Akita	1,279,835	26. Nagano	1,958,007
3. Aomori	1,416,591	27. Nagasaki	1,641,245
4. Chiba	2,701,770	28. Nara	825,965
5. Ehime	1,446,384	29. Niigata	2,398,931
6. Fukui	750,557	30. Oita	1,187,480
7. Fukuoka	3,964,611	31. Okayama	1,645,135
8. Fukushima	1,983,754	32. Okinawa	934,176
9. Gifu	1,700,365	33. Osaka	6,657,189
10. Gumma	1,605,584	34. Saga	871,885
11. Hiroshima	2,281,146	35. Saitama	3,014,983
12. Hokkaido	5,171,800	36. Shiga	853,385
13. Hyogo	4,309,944	37. Shimane	821,620
14. Ibaraki	2,056,154	38. Shizuoka	2,912,521
15. Ishikawa	980,499	39. Tochigi	1,521,656
16. Iwate	1,411,118	40. Tokushima	815,115
17. Kagawa	900,845	41. Tokyo	10,869,244
18. Kagoshima	1,853,541	42. Tottori	579,853
19. Kanagawa	4,430,743	43. Toyama	1,025,465
20. Kochi	812,714	44. Wakayama	1,026,975
21. Kumamoto	1,770,736	45. Yamagata	1,263,103
22. Kyoto	2,102,808	46. Yamaguchi	1,543,573
23. Mie	1,514,467	47. Yamanashi	763,194
24. Miyagi	1,753,126		

Source: Bureau of Statistics, Office of the Prime Minister

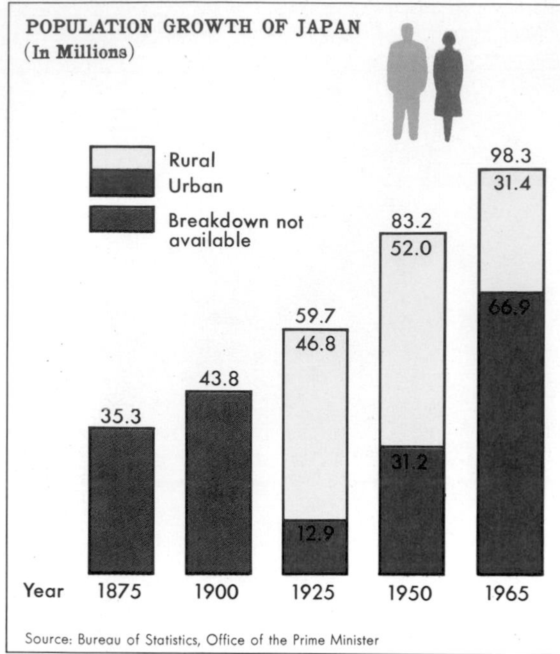

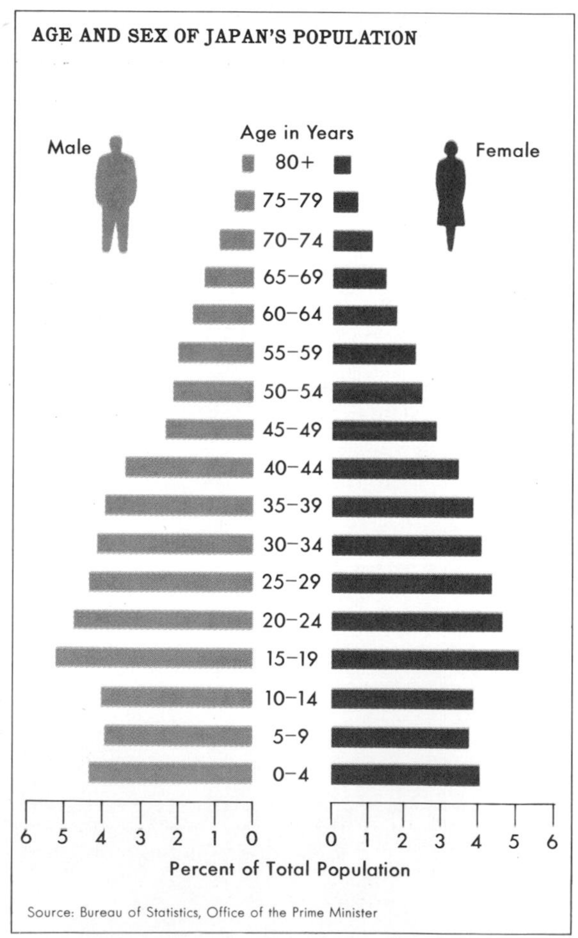

JAPAN—People

THE PEOPLE OF JAPAN

Japan is the seventh most populous nation in the world. At the time the 1965 census was taken, it had a population of 98,274,961, and in 1967 its population passed the 100 million mark. Yet Japan has one of the world's lowest rates of population growth—barely one percent per year.

Japanese population data is incomplete for the period before 1868, when the nation's modern era began. However, the population of Japan is believed to have reached 5 million in the 7th century and 10 million in the 14th century. Official estimates placed the number of Japanese in the mid-19th century at over 30 million. In 1920, when Japan's first census was taken, it had a population of 55,963,000. In 1940 its population was 73,114,000.

Japan experienced a brief baby boom after World War II, but then the nation's birthrate dropped from a high of 34 per 1,000 in 1947 to only 17 per 1,000 in 1962. This is one of the fastest declines that has ever been experienced by any nation. Japan's death rate has also fallen—to less than 10 per 1,000—largely because of improvements in public health measures, advances in medicine, and the greater availability of modern medical facilities. Average life expectancy in Japan reached 69 years for men and 74 years for women in 1968. In 1890 it was 43 years for men and 44 years for women.

The proportion of young people in Japan has been decreasing. Average family size has also been shrinking—it dropped from 4.97 in 1955 to 4.05 in 1965. This drop occurred in part because a growing number of young married couples were establishing their own households instead of living with their parents in the traditional fashion. Another reason was that young couples in Japan were having fewer children. In Japan, abortion is an accepted and widely used means of controlling family size. It is permitted under a 1952 law. Contraception, however, is not popular.

The Japanese are a fairly homogeneous people—both culturally and racially. They have a single language, and almost all are of Mongoloid racial stock. Koreans, the largest alien group in Japan, number less than one million. The Ainu, a native people of northern Japan, have been almost completely assimilated into the general population of the country.

Japan is one of the world's most thickly populated nations. The population density of the country as a whole is about 700 persons per square mile, but if only the agricultural and urban land area is counted, the density is more than six times greater. The bulk of Japan's people live in the coastal lowlands, which comprise a relatively small part of the nation's total area. The extensive mountainous interior is very sparsely populated.

Japan is the most urbanized major nation in Asia. In 1920, over four fifths of its people still lived in rural areas. By the 1960's, however, about two out of every three Japanese lived in cities.

Japan's greatest concentration of population is in a 350-mile-long belt that extends from Tokyo and the Kanto Plain westward along the Pacific coast through Nagoya and Kyoto to Osaka and Kobe on the eastern edge of the Inland Sea. Within this belt, called the Tokaido Megalopolis, live fully one half of Japan's people. The belt comprises the six largest cities and two thirds of the 130-odd cities with more than 100,000 population. A western extension of the Tokaido Megalopolis is growing along the Inland Sea to the city of Kitakyushu, in northern Kyushu.

The Tokaido Megalopolis includes the metropolitan clusters of Tokyo-Kawasaki-Yokohama, Nagoya, and Osaka-Kobe-Kyoto. The largest and fastest growing of these is the one around Tokyo. Population growth within the city limits of Tokyo has slowed, but in its suburbs—where open land is available for the construction of new homes and apartments—the number of people is increasing rapidly.

The Tokaido Megalopolis comprises the principal Japanese centers of industry, business, and finance and Japan's major international ports. It provides most of the job opportunities for migrants from the farms and small towns of Japan. For this reason, perhaps, Japan's difficulties in providing adequate housing, transportation, and social services of all kinds are greatest in the Tokaido Megalopolis.

Many prefectures outside the Tokaido Megalopolis and the few other large metropolitan centers have been losing population through out-migration, especially since 1950. The heaviest losses have occurred along the Sea of Japan coast and in the north of Honshu, in southern Kyushu, and on Shikoku. Hokkaido, an area of pioneer settlement until the 1930's, has the lowest population density of any prefecture and only one fourth that of the entire nation.

Three fourths of Japan's people—71,354,000 according to the 1965 census—live on the island of Honshu. Three other major islands of Japan's—Kyushu, Hokkaido, and Shikoku—have populations of 12,904,000, 5,039,000, and 4,121,000, respectively.

EVERYDAY LIFE IN JAPAN

Japan has been modernizing rapidly. Yet there are still great contrasts in the everyday life of the Japanese people. Especially striking are the contrasts between the tradition-bound countryside and the bustling urban centers.

Life in the Countryside

About one third of the Japanese people live in small farming villages called *buraku*. The way of life of these people is changing, but the traditional patterns established centuries ago are still widespread.

Rural homes are generally small. The walls are made of clay. Some rooms have earthen floors, while the floors of others are covered with wood or straw

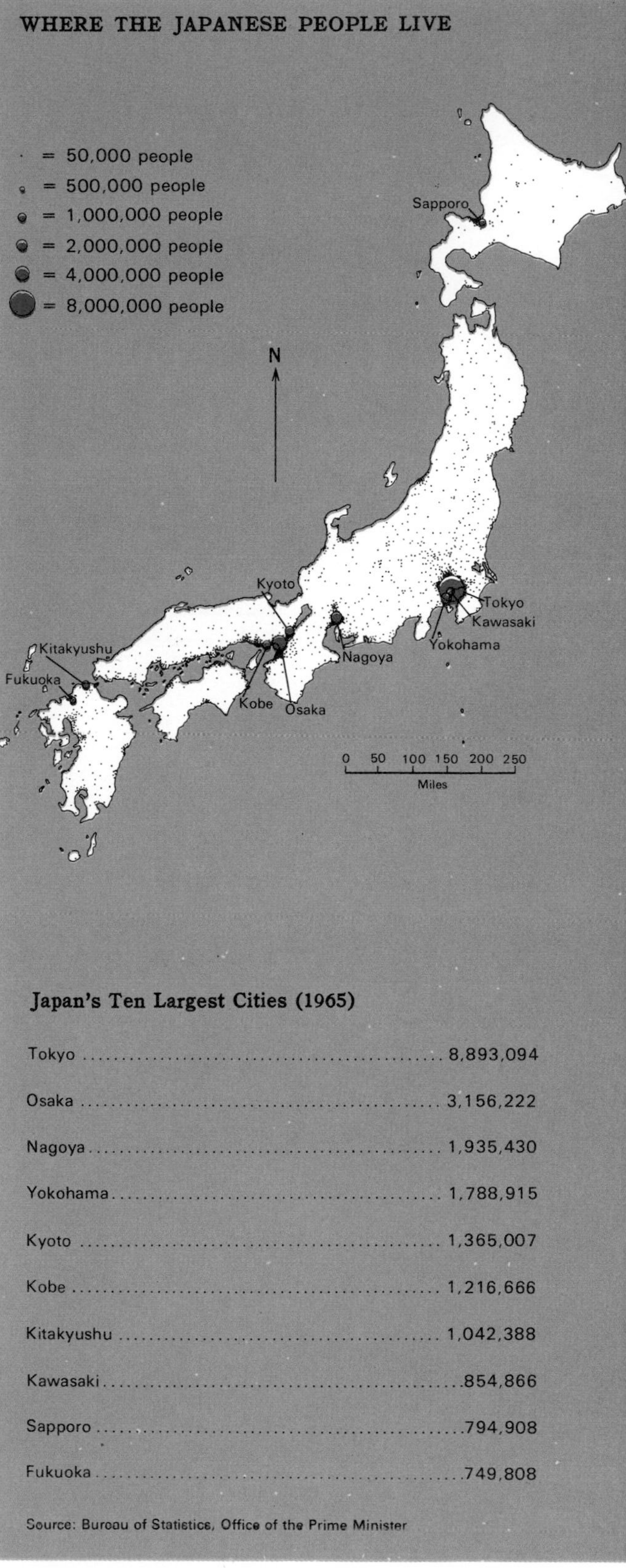

Japan's Ten Largest Cities (1965)

Tokyo	8,893,094
Osaka	3,156,222
Nagoya	1,935,430
Yokohama	1,788,915
Kyoto	1,365,007
Kobe	1,216,666
Kitakyushu	1,042,388
Kawasaki	854,866
Sapporo	794,908
Fukuoka	749,808

Source: Bureau of Statistics, Office of the Prime Minister

Continued on page 370

Akira finds chatting with a friend in a Tokyo park a fine way to spend a sunny winter afternoon.

A Western-style bunk bed, a miniature television, and casual clothes help make Akira's weekend studies more comfortable.

Akira's family enjoys *sushi* (rice balls with fish). An electric heater under the low table is concealed by the quilt.

Akira—Young Man of Japan

by Michael Berger

Akira Kobayashi of Tokyo is a modern city boy. (In Japan, where family names are put first, he is called Kobayashi Akira.) Now 16, Akira has far more personal freedom than his father did as a youth. Yet he is also very much a part of the traditional society that still endures in Japan.

As a boy, Akira is favored almost unconsciously by his parents, who want him to attend college and to succeed in Japan's competitive economy. But as a second son, Akira does not receive nearly as much attention as his 20-year-old brother, Hiroyasu. "I'm sort of glad," says Akira, "because I like to be by myself once in a while. My brother is the first in our family to go to college. He's pampered."

Akira's parents indulge their children and make great sacrifices for them. Mr. Kobayashi, an assistant supervisor in a large trading company, has saved money for years for his children's education. Mrs. Kobayashi rises early in the morning to prepare breakfast and box lunches for her family.

Though Hiroyasu may be pampered, he must still share his small bedroom with Akira. When relatives or special friends stay overnight, their 14-year-old sister, Yoshiko, also sleeps in the boys' room.

"We're not unusual," says Akira. "I have friends whose houses are smaller than ours. We have only six rooms for my parents, my grandmother, and the three children, but there isn't even a bath in my best friend's house. His family goes to a public bath every evening."

Akira's home has both foreign and Japanese furnishings—and this is not unusual either. The children sleep in beds, but Akira's parents and his grandmother sleep on the traditional padded mattresses over *tatami* (straw mats), laid out on the floor. A Western dish—hamburgers, perhaps—may be served for dinner, but such Japanese foods as soybean soup, dried fish, and steamed rice are eaten with it. The family eats seated on cushions, not chairs, before low tables. Some rooms are separated by doors, others by sliding panels made of paper and wood. The dining-room windows are curtained, but screens are placed in front of the living-room windows.

Though Akira likes new clothes, he wears the same thing to school every day—a black uniform consisting of pants, a jacket with a high collar, and a cap. Schoolgirls wear dark skirts hemmed at or below the knees, white blouses, and dark jackets. The school authorities allow no exceptions, because they believe that one way to eliminate consciousness of social class from school life is for everyone to dress alike.

"They think that will make us better citizens," says Akira, "but most of my friends don't agree. We'd rather wear what we like."

Akira gets up at 7:00 every morning except Sunday. He rides the subway for a half hour to be at school by 8:30. Classes usually end around 3:00. A second-year high school student, Akira is taking courses in history, mathematics, philosophy, science, and English, as well as in the Japanese language.

Akira worries about being accepted by a university when he graduates from high school. "Competition to get into our top colleges is fierce," he explains. "There isn't much space, and they're overcrowded. I'd like to go to the University of Tokyo. It's the best in Japan, and most employers favor its graduates for positions in their companies.

"My sister, Yoshiko, doesn't have to worry like I do. Girls working in large companies like my father's don't have very important jobs. The girls at my school know this, so they don't look forward to working. Most of them just want to get married, and they try to have a good time."

Akira and his schoolmates often go to a movie or bowling or to one of the hundreds of coffeehouses in Tokyo where they can listen to music and talk. "My boyfriends and I talk about girls a lot," he laughs. "But we also like to talk about photography, movies, and jazz and rock music. Once in a while we discuss politics. I criticize my friends for not being serious enough about politics, but they're more interested in *kakko ii* things." Kakko ii means "groovy"—the latest, the most fashionable, the "in" things. Stylish clothes, for example.

"I like that sort of thing too," says Akira, "but I get only about 1,500 *yen* a month allowance—about 4 dollars—and I use it to save up for photo equipment or records or hiking or skiing gear.

"I like skiing best of all," he says. "To make sure we get a seat on a train to the mountains, my friends and I will wait at the station for hours, playing chess or singing and talking. We bring our sleeping bags and food, and we stay at inexpensive youth hostels. We ski all day and talk at night. After a day or two, it's back to Tokyo.

"My father says that I am lucky and that I should enjoy myself now because hard years are ahead. Many of my friends already know exactly what their lives will be like. They'll work for a large company and get married—maybe to girls their families choose for them. I'd like to be a photographer and have more freedom if I can, but I think it's all right for my parents to decide whom I should marry, as long as I like the girl and she likes me. My friends and I would like to try something different, but we don't know what. I guess we're like young people in other countries. They worry about their futures too, don't they?

"The thing that bothers me most," says Akira, "is that Japan is too crowded and too tense. My friends and I like many things about our Japanese tradition—the culture, the art—and we love the natural beauty of our country. But we don't like the rules. Foreigners find it hard to understand, but there are all sorts of rules in Japan for how you're supposed to act in all kinds of situations. I'd like to relax and be myself, but I know I can't very often. We don't like the rules, but we accept them. I guess we young Japanese aren't as different as some people think."

Akira and his classmates concentrate on schoolwork. Difficult college entrance examinations are not too far off.

Akira and several friends are looking forward to an exciting skiing holiday as they wait for a train at Tokyo's Ueno Station.

It is hard to decide where to go first in Shinjuku Kabuki-cho, one of Tokyo's liveliest entertainment districts.

In the late 1960's, nearly a million dwelling units were built in Japan each year with government aid. Much of the new housing was put up in the suburbs of the major cities.

mats. The stoves used for cooking are made of clay or brick. They are heated with such materials as straw or with compressed gas, which has come into widespread use. The toilet facilities are separate from the house. Water is usually obtained from wells.

The villagers usually live in households that include grandparents and grown sons with their families, as well as the farmer, his wife, and his younger children. When a farmer dies or grows old, his land is passed on to a son, traditionally the eldest. His other sons may inherit money and may stay on the farm. However, most enter occupations in the village or a city.

Each member of a farm family has certain responsibilities. The most important involve work in the fields. The men spend long days planting, tilling, and harvesting their crops. During the time in each growing season when the paddies are flooded, the men work knee-deep in water. Most farmers tend and harvest their crops by hand, but modern farm machinery is also being used. Rice is the principal food crop.

The women often help in the fields after they have finished their usual household tasks of cooking, cleaning, weaving straw mats, and gardening. Although older children go to school, they also work in the fields or take care of younger brothers and sisters. Grandparents no longer able to do field work weave mats and look after their grandchildren.

After a hard day's work, the entire family enjoys an evening bath. The large earthen or cedar bathtub stands in a bathhouse or in the kitchen near the stove. A fire kindled beneath the tub keeps the water hot. Then each family member in turn—beginning with the father—washes and rinses thoroughly before getting into the tub. The water in the tub is used only for soaking since it is shared by all members of the family. On winter days the hot bath gives the farm family its first chance to get really warm.

Japanese villagers are neighborly. They share many of their joys and sorrows. The whole village may partake in a wedding or a funeral. All the women prepare food for a village celebration, and every family brings its share. Most village business is handled through social and economic cooperatives. The farmers sell their produce in a common market.

Life in the Cities

Japanese city life is much more Westernized than that of the countryside. The cities have modern housing and modern transportation systems. Many Japanese city dwellers live in high-rise apartment buildings and take subways or buses to their jobs in offices and factories. The daily lives of city dwellers have been transformed by modern conveniences, such as automobiles, electric household appliances, and central heating. Yet many traditional practices survive. Bath facilities even in modern apartment houses may be much like those in the villages, and many city dwellers still use public bathhouses.

In the cities, fewer marriages are arranged by parents and fewer young people live with their parents after marriage. Since more of the young men and women attend universities or work away from home, they have more opportunities to meet socially and to choose their own husbands and wives.

Entertainment in the cities is not as dependent upon family activity as is that of the villages. Women enjoy shopping in markets and department stores. Men are attracted by teahouses and beer halls. Wealthy men may banquet friends and business associates in *geisha* restaurants. Here they are entertained by geisha, highly trained girls who dance, sing, recite poetry, play a banjolike instrument called the *samisen,* and chat with the guests. The geisha are gowned richly in silk costumes, and their hair is elaborately styled. City dwellers can also attend a wide variety of theatrical performances and sports events.

Growing Up in Japan

When a baby is about seven days old, his father places a paper bearing the child's name before a household shrine. He does this to inform the ancestors of the family that another member has been added to it. Friends and relatives attend, bringing gifts for the child. When the child is about a month old, he is taken to the nearest Shinto shrine. There the priest may record his name and birthday, and the child formally becomes a member of the community.

A Japanese baby is often carried on the back of his mother, grandmother, or sister, safely fastened with broad sashes. From early infancy a child is trained in obedience. Spankings are rarely used, but a child may be ridiculed and shamed if he acts badly.

After World War II, the status of Japanese men and women began to be equalized. Prior to that time, boys and girls were treated very differently. Parents thought it so important to have sons to carry on the family name that boys were preferred and pampered. They could "boss" their older sisters and even their mothers. Girls, on the other hand, had to defer not only to their elders but even to younger brothers. However, a father expected his sons to achieve more than his daughters, and boys were brought up with the obligation to do nothing to harm the family's reputation. Japanese boys are still often favored above their sisters and more is still expected of them, but the disparities in the treatment of boys and girls are not as great as they used to be.

When a boy is about 21, his family may take steps to find a suitable wife for him. When friends have recommended a young lady with a similar family background, the prospective couple are introduced. If neither the boy nor the girl objects strongly to the proposed marriage, the boy's family chooses a go-between to carry on discussions with the girl's parents and make arrangements for the exchange of presents.

There are religious and regional variations in the forms of the marriage ceremony in Japan. In the Shinto ceremony, the bride and groom take three sips of *sake*, a rice wine, from three cups. The bride wears the elaborate clothing and the complicated hairstyle that are traditional on this occasion. The marriage ceremony may be followed by feasting and dancing.

The Japanese mark a man's entry into old age with a special ceremony which occurs between his 59th and 60th birthdays. At that time he dons a red kimono, a color not usually worn by adult males, to signify that he has shed the responsibilities of maturity.

Most Japanese funerals are marked by Buddhist or Shinto rites. The body is borne in a procession to a crematory or a cemetery. The period of mourning may last as long as 50 days.

Inside a Japanese Home

Japanese homes are rather small by Western standards. They generally have a kitchen and three or four rooms that serve as living and sleeping quarters. The walls are lined with thin bamboo strips. The floors are covered with *tatami*, woven straw mats six feet by three feet in size. A room's size is stated in terms of the number of tatami required to cover the floor. Among the most common sizes are 6-, 8-, and 12-tatami rooms. To keep the tatami clean, the Japanese remove their shoes when entering a house.

Most houses perch on two-foot-high posts set on rock foundations. A narrow porch on the sunny side serves as a hall onto which the rooms open. Permanent partitions are rare. *Fusuma*, or sliding screens made of paper-covered frames, may be closed to create separate rooms or opened to convert the entire house into a single room. *Shoji*, or sliding outer doors, are pushed back on summer days to let in air and are shut for protection at night.

The light, open construction of such Japanese houses is well suited to a warm climate and to a region where earthquakes destroy heavier structures. However, these houses do not keep out the damp chill of winter. A *hibachi* (charcoal brazier) gives some warmth. Sometimes a *kotatsu* (burner) is set into the floor and a table draped with quilts is placed over it. The family gather around the table to warm their feet.

Furniture in the Japanese home generally consists only of storage chests and low tables. In most homes the family sit on *zabuton* (low cushions) and sleep on *futon* (cotton-filled mattresses about four inches thick). However, many city families have replaced the futon with beds. Both the zabuton and the futon are stored in wall closets when they are not being used.

Traditional dress may be worn in Shinto and Buddhist wedding rites. A *montsuki* (crested coat) tops the groom's kimono. A *tsunokakushi* (hood) accents the bride's elaborate hairdo.

The most important spot in the house is the *tokonoma*, an alcove containing a low platform which holds a flower arrangement. Above the platform hangs a painted scroll. When callers come, the most honored guest is seated near the tokonoma. Except for the embellished parchment doors between rooms, scrolls and flower arrangements are usually the only decoration found in Japanese homes.

Carefully tended gardens demonstrate the Japanese love of nature. The rooms of a home often open onto a garden through a sliding door. Many Japanese gardens are actually miniature landscapes, with small trees, flowering bushes, pools, streams, and bridges.

Food for the Japanese Family

Most Japanese eat three meals a day. Rice, the mainstay of the Japanese diet for centuries, is eaten at almost every meal. At breakfast it is usually supplemented by *misoshiru* (a bean-paste soup) and *tsukemono* (pickled vegetables). In the cities, some Japanese have replaced these dishes with bread, butter, and eggs. Lunch is a light meal and may consist of salted fish, tsukemono, and *tsukudani* (seafood or vegetables cooked and preserved in soy sauce), in addition to rice or noodles. Supper is the most important meal of the day. In most homes it includes fish, beef, pork, or chicken with vegetables and rice. Meat is usually cut into thin strips and fried. It is not as important in the Japanese diet as in that of Western nations. Until the late 19th century, Buddhist practice discouraged eating the flesh of four-legged animals. Fish is often served raw.

The two most popular beverages in Japan are tea and sake. Tea is drunk during and after meals. It is also served to guests with such snacks as *soba* (buck-

Continued on page 374

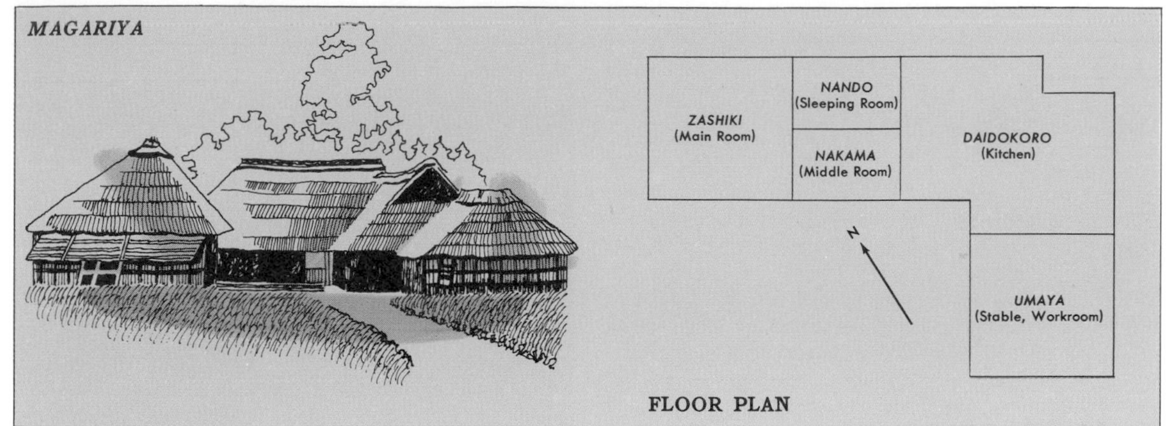

A stable to the right of the living quarters is the distinctive feature of the L-shaped magariya-style farmhouse. This type of Japanese home is common in the wild grasslands of mountainous areas in the Tohoku Region, where horse raising has been important. Linking the stable with the living quarters is a working and cooking area which provides warmth for the horses and storage space for their equipment. If the family has no horses, the stable is used as a workroom.

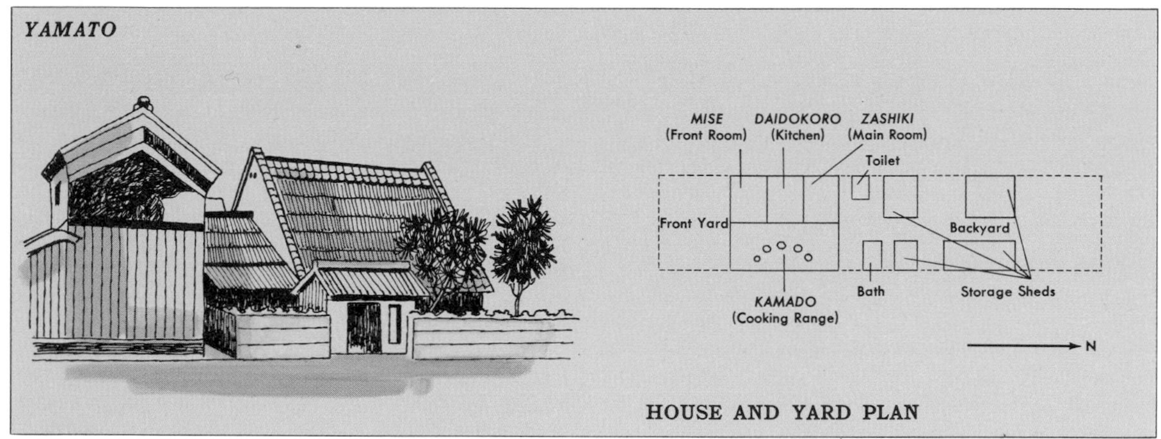

Yamato-style farmhouses are common in the Nara Basin and are generally found densely clustered in villages. In the string-shaped villages that wind along Japanese highways, the houses, outbuildings, and plots are unusually long and narrow. The gabled roofs of neighboring houses nearly touch one another. An important feature of the Yamato farmhouse is the large cooking area. It has a huge range, called a *kamado*, which may have as many as 11 cooking units of different sizes.

The small, simple Mitsunarabe-style farmhouse is generally found in southern Japan—particularly in Kagoshima Prefecture and on the Okinawa Islands. It is composed of a row of three individually roofed units enclosing living and sleeping quarters; a kitchen and dining area; and a stable, storage, and work area. The units may be joined, or they may be separated by narrow open spaces. Scattered outbuildings may house storage space and bath and toilet facilities.

The styles of traditional Japanese farmhouses were developed centuries ago and are adapted to the climate, economy, and customs of the regions in which they are located. As a result, the farmhouses in a given area tend to resemble one another. Japanese farmhouse styles include the *magariya,* the *Yamato,* and the *Mitsunarabe.*

The roof design of a traditional Japanese farmhouse expresses both the artistry of the architect and the individuality of the owner. Several distinct types of roofs have evolved. They include the *irimoya,* the *yosemune,* and the *kirizuma.* Like traditional Japanese house styles, individual roof types are often particularly common in certain regions. Thatch is the usual roof covering. Other roofing materials include wood shingles weighted by rocks, and decorative tiles—either alone or combined with thatch. *Chigi* (crossed ornamental rafters) may be placed on the roof crest. A ridge pole may run along the crest alone or supported by chigi.

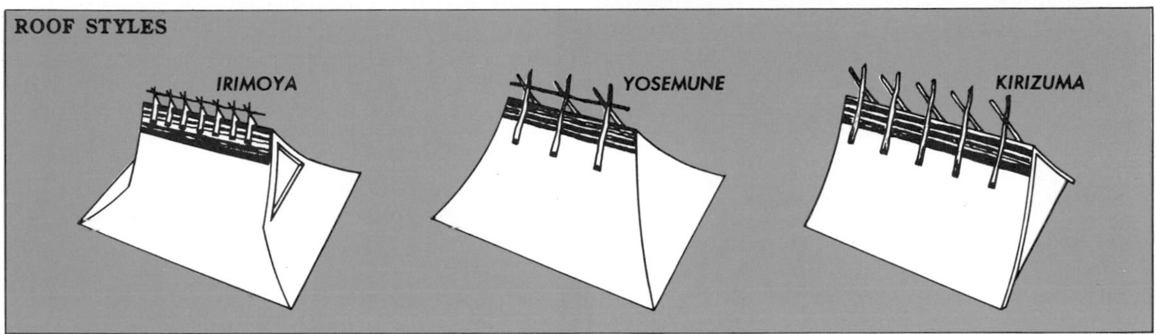

The irimoya (gabled-and-hipped) roof is found in Kinki Region, especially in the Kyoto area. It usually has long, low eaves and is large in relation to the rest of the building. Its crest is often beautifully ornamented.

The yosemune (hipped) roof is found throughout Japan. Its design, suited to areas with heavy rainfall, allows the rapid run-off of water in four directions. A variation of this roof type is slightly pyramidal or cone shaped.

The kirizuma (gabled) roof is common in central and western Honshu. Its structural simplicity shows the modesty which many Japanese believe to be proper for farmhouses. The gables are often ornamented with symbolic designs.

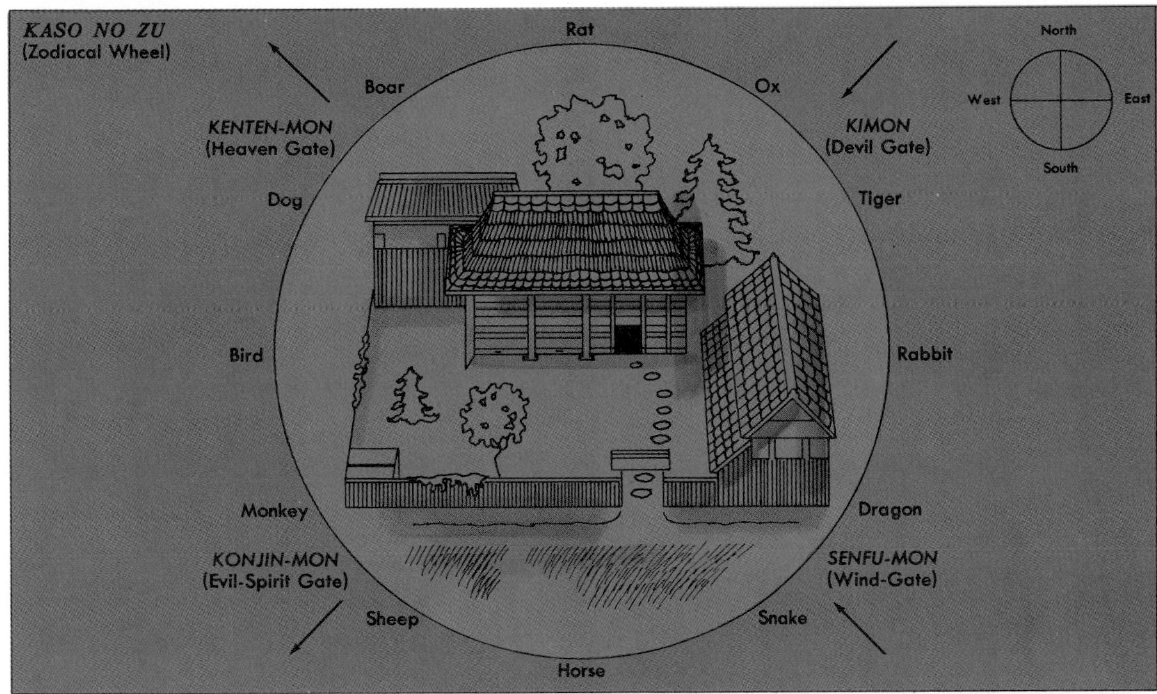

Many Japanese farmyards look alike because the buildings are arranged according to *hogaku,* a system of traditional rules governing lucky and unlucky directions. Twelve primary directions, each bearing the name of an animal, form a zodiacal wheel. The wheel, called *kaso no zu,* may be inscribed on the farmhouse's *daikokubashira,* or main supporting pillar.

No important part of the house should face northeast (*kimon,* or devil gate), considered an unfavorable direction. Since ill fortune is thought to flow from northeast to southwest (*konjin-mon,* or evil-spirit gate), spaces should be provided in these directions to allow bad influences to leave the farmyard. The southeast (*senfu-mon,* or wind gate) is considered a lucky direction. Income is believed to flow from southeast to northwest (*kenten-mon,* or heaven gate), where a strong room should be located to collect it.

In modern Japan the rules of hogaku are not always strictly followed. However, in many areas total disregard for hogaku may still invite public scorn.

Young pupils in modern Japanese schools are taught general science in well-equipped classrooms. About 30 percent of the college students specialize in some branch of the sciences.

wheat noodles) and *udon* (wheat noodles). Sake may be served before meals, but it is usually reserved for special occasions, such as weddings or holiday feasts.

Chopsticks are the only eating utensils—knives, forks, and spoons are not used. Food is served in china or lacquer bowls and in dishes. On important occasions, individual trays are provided. Usually a Japanese family sits around a low table for meals.

Japanese Clothing Styles

Modern Japanese dress incorporates both Eastern and Western styles. Western clothes, worn by both men and women, are seen most frequently on city streets. The traditional *kimono*, a loose-fitting garment with wide sleeves, is now worn principally at home. Men's kimono differ from women's primarily in color and fabric. Women wear their kimono at ankle length, bound with a sash called an *obi*. Men's kimono are shorter and on formal occasions are worn with a wide, divided skirt called a *hakama*. A kimono-shaped cloak called a *haori* may be worn over a kimono by both sexes.

The clothes Japanese children wear are much like those worn by children in the United States. Boys wear short or long pants and shirts or sweaters. Girls wear skirts with blouses or sweaters. Japanese girls still wear kimono for festivals, however.

The Japanese usually wear shoes like those worn in Western nations. However, *geta* (wooden clogs) and *zori* (rubber or straw sandals) are still worn with kimono. Socks called *tabi* are worn with geta and zori. The tabi have a separate place for the big toe—the geta or zori strap is held between it and the other toes.

Japanese men and women now wear Western hairstyles. The elaborate hairstyles Japanese women formerly wore are now used only at weddings or by entertainers in the theater and hostesses at geisha houses.

Education

Nearly all of Japan's school-age children attend school regularly. Attendance is compulsory through the lower level of secondary school. Children begin nursery school when they are about 3. At 6, they begin elementary school; at 12, lower-secondary school. Any student who has completed lower-secondary school may enroll in an upper-secondary school. The Japanese upper-secondary school is comparable to the United States high school. It offers either a technical or a college preparatory course of instruction.

Japanese students do not feel that they are in competition with other students for grades and honors. In school competitions, all participants usually receive some sort of recognition. All students are promoted at the end of each term.

To go beyond high school, however, a Japanese student must pass difficult college entrance examinations. Higher education is provided by junior colleges, four-year universities, and graduate schools. Before World War II Japanese colleges and universities stressed technical education. In recent decades, however, they have broadened their curricula and given greater emphasis to the liberal arts.

Recreation

Japanese recreational activities take place indoors and outdoors. Young children fly kites, spin tops, play baseball, watch television, and build plastic models. In the summer they watch fireworks, a pastime the Japanese have enjoyed for centuries.

With higher incomes and more leisure time, the Japanese have adopted a number of new outdoor sports. Blessed with high mountains and heavy snows, Japan has become one of the world's most popular ski areas. Most of the nation's major cities have indoor skating rinks. At Sapporo, outdoor ice-sculpture festivals attract many entrants each year.

Competitive sports have a wide following among the Japanese. Baseball—with two professional leagues—is one of Japan's most popular spectator sports. Other sports enjoyed by the Japanese include basketball, lawn and table tennis, volleyball, bicycling, hockey, and swimming. *Sumo, judo, kendo, karate,* and other traditional Japanese martial arts are now regarded primarily as competitive sports and as ways to keep physically fit.

The Japanese go on frequent family outings. Parents take their children to shrines and temples and to parks and zoos. Excursions into the country to view the spring cherry blossoms or the autumn foliage are very popular.

SCHOOL ENROLLMENT IN JAPAN

	Number of Students	
	1967	1968
Primary, elementary	9,452,071	9,383,190
General and vocational (high school, middle school, secondary school)	10,151,482	9,565,025
Higher professional school, teachers college, university	1,430,775	1,565,129
Total	21,034,328	20,513,344

Source: Ministry of Education

Religious Practices

Most Japanese people follow either the Buddhist or the Shinto religion. There are fewer than one million Christians in Japan. Many families combine Buddhist and Shinto practices. These families have two separate altars in their homes, one for the family ancestors, in accordance with Buddhist teachings, another for the Shinto gods. Upon awakening, members of the family burn incense in honor of the dead and clap their hands in tribute to the Shinto gods.

Shinto is the only religion that originated in Japan. Buddhism was introduced into Japan from Korea in the 6th century, and Portuguese and Spanish missionaries brought Christianity to Japan in the 16th century. Shinto received the support of the Japanese government until 1947, when the emperor disclaimed his divinity. The present Japanese constitution guarantees complete freedom of religion.

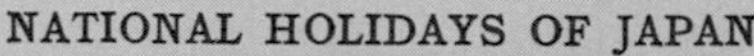

NATIONAL HOLIDAYS OF JAPAN

Jan. 1—Ganjitsu (New Year's Day). Celebrated by decorating the home, sending greeting cards, and visiting friends.

Jan. 15—Seijin-no-Hi (Adult's Day, or Coming-of-Age Day). Dedicated to those who reached the age of 20 during the previous year.

Feb. 11—Kenkoku Kinen-no-Hi (Day to Commemorate the Founding of the Nation).

March 20, 21, or 22—Shumbun-no-Hi (First Day of Spring).

April 29—Tenno Tanjobi (Emperor's Birthday).

May 3—Kempo Kinembi (Constitution Memorial Day). Marks the adoption of the 1947 constitution.

May 5—Kodomo-no-Hi (Children's Day). Dedicated to boys and girls, who celebrate it by decorating their homes with paper carp.

Sept. 15—Taiiku-no-Hi (Respect for the Aged Day). Honors senior citizens.

Sept. 23 or 24—Shubun-no-Hi (First Day of Autumn).

Oct. 10—Keiro-no-Hi (Health-Sports Day). Celebrates traditional sports and games.

Nov. 3—Bunka-no-Hi (Culture Day). Dedicated to the advancement of the arts.

Nov. 23—Kinro Kansha-no-Hi (Labor-Thanksgiving Day). Gives thanks to labor and for a successful harvest.

Health and Welfare Services

Japanese medicine is administered by the Ministry of Health and Welfare. The ministry operates health centers throughout the nation. At these centers doctors examine patients and, when necessary, refer them to hospitals for treatment. The health centers are also responsible for dealing with sanitation and public health problems.

At the November 15 Shichigosan Festival, parents give thanks at a shrine—these are at Tokyo's Meiji Shrine—that their children have safely reached ages three, five, and seven.

Most of the citizens of Japan are protected by a form of health insurance that is available on an occupational or a regional basis. The insured person pays a monthly premium. He is charged a small consulting fee for the treatment of each illness. The rest of his medical care is either furnished without charge or for only a fraction of its actual value. Members of the family other than the insured person are entitled to receive medical care for half the fees usually charged.

Words to Remember

buraku—a small farming village.
geisha—a female entertainer.
sake—a rice wine.
tatami—a straw mat, six feet by three feet in size.
fusuma—a sliding screen separating rooms.
shoji—a sliding outer door.
hibachi—a charcoal brazier.
kotatsu—a burner set into the floor.
zabuton—a low cushion used for seating.
futon—a cotton-filled mattress.
tokonoma—an ornamental alcove in a Japanese home.
tsukemono—pickled vegetables.
tsukudani—seafood or vegetables cooked and preserved in soy sauce.
kimono—a traditional loose-fitting garment worn by Japanese men and women.
obi—the sash used with a kimono.
geta—wooden clogs.
zori—rubber or straw sandals.
tabi—socks with the big toe separate, worn with geta and zori.

Questions to Think About

1. Give possible reasons why Japan has a low rate of population growth.
2. Which elements in traditional Japanese life may change as Japan continues to modernize? Which may remain unchanged? Why?
3. Half of the Japanese people live in the Tokaido Megalopolis. How might this urban concentration affect Japan's rural areas?
4. Give possible advantages and disadvantages in the way a traditional Japanese home is built and furnished.

IMPERIAL CREST

Source: Ministry of Foreign Affairs

The crest of the Japanese imperial family is a 16-petaled chrysanthemum. Most Japanese family crests have plant motifs.

NATIONAL ANTHEM

'Kimigayo'

♩= 69

p

mf

Ki - mi ga — yo — wa, Chi-yo ni — Ya-chi-yo ni

Ten thou-sand years of hap-py reign be thine: Rule on, my Lord,

f
mf
Sa - za - re - i - shi no, I - wa - o to na - ri te
till what are peb - bles now By ag - es u - nited to migh - ty

Ko - ke no mu - su — ma - - de.
rocks shall grow Whose ven - er - able sides the moss doth line.

Source: Ministry of Foreign Affairs

Kimigayo (Reign of Our Emperor) was adopted as the national anthem of Japan in 1888. Its words come from an ancient, anonymous Japanese poem. The Japanese court musician Hiromori Hayashi composed the melody. A revised version for Western instruments was written by Franz Eckert, a German who served as bandmaster of the Japanese army. Basil Hall Chamberlain, a British scholar at the Imperial University of Tokyo, translated the anthem into English.

JAPAN—Government

The present, Showa constitution of Japan became law on May 3, 1947, as an amendment to the Meiji constitution of 1889. It is based on a draft prepared in English by the Allied occupation forces after World War II. A Japanese version was debated and approved by the Japanese Diet, or parliament. In some quarters, the Showa constitution has been regarded as an American-imposed document, untrue to Japanese traditions and political realities. However, moves to revise it have made little headway.

Government Organization

Under the constitution the emperor is "the symbol of the State and of the unity of the people." His duties are largely ceremonial, such as opening the Diet or receiving ambassadors. The emperor acts only on the initiative of responsible government officials. His appearances in public are carefully directed by the Kunaicho, or Imperial Household Ministry.

The two-house Diet has the sole constitutional power to make laws. The upper house, or House of Councillors, has 250 members elected for six-year terms. Of these, 100 are elected by the nation at large and 150 by prefectural constituencies. The lower house, or House of Representatives, has 486 members elected for four-year terms. They represent districts that return from three to five members each.

All bills approved by both houses of the Diet become law, but a bill rejected in the upper house can become law if it is approved by a two-thirds majority in the lower house. A simple majority in the lower house is sufficient to ensure the selection of a prime minister or the ratification of a treaty even over the opposition of the upper house. In practice, however, the two houses are usually in agreement. The budget originates in the lower house.

The principal executive body is the cabinet. It is headed by the prime minister, who is chosen by the Diet. Ministers heading the major administrative agencies are named by the prime minister. They must all be civilians, and a majority of them must be members of the Diet. The cabinet is responsible to the Diet. If the House of Representatives passes a no-confidence resolution or rejects a confidence resolution, the cabinet must resign or the prime minister must dissolve the Diet and call a new election.

The judiciary is separate from both the legislative and executive branches. Fourteen Supreme Court justices are appointed by the cabinet, and the emperor appoints a chief justice nominated by the cabinet. An appointee to the Supreme Court is reviewed by the voters at the next general election for the House of Representatives. A Supreme Court justice is again reviewed at the elections following each of the ten-year periods that he remains on the bench. The Supreme Court has administrative control over lower courts. It is the court of last resort, with power to decide the constitutionality of laws, cabinet orders, regulations, and official acts.

Voters in each of Japan's 46 prefectures elect a governor and a one-house legislature. Voters in each city, town, and village elect a mayor and a one-house legislature. The governors and mayors can dissolve their legislatures, and the legislatures can, in turn, pass votes of no-confidence in their executives. Local governments adopt budgets and levy taxes. Local voters have the powers of initiative, referendum, and recall.

Routine national and local government business in Japan is handled by a professional civil service. Civil service appointments are based on written and oral examinations, efficiency, and other tests of ability. In 1960 one out of every 14 employed persons in Japan worked for a governmental agency.

Politics

Since the end of World War II, Japan's most successful political organization has been the conservative Liberal-Democratic party. In the 1969 general election it captured 48 percent of the vote and 288 seats in the House of Representatives. The opposition to the Liberal-Democrats includes the left-wing Socialist, Democratic Socialist, and Communist parties and the Komeito, or Clean Government, party, which is backed by a Buddhist sect, the Soka Gakkai.

Japanese political parties are mostly combinations of *habatsu*, or small factions centered on strong individual leaders. Local political organizations usually consist of small support groups for local Diet members. However, the Komeito party has a mass membership and an extensive organizational structure.

Japan has universal, equal, and direct suffrage. All Japanese 20 years of age and over have the right to vote. Participation in elections is high. In six national elections between 1949 and 1960 about 75 percent of those qualified voted, though in 1969 voter participation dropped to 68 percent. In local elections voter participation usually ranges from 85 to 95 percent. Candidates for office receive some financial aid from the government, but governmental attempts to limit campaign spending have been unsuccessful.

Interest groups play a major role in Japanese politics. National federations of labor unions are closely linked to the left-wing parties. Large industrial concerns, national federations of farm cooperatives, businessmen's associations, and professional groups have close links with the Liberal-Democrats. Interest groups provide electoral and financial support for political parties and individual politicians. They also lobby for laws or policies favorable to their memberships. The relations between special interests and government officials or political parties sometimes lead to bribery and corruption.

Demo, or mass demonstrations, are another means of influencing government policy. They are usually employed by the left-wing parties, which are able to mobilize the support of students and union members.

GOVERNMENT ORGANIZATION

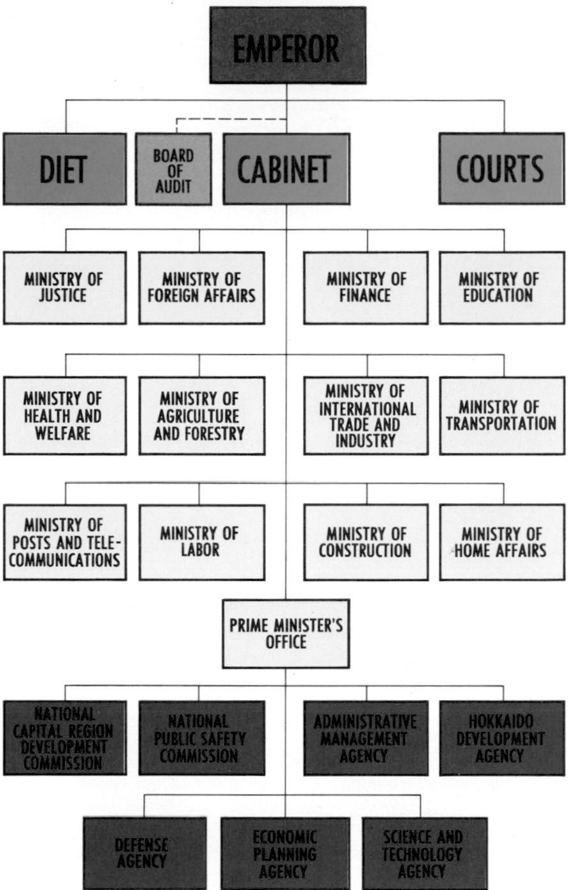

Source: Ministry of Foreign Affairs

Emperor Hirohito (seated) is Japan's head of state. In this official portrait of the imperial family Crown Prince Akihito is standing at the emperor's far right.

Elections to House of Representatives*

Party	Year	Number of Votes	Percent of Total Vote	Seats Won
Liberal-Democratic	1967	22,447,838	48.80	277
	1969	22,381,566	47.63	288
Socialist	1967	12,826,103	27.89	140
	1969	10,074,099	21.44	90
Democratic Socialist	1967	3,404,463	7.40	30
	1969	3,636,590	7.74	31
Komeito	1967	2,472,371	5.38	25
	1969	5,124,666	10.91	47
Communist	1967	2,190,563	4.76	5
	1969	3,199,031	6.81	14
Minor parties	1967	101,244	0.22	0
	1969	81,373	0.17	0
Independent	1967	2,553,988	5.55	9
	1969	2,492,559	5.30	16
TOTALS	1967	45,996,570	100.00	486
	1969	46,989,884	100.00	486

*Jan. 29, 1967, and Dec. 27, 1969.
Source: Election Bureau, Ministry of Home Affairs

In 1970 these Japanese students protested the renewal of the security treaty between the United States and Japan. Demonstrations on political issues are common in Japan.

Frequently, large delegations of workers demonstrate in front of the Diet building or government ministries. In 1960 massive demonstrations against the renewal of Japan's mutual security treaty with the United States led to the resignation of the cabinet.

The expression of public opinion is protected by the constitution. Japanese citizens are guaranteed freedom of speech, religion, assembly, and association and take full advantage of these rights. Newspapers and magazines are uncensored and are often critical of the government and of its policies.

The former, discredited nationalist ideology of Japan's military-imperial system was known as *kokutai*, or "national essence." It was based on deep devotion to the emperor and submission to authority.

Defense and Foreign Relations

The Japanese constitution renounces "war as a sovereign right of the nation and the threat or use of force as means of settling international disputes." Nevertheless, since 1950 Japan has developed its own land, naval, and air arms into a National Self-Defense Force. In 1969 the National Self-Defense Force consisted of about 250,000 men, supplied with modern weapons and equipment. All members of the force are volunteers.

Foreign affairs and the negotiation of treaties are handled by the cabinet. The prime minister reports on foreign relations to the Diet and must obtain its approval of treaties. Routine administrative business with foreign nations, such as granting visas, is handled by a professional diplomatic corps.

Japan is a member of the United Nations and many other international organizations. Since regaining full sovereignty in 1952, its foreign policy has been based on close ties with the United States. A mutual security treaty between the two countries affords Japan the protection of American nuclear weapons.

Words to Remember

Showa constitution—Japan's present constitution.
Diet—the Japanese parliament.
Soka Gakkai—the Buddhist sect which supports the Komeito (Clean Government) party.
habatsu—the factions that make up Japanese political parties.
kokutai—Japan's former nationalist ideology, based on submission to authority.
National Self-Defense Force—the armed services of Japan.

Questions to Think About

1. How are the Japanese Diet and the United States Congress similar? How do they differ?
2. What are the advantages and disadvantages of having voters review Supreme Court appointments?
3. Under what circumstances might Japan renounce the "no war" clause in its constitution?

JAPAN—Economy

The growth of the Japanese economy is one of the most remarkable success stories of recent decades. Though Japan was already a modern industrial nation in the 1930's, its economy was shattered by its defeat in World War II. Japan emerged from the war shorn of its colonial empire, shunned by its former trading partners, and occupied by foreign troops. Much of its industrial plant had been destroyed. Yet by the late 1960's Japan ranked third among the industrially advanced nations of the world, surpassed only by the United States and the Soviet Union.

Japan's gross national product soared to almost 170 billion dollars—about $1,640 per capita—in 1969. For the four-year period 1966–69 its annual economic growth rate averaged 13 percent. By the end of the 1960's the Japanese labor force totaled more than 50 million. The number employed in the primary industries (agriculture, fishing, forestry, and mining) fell from 17 million in 1955 to 10 million in 1968. However, the number employed in the secondary industries (manufacturing and construction) and the tertiary industries (trades and services) rose from 24 million in 1955 to 40 million in 1968. Despite the rapid growth of the labor force, Japan suffered from a labor shortage, especially of the skilled and the young and in small enterprises.

The Japanese economic miracle was based primarily on the application of modern technology and business methods and on a large, skilled, and hardworking labor force. In addition, the Japanese government encouraged new industry with subsidies, and more money was available for investments in industry and education because very little was being spent on defense. Japan's achievement was also spurred by a resurgence of national pride.

Agriculture

Japan has one of the world's most productive agricultural systems. Yet only 16 percent of the nation's total land area is under cultivation. A shift from subsistence to commercial farming has been taking place. Large crop surpluses in Hokkaido, northern and western Honshu, and central Kyushu are now shipped to the heavily populated, urbanized belt that stretches from Tokyo westward to northern Kyushu.

Rice, the staple food in Japan, is by far the largest crop in acreage, tonnage, and value. Irrigated rice fields, or paddies, occupy more than half the cultivated area of Japan. Most rice fields in Hokkaido and northern Honshu bear only one crop a year. To the south, where the winter is milder and the growing season longer, multiple cropping is used. Under this system, paddies produce a summer rice crop and a winter crop of dry grains or vegetables. As a result of government price supports and the use of modern farming methods, rice production rose steeply in the

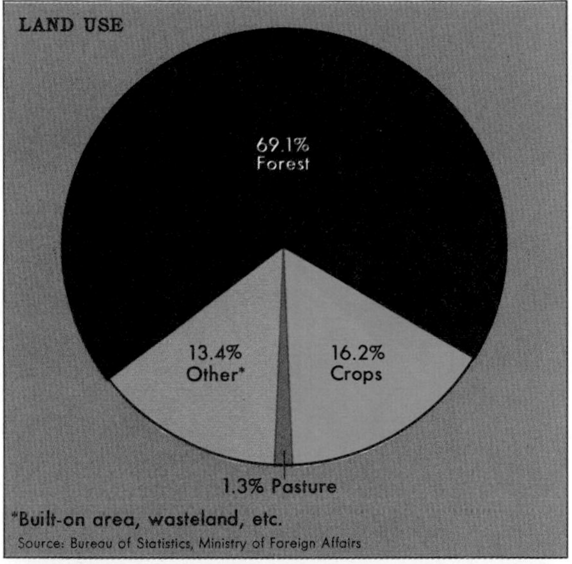

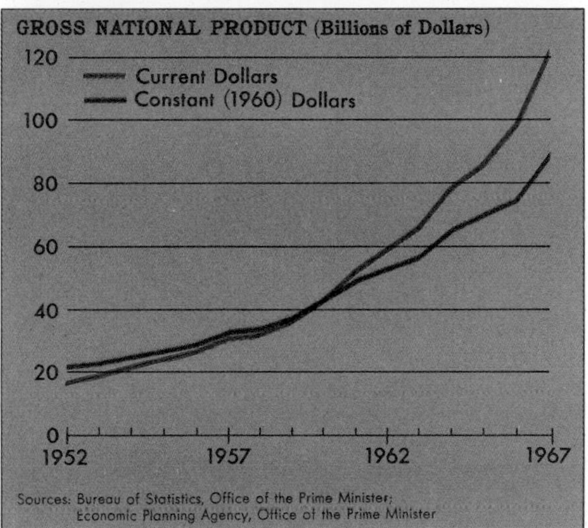

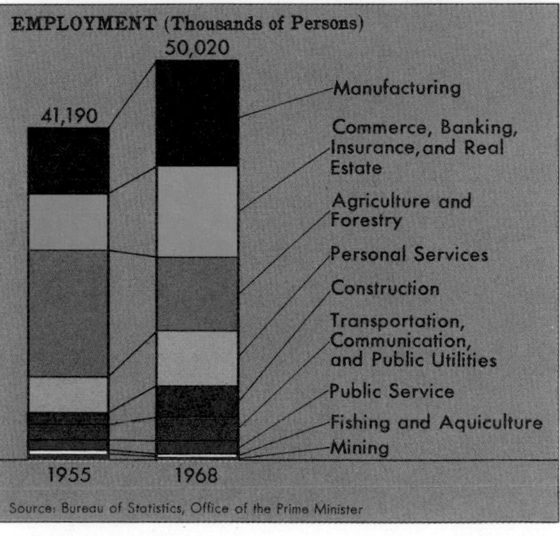

Tea production in Japan more than doubled between 1950 and 1967. These women are cutting quality tea leaves by hand. Tea is Japan's most popular drink.

1960's. Until the bumper harvests of the late 1960's, when 14 to 15 million tons were raised yearly, the Japanese consumed more rice than they produced. Now Japan has a rice surplus.

Leading Japanese crops in addition to rice include wheat, barley, soybeans, sweet potatoes, white potatoes, sugar beets, and vegetables. Mandarin oranges are a major Japanese fruit crop. Sericulture—the production of silk from silkworms—provides income to only 10 percent of all Japanese farm households, a sharp drop from the 50 percent of the 1930's. A small but growing number of cattle and hogs are raised. Farm mechanization, however, has brought a decline in the number of horses and draft cattle. Large market-gardening belts lie outside the main cities, and many agricultural districts specialize in industrial crops, such as tea, tobacco, pyrethrum, hops, and reeds.

The average size of Japanese farms is only about 2.5 acres. One third of all farms are less than 1.2 acres in size; only one twentieth, 5 acres or more in size. Average farm size increases from southwest to northeast. Only in Hokkaido, with its short growing season and relatively low productivity, does farm size average more than 12 acres. The typical Japanese farm consists of several small fields located at some distance from the farmhouse. Farmhouses are usually clustered in hamlets surrounded by the fields of their inhabitants.

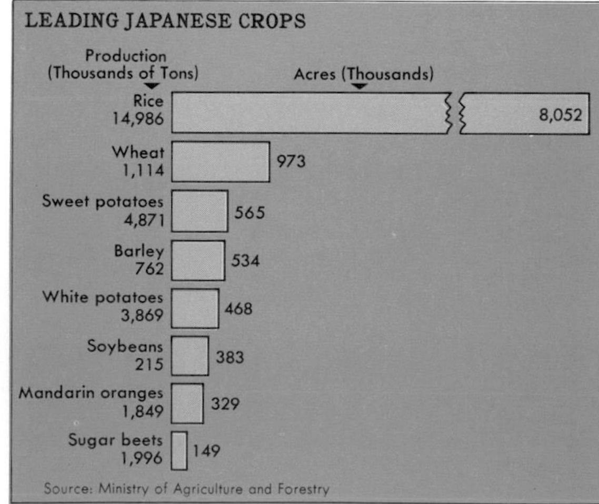

The percentage of the total labor force engaged in farming has been falling sharply. Before World War II, Japan's farmers comprised more than half of the total working population. Their proportion had declined to less than two fifths by 1955 and to less than a fifth by the late 1960's.

A large number of farm households are more dependent for a living on jobs in nearby cities than they are on farming. But many farmers who have taken city jobs are holding onto their farms because they regard them as a hedge against unemployment and inflation. The outflow of young men to the cities has been particularly great. This has led to an increase in the proportion of women and older men in the farm labor force. By 1965, women comprised 54 percent of all farm workers, and 25 percent of the men who worked on farms were at least 60 years old.

Prior to 1947, more than half of the farm families did not own the land they farmed. Under the Allied occupation, a Japanese government land reform abolished absentee ownership and transferred many farms to the tenant farmers who had been cultivating them. As a result, tenant-operated land was reduced to only 13 percent of the total cultivated area.

Farming was done mainly by manual labor before World War II, but since the 1950's mechanization has made spectacular headway. Most farm households now use power tillers or tractors; and power pumps, threshing machines, and other farm machinery have become commonplace. Mechanization has helped boost farm output despite the decline in the farm labor supply.

The amount of fertilizer used per acre by Japanese farmers is among the world's largest. Organic fertilizers—including night soil, or human waste—have been largely replaced by low-priced chemical fertilizers. Insecticides have reduced crop damage from insect pests such as the rice borer.

Funds needed by farmers to modernize their operations are provided by government agencies and by farm cooperatives. The cooperatives also help market the farmers' produce.

Fishing and Forestry

Japan is one of the world's major fishing nations. Its annual fish catch of more than 8 million tons is second only to Peru's. Japan leads the world in the value of its fish catch—more than 2 billion dollars a year.

Most Japanese fishermen work in shallow coastal waters. The typical coastal fishing craft have a capacity of less than ten tons. "Sea farming"—the culture in shallow coastal bays of prawns, sea bream, edible seaweed, oysters, pearls, and other marine products—has grown rapidly in recent years. The value of the coastal catch is about one third that of Japan's total catch. Offshore fishing, for which somewhat larger boats are used, accounts for one fourth the value of Japan's catch.

Pelagic, or deep-sea, fishing, which accounts for the balance, is done in waters far from Japan by large modern fleets. Mother ships serve the fleets as floating processing and canning plants. The Japanese government is a party to international treaties and conventions regulating the use of international waters for fishing.

The Japanese have traditionally depended on the sea for much of the protein in their diet. Though labor shortages are severe in the fishing industry, enough fish are caught to satisfy most domestic needs and to permit some exports. Many of the fish products used for fertilizer and animal feed are imported.

Forests occupy about two thirds of Japan's land area. About three fifths of the forested land is privately owned, mostly in small plots of less than ten acres. These are usually a part of normal farming operations and a source of household fuel.

Planted forests, many of them publicly owned, occupy about one fourth of the total forested area. Cedar, cypress, and pine are the leading species. Sawlogs are obtained mainly from Hokkaido, the mountains of northern and central Honshu, Shikoku, and Kyushu. Both conifers and broadleaf trees are harvested for pulpwood. Charcoal was formerly an important source of income for mountain villagers, but it has been largely replaced by gas and electricity as the main household fuel.

Lumber production has fallen below the peak years of the early 1960's. Since the demand for lumber continues to rise, Japan has relied increasingly on imports. The government has been trying to increase domestic production by opening roads to remote forest stands, securing top-grade tree seeds, promoting tree planting by private owners of woodland, and mechanizing tree-felling equipment.

Minerals and Energy

Japan's mineral and energy base is small compared with that of other major industrial nations. Its mineral deposits are limited both in quality and in quantity. The supply of ordinary coal, limestone, chromite, magnesium, pyrites, sulfur, lead, and zinc is nearly adequate, but large amounts of such minerals as iron ore, coking coal, petroleum, tin, nickel, nitrate, and phosphate must be imported.

In both volume and value, coal is the main domestic mineral resource. Northern Kyushu, Hokkaido, the east coast of central Honshu, and extreme southwestern Honshu account for most of Japan's coal output. Though Japan's total coal production declined gradually through the 1960's due to the growing popularity of petroleum as an energy source, its output of coking coal remained high. Nevertheless, more than

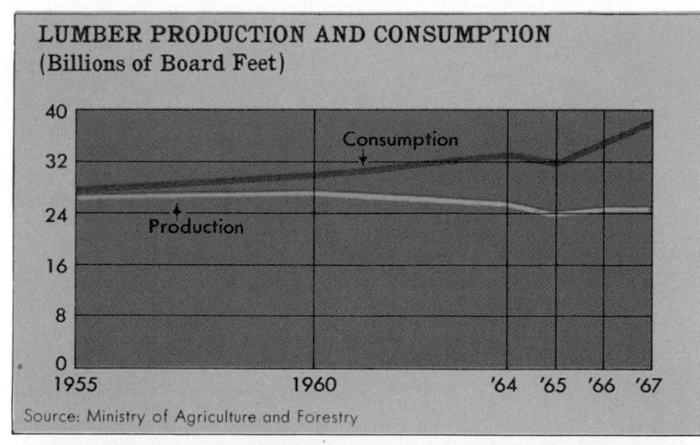

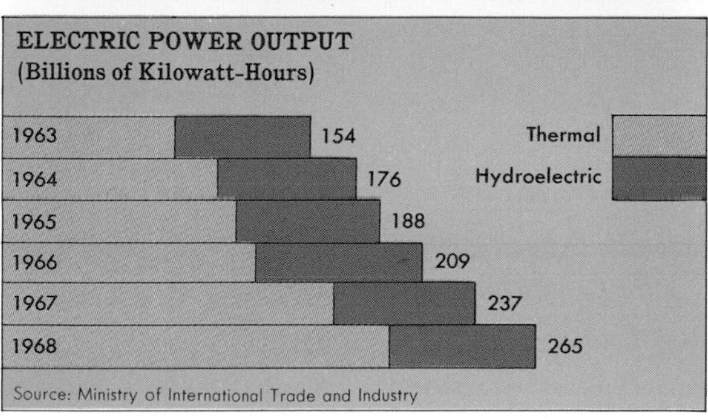

two thirds of the coking coal used by the nation's rapidly expanding iron and steel industry had to be imported. The small, scattered deposits of iron ore in Hokkaido and northern Honshu also met only a small part of the nation's needs.

The consumption of petroleum increased greatly during the 1960's. Japan's domestic reserves, largely in northwestern Honshu, are meager and must be supplemented with enormous imports from the Persian Gulf and other areas. Near Tokyo and on the central Sea of Japan coast are natural-gas deposits.

The availability of large supplies of electric power has been a key to Japan's industrial growth and rising living standards. Japan ranks third in the world in electric power output and fourth in installed capacity. Hydroelectric power made up almost

Small fishing boats unload on a beach near Tokyo. Fish, served at most meals, is the main source of protein in Japan. The average Japanese eats nearly 55 pounds of seafood a year.

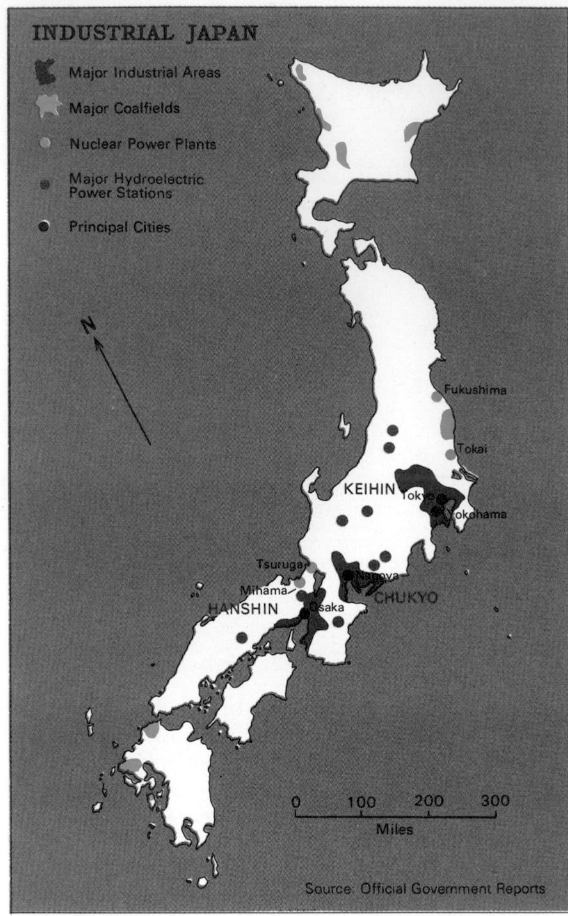

Famous throughout the world, Japan's electrical and electronic products contribute significantly to the nation's economy. Here delicate parts are soldered under microscopes.

two thirds of the total electric supply in the early 1950's. Since then, hydroelectric dams have continued to be built, mostly in central Honshu. However, there has been a much greater emphasis on the construction of coal- and oil-burning thermal power plants. Giant thermal power plants have been built along the coasts, near urban and industrial markets. Tokyo Bay has the largest concentrations of such plants. The first Japanese nuclear-powered thermal electric plant, situated at Tokai, went into full production in 1967. By the end of the 1960's thermal power plants were contributing about three fourths of the total electric power generated in Japan.

Manufacturing

More than one fourth of Japan's labor force is employed in manufacturing. Most Japanese manufacturing units are small workshops employing only up to three workers. These enterprises tend to be inefficient, to pay low wages, and to turn out goods of uncertain quality. But factories employing more than 300 workers—only 2 percent of the total number—account for more than two thirds of Japan's industrial production. Prior to the 1950's, Japan had a reputation for low-priced, shoddy goods. In recent years, however, the quality of Japanese merchandise has met the highest standards in world markets.

Many large manufacturing firms have merged into *zaibatsu* (giant business combines). In many cases—in the manufacture of machinery, for example—large factories subcontract to small workshops.

Manufacturing is heavily concentrated in the Tokaido Megalopolis—the heavily populated urban-industrial belt extending westward from Tokyo and the Kanto Plain along the Pacific coast and the Inland Sea to northern Kyushu. The megalopolis comprises 80 percent of Japan's workers and manufacturing plants and contributes 85 percent of the value of its manufactured goods. Japan's major international ports, its best overland transportation facilities, and the headquarters of its leading banks and trading companies are in the megalopolis. Most of the industrial complexes are on the coast where they have access to ocean shipping and imported fuel and raw materials.

Within the Tokaido Megalopolis are several major clusters of manufacturing activity. The largest—the Keihin industrial area—is centered upon the urban core of Tokyo, Kawasaki, and Yokohama, on the Kanto Plain. Within the Keihin area, large-scale heavy industry lines the western and northern shores of Tokyo Bay. The area is also a center for printing and publishing and for the manufacture of machinery. Yokohama provides international port services.

The Nagoya cluster—the Chukyo industrial area—is noted for its production of textiles, ceramics, and machinery. The postwar expansion of local automobile plants and the port of Nagoya, new steelworks, and a small-scale revival of the aircraft industry have provided a base for further growth. Here also, in the Kuwana-Yokkaichi area, is one of Japan's largest oil-refining and petrochemical centers.

The Hanshin industrial area includes the cities of Osaka and Kobe. It led the nation in industrial output until the 1930's and now ranks second. Osaka has chemical and textile plants and an electronics industry. Kobe is a major international port and produces ships and railway rolling stock.

Another industrial area is centered on Kitakyushu, in northern Kyushu. It developed around Japan's first steel mill, established in 1901, at Yawata. The Kitakyushu area specializes in the manufacture of iron and steel and has other heavy industries.

The Japanese government is encouraging the growth of industrial centers outside the Tokaido Megalopolis. Its aim is to diversify the economy of predominantly agricultural regions and to reduce the concentration of people and manufacturing capacity in the megalopolis.

Japanese industrial production increased fourfold between 1957 and 1970. Heavy industry, led by machinery, scored the biggest gains. In the late 1960's machinery—electrical and nonelectrical—accounted for one third of manufacturing output. The growing purchasing power of the Japanese people has led to a great increase in the production of consumer goods, such as electrical appliances and automobiles. The output of ceramics, glass, chemicals, rubber, and petroleum products has also increased greatly. However, the output of textiles and food products has not, reflecting the shift from light to heavy industry.

The Japanese iron and steel industry, vital to the development of all manufacturing, has grown spectacularly since the 1950's. Crude-steel output surpassed the prewar high of 7.6 million tons in 1953 and reached 28 million tons in 1961; 41 million tons in 1965; and 90 million tons in 1969. The industry's modern equipment helps make it a strong competitor in international trade. Its plants are among the largest and most efficient in the world. In 1969, 77 percent of Japan's steel was made in oxygen furnaces, 17 percent in electric furnaces. Specially designed ships deliver imported iron ore and coking coal directly to coastal steel mills.

Six corporations account for four fifths of Japan's steel output. The largest plants are in the Tokyo and Osaka areas of the main manufacturing belt; in Kamaishi in northern Honshu; and in Muroran in Hokkaido. The output of copper, aluminum, and titanium has also expanded. Aluminum output, which reached almost 600,000 tons in 1969, still fell short of domestic demand, however.

Great advances have been made in the manufacture of machinery, electrical goods, and transportation equipment. New factories use the latest assembly-line techniques for the mass production of high-quality goods. A home-electrification boom has resulted in a great demand for radios, televisions, rice cookers, washing machines, electric fans, refrigerators, vacuum cleaners, and other household appliances. Also widely used are stereophonic equipment, tape recorders, home freezers, hot-water heaters, air conditioners, and cameras. There is a large output of telephones, watches and clocks, sewing machines, fluorescent lamps; textile machinery, construction equipment, agricultural machinery, metalworking machinery; and electrical equipment, such as motors, generators, and transformers. Japan is the world's leading producer of pianos.

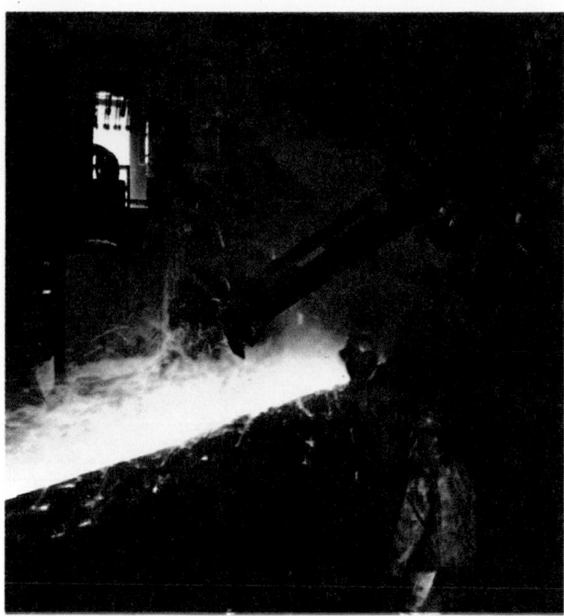

Japan's advanced and efficient iron and steel industry is largely dependent upon imported iron ore and coking coal. Japan is one of the world's leading steel producers.

The shipbuilding industry has thrived upon both the postwar worldwide demand for super oil tankers and specialty ships and government-sponsored programs for expanding the Japanese merchant fleet. Since the 1950's Japan has led the world in ship tonnage launched in many years building fully one half of the world total. Japanese ships are noted for their advanced design, automation, and high speeds. Japanese shipbuilders have won foreign contracts be-

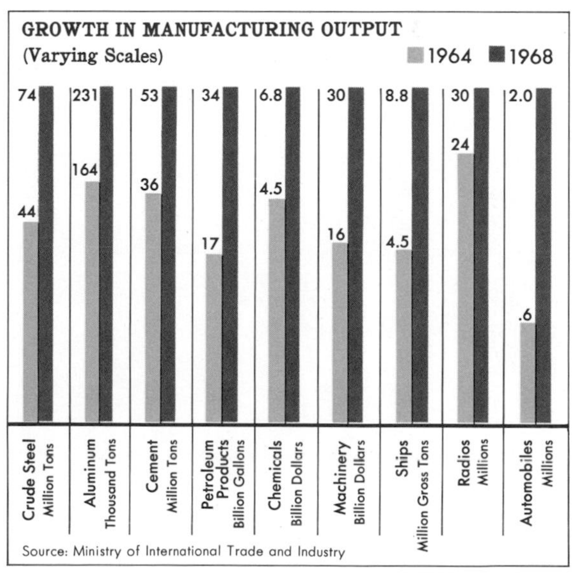

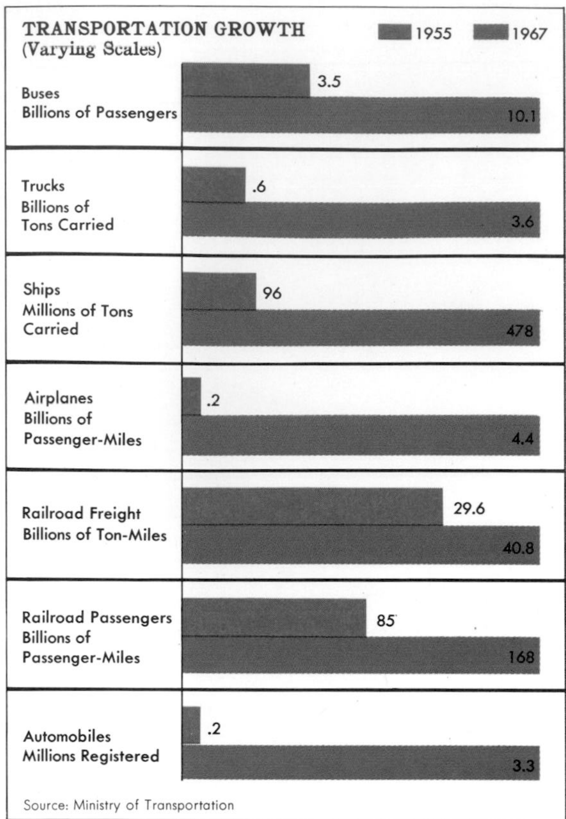

The growing use of the automobile has spurred the construction of such modern highway facilities as the Wakato Bridge (above), which spans Dokai Bay in Kitakyushu. Subways in Tokyo (below) and elsewhere serve Japan's city dwellers.

cause of their reputation for high quality, rapidity of construction, and relatively easy terms of payment.

It was not until the 1960's that Japan, already a major producer of trucks and buses, turned to the mass production of motorcycles and automobiles. American technology, styling, and selling methods were so successfully applied that by 1968 Japan ranked third behind the United States and West Germany in automobile output.

Japan is a leading producer of industrial chemicals, pharmaceuticals, chemical fertilizer, and petrochemical products, such as plastics, synthetic fibers, and synthetic rubber. Japanese oil-refining capacity is second to that of the United States. Japan is also a leading world producer of cement. Large amounts of Japanese-made plate glass, firebrick, asbestos products, fiberboard, and other construction materials find ready markets in the nation's fast-growing cities.

Textile manufacturing was Japan's first modern industry. As recently as the 1930's the textile industry employed one fourth of the Japanese industrial labor force. Outpaced by other industries, its relative position has slipped since then. Yet the textile industry remains Japan's leading employer. Cotton textiles, an early specialty, have lost ground to synthetics. Japan's output of synthetic fibers is second only to that of the United States and comprises one half of all Japanese textile production.

Transportation

Modern transportation facilities link all parts of Japan and facilitate the swift, efficient movement of people and goods. Railways are the main form of land transportation. Railway stations are the hubs of mass-transportation systems which also include buses, taxis, subways, and the vanishing trolleys.

The first Japanese railway was laid in 1872 between Tokyo and Yokohama. By 1930 a rail network covered the four main islands. Most private lines were nationalized in 1906 and passed to a public corporation, the Japan National Railways (JNR), in 1949. The JNR operates about three fourths of Japan's 17,000 miles of railway lines, including all long-distance trunk lines. It owns about 85 percent of all rolling stock. The private railways operate commuter lines in the metropolitan areas. Japanese railways use narrow-gauge track—3 feet 6 inches—and relatively small and light rolling stock. Almost one third of the JNR lines are double-tracked and electrified. Diesel and electric units have replaced coal-burning locomotives.

Postwar population and economic growth, most marked in the Tokyo-Osaka axis, has placed an enormous strain on the carrying capacity of Japan's railways. The high-speed, broad-gauge New Tokaido Line went into operation in 1964. Its fastest express trains make the 320-mile run from Tokyo to Osaka in a little more than three hours. An extension—the New Sanyo Line—was to be completed from Osaka to Okayama in 1972. The railways of Honshu are linked to Kyushu by undersea tunnel and to Hokkaido and

Shikoku by ferry service. Tokyo, Osaka, Nagoya, Kobe, and Yokohama have subways.

Modern highway construction has lagged badly behind the needs of automobile and truck traffic. Only one tenth of the total mileage of national, prefectural, and local roads is paved. The Japanese government's accelerated road-building program has been relying upon expressways to ease the intercity traffic problem. The Meishin Expressway (1964) from Kobe to Nagoya and the Tomei Expressway (1969) from Nagoya to Tokyo provide for uninterrupted high-speed movement through Japan's most densely settled area. City traffic is speeded by street widening and the construction of elevated expressways.

Domestic air service links all major cities. Japan Air Lines (JAL), the Japanese international flag carrier, operates round-the-world service. Tokyo International Airport, Haneda, built on reclaimed land on Tokyo Bay ten miles from downtown Tokyo, is the nation's busiest air terminal.

Retail Trade

About four fifths of Japan's retail stores have fewer than four employees each. These small stores, many of which have a small stock and make little profit, are usually operated by an owner and members of his family. They generally live in quarters to the rear of or over the store. In good weather, storefronts are open and goods are within easy reach from the street. Merchandise is also sold by peddlers who circulate in residential neighborhoods.

Western-style stores with plate-glass windows and window displays are becoming common in the cities. Supermarkets based on American models have also sprung up. Japanese department stores are among the largest in the world. They have prime locations in the downtown areas and near key railway terminals. The typical department store has a wide selection of goods and offers many services, including a children's playground on the roof, art displays and cultural events in specially designed rooms, beauty parlors, dining facilities, and home-delivery services.

Foreign Trade

Japan is one of the world's leading trading nations. The value of its annual exports and imports reached 30 billion dollars by the end of the 1960's. Japan imports a huge volume of fuels and raw materials, upon which its manufacturing industries are greatly dependent. It exports great quantities of manufactured goods. Japan's domestic market is too small to absorb its entire output of manufactured goods.

Manufactured items account for more than 90 percent of Japan's exports. Textiles comprised half of its exports before World War II but only about a sixth in the late 1960's. Machinery, transportation equipment, and metals—especially steel—now make up about three fifths of Japan's exports. Raw materials, such as iron ore, coking coal, and scrap metal account for about half the value of Japanese imports; foodstuffs, such as wheat and meat, for about 15 percent;

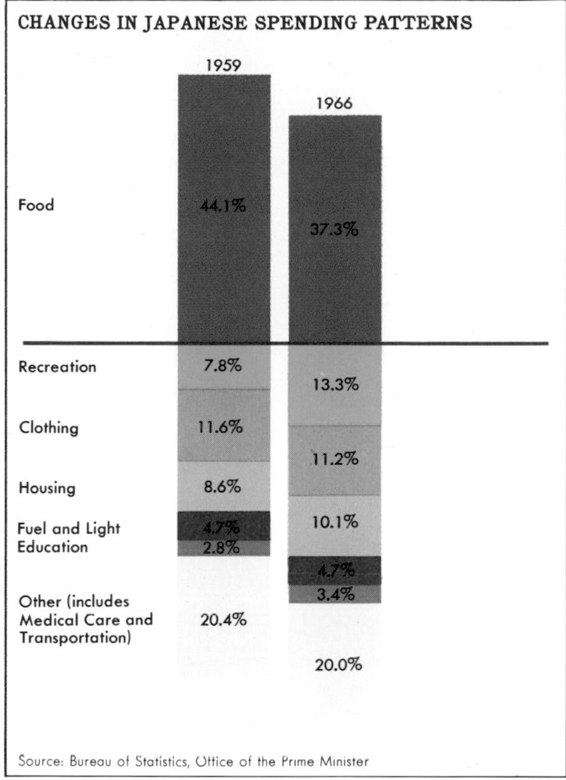

manufactured goods, including textiles, machinery, metals, and chemicals, for about 30 percent. Japan has had a favorable trade balance since 1964, exports having consistently exceeded imports.

Japan's principal trading partner is the United States, the supplier of about 30 percent of its imports and the market for about 30 percent of its exports. In this exchange, Japan's most important imports are machinery, foodstuffs, and sawlogs; its most important exports, iron and steel, machinery, and textiles. Nearly 30 percent of Japan's exports, largely machine-

Customers stroll in a covered shopping arcade in Osaka. Western-style department stores and supermarkets are providing strong competition for Japan's traditional small shops.

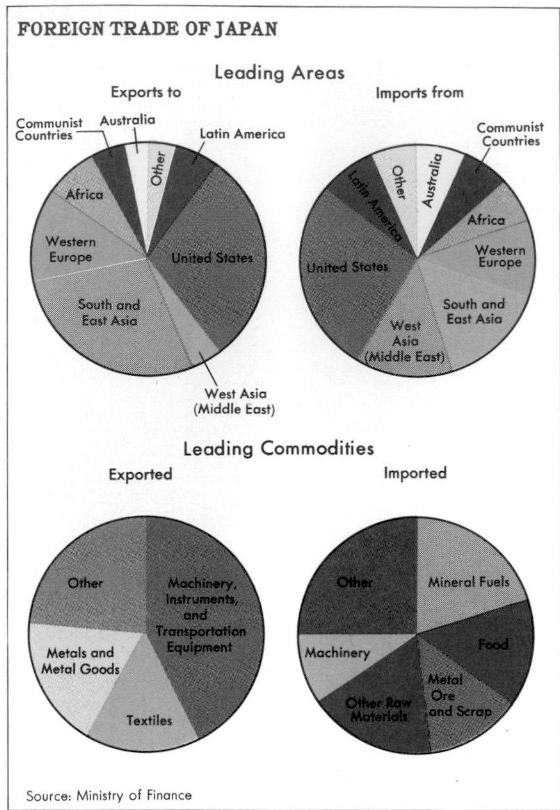

These merchant ships are berthed at Yokohama, Japan's busiest port. Japan has one of the world's largest merchant fleets and is the world's leading shipbuilder.

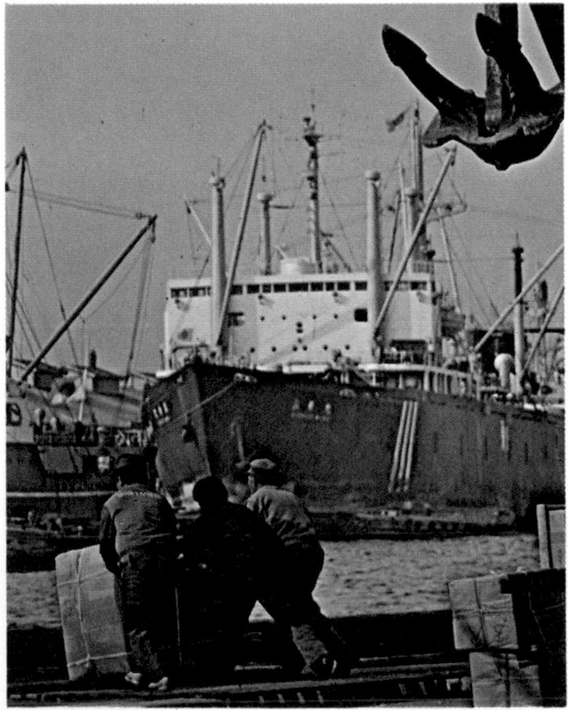

ry, textiles, chemicals, and iron and steel, go to the countries of southern and eastern Asia. Foodstuffs, sawlogs, and other agricultural products and raw materials from this region constitute about 15 percent of its imports. Japan's trade ties with Western Europe are also strong—the export of ships and the import of machinery being especially significant. The Middle East is a major source of oil.

Most of Japan's foreign trade is handled by large firms that are part of the zaibatsu. Shipping is channeled through ten main international ports: Kobe, Yokohama, Osaka, Nagoya, Tokyo, Shimizu, Yokkaichi, Shimonoseki, Moji, and Kokura. The deepwater ports of Kobe and Yokohama handle three fifths of Japan's exports and two fifths of its imports.

To guarantee its supply of raw materials, Japan has invested heavily in overseas developments. Its interests abroad include oil fields in Alaska and on Sakhalin and Sumatra; pulp mills in Alaska and British Columbia; copper mines in Peru, Canada, and South Africa; iron mines in Australia, Brazil, and India; and coking coal and bauxite mines in Australia. Japan gives other countries economic aid either directly or through the Asian Development Bank. It belongs to the Organization for Economic Cooperation and Development, the General Agreement on Tariffs and Trade, and other international economic organizations.

Communications and Information Media

Japan has one of the world's most advanced mass-communications systems. The Nippon Hoso Kyokai (NHK), or Japan Broadcasting Corporation, operates the nation's sole public broadcasting system. The NHK radio and television programs reach all parts of Japan through two television networks, three radio networks, and hundreds of local television and radio outlets. The television programs are financed through monthly license fees paid by each household owning a set—85 percent of all Japanese households. The NHK broadcasts emphasize cultural and educational topics. The more than 600 commercial broadcasting stations in Japan receive advertising revenue and stress entertainment in their programming. In most areas, viewers can watch television on three or more channels.

The Japanese are among the world's most ardent newspaper readers. Average daily newspaper circulation in Japan was about 47.5 million in 1967. The nation has more than 120 newspapers, two fifths of which publish both morning and evening editions. Magazines, books, and other reading matter are printed and sold in huge quantities.

Japan's government-owned telephone system is second only to that of the United States in size. Almost one fifth of its 21 million telephones are in the Tokyo metropolitan area. The government also operates the country's postal and telegraph services.

Finance, Labor, and Technology

The Bank of Japan is the core of Japan's banking system. The bank's purpose is to stabilize the value of the country's currency and to foster credit. The bank issues *yen* notes; the government mints coins. The country's commercial banks receive savings deposits and provide funds for private industry.

The Japanese government stimulates industry and foreign trade by providing funds through such agencies as the Japan Import-Export Bank, the Housing Finance Bank, and the Finance Bank for Small and Medium Enterprises. Credit associations, cooperatives, and the postal savings system are widely patronized by the Japanese people. There are large stock exchanges in Tokyo, Osaka, and Nagoya.

The Japanese labor movement flourished in the postwar period. About one third of all Japanese workers—11 million—are union members. Most unions are organized by single enterprises rather than by industry or craft. However, local unions have combined to form nationwide federations. The largest are Sohyo (the General Council of Trade Unions of Japan) and Domei (the Japanese Confederation of Labor). Management is organized in Nikkeiren (the Japan Federation of Employers Association).

Japanese businesses take a keen interest in their employees. They provide many benefits, including low-cost housing, medical care, insurance, paid vacations, and huge year-end bonuses. There is a rigid system of promotions and salary increases in Japanese industry. Employees are traditionally very loyal to their companies, and job turnover is low. A Japanese is likely to spend his entire working life on the job he takes when just out of school.

Japan's success in economic development is based in part upon its many highly trained scientists, engineers, and technicians. The Japanese keep abreast of scientific advances in other countries through professional journals, foreign study and inspection tours, and international conferences. Many large Japanese firms share technical information with companies in the United States and Europe—particularly in the chemical, communications, electronics, synthetic fiber, machinery, steel, and rubber industries.

Japan's investment in basic and applied research has lagged behind that of the leading Western nations despite governmental efforts to promote technological innovation. Japan has been playing a growing role, however, in transmitting modern technology to other Asian nations, especially in Southeast Asia. Many Japanese technicians go abroad to teach or to help assemble Japanese-made plants. Groups of Asians attend Japanese universities and receive advanced scientific and technical training from Japanese firms.

Tourism

The number of foreign visitors to Japan—especially from the United States—has been increasing steadily. Japan abounds in natural scenic beauty, offers a charming combination of traditional and modern facilities, and has a great variety of cultural attractions. Tourism is well organized. There are many modern high-rise hotels, especially in Tokyo, Osaka, and Kyoto, and *ryokan* (Japanese-style inns) may be found throughout the country.

Japan's scientists have contributed greatly to its economic development. Sin-itiro Tomonaga (1965) (left) and Hideki Yukawa (1949) both won the Nobel prize in physics.

An increasing number of international gatherings are being held in Japan. Special events have attracted many additional visitors. The most well received of these were the summer Olympic Games held at Tokyo in 1964 and Expo '70, Japan's first world's fair, held outside Osaka in 1970.

Tourists in search of unspoiled natural scenery can choose from among a large number of national and prefectural parks. There are sweeping views from mountaintops reached by ropeways, cable cars, and automobile toll roads. Other tourist attractions in Japan include the many ancient temples and shrines, the Japanese theater and festivals, and the restaurants and night life of the big cities.

Words to Remember

zaibatsu—the giant business combines of Japan.
Keihin—the industrial area centered upon Tokyo, Kawasaki, and Yokohama.
Chukyo—the industrial area centered upon Nagoya.
Hanshin—the industrial area centered upon Osaka and Kobe.
Sohyo—the General Council of Trade Unions of Japan.
Domei—the Japanese Confederation of Labor.
Nikkeiren—the Japan Federation of Employers Association.
ryokan—a Japanese-style inn.

Questions to Think About

1. What might be the effect of industrialization on living conditions in Japanese cities? In Japanese rural areas?
2. Spending money on defense is often thought to stimulate a nation's economy. Why then is Japanese industry believed to have benefited from *low* military expenditures?
3. How could the Japanese government induce industries to locate in areas other than the Tokaido Megalopolis?
4. Can Japan's economy continue to maintain its rapid rate of growth? Why or why not?

A Tour of Japan

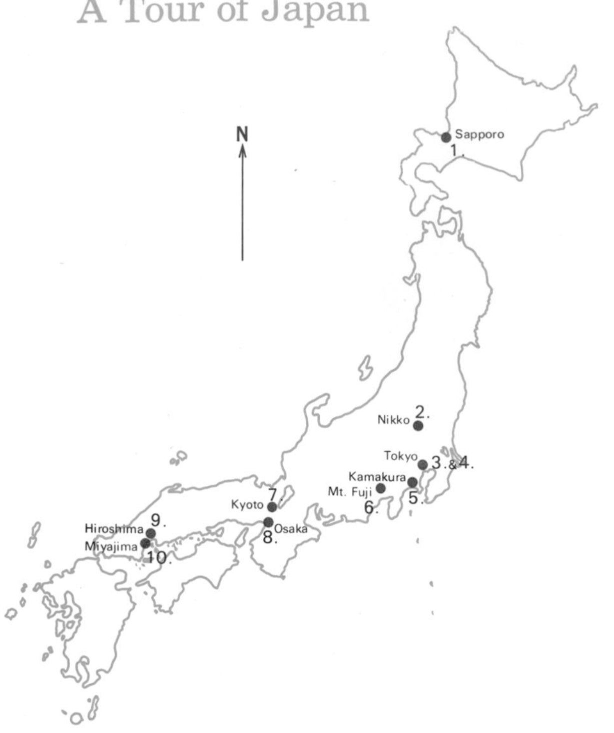

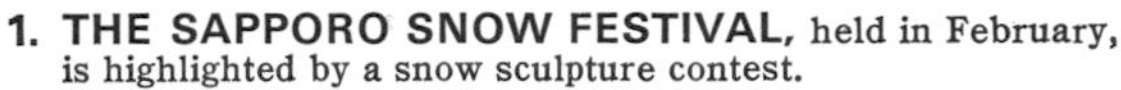

1. **THE SAPPORO SNOW FESTIVAL,** held in February, is highlighted by a snow sculpture contest.
2. **NIKKO NATIONAL PARK** is the site of spectacular Kegon Falls. Boating is popular on Lake Chuzenji.
3. **THE GINZA** is the world-famous entertainment and shopping district of Japan's capital city, Tokyo.
4. **THE IMPERIAL PALACE,** completed in 1968, replaced the Tokyo palace destroyed in World War II.
5. **THE GREAT BUDDHA** at Kamakura, a huge bronze sculpture, was cast in the mid-13th century.
6. **MOUNT FUJI,** Japan's sacred volcano, is a favorite subject of artists. A Tokaido express streaks past.
7. **THE KINKAKUJI TEMPLE** (Gold Pavilion) in Kyoto was a villa of the Muromachi period.
8. **THE TENJIN FESTIVAL** is held in Osaka each July. A sacred litter is carried to its boat procession.

1

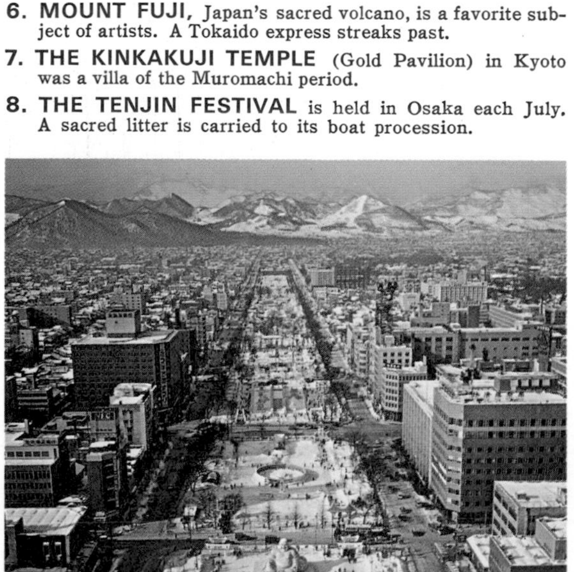

2

3

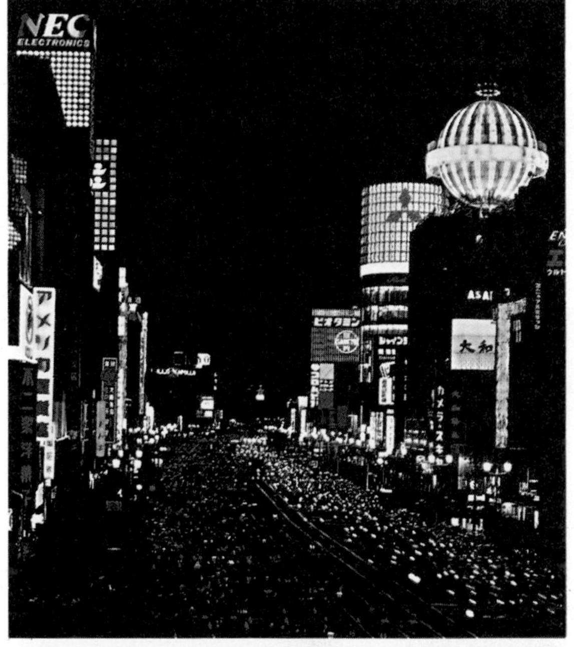

4

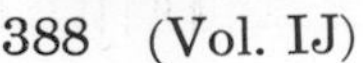

5

6

7

8

9

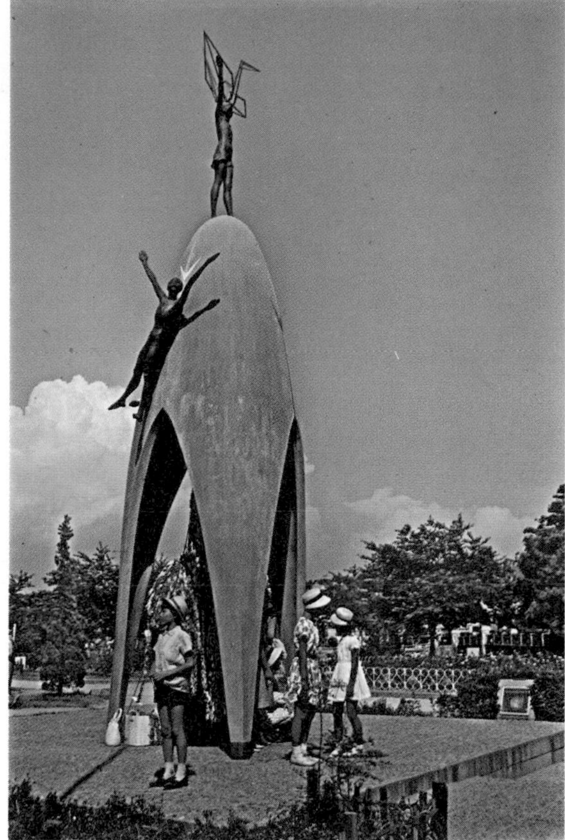

9. **THE CHILDREN'S PEACE MONUMENT** in Hiroshima commemorates the atomic bombing of the city at the end of World War II.

10. **THE TORII OF THE ITSUKUSHIMA SHRINE** is the largest shrine gateway in Japan. It was erected on Miyajima Island, near Hiroshima, in 1875. Ancient bugaku dances are performed at the shrine.

10

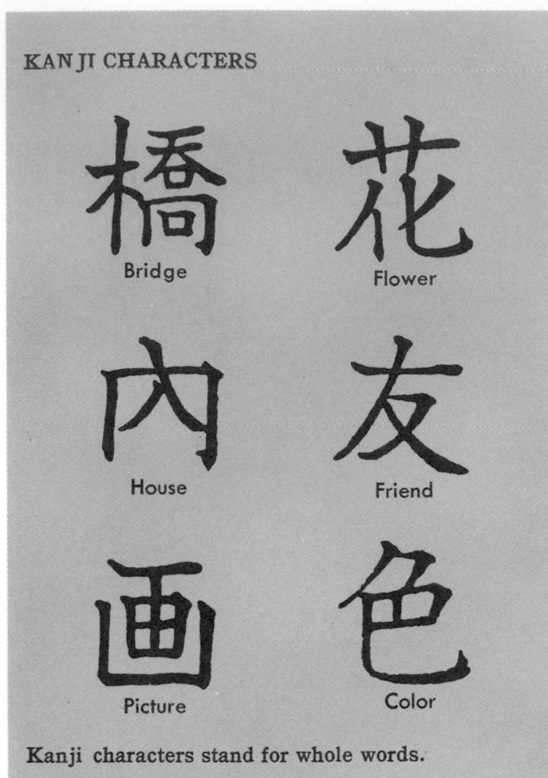

Kanji characters stand for whole words.

KANA CHARACTERS

	HIRAGANA	KATAKANA
ha	は	ハ
na	な	ナ
ta	た	タ
ba	ば	バ
mi	み	ミ
shi	し	シ
ru	る	ル
ku	く	ク

Kana characters stand for the sounds of syllables.

JAPAN—Culture

THE JAPANESE LANGUAGE

The language of Japan has many dialects, and speakers of different dialects do not always understand each other. But almost everyone in Japan uses standard Japanese as well as the dialect of his home area. Standard Japanese, originally the dialect spoken by the educated people of Tokyo, is now taught and understood throughout the country.

Broadly speaking, the accent in Japanese is musical. To say "bridge" (*hashi*) in standard Japanese, the voice begins with a low pitch on *ha* and rises on *shi*. If the voice is high for *ha* and low for *shi*, the word means "chopsticks." The pitch of a word can also change in a sentence. As a word, *hi* (fire) has a low pitch. But in the sentence *Hi ga deta* (Fire has broken out), the pitch pattern is high for *hi*, low for the rest of the sentence.

Japanese sentences are not put together in the same way as sentences in English. For one thing, the verb comes at the end of a statement in Japanese. In Japanese, the word order for "Kenji read the book" is "Kenji the book read." In addition, two language particles—*wa* and *wo*—are added. *Wa* often follows the subject of a clause (Kenji). *Wo* follows the direct object of a verb (the book). So the sentence in Japanese is *Kenji wa hon wo yomimashita.* To make a question of a statement, the particle *ka* is usually added. Thus *Kenji wa hon wo yomimashita ka* means "Did Kenji read the book?"

In Japanese, different styles of speech are used to show degrees of politeness and familiarity. A plain style is generally used in speaking to close friends. For strangers, a polite style may be used. To show honor and respect, a deferential style is often used toward parents, older people, teachers, and so on. Different styles are also used in talking *about* people and things. One of them, the exalted style, is almost entirely limited to references to the emperor and the imperial family.

The Japanese writing system is unique. Chinese characters, called *kanji,* were adopted by the Japanese more than 1,500 years ago. Because Japanese is very different from Chinese, however, additional sets of characters, called *kana,* were developed. After World War II the Japanese government modified the system of writing. Kanji were reduced from many thousands of characters to 1,850 basic characters, and their forms were simplified. Many words are written with kanji only. Some words are written with kana (*hiragana* or *katakana*) only. But most Japanese writing is a mixture of kanji and kana. In newspapers and magazines, Japanese is usually printed from top to bottom, in columns running from right to left. But in many textbooks, Japanese is printed horizontally from left to right.

THE LITERATURE OF JAPAN

Poetry is an important part of Japanese culture. Occasions of many kinds are celebrated with poems, and thousands of poems are submitted for the poetry prize awarded by the emperor each New Year. Most Japanese compose short poems, called *haiku* and *tanka*. Japanese poems, which usually do not rhyme, are based on a syllable count. A haiku is a three-line poem, with 5 syllables in the first line, 7 syllables in the second, and 5 syllables in the third. A tanka has five lines, with 5, 7, 5, 7, and 7 syllables. Because haiku and tanka are short, they can only suggest a mood or a picture; the listener or reader has to fill in the details. Matsuo Basho (1644–94), who has been regarded by many as Japan's greatest poet, was a master of haiku. A notable tanka poet was Ki no Tsurayuki (884–946), one of Japan's "thirty-six poetic immortals."

Japanese literature is noted for distinctive forms of drama as well as of poetry. The *no*, or *noh*, play combines recitation, music, and slow dancing. No plays can be considered scenes from the ceremonious life of lords and ladies during Japan's Middle Ages. The mood of these plays is usually serious—often tragic—and they are noted for their fine poetry, which is chanted by the actors and chorus. Because no plays are short, five different types of plays are presented at a time, each with its own music. The first is usually about a god, the second about a warrior, the third about a woman. Japan's outstanding no dramatists were Zeami (Seami) Motokiyo (1363–1443) and his father, Kanami Kiyotsugu (1333–84).

Like the no, the Japanese puppet play is serious drama combining words, music, and dancing. Perhaps the greatest writer of puppet drama, called *bunraku*, was Monzaemon Chikamatsu (1653–1725). His plays fall into two groups: heroic plays, often set in Japan's Middle Ages, and domestic tragedies—for example, 'The Love Suicides at Amijima'—which give a naturalistic picture of middle-class life.

For elaborate spectacle, *Kabuki* drama has no rival. Kabuki plays are distinguished by sensationalism and melodrama. One of the most famous Kabuki plays is 'Chushingura', about 47 *samurai* who avenge their lord's death and then commit *hara-kiri* as required by the law of the time. (*See also* subhead "The Performing Arts of Japan" later in this section.)

Japanese prose works tend to be series of loosely connected episodes. Diaries and books of random thoughts, which lend themselves to this style, are typical of Japanese prose literature. Early Japanese novels consisted of series of incidents, each incident built around a poem. Perhaps the greatest work of Japanese literature is 'The Tale of Genji', an episodic novel by Lady Shikibu Murasaki (975?–1025?). Most of the works of Ihara Saikaku (1642–93), the outstanding novelist of the Tokugawa period, are really collections of short stories based on one theme. In many modern novels it is common to find loosely related incidents.

Yasunari Kawabata (center, facing camera) was awarded the 1968 Nobel prize in literature. He is pictured at an outdoor tea ceremony in a Kyoto temple.

Shown below are part of a poem scroll by a 17th-century poet, a section from the 'Pages of Collected Poems by Thirty-Six Poetic Immortals', and an illustration from the novel 'The Tale of Genji'.

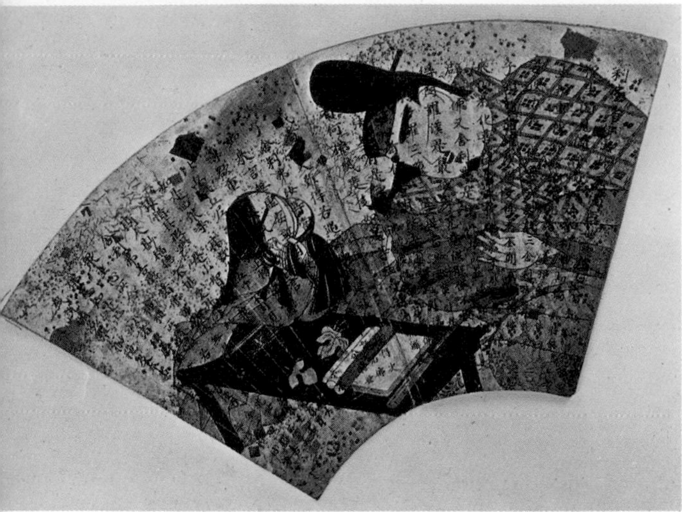

The 'Hokekyo Sutra', upon which the Nichiren sect of Buddhism is based, adorns this painted fan. A Japanese national treasure, it is kept at Shitennoji Temple in Osaka.

'Girl with a Maple Branch', by Katsukawa Shunsho (1726–93), is a kakemono painted on silk. Shunsho's famous paintings of Kabuki actors became woodcuts.

THE FINE ARTS OF JAPAN

The fine arts of modern Japan are similar to those of many Western countries. However, Japanese classical works of art are unique in the philosophy, methods, and materials used in their creation. These works include paintings and sculptures, as well as products of the decorative arts, such as pottery and porcelains, lacquers, textiles, and woodcuts.

Painting

In classical Japanese painting, black ink and watercolors were used on tissue-thin silk or *washi* (Japanese paper). Often the artist used only black ink, achieving a sense of color in the gradations from deep, luminous black to silvery gray. One-color paintings made in this way are called *sumi-e*.

Although classical Japanese paintings were realistic, they were never photographic. Instead, the artist used only a few brushstrokes to suggest the crumbly texture of a boulder; a hard-edged, rocky cliff; the gnarled trunk and rustling foliage of a tree; or the feathers of a bird. Unpainted areas of silk or paper created a sense of space and depth. Through economy of line and careful composition, the artist presented a distillation of his subject, leaving the viewer to fill in the details.

Classical Japanese paintings were "studio pictures." The artist did not go into the countryside with paints and easel. Instead, following a walk in the hills or along a stream, he returned to his studio to paint his impressions. The paintings usually took the form of hanging scrolls called *kakemono*, hand scrolls called *emakimono*, large folding screens, sliding doors, or fans. The hand scrolls, often 30 feet or more in length, are unrolled from right to left, the viewer enjoying only as much of the painting as may be exposed between his outstretched hands.

After Buddhism was introduced in Japan in the mid-6th century, great temples were built. These served not only as religious shrines but also as centers of art and learning. The numerous deities of Buddhism were depicted in paintings and sculptures. Artists, governed by precise descriptions in the *sutras* (holy texts) created likenesses of the Buddha, his disciples, and minor deities, as well as complex maplike representations of gods surrounding a central Buddha. These figures were painted or carved to embellish the temples and instruct the devout. Long narrative hand scrolls record in fine line and rich color the lives, journeys, and campaigns of important Buddhist priests and nobles. The names of most early painters, many of them priests, are no longer known.

Sumi-e developed rapidly during the Muromachi period (1392–1573) of Japanese art. It was fostered by Zen Buddhism, which stressed simplicity and was influenced by similar examples from China. However, while Japan was subjected over the centuries to successive waves of influence from China, the artists assimilated the foreign styles and in almost every instance made them uniquely their own.

During the Muromachi period and the Momoyama period (1573–1615), distinctive schools of painting emerged and individual artists established their fame. The Buddhist monk Sesshu (1420–1506) perfected black-and-white landscape painting in the Chinese tradition. The Kano school, founded by Masanobu Kano (1434–1530) and continued by his family, developed a distinctively Japanese style. Folding screens and sliding door panels in rich colors and patterns, often on a ground of gold or silver, were created to enliven the austere grandeur of 16th- and 17th-century castle interiors. The creators of these works were called "the great decorators." The Kano school remained dominant well into the Edo, or Tokugawa, period (1615–1867). It shared favor with traditional Chinese-style ink painting as well as a new artistic style called *ukiyo-e,* paintings depicting the life of common people.

Woodcuts

Woodcuts were made in Japan as early as the 11th century. But this art form enjoyed its greatest popularity from the mid-17th through the 19th centuries. The earliest woodcuts, which portrayed Buddhist patriarchs and deities, were executed in black with strong, rhythmic lines and areas of simple pattern. Occasionally, rich red-oranges, mustard yellows, and greens were added by hand. Early color prints, developed around 1740, were also restricted to three colors, usually green or pinkish-red, and sometimes yellow. True color prints, using many wood blocks and called *nishiki-e* (brocade pictures), were developed in 1765. A print bore the name of the artist who designed it. The carving and printing, however, were done by two other craftsmen.

Japanese woodcuts are probably the finest expression of the ukiyo-e movement. Courtesans, Kabuki actors, and scenes from Kabuki dramas were popular subjects. Moronobu Hishikawa (1618–94) is credited with beginning the ukiyo-e tradition of printmaking. The era of the full-color print starts with the work of Harunobu Suzuki (1725–70). The early 19th century brought both the full maturity and the gradual degeneration of this art form. The landscape artists Hokusai Katsushika (1760–1849) and Hiroshige Ando (1797–1858) were the last outstanding woodcut artists of the ukiyo-e. In the 20th century a modern movement in printmaking developed, called *sosaku hanga* (creative prints).

Sculpture

Japanese sculpture of the pre-Buddhist period is perhaps best represented by the *haniwa* (clay cylinders), which date from the 3d to the 5th century. These images of red clay were sometimes elaborately modeled in the forms of animals, birds, and human figures. Placed fencelike around tomb mounds of the imperial family and important court figures, the haniwa seem to have served the dual function of preventing soil erosion and providing the deceased with objects they had enjoyed during their lives.

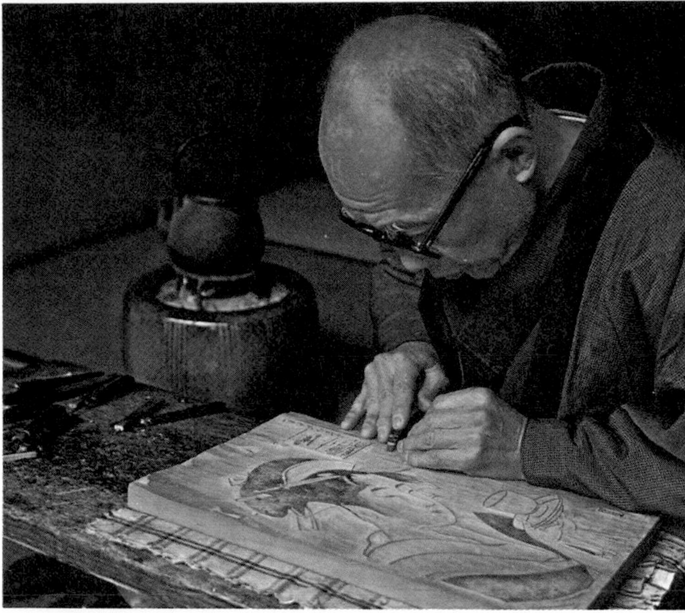

Traditional woodcuts are still produced in modern Japan. The printing blocks, usually cherry wood, are carved with the grain rather than across it as is done in Western nations.

This haniwa warrior figure dates from the 5th century A.D. The cylindrical bases of the haniwa were used to hold the images firmly in the ground.

Following the introduction of Buddhism to Japan, the development of sculpture paralleled that of painting. Numerous icons depicted the growing number of deities. Sculpture closely followed earlier Chinese examples which had been transmitted through Korea. Important images were cast in bronze, though wood was also favored. In later periods, wood and clay were increasingly preferred, as was dry lacquer. This consisted of successive coats of lacquer applied to cloth over a clay or wood core that was later removed. Since stone was scarce and of poor quality, it was almost never used in sculpture. Most of the best surviving sculptures were made by unknown masters.

A noteworthy 8th-century tendency, which continued through the Kamakura period (1185–1392), was the portraitlike quality of much of the sculpture. This may in part be attributed to the growing preference for the dry-lacquer technique, which allowed greater inventiveness on the part of the artist. The finished product was light but durable. An innovation in wood sculpture—the use of small blocks ingeniously fitted together, rather than a single block or log—also provided the artist with greater freedom of expression.

Japanese sculpture reached its peak during the Kamakura period. Although distinctive pieces were made in later eras, sculpture never again attained the position it had enjoyed in the preceding seven centuries. Most of the important sculptures have remained in the temples for which they were created.

Decorative Arts

The Japanese decorative arts include the making of pottery, porcelains, lacquers, and textiles. It is for such works that Japan is perhaps best known.

The earliest examples of Japanese artistic expression are earthenware vessels called *jomon* (rope-patterned) and the later, but still archaic, *yayoi* pottery. Some jomon specimens may date as far back as 6000 B.C. The style continued until about the 2d century B.C., when it was supplanted by the more finely executed yayoi.

The process of making true porcelain was not introduced into Japan until the 16th century. Elegantly patterned products found favor with the nobility and court circles. By contrast, native rough pottery enjoyed great popularity in intellectual circles and was especially favored for use in the tea ceremony.

Many well-known painters also applied their skills to allied arts. Koetsu Honnami (1558–1637), famed for his calligraphy, or decorative writing, was also a gifted potter and lacquer designer. Kenzan Ogata (1663–1743) executed in pottery the designs of his brother Korin (1658–1716), who was renowned for bold decorative paintings.

The dry-lacquer technique was used not only for sculpture but also for decorative accessories such as trays, tables, small chests, containers for tea and candy, and sumptuously fitted picnic boxes. Sprinklings of gold and silver powder and burnished and cut-gold foil—alone or combined with inlays of shell, mother-of-pearl, or metal—provided a bold contrast to the red, black, brown, and green lacquer surfaces. The 18th- and 19th-century love of splendor and rich decoration was mirrored in handsomely brocaded silks favored by the court and clergy. The latter, under vows of poverty, cut brocades into small squares and pieced them together again so that their fine garments would simulate the patched clothing of leaner years. Even the simple folk designs worn by the poor reflected the taste of Japanese weavers.

The woodcut 'Winter' was made by Kunihiro Amano in 1957. All but a small part is shown here. Modern Japanese printmakers carve and print their blocks as well as design them.

Architecture and Gardens

Japanese architecture, like painting and sculpture, made its greatest advances following the introduction of Buddhism. As with sculpture, wood was the primary material. The design of traditional Japanese architecture emphasizes horizontal lines. Even in taller structures like pagodas, the use of sloping roofs helps minimize the impression of height.

Great temples and monasteries and feudal castles and palaces are the major architectural monuments. The temples are characterized by vast halls and soaring roofs. Based on Chinese examples, the temples and storied pagodas feature elaborate bracketing systems to support their roofs. Major constructions mirror the taste of the periods which produced them. Horyuji Temple near Nara reflects the simple elegance favored in the 7th century. The Toshogu Shrine in Nikko illustrates the opulence of the Edo period.

Secular architecture of nearly all periods reveals the Japanese love for refined simplicity. Interior and exterior finishes depend on the fine grain of wood and textured stucco.

Origami—Japanese Paper Folding

Origami, the Japanese art of paper folding, may have originated in the 8th century in connection with the Dolls' Festival, now celebrated annually on March 3. On this day children would make paper dolls which they threw into a river to carry away the evil spirits hiding in their bodies. Today both adults and children enjoy making origami decorations, puppets, dolls, and animals.

Origami figures can be made with any thin, crisp paper that takes a sharp crease. Origami paper is usually square, brightly colored on one side, and lightly colored or white on the other side. Colored inks or paints may be used to decorate a completed origami figure. Origami figures can be so constructed that they seem to move and fly.

Modern origami is a symbolic art as well as a hobby. A paper crane or a tortoise attached to an important gift signifies a wish for good fortune and long life. Paper carps, signifying persistence and aspiration, are flown during the May 5 Children's Day festival.

HOW TO MAKE ORIGAMI FOLDS

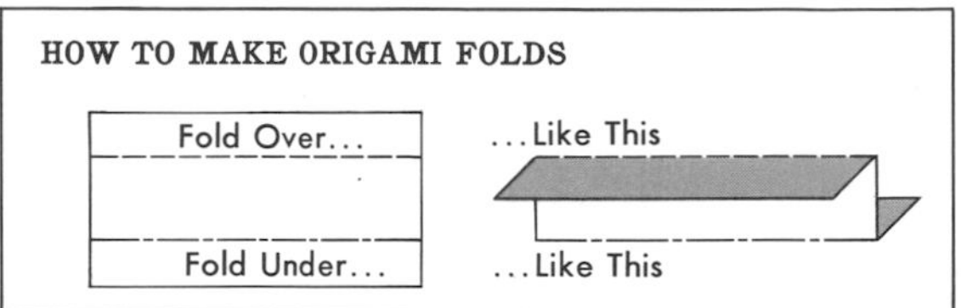

HOW TO MAKE AN ORIGAMI FISH

1. Place a sheet of square origami paper on a table with the light side up. Lettering may be added lightly as shown for aid in folding.

2. Fold the top half of the sheet over the bottom half so that the colored side appears. Fold the right side over the left side. Unfold, leaving creases IB and IF (in back). Fold corner D under so that it meets point F. Unfold, leaving creases IC and IE (in back).

3. Bring corner C up and over to corner A so that point D meets point B, refolding creases IB and IC. Press paper flat.

4. Turn paper over. Fold corner H under so that it meets point D. Unfold, leaving creases IG and IA (in back). Bring corner G up and over to corner E, refolding creases IF and IG.

5. Press paper flat.

6. Cut out shaded areas to form fins.

7. Decorate the completed figure if desired. Several fish can be fashioned into a mobile or used to make an ocean or aquarium scene.

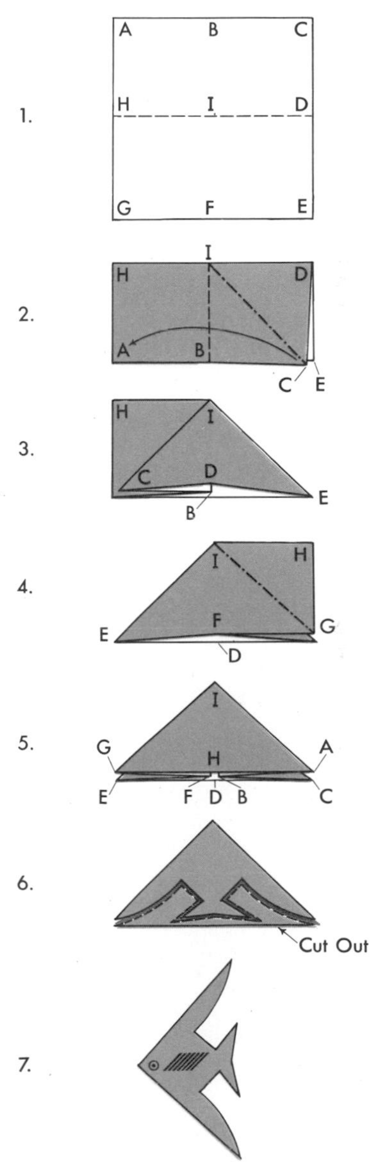

Handsome gardens are created to so complement the buildings they surround that the landscape and structures appear to be part of one another. Moss, trees, pebbles, and rocks may be combined with artificial hills, ponds, and a stream to suggest the natural beauty of a lake, seascape, or mountain waterfall. Profound simplicity is achieved in the garden of Ryoanji Temple near Kyoto, for example, by the use of five artfully placed rock formations set in moss in a patterned field of white sand. Whatever its proportions or the materials used, the Japanese garden is designed to invite entry and inspire meditation.

Interior Decoration and Home Arts

The art of raising *bonsai* (dwarfed potted trees) has enabled the Japanese to admire nature in an indoor setting. Bonsai are able to bear fruit and to drop their leaves in season, thus reproducing nature in miniature. A skillful bonsai artist can prune, bend, and shape branches to suggest trees standing tall and upright in a field or bent and gnarled by age or weather. The beauty of a natural landscape is evoked in the viewer's imagination.

Another means of enjoying nature in the home is through the arrangement of flowers, which has been refined in Japan to an art known as *ikebana*. Unlike Western arrangements which emphasize the color and form of flowers, ikebana favors the flowing lines of stems, leaves, and branches. In any arrangement, the plant materials used must convey a feeling of continuing growth as well as be symbolic of time and the season. Full blossoms might suggest the past; buds, the future. A full and spreading arrangement might suggest summer; a sparse one, autumn. A graceful floral design and a symbolic ornamental scroll often decorate the alcove called the *tokonoma*, the place of honor in a Japanese home.

Chanoyu, the ceremonial art of making tea, is a notable aesthetic discipline in Japan. Through the delicate flavor of the tea and the simplicity of the ceremony, participants in the ritual hope to achieve serenity and an understanding of true beauty. (*See also* Tea.)

THE PERFORMING ARTS OF JAPAN

The Japanese have great respect for their ancient, traditional performing arts. At the same time they are attracted by new, more modern forms. As a result, a Japanese who enjoys a performance of *bugaku*, an ancient musical dance of the imperial court, may also take pleasure in a concert of contemporary Western music played by an excellent Japanese symphony orchestra.

One reason for the vitality of the performing arts in Japan is that "performance" is an essential part of the nation's life. The ceremonies of the native Shinto religion include music and dance. A Japanese wanting to honor the gods pays for a performance of the sacred dance *kagura* at a shrine. During the *bon* festival, a Buddhist celebration for the souls of the dead, the young people of a community dance in a circle around a drum tower. In the summer, groups of young men carrying a portable shrine dance and chant through the city streets. All such dances are related to the Japanese love and worship of nature.

Rhythm, singing, and chanting are also part of everyday work in Japan—pulling a net from the sea, felling timber, even erecting a telephone pole. Ancient music and dance accompany the planting and harvesting of rice. Music and rhythmical movement closely combine dancing, acting, and instrumental and vocal music. In any traditional Japanese stage performance, it is difficult to say where the dancing stops and the acting begins.

The Japanese performing arts differ greatly from those of the West. Traditional Japanese music does not use Western keys and scales. The drums, stringed instruments, and flutes produce sounds not usually heard from Western instruments, though the *koto* (Japanese harp) comes close to sounding Western. Traditional Japanese singing uses a different system of voice production than that of the West, and the traditional dance employs patterns of body movement unfamiliar in the West. A traditional Japanese actor does not think he should look like a "real person" when he is performing. From his youth the Japanese performing artist is trained in the strict imitation of his teacher. This method insures that traditional techniques of performance are preserved in a continuous, almost unchanged, artistic heritage.

Before 1640, foreign influences on the Japanese performing arts came only from the Asian mainland. But, as is typical in Japan, the borrowed materials were refined into a principally Japanese expression.

Gagaku and Bugaku

Classical *gagaku* music was introduced into Japan from China in the 8th century A.D. It combined musical forms absorbed from Korea, Manchuria, Persia, India, and Indochina. Gagaku merged with Japanese music around 850.

Wind, stringed, and percussion instruments are used in gagaku performances, which are known as *kangen* when performed alone. When gagaku is accompanied by dancing, it is called bugaku. A single dancer or one or more pairs of dancers perform with great symmetry of movement. The dances may be slow or spirited depending on whether they are ceremonial dances, military dances, or dances for children. A bugaku may tell a story, but the story is generally not learned from a view of the dance alone.

No Plays

The medieval dance drama of the no theater came in part from Chinese sources. Actors in no plays perform on a usually bare stage about 18 feet square and on a narrow runway leading to the stage from the dressing room. They are accompanied by drums, a high-pitched flute, and chanting by a chorus of six or eight men. All parts, including female roles, are played by men and boys. There are only two important roles—the *shite* (principal character) and the *waki* (subordinate character).

Both the shite and the waki wear handsomely embroidered costumes patterned upon medieval court dress. The shite usually wears a painted mask carved from wood. Joy, sorrow, or anger may be represented by slightly changing the position of the mask on the actor's face. Different masks are used to represent men, women, elderly persons, gods, and demons. In most of the 240 no plays performed in Japan today, the shite changes his costume and mask for the second half of the performance to reveal his true character. He may change, for example, from a beautiful woman to a demon or from a boy to a warrior. Often, the waki is a Buddhist priest and the shite is the ghost of a person who, suffering for evil he committed during his lifetime, seeks and obtains help from the priest for the peace of his soul.

A no performance neither looks nor sounds like real life. Movement is extremely slow. If the play requires, for example, a boat or a hut, these are represented by a skeletal framework which only suggests their shape. A folding fan in the hands of an actor may represent a variety of objects—a sword, a letter, the rising moon, or falling rain. The text is ancient poetry, difficult even for many Japanese to understand.

The traditional no program consists of five plays with short comic pieces called *kyogen* performed between them. The usual program is now three plays, each lasting an hour or longer, and two kyogen. The kyogen are a complete contrast to the serious no plays, for they are acted vigorously and amusingly and deal with such matters as servants outwitting their masters or husbands their wives.

Hayashi-kata (no accompanists) sit before the rear stage wall, which is decorated with a painting of an ancient pine. The *ji-utai* (no chorus) sits to the left of the actors.

Bunraku

Toward 1700 a new form of theater appeared in Japan. Called bunraku, it combines the manipulation of puppets with a narrative accompanied by music played on the *samisen*, a three-stringed, banjo-shaped, plucked instrument. Each puppet is about half life-size and is handled by a team of three men in a fashion unique to Japan. By means of strings inside the puppet's head, the chief manipulator controls the movable mouth, eyebrows, and eyelids, as well as the right arm and hand of the doll. His assistants animate the rest of the puppet. The operators are silent but visible to the audience throughout the play.

Unlike the no stage, the bunraku stage uses elaborate scenery and various techniques and devices for changing scenes rapidly. At one side of the stage are seated one or more samisen players and the narrator-singer, who chants both the descriptive passages and the spoken words of all the characters. Such precise coordination and teamwork is demanded among the operators, the musician, and the narrator that they must all have many years of training.

Bunraku developed two kinds of plays. *Jidaimono* deals with historical materials and the warrior class, while *sewamono* is concerned with the life of the commoner. Some of the greatest Japanese dramatists wrote bunraku plays. Among them was Chikamatsu, who is sometimes called "the Shakespeare of Japan."

The body of a bunraku puppet is a hollow, cloth-covered bamboo frame. The puppet heads are varied to portray characters of different sexes, ages, and personalities.

The Kabuki drama 'Kagami-jishi' is patterned after a no play. A shy young maiden performs a lion dance and, overcome by the animal's spirit, becomes the lion itself.

Another was Izumo Takeda (1691–1756), whose 'Kanadehon Chushingura' (1748), or 'Chushingura' for short, is a popular Japanese play in both the bunraku and Kabuki theaters. Its theme—loyalty to a master—is a common one in the puppet theater.

Bunraku declined in popularity after the mid-1700's. It survives only in Osaka, though tours are made to other cities. It is regarded as a "cultural property" by the Japanese government, which supports it through the Japan Broadcasting Corporation.

Kabuki

Kabuki, a form of Japanese theater using live actors, began around the same time as bunraku. It originated in Kyoto with new kinds of dances performed by a woman named Okuni in the early 1600's. These became highly popular, and Okuni was imitated by other actresses and actors. But the Japanese government, deciding that the performances were immoral, decreed in 1629 that women could no longer appear on the stage. Women's roles were taken over by men, and this practice continues in modern Kabuki.

A typical Kabuki program may include a dance based upon a no play or a kyogen, part of doll theater jidaimono, and acts from plays written especially for the Kabuki in the 18th and 19th centuries. No important Kabuki plays were written after 1900, and this theater is in many ways a living museum of the Japanese performing arts. It is now based in Tokyo theaters and attracts large audiences.

The performance of a Kabuki program requires highly skilled actors, trained from childhood in dance, voice, and acrobatics, who are capable of playing a wide variety of parts, including female roles. An actor who plays the part of a woman is called an *onnagata*. Among the Kabuki characters are horses, foxes, dogs, and demons, all played by actors.

Kabuki visual effects are varied and spectacular. Huge settings change on a revolving stage in plain view of the audience. Scenery and actors rise from or disappear into the stage floor on elevators. Actors perform portions of the program in the midst of the audience on the *hanamichi*, a runway about six feet wide extending from the rear of the auditorium to the stage. Music, most frequently that of the samisen, is used throughout, the musicians performing either on the stage or in a room at the side of it.

In some Kabuki plays the actors wear striking white, red, and black makeup to create the effect of power and strength. Elaborate costumes, which can be changed on stage, may weigh as much as 50 pounds. Masses of warriors dance and somersault in scenes of battle. The dramatic poses of an actor are accompanied by the beating of wooden clappers on the stage.

Television, Western Music, and Motion Pictures

Thanks to television, no, bunraku, and Kabuki are now seen by larger audiences than ever. The Japanese government television station regularly broadcasts performances, from short excerpts to long Kabuki programs. The entire nine-hour bunraku production of the 11-act 'Kanadehon Chushingura' has been televised. The national network also televises modern plays, opera, modern dance, ballet, and the programs of its own symphony orchestra.

Western music, which has been taught in Japanese schools since the 1870's, is as popular as the traditional music of ancient Japan. Many Japanese cities have permanent orchestras and thriving musical conservatories. Internationally known orchestra, ballet, and opera companies visit Japan. Similarly, the works of contemporary Japanese composers trained in Western music, such as Toru Takemitsu and Toshiro Mayazumi, are played in Europe and the United States.

Motion pictures have been another Western influence on the Japanese performing arts. Film making in Japan began early in the 20th century with screen adaptations of traditional literary masterpieces and Kabuki drama. The cinematic art declined during the war years of the 1930's and 1940's.

After World War II many Japanese films became internationally famous for their artistic and technical quality. 'Rashomon', directed by Akira Kurosawa, won the grand prize at the Venice International Film Festival in 1951. Other notable Japanese films include 'Gate of Hell', 'The Rickshaw Man', and 'Bushido—A Samurai Saga', which received a grand prize at the 1963 Berlin Film Festival.

THE MARTIAL ARTS

The martial arts in Japan originated with medieval warriors, the samurai, who mastered at least one or two of them for use in battle. Today they are more important as competitive sports and as aids to physical and mental fitness. The martial arts were traditionally acquired through the family, but schools to teach them now thrive in Japan.

Sumo (Japanese wrestling) is one of the country's most popular sports. Professional sumo matches are held in rings of sand between two huge wrestlers dressed only in *mawashi* (loincloths). The actual bout is preceded by a ritual during which the wrestlers face each other, squatting and touching the ground with their fists. The match does not begin until both wrestlers come up at the same time. It ends only when a wrestler has been pushed out of the ring or when any part of a wrestler's body except his feet touches the ground. Several professional sumo tournaments are held each year in Japan. A grand champion wrestler is called *Yokozuna.*

Judo developed from *jujitsu,* an art of self-defense that was popular during the Tokugawa period. Judo has three basic strategies—attacking the opponent's vital points, throwing the opponent, and grappling. One referee and two assistants preside at a judo match. The winner is the first man to throw his opponent to the floor, to lift his opponent over his shoulders, to pin him down until he gives up, or to pin him for at least 30 seconds. If neither contestant accomplishes any of these goals, the match is awarded to the more aggressive of the two. Colored belts are worn to indicate degrees of mastery in judo.

During the Ashikaga period (1340–1540) kendo, then called *kata-kenjutsu,* stressed form over action. After about 1700, however, it became the lively sport that it is today.

Aikido also developed from jujitsu. In aikido, the purpose is to throw the opponent to the floor or to attack him at his weakest point by applying a painful hold. The opponent is then easier to overcome. Opponents in aikido, unlike judo contestants, try to stay apart from each other as much as possible. Aikido does not require great muscular strength. It is practiced to enhance body flexibility and to foster graceful movement.

Karate evolved in ancient China and was introduced into Japan in the 17th century. Only in the 20th century, however, did it gain wide popularity. Karate involves jabbing, hitting, and kicking at the most vulnerable parts of the opponent's body. One of the most destructive of the martial arts, karate is usually practiced on tiles, boards, and other hard objects rather than on human opponents.

Kendo (Japanese fencing) developed in ancient Japan. In kendo, two opponents hit or jab at each other with bamboo swords. Both wear protective bamboo armor, leg padding, and thick gloves. In a match, a point is given to the fencer who makes a clean hit on the throat, head, body, or hand of his opponent. The first to make two points is declared the winner.

Kyudo (Japanese archery) was used in early Japan for fishing and hunting. Later it became a military art. In medieval times, samurai displayed their skill as bowmen in exhibitions. After the introduction of firearms in the 16th century, however, kyudo declined as an effective technique of combat and became a sport. Kyudo archers use a seven-foot bow made of wood glued to bamboo. Arrows consist of a bamboo shaft, three feathers, and an arrowhead. Each contestant in a match usually shoots 10 to 20 arrows. The contestant hitting the target with the greatest number of arrows is the winner.

JAPANESE PHILOSOPHY AND RELIGION

Japan's religious philosophy derives from both native and foreign sources. Shinto originated in early Japan as a combination of nature and ancestor worship. Among its many gods were the creator, the moon, stars, mountains, rivers, seas, fire, and some animals and vegetables. Modern Shinto teaches that the gods are present in the mind of the individual.

Shinto became the state religion after the Meiji Restoration of 1868. As such, it assumed that the Japanese were descendants of the sun-goddess Amaterasu and members of one family headed by the emperor. The nationalists and militarists who rose to power in the 1930's adapted Shinto to their purposes, telling the Japanese that they were destined to rule the world. After World War II, state support of Shinto was abolished and the emperor disclaimed his divinity.

Shinto is now split among many sects. Some of them place greater stress on rituals than on philosophic content. Shinto is also valued because it is unique to Japan and creates a bond between the individual, his ancestors, and his nation.

Confucianism, which originated in China, was introduced into Japan from Korea around the 3d century A.D. Its ethical teachings were adopted primarily by the aristocracy, though the principles of absolute obedience to one's father and lord also greatly influenced the samurai. During World War II, Confucian rules of obedience were used to arouse patriotism. After the war, Confucianism was excluded from the Japanese educational curriculum. (*See also* Confucius.)

Buddhism arose in India and was introduced into Japan from Korea in the 6th century. Japanese Buddhism teaches that all men should aim to become Buddha. The worship of ancestors through funeral and memorial rites are the most universal practices of the many Buddhist sects.

Christianity was introduced into Japan in the 16th century by Francis Xavier, a Spanish Jesuit. During the Tokugawa shogunate, Japanese Christians were severely persecuted. After Japan was opened to the West in the 19th century, Japanese Christians became involved in social-welfare movements. Many prominent Japanese intellectuals are Christians.

A Buddhist monk meditates near a peaceful garden. There are more than ten leading Buddhist sects in Japan. Each differs in its rituals and its beliefs about the path to salvation.

Words to Remember

kana—Japanese characters for syllable sounds.
haiku—a 17-syllable Japanese poem.
tanka—a 31-syllable Japanese poem.
no, or *noh*—medieval Japanese dance drama.
bunraku—a Japanese puppet drama.
Kabuki—a traditional form of Japanese drama.
ukiyo-e—art movement of Edo period depicting everyday life, places, and people in Japan.
ikebana—the Japanese art of flower arrangement.
samisen—a banjolike, three-stringed instrument.
sumo—Japanese wrestling.
judo—a martial art based on holds.
karate—a martial art based on jabs and kicks.

Questions to Think About

1. In what ways do Japan's traditional fine arts resemble and differ from those of the West?
2. Give reasons why the traditional Japanese performing arts do not strive for realism.
3. Compare the traditional Japanese martial arts with those of the medieval European knights.
4. Has modernization made religion less important to the people of Japan?

JAPAN—Natural Features

Land

The islands of Japan are the exposed tops of massive undersea ridges that rise from the floor of the Pacific Ocean on the eastern edge of the Asian continental shelf. The islands lie between the Japan Deep—a north-south, 28,000-foot-deep trench in the Pacific—and the 10,000–12,000-foot-deep Sea of Japan. The Japan Deep is east of the islands; the Sea of Japan, west of the islands.

The islands of Japan are geologically young and unstable. They have been subjected to considerable folding, faulting, and volcanic activity. As a result, the land surface of the Japanese islands is dominated by mountains and hills which divide them into hundreds of subunits. This creates a landscape of great variety and beauty and gives Japanese life a small-scale compactness. The largest and highest mountain mass, part of which is known as the Japanese Alps, is in central Honshu. From it mountain chains extend northward to Hokkaido and southwest to Shikoku and Kyushu. These mountain chains are gouged by many short river valleys and interrupted by many small lowland plains.

Only one fourth of Japan's land surface has a slope of less than 15 degrees. Most Japanese plains have been formed by river deposits and lie along the seacoast. The largest lowland, the Kanto Plain of east-central Honshu, has an area of only 5,000 square miles. It contains the city of Tokyo. Among the nation's smaller plains are the Nobi (Nagoya) Plain and the Kansai (Osaka, Kyoto, and Kobe) Plain.

The numerous rivers of Japan are short and have small drainage basins. Only three of them are more than 200 miles long—the Shinano and the Tone, on Honshu, and the Ishikari, on Hokkaido. Of the three, the Shinano is the longest (229 miles) and the Tone drains the largest area (about 6,000 square miles).

Japan's rivers generally have steep gradients and carry heavy loads of sediment from the mountains to the lowlands. On the lowlands they are usually shallow and braided and flow through gravel-filled beds. Often they have built-up natural levees and are elevated above the river plains. Their flow rates vary greatly with the seasonal rain.

Although of little use for navigation, the rivers of Japan are used intensively for irrigation, urban water supply, and the generation of electricity. Floods are common, especially during the typhoon season, and are highly destructive in the heavily populated river valleys and plains. Japan has few lakes. The largest is Lake Biwa, in west-central Honshu.

Japan's coastline is unusually long in relation to the nation's total land area. The Pacific coast has many deep indentations, among them Tokyo and Ise bays on Honshu and the Inland Sea between Honshu and Shi-

TOPOGRAPHY OF JAPAN

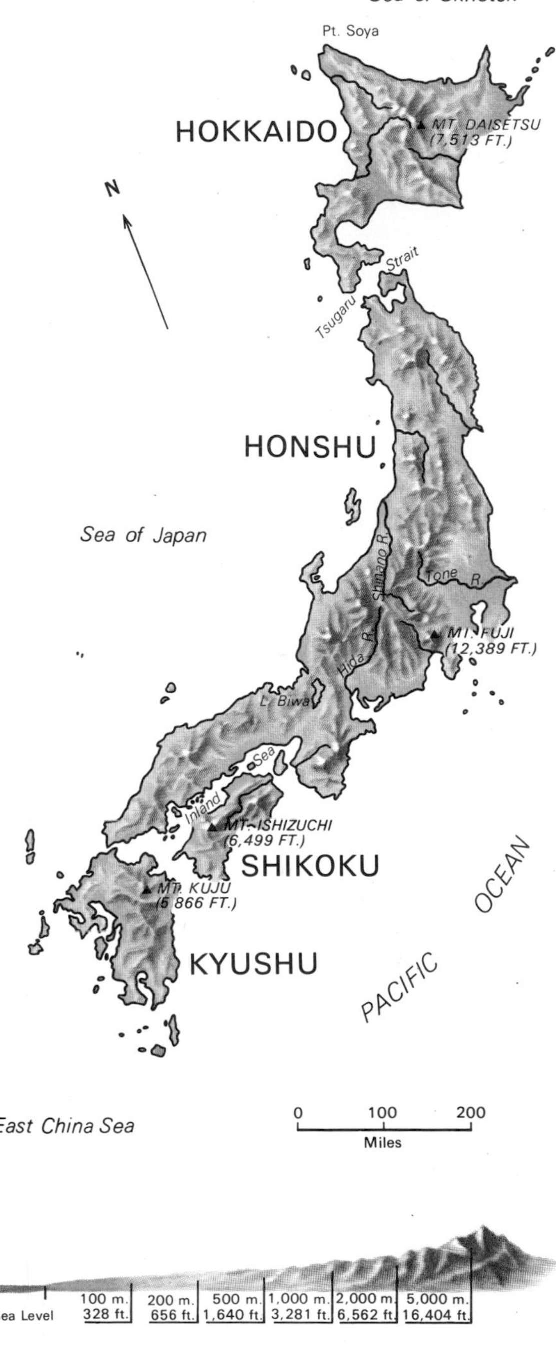

Much of Japan's coast is hilly and heavily forested. The country contains thousands of small islands, like these along the northwest coast of Kyushu.

koku. The indentations are separated by rugged peninsulas and headlands. Among them are the Boso and Izu peninsulas. The west coast of Kyushu is also deeply indented, and there are many small offshore islands. The Sea of Japan coast of Honshu, however, is much straighter and has long stretches of sand dunes and beach ridges. A major exception is the Noto Peninsula.

Japan's numerous volcanoes and frequent earthquakes are evidence of the instability of the rocks underlying the country. It has more than 150 volcanoes, of which more than 40 have been active in recent years. Some of the volcanoes are cone-shaped and rise to the highest elevations in Japan, while others are calderas, or lake-filled depressions where cones once stood.

Mount Fuji (12,389 feet), the famous volcanic cone, is the highest peak in Japan. It has been dormant since 1707. Mount Asama in central Honshu and Mount Sakurajima in southern Kyushu are well-known active volcanoes. Among the most notable calderas are Mount Aso in Kyushu and Mount Akan in Hokkaido. There are hot springs in the volcanic zones.

In Japan, the heaviest winter snows fall in mountain areas, on Hokkaido, and on the northwest coast of Honshu.

Undersea earthquakes in the northern Pacific basin stir up unusually large *tsunamis*, or "tidal waves," which are very destructive when they reach the Japanese coast. Severe earthquakes that do damage over small areas occur about every five or six years in Japan. One of the worst was the Great Kanto Earthquake of 1923, which combined with fire and tsunami to wipe out much of Tokyo and Yokohama. More than 100,000 lives were lost.

Climate

For a small nation, Japan has a great variety of climatic conditions. This is because its islands have a long latitudinal spread and are in the zone where the conflicting air masses of the Asian continent and of the Pacific Ocean meet and interact. The continental air masses make for more extreme temperatures, both in winter and in summer, and result in large annual temperature ranges. But their effect is moderated by the strong marine influence, which also produces high humidity and abundant rainfall. Japan's rugged topography also makes for many local variations in weather and climate.

During the winter, Japan is primarily under the influence of cold air masses moving out of Siberia, deep in the Asian interior. Biting northwest winds pass over the Sea of Japan and cross the islands of Japan. Moisture picked up over the Sea of Japan is deposited on Japan's west coast in the form of heavy snows that are among the deepest in the world.

During the summer, Japan is under the influence of air moving in from the Pacific Ocean. Southeast winds prevail, making the summer months warm and humid. The cycle of the seasons brings frequent, often sharp, changes in the weather, especially during the spring and autumn months.

Japan's climate, especially along the coasts, is also affected by two ocean currents—the warm Kuroshio, or Japan Current, from the south, and the cold Oyashio, or Okhotsk Current, from the north. The two currents meet off northeastern Honshu. The Kuroshio, on the lee side of Japan in winter, has little warming effect on land temperatures. The Tsushima Current, a branch of the Kuroshio, passes into the Sea of Japan by way of Korea Strait and slightly warms offshore waters. The Oyashio reduces summer temperatures and creates dense fog banks off the coasts of northeastern Honshu and Hokkaido.

Virtually all of Japan except parts of eastern Hokkaido averages more than 40 inches of precipitation annually. Several coastal mountain areas in Honshu get more than 120 inches. Areas around the Inland Sea, in eastern Honshu north of Tokyo Bay, and in western Hokkaido average 40 to 60 inches. The Sea of Japan coast gets more precipitation in winter, largely in the form of snow, than it does in summer. The reverse is true for the Pacific coast, where summer precipitation exceeds that of winter. In northern Hokkaido, snow falls an average of 130 days per year; along the Sea of Japan, 80 days; on the Pacific coast south and west of Tokyo Bay, only 10 days.

Climate Patterns of Japan

Japan has a wide range of climate. Winters are long and cold in Hokkaido and in the mountains of northern Honshu. They are short and mild along the southern and southwestern shores of Kyushu and Shikoku. Summers are short and cool in the far north but long and hot in the south. Winter snows are heavy along the north and central coasts of the Sea of Japan. Summer rains are heavy along the south and southwest coasts. In general the climate of Japan is much like that of the United States East coast, from the continental coolness of northern Maine to the humid subtropics of northern Florida.

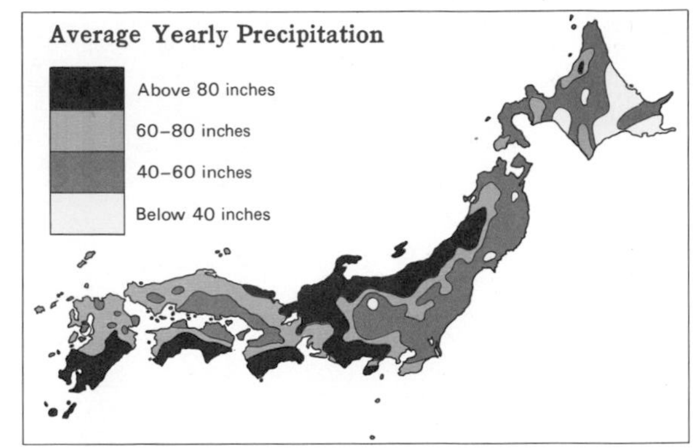

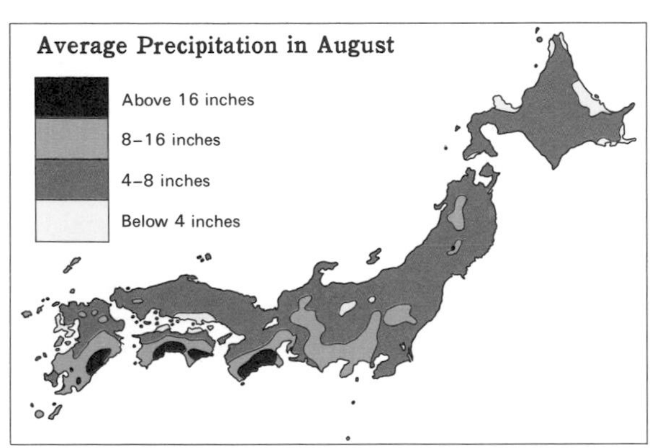

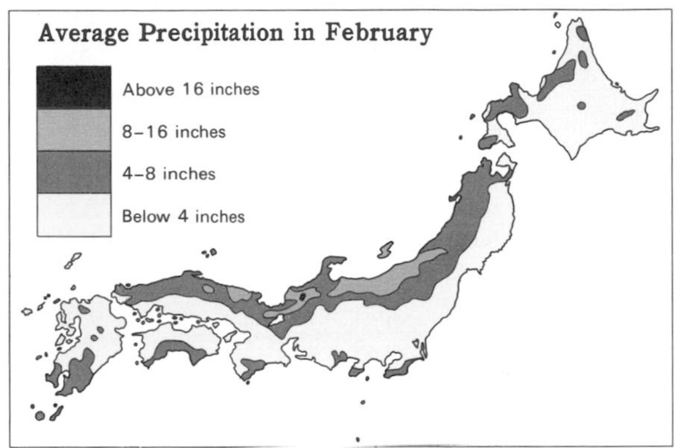

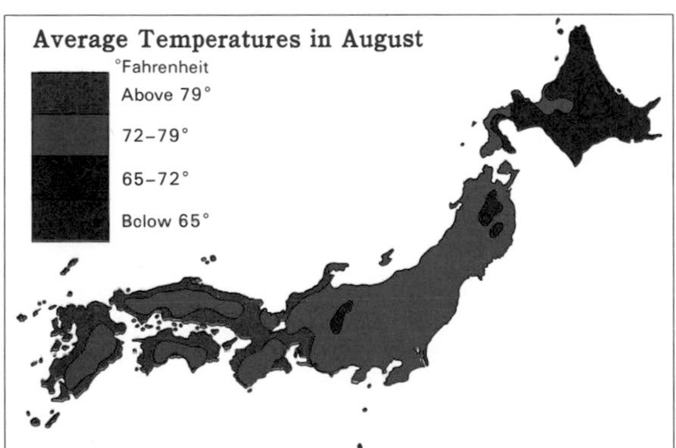

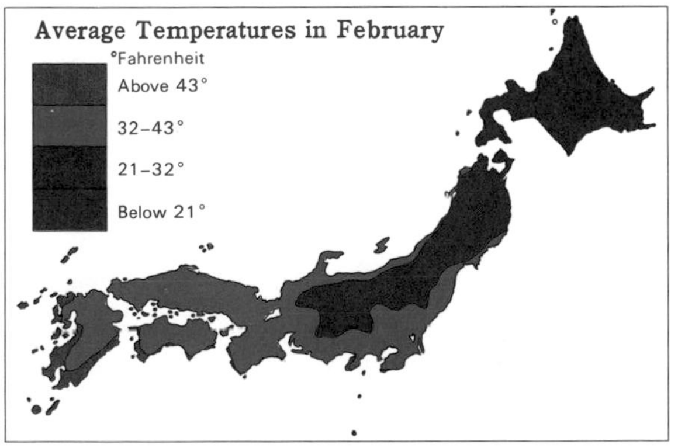

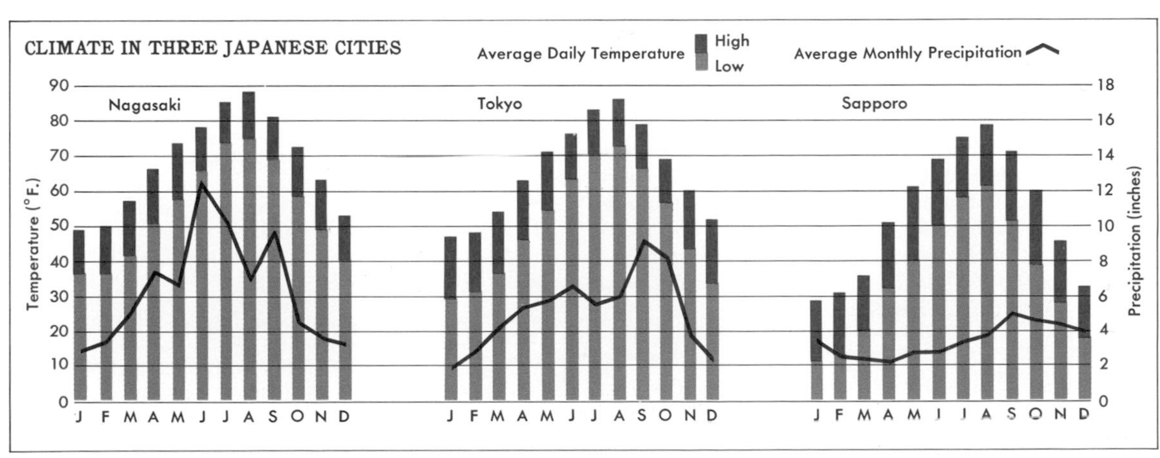

Japan contains hundreds of wild-bird species. Peacocks live in the southernmost part of the country.

Japan has rainy seasons in June and in September, though there is some precipitation throughout the year. The main, June rainy season is called the *baiu*, or *tsuyu*, and has many days of continuous rain. The September rainy season is called the *shurin*. It is associated with occasional typhoons, tropical storms like the hurricanes of southeastern North America. These move to the north and northeast in a clockwise arc from their spawning grounds east of the Philippines. When they strike Japan, their furious winds and heavy rains cause destructive floods and landslides. However, they also restore water levels in rivers and reservoirs, which drop during the dry days of late summer.

Typhoons bring roughly one third of the rain that falls annually on the Pacific coast. In 1959, one of the worst typhoons of modern times tore through the city of Nagoya and across central Honshu. Approaching typhoons are carefully watched by the Japan Meteorological Agency, and special radio and television bulletins are issued on their progress.

Seasonal temperatures in Japan increase from north to south. Average January temperatures are 15° to 20° F. in Hokkaido; 35° to 40° in central Honshu; and 45° in southern Kyushu. There is little difference in winter temperatures between the west and east coasts, though the skies are more overcast on the west coast and clearer and sunnier on the east coast. Summers are sultry throughout Japan. July temperatures average 77° to 80° in Kyushu, Shikoku, and southern and central Honshu; 72° to 75° in northern Honshu; and a cooler 65° to 70° in Hokkaido.

The clear, hot weather of summer arrives in mid-July, following the baiu rains. It is ended by the shurin rains. The length of the frost-free, or growing, season ranges from 250 days or more along the Pacific coast south from Tokyo Bay to only 120 days in central Hokkaido. Early autumn frosts in northern Japan and late spring frosts in central and southern Japan pose a seasonal threat to farming.

Plant and Animal Life

The trees, shrubs, and flowering plants of Japan are as varied as its topography and climate. Forests cover most of the land surface that has not been cleared by man. Coniferous, broadleaf, and mixed forests are the three main types. Among the conifers, pine, cypress, hemlock, cedar, fir, and spruce are commercially valuable. The numerous broadleafs include oak, maple, ash, birch, beech, poplar, chestnut, and horse chestnut. Subtropical forms such as bamboo and palms grow as far north as central Honshu.

The native plant life of Japan has been severely modified by man over the centuries. Many native species have been destroyed or reduced in extent, and new species from the Asian mainland have been introduced as a result of reforestation. Large virgin-forest areas have been preserved in parks.

Japan is rich in both land and marine animal life. Large mammals include bear, badger, otter, mink, deer, fox, and walrus. One monkey, the Japanese macaque, is found as far north as Hokkaido. Adjacent seas are the home of whales and porpoises. The hundreds of Japanese bird species include many water and wading birds, hawks, pheasants, peacocks, doves, owls, and woodpeckers. Among the reptiles are sea turtles, tortoises, lizards, and snakes. The sea abounds with hundreds of fish species. Salmon, sardine, sea bream, tuna, trout, mackerel, cod, and mullet are among those caught by commercial fishermen. Tropical varieties accompany the warm waters of the Kuroshio as far north as Tokyo Bay. The raising of goldfish for decorative purposes is a Japanese specialty.

Words to Remember

Kanto Plain—the lowland around Tokyo.
Shinano—Japan's longest river.
Biwa—Japan's largest lake.
Mount Fuji—Japan's highest mountain.
tsunami—a huge wave caused by an undersea earthquake.
Kuroshio and Oyashio—two major ocean currents which affect the climate of Japan.
baiu, or *tsuyu*—the June rainy season of Japan.
shurin—the September rainy season of Japan.

Questions to Think About

1. Japan and the United Kingdom are island nations situated just off continental mainlands. In what ways might this explain the industrialization of both nations?
2. How has the geologic instability of Japan influenced Japanese architecture?
3. Is Japan's varied climate more desirable than a climate that remains much the same all the time? Why or why not?

JAPAN—History

Ancient Japan (to 1185)

Men have lived in Japan since the Stone Age. The early Japanese were primitive hunters, gatherers, and farmers. They lived in small villages, growing rice in paddies and irrigated fields. They had no writing system, and they worshiped nature gods and family ancestors. Chieftains headed small, clanlike tribal units.

According to legend, the Japanese state was founded in 660 B.C. by Jimmu, the first emperor. In fact, it emerged by the 6th century A.D., when one family of chieftains became dominant. Their base was the Yamato region at the eastern end of the Inland Sea. Claiming the sun-goddess Amaterasu as their ancestor, this family founded the imperial dynasty which has reigned in Japan ever since.

The Japanese made borrowings from the civilization of the T'ang Dynasty in neighboring China. These included the Buddhist religion, Confucian ethics, and Chinese writing, art, architecture, and dress. In 604 the Yamato ruler Prince Shotoku (573–622) began to infuse the life of the imperial court with Chinese ideals, and in 607 the court's first official emissaries were sent to China.

The Chinese model of government was also imported. The Taika reforms, beginning in 645, transformed the Yamato ruler into an absolute sovereign —the emperor. An elaborate bureaucracy was established. Large landholdings were abolished; some farmland was redistributed among the peasants; and regular tax collections were begun. However, in order to encourage agricultural development, the Yamato regime allowed tax exemptions on newly cultivated land. This practice actually stimulated the growth of huge estates called *shoen*. Similar to the manors of medieval Europe, the shoen were owned by powerful families, court aristocrats, or religious institutions and worked by thousands of peasants.

In 710 an imperial capital was built at Nara on the model of Ch'ang-an, the Chinese capital. In 794 the capital was moved to Heian-kyo (Kyoto). From the 8th to the 11th century an aristocracy controlled by the Fujiwara family dominated Japan. This period was a classic age of art and literature. Japan's culture was no longer one largely borrowed from China but had become distinctively Japanese.

The Feudal Age (1185–1600)

Beginning in the 11th century the *samurai*, provincial warriors who resembled medieval European knights, began to assume power. They often managed the estates of aristocrats, and sometimes they held land in their own right. Rivalry between two warrior clans—the Taira and the Minamoto—led to the Heiji War (1159–60). The Taira won, but a revolt begun in 1180 ended in 1185 with the victory of the Minamoto.

Yoritomo Minamoto (1147–99) then established a new government at Kamakura, and in 1192 he was named *shogun*, or chief military commander, by the imperial court. He was authorized to appoint military governors (*shugo*) in the provinces and land stewards (*jito*) on many private estates. His administrative organization, called the *bakufu* (camp government), served as a model for a series of later regimes.

The Kamakura shogunate successfully repelled Mongol invasions in 1274 and in 1281. It was overthrown by a domestic revolt in 1333, and Takauji Ashikaga (1305–58) established a new regime. A dispute between rival families over the succession to the shogunate led to the Onin War (1467–77). Centralized control disappeared as the country was plunged into civil wars which lasted until the late 1500's.

During this period, warrior leaders fought each other for land and vassals. The emperor and shogun became politically insignificant. Local lords known as *daimyo* divided the country into feudal domains. Their vassals served both as warriors and as government officials. The daimyo taxed the peasantry, who made up the bulk of the population.

Mongols invading Japan in 1274 are shown in the medieval Japanese Mongol Scroll. Japanese archers and swordsmen triumphed despite the explosive missiles used by the invaders.

Before his death in 1616, Ieyasu Tokugawa defeated the forces of Hideyori, heir to Hideyoshi Toyotomi, at Osaka. Over two centuries of Tokugawa supremacy were thus ensured.

Meanwhile, Japan was developing trade contacts with the outside world. Official trade missions to China had begun in 1404. Japanese traders were active along the coasts of Korea and China. Japanese adventurers and pirates also operated in eastern Asian waters, some reaching Siam and the Philippines.

Later in the feudal period, the first Europeans arrived in Japan, known to them as Xipangu from the tales of Marco Polo. Portuguese traders came first, in 1543. They were soon followed by Spanish, English, and Dutch traders. In the hope of attracting European trade, the Japanese encouraged conversions to Christianity. After the arrival of the Jesuit priest Francis Xavier in 1549, the Christian missionary movement enjoyed great success in Japan.

National Unification (1600–1853)

Feudal division and disorder in Japan ended in the late 16th century. The powerful daimyo leader Nobunaga Oda (1534–82) began to subdue the smaller daimyo. By 1590 Hideyoshi Toyotomi (1536–98), one of his generals, succeeded in defeating the rival Hojo family. Although he never became shogun, Hideyoshi took control of the whole country. In 1592–93 and in 1597–98 he led invasions of Korea as part of an unsuccessful plan to conquer China.

The political consolidation of Japan continued under Ieyasu Tokugawa (1542–1616), one of several men chosen to govern the country after Hideyoshi's death in Korea in 1598. After winning a battle against his rivals at Sekigahara in 1600, Ieyasu organized the daimyo into a federation under a new bakufu at Edo, the present city of Tokyo. He was named shogun in 1603.

Mutsuhito became the emperor of Japan in 1867. As the Meiji emperor, he symbolized Japan's modernization.

For the next two centuries, under the Tokugawa shogunate, Japan enjoyed extraordinary peace and stability. Ieyasu and his successors built an elaborate system of controls over the daimyo, including limits on their military strength. The country was closed to all outside contact. Fearing that Japan was being prepared for foreign conquest, the government expelled the Christian missionaries, prohibited the Christian religion, and persecuted many Japanese converts to Christianity. It gradually cut back foreign trade until by 1641 only Dutch and Chinese merchants were permitted to trade—at the single port of Nagasaki. Japanese were forbidden under pain of death to leave the country.

As a result of internal peace, a national market developed and the economy flourished. New rice lands were cultivated, and advances were made in farming techniques. Osaka and Edo became great commercial centers. By the 18th century Edo, with a population of more than 500,000, was larger than any city in Europe. A new urban culture, reflecting the tastes of merchants, shopkeepers, and artisans, emerged in both Osaka and Edo. The cultural standards of the peasantry rose as well, and by the middle of the 19th century almost half of the entire male population of Japan could read and write.

The Modernization of Japan (1853–1905)

The seclusion of Japan ended in 1853 with the arrival of a United States naval fleet commanded by Commo. Matthew C. Perry. He had been instructed to open Japan to foreign trade and diplomatic contact. The Edo bakufu, afraid of United States military superiority, signed a treaty of friendship during a second visit by Perry in 1854.

The Netherlands, Russia, Great Britain, and France followed the lead of the United States. By 1859 the bakufu had been pressured into signing a series of "unequal treaties" opening several Japanese ports to foreign trade. Western nationals were given the right of extraterritoriality, or exemption from local law. Tariff rates that the Japanese government could not alter were established.

Many Japanese regarded the surrender to the West as a national humiliation, and the bakufu's authority declined rapidly. There were growing demands for the expulsion of the foreigners and for the restoration of political power to the emperor. These demands were supported by the court and two powerful daimyo domains in western Japan—Satsuma and Choshu. In 1868 the Tokugawa shogun was forced to abdicate. A new government was established under the young emperor Mutsuhito, who took the reign name of Meiji ("enlightened government"). This transfer of power from the Tokugawa shogunate to the Meiji emperor is known as the Meiji Restoration. It is regarded as the beginning of Japan's modern era.

Leaders of the new government were former samurai of Satsuma and Choshu, such as Toshimichi Okubo (1830–78), Koin Kido (1833–77), and Takamori Saigo (1827–77). They wished to end the "unequal treaties" and to catch up militarily with the Western nations. Their first task, however, was to create internal order. A centralized administration replaced the daimyo system; many class distinctions were abolished; and a conscript army was built up. In 1868 Edo was renamed Tokyo ("eastern capital") and designated the new imperial capital.

During the 1870's the army quelled a number of rebellions by former samurai who objected to rapid modernization. The ill-fated Satsuma rebellion of 1877 was led by Saigo, who had resigned from the government in 1873. It was the last major challenge to the new regime.

The imperial government also laid the foundations for an industrial economy. Modern money and banking systems were introduced. Railroads, telegraph and telephone lines, and factories using the newest technology were built. Private enterprises were subsidized, and laws permitting the private ownership of land were enacted.

Leaders like Arinori Mori (1847–89) helped create a modern educational system. Compulsory universal education was instituted in 1872. By 1905 nearly 95 percent of Japanese school-age children were in school, and Japan soon achieved one of the highest literacy rates in the world.

A constitution was drafted in the 1880's under the direction of the political leader Hirobumi Ito (1841–1909), who took as his model the institutions of the German empire. The constitution, finally promulgated in 1889, gave strong executive powers to the emperor and a privy council. A prime minister headed a cabinet whose members were individually responsible to the emperor. Legislative powers were exercised by a two-house parliament, or Diet. The upper house, or House of Peers, consisted mainly of a new nobility created in 1884. The lower house, or House of Representatives, was elected by male taxpayers over 25 years of age.

By the 1890's Japan's rapid modernization had made it the most powerful nation in Asia. Extraterritoriality was relinquished by Great Britain, the United States, and the other Western powers by 1899. But Meiji leaders like Ito and Aritomo Yamagata (1838–1922) remained suspicious of Western imperialism. Using its growing economic and military power, Japan sought to build an empire of its own.

To achieve this objective Japan fought two major wars. After its victory in the first, the Sino-Japanese War of 1894–95, Japan forced the enormous but weak Chinese empire to cede Taiwan (Formosa) and the Penghu Islands (Pescadores). Japan was also supposed to get the Liaotung Peninsula in Manchuria, but Russia forced Japan not to accept it. Instead, in 1898, Russia took the peninsula itself.

The second war was fought in 1904–5 against Russia, now Japan's chief rival in eastern Asia. Japan won from Russia the southern half of Sakhalin Island and a leasehold in Liaotung, together with the South Manchurian Railway. In 1910 Japan annexed Korea. In 1915 Japan extended its hold in Manchuria after presenting "Twenty-one Demands" to the Chinese government. The empire of Japan had become a recognized world power.

Imperial Japan (1905–45)

After 1905 Japan faced a change in national leadership. The Meiji emperor died on July 30, 1912, and was succeeded by his son Yoshihito, who became known as the Taisho emperor. Yoshihito soon showed signs of mental illness, and Crown Prince Hirohito served as regent from November 1921 until he became the Showa emperor on Dec. 25, 1926.

More important, the original Meiji leaders had all died by the early 1920's. At first they were replaced by younger protégés, such as Taro Katsura (1848–1913) and Kimmochi Saionji (1849–1940). Gradually, however, under the leadership of men like Kei Hara (1856–1921) and Komei Kato (1860–1926), political parties in the Diet gained increasing control over the government. Between 1918 and 1932 most Japanese prime ministers were leaders of political parties in the lower house of the Diet.

The emergence of party government was accompanied by a flourishing of democratic ideas. Intellectuals like Sakuzo Yoshino (1878–1933) advocated greater attention to the needs of the common man. Some social-welfare legislation was approved, and in 1925 universal manhood suffrage was instituted.

By the 1920's Japan had begun to encounter severe economic problems. The rate of economic development was beginning to slow down. Agricultural production had reached a plateau, and domestic food supplies were no longer adequate. Imports of rice had to be increased greatly. By the late 1920's and early 1930's the countryside faced hard times.

World War II ended with Japan's surrender to the Allies. General Yoshijiro Umezo signed the surrender document on Sept. 2, 1945, aboard the USS *Missouri* in Tokyo Bay.

Continued on page 410

Japan and China

by John Roderick

For nearly 2,000 years an intimate relationship existed between Japan and China. In the late 19th century and the first half of the 20th century that relationship was disrupted by Japanese wars of conquest waged against imperial and republican China. In recent years the rift between the two countries has been prolonged by basic political differences. How to normalize relations with Communist China is one of Japan's biggest unsettled problems.

Historical Background

During much of Japan's history its relationship to China was that of pupil to teacher. As early as the 1st century A.D., Japanese travelers visited the Chinese imperial court. They brought back treasures that enriched Japanese life—the Buddhist religion, Confucian ethics, written language, literature, art, architecture, music, and methods of government.

In the late 19th century the coming of the Industrial Revolution to Asia changed this relationship. Japan emerged from more than two centuries of isolation, recognizing that industrialization was a means of gaining equality with the Western powers. Mastering Western techniques, it soon built factories and created a modern army and navy.

China was slower in acquiring the new technology. It was hampered by the actions of competing industrial nations which, eager to get its markets and raw materials, carved China into spheres of influence.

In 1894–95, armed with modern weapons, Japan warred China and seized Taiwan (Formosa). In the 1930's Japanese armies conquered Manchuria and carved from it a puppet state called Manchukuo. Japan's greed for the resources of China led to its brutal conquest and occupation of a large part of northern and eastern China before and during World War II.

The Japanese today have mixed feelings toward China. They are grateful for their rich inheritance from ancient China. They are also torn by feelings of guilt and shame over the indignities Japan's armies committed against the Chinese during the past century. Some Japanese are convinced that their country's old associations with China make Japan the one nation that knows China best. Others believe that the Japanese do not truly understand the breed of men who now run China.

War—Japanese capture Shanghai, China (1937).

It is an irony of history that Japan is today the custodian of the old Chinese virtues, the elaborate system of interpersonal obligations prescribed by Confucius. Within this framework, the Japanese have built a stable industrial, political, and social structure. Their skills and hard work have helped Japan become the world's third-ranking industrial power.

The situation in China has been different. New ideas have stirred the Chinese imagination. First democracy and then Communism gained the ascendancy. Communism has been the sole political system since 1949. Under the leadership of Mao Tse-tung, China has been torn by revolutionary change. Confucianism, with its accent on the family, has been shattered on the Chinese mainland. It has survived, however, on the island of Taiwan, where the defeated Nationalist leader Chiang Kai-shek heads a Chinese government-in-exile—the Republic of China.

Present Relations

Japan's relations with Communist China have been complicated by its military alliance with the United States, its recognition of the Republic of China, and its economic expansion into Southeast Asia.

The Japanese are bound to the United States by a security treaty that guarantees Japan protection against outside attack. Air and naval bases authorized by the treaty have been established by the United States on Japanese soil.

The Communist Chinese contend that this treaty is aimed at them and that its objective is to permit Japan to rearm. They insist that the treaty be renounced and that Japan become instead a member of a Pacific security pact that would include Communist China, the United States, and the Soviet Union. The Japanese reaction to this demand has been cool.

The present conservative government of Japan seems inclined to continue a close relationship with the United States well into the 1970's, and perhaps beyond. It has taken steps to expand and strengthen Japan's military establishment, the National Self-Defense Force, from the 1970 level of about 250,000 men. However, Japan's leaders have refused to become upset over Communist China's possession of nuclear weapons, a situation that many observers believed would create new tensions between the two countries. The Japanese government has said that it would not retaliate by equipping Japan with nuclear weapons. Whatever Communist China believes about the possibility and danger of a remilitarized Japan, it cannot deny that since 1945 no Japanese soldier has been involved in an overseas conflict. And until Japan's no-war constitution is revised, none can be.

The Japanese government's major opposition—the Socialist party—wants the security treaty with the United States scrapped and an unarmed neutrality substituted. When Prime Minister Eisaku Sato's Liberal-Democratic party campaigned on this issue in the December 1969 general election, the Socialists were badly defeated.

A new ground for Communist China's fears regarding Japan arose in 1969. In November Sato signed an agreement with the United States providing for the return of Okinawa to Japan in 1972. As he did so, he said that the stability of Taiwan was vital to Japanese national interests. Communist China regarded his remark as an interference in its internal affairs.

Japan's continued recognition of the Republic of China has been deeply resented in Communist China. The Communist Chinese regard it as part of a maneuver to prevent the reunification of Taiwan with the mainland. They have been particularly angered by Japan's repeated, successful cosponsorship in the United Nations General Assembly of a rule that requires a two-thirds majority vote to grant Communist China membership and to expel Nationalist China. This rule has effectively blocked Communist China's admission to the United Nations for many years.

If the Communist Chinese have been uneasy about Japan's intentions, the same can also be said about the Japanese view of China. Japanese concern has been aroused by the frequency and harshness of Chinese attacks on their government. The Japanese have responded with anxiety to such events as Communist China's seizure of Tibet, its invasion of India, its border conflicts with the Soviet Union, and the excesses of its Great Proletarian Cultural Revolution.

Although Japan balks at official recognition of the People's Republic of China, its trade with mainland China was valued at more than 625 million dollars in 1969, the highest level since the end of World War II. In the late 1960's Japan's chief exports to China were iron and steel and chemical fertilizers; its chief imports from China were foodstuffs and soybeans.

Much of the exchange of goods is carried out through unofficial agreements between the Communist government in Peking and leading members of Japan's Liberal-Democratic party. This is known as "memorandum trade." The remainder of the trade between the two countries is done through Japanese firms friendly to the Chinese.

The Communist Chinese are irritated that Japan, though engaged in this large and profitable trade with them, refuses to make any political concessions. One of the reasons for Japan's refusal, aside from the Japanese government's insistence that politics and economics be kept separate, is that Japan has even greater trade links with the Nationalist Chinese. Its trade with Taiwan in 1969 was valued at almost 660 million dollars.

Despite the volume and importance of Japan's commercial relations with Communist China, human contacts have been few and one-sided. In 1969, when about 2,600 Japanese businessmen, politicians, writers, tourists, and members of goodwill delegations visited China, the Chinese allowed only two newsmen and eight trade negotiators to go to Japan. Under a 1964 agreement, the two countries initiated an exchange of journalists that began with the installation of nine journalists in each of their respective capitals. In 1970 there were only three.

Japan's widening trade with Southeast Asia could be another source of conflict with Communist China, as the Chinese also move more prominently into that market. Japanese businessmen say there is room in the area for both countries. But should Japan's vital lines of communication be threatened, there might be an outcry in Japan to protect its interests militarily. An armed collision with China could result.

Future Prospects

The conflict over Taiwan will probably continue to block a complete rapprochement between Japan and Communist China. Nevertheless, steps to lessen the tensions between the two nations can be taken. Much depends on Communist China's own experience. Its difficulties with the Soviet Union, for example, may force it to adopt a more flexible attitude toward both the United States and Japan.

Many scholars, diplomats, and politicians believe that the reemergence of a peace-loving China in the international community would be of immense benefit to the nations of Asia as well as to the United States. But many of them also believe that Communist China's domestic instability and its deeply rooted hostility to the West make any positive response on its part to peace overtures from Japan or the West unlikely in the near future. Some feel, however, that the likelihood of a relaxation of tensions and the eventual establishment of harmonious and cooperative relations between Japan and China would be increased if Japan took the lead. A first move toward those ends, they say, would be a clear, public acknowledgment by the Japanese government that the Communist regime in Peking is in effective control of the Chinese mainland.

Peace—Japanese visit a trade fair in Canton, China (1963).

The cities remained relatively prosperous, however, and industry continued to grow. Employees of the *zaibatsu*, large urban business combines, enjoyed secure jobs and rising wages. But in the midst of industrial prosperity there were also signs of unrest. Strikes and labor disputes increased sharply after 1919. The growth of labor unions led to the rise of a left-wing political movement in the 1920's. To curb left-wing activities, the Peace Preservation Law was passed in 1925.

The party governments of the 1920's tried to follow a peaceful foreign policy. Men like Foreign Minister Kijuro Shidehara (1872–1951) advocated cooperation with Great Britain and the United States and nonintervention in Chinese affairs. But Japanese economic interests in southern Manchuria seemed to be threatened by the Soviet Union and the Chinese Kuomintang government.

In September 1931 the Japanese army engineered a take-over of Manchuria, and in 1932 a puppet state, renamed Manchukuo, was established there. Ultranationalist military officers and civilians began to attack leading Japanese government officials. Prime Minister Tsuyoshi Inukai (1855–1932) was assassinated in 1932. A rebellion by military extremists in February 1936 was defeated, but the political parties were losing control of the government. Cabinets were increasingly dominated by militarists, and Japanese military involvement on the Asian mainland grew.

Undeclared war with China broke out in July 1937. Prime Minister Fumimaro Konoe (1891–1945) refused to negotiate with the Chinese government. But Japanese armies, penetrating deep into China, were unsuccessful in forcing a Chinese surrender. Japan moved troops into French Indochina in 1940. In September the Tripartite Pact was signed with Nazi Germany and Fascist Italy. The United States attempted, unsuccessfully, to curtail Japan's aggressive policy through economic sanctions. In October 1941 Gen. Hideki Tojo (1884–1948) became prime minister. Fearing that its plans to dominate eastern and southeastern Asia were in danger, the Japanese government decided to go to war against the United States. On Dec. 7, 1941, the Japanese air force attacked the United States fleet at Pearl Harbor, Hawaii.

By the middle of 1942, Japanese forces had occupied the Philippines, the Dutch East Indies, Malaya, and Burma and had reached into the Aleutian Islands of Alaska. Japan's leaders hoped to achieve a favorable negotiated peace with the United States by a series of quick victories.

But the United States was determined to win an unconditional surrender. Beginning with the loss of naval battles in the Coral Sea and off the Midway Islands in 1942, Japan's fortunes declined. The United States, enjoying a superior industrial capacity and employing a strategy of "island hopping," penetrated Japan's defense perimeter in the Pacific. In July 1944 the Tojo cabinet fell, and later in the year massive air raids from Pacific island bases began to destroy Japan's industry, cities, and military bases. (*See also* World War II.)

LEADERS OF MODERN JAPAN

Emperors Since the Meiji Restoration	
Mutsuhito	1867–1912 (Meiji Reign)
Yoshihito, son of Mutsuhito	1912–1926 (Taisho Reign)
Hirohito, son of Yoshihito	1926– (Showa Reign)

Prime Ministers After World War II	
Kijuro Shidehara	1945–1946
Shigeru Yoshida	1946–1947
Tetsu Katayama	1947–1948
Hitoshi Ashida	1948
Shigeru Yoshida	1948–1954
Ichiro Hatoyama	1954–1956
Tanzan Ishibashi	1956–1957
Nobusuke Kishi	1957–1960
Hayato Ikeda	1960–1964
Eisaku Sato	1964–

Postwar Japan (1945–)

Japan surrendered in 1945 after United States atomic bombs had destroyed the cities of Hiroshima (August 6) and Nagasaki (August 9). The Soviet Union had entered the war against Japan on August 8. Under the terms of surrender, all territory acquired by Japan since 1895 was given up and Japan was restricted to its four home islands. United States forces under the command of Gen. Douglas MacArthur began a military occupation of Japan.

The United States demobilized Japan's military forces and destroyed its arms. Many civilian and military leaders were tried as war criminals. Seven of the chief wartime leaders, including Tojo, were convicted and executed in December 1948. Thousands of lesser officials, military officers, and business executives were removed from their jobs because they had supported Japan's war policies.

To encourage the growth of democracy in Japan, the United States occupation authorities pressured the new Japanese government into accepting a series of political, social, and educational reforms. A new constitution became effective in 1947, and the educational system was reorganized. The new leaders of Japan generally cooperated not only because of the United States military occupation but also because they themselves had advocated many of the same reforms before the war.

On Sept. 8, 1951, Japan signed a peace treaty at San Francisco, Calif., with the United States and 47 other nations. The occupation formally ended when the treaty went into effect on April 28, 1952. Only Okinawa and several smaller Japanese islands remained under United States control. Shigeru Yoshida (1878–1967), prime minister during much of the occupation, was instrumental in the negotiation of the treaty. In 1956 Japan joined the United Nations.

When Japan regained full sovereignty in 1952, the political reforms of the occupation had taken effect. Political leadership rested in a cabinet based on a popularly elected Diet. Conservative political parties, which had led the country almost continuously since 1947, combined in 1955 to form the Liberal-Democratic party.

The occupation reforms also strengthened the labor unions and the Socialists. In May 1947 Tetsu Katayama, a prominent Socialist leader, became prime minister, holding office until February 1948. The Socialists' popular vote and strength in the Diet increased during the 1950's and the early 1960's. Although the Socialists were unable to capture a Diet majority, they were a strong and active opposition to the ruling conservatives.

A main political issue during much of the 1950's and 1960's was the Japanese alliance with the United States. A bilateral security treaty signed on Sept. 8, 1951, permitted the United States to retain military bases and troops in Japan. The treaty enabled Japan to rely on the "atomic umbrella" of the United States for effective defense. The Socialists and other left-wing groups objected to the treaty and demanded that Japan adopt a policy of neutrality. In 1960, after the Liberal-Democratic government of Prime Minister Nobusuke Kishi had agreed to a renewal of the security treaty, there were widespread riots and demonstrations. Nevertheless, the treaty was again renewed in 1970.

The most far-reaching developments in postwar Japan were economic. Freed from the burden of heavy military expenditures, the Japanese could pour most of their resources into peacetime industrial production. An economic boom began in the mid-1950's. Between 1955 and 1967 the economy more than tripled in size. By 1970 Japan had become the world's third largest industrial nation, outranked only by the United States and the Soviet Union. Although national income lagged, most Japanese enjoyed steadily rising living standards.

Economic progress helped bring a return of Japanese national confidence, which had been greatly dampened by the defeat in World War II. The 1964 summer Olympics at Tokyo, the Meiji Centennial of 1968, and the world exposition held near Osaka in 1970 were all official expressions of renewed national pride. So too was the successful effort of Prime Minister Eisaku Sato to negotiate the return of Okinawa to Japanese sovereignty. In November 1969 the United States agreed to evacuate Okinawa by 1972.

Economic progress and reviving nationalism served to weaken the Japanese Socialists. In the 1969 election, their popular vote declined and they lost a large number of seats in the Diet. The conservatives continued to govern Japan, but it was predicted that during the 1970's the Liberal-Democrats would have to form coalition cabinets with new political groups like the Komeito. This party, based on the Soka Gakkai, a Buddhist religious sect, became Japan's third largest party in the 1969 election.

National Stadium in Tokyo was the main arena for the 1964 summer Olympic Games (top). A world exposition, Expo '70, was held on a site in the Senri Hills outside Osaka.

Words to Remember

Jimmu—the mythical first emperor and founder of the Japanese nation.
Amaterasu—the mythical sun-goddess claimed as ancestor of Japan's imperial dynasty.
shoen—a large medieval agricultural estate.
samurai—a medieval provincial warrior.
shogun—the chief military ruler and commander in Japan from 1192 to 1868.
bakufu—the military government of a shogun.
daimyo—a feudal lord of medieval Japan.

Questions to Think About

1. How has Japan's island location affected its history?
2. In what ways were civil and military authority linked throughout Japanese history?
3. Would Japan have modernized if the Meiji Restoration had never occurred? Explain.
4. What reasons could the Japanese government have given for its expansion into Asia in the 1930's and 1940's?
5. How has the influence of the United States on Japan since 1945 been helpful? How has it been harmful?

Notable Events in Japan's History

A.D. 593–622—Prince Shotoku rules Japan. In 604, reforms are begun to establish a Chinese-style form of government.

1854—Commodore Matthew C. Perry negotiates treaty opening ports of Shimoda and Hakodate to United States ships; treaty of 1858 opens more Japanese ports to United States.

600 1150 1850

1159–60—Taira family defeats Minamoto family in Heiji War; Taira then control Japanese imperial court for 20 years; Minamoto revolt, launched in 1180, destroys Taira in 1185.

1889—Meiji constitution is promulgated on February 11, anniversary of legendary founding of Japan in 660 B.C.; it creates the Diet, Japan's first representative national assembly.

THE JAPANESE PEOPLE BUILD THEIR NATION

A.D. 300–500—Yamato state established.
600–622—Japan makes extensive borrowings from Chinese culture under Prince Shotoku.
710—Imperial capital established at Nara; moved to Heian-kyo (Kyoto), 794.
1156–85—Conflicts between Taira and Minamoto families: Heiji War (1159–60), Minamoto revolt (1180–85).
1192—Yoritomo Minamoto establishes Kamakura shogunate.
1274–81—Mongol invasions repelled.
1333—Kamakura shogunate overthrown.
1400–1500—Daimyo regimes emerge.
1543—Portuguese land in Japan.
1560–90—Military reunification achieved under Nobunaga Oda and Hideyoshi Toyotomi.
1592–98—Hideyoshi conducts expeditions against Korea.
1600—Ieyasu Tokugawa victorious at Sekigahara.
1603—Ieyasu establishes Tokugawa shogunate.
1633–41—Japan's seclusion policy isolates it from outside world.
1853—United States Commo. Matthew C. Perry arrives in Japan.

1905—Japan defeats Russia at Mukden, Manchuria, in final battle of Russo-Japanese War, 1904-5.

1970—Expo '70, Asia's first universal exposition, is held near Osaka; Tower of the Sun symbolizes exposition's theme—"Progress and Harmony for Mankind."

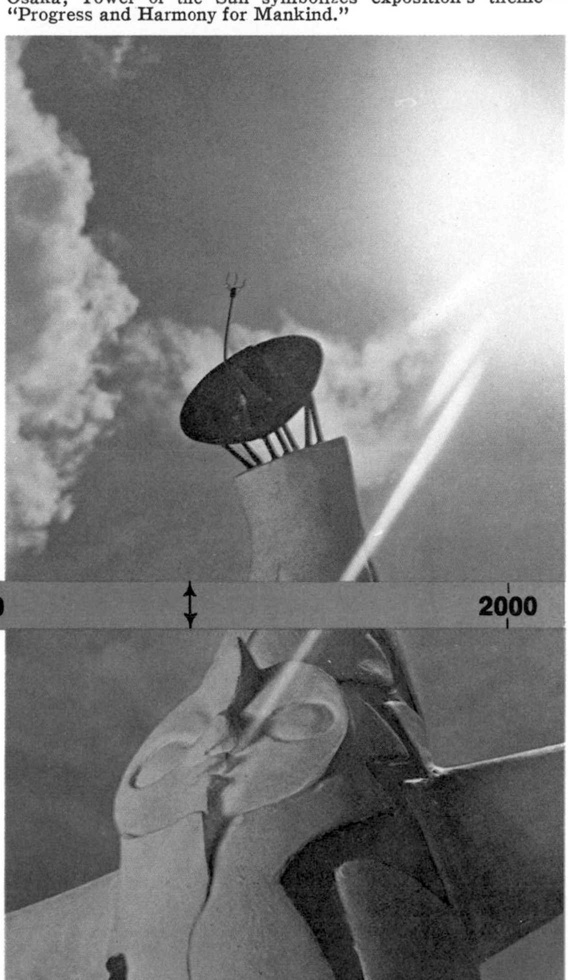

1900 1950 2000

1944–45—Tokyo is nearly destroyed by Allied air raids during World War II; Japan's defeat in war is followed by United States military occupation.

1854—Japan signs treaty of friendship with United States; treaty of trade, 1858.
1867—Mutsuhito becomes emperor; Meiji Restoration ends Tokugawa shogunate, Edo (Tokyo) replaces Kyoto as capital, 1868.
1877—Satsuma rebellion put down.
1889—Meiji constitution promulgated.
1894–95—China defeated in Sino-Japanese War.
1904–5—Russia defeated in Russo-Japanese War.
1926—Hirohito becomes Showa emperor.
1931–32—Japan occupies Manchuria.
1936—February Rebellion defeated.
1937—War with China begins.
1940—Japan concludes alliance with Germany and Italy; enters World War II on side of Germany and Italy, 1941; defeated, 1945.
1945–52—Japan occupied by United States troops.
1956—Japan admitted to United Nations.
1960—Widespread demonstrations against U.S.-Japan mutual security treaty.
1964—Olympic Games held in Tokyo.
1970—Expo '70 held near Osaka.

JAPAN—Fact Summary

HOW JAPAN COMPARES . . .
. . . IN AREA AND POPULATION

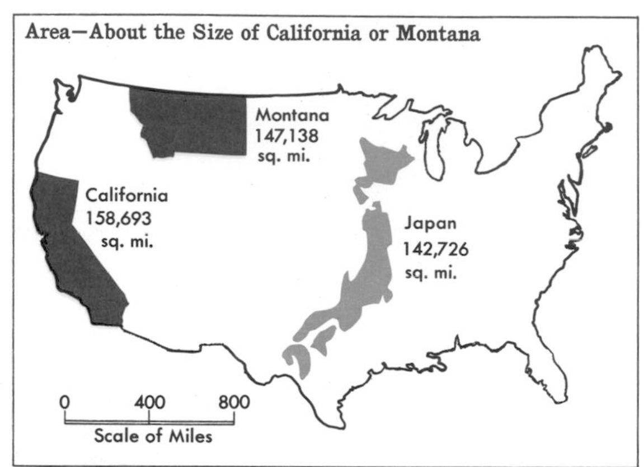

Population—7th Largest Country

1. People's Republic of China	730,000,000
2. India	523,893,000
3. U.S.S.R.	237,798,000
4. United States	201,152,000
5. Indonesia	112,825,000
6. Pakistan	109,520,000
7. Japan	101,090,000
8. Brazil	88,209,000

Source: Statistical Office, United Nations

—Near the Top in Population Density [2]

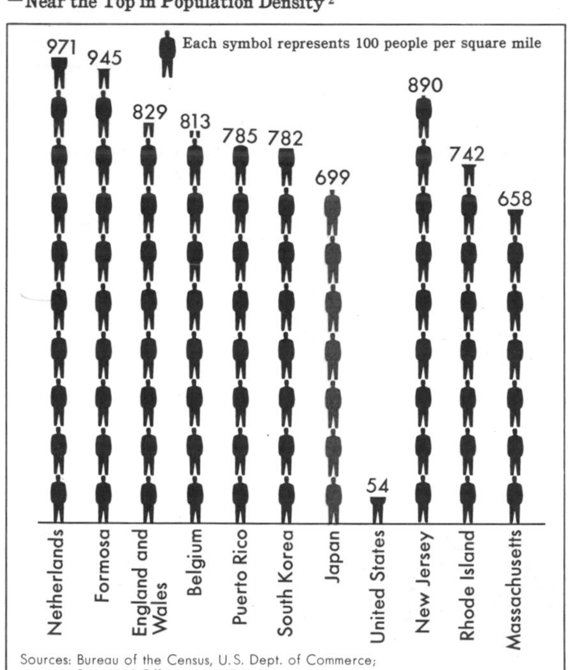

HOW JAPAN COMPARES . . .

Rapid Increase in Gross National Product (GNP) [3,4]

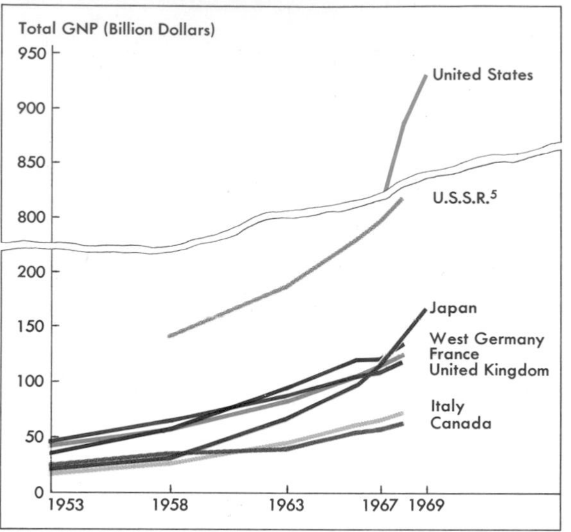

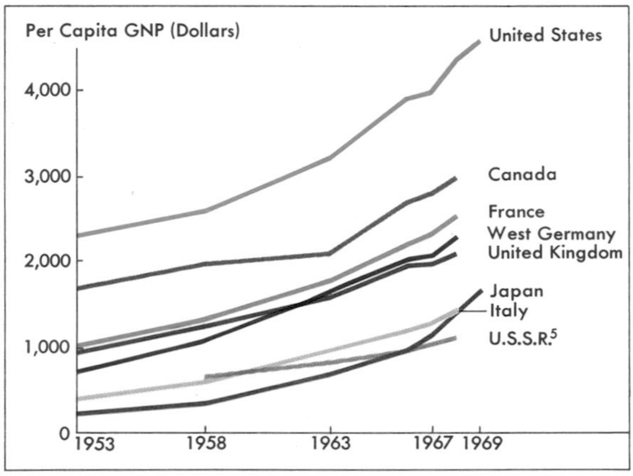

Source: Statistical Office, United Nations

Annual Rate of GNP Growth Outstrips Rivals [4,6]

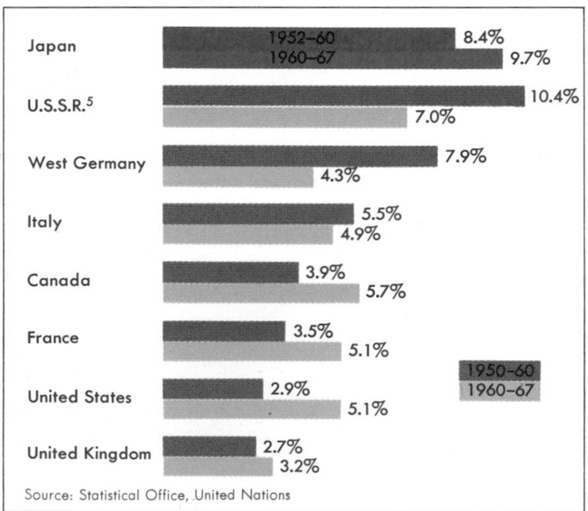

. . . IN ECONOMIC POWER

How have the Japanese been able to achieve such a high rate of economic growth?

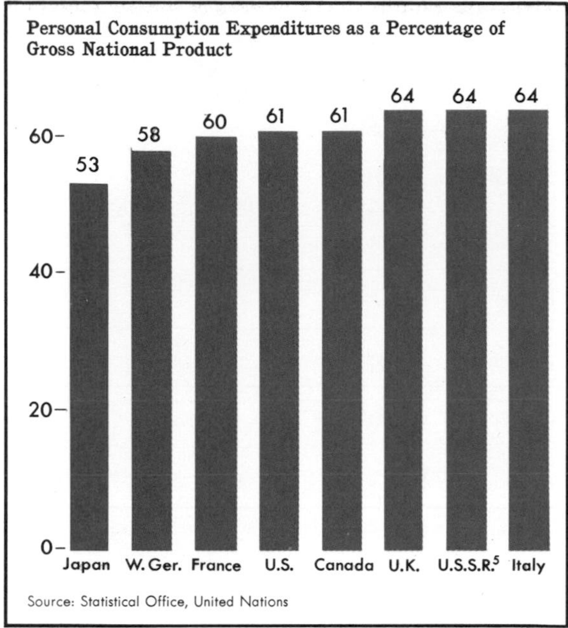

A smaller proportion of Japan's gross national product than that of other leading industrial nations is used for personal expenditures. Thus more money is available for investments in industrial plant and equipment.

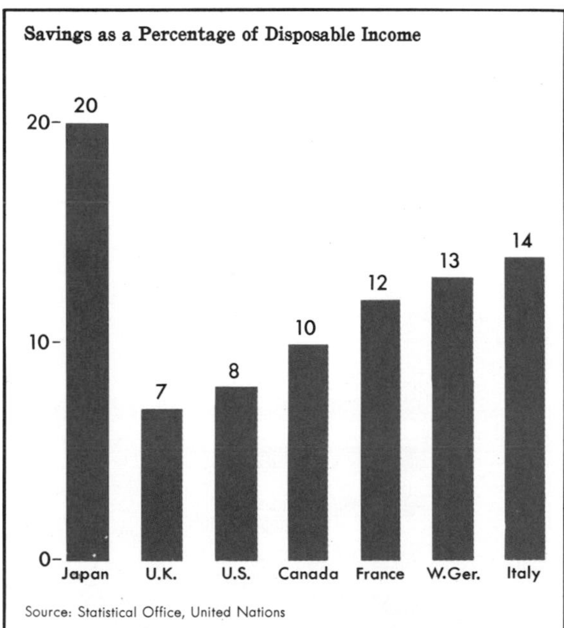

The Japanese save a larger proportion of their disposable income than the people of other leading industrial nations. These savings are then used for further investments in industrial plant and equipment.

Japan Ranks High in the Output of Many Products[8]

Product	Japan's World Rank	Japan's Share of World Output
Commercial vehicles	1	31.4%
Merchant vessels	1	51.1%
Radios	1	9
Caustic soda	2	9
Eggs	2	7.3%
Fish catch	2	12.9%
Plastics and resins	2	14.9%
Rayon and acetate	2	14.4%
Television sets	2	9
Whale catch	2	38.9%
Cement	3	9.5%
Electric power	3	6.4%
Newsprint	3	7.8%
Nitrogen fertilizer	3	8.4%
Passenger cars	3	9.5%
Steel, crude	3	13.0%
Sulfuric acid	3	9
Zinc, primary	3	15.6%
Aluminum, primary	4	7.1%
Copper, refined	4	12.0%
Cotton yarn	4	9
Hydroelectric power	4	9
Lumber	4	9.5%
Rice	4	6.8%
Tea	4	8.6%

Source: Statistical Office, United Nations

Notes for Fact Summary

1. United Nations 1968 midyear estimate.
2. Based on 1967 population estimates of selected countries, regions, and states.
3. Leading countries in gross national product.
4. Excludes the People's Republic of China.
5. Includes production of goods, not services.
6. Less net income from abroad.
7. Selected countries.
8. Based on latest available data.
9. Data not available.
10. Excludes Hawaii.
11. Excludes Northern Ireland.

HOW JAPAN COMPARES . . . IN TRANSPORTATION, COMMUNICATION, DEFENSE

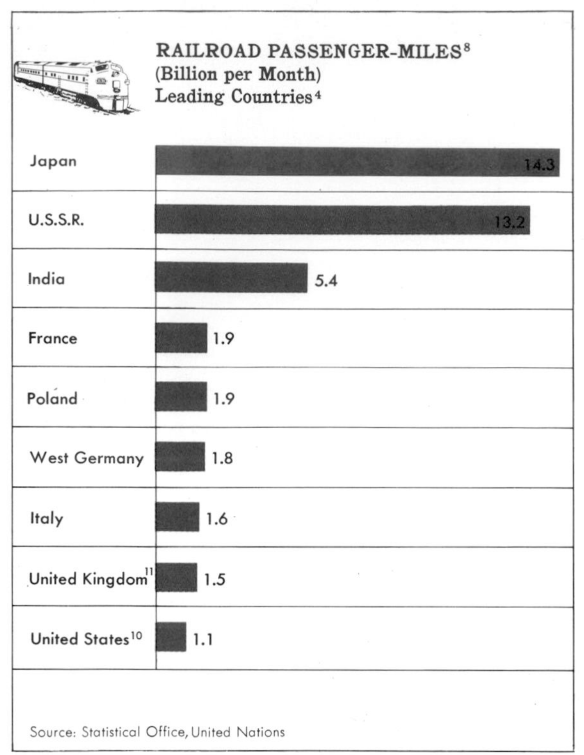
RAILROAD PASSENGER-MILES[8]
(Billion per Month)
Leading Countries[4]
Japan 14.3
U.S.S.R. 13.2
India 5.4
France 1.9
Poland 1.9
West Germany 1.8
Italy 1.6
United Kingdom[11] 1.5
United States[10] 1.1
Source: Statistical Office, United Nations

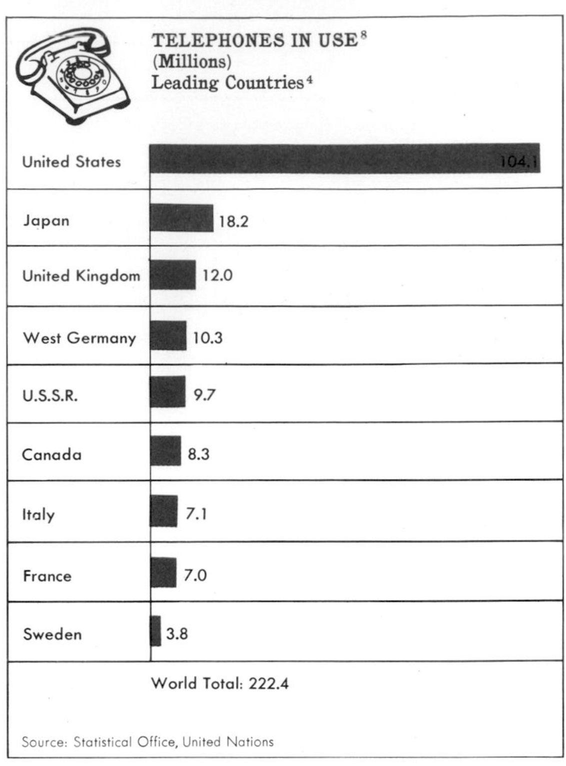
TELEPHONES IN USE[8]
(Millions)
Leading Countries[4]
United States 104.1
Japan 18.2
United Kingdom 12.0
West Germany 10.3
U.S.S.R. 9.7
Canada 8.3
Italy 7.1
France 7.0
Sweden 3.8
World Total: 222.4
Source: Statistical Office, United Nations

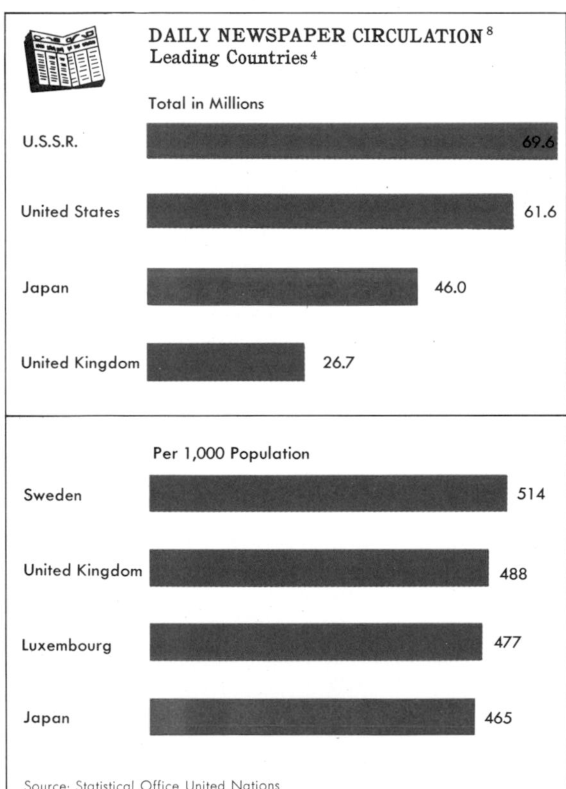
DAILY NEWSPAPER CIRCULATION[8]
Leading Countries[4]
Total in Millions
U.S.S.R. 69.6
United States 61.6
Japan 46.0
United Kingdom 26.7
Per 1,000 Population
Sweden 514
United Kingdom 488
Luxembourg 477
Japan 465
Source: Statistical Office, United Nations

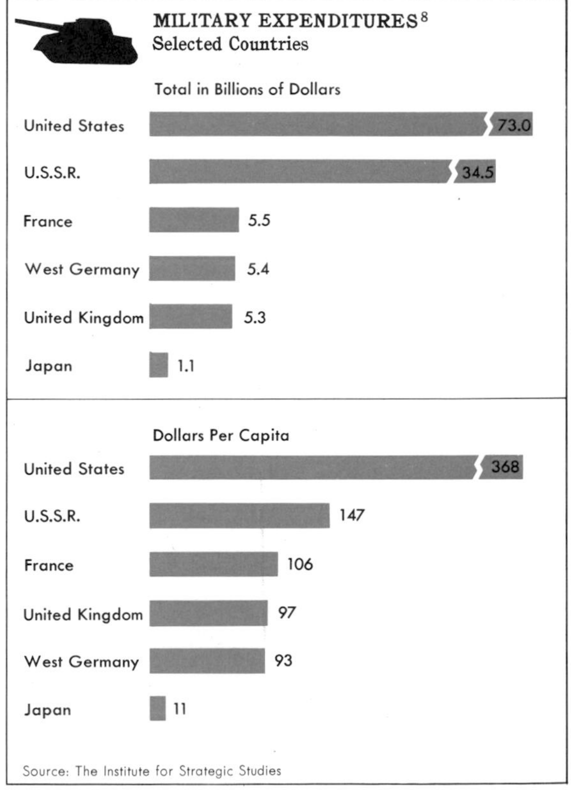
MILITARY EXPENDITURES[8]
Selected Countries
Total in Billions of Dollars
United States 73.0
U.S.S.R. 34.5
France 5.5
West Germany 5.4
United Kingdom 5.3
Japan 1.1
Dollars Per Capita
United States 368
U.S.S.R. 147
France 106
United Kingdom 97
West Germany 93
Japan 11
Source: The Institute for Strategic Studies

JAPAN*

JAPAN

PREFECTURES

Name	Population	Key
Aichi	4,798,653	H 6
Akita	1,279,835	J 4
Aomori	1,416,591	K 3
Chiba	2,701,770	P 2
Ehime	1,446,384	F 7
Fukui	750,557	G 5
Fukuoka	3,964,611	D 7
Fukushima	1,983,754	K 5
Gifu	1,700,365	H 6
Gumma	1,605,584	J 5
Hiroshima	2,281,146	E 6
Hokkaido	5,171,800	K 2
Hyogo	4,309,944	H 7
Ibaraki	2,056,154	K 5
Ishikawa	980,499	H 5
Iwate	1,411,118	K 4
Kagawa	900,845	G 6
Kagoshima	1,853,541	E 8
Kanagawa	4,430,743	O 2
Kochi	812,714	F 7
Kumamoto	1,770,736	E 7
Kyoto	2,102,808	J 7
Mie	1,514,467	H 6
Miyagi	1,753,126	F 4
Miyazaki	1,080,692	E 8
Nagano	1,958,007	J 5
Nagasaki	1,641,245	D 7
Nara	825,965	J 8
Niigata	2,398,931	J 5
Oita	1,187,480	E 7
Okayama	1,645,135	F 6
Osaka	6,657,189	J 8
Saga	871,885	E 7
Saitama	3,014,983	O 2
Shiga	853,385	J 7
Shimane	821,620	F 6
Shizuoka	2,912,521	H 6
Tochigi	1,521,656	K 5
Tokushima	815,115	G 7
Tokyo	10,869,244	O 2
Tottori	579,853	G 6
Toyama	1,025,465	H 5
Wakayama	1,026,975	G 6
Yamagata	1,263,103	K 4
Yamaguchi	1,543,573	E 6
Yamanashi	763,194	J 6

CITIES, PLACES, AND GEOGRAPHICAL FEATURES

Name	Population	Key
Abashiri	44,195	M 1
Abashiri (river)		M 1
Abukama (river)		K 4
Agano (river)		J 4
Ageo	54,776	O 2
Aikawa	16,454	H 4
Aizuwakamatsu	102,239	J 5
Ajigasawa	20,504	J 3
Akabira	46,646	K 2
Akan National Park		M 2
Akashi	159,299	H 8
Aki	26,605	F 7
Akita	216,607	J 4
Akkeshi	19,039	M 2
Akune	36,026	E 7
Amagasaki	500,990	H 8
Amaha	18,062	O 3
Amakusa (isls.)	223,465	D 7
Amami (isls.)	186,193	N 5
Amami-O-Shima (isl.)	94,348	N 5
Anamizu	16,695	H 5
Anan	59,105	G 7
Aomori	224,433	K 3
Ara (river)		O 2
Asahi	31,063	K 6
Asahi (mt.)		J 4
Asahikawa	245,246	L 2
Asama (mt.)		J 5
Ashibetsu	52,123	L 2
Ashikaga	150,259	J 5
Ashiya	63,195	H 8
Ashizuri (point)		F 7
Aso (mt.)		E 7
Aso National Park		E 7
Atami	54,540	J 6
Atsugi	61,383	O 2
Atsumi (bay)		H 6
Awa (isl.)	771	J 4
Awaji	9,972	H 8
Awaji (isl.)	185,473	H 8
Ayabe	48,339	G 6
Bandai (mt.)		K 5
Bandai-Asahi National Park		J 4
Bekkai	19,502	M 2
Beppu	118,938	E 7
Bibai	63,051	L 2
Biratori	12,930	L 2
Biwa (lake)		H 6
Bonin (isls.)	203	M 3
Bungo (strait)		F 7
Chiba	332,188	P 2
Chichi (isl.)	203	M 3
Chichibu	60,330	J 6
Chichibu-Tama National Park		J 6
Chigasaki	100,081	O 3
Chitose	51,243	K 2
Chofu	118,004	O 2
Chokai (mt.)		J 4
Choshi	91,492	K 6
Chubu Sangaku National Park		H 5
Dai (mt.)		F 6
Daio (cape)		H 6
Daisen-Oki National Park		F 6
Daisetsu (mt.)		L 2
Daisetsu-Zan National Park		L 2
Daito	57,107	J 8
Dogo (isl.)	23,669	F 5
Dozen (isls.)	12,516	F 5
East China (sea)		C 8
Ebetsu	44,510	K 2
Edo (river)		P 2
Erabu (isl.)	22,049	N 5
Erimo (cape)		L 3
Esan (point)		K 3
Esashi, Hokkaido	15,380	J 3
Esashi, Hokkaido	11,401	L 1
Esashi, Iwate	42,666	K 4
Etorofu (isl.)		N 1
Fuchu, Hiroshima	45,341	F 6
Fuchu, Tokyo	126,519	O 2
Fuji	143,471	J 6
Fuji (mt.)		J 6
Fuji (river)		J 6
Fuji-Hakaone-Izu National Park		H 6
Fujisawa	175,183	O 3
Fukuchiyama	58,223	G 6
Fukue	38,876	D 7
Fukui	169,636	G 5
Fukuoka	749,808	D 7
Fukushima, Fukushima	173,678	K 5
Fukushima, Nagano	9,373	H 6
Fukuyama	204,768	F 6
Funabashi	223,989	P 2
Furukawa	52,853	K 4
Futtsu	16,445	O 3
Gassan (mt.)		J 4
Gifu	358,190	H 6
Gobo	30,040	G 7
Gose	35,788	J 8
Gosen	38,113	J 5
Goshogawara	47,433	K 3
Goto (isls.)	159,190	D 7
Gotsu	30,209	F 6
Habikino	50,333	J 8
Habomai (isls.)		N 2
Haboro	30,266	K 1
Hachinohe	189,387	K 3
Hachioji	207,753	O 2
Hachiro (lagoon)		J 3
Hagi	53,905	E 6
Haha (isl.)		M 3
Hakken (mt.)		H 6
Hakodate	243,418	K 3
Haku (mt.)		H 5
Hakui	29,090	H 5
Hakusan National Park		H 5
Hamada	44,439	E 6
Hamamatsu	392,632	H 6
Hamasaka	14,466	G 6
Hanamaki	62,710	K 4
Hanno	47,825	O 2
Haramachi	40,643	K 5
Harima (sea)		G 6
Hayama	17,617	O 3
Hida (river)		H 6
Higashiosaka	443,081	J 8
Hikone	62,740	H 6
Himeji	367,807	G 6
Himi	62,452	H 5
Hirakata	127,520	J 7
Hirata	33,128	F 6
Hiratsuka	134,931	O 3
Hiroo	13,598	L 2
Hirosaki	151,624	K 3
Hiroshima	504,245	E 6
Hitachi	179,703	K 5
Hitachiota	36,974	K 5
Hitoyoshi	44,831	E 7
Hodaka (mt.)		H 5
Hofu	94,342	E 6
Hokkaido (isl.)	5,171,800	L 2
Hokota	26,939	K 5
Hondo	39,790	E 7
Honjo	38,361	J 4
Honshu (isl.)	76,757,913	J 5
Hyuga	43,678	E 7
Ibaraki	115,136	J 7
Ibusuki	32,386	E 8
Ichihara	86,475	P 2
Ichikawa	207,988	P 2
Ichinohe	25,165	K 3
Ichinomiya	203,743	H 6
Ichinoseki	57,238	K 4
Iida	79,145	H 6
Iizuka	82,033	E 7
Ikeda, Hokkaido	15,529	L 2
Ikeda, Osaka	82,478	H 7
Iki (isl.)	45,654	D 7
Ikuno	9,466	G 6
Imabari	104,470	F 6
Imari	67,316	D 7
Imazu	11,245	G 6
Ina	51,944	H 6
Inawashiro (lake)		K 5
Inubo (cape)		K 6
Iro (point)		J 6
Isahaya	63,886	D 7
Ise	102,395	H 6
Ise (bay)		H 6
Ise-Shima National Park		H 6
Ishige	18,481	P 2
Ishikari (bay)		K 2
Ishikari (river)		L 2
Ishinomaki	89,284	K 4
Ishizuchi (mt.)		F 7
Itami	121,380	H 7
Ito	59,404	J 6
Itoigawa	39,332	H 5
Iwaki	333,881	K 5
Iwaki (mt.)		K 3
Iwakuni	105,931	E 6
Iwamisawa	65,508	L 2
Iwanai	25,405	K 2
Iwasaki	5,432	J 3
Iwate (mt.)		K 4
Iwatsuki	41,946	O 2
Iwo (isl.)		M 4
Iyo	28,611	F 7
Iyo (sea)		E 7
Izu (isls.)	35,592	J 6
Izuhara	21,989	D 6
Izumi	84,771	J 8
Izumiotsu	53,312	J 8
Izumisano	66,521	G 6
Izumo	68,765	F 6
Japan (sea)		G 4
Joshinetsu-Kogen National Park		J 5
Kaga	54,860	H 5
Kagoshima	371,329	E 8
Kagoshima (bay)		E 8
Kaizuka	69,365	H 8
Kakogawa	101,841	G 6
Kamaishi	82,104	L 4
Kamakura	118,329	O 3
Kameoka	43,335	J 7
Kaminoyama	38,679	J 4
Kamiyaku	12,458	O 4
Kamo	38,937	J 5
Kamui (cape)		K 2
Kanazawa	335,828	H 5
Kanonji	44,200	F 6
Kanoya	70,519	E 8
Kanuma	77,240	J 5
Karatsu	73,999	D 7
Kariba (mt.)		K 2
Kashihara, Nara	57,065	J 8
Kashihara, Osaka	44,972	J 8
Kashiwa	109,237	P 2
Kashiwazaki	71,465	J 5
Kasukabe	42,460	O 2
Kasumiga (lagoon)		K 5
Katsuura	29,133	K 6
Kawachi	91,853	J 8
Kawachinagano	40,109	J 8
Kawagoe	127,155	O 2
Kawaguchi	249,112	O 2
Kawanishi	61,282	H 7
Kawasaki	854,866	O 2
Kazan-Retto (Volcano) (isls.)		M 4
Kazusa	12,787	P 3
Kembuchi	8,013	L 1
Kesennuma	59,884	K 4
Kii (channel)		G 7
Kikai (isl.)	14,231	O 5
Kikonai	11,353	K 3
Kino (river)		G 6
Kirishima National Park		E 8
Kiryu	127,880	J 5
Kisarazu	54,928	P 3
Kishiwada	143,710	J 8
Kitaibaraki	55,334	K 5
Kitakami (river)		K 4
Kitakata	40,424	J 5
Kitakyushu	1,100,000	E 6
Kitami	74,841	L 2
Kizu	10,814	J 7
Kobayashi	41,922	E 8
Kobe	1,200,000	H 7
Kochi	217,889	F 7
Kofu	172,457	J 6
Kokubu	31,249	E 8
Koma (mt.)		K 2
Komatsu	91,163	H 5
Komoro	38,830	J 5
Koriyama	223,183	K 5
Kosaka	15,280	K 3
Koshiki (isls.)	16,301	D 8
Kuchino (isl.)		O 4
Kuji	38,374	K 3
Kuju (mt.)		E 7
Kuki	26,773	O 2
Kumagaya	109,575	J 5
Kumamoto	407,052	E 7
Kunashiri (isl.)		N 1
Kurashiki	275,336	F 6
Kurayoshi	50,114	F 6
Kure	225,013	F 6
Kuroiso	32,268	K 5
Kurume	158,974	E 7
Kusatsu	8,867	J 5
Kushikino	31,781	E 8
Kushima	36,425	E 8
Kushimoto	20,252	G 7
Kushiro	174,405	M 2
Kutchan	19,738	K 2
Kutcharo (lake)		M 2
Kyoto	1,400,000	J 7
Kyushu (isl.)	12,370,190	E 7
Machida	115,918	O 2
Maebashi	198,745	J 5
Maibara	13,415	G 6
Maizuru	96,641	G 6
Makurazaki	31,464	O 3
Marugame	58,826	G 6
Mashike	13,063	K 2
Masuda	52,729	E 6
Matsubara	71,406	H 8
Matsudo	160,001	P 2
Matsue	110,534	F 6
Matsumae	19,111	J 3
Matsumoto	154,131	H 5
Matsusaka	99,814	H 6
Matsuyama	282,651	F 7
Meakan (mt.)		L 2

*All population figures are taken from the latest official census or estimate available. †City and suburbs.

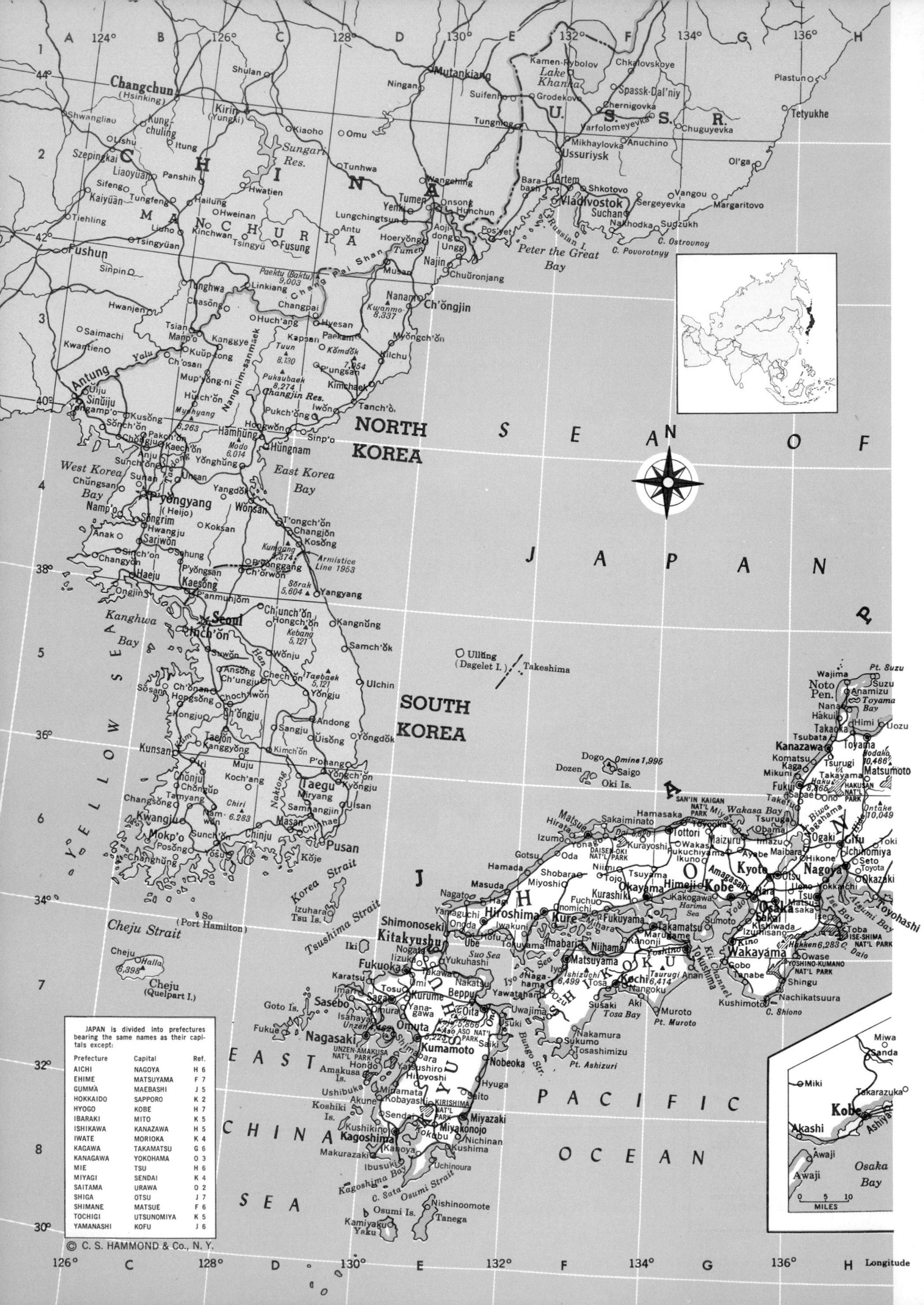

JAPAN is divided into prefectures bearing the same names as their capitals except:

Prefecture	Capital	Ref.
AICHI	NAGOYA	H 6
EHIME	MATSUYAMA	F 7
GUMMA	MAEBASHI	J 5
HOKKAIDO	SAPPORO	K 2
HYOGO	KOBE	H 7
IBARAKI	MITO	K 5
ISHIKAWA	KANAZAWA	H 5
IWATE	MORIOKA	K 4
KAGAWA	TAKAMATSU	G 6
KANAGAWA	YOKOHAMA	O 3
MIE	TSU	H 6
MIYAGI	SENDAI	K 4
SAITAMA	URAWA	O 2
SHIGA	OTSU	J 7
SHIMANE	MATSUE	F 6
TOCHIGI	UTSUNOMIYA	K 5
YAMANASHI	KOFU	J 6

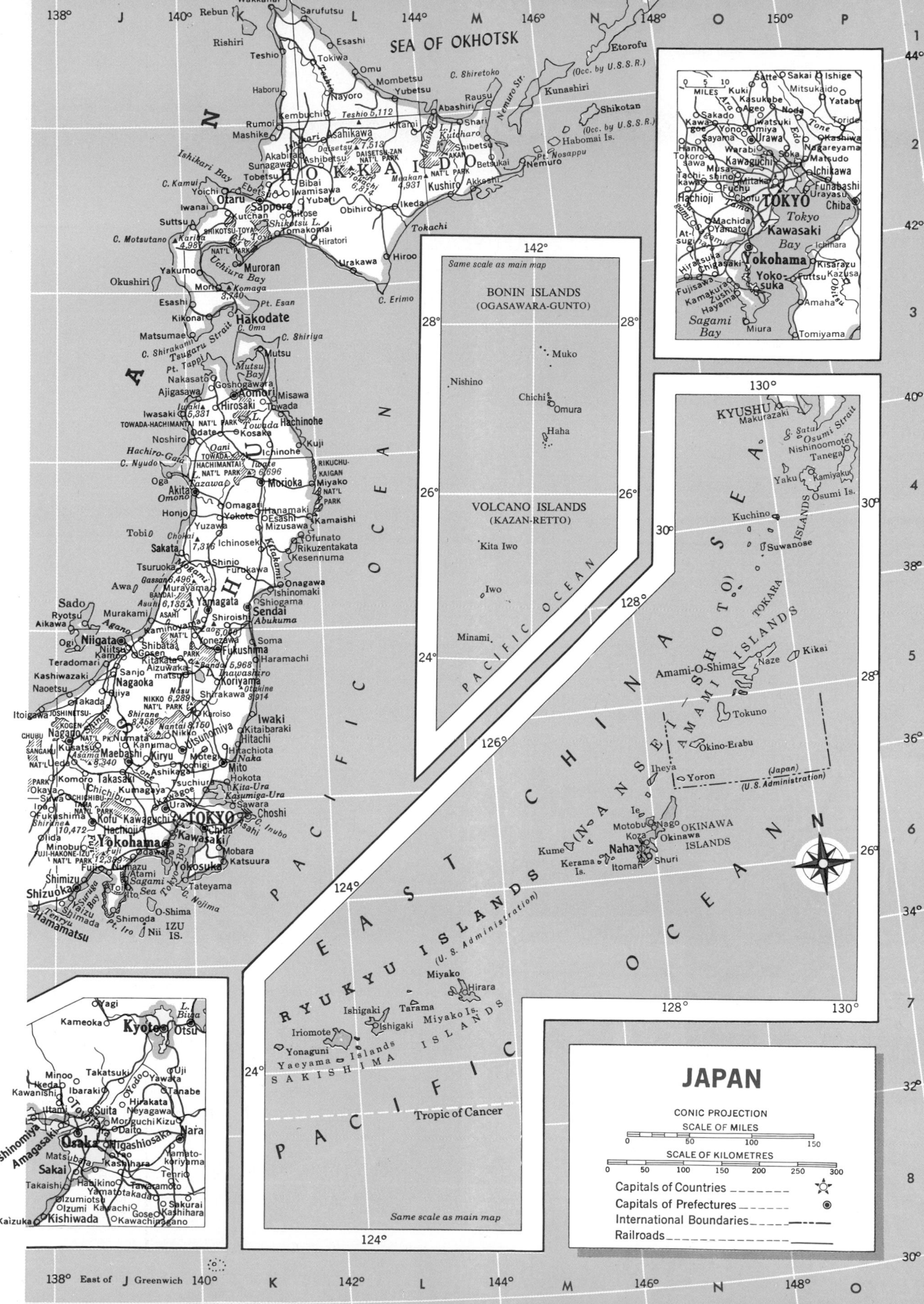

JAPAN
CONIC PROJECTION
SCALE OF MILES
SCALE OF KILOMETRES
Capitals of Countries
Capitals of Prefectures
International Boundaries
Railroads
SEA OF OKHOTSK
SEA OF JAPAN
PACIFIC OCEAN
EAST CHINA SEA
HOKKAIDO
HONSHU
TOKYO
Sapporo
Hakodate
Aomori
Sendai
Niigata
Yokohama
Kyoto
Osaka
Nara
Kobe
BONIN ISLANDS (OGASAWARA-GUNTO)
VOLCANO ISLANDS (KAZAN-RETTO)
Same scale as main map
RYUKYU ISLANDS (U. S. Administration)
NANSEI-SHOTO
AMAMI ISLANDS
OKINAWA ISLANDS
SAKISHIMA ISLANDS
KYUSHU
Tropic of Cancer
East of Greenwich
(Occ. by U.S.S.R.)

JAPAN—*Continued*

Mihara	82,175	F 6
Miki	38,542	H 7
Mikuni	22,135	G 5
Minamata	45,577	E 7
Minobu	12,250	J 6
Minoo	43,851	J 7
Misawa	36,326	K 3
Mitaka	135,873	O 2
Mito	154,983	K 5
Mitsukaido	36,584	P 2
Miura	42,601	O 3
Miwa		H 7
Miyako	56,575	L 4
Miyakonojo	108,220	E 8
Miyazaki	182,870	E 8
Miyazu	33,285	G 6
Miyoshi	37,871	F 6
Mizusawa	45,985	K 4
Mobara	42,486	K 6
Mogami (river)		K 4
Mombetsu	40,389	L 1
Mori	18,330	K 2
Moriguchi	138,856	J 7
Morioka	176,967	K 4
Motegi	24,106	K 5
Motsutano (cape)		J 2
Murakami	32,651	J 4
Murayama	36,423	J 4
Muroran	161,252	K 2
Muroto	28,746	G 7
Muroto (point)		G 7
Musashino	133,516	O 2
Mutsu	39,282	K 3
Mutsu (bay)		K 3
Nachikatsuura	24,889	H 7
Nagahama, Ehime	16,193	F 7
Nagahama, Shiga	49,871	H 6
Nagano	243,957	J 5
Nagaoka	154,752	J 5
Nagareyama	39,168	P 2
Nagasaki	405,479	D 7
Nagato	29,246	E 6
Nagoya	2,000,000	H 6
Naka (river)		J 5
Nakamura	35,717	F 7
Nakasato	15,898	K 3
Nakatsu	58,371	E 7
Nanao	48,715	H 5
Nangoku	41,237	F 7
Nantai (mt.)		J 5
Naoetsu	45,650	H 5
Nara	160,641	J 8
Nasu (mt.)		J 5
Nayoro	36,106	L 1
Naze	44,111	O 5
Nemuro	45,149	M 2
Nemuro (strait)		M 1
Neyagawa	113,576	J 7
Nichinan	57,612	E 8
Nii (isl.)	3,913	J 6
Niigata	356,302	J 5
Niihama	125,155	F 6
Niimi	34,063	F 6
Niitsu	56,594	J 5
Nikko	32,031	J 5
Nikko National Park		J 5
Nishinomiya	336,873	H 8
Nishinoomote	30,490	E 8
Nobeoka	124,000	E 7
Noda	59,799	P 2
Nogata	57,839	E 7
Nojima (cape)		K 6
Noshappu (point)		N 2
Noshiro	61,921	J 3
Noto (pen.)		H 5
Numata	44,347	J 5
Numazu	159,880	J 6
Nyudo (cape)		J 4
Oani (river)		K 3
Obama	35,160	G 6
Obihiro	117,253	L 2
Obitsu (river)		B 3
Oda	42,322	F 6
Odate	59,662	K 3
Odawara	143,377	J 6
Ofunato	38,347	K 4
Oga	43,333	J 4
Ogaki	113,671	H 6
Ogasawara-Gunto (Bonin) (isls.)	203	M 3
Ogi	5,500	J 5
Oita	226,417	E 7
Ojiya	47,376	J 5
Okaya	56,986	H 5
Okayama	291,825	F 6
Okazaki	194,409	H 6
Okhotsk (sea)		M 1
Oki (isls.)	36,185	F 5
Okushiri (isl.)	7,142	J 2
Oma (cape)		K 3
Omagari	39,900	K 4
Omiya	215,646	O 2
Omono (river)		J 4
Omu	9,494	L 1
Omura, Nagasaki	56,425	E 7
Omura, Tokyo	203	M 3
Omuta	193,875	E 7
Onagawa	18,080	K 4
Ono	43,747	H 6
Ono (river)		E 7
Onoda	43,584	E 6
Onomichi	90,740	F 6
Ontake (mt.)		H 6
Osaka	3,100,000	J 8
Osaka (bay)		H 8
O-Shima (isl.)	11,840	J 6
Osumi (isls.)	82,372	E 8
Osumi (strait)		E 8
Otakine (mt.)		K 5
Otaru	196,771	K 2
Otsu	121,041	J 7
Owase	34,019	H 6
Ozu	40,165	F 7
Rausu	8,931	M 1
Rebun (isl.)	8,374	K 1
Rikuchu-Kaigan National Park		L 4
Rikuzentakata	31,040	K 4
Rishiri (isl.)	17,663	K 1
Rumoi	40,231	K 2
Ryotsu	26,494	J 4
Sabae	50,114	H 5
Sado (isl.)	102,925	J 4
Saga	134,575	E 7
Sagami (bay)		O 3
Sagami (river)		O 2
Sagami (sea)		J 6
Sagamihara	163,381	O 2
Saigo	16,569	F 5
Saiki	51,145	E 7
Saito	42,543	E 7
Sakado	24,854	O 2
Sakai, Ibaraki	21,689	P 1
Sakai, Osaka	466,412	J 8
Sakaiminato	32,846	F 6
Sakata	95,982	J 4
Sakurai	49,939	J 8
Sanda	32,265	H 7
San'in Kaigan National Park		G 6
Sanjo	74,080	J 5
Sapporo	794,908	K 2
Sarufutsu	7,450	L 1
Sasebo	247,069	D 7
Sata (cape)		E 8
Satte	25,169	O 1
Sawara	47,561	K 6
Sayama	40,183	O 2
Sendai, Kagoshima	67,142	E 8
Sendai, Miyagi	480,925	K 4
Seto	86,424	H 6
Shari	18,015	M 2
Shibata	73,992	J 5
Shibetsu	36,502	M 2
Shikoku (isl.)	3,975,058	F 7
Shikotan (isl.)		N 2
Shikotsu (lake)		K 2
Shikotsu-Toya National Park		K 2
Shimabara	44,175	E 7
Shimada	63,493	J 6
Shimizu	210,559	J 6
Shimoda	28,645	J 6
Shimonoseki	254,376	E 6
Shinano (river)		J 5
Shingu	40,051	H 7
Shinjo	43,037	K 4
Shiogama	58,363	K 4
Shiono (cape)		H 7
Shirakami (cape)		J 3
Shirakawa	40,747	K 5
Shirane (mt.)		H 6
Shirane (mt.)		J 5
Shiretoko (cape)		M 1
Shiriya (cape)		K 3
Shiroishi	41,928	K 4
Shizuoka	367,705	H 6
Shobara	26,515	F 6
Soka	80,707	O 2
Soma	38,430	K 5
Soya (point)		L 1
Suita	196,779	J 7
Sukumo	26,992	F 7
Sumoto	46,313	G 6
Sunagawa	30,205	K 2
Suo (sea)		E 7
Suruga (bay)		J 6
Susaki	32,020	F 7
Suttsu	8,043	J 2
Suwa	46,276	H 6
Suwanose (isl.)		O 4
Suzu	32,122	H 5
Suzu (point)		H 5
Tachikawa	100,719	O 2
Takada	73,668	J 5
Takaishi	45,679	H 7
Takamatsu	243,444	G 6
Takaoka	139,502	H 5
Takarazuka	91,486	H 7
Takasaki	173,887	J 5
Takatsuki	130,735	J 7
Takawa	74,063	E 7
Takayama	53,399	H 5
Takefu	62,588	G 6
Takeshima (isls.)		F 5
Tama (river)		O 2
Tanabe, Kyoto	17,333	J 7
Tanabe, Wakayama	62,276	G 7
Tanega (isl.)	60,130	E 8
Tappi (point)		K 3
Tateyama	55,866	K 6
Tawaramoto	20,150	J 8
Tazawa (lake)		K 4
Tenri	54,169	J 8
Tenryu (river)		J 6
Teradomari	14,922	J 5
Teshio	9,493	K 1
Teshio (mt.)		L 1
Teshio (river)		L 1
Toba	30,098	H 6
Tobetsu	19,406	K 2
Tobi (isl.)		J 4
Tochigi	74,671	J 5
Toi	8,004	J 6
Tojo	16,866	F 6
Tokachi (mt.)		L 2
Tokachi (river)		L 2
Tokara (arch.)	2,722	O 5
Toki	59,038	H 6
Tokiwa	3,970	L 1
Tokorosawa	89,346	O 2
Tokuno (isl.)	18,920	O 5
Tokushima	193,233	G 7
Tokuyama	84,687	F 6
Tokyo (capital)	9,000,000	O 2
Tokyo	†11,005,000	O 2
Tokyo (bay)		O 2
Tomakomai	81,812	K 2
Tomiyama	7,863	O 3
Tone (river)		J 5
Toride	26,179	P 2
Tosa	30,772	F 7
Tosa (bay)		F 7
Tosashimizu	26,725	F 7
Tosu	44,419	E 7
Tottori	108,860	G 6
Towada	46,713	K 3
Towada (lake)		K 3
Towada-Hachimantai National Park		K 3
Toya (lake)		K 2
Toyama	239,810	H 5
Toyama (bay)		H 5
Toyohashi	238,672	H 6
Toyonaka	291,936	J 7
Toyooka	43,259	G 6
Toyota	107,455	H 6
Tsu	117,214	H 6
Tsubata	21,113	H 5
Tsuchiura	78,971	J 5
Tsugaru (strait)		K 3
Tsuruga	54,508	G 6
Tsurugi	12,229	H 5
Tsurugi (mt.)		G 7
Tsuruoka	95,615	J 4
Tsushima (isls.)	65,304	D 6
Tsushima (strait)		D 7
Tsuyama	76,007	F 6
Ube	158,986	E 6
Uchinoura	10,036	E 8
Uchiura (bay)		K 2
Ueda	73,940	J 5
Ueno	58,915	H 6
Uji	68,934	J 7
Umi	19,390	E 7
Unzen (mt.)		D 7
Unzen-Amakusa National Park		D 7
Uozu	46,854	H 5
Urakawa	21,552	L 2
Urawa	221,337	O 2
Urayasu	18,463	P 2
Ushibuka	30,995	D 7
Usuki	42,731	F 7
Utsunomiya	265,696	K 5
Uwajima	66,484	F 7
Volcano (isls.)		M 4
Wajima	35,798	H 5
Wakasa	8,455	G 8
Wakasa (bay)		G 6
Wakayama	328,657	G 6
Wakkanai	51,539	K 1
Warabi	69,715	O 2
Yagi	10,693	J 7
Yaizu	77,008	J 6
Yaku (isl.)	22,242	E 8
Yakumo	22 487	J 2
Yamagata	193,737	K 4
Yamaguchi	98,977	E 6
Yamato	64,991	O 2
Yamatokoriyama	45,765	J 8
Yamatotakada	47,371	J 8
Yanagawa	47,549	E 7
Yao	170,248	J 8
Yatabe	20,093	P 2
Yatsushiro	102,511	E 7
Yawata	19,204	J 7
Yawatahama	50,005	F 7
Yodo (river)		J 7
Yoichi	26,154	K 2
Yokkaichi	218,981	H 6
Yokohama	2,000,000	O 3
Yokosuka	317,411	O 3
Yokote	44,331	K 4
Yonago	99,484	F 6
Yonezawa	94,435	K 5
Yono	51,746	O 2
Yoron (isl.)	7,181	N 6
Yoshino (river)		G 8
Yoshino-Kumano National Park		H 7
Yubari	85,141	L 2
Yubetsu	9,720	L 1
Yukuhashi	47,495	E 7
Yuzawa	39,879	K 4
Zao (mt.)		K 5
Zushi	43,211	O 3

RYUKYU ISLANDS

Hirara	32,591	L 7
Ie (isl.)	7,059	N 6
Iheya (isl.)	3,083	N 6
Iriomote (isl.)	7,026	K 7
Ishigaki	41,315	L 7
Ishigaki (isl.)	41,315	L 7
Itoman	34,065	N 6
Kerama (isls.)	2,467	M 6
Koza	55,923	N 6
Kume (isl.)	5,922	M 6
Miyako (isl.)	47,150	L 7
Miyako (isls.)	69,825	L 7
Motobu	15,068	N 6
Nago	19,601	N 6
Naha (capital)	257,177	N 6
Okinawa (isl.)	782,267	N 6
Okinawa (isls.)	812,339	N 6
Sakishima (isls.)	121,837	K 7
Shuri	28,282	N 6
Tarama (isl.)	2,603	L 7
Yaeyama (isls.)	52,012	K 7
Yonaguni (isl.)	3,671	K 7

Index

This index is arranged in alphabetical order. Words beginning with "Mc" are alphabetized as "Mac," and "St." is alphabetized as "Saint."

The figures in brackets [67, 69] indicate earlier editions of THE COMPTON YEARBOOK in which the topic has appeared since 1967.

The first page reference is the main discussion.

Cross-references refer to index entries in this volume.

The reprints from the 1971 COMPTON'S ENCYCLOPEDIA are usually indexed by title only unless they contain events of 1970.

Major sections of the Yearbook appear on the following pages:

Compton's Pictured Highlights and Chronology of 1970, 12–31

Feature articles—Women in Society: the Search for "Personhood" by Jacqueline Wexler, 32–47; Let's Travel, by Horace Sutton, 48–57; The Need for Population Control, by Paul R. Ehrlich, 58–67; The Art of Photography, by John Szarkowski, 68–95; Drugs and Youth, by Dr. Stanley Fausst Yolles, 96–107

Special reports—Business and Industry: Franchising, 164–65; Conservation: The Alaska Pipeline, 205–07; Germany: East Meets West, 269–71; Housing: Tenants on the Move, 286–88; Ireland: The Two Irelands, 307–09; Law: Chicago Conspiracy Trial, 325–26; Religion: The New English Bible, 410–11; Space Exploration: After Apollo, 430–32; Television and Radio: News and Views, 454–55

Events of the Year 1970, 107–497

Calendar for 1971, 498–500

New Words, 501–06

Reprints from the 1971 edition of COMPTON'S ENCYCLOPEDIA, 523–592

The Family Record follows the index.

V

W

OUR FAMILY RECORD FOR 1971

What we did and how we looked

This space for family group photo

Each year important events highlight the life of every family. Year after year these events may be noted in the Family Record pages of your Compton Yearbooks. You will then have a permanent record of your family's significant achievements, celebrations, and activities.

OUR FAMILY TREE

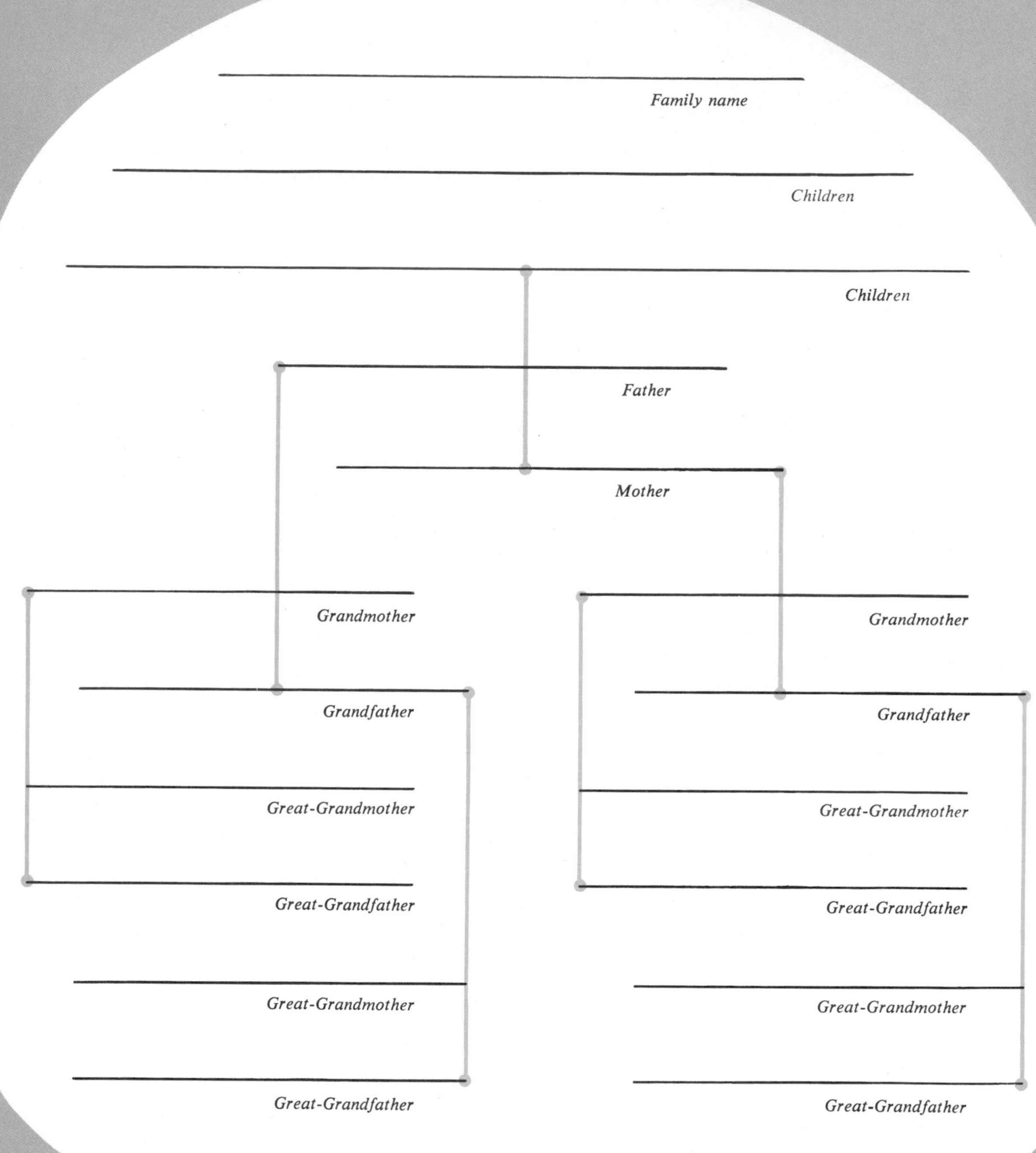

DATES TO REMEMBER

Birthdays, weddings, anniversaries, graduations, gifts sent

JANUARY	FEBRUARY	MARCH
APRIL	MAY	JUNE
JULY	AUGUST	SEPTEMBER
OCTOBER	NOVEMBER	DECEMBER

FAMILY CELEBRATIONS IN 1971

PASTE PHOTO HERE

BIRTHDAYS

NAME ______

DATE ______

______

______

NAME ______

DATE ______

______

______

NAME ______

DATE ______

______

______

NAME ______

DATE ______

______

______

NAME ______

DATE ______

______

______

NAME ______

DATE ______

______

______

______

WEDDINGS

NAMES ______

______

DATE ______

NAMES ______

______

DATE ______

NAMES ______

______

DATE ______

ANNIVERSARIES

NAMES ______

DATE ______

______

NAMES ______

DATE ______

______

PROMOTIONS

FIRM ______

TITLE ______

DATE ______

FIRM ______

TITLE ______

DATE ______

HOLIDAYS

OCCASION

OCCASION

OCCASION

OCCASION

BIRTHS

NAME
DATE
PARENTS

NAME
DATE
PARENTS

NAME
DATE
PARENTS

NAME
DATE
PARENTS

SPIRITUAL MILESTONES

NAME
MILESTONE

NAME
MILESTONE

NAME
MILESTONE

NAME
MILESTONE

NAME
MILESTONE

NAME
MILESTONE

NAME
MILESTONE

NAME
MILESTONE

PASTE PHOTO HERE

SCHOOL ACTIVITIES AND ACHIEVEMENTS

NAME ______________________

SCHOOL ______________ GRADE ____

NAME ______________________

SCHOOL ______________ GRADE ____

SPORTS

NAME ______________________

SPORT ______________________

ACHIEVEMENT ______________________

NAME ______________________

SPORT ______________________

ACHIEVEMENT ______________________

NAME ______________________

SPORT ______________________

ACHIEVEMENT ______________________

NAME ______________________

SPORT ______________________

ACHIEVEMENT ______________________

NAME ______________________

SPORT ______________________

ACHIEVEMENT ______________________

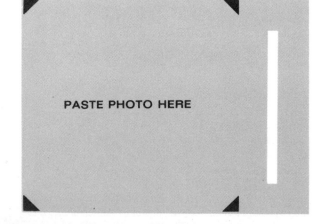

PASTE PHOTO HERE

CLUB ACTIVITIES

NAME ______________________

CLUB ______________________

ACHIEVEMENT ______________________

NAME ______________________

CLUB ______________________

ACHIEVEMENT ______________________

NAME ______________________

CLUB ______________________

ACHIEVEMENT ______________________

NAME ______________________

CLUB ______________________

ACHIEVEMENT ______________________

NAME ______________________

CLUB ______________________

ACHIEVEMENT ______________________

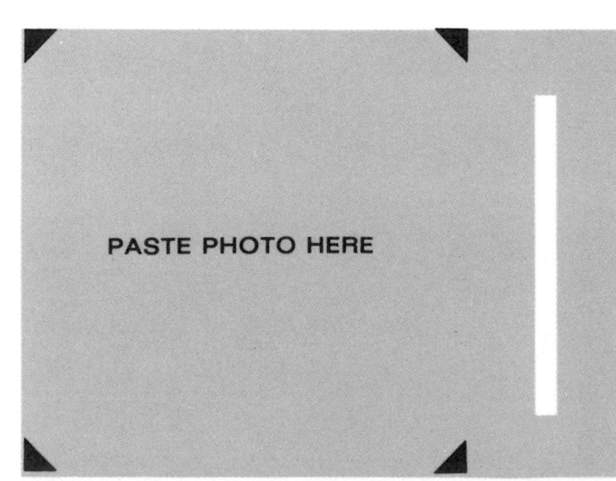

NAME ____________

SCHOOL ____________ GRADE ____

NAME ____________

SCHOOL ____________ GRADE ____

PASTE PHOTO HERE

SCHOOL PARTIES

DATE ____________

OCCASION ____________

____

DATE ____________

OCCASION ____________

____

DATE ____________

OCCASION ____________

____

DATE ____________

OCCASION ____________

____

DATE ____________

OCCASION ____________

____

DATE ____________

OCCASION ____________

____

DATE ____________

OCCASION ____________

____

DATE ____________

OCCASION ____________

____

____

EDUCATIONAL HONORS AND PRIZES

Scholarships, Awards, Honor Societies

NAME ____________

GRADE ____________

HONOR ____________

NAME ____________

GRADE ____________

HONOR ____________

NAME ____________

GRADE ____________

HONOR ____________

NAME ____________

GRADE ____________

HONOR ____________

GRADUATIONS

NAME ____________

SCHOOL ____________

NAME ____________

SCHOOL ____________

NAME ____________

SCHOOL ____________

DOCTOR'S NAME ______

ADDRESS ______

______

TELEPHONE NUMBER ______

DOCTOR'S NAME ______

ADDRESS ______

______

TELEPHONE NUMBER ______

______

DENTIST'S NAME ______

ADDRESS ______

______

TELEPHONE NUMBER ______

______

DENTIST'S NAME ______

ADDRESS ______

______

TELEPHONE NUMBER ______

RECORD OF GROWTH IN HEIGHT

FEET

	Feet	
	6	
	5	
	4	
	3	
	2	
	1	
Check Height on This Scale, Write Name and Date Opposite It		

RECORD OF WEIGHT

POUNDS

	Pounds	
	225	
	200	
	175	
	150	
	125	
	100	
	75	
	50	
	25	
Check Weight on This Scale, Write Name and Date Opposite It		

NAME ____________________

HEIGHT ____________ WEIGHT ________

VISITS TO DENTIST ____________________

VISITS TO DOCTOR ____________________

INOCULATIONS ____________________

TYPE ____________ DATE ________

TYPE ____________ DATE ________

ACCIDENTS, ILLNESSES ____________________

OPERATIONS ____________________

NAME ____________________

HEIGHT ____________ WEIGHT ________

VISITS TO DENTIST ____________________

VISITS TO DOCTOR ____________________

INOCULATIONS ____________________

TYPE ____________ DATE ________

TYPE ____________ DATE ________

ACCIDENTS, ILLNESSES ____________________

OPERATIONS ____________________

NAME ____________________

HEIGHT ____________ WEIGHT ________

VISITS TO DENTIST ____________________

VISITS TO DOCTOR ____________________

INOCULATIONS ____________________

TYPE ____________ DATE ________

TYPE ____________ DATE ________

ACCIDENTS, ILLNESSES ____________________

OPERATIONS ____________________

NAME ____________________

HEIGHT ____________ WEIGHT ________

VISITS TO DENTIST ____________________

VISITS TO DOCTOR ____________________

INOCULATIONS ____________________

TYPE ____________ DATE ________

TYPE ____________ DATE ________

ACCIDENTS, ILLNESSES ____________________

OPERATIONS ____________________

LEISURE HOURS INDOORS

BOOKS WE ENJOYED

AUTHOR

TITLE

WHO READ IT

WHY IT WAS LIKED

AUTHOR

TITLE

WHO READ IT

WHY IT WAS LIKED

AUTHOR

TITLE

WHO READ IT

WHY IT WAS LIKED

FAVORITE RECORDS

FAVORITE PLAYS, MOVIES, TV PROGRAMS

NAME

WHO SAW IT

WHY IT WAS LIKED

NAME

WHO SAW IT

WHY IT WAS LIKED

NAME

WHO SAW IT

WHY IT WAS LIKED

HOBBIES AND GAMES WE LIKED

COMPTON ARTICLES WE LIKED